2012 EDITION | PRIDE & FERRELL
marketing

William M. Pride
Texas A&M University

O. C. Ferrell
University of New Mexico

SOUTH-WESTERN
CENGAGE Learning™

Australia • Brazil • Japan • Korea • Mexico • Singapore • Spain • United Kingdom • United States

SOUTH-WESTERN
CENGAGE Learning™

Marketing, 16th Edition
William M. Pride , O. C. Ferrell

Vice President of Editorial, Business:
Jack W. Calhoun

Editor-in-Chief: Melissa Acuña

Acquisitions Editor: Mike Roche

Developmental Editor: Suzanna Bainbridge

Editorial Assistant: Kayti Purkiss

Marketing Coordinator: Shanna Shelton

Content Project Manager: Scott Dillon

Media Editor: John Rich

Frontlist Buyer, Manufacturing:
Miranda Klapper

Sr. Marketing Communications Manager:
Jim Overly

Project Management: Elm Street Publishing
Services

Composition: Integra Software Services
Pvt. Ltd.

Sr. Art Director: Stacy Jenkins Shirley

Cover/Internal Designer: Craig Ramsdell

Cover Image: © Getty Images/George Diebold

Rights Acquisitions Specialist: Deanna Ettinger

> For product information and technology assistance, contact us at
> **Cengage Learning Customer & Sales Support, 1-800-354-9706**
>
> For permission to use material from this text or product,
> submit all requests online at **www.cengage.com/permissions**
> Further permissions questions can be emailed to
> **permissionrequest@cengage.com**

ExamView® is a registered trademark of eInstruction Corp. Windows is a registered trademark of the Microsoft Corporation used herein under license. Macintosh and Power Macintosh are registered trademarks of Apple Computer, Inc. used herein under license.
© 2012 Cengage Learning. All Rights Reserved.

Cengage Learning WebTutor™ is a trademark of Cengage Learning.

Library of Congress Control Number: 2010934025

Library Edition: ISBN-13: 978-0-538-47540-2

Library Edition: ISBN-10: 0-538-47540-4

Paperback Edition: ISBN-13: 978-1-111-52619-1

Paperback Edition: ISBN-10: 1-111-52619-2

South-Western Cengage Learning
5191 Natorp Boulevard
Mason, OH 45040
USA

Cengage Learning products are represented in Canada by Nelson Education, Ltd.

For your course and learning solutions, visit **www.cengage.com**

Purchase any of our products at your local college store or at our preferred online store **www.cengagebrain.com**

Printed in the United States of America
1 2 3 4 5 6 7 15 14 13 12 11

brief contents

contents

Part 4: Customer Behavior and E-Marketing 189

Part 6: Distribution Decisions 427

Part 7: Promotion Decisions 503

Part 8: Pricing Decisions 597

preface

Marketing in a Changing World

The challenges of developing and implementing marketing strategies continue to increase in today's complex business environment. This new edition provides comprehensive coverage of relevant concepts and best practices to help navigate marketing's role in organizations and society. Marketing is being complicated by environmental challenges related to economic fluctuations, advances in technology, concerns about the natural environment and sustainability, and increased global competition. In addition, advances in information technology are creating opportunities for marketers to use digital media in their marketing strategies. We have carefully analyzed these developments and revised the content of this new edition to reflect major changes in the marketing environment.

Online social networking has become an increasingly powerful tool for marketers. Most discussions about marketing today necessarily bring up issues such as how digital media can lower costs, improve communications, provide better customer support, and achieve improved marketing research. All elements of the marketing mix should be considered when using digital media and in e-marketing. To address these changes in the marketing environment, this edition provides a new chapter: E-Marketing, Digital Media, and Social Networking (Chapter 10). The new chapter addresses important e-marketing strategies and the use of digital media to achieve addressability, interactivity, connectivity, control, and accessibility and how they differ from traditional marketing efforts. In addition, the entire book integrates important digital marketing concepts and examples where appropriate.

In developing a Principles of Marketing text, it is important to maintain balance in all main conceptual areas. Therefore, in this extensive revision, we have updated all key concepts and topics, not just by updating examples. The new *Marketing in Transition* boxes reflect how marketing is changing and adapting to new technology, competitive forces, and to the global economy. With carbon emissions becoming a focal point of most reports on how to minimize global warming, the need to reduce, reuse, and recycle has become a source of green initiatives for many businesses. Each chapter has a *Sustainable Marketing* box that relates marketing activities to sustainability and the natural environment.

We have paid careful attention to enhancing all key concepts in marketing and have built this revision to be current and to reflect important changes in marketing. Our book is a market leader because students find it readable and relevant. Our text reflects the real world of marketing and provides the most comprehensive coverage possible of important marketing topics.

Specific details of this extensive revision are available in the transition guide in the *Instructor's Resource Manual.* We have also made efforts to improve all teaching ancillaries and student learning tools. PowerPoints continue to be a very popular teaching device, and a special effort has been made to upgrade the PowerPoint program to enhance classroom teaching. The *Instructor's Manual* continues to be a valuable tool updated with engaging in-class activities and projects. The authors and publisher have worked together to provide a competent teaching package and ancillaries that are unsurpassed in the marketplace.

The authors have maintained a hands-on approach to teaching this material and revising the text and its ancillaries. This results in an integrated teaching package and approach that is accurate, sound, and successful in reaching students. The outcome of this involvement fosters trust and confidence in the teaching package and in student learning outcomes.

Keeping Pace with the Challenges and the Changing World

We believe that marketing students are changing as rapidly as the marketing environment. Today's students are looking for knowledge that is timely, relevant, and application oriented. We also know that a concise feature or application such as a box or exercise can enliven foundational marketing concepts. In this edition, we start each chapter with an opening vignette that captures the excitement and challenges of marketing. We have two boxes that include sustainable marketing and marketing in transition. In addition, we have two shorter student engagement features relating to responsible marketing and entrepreneurship in marketing: *Responsible Marketing?* and *Entrepreneurial Marketing.*

The new Chapter 10 focuses on e-marketing, digital media, and social networking and is tied directly to strategic planning and developing marketing strategies. It is important to identify and understand the role of digital media in marketing strategy implementation and how digital media are used as effective marketing tools to build customer relationships. Digital media have had an important impact on consumer behavior and have opened new avenues for marketing research.

We continue to emphasize global marketing, ethics, and social responsibility by using integrated concepts and examples in most of the chapters. The role of the United States and our world economy has become challenging and, at times, controversial. And, with the economies of developing countries accelerating at a fast pace, global economic resources are under strain. Nearly every business decision has to consider global competition and environmental implications as they shape marketing strategies. The recent downturn in the world economy created new marketing challenges that are reflected in this revision. We address these issues and provide examples to help students understand the marketing implications.

Features of the Book

As with previous editions, this edition of the text provides a comprehensive and practical introduction to marketing that is both easy to teach and to learn. *Marketing: Concepts and Strategies* continues to be one of the most widely adopted introductory textbooks in the world. We appreciate the confidence that adopters have placed in our textbook and continue to work hard to make sure that, as in previous editions, this edition keeps pace with changes. The entire text is structured to excite students about the subject and to help them learn completely and efficiently:

- An *organizational model* at the beginning of each part provides a "road map" of the text and a visual tool for understanding the connection among various components.
- *Objectives* at the start of each chapter present concrete expectations about what students are to learn as they read the chapter.
- Every chapter begins with an opening vignette. This feature provides an example of the real world of marketing that relates to the topic covered in the chapter. After reading the vignette, the student should be motivated to want to learn more about concepts and strategies that relate to the varying topics. Students will learn about topics such as the recent BP oil spill, the ethics of sports marketing, and marketing to changing demographics. Students will also be introduced to such companies as Vizio, NASCAR, Google, and Harley-Davidson.

- Boxed features—*Marketing in Transition* and *Sustainable Marketing*—capture dynamic changes in marketing. These changes are influencing marketing strategies and customer behavior. Strong feedback from adopters indicated the need for coverage in these areas.

    The *Marketing in Transition* boxes cover such marketing phenomena as consumer-created marketing campaigns, digital word-of-mouth marketing, marketing biofuels, digital advertising, and virtual products. Featured companies include Hulu.com, Pantone, Facebook, Twitter, and Guitar Affair.

    The *Sustainable Marketing* boxes introduce students to such topics as paperless marketing, the organic movement, global green efforts, ecotourism, and zero waste. Featured companies include Zipcar, Trader Joe's, Ecco Restaurant, Rainforest Expeditions, Frito Lay, and Patagonia.

- In every chapter, there are two mini-features. The *Responsible Marketing?* marginal feature discusses controversial issues related to ethics and social responsibility, such as digital rights management technology, marketing practices of the tobacco industry, advertising puffery in the pharmaceutical industry, credit card practices, carbon reduction of power companies, and guerilla marketing issues.

    The *Entrepreneurial Marketing* feature focuses on the role of entrepreneurship and the need for creativity in developing successful marketing strategies by featuring successful entrepreneurial companies such as Crocs, Spanx, Cirque du Soleil, Womenkind, and Terracycle.

- *Key term definitions* appear in the margins to help students build their marketing vocabulary.

- Figures, tables, photographs, advertisements, and Snapshot features increase comprehension and stimulate interest.

- A complete *chapter summary* reviews the major topics discussed, and the list of important terms provides another end-of-chapter study aid to expand students' marketing vocabulary.

- *Discussion and review questions* at the end of each chapter encourage further study and exploration of chapter content, and *application questions* enhance students' comprehension of important topics.

- An *Internet exercise* at the end of each chapter asks students to examine a website and assess one or more strategic issues associated with the site. This section also points students toward the various learning tools that are available on the text's website.

- *Developing Your Marketing Plan* ties the chapter concepts into an overall marketing plan that can be created by completing the Interactive Marketing Plan activity found at **www.cengagebrain.com**. The *Developing Your Marketing Plan* feature allows students to explore each chapter topic in relation to developing and implementing a marketing campaign.

- Two *cases* at the end of each chapter help students understand the application of chapter concepts. One of the end-of-chapter cases is related to a video segment. Some examples of companies highlighted in the cases are Raleigh, Trek, Netflix, Bombardier, Lonely Planet, RogueSheep, Washburn Guitars, New Belgium Brewery, and Vans.

- A *strategic case* at the end of each part helps students integrate the diverse concepts that have been discussed within the related chapters. Examples include Monsanto, Shutterfly, GameStop, and Indy Racing League.

- *Appendixes* discuss marketing career opportunities, explore financial analysis in marketing, and present a sample marketing plan.

- A comprehensive *glossary* defines more than 625 important marketing terms.

Text Organization

We have organized the eight parts of *Marketing: Concepts and Strategies* to give students a theoretical and practical understanding of marketing decision making.

Part 1   **Marketing Strategy and Customer Relationships**
In **Chapter 1,** we define marketing and explore several key concepts: customers and target markets, the marketing mix, relationship marketing, the marketing concept, and value-driven marketing. In **Chapter 2,** we look at an overview of strategic marketing issues, such as the role of the mission statement; corporate, business-unit, and marketing strategies; and the creation of the marketing plan.

Part 2   **Environmental Forces and Social and Ethical Responsibilities**
We examine competitive, economic, political, legal, regulatory, technological, and sociocultural forces that can have profound effects on marketing strategies in **Chapter 3.** In **Chapter 4,** we explore social responsibility and ethical issues in marketing decisions.

Part 3   **Marketing Research and Target Market Analysis**
In **Chapter 5,** we provide a foundation for analyzing buyers with a look at marketing information systems and the basic steps in the marketing research process. We look at elements that affect buying decisions to better analyze customers' needs and evaluate how specific marketing strategies can satisfy those needs. In **Chapter 6,** we deal with how to select and analyze target markets—one of the major steps in marketing strategy development.

Part 4   **Customer Behavior and E-Marketing**
We examine consumer buying decision processes and factors that influence buying decisions in **Chapter 7.** In **Chapter 8,** we explore business markets, business customers, the buying center, and the business buying decision process. **Chapter 9** focuses on the actions, involvement, and strategies of marketers that serve international customers. In **Chapter 10,** we discuss e-marketing, social media, and social networking.

Part 5   **Product Decisions**
In **Chapter 11,** we introduce basic concepts and relationships that must be understood to make effective product decisions. We analyze a variety of dimensions regarding product management in **Chapter 12,** including line extensions and product modification, new-product development, and product deletions. **Chapter 13** discusses branding, packaging, and labeling. In **Chapter 14,** we explore the nature, importance, and characteristics of services.

Part 6   **Distribution Decisions**
In **Chapter 15,** we look at supply-chain management, marketing channels, and the decisions and activities associated with the physical distribution of products, such as order processing, materials handling, warehousing, inventory management, and transportation. **Chapter 16** explores retailing and wholesaling, including types of retailers and wholesalers, direct marketing and selling, and strategic retailing issues.

Part 7   **Promotion Decisions**
We discuss integrated marketing communications in **Chapter 17.** The communication process and major promotional methods that can be included in promotions mixes are described. In **Chapter 18,** we analyze the major steps in developing an advertising campaign. We also define public relations and how it can be used. **Chapter 19** deals with personal selling and the role it can play in a firm's promotional efforts. We also

explore the general characteristics of sales promotion and describe sales promotion techniques.

Part 8 **Pricing Decisions**
In **Chapter 20,** we discuss the importance of price and look at some characteristics of price and nonprice competition. We explore fundamental concepts such as demand, elasticity, marginal analysis, and break-even analysis. We then examine the major factors that affect marketers' pricing decisions. In **Chapter 21,** we look at the six major stages of the process marketers use to establish prices.

What's New to This Edition?

This edition is revised and updated to address the dynamic issues emerging in the marketing field, while continuing to stress the importance of traditional marketing issues. These revisions assist students in gaining a full understanding of marketing practices pertinent today and in helping them anticipate increasing future changes.

General Text Changes

- *New Chapter 10, E-Marketing, Digital Media, and Social Networking* focuses on how consumers and marketers are changing their information searching and consumption behavior to benefit from emerging technology trends. We describe how marketing can use digital media to create effective e-marketing strategies. A complete description of social networking methods useful in developing marketing strategies helps students connect their own knowledge with the application of digital media in marketing practice.
- *Reorganization.* We have moved the services marketing chapter ahead of the discussion of branding because the marketing of services relies heavily on branding.
- *Theme-related coverage.* To discuss changes in marketing practices, we have retained a boxed feature entitled *Marketing in Transition.* The topics covered in these features are new to this edition. In addition, most of the green-related topics covered in our *Sustainable Marketing* features are new and include theme-specific boxes on green marketing and entertainment marketing throughout the chapter. To bring the concept of responsible marketing to life, we present a controversial issue in our *Responsible Marketing?* feature and ask students to look at several dimensions of today's real-world marketing changes.

Changes in Every Chapter

- *Opening vignettes.* All of the chapter-opening vignettes are new. They are written to introduce the theme of each chapter by focusing on actual entrepreneurial companies and how they deal with real-world situations.
- *Boxed features.* Each chapter includes two new boxed features that highlight sustainable marketing and marketing in transition. The majority of the boxed features are new to this edition; a few have been significantly updated and revised to fit the themes of this edition.
- *New Snapshot features.* Many of the Snapshot features are new and engage students by highlighting interesting, up-to-date statistics that link marketing theory to the real world.
- *New research.* Throughout the text we have updated content with the most recent research that supports the frameworks and best practices for marketing.
- *New illustrations and examples.* New advertisements from well-known firms are employed to illustrate chapter topics. Experiences of real-world companies are used to exemplify marketing concepts and strategies throughout the text. Most

examples are new or updated to include e-marketing concepts as well as several new sustainable marketing illustrations.

- *End-of-chapter cases.* Each chapter contains two cases, including a video case, profiling firms to illustrate concrete application of marketing strategies and concepts. The vast majority of our video cases are new to this edition and supported by current and engaging videos.

A Comprehensive Instructional Resource Package

For instructors, this edition of *Marketing* includes an exceptionally comprehensive package of teaching materials.

INSTRUCTOR'S MANUAL

The *Instructor's Manual* has been revamped to meet the needs of an engaging classroom environment. It has been updated with diverse and dynamic discussion starters, classroom activities, and group exercises. It includes such tools as:

- Quick Reference Guide
- Purpose Statement
- Integrated Lecture Outline with features and multimedia (e.g. PowerPoint call-outs) incorporated
- Discussion Starter recommendations that encourage active exploration of the in-text examples
- Class Exercises, Semester Project Activities (tied to the Interactive Marketing Plan), and Chapter Quizzes
- Suggested Answers to end-of-chapter exercises, cases, and strategic cases

TEST BANK (DR. KATHY SMITH, TEXAS A&M UNIVERSITY)

The test bank provides more than 4,000 test items including true/false, multiple-choice, and essay questions. Each objective test item is accompanied by the correct answer, appropriate Learning Objective, level of difficulty, main text page reference, and AACSB standard coding. Instructors are able to select, edit, and add questions, or generate randomly selected questions to produce a test master for easy duplication.

POWERPOINT® SLIDES

PowerPoint® continues to be a very popular teaching device, and a special effort has been made to upgrade the PowerPoint program to enhance classroom teaching. Premium lecture slides, containing such content as advertisements, web links, and unique graphs and data, have been created to provide instructors with up-to-date unique content to increase student application and interest.

ONLINE TEACHING RESOURCES

To access additional course materials, including Marketing CourseMate, please visit **www.cengagebrain.com.** At the CengageBrain.com home page, search for the ISBN of your title (from the back cover of your book) using the search box at the top of the page. This will take you to the product page where the following resources can be found:

- An interactive eBook
- Interactive teaching and learning tools including:
  - Quizzes
  - PowerPoint® presentation
  - eLectures
  - Flashcards
  - Videos
  - Simulations
  - An Interactive Marketing Plan

■ Engagement Tracker, a first-of-its-kind tool that monitors student engagement in the course

COURSEMATE

Interested in a simple way to complement your text and course content with study and practice materials? Cengage Learning's Marketing CourseMate brings course concepts to life with interactive learning, study, and exam preparation tools that support the printed textbook. Watch student comprehension soar as your class works with the printed textbook and the textbook-specific website. Marketing CourseMate goes beyond the book to deliver what you need! Marketing CourseMate includes an interactive eBook as well as interactive teaching and learning tools including quizzes, flashcards, homework video cases, simulations, and more. Engagement Tracker monitors student engagement in the course.

WEBTUTOR™ (FOR WEBCT® AND BLACKBOARD®)

Online learning is growing at a rapid pace. Whether you are looking to offer courses at a distance or in a Web-enhanced classroom, South-Western, a part of Cengage Learning, offers you a solution with WebTutor. WebTutor provides instructors with text-specific content that interacts with the two leading systems of higher education course management: WebCT and Blackboard.

WebTutor is a turnkey solution for instructors who want to begin using technology like Blackboard or WebCT but do not have Web-ready content available or do not want to be burdened with developing their own content. WebTutor uses the Internet to turn everyone in your class into a front-row student. WebTutor offers interactive study guide features including quizzes, concept reviews, animated figures, discussion forums, video clips, and more. Instructor tools are also provided to facilitate communication between students and faculty.

CENGAGENOW (FOR WEBCT® AND BLACKBOARD®)

Ensure that your students have the understanding they need of marketing procedures and concepts they need to know with CengageNOW. This integrated, online course management and learning system combines the best of current technology to save time in planning and managing your course and assignments. You can reinforce comprehension with customized student learning paths and efficiently test and automatically grade assignments.

MARKETING VIDEO CASE SERIES

This series contains videos specifically tied to the video cases found at the end of the book. The videos include information about exciting companies such as Netflix, Harley-Davidson, Lonely Planet, Washburn Guitars, and Vans.

INTERACTIVE MARKETING PLAN

The Marketing Plan Worksheets have been revamped and reproduced within an interactive and multimedia environment. A video program has been developed around the worksheets, allowing students to follow a company through the trials and tribulations of launching a new product. This video helps place the conceptual marketing plan into an applicable light and is supported by a summary of the specific stages of the marketing plan as well as a sample plan based on the events of the video. These elements act as the 1-2-3 punch supporting the student while completing his or her own plan, the last step of the Interactive Marketing Plan. The Plan is broken up into three functional sections that can either be completed in one simple project or carried over throughout the semester.

Supplements to Meet Student Needs

The complete package available with *Marketing: Concepts and Strategies* includes support materials that facilitate student learning.

Online Learning Resources

To access additional course materials, including Marketing CourseMate, please visit www.cengagebrain.com. At the CengageBrain.com home page, search for the ISBN of your title (from the back cover of your book) using the search box at the top of the page. This will take you to the product page where the following resources can be found:

- Interactive teaching and learning tools, including:
  - Quizzes
  - eLectures
  - Flashcards
  - Videos
  - Simulations
  - An Interactive Marketing Plan
  - And more!
- Online homework—Homework is auto-graded and provides instant feedback for students.
- Full-color eBook—Allows you to highlight and search for key terms.
- Flexibility and control—Your instructor has the ability to customize assignments and grade-book options to best suit the needs of the class as you progress through the course.
- Better course results—Many CengageNow products include a diagnostic Personalized Study Plan to accompany your text (featuring a chapter-specific Pretest, Study Plan, and Posttest), allowing you to master concepts, prepare for exams, and get a better grade.

Your Comments and Suggestions Are Valued

As authors, our major focus has been on teaching and preparing learning material for introductory marketing students. We have both traveled extensively to work with students and understand the needs of professors of introductory marketing courses. We both teach this marketing course on a regular basis and test the materials included in the book, Test Bank, and other ancillary materials to make sure they are effective in the classroom.

Through the years, professors and students have sent us many helpful suggestions for improving the text and ancillary components. We invite your comments, questions, and criticisms. We want to do our best to provide materials that enhance the teaching and learning of marketing concepts and strategies. Your suggestions will be sincerely appreciated. Please write us, or e-mail us at **w-pride@tamu.edu** or **OCFerrell@mgt. unm.edu**, or call 979-845-5857 (Bill Pride) or 505-277-3468 (O.C. Ferrell).

Acknowledgments

Like most textbooks, this one reflects the ideas of many academicians and practitioners who have contributed to the development of the marketing discipline. We appreciate the opportunity to present their ideas in this book.

A number of individuals have made helpful comments and recommendations in their reviews of this or earlier editions. We appreciate the generous help of these reviewers:

Zafar U. Ahmed
Minot State University

Thomas Ainscough
University of Massachusetts—Dartmouth

Sana Akili
Iowa State University

Katrece Albert
Southern University

Joe F. Alexander
University of Northern Colorado

Mark I. Alpert
University of Texas at Austin

David M. Ambrose
University of Nebraska

David Andrus
Kansas State University

Linda K. Anglin
Minnesota State University

George Avellano
Central State University

Emin Babakus
University of Memphis

Julie Baker
Texas Christian University

Siva Balasubramanian
Southern Illinois University

Joseph Ballenger
Stephen F. Austin State University

Guy Banville
Creighton University

Frank Barber
Cuyahoga Community College

Joseph Barr
Framingham State College

Thomas E. Barry
Southern Methodist University

Charles A. Bearchell
California State University—Northridge

Richard C. Becherer
University of Tennessee—Chattanooga

Walter H. Beck, Sr.
Reinhardt College

Russell Belk
University of Utah

John Bennett
University of Missouri—Columbia

W. R. Berdine
California State Polytechnic Institute

Karen Berger
Pace University

Bob Berl
University of Memphis

Stewart W. Bither
Pennsylvania State University

Roger Blackwell
Ohio State University

Peter Bloch
University of Missouri—Columbia

Wanda Blockhus
San Jose State University

Nancy Bloom
Nassau Community College

Paul N. Bloom
University of North Carolina

James P. Boespflug
Arapahoe Community College

Joseph G. Bonnice
Manhattan College

John Boos
Ohio Wesleyan University

Peter Bortolotti
Johnson & Wales University

Jenell Bramlage
University of Northwestern Ohio

James Brock
Susquehanna College

John R. Brooks, Jr.
Houston Baptist University

William G. Browne
Oregon State University

John Buckley
Orange County Community College

Gul T. Butaney
Bentley College

James Cagley
University of Tulsa

Pat J. Calabros
University of Texas—Arlington

Linda Calderone
*State University of New York
College of Technology at Farmingdale*

Joseph Cangelosi
University of Central Arkansas

William J. Carner
University of Texas—Austin

James C. Carroll
University of Central Arkansas

Terry M. Chambers
Westminster College

Lawrence Chase
Tompkins Cortland Community College

Larry Chonko
Baylor University

Barbara Coe
University of North Texas

Ernest F. Cooke
Loyola College—Baltimore

Robert Copley
University of Louisville

John I. Coppett
University of Houston—Clear Lake

Robert Corey
West Virginia University

Deborah L. Cowles
Virginia Commonwealth University

Sandra Coyne
Springfield College

Melvin R. Crask
University of Georgia

William L. Cron
Texas Christian University

Gary Cutler
Dyersburg State Community College

Bernice N. Dandridge
Diablo Valley College

Tamara Davis
Davenport University

Lloyd M. DeBoer
George Mason University

Sally Dibb
University of Warwick

Ralph DiPietro
Montclair State University

Paul Dishman
Idaho State University

Suresh Divakar
State University of New York—Buffalo

Casey L. Donoho
Northern Arizona University

Todd Donovan
Colorado State University

Peter T. Doukas
Westchester Community College

Kent Drummond
University of Wyoming

Tinus Van Drunen
University Twente (Netherlands)

Lee R. Duffus
Florida Gulf Coast University

Robert F. Dwyer
University of Cincinnati

Roland Eyears
Central Ohio Technical College

Thomas Falcone
Indiana University of Pennsylvania

James Finch
University of Wisconsin—La Crosse

Letty C. Fisher
SUNY/Westchester Community College

Renée Florsheim
Loyola Marymount University

Charles W. Ford
Arkansas State University

John Fraedrich
Southern Illinois University, Carbondale

David J. Fritzsche
University of Washington

Donald A. Fuller
University of Central Florida

Terry Gable
Truman State University

Ralph Gaedeke
California State University, Sacramento

Robert Garrity
University of Hawaii

Cathy Goodwin
University of Manitoba

Geoffrey L. Gordon
Northern Illinois University

Robert Grafton-Small
University of Strathclyde

Harrison Grathwohl
California State University—Chico

Alan A. Greco
North Carolina A&T State University

Blaine S. Greenfield
Bucks County Community College

Thomas V. Greer
University of Maryland

Sharon F. Gregg
Middle Tennessee University

Jim L. Grimm
Illinois State University

Charles Gross
University of New Hampshire

Joseph Guiltinan
University of Notre Dame

John Hafer
University of Nebraska at Omaha

David Hansen
Texas Southern University

Richard C. Hansen
Ferris State University

Nancy Hanson-Rasmussen
*University of Wisconsin—
Eau Claire*

Robert R. Harmon
Portland State University

Mary C. Harrison
Amber University

Lorraine Hartley
Franklin University

Michael Hartline
Florida State University

Timothy Hartman
Ohio University

Salah S. Hassan
George Washington University

Manoj Hastak
American University

Del I. Hawkins
University of Oregon

Dean Headley
Wichita State University

Esther Headley
Wichita State University

Debbora Heflin-Bullock
*California State Polytechnic University—
Pomona*

Merlin Henry
Rancho Santiago College

Tony Henthorne
University of Southern Mississippi

Lois Herr
Elizabethtown College

Charles L. Hilton
Eastern Kentucky University

Elizabeth C. Hirschman
Rutgers, State University of New Jersey

George C. Hozier
University of New Mexico

John R. Huser
Illinois Central College

Joan M. Inzinga
Bay Path College

Deloris James
University of Maryland

Theodore F. Jula
Stonehill College

Peter F. Kaminski
Northern Illinois University

Yvonne Karsten
Minnesota State University

Jerome Katrichis
Temple University

Garland Keesling
Towson University

James Kellaris
University of Cincinnati

Alvin Kelly
Florida A&M University

Philip Kemp
DePaul University

Sylvia Keyes
Bridgewater State College

William M. Kincaid, Jr.
Oklahoma State University

Roy Klages
State University of New York at Albany

Hal Koenig
Oregon State University

Douglas Kornemann
Milwaukee Area Technical College

Kathleen Krentler
San Diego State University

Ron Johnson
Colorado Mountain College

John Krupa, Jr.
Johnson & Wales University

Barbara Lafferty
University of South Florida

Patricia Laidler
Massasoit Community College

Bernard LaLond
Ohio State University

Richard A. Lancioni
Temple University

Irene Lange
California State University—Fullerton

Geoffrey P. Lantos
Stonehill College

Charles L. Lapp
University of Texas—Dallas

Virginia Larson
San Jose State University

John Lavin
Waukesha County Technical Institute

Marilyn Lavin
University of Wisconsin—Whitewater

Hugh E. Law
East Tennessee University

Monle Lee
Indiana University—South Bend

Ron Lennon
Barry University

Richard C. Leventhal
Metropolitan State College

Marilyn L. Liebrenz-Himes
George Washington University

Jay D. Lindquist
Western Michigan University

Terry Loe
Kennesaw State University

Mary Logan
Southwestern Assemblies of God College

Paul Londrigan
Mott Community College

Anthony Lucas
Community College of Allegheny County

George Lucas
U.S. Learning, Inc.

William Lundstrom
Cleveland State University

Rhonda Mack
College of Charleston

Stan Madden
Baylor University

Patricia M. Manninen
North Shore Community College

Gerald L. Manning
Des Moines Area Community College

Lalita A. Manrai
University of Delaware

Franklyn Manu
Morgan State University

Allen S. Marber
University of Bridgeport

Gayle J. Marco
Robert Morris College

Carolyn A. Massiah
University of Central Florida

James McAlexander
Oregon State University

Donald McCartney
University of Wisconsin—Green Bay

Anthony McGann
University of Wyoming

Jack McNiff
*State University of New York
College of Technology at Farmington*

Lee Meadow
Eastern Illinois University

Carla Meeske
University of Oregon

Jeffrey A. Meier
Fox Valley Technical College

James Meszaros
County College of Morris

Brian Meyer
Minnesota State University

Martin Meyers
University of Wisconsin—Stevens Point

Stephen J. Miller
Oklahoma State University

William Moller
University of Michigan

Kent B. Monroe
University of Illinois

Carlos W. Moore
Baylor University

Carol Morris-Calder
Loyola Marymount University

David Murphy
Madisonville Community College

Keith Murray
Bryant College

Sue Ellen Neeley
University of Houston—Clear Lake

Carolyn Y. Nicholson
Stetson University

Francis L. Notturno, Sr.
Owens Community College

Terrence V. O'Brien
Northern Illinois University

James R. Ogden
Kutztown University of Pennsylvania

Lois Bitner Olson
San Diego State University

Mike O'Neill
California State University—Chico

Robert S. Owen
State University of New York—Oswego

Allan Palmer
University of North Carolina at Charlotte

Terry Paul
Ohio State University

David P. Paul III
Monmouth University

Teresa Pavia
University of Utah

John Perrachione
Truman State University

Michael Peters
Boston College

Linda Pettijohn
Missouri State University

Lana Podolak
Community College of Beaver County

Raymond E. Polchow
Muskingum Area Technical College

Thomas Ponzurick
West Virginia University

William Presutti
Duquesne University

Kathy Pullins
Columbus State Community College

Edna J. Ragins
North Carolina A&T State University

Daniel Rajaratnam
Baylor University

Mohammed Rawwas
University of Northern Iowa

James D. Reed
Louisiana State University—Shreveport

William Rhey
University of Tampa

Glen Riecken
East Tennessee State University

Winston Ring
University of Wisconsin—Milwaukee

Ed Riordan
Wayne State University

Bruce Robertson
San Francisco State University

Robert A. Robicheaux
University of Alabama—Birmingham

Linda Rose
Westwood College Online

Bert Rosenbloom
Drexel University

Robert H. Ross
Wichita State University

Tom Rossi
Broome Community College

Vicki Rostedt
The University of Akron

Michael L. Rothschild
University of Wisconsin—Madison

Kenneth L. Rowe
Arizona State University

Don Roy
Middle Tennessee State University

Catherine Ruggieri
St. John's University

Elise Sautter
New Mexico State University

Ronald Schill
Brigham Young University

Bodo Schlegelmilch
Vienna University of Economics and Business Administration

Edward Schmitt
Villanova University

Thomas Schori
Illinois State University

Donald Sciglimpaglia
San Diego State University

Stanley Scott
University of Alaska—Anchorage

Harold S. Sekiguchi
University of Nevada—Reno

Gilbert Seligman
Dutchess Community College

Richard J. Semenik
University of Utah

Beheruz N. Sethna
Lamar University

Morris A. Shapero
Schiller International University

Terence A. Shimp
University of South Carolina

Mark Siders
Southern Oregon University

Carolyn F. Siegel
Eastern Kentucky University

Dean C. Siewers
Rochester Institute of Technology

Lyndon Simkin
University of Warwick

Roberta Slater
Cedar Crest College

Paul J. Solomon
University of South Florida

Sheldon Somerstein
City University of New York

Eric R. Spangenberg
University of Mississippi

Rosann L. Spiro
Indiana University

William Staples
University of Houston—Clear Lake

Bruce Stern
Portland State University

Carmen Sunda
University of New Orleans

Claire F. Sullivan
Metropolitan State University

Robert Swerdlow
Lamar University

Crina Tarasi
Central Michigan University

Ruth Taylor
Texas State University

Steven A. Taylor
Illinois State University

Hal Teer
James Madison University

Ira Teich
Long Island University—C.W. Post

Debbie Thorne
Texas State University

Dillard Tinsley
Stephen F. Austin State University

Sharynn Tomlin
Angelo State University

Hale Tongren
George Mason University

James Underwood
University of Southwest Louisiana—Lafayette

Barbara Unger
Western Washington University

Dale Varble
Indiana State University

Bronis Verhage
Georgia State University

R. Vish Viswanathan
University of Northern Colorado

Charles Vitaska
Metropolitan State College

Kirk Wakefield
Baylor University

Harlan Wallingford
Pace University

Jacquelyn Warwick
Andrews University

James F. Wenthe
Georgia College

Sumner M. White
Massachusetts Bay Community College

Janice Williams
University of Central Oklahoma

Alan R. Wiman
Rider College

John Withey
Indiana University—South Bend

Ken Wright
West Australia College of Advanced

We would like to thank Charlie Hofacker and Michael Hartline, both of Florida State University, for many helpful suggestions and insights in developing the new chapter on e-marketing, digital media, and social networking. Michael Hartline also assisted in the development of the marketing plan outline and the sample marketing plan in Appendix C, as well as the career worksheets on the website. We are grateful to Tomas Hult for revising Chapter 2: Planning, Implementing, and Controlling Marketing Strategies.

We would like to acknowledge Jennifer Jackson, who provided editorial oversight in developing Chapter 10: E-Marketing, Digital Media, and Social Networking, and assisted in the development of a number of other chapters in the revision process as well as the *Instructor's Manual* and PowerPoint program. Jennifer Sawayda also updated a number of chapters as well as reviewed and revised the manuscript during all stages of the production process. In addition, we are grateful to Katherine Smith for her work on the test bank. We thank Stacey Massey and Marian Wood for developing some of the examples and boxed features. We deeply appreciate the assistance of Courtney Bohannon, Laurie Marshall, Clarissa Means, Tyler Sorensen, Saleha Amin, Brenda Lake, Alexi Sherrill, and Harper Baird for providing editorial technical assistance and support.

We express appreciation for the support and encouragement given to us by our colleagues at Texas A&M University and University of New Mexico. We are also grateful for the comments and suggestions we receive from our own students, student focus groups, and student correspondents who provide ongoing feedback through the website.

A number of talented professionals at Cengage Learning and Elm Street Publishing Services have contributed to the development of this book. We are especially grateful to Mike Roche, Suzanna Bainbridge, Scott Dillon, Susan Nodine, Deanna Ettinger, Terri Miller, Stacy Shirley, Jim Overly, and Sarah Greber. Their inspiration, patience, support, and friendship are invaluable.

William M. Pride
O. C. Ferrell

About the Authors

William M. Pride is Professor of Marketing, Mays Business School, at Texas A&M University. He received his Ph.D. from Louisiana State University. In addition to this text, he is the co-author of Cengage Learning's *Business* text, a market leader.

Dr. Pride's research interests are in advertising, promotion, and distribution channels. His research articles have appeared in major journals in the fields of marketing such as the *Journal of Marketing*, the *Journal of Marketing Research*, the *Journal of the Academy of Marketing Science*, and the *Journal of Advertising*.

Dr. Pride is a member of the American Marketing Association, Academy of Marketing Science, Society for Marketing Advances, and the Marketing Management Association. He has received the Marketing Fellow Award from the Society for Marketing Advances and the Marketing Innovation Award from the Marketing Management Association. Both of these are lifetime achievement awards.

Dr. Pride has taught principles of marketing and other marketing courses for more than 30 years at both the undergraduate and graduate levels.

O. C. Ferrell is Professor of Marketing and Bill Daniels Professor of Business Ethics, Anderson School of Management, University of New Mexico. He has also been on the faculties of the University of Wyoming, Colorado State University, University of Memphis, Texas A&M University, and Illinois State University. He received his Ph.D. in Marketing from Louisiana State University.

He is past president of the Academic Council of the American Marketing Association and chaired the American Marketing Association Ethics Committee. Under his leadership, the committee developed the AMA Code of Ethics and the AMA Code of Ethics for Marketing on the Internet. He is currently a member of the advisory committee for the AMA marketing certification program. In addition, he is a former member of the Academy of Marketing Science Board of Governors and is a Society of Marketing Advances and Southwestern Marketing Association Fellow. He is the Academy of Marketing Science's Vice President of Publications. In 2010, he received a Lifetime Achievement Award from the Macromarketing Society and a special award for service to doctoral students from the Southeast Doctoral Consortium.

Dr. Ferrell is the co-author of 20 books and approximately 80 articles. His articles have been published in the *Journal of Marketing Research*, the *Journal of Marketing*, the *Journal of Business Ethics*, the *Journal of Business Research*, the *Journal of the Academy of Marketing Science*, and the *Journal of Public Policy Marketing*, as well as other journals.

Part I

Marketing Strategy and Customer Relationships

PART ONE introduces the field of marketing and offers a broad perspective from which to explore and analyze various components of the marketing discipline. **CHAPTER 1** defines *marketing* and explores several key concepts, including customers and target markets, the marketing mix, relationship marketing, the marketing concept, and value-driven marketing. **CHAPTER 2** provides an overview of strategic marketing issues, such as the role of the mission statement; corporate, business-unit, and marketing strategies; and the creation of the marketing plan.

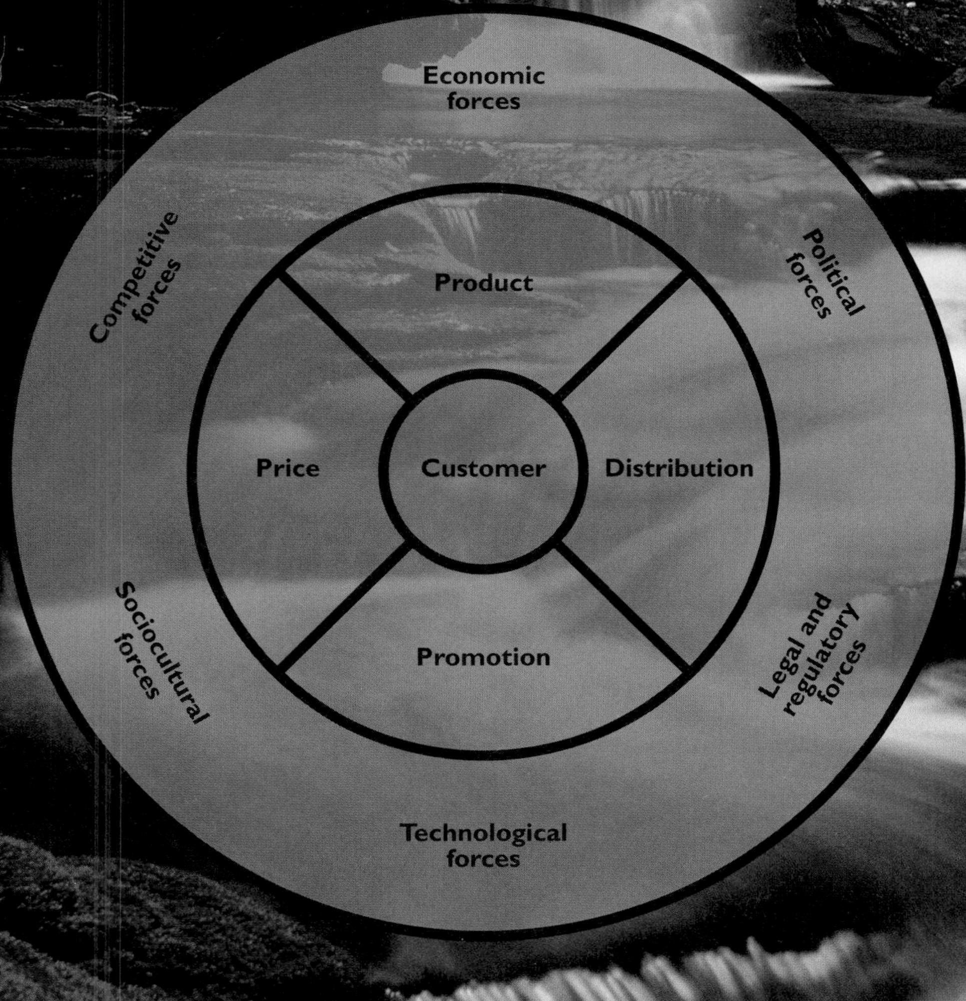

Economic forces

Competitive forces

Political forces

Product

Price   Customer   Distribution

Promotion

Sociocultural forces

Legal and regulatory forces

Technological forces

Chapter 1

An Overview of Strategic Marketing

OBJECTIVES

1. To be able to define marketing as focused on customers

2. To identify some important marketing terms, including *target market*, *marketing mix*, *marketing exchanges*, and *marketing environment*

3. To become aware of the marketing concept and market orientation

4. To understand the importance of building customer relationships

5. To learn about the process of marketing management

6. To recognize the role of marketing in our society

Vizio Tunes into Television Marketing

How does an unknown company catapult itself into the top tier of a highly competitive industry and establish its high-tech products as consumer favorites in less than a decade? Vizio has grown into one of the country's leading marketers of high-definition flat-screen televisions because its entrepreneurial founder, William Wang, pays close attention to the needs of the customers.

Wang came up with the idea for Vizio as the 1990s drew to a close. He had learned about a new U.S. law requiring television stations to begin a slow transition to all-digital broadcasting. Philips and other major multinationals were already introducing pricey, large-screen digital televisions suited to affluent home-theater enthusiasts. "At the time, most digital television sets were going for around $8,000," he remembers, "so what I saw was a great opportunity: a legal mandate and a wide-open market for more affordable televisions to fit that mandate."

screen images simulated

By 2003, Wang's new company, Vizio, was ready to launch a 46-inch, high-definition digital television, providing a great viewing experience at consumer-friendly prices. Knowing that Costco's customers sought out quality merchandise at reasonable prices, Wang asked the retailer to try stocking this product. Vizio broke Costco sales records and helped establish the retailer's reputation as a prime shopping destination for consumer electronics. Vizio then began to make its brand name more prominent through advertising and sports sponsorship.

Today, thanks to a winning combination of full-featured products with affordable price tags, convenient distribution, and brand-building communications, Vizio is among the leaders in the U.S. television market. Every year, it sells more than 6 million units, rings up more than $2 billion in revenue, and keeps up with customer needs by introducing new televisions, DVD players, and related items. Ask William Wang about Vizio's success, and he will tell you: "First, you must learn about your customers—what they like and dislike. The customer is always first."[1]

Like all organizations, Vizio attempts to develop products that customers want, communicate useful information about them to excite interest, price them appropriately, and make them available when and where customers want to buy them. Even if an organization does all these things well, however, competition from marketers of similar products, economic conditions, and other factors can impact the company's success. Such factors influence the decisions that all organizations must make in strategic marketing.

This chapter introduces the strategic marketing concepts and decisions that will be discussed throughout the book. First, we develop a definition of *marketing* and explore each element of the definition in detail. Next, we introduce the marketing concept and consider several issues associated with implementing it. We also take a brief look at the management of customer relationships and then at the concept of value, which customers are demanding today more than ever before. We next explore the process of marketing management, which includes planning, organizing, implementing, and controlling marketing activities to encourage marketing exchanges. Finally, we examine the importance of marketing in our global society.

Defining *Marketing*

marketing The process of creating, distributing, promoting, and pricing goods, services, and ideas to facilitate satisfying exchange relationships with customers and develop and maintain favorable relationships with stakeholders in a dynamic environment

If you ask several people what *marketing* is, you are likely to hear a variety of definitions. Although many people think marketing is advertising or selling, marketing actually encompasses many more activities. In this book, we define **marketing** as the process of creating, distributing, promoting, and pricing goods, services, and ideas to facilitate satisfying exchange relationships with customers and develop and maintain favorable relationships with stakeholders in a dynamic environment. Our definition is consistent with the American Marketing Association (AMA), which defines marketing as "the activity, set of institutions, and processes for creating, communicating, delivering, and exchanging offerings that have value for customers, clients, partners, and society at large."[2]

FIGURE 1.1 Components of Strategic Marketing

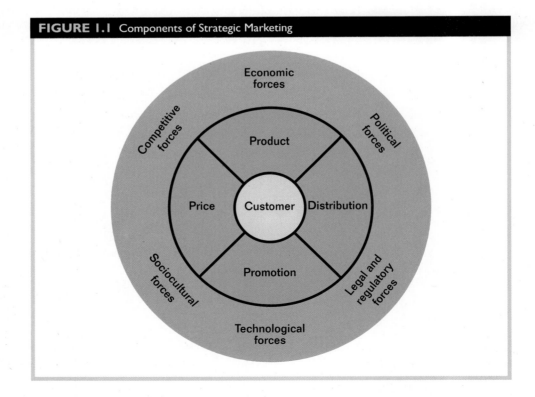

Marketing Focuses on Customers

As the purchasers of the products that organizations develop, promote, distribute, and price, **customers** are the focal point of all marketing activities (see Figure 1.1). Organizations must define their products not according to what they produce but according to how they satisfy customers. The Walt Disney Company, for example, is not in the business of establishing theme parks; it is in the business of making people happy. At Disney World, customers are the guests, the crowd is the audience, and the employees are the cast members. Customer satisfaction and enjoyment can come from anything experienced when buying and using a product.

The essence of marketing is to develop satisfying exchange relationships from which both customers and marketers benefit. The customer expects to gain a reward or benefit in excess of the costs incurred in a marketing transaction. The marketer expects to gain something of value in return—generally the price charged for the product. Through buyer–seller interactions, a customer develops expectations about the seller's future behavior. To fulfill these expectations, the marketer must deliver on promises made. Over time, this interaction results in interdependencies between the two parties. Fast-food restaurants such as Wendy's and Burger King depend on repeat purchases from satisfied customers, many of whom live or work a few miles from these restaurants, whereas customer expectations revolve around high-quality food, good value, and dependable service.

Organizations generally focus their marketing efforts on a specific group of customers, called a **target market**. Marketing managers may define a target market as a vast number of people or a relatively small group. Firefly Mobile, for example, targets its FlyPhone cellular phone at a young part of the cellular phone market: 13- to 17-year-olds who want a phone with which they can take photos, play MP3 tunes, and play games.[3] Other companies target multiple markets with different products, promotions, prices, and distribution systems for each one. Nike uses this strategy, marketing different types of shoes and apparel to meet specific needs of cross-trainers, rock climbers, basketball players, aerobics enthusiasts, and other athletic shoe buyers. Nike has even developed an athletic shoe for a single ethnicity: the Air Native N7 for Native Americans.[4]

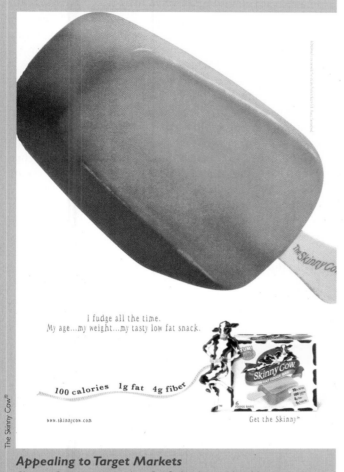

Appealing to Target Markets
Skinny Cow targets its low-fat fudge bar at health-conscious consumers.

Marketing Deals with Products, Distribution, Promotion, and Price

Marketing is more than just advertising or selling a product; it involves developing and managing a product that will satisfy customer needs. It focuses on making the product available in the right place and at a price that buyers are willing to pay. It also requires communicating information that helps customers determine if the product will satisfy their needs. These activities are planned, organized, implemented, and controlled to meet the needs of customers within the target market. Marketers refer to these elements—product, distribution, promotion, and pricing—as the **marketing mix** because they decide what type of each variable to use and in what amounts. A primary goal of a marketing manager is to create and maintain the right mix of these elements to satisfy customers' needs for a general product type. Note in Figure 1.1 that the marketing mix is built around the customer.

customers The purchasers of organizations' products; the focal point of all marketing elements

target market The group of customers on which marketing efforts are focused

marketing mix Four marketing elements—product, distribution, promotion, and pricing—that a firm can control to meet the needs of customers within its target markets

When You Are 12 to 17 Years Old, What Is a Necessity?

Cell phone	47%
TV	42%
Microwave	27%
Google	22%
Video games	22%

Source: Lemelson-MIT Invention Index Survey of 500 teens.

Marketing managers strive to develop a marketing mix that matches the needs of customers in the target market. The Nissan Cube, for example, definitely has features to attract the teens and early 20-somethings, including an upgraded Rockford Fosgate subwoofer, an interface system for iPods, smaller cup holders for energy drinks, and the option to add more than 40 accessories. Nissan also ensured that its promotion, price, and distribution were appropriate for this target market. The price point for the Cube starts at just under $14,000. Ideas for promoting this vehicle came straight from U.S. college students who competed to have their marketing strategy adopted by Nissan and are part of this vehicle's target market.[5]

Before marketers can develop a marketing mix, they must collect in-depth, up-to-date information about customer needs. Such information might include data about the age, income, ethnicity, gender, and educational level of people in the target market; their preferences for product features; their attitudes toward competitors' products; and the frequency with which they use the product. Armed with such data, marketing managers are better able to develop a marketing mix that satisfies a specific target market. Let's look more closely at the decisions and activities related to each marketing mix variable.

THE PRODUCT VARIABLE

Successful marketing efforts result in products that become a part of everyday life. Consider the satisfaction customers have had over the years from Coca-Cola, Levi's

---

Marketing in Transition
Marketing by the People, for the People

Got an idea for a clever ad or new product? Some of the best-known companies may want to hear from you. Doritos, Dell, Starbucks, and other companies are actively seeking submissions of user-generated marketing. By inviting customers to create commercials or suggest product ideas, marketers gain insights into customers' likes and dislikes. User-generated marketing also gets people talking about and involved with the company's brand, which also builds excitement and strengthens customer relationships.

Doritos has held a number of annual contests in which customers script and shoot eye-catching, humorous 30-second commercials about its snacks. After reviewing all submissions, Doritos posts the best online and puts them to a public vote. In addition to receiving cash prizes, the top vote-getters enjoy the thrill of seeing their ads air during the Super Bowl.

Dell's IdeaStorm site serves as a nerve-center for user-generated product ideas. In its first three years, IdeaStorm received 14,000 messages about creating or tweaking a computer product. Site visitors can also comment on each other's ideas, which helps Dell understand what customers think and feel about potential products and improvements.

Starbucks asks customers to share their thoughts about products, communications, and services on the MyStarbucksIdea site. Visitors click to vote "thumbs up" or "thumbs down" on ideas. Later, Starbucks will indicate, with a check mark, which user-generated ideas are actually implemented.[a]

jeans, Visa credit cards, Tylenol pain relievers, and 3M Post-it Notes. The product variable of the marketing mix deals with researching customers' needs and wants and designing a product that satisfies them. A **product** can be a good, a service, or an idea. A good is a physical entity you can touch. A Toyota Yaris, an iPod, a Duracell battery, and a puppy available for adoption at an animal shelter are examples of goods. A service is the application of human and mechanical efforts of people or objects to provide intangible benefits to customers. Air travel, dry cleaning, hair cutting, banking, insurance, medical care, and day care are examples of services. Ideas include concepts, philosophies, images, and issues. For instance, a marriage counselor, for a fee, gives spouses ideas to help improve their relationship. Other marketers of ideas include political parties, churches, and schools. Note, however, that the actual production of tangible goods is not a marketing activity.

The product variable also involves creating or modifying brand names and packaging, and it may also include decisions regarding warranty and repair services. Even one of the world's best soccer players is a global brand. David Beckham, who now plays for the Major League Soccer team the Los Angeles Galaxy, has promoted or endorsed products from Adidas, Emporio Armani, and Motorola, and his celebrity standing helps sell out soccer stadiums.[6]

Product variable decisions and related activities are important because they are directly involved in creating products that address customers' needs and wants. To maintain an assortment of products that helps an organization achieve its goals, marketers must develop new products, modify existing ones, and eliminate those that no longer satisfy enough buyers or that yield unacceptable profits.

product A good, service, or idea

Product
Welch's products are examples of tangible goods. Alamo Rental Car provides a product that is a service.

THE DISTRIBUTION VARIABLE

To satisfy customers, products must be available at the right time and through convenient distribution methods. In the video rental industry, there have been significant changes in how videos are distributed. Currently, vending machines like Redbox make up 19 percent of the video rental market, mail rental services like Netflix have 36 percent, and brick-and-mortar stores like Blockbuster own 45 percent. Fifteen years ago, almost all videos were distributed through brick-and-mortar stores.[7]

In dealing with the distribution variable, a marketing manager makes products available in the quantities desired to as many target market customers as possible, keeping total inventory, transportation, and storage costs as low as possible. A marketing manager may also select and motivate intermediaries (wholesalers and retailers), establish and maintain inventory control procedures, and develop and manage transportation and storage systems. The Internet and other technologies have also dramatically influenced the distribution variable. Companies can now make their products available throughout the world without maintaining facilities in each country.

THE PROMOTION VARIABLE

The promotion variable relates to activities used to inform individuals or groups about the organization and its products. Promotion can aim to increase public awareness of the organization and of new or existing products. The band Weezer, for example, promoted its album by featuring it on their website, by offering a discount to fans who purchased the CD on Amazon.com, and by creating a Weezer Snuggie that could only be purchased as a bundle with the CD. The band made a parody video of the famous Snuggie infomercial, featuring band members wearing the Weezer Snuggie, and uploaded the video to their website as well as to YouTube.[8]

Promotional activities can also educate customers about product features or urge people to take a particular stance on a political or social issue, such as smoking or drug abuse. Verizon has taken a stand on what the company feels is a very dangerous action: text messaging while driving. Verizon created the "Don't Text and Drive" campaign, which utilized television, radio, print, Internet, billboards, and other media vehicles. As the executive vice president and chief operating officer at Verizon Wireless said, "sending a text message isn't worth losing a life."[9]

Promotion can also help sustain interest in established products that have been available for decades, such as Arm & Hammer baking soda or Ivory soap. Many companies are using the Internet to communicate information about themselves and their products. Ragu's website, for example, offers tips, recipes, and a sweepstakes, and Southwest Airlines' website enables customers to make flight reservations.

THE PRICE VARIABLE

The price variable relates to decisions and actions associated with establishing pricing objectives and policies and determining product prices. Price is a critical component of the marketing mix because customers are concerned about the value obtained in an exchange. Apple, for example, began using variable pricing in its iTunes music store when it stopped selling all songs at 99 cents each. The company's new price structure has three tiers: 69 cents for older, less popular songs, $1.29 for popular songs or new hits, and 99 cents for all other songs.[10]

Price is often used as a competitive tool, and intense price competition sometimes leads to price wars. Airlines, for example, develop complex systems for determining the right price for each seat on a specific flight. High prices can be used competitively to establish a product's image. Waterman and Mont Blanc pens, for example, have an image of high quality and high price that has given them significant status.

The marketing mix variables are often viewed as controllable because they can be modified. However, there are limits to how much marketing managers can alter them. Economic conditions, competitive structure, or government regulations may prevent a manager from adjusting prices frequently or significantly. Making changes in the size, shape, and design of most tangible goods is expensive, so such product features cannot be altered very often. In addition, promotional campaigns and methods used to distribute products ordinarily cannot be rewritten or revamped overnight.

Marketing Builds Relationships with Customers and Other Stakeholders

Individuals and organizations engage in marketing to facilitate **exchanges**—the provision or transfer of goods, services, or ideas in return for something of value. Any product (good, service, or even idea) may be involved in a marketing exchange. We assume only that individuals and organizations expect to gain a reward in excess of the costs incurred.

For an exchange to take place, four conditions must exist. First, two or more individuals, groups, or organizations must participate, and each must possess something of value that the other party desires. Second, the exchange should provide a benefit or satisfaction to both parties in the transaction. Third, each party must have confidence in the promise of the "something of value" held by the other. If you go to a Coldplay concert, for example, you go with the expectation of a great performance. Finally, to build trust, the parties to the exchange must meet expectations.

Figure 1.2 depicts the exchange process. The arrows indicate that the parties communicate that each has something of value available to exchange. An exchange will not necessarily take place just because these conditions exist; marketing activities can occur even without an actual transaction or sale. You may see an ad for a plasma TV, for instance, but you may never buy the product. When an exchange occurs, products are traded for other products or for financial resources.

Marketing activities should attempt to create and maintain satisfying exchange relationships. To maintain an exchange relationship, buyers must be satisfied with the obtained good, service, or idea, and sellers must be satisfied with the financial reward or something else of value received. A dissatisfied customer who lacks trust in the relationship often searches for alternative organizations or products.

Marketers are concerned with building relationships not only with customers but also with relevant stakeholders. **Stakeholders** include those constituents who have a "stake," or claim, in some aspect of a company's products, operations, markets, industry, and outcomes. Stakeholders include customers, employees, investors and shareholders, suppliers, governments, communities, and many others. Stakeholders have the power to provide or withdraw needed resources or influence customer opinion about a firm's marketing strategy and products. Developing and maintaining favorable relations with stakeholders is crucial to the long-term growth of an organization and its products.

Marketing Occurs in a Dynamic Environment

Marketing activities do not take place in a vacuum. The **marketing environment**, which includes competitive, economic, political, legal and regulatory, technological, and

exchanges The provision or transfer of goods, services, or ideas in return for something of value

stakeholders Constituents who have a "stake," or claim, in some aspect of a company's products, operations, markets, industry, and outcomes

marketing environment The competitive, economic, political, legal and regulatory, technological, and sociocultural forces that surround the customer and affect the marketing mix

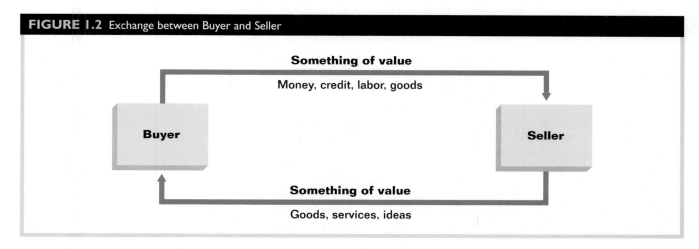

FIGURE 1.2 Exchange between Buyer and Seller

sociocultural forces, surrounds the customer and affects the marketing mix (see Figure 1.1). The effects of these forces on buyers and sellers can be dramatic and difficult to predict. We all know that advances in technology are changing the way we live our day-to-day lives, but years ago, very few people would have predicted that consumers would have no need for their daily newspaper. However, that day has come; with 24-hour up-to-the-second news online, fewer people are buying newspapers. Consumers want today's news now and are able to access it, usually for free, from computers and smartphones and other devices with Internet access.[11] Environmental forces can create threats to marketers, but they can also generate opportunities for new products and new methods of reaching customers.

The forces of the marketing environment affect a marketer's ability to facilitate exchanges in three general ways. First, they influence customers by affecting their lifestyles, standards of living, and preferences and needs for products. Because a marketing manager tries to develop and adjust the marketing mix to satisfy customers, effects of environmental forces on customers also have an indirect impact on marketing mix components. Second, marketing environment forces help determine whether and how a marketing manager can perform certain marketing activities. Finally, environmental forces may affect a marketing manager's decisions and actions by influencing buyers' reactions to the firm's marketing mix. Marketing environment forces can fluctuate quickly and dramatically, which is one reason that marketing is so interesting and challenging. Because these forces are closely interrelated, changes in one may cause changes in others. For instance, evidence linking children's consumption of soft drinks, fast foods, and other junk foods to health issues such as obesity, diabetes, and osteoporosis has exposed marketers of such products to negative publicity and generated calls for legislation regarding the sale of unhealthy foods in public schools. Some companies have responded to these concerns by reformulating products to make them healthier or even replacing unhealthy menu items with better alternatives. Denny's, for example, recently removed French toast sticks and hot dogs from its children's menus and added carrots, cucumbers, celery, and vanilla yogurt with strawberry topping. Recently, the Council of Better Business Bureaus created the Children's Food and Beverage Initiative in an effort to limit food advertising to children. Coca-Cola, Mars, and Hershey all joined the program, saying they would not advertise their products to children at all. Other companies announced that they would not advertise products that fell below a certain nutritional level.[12]

Changes in the marketing environment produce uncertainty for marketers and at times hurt marketing efforts, but they also create opportunities. Marketers who are alert to changes in environmental forces can adjust to and influence these changes and can capitalize on the opportunities such changes provide. Marketing mix elements— product, distribution, promotion, and price—are factors over which an organization has control; the forces of the environment, however, are more

Responsible Marketing?
Partnerships and Sustainability Strategies

CRITICAL THINKING

ISSUE: Should companies partner in managing their environmental and social responsibility issues, or should they maintain independence, making this a competitive marketing strategy?

What does *sustainability* mean to marketers? Is it good business and marketing strategy, good shareholder relations, or the creation of sustainable competitive advantage? Would it surprise you to learn that many of the nation's largest companies have begun to work together to address global warming and other environmental sustainability issues? Ford, Walmart, McDonald's, Time Inc., Walgreens, Dow, Anheuser-Busch, Kimberly-Clark, PG&E, BP, and Abbott all provided speakers at a Corporate Climate Response Conference to share information on their experiences with what works and what does not.

Some of the topics discussed at the conference were fundamentals of corporate climate change strategy, carbon footprint and life-cycle analysis, energy efficiency, waste management, fleet management, green power and RECs (Renewable Energy Certificate products), carbon offsetting and emissions trading, climate adaptation, and ways to engage consumers and the public in the dialogue on climate change. If you were an executive with one of these firms or a competing firm, would you feel at a competitive disadvantage sharing your personal experiences on successes and failures in this area? How would you defend involvement? If consumers want these initiatives, why would you not use sustainability as a key competitive advantage?[b]

difficult to control. But even though marketers know they cannot predict changes in the marketing environment with certainty, they must nevertheless plan for them.

Understanding the Marketing Concept

Some firms have sought success by buying land, building a factory, equipping it with people and machines, and then making a product they believe buyers want and need. However, these firms frequently fail to attract customers with what they have to offer because they defined their business as "making a product" rather than as "helping potential customers satisfy their needs and wants." For example, when compact discs became more popular than vinyl records, turntable manufacturers had an opportunity to develop new products to satisfy customers' needs for home entertainment. Companies that did not pursue this opportunity, such as Dual and Empire, are no longer in business. Such organizations failed to implement the marketing concept. Likewise, the growing popularity of MP3 technology has enabled firms such as Apple and Microsoft to develop products like the iPod and Zune to satisfy the consumer desire of being able to store customized music libraries. Instead of buying CDs, a consumer can download individual songs from Apple's iTunes.

According to the **marketing concept**, an organization should try to provide products that satisfy customers' needs through a coordinated set of activities that also allows the organization to achieve its goals. Customer satisfaction is the major focus of the marketing concept. To implement the marketing concept, an organization strives to determine what buyers want and uses this information to develop satisfying products. It focuses on customer analysis, competitor analysis, and integration of the firm's resources to provide customer value and satisfaction as well as generate long-term profits. The firm must also continue to alter, adapt, and develop products to keep pace with customers' changing desires and preferences. Ben & Jerry's Homemade Ice Cream, for example,

marketing concept A philosophy that an organization should try to provide products that satisfy customers' needs through a coordinated set of activities that also allows the organization to achieve its goals

The Marketing Concept
A part of the marketing concept involves being focused on satisfying customers.

© Stew Leonard's

continuously assesses customer demand for ice cream and sorbet. On its website, it maintains a "flavor graveyard" that lists combinations that were tried and ultimately failed. It also lists its top ten flavors each month.

Thus, the marketing concept emphasizes that marketing begins and ends with customers. Researchers have found a positive association between customer satisfaction and shareholder value,[13] and high levels of customer satisfaction also tend to attract and retain high-quality employees and managers.[14]

The marketing concept is not a second definition of *marketing*. It is a management philosophy that guides an organization's overall activities and affects all organizational activities, not just marketing. Production, finance, accounting, human resources, and marketing departments must work together.

The marketing concept is also not a philanthropic philosophy aimed at helping customers at the expense of the organization. A firm that adopts the marketing concept must satisfy not only its customers' objectives but also its own, or it will not stay in business long. The overall objectives of a business might relate to increasing profits, market share, sales, or a combination of the three. The marketing concept stresses that an organization can best achieve these objectives by being customer oriented. Thus, implementing the marketing concept should benefit the organization as well as its customers.

It is important for marketers to consider not only their current buyers' needs but also the long-term needs of society. Striving to satisfy customers' desires by sacrificing society's long-term welfare is unacceptable. For instance, there is significant demand for large SUVs and trucks. However, environmentalists and federal regulators are challenging automakers to produce more fuel-efficient vehicles with increased mpg standards. The question that remains is whether or not Americans are willing to give up their spacious SUVs for the good of the environment.[15]

Evolution of the Marketing Concept

The marketing concept may seem to be an obvious approach to running a business. However, businesspeople have not always believed that the best way to make sales and profits is to satisfy customers (see Figure 1.3).

THE PRODUCTION ORIENTATION

During the second half of the nineteenth century, the Industrial Revolution was in full swing in the United States. Electricity, rail transportation, division of labor, assembly lines, and mass production made it possible to produce goods more efficiently. With new technology and new ways to use labor, products poured into the marketplace, where demand for manufactured goods was strong.

THE SALES ORIENTATION

In the 1920s, strong demand for products subsided, and businesses realized they would have to "sell" products to buyers. From the mid-1920s to the early 1950s, businesses viewed sales as the major means of increasing profits and came to adopt a sales orientation. Businesspeople believed the most important marketing activities were personal selling, advertising, and distribution. Today, some people incorrectly equate marketing with a sales orientation.

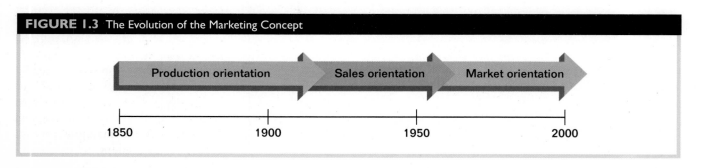

FIGURE 1.3 The Evolution of the Marketing Concept

Production orientation → Sales orientation → Market orientation

1850   1900   1950   2000

THE MARKET ORIENTATION

By the early 1950s, some businesspeople began to recognize that efficient production and extensive promotion did not guarantee that customers would buy products. These businesses, and many others since, found they must first determine what customers want and then produce these products, rather than make the products first and then try to convince customers they needed them. As more organizations realized the importance of satisfying customers' needs, U.S. businesses entered the marketing era, one of market orientation.

A **market orientation** requires the "organizationwide generation of market intelligence pertaining to current and future customer needs, dissemination of the intelligence across departments, and organizationwide responsiveness to it."[16] Market orientation is linked to new-product innovation by developing a strategic focus to explore and develop new products to serve target markets.[17] Top management, marketing managers, nonmarketing managers (those in production, finance, human resources, and so on), and customers are all important in developing and carrying out a market orientation. Trust, openness, honoring promises, respect, collaboration, and recognizing the market as the raison d'être are six values required by organizations that want to become more marketing oriented.[18] Unless marketing managers provide continuous customer-focused leadership with minimal interdepartmental conflict, achieving a market orientation will be difficult. Nonmarketing managers must share with marketing managers any information that is pertinent to understanding the customer. Finally, a market orientation involves being responsive to ever-changing customer needs and wants. For example, to accomplish this, Amazon.com follows buyers' online purchases and recommends related purchases. Trying to assess what customers want, a difficult task to begin with, is further complicated by the speed with which fashions and tastes can change. Today, businesses want to satisfy customers and build meaningful, long-term buyer–seller relationships. Doing so helps a company boost its own financial value.[19]

Implementing the Marketing Concept

A philosophy may sound reasonable and look good on paper, but that does not mean it can be put into practice easily. To implement the marketing concept, a marketing-oriented organization must accept some general conditions and recognize and deal with several problems. Consequently, the marketing concept has yet to be fully accepted by all U.S. businesses. Management must first establish an information system to discover customers' real needs and then use the information to create satisfying products. An information system is usually expensive; management must commit money and time for its development and maintenance. However, without an adequate information system, an organization cannot be marketing oriented.

To satisfy customers' objectives as well as its own, a company must also coordinate all its activities. This may require restructuring the internal operations and overall objectives of one or more departments. Walmart, for example, began using bar-code technology in its distribution centers and stores in 1984, and many other retailers and producers embraced the technology within a few years. In 2003, however, Walmart shifted to radio frequency identification (RFID) technology, investing significant resources in RFID readers throughout its system and demanding that its larger suppliers adopt the technology

market orientation An organizationwide commitment to researching and responding to customer needs

Entrepreneurial Marketing

Leatherman's Marketing Appeals to Survivalists

Timothy S. Leatherman developed the idea for the Pocket Survival Tool when his car broke down on a driving tour of Europe with his wife. Leatherman's generic pocketknife lacked the tools he needed to repair the car. He wondered, why couldn't he just add pliers to a pocketknife? After he returned home, he worked on developing a prototype. When he took it to a Portland knife business, they looked at it and said, "This isn't a knife; it's a tool." Leatherman then decided to name his invention the Pocket Survival Tool to appeal to the outdoor survivalist market. Making his products available through mail order catalogs also helped him find the right market. It wasn't too long before Tim Leatherman and his partner were selling more than 1 million units per year. Leatherman succeeded in marketing by understanding his customers' needs and finding out how to reach them.[c]

as well. After suppliers balked at RFID's cost and poor return on investment, Walmart was forced to drop the supplier initiative. If the head of the marketing unit is not a member of the organization's top-level management, a new technology may fail to sufficiently address actual customer needs and desires. Implementing the marketing concept demands the support not only of top management but also of managers and staff across all functions and levels of the organization.

Managing Customer Relationships

Achieving the full profit potential of each customer relationship should be the fundamental goal of every marketing strategy. Marketing relationships with customers are the lifeblood of all businesses. At the most basic level, profits can be obtained through relationships by (1) acquiring new customers, (2) enhancing the profitability of existing customers, and (3) extending the duration of customer relationships. Implementing the marketing concept means optimizing the exchange relationship: the relationship between a company's investment in customer relationships and the return generated by customers' loyalty and retention.[20]

Maintaining positive relationships with customers is an important goal for marketers. The term **relationship marketing** refers to "long-term, mutually beneficial arrangements in which both the buyer and seller focus on value enhancement through the creation of more satisfying exchanges."[21] Relationship marketing continually deepens the buyer's trust in the company, which, as the customer's confidence grows, in turn increases the firm's understanding of the customer's needs. Successful marketers respond to customer needs and strive to increase value to buyers over time. Eventually this interaction becomes a solid relationship that allows for cooperation and mutual dependency.

Customer-centric marketing involves developing collaborative relationships with customers based on focusing on their individual needs and concerns. It adopts the view that customers buy offerings that provide value and prefer a relationship rather than a transactional orientation. The focus is on the individual. Collaborating with and learning from customers leads to a "sense-and-respond" approach rather than a produce-and-sell approach.[22] OfficeMax, for example, is typically considered to be in a not-so-dazzling industry with a very broad definition for its target market (people and businesses that need office supplies), and so the company decided to completely reposition itself. No longer is it a dull office supply store, but instead a fun, more intimate retail outlet that appeals to women. The company has repositioned itself through its campaign called "Life is Beautiful, Work Can Be Too," stylish new private-label product lines, a spiced-up catalogue, and appearances at venues like Mercedes-Benz Fashion Week in New York. OfficeMax has made a huge effort to separate itself from other office supply stores by further defining its target market and centering all of its marketing around "her."[23]

To build long-term customer relationships, marketers are increasingly turning to marketing research and information technology. **Customer relationship management (CRM)** focuses on using information about customers to create marketing strategies that develop and sustain desirable customer relationships. Organizations attempt to increase long-term profitability by building customer loyalty, which results from increasing customer value. Barnes and Noble, for example, offers a membership program that costs $25 per year but gives the member access to members-only coupons and special offers, as well as discounts of 10 to 40 percent off items purchased. Sears likewise offers a free rewards program that allows frequent shoppers to earn rewards on purchases that can be used later.[24] Such initiatives give stores the opportunity to acquire a greater share of each customer's business.

Managing customer relationships requires identifying patterns of buying behavior and then using that information to focus on the most promising and profitable customers. Companies must be sensitive to customers' requirements and desires, and establish communication to build customers' trust and loyalty. The lifetime value of a Lexus customer may be about 50 times that of a Taco Bell customer, but there are a lot

relationship marketing Establishing long-term, mutually satisfying buyer-seller relationships

customer-centric marketing Developing collaborative relationships with customers based on focusing on their individual needs and concerns

customer relationship management (CRM) Using information about customers to create marketing strategies that develop and sustain desirable customer relationships

more Taco Bell customers! For either organization, however, a customer is important. A customer's lifetime value results from his or her frequency of purchases, average value of purchases, and brand-switching patterns.[25] A customer's value over a lifetime represents an intangible asset to a marketer that can be augmented by addressing the customer's varying needs and preferences at different stages in his or her relationship with the firm.[26] Because the loss of a loyal, potential lifetime customer can result in lower profits, managing customer relationships has become a major focus of strategic marketing today.

Through the use of Internet-based marketing strategies (e-marketing), companies can personalize customer relationships on a nearly one-on-one basis. A wide range of products, such as computers, jeans, golf clubs, cosmetics, and greeting cards, can be tailored for specific customers. CRM provides a strategic link between information technology and marketing efforts to foster relationships with customers. Thus, information technology helps organizations manage customer relationships to build value, increase sales, and enhance customer satisfaction.

Value-Driven Marketing

value A customer's subjective assessment of benefits relative to costs in determining the worth of a product

Value is an important element of managing long-term customer relationships and implementing the marketing concept. We view **value** as a customer's subjective assessment of benefits relative to costs in determining the worth of a product (customer value = customer benefits − customer costs). Consumers develop a concept of value through the integration of their perceptions of product quality and financial sacrifice.[27] From a company's perspective, there is a trade-off between increasing the value offered to a customer and maximizing the profits from a transaction.[28]

Customer benefits include anything a buyer receives in an exchange. Hotels and motels, for example, basically provide a room with a bed and a bathroom, but each firm provides a different level of service, amenities, and atmosphere to satisfy its guests. Hampton Inns offers the minimum services necessary to maintain a quality, efficient, low-priced overnight accommodation. In contrast, the Ritz-Carlton provides every imaginable service a guest might desire and strives to ensure that all service is of the highest quality. Customers judge which type of accommodation offers the best value according to the benefits they desire and their willingness and ability to pay for the costs associated with those benefits.

Customer costs include anything a buyer must give up to obtain the benefits the product provides. The most obvious cost is the monetary price of the product, but nonmonetary costs can be equally important in a customer's determination of value. Two nonmonetary costs are the time and effort customers expend to find and purchase desired products. To reduce time and effort, a company can increase product availability, thereby making it more convenient for buyers to purchase the firm's products. Another nonmonetary cost is risk, which can be reduced by offering good basic warranties or extended warranties for an additional charge. Another risk reduction strategy is the offer of a 100 percent satisfaction guarantee. This strategy is increasingly popular in today's catalog/telephone/Internet shopping environment. L.L.Bean, for example, uses such a guarantee to reduce the risk involved in ordering merchandise from its catalogs and online store.

Courtesy of Susan Van Etten

The best Maxwell House ever is less than 5¢ a cup.

Now that's something to smile about.

Today's Maxwell House is made with 100% Arabica beans for a full flavor without bitterness. It's our best coffee ever, all for a great price.

Good just got Great.

Value-Driven Marketing
This Maxwell House ad focuses on value, high quality, and a reasonable price.

The process people use to determine the value of a product is not highly scientific. We all tend to get a feel for the worth of products based on our own expectations and previous experiences. We can, for example, compare the value of tires, batteries, and computers directly with the value of competing products. We evaluate movies, sporting events, and performances by entertainers on the more subjective basis of personal preferences and emotions. For most purchases, we do not consciously try to calculate the associated benefits and costs. It becomes an instinctive feeling that Kellogg's Corn Flakes are a good value or that McDonald's is a good place to take children for a quick lunch. The purchase of an automobile or a mountain bike may have emotional components, but more conscious decision making may also figure in the process of determining value.

In developing marketing activities, it is important to recognize that customers receive benefits based on their experiences. For example, many computer buyers consider services such as fast delivery, ease of installation, technical advice, and training assistance to be important elements of the product. Customers also derive benefits from the act of shopping and selecting products. These benefits can be affected by the atmosphere or environment of a store, such as Red Lobster's nautical theme. Even the ease of navigating a website can have a tremendous impact on perceived value. For this reason, General Motors has developed a user-friendly way to navigate its website for researching and pricing vehicles. Using the Internet to compare a Chevrolet to a Mercedes could result in different customers viewing each automobile as an excellent value. Owners have rated the Chevrolet as providing reliable transportation and having dealers who provide acceptable service. A Mercedes may cost twice as much but has been rated as a better-engineered automobile that also has a higher social status than the Chevrolet. Different customers may view each car as being an exceptional value for their own personal satisfaction.

The marketing mix can be used to enhance perceptions of value. A product that demonstrates value usually has a feature or an enhancement that provides benefits. Promotional activities can also help create an image and prestige characteristics that customers consider in their assessment of a product's value. In some cases, value may simply be perceived as the lowest price. Many customers may not care about the quality of the paper towels they buy; they simply want the cheapest ones for use in cleaning up spills because they plan to throw them in the trash anyway. On the other hand, more people are looking for the fastest, most convenient way to achieve a certain goal and therefore become insensitive to pricing. Evidence of this lies in the fact that many busy customers are buying more prepared meals in supermarkets to take home and serve quickly, even though these meals cost considerably more than meals prepared from scratch. In such cases, the products with the greatest convenience may be perceived as having the greatest value. The availability or distribution of products can also enhance their value. Taco Bell, for example, wants to have its Mexican fast-food products available at any time and any place people are thinking about consuming food. It has therefore introduced Taco Bell products into supermarkets, vending machines, college campuses, and other convenient locations. Thus, the development of an effective marketing strategy requires understanding the needs and desires of customers and designing a marketing mix to satisfy them and provide the value they want.

Marketing Management

marketing management
The process of planning, organizing, implementing, and controlling marketing activities to facilitate exchanges effectively and efficiently

Marketing management is the process of planning, organizing, implementing, and controlling marketing activities to facilitate exchanges effectively and efficiently. Effectiveness and efficiency are important dimensions of this definition. *Effectiveness* is the degree to which an exchange helps achieve an organization's objectives. *Efficiency* refers to minimizing the resources an organization must spend to achieve a specific level of desired exchanges. Thus, the overall goal of marketing management is to facilitate highly desirable exchanges and to minimize the costs of doing so.

Planning is a systematic process of assessing opportunities and resources, determining marketing objectives, and developing a marketing strategy and plans for implementation and control. Planning determines when and how marketing activities are performed and who performs them. It forces marketing managers to think ahead, establish objectives, and consider future marketing activities and their impact on society. Effective planning also reduces or eliminates daily crises.

Organizing marketing activities involves developing the internal structure of the marketing unit. The structure is the key to directing marketing activities. The marketing unit can be organized by functions, products, regions, types of customers, or a combination of all four. Proper implementation of marketing plans hinges on coordination of marketing activities, motivation of marketing personnel, and effective communication within the unit. Marketing managers must motivate marketing personnel, coordinate their activities, and integrate their activities both with those in other areas of the company and with the marketing efforts of personnel in external organizations, such as advertising agencies and research firms. For example, in its recent Super Bowl marketing debut, Denny's Restaurant offered a free Grand Slam breakfast to every patron visiting a Denny's over an eight-hour period. To properly implement this campaign, executives traveled to franchisees to ensure that each restaurant had enough staff and product to handle the increased demand. In anticipation of the increased demand, Denny's executives even administered a "rain check" policy that allowed patrons to get a free Grand Slam at a later date if they were not able to place their orders by the 2:00 p.m. cut-off.[29]

An organization's communication system must allow the marketing manager to stay in contact with high-level management, with managers of other functional areas within the firm, and with personnel involved in marketing activities both inside and outside the organization.

The marketing control process consists of establishing performance standards, comparing actual performance with established standards, and reducing the difference between desired and actual performance. An effective control process has four requirements. First, it should ensure a rate of information flow that allows the marketing manager to quickly detect any differences between actual and planned levels of performance. Second, it must accurately monitor various activities and be flexible enough to accommodate changes. Third, the costs of the control process must be low relative to costs that would arise without controls. Finally, the control process should be designed so that both managers and subordinates can understand it. We examine the development, organization, implementation, and controlling of marketing strategies in greater detail in the next chapter.

The Importance of Marketing in Our Global Economy

Our definition of *marketing* and discussion of marketing activities reveal some of the obvious reasons the study of marketing is relevant in today's world. In this section, we look at how marketing affects us as individuals and at its role in our increasingly global society.

Marketing Costs Consume a Sizable Portion of Buyers' Dollars

Studying marketing will make you aware that many marketing activities are necessary to provide satisfying goods and services. Obviously these activities cost money. About one-half of a buyer's dollar goes toward marketing costs. If you spend $14 on a new CD, 50 to 60 percent goes toward marketing expenses, including promotion and distribution, as well as profit margin. The production (pressing) of the CD represents about $1, or 6.25 percent of its price. A family with a monthly income of $3,000 that allocates $600 to taxes and savings spends about $2,400 for goods and services. Of this amount, $1,200 goes for marketing activities. If marketing expenses consume that much of your dollar, you should know how this money is used.

Marketing Is Used in Nonprofit Organizations

Although the term *marketing* may bring to mind advertising for Burger King, Toyota, and Apple, marketing is also important in organizations working to achieve goals other than ordinary business objectives (such as profit). Government agencies at the federal, state, and local levels engage in marketing activities to fulfill their mission and goals. The U.S. armed forces, for instance, use promotion, including television advertisements and event sponsorships, to communicate the benefits of enlisting to potential recruits. The American Red Cross relies on marketing to inform citizens of the services the organization provides to people all over the world during times of need. After the earthquake in Haiti in January 2010, the American Red Cross reached out to the American people asking for donations and promoting its mobile text messaging donation tool. The public was encouraged to text message the word "HAITI" to 90999 to make a $10 donation to the American Red Cross Relief and Development Fund.[30]

Universities and colleges also engage in marketing activities to recruit new students as well as donations from alumni and businesses.

In the private sector, nonprofit organizations employ marketing activities to create, distribute, promote, and even price programs that benefit particular segments of society. Habitat for Humanity, for example, must promote its philosophy of low-income housing to the public. These promotions help the organization raise funds and receive donations of supplies to build or renovate housing for low-income families, who contribute "sweat equity" to the construction of their own homes. In a recent year, such activities helped nonprofit organizations raise more than $292 billion in philanthropic contributions to assist them in fulfilling their missions.[31]

Marketing Is Important to Business and the Economy

Businesses must sell products to survive and grow, and marketing activities help sell their products. Financial resources generated from sales can be used to develop innovative products. New products allow a firm to better satisfy customers' changing needs, which in turn enables the firm to generate more profits. Even nonprofit businesses need to "sell" to survive.

Marketing activities help produce the profits that are essential not only to the survival of individual businesses but also to the health and ultimate survival of the global economy. Profits drive economic growth because without them businesses find it difficult, if not impossible, to buy more raw materials, hire more employees, attract more capital, and create additional products that in turn make more profits. Without profits, marketers cannot continue to provide jobs and contribute to social causes.

Marketing Fuels Our Global Economy

Profits from marketing products contribute to the development of new products and technologies. Advances in technology, along with falling political and economic barriers and the universal desire for a higher standard of living, have made marketing across national borders commonplace while stimulating global economic growth. As a result of worldwide communications and increased international travel, many U.S. brands have achieved

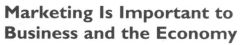

Nonprofit Organizations
The United Negro College Fund uses marketing to promote its cause.

widespread acceptance around the world. At the same time, customers in the United States have greater choices among the products they buy as foreign brands such as Toyota (Japan), Bayer (Germany), and BP (Great Britain) now sell alongside U.S. brands such as Ford, Tylenol, and Chevron. People around the world watch CNN and MTV on Toshiba and Sony televisions they purchased at Walmart. Electronic commerce via the Internet now enables businesses of all sizes to reach buyers worldwide. We explore the international markets and opportunities for global marketing in Chapter 9.

Marketing Knowledge Enhances Consumer Awareness

Besides contributing to the well-being of our economy, marketing activities improve the quality of our lives. For instance, recent research findings suggest that low-fat nutrition claims for a food product can actually increase the intake of that product, thus countering the desired effects of consuming low-fat snacks to lose weight.[32] Studying marketing allows us to assess a product's value, flaws, and marketing strategy more effectively. Thus, we can determine which marketing efforts need improvement. For example, an unsatisfactory experience with a warranty may make you wish for stricter law enforcement so sellers would fulfill their promises. You may also wish you had more accurate information about a product before you purchased it. Understanding marketing enables us to evaluate corrective measures (such as laws, regulations, and industry guidelines) that could stop unfair, damaging, or unethical marketing practices. Thus, understanding how marketing activities work can help you be a better consumer.

Sustainable Marketing
Are Athletic Shoes Walking or Running toward Sustainability?

All around the world, athletic shoe marketers are trying to go green. Making sustainability a high priority is a matter of competitive pride. It also demonstrates that these companies understand their customers' changing needs and the expectations of society.

Brooks Sports, based near Seattle, is steadily increasing the amount of biodegradable components in its running and hiking shoes. "We view increasing our sustainability as a necessity, not an option," says the chief executive officer (CEO). The company has switched to packaging made from recycled materials and recently introduced Green Silence, an eco-friendly concept running shoe. "Sustainability is part of our brand value," the CEO states. "It's important to our customers and our employees."

The German company Adidas markets a line of fashionable performance shoes created with sustainability in mind. In addition to incorporating recycled and natural fabrics as well as earth-friendly dyes, the athletic shoes are manufactured using processes that minimize their environmental impact.

Nike, the world's largest shoe company, has been pursuing sustainability goals for two decades. Its Nike Considered products require less energy to manufacture and result in less waste than conventional athletic footwear. Through the Nike Grind initiative, the company has collected 25 million used athletic shoes and ground them into material for running tracks, tennis courts, and other sports surfaces.

Despite being in the same race for sales and profits, athletic shoe marketers are interested in finding industrywide solutions to the kinds of environmental concerns that they and their competitors face. This is why Nike has become a founding partner of the GreenXchange, an online marketplace for sharing green ideas in the business world. "Our hope is [that] this will unleash new innovation to help solve current obstacles to sustainability issues," Nike's CEO explains.[d]

Marketing Connects People through Technology

Technology, especially computers and telecommunications, helps marketers understand and satisfy more customers than ever before. Over the phone and online, customers can provide feedback about their experiences with a company's products. Even products such as Dasani bottled water provide a customer service number and a website for questions or comments. This feedback helps marketers refine and improve their products to better satisfy customer needs. Today marketers must recognize the impact not only of websites but of instant messaging, blogs, online forums, online games, mailing lists, and wikis, as well as text messaging via cell phones and podcasts via MP3 players. Increasingly, these tools are facilitating marketing exchanges. Some restaurants, for example, are permitting customers to preorder their food and coffee products by sending text messages to the restaurants via their cell phones. Other companies are utilizing text messages to offer coupons, allowing for a more targeted way of offering discounts. One particular chain restaurant saw a 4 percent redemption rate with mobile coupons on Yowza, a free mobile application for smartphones. This was four times the redemption rate the chain saw with direct mail coupons.[33]

The Internet allows companies to provide tremendous amounts of information about their products to consumers and to interact with them through e-mail and websites. A consumer who is shopping for a new car, for example, can access automakers' webpages, configure an ideal vehicle, and get instant feedback on its price. They can visit Autobytel, Edmund's, and other websites to find professional reviews and obtain comparative pricing information on both new and used cars to help them find the best value. They can also visit a consumer opinion site, such as Epinions.com, to read other consumers' reviews of the products. They can then purchase a vehicle online or at a dealership. A number of companies employ social media to connect with their customers, utilizing blogs and social networking sites, such as Facebook and Twitter.

Marketers of everything from computers to travel reservations use the Internet for transactions. Southwest Airlines, for example, now books 81 percent of its passenger revenue online.[34] The Internet has also become a vital tool for marketing to other businesses. Successful companies are using technology in their marketing strategies to develop profitable relationships with these customers. Table 1.1 shows the most common online activities.

Marketing Connects People through Technology
Apple manages the development of technology to produce customer satisfaction and loyalty.

Socially Responsible Marketing: Promoting the Welfare of Customers and Society

The success of our economic system depends on marketers whose values promote trust and cooperative relationships in which customers are treated with respect. The public is increasingly insisting that social responsibility and ethical concerns be considered in planning and implementing marketing activities. Although some marketers' irresponsible or unethical

TABLE 1.1 Leading Internet Activities

Activity	Percent of U.S. Adults Who Have Engaged in Online Activity
Using e-mail	89
Using a search engine to find information	88
Searching for a map or driving directions	86
Looking for information on a hobby or interest	83
Looking for medical/health information	83
Researching products before making a purchase	81
Checking the weather	76
Making online purchases	75
Getting news	72
Getting travel information	66

Source: "Online Activities, Total" Pew Internet & American Life Project, December 2009. www.pewinternet.org/Trend-Data/Online-Activites-Total.aspx (accessed June 3, 2010).

activities end up on the front pages of *USA Today* or the *Wall Street Journal*, more firms are working to develop a responsible approach to developing long-term relationships with customers and other stakeholders. In one such instance, OfficeMax recently partnered with Adopt-A-Classroom, a nonprofit organization, to create an event to end teacher-funded classrooms called A Day Made Better. Once a year, OfficeMax makes 1,000 teachers' days better all across the United States by surprising them at school with more than $1,000 in school supplies.[35]

In the area of the natural environment, companies are increasingly embracing the notion of **green marketing**, which is a strategic process involving stakeholder assessment to create meaningful long-term relationships with customers while maintaining, supporting, and enhancing the natural environment. Coca-Cola, for example, pledged to be a zero-waste carbon neutral sponsor of the Olympic Games in Vancouver. The company planned to have all beverages delivered to the facility with diesel-electric hybrid heavy-duty vehicles, provide staff uniforms completely made from recycled bottles, and place recycling bins throughout the venue as well as carbon offsets for air and land travel. These are just a few of the initiatives the company has planned to be a more green company and reduce its impact on the environment.[36]

By addressing concerns about the impact of marketing on society, a firm can protect the interests of the general public and the natural environment. We examine these issues and many others as we develop a framework for understanding more about marketing in the remainder of this book.

Marketing Offers Many Exciting Career Prospects

From 25 to 33 percent of all civilian workers in the United States perform marketing activities. The marketing field offers a variety of interesting and challenging career opportunities throughout the world, such as personal selling, advertising, packaging, transportation, storage, marketing research, product development, wholesaling, and retailing. In addition, many individuals working for nonbusiness organizations engage in marketing activities to promote political, educational, cultural, church, civic, and charitable activities. Whether a person earns a living through marketing activities or performs them voluntarily for a nonprofit group, marketing knowledge and skills are valuable personal and professional assets.

green marketing A strategic process involving stakeholder assessment to create meaningful long-term relationships with customers while maintaining, supporting, and enhancing the natural environment

summary

1. To be able to define marketing as focused on customers

Marketing is the process of creating, distributing, promoting, and pricing goods, services, and ideas to facilitate satisfying exchange relationships with customers and develop and maintain favorable relationships with stakeholders in a dynamic environment. As the purchasers of the products that organizations develop, promote, distribute, and price, customers are the focal point of all marketing activities. The essence of marketing is to develop satisfying exchanges from which both customers and marketers benefit. Organizations generally focus their marketing efforts on a specific group of customers called a target market.

2. To identify some important marketing terms, including *target market, marketing mix, marketing exchanges,* and *marketing environment*

Marketing involves developing and managing a product that will satisfy customer needs, making the product available in the right place and at a price acceptable to customers, and communicating information that helps customers determine if the product will satisfy their needs. These activities—product, distribution, promotion, and pricing—are known as the marketing mix because marketing managers decide what type of each element to use and in what amounts. Marketing managers strive to develop a marketing mix that matches the needs of customers in the target market. Before marketers can develop a marketing mix, they must collect in-depth, up-to-date information about customer needs. The product variable of the marketing mix deals with researching customers' needs and wants and designing a product that satisfies them. A product can be a good, a service, or an idea. In dealing with the distribution variable, a marketing manager tries to make products available in the quantities desired to as many customers as possible. The promotion variable relates to activities used to inform individuals or groups about the organization and its products. The price variable involves decisions and actions associated with establishing pricing policies and determining product prices. These marketing mix variables are often viewed as controllable because they can be changed, but there are limits to how much they can be altered.

Individuals and organizations engage in marketing to facilitate exchanges—the provision or transfer of goods, services, and ideas in return for something of value. Four conditions must exist for an exchange to occur. First, two or more individuals, groups, or organizations must participate, and each must possess something of value that the other party desires. Second, the exchange should provide a benefit or satisfaction to both parties involved in the transaction. Third, each party must have confidence in the promise of the "something of value" held by the other. Finally, to build trust, the parties to the exchange must meet expectations. Marketing activities should attempt to create and maintain satisfying exchange relationships.

The marketing environment, which includes competitive, economic, political, legal and regulatory, technological, and sociocultural forces, surrounds the customer and the marketing mix. These forces can create threats to marketers, but they also generate opportunities for new products and new methods of reaching customers. These forces can fluctuate quickly and dramatically.

3. To become aware of the marketing concept and market orientation

According to the marketing concept, an organization should try to provide products that satisfy customers' needs through a coordinated set of activities that also allows the organization to achieve its goals. Customer satisfaction is the marketing concept's major objective. The philosophy of the marketing concept emerged in the United States during the 1950s after the production and sales eras. Organizations that develop activities consistent with the marketing concept become marketing-oriented organizations. To implement the marketing concept, a marketing-oriented organization must establish an information system to discover customers' needs and use the information to create satisfying products. It must also coordinate all its activities and develop marketing mixes that create value for customers in order to satisfy their needs.

4. To understand the importance of building customer relationships

Relationship marketing involves establishing long-term, mutually satisfying buyer–seller relationships. Customer-centric marketing requires developing collaborative relationships with customers based on focusing on their individual needs and concerns. Customer relationship management (CRM) focuses on using information about customers to create marketing strategies that develop and sustain desirable customer relationships. Managing customer relationships requires identifying patterns of buying behavior and using that information to focus on the most promising and profitable customers.

Value is a customer's subjective assessment of benefits relative to costs in determining the worth of a product. Benefits include anything a buyer receives in an exchange; costs include anything a buyer must give up to obtain the benefits the product provides. The marketing mix can be used to enhance perceptions of value.

5. To learn about the process of marketing management

Marketing management is the process of planning, organizing, implementing, and controlling marketing activities to facilitate effective and efficient exchanges. Planning is a systematic process of assessing opportunities and resources, determining marketing objectives, developing a marketing strategy, and preparing for implementation and control. Organizing marketing activities involves developing the marketing unit's internal structure. Proper implementation of marketing plans depends on coordinating marketing activities, motivating marketing personnel, and communicating

effectively within the unit. The marketing control process consists of establishing performance standards, comparing actual performance with established standards, and reducing the difference between desired and actual performance.

6. To recognize the role of marketing in our society

Marketing is important in our society in many ways. Marketing costs absorb about half of each buyer's dollar. Marketing activities are performed in both business and nonprofit organizations. Marketing activities help business organizations generate profits and help fuel the increasingly global economy. Knowledge of marketing enhances consumer awareness. New technology improves marketers' ability to connect with customers. Socially responsible marketing can promote the welfare of customers and society. Green marketing is a strategic process involving stakeholder assessment to create meaningful long-term relationships with customers while maintaining, supporting, and enhancing the natural environment. Finally, marketing offers many exciting career opportunities.

Go to www.cengagebrain.com for resources to help you master the content in this chapter as well as materials that will expand your marketing knowledge!

important terms

marketing, 4
customers, 5
target market, 5
marketing mix, 5
product, 7
exchanges, 9

stakeholders, 9
marketing environment, 9
marketing concept, 11
market orientation, 13
relationship marketing, 14

customer-centric marketing, 14
customer relationship management (CRM), 14
value, 15

marketing management, 16
green marketing, 21

discussion and review questions

1. What is *marketing*? How did you define the term before you read this chapter?
2. What is the focus of all marketing activities? Why?
3. What are the four variables of the marketing mix? Why are these elements known as variables?
4. What conditions must exist before a marketing exchange can occur? Describe a recent exchange in which you participated.
5. What are the forces in the marketing environment? How much control does a marketing manager have over these forces?
6. Discuss the basic elements of the marketing concept. Which businesses in your area use this philosophy? Explain why.
7. How can an organization implement the marketing concept?
8. What is customer relationship management? Why is it so important to "manage" this relationship?
9. What is *value*? How can marketers use the marketing mix to enhance customers' perception of value?
10. What types of activities are involved in the marketing management process?
11. Why is marketing important in our society? Why should you study marketing?

application questions

1. Identify several businesses in your area that have *not* adopted the marketing concept. What characteristics of these organizations indicate nonacceptance of the marketing concept?
2. Identify possible target markets for the following products:
   a. Kellogg's Corn Flakes
   b. Wilson tennis rackets
   c. Disney World
   d. Diet Pepsi
3. Discuss the variables of the marketing mix (product, price, promotion, and distribution) as they might relate to each of the following:
   a. A trucking company
   b. A men's clothing store
   c. A skating rink
   d. A campus bookstore

internet exercise

The American Marketing Association

The American Marketing Association (AMA) is the marketing discipline's primary professional organization. In addition to sponsoring academic research, publishing marketing literature, and organizing meetings of local businesspeople with student members, it helps individual members find employment in member firms. To see what the AMA has to offer you, visit the AMA website at **www.marketingpower.com**.

1. What type of information is available on the AMA website to assist students in planning their careers and finding jobs?
2. If you joined a student chapter of the AMA, what benefits would you receive?
3. What marketing mix variable does the AMA's Internet marketing efforts exemplify?

developing your marketing plan

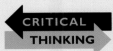
CRITICAL THINKING

Successful companies develop strategies for marketing their products. The strategic plan guides the marketer as it makes decisions about the attributes of the product, its distribution, promotional activities, and pricing. A clear understanding of the foundations of marketing is essential in formulating a strategy and in the development of a specific marketing plan. To guide you in relating the information in this chapter to the development of your marketing plan, consider the following:

I. Discuss how the marketing concept contributes to a company's long-term success.

2. Describe the level of market orientation that currently exists in your company. How will a market orientation contribute to the success of your new product?

3. What benefits will your product provide to the customer? How will these benefits play a role in determining the customer value of your product?

The information obtained from these questions should assist you in developing various aspects of your marketing plan found in the *Interactive Marketing Plan* exercise at **www. cengagebrain.com.**

VIDEO CASE 1.1

Method for Success: Marketing Beyond Green

CRITICAL THINKING

"People against dirty" is the intriguing slogan of the San Francisco–based home and body care brand Method. The founders say that they seek not only to clean our homes and bodies, but to remove harmful chemicals from our lives as well. All Method products are chemical-free and made with natural, safe ingredients. However, Method has not become one of the fastest-growing brands in the United States (sold in more than 25,000 retail outlets) by focusing only on a green philosophy. The company has attracted customers with hip, eye-catching packaging and edgy marketing communications in online and traditional media.

Method was founded in 2000 by former roommates and high school friends Adam Lowry and Eric Ryan. Lowry was a chemical engineer who worked as a climatologist for the Carnegie Institute before becoming Method's "chief greens keeper." Ryan was a marketing expert with experience designing campaigns for The Gap and others before becoming Method's

"chief brand architect." Joining forces to help wean people off of the harmful chemicals used to clean homes and bodies, Lowry and Ryan set out to develop products that were effective and natural, as well as packaged in great-looking containers.

Method's concept is not new. Companies such as Seventh Generation have been around for years, but they had difficulty breaking into the mainstream. When choosing distribution channels, Lowry and Ryan decided to steer away from co-ops and health food stores and instead sought mass recognition and distribution at Target, Amazon.com, and other large retailers. To make this channel strategy work, the founders knew that they could not charge the high prices established by other companies marketing eco-friendly cleaning products. They needed to compete head-on with the major cleaning brands.

Although they're dedicated to creating products that adhere to strict green standards, Lowry and Ryan agreed from the beginning that taking the green slant would not be the best way to sell their products. With deep-pocketed rivals such as Procter & Gamble and Clorox, the fight to get

© Terri Miller/E-Visual Communications, Inc. / © Comstock Images/Getty Images noticed on the shelf is fierce. This is why packaging has always been a major marketing emphasis for Method.

To help their products stand out, they enlisted designer Karim Rashid (who has also designed for the likes of Prada and Dirt Devil) to create visually appealing packaging. The result is affordable cleaning products in highly attractive, recyclable bottles made from recycled materials. Customers drawn to the product for its looks or the all-natural scents will be purchasing more nonpolluting green products for their home without even knowing it. In the end, Lowry and Ryan want their approach to create a change in perspective among consumers previously uninterested in going green or unable to afford to do so.

In addition, Method has been ahead of the curve in developing new kinds of cleaning products. The company became an industry leader when it created a triple-concentrated laundry detergent long before major companies began doing so. Method has also taken stock of competitive products already on the market and continually works on making its own brand's versions more eco-friendly. Cases in point are dryer sheets and the Omop.

Conventional dryer sheets are coated in beef fat in order to create soft clothing, but this was unacceptable to Lowry. Looking for a vegetarian solution, the company developed dryer sheets coated with canola oil instead. The Omop, Method's answer to the Swiffer floor cleaner, is a stylish mop using cloths created from a corn-based plastic product. Unlike Swiffer's cloths, which are synthetic, the Omop's cloths are completely biodegradable.

Now, Method's annual revenues are nearing $100 million, and the company is using multimedia advertising to turn its brand into a household name. One recent print and online campaign contrasted Method's products and packaging with those of the major brands, urging consumers to "Say no to jugs" (the large containers of detergent marketed by competitors) and "Get off the jugs and get clean." The ads communicated the benefits of measuring precise amounts of Method's concentrated detergent from the easy-to-use pump bottle. They also highlighted the eco-friendly, low carbon footprint of Method's detergent.

Product quality, innovation, value, design, convenience, availability, and competitive advantage have all helped Method grow from a small, unknown company to a profitable mainstream business. Its founders have learned that smart marketing may be the best way to help the environment in the long run. The combination of targeting a fast-growing market segment and cultivating a unique, distinct personality for their green products has allowed Lowry and Ryan to keep Method growing year after year.[37]

QUESTIONS FOR DISCUSSION

1. How has Method implemented the marketing concept?
2. Why is Method successful in a highly competitive industry?
3. Does the success of Method provide insights about the future of green marketing?

CASE 1.2

Healthy Activia Grows Healthy U.S. Sales

When Groupe Danone launched Activia yogurt, it started a new and highly successful marketing chapter in the Paris-based company's long, profitable business life. With annual revenues topping $18 billion, Danone was already a major global force in the yogurt industry, responsible for such well-known brands as Dannon and Stonyfield Farm. It also marketed bottled water under Evian and other brands. Danone's marketers were aiming to boost sales and profits when they developed Activia as the firm's leading yogurt for consumers interested in healthy eating.

In recent years, consumers have been increasingly aware of the health implications of eating properly. Studying the market, Danone's marketers found that many consumers would be willing to pay premium prices for foods with special nutritional benefits. They decided to position Activia as a yogurt that aids digestion, thanks to its patented probiotic bacteria. They also secured the right to label Activia as having live and active bacterial cultures, based on the National Yogurt Association's standards. This labeling reassures consumers of the high quality of Activia's bacterial ingredients.

Activia's health message struck a chord with consumers, and the brand became an instant sensation, ringing up more than $100 million in sales during its first year alone. Within a few years, Activia was delivering $2 billion in sales worldwide and spearheading Danone's aggressive expansion into healthy foods. Company research suggests that with the right marketing, Danone can unlock even more profit potential in the U.S. market for yogurt products.

Today, the average annual per capita consumption of yogurt in the United States is 12 pounds. In Europe, however, where consumers are accustomed to yogurt's tangy taste and its health benefits, yogurt consumption is significantly higher. For example, the average annual per capita consumption of yogurt is 35 pounds of yogurt in Germany and 40 pounds in France. If U.S. consumers start to eat more yogurt, Activia's sales are very likely to grow as the market expands. In fact, retailers have noticed higher demand for yogurt, causing them to devote more shelf space in refrigerated sections to such products and set up special displays in high-traffic areas to attract attention.

Danone is doing its part to fill that added shelf space in supermarkets and grocery stores worldwide with new Activia flavor and size variations. In the United States, Danone offers Activia yogurt with extra fiber and a wide range of Activia fruit-flavored yogurt drinks, all enriched with the brand's patented probiotics. In Brazil, Danone appeals to novelty seekers with limited edition flavors such as Activia yogurt with cashews, honey, and oats. In Europe, Danone is selling Activia in single-serving containers for on-the-go convenience. Despite challenging economic circumstances, healthy competition, and a premium price, Activia has succeeded in boosting its sales throughout the Americas and Europe.

Danone targets consumers with television, print, and online advertising messages about the Activia brand and the health benefits of its probiotics. It also targets health professionals with messages that cite scientific studies showing the effects of probiotics on digestion. By sending Activia representatives to major medical conferences, Danone gains valuable

opportunities to discuss the health benefits of probiotics with doctors to encourage them to continue the discussion with consumers.

Activia and two other yogurt brands, Actimel and Danonino, have now become indispensable ingredients in Danone's portfolio of products and its corporate recipe for continued success. Already the global market leader in fresh dairy products, the company has established 16 Danone Institutes to study nutrition and pursue health-related patents for new dairy foods. It also maintains a "biobank" with 3,500 strains of bacteria for research purposes. Moreover, Danone has stepped up its sustainability efforts by changing some of Activia's packaging to reduce waste without compromising either safety or quality.

Looking ahead, Danone's dairy unit, which includes Activia, will continue to be the company's biggest revenue generator and the driving force in its strategy of focusing on foods and beverages that enhance health and wellness. New Activia yogurt products geared to local and regional tastes are in the works, based on research into consumer preferences and purchasing patterns. Danone's marketers are also preparing new communications to explain how Activia's probiotics work and why they're important to a healthy lifestyle. What additional marketing activities are needed to push Activia to new market-share heights in the coming years?[38]

QUESTIONS FOR DISCUSSION

1. Describe the target market for Activia probiotic yogurt.
2. What forces in the marketing environment represent possible opportunities for Danone's Activia brand? What forces represent potential threats to the Activia brand?
3. How might a customer assess the value of Activia yogurt? Be as specific as possible in your answer.

Chapter 2

Planning, Implementing, and Controlling Marketing Strategies

OBJECTIVES

1. To describe the strategic planning process

2. To explain how organizational resources and opportunities affect the planning process

3. To understand the role of the mission statement in strategic planning

4. To examine corporate, business-unit, and marketing strategies

5. To understand the process of creating the marketing plan

6. To describe the marketing implementation process and the major approaches to marketing implementation

BP Utilizes Questionable Risk Management

BP has become synonymous with the worst oil leak disaster in U.S. history. The event makes it easy to forget that BP was being praised for investing millions in renewable energy before the disaster in the Gulf of Mexico. To promote a sustainable reputation, BP contributed around 4 percent of its total capital investment into renewable energy exploration.

Like many companies, BP failed to adequately prepare for the worst-case scenario. When the oil rig exploded, killing 11 workers and pouring millions of gallons of oil into the Gulf of Mexico, BP had no contingency plan prepared to address the emergency. The crisis immediately spun out of control. BP had not developed a plan to deal with a well failure or explosion.

Not only did BP's strategy underestimate the risks, but some suggest that the company willfully cut corners to save money. One of the technicians on the Deepwater Horizon oil rig accused BP of knowing that the rig's blowout preventer was leaking weeks before the explosion but did not halt production. Two months into the disaster, it was revealed that one-third of BP's deep water oil rigs were deemed risky by government inspectors, a significantly higher percentage than other oil companies.

Firms need to assess their strengths, weaknesses, opportunitie, and threats in strategic planning. BP failed to acknowledge the risks it was taking in using a less expensive well design. The disaster has undermined its reputation and its marketing strategy. Some consumers responded by boycotting BP filling stations and products. BP has a long history of environmental disasters and violations. With its past reputation of safety violations, a leak that took months to stop, billions of dollars in environmental damage, and the wrath of citizens and government, things have taken a downward spiral for BP.[1]

With competition increasing, Apple, EOS Converge, Nikon, and RCA, among many companies in the marketplace, are spending more time and resources on strategic planning—that is, on determining how to use their resources and capabilities to achieve their objectives and satisfy their customers. Often, the most innovative ideas come from the most creative and innovative entrepreneurs. The truly successful entrepreneurs also market their products effectively—a marketing plan is the key roadmap to success.

Although most of this book deals with specific marketing decisions and strategies, this particular chapter focuses on "the big picture": all the functional areas and activities—finance, production, human resources, and research and development, as well as marketing—that must be coordinated to reach organizational goals. To effectively implement the marketing concept of satisfying customers and achieving organizational goals, all organizations must engage in strategic planning.

We begin this chapter with an overview of the strategic planning process. Next, we examine how organizational resources and opportunities affect strategic planning and the role played by the organization's mission statement. After discussing the development of both corporate and business-unit strategy, we explore the nature of marketing strategy and the creation of the marketing plan. These elements provide a framework for the development and implementation of marketing strategies, as we will see throughout the remainder of this book.

Understanding the Strategic Planning Process

strategic planning The process of establishing an organizational mission and formulating goals, corporate strategy, marketing objectives, marketing strategy, and a marketing plan

Through the process of **strategic planning**, a company establishes an organizational mission and formulates goals, a corporate strategy, marketing objectives, a marketing strategy, and, finally, a marketing plan.[2] A market orientation should guide the process

---

FIGURE 2.1 Components of Strategic Planning

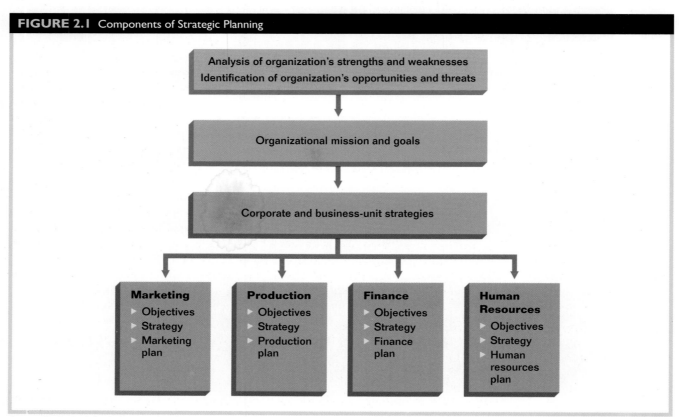

Source: Figure adapted from *Marketing Strategy*, Third Edition, by O. C. Ferrell and Michael Hartline. Reprinted with permission of South-Western, a division of Cengage Learning: www.cengage.com/permissions/.

The Marketing Strategy
Apple has a great understanding of its target markets as well as the need to develop innovative products to stay relevant to its customers.

of strategic planning to ensure that a concern for customer satisfaction is an integral part of the process and permeates the entire company. A market orientation is also important for the successful implementation of marketing strategies.[3] Figure 2.1 shows the components of strategic planning.

The process begins with a detailed analysis of the organization's strengths and weaknesses and with the identification of opportunities and threats within the marketing environment and industry. Based on this analysis, the company can establish or revise its mission and goals, and then develop corporate strategies to achieve those goals. Next, each functional area of the organization (marketing, production, finance, human resources, etc.) establishes its own objectives and develops strategies to achieve them that are in line with the company's corporate strategy. Thus, the objectives and strategies of each functional area must support the organization's overall goals and mission, and should also be coordinated with a focus on market orientation.

Because our focus is marketing, we are, of course, most interested in the development of marketing objectives and strategies. Marketing objectives should be designed so their achievement will contribute to the corporate strategy and so they can be accomplished through efficient use of the company's marketing and nonmarketing resources. To achieve its marketing objectives, an organization must develop a **marketing strategy**, which includes identifying and analyzing a target market and developing a marketing mix to meet the needs of individuals in that market or segment of particular interest.

A marketing strategy includes a plan of action for developing, distributing, promoting, and pricing products that meet the needs of the target market. Marketing strategy is best formulated when it reflects the overall direction of the organization and is coordinated with all of the company's functional areas. When properly implemented and controlled, a marketing strategy will contribute to the achievement not only of marketing objectives but also of the organization's overall goals. Consider that Apple's successful marketing strategy for its iPhone smartphone helped revitalize the computer company's reputation for excellent design, which transfers to other Apple products such as the iPad tablet.

The strategic planning process ultimately yields a marketing strategy that is the framework for a **marketing plan**, a written document that specifies the marketing activities to be performed to implement and control the organization's marketing activities. In the remainder of this chapter, we discuss the major components of the strategic planning process: organizational opportunities and resources, organizational mission and goals, corporate and business-unit strategy, marketing strategy, and the role of the marketing plan.

marketing strategy A plan of action for identifying and analyzing a target market and developing a marketing mix to meet the needs of that market

marketing plan A written document that specifies the activities to be performed to implement and control the organization's marketing activities

Assessing Organizational Resources and Opportunities

The strategic planning process begins with an analysis of the marketing environment, including a thorough analysis of the industry in which the company is operating or intends to sell its products. As we will see in Chapter 3, economic, competitive,

core competencies Things a company does extremely well, which sometimes give it an advantage over its competition

market opportunity A combination of circumstances and timing that permits an organization to take action to reach a particular target market

strategic windows Temporary periods of optimal fit between the key requirements of a market and the particular capabilities of a company competing in that market

competitive advantage The result of a company matching a core competency to opportunities it has discovered in the marketplace

political, legal and regulatory, sociocultural, and technological forces can threaten an organization and influence its overall goals; they also affect the amount and type of resources the company can acquire. However, these environmental forces can create favorable opportunities as well—opportunities that can be translated into overall organizational goals and marketing objectives. The organization's culture and the knowledge it has about the environment affect the extent to which managers perceive such opportunities as situations on which they can successfully capitalize in the marketplace.

Any strategic planning effort must assess the organization's available financial and human resources and capabilities as well as how the level of these factors is likely to change in the future, because additional resources may be needed to achieve the organization's goals and mission. Resources indirectly affect marketing and financial performance by helping to create customer satisfaction and loyalty. Resources can also include goodwill, reputation, and brand names. The reputation and well-known brand names of Rolex watches and BMW automobiles, for example, are resources that give these companies an advantage over their competitors. Such strengths also include **core competencies**, things a company does extremely well—sometimes so well that they give the company an advantage over its competition. Walmart's core competency, which is efficiency in supply chain management, has enabled the chain to build a strong reputation for low prices at high quality levels on a wide variety of goods.

Analysis of the marketing environment involves not only an assessment of resources but also identification of opportunities in the marketplace. An aspect of this environmental analysis is to understand the company's own industry or industries in which it markets its products and services. When the right combination of circumstances and timing permits an organization to take action to reach a particular target market, a **market opportunity** exists. For example, after consumers began to perceive bottled water as having a negative impact on the natural environment because of their plastic containers, Sigg USA recognized a market opportunity for its reusable aluminum water bottles. The bottles can be refilled with tap water (or any filtered water) and carried easily, making them both more environmentally friendly and economical than bottled water.[3] Such opportunities are often called **strategic windows**, temporary periods of optimal fit between the key requirements of a market and the particular capabilities of a company competing in that market.[5] When a company matches a core competency to opportunities it has discovered in the marketplace, it is said to have a **competitive advantage**. In

Competitive Advantage
Organic ingredients have become widely used to create a competitive advantage for companies like Stonyfield Farms.

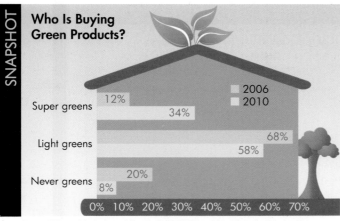

SNAPSHOT

Who Is Buying Green Products?

- Super greens: 12% (2006), 34% (2010)
- Light greens: 68% (2006), 58% (2010)
- Never greens: 20% (2006), 8% (2010)

Legend: 2006, 2010

Source: "Green Marketing—US—April 2010," Mintel, http:// academic.mintel.com. libproxy.unm.edu/sinatra/oxygen_academic/search_results/show&/display/id=482522/ displaytables/id=482522 (accessed September 13, 2010).

some cases, a company may possess manufacturing, technical, or marketing skills that it can match to market opportunities to create a competitive advantage. For instance, Tesco, a large-scale grocery chain from the United Kingdom, entered the western U.S. market with its Fresh & Easy Neighborhood Markets. The company seeks competitive advantage by offering cheap, healthy food options such as 98-cent produce packages and cheap cuts of meat. In addition to being a good value, the stores seek to source produce and meats locally as much as possible, offer organic and hormone-free foods, and use less energy than typical grocery stores.[6]

SWOT Analysis

One tool marketers use to assess an organization's strengths, weaknesses, opportunities, and threats is the **SWOT analysis**. Strengths and weaknesses are internal factors that can influence an organization's ability to satisfy its target markets. *Strengths* refer to competitive advantages or core competencies that give the company an advantage in meeting the needs of its target markets. John Deere, for example, promotes its service, experience, and reputation in the farm equipment business to emphasize the craftsmanship used in its lawn tractors and mowers for city dwellers. *Weaknesses* refer to any limitations a company faces in developing or implementing a marketing strategy. Consider that AOL, once the leading Internet service provider, watched its customer base shrivel as consumers opted for low-priced and free Internet service providers. Both strengths and weaknesses should be examined from a customer perspective because they are meaningful only when they help or hinder the company in meeting customer needs. Only those strengths that relate to satisfying customers should be considered true competitive advantages. Likewise, weaknesses that directly affect customer satisfaction should be considered competitive disadvantages. To boost profits, AOL altered its marketing model, effectively ending paid subscribership in favor of advertising-driven revenues. To achieve its goals, the Internet provider made much of its content, including e-mail, free.[7]

Opportunities and threats exist independently of the company and therefore represent issues to be considered by all organizations, even those that do not compete with the company. *Opportunities* refer to favorable conditions in the environment that could produce rewards for the organization if acted on properly. That is, opportunities are situations that exist but must be exploited for the company to benefit from them. *Threats*, on the other hand, refer to conditions or barriers that may prevent the company from reaching its objectives. For example, although Chrysler has improved the quality of its vehicles in recent years, it continues to face the threat of consumer perceptions that its vehicles are not as reliable as import brands such as Toyota and Lexus.[8] Threats must be acted upon to prevent them from limiting the organization's capabilities. To counter this particular problem, Chrysler launched an initiative to clarify the Chrysler marquee's premium identity. Along with new promotional campaigns, the company is

SWOT analysis Assessment of an organization's strengths, weaknesses, opportunities, and threats

Market Opportunity

Southwest Airlines responded to competitors charging for checked bags with an effective "Bags Fly Free" ad campaign.

FIGURE 2.2 The Four-Cell SWOT Matrix

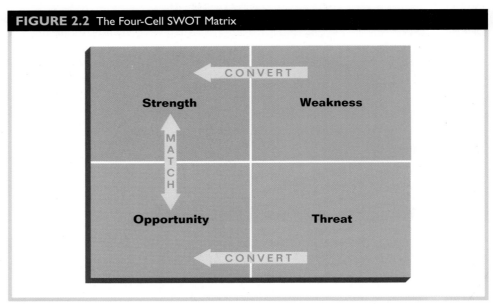

Source: Adapted from Nigel F. Piercy, *Market-Led Strategic Change*. Copyright © 1992 Butterworth-Heinemann Ltd., p. 371. Reprinted with permission.

spending more resources to identify, via feedback from dealers and customers, ways to make its cars more appealing to import buyers.[9] Opportunities and threats can stem from many sources within the environment. When a competitor's introduction of a new product threatens a company, a defensive strategy may be required. If the company can develop and launch a new product that meets or exceeds the competition's offering, it can transform the threat into an opportunity.[10]

Figure 2.2 depicts a four-cell SWOT matrix that can help managers in the planning process. When an organization matches internal strengths to external opportunities, it creates competitive advantages in meeting the needs of its customers. In addition, an organization should act to convert internal weaknesses into strengths and external threats into opportunities. Procter & Gamble, for instance, converted the weaknesses of not having competitive advantages in five areas that are essential to succeeding in consumer products—consumer understanding, brand-building, innovation, go-to-market capability, and scale—into strengths by investing billions of dollars into areas such as marketing research and supply-chain management. Indeed, the company's research and development program has become a core competency that fosters significant innovation in areas such as enzymes, perfumes, flavors, polymers, substrates, and surfactants.[11] A company that lacks adequate marketing skills can hire outside consultants to help convert a weakness into a strength.

Establishing an Organizational Mission and Goals

Once an organization has assessed its resources and opportunities, it can begin to establish goals and strategies to take advantage of those opportunities. The goals of any organization should derive from its **mission statement**, a long-term view of what the organization wants to become. Herbal tea marketer Celestial Seasonings, for example, has a stated commitment to social responsibility, truth, beauty, quality and goodness when it comes to its product.[12]

mission statement A long-term view, or vision, of what the organization wants to become

When an organization decides on its mission, it really answers two questions. Who are our customers? What is our core competency? Although these questions appear very simple, they are two of the most important questions any company must answer. Defining customers' needs and wants gives direction to what the company must do to satisfy them.

Companies try to develop and manage their *corporate identity*—their unique symbols, personalities, and philosophies—to support all corporate activities, including marketing. Managing identity requires broadcasting mission goals and values, sending a consistent image, and implementing visual identity with stakeholders. Mission statements, goals, and objectives must be properly implemented to achieve the desired corporate identity. Johnson & Johnson developed a credo and identity-based principles of responsibility to consumers, employees, the community, and shareholders worldwide. An organization's goals and objectives, derived from its mission statement, guide the remainder of its planning efforts. Goals focus on the end results the organization seeks. Johnson Controls, for example, developed a new mission—"a more comfortable, safe and sustainable world"—to highlight its goal of helping customers add value to their daily lives by using its diverse industrial products. The industrial conglomerate also revamped its corporate logo and introduced a new slogan, "Ingenuity Welcome." In addition to a new advertising campaign, the firm will add the new corporate logo to a number of the company's well-known brands, including HomeLink (garage door openers), York (air-conditioning and heating products), Optima (batteries), and Varta (auto batteries).[13]

A **marketing objective** states what is to be accomplished through marketing activities. These objectives can be stated in terms of product introduction, product improvement or innovation, sales volume, profitability, market share, pricing, distribution, advertising, or employee training activities. A marketing objective of Ritz-Carlton hotels, for example, is to have more than 90 percent of its customers indicate that they had a memorable experience at the hotel. Marketing objectives should be based on a careful study of the SWOT analysis and should relate to matching strengths to opportunities and/or eliminating weaknesses or threats. With nearly one out of four consumer airline flights delayed, making significant improvements in on-time performance—such as having 90 percent on-time arrivals—would be a good marketing objective for an airline.

Marketing objectives should possess certain characteristics. First, a marketing objective should be expressed in clear, simple terms so all marketing and nonmarketing personnel in the company understand exactly what they are trying to achieve. Second, an objective should be written so it can be measured accurately. This allows the organization to determine if and when the objective has been achieved. For instance, if an objective is to increase market share by 10 percent in the U.S. marketplace, the company should be able to measure market share changes accurately in the United States. Third, a marketing objective should specify a time frame for its accomplishment. A company that sets an objective of introducing a new product should state the time period in which to do this. Finally, a marketing objective should be consistent with both business-unit and corporate strategy. This ensures that the company's mission is carried out at all levels of the organization and by both marketing and nonmarketing personnel.

Developing Corporate, Business-Unit, and Marketing Strategies

marketing objective A statement of what is to be accomplished through marketing activities

In most organizations, strategic planning typically begins at the corporate level and proceeds downward to the business-unit and marketing levels. However, more and more, organizations are developing strategies and conducting strategic planning both

Sustainable Marketing
Zipcar: A Car Sharing Service Strategy

Going green is not only trendy, smart, and timely—it can also be part of a company's marketing strategy. Zipcar uses the popularity of emissions-reduction initiatives to promote its car sharing business. Founded in 2000 by Robin Chase and Antje Danielson, Zipcar is based on a car-sharing model that has been popular in Europe for many years. CEO Scott Griffith raised $35 million in funding and utilized strategic planning to develop and expand Zipcar services in existing markets, which are primarily major metropolitan areas and college towns across the United States, before expanding to new markets. Zipcar does have competition, mostly from nonprofit agencies focusing on the environmental aspect of car sharing. Although Griffith endorses that focus, he's also dedicated to making Zipcar profitable by incorporating BMWs, and other desirable but less eco-friendly cars, to attract a broader range of consumers. Critics do not always agree with Griffith's for-profit strategy, but he has helped the business to grow. Zipcar boasts annual revenues of more than $130 million and a growth rate of 30 percent.

To join Zipcar, users register online and receive a Zipcard, an electronic keycard, in the mail. Members reserve a car and unlock the car using their Zipcards. Cars are available at multiple off-street locations in each city, making it easy to locate a vehicle. Members may rent by the hour or by the day, and gas and insurance are included (for up to 180 daily miles). The most recent economic recession helped boost the popularity of this kind of service, to

more than 350,000 members, as people looked for ways to reduce expenses. The company claims that drivers can save $300 to $600 per month using Zipcar, rather than driving their own cars.

Zipcar is spawning imitators as well. Rental companies such as Hertz have launched car-sharing extensions. Auto makers are also exploring Zipcar's concept in an effort to find out how they can become involved. Innovation is an important part of Zipcar's strategy; it allows them to stay ahead of the curve. For example, the company is exploring a plug-in hybrid test program in San Francisco that may offer another sustainable way to travel on the roads.[a]

from the top-down and from the bottom-up. This means that companies often seek out the best expertise from multiple levels of the organization, not just from the corporate leadership, to do strategic planning. Corporate strategy is the broadest of the three levels of strategy (i.e., corporate, business unit, and marketing) and should be developed with the organization's overall mission in mind. Business-unit strategy should be consistent with the corporate strategy, and marketing strategy should be consistent with both the business-unit and corporate strategies. Figure 2.3 shows the relationships among these planning levels.

Corporate Strategy

Corporate strategy determines the means for utilizing resources in the functional areas of marketing, production, finance, research and development, and human resources to reach the organization's goals. A corporate strategy determines not only the scope of the business but also its resource deployment, competitive advantages, and overall coordination of functional areas. In particular, top management's marketing expertise and deployment of resources for addressing markets contribute to sales growth and profitability.[14] Corporate strategy addresses the two questions posed in the organization's mission statement. Who are our customers? What is our core competency? The term *corporate* in this context does not apply solely to corporations; corporate strategy is used by all organizations, from the smallest sole proprietorship to the largest multinational corporation. Corporate strategy simply refers to the top-level (i.e., highest) strategy developed within an organization.

corporate strategy A strategy that determines the means for utilizing resources in the various functional areas to reach the organization's goals

strategic business unit (SBU) A division, product line, or other profit center within the parent company

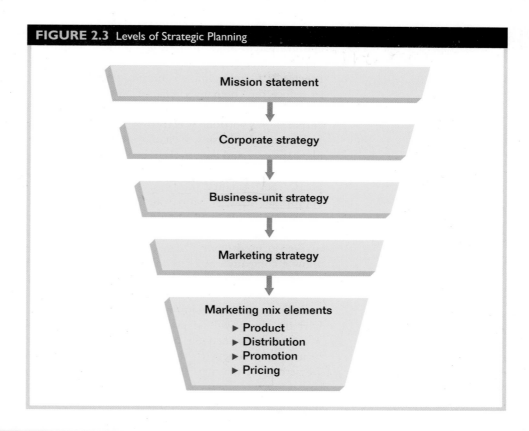

FIGURE 2.3 Levels of Strategic Planning

Mission statement

Corporate strategy

Business-unit strategy

Marketing strategy

Marketing mix elements
► Product
► Distribution
► Promotion
► Pricing

Corporate Strategy

Marriott's corporate strategy involves appealing to business travelers who want comfortable and relaxing accommodations.

Corporate strategy planners are concerned with broad issues such as corporate culture, competition, differentiation, diversification, interrelationships among business units, and environmental and social issues. They attempt to match the resources of the organization with the opportunities and threats in the environment. Google, for example, purchased YouTube for $1.65 billion after recognizing that the video-sharing website's rapid growth represented a shift in how consumers view videos.[15] Corporate strategy planners are also concerned with defining the scope and role of the company's business units so the units are coordinated to reach the ends desired. A company's corporate strategy may affect its technological competence and ability to innovate.[16]

Business-Unit Strategy

After analyzing corporate operations and performance, the next step in strategic planning is to determine future business directions and develop strategies for individual business units. A **strategic business unit (SBU)** is a division, product line, or other profit center within the parent company. Borden's strategic business units, for example, consist of dairy products, snacks, pasta, niche grocery products like ReaLemon juice and Cremora coffee creamer, and other units such as glue and paints. Each of these units sells a distinct set of products to an identifiable group of customers, and each competes with a well-defined set of competitors. The revenues, costs, investments, and strategic plans of each SBU can be separated from those of the parent company and evaluated. SBUs operate in a variety of markets, all with differing growth rates, opportunities, degrees of competition, and profit-making potential. Recognizing this, Procter & Gamble implemented business strategies in the 1990s that were intended to reduce the company's reliance on two SBUs that had accounted for 85 percent of P&G's value in the 1990s, but were declining. By the 21st century, the multinational corporation's portfolio was spread across 22 different categories to balance fast-growing, high-margin businesses, such as home and beauty products, with foundational segments like baby care and laundry.[17] (see Figure 2.4) Business strategy is fundamentally focused on the measures required to create value for the company's target markets and achieve greater performance. Marketing research suggests that this requires implementing appropriate strategic actions and targeting appropriate market segments.[18]

Strategic planners should recognize the strategic performance capabilities of each SBU and carefully allocate scarce resources among those divisions. This requires market-focused flexibility in considering changes in the environment.[19] Several tools allow a company's portfolio of strategic business units, or even individual products, to be classified and visually displayed according to the attractiveness of various markets and the business's relative market share within those markets. A **market** is a group of individuals and/or organizations that have needs for products in a product class and have the ability, willingness, and authority to purchase those products. The percentage of a market that actually buys a specific product from a particular company is referred to as that product's (or business unit's) **market share**. Apple, for example, controls 74 percent of the market for digital music players in the United States with its iPod

market A group of individuals and/or organizations that have needs for products in a product class and have the ability, willingness, and authority to purchase those products

market share The percentage of a market that actually buys a specific product from a particular company

FIGURE 2.4 Developing Strategic Business Units for Performance at Procter & Gamble

Leadership and Integrity
High integrity, experienced management, market-focused

Discipline and Value
Strategic, operational, and financial discipline to foster stakeholder value

Strengths and Innovation
Strengths needed to succeed: consumer understanding, brand building, innovation, go-to market capability, and scale

Portfolio of Strategic Business Units
Diversified portfolio of businesses reduces exposure to economic and competitive risks while maximizing growth opportunities

Source: Adapted from "Designed to Grow," 2007 Annual Report, Procter & Gamble, p. 5.

line, and SanDisk and Microsoft command 7.2 percent and 1.1 percent, respectively.[20] Product quality, order of entry into the market, and market share have been associated with SBU success.[21]

One of the most helpful tools is the **market growth/market share matrix**, the Boston Consulting Group (BCG) approach, which is based on the philosophy that a product's market growth rate and its market share are important considerations in determining its marketing strategy. All the company's SBUs and products should be integrated into a single, overall matrix and evaluated to determine appropriate strategies for individual products and overall portfolio strategies. Managers can use this model to determine and classify each product's expected future cash contributions and future cash requirements. The BCG analytical approach is more of a diagnostic tool than a guide for making strategy prescriptions.

Figure 2.5, which is based on work by the BCG, enables the strategic planner to classify a company's products into four basic types: stars, cash cows, dogs, and question marks. *Stars* are products with a dominant share of the market and good prospects for growth. However, they use more cash than they generate to finance growth, add capacity, and increase market share. An example of a star might be Sony's Wii video game system. *Cash cows* have a dominant share of the market but low prospects for growth; typically they generate more cash than is required to maintain market share. Bounty, the best-selling paper towels in the United States, represents a cash cow for Procter & Gamble. *Dogs* have a subordinate share of the market and low prospects for growth; these products are often found in established markets. Conventional cathode-ray tube televisions (CRTs) may be considered dogs at Sony, Toshiba, and Panasonic; the popularity of flat-screen plasma and LCD televisions, especially high-definition televisions, has resulted in plummeting profits and market share for CRTs, and many manufacturers are phasing them out. *Question marks,* sometimes called "problem children," have a small share of a growing market and generally require a large amount of cash to build market share. Mercedes carbon racing bikes, for example, are a question mark relative to Mercedes' automobile products.

The long-term health of an organization depends on having some products that generate cash (and provide acceptable profits) and others that use cash to support growth. Among the indicators of overall health are the size and vulnerability of the cash cows; the prospects for the stars, if any; and the number of question marks and dogs. Particular attention should be paid to those products with large cash appetites. Unless

market growth/market share matrix A helpful business tool, based on the philosophy that a product's market growth rate and its market share are important considerations in determining its marketing strategy

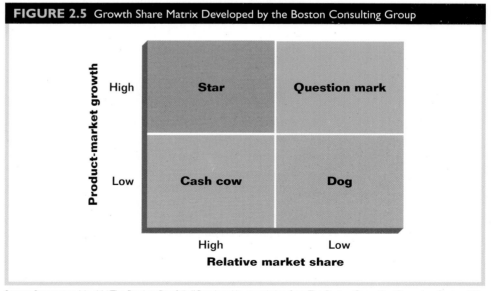

FIGURE 2.5 Growth Share Matrix Developed by the Boston Consulting Group

the company has an abundant cash flow, it cannot afford to sponsor many such products at one time. If resources, including debt capacity, are spread too thin, the company will end up with too many marginal products and will be unable to finance promising new-product entries or acquisitions in the future.

Marketing Strategy

The next phase in strategic planning is the development of sound strategies for each functional area of the organization, including marketing. Corporate strategy and marketing strategy must balance and synchronize the organization's mission and goals with stakeholder relationships. This means that marketing must deliver value and be responsible in facilitating effective relationships with all relevant stakeholders.[22] Consider that customers depend on the Coca-Cola Company to provide a standardized, reliable, satisfying soft drink or beverage any place in the world. Due to its efforts to expand distribution to every possible location, 75 percent of Coca Cola's revenue comes from sales that occur outside the United States and 25 percent within the United States.[23] The company continues to introduce new products, expand distribution, and maintain a high-quality product. Coca-Cola is also a good "corporate citizen," donating millions of dollars to education, health and human services, and disaster-plagued regions each year. An effective marketing strategy must gain the support of key stakeholders including employees, investors, and communities, as well as channel members. The complexity of marketing strategy decisions requires the identification of key stakeholders and their support or reaction to marketing activities.[24] A need exists in marketing to develop more of a stakeholder orientation to go beyond markets, competitors, and channel members to understand and address all stakeholder concerns.[25]

Within the marketing area, a strategy is typically designed around two components: the selection of a target market and the creation of a marketing mix (considered marketing's tactical variables or action elements) that will satisfy the needs of the chosen target market. A marketing strategy articulates the best use of the company's resources and tactics to achieve its marketing objectives. It should also match customers' desire for value with the organization's distinctive capabilities. Internal capabilities should be used to maximize external opportunities. The planning process should be guided by market-oriented organizational culture and procedures.[26] A comprehensive strategy involves a thorough search for information, the analysis of many potential courses of action, and the use of specific criteria for making decisions regarding strategy development and implementation.[27] When properly implemented, a sound marketing strategy enables a company to achieve its business-unit and corporate objectives. Although corporate, business-unit, and marketing strategies all overlap to some extent, the marketing strategy is the most detailed and specific of the three. Marketing strategy gets the company the closest to the customers and specifies in great detail what the company should do to satisfy the needs and wants of the customers.

TARGET MARKET SELECTION

Selecting an appropriate target market may be the most important decision a company makes in the strategic planning process. The target market must be chosen before the organization can adapt its marketing mix to meet the customers' needs and preferences. Defining the target market and developing an appropriate marketing mix are the keys to strategic success. Toyota, for example, designed its Yaris sedan to appeal to 18- to 34-year-olds by giving the compact cars a "mischievous" personality to complement their quirky styling and then promoting them where Generation Y consumers were likely to be. Toyota used Facebook, a user-generated-content website, and "mobisodes" (short mobile-phone episodes of popular television shows) to attract the attention of younger consumers. If a company selects the wrong target market, all other marketing decisions are likely to be made in vain.

Target Market Selection
The Gap Company's Piperlime targets a larger market with its more affordable handbags, whereas Dooney & Bourke produces higher-end, more expensive, luxury handbags.

Careful and accurate target market selection is crucial to productive marketing efforts. Products, and even whole companies, sometimes fail because marketers do not identify appropriate customer groups at whom to aim their efforts. Organizations that try to be all things to all people rarely satisfy the needs of any customer group very well. An organization's management therefore should designate which customer and stakeholder groups the company is trying to serve and gather adequate information about those groups. Identification and analysis of a target market provide a foundation on which the company can develop a marketing mix.

When exploring possible target markets, marketing managers try to evaluate how entering them would affect the company's sales, costs, and profits. Marketing information should be organized to facilitate a focus on the chosen target customers. Accounting and information systems, for example, can be used to track revenues and costs by customer (or group of customers). In addition, managers and employees need to be rewarded for focusing on profitable customers. Teamwork skills can be developed with organizational structures that promote a customer orientation that allows quick responses to changes in the marketing environment.[28]

Marketers should also assess whether the company has the resources to develop the right mix of product, price, promotion, and distribution (i.e., marketing mix) to meet the needs of a particular target market. In addition, they should determine if satisfying those needs is consistent with the company's overall mission and objectives. The size and number of competitors already marketing products in potential target markets are concerns as well. When Amazon.com, the number one Internet bookseller, began selling electronic products on its website, it made a strategic decision with the belief that efforts to target this larger customer market would increase profits and be consistent with the company's objective to be the largest online retailer. The company's marketing mix reflects this broad market by offering the latest products, attractive prices, effective promotions, and a website that facilitates distribution.

CREATING THE MARKETING MIX

The selection of a target market serves as the basis for creating a marketing mix to satisfy the needs of that market. The decisions made in creating a marketing mix are only as good as the organization's understanding of its target market. This understanding typically comes from careful, in-depth research into the characteristics of the target market. Thus, although demographic information is important, the organization should also analyze customer needs, preferences, and behaviors with respect to product design, pricing, distribution, and promotion. Such is the case for Kimberly-Clark; its marketing researchers found that customers who buy Kleenex tissues have varied needs, so the company introduced a variety of packages, colors, and tissue types to meet the needs of its diverse target markets. These products ranged from tissues that are anti-viral; for everyday use; with lotion; with different expressions; and ultra soft. The box shapes come in square, rectangle, oval, and even triangle.

Marketing mix decisions should have two additional characteristics: consistency and flexibility. All marketing mix decisions should be consistent with the business-unit and corporate strategies. Such consistency allows the organization to achieve its objectives on all three levels of planning. Flexibility, on the other hand, permits the organization to alter the marketing mix in response to changes in market conditions, competition, and customer needs. Marketing strategy flexibility has a positive influence on organizational performance. Market orientation and strategic flexibility complement each other to help the organization manage varying environmental conditions.[29]

The concept of the four marketing mix variables has stood the test of time, providing marketers with a rich set of questions for the four most important decisions in strategic marketing. Consider the efforts of Harley-Davidson to improve its competitive position. The company worked to improve its product by eliminating oil leaks and other problems, and set prices that customers consider fair. The company used promotional tools to build a community of Harley riders renowned for their camaraderie. Harley-Davidson also fostered strong relationships with the dealers that distribute the company's motorcycles and related products and that reinforce the company's promotional messages.[30]

At the marketing mix level, a company can detail how it will achieve a competitive advantage. To gain an advantage, the company must do something better than its competition. In other words, its products must be of higher quality, its prices must be consistent with its products' level of quality (value), its distribution methods must be efficient and cost as little as possible, and its promotion must be more effective than the competition's. It is also important that the company attempt to make these advantages sustainable. A **sustainable competitive advantage** is one that the competition cannot copy in the foreseeable future. Walmart, for example, maintains a sustainable competitive advantage in groceries over supermarkets because of its highly efficient and low-cost distribution system. This advantage allows Walmart to offer lower prices and helps it gain the largest share of the supermarket business. Maintaining a sustainable competitive advantage requires flexibility in the marketing mix when facing uncertain competitive environments.[31]

sustainable competitive advantage An advantage that the competition cannot copy

marketing planning The systematic process of assessing marketing opportunities and resources, determining marketing objectives, defining marketing strategies, and establishing guidelines for implementation and control of the marketing program

Creating the Marketing Plan

A major concern in the strategic planning process is **marketing planning**, the systematic process of assessing marketing opportunities and resources, determining marketing objectives, defining marketing strategies, and establishing guidelines for implementation and control of the marketing program. A key component of marketing planning is the development of a marketing plan. As noted earlier, a marketing plan is a written document that outlines and explains all the activities necessary to implement marketing strategies. The document is intended for both marketing and nonmarketing personnel in the company. It describes the company's current position or situation, establishes marketing objectives for the product or product group, and specifies how the organization will attempt to achieve those objectives. For example, Flexpetz's "time-share pet" marketing plan for targeting dog lovers who do not have enough time to care for a pet full time includes rental and registration fees of $120 per month, and part-time owners can book their time with "their" pet online or by telephone. Each dog has an embedded GPS chip in case it strays and brings its own leash, chew toys, bed, bowls, and dog food to the customer's home. Customers are required to attend an hour-long training session and to rent their dog at least twice a month. The company's objectives also include expansion from San Diego and Los Angeles to 50 more cities and $6 million in annual revenues.[32]

Developing a clear, well-written marketing plan, though time consuming, is important. The plan is the basis for internal communication among employees. It covers the assignment of responsibilities and tasks, as well as schedules for implementation. It presents objectives and specifies how resources are to be allocated to achieve those objectives. Finally, the marketing plan helps marketing managers monitor and evaluate the performance of a marketing strategy.

Marketing planning and implementation are inextricably linked in successful companies. The marketing plan provides a framework to stimulate thinking and provide strategic direction, whereas implementation occurs as an adaptive response to day-to-day issues, opportunities, and unanticipated situations—for example, increasing interest rates or an economic slowdown—that cannot be incorporated into marketing plans. Implementation-related adaptations directly affect an organization's market orientation, rate of growth, and strategic effectiveness.[33]

Organizations use many different formats when devising marketing plans. Plans may be written for strategic business units, product lines, individual products or brands, or specific markets. The key, however, is to make sure that the marketing plan is written in alignment with corporate and business-unit strategies and is accessible to and shared with all key employees. Marketing plans are critical parts of a company's overall strategy

Marketing in Transition
Target Changes Its Strategy to Compete with Walmart

Target enjoyed great success during the decade beginning in 2000. The company found the perfect mix of low prices, hip styling, and a fun image. Walmart, in spite of its ongoing success, has not been able to replicate the cheap-chic image attained by Target. However, during the most recent recession consumers were more concerned about simply cheap, and less so about chic. The tide turned in Walmart's favor, leaving Target to follow Walmart's lead. Thanks to the unstable economy, many consumers turned to Walmart for their shopping needs. In a change of strategy, Walmart began focusing its promotion on good values instead of cheap prices. Walmart stores have the added advantage of offering fresh grocery goods, making it a one-stop shopping location. Walmart saw sales continue to rise during the recession, while Target and other big box retailers watched them fall.

Target executives acknowledge that they have lost some ground to Walmart but insist that they have learned from the experience. Target has redesigned its marketing strategy to acknowledge the changing needs of modern consumers. Super Targets seek to imitate the one-stop shopping appeal of Walmart. The company eventually plans to offer full-service grocery sections in all stores. Starting in 2010, Target slowed its expansion efforts in order to concentrate on enhancing consumers' experiences at current locations. Walmart responded

by unveiling its own revamped stores that improve the shopping experience. Both retailers also have plans for smaller stores in urban markets. To make this succeed, Target and Walmart must consider the differing needs of urban dwellers versus suburbanites and choose their merchandise accordingly. It will take years for both chains to implement their new strategies, and until then it's anyone's guess which company will end up on top.[b]

TABLE 2.1 Components of the Marketing Plan

Plan Component	Component Summary	Highlights
Executive Summary	One- to two-page synopsis of the entire marketing plan	1. Stress key points 2. Include 1–3 key points that make the company unique
Environmental Analysis	Information about the company's current situation with respect to the marketing environment	1. Assessment of marketing environment factors 2. Assessment of target market(s) 3. Assessment of current marketing objectives and performance
SWOT Analysis	Assessment of the organization's strengths, weaknesses, opportunities, and threats	1. Strengths of the company 2. Weaknesses of the company 3. Opportunities in the environment and industry 4. Threats in the environment and industry
Marketing Objectives	Specification of the company's marketing objectives	Qualitative measures of what is to be accomplished
Marketing Strategies	Outline of how the company will achieve its objectives	1. Target market(s) 2. Marketing mix
Marketing Implementation	Outline of how the company will implement its marketing strategies	1. Marketing organization 2. Activities and responsibilities 3. Implementation timetable
Evaluation and Control	Explanation of how the company will measure and evaluate the results of the implemented plan	1. Performance standards 2. Financial controls 3. Monitoring procedures (audits)

development, and they should go beyond the interests of marketing personnel to permeate the company's culture and all functional specialists in the company. Most plans share some common ground by including many of the same components. Table 2.1 describes the major parts of a typical marketing plan.

Implementing Marketing Strategies

Marketing implementation is the process of putting marketing strategies into action. Although implementation is often neglected in favor of strategic planning, the implementation process itself can determine whether a marketing strategy succeeds. It is also important to recognize that marketing strategies almost always turn out differently than expected. In essence, all organizations have two types of strategy: intended strategy and realized strategy.[34] The **intended strategy** is the strategy the organization decides on during the planning phase and wants to use, whereas the **realized strategy** is the strategy that actually takes place. The difference between the two is often the result of how the intended strategy is implemented. When Japanese fast-food restaurants were first introduced in the United States, they were generally located in food courts. However, Japanese- and Asian-fare fast-food chains such as Yoshinoya and Hibachi-San Japanese Grill are growing at three times the rate of other fast-food restaurants in the United States. Yoshinoya is Japan's largest beef-bowl restaurant franchise and has benefited from increasing numbers of global consumers seeking filling, tasty, budget-conscious meals.[35] The realized strategy, though not necessarily any better or worse than the intended strategy, often does not live up to planners' expectations.

Approaches to Marketing Implementation

Just as organizations can achieve their goals by using different marketing strategies, they can also implement their marketing strategies by using different approaches. In this section, we discuss three general approaches to marketing implementation: customer relationship

marketing implementation The process of putting marketing strategies into action

intended strategy The strategy the organization decides on during the planning phase and wants to use

realized strategy The strategy that actually takes place

Entrepreneurial Marketing

Crocs' Strategy to Break into the Mainstream

Have you ever wondered how Crocs became such a popular trend? Three friends from Boulder, Colorado, got the idea from a Canadian company that made boating shoes. The friends purchased Foam Creations, the company that created the original clogs, and began marketing and distributing the products in the United States under the Crocs brand. The shoes are made of Crosslite™, a proprietary closed-cell resin that makes the shoes anti-microbial, lightweight, and odor-resistant while providing flexibility and support. Despite an initial lack of funding and the derision of many consumers (not everyone thinks they are fashionable), the multicolored Crocs—with their vent holes and lightweight, skid-resistant, nonmarking soles—quickly became a global phenomenon.[c]

management, internal marketing, and total quality management. Each approach represents a mindset that marketing managers may adopt when organizing and planning marketing activities. These approaches are not mutually exclusive; indeed, many companies adopt more than one when designing marketing activities.

CUSTOMER RELATIONSHIP MANAGEMENT

As we saw in Chapter 1, customer relationship management (CRM) focuses on using information about customers to create marketing strategies that develop and sustain desirable long-term customer relationships. The airline industry is a key player in CRM efforts with its frequent-flyer programs. In some sense, an argument can be made that the airline industry exemplifies the best (and, some would say, also the worst) of CRM practices. It all started in 1981 with American Airlines and the launch of their AAdvantage Program. Now most airlines have their own or even shared frequent-flyer programs. These programs track individual information about customers, using databases that can help airlines understand what different customers want and treat customers differently depending on their flying habits. Relationship-building efforts like frequent-flyer programs have been shown to increase customer value.[36]

CRM strives to build satisfying exchange relationships between buyers and sellers by gathering useful data at all customer-contact points—telephone, fax, Internet, and personal—and analyzing that data to better understand customers' needs, desires, and habits. It focuses on building and using databases and leveraging technologies to identify strategies and methods that will maximize the lifetime value of each desirable customer to the company. It is imperative that marketers educate themselves about their customers' expectations if they are to satisfy their needs; customer dissatisfaction will only lead to defection.[37]

CRM technologies help marketers to identify specific customers, establish interactive dialogues with them to learn about their needs, and combine this information with their purchase histories to customize products to meet those needs. Like many online retailers, Amazon.com stores analyze purchase data to understand each customer's interests. This information helps the retailer improve its ability to satisfy individual customers and thereby increase sales of books, music, movies, and other products to each customer. The ability to identify individual customers allows marketers to shift their focus from targeting groups of similar customers to increasing their share of an individual customer's purchases. Thus, the emphasis changes from *share of market* to *share of customer*.

Focusing on share of customer requires recognizing that all customers have different needs and that not all customers weigh the value of a company equally. CRM technologies help marketers analyze individual customers' purchases and identify the most profitable and loyal customers. The most basic application of this idea is the 80/20 rule: 80 percent of business profits come from 20 percent of customers. The goal is to assess the worth of individual customers and thus estimate their lifetime value to the company. The concept of *customer lifetime value* (CLV) may include not only an individual's propensity to engage in purchases but also his or her strong word-of-mouth communication about the company's products. Some customers—those who require considerable hand-holding or who return products frequently—may simply be too expensive to retain due to the low level of profits they generate. Companies can discourage these unprofitable customers by requiring them to pay higher fees for additional services.

CLV is a key measurement that forecasts a customer's lifetime economic contribution based on continued relationship marketing efforts. It can be calculated by taking the sum of the customer's present value contributions to profit margins over a specific time frame. For example, the lifetime value of a Lexus customer could be predicted by how many new automobiles Lexus could sell the customer over a period of years and a summation of the contribution to margins across the time period. Although this is not an exact science, knowing a customer's potential lifetime value can help marketers determine how best to allocate resources to marketing strategies to sustain that customer over a lifetime.

INTERNAL MARKETING

External customers are the individuals who patronize a business—the familiar definition of "customers"—whereas **internal customers** are the company's employees. For implementation to succeed, the needs of both groups of customers must be met. If internal customers are not satisfied, it is likely that external customers will not be satisfied either. Thus, in addition to targeting marketing activities at external customers, a company uses internal marketing to attract, motivate, and retain qualified internal customers by designing internal products (jobs) that satisfy their wants and needs. **Internal marketing** is a management philosophy that coordinates internal exchanges between the organization and its employees to achieve successful external exchanges between the organization and its customers.

Generally speaking, internal marketing refers to the managerial actions necessary to make all members of the organization understand and accept their respective roles in implementing the marketing strategy. Thus, marketing managers need to focus internally on employees as well as externally on customers. This means that all internal customers, from the president of the company down to the hourly workers on the shop floor, must understand the roles they play in carrying out their jobs and implementing the marketing strategy. At Starbucks, all employees receive training and support—including health-care benefits—that foster an organizational culture founded on product quality and environmental concern. In short, anyone invested in the company, both marketers and those who perform other functions that are a part of the company's value chain, must recognize the tenet of customer orientation and service that underlies the marketing concept. Being market-oriented as a company is not a marketing responsibility; it is a companywide activity that engages all employees (marketing and nonmarketing).

Like external marketing activities, internal marketing may involve all the elements of the marketing mix: product, price, promotion, and distribution. For instance, an organization may sponsor sales contests to inspire sales personnel to boost their selling efforts. Such efforts help employees (and ultimately the company) understand customers' needs and problems, foster communication between employees and management, teach valuable new skills, and heighten the employees' enthusiasm for their jobs. In addition, many companies use planning sessions, websites, e-mail, workshops, letters, formal reports, and personal conversations to ensure that employees comprehend the corporate mission, the organization's goals, and the marketing strategy. The ultimate results are more satisfied employees and improved customer relations.

DELIVERING ON QUALITY

Quality is a major concern in most organizations, particularly in light of intense foreign competition, more demanding customers, and poorer profit performance owing to reduced market share and higher costs. To regain a competitive edge, a number of companies have adopted a total quality management approach that follows standards established by the ISO (International Organization for Standardization).

Total quality management (TQM) is a philosophy that uniform commitment to quality in all areas of the organization will promote a culture that meets customers'

external customers
Individuals who patronize a business—the familiar definition of "customers"

internal customers The company's employees

internal marketing A management philosophy that coordinates internal exchanges between the organization and its employees to achieve successful external exchanges between the organization and its customers

total quality management (TQM) A philosophy that uniform commitment to quality in all areas of the organization will promote a culture that meets customers' perceptions of quality

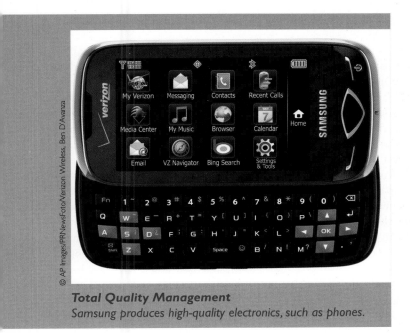

Total Quality Management
Samsung produces high-quality electronics, such as phones.

© AP Images/PRNewsFoto/Verizon Wireless, Ben D'Avanza

perceptions of quality. Indeed, research has shown that quality orientation and market orientation are complementary and together are sources of superior performance.[38] TQM involves coordinating efforts to improve customer satisfaction, increasing employee participation, forming and strengthening supplier partnerships, and facilitating an organizational culture of continuous quality improvement. It requires constant improvements in all areas of the company as well as employee empowerment.

Continuous improvement of an organization's goods and services is built around the notion that quality is free; in contrast, *not* having high-quality goods and services can be very expensive, especially in terms of dissatisfied customers.[39] A primary tool of the continuous improvement process is **benchmarking**, comparing the quality of the organization's goods, services, or processes with that of the best-performing companies in the industry.[40] Benchmarking fosters organizational "learning" by helping companies identify and enhance valuable marketing capabilities.[41] Benchmarking lets the organization assess where it stands competitively in its industry, thus giving it a goal to aim for over time. Many companies adhere to the quality standards developed by the International Organization for Standardization. ISO has developed about 18,000 quality standards across all industries since 1947.

Ultimately the success or failure of a quality program is due to the efforts of the organization's employees. Thus, employee recruitment, selection, and training are critical to the success of marketing implementation. **Empowerment** gives customer-contact employees the authority and responsibility to make marketing decisions without seeking the approval of their supervisors.[42] Although employees at any level in an organization can be empowered to make decisions, empowerment is used most often at the frontline, where employees interact daily with customers.

One characteristic of empowerment is that employees can perform their jobs the way they see fit, as long as their methods and outcomes are consistent with the organization's mission. However, empowering employees is successful only if the organization is guided by an overall corporate vision, shared goals, and a culture that supports the quality effort. For instance, Ritz-Carlton hotels give each customer-contact employee permission to take care of customer needs as he or she observes issues. A great deal of time, effort, and patience is needed to develop and sustain a quality-oriented culture in an organization.

Organizing Marketing Activities

The structure and relationships of a marketing unit, including lines of authority and responsibility that connect and coordinate individuals, strongly affect marketing activities. Companies that truly adopt the marketing concept develop a distinct organizational culture: a culture based on a shared set of beliefs that makes the customer's needs the pivotal point of the company's decisions about strategy and operations.[43] Instead of developing products in a proverbial vacuum and then trying to persuade customers to purchase those products, companies that use the marketing concept begin with an orientation toward their customers' needs and desires. Recreational Equipment Inc. (REI), for example, gives customers a chance to try out sporting goods in conditions that approximate how the products will actually be used. Customers can try out hiking boots on a simulated hiking path with a variety of trail surfaces and inclines or test climbing gear on an indoor climbing wall. In addition, REI

benchmarking Comparing the quality of the company's goods, services, or processes with that of its best-performing competitors

empowerment Giving customer-contact employees authority and responsibility to make marketing decisions without seeking approval of their supervisors

offers clinics to customers, such as "Rock Climbing Basics," "Basic Backpacking," and "REI's Outdoor School."

If the marketing concept serves as a guiding philosophy, the marketing unit will be closely coordinated with other functional areas such as production, finance, and human resources. Marketing must interact with other departments in a number of key areas. It needs to work with manufacturing in determining the volume and variety of the company's products. Those in charge of production rely on marketers for accurate sales forecasts. Research and development departments depend heavily on information gathered by marketers regarding the product features and benefits that consumers desire. Decisions made by the physical distribution department hinge on information about the urgency of delivery schedules and cost/service tradeoffs.

How effectively a company's marketing management can plan and implement marketing strategies also depends on how the marketing unit is organized. Organizing marketing activities in ways that mesh with a company's strategic marketing approach enhances performance.[44] Effective organizational planning can give the company a competitive advantage. The organizational structure of a marketing department establishes the authority relationships among marketing personnel and specifies who is responsible for making certain decisions and performing particular activities. This internal structure helps direct marketing activities.

One crucial decision regarding structural authority is centralization versus decentralization. In a **centralized organization**, top-level managers delegate little authority to lower levels. In a **decentralized organization**, decision-making authority is delegated as far down the chain of command as possible. The decision to centralize or decentralize the organization directly affects marketing. Most traditional organizations are highly centralized. In these organizations, most, if not all, marketing decisions are made at the top levels. However, as organizations become more marketing oriented, centralized decision making proves somewhat ineffective. In these organizations, decentralized authority allows the company to respond to customer needs more quickly.

No single approach to organizing a marketing unit works equally well in all businesses. The best approach or approaches depend on the number and diversity of the company's products, the characteristics and needs of the people in the target market, and many other factors. A marketing unit can be organized according to (1) functions, (2) products, (3) regions, or (4) types of customers. Companies often use some combination of these organizational approaches. Product features may dictate that the marketing unit be structured by products, whereas customer characteristics may require that it be organized by geographic region or by types of customers. By using more than one type of structure, a flexible marketing unit can develop and implement marketing plans to match customers' needs precisely.

ORGANIZING BY FUNCTIONS

Some marketing departments are organized by general marketing functions, such as marketing research, product development, distribution, sales, advertising, and customer relations. The personnel who direct these functions report directly to the top-level marketing executive. This structure is fairly common because it works well for some businesses with centralized marketing operations, such as Ford and General Motors. In more decentralized companies, such as grocery store chains, functional organization can cause serious coordination problems. However, the functional approach may suit a large, centralized company whose products and customers are neither numerous nor diverse.

ORGANIZING BY PRODUCTS

An organization that produces and markets diverse products may find the functional approach inadequate. The decisions and problems related to a single marketing function for one product may be quite different from those related to the same marketing function for another product. As a result, businesses that produce diverse products sometimes organize their marketing units according to product groups. Organizing by product

centralized organization A structure in which top-level managers delegate little authority to lower levels

decentralized organization A structure in which decision-making authority is delegated as far down the chain of command as possible

Responsible Marketing?

McDonald's: The Case for Customization of Corporate Social Responsibility Around the World

CRITICAL THINKING

ISSUE: Which stakeholders' interests should dominate in determining CSR focus: local or global interests?

When McDonald's evaluated its approach to green marketing, the company was attempting to develop a plan that would encompass more than 31,000 restaurants operating in 118 countries. What McDonald's learned in the process was that a wide variety of environmental interests existed around the world. Although McDonald's has centralized many of its strategic decisions to provide consistency, guidance, and some level of control, the decision with respect to green marketing was to decentralize the decision process as much as possible. This strategic decision would allow greater customization of the initiatives in each market and allow for greater "buy-in" among franchisees and corporate-owned restaurants.

McDonald's has moved forward with implementing this strategy on a local basis. In Japan, which has a high population density, waste and recycling are significant concerns. In Australia, water conservation is a major issue. In Pensacola, Florida, one restaurant is digging fifty-five 350-foot-deep holes to heat and cool the new location, using geothermal energy. Bob Langert, vice president of Corporate Social Responsibility, notes that restaurants in these markets are functioning as "laboratories of green experimentation." In addition, as part of its global commitment to CSR, McDonald's is working to manage and reduce energy consumption in its restaurants around the world. McDonalds's earned an "A" for the quality of its voluntary reporting on environmental and social issues from the Roberts Environmental Center at Claremont McKenna College, the only company in its sector to do so.[d]

groups gives a company the [...] to develop special marketing m[...] for different products. Procter & Gamble, like many companies in the consumer packaged goods industry, is organized by product group. Although organizing by products allows a company to remain flexible, this approach can be rather expensive unless efficient categories of products are grouped together to reduce duplication and improve coordination of product management.

ORGANIZING BY REGIONS

A large company that markets products nationally (or internationally) may organize its marketing activities by geographic regions. Managers of marketing functions for each region report to their regional marketing manager; all the regional marketing managers report directly to the executive marketing manager. Frito-Lay, for example, is organized into four regional divisions, allowing the company to get closer to its customers and respond more quickly and efficiently to regional competitors. This form of organization is especially effective for a company whose customers' characteristics and needs vary greatly from one region to another. Companies that try to penetrate the national market intensively may divide regions into subregions.

ORGANIZING BY TYPES OF CUSTOMERS

Sometimes a company's marketing unit is organized according to types of customers. This form of internal organization works well for a company that has several groups of customers whose needs and problems differ significantly. For example, Home Depot targets home builders and contractors as well as do-it-yourself customers and consumers who desire installation and service. Retailers may want more rapid delivery of small shipments and more personal selling by the producer than do either wholesalers or institutional buyers. Because the marketing decisions and activities required for these two groups of customers differ considerably, the company may find it efficient to organize its marketing unit by types of customers.

marketing control process
Establishing performance standards, evaluating actual performance by comparing it with established standards, and reducing the differences between desired and actual performance

Controlling Marketing Activities

To achieve both marketing and general organizational objectives, marketing managers must effectively control marketing efforts. The **marketing control process** consists of establishing performance standards, evaluating actual performance by comparing it with established standards, and reducing the differences between desired and actual performance by taking corrective actions.

Although the control function is a fundamental management activity, it has received little attention in marketing. Organizations have both formal and informal control systems. The formal marketing control process, as mentioned earlier, involves performance standards, evaluation of actual performance, and corrective action to remedy shortfalls (see Figure 2.6). The informal control process involves self-control, social or group control, and cultural control through acceptance of the company's value system. Which type of control system dominates depends on the environmental context of the company.[45] We now discuss these steps in the formal control process and consider the major problems they involve.

ESTABLISHING PERFORMANCE STANDARDS

Planning and controlling are closely linked because plans include statements about what is to be accomplished. For purposes of control, these statements function as performance standards. A **performance standard** is an expected level of performance against which actual performance can be compared. A performance standard might be a 20 percent reduction in customer complaints, a monthly sales quota of $150,000, or a 10 percent increase per month in new-customer accounts.

EVALUATING ACTUAL PERFORMANCE

To compare actual performance with performance standards, marketing managers must know what employees within the company are doing and have information about the activities of external organizations that provide the

Organizing by Types of Customers
Garmin organizes its marketing activities based on customer needs in such things as automotive, marine, aviation, and outdoor recreation.

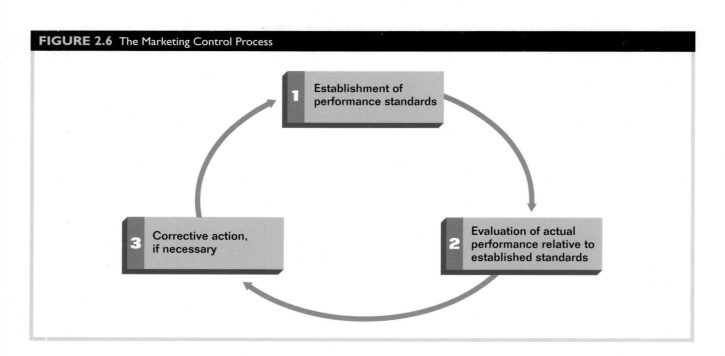

FIGURE 2.6 The Marketing Control Process

1 Establishment of performance standards

2 Evaluation of actual performance relative to established standards

3 Corrective action, if necessary

company with marketing assistance. Such is the case with Cadillac, which, like many automakers, uses many measures to evaluate its product and service levels, including how well it ranks on the J. D. Power & Associates Customer Service Index. In 2009, Cadillac ranked number three in overall quality, only behind Lexus and Porsche.[46] Records of actual performance are compared with performance standards to determine whether and how much of a discrepancy exists. For example, if GM determines that only 9.6 million vehicles were sold in 2009, a discrepancy would have existed because its goal was 9.85 million vehicles.

TAKING CORRECTIVE ACTIONS

Marketing managers have several options for reducing a discrepancy between established performance standards and actual performance. They can take steps to improve actual performance, reduce or totally change the performance standard, or do both. For example, facing intense competition and tight profit margins, HDTV makers have begun to add new features, such as LED backlighting, screen refresh (to prevent motion blur in sporting events), proprietary color-processing technology, and easier connections, to engage customers. To improve actual performance, the marketing manager may have to use better methods of motivating marketing personnel or find more effective techniques for coordinating marketing efforts.

PROBLEMS IN CONTROLLING MARKETING ACTIVITIES

In their efforts to control marketing activities, marketing managers frequently run into several problems. Often the information required to control marketing activities is unavailable or is available only at a high cost. Although marketing controls should be flexible enough to allow for environmental changes, the frequency, intensity, and unpredictability of such changes may hamper control. In addition, the time lag between marketing activities and their results limits a marketing manager's ability to measure the effectiveness of specific marketing activities. This is especially true for all advertising activities.

Because marketing and other business activities overlap, marketing managers cannot determine the precise costs of marketing activities. Without an accurate measure of marketing costs, it is difficult to know if the outcome of marketing activities is worth the expense. Finally, marketing control may be difficult because it is very hard to develop exact performance standards for marketing personnel.

performance standard An expected level of performance against which actual performance can be compared

summary

1. To describe the strategic planning process

Through the process of strategic planning, a company identifies or establishes an organizational mission and goals, corporate strategy, marketing goals and objectives, marketing strategy, and a marketing plan. To achieve its marketing objectives, an organization must develop a marketing strategy, which includes identifying a target market and developing a plan of action for developing, distributing, promoting, and pricing products that meet the needs of customers in that target market. The strategic planning process ultimately yields the framework for a marketing plan, a written document that specifies the activities to be performed for implementing and controlling an organization's marketing activities.

2. To explain how organizational resources and opportunities affect the planning process

The marketing environment, including economic, competitive, political, legal and regulatory, sociocultural, and technological forces, can affect the resources a company can acquire and use to create favorable opportunities. Resources may include core competencies, which are things that a company does extremely well, sometimes so well that it gives the company an advantage over its competition. When the right combination of circumstances and timing permits an organization to take action toward reaching a particular target market, a market opportunity exists. Strategic windows are temporary periods of optimal fit between the key requirements of a market and the particular capabilities of a company competing in that market. When a company matches a core competency to opportunities it has discovered in the marketplace, it is said to have a competitive advantage.

3. To understand the role of the mission statement in strategic planning

An organization's goals should be derived from its mission statement—a long-term view, or vision, of what the organization wants to become. A well-formulated mission statement helps give an organization a clear purpose and direction, distinguish it from competitors, provide direction for strategic planning, and foster a focus on customers. An organization's goals and objectives, which focus on the end results sought, guide the remainder of its planning efforts.

4. To examine corporate, business-unit, and marketing strategies

Corporate strategy determines the means for utilizing resources in the areas of production, finance, research and development, human resources, and marketing to reach the organization's goals. Business-unit strategy focuses on strategic business units (SBUs)—divisions, product lines, or other profit centers within the parent company used to define areas for consideration in a specific strategic market plan. The Boston Consulting Group's market growth/market share matrix integrates a company's products or SBUs into a single, overall matrix for evaluation to determine appropriate strategies for individual products and business units. Marketing strategies, the most detailed and specific of the three levels of strategy, are composed of two elements: the selection of a target market and the creation of a marketing mix that will satisfy the needs of the chosen target market. The selection of a target market serves as the basis for the creation of the marketing mix to satisfy the needs of that market. Marketing mix decisions should also be consistent with business-unit and corporate strategies and be flexible enough to respond to changes in market conditions, competition, and customer needs. Different elements of the marketing mix can be changed to accommodate different marketing strategies.

5. To understand the process of creating the marketing plan

A key component of marketing planning is the development of a marketing plan, which outlines all the activities necessary to implement marketing strategies. The plan fosters communication among employees, assigns responsibilities and schedules, specifies how resources are to be allocated to achieve objectives, and helps marketing managers monitor and evaluate the performance of a marketing strategy.

6. To describe the marketing implementation process and the major approaches to marketing implementation

Marketing implementation is the process of executing marketing strategies. Marketing strategies do not always turn out as expected. Realized marketing strategies often differ from the intended strategies because of issues related to implementation. Proper implementation requires efficient organizational structures and effective control and evaluation.

One major approach to marketing implementation is customer relationship management (CRM), which focuses on using information about customers to create marketing strategies that develop and sustain desirable long-term customer relationships. CRM employs database marketing techniques to identify different types of customers and develop specific strategies for interacting with each customer. Another approach is internal marketing, a management philosophy that coordinates internal exchanges between the organization and its employees to achieve successful external exchanges between the organization and its customers. For strategy implementation to be successful, the needs of both internal and external customers must be met.

The organization of marketing activities involves the development of an internal structure for the marketing unit. In a centralized organization, top-level managers delegate very little authority to lower levels, whereas in decentralized organizations, decision-making authority is delegated as far down the chain of command as possible. The marketing unit can be organized by functions, products, regions, or types of customers, or some combination of those elements.

The marketing control process consists of establishing performance standards, evaluating actual performance by comparing it with established standards, and reducing the discrepancy between desired and actual performance. When actual performance is compared with performance standards, marketers must determine whether a discrepancy exists and, if so, whether it requires corrective action, such as changing the performance standard or improving actual performance. Problems encountered in controlling marketing activities include lack of information, environmental changes, time lags between marketing activities and their effects, and difficulty in determining the costs of marketing activities.

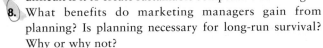

Go to www.cengagebrain.com for resources to help you master the content in this chapter as well as materials that will expand your marketing knowledge!

important terms

strategic planning, 30
marketing strategy, 31
marketing plan, 31
core competencies, 32
market opportunity, 32
strategic windows, 32
competitive
    advantage, 32
SWOT analysis, 33
mission statement, 34

marketing objective, 35
corporate strategy, 36
strategic business unit
    (SBU), 36
market, 38
market share, 38
market growth/market
    share matrix, 39
sustainable competitive
    advantage, 42
marketing planning, 42

marketing
    implementation, 44
intended strategy, 44
realized strategy, 44
external customers, 46
internal customers, 46
internal marketing, 46
total quality
    management
    (TQM), 46
benchmarking, 47

empowerment, 47
centralized
    organization, 48
decentralized
    organization, 48
marketing control
    process, 49
performance standard, 51

discussion and review questions

1. Identify the major components of strategic planning, and explain how they are interrelated.

2. What are the two major parts of a marketing strategy?

3. What are some issues to consider in analyzing a company's resources and opportunities? How do these issues affect marketing objectives and marketing strategy?

4. How important is the SWOT analysis to the marketing planning process?

5. How should organizations set marketing objectives?

6. Explain how an organization can create a competitive advantage at the corporate, business-unit, and marketing strategy levels.

7. Refer to question 6. How can an organization make its competitive advantages sustainable over time? How difficult is it to create sustainable competitive advantages?

8. What benefits do marketing managers gain from planning? Is planning necessary for long-run survival? Why or why not?

9. Why does an organization's intended strategy often differ from its realized strategy?

10. Why might an organization use multiple bases for organizing its marketing unit?

11. What are the major steps of the marketing control process?

application questions

1. Contact three companies that appear to be successful. Ask one of the company's managers if he or she would share with you the company's mission statement or organizational goals. For many companies, the mission statement and organizational goals can also be found on the company's webpage. Obtain as much information as possible about the mission statement and organizational goals. Discuss how the statement matches the criteria outlined in the text.

2. Assume you own a new, family-style restaurant that will open for business in the coming year. Formulate a long-term goal for the restaurant, and then develop short-term goals to help you achieve the long-term goal.

3. Amazon.com identified an opportunity to capitalize on a desire of many consumers to shop at home. This strategic window gave Amazon.com a very competitive position in a new market. Consider the opportunities that may be present in your city or your region. Identify a strategic window, and discuss how a company could take advantage of this opportunity. What types of core competencies are necessary?

4. Marketing units may be organized according to functions, products, regions, or types of customers. Describe how you would organize the marketing units for the following:
a. A toothpaste with whitener; a toothpaste with sensitivity protection; a toothpaste with cinnamon flavor
b. A national line offering all types of winter and summer sports clothing for men and women
c. A life insurance company that provides life, health, and disability insurance

internet exercise

Sony

Internet analysts have praised Sony's website as one of the best organized and most informative on the Internet. See why by accessing **www.sony.com**.

1. Based on the information provided on the website, describe Sony's SBUs. Does Sony have SBUs that are divisions, product lines, or some other profit center structure within the parent company Sony?

2. Based on your existing knowledge of Sony as an innovative leader in the consumer electronics industry, describe the company's primary competitive advantage (i.e., what makes Sony strategically unique?). How does Sony's website support this competitive advantage?

3. Assess the quality and effectiveness of Sony's website. Specifically, perform a preliminary SWOT analysis comparing Sony's website with other high-quality websites you have visited.

developing your marketing plan

One of the foundations of a successful marketing strategy is a thorough analysis of your company. To make the best decisions about what products to offer, which markets to target, and how to reach those targets, you must recognize your company's strengths and weaknesses. The information collected in this analysis should be referenced when making many of the decisions in your marketing plan. While writing the beginning of your plan, the information in this chapter can help you with the following issues:

1. Can you identify the core competencies of your company? Do they currently contribute to a competitive advantage? If not, what changes could your company make to establish a competitive advantage?

2. Conduct a SWOT analysis of your company to identify its strengths and weaknesses. Continue your analysis to include the business environment, discovering any opportunities that exist or threats that may impact your company.

3. Using the information from your SWOT analysis, have you identified any opportunities that are a good match with your company's core competencies? Likewise, have you discovered any weaknesses that could be converted to strengths through careful marketing planning?

The information obtained from these questions should assist you in developing various aspects of your marketing plan found in the *Interactive Marketing Plan* exercise at **www.cengagebrain.com**.

White Rock Uses Marketing Strategies to Revitalize Company

Larry Bodkin had a tough road ahead of him when he became president of White Rock Beverages. Founded in the late 1800s, White Rock's sparkling water reached its heyday in the early 20th century as the water of the upper class. However, by the end of the century, White Rock was struggling to survive. Growth had stagnated, and new strategies were needed to keep the White Rock brand alive.

White Rock used a combination of different marketing strategies to revitalize the company. For years it utilized a hybrid distribution system to sell directly to distributors in some markets and to retailers in other markets. In the process, White Rock uses customer service as a differentiator between its beverages and its competitors. White Rock customers feel like the company is responsive to their needs, with many becoming loyal to the White Rock brand.

Another way in which White Rock differentiates itself from companies like Coca-Cola and Pepsi is by its branding strategy. The company recognizes that one of its key strengths is as a premium brand for a niche market segment. White Rock targets the health-food segment by marketing itself as a unique, healthy brand. It also capitalizes on its history as one of the oldest sparkling beverage companies in America. This brand appeal has become so important that White Rock challenged Coca-Cola after Coke claimed that it created today's modern image of Santa Claus. Bodkin demanded an apology from Coca-Cola when it was revealed that White Rock had been using the modern Santa Claus ad two decades prior to Coca-Cola's Santa ads. By developing a strong, authentic brand image, White Rock is attempting to re-assert its brand into the minds of consumers.

White Rock's efforts have been successful in stimulating growth. The company grew 10 percent in 2009. However, since White Rock recognizes that its brand has matured (meaning that growth will likely be minimal), the company is adapting its strategy by introducing White Rock in new containers and sizes. For instance, it developed the White Rock Punch 'n' Fruity juice boxes, which are meant to appeal to on-the-go consumers and parents. Additionally, White Rock is breaking into the organic industry with its line of White Rock organics, made with cane sugar and natural fruit extracts.

White Rock is also pursuing an acquisition strategy of other brands. In addition to the White Rock brand, the company owns the Sioux City and Olde Brooklyn brands. Both brand names appeal to a bygone era. White Rock credits its nationally distributed Sioux City brand as one of the first brand of soft drinks to carry a Western theme. Olde Brooklyn's flavors are named after Brooklyn neighborhoods that imbue the brand with a sense of authenticity. Olde Brooklyn also lacks preservatives, which appeal more to the health food market. By using brands such as Olde Brooklyn to gain entry into health-food stores like Trader Joe's, White Rock hopes to expand its market of distribution and secure more growth for the company.[47]

QUESTIONS FOR DISCUSSION

1. What do you think White Rock's core competency is to reach a particular target market or market opportunity?
2. What do you think White Rock should do to gain competitive advantage?
3. What elements of the marketing mix could White Rock change to improve its marketing strategy?

CASE 2.2

Ford Develops a Strategy for Competitive Advantage

Ford Motor Company was founded and incorporated by Henry Ford in 1903. Headquartered in Dearborn, Michigan, Ford today comprises many global brands. Traditionally, the automaker has been one of the world's top 10 corporations by revenue, and as recently as seven years ago, it ranked as one of the world's most profitable corporations. In recent years, however, Ford and the automobile industry have not fared so well. In 2009, both General Motors and Chrysler declared bankruptcy and ended up with the U.S. government as a major shareholder. Ford avoided bankruptcy, but the company faced declining sales, with a 23.4 percent decrease in sales from 2008 to 2009.

In 2006, Bill Ford resigned as CEO (but remained chairman), and Alan Mulally, a former executive vice president of Boeing, took the reins with a new corporate strategy. Mulally has been credited with turning around Boeing's commercial airlines unit after 9/11, and many people hope that he will be able to do the same for Ford. Mulally has made reducing capacity, pricing strategy, and innovation the number one priority for Ford vehicles.

In an attempt to jump-start sales, Ford Motor Company embarked on a new strategy—"The Way Forward"—to reduce costs while maintaining a focus on customers as the foundation for everything the company does. The plan also included an emphasis on cars and car-based crossover vehicles. It required closing 16 factories and eliminating around 30,000 jobs over six years. Ford's executives believe that refocusing the company's business model on customers will lead to stronger brands and products that are targeted more precisely for specific market segments. For example, Ford aimed its new Fusion auto at women using a unique promotional campaign, the Fusion Studio. The Fusion Studio is a "pop-up store" that traveled to 10 malls across the United States where women could interact with the Fusion while they were being treated to beauty services, fitness training, and music. They were also given an opportunity to test-drive the car. Although Ford's overall sales decreased from 2008 to 2009, the Fusion model increased in sales from 2008 to 2009.

Ford is also implementing a global strategy, the first of its kind for the company. The company recently introduced the Ford Fiesta as a global car. Previously, Ford changed the names and the designs of its models to suit different countries, but now the company is introducing a car that it hopes will become popular throughout the world. According to CEO Mullaly, the Ford Fiesta is meant to become "a world standard for car quality, design and comfort." The Ford Fiesta is one step in Ford's strategic plan to use its global development process to create car models that will be accepted throughout the world. Ford has also shifted its focus on the growing Asian market rather than the luxury market in Europe as it has done historically. Most recently, Ford sold its Volvo Cars subsidiary to Zehjiang Geely of China in a strategic move to offer smaller, fuel-efficient cars to the Chinese and Indian markets, Asia's two largest growing economies. Ford is continually increasing its manufacturing capacities as dealers in the Chinese and Indian markets are challenged to keep pace with the rapid demand from consumers. For instance, the Ford Figo, a four-door subcompact hatchback sold in India, costs $7,700, and 10,000 orders were received in the first month of its launch. In one year, this tripled Ford's sales in India.

Furthermore, in the auto industry, hybrid sales were down by 14 percent but Ford's hybrid models sales were up by 73 percent from 2008 to 2009. In Ford's ongoing effort to focus on the customer through innovative product design, electric vehicles are part of its strategy. Nancy Gioia, Ford's Director of Sustainable Mobility, stated at Ford's Drive Green Media Forum in 2009, "Electrification is not an option, it is the way forward."

Another part of "The Way Forward" plan is a return to clear, simple pricing—bringing its sticker prices more in line with actual transaction prices to reduce the number of rebates as it introduces new cars and trucks into the marketplace. Ford made it though the worst recession in 80 years because it has a good strategy. In the future the way forward will require a creative and dynamic focus on leadership that promotes quality, innovation, and consumers.

So far, it appears that Ford has been successful in its "The Way Forward" strategy. By focusing on the global market with stronger brands, new models, and high-quality, fuel-efficient vehicles such as the Fiesta and the Fusion, Ford's future looks bright. By scaling back in the luxury market, particularly in

Europe, and by selling its Volvo cars subsidiary, Ford is implementing its new strategy to focus on the largest markets in the global economy. Ford has gained status in the United States as the only major auto manufacturer not to have gone into bankruptcy or receive a financial bailout during the last recession. As Ford was gaining on competitors in 2010, it also benefited from a series of recalls from the Toyota Motor Corporation. Toyota was fined $16.4 million for allegedly hiding safety defects from consumers. A number of recalls followed over the next few months, resulting in Ford becoming number one in auto sales in the United States during this period. In this case, environmental developments and a loss in consumer confidence in Toyota resulted in even more success for "The Way

Forward" strategy. Ford had positioned itself to be able to take advantage of opportunities by building a solid strategic foundation.[48]

QUESTIONS FOR DISCUSSION

1. How did Ford's "The Way Forward" strategy help to save the company during the 2008 recession?
2. How has Ford linked its domestic strategy with its global strategy to create success?
3. Evaluate Ford's strategy to focus on global markets with stronger brands and scale back or exit the luxury car market.

Monsanto: Linking Core Competencies to Market Opportunity

The Monsanto Co. is the world's largest seed company, with annual sales of $11.7 billion. It specializes in biotechnology, or the genetic manipulation of organisms. Monsanto scientists have spent the last few decades modifying crops, often by inserting new genes or adapting existing genes within plant seeds, to better meet certain aims like higher crop yields or insect resistance. Monsanto's genetically modified (GM) seeds have increased the quantity and availability of crops, helping farmers worldwide increase food production and revenues.

History: From Chemicals to Food

Monsanto was started by John F. Queeny in 1901 in St. Louis. The company started off by selling food additives, food extracts, and artificial sweeteners to companies like Coca-Cola. However, at the start of World War I company leaders realized the growth opportunities in the industrial chemicals industry. The company began specializing in plastics, agricultural chemicals, and synthetic rubbers.

During the 1970s, Monsanto marketed its first Roundup herbicide, a product that would propel the company even more into the public's consciousness. However, a few years later, Monsanto hit a legal snare regarding a chemical it had produced called Agent Orange. Used during the Vietnam War to deforest jungles, Agent Orange contained the carcinogenic chemical dioxin. In 1979, a lawsuit was filed against Monsanto by hundreds of veterans claiming they were harmed by the chemical. Monsanto and other manufacturers agreed to settle for $180 million.

In 1981, Monsanto leaders determined that biotechnology would be the company's new strategic focus, a dynamic change for the company. The quest for biotechnology was on. Soon the company was selling soybean, cotton, and canola seeds that could tolerate Monsanto's Roundup Ready herbicide. Roundup Ready seeds allowed farmers to use the herbicide to eliminate weeds while sparing the crop.

When CEO Hugh Grant took over in 2003, the price of Monsanto's stock had fallen by almost 50 percent. The company had lost $1.7 billion the previous year. By assessing organizational resources and opportunities, a new corporate strategy was developed for the company's core competencies. Under Grant's leadership and through a strategic focus on GM seeds, the company has recovered and is now prospering. Today, Monsanto is a global leader in the seed industry and employs nearly 20,000 people in 160 countries.

The Seeds of Change: A Strategic Emphasis on Biotechnology

While the original Monsanto made a name for itself through the manufacturing of chemicals, the new Monsanto switched its emphasis from chemicals to food. Today's Monsanto owes its $11.7 billion in sales to biotechnology, specifically to sales of genetically modified plant seeds and from licensing them to other companies. These seeds have revolutionized the general and task environments of Monsanto.

Monsanto prides itself on its quest for technological innovations in biotechnology. Its first major success in this field was its herbicide. Throughout history, weeds and insects have been the bane of the farmer's existence. Herbicides and pesticides were invented to ward off pests, but applying these chemicals to crops was costly and time-consuming. Then Monsanto scientists, through biotechnology, were able to create seeds containing the herbicide Roundup Ready, which kills weeds but spares crops. They also implanted seeds with genes that allow the plants themselves to kill bugs.

Monsanto continues to expend great effort in technological innovation. It spends about $1 billion on research and development per year and uses its technology to gain the support of stakeholders. For example, Monsanto has a laboratory in St. Louis that gives tours to farmers. One of the technologies that farmers are shown is a technology known as the corn chipper, a machine that picks up seeds and takes genetic material from them. That

material is then analyzed to see how well the seed will do if planted. The "best" seeds are the ones Monsanto sells for planting. Impressing farmers with its technology and the promise of better yields is one way that Monsanto attracts potential customers.

Monsanto also transplants genetic material into seeds to make them better able to withstand natural conditions. In Monsanto's latest projects, it is working on such innovative products as an omega-3 soybean (omega-3 is a nutritional fatty acid commonly found in fish) and drought-tolerant technology. If successful, this latter technology will be helpful in dry areas like Africa.

Monsanto has developed sound strategies for each functional area of its organization, including marketing. The company has synchronized its corporate strategy and marketing strategy with the organization's mission and goals. For marketing strategies all elements of the marketing mix have been developed based on the respective target market. The company serves both business and consumer markets. This requires careful analysis to provide products at the right price and through the right marketing channel. For example, some products such as Roundup are sold in retail stores such as Home Depot and Lowes. Other products are sold directly to large agricultural corporations and even governments.

Stakeholder Perspectives and Monsanto's Environment

Critics believe that influencing the gene pool of plants could result in negative health consequences. CEO Hugh Grant decided to curtail criticism by focusing biotechnology on products that would be used to produce goods like animal feed and corn syrup. Today, the company invests largely in four crops: corn, cotton, soybeans, and canola.

Monsanto owes about 60 percent of its revenue to its work in GM seeds, and more than half of U.S. crops are genetically modified. Approximately 282 million acres worldwide are devoted to biotech crops, with the fastest growth in developing countries. On a global dimension, Monsanto sells more GM cotton to India than in the United States.

Farmers who purchase GM seeds (primary stakeholders) can now grow more crops on less land and with less left to chance. For example, in 1970 the average corn harvest yielded about 70 bushels an acre. With the introduction of biotech crops, the average corn harvest has increased to roughly 150 bushels an acre. Monsanto predicts even higher yields in the future, possibly up to 300 bushels an acre by 2030.

According to company statistics, the cotton yield of Indian farmers rose by 50 percent, doubling their income in one year. Monsanto also claims that its insect-protected corn has raised the income level in the Philippines to above poverty level. However, critics argue that these numbers are inflated; they say the cost of GM seeds is dramatically higher than that of traditional seeds, and therefore they actually reduce farmers' take-home profits.

Monsanto's GM seeds have not been accepted everywhere. Attempts to introduce them into Europe have met with consumer backlash. It appears that every time Monsanto tries to test GM seeds in Britain, for instance, protestors destroy the experiments. Greenpeace, a secondary stakeholder, has fought Monsanto for years, especially in the company's efforts to promote GM crops in developing countries. This animosity toward Monsanto's products is generated by two main concerns: worries about the safety of GM food and concerns about environmental effects.

Of great concern for many stakeholders are the moral and safety implications of GM food. Many skeptics see biotech crops as unnatural, with Monsanto controlling what goes into seeds. Also, because GM crops are relatively new, critics maintain that the health implications of biotech food may not be known for years. Some geneticists believe the splicing of genes into seeds could create small changes that might negatively impact the health of the humans and animals that eat them.

Social Responsibility at Monsanto

It is a common expectation today for companies to take actions to advance the well-being of the people in the countries in which they do business. No less is expected of Monsanto. The company has given millions of dollars to programs to help improve the communities in developing countries. Corporate Responsibility Magazine ranked Monsanto number 20 on its 100 Best Corporate Citizens list of 2009.

As an agricultural company, Monsanto must address the grim reality facing the world: The population is increasing at a fast rate, and available land and water for agriculture is decreasing. Some feel the planet will have to produce more food in the next 50 years to feed the world's population than it has grown in the past 10,000 years.

To address these problems, Monsanto has developed a three-tiered commitment policy: (1) produce more crop yields, (2) conserve more resources, and (3) improve farmers' lives. It hopes to meet these goals with sustainable agriculture initiatives.

STRATEGIC CASE 1

Monsanto still has many challenges to face that go beyond legal or technological factors. These challenges involve the problem of feeding a growing population. Monsanto points out that its biotech products added more than 100 million tons to worldwide agriculture production between 1996 and 2006. It has also created partnerships to enrich the lives of farmers in developing countries, including India and Africa.

Biotech crops have helped to improve the size of yields in India, and Monsanto estimates that Indian cotton farmers using biotech crops earn about $176 more in revenues per acre than their non-biotech contemporaries. In 2009, Monsanto stated that it would launch Project SHARE, a sustainable yield initiative done in conjunction with a nonprofit organization to improve the lives of 10,000 cotton farmers in 1,100 villages.

In Africa, Monsanto has helped farmers survive through difficult periods. For instance, Monsanto has participated in Project Malawi, a program to improve food security and health care to thousands of Malawians. Monsanto has provided the program with hybrid maize seed and has sent experts from the company to provide training for farmers in how to use the seed. Monsanto has also agreed to donate 240 tons of hybrid corn seed to villages in Malawi, Tanzania, and Kenya. Monsanto's goal is to improve farmers' lives in a way that will help them become self-sufficient.

Not all view Monsanto's presence in Africa as socially responsible. Critics see Monsanto as trying to control African agriculture and destroy thousand-year-old agricultural practices. Others agree, but take a more utilitarian view: the benefits (combating starvation in Africa) outweigh these disadvantages. There is no denying that Monsanto has positively affected African farmers' lives, along with increasing the company's profits for shareholders. As CEO Hugh Grant writes, "This initiative isn't simply altruistic; we see it as a unique business proposition that rewards farmers and shareowners." These emerging industries are a major opportunity for company growth.

The Future Challenges Facing Monsanto

Monsanto faces challenges that it needs to address, including lingering concerns over the safety and the environmental impact of its products. This requires a SWOT analysis that examines the company's strengths, weaknesses, opportunities and threats. Monsanto is also facing the threat of increased competition. The seed company Pioneer Hi-Bred International Inc. uses pricing strategies and seed sampling to attract price-conscious customers. Additionally, lower grain prices may convince farmers to switch from Monsanto to less expensive brands.

Monsanto most recently faces generic weed killer competition and a farmer backlash against high-priced, genetically modified seeds. Monsanto is slashing its prices of Roundup, which is based on the active ingredient glyphosate, to cope with a flood of cheap glyphosate from factories in China that have the capacity to make twice as much of the herbicide as the world needs. The company is also planning to lower prices for two recently introduced lines of genetically modified seeds to spur broader adoption by U.S. farmers, who bought far fewer of the seeds in 2010. The decrease in sales of Monsanto may relate to environmental concerns and the fear that these products may inflict harm on the environment, such as killing harmless insects, butterflies, and other forms of life.

Despite these challenges, Monsanto has numerous opportunities to thrive. The company is currently working on new innovations that could increase its competitive edge and provide enormous benefits to farmers worldwide. In a further act of social responsibility, Monsanto is donating intellectual property and seeds to aid in developing drought-tolerant white corn seeds for Africa.

Although Monsanto has made mistakes in the past, it is trying to portray itself as a responsible company that is helping society with sustainable agriculture. It is using its technology and market share to meet challenges, including the global and political-legal factors facing the company. With the growing popularity of organic food and staunch criticism from opponents, Monsanto has to continue working with stakeholders to promote its technological innovations and eliminate challenges concerning its industry.[49]

QUESTIONS FOR DISCUSSION

1. What are the major strengths, weaknesses, opportunities, and threats (SWOT) associated with Monsanto?

2. Explain how Monsanto has utilized the marketing concept and developed a market orientation.

3. What is the importance of gaining the support of Monsanto's stakeholders in achieving long-term success?

© Comstock Images/Getty Images

Part 2

Environmental Forces and Social and Ethical Responsibilities

PART TWO deals with the marketing environment, examining concepts, influences, and trends both in the United States and abroad. **CHAPTER 3** examines competitive, economic, political, legal and regulatory, technological, and sociocultural forces in the marketing environment, which can have profound effects on marketing strategies. **CHAPTER 4** explores the role of social responsibility and ethical issues in marketing decisions.

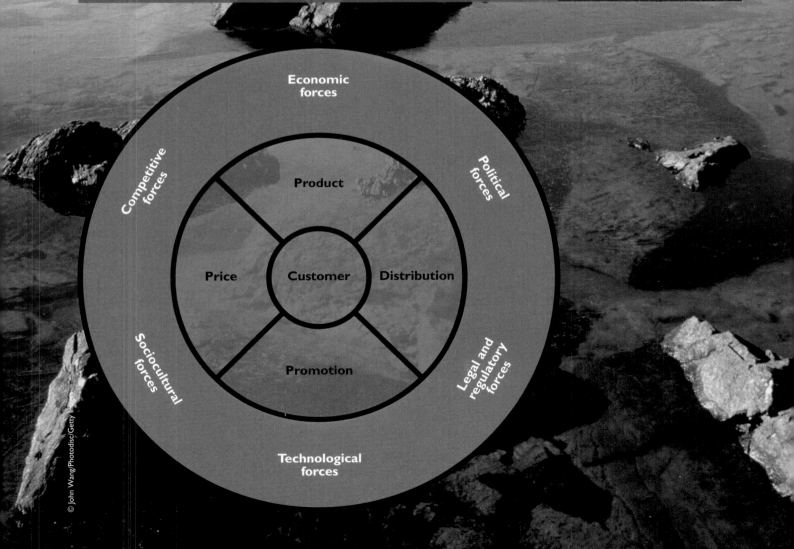

© John Wang/Photodisc/Getty Images

Chapter 3

The Marketing Environment

OBJECTIVES

1. To recognize the importance of environmental scanning and analysis

2. To understand how competitive and economic factors affect an organization's ability to compete and a customer's ability and willingness to buy products

3. To identify the types of political forces in the marketing environment

4. To understand how laws, government regulations, and self-regulatory agencies affect marketing activities

5. To explore the effects of new technology on society and on marketing activities

6. To analyze sociocultural issues marketers must deal with as they make decisions

Geox Puts Best Foot Forward in World Shoe Markets

Italian winemaker Mario Polegato was walking in the desert heat of Reno, Nevada, when he got an unusual idea for a new type of shoe. His feet felt overheated, but fresh air couldn't penetrate the shoes he was wearing. On the spur of the moment, he poked a few holes in his rubber soles—and his feet cooled off right away. Polegato's entrepreneurial instincts kicked in as he realized that following up on this brainstorm could lead to new marketing possibilities.

Returning home to Italy, Polegato consulted experts at local universities for assistance in developing new shoe technology. Ultimately, he patented a design for a sturdy sole that would let air circulate around the foot while keeping out moisture and dirt. Although he presented his "breathable shoe" innovation to several major footwear firms, none were interested.

Convinced that consumers would embrace the benefits, Polegato negotiated a bank loan and founded his own company to market shoes equipped with the new sole. He chose the company and brand name Geox, combining the Greek word for Earth (Geo) with an x to represent new technology. Soon Geox was marketing breathable shoes with Italian styling and high-tech soles.

With the introduction of company stores in 2003, Geox stepped up the pace of its marketing and expanded its brand around the world. Today, the company operates a global network of 1,000 stores and annually sells 20 million pairs of shoes for men, women, and children. Although Europe accounts for more than 80 percent of Geox's sales, demand in North America and Asia is increasing as the company brings its stores to major cities in new markets. With brand fans like Angelina Jolie, Paul McCartney, and Pope Benedict XVI, Geox is putting its best foot forward and positioning itself to race toward higher sales in the future.[1]

Companies like Geox are modifying marketing strategies in response to changes in the marketing environment. Because recognizing and addressing such changes in the marketing environment are crucial to marketing success, we will focus in detail on the forces that contribute to these changes.

This chapter explores the competitive, economic, political, legal and regulatory, technological, and sociocultural forces that constitute the marketing environment. First, we define the marketing environment and consider why it is critical to scan and analyze it. Next, we discuss the effects of competitive forces and explore the influence of general economic conditions: prosperity, recession, depression, and recovery. We also examine buying power and look at the forces that influence consumers' willingness to spend. We then discuss the political forces that generate government actions that affect marketing activities and examine the effects of laws and regulatory agencies on these activities. After analyzing the major dimensions of the technological forces in the environment, we consider the impact of sociocultural forces on marketing efforts.

Examining and Responding to the Marketing Environment

The marketing environment consists of external forces that directly or indirectly influence an organization's acquisition of inputs (human, financial, natural resources and raw materials, and information) and creation of outputs (goods, services, or ideas). As we saw in Chapter 1, the marketing environment includes six such forces: competitive, economic, political, legal and regulatory, technological, and sociocultural.

Whether fluctuating rapidly or slowly, environmental forces are always dynamic. Changes in the marketing environment create uncertainty, threats, and opportunities for marketers. Consider that after uncertainty in the Middle East and the effects of Hurricanes Katrina and Rita led to escalating fuel costs, many automakers saw sales of their gas-guzzling sport utility vehicles plummet while more fuel-efficient vehicles saw an increase in sales. Soon after these events, the United States entered a recession, boosting the sales of more economically priced vehicles. Of all the cars sold in the United States in a recent year, the only brands with increased sales were Kia, Subaru, and Hyundai.[2] Although the future is not very predictable, marketers try to forecast what may happen. We can say with certainty that marketers continue to modify their marketing strategies and plans in response to dynamic environmental forces. Consider how technological changes have affected the products offered by computer companies and how the public's growing concern with health and fitness has influenced the products of clothing, food, exercise equipment, and health-care companies. Marketing managers who fail to recognize changes in environmental forces leave their firms unprepared to capitalize on marketing opportunities or to cope with threats created by those changes. Monitoring the environment is crucial to an organization's survival and to the long-term achievement of its goals.

Environmental Scanning and Analysis

To monitor changes in the marketing environment effectively, marketers engage in environmental scanning and analysis. **Environmental scanning** is the process of collecting information about forces in the marketing environment. Scanning involves observation; secondary sources such as business, trade, government, and general-interest publications; and marketing research. The Internet has become a popular scanning tool because it makes data more accessible and allows companies to gather needed information quickly. Environmental scanning gives companies an edge over competitors in allowing them to take advantage of current trends. However, simply gathering information about competitors and customers is not enough; companies must know *how* to use that information in the strategic planning process. Managers must be careful not to gather so much information that sheer volume makes analysis impossible.

environmental scanning The process of collecting information about forces in the marketing environment

Environmental analysis is the process of assessing and interpreting the information gathered through environmental scanning. A manager evaluates the information for accuracy, tries to resolve inconsistencies in the data, and, if warranted, assigns significance to the findings. Evaluating this information should enable the manager to identify potential threats and opportunities linked to environmental changes. Understanding the current state of the marketing environment and recognizing threats and opportunities that might arise from changes within it help companies in their strategic planning. In particular, it can help marketing managers assess the performance of current marketing efforts and develop future marketing strategies.

Responding to Environmental Forces

Marketing managers take two general approaches to environmental forces: accepting them as uncontrollable or attempting to influence and shape them. An organization that views environmental forces as uncontrollable remains passive and reactive toward the environment. Instead of trying to influence forces in the environment, its marketing managers adjust current marketing strategies to environmental changes. They approach with caution market opportunities discovered through environmental scanning and analysis. On the other hand, marketing managers who believe environmental forces can be shaped adopt a more proactive approach. For example, if a market is blocked by traditional environmental constraints, proactive marketing managers may apply economic, psychological, political, and promotional skills to gain access to and operate within it. Once they identify what is constraining a market opportunity, they assess the power of the various parties involved and develop strategies to overcome the obstructing environmental forces. Microsoft, Intel, and Google, for example, have responded to political, legal, and regulatory concerns about their power in the computer industry by communicating the value of their competitive approaches to various publics. The computer giants contend that their competitive success results in superior products for their customers.

A proactive approach can be constructive and bring desired results. To influence environmental forces, marketing managers seek to identify market opportunities or to extract greater benefits relative to costs from existing market opportunities. Consider a firm that is losing sales to competitors with lower-priced products. If this firm develops a technology that makes its production processes more efficient, it will be able to lower the prices of its own products. Political action is another way to affect environmental forces. The pharmaceutical industry, for example, has lobbied very effectively for fewer restrictions on prescription drug marketing. However, managers must recognize that there are limits to the degree that environmental forces can be shaped. Although an organization may be able to influence legislation through lobbying, it is unlikely that a single organization can significantly increase the national birthrate or move the economy from recession to prosperity.

We cannot say whether a reactive or a proactive approach to environmental forces is better. For some organizations the passive, reactive approach is more appropriate, but for others the aggressive approach leads to better performance. Selection of a particular approach depends on an organization's managerial philosophies,

environmental analysis The process of assessing and interpreting the information gathered through environmental scanning

© American Academy of Orthopaedic Surgeon (AAOS)/Orthopaedic Trauma Association (OTA)

GET THE MESSAGE.
TEXTING WHILE DRIVING IS A DEADLY DISTRACTION.

Spread the word, save a friend.
Visit ota.org/donttext and aaos.org/donttext.

Responding to the Marketing Environment
Sponsors of this advertisement encourage drivers to not text when they are behind the wheel. By attempting to shape public opinion regarding texting while driving, these organizations may indirectly encourage lawmakers to enact laws that prohibit texting while driving.

objectives, financial resources, customers, and human skills, as well as on the environment within which the organization operates. Both organizational factors and managers' personal characteristics affect the variety of responses to changing environmental conditions. Microsoft, for example, can take a proactive approach because of its financial resources and the highly visible image of its founder, Bill Gates.

In the remainder of this chapter, we explore in greater detail the six environmental forces—competitive, economic, political, legal and regulatory, technological, and sociocultural—that interact to create opportunities and threats that must be considered in strategic planning.

Competitive Forces

Few firms, if any, operate free of competition. In fact, for most goods and services, customers have many alternatives from which to choose. For example, although the five best-selling soft drinks are Coke, Pepsi-Cola, Diet Coke, Mountain Dew, and Dr Pepper, soft-drink sales in general have flattened as consumers have turned to alternatives such as bottled water, flavored water, fruit juice, and iced tea products.[3] Thus, when marketing managers define the target market(s) their firm will serve, they simultaneously establish a set of competitors.[4] In addition, marketing managers must consider the type of competitive structure in which the firm operates. In this section, we examine types of competition and competitive structures, as well as the importance of monitoring competitors' actions.

Types of Competitors

Broadly speaking, all firms compete with one another for customers' dollars. More practically, however, a marketer generally defines **competition** as other firms that market products that are similar to or can be substituted for its products in the same geographic area. These competitors can be classified into one of four types. **Brand competitors** market products with similar features and benefits to the same customers at similar prices. For instance, a thirsty, calorie-conscious customer may choose a diet soda such as Diet Coke or Diet Pepsi from the soda machine. However, these sodas face competition from other types of beverages. **Product competitors** compete in the same product class but market products with different features, benefits, and prices. The thirsty dieter, for instance, might purchase iced tea, juice, mineral water, or bottled water instead of a soda. Google Inc., parent company of the most popular Internet search engine, has decided to venture into several new markets, including the cell phone industry. The company has teamed up with T-Mobile to enter the lucrative smartphone market with the Nexus One, which is competing with other smartphones like the Apple iPhone and the BlackBerry.[5]

Generic competitors provide very different products that solve the same problem or satisfy the same basic customer need. Our dieter, for example, might simply have a glass of water from the kitchen tap to satisfy her thirst. **Total budget competitors** compete for the limited financial resources of the same customers.[6] Total budget competitors for Diet Coke, for example, might include gum, a newspaper, and bananas. Although all four types of competition can affect a firm's marketing performance, brand competitors are the most significant because buyers typically see the different products of these firms as direct substitutes for one another. Consequently marketers tend to concentrate environmental analyses on brand competitors.

Types of Competitive Structures

The number of firms that supply a product may affect the strength of competitors. When just one or a few firms control supply, competitive factors exert a different form of influence on marketing activities than when many competitors exist. Table 3.1 presents four general types of competitive structures: monopoly, oligopoly, monopolistic competition, and pure competition.

competition Other organizations that market products that are similar to or can be substituted for a marketer's products in the same geographic area

brand competitors Firms that market products with similar features and benefits to the same customers at similar prices

product competitors Firms that compete in the same product class but market products with different features, benefits, and prices

generic competitors Firms that provide very different products that solve the same problem or satisfy the same basic customer need

total budget competitors Firms that compete for the limited financial resources of the same customers

TABLE 3.1 Selected Characteristics of Competitive Structures

Type of Structure	Number of Competitors	Ease of Entry into Market	Product	Example
Monopoly	One	Many barriers	Almost no substitutes	Fort Collins (Colorado) Water Utilities
Oligopoly	Few	Some barriers	Homogeneous or differentiated (with real or perceived differences)	General Motors (autos)
Monopolistic competition	Many	Few barriers	Product differentiation, with many substitutes	Levi Strauss (jeans)
Pure competition	Unlimited	No barriers	Homogeneous products	Vegetable farm (sweet corn)

monopoly A competitive structure in which an organization offers a product that has no close substitutes, making that organization the sole source of supply

oligopoly A competitive structure in which a few sellers control the supply of a large proportion of a product

monopolistic competition A competitive structure in which a firm has many potential competitors and tries to develop a marketing strategy to differentiate its product

pure competition A market structure characterized by an extremely large number of sellers, none strong enough to significantly influence price or supply

A **monopoly** exists when an organization offers a product that has no close substitutes, making that organization the sole source of supply. Because the organization has no competitors, it controls the supply of the product completely and, as a single seller, can erect barriers to potential competitors. In reality, most monopolies surviving today are local utilities, which are heavily regulated by local, state, or federal agencies. These monopolies are tolerated because of the tremendous financial resources needed to develop and operate them. For example, few organizations can obtain the financial or political resources to mount any competition against a local water supplier. On the other hand, competition is increasing in the electric and cable television industries.

An **oligopoly** exists when a few sellers control the supply of a large proportion of a product. In this case, each seller considers the reactions of other sellers to changes in marketing activities. Products facing oligopolistic competition may be homogeneous, such as aluminum, or differentiated, such as automobiles. Usually barriers of some sort make it difficult to enter the market and compete with oligopolies. For example, because of the enormous financial outlay required, few companies or individuals could afford to enter the oil-refining or steel-producing industry. Moreover, some industries demand special technical or marketing skills, a qualification that deters entry of many potential competitors.

Monopolistic competition exists when a firm with many potential competitors attempts to develop a marketing strategy to differentiate its product. Consider Levi Strauss, which has established an advantage for its blue jeans through a well-known trademark, recognizable design, aggressive advertising, and a reputation for quality. Although many competing brands of blue jeans are available, this firm has carved out a market niche by emphasizing differences in its products.

Pure competition, if it existed at all, would entail an extremely large number of sellers, none of which could significantly influence price or supply. Products would be homogeneous, and entry into the market would be easy. The closest thing to an example of pure competition is an unregulated farmers' market, where local growers gather to sell their produce.

THE FIRST CAR TO STOP TRAFFIC. AND ITSELF.

INTRODUCING THE NEW 2010 VOLVO XC60 WITH CITY SAFETY.

Volvo. for life

Oligopoly
The auto industry is an example of an oligopoly.

Pure competition is an ideal at one end of the continuum, and a monopoly is at the other end. Most marketers function in a competitive environment somewhere between these two extremes.

Monitoring Competition

Marketers need to monitor the actions of major competitors to determine what specific strategies competitors are using and how those strategies affect their own. Competitive intensity influences a firm's strategic approach to markets.[7] Price is one marketing strategy variable that most competitors monitor. When AirTran or Southwest Airlines lowers its fare on a route, most major airlines attempt to match the price. Monitoring guides marketers in developing competitive advantages and in adjusting current marketing strategies and planning new ones.

In monitoring competition, it is not enough to analyze available information; the firm must develop a system for gathering ongoing information about competitors and potential competitors. Information about competitors allows marketing managers to assess the performance of their own marketing efforts and to recognize the strengths and weaknesses in their own marketing strategies. In addition, organizations are rewarded for taking risks and dealing with the uncertainty created by inadequate information.[8] Data about market shares, product movement, sales volume, and expenditure levels can be useful. However, accurate information on these matters is often difficult to obtain.

Economic Forces

Economic forces in the marketing environment influence both marketers' and customers' decisions and activities. In this section, we examine the effects of general economic conditions as well as buying power and the factors that affect people's willingness to spend.

Economic Conditions

The overall state of the economy fluctuates in all countries. Changes in general economic conditions affect (and are affected by) supply and demand, buying power, willingness to spend, consumer expenditure levels, and intensity of competitive behavior. Therefore, current economic conditions and changes in the economy have a broad impact on the success of organizations' marketing strategies.

Fluctuations in the economy follow a general pattern, often referred to as the **business cycle**. In the traditional view, the business cycle consists of four stages: prosperity, recession, depression, and recovery. From a global perspective, different regions of the world may be in different stages of the business cycle during the same period. Throughout much of the 1990s, for example, the United States experienced booming growth (prosperity). The U.S. economy began to slow in 2000, with a brief recession, especially in high-technology industries, in 2001. Japan, however, endured a recession during most of the 1990s and into the early 2000s. Economic variation in the global marketplace creates a planning challenge for firms that sell products in multiple markets around the world. In 2008, the United States experienced an economic downturn due to higher energy prices, falling home values, increasing unemployment, the financial crisis in the banking industry, and fluctuating currency values.

During **prosperity**, unemployment is low and total income is relatively high. Assuming a low inflation rate, this combination ensures high buying power. If the economic outlook remains prosperous, consumers generally are willing to buy. In the prosperity stage, marketers often expand their product offerings to take advantage of increased buying power. They can sometimes capture a larger market share by intensifying distribution and promotion efforts.

Because unemployment rises during a **recession**, total buying power declines. These factors, usually accompanied by consumer pessimism, often stifle both consumer and business spending. As buying power decreases, many customers may become more price and value conscious, and look for basic, functional products. For example, when buying

business cycle A pattern of economic fluctuations that has four stages: prosperity, recession, depression, and recovery

prosperity A stage of the business cycle characterized by low unemployment and relatively high total income, which together ensure high buying power (provided the inflation rate stays low)

recession A stage of the business cycle during which unemployment rises and total buying power declines, stifling both consumer and business spending

power decreased during the recession, luxury car sales dropped sharply. Consumers began looking for functionality when purchasing a vehicle rather than frills and flashy gadgets, forcing luxury carmakers to adapt. Mercedes is trying to increase sales during the recession by offering a four-cylinder engine option for certain models and highlighting cutting edge safety features like a fatigue warning system.[9]

During a recession, some firms make the mistake of drastically reducing their marketing efforts, thus damaging their ability to survive. Obviously, however, marketers should consider some revision of their marketing activities during a recessionary period. Because consumers are more concerned about the functional value of products, a company should focus its marketing research on determining precisely what functions buyers want and make sure those functions become part of its products. Promotional efforts should emphasize value and utility.

A prolonged recession may become a **depression**, a period in which unemployment is extremely high, wages are very low, total disposable income is at a minimum, and consumers lack confidence in the economy. A depression usually lasts for an extended period, often years, and has been experienced by Russia, Mexico, and Brazil in the 2000s. Although evidence supports maintaining or even increasing spending during economic slowdowns, marketing budgets are more likely to be cut in the face of an economic downturn.

During **recovery**, the economy moves from recession or depression toward prosperity. During this period, high unemployment begins to decline, total disposable income increases, and the economic gloom that reduced consumers' willingness to buy subsides. Both the ability and the willingness to buy rise. Marketers face some problems during recovery; for example, it is difficult to ascertain how quickly and to what level prosperity will return. In this stage, marketers should maintain as much flexibility in their marketing strategies as possible so they can make the needed adjustments.

Buying Power

The strength of a person's **buying power** depends on economic conditions and the size of the resources—money, goods, and services that can be traded in an exchange—that enable the individual to make purchases. The major financial sources of buying power are income, credit, and wealth. For an individual, **income** is the amount of money received through wages, rents, investments, pensions, and subsidy payments for a given period, such as a month or a year. Normally this money is allocated among taxes, spending for goods and services, and savings. The median annual household income in the United States is approximately $50,300.[10] However, because of differences in people's educational levels, abilities, occupations, and wealth, income is not equally distributed in this country.

Marketers are most interested in the amount of money left after payment of taxes because this **disposable income** is used for spending or saving. Because disposable income is a ready source of buying power, the total amount available in a nation is important to marketers. Several factors determine the size of total disposable income. One is the total amount of income, which is affected by wage levels, the rate of unemployment, interest rates, and dividend rates. Because disposable income is income left after taxes are paid, the number and amount of taxes directly affect the size of total disposable income. When taxes rise, disposable income declines; when taxes fall, disposable income increases.

Disposable income that is available for spending and saving after an individual has purchased the basic necessities of food, clothing, and shelter is called **discretionary income**. People use discretionary income to purchase entertainment, vacations, automobiles, education, pets, furniture, appliances, and so on. Changes in total discretionary income affect sales of these products, especially automobiles, furniture, large appliances, and other costly durable goods.

Credit enables people to spend future income now or in the near future. However, credit increases current buying power at the expense of future buying power. Several factors determine whether people use or forgo credit. First, credit must be available. Interest rates also affect buyers' decisions to use credit, especially for expensive purchases such as homes, appliances, and automobiles. When interest rates are low, the total cost of automobiles and houses becomes more affordable. In the United States, low interest rates in the 2000s induced many buyers to take on the high level of debt necessary to own

depression A stage of the business cycle when unemployment is extremely high, wages are very low, total disposable income is at a minimum, and consumers lack confidence in the economy

recovery A stage of the business cycle in which the economy moves from recession or depression toward prosperity

buying power Resources, such as money, goods, and services, that can be traded in an exchange

income For an individual, the amount of money received through wages, rents, investments, pensions, and subsidy payments for a given period

disposable income After-tax income

discretionary income Disposable income available for spending and saving after an individual has purchased the basic necessities of food, clothing, and shelter

A CITY SLICKER EMAILED IN THE STICKS.

Introducing the new Dell Inspiron™ notebook. Now with the option of eight exciting colors, HD widescreen, and fast, long-range wireless. If you want to stay connected, even when you're in the sticks, yours is here.

Starting at $799

DELL™
YOURS IS HERE

Discretionary Income
A consumer uses discretionary income when he or she purchases a laptop computer for personal use.

a home, fueling a tremendous boom in the construction of new homes and the sale of older homes. In contrast, when interest rates are high, consumers are more likely to delay buying such expensive items. Use of credit is also affected by credit terms, such as size of the down payment and amount and number of monthly payments.

Wealth is the accumulation of past income, natural resources, and financial resources. It exists in many forms, including cash, securities, savings accounts, jewelry, and real estate. Global wealth is increasing, with 9.5 million millionaires worldwide, double the number ten years ago.[11] Like income, wealth is unevenly distributed. A person can have a high income and very little wealth. It is also possible, but not likely, for a person to have great wealth but little income. The significance of wealth to marketers is that as people become wealthier, they gain buying power in three ways: they can use their wealth to make current purchases, to generate income, and to acquire large amounts of credit.

Income, credit, and wealth equip consumers with buying power to purchase goods and services. Marketing managers must be aware of current levels and expected changes in buying power in their own markets because buying power directly affects the types and quantities of goods and services customers purchase. Information about buying power is available from government sources, trade associations, and research agencies. One of the most current and comprehensive sources of buying power data is the Sales & Marketing Management Survey of Buying Power, published annually by Sales & Marketing Management magazine. Having buying power, however, does not mean consumers will buy. They must also be willing to use their buying power.

Willingness to Spend

People's **willingness to spend**—their inclination to buy because of expected satisfaction from a product—is, to some degree, related to their ability to buy. That is, people are sometimes more willing to buy if they have the buying power. However, a number of other elements also influence willingness to spend. Some elements affect specific products; others influence spending in general. A product's price and value influence almost all of us. Cross pens, for example, appeal to customers who are willing to spend more for fine writing instruments even when lower-priced pens are readily available. The amount of satisfaction received from a product already owned may also influence customers' desire to buy other products. Satisfaction depends not only on the quality of the currently owned product but also on numerous psychological and social forces. The American Customer Satisfaction Index, computed by the National Quality Research Center at the University of Michigan (see Figure 3.1), offers an indicator of customer satisfaction with a wide variety of businesses.

Factors that affect consumers' general willingness to spend are expectations about future employment, income levels, prices, family size, and general economic conditions. Willingness to spend ordinarily declines if people are unsure whether or how long they will be employed, and it usually increases if people are reasonably certain of higher incomes in the future. Expectations of rising prices in the near future may also increase willingness to spend in the present. For a given level of buying power, the larger the family, the greater the willingness to spend. One reason for this relationship is that as the size of a family increases, more dollars must be spent to provide the basic necessities to sustain family members.

wealth The accumulation of past income, natural resources, and financial resources

willingness to spend An inclination to buy because of expected satisfaction from a product, influenced by the ability to buy and numerous psychological and social forces

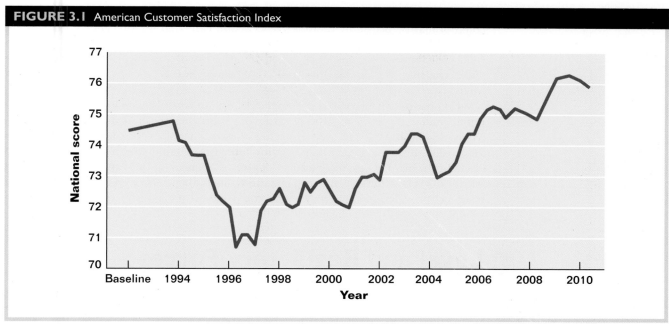

FIGURE 3.1 American Customer Satisfaction Index

Source: "National Quartely Scores," American Customer Satisfaction Index, University of Michigan Business School, www.theacsi.org/index.php?option=com_content&task=view&id=31&Itemid=35 (accessed September 1, 2010).

Political Forces

Political, legal, and regulatory forces of the marketing environment are closely interrelated. Legislation is enacted, legal decisions are interpreted by courts, and regulatory agencies are created and operated, for the most part, by elected or appointed officials. Legislation and regulations (or the lack thereof) reflect the current political outlook. For instance, after the expansive salmonella peanut butter recall in January of 2009, the Food Safety Modernization Act was proposed. This would create an agency under the Department of Health and Human Services that would solely regulate food and would have the authority to require recalls in the food industry. The bill would also set higher standards for producers in the food industry.[12] Consequently, the political forces of the marketing environment have the potential to influence marketing decisions and strategies.

Marketing organizations strive to maintain good relations with elected and appointed political officials for several reasons. Political officials well disposed toward particular firms or industries are less likely to create or enforce laws and regulations unfavorable to those companies. For example, political officials who believe oil companies are making honest efforts to control pollution are unlikely to create and enforce highly restrictive pollution-control laws. In addition, governments are big buyers, and political officials can influence how much a government agency purchases and from whom. Finally, political officials can play key roles in helping organizations secure foreign markets.

Many marketers view political forces as beyond their control and simply adjust to conditions that arise from those forces. Some firms, however, seek to influence the political process. In some cases, organizations publicly protest the actions of legislative bodies. More often, organizations help elect individuals to political offices who regard them positively. Much of this help is in the form of campaign contributions. AT&T is an example of a company that has attempted to influence legislation and regulation over a long period of time. Since 1990, AT&T has made more than $44 million in corporate donations for use in supporting the campaign funds of political candidates. Some companies choose to donate to the campaign funds of opponents when it is believed to be a close race. Until recently, laws have limited corporate contributions to political campaign funds for specific candidates, and company-sponsored political advertisements could primarily focus only on topics (e.g., health care) and not on candidates. A recent U.S. Supreme Court decision has nullified federal laws that restrict political campaign fund contributions for corporate labor unions. This decision will likely affect similar state laws that restrict corporate and labor union contributions to political campaign funds.

Companies can also participate in the political process through lobbying to persuade public and/or government officials to favor a particular position in decision making. Many organizations concerned about the threat of legislation or regulation that may negatively affect their operations employ lobbyists to communicate their concerns to elected officials. For instance, when Congress was debating the Patient Protection and Affordable Care Act, several organizations, including medical associations, private insurance providers, and pharmaceutical companies, sent lobbyists to give their respective viewpoints regarding the health-care bill.[13]

Legal and Regulatory Forces

A number of federal laws influence marketing decisions and activities. Table 3.2 lists some of the most important laws. In addition to discussing these laws, which deal with competition and consumer protection, this section examines the effects of regulatory agencies and self-regulatory forces on marketing efforts.

Procompetitive Legislation

Procompetitive laws are designed to preserve competition. Most of these laws were enacted to end various antitrade practices deemed unacceptable by society. The Sherman Antitrust Act, for example, was passed in 1890 to prevent businesses from restraining trade and monopolizing markets. Examples of illegal anticompetitive practices include stealing trade secrets or obtaining other confidential information from a competitor's employees, trademark and copyright infringement, price fixing, false advertising, and deceptive selling methods such as "bait and switch" and false representation of products. For example, the Lanham Act (1946) and the Federal Trademark Dilution Act (1995) help companies protect their trademarks (brand names, logos, and other registered symbols) against infringement. The latter also requires users of names that match or parallel existing trademarks to relinquish them to prevent confusion among consumers. Antitrust laws also authorize the government to punish companies that engage in such anticompetitive practices. For instance, the European Commission recently fined Intel a record $1.45 billion (1.06 billion euros) for engaging in anticompetitive behavior in the computer chip market. Among other violations, Intel had been offering computer companies rebates if they bought less of a rival's product or even none at all.[14]

Consumer Protection Legislation

Consumer protection legislation is not a recent development. During the mid-1800s, lawmakers in many states passed laws to prohibit adulteration of food and drugs. However, consumer protection laws at the federal level mushroomed in the mid-1960s and early 1970s. A number of them deal with consumer safety, such as the food and drug acts, and are designed to protect people from actual and potential physical harm caused by adulteration or mislabeling. Other laws prohibit the sale of various hazardous products, such as flammable fabrics and toys that may injure children. Others concern automobile safety. Congress has also passed several laws concerning information disclosure. Some require that information about specific products, such as textiles, furs, cigarettes, and automobiles, be provided on labels. Other laws focus on particular marketing activities: product development and testing, packaging, labeling, advertising, and consumer financing. For example, concerns about companies' online collection

TABLE 3.2 Major Federal Laws That Affect Marketing Decisions

Name and Date Enacted	Purpose
Sherman Antitrust Act (1890)	Prohibits contracts, combinations, or conspiracies to restrain trade; establishes as a misdemeanor monopolizing or attempting to monopolize
Clayton Act (1914)	Prohibits specific practices such as price discrimination, exclusive-dealer arrangements, and stock acquisitions whose effect may noticeably lessen competition or tend to create a monopoly
Federal Trade Commission Act (1914)	Created the Federal Trade Commission; also gives the FTC investigatory powers to be used in preventing unfair methods of competition
Robinson-Patman Act (1936)	Prohibits price discrimination that lessens competition among wholesalers or retailers; prohibits producers from giving disproportionate services or facilities to large buyers
Wheeler-Lea Act (1938)	Prohibits unfair and deceptive acts and practices regardless of whether competition is injured; places advertising of foods and drugs under the jurisdiction of the FTC
Lanham Act (1946)	Provides protections for and regulation of brand names, brand marks, trade names, and trademarks
Celler-Kefauver Act (1950)	Prohibits any corporation engaged in commerce from acquiring the whole or any part of the stock or other share of the capital assets of another corporation when the effect would substantially lessen competition or tend to create a monopoly
Fair Packaging and Labeling Act (1966)	Prohibits unfair or deceptive packaging or labeling of consumer products
Magnuson-Moss Warranty (FTC) Act (1975)	Provides for minimum disclosure standards for written consumer product warranties; defines minimum consent standards for written warranties; allows the FTC to prescribe interpretive rules in policy statements regarding unfair or deceptive practices
Consumer Goods Pricing Act (1975)	Prohibits the use of price maintenance agreements among manufacturers and resellers in interstate commerce
Trademark Counterfeiting Act (1980)	Imposes civil and criminal penalties against those who deal in counterfeit consumer goods or any counterfeit goods that can threaten health or safety
Trademark Law Revision Act (1988)	Amends the Lanham Act to allow brands not yet introduced to be protected through registration with the Patent and Trademark Office
Nutrition Labeling and Education Act (1990)	Prohibits exaggerated health claims; requires all processed foods to contain labels with nutritional information
Telephone Consumer Protection Act (1991)	Establishes procedures to avoid unwanted telephone solicitations; prohibits marketers from using an automated telephone dialing system or an artificial or prerecorded voice to certain telephone lines
Federal Trademark Dilution Act (1995)	Grants trademark owners the right to protect trademarks and requires relinquishment of names that match or parallel existing trademarks
Digital Millennium Copyright Act (1996)	Refined copyright laws to protect digital versions of copyrighted materials, including music and movies
Children's Online Privacy Protection Act (2000)	Regulates the collection of personally identifiable information (name, address, e-mail address, hobbies, interests, or information collected through cookies) online from children under age 13
Do Not Call Implementation Act (2003)	Directs the FCC and FTC to coordinate so their rules are consistent regarding telemarketing call practices including the Do Not Call Registry and other lists, as well as call abandonment; in 2008, the FTC amended its rules and banned prerecorded sales pitches for all but a few cases
Credit Card Act (2009)	Implemented strict rules on credit card companies regarding topics such as issuing credit to youth, terms disclosure, interest rates, and fees

and use of personal information, especially about children, resulted in the passage of the Children's Online Privacy Protection Act, which prohibits websites and Internet providers from seeking personal information from children under age 13 without parental consent.

An example of more recent consumer protection legislation is the Credit Card Accountability, Responsibility and Disclosure (or Credit CARD) Act of 2009, which restricts credit card companies' ability to change interest rates, charge unfair late fees, use complicated or unclear wording in their terms, and issue credit to individuals under 21.[15]

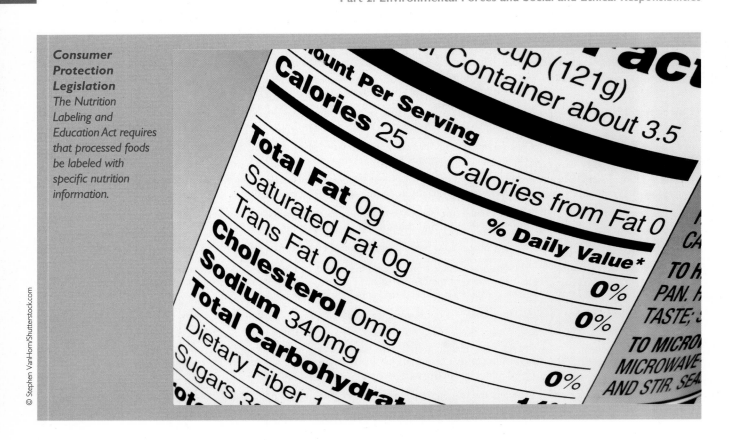

Consumer Protection Legislation *The Nutrition Labeling and Education Act requires that processed foods be labeled with specific nutrition information.*

Encouraging Compliance with Laws and Regulations

Marketing activities are sometimes at the forefront of organizational misconduct, with fraud and antitrust violations the most frequently sentenced organizational crimes. Legal violations usually begin when marketers develop programs that unwittingly overstep legal bounds. Many marketers lack experience in dealing with complex legal actions and decisions. Some test the limits of certain laws by operating in a legally questionable way to see how far they can get with certain practices before being prosecuted. Other marketers interpret regulations and statutes very strictly to avoid violating a vague law. When marketers interpret laws in relation to specific marketing practices, they often analyze recent court decisions both to better understand what the law is intended to do and to predict future court interpretations.

The current trend is away from legally based organizational compliance programs to providing incentives that foster a culture of ethics and responsibility that encourages compliance with laws and regulations. Developing best practices and voluntary compliance creates rules and principles that guide decision making. Many companies are encouraging their employees to take responsibility for avoiding legal misconduct themselves. The New York Stock Exchange, for example, requires all member companies to have a code of ethics, and some firms try to go beyond what is required by the law. For example, many firms are seeking out and implementing alternative energy solutions before stricter laws are enacted to protect the environment.

Regulatory Agencies

Federal regulatory agencies influence many marketing activities, including product development, pricing, packaging, advertising, personal selling, and distribution. Usually these bodies have the power to enforce specific laws, as well as some discretion in establishing operating rules and regulations to guide certain types of industry practices. Because of this discretion and overlapping areas of responsibility, confusion or conflict regarding which agencies have jurisdiction over which marketing activities is common.

Marketing in Transition
Truth in Tweeting

Not so long ago, the World Wide Web was the Wild West of marketing. Customers might see a YouTube video of a celebrity praising a product or a blog entry trumpeting a brand without knowing that these activities were part of a coordinated marketing campaign. Now marketing is becoming more transparent, thanks to new Federal Trade Commission rules that require public disclosure of who's behind the message.

These days, when companies pay celebrities to promote their products in social media, the financial connections must be clear. Also, if celebrities blog or tweet things about products that they know (or should know) are untrue, the FTC can hold them personally accountable for making misleading statements. Moreover, bloggers who receive freebies for product reviews have to make this clear, even when the deal is that bloggers can write whatever they wish about the goods or services. Nor can a marketer set up a website, post a blog entry, or send a tweet that appears to be the work of an enthusiastic brand fan unrelated to the business. When a company or its communications agency is actually the driving force, this fact must be disclosed.

However, openly identifying online messages as marketing can be a challenge when space is limited, as with Twitter posts, which

are only 140 characters long. That's why the Word of Mouth Marketing Association, an industry group, suggests using the tag *#spon* within the message to indicate a sponsored tweet (paid for by a marketer) and *#paid* or *#samp* to indicate that someone was paid or received a sample in exchange for tweeting.[a]

© AP Images/Larry Crowe / © iStockphoto.com/Marcus Lindström

Federal Trade Commission (FTC) An agency that regulates a variety of business practices and curbs false advertising, misleading pricing, and deceptive packaging and labeling

Of all the federal regulatory units, the **Federal Trade Commission (FTC)** most heavily influences marketing activities. Although the FTC regulates a variety of business practices, it allocates a large portion of resources to curbing false advertising, misleading pricing, and deceptive packaging and labeling. When it has reason to believe a firm is violating a law, the commission typically issues a complaint stating that the business is in violation and takes appropriate action. For instance, the FTC recently settled charges against LifeLock for making false claims regarding levels of consumer protection and internal data security in advertisements. LifeLock's commercials featured the company's CEO's Social Security number on the side of a truck, as LifeLock promised customers its services could protect them from all types of identity theft, and that customers' data was encrypted and properly secured in the company's internal records. The FTC, however, found that LifeLock's services did not fully protect consumers from several types of identity theft, and the company's internal records of users' personal data were not encrypted and could be accessed easily without authorization. The settlement required LifeLock to pay $12 million (which included customer refunds), to no longer misrepresent its services or the scope of their protection in advertisements, and to take more measures to improve internal data security.[16] If, after it is issued a complaint, a company continues the questionable practice, the FTC can issue a cease-and-desist order demanding that the business stop doing whatever caused the complaint. The firm can appeal to the federal courts to have the order rescinded. However, the FTC can seek civil penalties in court, up to a maximum penalty of $10,000 a day for each infraction if a cease-and-desist order is violated. The commission can require companies to run corrective advertising in response to previous ads deemed misleading (see Figure 3.2).

FIGURE 3.2 Federal Trade Commission Enforcement Tools

Cease-and-desist order	Consent decree	Redress	Corrective advertising	Civil penalties
A court order to a business to stop engaging in an illegal practice	An order for a business to stop engaging in questionable activities to avoid prosecution (In 2005, 10,021 were issued)	Money paid to customer to settle or resolve a complaint	A requirement that a business make new advertisement to correct misinformation	Court-ordered civil fines for up to $10,000 per day for violating a cease-and-desist order

Source: www.ftc.gov.

The FTC also assists businesses in complying with laws and evaluates new marketing methods every year. For example, the agency has held hearings to help firms establish guidelines for avoiding charges of price fixing, deceptive advertising, and questionable telemarketing practices. It has also held conferences and hearings on electronic (Internet) commerce, identity theft, and childhood obesity. When general sets of guidelines are needed to improve business practices in a particular industry, the FTC sometimes encourages firms within that industry to establish a set of trade practices voluntarily. The FTC may even sponsor a conference that brings together industry leaders and consumers for this purpose.

Unlike the FTC, other regulatory units are limited to dealing with specific products, services, or business activities. Consider the Food and Drug Administration (FDA), which enforces regulations that prohibit the sale and distribution of adulterated, misbranded, or hazardous food and drug products. A popular birth control pill, Yaz, recently had a run-in with the FDA regarding claims made in commercials that use of their product could result in acne reduction and improvements in mood. After investigating these claims, the FDA required corrective advertising totaling $20 million be made over a six-year period as well as screening of the brand's marketing communications before they are released.[17] Table 3.3 outlines the areas of responsibility of six federal regulatory agencies.

In addition, all states, as well as many cities and towns, have regulatory agencies that enforce laws and regulations regarding marketing practices within their states or

TABLE 3.3 Major Federal Regulatory Agencies

Agency	Major Areas of Responsibility
Federal Trade Commission (FTC)	Enforces laws and guidelines regarding business practices; takes action to stop false and deceptive advertising, pricing, packaging, and labeling
Food and Drug Administration (FDA)	Enforces laws and regulations to prevent distribution of adulterated or misbranded foods, drugs, medical devices, cosmetics, veterinary products, and potentially hazardous consumer products
Consumer Product Safety Commission (CPSC)	Ensures compliance with the Consumer Product Safety Act; protects the public from unreasonable risk of injury from any consumer product not covered by other regulatory agencies
Federal Communications Commission (FCC)	Regulates communication by wire, radio, and television in interstate and foreign commerce
Environmental Protection Agency (EPA)	Develops and enforces environmental protection standards and conducts research into the adverse effects of pollution
Federal Power Commission (FPC)	Regulates rates and sales of natural gas producers, thereby affecting the supply and price of gas available to consumers; also regulates wholesale rates for electricity and gas, pipeline construction, and U.S. imports and exports of natural gas and electricity

municipalities. State and local regulatory agencies try not to establish regulations that conflict with those of federal regulatory agencies. They generally enforce laws dealing with the production and sale of particular goods and services. The utility, insurance, financial, and liquor industries are commonly regulated by state agencies. Among these agencies' targets are misleading advertising and pricing. Recent legal actions suggest that states are taking a firmer stance against perceived deceptive pricing practices and are using basic consumer research to define deceptive pricing.

State consumer protection laws offer an opportunity for state attorneys general to deal with marketing issues related to fraud and deception. Most states have consumer protection laws that are very general in nature and provide enforcement when new schemes evolve that injure consumers. For example, the New York Consumer Protection Board is very proactive in monitoring consumer protection and providing consumer education. New York also became the first state to implement an airline passenger rights law in 2008.

Self-Regulatory Forces

In an attempt to be good corporate citizens and prevent government intervention, some businesses try to regulate themselves. Similarly, a number of trade associations have developed self-regulatory programs. Though these programs are not a direct outgrowth of laws, many were established to stop or stall the development of laws and governmental regulatory groups that would regulate the associations' marketing practices. Sometimes trade associations establish ethics codes by which their members must abide or risk censure or exclusion from the association. For instance, the Pharmaceutical Research and Manufacturers of America released its "Guiding Principles" to function as a set of voluntary industry rules for drug companies to follow when advertising directly to consumers. Some of the key guidelines are explained in detail in Table 3.4.[18]

Perhaps the best-known self-regulatory group is the **Better Business Bureau (BBB)**, which is a system of nongovernmental, independent, local regulatory agencies that are supported by local businesses. More than 150 bureaus help settle problems between consumers and specific business firms. Each bureau also acts to preserve good business practices in a locality, although it usually lacks strong enforcement tools for dealing with firms that employ questionable practices. When a firm continues to violate what the Better Business Bureau believes to be good business practices, the bureau warns consumers through local newspapers or broadcast media. If the offending organization is a BBB member, it may be expelled from the local bureau. For example, the Better Business Bureau of Upstate New York expelled two building contractors for having too many unresolved complaints on file.[19]

The Council of Better Business Bureaus is a national organization composed of all local Better Business Bureaus. The National Advertising Division (NAD) of the Council operates a self-regulatory program that investigates claims regarding alleged deceptive advertising. The long time rivals Coca-Cola and Pepsi are familiar names to

Better Business Bureau (BBB) A system of nongovernmental, independent, local regulatory agencies supported by local businesses that helps settle problems between customers and specific business firms

TABLE 3.4 Selected Direct-to-Consumer Pharmaceutical Guidelines

Doctor information	Doctors must be informed about a product before it is marketed to consumers.
Schedule of advertisements	Advertisements must be aired at times for age-appropriate viewers. (Ads for Viagra and similar medications, for example, must appear at later hours.)
Identification of health condition	Advertisements must include the health condition the drug treats and include more than only the product name.
Advertisement review by FDA	All new television advertising must be submitted to the FDA before being broadcast.
Accurate claims	Information should not be misleading, and claims must be supported by substantial evidence.

Encouraging Compliance with Regulations
The U.S. Department of Health & Human Services regulatory agency encourages compliance by facilitating the reporting of fraud.

the NAD, as both companies are constantly monitoring the other's marketing and product claims. A recent complaint ruled on by the NAD was in regards to a Powerade Zero commercial (by Coca-Cola) showing two mountain climbers hanging by a rope. The climber drinking the higher-calorie Gatorade (by Pepsi) falls after his rope tears. The NAD ruled in favor of Coca-Cola on the Powerade Zero commercial.[20]

Another self-regulatory entity, the **National Advertising Review Board (NARB)**, considers cases in which an advertiser challenges issues raised by the NAD about an advertisement. Cases are reviewed by panels drawn from NARB members that represent advertisers, agencies, and the public. For example, General Mills appealed to the NARB about an NAD order to abandon its claim "Betcha Can't Taste the Difference" between its Malt-O-Meal cereal and those of other manufacturers; the NAD had said the claim couldn't be substantiated. The NARB concurred with the NAD on the issue.[21] The NARB, sponsored by the Council of Better Business Bureaus and three advertising trade organizations, has no official enforcement powers. However, if a firm refuses to comply with its decision, the NARB may publicize the questionable practice and file a complaint with the FTC.

Self-regulatory programs have several advantages over governmental laws and regulatory agencies. Establishment and implementation are usually less expensive, and guidelines are generally more realistic and operational. In addition, effective self-regulatory programs reduce the need to expand government bureaucracy. However, these programs have several limitations. When a trade association creates a set of industry guidelines for its members, nonmember firms do not have to abide by them. Furthermore, many self-regulatory programs lack the tools or authority to enforce guidelines. Finally, guidelines in self-regulatory programs are often less strict than those established by government agencies.

Technological Forces

The word *technology* brings to mind scientific advances such as information technology and biotechnology, which have resulted in the Internet, cell phones, cloning, stem-cell research, pharmaceutical products, lasers, and more. Technology has revolutionized the products created and offered by marketers and the channels by which they communicate about those products. However, even though these innovations are outgrowths of technology, none of them *are* technology. **Technology** is the application of knowledge and tools to solve problems and perform tasks more efficiently. Technology grows out of research performed by businesses, universities, government agencies, and nonprofit organizations. More than half of this research is paid for by the federal government, which supports research in such diverse areas as health, defense, agriculture, energy, and pollution.

The rapid technological growth of the last several decades is expected to accelerate. It has transformed the U.S. economy into the most productive in the world and provided Americans with an ever-higher standard of living and tremendous opportunities for sustained business expansion. Technology and technological advancements clearly influence buyers' and marketers' decisions, so let's take a closer look at the impact of technology and its use in the marketplace.

National Advertising Review Board (NARB) A self-regulatory unit that considers challenges to issues raised by the National Advertising Division (an arm of the Council of Better Business Bureaus) about an advertisement

technology The application of knowledge and tools to solve problems and perform tasks more efficiently

Sustainable Marketing
Greenlight for Green Lights

How many marketers does it take to change a light bulb? To save energy and promote sustainability, a growing number of countries are mandating the gradual phase-out of traditional incandescent light bulbs. Some European nations have already begun restricting the retail sale of incandescents, the type of light bulb invented by Thomas Edison more than a century ago. U.S. law calls for all incandescents to be removed from store shelves by the end of 2014.

The coming ban on incandescents, coupled with increasingly positive consumer attitudes toward earth-friendly innovations, has created a lucrative marketing opportunity for companies that make energy-sipping lighting products. The three leaders of the global lighting industry (General Electric, OSRAM, and Philips) are not the only marketers with bright ideas for new bulbs. Dozens of firms now compete for the attention of consumers and businesses that want or need to change their light bulbs.

In particular, marketers are promoting two types of energy-efficient bulbs, compact fluorescent lights (CFLs) and light-emitting diodes (LEDs). Both have a higher purchase price than incandescents. However, because they require little power to operate and last much longer than incandescents, CFLs and LEDs actually save money in the long run. Not surprisingly, many budget-conscious consumers are postponing their CFL and LED purchases until forced to switch. Business buyers, meanwhile, are already placing orders because the bulb marketers have clearly articulated the long-term benefits. Replacing incandescents with CFLs or LEDs is not only a good way to slash the business's electrical bills, it's a good way to demonstrate commitment to sustainability.[b]

Impact of Technology

Technology determines how we, as members of society, satisfy our physiological needs. In various ways and to varying degrees, eating and drinking habits, sleeping patterns, sexual activities, health care, and work performance are all influenced by both existing technology and changes in technology. Because of the technological revolution in communications, for example, marketers can now reach vast numbers of people more efficiently through a variety of media. E-mail, voice mail, cell phones, pagers, and PDAs help marketers stay in touch with clients, make appointments, and handle last-minute orders or cancellations. A growing number of U.S. households, as well as many businesses, have given up their "land lines" in favor of using cell phones as their primary phones, and growth in wireless subscriptions has continued to increase. A company that has made note of this shift is Vonage, a phone company that emphasizes its flat-rate, unlimited local and long distance plans. Vonage now has

SNAPSHOT

Phone Use by Adults Who Have Both Land-Line and Cell Phones

Primarily land line 35%

Primarily cell phone 32%

Both equally 32%

Source: CARAVAN Opinion Research Corp. Survey of 2,005 adults for New Millennium Research Council..

Impact of Technology
Technology creates opportunities for new products and for the ways that customers can purchase them, such as digital audiobooks through Audible.com.

an app available on the iPhone and BlackBerry that allows customers to make long-distance phone calls at discounted Vonage rates from their cell phone without using any minutes from their cellular provider.[22]

The proliferation of cell phones, most with text-message capabilities, has led experts to project that an increasing number of brands will employ text and multimedia messaging on cell phones to reach their target markets. Increasing numbers of restaurants now accept customers' take-out orders via cell phone text messaging. Indeed, Papa John's Pizza projects that text ordering will soon rival ordering online, which currently is about 20 percent of the pizza chain's sales.[23]

Personal computers are now in three-quarters of U.S. consumers' homes, and most of them include broadband or modems for accessing the Internet. The Internet has become a major tool in most households for communicating, researching, shopping, and entertaining. Last year, Internet users in the United States watched 40 percent more videos online than they did the previous year. These videos are viewed primarily on sites like YouTube and Hulu.[24]

Though technology has had many positive impacts on our lives, there are also many negative impacts to consider. We enjoy the benefits of communicating through the Internet; however, we are increasingly concerned about protecting our privacy and intellectual property. Likewise, technological advances in the areas of health and medicine have led to the creation of new drugs that save lives; however, such advances have also led to cloning and genetically modified foods that have become controversial issues in many segments of society. Consider the impact of cell phones. The ability to call from almost any location has many benefits, but it also has negative side effects, including increases in traffic accidents, increased noise pollution, and fears about potential health risks.[25]

The effects of technology relate to such characteristics as dynamics, reach, and the self-sustaining nature of technological progress. The *dynamics* of technology involve the constant change that often challenges the structures of social institutions, including social relationships, the legal system, religion, education, business, and leisure. *Reach* refers to the broad nature of technology as it moves through society.

The *self-sustaining* nature of technology relates to the fact that technology acts as a catalyst to spur even faster development. As new innovations are introduced, they stimulate the need for more advancement to facilitate further development. For example, the Internet has created the need for ever-faster transmission of signals through broadband connections such as high-speed phone lines (DSL), satellites, and cable. Technology initiates a change process that creates new opportunities for new technologies in every industry segment or personal life experience that it touches. At some point, there is a multiplier effect that causes still greater demand for more change to improve performance.[26]

The expanding opportunities for e-commerce, the sharing of business information, the ability to maintain business relationships, and the ability to conduct business transactions via digital networks are changing the relationship between businesses and consumers.[27] Many people use the Internet to purchase consumer electronics, clothing, software, books, furniture, and music. More people now opt to purchase music online or simply listen for free on social networking sites. Recently, CD sales dropped 19 percent in one year alone.[28] In addition, consumers go online to acquire travel-related services,

Responsible Marketing?
Dyson's Airblade: Out with the Old and in with the New

 **CRITICAL THINKING**

ISSUE: When should organizations abandon existing technology in light of new, more energy-efficient options?

James Dyson has built a career on making everyday products work better. His line of vacuum cleaners has taken a unique market position by providing greater suction and cleaning ability than major competitors. One of Dyson's innovations is the Airblade. The Airblade is a hand dryer like the ones you see in public and corporate restrooms that blows filtered, unheated air through a narrow opening the width of an eyelash at 400 miles per hour. Your hands are dried in just 12 seconds, and the Airblade uses 80 percent less energy than conventional dryers. The downside is that each unit costs $1,400—about three times as much as traditional hand dryers.

Dyson admits to the unique challenge in marketing the Airblade. If you want a better vacuum cleaner, for example, you go out and buy one. But what business wants to remove perfectly adequate, functioning technology in their restrooms and replace them with "superior" technology? To spur interest and create some buzz about the product, Dyson gave away 1,000 machines (costing $840 each to manufacture). These giveaways were placed in high-traffic locations, such as the London Eye, a popular tourist spot. Current Airblade customers include the Le Parker Meridien New York Hotels; Advocate Lutheran General Hospital in Park Ridge, Illinois; and AMC movie theaters. The National Sanitation Foundation called the Airblade the world's first "hygienic hand dryer," thanks to its HEPA filter. The challenge for Dyson was selling its better, cleaner product at a higher price when capital expenditures on such an item were not necessary. Should other companies feel pressured to innovate in this way?[c]

financial services, and information. The forces unleashed by the Internet are particularly important in business-to-business relationships, where uncertainties are being reduced by improving the quantity, reliability, and timeliness of information.

Adoption and Use of Technology

Many companies lose their status as market leaders because they fail to keep up with technological changes. It is important for firms to determine when a technology is changing the industry and to define the strategic influence of the new technology. For example, wireless devices in use today include radios, cell phones, laptop computers, TVs, pagers, and car keys. To remain competitive, companies today must keep up with and adapt to technological advances.

The extent to which a firm can protect inventions that stem from research also influences its use of technology. How secure a product is from imitation depends on how easily others can copy it without violating its patent. If groundbreaking products and processes cannot be protected through patents, a company is less likely to market them and make the benefits of its research available to competitors.

Through a procedure known as *technology assessment*, managers try to foresee the effects of new products and processes on their firm's operations, on other business organizations, and on society in general. With information obtained through a technology assessment, management tries to estimate whether benefits of adopting a specific technology outweigh costs to the firm and to society at large. The degree to which a business is technologically based also influences its managers' response to technology.

Sociocultural Forces

sociocultural forces The influences in a society and its culture(s) that change people's attitudes, beliefs, norms, customs, and lifestyles

Sociocultural forces are the influences in a society and its culture(s) that bring about changes in people's attitudes, beliefs, norms, customs, and lifestyles. Profoundly affecting how people live, these forces help determine what, where, how, and when people buy products. Like the other environmental forces, sociocultural forces present marketers with both challenges and opportunities. For a closer look at sociocultural forces, we examine three major issues: demographic and diversity characteristics, cultural values, and consumerism.

Retired *but busy.*

Wireless *but easy.*

Introducing the Coupe.™ Exclusively from
Verizon Wireless. With a large, easy-to-read screen and
keypad, plus dedicated buttons for emergency contacts.
It's everything you need, and nothing you don't.
Backed by the Good Housekeeping Seal and
America's most reliable wireless network.

verizonwireless.com

See verizonwireless.com/bestnetwork for details.

© Verizon Wireless

Demographic Changes
*Verizon Wireless often targets older customers with
phones that are easier to use.*

Demographic and Diversity Characteristics

Changes in a population's demographic characteristics—
age, gender, race, ethnicity, marital and parental status,
income, and education—have a significant bearing on
relationships and individual behavior. These shifts lead
to changes in how people live and ultimately in their
consumption of such products as food, clothing, housing,
transportation, communication, recreation, education,
and health services. We look at a few of the changes in
demographics and diversity that are affecting marketing
activities.

One demographic change that is affecting the
marketplace is the increasing proportion of older
consumers. According to the U.S. Bureau of the Census,
the number of people age 65 and older is expected to
more than double by the year 2050, reaching 88 million.[29]
Consequently, marketers can expect significant increases
in the demand for health-care services, recreation, tourism,
retirement housing, and selected skin-care products. Even
online companies are trying to take advantage of the
opportunities baby boomers present. For example, several
online dating sites directed toward boomers were recently
launched, such as BabyBoomerPeopleMeet.com and
SeniorPeopleMeet.com.[30]

To reach older customers effectively, of course,
marketers must understand the diversity within the mature
market with respect to geographic location, income,
marital status, and limitations in mobility and self-care.

The number of singles is also on the rise. Nearly 41
percent of U.S. adults are single, and many plan to remain
that way. Moreover, single men who live alone comprise
11 percent of all households (up from 3.5 percent in 1970),
and single women who live alone make up nearly 15 percent (up from 7.3 percent in
1970).[31] Single people have quite different spending patterns than couples and families
with children. They are less likely to own homes and thus buy less furniture and
fewer appliances. They spend more heavily on convenience foods, restaurants, travel,
entertainment, and recreation. In addition, they tend to prefer smaller packages, whereas
families often buy bulk goods and products packaged in multiple servings.

The United States is entering another baby boom, with more than 84 million
Americans age 19 or younger. The new baby boom represents 27.1 percent of the total
population; the original baby boomers, born between 1946 and 1964, account for
nearly 26 percent.[32] The children of the original baby boomers differ from one another
radically in terms of race, living arrangements, and socioeconomic status. Thus, the
newest baby boom is much more diverse than in previous generations.

Another noteworthy population trend is the increasingly multicultural nature of U.S.
society. Because of this, the federal government decided to produce the advertisements for
the 2010 Census in 28 different languages rather than only in English.[33] The number of
immigrants into the United States has steadily risen during the last 40 years. In the 1960s,
3.3 million people immigrated to the United States; in the 1970s, 4.4 million immigrated;
in the 1980s, 7.3 million arrived; in the 1990s, the United States received 9.1 million
immigrants; and in the 2000s, more than 8.3 million people have immigrated to the
United States.[34] In contrast to earlier immigrants, very few recent ones are of European
origin. Another reason for the increasing cultural diversification of the United States
is that most recent immigrants are relatively young, whereas U.S. citizens of European

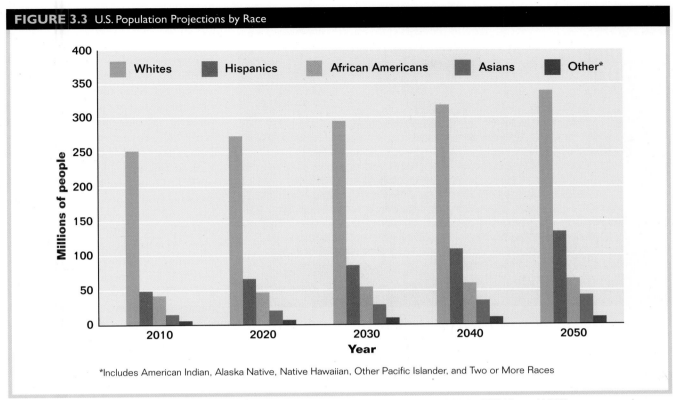

FIGURE 3.3 U.S. Population Projections by Race

*Includes American Indian, Alaska Native, Native Hawaiian, Other Pacific Islander, and Two or More Races

Source: U.S. Bureau of the Census, "Projections of the Population by Sex, Race, and Hispanic Origin for the United States: 2010 to 2050," August 14, 2008. www.census.gov/population/www/projections/summarytables.html.

origin are growing older. These younger immigrants tend to have more children than their older counterparts, further shifting the population balance. By the turn of the 20th century, the U.S. population had shifted from one dominated by whites to one consisting largely of three racial and ethnic groups: whites, blacks, and Hispanics. The U.S. government projects that by the year 2050, more than 133 million Hispanics, 66 million blacks, and 41 million Asians will call the United States home.[35] Figure 3.3 depicts how experts believe the U.S. population will change over the next 40 years.

Marketers recognize that these profound changes in the U.S. population bring unique problems and opportunities. But a diverse population means a more diverse customer base, and marketing practices must be modified—and diversified—to meet its changing needs. For example, Hispanics wield about $862 billion in annual buying power, and experts project that figure will grow to $1.3 trillion by 2015.[36] In an effort to target this expanding demographic, Hewlett-Packard has been studying the Hispanic population to identify trends and opportunities. According to HP, children have a large impact on brand choice for technological products in Hispanic families. Therefore, when marketing to this demographic, the company highlights the benefits of the product for parents while also displaying the popular features for children.[37]

Cultural Values

Changes in cultural values have dramatically influenced people's needs and desires for products. Although cultural values do not shift overnight, they do change at varying speeds. Marketers try to monitor these changes, knowing this information can equip them to predict changes in consumers' needs for products, at least in the near future.

Starting in the late 1980s, issues of health, nutrition, and exercise grew in importance. People today are more concerned about the foods they eat and thus are choosing healthier

Entrepreneurial Marketing

Entrepreneurs Fight Hunger with Plumpy'nut

More than 850 million people live in a state of hunger today, killing more people annually than AIDS, malaria, and tuberculosis combined. The nonprofit organization Nutriset has been selling food products to combat hunger and malnutrition since 1986. The company launched "Plumpy'nut," a three-ounce peanut butter–based food packet with 500 calories that does not require clean water and can be consumed by a child without assistance from an adult, a true revolution in the management of severe malnutrition. A day's worth of the product costs about $1 per child. Nutriset has partnered with entrepreneurs in Africa and the Caribbean to make the product locally, even using local ingredients when possible. Nutriset has found a way to combine entrepreneurship and social responsibility.[d]

products. Compared to those in the previous two decades, Americans today are more likely to favor smoke-free environments and to consume less alcohol. They have also altered their sexual behavior to reduce the risk of contracting sexually transmitted diseases. Marketers have responded with a proliferation of foods, beverages, and exercise products that fit this new lifestyle, as well as with programs to help people quit smoking and contraceptives that are safer and more effective. Americans are also becoming increasingly open to alternative medicines and nutritionally improved foods. As a result, sales of organic foods, herbs and herbal remedies, vitamins, and dietary supplements have escalated. In addition to the proliferation of new organic brands, such as Earthbound Farm, Horizon Dairy, and Whole Foods' 365, many conventional marketers have introduced organic versions of their products, including Orville Redenbacher, Heinz, and even Walmart.

The major source of cultural values is the family. For years, when asked about the most-important aspects of their lives, adults specified family issues and a happy marriage. Today, however, only one out of two marriages is predicted to last. Values regarding the permanence of marriage are changing. Because a happy marriage is prized so highly, more people are willing to give up an unhappy one and seek a different marriage partner or opt to stay single.

Children continue to be very important. Marketers have responded with safer, upscale baby gear and supplies, children's electronics, and family entertainment products. Marketers are also aiming more marketing efforts directly at children because children often play pivotal roles in purchasing decisions. A recent study in Austria reported that children influence twice as many purchase decisions in the supermarket than parents are aware of, and the majority of items children requested are products positioned at their eye-level.[38]

Children and family values are also factors in the trend toward more eat-out and take-out meals. Busy families in which both parents work generally want to spend less time in the kitchen and more time together enjoying themselves. Beneficiaries of this trend have primarily been fast-food and casual restaurants like McDonald's, Taco Bell, and Applebee's, but most supermarkets have added more ready-to-cook and ready-to-serve meal components to meet the needs of busy customers. Some also offer dine-in cafés.

Green marketing helps establish long-term consumer relationships by maintaining, supporting, and enhancing the natural environment. One of society's environmental hurdles is proper disposal of waste, especially of nondegradable materials such as disposable diapers and polystyrene packaging. Companies have responded by developing more environmentally sensitive products and packaging. Procter & Gamble, for example, uses recycled materials in some of its packaging and sells environment-friendly refills. Companies like Seventh Generation, which sells products like paper towels and bathroom tissue made from recycled paper as well as eco-friendly cleaning products, have entered the mainstream. Everything the company produces is as environmentally friendly as it can be, in hopes of having as little impact on the next seven generations as possible.[39] A number of marketers sponsor recycling programs and encourage their customers to take part in them.

Consumerism

Consumerism involves organized efforts by individuals, groups, and organizations to protect consumers' rights. The movement's major forces are individual consumer advocates, consumer organizations and other interest groups, consumer education, and consumer laws.

To achieve their objectives, consumers and their advocates write letters or send e-mails to companies, lobby government agencies, broadcast public service announcements, and boycott companies whose activities they deem irresponsible. Consider that a number of consumers would like to eliminate telemarketing and e-mail spam, and some of them have joined organizations and groups attempting to stop these activities. As discussed earlier, telemarketing activities have been significantly restricted through regulation. Businesses that engage in questionable practices invite additional regulation. For example, several organizations evaluate children's products for safety, often announcing dangerous products before Christmas so parents can avoid them. Other actions by the consumer movement have resulted in seat belts and air bags in automobiles, dolphin-free tuna, the banning of unsafe three-wheel motorized vehicles, and numerous laws regulating product safety and information. We take a closer look at consumerism in the next chapter.

consumerism Organized efforts by individuals, groups, and organizations to protect consumers' rights

summary

1. To recognize the importance of environmental scanning and analysis

The marketing environment consists of external forces that directly or indirectly influence an organization's acquisition of inputs (personnel, financial resources, raw materials, and information) and generation of outputs (goods, services, and ideas). The marketing environment includes competitive, economic, political, legal and regulatory, technological, and sociocultural forces.

Environmental scanning is the process of collecting information about forces in the marketing environment; environmental analysis is the process of assessing and interpreting information obtained in scanning. This information helps marketing managers predict opportunities and threats associated with environmental fluctuation. Marketing managers may assume either a passive, reactive approach or a proactive, aggressive approach in responding to these environmental fluctuations. The choice depends on the organization's structures and needs and on the composition of environmental forces that affect it.

2. To understand how competitive and economic factors affect an organization's ability to compete and a customer's ability and willingness to buy products

All businesses compete for customers' dollars. A marketer, however, generally defines *competition* as other firms that market products that are similar to or can be substituted for its products in the same geographic area. These competitors can be classified into one of four types: brand competitors, product competitors, generic competitors, and total budget competitors. The number of firms controlling the supply of a product may affect the strength of competitors. The four general types of competitive structures are monopoly, oligopoly, monopolistic competition, and pure competition. Marketers monitor what competitors are currently doing and assess changes occurring in the competitive environment.

General economic conditions, buying power, and willingness to spend can strongly influence marketing decisions and activities. The overall state of the economy fluctuates in a general pattern known as the business cycle, which consists of four stages: prosperity, recession, depression, and recovery. Consumers' goods, services, and financial holdings make up their buying power, or ability to purchase. Financial sources of buying power are income, credit, and wealth. After-tax income used for spending or saving is disposable income. Disposable income left after an individual has purchased the basic necessities of food, clothes, and shelter is discretionary income. Factors affecting buyers' willingness to spend include product price; level of satisfaction obtained from currently used products; family size; and expectations about future employment, income, prices, and general economic conditions.

3. To identify the types of political forces in the marketing environment

The political, legal, and regulatory forces of the marketing environment are closely interrelated. Political forces may determine what laws and regulations affecting specific marketers are enacted and how much the government purchases and from which suppliers. They can also be important in helping organizations secure foreign markets. Companies influence political forces in several ways, including maintaining good relationships with political officials, protesting the actions of legislative bodies, helping elect individuals who regard them positively to public office through campaign contributions, and employing lobbyists to communicate their concerns to elected officials.

4. To understand how laws, government regulations, and self-regulatory agencies affect marketing activities

Federal legislation affecting marketing activities can be divided into procompetitive legislation—laws designed to preserve and encourage competition—and consumer protection laws, which generally relate to product safety and information disclosure. Actual effects of legislation are determined by how marketers and courts interpret the laws. Federal guidelines for sentencing violations of these laws represent an attempt to force marketers to comply with the laws.

Federal, state, and local regulatory agencies usually have power to enforce specific laws. They also have some discretion in establishing operating rules and drawing up regulations to guide certain types of industry practices. Industry self-regulation represents another regulatory force; marketers view this type of regulation more favorably than government action because they have more opportunity to take part in creating guidelines. Self-regulation may be less expensive than government regulation, and its guidelines are generally more realistic. However, such regulation generally cannot ensure compliance as effectively as government agencies.

5. To explore the effects of new technology on society and on marketing activities

Technology is the application of knowledge and tools to solve problems and perform tasks more efficiently.

Consumer demand, buyer behavior, product development, packaging, promotion, prices, and distribution systems are all influenced directly by technology. The rapid technological growth of the last few decades is expected to accelerate. Revolutionary changes in communication technology have allowed marketers to reach vast numbers of people; however, with this expansion of communication has come concern about privacy and intellectual property. And while science and medical research have brought many great advances, cloning and genetically modified foods are controversial issues in many segments of society. Home, health, leisure, and work are all influenced to varying degrees by technology and technological advances. The *dynamics* of technology involves the constant change which challenges every aspect of our society. *Reach* refers to the broad nature of technology as it moves through and affects society.

Many companies lose their status as market leaders because they fail to keep up with technological changes. The ability to protect inventions from competitor imitation is also an important consideration when making marketing decisions.

6. To analyze sociocultural issues marketers must deal with as they make decisions

Sociocultural forces are the influences in a society and its culture that result in changes in attitudes, beliefs, norms, customs, and lifestyles. Major sociocultural issues directly affecting marketers include demographic and diversity characteristics, cultural values, and consumerism.

Changes in a population's demographic characteristics, such as age, income, race, and ethnicity, can lead to changes in that population's consumption of products. Changes in cultural values, such as those relating to health, nutrition, family, and the natural environment, have had striking effects on people's needs for products and therefore are closely monitored by marketers. Consumerism involves the efforts of individuals, groups, and organizations to protect consumers' rights. Consumer rights organizations inform and organize other consumers, raise issues, help businesses develop consumer-oriented programs, and pressure lawmakers to enact consumer protection laws.

Go to www.cengagebrain.com for resources to help you master the content in this chapter as well as materials that will expand your marketing knowledge!

important terms

environmental
scanning, 64

environmental
analysis, 65

competition, 66

brand competitors, 66

product competitors, 66

generic competitors, 66

total budget
competitors, 66

monopoly, 67

oligopoly, 67

monopolistic
competition, 67

pure competition, 67

business cycle, 68

prosperity, 68

recession, 68

depression, 69

recovery, 69

buying power, 69

income, 69

disposable income, 69

discretionary income, 69

wealth, 70

willingness to spend, 70

Federal Trade
Commission (FTC), 75

Better Business Bureau
(BBB), 77

National Advertising
Review Board
(NARB), 78

technology, 78

sociocultural forces, 81

consumerism, 85

discussion and review questions

1. Why are environmental scanning and analysis important to marketers?
2. What are the four types of competition? Which is most important to marketers?
3. In what ways can each of the business cycle stages affect consumers' reactions to marketing strategies?
4. What business cycle stage are we experiencing currently? How is this stage affecting business firms in your area?
5. Define *income, disposable income,* and *discretionary income.* How does each type of income affect consumer buying power?
6. How do wealth and consumer credit affect consumer buying power?
7. What factors influence a buyer's willingness to spend?
8. Describe marketers' attempts to influence political forces.
9. What types of problems do marketers experience as they interpret legislation?
10. What are the goals of the Federal Trade Commission? List the ways in which the FTC affects marketing activities.

Do you think a single regulatory agency should have such broad jurisdiction over so many marketing practices? Why or why not?

11. Name several nongovernmental regulatory forces. Do you believe self-regulation is more or less effective than governmental regulatory agencies? Why?
12. What does the term *technology* mean to you? Do the benefits of technology outweigh its costs and potential dangers? Defend your answer.
13. Discuss the impact of technology on marketing activities.
14. What factors determine whether a business organization adopts and uses technology?
15. What evidence exists that cultural diversity is increasing in the United States?
16. In what ways are cultural values changing? How are marketers responding to these changes?
17. Describe consumerism. Analyze some active consumer forces in your area.

application questions

1. Assume you are opening one of the following retail stores. Identify publications at the library or online that provide information about the environmental forces likely to affect the store. Briefly summarize the information each source provides.
   a. Convenience store
   b. Women's clothing store
   c. Grocery store
   d. Fast-food restaurant
   e. Furniture store

2. For each of the following products, identify brand competitors, product competitors, generic competitors, and total budget competitors.
   a. Chevrolet Tahoe
   b. Levi's jeans
   c. Travelocity

3. Technological advances and sociocultural forces have a great impact on marketers. Identify at least one technological advance and one sociocultural change that has affected you as a consumer. Explain the impact of each change on your needs as a customer.

internet exercise

The Federal Trade Commission

To learn more about the Federal Trade Commission and its functions, look at the FTC's website at **www.ftc.gov**.

I. Based on information on the website, describe the FTC's impact on marketing.

2. Examine the sections entitled Newsroom and Formal Actions. Describe three recent incidents of illegal or inappropriate marketing activities and the FTC's response to those actions.

3. How could the FTC's website assist a company in avoiding misconduct?

developing your marketing plan

CRITICAL THINKING

A marketing strategy is dynamic. Companies must constantly monitor the marketing environment not only to create their marketing strategy but to revise it if necessary. Information about various forces in the marketplace is collected, analyzed, and used as a foundation for several marketing plan decisions. The following questions will help you to understand how the information in this chapter contributes to the development of your marketing plan.

I. Describe the current competitive market for your product. Can you identify the number of brands or market share they hold? Expand your analysis to include other products that are similar or could be substituted for yours.

2. Using the business cycle pattern, in which of the four stages is the current state of the economy? Can you

identify any changes in consumer buying power that would affect the sale and use of your product?

3. Referring to Tables 3.2 and 3.3, do you recognize any laws or regulatory agencies that would have jurisdiction over your type of product?

4. Conduct a brief technology assessment, determining the impact that technology has on your product, its sale, or use.

5. Discuss how your product could be affected by changes in social attitudes, demographic characteristics, or lifestyles.

The information obtained from these questions should assist you in developing various aspects of your marketing plan found in the *Interactive Marketing Plan* exercise at **www.cengagebrain.com.**

VIDEO CASE 3.1

The Ever-Changing Environment of Organic Valley

CRITICAL THINKING

Founded in 1988, Organic Valley is one of the nation's largest organic dairy cooperatives with more than 1,600 farm families in 32 states. Organic Valley works with small, independent organic dairy farmers, ensuring a high standard of quality and a fair price for farmer

output. The cooperative produces an ever-expanding line of 200 Organic Valley–branded dairy foods and beverages, including milks, cheeses, yogurts, and eggs. Some Organic Valley farmers also market meats, juices, butter, fruits, and vegetables under the cooperative's brand.

Paul Deutsch of Sweet Ridge Organic Dairy Farm is a member of the Organic Valley cooperative. After working for some time at a conventional commercial dairy farm, Deutsch became fed up over the condition of the animals, the drugs administered to animals, and the amount of pollution that the factory farms caused. He determined that large conventional farms produced an inferior product with less taste and less nutritional value. Deutsch purchased his own land so he could work on his own terms—cultivating healthier land and healthier, more productive cows. By the late 1990s, his farm was certified organic and soon after, he became a member of Organic Valley. Deutsch now benefits from the good reputation and extensive distribution channels of Organic Valley as well as the large network of knowledge and support of fellow organic farmers.

The life of an organic farmer is not easy: keeping plants and animals healthy without chemicals can be labor intensive and complicated, and ensuring compliance with the myriad of regulatory standards that govern organic foods can be daunting. Yet as organics move into the mainstream, marketing such products has become considerably easier. Changing consumer attitudes toward organic products has profoundly affected how, when, where, and what people buy. As consumers hear news of salmonella-tainted vegetables, infected meat, and the harmful environmental

effects of conventional farming, they are more likely to buy and eat organic foods. Media coverage has built public awareness of organic products as a nutritious and environmentally friendly alternative to conventionally produced foods.

For nearly 15 years, the entire organic industry enjoyed 20 percent annual growth rates. During the same period, sales of organic dairy products grew by 27 percent annually. However, while the global economy was in recession, sales of organic dairy goods barely grew. Organic Valley has felt the effects of this challenging situation. After 21 consecutive years of steady sales growth, Organic Valley's annual revenue experienced a slight dip for the first time in 2009, to $520 million.

On the other hand, thanks to the "buy local" movement and heightened knowledge of organic products' benefits, community farmers' markets have never been so popular. Organic grocers, like Whole Foods, are as large as and more profitable than conventional supermarkets. Organic food brands, once

available only in specialty shops and health food stores, are showing up in all supermarkets. Also, farmers benefit from higher profit margins and healthier, chemical-free work environments.

While organic has not caught on in all parts of the country, it is a growing trend that has afforded the likes of Deutsch a means of doing what he loves while supplying the marketplace with nutritious, safe products. Consumer demand is driving the expansion of the organic industry and providing brands like Organic Valley with increased distribution opportunities. Because Organic Valley is a cooperative, as it expands and takes on new members, farmers like Deutsch can directly benefit from growth of Organic Valley as well as the industry at large. The cooperative model also encourages collaboration, not competition, between other members of the co-op. For example, to learn from each other, Deutsch and other farmers in the region get together periodically to share advice, knowledge, and methods so that they can all benefit from the best practices of their peers.

Organic Valley and other co-ops like it are concerned not only about the health of the cows and the environment but also with the well-being of small farmers and their communities. Therefore, the Organic Valley cooperative has developed a profit-sharing model in which farmers and employees each receive 45 percent of the profits and their communities receive the remaining 10 percent. This model not only builds loyal producers; it also encourages a growing base of loyal consumers as more people recognize the health benefits of organic products and the good things the cooperative does for small farming communities. These trends are opening doors and providing competitive advantages for Deutsch and for all of Organic Valley's members.[40]

QUESTIONS FOR DISCUSSION

1. Has Organic Valley differentiated its product offerings from those of traditional dairies?

2. How do economic forces appear to be affecting Organic Valley's marketing performance?

3. What role do legal and regulatory forces seem to be playing in the marketing environment for organic foods and Organic Valley?

CASE 3.2

First Solar Power Profits by Marketing Sun Power

CRITICAL THINKING

First Solar wants to meet the world's vast energy needs with the power of the sun. Given gyrating oil prices and concerns over the long-term environmental effects of fossil fuels, alternative energy is now recognized as a responsible and economical option for consumers and businesses. That's good news for First Solar, based in Tempe, Arizona, a leading designer, manufacturer, and marketer of solar energy equipment and utility-sized power plants.

Founded in 1999, the company was originally funded by the Walton family of Walmart fame. Its mission is "to create enduring value by enabling a world powered by clean, affordable solar electricity." The company has become known for its razor-thin cadmium telluride solar cells and panels, which are specially designed to produce electricity efficiently, even on cloudy days. During the 2000s, First Solar has steadily reduced the cost of manufacturing a watt of solar power, bringing it below $1 per watt for the first time in 2008. By 2014, the company aims to slash the cost to little more than 50 cents per watt, making solar power a highly price-competitive alternative to traditional energy.

Among First Solar's products are modules designed for use in large-scale, grid-connected solar power plants. These molecules are sold to major solar project developers for use in commercial projects. The company is also expanding into the construction of entire power plants equipped with its wafer-thin solar panels, such as the massive plant it recently began building in China. When completed in 2019, this 25-square-mile facility in China will cover more space than the island of Manhattan. Such installations are complex, multiyear projects, requiring First Solar's engineers to work closely with the firm's project development partners in planning the optimal balance of systems and solutions for solar energy generation at each site.

One of First Solar's key advantages is that its main product is not dependent on the silicon wafers used by most of the solar industry. Silicon is in short supply and quite expensive, creating a bottleneck for many competitors. This advantage enables First Solar to be aggressive in growing its production capabilities and planning to serve markets that are undersupplied.

The company also maintains a global perspective to enhance marketing opportunities, achieve market penetration, and achieve maximum production efficiency. Not long ago, First Solar's primary target market was Germany. This is because Europe remains slightly ahead of the United States in seeking renewable energy alternatives and tackling the environmental pollution concerns associated with fossil fuels. Germany, among other European nations, has encouraged the development of alternative energy sources by subsidizing electrical rates for energy from solar power. With the German government's subsidies soon to be reduced, however, First Solar and its competitors will face a vastly different marketing environment in Germany and elsewhere, making price more important than ever before.

Although First Solar continues to target European customers, its marketers have also noticed dramatically higher demand for the installation of solar modules on commercial and residential rooftops around the United States and Canada. In addition, North American utilities are rapidly going green by harnessing solar power, wind power, and other clean alternatives to fossil fuels. Now, by targeting North American utilities, First Solar can move into the mainstream of providing cells and panels for power that can reach everyone, not just those individuals and businesses that have their own solar generators. Among other projects, the company has reached an agreement to design and build a sizable solar power plant for Southern California Edison.

First Solar is strategically positioned to use the unique technology associated with its cadmium telluride cells plus its knowledge of the marketing environment to power its way to profits in the emerging alternative energy industry. For future growth, the company will have to continue assessing ever-changing factors such as competition, fossil fuel prices, governmental subsidies, technological innovations, customer behavior, and social attitudes. Population growth and

© iStockphoto.com/Andreas Weber / © John Wang/Photodisc/Getty Images infrastructure development are also vital influences on First Solar's marketing plans because they determine how much additional energy a city or nation will require.

In the coming years, customer attitudes and the willingness of businesses and consumers to adopt (and pay for) renewable energy practices will only become more important to increased demand for solar power. Given the combined effect of all these environmental trends, can First Solar maintain its marketing momentum in the global marketplace?[41]

QUESTIONS FOR DISCUSSION

1. Which forces in the marketing environment are likely to have the greatest influence on First Solar's marketing in the short term? In the long term?

2. What should First Solar do to scan the marketing environment in search of potential opportunities and threats?

3. Do you think that First Solar should pay the most attention to brand competition, product competition, generic competition, or total budget competition? Explain your answer.

Chapter 4

Social Responsibility and Ethics in Marketing

OBJECTIVES

1. To understand the concept and dimensions of social responsibility

2. To define and describe the importance of marketing ethics

3. To become familiar with ways to improve ethical decisions in marketing

4. To understand the role of social responsibility and ethics in improving marketing performance

The Ethics and Social Responsibility of Sports Marketing

The National Collegiate Athletic Association (NCAA) is a governing body that creates rules meant to protect student athletes and their colleges. For example, an enrolled student is not allowed to permit an agent to pursue professional engagements on the student's behalf. Students are also forbidden to accept money from agents or marketers. Additionally, advertisers/marketers are forbidden to pay to use student athlete images, unless the usage is sanctioned by the NCAA. Students and colleges that break these rules face consequences from the NCAA such as probation, loss of scholarships, or even bans on particular sports.

Some college athletics departments have had trouble adhering to these guidelines. In 2006, University of Southern California (USC) football player Reggie Bush was accused of accepting cash and gifts from agents. Bush denied the charges. Former USC basketball coach Tim Floyd resigned after accusations surfaced that alleged Floyd had paid an individual to recruit basketball superstar O. J. Mayo. The NCAA responded by investigating the entire USC athletics program, and USC self-imposed sanctions on its basketball team.

College athletics also face a threat from outside companies looking to capitalize on their success. Some of these companies create ethical issues for underage students. For instance, Anheuser-Busch was reprimanded for its Bud Light Fan Can campaign, which featured beer cans sporting the colors of 26 top teams. The Federal Trade Commission's alcohol attorney, Janet Evan, along with universities such as The University of Michigan and Boston College, argued, that the promotion could encourage underage drinking among students. Anheuser-Busch countered that its cans were sold only to customers 21 and over. However, this argument was not enough to alleviate concerns, and Anheuser-Busch finally agreed to stop the program.

Determined to boost revenue, many college and professional sports teams are selling ad placements to the highest bidder, resulting in an overwhelming amount of ads in most stadiums. The NCAA has become concerned about whether schools are too willing to compromise their integrity in exchange for marketing dollars. Certainly, colleges should be allowed to promote their teams, but where should the NCAA draw the line? Although it is challenging, and schools and individuals will hit road blocks along the way, behaving ethically and responsibly is the key to maintaining the integrity of schools, teams, and collegiate sports.[1]

Most businesses operate responsibly and within the limits of the law, but organizations often walk a fine line between acting ethically and engaging in questionable behavior. Certain activities, such as a coach paying individuals to recruit skilled players or a player who accepts bribes from agents, are a direct violation of governing bodies like the NCAA. Other questionable activities, however, are not necessarily illegal. For example, Anheuser-Busch's Bud Light Fan Can campaign was not against the law but could be construed as unethical if it encouraged underage drinking. Ethics often goes above and beyond the law and should therefore be a critical concern of marketers.

Some of the most common types of unethical practices among companies include questionable selling practices, bribery, price discrimination, deceptive advertising, misleading packaging, and marketing defective products. Deceptive advertising in particular causes consumers to become defensive toward all promotional messages and distrustful of all advertising, so it hurts not only consumers but the marketers as well.[2] Practices of this kind raise questions about marketers' obligations to society. Inherent in these questions are the issues of social responsibility and marketing ethics.

Because social responsibility and ethics often have profound impacts on the success of marketing strategies, we devote this chapter to their role in marketing decision making. We begin by defining social responsibility and exploring its dimensions. We then discuss social responsibility issues, such as the natural environment and the marketer's role as a member of the community. Next, we define and examine the role of ethics in marketing decisions. We consider ethical issues in marketing, the ethical decision-making process, and ways to improve ethical conduct in marketing. Finally, we incorporate social responsibility and ethics into strategic market planning.

social responsibility An organization's obligation to maximize its positive impact and minimize its negative impact on society

The Nature of Social Responsibility

In marketing, **social responsibility** refers to an organization's obligation to maximize its positive impact and minimize its negative impact on society. Social responsibility thus deals with the total effect of all marketing decisions on society. In marketing, social responsibility includes the managerial processes needed to monitor, satisfy, and even exceed stakeholder expectations and needs.[3] Remember from Chapter 1 that stakeholders are groups that have a "stake," or claim, in some aspect of a company's products, operations, markets, industry, and outcomes. CEOs such as Indra Nooyi, chairperson and CEO of PepsiCo, are increasingly recognizing that in the future companies will have to "do better by doing better." She goes on to say that "performance without purpose is not a long-term sustainable formula."[4]

Ample evidence demonstrates that ignoring stakeholders' demands for responsible marketing can destroy customers' trust and even prompt government regulations. Irresponsible actions that anger customers, employees, or competitors may not only jeopardize a marketer's financial standing but have legal repercussions as well. For instance, General Electric was ordered to pay $11.3 million for making false advertising claims. The judge ruled that the company misconstrued a competitor's product when a GE-owned company claimed that its

© AP Images/PRNewsFoto/WWF

The Nature of Social Responsibility
Nonprofit organizations like the World Wildlife Foundation create awareness of environmental concerns for businesses and consumers.

X-ray contrast agent caused fewer heart and kidney problems than a competitor's contrast agent. The GE-owned company lacked sufficient evidence to back up its claims. The judge determined that GE had violated the Lanham Act, an act passed to prevent false advertising, and forced GE to reimburse its competitor for past and future expenses incurred to mitigate the damage.[5]

In contrast, socially responsible activities can generate positive publicity and boost sales. The Avon Products–sponsored Breast Cancer Awareness Crusade, for example, has helped raise nearly $640 million to fund community-based breast cancer education and early-detection services. Within the first few years of the Awareness Crusade, hundreds of stories about Avon's efforts appeared in major media, which contributed to an increase in company sales. Avon, a marketer of women's cosmetics, is also known for employing a large number of women and promoting them to top management; more than half of the firm's top management consists of women (55 percent worldwide), prompting the National Association for Female Executives to rank Avon in the top 10 businesses dedicated to the advancement of women.[6]

Socially responsible efforts like Avon's have a positive impact on local communities; at the same time, they indirectly help the sponsoring organization by attracting goodwill, publicity, and potential customers and employees. Thus, although social responsibility is certainly a positive concept in itself, most organizations embrace it in the expectation of indirect long-term benefits. Our own research suggests that an organizational culture that is conducive to social responsibility engenders greater employee commitment and improved business performance.[7] Table 4.1 provides a sampling of companies that have chosen to make social responsibility a strategic long-term objective.

TABLE 4.1 Best Corporate Citizens

1	Bristol Myers-Squibb
2	General Mills Inc.
3	IBM Corp.
4	Merck & Co. Inc.
5	HP Co. L.P.
6	Cisco Systems Inc.
7	Mattel Inc.
8	Abbott Laboratories
9	Kimberly-Clark Corp.
10	Entergy Corp.
11	ExxonMobil Corp.
12	Wisconsin Energy Corp.
13	Intel Corp.
14	Procter & Gamble Co.
15	Hess Corp.
16	Xerox Corp.
17	3M Co.
18	Avon Products Inc.
19	Baxter International Inc.
20	Monsanto Co.

Source: "CRO's 100 Best Corporate Citizens 2009," *CRO*, http:// thecro.com/files/CRO100BestCorporateCitizensList2009.pdf (accessed February 10, 2010).

The Dimensions of Social Responsibility

Socially responsible organizations strive for **marketing citizenship** by adopting a strategic focus for fulfilling the economic, legal, ethical, and philanthropic social responsibilities that their stakeholders expect of them. Companies that consider the diverse perspectives of stakeholders in their daily operations and strategic planning are said to have a *stakeholder orientation,* an important element of social responsibility.[8] A stakeholder orientation in marketing goes beyond customers, competitors, and regulators to include understanding and addressing the needs of all stakeholders, including communities and special-interest groups. As a result, organizations are now under pressure to undertake initiatives that demonstrate a balanced perspective on stakeholder interests.[9] Pfizer, for example, has secured stakeholder input on a number of issues including rising health-care costs and health-care reform.[10] As Figure 4.1 shows, the economic, legal, ethical, and philanthropic dimensions of social responsibility can be viewed as a pyramid.[11] The economic and legal aspects have long been acknowledged, whereas ethical and philanthropic issues have gained recognition more recently.

At the most basic level, all companies have an economic responsibility to be profitable so that they can provide a return on investment to their owners and investors, create jobs for the community, and contribute goods and services to the economy. How organizations relate to shareholders, employees, competitors, customers, the community, and the natural environment affects the economy. When economic downturns or poor decisions lead companies to lay off employees, communities often suffer as they attempt to absorb the displaced employees. Customers may experience diminished levels of service as a result of fewer experienced employees. Stock prices often decline when layoffs are announced, reducing the value of shareholders' investment portfolios. Moreover, stressed-out employees facing demands to reduce expenses may make

marketing citizenship The adoption of a strategic focus for fulfilling the economic, legal, ethical, and philanthropic social responsibilities expected by stakeholders

FIGURE 4.1 The Pyramid of Corporate Social Responsibility

RESPONSIBILITIES

Philanthropic
Be a good corporate citizen
► Contribute resources to the community; improve quality of life

Ethical
Be ethical
► Obligation to do what is right, just, and fair
► Avoid harm

Legal
Obey the law
► Law is society's codification of right and wrong
► Play by the rules of the game

Economic
Be profitable
► The foundation upon which all others rest

Source: From Archie B. Carroll, "The Pyramid of Corporate Social Responsibility: Toward the Moral Management of Organizational Stakeholders," adaptation of Figure 3, p. 42. Reprinted from *Business Horizons,* July/August 1991. Copyright © 1991 by the Foundation for the School of Business at Indiana University. Reprinted with permission.

poor decisions that affect the natural environment, product quality, employee rights, and customer service. An organization's sense of economic responsibility is especially significant for employees, raising such issues as equal job opportunities, workplace diversity, job safety, health, and employee privacy. Economic responsibilities require finding a balance between society's demand for social responsibility and investors' desire for profits.

Marketers also have an economic responsibility to compete fairly. Size frequently gives companies an advantage over rivals. Large firms can often generate economies of scale that allow them to put smaller firms out of business. Consequently small companies and even whole communities may resist the efforts of firms like Walmart, Home Depot, and Best Buy to open stores in their vicinity. These firms are able to operate at such low costs that small, local firms find it difficult to compete. Though consumers appreciate lower prices, the failure of small businesses creates unemployment for some members of the community. Such issues create concerns about social responsibility for organizations, communities, and consumers.

Marketers are also expected, of course, to obey laws and regulations. The efforts of elected representatives and special-interest groups to promote responsible corporate behavior have resulted in laws and regulations designed to keep U.S. companies' actions within the range of acceptable conduct. When marketers engage in deceptive practices to advance their own interests over those of others, charges of fraud may result. In general, fraud is any purposeful communication that deceives, manipulates, or conceals facts to create a false impression. It is considered a crime, and convictions may result in fines, imprisonment, or both. One study revealed that fraud costs U.S. retailers more than $191 billion each year. Other types of fraud include tax fraud, where the individual or organization avoids paying taxes owed to the government, and healthcare fraud, which often involves filing false claims to insurance companies.[12]

When customers, interest groups, or businesses become outraged over what they perceive as irresponsibility on the part of a marketing organization, they may urge their legislators to draft new legislation to regulate the behavior or engage in litigation to force the organization to "play by the rules." The semiconductor manufacturer Advanced Micro Devices (AMD), for example, filed a lawsuit against Intel, accusing the company of using its influence to discourage computer makers not to carry AMD's chips. Intel settled with AMD by paying its competitor $125 billion.[13]

Economic and legal responsibilities are the most basic levels of social responsibility for a good reason: failure to consider them may mean that a marketer is not around long enough to engage in ethical or philanthropic activities. Beyond these dimensions is **marketing ethics**, principles and standards that define acceptable conduct in marketing as determined by various stakeholders, including the public, government regulators, private-interest groups, consumers, industry, and the organization itself. The most basic of these principles have been codified as laws and regulations to encourage marketers to conform to society's expectations for conduct. However, marketing ethics goes beyond legal issues. Ethical marketing decisions foster trust, which helps build long-term marketing relationships. We take a more detailed look at the ethical dimension of social responsibility later in this chapter.

At the top of the pyramid of corporate responsibility (see Figure 4.1) are philanthropic responsibilities. These responsibilities, which go beyond marketing ethics, are not required of a company, but they promote human welfare or goodwill, as do the economic, legal, and ethical dimensions of social responsibility. That many companies have demonstrated philanthropic responsibility is evidenced by the nearly $14.5 billion in annual corporate donations and contributions to environmental and social causes.[14] After natural disasters such as the earthquake in Haiti, for example, many corporations—including Coca-Cola, Target, Hewlett-Packard, Microsoft, Visa, Unilever, General Mills, FedEx, The Walt Disney Company, and Pfizer—donated millions of dollars in cash, supplies, equipment, food, and medicine to help victims.[15] Even small companies participate in philanthropy through donations and volunteer support of local causes and national charities, such as

marketing ethics Principles and standards that define acceptable marketing conduct as determined by various stakeholders

So-called "free goods" such as sunshine and fresh air may be of more real worth than most economic goods.

– Walter J. Kohler, 1934

Bold. Conservation.

Sometimes boldness is about clarity – about knowing what's important. For us, it's creating water-saving products people love to use. Products that can help a household save tens of thousands of gallons of water every year. Together, we make a world of difference.

WaterSense 2009 PARTNER OF THE YEAR | THE BOLD LOOK OF KOHLER.

SaveWaterAmerica.com

© Kohler Co.

Strategic Philanthropy
Kohler, as a WaterSense Partner, has started the Save Water America program. Through this campaign, Kohler contributes $1 (up to a total of $2 million) in water-saving products to Habitat for Humanity every time a customer completes a web quiz established to spread awareness.

the Red Cross and the United Way. For example, Austin-based Kerbey Lane Café strives to give back to the Austin community, with staff volunteering for charities such as the Special Olympics and the *Austin Race for the Cure*. The café also provides gift card and cash donations to charities like Habitat for Humanity, the American Cancer Society's Relay for Life, and the Sustainable Food Center, along with sponsoring four local schools.[16]

More companies than ever are adopting a strategic approach to corporate philanthropy. Many firms link their products to a particular social cause on an ongoing or short-term basis, a practice known as **cause-related marketing**. The yogurt company Yoplait, for example, launched its "Save Lids to Save Lives" campaign, where it placed pink lids on some of its yogurt products sold in stores. Consumers were encouraged to mail in the pink lids to Yoplait. The company promised to donate 10 cents to Susan G. Komen for the Cure (a breast cancer foundation) for every pink lid it received, up to $1.5 million.[17] Such cause-related programs tend to appeal to consumers because they provide an additional reason to "feel good" about a particular purchase. Marketers like the programs because well-designed ones increase sales and create feelings of respect and admiration for the companies involved. Indeed, research suggests that 85 percent of American consumers have a more positive opinion of an organization when it supports causes that they care about.[18] On the other hand, some companies are beginning to extend the concept of corporate philanthropy beyond financial contributions by adopting a **strategic philanthropy** approach, the synergistic use of organizational core competencies and resources to address key stakeholders' interests and achieve both organizational and social benefits. Strategic philanthropy involves employees, organizational resources and expertise, and the ability to link those assets to the concerns of key stakeholders, including employees, customers, suppliers, and social needs. Strategic philanthropy involves both financial and nonfinancial contributions to stakeholders (employee time, goods and services, and company technology and equipment, as well as facilities), but it also benefits the company.[19] Home Depot, for example, has been progressive in aligning its expertise and resources to address community needs. Its relationship with Habitat for Humanity gives employees a chance to improve their skills and bring direct knowledge back into the workplace to benefit customers. Home Depot has also embarked on sustainability initiatives that support green housing. The Home Depot Foundation has partnered with Habitat for Humanity to help build 5,000 green homes that will consume less energy, use less water, and emit lower levels of greenhouse gases. Home Depot also responds to customers' needs during disasters. During natural disasters, some home-building supply and hardware stores have taken advantage of customers by inflating prices on emergency materials, but Home Depot has opened its stores 24 hours a day and made materials available at reduced costs to help customers survive the disaster.[20]

Social Responsibility Issues

Although social responsibility may seem to be an abstract ideal, managers make decisions related to social responsibility every day. To be successful, a business must determine

cause-related marketing The practice of linking products to a particular social cause on an ongoing or short-term basis

strategic philanthropy The synergistic use of organizational core competencies and resources to address key stakeholders' interests and achieve both organizational and social benefits

TABLE 4.2 Social Responsibility Issues

Issue	Description	Major Social Concerns
Natural environment	Consumers insisting not only on a good quality of life but on a healthful environment so they can maintain a high standard of living during their lifetimes	Conservation Water pollution Air pollution Land pollution
Consumerism	Activities undertaken by independent individuals, groups, and organizations to protect their rights as consumers	The right to safety The right to be informed The right to choose The right to be heard
Community relations	Society eager to have marketers contribute to its well-being, wishing to know what marketers do to help solve social problems	Equality issues Disadvantaged members of society Safety and health Education and general welfare

sustainability The potential for the long-term well-being of the natural environment, including all biological entities, as well as the interaction among nature and individuals, organizations, and business strategies

what customers, government regulators, and competitors, as well as society in general, want or expect in terms of social responsibility. Table 4.2 summarizes three major categories of social responsibility issues: the natural environment, consumerism, and community relations.

SUSTAINABILITY

One of the more common ways marketers demonstrate social responsibility is through programs designed to protect and preserve the natural environment. **Sustainability** is the potential for the long-term well-being of the natural environment, including all

Sustainable Marketing
Fifth Group Strives for Zero Waste

As society becomes more environmentally conscious, consumers are starting to push businesses toward accountability in this area. Fifth Group, owner of several restaurants in Georgia, is stepping up to the challenge. In one year, Fifth Group has taken its restaurant Ecco from 100 percent waste to zero waste. All food left on plates is put directly into industrial composting bins, eliminating 30 percent of the restaurant's waste. The other 70 percent is taken care of via recycling. Only biodegradable and eco-friendly products are used in the kitchen. Fifth Group is so certain it can maintain zero waste that Ecco has no dumpsters. The company views its move as a shifting of habits rather than an expense, with a corporate culture that firmly supports such a shift.

Due to its environmental efforts, Fifth Group's Ecco has been awarded Green Foodservice Certification through the Green Foodservice Alliance (an organization dedicated to helping food service companies decrease waste). To achieve certification, a company must recycle all allowable materials, send used grease to be converted into local biofuel, avoid polystyrene, give all unsold food to charities, and have a plan in place to conserve energy. This is a tall order, but Ecco has been

able to fill it. Fifth Group is now moving its other restaurants in the same direction, aiming to comply with zero waste across the board.

Of course, in addition to reducing waste, Fifth Group's green marketing efforts can also have a profound financial effect. Consumers are showing increasing support for businesses living up to their social responsibilities, and individuals who share Fifth Group's environmental concerns may be more likely to patronize its restaurants. As environmental concern shows no signs of abating, going green may be not only the right thing but the profitable thing for businesses to do.[a]

© Iwona Grodzka/Shutterstock.com / © iStockphoto.com/Kutay Tanir

Top Eco-Actions Taken to Help the Environment

Survey respondents say recycling trash, reducing waste, and reusing materials make the biggest difference in protecting the environment

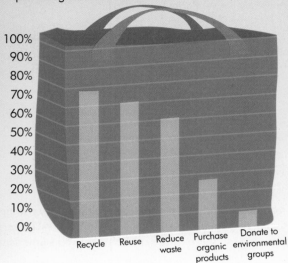

Source: Kelton Research.

Green Marketing
Climate Master assists consumers interested in energy efficiency with home improvement products that cut energy costs up to 80 percent.

biological entities, as well as the interaction among nature and individuals, organizations, and business strategies. Sustainability includes the assessment and improvement of business strategies, economic sectors, work practices, technologies, and lifestyles—all while maintaining the natural environment. Many companies are making contributions to environmental protection organizations, sponsoring and participating in cleanup events, promoting recycling, retooling manufacturing processes to minimize waste and pollution, and generally reevaluating the effects of their products on the natural environment. Procter & Gamble, for example, uses recycled materials in some of its packaging and sells refills for some products, which reduces packaging waste. Walmart provides on-site recycling for customers and encourages its suppliers to reduce wasteful packaging. It has also opened "green" prototype stores around the country, saved tens of millions of dollars in gas savings by overhauling its truck fleet, and announced an ambitious plan to implement a "green" labeling system for all of its products. The labels would inform consumers of each product's carbon footprint, as well as other information such as the amount of water used in manufacturing. The plan is ambitious, and detractors worry that it will increase costs for suppliers and consumers alike. Nevertheless, such a plan marks Walmart's continued push to be perceived as an environmentally responsible business.[21] Such efforts generate positive publicity and often increase sales for the companies involved.

Green marketing is a strategic process involving stakeholder assessment to create meaningful long-term relationships with customers while maintaining, supporting, and enhancing the natural environment. Toyota, Honda, and Ford, for example, have succeeded in marketing "hybrid" cars that use electric motors to augment their internal combustion engines, improving the vehicles' fuel economy without reducing their power. Benjamin Moore & Co. has introduced a line of paint called Aura that emits only about one-third as much in harmful volatile organic compounds (VOCs) as regular paint does.[22] Hewlett-Packard (HP) has taken a leadership role in the recycling of electronic waste by creating drop-off locations for rechargeable batteries and recycling programs for InkJet and LaserJet cartridges, computer hardware, and other electronic equipment.[23]

Many products have been certified as "green" by environmental organizations such as Green Seal and carry a special logo identifying their organization as green marketers. Lumber products at Home Depot, for example, may carry a seal from the Forest Stewardship Council to indicate that they were harvested from sustainable forests using environmentally friendly methods.[24] Likewise, most Chiquita bananas are certified through the Rainforest Alliance's Better Banana Project as having been grown with more environmentally and labor-friendly practices.[25] In Europe, companies can

FIGURE 4.2 The EU Ecolabel

© EU Ecolabel

voluntarily apply for the EU Ecolabel to indicate that their products are less harmful to the environment than competing products, based on scientifically determined criteria (see Figure 4.2).

Although demand for economic, legal, and ethical solutions to environmental problems is widespread, the environmental movement in marketing includes many different groups whose values and goals often conflict. Some environmentalists and marketers believe companies should work to protect and preserve the natural environment by implementing the following goals:

1. *Eliminate the concept of waste.* Recognizing that pollution and waste usually stem from inefficiency, the question is not what to do with waste but how to make things without waste.

2. *Reinvent the concept of a product.* Products should be reduced to only three types and eventually just two. The first type is consumables, which are eaten or, when placed in the ground, turn into soil with few harmful side effects. The second type is durable goods—such as cars, televisions, computers, and refrigerators—that should be made, used, and returned to the manufacturer within a closed-loop system. Such products should be designed for disassembly and recycling. The third category is unsalables and includes such products as radioactive materials, heavy metals, and toxins. These products should always belong to the original makers, who should be responsible for the products and their full life-cycle effects. Reclassifying products in this way encourages manufacturers to design products more efficiently.

3. *Make prices reflect the cost.* Every product should reflect or at least approximate its actual cost—not only the direct cost of production but also the cost of air, water, and soil. For example, the cost of a gallon of gasoline, according to the World Resources Institute in Washington, DC, is significantly more when pollution, waste disposal, health effects, and defense expenditures like those of the Persian Gulf and Iraq wars are

green marketing A strategic process involving stakeholder assessment to create meaningful long-term relationships with customers while maintaining, supporting, and enhancing the natural environment

factored in. Major disasters like the BP oil leak in the Gulf of Mexico also impact the price of gas.

4. *Make environmentalism profitable.* Consumers are beginning to recognize that competition in the marketplace should not occur between companies that are harming the environment and those that are trying to save it.[26]

CONSUMERISM

Another significant issue in socially responsible marketing is consumerism, which we defined in Chapter 3 as the efforts of independent individuals, groups, and organizations to protect the rights of consumers. A number of interest groups and individuals have taken action against companies they consider irresponsible by lobbying government officials and agencies, engaging in letter-writing campaigns and boycotts, and making public-service announcements. Some consumers choose to boycott firms and products out of a desire to support a cause and make a difference.[27] How a firm handles customer complaints affects consumer evaluations and in turn customer satisfaction and loyalty.[28] The consumer movement has been helped by news-format television programs, such as *Dateline, 60 Minutes,* and *Prime Time Live,* as well as by 24-hour news coverage from CNN, MSNBC, and Fox News. The Internet too has changed the way consumers obtain information about companies' goods, services, and activities. Consumers can share their opinions about goods and services and about companies they see as irresponsible at consumer-oriented websites, such as epinions.com and ConsumerReview.com, and through blogs and social networking sites. Large retailers like Best Buy have helped their reputations and the environment by offering recycling programs. Best Buy began offering a free recycling program in early 2009, and it quickly became the country's largest collector of electronic trash. Customers who do not know how to dispose of their outmoded electronics appreciate the service, and it creates opportunities for them to stop by Best Buy and perhaps purchase something new. The program, which was started at the request of employees and customers, has been a win-win for both the retailer and society.[29]

Ralph Nader, one of the best-known consumer activists, continues to crusade for consumer rights. Consumer activism by Nader and others has resulted in legislation requiring many features that make cars safer: seat belts, air bags, padded dashboards, stronger door latches, head restraints, shatterproof windshields, and collapsible steering columns. Activists' efforts have also facilitated the passage of several consumer protection laws, including the Wholesome Meat Act of 1967, the Radiation Control for Health and Safety Act of 1968, the Clean Water Act of 1972, and the Toxic Substance Act of 1976.

Also of great importance to the consumer movement are four basic rights spelled out in a consumer "bill of rights" that was drafted by President John F. Kennedy. These rights include the right to safety, the right to be informed, the right to choose, and the right to be heard.

Ensuring consumers' *right to safety* means marketers are obligated not to market a product that they know could harm consumers. This right can be extended to imply that all products must be safe for their intended use, include thorough and explicit instructions for proper and safe use, and have been tested to ensure reliability and quality.

Consumers' *right to be informed* means consumers should have access to and the opportunity to review all relevant information about a product before buying it. Many laws require specific labeling on product packaging to satisfy this right. In addition, labels on alcoholic and tobacco products must inform consumers that these products may cause illness and other problems.

The *right to choose* means consumers should have access to a variety of products and services at competitive prices. They should also be assured of satisfactory quality and

Responsible Marketing?

Who Pays for Corporate Social Responsibility Activities: The Economic Issue

CRITICAL THINKING

ISSUE: Who should pay for corporate social responsibility activities?

Many companies today engage in significant social responsibility activities. Avon raises money for breast cancer research, many homebuilders work with Habitat for Humanity (donating materials and employee time), Starbucks invests in fair trade activities, and other companies transfer significant corporate dollars to social activities with little concern for shareholders' interests. If foundational economists were to discuss the positives and negatives of these CSR activities, they would weigh heavily on the negative side, noting that this raises the cost of doing business and lowers corporate productivity. On the positive side, billions of dollars are being allocated to worthy social causes, impacting the greater overall good of our society.

Should consumers be allowed to buy products that are devoid of a heavy social cost and make decisions to give on an individual basis? Massachusetts gave taxpayers the option of donating to social services by simply checking a box on their tax return. The message that came back was clear: $100 million was generated for social services. What if Dell sold one notebook computer for $1,000 and the same computer for $1,150, with the notation that the purchase of the more expensive computer would support the fight against AIDS around the world? Dell and Microsoft created products for the Product (Red) campaign, joining other large corporate companies such as The Gap, Apple, and Motorola in support of The Global Fund, an international organization devoted to fighting AIDS, tuberculosis, and malaria. How many consumers do you think would support the companies' AIDS donation from their product purchases? How many would prefer to purchase a less-expensive product and just donate the money themselves? Should consumers have the right to decide if they support the social causes of a company, or should companies assume that many consumers are not as charitable as they could be and make these decisions for them?[b]

service at a fair price. Activities that reduce competition among businesses in an industry might jeopardize this right.

The *right to be heard* ensures that consumers' interests will receive full and sympathetic consideration in the formulation of government policy. The right to be heard also promises consumers fair treatment when they complain to marketers about products. This right benefits marketers too because when consumers complain about a product, the manufacturer can use this information to modify the product and make it more satisfying.

The Federal Trade Commission provides a wealth of consumer information at its website (**www.ftc. gov/bcp/consumer.shtm**) on a variety of topics ranging from automobiles and the Internet to diet, health, and fitness to identity theft.

COMMUNITY RELATIONS

Social responsibility also extends to marketers' roles as community members. Individual communities expect marketers to make philanthropic contributions to civic projects and institutions and to be "good corporate citizens." The Weaver Street Market Cooperative in Carrboro, North Carolina, for example, serves as a community hub and live music venue, as well as a farmers' market and food store that emphasizes sustainable and local food products. It also supports eco-friendly practices through its use of green resources such as bio-diesel for its trucks, energy-saving technologies, and biodegradable containers.[30]

Although most charitable donations come from individuals, corporate philanthropy is on the rise. Target, for example, contributes significant resources to education, including fundraising and scholarship programs that assist teachers and students, as well as direct donations of more than $200 million to schools. Through the retailer's Take Charge of Education program, customers who use a Target REDcard can designate a specific school to which Target donates 1 percent of their total purchase. This program is designed to make customers feel that their purchases are benefiting their community while increasing the use of Target REDcards.[31]

Smaller firms can also make positive contributions to their communities. For example, Colorado-based New Belgium Brewing Company donates $1 for every barrel of beer brewed to charities within the markets it serves. The brewery divides the funds among states in proportion to interests and needs, considering environmental, human services, drug and alcohol awareness, and cultural issues.[32] From a positive perspective, a marketer can significantly improve its community's quality of life through employment opportunities, economic development, and financial contributions to educational, health, cultural, and recreational causes.

Marketing Ethics

As noted earlier, marketing ethics is a dimension of social responsibility that involves principles and standards that define acceptable conduct in marketing. Acceptable standards of conduct in making individual and group decisions in marketing are determined by various stakeholders and by an organization's ethical climate. Marketers must also use their own values and knowledge of ethics to act responsibly and provide ethical leadership for others.

Marketers should be aware of ethical standards for acceptable conduct from several viewpoints: company, industry, government, customers, special-interest groups, and society at large. When marketing activities deviate from accepted standards, the exchange process can break down, resulting in customer dissatisfaction, lack of trust, and lawsuits. In recent years, a number of ethical scandals have resulted in a massive loss of confidence in the integrity of U.S. businesses. In fact, a recent study revealed that 77 percent of respondents in the United States trusted businesses less than the year before.[33] The most recent worldwide financial crisis led to even more distrust of business. For instance, Countrywide Financial was sharply criticized for providing liar loans, a situation in which borrowers overstated their income by as much as 50 percent in order to secure loans, sometimes with the lender's knowledge. Countrywide's CEO Angelo Mozilo was also investigated by the Securities and Exchange Commission and was the defendant of many lawsuits accusing him of negligence, lack of fiduciary duties, and improper financial reporting. Countrywide's reputational damage and major losses led to its acquisition by Bank of America.[34] When companies like Countrywide engage in activities that deviate from accepted principles, continued marketing exchanges become difficult, if not impossible. Once trust is lost, it can take a lifetime to rebuild. The way to deal with ethical issues is proactively during the strategic planning process, not after major problems materialize.

As we already noted, marketing ethics goes beyond legal issues. Marketing decisions based on ethical considerations foster mutual trust in marketing relationships. Although we often try to draw a boundary between legal and ethical issues, the distinction between the two is frequently blurred in decision making. Marketers operate in an environment in which overlapping legal and ethical issues color many decisions. To separate legal and ethical decisions, one must assume that marketing managers can instinctively differentiate legal and ethical issues. However, although the legal ramifications of some issues and problems may be very obvious, others are not. Questionable decisions and actions often result in disputes that must be resolved through litigation. The legal system therefore provides a formal venue for marketers to resolve ethical disputes as well as legal ones. For example, the U.S. government joined in a lawsuit against Johnson & Johnson's Scios unit for marketing a drug for uses that were not approved by the U.S. Food and Drug Administration. The drug, Natrecor, was approved to treat patients with severe congestive heart failure. However, Scios is accused of promoting the drug to patients with less serious heart problems, a market for which the drug was not originally intended. J&J's Scios unit was accused of misleading consumers and causing false claims to be submitted to federal health care programs.[35] Such fraud could have significant legal repercussions on a company. Indeed, most ethical disputes reported in the media involve the legal system at some level. In many cases, however, settlements are reached without requiring the decision of a judge or jury.

Before we proceed with our discussion of ethics in marketing, it is important to state that it is not our purpose to question anyone's ethical beliefs or personal

Marketing Ethics
Companies like Goldman Sachs were questioned in congressional meetings to better understand the causes of the global financial crisis.

convictions. Nor is it our purpose to examine the conduct of consumers, although some do behave unethically (engaging, for instance, in coupon fraud, shoplifting, returning clothing after wearing it, and other abuses). Instead, our goal here is to underscore the importance of resolving ethical issues in marketing and to help you learn about marketing ethics.

Ethical Issues in Marketing

An **ethical issue** is an identifiable problem, situation, or opportunity that requires an individual or organization to choose from among several actions that must be evaluated as right or wrong, ethical or unethical. Any time an activity causes marketing managers or customers in their target market to feel manipulated or cheated, a marketing ethical issue exists, regardless of the legality of that activity. For instance, Unilever's "I Can't Believe It's Not Butter" brand was criticized for containing trace amounts of trans fat in its fat-free butter, even though by law companies are allowed to label their food products as containing zero percent trans fat as long as the product contains less than 0.5 gram of trans fat per serving. Rival company Smart Balance used the trans fat issue to promote its own brand of healthier spreads over those of Unilever and other competitors. Unilever later announced that it was eradicating all artificial trans fats from its spreads.[36]

Regardless of the reasons behind specific ethical issues, marketers must be able to identify those issues and decide how to resolve them. Doing so requires familiarity with the many kinds of ethical issues that may arise in marketing. Research suggests that the greater the consequences associated with an issue, the more likely it will be recognized as an ethics issue and the more important it will be in making an ethical decision.[37] Some examples of ethical issues related to product, promotion, price, and distribution (the marketing mix) appear in Table 4.3.

Product-related ethical issues generally arise when marketers fail to disclose risks associated with a product or information regarding the function, value, or use of a product. Most automobile and many toy companies have experienced negative publicity associated with design or safety issues that resulted in a government-required recall of specific models. Pressures can build to substitute inferior materials or product components to reduce costs. Ethical issues also arise when marketers fail to inform

ethical issue An identifiable problem, situation, or opportunity requiring a choice among several actions that must be evaluated as right or wrong, ethical or unethical

TABLE 4.3 Sample Ethical Issues Related to the Marketing Mix

Product Issue *Product information*	Covering up defects that could cause harm to a consumer; withholding critical performance information that could affect a purchase decision.
Distribution Issue *Counterfeiting*	Counterfeit products are widespread, especially in the areas of computer software, clothing, and audio and video products. The Internet has facilitated the distribution of counterfeit products.
Promotion Issue *Advertising*	Deceptive advertising or withholding important product information in a personal selling situation.
Pricing Issue *Pricing*	Indicating that an advertised sale price is a reduction below the regular price when in fact that is not the case.

customers about existing conditions or changes in product quality; such failure is a form of dishonesty about the nature of the product. For instance, Johnson & Johnson, a company long known for its high ethical standards, has more recently received criticism for not adequately disclosing the dangers of acetaminophen, a key ingredient in Tylenol. Unaware of the dangers, some consumers were overdosing on the drug. Johnson & Johnson was forced to pay damages in a wrongful death lawsuit after a judge determined that the company knew about the product's risks but did not sufficiently inform consumers about them.[38]

Promotion can create ethical issues in a variety of ways, among them false or misleading advertising and manipulative or deceptive sales promotions, tactics, and publicity. One controversial issue in the area of promotion is the promotion of pharmaceuticals that require a doctor's prescription directly to consumers. Proponents of the practice argue that it arms consumers with more information about products that may be beneficial for their conditions. Critics worry about the potential for overtreatment and have called for tighter guidelines on the promotion of drugs. With studies suggesting that pharmaceutical ads strongly influence both doctors and consumers, timely and accurate information is important. Consumers have grown increasingly wary of the veracity of such prescription drug ads, so the Pharmaceutical Researchers and Manufacturers of America created voluntary guidelines to which member companies are encouraged to adhere. These guidelines are meant to create more accuracy and transparency in direct-to-consumer drug advertising.[39] Another major ethical issue in promotion pertains to the marketing of allegedly violent video games to children. Many other ethical issues are linked to promotion, including the use of bribery in personal selling situations. Even a bribe that is offered to benefit the organization is usually considered unethical. Because it jeopardizes trust and fairness, it hurts the organization in the long run.

In pricing, common ethical issues are price fixing, predatory pricing, and failure to disclose the full price of a purchase. The emotional and subjective nature of price creates many situations in which misunderstandings between the seller and buyer cause ethical problems. Marketers have the right to price their products to earn a reasonable profit, but ethical issues may crop up when a company seeks to earn high profits at the expense of its customers. Some pharmaceutical companies, for example, have been accused of pricing products at exorbitant levels and taking advantage of customers who must purchase the medicine to survive or to maintain their quality of life. Another issue relates to quantity surcharges that occur when consumers are effectively overcharged for buying a larger package size of the same grocery product.[40]

Ethical issues in distribution involve relationships among producers and marketing intermediaries. Marketing intermediaries, or middlemen (wholesalers and retailers), facilitate the flow of products from the producer to the ultimate customer. Each intermediary performs a different role and agrees to certain rights, responsibilities, and rewards associated with that role. For example, producers expect wholesalers and retailers to honor agreements and keep them informed of inventory needs. Serious ethical issues

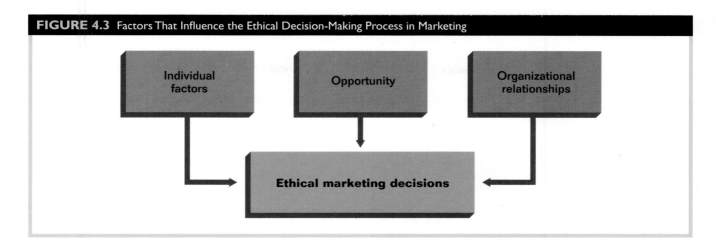

FIGURE 4.3 Factors That Influence the Ethical Decision-Making Process in Marketing

with regard to distribution include manipulating a product's availability for purposes of exploitation and using coercion to force intermediaries to behave in a specific manner. Several companies have been accused of channel stuffing, which involves shipping surplus inventory to wholesalers and retailers at an excessive rate, typically before the end of a quarter. The practice may conceal declining demand for a product or inflate financial statement earnings, misleading investors.[41] When companies outsource production and other functions, managing the supply chain becomes increasingly complicated and difficult to monitor. For instance, melamine-tainted milk from China found its way into thousands of products around the world, sickened 300,000 people, and killed six infants before the problem was contained. The same issue resurfaced a little more than a year later. Companies that source their milk from China suffered blows to their reputations and their profits in the wake of these scandals.[42]

The Nature of Marketing Ethics

To grasp the significance of ethics in marketing decision making, it is helpful to examine the factors that influence the ethical decision-making process. As Figure 4.3 shows, individual factors, organizational relationships, and opportunity interact to determine ethical decisions in marketing.

INDIVIDUAL FACTORS

When people need to resolve ethical conflicts in their daily lives, they often base their decisions on their own values and principles of right or wrong. For example, a study by the Josephson Institute of Ethics reported that 64 percent of students admitted to cheating on an exam at least once in the past year, and 42 percent admitted to lying to save money in the past year. Thirty percent of students confessed to stealing from a store in the same period.[43] People learn values and principles through socialization by family members, social groups, religion, and formal education. In the workplace, however, research has established that an organization's culture often has more influence on marketing decisions than an individual's own values.[44]

ORGANIZATIONAL RELATIONSHIPS

Although people can and do make ethical choices pertaining to marketing decisions, no one operates in a vacuum.[45] Ethical choices in marketing are most often made jointly, in work groups and committees, or in conversations and discussions with coworkers. Marketing employees resolve ethical issues based not only on what they learned from their own backgrounds but also on what they learn from others in the organization. The outcome of this learning process depends on the strength of each individual's personal values, opportunity for unethical behavior, and exposure to others who behave ethically or unethically. Superiors, peers, and subordinates in the organization influence the ethical decision-making process. Although people outside the organization, such as family

Organizational Culture
Bayer's corporate culture focuses on implementing scientific solutions to environmental conservation.

organizational (corporate) culture A set of values, beliefs, goals, norms, and rituals that members of an organization share

members and friends, also influence decision makers, organizational culture and structure operate through organizational relationships to influence ethical decisions.

Organizational, or **corporate, culture** is a set of values, beliefs, goals, norms, and rituals that members of an organization share. These values also help shape employees' satisfaction with their employer, which may affect the quality of the service they provide to customers. A firm's culture may be expressed formally through codes of conduct, memos, manuals, dress codes, and ceremonies, but it is also conveyed informally through work habits, extracurricular activities, and anecdotes. An organization's culture gives its members meaning and suggests rules for how to behave and deal with problems within the organization.

With regard to organizational structure, most experts agree that the chief executive officer or vice president of marketing sets the ethical tone for the entire marketing organization. Lower-level managers obtain their cues from top managers, but they too impose some of their personal values on the company. This interaction between corporate culture and executive leadership helps determine the firm's ethical value system.

Coworkers' influence on an individual's ethical choices depends on the person's exposure to unethical behavior. Especially in gray areas, the more a person is exposed to unethical activity by others in the organizational environment, the more likely he or she is to behave unethically. Most marketing employees take their cues from coworkers in learning how to solve problems, including ethical problems.[46] For instance, the most recent National Business Ethics Survey (NBES) found that 49 percent of employees had observed at least one type of misconduct in the past year; about 37 percent of them had chosen not to report the misconduct to management.[47] Table 4.4 compares the percentage of observed misconduct in the United States between 2007 and 2009. Moreover, research suggests that marketing employees

TABLE 4.4 Percentage of U.S. Workforce Observing Specific Forms of Misconduct

Behaviors	2007 (%)	2009 (%)
Company resource abuse	n/a	23
Abusive behavior	21	22
Lying to employees	20	19
E-mail or Internet abuse	18	18
Conflicts of interest	22	16
Discrimination	12	14
Lying to outside stakeholders	14	12
Employee benefit violations	n/a	11
Health or safety violations	15	11
Employee privacy breach	n/a	10
Improper hiring practices	10	10
Falsifying time or expenses	n/a	10

Source: Ethics Resource Center, *2009 National Business Ethics Survey.*

who perceive their work environment as ethical experience less role conflict and ambiguity, are more satisfied with their jobs, and are more committed to their employer.[48]

Organizational pressure plays a key role in creating ethical issues. For example, because of pressure to meet a schedule, a superior may ask a salesperson to lie to a customer over the phone about a late product shipment. Similarly, pressure to meet a sales quota may result in overly aggressive sales tactics. Research in this area indicates that superiors and coworkers can generate organizational pressure, which plays a key role in creating ethical issues. Nearly all marketers face difficult issues whose solutions are not obvious or that present conflicts between organizational objectives and personal ethics.

OPPORTUNITY

Another factor that may shape ethical decisions in marketing is opportunity—that is, conditions that limit barriers or provide rewards. A marketing employee who takes advantage of an opportunity to act unethically and is rewarded or suffers no penalty may repeat such acts as other opportunities arise. For instance, a salesperson who receives a raise after using a deceptive sales presentation to increase sales is being rewarded and thus will probably continue the behavior. Indeed, opportunity to engage in unethical conduct is often a better predictor of unethical activities than are personal values.[49] Beyond rewards and the absence of punishment, other elements in the business environment may create opportunities. Professional codes of conduct and ethics-related corporate policy also influence opportunity by prescribing what behaviors are acceptable, as we will see later. The larger the rewards and the milder the punishment for unethical conduct, the greater is the likelihood that unethical behavior will occur.

However, just as the majority of people who go into retail stores do not try to shoplift at each opportunity, most marketing managers do not try to take advantage of every opportunity for unethical behavior in their organizations. Although marketing managers often perceive many opportunities to engage in unethical conduct in their companies and industries, research suggests that most refrain from taking advantage of such opportunities. Moreover, most marketing managers do not believe that unethical conduct in general results in success.[50] Individual factors as well as organizational culture may influence whether an individual becomes opportunistic and tries to take advantage of situations unethically.

Improving Ethical Conduct in Marketing

It is possible to improve ethical conduct in an organization by hiring ethical employees and eliminating unethical ones, and by improving the organization's ethical standards. One way to approach improvement of an organization's ethical standards is to use a "bad apple–bad barrel" analogy. Some people always do things in their own self-interest, regardless of organizational goals or accepted moral standards; they are sometimes called "bad apples." To eliminate unethical conduct, an organization must rid itself of bad apples through screening techniques and enforcement of the firm's ethical standards. However, organizations sometimes become "bad barrels" themselves, not because the individuals within them are unethical but because the pressures to survive and succeed create conditions (opportunities) that reward unethical behavior. One way to resolve the problem of the bad barrel is to redesign the organization's image and culture so that it conforms to industry and societal norms of ethical conduct.[51]

If top management develops and enforces ethical and legal compliance programs to encourage ethical decision making, it becomes a force to help individuals make better decisions. According to a recent National Business Ethics Survey, a company's ethical culture is the greatest determinant of future misconduct. Thus, a well-implemented formal ethics and compliance program and a strong corporate culture result in the greatest reduction in ethical risks for an organization. Companies that wish to improve their ethics, then, should implement a strong ethics and compliance program and encourage organization-wide commitment to an ethical culture.[52] Ethics programs that include written standards of conduct, ethics training, ethics advice lines or offices, and systems for anonymous reporting increase the likelihood that employees will report misconduct observed in the workplace. When top managers talk about the importance

TABLE 4.5 Types of Misconduct Employees Are Not Likely to Report

Use of competitor information
Anti-competitive practices
Bribing public officials
Insider trading
Illegal political contributions

Source: Ethics Resource Center, "The Ethics Resource Center's 2009 *National Business Ethics Survey: Ethics in the Recession*" (Washington, DC: Ethics Resource Center, 2009), p. 34.

of ethics, inform employees, keep promises, and model ethical behavior, employees observe significantly fewer instances of unethical conduct. When marketers understand the policies and requirements for ethical conduct, they can more easily resolve ethical conflicts. However, marketers can never fully abdicate their personal ethical responsibility in making decisions. Claiming to be an agent of the business ("the company told me to do it") is unacceptable as a legal excuse and is even less defensible from an ethical perspective.[53] It is also unacceptable for managers to punish those who do report ethical misconduct, although retaliation is still fairly prevalent. The NBES survey stated that 15 percent of respondents who reported misconduct said they experienced retaliation, from getting the cold shoulder from other employees to being demoted.[54] Table 4.5 lists some of the types of misconduct that employees are unlikely to report.

CODES OF CONDUCT

Without compliance programs and uniform standards and policies regarding conduct, it is hard for employees to determine what conduct is acceptable within the company. In the absence of such programs and standards, employees will generally make decisions based on their observations of how coworkers and superiors behave. To improve ethics, many organizations have developed **codes of conduct** (also called *codes of ethics*) that consist of formalized rules and standards that describe what the company expects of its employees. Most large corporations have formal codes of conduct. After CEO Dennis Kozlowski was imprisoned for stealing millions of dollars from the company, Tyco International established a Guide to Ethical Conduct as part of a major corporate overhaul. The overhaul involved forcing out nearly 300 managers, making dramatic changes in reporting relationships, and enforcing many more initiatives to ensure that Tyco developed an ethical corporate culture. Tyco's new ethical climate was implemented to ensure that widespread misconduct would not occur again within the company.[55] Codes of conduct promote ethical behavior by reducing opportunities for unethical behavior; employees know both what is expected of them and what kind of punishment they face if they violate the rules. Codes help marketers deal with ethical issues or dilemmas that develop in daily operations by prescribing or limiting specific activities. At Hospital Corporation of America (HCA), for example, the code of conduct specifies that any violation of the code may trigger an oral warning, written warning, written reprimand, suspension, termination, and/or restitution, depending on the nature, severity, and frequency of the violation.[56] Codes of conduct have also made companies that subcontract manufacturing operations abroad more aware of the ethical issues associated with supporting facilities that underpay and even abuse their workforce. The American Apparel & Footwear Association, for example, has endorsed the principles and certification program of Worldwide Responsible Apparel Production (WRAP), a nonprofit organization dedicated to promoting and certifying "lawful, humane, and ethical manufacturing throughout the world." Companies that endorse the principles are expected to allow independent monitoring to ensure that their contractors are complying with the principles.[57]

codes of conduct Formalized rules and standards that describe what the company expects of its employees

Codes of conduct do not have to be so detailed that they take every situation into account, but they should provide guidelines that enable employees to achieve organizational objectives in an ethical, acceptable manner. The American Marketing Association Code of Ethics, reprinted in Table 4.6, does not cover every possible ethical

TABLE 4.6 Code of Ethics of the American Marketing Association

Ethical Norms and Values for Marketers

PREAMBLE

The American Marketing Association commits itself to promoting the highest standard of professional ethical norms and values for its members. Norms are established standards of conduct expected and maintained by society and/or professional organizations. Values represent the collective conception of what people find desirable, important, and morally proper. Values serve as the criteria for evaluating the actions of others. Marketing practitioners must recognize that they serve not only their enterprises but also act as stewards of society in creating, facilitating, and executing the efficient and effective transactions that are part of the greater economy. In this role, marketers should embrace the highest ethical norms of practicing professionals as well as the ethical values implied by their responsibility toward stakeholders (e.g., customers, employees, investors, channel members, regulators, and the host community).

GENERAL NORMS

1. Marketers must first do no harm. This means doing work for which they are appropriately trained or experienced so they can actively add value to their organizations and customers. It also means adhering to all applicable laws and regulations, as well as embodying high ethical standards in the choices they make.

2. Marketers must foster trust in the marketing system. This means that products are appropriate for their intended and promoted uses. It requires that marketing communications about goods and services are not intentionally deceptive or misleading. It suggests building relationships that provide for the equitable adjustment and/or redress of customer grievances. It implies striving for good faith and fair dealing so as to contribute toward the efficacy of the exchange process.

3. Marketers should embrace, communicate, and practice the fundamental ethical values that will improve consumer confidence in the integrity of the marketing exchange system. These basic values are intentionally aspirational and include: Honesty, Responsibility, Fairness, Respect, Openness, and Citizenship.

Ethical Values

Honesty—this means being truthful and forthright in our dealings with customers and stakeholders.

We will tell the truth in all situations and at all times.

We will offer products of value that do what we claim in our communications.

We will stand behind our products if they fail to deliver their claimed benefits.

We will honor our explicit and implicit commitments and promises.

Responsibility—this involves accepting the consequences of our marketing decisions and strategies.

We will make strenuous efforts to serve the needs of our customers.

We will avoid using coercion with all stakeholders.

We will acknowledge the social obligations to stakeholders that come with increased marketing and economic power.

We will recognize our special commitments to economically vulnerable segments of the market such as children, the elderly, and others who may be substantially disadvantaged.

Fairness—this has to do with justly trying to balance the needs of the buyer with the interests of the seller.

We will clearly represent our products in selling, advertising, and other forms of communication; this includes the avoidance of false, misleading, and deceptive promotion.

We will reject manipulations and sales tactics that harm customer trust.

We will not engage in price fixing, predatory pricing, price gouging, or "bait and switch" tactics.

We will not knowingly participate in material conflicts of interest.

Respect—this addresses the basic human dignity of all stakeholders.

(continued)

TABLE 4.6 Code of Ethics of the American Marketing Association (*continued*)

We will value individual differences even as we avoid customer stereotyping or depicting demographic groups (e.g., gender, race, sexual) in a negative or dehumanizing way in our promotions.
We will listen to the needs of our customers and make all reasonable efforts to monitor and improve their satisfaction on an ongoing basis.
We will make a special effort to understand suppliers, intermediaries, and distributors from other cultures.
We will appropriately acknowledge the contributions of others, such as consultants, employees, and coworkers, to our marketing endeavors.
Openness—this focuses on creating transparency in our marketing operations.
We will strive to communicate clearly with all our constituencies.
We will accept constructive criticism from our customers and other stakeholders.
We will explain significant product or service risks, component substitutions, or other foreseeable eventualities affecting the customer or their perception of the purchase decision.
We will fully disclose list prices and terms of financing as well as available price deals and adjustments.
Citizenship—this involves a strategic focus on fulfilling the economic, legal, philanthropic, and societal responsibilities that serve stakeholders.
We will strive to protect the natural environment in the execution of marketing campaigns.
We will give back to the community through volunteerism and charitable donations.
We will work to contribute to the overall betterment of marketing and its reputation.
We will encourage supply-chain members to ensure that trade is fair for all participants, including producers in developing countries.

Implementation

Finally, we recognize that every industry sector and marketing subdiscipline (e.g., marketing research, e-commerce, direct selling, direct marketing, advertising, etc.) has its own specific ethical issues that require policies and commentary. An array of such codes can be accessed via links on the AMA website. We encourage all such groups to develop and/or refine their industry and discipline-specific codes of ethics in order to supplement these general norms and values.

Source: Copyright © 2010 by the American Marketing Association, www.marketingpower.com/AboutAMA/Pages/Statement%20 of%20Ethics.aspx (accessed July 10, 2010).

issue, but it provides a useful overview of what marketers believe are sound principles for guiding marketing activities. This code serves as a helpful model for structuring an organization's code of conduct.

ETHICS OFFICERS

Organizational compliance programs must also have oversight by high-ranking persons in the organization who are known to respect legal and ethical standards. Ethics officers are typically responsible for creating and distributing a code of conduct, enforcing the code, and meeting with organizational members to discuss or provide advice about ethical issues. Many firms have created ethics officer positions, including Best Buy, Walmart, Merck, and Starbucks. Best Buy's chief ethics officer Kathleen Edmond made *Ethisphere*'s 100 Most Influential People in Business Ethics list for creating a Chief Ethics Officer Blog in which she uses case studies of recent unethical events within the company to teach employees about ethical conduct.[58]

Many ethics officers also employ toll-free telephone "hotlines" to provide advice, anonymously when desired, to employees who believe they face an ethical

Implementing Ethical Compliance
The Ethics & Safety Compliance Standards Initiative is designed to help enact attainable guidelines and standards for personal trainers and fitness professionals to support ethical conduct.

issue. Since the passage of the 2002 Sarbanes-Oxley Act, more companies have implemented anonymous hotlines for employees to report misconduct; many companies have contracted the operation of these hotlines to third parties, such as EthicsPoint, Global Compliance Services, National Hotline Services, and Pinkerton Consulting & Investigations.

IMPLEMENTING ETHICAL AND LEGAL COMPLIANCE PROGRAMS

To nurture ethical conduct in marketing, open communication and coaching on ethical issues are essential. This requires providing employees with ethics training, clear channels of communication, and follow-up support throughout the organization.

It is important that companies consistently enforce standards and impose penalties or punishments on those who violate codes of conduct and ethics policies. Wells Fargo, for example, fired a senior vice president after she used a bank-owned home to entertain family and friends. Company policy prohibited the personal use of bank-owned property.[59] In addition, companies must take reasonable steps in response to violations of standards and, as appropriate, revise their compliance programs to diminish the likelihood of future misconduct. To succeed, a compliance program must be viewed as a part of the overall marketing strategy implementation. If ethics officers and other executives are not committed to the principles and initiatives of marketing ethics and social responsibility, the program's effectiveness will be in question.

Although the virtues of honesty, fairness, and openness are often assumed to be self-evident and universally accepted, marketing strategy decisions involve complex and detailed matters in which correctness may not be so clear-cut. A high level of personal morality may not be sufficient to prevent an individual from violating the law in an organizational context in which even experienced lawyers debate the exact meaning of the law. Because it is impossible to train all members of an organization as lawyers, the identification of ethical issues and implementation of compliance programs and codes of conduct that incorporate both legal and ethical concerns constitute the best approach to preventing violations and avoiding litigation. Codifying ethical standards into meaningful policies that spell out what is and is not acceptable gives marketers an opportunity to reduce the probability of behavior that could create legal problems. Without proper ethical training and guidance, it is impossible for the average marketing manager to understand the exact boundaries of illegality in the areas of price fixing, copyright violations, fraud, export/import violations, and so on. A corporate focus on ethics helps create a buffer zone around issues that could trigger serious legal complications for the company.

Incorporating Social Responsibility and Ethics into Strategic Planning

Although the concepts of marketing ethics and social responsibility are often used interchangeably, it is important to distinguish between them. *Ethics* relates to individual and group decisions—judgments about what is right or wrong in a particular

TABLE 4.7 Organizational Audit of Social Responsibility and Ethics Control Mechanisms

		Answer True or False for Each Statement
T	F	1. No mechanism exists for top management to detect social responsibility and ethical issues relating to employees, customers, the community, and society.
T	F	2. There is no formal or informal communication within the organization about procedures and activities that are considered acceptable behavior.
T	F	3. The organization fails to communicate its ethical standards to suppliers, customers, and groups that have a relationship with the organization.
T	F	4. There is an environment of deception, repression, and cover-ups concerning events that could be embarrassing to the company.
T	F	5. Compensation systems are totally dependent on economic performance.
T	F	6. The only concerns about environmental impact are those that are legally required.
T	F	7. Concern for the ethical value systems of the community with regard to the firm's activities is absent.
T	F	8. Products are described in a misleading manner, with no information on negative impact or limitations communicated to customers.

True answers indicate a lack of control mechanisms, which, if implemented, could improve ethics and social responsibility.

decision-making situation—whereas *social responsibility* deals with the total effect of marketing decisions on society. The two concepts are interrelated because a company that supports socially responsible decisions and adheres to a code of conduct is likely to have a positive effect on society. Because ethics and social responsibility programs can be profitable as well, an increasing number of companies are incorporating them into their overall strategic market planning.

As we have emphasized throughout this chapter, ethics is one dimension of social responsibility. Being socially responsible relates to doing what is economically sound, legal, ethical, and socially conscious. One way to evaluate whether a specific activity is ethical and socially responsible is to ask other members of the organization if they approve of it. Contact with concerned consumer groups and industry or government regulatory groups may be helpful. A check to see whether there is a specific company policy about an activity may help resolve ethical questions. If other organizational members approve of the activity and it is legal and customary within the industry, chances are that the activity is acceptable from both an ethical and a social responsibility perspective. Table 4.7 provides an audit of mechanisms to help control ethics and social responsibility in marketing.

A rule of thumb for resolving ethical and social responsibility issues is that if an issue can withstand open discussion that results in agreement or limited debate, an acceptable solution may exist. Nevertheless, even after a final decision is reached, different viewpoints on the issue may remain. Openness is not the end-all solution to the ethics problem. However, it creates trust and facilitates learning relationships.[60]

The Challenge of Ethical and Socially Responsible Behavior

To promote socially responsible and ethical behavior while achieving organizational goals, marketers must monitor changes and trends in society's values. Consider that as aging baby boomers face increased rates of obesity, diabetes, heart conditions, and other

Marketing in Transition
Are Biofuels Socially Responsible?

Touted as a panacea to climate change, governments and business have been encouraging the use of biofuels. Replacing fossil fuels with biofuels may seem like a good idea, but they create new problems too—for the environment and for marketers. From an environmental standpoint, even though biofuels generate fewer emissions when burned, they can be more polluting to produce. From a marketing standpoint, cars that run on biofuels can be a major selling point, but also a dilemma. In smaller markets, biofuel availability may be limited, reducing the attractiveness of such vehicles. On the other hand, consumers who are concerned about the environment may be interested in these cars. Despite the possible downsides of biofuels, government incentives and public interest have made biofuels big business in companies such as Boeing and Honeywell.

Different crops are used to produce biofuel. In Brazil, ethanol from sugarcane is common. In the United States, corn is the go-to source. However, corn is more energy-intensive to process than sugar. Critics also argue that increased biofuel production has forced up the commodity price of corn (more than 50 percent since 2006), which increases food prices. Scientists also worry that corn-based fuel will do more harm to the environment than fossil fuels as new land is cultivated for agriculture. One crop appears to be a bit more environmentally friendly: sorghum. Its plant stalks can be used to create green fuel needed for ethanol production, while the grain can be used

for food. However, given that all these crops require land, the potential deforestation looms large as a huge negative for any of these fuel stocks.

The United Nations Environment Programme performed a study of biofuels, which concluded that biofuel production is only beneficial when the crops are grown on abandoned or degraded land. UN Under-Secretary General Achim Steiner says that biofuels are, on their own, neither good nor bad—the challenge is balancing the pros and cons. However, biofuels are starting to look like they are not the cure-all that they were originally touted as being.[c]

chronic illnesses, many companies in the food industry are responding by introducing or adapting products to address their needs. Their approaches range from special brands and labels to introducing low-fat, low-sugar, whole-grain, and other specialty-food requirements to maintaining separate shelf space for products that target these conditions. Developing a more user-friendly grocery store for these consumers is both socially responsible and lucrative.[61] An organization's top management must assume some responsibility for employees' conduct by establishing and enforcing policies that address society's desires.

After determining what society wants, marketers must attempt to predict the long-term effects of decisions pertaining to those wants. Specialists outside the company, such as doctors, lawyers, and scientists, are often consulted, but sometimes there is a lack of agreement within a discipline as to what is an acceptable marketing decision. Forty years ago, for example, tobacco marketers promoted cigarettes as being good for one's health. Today, years after the discovery that cigarette smoking is linked to cancer and other medical problems, society's attitude toward smoking has changed, and marketers face new social responsibilities as well as heavy regulation. For example, cigarette marketers are not allowed to use cartoon characters in their advertisements (as it is believed that these encourage child smoking), are banned from most outdoor and transit advertising, and cannot sell apparel and merchandise with brand-name logos. The recent passage of the FDA Tobacco Regulation Bill will also create significant challenges for cigarette manufacturers, as the Federal Drug Administration now has authority over product ingredients and possesses the ability to overrule new cigarette products.[62]

Many of society's demands impose costs. For example, society wants a cleaner environment and the preservation of wildlife and their habitats, but it also wants low-priced products. Consider the plight of the gas station owner who asked his customers if they would be willing to spend an additional 1 cent per gallon if he instituted an air filtration system to eliminate harmful fumes. The majority indicated they supported his plan. However, when the system was installed and the price increased, many customers switched to a lower-cost competitor across the street. Thus, companies must carefully balance the costs of providing low-priced products against the costs of manufacturing, packaging, and distributing their products in an environmentally responsible manner.

In trying to satisfy the desires of one group, marketers may dissatisfy others. Regarding the smoking debate, for example, marketers must balance nonsmokers' desire for a smoke-free environment against smokers' desires, or needs, to continue to smoke. Some anti-tobacco crusaders call for the complete elimination of tobacco products to ensure a smoke-free world. However, this attitude fails to consider the difficulty smokers have in quitting (now that tobacco marketers have admitted their product is addictive) and the impact on U.S. communities and states that depend on tobacco crops for their economic survival. Thus, this issue, like most ethical and social responsibility issues, cannot be viewed in black and white.

Balancing society's demands to satisfy all members of society is difficult, if not impossible. Marketers must evaluate the extent to which members of society are willing to pay for what they want. For instance, customers may want more information about a product but be unwilling to pay the costs the firm incurs in providing the data. Marketers who want to make socially responsible decisions may find the task a challenge because, ultimately, they must ensure their economic survival.

Social Responsibility and Ethics Improve Marketing Performance

Do not think, however, that the challenges of ethical conduct are not worth the effort. On the contrary, increasing evidence indicates that being socially responsible and ethical pays off. Research suggests that a relationship exists between a market orientation and an organizational climate that supports marketing ethics and social responsibility. This relationship implies that being ethically and socially concerned is consistent with meeting the demands of customers and other stakeholders. By encouraging employees to understand their markets, companies can help them respond to stakeholders' demands.[63]

A direct association exists between corporate social responsibility and customer satisfaction, profits, and market value.[64] In a survey of consumers, about three-fourths of respondents indicated that they would pay more for a product that came from a socially responsible company. In addition, almost half of young adults aged 18 to 25 said they would take a pay cut to work for a socially responsible company.[65]

© SIEMENS

Social Responsibility Improves Marketing Performance
Siemens works to communicate its focus on corporate social responsibility while maintaining its brand position as a company answering the world's toughest questions.

Thus, recognition is growing that the long-term value of conducting business in a socially responsible manner far outweighs short-term costs.[66] Companies that fail to develop strategies and programs to incorporate ethics and social responsibility into their organizational culture may pay the price with poor marketing performance and the potential costs of legal violations, civil litigation, and damaging publicity when questionable activities are made public. Because marketing ethics and social responsibility are not always viewed as organizational performance issues, many managers do not believe they need to consider them in the strategic planning process. Individuals also have different ideas as to what is ethical or unethical, leading them to confuse the need for workplace ethics and the right to maintain their own personal values and ethics. Although the concepts are undoubtedly controversial, it is possible—and desirable—to incorporate ethics and social responsibility into the planning process.

summary

1. To understand the concept and dimensions of social responsibility

Social responsibility refers to an organization's obligation to maximize its positive impact and minimize its negative impact on society. It deals with the total effect of all marketing decisions on society. Although social responsibility is a positive concept, most organizations embrace it in the expectation of indirect long-term benefits. Marketing citizenship involves adopting a strategic focus for fulfilling the economic, legal, ethical, and philanthropic social responsibilities expected of organizations by their stakeholders, those constituents who have a stake, or claim, in some aspect of the company's products, operations, markets, industry, and outcomes. At the most basic level, companies have an economic responsibility to be profitable so that they can provide a return on investment to their stockholders, create jobs for the community, and contribute goods and services to the economy. Marketers are also expected to obey laws and regulations. Marketing ethics refers to principles and standards that define acceptable conduct in marketing as determined by various stakeholders, including the public, government regulators, private-interest groups, industry, and the organization itself. Philanthropic responsibilities go beyond marketing ethics; they are not required of a company, but they promote human welfare or goodwill. Many firms use cause-related marketing, the practice of linking products to a social cause on an ongoing or short-term basis. Strategic philanthropy is the synergistic use of organizational core competencies and resources to address key stakeholders' interests and achieve both organizational and social benefits.

Three major categories of social responsibility issues are the natural environment, consumerism, and community relations. One of the more common ways marketers demonstrate social responsibility is through programs designed to protect and preserve the natural environment. Green marketing refers to the specific development, pricing, promotion, and distribution of products that do not harm the environment. Consumerism consists of the efforts of independent individuals, groups, and organizations to protect the rights of consumers. Consumers expect to have the right to safety, the right to be informed, the right to choose, and the right to be heard. Many marketers view social responsibility as including contributions of resources (money, products, and time) to community causes such as the natural environment, arts and recreation, disadvantaged members of the community, and education.

2. To define and describe the importance of marketing ethics

Whereas social responsibility is achieved by balancing the interests of all stakeholders in the organization, ethics relates to acceptable standards of conduct in making individual and group decisions. Marketing ethics goes beyond legal issues. Ethical marketing decisions foster mutual trust in marketing relationships.

An ethical issue is an identifiable problem, situation, or opportunity requiring an individual or organization to choose from among several actions that must be evaluated as right or wrong, ethical or unethical. A number of ethical issues relate to the marketing mix (product, promotion, price, and distribution).

Individual factors, organizational relationships, and opportunity interact to determine ethical decisions in marketing. Individuals often base their decisions on their own values and principles of right or wrong. However, ethical choices in marketing are most often made jointly, in work groups and committees or in conversations and discussions with coworkers. Organizational culture and structure operate through organizational relationships (with superiors, peers, and subordinates) to influence ethical decisions. Organizational, or corporate, culture is a set of values, beliefs, goals, norms, and rituals that members of an organization share. The more a person is exposed to unethical activity by others in the organizational environment, the more likely he or she is to behave unethically. Organizational pressure plays a key role in creating ethical issues, as do opportunity and conditions that limit barriers or provide rewards.

3. To become familiar with ways to improve ethical decisions in marketing

It is possible to improve ethical behavior in an organization by hiring ethical employees and eliminating unethical ones, and by improving the organization's ethical standards. If top management develops and enforces ethics and legal compliance programs to encourage ethical decision making, it becomes a force to help individuals make better decisions. To improve company ethics, many organizations have developed codes of conduct, formalized rules and standards that describe what the company expects of its employees. A marketing compliance program must have oversight by a high-ranking organizational member known to abide by legal and common ethical standards; this person is usually called an ethics officer. To nurture ethical conduct in marketing, open communication and

coaching on ethical issues are essential. This requires providing employees with ethics training, clear channels of communication, and follow-up support throughout the organization. Companies must consistently enforce standards and impose penalties or punishment on those who violate codes of conduct.

4. To understand the role of social responsibility and ethics in improving market performance

An increasing number of companies are incorporating ethics and social responsibility programs into their overall strategic market planning. To promote socially responsible and ethical behavior while achieving organizational goals, marketers must monitor changes and trends in society's values. They must determine what society wants and attempt to predict the long-term effects of their decisions. Costs are associated with many of society's demands, and balancing those demands to satisfy all of society is difficult. However, increasing evidence indicates that being socially responsible and ethical results in valuable benefits: an enhanced public reputation (which can increase market share), costs savings, and profits.

Go to www.cengagebrain.com for resources to help you master the content in this chapter as well as materials that will expand your marketing knowledge!

important terms

social responsibility, 94
marketing citizenship, 96
marketing ethics, 97

cause-related marketing, 98
strategic philanthropy, 98

sustainability 99
green marketing, 101
ethical issue, 105

organizational (corporate) culture, 108
codes of conduct, 110

discussion and review questions

1. What is social responsibility? Why is it important?
2. What are stakeholders? What role do they play in strategic marketing decisions?
3. What are four dimensions of social responsibility? What impact do they have on marketing decisions?
4. What is strategic philanthropy? How does it differ from more traditional philanthropic efforts?

5. What are some major social responsibility issues? Give an example of each.
6. What is the difference between ethics and social responsibility?
7. Why is ethics an important consideration in marketing decisions?

8. How do the factors that influence ethical or unethical decisions interact?

9. What ethical conflicts may exist if business employees fly on certain airlines just to receive benefits for their personal frequent-flyer programs?

10. Give an example of how ethical issues can affect each component of the marketing mix.

11. How can the ethical decisions involved in marketing be improved?

12. How can people with different personal values work together to make ethical decisions in organizations?

13. What trade-offs might a company have to make to be socially responsible and responsive to society's demands?

14. What evidence exists that being socially responsible and ethical is worthwhile?

application questions

CRITICAL THINKING

1. Some organizations promote their social responsibility. These companies often claim that being ethical is good business and that it pays to be a "good corporate citizen." Identify an organization in your community that has a reputation for being ethical and socially responsible. What activities account for this image? Is the company successful? Why or why not?

2. If you had to conduct a social audit of your organization's ethics and social responsibility, what information would most interest you? What key stakeholders would you want to communicate with? How could such an audit assist the company in improving its ethics and social responsibility?

3. Suppose that in your job you face situations that require you to make decisions about what is right or wrong and then act on these decisions. Describe such a situation. Without disclosing your actual decision, explain what you based it on. What and whom did you think of when you were considering what to do? Why did you consider them?

4. Consumers interact with many businesses daily and weekly. Not only do companies in an industry acquire a reputation for being ethical or unethical; entire industries also become known as ethical or unethical. Identify two types of businesses with which you or others you know have had the most conflict involving ethical issues. Describe those ethical issues.

internet exercise

Business for Social Responsibility

Business for Social Responsibility (BSR) is a nonprofit organization for companies who want to operate responsibly and demonstrate respect for ethical values, people, communities, and the natural environment. Founded in 1992, BSR offers members practical information, research, educational programs, and technical assistance, as well as the opportunity to network with peers on current social responsibility issues. To learn more about this organization and access its many resources, visit **www.bsr.org**.

1. What types of businesses join BSR, and why?

2. Describe the services available to member companies. How can these services help companies improve their performances?

3. Peruse the "Conference Overview" link, located at the top of the home page. What are some advantages to attending the BSR conference and listening to industry leaders and experts in corporate social responsibility?

developing your marketing plan

 **CRITICAL THINKING**

When developing a marketing strategy, companies must consider that their decisions affect not only their own company but also society in general. Many socially responsible and ethical companies identify their intentions as part of their mission statement, which serves as a guide for making all decisions about the company, including those in the marketing plan. To assist you in relating the information in this chapter to the development of your marketing plan, consider the following:

1. Determine the level of importance that marketing citizenship holds in your company. Identify the various stakeholders who would be affected by your strategic decisions.

2. Referring to Table 4.2 as a guide, discuss how the negative impact of your product's production and use could be minimized.

3. Using Table 4.3, identify additional issues related to your product for each of the 4Ps.

The information obtained from these questions should assist you in developing various aspects of your marketing plan found in the *Interactive Marketing Plan* exercise **www.cengagebrain.com.**

VIDEO CASE 4.1

The Putting Lot: Building a Miniature Golf Course to Support Sustainability

 **CRITICAL THINKING**

The Putting Lot is a unique miniature golf course located in Bushwick, a former industrial neighborhood in Brooklyn. The course opened in the summer of 2009 as a temporary installation in one of the neighborhood's many empty lots. Co-organizers Gabriel Fries-Briggs and Rachel Himmelfarb created the lot to preserve Bushwick's local culture while providing a place for residents to learn and have fun.

The idea to create a miniature golf course in the middle of the city came from the creators' own childhood experiences. One creator says, "A lot of us are not from the city and have very fond childhood memories of playing mini golf. There is a lack of affordable recreational activities that are appropriate for all ages in New York, so building a mini golf course in the city seemed like a great idea." The creators also wanted a space that would help anchor the neighborhood as more and more established families left the area. The land utilization and construction provided an opportunity to demonstrate neighborhood sustainability. The organizers of

the Putting Lot recognized that in the buying decision process, situational influences such as time and location would encourage local residents to visit the mini golf course. The physical and social surroundings are especially important in a decision to engage in recreational activities.

The Putting Lot was also designed to help people to think about the possibilities of vacant spaces in neighborhoods that support sustainability. Bushwick is the 21st emptiest neighborhood in New York City. The Putting Lot's creators believe filling the empty spaces will help the neighborhood transition from an industrial district to a residential area. According to the Putting Lot's creators, "Vacant spaces are often places where developers, neighbors, and city workers come into conflict, but they can also be rich places for residents to imagine what they would like to see in the city." This is an attempt to change attitudes about the neighborhood and the possibilities for vacant land to be used in a responsible manner.

© Scott Sanders/Shutterstock.com / © Comstock Images/Getty Images

Despite the large number of vacant spaces in Bushwick, the Putting Lot team had a difficult time finding a space to put their mini golf course. They say, "Even though the zoning of the neighborhood specifically permits our use as a right, most landlords did not want to deviate from standard, most common land-uses. In the end, we did find one who has been very supportive and is excited about the project and the possibilities it brings to the neighborhood." They recognized that family influences would be important in supporting the Putting Lot because, once children enjoyed playing there, they could have a very supportive impact on decisions to use the course.

The Putting Lot focuses on sustainability, using recycled and reclaimed materials in its design. Additionally, the designs cannot be permanent or damage the land in any away. Before the course opened, the creators called for design submissions for the holes. The winners received $500 to cover the cost of materials for their hole. One hole includes scrap-car doors and was inspired by the hazards of city cycling. Other holes include a water feature made with recycled plastic bottles and an obstacle course composed of boxes and milk crates. These hazards of the city represent an attempt to relate to the local culture and changes in attitudes toward sustainability.

Additionally, Fries-Briggs and Himmelfarb searched for additional materials online and throughout New York City. Examples of materials used to create the Putting Lot include wooden shipping pallets from a local factory and old sails for the awnings. The golf equipment was acquired from a miniature golf course in Canada that was going out of business. The emphasis on developing a mini golf course based on sustainability appealed to neighborhood residents who want to exhibit a sustainable lifestyle through their activities, interests, and opinions.

The Putting Lot became an important space for the Bushwick neighborhood. The Putting Lot's organizers say, "Through the transformation of the lot, the construction of the holes, and a series of events held in the public area, we hope to provide a forum for discussing urban sustainability in a new context." Therefore, the organizers were involved in socializing neighborhood members to patronize the course and communicate with others positively in their reference groups. They hoped that some neighborhood members would become opinion leaders and influence others to become involved with the Putting Lot as a role model for community sustainability.[67]

QUESTIONS FOR DISCUSSION

1. How did the creators of the Putting Lot incorporate sustainability into their business concept?

2. How do you think the creators of the Putting Lot used marketing concepts to emphasize the advantages of a miniature golf course based on sustainability?

3. Based on the successful creation of the Putting Lot, can you think of other similar products that could be developed around the concept of sustainability?

CASE 4.2

PETCO: Putting Pets First Earns Loyal Customers

CRITICAL THINKING

PETCO Animal Supplies is the nation's number two specialty pet supply retailer, with more than 1,000 stores in all 50 states and the District of Columbia. Its pet-related products include pet food, pet supplies, grooming products, toys, novelty items, vitamins, veterinary supplies, and small pets such as fish, birds, and hamsters. It does not sell cats or dogs. PETCO strives to offer customers a complete assortment of pet-related products and services at competitive prices at convenient locations and through its website, **www.petco.com**, with a high level of customer service.

Most PETCO stores are 12,000 to 15,000 square feet and are conveniently located near local neighborhood shopping destinations, such as supermarkets, bookstores, coffee shops, dry cleaners, and video stores, where its target customers make regular weekly shopping trips. PETCO executives believe the company is well positioned, in terms of both product offerings and location, to benefit from favorable long-term demographic trends: a growing pet population and an increasing willingness of "pet parents" to spend on their pets. Indeed, the U.S. pet population has now reached 411.8 million animals, including 171.1 million cats and dogs. An estimated 62 percent of all U.S. households own at least one pet, and three-quarters of those households have two or more pets. The trend to have more pets and the number of pet-owning households will continue to grow, driven by an increasing number of children under 18 as well as a growing population of empty nesters whose pets become their new children. U.S. retail sales of pet food, supplies, small animals (excluding cats and dogs), and services grew to approximately $47.7 billion in 2010.

PETCO was founded on the principle of "connecting with the community." One of its most important missions is to promote the health, well-being, and humane treatment of animals. It strives to carry out this mission through vendor-selection programs, pet-adoption programs, and partnerships with animal welfare organizations. The company is involved every year in a number of programs to raise money for local communities and local animal initiatives.

Recognizing that more than 4 million pets are euthanized in the United States every year, PETCO launched an annual "Spay Today" initiative to address the growing problem of pet overpopulation in the United States. The "Spay Today" funds come from customer donations at PETCO stores, where customers are encouraged to round up their purchases to the nearest dollar or more. In addition, PETCO launched the "Think Adoption First" program, which supports and promotes the human–animal bond. It is a program that sets the standard for responsibility and community involvement for the industry. The "Spring a Pet" fundraiser encourages pet lovers to donate $1, $5, $10, or $20 to animal welfare causes. Donors received a personalized cutout bunny as a reminder of their generosity. In 2009, PETCO's annual Tree of Hope program raised $4 million—up 30 percent from the prior year—which encourages customers to think of animals during the Christmas season. Customers who visit PETCO during the Christmas season can purchase card ornaments, the proceeds of which go to animal welfare charities. The PETCO Foundation also sponsors "Kind News," a Humane Education Program that educates children about humane treatment of companion animals and fellow human beings. It features stories about responsible pet environmental concerns and issues as well as information on all types of animals.

Like all companies, PETCO operates in an environment in which a single negative incident can influence customers' perceptions of a firm's image and reputation instantly and potentially for years afterward. Because pets engender such strong emotional attachments, it is especially important for companies that sell pets and pet products to provide a rapid response to justify or to correct activities that may arouse potentially negative perceptions. The focus should be on a commitment to make correct decisions and to continually assess and address the risks of operating the business.

All retailers are subject to criticisms and must remain vigilant to maintain internal controls that provide assurance that employees and other partners follow ethical codes. PETCO accomplishes this through an ethics office and by developing an ethical corporate culture. PETCO has also developed and implemented a comprehensive code of ethics, which addresses all areas of organizational risk associated with human resources, conflicts of interests, and appropriate behavior in the workplace. The code's primary emphasis is that animals always come first. PETCO insists that the well-being of animals in its care is of paramount importance. In the case of PETCO, a desire to do the right thing and to train all organizational members to make ethical decisions ensures not only success in the marketplace but a significant contribution to society.[68]

QUESTIONS FOR DISCUSSION

1. How does PETCO's ethics program help manage the risks associated with the pet industry?
2. How can PETCO's social responsibility programs advance its marketing strategy?
3. Why is it important for PETCO to train all of its employees to understand and implement its ethical policies?

At Timberland, Doing Well and Doing Good Are Laced Together

Timberland's well-known name and tree logo are good clues as to how much this multinational firm cares about sustainability. The company, headquartered in Stratham, New Hampshire, started out manufacturing shoes and boots and later expanded into apparel and accessories. Today Timberland sells through its own network of stores as well as through thousands of department and specialty stores worldwide. It also operates e-business websites in the United States, the United Kingdom, Japan, and France.

Nearly half of Timberland's $1.3 billion in revenue comes from North America; Europe accounts for 40 percent and Asia accounts for 11 percent of its sales. To stay on top of fast-changing trends in the world of fashion, Timberland maintains an international design center in London. Its mission is "to equip people to make a difference in their world. We do this by creating outstanding products and by trying to make a difference in the communities where we live and work while doing it." As a result, the company's long-term strategy for success combines a comprehensive social responsibility agenda with careful planning for the ever-changing marketing environment.

Four Pillars of Social Responsibility

Timberland's social responsibility agenda rests on the four "pillars" of energy, products, workplaces, and service. Each pillar is associated with specific short- and long-term targets that Timberland has established with the input of its stakeholders. Under the first pillar— energy—the company has reduced energy consumption, slashed harmful greenhouse gas emissions, and increased its use of power from renewable sources. It is also increasing the use of virtual meetings to cut down on employee travel, which saves energy as well as time and money.

The second pillar, earth-friendly products, is a key element in Timberland's social responsibility agenda.

More than one-third of its shoes contain some recycled material. Its Earthkeepers shoes have been specially designed to incorporate a combination of organic, renewable, and recyclable materials. Some Earthkeepers are not only made from old plastic bottles and other recycled content, they can be completely disassembled and the components can be reworked into new Timberland shoes. Soon, all Timberland products will be labeled to show their impact on the planet.

The third pillar relates to the workplace. Timberland sets tough standards for fair and safe working conditions at all the factories and facilities that make its shoes and clothing products. Although it owns and operates a factory in the Dominican Republic, the company buys most of its products from a global network of suppliers that employs 175,000 workers in 290 factories spread across 35 countries. Suppliers are required to comply with Timberland's detailed code of conduct, which forbids discrimination, child labor, and unsafe practices. Factories are audited regularly and when violations are found, Timberland follows up to be sure that the necessary workplace improvements are made. Timberland employees are encouraged to call the Integrity Line, a 24-hour hotline answered by a third party, whenever they want to report workplace concerns, submit ideas, or ask questions.

The fourth pillar, service, has long been part of Timberland's cultural fabric. Every full-time Timberland employee can take up to 40 hours, with pay, to volunteer in his or her community. In addition, Timberland's CEO began the tradition of Serv-a-palooza in 1998 when he set aside one work day for global volunteerism. Today, employees are encouraged (but not required) to devote this annual day of service to volunteering in their communities.

Some employees use the day to clear nature trails, some pick up trash from riverbanks, and others grab their

STRATEGIC CASE 2

tool belts to build arts facilities or repair neighborhood schools. In more than a decade with Timberland, the vice president of corporate culture has enthusiastically laced up his Timberland boots and volunteered on three continents, doing everything from protecting the rainforest to improving the gardens around a senior center. He explains that the company's philosophy is to make local communities better, which makes Timberland better: "Our CEO believes that doing well and doing good are inextricably linked. It engages your employees, customers, and suppliers."

The Changing Marketing Environment

Because Timberland has a diverse product portfolio and is active in retailing and wholesaling as well as manufacturing, it has to keep an eye on competitors in several industries. The outdoor retailer L.L.Bean, headquartered in Maine, is a powerful competitor, with its wide variety of private-branded footwear and clothing products. Another strong U.S.-based rival is Wolverine World Wide, which manufactures Hush Puppies, Sebago, Merrell, Patagonia Footwear, and other brands of casual and work shoes. Like Timberland, Wolverine operates company stores in the United States and the United Kingdom. The U.K.-based R. Griggs Group, maker of Doc Martens boots, shoes, and sandals, is a key competitor. Finally, particular Timberland shoes styles compete directly with footwear marketed by the world's largest athletic shoe companies.

Economic conditions can also affect Timberland's marketing situation. During the recent recession, when many consumers held back on discretionary purchases, the company's overall revenue fell. However, sales of its work boots remained flat, even as some competitors saw their sales drop. Timberland's marketing executives realized that the brand was holding its own among construction workers and other buyers who need tough, reliable footwear to use day in and day out.

Timberland's marketers have also noticed that the challenging global economic situation is influencing the way consumers think and feel about buying products such as shoes and clothing. When unemployment was low and buying power was high, consumers often used such purchases as a way to display their wealth. As the economy moved into recession, however, many cash-strapped consumers cut back on purchases of showy, expensive items, in favor of products that conveyed a more subtle message about cultural values such as concern for the environment. Today, "self worth is tied to thoughtful purchases as a way to impress your peers, instead of conspicuous consumption," states Timberland's senior director of merchandising.

In addition to its international marketing initiatives in China and Europe, Timberland sees promising opportunities for growth in India. It recently signed a strategic alliance with Reliance Industries, a local company known for marketing international brands. Reliance will distribute shoes, boots, and clothing through Timberland-branded stores and through selected department stores in major Indian cities. Timberland's CEO says that Reliance has "a clear understanding of the Timberland brand and consumer" and, just as important, it's "as committed as we are to our ideology and passion for the outdoors."

High-Tech Shoes and Communications

Timberland is applying technological advances to improve its footwear products and to reach out to customers through digital media. For example, to satisfy customers' needs for comfort, the company has introduced patented "Smart Comfort" footbeds in its shoes. As part of its commitment to sustainability, Timberland makes Green Rubber soles from recycled rubber and is designing its new footwear products for easy disassembly and recycling at the end of their useful lives.

Moving into digital media is helping Timberland bring its marketing messages to the attention of consumers who use the Web. Through brand-specific sites, Facebook fan pages, blog entries, a Twitter feed, YouTube videos, and online games, Timberland supplements its traditional marketing activities and engages consumers who seek a deeper level of involvement with their favorite brands.[69]

QUESTIONS FOR DISCUSSION

1. What forces in the marketing environment appear to pose the greatest challenges to Timberland's marketing performance? Explain.

2. What kinds of ethical issues does Timberland face in its marketing? What is the company doing to address these issues?

3. How does Timberland's reputation for social responsibility serve as a strength when consumers are turning away from showy, expensive products?

4. Over time, Timberland plans to add labels to show how eco-friendly each of its products really is. What are the marketing advantages and disadvantages of this move?

Part 3

Marketing Research and Target Market Analysis

PART THREE examines how marketers use information and technology to better understand and reach customers. **CHAPTER 5** provides a foundation for analyzing buyers through a discussion of marketing information systems and the basic steps in the marketing research process. Understanding elements that affect buying decisions enables marketers to better analyze customers' needs and to evaluate how specific marketing strategies can satisfy those needs. **CHAPTER 6** deals with selecting and analyzing target markets, which is one of the major steps in marketing strategy development.

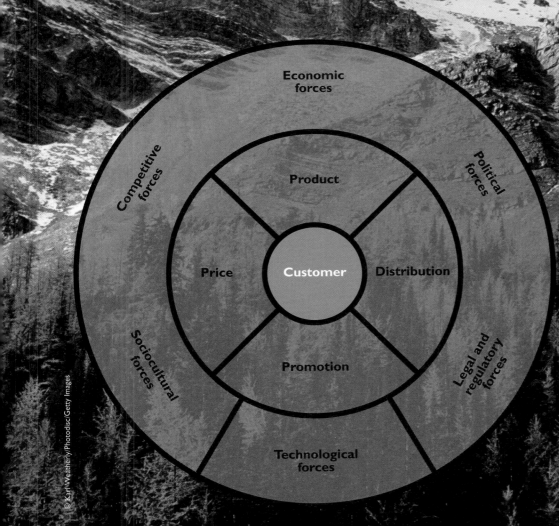

Economic forces

Competitive forces

Political forces

Sociocultural forces

Legal and regulatory forces

Product

Price

Customer

Distribution

Promotion

Technological forces

Chapter 5

Marketing Research and Information Systems

OBJECTIVES

1. To describe the basic steps in conducting marketing research

2. To explore the fundamental methods of gathering data for marketing research

3. To describe the nature and roles of tools such as databases, decision support systems, and the Internet in marketing decision making

4. To identify key ethical and international considerations in marketing research

Kimberly Clark Helps Retailers Understand Senior Shoppers

According to a Research and Markets report, individuals 65 and over will comprise 14 percent of the U.S. population by 2014. The Federal Interagency Forum on Aging-Related Statistics reports that there will be 71.5 million senior citizens by 2030—one-fifth of the population. As boomers age, their shopping needs and wants are changing. Kimberly Clark—the company that makes Kleenex, feminine products, and Depends—is on the forefront in terms of understanding, dealing with, and marketing for an aging population.

After conducting marketing research, Kimberly Clark developed a program for training retailers to understand their changing markets. As part of the program, company executives and managers are asked to alter their own capabilities by wearing sight blurring glasses, placing popcorn kernels in their shoes, and taping their thumbs to their fingers or wearing gloves. These adjustments mimic the changes felt by senior citizens. The company members are then asked to shop for items often purchased by the 65-and-over crowd. Kimberly Clark and its program participants have discovered that shelf placement of items, type size on packing and store fliers, dim lighting, and other factors contribute to a challenging shopping experience for older consumers.

As a result, participating companies such as Rite Aid, Family Dollar Stores, and Walgreens are making changes. Rite Aid intends to increase the type size on packaging, and Family Dollar is considering changing its lighting and improving its in-store labeling. Walgreens plans to place call buttons near heavy items so that shoppers can get assistance. The company has also improved signage and provided magnifying glasses. Analysts suggest that companies also consider offering special parking, stores that are easier to navigate, and shopping carts that are easier to manage.

Kimberly Clark is also making changes so that its products are more accessible to seniors. Depends, a division of Kimberly Clark, has a highly trafficked website that offers a "Lifestyle & Community" section with popular discussion boards. With such a large section of the population set to enter the 65-or-older age group, Kimberly Clark is smart to position itself to serve and thereby profit from this growing population segment.[1]

Marketing research, like that conducted at Kimberly Clark, enables marketers to implement the marketing concept by helping them acquire information about whether and how their goods and services satisfy the desires of target market customers. When used effectively, such information facilitates relationship marketing by helping marketers focus their efforts on meeting and even anticipating the needs of their customers. Marketing research and information systems that can provide practical and objective information to help firms develop and implement marketing strategies are therefore essential to effective marketing.

In this chapter, we focus on how marketers gather information needed to make marketing decisions. First, we define marketing research and examine the individual steps of the marketing research process, including various methods of collecting data. Next, we look at how technology aids in collecting, organizing, and interpreting marketing research data. Finally, we consider ethical and international issues in marketing research.

The Importance of Marketing Research

Marketing research is the systematic design, collection, interpretation, and reporting of information to help marketers solve specific marketing problems or take advantage of marketing opportunities. As the word *research* implies, it is a process for gathering information that is not currently available to decision makers. The purpose of marketing research is to inform an organization about customers' needs and desires, marketing opportunities for particular goods and services, and changing attitudes and purchase patterns of customers. Market information increases the marketer's ability to respond to customer needs, which leads to improved organizational performance. Detecting shifts in buyers' behaviors and attitudes helps companies stay in touch with the ever-changing marketplace. Organic food marketers, for example, would be interested to know that demand for high-end organic food brands is declining, while demand for private label organic brands, such as those sold by Albertsons, Trader Joe's, and Whole Foods, is growing. In fact, consumer confidence in private label organic brands has boosted confidence in private label brands overall.[2] Strategic planning requires marketing research to facilitate the process of assessing such opportunities or threats.

marketing research The systematic design, collection, interpretation, and reporting of information to help marketers solve specific marketing problems or take advantage of marketing opportunities

Importance of Marketing Research
Irwin provides services to help companies better understand their customers' needs.

Is your new product right on target? We'll let you know.

"You need an on-site focus group facility with corporate integrity, effective partnerships, and industry experts who get the job done right the first time. For over 35 years, Irwin has been – and still is – the premier focus group facility in the Southeast for all of these reasons. Call us to discuss your next project today."

-Kathryn Blackburn
President
kblackburn@irwin-jx.com

Irwin
Building integrity one job at a time

9250 Baymeadows Road, Suite 350 | Jacksonville, FL 32256
904.731.1811 F. 904.731.1225 | www.irwin-jx.com

Additional Services: Door-to-Door Interviewing • Executive Interviewing • Medical Interviews • Mystery Shopping • Store Intercepts • Focus Groups • Auditing

Marketing research can help a firm better understand market opportunities, ascertain the potential for success for new products, and determine the feasibility of a particular marketing strategy. Marketing research has consistently shown Google to be at the top of the pack in terms of market share and market valuation among competing search engine providers. However, Microsoft and Yahoo! have conducted marketing research to understand consumers' habits and needs in order to develop rival products that are now challenging Google as never before. As more consumers purchase smartphones, Microsoft has been able to gain inroads against Google by offering its "decision engine" Bing, which Microsoft claims is far better than Google at performing searches and delivering consumers the information they seek.[3]

Many types of organizations use marketing research to help them develop marketing mixes to match the needs of customers. Supermarkets, for example, have learned from marketing research that roughly half of all Americans prefer to have their dinners ready in 15 to 30 minutes. Such information highlights a tremendous opportunity for supermarkets to offer high-quality "heat-and-eat" meals to satisfy this growing segment of the food market. Political candidates also depend on marketing research to understand the scope of issues their constituents view as important. National political candidates may spend millions surveying voters to better understand issues and craft their images accordingly.

Changes in the economy, especially the most recent recession, have dramatically changed marketers' decision-making strategies. Increasingly, businesses need speed and agility to survive and to react quickly to changing consumer behavior. Marketing research has shifted focus on smaller studies like test marketing, small-scale surveys, and short-range forecasting in order to learn about changing dynamics in the marketplace. However, large, high-value research projects remain necessary for long-term success. While it is acceptable to conduct studies that take six months or more, many companies need real-time information to help them make good decisions. Firms may benefit from historical or secondary data, but due to changes in the economy and buyer behavior, this data is not as useful in today's decision-making environment. As will be discussed in this chapter, as well as in Chapter 10, online research services are helping to supplement and integrate findings in order to help companies make tactical and strategic decisions. In the future, the marketing researcher will need to be able to identify the most efficient and effective ways of gathering information.[4]

The real value of marketing research is measured by improvements in a marketer's ability to make decisions. For example, Coach, a high-end handbag company, invests $5 million per year on customer research and conducts regular customer surveys. During the most recent recession, Coach made two important discoveries using its research tools. The company learned that high-end shoppers were spending less and were less willing to purchase the average Coach bag than before. More importantly, Coach also discovered that its customers still wanted to occasionally purchase specialty items that made them feel happy. This inspired the company to create a new, less expensive, fun-focused bag line called Poppy.[5] Marketers should treat information the same way as other resources, and they must weigh the costs and benefits of obtaining information. Information should be considered worthwhile if it results in marketing activities that better satisfy the firm's target customers, lead to increased sales and profits, or help the firm achieve some other goal.

The Marketing Research Process

To maintain the control needed to obtain accurate information, marketers approach marketing research as a process with logical steps: (1) locating and defining problems or issues, (2) designing the research project, (3) collecting data, (4) interpreting research findings, and (5) reporting research findings (see Figure 5.1). These steps should be viewed as an overall approach to conducting research rather than as a rigid set of rules to be followed in each project. In planning research projects, marketers must consider each step carefully and determine how they can best adapt the steps to resolve the particular issues at hand.

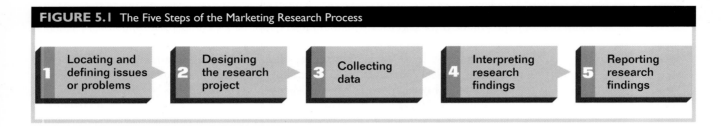

FIGURE 5.1 The Five Steps of the Marketing Research Process

1 Locating and defining issues or problems → 2 Designing the research project → 3 Collecting data → 4 Interpreting research findings → 5 Reporting research findings

Locating and Defining Problems or Research Issues

The first step in launching a research study is problem or issue definition, which focuses on uncovering the nature and boundaries of a situation or question related to marketing strategy or implementation. The first sign of a problem is typically a departure from some normal function, such as the failure to attain objectives. If a corporation's objective is a 12 percent sales increase and the current marketing strategy resulted in a 6 percent increase, this discrepancy should be analyzed to help guide future marketing strategies. Declining sales, increasing expenses, and decreasing profits also signal problems. Customer relationship management (CRM) is frequently based on analysis of existing customers. However, researchers have found that this information could be biased and therefore misleading when making decisions related to identifying and acquiring new customers.[6] Armed with this knowledge, a firm could define a problem as finding a way to adjust for biases stemming from existing customers when gathering data or to develop methods for gathering information to help find new customers. Conversely, when an organization experiences a dramatic rise in sales or some other positive event, it may conduct marketing research to discover the reasons and maximize the opportunities stemming from them.

Marketing research often focuses on identifying and defining market opportunities or changes in the environment. When a firm discovers a market opportunity, it may need to conduct research to understand the situation more precisely so it can craft an appropriate marketing strategy. For instance, AT&T's mobile phone service has a bad reputation for quality, particularly as it applies to the popular iPhone. To help combat increasing customer dissatisfaction, AT&T has created a free "Mark the Spot" app that allows iPhone users to identify problem areas as they are experiencing difficulty. AT&T is using the data to improve its service, thereby retaining more customers.[7]

To pin down the specific boundaries of a problem or an issue through research, marketers must define the nature and scope of the situation in a way that requires probing beneath the superficial symptoms. The interaction between the marketing manager and the marketing researcher should yield a clear definition of the research needed. Researchers and decision makers should remain in the problem or issue definition stage until they have determined precisely what they want from marketing research and how they will use it. Deciding how to refine a broad, indefinite problem or issue into a precise, researchable statement is a prerequisite for the next step in the research process.

Designing the Research Project

Once the problem or issue has been defined, the next step is to create a **research design**, an overall plan for obtaining the information needed to address it. This step requires formulating a hypothesis and determining what type of research is most appropriate for testing the hypothesis to ensure the results are reliable and valid.

DEVELOPING A HYPOTHESIS

The objective statement of a marketing research project should include a hypothesis based on both previous research and expected research findings. A **hypothesis** is an informed guess or assumption about a certain problem or set of circumstances. It is based

research design An overall plan for obtaining the information needed to address a research problem or issue

hypothesis An informed guess or assumption about a certain problem or set of circumstances

on all the insight and knowledge available about the problem or circumstances from previous research studies and other sources. As information is gathered, the researcher can test the hypothesis. For example, a food marketer such as H. J. Heinz might propose the hypothesis that children today have considerable influence on their families' buying decisions regarding ketchup and other grocery products. A marketing researcher would then gather data, perhaps through surveys of children and their parents, and draw conclusions as to whether the hypothesis is correct. Movie theater, sports arena, and concert venue owners who may be wondering why sales are down have hypothesized that consumers are staying home more because of rising event prices, widespread availability of home theater systems and broadband Internet access, and families' increasingly busy schedules. Marketers could test this hypothesis by manipulating prices or offering strong incentives for consumers to return. Sometimes several hypotheses are developed during an actual research project; the hypotheses that are accepted or rejected become the study's chief conclusions.

TYPES OF RESEARCH

The nature and type of research vary based on the research design and the hypotheses under investigation. Marketers may elect to conduct either exploratory research or conclusive research. Although each has a distinct purpose, the major differences between them are formalization and flexibility rather than the specific research methods used. Table 5.1 summarizes the differences.

Exploratory Research When marketers need more information about a problem or want to make a tentative hypothesis more specific, they may conduct **exploratory research**. The main purpose of exploratory research is to better understand a problem or situation and/or to help identify additional data needs or decision alternatives.[8] Consider that until recently, there was no research available to help marketers understand how consumers perceive the terms *clearance* versus *sale* in describing a discounted price event. An exploratory study asked one group of 80 consumers to write down their thoughts about a store window sign that said "sale" and another group of 80 consumers to write about a store window sign that read "clearance." The results revealed that consumers expected deeper discounts when the term *clearance* was used, and they expected the quality of the clearance products to be lower than that of products on sale.[9] This exploratory research

exploratory research
Research conducted to gather more information about a problem or to make a tentative hypothesis more specific

TABLE 5.1 Differences between Exploratory and Conclusive Research

Research Project Components	Exploratory Research	Conclusive Research
Research purpose	General: to generate insights about a situation	Specific: to verify insights and aid in selecting a course of action
Data needs	Vague	Clear
Data sources	Ill-defined	Well-defined
Data collection form	Open-ended, rough	Usually structured
Sample	Relatively small; subjectively selected to maximize generalization of insights	Relatively large; objectively selected to permit generalization of findings
Data collection	Flexible; no set procedure	Rigid; well-laid-out procedure
Data analysis	Informal; typically nonquantitative	Formal; typically quantitative
Inferences/recommendations	More tentative than final	More final than tentative

Source: A. Parasuraman, Dhruv Grewal, and R. Krishnan, *Marketing Research*, p. 64. Copyright © 2004 by Houghton Mifflin Company. Used by permission.

helped marketers better understand how consumers view these terms and opened up the opportunity for additional research hypotheses about decision alternatives for retail pricing.

Conclusive Research **Conclusive research** is designed to verify insights through an objective procedure to help marketers make decisions. It is used when the marketer has one or more alternatives in mind and needs assistance in the final stages of decision making. Consider exploratory research that has revealed that the terms *clearance* and *sale* send different signals to consumers. To make a decision about how to use this information, marketers would benefit from a well-defined and structured research project that will help them decide which approach is best for a specific set of products and target consumers. The typically quantitative study should be specific in selecting a course of action and using methods that can be verified. Two such types of conclusive research are descriptive research and experimental research.

If marketers need to understand the characteristics of certain phenomena to solve a particular problem, **descriptive research** can aid them. Descriptive studies may range from general surveys of customers' educations, occupations, or ages to specifics on how often teenagers consume sports drinks or how often customers buy new pairs of athletic shoes. For example, if Nike and Reebok want to target more young women, they might ask 15- to 35-year-old females how often they work out, how frequently they wear athletic shoes for casual use, and how many pairs of athletic shoes they buy in a year. Such descriptive research can be used to develop specific marketing strategies for the athletic-shoe market. Descriptive studies generally demand much prior knowledge and assume that the problem or issue is clearly defined. Some descriptive studies require statistical analysis and predictive tools. The marketer's major task is to choose adequate methods for collecting and measuring data.

Descriptive research is limited in providing evidence necessary to make causal inferences (i.e., that variable X causes a variable Y). **Experimental research** allows marketers to make causal deductions about relationships. Such experimentation requires that an independent variable (one not influenced by or dependent on other variables) be manipulated and the resulting changes in a dependent variable (one contingent on, or restricted to, one value or set of values assumed by the independent variable) be measured. For instance, when Coca-Cola introduced Dasani flavored waters, managers needed to estimate sales at various potential price points. In some markets, Dasani was introduced at $6.99 per six-pack. By holding variables such as advertising and shelf position constant, Coca-Cola could manipulate the price variable to study its effect on sales. If sales increased 40 percent when the price was reduced by $2, then managers could make an informed decision about the effect of price on sales. Coca-Cola could also use experimental research to manipulate other variables such as advertising or in-store shelf position to determine their effect on sales. Manipulation of the causal variable and control of other variables are what make experimental research unique. As a result, they can provide much stronger evidence of cause and effect than data collected through descriptive research.

RESEARCH RELIABILITY AND VALIDITY

In designing research, marketing researchers must ensure that research techniques are both reliable and valid. A research technique has **reliability** if it produces almost identical results in repeated trials. However, a reliable technique is not necessarily valid. To have **validity**, the research method must measure what it is supposed to measure, not something else. For example, although a group of customers may express the same level of satisfaction based on a rating scale, as individuals they may not exhibit the same repurchase behavior because of different personal characteristics. If the purpose of rating satisfaction was to estimate potential repurchase behavior, this result may cause the researcher to question the validity of the satisfaction scale.[10] A study to measure the effect of advertising on sales would be valid if advertising could be isolated from other factors or from variables that affect sales. The study would be reliable if replications of it produced the same results.

conclusive research
Research designed to verify insights through objective procedures and to help marketers in making decisions

descriptive research
Research conducted to clarify the characteristics of certain phenomena to solve a particular problem

experimental research
Research that allows marketers to make causal inferences about relationships

reliability A condition that exists when a research technique produces almost identical results in repeated trials

validity A condition that exists when a research method measures what it is supposed to measure

Collecting Data
Toluna assists clients in collecting primary data to gain insight into customer behaviors and needs.

Collecting Data

The next step in the marketing research process is collecting data to help prove (or disprove) the research hypothesis. The research design must specify what types of data to collect and how they will be collected.

TYPES OF DATA

Marketing researchers have two types of data at their disposal. **Primary data** are observed and recorded or collected directly from respondents. This type of data must be gathered by observing phenomena or surveying people of interest. **Secondary data** are compiled both inside and outside the organization for some purpose other than the current investigation. Secondary data include general reports supplied to an enterprise by various data services and internal and online databases. Such reports might concern market share, retail inventory levels, and customers' buying behavior. Commonly, secondary data are already available in private or public reports or have been collected and stored by the organization itself. Due to the opportunity to obtain data via the Internet, more than half of all marketing research now comes from secondary sources.

SOURCES OF SECONDARY DATA

Marketers often begin the data-collection phase of the marketing research process by gathering secondary data. They may use available reports and other information from both internal and external sources to study a marketing problem.

Internal sources of secondary data can contribute tremendously to research. An organization's own database may contain information about past marketing activities, such as sales records and research reports, which can be used to test hypotheses and pinpoint problems. From sales reports, for example, a firm may be able to determine not only which product sold best at certain times of the year but also which colors and sizes customers preferred. Such information may have been gathered using customer-relationship management tools for marketing, management, or financial purposes.

Procter & Gamble launched an online store to sell key brands in order to obtain data on consumer buying habits. Sales data can be used to determine trends in the purchase of certain brands, which can be used to formulate hypotheses or to uncover marketing opportunities. Additional secondary data is available from large retailers like Walmart, which shares some of its sales data with Procter & Gamble.[11]

Accounting records are also an excellent source of data but, surprisingly, are often overlooked. The large volume of data an accounting department collects does not automatically flow to other departments. As a result, detailed information about costs, sales, customer accounts, or profits by product category may not be easily accessible to the marketing area. This condition develops particularly in organizations that do not store marketing information on a systematic basis. A third source of internal secondary data is competitive information gathered by the sales force.

External sources of secondary data include trade associations, periodicals, government publications, unpublished sources, and online databases. Trade associations such as the American Marketing Association offer guides and directories that are full of information. Periodicals such as *Bloomberg BusinessWeek*, the *Wall Street Journal*, *Sales & Marketing Management*, *Advertising Age*, *Marketing Research*, and *Industrial*

primary data Data observed and recorded or collected directly from respondents

secondary data Data compiled both inside and outside the organization for some purpose other than the current investigation

Marketing publish general information that can help marketers define problems and develop hypotheses. *Survey of Buying Power,* an annual supplement to *Sales & Marketing Management,* contains sales data for major industries on a county-by-county basis. Many marketers also consult federal government publications such as the *Statistical Abstract of the United States,* the *Census of Business,* the *Census of Agriculture,* and the *Census of Population;* most of these government publications are available online. Although the government still conducts its primary census every ten years, it also conducts the American Community Survey, an ongoing survey sent to population samples on a regular basis.[12] This provides marketers with a more up-to-date demographic picture of the nation's population every year. A company might use survey census data to determine, for example, whether or not to construct a shopping mall in a specific area.[13]

In addition, companies may subscribe to services, such as ACNielsen or Information Resources Inc. (IRI), that track retail sales and other information. For example, IRI tracks consumer purchases using in-store, scanner-based technology. Marketing firms can purchase information from IRI about a product category, such as frozen orange juice, as secondary data.[14] Small businesses may be unable to afford such services, but they can still find a wealth of information through industry publications and trade associations.

Companies such as TiVo are challenging services like ACNielson by offering year-round second-by-second information about the show and advertising viewing habits of consumers who own the company's DVRs. The data are anonymous and are recorded by the TV viewers' boxes. ACNielson, on the other hand, only measures local program viewing for four months a year. However, TiVo's data gathering is limited. Its privacy-protection policies prevent the company from collecting information that Nielson can provide, such as demographic breakdowns and the number of people watching each TV set. On the other hand, TiVo information can aid local TV news programs in their programming decisions by helping them choose when to air sports and weather and how much time to devote to each segment.[15]

The Internet can be especially useful to marketing researchers. Search engines such as Google can help marketers locate many types of secondary data or to research topics of interest. Of course, companies can mine their own websites for useful information by using CRM tools. Amazon.com, for example, has built a relationship with its customers by tracking the types of books, music, and other products they purchase. Each time a customer logs on to the website, the company can offer recommendations based on the customer's previous purchases. Such a marketing system helps the company track the changing desires and buying habits of its most valued customers. Furthermore, marketing researchers are increasingly monitoring blogs to discover what consumers are saying about their products—both positive and negative. Some, including yogurt maker Stonyfield Farms, have even established their own blogs as a way to monitor consumer dialog on issues of their choice. There are many reasons people go online, which can make the job of using the Internet complicated for marketers. Table 5.2 lists the main reasons people go online, and Table 5.3 summarizes the external sources of secondary data, excluding syndicated services.

METHODS OF COLLECTING PRIMARY DATA

Collecting primary data is a lengthier, more expensive, and more complex process than collecting secondary data. To gather primary data, researchers use sampling procedures, survey methods, and observation. These efforts can be handled in-house by the firm's own research department or contracted to a private research firm such as ACNielsen, Information Resources Inc., or IMS International.

Sampling Because the time and resources available for research are limited, it is almost impossible to investigate all the members of a target market or other population. A **population**, or "universe," includes all the elements, units, or individuals of interest to researchers for a specific study. Consider a Gallup poll designed to predict the results of a presidential election. All registered voters in the United States would constitute the population. By systematically choosing a limited number of units—a **sample**—to represent the characteristics of a total population, researchers can project the reactions of a total market or market segment. (In the case of the presidential poll, a representative national sample of several thousand registered voters would be selected and surveyed to project the probable

population All the elements, units, or individuals of interest to researchers for a specific study

sample A limited number of units chosen to represent the characteristics of a total population

Table 5.2 Top 10 Online Pursuits by Generation

Rank	Gen Y	Gen X	Younger Boomers	Older Boomers	Silent Generation	G.I. Generation
1	E-mail	E-mail	E-mail	E-mail	E-mail	E-mail
2	Search	Search	Search	Search	Search	Search
3	Research product	Research product	Research product	Get health info	Research product	Get health info
4	Get news	Get health info	Get health info	Research product	Get health info	Make travel reservations
5	Watch video	Buy something	Get news	Buy something	Make travel reservations	Research product
6	Buy something	Get news	Make travel reservations	Get news	Visit gov't site	Buy something
7	Get health info	Make travel reservations	Buy something	Make travel reservations	Buy something	Get news
8	Visit SNS	Bank	Visit gov't site	Visit gov't site	Get news	Visit gov't site
9	Make travel reservations	Visit gov't site	Research for job	Bank	Bank	Get religious info
10	Research for job	Research for job	Bank	Research for job	Research for job	Bank

Source: "Generations Online Charts," Pew Research Center by Sydney Jones and Susannah Fox, January 28, 2009, www.pewinternet.org/Presentations/2009/Generations-Online-in-2009.aspx.

Table 5.3 External Sources of Secondary Data

Government Sources	
Economic Census	www.census.gov/econ/census02/index.html
Export.gov—country and industry market research	www.export.gov/index/asp
National Technical Information Services	www.ntis.gov
STAT-USA	www.statusa.gov
Industry Canada	www.strategis.ic.gc.ca/engdoc/main.html
Trade Associations and Shows	
American Society of Association Executives	www.asaecenter.org
Directory of Associations	www.marketingsource.com/products/directories/usassociations/index.php
Trade Show News Network	www.tsnn.com
Tradeshow Week	www.tradeshowweek.com
Magazines, Newspapers, Video, Audio News Programming	
Blinkx	www.blinkx.com/home?safefilter=off
FindArticles.com	http://findarticles.com
Google Video Search	http://video.google.com
Corporate Information	
Annual Report Service	www.annualreportservice.com
Bitpipe	www.bitpipe.com
Business Wire	www.businesswire.com/portal/site/home/welcome
Hoover's Online	www.hoovers.com
Open Directory Project	http://dmoz.org

(All websites accessed February 22, 2010.)

sampling The process of selecting representative units from a total population

probability sampling A type of sampling in which every element in the population being studied has a known chance of being selected for study

random sampling A form of probability sampling in which all units in a population have an equal chance of appearing in the sample, and the various events that can occur have an equal or known chance of taking place

stratified sampling A type of probability sampling in which the population is divided into groups with a common attribute and a random sample is chosen within each group

voting outcome.) **Sampling** in marketing research, therefore, is the process of selecting representative units from a total population. Sampling techniques allow marketers to predict buying behavior fairly accurately on the basis of the responses from a representative portion of the population of interest. Most types of marketing research employ sampling techniques.

There are two basic types of sampling: probability sampling and nonprobability sampling. With **probability sampling**, every element in the population being studied has a known chance of being selected for study. Random sampling is a form of probability sampling. When marketers employ **random sampling**, all the units in a population have an equal chance of appearing in the sample. The various events that can occur have an equal or known chance of taking place. For example, a specific card in a regulation deck should have a 1 in 52 probability of being drawn at any one time. Sample units are ordinarily chosen by selecting from a table of random numbers statistically generated so that each digit, 0 through 9, will have an equal probability of occurring in each position in the sequence. The sequentially numbered elements of a population are sampled randomly by selecting the units whose numbers appear in the table of random numbers.

Another type of probability sampling is **stratified sampling**, in which the population of interest is divided into groups according to a common attribute, and a random sample is then chosen within each group. The stratified sample may reduce some of the error that could occur in a simple random sample. By ensuring that each major group or segment of the population receives its proportionate share of sample units, investigators

Marketing in Transition
Companies Use Online Research Communities to Understand Consumers

Traditional market research can be expensive. Businesses large and small are always on the lookout for ways to conduct marketing research that help their companies while saving money. Many companies are realizing that online social media can be powerful marketing tools. According to Jeremiah Owyang of *Forbes* magazine, 67 percent of the worldwide population spends time on social networking sites.

For help, some companies turn to organizations such as Communispace and Passenger. These services create online communities, recruit participants, and manage the sites and all marketing communication. Communispace runs private online research communities for clients such as Best Buy and Reebok. The site is a recipient of the Forrester Groundswell award for excellent and effective use of social technologies. Passenger serves clients such as Starbucks, Adidas, and Mercedes. Mercedes recently used its online community to pre-screen a commercial, which the community loved. Mercedes aired the ad.

Advantages to online research communities are lower costs and the detailed understanding of participants through profiles and long-term interaction. Online communities often take on lives of their own, and conversations develop in ways impossible to replicate through traditional methods. The disadvantages include smaller sample sizes that may not be demographically representative of target markets compared to traditional surveys.

Although many companies are experiencing success with Internet marketing and research, recent information collected from an online research community-based project for Mars Food Australia revealed

that overall participant satisfaction was under 35 percent (although 80 percent did say they would gladly participate in additional projects), indicating the need to refine the process. As the use of online social media continues to expand, will more companies convert to this cost-saving form of market research?[a]

avoid including too many or too few sample units from each group. Samples are usually stratified when researchers believe there may be variations among different types of respondents. For instance, many political opinion surveys are stratified by gender, race, age, and/or geographic location.

The second type of sampling, **nonprobability sampling**, is more subjective than probability sampling because there is no way to calculate the likelihood that a specific element of the population being studied will be chosen. Quota sampling, for example, is highly judgmental because the final choice of participants is left to the researchers. In **quota sampling**, researchers divide the population into groups and then arbitrarily choose participants from each group. In quota sampling, there are some controls—usually limited to two or three variables, such as age, gender, or race—over the selection of participants. The controls attempt to ensure that representative categories of respondents are interviewed. A study of people who wear eyeglasses, for example, may be conducted by interviewing equal numbers of men and women who wear eyeglasses. Because quota samples are not probability samples, not everyone has an equal chance of being selected, and sampling error therefore cannot be measured statistically. Quota samples are used most often in exploratory studies, when hypotheses are being developed. Often a small quota sample will not be projected to the total population, although the findings may provide valuable insights into a problem. Quota samples are useful when people with some common characteristic are found and questioned about the topic of interest. A probability sample used to study people who are allergic to cats, for example, would be highly inefficient.

Survey Methods Marketing researchers often employ sampling to collect primary data through mail, telephone, online, or personal interview surveys. The results of such surveys are used to describe and analyze buying behavior. The survey method chosen depends on the nature of the problem or issue; the data needed to test the hypothesis; and the resources, such as funding and personnel, available to the researcher. Marketers may employ more than one survey method depending on the goals of the research. Surveys can be quite expensive (Procter & Gamble spends about $350 million on consumer understanding and conducts over 15,000 research studies annually), but small businesses can turn to sites such as SurveyMonkey.[16] com and zoomerang.com for inexpensive or even free online surveys. Table 5.4 summarizes and compares the advantages of the various survey methods.

Gathering information through surveys is becoming increasingly difficult because fewer people are willing to participate. Many people believe responding to surveys requires too much scarce personal time, especially as surveys become longer and more detailed. Others have concerns about how much information marketers are gathering and whether their privacy is being invaded. The unethical use of selling techniques disguised as marketing surveys has also led to decreased cooperation. These factors contribute to nonresponse rates for any type of survey.

In a **mail survey**, questionnaires are sent to respondents, who are encouraged to complete and return them. Mail surveys are used most often when the individuals in the sample are spread over a wide area and funds for the survey are limited. A mail survey is less expensive than a telephone or personal interview survey as long as the response rate is high enough to produce reliable results. The main disadvantages of this method are the possibility of a low response rate and of misleading results if respondents differ significantly from the population being sampled.

nonprobability sampling
A sampling technique in which there is no way to calculate the likelihood that a specific element of the population being studied will be chosen

quota sampling A nonprobability sampling technique in which researchers divide the population into groups and then arbitrarily choose participants from each group

mail survey A research method in which respondents answer a questionnaire sent through the mail

Sampling
Companies like uSamp assist customers in creating samples and panels.

Table 5.4 Comparison of the Four Basic Survey Methods

	Mail Surveys	**Telephone Surveys**	**Online Surveys**	**Personal Interview Surveys**
Economy	Potentially lower in cost per interview than telephone or personal surveys if there is an adequate response rate.	Avoids interviewers' travel expenses; less expensive than in-home interviews.	The least expensive method if there is an adequate response rate.	The most expensive survey method; shopping mall and focus-group interviews have lower costs than in-home interviews.
Flexibility	Inflexible; questionnaire must be short and easy for respondents to complete.	Flexible because interviewers can ask probing questions, but observations are impossible.	Less flexible; survey must be easy for online users to receive and return; short, dichotomous, or multiple-choice questions work best.	Most flexible method; respondents can react to visual materials; demographic data are more accurate; in-depth probes are possible.
Interviewer bias	Interviewer bias is eliminated; questionnaires can be returned anonymously.	Some anonymity; may be hard to develop trust in respondents.	Interviewer bias is eliminated, but e-mail address on the return eliminates anonymity.	Interviewers' personal characteristics or inability to maintain objectivity may result in bias.
Sampling and respondents' cooperation	Obtaining a complete mailing list is difficult; nonresponse is a major disadvantage.	Sample limited to respondents with telephones; devices that screen calls, busy signals, and refusals are a problem.	Sample limited to respondents with computer access; the available e-mail address list may not be a representative sample for some purposes.	Not-at-homes are a problem, which may be overcome by focus-group and shopping mall interviewing.

One method of improving response rates involves attaching a brief personal message on a Post-it® Note to the survey packet. Response rates to these surveys are higher, and the quality and timeliness of the responses are also improved.[17] As a result of these issues, companies are increasingly moving to Internet surveys and automated telephone surveys.

Premiums or incentives that encourage respondents to return questionnaires have been effective in developing panels of respondents who are interviewed regularly by mail. Such mail panels, selected to represent a target market or market segment, are especially useful in evaluating new products and providing general information about customers, as well as records of their purchases (in the form of purchase diaries). Mail panels and purchase diaries are much more widely used than custom mail surveys, but both panels and purchase diaries have shortcomings. People who take the time to fill out a diary may differ from the general population based on income, education, or behavior, such as the time available for shopping activities. Internet surveys have also greatly gained in popularity, although they are similarly limited as well—given that not all demographics utilize the internet equally.

In a **telephone survey**, an interviewer records respondents' answers to a questionnaire over a phone line. A telephone survey has some advantages over a mail survey. The rate of response is higher because it takes less effort to answer the telephone and talk than to fill out and return a questionnaire. If enough interviewers are available, a telephone survey can be conducted very quickly. Thus, political candidates or organizations that want an immediate reaction to an event may choose this method. In addition, a telephone survey permits interviewers to gain rapport with respondents and ask probing questions. Automated telephone surveys, also known as interactive voice response or "robosurveys," rely on a recorded voice to ask the questions while a computer program records respondents' answers. The primary benefit of automated surveys is the elimination of any bias that might be introduced by a live researcher.

However, only a small proportion of the population likes to participate in telephone surveys. This can significantly limit participation and distort representation in a telephone survey. Moreover, telephone surveys are limited to oral communication; visual aids or observation cannot be included. Interpreters of results must make adjustments for individuals who are not at home or do not have telephones. Many households are excluded from

telephone survey A research method in which respondents' answers to a questionnaire are recorded by an interviewer on the phone

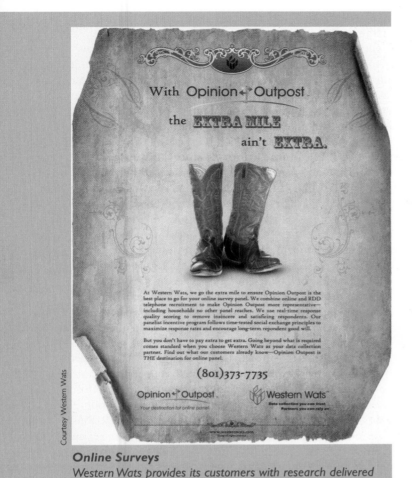

Online Surveys
Western Wats provides its customers with research delivered by a readily available online survey panel.

Courtesy Western Wats

telephone directories by choice (unlisted numbers) or because the residents moved after the directory was published. Potential respondents often use telephone answering machines, voice mail, or caller ID to screen or block calls; additionally, millions have signed up for "Do Not Call Lists." Moreover, an increasing number of younger Americans are giving up their fixed telephone lines in favor of cellular or wireless phones. These issues have serious implications for the use of telephone samples in conducting surveys. Some adjustment must be made for groups of respondents that may be undersampled because of a smaller-than-average incidence of telephone listings. Nondirectory telephone samples can overcome such bias. Various methods are available, including random-digit dialing (adding random numbers to the telephone prefix) and plus-one telephone sampling (increasing the last digit of a directory number by 1).

Online surveys are evolving as an alternative to telephone surveys. In an **online survey**, questionnaires can be transmitted to respondents who have agreed to be contacted and have provided their e-mail addresses. Because e-mail is semi-interactive, recipients can ask for clarification of specific questions or pose questions of their own. The potential advantages of e-mail surveys are quick response and lower cost than traditional mail, telephone, and personal interview surveys if the response rate is adequate. In addition, more firms use their websites to conduct surveys. Online surveys can also use online communities—such as chat rooms, web-based forums, blogs, newsgroups, social networking sites, and research communities—to identify trends in interests and consumption patterns. Movies, consumer electronics, food, and computers are popular topics in many online communities. Indeed, by "listening in" on these ongoing conversations, marketers may be able to identify new product opportunities and consumer needs. Moreover, this type of online data can be gathered at little incremental cost compared to alternative data sources. Evolving technology and the interactive nature of the Internet allow for considerable flexibility in designing online questionnaires. **Crowdsourcing** combines the words *crowd* and *outsourcing* and calls for taking tasks usually performed by a marketer or researcher and outsourcing them to a crowd, or potential market, through an open call. Consider Procter & Gamble, which has used social networking sites to solicit new ideas and suggestions straight from consumers when developing new products. Crowdsourcing is a way for marketers to gather input straight from willing consumers and to actively listen and engage with people's ideas and evaluations on products. The computer company Dell Inc. has used crowdsourcing to tap into consumer insights and to spur innovations in everything from new products to website design and marketing improvements. Seventy-five percent of respondents to a recent survey indicate that crowdsourcing is an effective way to approach innovations in products and services.[18]

Given the growing number of households that have computers with Internet access, marketing research is likely to rely heavily on online surveys and crowdsourcing in the future. Furthermore, as negative attitudes toward telephone surveys render that technique less representative and more expensive, the integration of e-mail and voice mail functions into one computer-based system provides a promising alternative for survey research. E-mail surveys have especially strong potential within organizations whose employees are networked and for associations that publish members' e-mail addresses. However, there are some ethical issues to consider when using e-mail for marketing research, such as unsolicited e-mail, which could be viewed as "spam," and

online survey A research method in which respondents answer a questionnaire via e-mail or on a website

crowdsourcing Combines the words *crowd* and *outsourcing* and calls for taking tasks usually performed by a marketer or researcher and outsourcing them to a crowd, or potential market, through an open call

privacy, as some potential survey respondents fear their personal information will be given or sold to third parties without their knowledge or permission.

In a **personal interview survey**, participants respond to questions face-to-face. Various audiovisual aids—pictures, products, diagrams, or prerecorded advertising copy—can be incorporated into a personal interview. Rapport gained through direct interaction usually permits more in-depth interviewing, including probes, follow-up questions, or psychological tests. In addition, because personal interviews can be longer, they may yield more information. Finally, respondents can be selected more carefully, and reasons for nonresponse can be explored.

One such research technique is the **in-home (door-to-door) interview**. The in-home interview offers a clear advantage when thoroughness of self-disclosure and elimination of group influence are important. In an in-depth interview of 45 to 90 minutes, respondents can be probed to reveal their true motivations, feelings, behaviors, and aspirations.

The object of a **focus-group interview** is to observe group interaction when members are exposed to an idea or a concept. Focus-group interviews are often conducted informally, without a structured questionnaire, in small groups of 8 to 12 people. They allow customer attitudes, behaviors, lifestyles, needs, and desires to be explored in a flexible and creative manner. Questions are open-ended and stimulate respondents to answer in their own words. Researchers can ask probing questions to clarify something they do not fully understand or something unexpected and interesting that may help explain buying behavior. For example, Ford may use focus groups to determine whether to change its advertising to emphasize a vehicle's safety features rather than its style and performance. On the other hand, focus-group participants do not always tell the truth. Some participants may be less than honest in an effort to be sociable or to receive money and/or food in exchange for their participation.[19] However, they generally provide only qualitative, not quantitative, data, and are thus best used to uncover issues that can then be explored using quantifiable marketing research techniques.

Online focus groups can gather data from large and geographically diverse groups in a less intensive manner than focus-group interviews. Online focus groups are less expensive than traditional sit down groups, but they do not allow for as much interaction, the ability to observe body language, or the spontaneity to quickly make changes in the discussion. Having a person on-site to interact with participants and to observe and manipulate verbal and nonverbal responses tends to be most effective. Ford Motor Company, for instance, prefers traditional live focus groups because of the advantages listed above.[20]

More organizations are starting **customer advisory boards**, which are small groups of actual customers who serve as sounding boards for new-product ideas and offer insights into their feelings and attitudes toward a firm's products, promotion, pricing, and other elements of marketing strategy. While these advisory boards help companies maintain strong relationships with valuable customers, they can also provide great insight into marketing research questions. Maxine Clark, CEO and founder of Build-A-Bear Workshop, runs a customer advisory board with the purpose of staying in tune with what her customers want. She highly recommends that startups, in particular, found advisory boards, stating that this technique allows a company to focus immediately on what its consumer base truly wants.[21]

Still another option is the **telephone depth interview**, which combines the traditional focus group's ability to probe with the confidentiality provided by a telephone survey. This type of interview is most appropriate for qualitative research projects among a small targeted group that is difficult to bring together for a traditional focus group because of members' professions, locations, or lifestyles. Respondents can choose the time and day for the interview. Although this method is difficult to implement, it can yield revealing information from respondents who otherwise would be unwilling to participate in marketing research.

personal interview survey A research method in which participants respond to survey questions face-to-face

in-home (door-to-door) interview A personal interview that takes place in the respondent's home

focus-group interview An interview that is often conducted informally, without a structured questionnaire, in small groups of 8 to 12 people, to observe interaction when members are exposed to an idea or a concept

customer advisory boards Small groups of actual customers who serve as sounding boards for new-product ideas and offer insights into their feelings and attitudes toward a firm's products and other elements of its marketing strategy

telephone depth interview An interview that combines the traditional focus group's ability to probe with the confidentiality provided by telephone surveys

InterVu...It's like being there only better.

Conduct Live Focus Groups Online with a Webcam

Sometimes you need to go outside a research facility to broaden the respondent pool. InterVu Online Focus Groups enable you to reach participants anywhere in the world at any time.

With InterVu, you can get the same face-to-face exchange you get from traditional focus groups. Moderators and respondents log in to the InterVu web portal through their computer and transmit their image with a personal web cam.

This *live* focus group exchange allows all participants to see, hear and react to each other in the same way as a traditional group interview only online. InterVu Focus Groups are transmitted in real-time to any number of viewers, world wide.

FocusVision
WORLDWIDE

Schedule a Demo or Book a Project today.

For more information, call 888-536-2878
or email request@focusvision.com

STAMFORD   LONDON   SINGAPORE
www.focusvision.com

© FocusVision Worldwide, Inc.

Focus Groups
Companies like FocusVision help administer video-enabled online focus groups with the use of such platforms as InterVu.

The nature of personal interviews has changed. In the past, most personal interviews, which were based on random sampling or prearranged appointments, were conducted in the respondent's home. Today many personal interviews are conducted in shopping malls. **Shopping mall intercept interviews** involve interviewing a percentage of individuals who pass by an "intercept" point in a mall. Like any face-to-face interviewing method, mall intercept interviewing has many advantages. The interviewer is in a position to recognize and react to respondents' nonverbal indications of confusion. Respondents can view product prototypes, videotapes of commercials, and the like, and provide their opinions. The mall environment lets the researcher deal with complex situations. For instance, in taste tests, researchers know that all the respondents are reacting to the same product, which can be prepared and monitored from the mall test kitchen. In addition to the ability to conduct tests requiring bulky equipment, lower cost and greater control make shopping mall intercept interviews popular.

An **on-site computer interview** is a variation of the shopping mall intercept interview in which respondents complete a self-administered questionnaire displayed on a computer monitor. A computer software package can be used to conduct such interviews in shopping malls. After a brief lesson on how to operate the software, respondents proceed through the survey at their own pace. Questionnaires can be adapted so that respondents see only those items (usually a subset of an entire scale) that may provide useful information about their attitudes.

Questionnaire Construction   A carefully constructed questionnaire is essential to the success of any survey. Questions must be clear, easy to understand, and directed toward a specific objective; that is, they must be designed to elicit information that meets the study's data requirements. Researchers need to define the objective before trying to develop a questionnaire because the objective determines the substance of the questions and the amount of detail. A common mistake in constructing questionnaires is to ask questions that interest the researchers but do not yield information useful in deciding whether to accept or reject a hypothesis. Finally, the most important rule in composing questions is to maintain impartiality.

The questions are usually of three kinds: open-ended, dichotomous, and multiple-choice.

shopping mall intercept interview A research method that involves interviewing a percentage of individuals passing by "intercept" points in a mall

on-site computer interview A variation of the shopping mall intercept interview in which respondents complete a self-administered questionnaire displayed on a computer monitor

Open-Ended Question
What is your opinion of British Petroleum (BP)?

_____

_____

_____

Dichotomous Question
Do you plan to purchase gasoline from a BP service station within the next 12 months?
Yes _____ No _____

Multiple-Choice Question

What age group are you in?

Under 20 _____
20–29 _____
30–39 _____
40–49 _____
50–59 _____
60 and over _____

Problems may develop in the analysis of dichotomous or multiple-choice questions when responses for one outcome outnumber others. For example, a dichotomous question that asks respondents to choose between "buy" or "not buy" might require additional sampling from the disproportionately smaller group if there were not enough responses to analyze.[22]

Researchers must also be very careful about questions that a respondent might consider too personal or that might require an admission of activities that other people are likely to condemn. Questions of this type should be worded to make them less offensive.

Observation Methods In using observation methods, researchers record individuals' overt behavior, taking note of physical conditions and events. Direct contact with them is avoided; instead, their actions are examined and noted systematically. For instance, researchers might use observation methods to answer the question, "How long does the average McDonald's restaurant customer have to wait in line before being served?" Observation may include the use of ethnographic techniques, such as watching customers interact with a product in a real-world environment.

After decades of using the same familiar red label, Campbell's Soup used observation methods to help develop an updated and eye-catching label. For years, researchers at Campbell's observed and tested consumers' reactions to the labels in order to determine what they find appealing. The end result is a label that preserves the familiar red coloring but that features steaming soup in updated bowls meant to trigger stronger emotional responses in consumers. A challenge for the company was to preserve the familiar look of the soup label while also making it more eye-catching and interesting to consumers who may feel overwhelmed by the large number of options on the shelves.[23] Observation may also be combined with interviews. For instance, during a personal interview, the condition of a respondent's home or other possessions may be observed and recorded. The interviewer can also directly observe and confirm such demographic information as race, approximate age, and gender.

Data gathered through observation can sometimes be biased if the subject is aware of the observation process. However, an observer can be placed in a natural market environment, such as a grocery store, without influencing shoppers' actions. If the presence of a human observer is likely to bias the outcome or if human sensory abilities are inadequate, mechanical means may be used to record behavior. Mechanical observation devices include cameras, recorders, counting machines, scanners, and equipment that records physiological changes. A special camera can be used to record the eye movements of people as they look at an advertisement; the camera detects the sequence of reading and the parts of the advertisement that receive the greatest attention. The electronic scanners used in supermarkets are very useful in marketing research: they provide accurate data on sales and customers' purchase patterns, and marketing researchers may buy such data from the supermarkets.

Observation is straightforward and avoids a central problem of survey methods: motivating respondents to state their true feelings or opinions. However, observation tends to be descriptive. When it is the only method of data collection, it may not provide insights into causal relationships. Another drawback is that analyses based on observation are subject to the observer's biases or the limitations of the mechanical device.

Interpreting Research Findings

After collecting data to test their hypotheses, marketers need to interpret the research findings. Interpretation of the data is easier if marketers carefully plan their data analysis methods early in the research process. They should also allow for continual evaluation of the data during the entire collection period. Marketers can then gain valuable insights into areas that should be probed during the formal analysis.

The first step in drawing conclusions from most research is to display the data in table format. If marketers intend to apply the results to individual categories of the things or people being studied, cross-tabulation may be useful, especially in tabulating joint occurrences. For example, using the two variables of gender and purchase rates of automobile tires, a cross-tabulation could show how men and women differ in purchasing automobile tires.

After the data are tabulated, they must be analyzed. **Statistical interpretation** focuses on what is typical and what deviates from the average. It indicates how widely responses vary and how they are distributed in relation to the variable being measured. When marketers interpret statistics, they must take into account estimates of expected error or deviation from the true values of the population. The analysis of data may lead researchers to accept or reject the hypothesis being studied. Data require careful interpretation by the marketer. If the results of a study are valid, the decision maker should take action; if a question has been incorrectly or poorly worded, however, the results may produce poor decisions. Consider the research conducted for a food marketer that asked respondents to rate a product on criteria such as "hearty flavor," as well as how important each criterion was to the respondent. Although such results may have had utility for advertising purposes, they are less helpful in product development because it is not possible to discern each respondent's meaning of the phrase "hearty flavor." Managers must understand the research results and relate them to a context that permits effective decision making.

Reporting Research Findings

The final step in the marketing research process is to report the research findings. Before preparing the report, the marketer must take a clear, objective look at the findings to

statistical interpretation
Analysis of what is typical and what deviates from the average

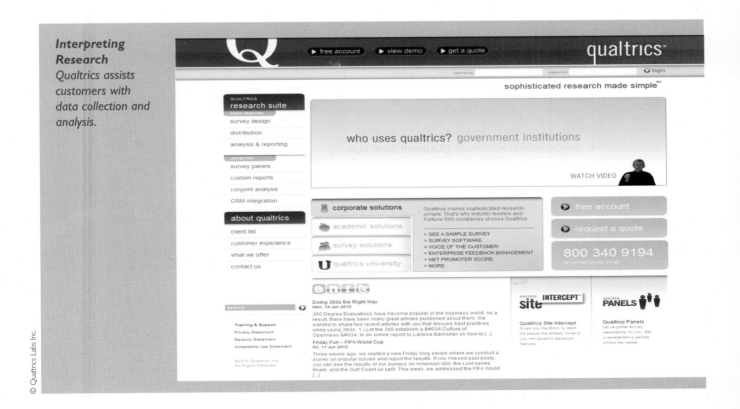

Interpreting Research
Qualtrics assists customers with data collection and analysis.

see how well the gathered facts answer the research question or support or negate the initial hypotheses. In most cases, it is extremely doubtful that the study can provide everything needed to answer the research question. Thus, the researcher must point out the deficiencies in the research and their causes in the report. Research should be meaningful to all participants, especially top managers who develop strategy. Therefore, researchers must try to make certain that their findings are relevant and not just interesting. Research is not useful unless it supports the organization's overall strategy objectives. The more knowledge researchers have about the opportunities and challenges facing an organization, the more meaningful their research report will be. If an outside research agency conducts research, it is even more important to understand the client's business. After conducting research, a research report is the next step. Those responsible for preparing the report must facilitate adjusting the findings to the environment, as elements change over time. Most importantly, the report should be helpful to marketers and managers on an ongoing basis.[24]

The report of research results is usually a formal, written document. Researchers must allow time for the writing task when they plan and schedule the project. Because the report is a means of communicating with the decision makers who will use the research findings, researchers need to determine beforehand how much detail and supporting data to include. They should keep in mind that corporate executives prefer reports that are short, clear, and simply expressed. Researchers often give their summary and recommendations first, especially if decision makers do not have time to study how the results were obtained. A technical report allows its users to analyze data and interpret recommendations because it describes the research methods and procedures and the most important data gathered. Thus, researchers must recognize the needs and expectations of the report user and adapt to them.

Sustainable Marketing
Arbitron's People Meter Replaces Diary-Based Audience Measurement

For years, radio stations have measured when and to what people are listening. Until a few years ago, populations selected for sampling used paper diaries to record their habits. Arbitron, a media research firm, is changing that practice with its Portable People Meter, a device that records people's radio listening habits by monitoring radio signals. Many companies are embracing this new method as an easier-to-use, more reliable, and more accurate way to gather information and understand how to best market their products or services to listeners.

The People Meter is more accurate than a person writing down his or her habits. It also reduces paper waste. Most importantly, advertisers can determine exactly when listeners tune in to a particular station and for how long. This allows advertisers and station directors to customize their content and retain listeners longer. As a result, many stations are changing their formulas. If advertisers can hold listeners' attention, it can make a tremendous difference to their bottom lines.

Although gaining popularity, the People Meter and the ethical behavior of Arbitron are under scrutiny. A House committee investigated the company due to accusations that the People Meter under-counts minorities. As of January 2010, however, reports showed that Arbitron had improved its People Meter's reach,

recording more information from minorities. Arbitron's rising stock value that month showed that investors had more confidence in the company. Arbitron also received an Emmy award for the People Meter. As with many new technologies, it can take time to work out the kinks, but companies seem excited to embrace the People Meter and eliminate old-fashioned paper diaries.[b]

Bias and distortion can be a major problem if the researcher is intent on obtaining favorable results. For example, research analyzing consumers' reports of their frequency of using long-distance telephone calls, letters, cards, and visits for personal communication found that some groups underreport their usage, whereas other groups overreport it. In particular, researchers found that consumers underestimate the duration of lengthy telephone calls but overestimate the length of short ones; in general, people tend to overestimate both the frequency and duration of their telephone calls. Without this information, companies relying on survey results may get a distorted view of the market for long-distance telephone services by mistakenly judging it to be larger and more homogeneous than it really is.[25]

Marketing researchers want to know about behavior and opinions, and they want accurate data to help them in making decisions. Careful wording of questions is very important because a biased or emotional word can dramatically change the results. Marketing research and marketing information systems can provide an organization with accurate and reliable customer feedback, which a marketer must have to understand the dynamics of the marketplace. As managers recognize the benefits of marketing research, they assign it a much larger role in decision making.

Using Technology to Improve Marketing Information Gathering and Analysis

Technology makes information for marketing decisions increasingly accessible. The ability of marketers to track customer buying behavior and to better discern what buyers want is changing the nature of marketing. Customer relationship management is being enhanced by integrating data from all customer contacts and combining that information to improve customer retention. Information technology permits internal research and quick information gathering to help marketers better understand and satisfy customers. For instance, company responses to e-mail complaints as well as to communications through mail, telephone, and personal contact can be used to improve customer satisfaction, retention, and value. Armed with such information, marketers can fine-tune marketing mixes to satisfy their customers' needs.

The integration of telecommunications and computer technologies allows marketers to access a growing array of valuable information sources related to industry forecasts, business trends, and customer buying behavior. Electronic communication tools can be effectively used to gain accurate information with minimal customer interaction. Most marketing researchers have e-mail, voice mail, teleconferencing, and fax machines at their disposal. In fact, many firms use marketing information systems and customer relationship management technologies to network all these technologies and organize all the marketing data available to them. In this section, we look at marketing information systems and specific technologies that are helping marketing researchers obtain and manage marketing research data.

Marketing Information Systems

A **marketing information system (MIS)** is a framework for the day-to-day management and structuring of information gathered regularly from sources both inside and outside the organization. As such, an MIS provides a continuous flow of information about prices, advertising expenditures, sales, competition, and distribution expenses. Anheuser-Busch, for example, uses a system called BudNet that compiles information about past sales at individual stores, the company's inventory, their competitors' displays and prices, and a host of other information collected by distributors' sales representatives on handheld computers. BudNet allows managers to respond quickly to changes in competitors' strategies with an appropriate promotional message, package, display, or discount.[26]

marketing information system (MIS) A framework for managing and structuring information gathered regularly from sources inside and outside the organization

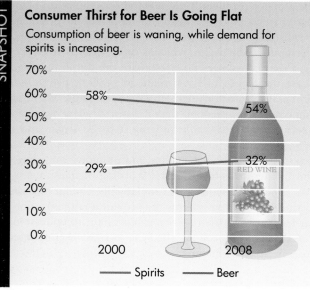

SNAPSHOT

Consumer Thirst for Beer Is Going Flat

Consumption of beer is waning, while demand for spirits is increasing.

58%
54%
29%
32%

—— Spirits —— Beer

2000   2008

Source: Beer Marketer's Insights.

This is important information for Budweiser in an increasingly competitive market where consumers' taste for beer appears to be on the decline (see Snapshot).

The main focus of the MIS is on data storage and retrieval, as well as on computer capabilities and management's information requirements. Regular reports of sales by product or market categories, data on inventory levels, and records of salespeople's activities are examples of information that is useful in making decisions. In the MIS, the means of gathering data receive less attention than do the procedures for expediting the flow of information.

An effective MIS starts by determining the objective of the information—that is, by identifying decision needs that require certain information. The firm can then specify an information system for continuous monitoring to provide regular, pertinent information on both the external and internal environment. Federal Express, for example, has interactive marketing systems that provide instantaneous communication between the company and customers. Customers can track their packages and receive immediate feedback concerning delivery via the Internet. The company's website provides information about customer usage and allows customers to convey what they think about company services. The evolving telecommunications and computer technologies allow marketers to use information systems to cultivate one-to-one relationships with customers.

Databases

Most marketing information systems include internal databases. A **database** is a collection of information arranged for easy access and retrieval. Databases allow marketers to tap into an abundance of information useful in making marketing decisions: internal sales reports, newspaper articles, company news releases, government economic reports, bibliographies, and more, often accessed through a computer system. Information technology has made it possible to develop databases to guide strategic planning and help improve customer services. Customer relationship management (CRM) employs database marketing techniques to identify different types of customers and develop specific strategies for interacting with each customer. CRM incorporates these three elements:

1. Identifying and building a database of current and potential consumers, including a wide range of demographic, lifestyle, and purchase information
2. Delivering differential messages according to each consumer's preferences and characteristics through established and new media channels
3. Tracking customer relationships to monitor the costs of retaining individual customers and the lifetime value of their purchases[27]

It is important for marketers to distinguish *active* customers—those who are likely to continue buying from the firm—from *inactive* customers—those who are likely to defect and those who have already defected. This information should help to (1) identify profitable inactive customers who can be reactivated; (2) remove inactive, unprofitable customers from the customer database; and (3) identify active customers who should be targeted with regular marketing activities.[28]

Many commercial websites require consumers to register and provide personal information to access the site or to make a purchase. Frequent-flyer programs permit airlines to ask loyal customers to participate in surveys about their needs and desires and to track their best customers' flight patterns by time of day, week, month, and year. Supermarkets gain a significant amount of data through checkout scanners tied to store discount cards. In fact, one of the best ways to predict market behavior is the use of

database A collection of information arranged for easy access and retrieval

single-source data Information provided by a single marketing research firm

marketing decision support system (MDSS) Customized computer software that aids marketing managers in decision making

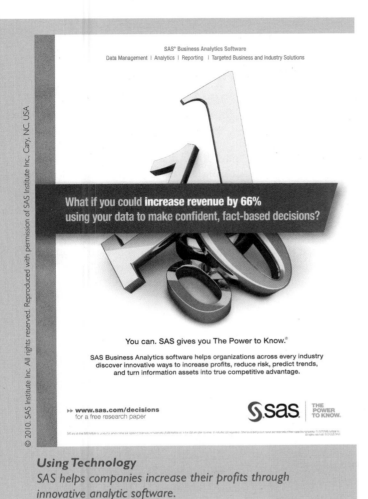

SAS® Business Analytics Software

Data Management | Analytics | Reporting | Targeted Business and Industry Solutions

What if you could increase revenue by 66% using your data to make confident, fact-based decisions?

You can. SAS gives you The Power to Know.®

SAS Business Analytics software helps organizations across every industry discover innovative ways to increase profits, reduce risk, predict trends, and turn information assets into true competitive advantage.

▸▸ www.sas.com/decisions
for a free research paper

§sas. THE POWER TO KNOW.

Using Technology
SAS helps companies increase their profits through innovative analytic software.

database information gathered through loyalty programs or other transaction-based processes.[29]

Marketing researchers can also use databases, such as Lexis-Nexis, to obtain useful information for marketing decisions. Many commercial databases are accessible online for a fee. Sometimes, they can be obtained in printed form or on computer compact discs. With most commercial databases, the user typically conducts a computer search by keyword, topic, or company, and the database service generates abstracts, articles, or reports that can then be printed out. Accessing multiple reports or a complete article may cost extra.

Information provided by a single firm on household demographics, purchases, television viewing behavior, and responses to promotions such as coupons and free samples is called **single-source data**. For example, Behavior Scan, offered by Information Resources Inc. screens populations between 75,000 and 200,000.[30] This single-source information service monitors consumer household televisions and records the programs and commercials watched. When buyers from these households shop in stores equipped with scanning registers, they present Hotline cards (similar to credit cards) to cashiers. This enables each customer's identification to be electronically coded so the firm can track each product purchased and store the information in a database. It is important to gather longitudinal (long-term) information on customers to maximize the usefulness of single-source data.

Marketing Decision Support Systems

A **marketing decision support system (MDSS)** is customized computer software that aids marketing managers in decision making by helping them anticipate the effects of certain decisions. Some decision support systems have a broader range and offer greater computational and modeling capabilities than spreadsheets; they let managers explore a greater number of alternatives. For instance, an MDSS can determine how sales and profits might be affected by higher or lower interest rates or how sales forecasts, advertising expenditures, production levels, and the like might affect overall profits. For this reason, MDSS software is often a major component of a company's marketing information system. Customized decision support systems can support customer orientation and customer satisfaction in business marketing.[31] Some decision support systems incorporate artificial intelligence and other advanced computer technologies.

Entrepreneurial Marketing

iModerate Uses Text Messaging to Research Consumer Feelings

iModerate LLC, a marketing research company, is attempting to address a weakness in online surveys. Traditional online surveys only provide one-way communication without offering any insight into feelings and attitudes beneath the surface of respondents. Carl Rosso co-founded iModerate with Joel Bensensen after working in polling for President Clinton's administration. He observed that Internet surveys simply did not provide enough information on the thoughts and feelings of each respondent, so he created an interactive online questionnaire that helps to expose feelings, uncover connections, and enhance survey data. iModerate is an example of using evolving technology and the Internet to allow for considerable flexibility in designing online questionnaires.[c]

Issues in Marketing Research

The Importance of Ethical Marketing Research

Marketing managers and other professionals are relying more and more on marketing research, marketing information systems, and new technologies to make better decisions. It is therefore essential that professional standards be established by which to judge the reliability of marketing research. Such standards are necessary because of the ethical and legal issues that develop in gathering marketing research data. In the area of online interaction, for example, consumers remain wary of how the personal information collected by marketers will be used, especially whether it will be sold to third parties. In addition, the relationships between research suppliers, such as marketing research agencies, and the marketing managers who make strategy decisions require ethical behavior. Organizations such as the Marketing Research Association have developed codes of conduct and guidelines to promote ethical marketing research. To be effective, such guidelines must instruct marketing researchers on how to avoid misconduct. Here are nine guidelines interviewers should follow when introducing a questionnaire.

1. Allow interviewers to introduce themselves by name.
2. State the name of the research company.
3. Indicate that this is a marketing research project.
4. Explain that there will be no sales involved.
5. Note the general topic of discussion (if this is a problem in a "blind" study, a statement such as "consumer opinion" is acceptable).
6. State the likely duration of the interview.
7. Assure the anonymity of the respondent and confidentiality of all answers.
8. State the honorarium if applicable (for many business-to-business and medical studies, this is done up front for both qualitative and quantitative studies).
9. Reassure the respondent with a statement such as "There are no right or wrong answers, so please give thoughtful and honest answers to each question" (recommended by many clients).

International Issues in Marketing Research

As we shall see in Chapter 9, sociocultural, economic, political, legal, and technological forces vary in different regions of the world. These variations create challenges for the

---

Responsible Marketing?

Marketing Research to Measure Business Ethics

CRITICAL THINKING

ISSUE: Can you measure marketing ethics?

Ethisphere magazine conducts marketing research to measure the world's most ethical companies. The editors and writers for the magazine try to distinguish absolute behaviors that can be used to differentiate one organization from another. The magazine also attempts to examine companies to make certain that their claims are translated into ethical actions. The methodology for this research involves an eight-step process of collecting and screening information. Several criteria are explored in this research, including litigation and controversy/conflict analysis; ethical tone analysis; innovation and industry leadership analysis; corporate citizenship analysis; industry effort and participation analysis; governance and transparency analysis; public and trade partner perception analysis; and ethics/compliance program system analysis. Companies highlighted in the study included Alcoa, Eaton Corporation, Kiplingers, GE, Kellogg's, and John Deere.

Fortune magazine conducts research to find the Most Admired Companies. The Hay Group assists the magazine in assessing companies based on nine criteria: attraction and retention of talent; corporate culture; leadership development; performance measurement; strategy implementation; responses to economic uncertainty; innovation; effectiveness of managing globally; and board governance and effectiveness. Some of *Fortune*'s Most Admired Companies include Apple, Berkshire Hathaway, GE, Google, Toyota, Starbucks, Federal Express, P&G, Johnson & Johnson, Goldman Sachs, Target, and Southwest Airlines. Admiration is a function of effectively managing your risks and relating to consumers and the public. Which measurement approach do you feel generates the greatest accuracy in measuring organizational ethics related to marketing?[d]

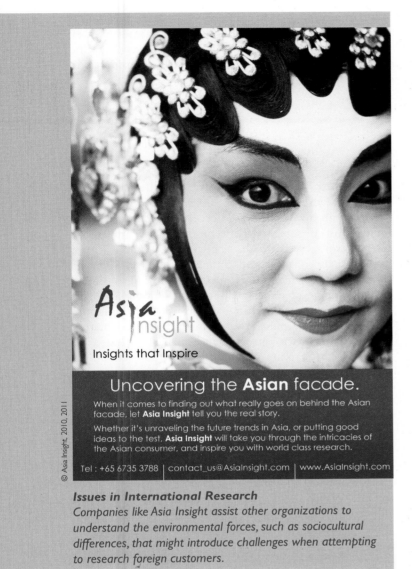

Issues in International Research
Companies like Asia Insight assist other organizations to understand the environmental forces, such as sociocultural differences, that might introduce challenges when attempting to research foreign customers.

organizations that are attempting to understand foreign customers through marketing research. The marketing research process we describe in this chapter is used globally, but to ensure the research is valid and reliable, data-gathering methods may have to be modified to allow for regional differences. For example, experts have found that Latin Americans do not respond well to focus groups or in-depth interviews that are longer than 90 minutes. Researchers therefore need to adjust their tactics to generate information that is useful for marketing products in Latin America.[32] To make certain that global and regional differences are satisfactorily addressed, many companies retain a research firm with experience in the country of interest. Most of the largest marketing research firms derive a significant share of their revenues from research conducted outside the United States. As Table 5.5 indicates, the Nielsen Company, the largest marketing research firm in the world, received nearly half of its revenues from outside the United States.[33]

Experts recommend a two-pronged approach to international marketing research. The first phase involves a detailed search for and analysis of secondary data to gain a greater understanding of a particular marketing environment and to pinpoint issues that must be taken into account in gathering primary research data. Secondary data can be particularly helpful in building a general understanding of the market, including economic, legal, cultural, and demographic issues, as well as in assessing the risks of doing business in that market and in forecasting demand. Marketing researchers often begin by studying country trade reports from the U.S. Department of Commerce, as well as country-specific information from local sources, such as a country's website, and trade and general business publications such as the *Wall Street Journal*. These sources can offer insights into the marketing environment in a particular country and can even indicate untapped market opportunities abroad.

The second phase involves field research using many of the methods described earlier, including focus groups and telephone surveys, to refine a firm's understanding of specific customer needs and preferences. Specific differences among countries can have a profound influence on data gathering. For instance, in-home (door-to-door) interviews are illegal in some countries. In developing countries, few people have land-line telephones, as many opt for cell phones, making telephone surveys less practical and less representative of the total population. Primary data gathering may have a greater chance of success if the firm employs local

Table 5.5 Top U.S. Marketing Research Firms

Company	Global Revenues (in Millions of U.S. Dollars)	Percent of Revenues from Outside the United States
1. The Nielsen Co.	4,575.0	51.2
2. The Kantar Group	3,616.1	74.1
3. IMS Health Inc.	2,392.6	63.9
4. GfK USA	1,797.2	82.6
5. Ipsos	1,442.1	78.7

Source: "Top 50 U.S. Market Research Organizations," *Marketing News*, June 30, 2009, p. 19.

researchers who better understand how to approach potential respondents and can do so in their own languages.[34] Regardless of the specific methods used to gather primary data, whether in the United States or abroad, the goal is to recognize the needs of specific target markets to craft the best marketing strategy to satisfy the needs of customers in each market, as we will see in the next chapter.

summary

I. To describe the basic steps in conducting marketing research

Marketing research is the systematic design, collection, interpretation, and reporting of information to help marketers solve specific marketing problems or take advantage of marketing opportunities. It is a process for gathering information not currently available to decision makers. Marketing research can help a firm better understand market opportunities, ascertain the potential for success for new products, and determine the feasibility of a particular marketing strategy. The value of marketing research is measured by improvements in a marketer's ability to make decisions.

To maintain the control needed to obtain accurate information, marketers approach marketing research as a process with logical steps: (1) locating and defining problems or issues, (2) designing the research project, (3) collecting data, (4) interpreting research findings, and (5) reporting research findings.

2. To explore the fundamental methods of gathering data for marketing research

The first step in launching a research study, the problem or issue definition, focuses on uncovering the nature and boundaries of a situation or question related to marketing strategy or implementation. When a firm discovers a market opportunity, it may need to conduct research to understand the situation more precisely so it can craft an appropriate marketing strategy. In the second step, marketing researchers design a research project to obtain the information needed to address it. This step requires formulating a hypothesis and determining what type of research to employ to test the hypothesis so the results are reliable and valid. A hypothesis is an informed guess or assumption about a problem or set of circumstances. Marketers conduct exploratory research when they need more information about a problem or want to make a tentative hypothesis more specific; they use conclusive research to verify insights through an objective procedure. Research is considered reliable if it produces almost identical results in repeated trials; it is valid if it measures what it is supposed to measure.

For the third step of the research process, collecting data, two types of data are available. Primary data are observed and recorded or collected directly from respondents; secondary data are compiled inside or outside the organization for some purpose other than the current investigation. Sources of secondary data include an organization's own database and other internal sources, periodicals, government publications, unpublished sources, and online databases. Methods of collecting primary data include sampling, surveys, observation, and experimentation. Sampling involves selecting representative units from a total population. In probability sampling, every element in the population being studied has a known chance of being selected for study. Nonprobability sampling is more subjective than probability sampling because there is no way to calculate the likelihood that a specific element of the population being studied will be chosen. Marketing researchers employ sampling to collect primary data through mail, telephone, online, or personal interview surveys. A carefully constructed questionnaire is essential to the success of any survey. In using observation methods, researchers record respondents' overt behavior and take note of physical conditions and events. In an experiment, marketing researchers attempt to maintain certain variables while measuring the effects of experimental variables.

To apply research data to decision making, marketers must interpret and report their findings properly—the final two steps in the marketing research process. Statistical interpretation focuses on what is typical or what deviates from the average. After interpreting the research findings, the researchers must prepare a report on the findings that the decision makers can understand and use. Researchers must also take care to avoid bias and distortion.

3. To describe the nature and role of tools such as databases, decision support systems, and the Internet in marketing decision making

Many firms use computer technology to create a marketing information system (MIS), a framework for managing and structuring information gathered regularly from sources both inside and outside the organization. A database is a collection of information arranged for easy access and retrieval. A marketing decision support system (MDSS) is customized computer software that aids marketing managers in decision making by helping them anticipate the effects of certain decisions. Online information services and the Internet also enable marketers to communicate with customers and obtain information.

4. To identify key ethical and international considerations in marketing research

Eliminating unethical marketing research practices and establishing generally acceptable procedures for conducting research are important goals of marketing research.

Both domestic and international marketing use the same marketing research process, but international marketing may require modifying data-gathering methods to address regional differences.

Go to www.cengagebrain.com for resources to help you master the content in this chapter as well as materials that will expand your marketing knowledge!

important terms

marketing research, 128
research design, 130
hypothesis, 130
exploratory research, 131
conclusive research, 132
descriptive research, 132
experimental research, 132
reliability, 132
validity, 132
primary data, 133
secondary data, 133

population, 134
sample, 134
sampling, 136
probability sampling, 136
random sampling, 136
stratified sampling, 136
nonprobability sampling, 137
quota sampling, 137
mail survey, 137
telephone survey, 138
online survey, 139

crowdsourcing, 139
personal interview survey, 140
in-home (door-to-door) interview, 140
focus-group interview, 140
customer advisory boards, 140
telephone depth interview, 140
shopping mall intercept interview, 141

on-site computer interview, 141
statistical interpretation, 143
marketing information system (MIS), 145
database, 146
single-source data, 146
marketing decision support system (MDSS), 146

discussion and review questions

1. What is marketing research? Why is it important?
2. Describe the five steps in the marketing research process.
3. What is the difference between defining a research problem and developing a hypothesis?
4. Describe the different types of approaches to marketing research, and indicate when each should be used.
5. Where are data for marketing research obtained? Give examples of internal and external data.
6. What is the difference between probability sampling and nonprobability sampling? In what situation would random sampling be best? Stratified sampling? Quota sampling?
7. Suggest some ways to encourage respondents to cooperate in mail surveys.

8. If a survey of all homes with listed telephone numbers is to be conducted, what sampling design should be used?
9. Describe some marketing problems that could be solved through information gained from observation.
10. What is a marketing information system, and what should it provide?
11. Define a database. What is its purpose, and what does it include?
12. How can marketers use online services and the Internet to obtain information for decision making?
13. What role do ethics play in marketing research? Why is it important that marketing researchers be ethical?
14. How does marketing research in other countries differ from marketing research in the United States?

application questions

1. After observing customers' traffic patterns, Bashas' Markets repositioned the greeting card section in its stores, and card sales increased substantially. To increase sales for the following types of companies, what information might marketing researchers want to gather from customers?

a. Furniture stores
b. Gasoline outlets service stations
c. Investment companies
d. Medical clinics

2. When a company wants to conduct research, it must first identify a problem or possible opportunity to market its goods or services. Choose a company in your city that you think might benefit from a research project. Develop a research question and outline a method to approach this question. Explain why you think the research question is relevant to the organization and why the particular methodology is suited to the question and the company.

3. Input for marketing information systems can come from internal or external sources. ACNielsen Corporation is the largest provider of single-source marketing research in the world. Identify two firms in your city that might benefit from internal sources and two that might benefit from external sources. Explain why these sources would be useful to these companies. Suggest the type of information each company should gather.

4. Suppose you are opening a health insurance brokerage firm and want to market your services to small businesses with fewer than 50 employees. Determine which database for marketing information you will use in your marketing efforts, and explain why you will use it.

internet exercise

World Association of Opinion and Marketing Research Professionals

ESOMAR, the European Society for Opinion and Marketing Research, was founded in 1948. It is a nonprofit association for marketing research professionals. ESOMAR promotes the use of opinion and marketing research to improve marketing decisions in companies worldwide and works to protect personal privacy in the research process. Visit the association's website at **www.esomar.org**.

1. How can ESOMAR help marketing professionals conduct research to guide marketing strategy?

2. How can ESOMAR help marketers to protect the privacy of research subjects when conducting marketing research in other countries?

3. ESOMAR introduced the first professional code of conduct for marketing research professionals in 1948. The association continues to update the document to address new technology and other changes in the marketing environment. According to ESOMAR's code, what are the specific professional responsibilities of marketing researchers?

developing your marketing plan

Decisions about which market opportunities to pursue, what customer needs to satisfy, and how to reach potential customers are not made in a vacuum. The information provided by marketing research activities is essential in developing both the strategic plan and the specific marketing mix. Focus on the following issues as you relate the concepts in this chapter to the development of your marketing plan.

1. Define the nature and scope of the questions you must answer with regard to your market. Identify the types of information you will need about the market to answer those questions. For example, do you need to know about the buying habits, household income levels, or attitudes of potential customers?

2. Determine whether or not this information can be obtained from secondary sources. Visit the websites provided in Table 5.3 as possible resources for the secondary data.

3. Using Table 5.4, choose the appropriate survey method(s) you would use to collect primary data for one of your information needs. What sampling method would you use?

The information obtained from these questions should assist you in developing various aspects of your marketing plan found in the *Interactive Marketing Plan* exercise at **www.cengagebrain.com**.

© Comstock Images/Getty Images

VIDEO CASE 5.1

Marketing Research and Sales Forecasting at Ogden Publications

CRITICAL THINKING

Understanding customers is the key to success at Ogden Publications. The Tulsa, Oklahoma–based company publishes magazines and books for people interested in self-sufficiency, sustainability, rural lifestyles, and farm memorabilia. Ogden publishes 10 magazines, including *Mother Earth News,* Utne *Reader,* and *Natural Home.*

Ogden Publications uses extensive market research in order to keep their customers happy and continue to grow their audience. According to Bryan Welch, publisher and editorial director at Ogden Publications, "We have become really dedicated to constantly and persistently surveying the audiences to make sure that we understand what turns them on." The results of surveys are used to describe and analyze buying behavior and ever-changing customers' needs and wants. Ogden uses the survey method when the nature of the problem or issue relates to relationships that can be translated into hypotheses that can be tested to see if these assumptions are correct. For example, decreased readership of magazines is associated with increased use of information technology within the target market (such as iPads, netbooks, and PDAs).

"We like to try to find out various things from an editorial perspective and advertising sales perspective that will help improve the content we are providing to our readers to make sure we are reaching the audience that our advertisers would like to reach," says Cherilyn Olmstead, Ogden Publications' circulation and marketing director. Ogden's marketing team uses SurveyMonkey, an online survey system, to collect and store data from the many online surveys that Ogden presents to its readers. SurveyMonkey allows the marketing team to reduce their costs and increase their response rate. The system gives the marketing team more control over their surveys. Olmstead says, "We determine what questions we want to ask." Online surveys allow for quicker collection of audience responses and can be inexpensive compared to other data collection methods.

Ogden Publications also creates online companion websites for each of their magazines. In addition to offering customers additional resources, the online companions to the magazines also provide Ogden with valuable information about their readers. Once a customer visits the magazine's site, Ogden can track several activities, including the number of clicks on advertising links and how many minutes the customer spends on a particular page. With a traditional magazine, Ogden Publications would have to wait several months to get reader and advertiser feedback. With the companion sites, they can see if they need to change their content and make adjustments to future editions of the print and web products. Internal primary data collection through the companion websites allows Ogden to further customize online content to better meet readers' needs.

"One thing we do differently here than people do in most businesses is that we don't budget, we forecast," says Welch. Olmstead and her team use information from past years and the reception from various new marketing projects to forecast future sales, both at the subscription and newsstand level and with advertisers. However, the forecasts often serve as general guidelines for Ogden Publications. "I will tell you, without a shadow of a doubt, that the five-year forecast is accurate six months out. Beyond that, it is wildly inaccurate," says Welch. "The reason you do it is because it is a strategic tool. It makes everyone think about what we will need to do to be successful in five years." Forecasting represents a critical stage in strategic planning that attempts to understand external and internal forces and their impact on sales over time. When interpreting statistical information such as forecasts, it is important to reflect on any changes that affect the assumptions of the forecast.

Ogden's readership continues to grow, thanks to the increased interest in sustainable lifestyles. Market research helps the company to tailor the magazine to readers' evolving desires. Welch says, "Our knowledge of how effective our medium is is extremely powerful today." Without marketing research, companies would struggle to determine changing market and consumer needs.[35]

QUESTIONS FOR DISCUSSION

1. Why is marketing research an important marketing activity for Ogden Publications?

2. What types of market research (exploratory, conclusive, descriptive, and experimental) does Ogden Publications conduct?

3. Why does Ogden Publications create long-term forecasts if they often become inaccurate after six months?

© olly/Shutterstock.com / © Comstock Images/Getty Images

CASE 5.2

Look-Look Provides Market Research for Teens and Young Adults

CRITICAL THINKING

Look-Look.com is an online, real-time service that provides accurate and reliable information, research, and news about trendsetting youths ages 14 to 30. With this age group spending an estimated $140 billion a year, many companies are willing to shell out an annual subscription fee of about $20,000 for access to this valuable data.

Look-Look was founded in 1999 by Sharon Lee and DeeDee Gordon, who wanted to identify current and future trends of the youth market. The challenge is that market preferences for this segment of the population change rapidly, sometimes in a matter of days or weeks. This makes it difficult for marketers to target this age group. Lee and Gordon also felt that young people themselves were not given a very large part to play in the market research process, despite the fact that they are in the best position to give detailed, accurate information on youth trends. Lee and Gordon's solution was to create an Internet communication system and recruit young people to provide up-to-date information straight from the source.

Look-Look pays more than 35,000 handpicked, pre-screened young people from all over the world to e-mail the company information about their styles, trends, opinions, and ideas. This group of selected youth represents the trendsetters—forward-thinking innovators who influence their peers. (Although trendsetters account for only about 20 percent of the youth population, they influence the other 80 percent.) Individuals who join the Look-Look Team are recruited by peers through a viral network. The Look-Look network consists of three different types of market researchers: survey respondents, field correspondents, and photojournalists. Look-Look's survey respondents are available to respond 24 hours a day. Its field correspondents go out into the community and create reports based on the latest trends. Look-Look's photographers travel the globe capturing youth trends in photos. This information is collected in an online database that not only allows subscribers to access the information but also to communicate with the correspondent.

Through the Internet and the company's intranet, Look-Look clients have access to results of surveys and polls. These clients can uncover information on the latest fashion and technology trends, entertainment, preferences, eating and drinking habits, and health and beauty issues of today's young people. They can also access the City Guide, which lists the most preferred shops, hangouts, and restaurants in selected cities. Clients who may want to know the answer to a specific question can key that question into a search feature and reach a worldwide focus group 24 hours a day. Gordon and Lee believe that a full understanding of the youth culture requires a constant dialogue with young people—an understanding not achieved by a once- or twice-a-year focus group or by traditional market research.

This dialogue is so important to the company that Look-Look has created a variety of ways for young people to get involved. For instance, Look-Look engages in social networking with its own blog and MySpace page. However, its most popular way to connect with young people, and consequently gather consumer information, is through its online community forum Team Look-Look. Its online community is broken up into three sections: Think, Speak, and Do. In the Think section, Look-Look's bloggers create weekly postings that encourage discussion among community members. The Speak forum is where Look-Look conducts polls, discussion boards, and surveys. It also allows members to view other correspondents' opinions on particular topics. The Do section provides images and instructions for "cool" things for its members to do.

Although Team Look-Look seems like a social networking community, it is clear that every section can be used by the company to collect market research from its users. For example, by encouraging discussion through its Do section, Look-Look can garner insight into the opinions of its young community members—an important component to understanding this market segment. The Speak section allows Look-Look to directly gather marketing research through polls, posting of opinions, discussion boards, and surveys. Finally, by observing which activities interest community members and by encouraging

© Yuri Arcurs/Shutterstock.com / © John Wang/Photodisc/Getty Images

members to post their own pictures of fun activities, Look-Look gets an in-depth view of what young people like to do.

This marketing research is so valuable that Look-Look has caught the attention of *Fortune* 500 companies. Clients of Look-Look have included Coca-Cola, Virgin Mobile, Nordstrom, and Kellogg's. By choosing to engage the youth market through unique information gathering processes, Look-Look has successfully carved out a niche for itself in the market research industry.[36]

QUESTIONS FOR DISCUSSION

1. How does Look-Look use technology to gain insights on the teen and young adult markets?
2. Why does Look-Look focus on trendsetters when they represent only 20 percent of the youth population?
3. Besides the companies mentioned above, who would you recommend Look-Look contact to potentially engage as clients?

Chapter 6

Target Markets: Segmentation, Evaluation, and Positioning

OBJECTIVES

1. To learn what a *market* is
2. To understand the differences among general targeting strategies
3. To become familiar with the major segmentation variables
4. To know what segment profiles are and how they are used
5. To understand how to evaluate market segments
6. To identify the factors that influence the selection of specific market segments for use as target markets
7. To understand positioning
8. To become familiar with sales forecasting methods

Kia Motors Uses Target Marketing to Drive Sales

When Kia Motors entered the U.S. market during the 1990s, it went after budget-minded buyers by offering little cars at low prices. Now the company, owned by South Korea's Hyundai, is accelerating its marketing activities with a special focus on value-conscious young consumers who have busy lifestyles, growing families, and a distinct sense of style.

Take the Soul, which Kia calls its "urban passenger vehicle." The company designed the Soul as a compact, fashionably boxy model for hip city dwellers who need or want the cargo space and ride of a sport-utility vehicle. The size gives city drivers the maneuverability they need to get into tight parking spots and navigate narrow streets. It's also geared to the personalities of twenty-something consumers who want to express their individuality. Buyers can customize their Souls, inside and out, or order one of three eye-catching special edition models. Just as important, the Soul carries on Kia's pricing tradition of offering "a really good package of value for the money," says the vice president for sales.

For young drivers seeking peppy yet fuel-efficient performance at an affordable price, Kia developed the Forte Koup sedan. The company is emphasizing the sporty driving experience this group craves by entering specially equipped Koups in auto races around the United States. It recently created an environmentally friendly electric version of the Forte, the Kia Ray, as a concept car. This experimental model is a futuristic blend of function and form, complete with aerodynamic styling, a hybrid electric-gasoline engine, and roof-mounted solar cells. Even if the Ray remains a concept car, it demonstrates that Kia has the technology and drive to pursue sustainability, yet another way to show its understanding of buyers' attitudes and interests.

Knowing how to appeal to specific customer groups has helped Kia achieve 15 consecutive years of sales growth in the U.S. market. Can the company maintain its marketing speed and momentum in the coming years?[1]

Like most organizations that are trying to compete effectively, Kia has identified specific customer groups toward which it will direct its marketing efforts. Any organization that wants to succeed must identify its customers and develop and maintain marketing mixes that satisfy the needs of those customers.

In this chapter, we explore markets and market segmentation. Initially we define the term *market* and discuss the major requirements of a market. Then we examine the steps in the target market selection process, including identifying the appropriate targeting strategy, determining which variables to use for segmenting consumer and business markets, developing market segment profiles, evaluating relevant market segments, and selecting target markets. Then we examine the concept of positioning products in customers' minds. Finally, we discuss various methods for developing sales forecasts.

What Are Markets?

In Chapter 2 we defined a *market* as a group of people who, as individuals or as organizations, have needs for products in a product class and have the ability, willingness, and authority to purchase such products. Students, for example, are part of the market for textbooks, as well as for computers, clothes, food, music, and other products. Individuals can have the desire, the buying power, and the willingness to purchase certain products, but may not have the authority to do so. For example, teenagers may have the desire, the money, and the willingness to buy liquor, but a liquor producer does not consider them a market because teenagers are prohibited by law from buying alcoholic beverages. A group of people that lacks any one of the four requirements thus does not constitute a market.

Markets fall into one of two categories: consumer markets and business markets. These categories are based on the characteristics of the individuals and groups that make up a specific market and the purposes for which they buy products. A **consumer market** consists of purchasers and household members who intend to consume or benefit from the purchased products and do not buy products for the main purpose of making a profit. Consumer markets are sometimes also referred to as *business-to-consumer (B2C) markets*. Each of us belongs to numerous consumer markets. The millions of individuals with the ability, willingness, and authority to buy make up a multitude of consumer markets for products such as housing, food, clothing, vehicles, personal services, appliances, furniture, recreational equipment, and so on, as we shall see in Chapter 7.

A **business market** consists of individuals or groups that purchase a specific kind of product for one of three purposes: resale, direct use in producing other products, or use in general daily operations. For instance, a lamp producer that buys electrical wire to use in the production of lamps is part of a business market for electrical wire. This same firm purchases dust mops to clean its office areas. Although the mops are not used in the direct production of lamps, they are used in the operations of the firm; thus, this manufacturer is part of a business market for dust mops. Business markets also may be called *business-to-business (B2B), industrial, or organizational markets*. They also can be classified into producer, reseller, government, and institutional markets, as we shall see in Chapter 8.

consumer market Purchasers and household members who intend to consume or benefit from the purchased products and do not buy products to make profits

business market Individuals or groups that purchase a specific kind of product for resale, direct use in producing other products, or use in general daily operations

Target Market Selection Process

In Chapter 1, we pointed out that the first of two major components of developing a marketing strategy is to select a target market. Although marketers may employ several methods for target market selection, generally they use a five-step process. This process is shown in Figure 6.1, and we discuss it in the following sections.

FIGURE 6.1 Target Market Selection Process

Step 1: Identify the Appropriate Targeting Strategy

Recall from Chapter 1 that a target market is a group of people or organizations for which a business creates and maintains a marketing mix specifically designed to satisfy the needs of group members. The strategy used to select a target market is affected by target market characteristics, product attributes, and the organization's objectives and resources. Figure 6.2 illustrates the three basic targeting strategies: undifferentiated, concentrated, and differentiated.

Undifferentiated Targeting Strategy

An organization sometimes defines an entire market for a particular product as its target market. When a company designs a single marketing mix and directs it at the entire market for a particular product, it is using an **undifferentiated targeting strategy**. As Figure 6.2 shows, the strategy assumes that all customers in the target market for a specific kind of product have similar needs, and thus the organization can satisfy most customers with a single marketing mix. This mix consists of one type of product with little or no variation, one price, one promotional program aimed at everybody, and one distribution system to reach most customers in the total market. Products marketed successfully through the undifferentiated strategy include commodities and staple food items, such as sugar and salt, and certain kinds of farm produce.

The undifferentiated targeting strategy is effective under two conditions. First, a large proportion of customers in a total market must have similar needs for the product, a situation termed a **homogeneous market**. A marketer using a single marketing mix for a total market of customers with a variety of needs would find that the marketing mix satisfies very few people. A "universal car" meant to suit everyone would fulfill very few customers' needs for cars because it would not provide the specific combination of attributes sought by a particular person. Second, the organization must be able to develop and maintain a single marketing mix that satisfies customers' needs. The company must be able to identify a set of needs common to most customers in a total market and have the resources and managerial skills to reach a sizable portion of that market.

The reality is that although customers may have similar needs for a few products, for most products their needs decidedly differ. In such instances, a company should use a concentrated or a differentiated strategy.

Concentrated Targeting Strategy through Market Segmentation

A market made up of individuals or organizations with diverse product needs is called a **heterogeneous market**. Not everyone wants the same type of car, furniture, or clothes. For example, some individuals want an economical car, whereas others desire a status symbol, and still others seek a roomy and comfortable or fuel-efficient vehicle. The automobile market thus is heterogeneous.

undifferentiated targeting strategy A strategy in which an organization designs a single marketing mix and directs it at the entire market for a particular product

homogeneous market A market in which a large proportion of customers have similar needs for a product

heterogeneous market A market made up of individuals or organizations with diverse needs for products in a specific product class

FIGURE 6.2 Targeting Strategies

Undifferentiated strategy

Organization → Single marketing mix (Product, Price, Distribution, Promotion) → Target market

Concentrated strategy

Organization → Single marketing mix (Product, Price, Distribution, Promotion) → Target market

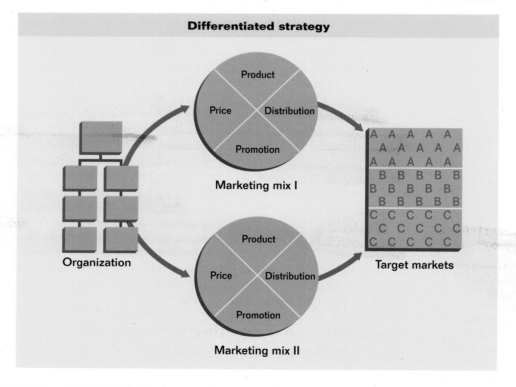

Differentiated strategy

Organization → Marketing mix I (Product, Price, Distribution, Promotion) and Marketing mix II (Product, Price, Distribution, Promotion) → Target markets

The letters in each target market represent potential customers. Customers with the same letters have similar characteristics and similar product needs.

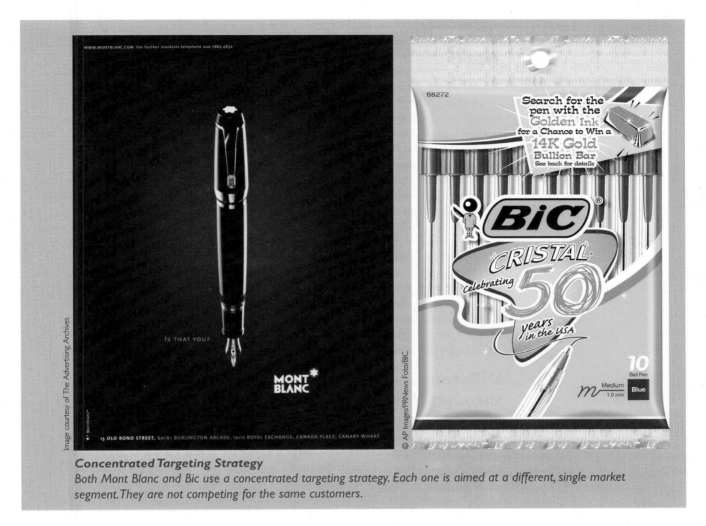

Concentrated Targeting Strategy

Both Mont Blanc and Bic use a concentrated targeting strategy. Each one is aimed at a different, single market segment. They are not competing for the same customers.

For such heterogeneous markets, market segmentation is appropriate. **Market segmentation** is the process of dividing a total market into groups, or segments, that consist of people or organizations with relatively similar product needs. The purpose is to enable a marketer to design a marketing mix that more precisely matches the needs of customers in the selected market segment. A **market segment** consists of individuals, groups, or organizations that share one or more similar characteristics that cause them to have relatively similar product needs. The automobile market is divided into many different market segments. Consider the Lexus 660h L, a luxury hybrid with a base price just over $100,000. This car targets high-income individuals who are environmentally conscious. This is not a vehicle that is purchased by the masses.[2]

The main rationale for segmenting heterogeneous markets is that a company is better able to develop a satisfying marketing mix for a relatively small portion of a total market than to develop a mix that meets the needs of all people. Market segmentation is widely used. Fast-food chains, soft-drink companies, magazine publishers, hospitals, and banks are just a few types of organizations that employ market segmentation.

For market segmentation to succeed, five conditions must exist. First, customers' needs for the product must be heterogeneous; otherwise, there is little reason to segment the market. Second, segments must be identifiable and divisible. The company must find a characteristic or variable for effectively separating individuals in a total market into groups containing people with relatively uniform needs for the product. Third, the total market should be divided so segments can be compared with respect to estimated sales potential, costs, and profits. Fourth, at least one segment must have enough profit potential to justify developing and maintaining a special marketing mix for that segment.

market segmentation The process of dividing a total market into groups with relatively similar product needs to design a marketing mix that matches those needs

market segment Individuals, groups, or organizations sharing one or more similar characteristics that cause them to have similar product needs

Finally, the company must be able to reach the chosen segment with a particular marketing mix. Some market segments may be difficult or impossible to reach because of legal, social, or distribution constraints. For instance, marketers of Cuban rum and cigars cannot market to U.S. consumers because of political and trade restrictions.

When an organization directs its marketing efforts toward a single market segment using one marketing mix, it is employing a **concentrated targeting strategy**. Porsche focuses on the luxury sports car segment and directs almost all of its marketing efforts toward high-income individuals who want to own high-performance sports cars. Notice in Figure 6.2 that the organization that is using the concentrated strategy is aiming its marketing mix only at "B" customers.

The chief advantage of the concentrated strategy is that it allows a firm to specialize. The firm analyzes the characteristics and needs of a distinct customer group and then focuses all its energies on satisfying that group's needs. A firm may generate a large sales volume by reaching a single segment. Also, concentrating on a single segment permits a firm with limited resources to compete with larger organizations that may have overlooked smaller segments.

Specialization, however, means that a company puts all its eggs in one basket, which can be hazardous. If a company's sales depend on a single segment and the segment's demand for the product declines, the company's financial strength also deteriorates. Moreover, when a firm penetrates one segment and becomes well entrenched, its popularity may keep it from moving into other segments. For example, it is very unlikely that Mont Blanc could or would want to compete with Bic in the low-end, disposable-pen market segment.

Differentiated Targeting Strategy through Market Segmentation

With a **differentiated targeting strategy**, an organization directs its marketing efforts at two or more segments by developing a marketing mix for each segment (refer to Figure 6.2). After a firm uses a concentrated strategy successfully in one market segment, it sometimes expands its efforts to include additional segments. For instance, Dove has traditionally been aimed at one segment: women. However, the company now also markets care and cleansing products to men, including face washes, soap, and a dual-sided shower tool.[3]

Marketing mixes for a differentiated strategy may vary as to product features, distribution methods, promotion methods, and prices. A firm may increase sales in the aggregate market through a differentiated strategy because its marketing mixes are aimed at more people. For example, Victoria's Secret has a variety of lingerie collections in its stores, but one collection has seen a huge success with the younger target market: PINK. The line was doing so well, Victoria's Secret gave the collection its own stores, which opened in the United States and Canada.[4] A company with excess production capacity may find a differentiated strategy advantageous because the sale of products to additional segments may absorb excess capacity. On the other hand, a differentiated strategy often demands more production processes, materials, and people. Thus, production costs may be higher than with a concentrated strategy.

Step 2: Determine Which Segmentation Variables to Use

Segmentation variables are the characteristics of individuals, groups, or organizations used to divide a market into segments. For instance, location, age, gender, and rate of product usage can all be bases for segmenting markets. Most marketers use several variables in combination. NutriSystem Silver, for example, is a weight loss program just for men (gender) over the age of 60 (age), and it is targeted through advertisements that use older sports celebrities, such as ex-NFL coach Don Shula, who have had success using the program.[5] To select a segmentation variable, several factors are considered. The segmentation variable should relate to customers' needs for, uses of, or behavior

concentrated targeting strategy A market segmentation strategy in which an organization targets a single market segment using one marketing mix

differentiated targeting strategy A strategy in which an organization targets two or more segments by developing a marketing mix for each segment

segmentation variables Characteristics of individuals, groups, or organizations used to divide a market into segments

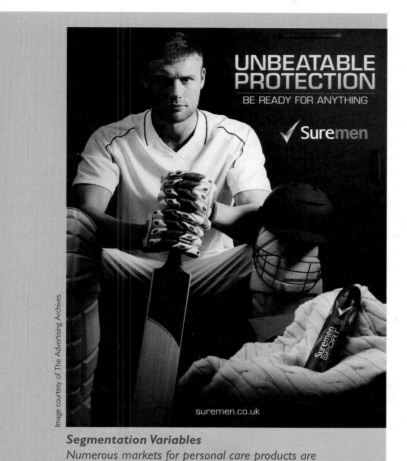

toward the product. Television marketers might segment the television market based on income and age but not on religion because people's television needs do not differ due to religion. Furthermore, if individuals or organizations in a total market are to be classified accurately, the segmentation variable must be measurable. Age, location, and gender are measurable because such information can be obtained through observation or questioning. In contrast, segmenting a market on the basis of, say, intelligence is extremely difficult because this attribute is harder to measure accurately.

A company's resources and capabilities affect the number and size of segment variables used. The type of product and degree of variation in customers' needs also dictate the number and size of segments targeted. In short, there is no best way to segment markets.

Choosing one or more segmentation variables is a critical step in targeting a market. Selecting an inappropriate variable limits the chances of developing a successful marketing strategy. To help you better understand potential segmentation variables, we next examine the major types of variables used to segment consumer markets and the types used to segment business markets.

Variables for Segmenting Consumer Markets

A marketer that is using segmentation to reach a consumer market can choose one or several variables from an assortment of possibilities. As Figure 6.3 shows, segmentation variables can be grouped into four categories: demographic, geographic, psychographic, and behavioristic.

Segmentation Variables
Numerous markets for personal care products are segmented based on gender.

Image courtesy of The Advertising Archives

FIGURE 6.3 Segmentation Variables for Consumer Markets

Demographic variables
- Age
- Gender
- Race
- Ethnicity
- Income
- Education
- Occupation
- Family size
- Family life cycle
- Religion
- Social class

Geographic variables
- Region
- Urban, suburban, rural
- City size
- County size
- State size
- Market density
- Climate
- Terrain

Psychographic variables
- Personality attributes
- Motives
- Lifestyles

Behavioristic variables
- Volume usage
- End use
- Benefit expectations
- Brand loyalty
- Price sensitivity

DEMOGRAPHIC VARIABLES

Demographers study aggregate population characteristics such as the distribution of age and gender, fertility rates, migration patterns, and mortality rates. Demographic characteristics that marketers commonly use in segmenting markets include age, gender, race, ethnicity, income, education, occupation, family size, family life cycle, religion, and social class. Marketers rely on these demographic characteristics because they are often closely linked to customers' needs and purchasing behaviors and can be readily measured. Like demographers, a few marketers even use mortality rates. Service Corporation International (SCI), the largest U.S. funeral services company, attempts to locate its facilities in higher-income suburban areas with high mortality rates. SCI operates more than 1,600 funeral service locations, cemeteries, and crematoriums.[6]

Age is a commonly used variable for segmentation purposes. A trip to the shopping mall highlights the fact that many retailers, including Abercrombie & Fitch, Aeropostale, and American Eagle Outfitters, target teens and very young adults. Some of these retailers are now looking to create new marketing mixes for their customers as they age by opening new concept stores with new brand names. Several clothing companies, for example, created new brands for their own stores to provide more mature clothing options to aging Generation Y customers (born between 1980 and 1996). Marketers need to be aware of age distribution and how that distribution is changing. All age groups under 55 are expected to decrease by the year 2025, whereas all age categories 55 and older are expected to increase. In 1970, the average age of a U.S. citizen was 27.9; currently it is about 36.6.[7] As Figure 6.4 shows, Americans 65 and older spend as much or more on food, housing, and health care compared to Americans in the two younger age groups.

FIGURE 6.4 Spending Levels of Three Age Groups for Selected Product Categories

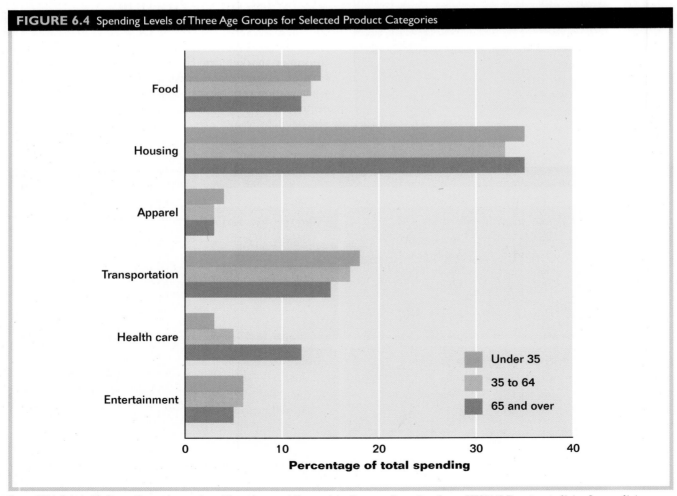

Source: "Table 3: Age of Reference Person: Average Annual Expenditures and Characteristics, Consumer Expenditure Survey, 2008," U.S. Department of Labor, Bureau of Labor Statistics, 2008, www.bls.gov/cex/2008/Standard/age.pdf.

Many marketers recognize the purchase influence of children and are targeting more marketing efforts at them. Disney, for example, partnered with Asus to create the Disney Netpal, a netbook computer for children that is durable, has easy-to-use software, and allows parents to set time restrictions and control their children's online activity.[8] As a group, parents of children ages from 4 to 12 have annual incomes in excess of $40 billion. Numerous products are aimed specifically at children—toys, clothing, food and beverages, and entertainment such as movies and TV cable channels. In addition, children in this age group influence $670 billion of parental spending yearly.[9] In households with only one parent or those in which both parents work, children often take on additional responsibilities such as cooking, cleaning, and grocery shopping, and thus influence the types of products and brands these households purchase.

Gender is another demographic variable that is commonly used to segment markets, including the markets for clothing, soft drinks, nonprescription medications, toiletries, magazines, and even cigarettes. The U.S. Census Bureau reports that girls and women account for 49.3 percent and boys and men for 50.7 percent of the total U.S. population.[10] Some deodorant marketers use gender segmentation: Secret and Soft & Dri are targeted specifically at women, whereas Degree and Mitchum are directed toward men. Food and beverage companies are paying close attention to women and have determined that all important food marketing trends are partially the result of women's influence in the home.[11]

Marketers also use race and ethnicity as variables for segmenting markets for such products as food, music, clothing, cosmetics, banking, and insurance. Mattel, for example, has designed Barbie to be a doll of many hobbies and professions. Mattel is making a greater effort to reach the multicultural market with its new line of dolls called So In Style, which are designed to have an African American appearance. These changes were made in hopes of reaching, relating to, and inspiring more young girls.[12]

Because income strongly influences people's product needs, it often provides a way to divide markets. Income affects people's ability to buy and their desires for certain lifestyles. Product markets segmented by income include sporting goods, housing, furniture, cosmetics, clothing, jewelry, home appliances, automobiles, and electronics. Although many retailers choose to target higher-income consumers, some marketers are instead going after lower-income consumers.

Among the factors that influence household income and product needs are marital status and the presence and age of children. These characteristics, often combined and called the *family life cycle*, affect needs for housing, appliances, food and beverages, automobiles, and recreational equipment.

Marketers also use many other demographic variables. For instance, dictionary publishing companies segment markets by education level. Some insurance companies segment markets using occupation, targeting health insurance at college students and young workers with employers that do not provide health coverage. Family life cycles can be broken down in various ways. Figure 6.5 shows a breakdown into nine categories. The composition of the U.S. household in relation to the family life cycle has changed considerably over the last several decades.

Single-parent families are on the rise, meaning that the "typical" family no longer consists of a married couple with children. Since 1970, the number of households headed by a

Entrepreneurial Marketing

Tasty Bite: Coming to America

Featuring authentic Indian recipes and all-natural ingredients, Tasty Bite meals, which were originally made in Pune, India, were introduced to the U.S. market when Ashok Vasudevan and his wife, Meera, bought the company. Now a $15 million business, Tasty Bite produces nonrefrigerated, heat-and-eat meals that combine quality food with convenience.

To appeal to American consumers, Vasudevan and Meera first renamed the dishes. For example, what was once "Palak Paneer" became "Kashmir Spinach." Then, they packaged the products in colorful boxes to attract attention.

By playing up Tasty Bite's natural ingredients, the new owners got placement in specialty stores like Whole Foods and Trader Joe's. To change the misperception that Indian food is overly spicy, they held hundreds of in-store taste demonstrations, with great results, which persuaded bigger supermarket chains to stock the product line. The company continues to expand into other ethnic specialties.[a]

FIGURE 6.5 Family Life Cycle Stages as a Percentage of all Households

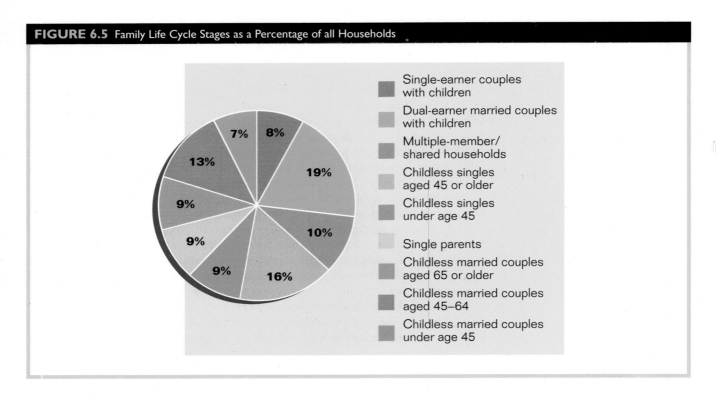

single mother increased from 12 percent to 23 percent of total family households, and that number grew from 1 percent to 3 percent for families headed by a single father. Another factor that influences the family life cycle is that the increase in median marrying age for women has increased from 20.8 years to 25.9 years since 1970, while for men it increased from 23.2 years to 28.1 years. Additionally, the proportion of women ages 20 to 24 who have never been married has more than doubled over this time, and for women ages 30 to 34 this number has nearly tripled. Other important changes in the family life cycle include the rise in the number of people living alone and the number of unmarried couples living together.[13] Tracking these changes helps marketers satisfy the needs of particular target markets through new marketing mixes.

GEOGRAPHIC VARIABLES

Geographic variables—climate, terrain, city size, population density, and urban/rural areas—also influence consumer product needs. Markets may be divided into regions because one or more geographic variables can cause customers to differ from one region to another. Consumers in the South, for instance, rarely have need for snow tires. A company that sells products to a national market might divide the United States into the following regions: Pacific, Southwest, Central, Midwest, Southeast, Middle Atlantic, and New England. A firm that is operating in one or several states might regionalize its market by counties, cities, zip code areas, or other units.

City size can be an important segmentation variable. Some marketers focus efforts on cities of a certain size. Consider one franchised restaurant organization that will not locate in cities of fewer than 200,000 people. It concluded that a smaller population base would result in inadequate profits. Other firms actively seek opportunities in smaller towns. A classic example is Walmart, which initially was located only in small towns.

Because cities often cut across political boundaries, the U.S. Census Bureau developed a system to classify metropolitan areas (any area with a city or urbanized area with a population of at least 50,000 and a total metropolitan population of at least 100,000). Metropolitan areas are categorized as one of the following: a metropolitan statistical area (MSA), a primary metropolitan statistical area (PMSA), or a consolidated metropolitan statistical area (CMSA). An MSA is an urbanized area encircled by nonmetropolitan counties and is neither socially nor economically dependent on any other metropolitan area. A metropolitan area within a complex of at least 1 million inhabitants can elect to be named a PMSA. A CMSA is a metropolitan area of at least 1 million that has two or more PMSAs. Of the 20 CMSAs, the 5 largest—New York, Los Angeles, Chicago, San Francisco, and Philadelphia—account for 20 percent of the U.S. population. The federal government provides a considerable amount of socioeconomic information about MSAs, PMSAs, and CMSAs that can aid in market analysis and segmentation.

Market density refers to the number of potential customers within a unit of land area, such as a square mile. Although market density relates generally to population density, the correlation is not exact. For example, in two different geographic markets of approximately equal size and population, market density for office supplies would be much higher in one area if it contained a much greater proportion of business customers than the other area. Market density may be a useful segmentation variable because low-density markets often require different sales, advertising, and distribution activities than do high-density markets.

A number of marketers are using geodemographic segmentation. **Geodemographic segmentation** clusters people in zip code areas and even smaller neighborhood units based on lifestyle and demographic information. These small, precisely described population clusters help marketers isolate demographic units as small as neighborhoods where the demand for specific products is strongest. Information companies such as Donnelley Marketing Information Services, Claritas, and C.A.C.I. Inc. provide geodemographic data services called Prospect Zone, PRIZM, and Acorn, respectively. PRIZM is based on a classification of the more than 500,000 U.S. neighborhoods into one of 40 cluster types, such as "shotguns and pickups," "money and brains," and "gray power."

Geodemographic segmentation allows marketers to engage in micromarketing. **Micromarketing** is the focusing of precise marketing efforts on very small geographic markets, such as community and even neighborhood markets. Providers of financial and health-care services, retailers, and consumer products companies use micromarketing. Special advertising campaigns, promotions, retail site location analyses, special pricing, and unique retail product offerings are a few examples of micromarketing facilitated through geodemographic segmentation. Many retailers use micromarketing to determine the merchandise mix for individual stores.

market density The number of potential customers within a unit of land area

geodemographic segmentation A method of market segmentation that clusters people in zip code areas and smaller neighborhood units based on lifestyle and demographic information

micromarketing An approach to market segmentation in which organizations focus precise marketing efforts on very small geographic markets

Climate is commonly used as a geographic segmentation variable because of its broad impact on people's behavior and product needs. Product markets affected by climate include air-conditioning and heating equipment, fireplace accessories, clothing, gardening equipment, recreational products, and building materials.

PSYCHOGRAPHIC VARIABLES

Marketers sometimes use psychographic variables, such as personality characteristics, motives, and lifestyles, to segment markets. A psychographic dimension can be used by itself to segment a market or it can be combined with other types of segmentation variables.

Personality characteristics can be useful for segmentation when a product resembles many competing products and consumers' needs are not significantly related to other segmentation variables. However, segmenting a market according to personality traits can be risky. Although marketing practitioners have long believed consumer choice and product use vary with personality, until recently marketing research had indicated only weak relationships. It is hard to measure personality traits accurately, especially since most personality tests were developed for clinical use, not for segmentation purposes.

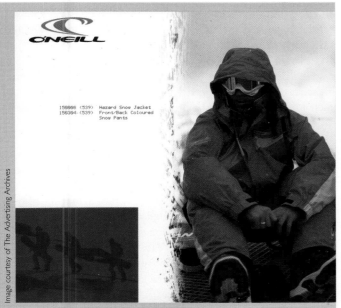

Image courtesy of The Advertising Archives

Geographic Variables
Markets for sports equipment and sport-related clothing can be segmented based on climate.

When appealing to a personality characteristic, a marketer almost always selects one that many people view positively. Individuals with this characteristic, as well as those who would like to have it, may be influenced to buy that marketer's brand. Marketers taking this approach do not worry about measuring how many people have the positively valued characteristic; they assume a sizable proportion of people in the target market either have it or want to have it.

When motives are used to segment a market, the market is divided according to consumers' reasons for making a purchase. Personal appearance, affiliation, status, safety, and health are examples of motives affecting the types of products purchased and the choice of stores in which they are bought. Marketing efforts based on health and fitness motives can be a point of competitive advantage. For instance, Taco Bell, Jack in the Box, and Starbucks each introduced new "light" products at the beginning of the year to target consumers who overindulged during the holidays or set weight-loss resolutions. Jack in the Box launched a 300-calorie chicken fajita pita and grilled chicken strips with a teriyaki dipping sauce. Taco Bell introduced a "Fresco menu" with nine items with 350 or fewer calories.[14]

Lifestyle segmentation groups individuals according to how they spend their time, the importance of things in their surroundings (homes or jobs, for example), beliefs about themselves and broad issues, and some demographic characteristics, such as income and education.[15] Lifestyle analysis provides a broad view of buyers because it encompasses numerous characteristics related to people's activities (work, hobbies, entertainment, sports), interests (family, home, fashion, food, technology), and opinions (politics, social issues, education, the future).

One of the most popular consumer frameworks is VALS™ from SRI Consulting Business Intelligence. VALS classifies consumers based on psychological characteristics (personality characteristics) that are correlated with purchase behavior and key demographics. The VALS classification questionnaire, which is used to determine a consumers' VALS type, can be integrated into larger questionnaires to find out about consumers' lifestyle choices. Figure 6.6 is an example of VALS data that shows the proportion of each VALS group that purchased a mountain bike, purchased golf clubs, owns a fishing rod, and goes hunting. VALS research is also used to create new products as well as to segment existing markets. VALS systems have been developed for the United States, Japan, and the United Kingdom with plans to develop new VALS systems in a few Latin American countries.[16] Many other lifestyle classification systems exist. Several companies, such as Hesperian's Behavior Bank, collect lifestyle data on millions of consumers.

BEHAVIORISTIC VARIABLES

Firms can divide a market according to some feature of consumer behavior toward a product, commonly involving some aspect of product use. For example, a market may be separated into users—classified as heavy, moderate, or light—and nonusers. To satisfy a specific group, such as heavy users, marketers may create a distinctive product, set special prices, or initiate special promotion and distribution activities. Per capita consumption data help identify different levels of usage.

How customers use or apply products may also determine the method of segmentation. To satisfy customers who use a product in a certain way, some feature—say, packaging, size, texture, or color—may be designed precisely to make the product easier to use, safer, or more convenient.

Lifestyle Segmentation
Lifestyle segmentation is based on people's activities, interests, and opinions.

FIGURE 6.6 VALS Types and Sports Preferences

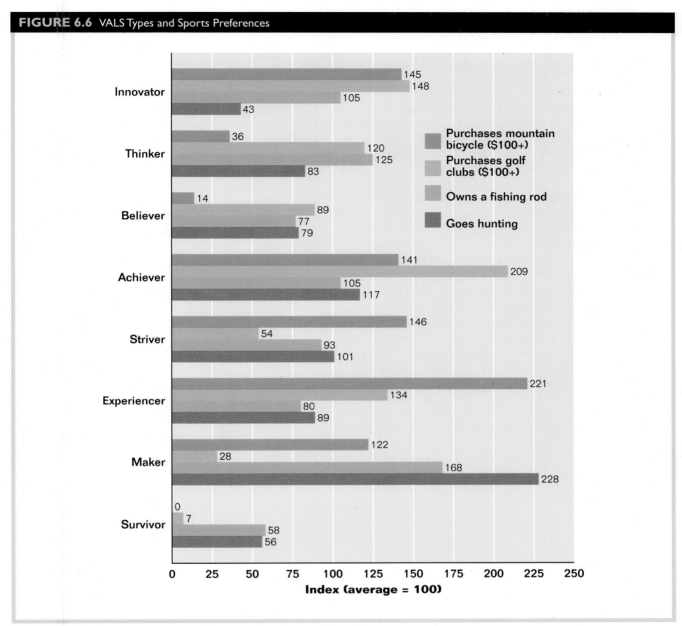

Source: VALS™ Program. SRI Consulting Business Intelligence (SRIC-BI). Reprinted with permission.

Benefit segmentation is the division of a market according to benefits that consumers want from the product. Although most types of market segmentation assume a relationship between the variable and customers' needs, benefit segmentation differs in that the benefits customers seek *are* their product needs. Consider that a customer who purchases over-the-counter cold relief medication may be specifically interested in two benefits: stopping a runny nose and relieving chest congestion. Thus, individuals are segmented directly according to their needs. By determining the desired benefits, marketers may be able to divide people into groups seeking certain sets of benefits. The effectiveness of such segmentation depends on three conditions: (1) the benefits sought must be identifiable; (2) using these benefits, marketers must be able to divide people into recognizable segments; and (3) one or more of the resulting segments must be accessible to the firm's marketing efforts. Both Timberland and Avia, for example, segment the foot apparel market based on benefits sought.

benefit segmentation The division of a market according to benefits that consumers want from the product

Marketing in Transition
Mobile Banking Gets the Call

No longer do bank customers have to visit a branch, find an ATM, or use a computer to check account balances and make payments. Wells Fargo, among other banks, is taking anytime, anywhere convenience to the next level by segmenting the market for financial services according to cell phone behavior.

In the past, Wells Fargo required customers to sign up for its web-based banking services if they wanted to access their accounts by cell phone. Research showed, however, that a number of customers are on the go so often that they rarely get near a computer keyboard. Instead, these customers rely on cell phones to manage their busy lifestyles. "There's a whole group of customers for whom text banking is very attractive, and these are customers whose lives don't revolve around a PC," explains the head of Wells Fargo's retail mobile banking group.

Wells Fargo therefore revamped its offerings so customers could bypass online banking, send text messages directly to their accounts, and receive text answers right away. Mobile banking is not only convenient, it's also secure: No account numbers or passwords appear in any of the text messages. Customers with iPhones can even download a special app to speed the process. Mobile banking clearly meets an important need: Wells Fargo has found that its average mobile banking customer now sends 19 text messages per month.[b]

As this discussion shows, consumer markets can be divided according to numerous characteristics. Business markets are segmented using different variables, as we will see in the following section.

Variables for Segmenting Business Markets

Like consumer markets, business markets are frequently segmented, often by multiple variables in combination. Marketers segment business markets according to geographic location, type of organization, customer size, and product use.

GEOGRAPHIC LOCATION

Earlier we noted that the demand for some consumer products can vary considerably among geographic areas because of differences in climate, terrain, customer preferences, and similar factors. Demand for business products also varies according to geographic location. For instance, producers of certain types of lumber divide their markets geographically because their customers' needs vary from region to region. Geographic segmentation may be especially appropriate for reaching industries concentrated in certain locations. Furniture and textile producers, for example, are concentrated in the Southeast.

TYPE OF ORGANIZATION

A company sometimes segments a market by types of organizations within that market. Different types of organizations often require different product features, distribution systems, price structures, and selling strategies. Given these variations, a firm may either concentrate on a single segment with one marketing mix (a concentration targeting strategy) or focus on several groups with multiple mixes (a differentiated targeting strategy). A carpet producer, for example, could segment potential customers into several groups, such as automobile makers, commercial carpet contractors (firms that carpet large commercial buildings), apartment complex developers, carpet wholesalers, and large retail carpet outlets.

CUSTOMER SIZE

An organization's size may affect its purchasing procedures and the types and quantities of products it wants. Size can thus be an effective variable for segmenting a business market. To reach a segment of a particular size, marketers may have to adjust one or more marketing mix components. For example, customers who buy in extremely large quantities are sometimes offered discounts. In addition, marketers often must expand personal selling efforts to serve large organizational buyers properly. Because the needs of large and small buyers tend to be quite distinct, marketers frequently use different marketing practices to reach various customer groups.

PRODUCT USE

Certain products, especially basic raw materials like steel, petroleum, plastics, and lumber, are used in numerous ways. How a company uses products affects the types and amounts of products purchased, as well as the purchasing method. Consider computers, which are used for engineering purposes, basic scientific research, and business operations such as word processing, accounting, and telecommunications. A computer maker therefore may segment the computer market by types of use because organizations' needs for computer hardware and software depend on the purpose for which products are purchased.

Step 3: Develop Market Segment Profiles

A market segment profile describes the similarities among potential customers within a segment and explains the differences among people and organizations in different segments. A profile may cover such aspects as demographic characteristics, geographic factors, product benefits sought, lifestyles, brand preferences, and usage rates. Individuals and organizations within segments should be relatively similar with respect to several characteristics and product needs, and differ considerably from those within other market segments. Marketers use market segment profiles to assess the degree to which their possible products can match or fit potential customers' product needs. Market segment profiles help marketers understand how a business can use its capabilities to serve potential customer groups.

The use of market segment profiles benefits marketers in several ways. Such profiles help a marketer determine which segment or segments are most attractive to the organization relative to the firm's strengths, weaknesses, objectives, and resources. Although marketers may initially believe certain segments are quite attractive, development of market segment profiles may yield information that indicates the opposite. For the market segment or segments chosen by the organization, the information included in market segment profiles can be highly useful in making marketing decisions.

Step 4: Evaluate Relevant Market Segments

After analyzing the market segment profiles, a marketer is likely to identify several relevant market segments that require further analysis and eliminate certain segments from consideration. To further assess relevant market segments, several important factors, including sales estimates, competition, and estimated costs associated with each segment, should be analyzed.

Sales Estimates

Potential sales for a market segment can be measured along several dimensions, including product level, geographic area, time, and level of competition.[17] With respect to product level, potential sales can be estimated for a specific product item (e.g., Diet Coke) or an entire product line (Coca-Cola Classic, Caffeine-Free Coke, Diet Coke, Caffeine-Free Diet Coke, Vanilla Coke, Diet Vanilla Coke, Cherry Coca-Cola, and Diet Cherry Coca-Cola comprise one product line). A manager must also determine the geographic area to include in the estimate. In relation to time, sales estimates can be short range (one year or less), medium range (one to five years), or long range (longer than five years). The competitive level specifies whether sales are being estimated for a single firm or for an entire industry.

Market potential is the total amount of a product that customers will purchase within a specified period at a specific level of industrywide marketing activity. Market potential can be stated in terms of dollars or units. A segment's market potential is affected by economic, sociocultural, and other environmental forces. Marketers must assume a certain general level of marketing effort in the industry when they estimate market potential. The specific level of marketing effort varies from one firm to another, but the sum of all firms' marketing activities equals industrywide marketing efforts. A marketing manager must also consider whether and to what extent industry marketing efforts will change.

Company sales potential is the maximum percentage of market potential that an individual firm within an industry can expect to obtain for a specific product. Several factors influence company sales potential for a market segment. First, the market potential places absolute limits on the size of the company's sales potential. Second, the magnitude of industrywide marketing activities has an indirect but definite impact on the company's sales potential. Those activities have a direct bearing on the size of the market potential. When Domino's Pizza advertises home-delivered pizza, for example, it indirectly promotes pizza in general; its commercials may indirectly help sell Pizza Hut's and other competitors' home-delivered pizza. Third, the intensity and effectiveness of a company's marketing activities relative to competitors' affect the size of the company's sales potential. If a company spends twice as much as any of its competitors on marketing efforts and if each dollar spent is more effective in generating sales, the firm's sales potential will be quite high compared to competitors'.

Two general approaches that measure company sales potential are breakdown and buildup. In the **breakdown approach**, the marketing manager first develops a general economic forecast for a specific time period. Next, the manager estimates market potential based on this economic forecast. Then the manager derives the company's sales potential from the general economic forecast and estimate of market potential. In the **buildup approach**, the marketing manager begins by estimating how much of a product a potential buyer in a specific geographic area, such as a sales territory, will purchase in a given period. The manager then multiplies that amount by the total number of potential buyers in that area. The manager performs the same calculation for each geographic area in which the firm sells products and then adds the totals for each area to calculate market potential. To determine company sales potential, the manager must estimate, based on planned levels of company marketing activities, the proportion of the total market potential the company can obtain.

Competitive Assessment

Besides obtaining sales estimates, it is crucial to assess competitors that are already operating in the segments being considered. Without competitive information, sales estimates may be misleading. A market segment that initially seems attractive based on sales estimates may turn out to be much less so after a competitive assessment. Such an assessment should ask several questions about competitors: How many exist? What are their strengths and weaknesses? Do several competitors have major market shares and together dominate the segment? Can our company create a marketing mix to compete effectively against competitors' marketing mixes? Is it likely that new competitors will enter this segment? If so, how will they affect our firm's ability to compete successfully? Answers to such questions are important for proper assessment of the competition in potential market segments.

market potential The total amount of a product that customers will purchase within a specified period at a specific level of industrywide marketing activity

company sales potential The maximum percentage of market potential that an individual firm within an industry can expect to obtain for a specific product

breakdown approach Measuring company sales potential based on a general economic forecast for a specific period and the market potential derived from it

buildup approach Measuring company sales potential by estimating how much of a product a potential buyer in a specific geographic area will purchase in a given period, multiplying the estimate by the number of potential buyers, and adding the totals of all the geographic areas considered

The actions of a national food company that considered entering the dog food market illustrate the importance of competitive assessment. Through a segmentation study, the company determined that dog owners could be divided into three segments according to how they viewed their dogs and dog foods. One group treated their dogs as companions and family members. These individuals were willing to pay relatively high prices for dog foods and wanted a variety of types and flavors so their dogs would not get bored. The second group saw their dogs as performing a definite utilitarian function, such as protecting family members, playing with children, guarding the property, or herding farm animals. These people wanted a low-priced, nutritious dog food and were not interested in a wide variety of flavors. Dog owners in the third segment were found to actually hate their dogs. These people wanted the cheapest dog food they could buy and were not concerned with nutrition, flavor, or variety. The food company examined the extent to which competitive brands were serving all these dog owners and found that each segment contained at least three well-entrenched competing brands, which together dominated the segment. The company's management decided not to enter the dog food market because of the strength of the competing brands.

Cost Estimates

To fulfill the needs of a target segment, an organization must develop and maintain a marketing mix that precisely meets the wants and needs of individuals and organizations in that segment. Developing and maintaining such a mix can be expensive. Distinctive product features, attractive package design, generous product warranties, extensive advertising, attractive promotional offers, competitive prices, and high-quality personal service consume considerable organizational resources. Indeed, to reach certain segments, the costs may be so high that a marketer concludes the segment is inaccessible. Another cost consideration is whether the organization can effectively reach a segment at costs equal to or below competitors' costs. If the firm's costs are likely to be higher, it will be unable to compete in that segment in the long run. For example, when Microsoft considered entering the MP3 market, the company had to consider its very strong competitor, the Apple iPod. The Microsoft Zune was created to be competition for the iPod, including additional features like access to FM radio and the ability to wirelessly share songs with other Zune users. Microsoft also had to consider its cost when deciding to take this product to market; for the Zune, it was important to position it as a cheaper substitute to the iPod. In order for Microsoft to accomplish this objective, Microsoft was forced to keep the Zune's production costs at a low level.[18]

Step 5: Select Specific Target Markets

An important initial consideration in selecting a target market is whether customers' needs differ enough to warrant the use of market segmentation. If segmentation analysis shows customer needs to be fairly homogeneous, the firm's management may decide to use the undifferentiated approach, discussed earlier. However, if customer needs are heterogeneous, which is much more likely, one or more target markets must be selected. On the other hand, marketers may decide not to enter and compete in any of the segments.

Assuming one or more segments offer significant opportunities to achieve organizational objectives, marketers must decide in which segments to participate. Ordinarily information gathered in the previous step—about sales estimates, competitors, and cost estimates—requires careful consideration in this final step to determine long-term profit opportunities. Also, the firm's management must investigate whether the organization has the financial resources, managerial skills, employee expertise, and facilities to enter and compete effectively in selected segments. Furthermore, the requirements of some market segments may be at odds with the firm's overall objectives, and the possibility of legal problems, conflicts with interest groups, and technological advancements could make certain segments unattractive. In addition, when prospects for long-term growth are taken into account, some segments may appear very attractive and others less desirable.

Selecting appropriate target markets is important to an organization's adoption and use of the marketing concept philosophy. Identifying the right target market is the key to implementing a successful marketing strategy, whereas failure to do so can lead to low sales, high costs, and severe financial losses. A careful target market analysis places an organization in a better position to both serve customers' needs and achieve its objectives.

Product Positioning and Repositioning

Once a target market is selected, a firm must consider how to position its product. **Product positioning** refers to the decisions and activities intended to create and maintain a certain concept of the firm's product (relative to competitive brands) in customers' minds. When marketers introduce a product, they try to position it so that it appears to have the characteristics that the target market most desires. This projected image is crucial. Crest is positioned as a fluoride toothpaste that fights cavities, whereas Close-Up is positioned as a whitening toothpaste that enhances the user's sex appeal, as shown in Figure 6.7.

Perceptual Mapping

A product's position is the result of customers' perceptions of the product's attributes relative to those of competitive brands. Buyers make numerous purchase decisions on a regular basis. To avoid a continuous reevaluation of numerous products, buyers tend to group, or "position," products in their minds to simplify buying decisions. Rather than allowing customers to position products independently, marketers often try to influence and shape consumers' concepts or perceptions of products through advertising. Marketers sometimes analyze product positions by developing perceptual maps, as shown

product positioning
Creating and maintaining a certain concept of a product in customers' minds

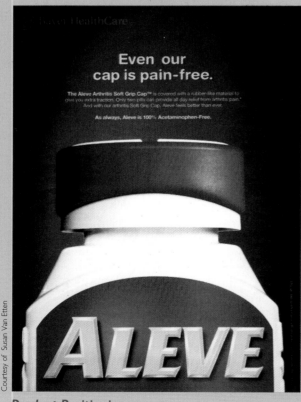

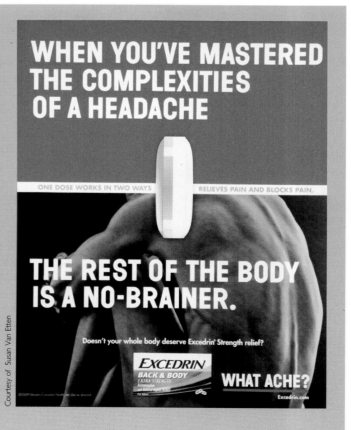

Product Positioning
These two competing brands of pain relievers are positioned differently by their respective manufacturers.

FIGURE 6.7 Toothpaste Product Positions

Brand	Product Position
Colgate Total	Fights full range of oral health problems
Close-Up	Sexy, whitener, great breath for kissing
Crest	Powerful fluoride cavity fighter
Aim	Milder taste than other brands, kid-friendly
Arm & Hammer	Popular baking soda mixed with toothpaste
AquaFresh	Kills germs, for young adults
Biotene	Reduces bacteria and germs in mouth
Oral-B	High quality, dentist approved
Rembrandt	Higher-quality whitening
Sensodyne	Especially for sensitive teeth
Mentadent	Baking soda and peroxide for fresh breath
Ultrabrite	Low-priced whitener, removes stains

in Figure 6.8. Perceptual maps are created by questioning a sample of consumers about their perceptions of products, brands, and organizations with respect to two or more dimensions. To develop a perceptual map like the one in Figure 6.8, respondents would be asked how they perceive selected pain relievers in regard to price and type of pain for which the products are used. Also, respondents would be asked about their preferences for product features to establish "ideal points" or "ideal clusters," which represent a consensus about what a specific group of customers desires in terms of product features. Then marketers can compare how their brand is perceived compared with the ideal points.

Bases for Positioning

Marketers can use several bases for product positioning. A common basis for positioning products is to use competitors. A firm can position a product to compete head-on with another brand, as PepsiCo has done against Coca-Cola, or to avoid competition, as 7UP has done relative to other soft-drink producers. Head-to-head competition may be a marketer's positioning objective if the product's performance characteristics are at least equal to those of competitive brands and if the product is priced lower. Head-to-head positioning may be appropriate even when the price is higher if the product's performance characteristics are superior. In hopes of providing legitimate competition to AT&T's Apple iPhone smartphone, Verizon is offering the Motorola Droid. There is no doubt in its advertising which phone it is competing against. With statements about its competition like "iDon't have a real keyboard, iDon't allow open development, and iDon't take pictures in the dark," it is very clear that the Droid is positioned head to head with the iPhone.[19]

Conversely, positioning to avoid competition may be best when the product's performance characteristics do not differ significantly from competing brands. Moreover,

FIGURE 6.8 Hypothetical Perceptual Map for Pain Relievers

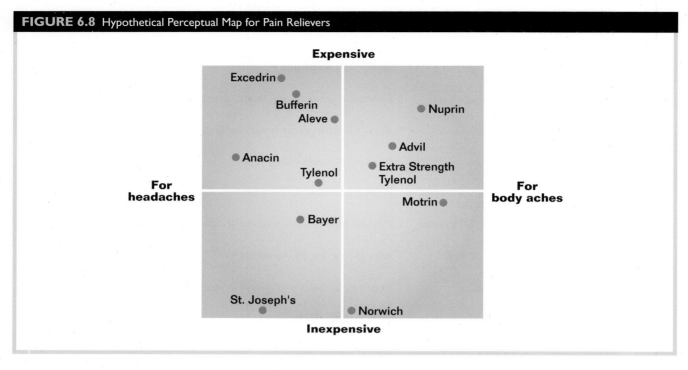

positioning a brand to avoid competition may be appropriate when that brand has unique characteristics that are important to some buyers. Volvo, for example, has for years positioned itself away from competitors by focusing on the safety characteristics of its cars. Whereas some auto companies mention safety issues in their advertisements, many are more likely to focus on style, fuel efficiency, performance, or terms of sale. Avoiding competition is critical when a firm introduces a brand into a market in which the company already has one or more brands. Marketers usually want to avoid cannibalizing sales of their existing brands, unless the new brand generates substantially larger profits.

A product's position can be based on specific product attributes or features. For instance, Apple's iPhone is positioned based on product attributes such as its unique shape, easy-to-use touchscreen, and its access to iTunes' music store. If a product has been planned properly, its features will give it the distinct appeal needed. Style, shape, construction, and color help create the image and the appeal. If buyers can easily identify the benefits, they are, of course, more likely to purchase the product. When the new product does not offer certain preferred attributes, there is room for another new product.

Other bases for product positioning include price, quality level, and benefits provided by the product. For example, Era detergent provides stain treatment and stain removal. Also, a positioning basis employed by

Responsible Marketing?
Cigarettes' Smoking Markets

CRITICAL THINKING

ISSUE: Do cigarette makers target minors?

Tobacco companies are believed to spend substantial promotional dollars to recruit "replacement smokers." This target market of replacements consists mostly of 14- to 20-year-olds. In a recent decision, Judge Gladys Kessler released her opinion on the government's case against tobacco companies, stating, "The defendants [tobacco companies] spent enormous resources tracking the preferences and behaviors of youth under 21...to start young people smoking and keep them smoking." Although the tobacco companies claim they do not intentionally market their products to minors, they continue to advertise in ways that reach this vulnerable age group. Almost 90 percent of all smokers begin before age 18. Thus, without this young market, the tobacco companies' sales would significantly decline. Each day, about 4,000 kids try smoking for the first time.

One of the major reasons that teens begin smoking is to look more mature. Some tobacco critics point out that tobacco companies promote their products to young adults (over 21) to reach teens. Do you believe that cigarette makers use advertisements aimed at young adults to reach teens that are under 18? Short of banning all cigarette advertising, how can government regulators deal with this type of advertising that may encourage teens to start smoking?[c]

some marketers is the target market. This type of positioning relies heavily on promoting the types of people who use the product.

Repositioning

Positioning decisions are not just for new products. Evaluating the positions of existing products is important because a brand's market share and profitability may be strengthened by product repositioning. Sometimes companies find it beneficial to reposition their products to align with current trends in the marketplace. In the United States, we've seen a growing concern for eating healthy. Fortunately for Quaker Oats, its products can easily be repositioned to attract these consumers by highlighting its whole grain oats, or as the company refers to them, super grains.[20] When introducing a new product into a product line, one or more existing brands may have to be repositioned to minimize cannibalization of established brands and ensure a favorable position for the new brand.

Repositioning can be accomplished by physically changing the product, its price, or its distribution. Rather than making any of these changes, marketers sometimes reposition a product by changing its image through promotional efforts. Finally, a marketer may reposition a product by aiming it at a completely different target market.

Developing Sales Forecasts

sales forecast The amount of a product a company expects to sell during a specific period at a specified level of marketing activities

After a company targets its market and positions its product, it needs a **sales forecast**—the amount of a product the company expects to sell during a specific period at a specified level of marketing activities. The sales forecast differs from the company sales potential. It concentrates on what actual sales will be at a certain level of company marketing effort, whereas the company sales potential assesses what sales are possible at various levels of marketing activities, assuming certain environmental conditions will exist. Businesses use the sales forecast for planning, organizing, implementing, and controlling their activities. The success of numerous activities depends on this forecast's accuracy. Common problems

Sustainable Marketing
Green Positioning for Tourism

Think green. That's the positioning of ecotourism companies that target consumers interested in environmentally friendly travel adventures to regions of natural beauty. Whether their ecotourism positioning is based on a bare-bones, back-to-nature experience (such as staying at a lodge deep in the South American rainforest) or a high-end vacation (such as a luxurious safari through an African wildlife preserve), the common theme is sustainability.

For more than 20 years, Rainforest Expeditions has positioned its services on the basis of ecologically sound tourism. The company markets accommodations at several lodges it built in the Peruvian rainforest, coupled with activities such as jungle tours and bird-watching trips. The lodges are built from renewable materials and the trips are led by local guides who share what they know and love about rainforest flora and fauna. Rainforest Expeditions has become a model of ecotourism marketing by doing its part to save the rainforest and, in the process, providing much-needed jobs deep in the Amazon.

Many marketers of African safaris highlight their green side by emphasizing how they protect fragile ecosystems. Although

most take customers out in four-wheel-drive vehicles, a growing number offer no-emissions alternatives such as walking, horseback, or elephant safaris. Even the cuisine is green, featuring foods from nearby farms and villages. Just as important, these unique ecotourism experiences encourage customers to think green long after they return home.[d]

in failing companies are improper planning and lack of realistic sales forecasts. Overly ambitious sales forecasts can lead to overbuying, overinvestment, and higher costs.

To forecast sales, a marketer can choose from a number of forecasting methods, some arbitrary and others more scientific, complex, and time consuming. A firm's choice of method or methods depends on the costs involved, type of product, market characteristics, time span of the forecast, purposes of the forecast, stability of the historical sales data, availability of required information, managerial preferences, and forecasters' expertise and experience.[21] Common forecasting techniques fall into five categories: executive judgment, surveys, time series analysis, regression analysis, and market tests.

Executive Judgment

At times, a company forecasts sales chiefly on the basis of **executive judgment**: the intuition of one or more executives. This approach is unscientific but expedient and inexpensive. Executive judgment may work reasonably well when product demand is relatively stable and the forecaster has years of market-related experience. However, because intuition is swayed most heavily by recent experience, the forecast may be overly optimistic or overly pessimistic. Another drawback to intuition is that the forecaster has only past experience as a guide for deciding where to go in the future.

Surveys

Another way to forecast sales is to question customers, sales personnel, or experts regarding their expectations about future purchases. In a **customer forecasting survey**, marketers ask customers what types and quantities of products they intend to buy during a specific period. This approach may be useful to a business with relatively few customers. Consider Intel, which markets to a limited number of companies (primarily computer manufacturers). Intel could conduct customer forecasting surveys effectively. PepsiCo, in contrast, has millions of customers and could not feasibly use a customer survey to forecast future sales.

Customer surveys have several drawbacks. Customers must be able and willing to make accurate estimates of future product requirements. Although some organizational buyers can estimate their anticipated purchases accurately from historical buying data and their own sales forecasts, many cannot make such estimates. In addition, customers may not want to take part in a survey. Occasionally, a few respondents give answers they know are incorrect, making survey results inaccurate. Moreover, customer surveys reflect buying intentions rather than actual purchases. Customers' intentions may not be well formulated, and even when potential purchasers have definite buying intentions, they do not necessarily follow through on them. Finally, customer surveys consume much time and money.

In a **sales force forecasting survey**, the firm's salespeople estimate anticipated sales in their territories for a specified period. The forecaster combines these territorial estimates to arrive at a tentative forecast. A marketer may survey the sales staff for several reasons. The most important is that the sales staff is closer to customers on a daily basis than other company personnel and therefore should know more about customers' future product needs. Moreover, when sales representatives assist in developing the forecast, they are more likely to work toward its achievement. In addition, forecasts can be prepared for single territories, divisions consisting of several territories, regions made up of multiple divisions, and the total geographic market. Thus, the method provides sales forecasts from the smallest geographic sales unit to the largest.

executive judgment A sales forecasting method based on the intuition of one or more executives

customer forecasting survey A survey of customers regarding the types and quantities of products they intend to buy during a specific period

sales force forecasting survey A survey of a firm's sales force regarding anticipated sales in their territories for a specified period

SNAPSHOT

Sales Forecasting: Is it the Heat or the Holiday That Affects Beer Sales?

Millions of cases sold

1. July 4th	63.5
2. Memorial Day	61.0
3. Labor Day	60.2
4. Father's Day	57.7
5. Cinco de Mayo	54.0
6. Thanksgiving	52.8
7. Christmas	52.8
8. Halloween	50.9
9. Easter	50.7
10. Super Bowl	49.2

Source: The Nielsen Company.

A sales force survey also has limitations. Salespeople may be too optimistic or pessimistic due to recent experiences. In addition, salespeople tend to underestimate sales potential in their territories when they believe their sales goals will be determined by their forecasts. They also dislike paperwork because it takes up time that could be spent selling. If preparation of a territorial sales forecast is time consuming, the sales staff may not do the job adequately.

Nonetheless, sales force surveys can be effective under certain conditions. The salespeople as a group must be accurate, or at least consistent, estimators. If the aggregate forecast is consistently over or under actual sales, the individual who develops the final forecast can make the necessary adjustments. Assuming the survey is well administered, the sales force can have the satisfaction of helping to establish reasonable sales goals and the assurance that its forecasts are not being used to set sales quotas.

When a company wants an **expert forecasting survey**, it hires professionals to help prepare the sales forecast. These experts are usually economists, management consultants, advertising executives, college professors, or other individuals outside the firm with solid experience in a specific market. Drawing on this experience and their analyses of available information about the company and the market, experts prepare and present forecasts or answer questions regarding a forecast. Using experts is expedient and relatively inexpensive. However, because they work outside the firm, these forecasters may be less motivated than company personnel to do an effective job.

A more complex form of the expert forecasting survey incorporates the Delphi technique. In the **Delphi technique**, experts create initial forecasts, submit them to the company for averaging, and have the results returned to them so they can make individual refined forecasts. The premise is that the experts will use the averaged results when making refined forecasts and these forecasts will be in a narrower range. The procedure may be repeated several times until the experts, each working separately, reach a consensus on the forecasts. The ultimate goal in using the Delphi technique is to develop a highly accurate sales forecast.

Time Series Analysis

With **time series analysis**, the forecaster uses the firm's historical sales data to discover a pattern or patterns in the firm's sales over time. If a pattern is found, it can be used to forecast sales. This forecasting method assumes that past sales patterns will continue in the future. The accuracy, and thus usefulness, of time series analysis hinges on the validity of this assumption.

In a time series analysis, a forecaster usually performs four types of analyses: trend, cycle, seasonal, and random factor. **Trend analysis** focuses on aggregate sales data, such as the company's annual sales figures, covering a period of many years to determine whether annual sales are generally rising, falling, or staying about the same. Through **cycle analysis**, a forecaster analyzes sales figures (often monthly sales data) for a three- to five-year period to ascertain whether sales fluctuate in a consistent, periodic manner. When performing a **seasonal analysis**, the analyst studies daily, weekly, or monthly sales figures to evaluate the degree to which seasonal factors, such as climate and holiday activities, influence sales. In a **random factor analysis**, the forecaster attempts to attribute erratic sales variations to random, nonrecurrent events, such as a regional power failure, a natural disaster, or political unrest in a foreign market. After performing each of these analyses, the forecaster combines the results to develop the sales forecast. Time series analysis is an effective forecasting method for products with reasonably stable demand, but not for products with highly erratic demand.

Regression Analysis

Like time series analysis, regression analysis requires the use of historical sales data. In **regression analysis**, the forecaster seeks to find a relationship between past sales (the dependent variable) and one or more independent variables, such as population, per capita income, or gross domestic product. Simple regression analysis uses one

---

expert forecasting survey Sales forecasts prepared by experts outside the firm, such as economists, management consultants, advertising executives, or college professors

Delphi technique A procedure in which experts create initial forecasts, submit them to the company for averaging, and then refine the forecasts

time series analysis A forecasting method that uses historical sales data to discover patterns in the firm's sales over time and generally involves trend, cycle, seasonal, and random factor analyses

trend analysis An analysis that focuses on aggregate sales data over a period of many years to determine general trends in annual sales

cycle analysis An analysis of sales figures for a three- to five-year period to ascertain whether sales fluctuate in a consistent, periodic manner

seasonal analysis An analysis of daily, weekly, or monthly sales figures to evaluate the degree to which seasonal factors influence sales

random factor analysis An analysis attempting to attribute erratic sales variations to random, nonrecurrent events

regression analysis A method of predicting sales based on finding a relationship between past sales and one or more independent variables, such as population or income

independent variable, whereas multiple regression analysis includes two or more independent variables. The objective of regression analysis is to develop a mathematical formula that accurately describes a relationship between the firm's sales and one or more variables; however, the formula indicates only an association, not a causal relationship. Once an accurate formula is established, the analyst plugs the necessary information into the formula to derive the sales forecast.

Regression analysis is useful when a precise association can be established. However, a forecaster seldom finds a perfect correlation. Furthermore, this method can be used only when available historical sales data are extensive. Thus, regression analysis is futile for forecasting sales of new products.

Market Tests

A **market test** involves making a product available to buyers in one or more test areas and measuring purchases and consumer responses to distribution, promotion, and price. Test areas are often cities with populations of 200,000 to 500,000, but they can be larger metropolitan areas or towns with populations of 50,000 to 200,000. For example, Nielsen, a marketing research firm, conducts market tests for client firms in Boise, Tucson, Colorado Springs, Peoria, Evansville, Charleston, and Portland, in addition to custom test markets in cities chosen by clients.[22] A market test provides information about consumers' actual rather than intended purchases. In addition, purchase volume can be evaluated in relation to the intensity of other marketing activities such as advertising, in-store promotions, pricing, packaging, and distribution. Motorola conducted market tests for its new Mobile Loyalty Solution service in Raleigh, North Carolina, before launching the program nationwide a couple of months later. The company hopes that its new service, which allows retailers to send offers and coupons to customers' mobile phones, will eliminate the need for membership cards and paper coupons and replace it with a digital system that is easier to use, faster, and more environmentally friendly. However, the company needed to assess consumer reaction to the service beforehand.[23] Forecasters base their sales estimates for larger geographic units on customer response in test areas.

market test Making a product available to buyers in one or more test areas and measuring purchases and consumer responses to marketing efforts

Sales Forecasting
A business organization can obtain the services of other organizations, like salesforce.com, to help with sales forecasting efforts.

Because it does not require historical sales data, a market test is effective for forecasting sales of new products or sales of existing products in new geographic areas. A market test also gives a marketer an opportunity to test various elements of the marketing mix. However, these tests are often time consuming and expensive. In addition, a marketer cannot be certain that consumer response during a market test represents the total market response or that such a response will continue in the future.

Using Multiple Forecasting Methods

Although some businesses depend on a single sales forecasting method, most firms use several techniques. Sometimes a company is forced to use multiple methods when marketing diverse product lines, but even a single product line may require several forecasts, especially when the product is sold to different market segments. Thus, a producer of automobile tires may rely on one technique to forecast tire sales for new cars and on another to forecast sales of replacement tires. Variation in the length of needed forecasts may call for several forecasting methods. A firm that employs one method for a short-range forecast may find it inappropriate for long-range forecasting. Sometimes a marketer verifies results of one method by using one or more other methods and comparing outcomes.

summary

1. To learn what a market is

A market is a group of people who, as individuals or as organizations, have needs for products in a product class and have the ability, willingness, and authority to purchase such products. Markets can be categorized as consumer markets or business markets based on the characteristics of the individuals and groups that make up a specific market and the purposes for which they buy products. A consumer market, also known as a *business-to-consumer (B2C) market*, consists of purchasers and household members who intend to consume or benefit from the purchased products and do not buy products for the main purpose of making a profit. A business market, also known as *business-to-business (B2B)*, *industrial*, or *organizational market*, consists of individuals or groups that purchase a specific kind of product for one of three purposes: resale, direct use in producing other products, or use in general daily operations.

2. To understand the differences among general targeting strategies

In general, marketers employ a five-step process when selecting a target market. Step 1 is to identify the appropriate targeting strategy. When a company designs a single marketing mix and directs it at the entire market for a particular product, it is using an undifferentiated targeting strategy. The undifferentiated strategy is effective in a homogeneous market, whereas a heterogeneous market needs to be segmented through a concentrated targeting strategy or a differentiated targeting strategy. Both these strategies divide markets into segments consisting of individuals, groups, or organizations that have one or more similar characteristics and thus can be linked to similar product needs. When using a concentrated strategy, an organization directs marketing efforts toward a single market segment through one marketing mix. With a differentiated targeting strategy, an organization directs customized marketing efforts at two or more segments.

Certain conditions must exist for effective market segmentation. First, customers' needs for the product should be heterogeneous. Second, the segments of the market should be identifiable and divisible. Third, the total market should be divided so segments can be compared with respect to estimated sales, costs, and profits. Fourth, at least one segment must have enough profit potential to justify developing and maintaining a special marketing mix for that segment. Fifth, the firm must be able to reach the chosen segment with a particular marketing mix.

3. To become familiar with the major segmentation variables

Step 2 is determining which segmentation variables to use. Segmentation variables are the characteristics of individuals, groups, or organizations used to divide a total market into segments. The segmentation variable should relate to customers' needs for, uses of, or behavior toward the product. Segmentation variables for consumer markets can be grouped into four categories: demographic (e.g., age, gender, income, ethnicity, family life cycle), geographic (population, market density, climate), psychographic (personality traits, motives, lifestyles), and behavioristic (volume usage, end use, expected benefits, brand loyalty, price sensitivity). Variables for segmenting business markets include geographic location, type of organization, customer size, and product use.

4. To know what segment profiles are and how they are used

Step 3 in the target market selection process is to develop market segment profiles. Such profiles describe the similarities among potential customers within a segment and explain the differences among people and organizations in different market segments. They are used to assess the degree to which the firm's products can match potential customers' product needs. Segments, which may seem at first quite attractive, may be shown to be quite the opposite after a market segment profile is completed.

5. To understand how to evaluate market segments

Step 4 is evaluating relevant market segments. Marketers analyze several important factors, such as sales estimates, competition, and estimated costs associated with each segment. Potential sales for a market segment can be measured along several dimensions, including product level, geographic area, time, and level of competition. Besides obtaining sales estimates, it is crucial to assess competitors that are already operating in the segments being considered. Without competitive information, sales estimates may be misleading. The cost of developing a marketing mix which meets the wants and needs of individuals in that segment must also be considered. If the firm's costs to compete in that market are very high, it may be unable to compete in that segment in the long run.

6. To identify the factors that influence the selection of specific market segments for use as target markets

Step 5 involves the actual selection of specific target markets. In this final step, the company considers whether customers' needs differ enough to warrant segmentation and which segments to target. If customers' needs are heterogeneous, the decision must be made which segment to target, or whether to enter the market at all. Considerations such as resources, managerial skills, employee expertise, facilities, the firm's overall objectives, possible legal problems, conflicts with interest groups, and technological advancements must be considered when deciding which segments to target.

7. To understand positioning

Product positioning relates to the decisions and activities that create and maintain a certain concept of the firm's product in customers' minds. Buyers tend to group, or "position," products in their minds to simplify buying decisions. Marketers try to position a new product so that it appears to have all the characteristics that the target market most desires. Positioning plays a role in market segmentation. Organizations can position a product to compete head-to-head with another brand or to avoid competition. Positioning a product away from competitors by focusing on a specific attribute not emphasized by competitors is one strategy. Other bases for positioning include price, quality level, and benefits provided by the product. Repositioning by making physical changes in the product, changing its price or distribution, or changing its image can boost a brand's market share and profitability.

8. To become familiar with sales forecasting methods

A sales forecast is the amount of a product the company actually expects to sell during a specific period at a specified level of marketing activities. To forecast sales, marketers can choose from a number of methods. The choice depends on various factors, including the costs involved, type of product, market characteristics, and time span and purposes of the forecast. There are five categories of forecasting techniques: executive judgment, surveys, time series analysis, regression analysis, and market tests. Executive judgment is based on the intuition of one or more executives. Surveys include customer, sales force, and expert forecasting surveys. Time series analysis uses the firm's historical sales data to discover patterns in the firm's sales over time and employs four major types of analyses: trend, cycle, seasonal, and random factor. With regression analysis, forecasters attempt to find a relationship between past sales and one or more independent variables. Market testing involves making a product available to buyers in one or more test areas and measuring purchases and consumer responses to distribution, promotion, and price. Many companies employ multiple forecasting methods.

Go to www.cengagebrain.com for resources to help you master the content in this chapter as well as materials that will expand your marketing knowledge!

important terms

consumer market, 158

business market, 158

undifferentiated targeting strategy, 159

homogeneous market, 159

heterogeneous market, 159

market segmentation, 161

market segment, 161

concentrated targeting strategy, 162

differentiated targeting strategy, 162

segmentation variables, 162

market density, 167

geodemographic segmentation, 167

micromarketing, 167

benefit segmentation, 169

market potential, 172

company sales potential, 172

breakdown approach, 172

buildup approach, 172

product positioning, 174

sales forecast, 177

executive judgment, 178

customer forecasting survey, 178

sales force forecasting survey, 178

expert forecasting survey, 179

Delphi technique, 179

time series analysis, 179

trend analysis, 179

cycle analysis, 179

seasonal analysis, 179

random factor analysis, 179

regression analysis, 179

market test, 180

discussion and review questions

1. What is a market? What are the requirements for a market?
2. In your local area, identify a group of people with unsatisfied product needs who represent a market. Could this market be reached by a business organization? Why or why not?
3. Outline the five major steps in the target market selection process.
4. What is an undifferentiated strategy? Under what conditions is it most useful? Describe a present market situation in which a company is using an undifferentiated strategy. Is the business successful? Why or why not?
5. What is market segmentation? Describe the basic conditions required for effective segmentation. Identify several firms that use market segmentation.
6. List the differences between concentrated and differentiated strategies, and describe the advantages and disadvantages of each.
7. Identify and describe four major categories of variables that can be used to segment consumer markets. Give examples of product markets that are segmented by variables in each category.
8. What dimensions are used to segment business markets?

9. Define *geodemographic segmentation*. Identify several types of firms that might employ this type of market segmentation, and explain why.
10. What is a market segment profile? Why is it an important step in the target market selection process?
11. Describe the important factors that marketers should analyze to evaluate market segments.
12. Why is a marketer concerned about sales potential when trying to select a target market?
13. Why is selecting appropriate target markets important for an organization that wants to adopt the marketing concept philosophy?
14. What is product positioning? Under what conditions would head-to-head product positioning be appropriate? When should head-to-head positioning be avoided?
15. What is a sales forecast? Why is it important?
16. What are the two primary types of surveys a company might use to forecast sales? Why would a company use an outside expert forecasting survey?
17. Under what conditions are market tests useful for sales forecasting? What are the advantages and disadvantages of market tests?
18. Under what conditions might a firm use multiple forecasting methods?

application questions

1. Cable channels such as Lifetime and Spike TV each target a specific market segment. Identify another product marketed to a distinct target market. Describe the target market, and explain how the marketing mix appeals specifically to that group.

2. Generally marketers use one of three basic targeting strategies to focus on a target market: undifferentiated, concentrated, or differentiated. Locate an article that discusses the target market for a specific product. Describe the target market, and explain the targeting strategy used to reach that target market.

3. The car market may be segmented according to income and age. Discuss two ways the market for each of the following products might be segmented.
   a. Candy bars
   b. Travel services
   c. Bicycles
   d. Cell phones
4. Product positioning aims to create a certain concept of a product in consumers' minds relative to its competition. For instance, Pepsi is positioned in direct competition with Coca-Cola, whereas Volvo has traditionally positioned itself away from competitors by emphasizing its cars' safety features. Following are several distinct positions in which an organization may place its product. Identify a product that would fit into each position.
   a. High price/high quality
   b. Low price
   c. Convenience
   d. Uniqueness
5. If you were using a time series analysis to forecast sales for your company for the next year, how would you use the following sets of sales figures?

a.

2001	$145,000	2006	$149,000
2002	$144,000	2007	$148,000
2003	$147,000	2008	$180,000
2004	$145,000	2009	$191,000
2005	$148,000	2010	$227,000

b.

	2008	2009	2010
Jan.	$12,000	$14,000	$16,000
Feb.	$13,000	$14,000	$15,500
Mar.	$12,000	$14,000	$17,000
Apr.	$13,000	$15,000	$17,000
May	$15,000	$17,000	$20,000
June	$18,000	$18,000	$21,000
July	$18,500	$18,000	$21,500
Aug.	$18,500	$19,000	$22,000
Sep.	$17,000	$18,000	$21,000
Oct.	$16,000	$15,000	$19,000
Nov.	$13,000	$14,000	$19,000
Dec.	$14,000	$15,000	$18,000

c. 2008 sales increased 21.2 percent (opened an additional store in 2008)
2009 sales increased 18.8 percent (opened another store in 2009)

internet exercise

iExplore

iExplore is an Internet company that offers a variety of travel and adventure products. Learn more about its goods, services, and travel advice through its website at **www.iexplore.com**.

1. Based on the information provided at the website, what are some of iExplore's basic products?

2. What market segments does iExplore appear to be targeting with its website? What segmentation variables is the company using to segment these markets?

3. How does iExplore appeal to comparison shoppers?

developing your marketing plan

Identifying and analyzing a target market is a major component of formulating a marketing strategy. A clear understanding and explanation of a product's target market is crucial to developing a useful marketing plan. References to various dimensions of a target market are likely to appear in several locations in a marketing plan. To assist you in understanding how information in this chapter relates to the creation of your marketing plan, focus on the following considerations:

1. What type of targeting strategy is being used for your product? Should a different targeting strategy be employed?
2. Select and justify the segmentation variables that are most appropriate for segmenting the market for your product.

If your product is a consumer product, use Figure 6.3 for ideas regarding the most appropriate segmentation variables. If your marketing plan focuses on a business product, review the information in the section entitled "Variables for Segmenting Business Markets."

3. Using Figure 6.7 as a guide, discuss how your product should be positioned in the minds of customers in the target market relative to the product positions of competitors.

The decisions and discussions of these dimensions should help you to answer some of the questions that are a part of the online interactive marketing plan exercise at **www.cengagebrain.com**.

VIDEO CASE 6.1

Raleigh Wheels Out Steel Bicycle Marketing

CRITICAL THINKING

From its 19th-century roots as a British bicycle company, Raleigh has developed a worldwide reputation for marketing sturdy, comfortable, steel-frame bicycles. The firm, named for the street in Nottingham, England, where it was originally located, was a trend-setter in designing and manufacturing bicycles. When Raleigh introduced steel-frame bicycles equipped with three-speed gear hubs in 1903, it revolutionized the industry and set off a never-ending race to improve the product's technology. In the pre-auto era, its bicycles became a two-wheeled status symbol for British consumers, and the brand maintained its cachet for decades. Although Raleigh's chopper-style bicycles were hugely popular in the 1970s, international competition and changing consumer tastes have taken a toll during the past few decades.

Now Raleigh markets a wide variety of bicycles to consumers in Europe, Canada, and the United States. Its U.S. division, based in Kent, Washington, has been researching new bicycles for contemporary consumers and developing models that are lighter, faster, and better. Inspired by the European lifestyle and tradition of getting around on bicycles, and its long history in the business, Raleigh is looking to reinvigorate sales and capture a larger share of the $6 billion U.S. bicycle market.

Raleigh's U.S. marketers have been observing the "messenger market," customers who ride bicycles through downtown streets to deliver documents and small packages to businesses and individuals. They have also noted that many everyday bicycle riders dress casually, in T-shirts and jeans, rather than in special racing outfits designed for speed. Targeting consumers who enjoy riding bicycles as a lifestyle, Raleigh's marketers are focusing on this segment's specific needs and preferences as they develop, price, promote, and distribute new models.

In recent years, Raleigh's marketers have stepped up the practice of bringing demonstration fleets to public places where potential buyers can hop on one of the company's bicycles and pedal for a few minutes. The idea is to allow consumers who enjoy bicycling to actually experience the fun feeling of riding a Raleigh. The marketers are also fanning out to visit bicycle races and meet bicyclists in cities and towns across America, encouraging discussions about Raleigh and about bicycling in general and seeking feedback about particular Raleigh products.

Listening to consumers, Raleigh's marketers recognized that many had misperceptions about the weight of steel-frame bicycles. Although steel can be quite heavy, Raleigh's bicycles are solid yet light, nimble, and easy to steer. Those who have been on bicycles with steel frames praise the quality of the ride, saying that steel "has a soul," according to market research.

To stay in touch with its target market, Raleigh is increasingly active in social media. It has several thousand fans who visit its Facebook page to see the latest product concepts and post their own photos and comments about Raleigh bicycles. It also uses Twitter to keep customers informed and answer questions about its bicycles and upcoming demonstration events. The company's main blog communicates the latest news about everything from frame design and new bike colors under consideration to product awards and racing activities. It has a separate blog about both the fun and the challenges of commuting on bicycle, a topic in which its customers are intensely interested because so many do exactly that. By listening to customers and showing that it understands the daily life of its target market, Raleigh is wheeling toward higher sales in a highly competitive marketplace.[24]

QUESTIONS FOR DISCUSSION

1. Of the four categories of variables, which is most important to Raleigh's segmentation strategy, and why?
2. How would you describe Raleigh's positioning for its steel-frame bicycles?
3. Raleigh sells exclusively through retail dealers, not directly to consumers. How does this affect its ability to segment the bicycle market using geographic variables?

CASE 6.2

Is There a Trek Bicycle for Everybody?

Trek Bicycle, founded in 1976, gets a marketing boost whenever Lance Armstrong and other high-profile pros speed off on their Trek bikes or world-class cyclists power through dirt-bike races. Based in Waterloo, Wisconsin, Trek is North America's largest bicycle manufacturer, with more than $600 million in annual sales and a worldwide network of 1,000 dealers. Knowing it can't be all things to all cyclists, Trek focuses its marketing efforts on satisfying the needs of serious cyclists seeking top-quality, high-performance bicycles for athletic training and competition, recreation, or commuting.

For example, Trek has found that the lifestyles and behavior of consumers who like mountain biking are distinctly different from those of consumers who ride in city streets. Even among mountain bikers, some consumers prefer to feel the rough terrain under their wheels, while others want a smoother ride. Similarly, some urban riders are interested in style, while others care about a bike's environmental impact. Professional athletes want the very best performance, whether they're competing in a fast-paced triathlon or the grueling Tour de France.

Targeting the segments it can satisfy most effectively, Trek now offers two separate lines of mountain bikes, "hardtails" for feeling the ride and "full-suspension" for comfort. For urban riders, it markets seven models of pedal-power bikes and five bikes equipped with electric motors. For consumers who wheel around on bike paths or take a spin on city streets, Trek offers a wide variety of options, including one tandem model. The company's triathlon bicycles are designed with aerodynamics in mind, to help speed cyclists on their way to victory or through a high-powered workout.

Because one size does not fit all cyclists, Trek also designs bikes specifically for women. In addition, customers can design and equip their own bikes online using Trek's Project One configuration tool. To ensure proper fit, customers must visit a local dealer to be measured before their bikes are manufactured and delivered.

Trek's choices of product names reflect the interests of each targeted segment. For example, the Madone product line, for dedicated athletes, is named for Col de la Madone, a French mountain where Lance Armstrong has famously tested his cycling strength. Some of the commuter models are named after cities where cyclists can be seen pedaling along downtown, such as the Portland (Washington) and the Soho (New York).

Prices for Trek's high-end Madone models can top $8,000, depending on exact specifications and customizing touches. The urban bikes range in price from $500 to more than $1,000. Many of its children's bicycles are priced above $200. These are well-made bicycles for people who want advanced engineering, stylish looks, and a great riding experience—and are willing to pay for it.

Just as Trek tailors its bikes to the needs of each customer group, it also tailors its promotional efforts. These include targeted advertising, training programs to help cyclists build their skills, and product demonstrations at parks and sporting events. Trek uses Facebook, blogs, Twitter, online videos, and e-mail newsletters to stay in touch with customers, answer questions, and gather feedback.

Supporting charitable groups such as the Lance Armstrong Foundation and the Breast Cancer Research Foundation helps the company show its commitment to social responsibility. Trek also funds DreamBikes, a nonprofit organization that recycles used bikes and trains teenagers in repair and retail sales techniques. DreamBikes asks for donations of bicycles that are unwanted or in disrepair and hires high school students to refurbish and resell the bikes, which are priced for affordability. Currently, DreamBikes has two stores in Wisconsin and plans additional stores in Buffalo, Chicago, Tulsa, and Omaha.

Trek started with the mission of building the world's best bicycle. Today, it markets the bicycle as a way to be fit, reduce traffic, and make the world a greener place. Its Eco Design bicycles incorporate environmentally friendly materials and can be disassembled to recycle the parts at the end of their useful lives. The company practices what it preaches about environmental issues, using renewable power to run its manufacturing plant and providing convenient parking for employees who bicycle to work. Green targeting helps Trek attract like-minded customers as well as employees. Where will targeting take Trek next?[25]

QUESTIONS FOR DISCUSSION

1. Is Trek using an undifferentiated, concentrated, or differentiated strategy for targeting? How do you know?
2. Identify the segmentation variables that Trek is applying to consumer markets. What additional variables would you suggest that it apply, and why?
3. If you were creating a perceptual map for the kind of bicycles Trek markets, such as mountain bikes, what two attributes would you choose? Explain your reasoning.

© John Wang/Photodisc/Getty Images

Marriott: Getting Down to Business with Business Travelers

Imagine marketing more than 3,000 hotels and resorts under 16 brands in 68 countries. That's the challenge facing Marriott, a multinational marketer that provides lodging services to millions of customers every day. The company, founded by J. Willard Marriott in 1927, started with a single root-beer stand and the "spirit to serve." Today it rings up $11 billion in global sales from guest room revenue, meals, meeting and special-event revenue, and other services.

Each of Marriott's brands has its own positioning. The flagship Marriott brand, for example, stands for full service. Its properties have restaurants, meeting rooms, fitness centers, and other facilities. The JW Marriott brand is more upscale, and the Ritz-Carlton brand is known for top-quality service. Marriott's newest hotel brand is Edition, a chain of stylish, luxury hotels. TownePlace Suites are mid-priced suite hotels for customers who plan an extended stay away from home. Fairfield Inn & Suites are for businesspeople and vacationers seeking value-priced accommodations.

Sluggish economic conditions have only intensified rivalry within the hyper-competitive hotel industry. Major hotel companies such as Hilton, Hyatt, InterContinental, and Starwood all offer a wide range of hotel and resort brands for different customers' needs and tastes. In addition, local hotels and regional chains compete on the basis of location, ambience, price, amenities, and other elements. To compete effectively in this pressured environment, Marriott is relying on extensive marketing research, expert segmentation, and careful targeting.

Focus on the Customer

What exactly do hotel customers want? Marriott uses a variety of research techniques to find out about customer needs and behavior, including focus groups, online surveys, and in-room questionnaires. For example, when it conducted focus groups with customers who had stayed at its Marriott and Renaissance properties, it discovered some interesting differences. Renaissance customers said they like to open the curtains and look out the window when they first enter their rooms. In contrast, Marriott

guests said they get unpacked quickly and get right to work in their rooms. "That's when we started making connections about the individual personalities that gravitate toward the Marriott brand," says the vice president of marketing strategy.

With this research in hand, marketers for the Marriott hotel brand targeted a segment they call "achievers," business travelers who feel driven to get a lot done in a short time. They created an advertising campaign to communicate that "Marriott is about productivity and performance," according to one marketing executive. The print and online ads featured interviews with six real customers, who discussed their drive to accomplish personal and professional goals.

When Marriott looked at visitors who prefer SpringHill Suites, one of its suite hotel brands, it found a slightly different profile. These are businesspeople who travel often and see a suite hotel as a place to spread out, feel refreshed, and take a break from the stress of being on the road. These customers are also heavy users of technology, especially mobile communication devices such as smartphones. In reaching out to this target market, Marriott uses mobile marketing as well as traditional media to get its message across. It invites business travelers to download its iPhone app, for example, and runs ads designed especially for viewing on smartphone screens. Customers can click on the mobile ad to check availability online or to speak with the reservations department.

More Business from Businesses Customers

Marriott also targets companies that need hotel space to hold meetings and seminars. In most cases, these companies bring in attendees from outside the immediate area, which means Marriott can fill more guest rooms during meetings. Meetings usually involve additional purchases, such as snacks or meals, another profitable reason to target businesses. Sales reps at major Marriott properties are ready to help companies plan employee workshops, supplier and distributor events, and other meetings for a handful to a ballroom full of people.

Studying the needs and buying patterns of companies that hold business meetings, Marriott's marketers

STRATEGIC CASE 3

have found that a growing number are interested in videoconferencing and other high-tech extras. To appeal to this segment, Marriott has equipped many of its meeting rooms with the latest in recording and communications technology. It has also partnered with AT&T and Cisco to offer "virtual meeting" capabilities in its Marriott, JW Marriott, and Renaissance Hotels. This teleconferencing technology allows a group gathered in one of Marriott's hotel meeting rooms to collaborate with coworkers, clients, or others anywhere in the world.

Because planning and managing a business meeting of any size can be a complicated process, Marriott offers online special tools for one-stop assistance. Meeting planners can log on to view photos and floor plans of different meeting rooms, reserve space, and book hotel rooms for individual attendees. They can also use Marriott's web-based calculators to determine how large a meeting space they'll need and estimate costs. Downloadable checklists guide companies through every step, from selecting a site to promoting their meetings to attendees. Marriott understands that when a business meeting goes smoothly, the company is more likely to pick a Marriott meeting place next time around.

Targeting Green Travelers

The segment of consumers and business travelers who care about the environment is sizable these days, and Marriott wants its share of this growing market. The company has developed prototype green hotels for several of its brands, designing the public space and guest rooms with an eye toward conserving both water and energy. Marriott will build hundreds of these green hotels during the next decade. Thanks to the company's emphasis on saving power, 275 of its hotels already qualify for the U.S. Environmental Protection Agency's Energy Star designation.

Marriott is also going green by working with suppliers that operate in environmentally friendly ways. It provides pads made from recycled paper for attendees of business meetings held at its properties, for example,

and buys key cards made from recycled plastic. Even the pillows in guest rooms are made from recycled plastic bottles.

Getting the Database Details Right

Marriott set up a central database to capture details such as how long customers stay and what they purchase when they stay at any of its hotels or resorts. It also stores demographic data and tracks individual preferences so it can better serve customers. By analyzing the information in this huge database, Marriott discovered that many of its customers visit more than one of its brands.

Therefore, the company created sophisticated statistical models to target customers for future marketing offers based on their history with Marriott. In one campaign, for instance, Marriott sent out 3 million e-mail messages customized according to each recipient's unique history with the hotel chain. Because of its database capabilities, Marriott was able to track whether recipients returned to one of its properties after this campaign—and actual sales results exceeded corporate expectations. This database technology has paid for itself many times over with improved targeting efficiency and higher response rates.

Watch for Marriott to continue its expansion into new markets and new brands with marketing initiatives targeting vacationers, business travelers, and meeting planners.[26]

QUESTIONS FOR DISCUSSION

1. How is Marriott segmenting the market for hotel services?
2. Which of the three targeting strategies is Marriott using? Explain your answer.
3. As Marriott builds more green hotels, should it reposition its hotel brands as being environmentally friendly? Why or why not?
4. What specific types of data should Marriott have in its customer database for segmentation purposes?

© Karl Weatherly/Photodisc/Getty Images

Part 4

Customer Behavior and E-Marketing

PART FOUR focuses on the buyer. The development of a marketing strategy begins with the customer. Understanding elements that affect buying decisions enables marketers to better analyze customers' needs and evaluate how specific marketing strategies can satisfy those needs. **CHAPTER 7** examines consumer buying decision processes and factors that influence buying decisions. **CHAPTER 8** explores business markets, business customers, the buying center, and the business buying decision process. **CHAPTER 9** focuses on the actions, involvement, and strategies of marketers that serve international customers. **CHAPTER 10** examines digital marketing strategies, new communication channels such as social networking, and customer behavior related to these emerging technologies and trends.

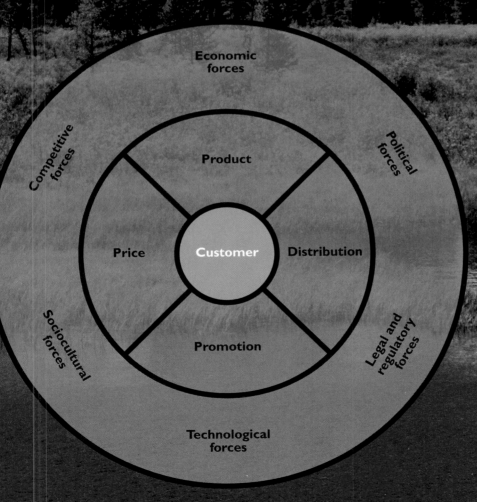

Chapter 7

Consumer Buying Behavior

OBJECTIVES

1. To recognize the stages of the consumer buying decision process

2. To explore how situational influences may affect the consumer buying decision process

3. To understand the psychological influences that may affect the consumer buying decision process

4. To understand consumers' level of involvement with a product and describe the types of consumer problem-solving processes

5. To examine the social influences that may affect the consumer buying decision process

Pet Ownership Lifestyle Creates New Marketing Opportunities

Marketers often study consumer lifestyles in order to hone their marketing strategies. As more and more consumers appear eager to spend money on their pets, marketers are taking notice. According to the American Pet Products Association, an estimated 62 percent of American households own a pet. The percentage will likely increase because children and retirees are fueling the demand. Owners spend more than $45 billion annually on their pets. This growing market creates new business opportunities in areas such as pet insurance and pet-specialized travel.

As consumer spending on pets increases, pet medical costs are rising too, as owners go to greater lengths to keep their furry friends healthy. Today's pet owners have greater access to treatments such as chemotherapy and dialysis, and as a result, the pet insurance market has grown rapidly. About 1 million pets, mostly dogs, are insured in the

United States. Around 19 percent of companies offer pet insurance to their employees as an optional benefit. Veterinary Pet Insurance (part of Nationwide Insurance), Pets Best LLC, and Pet Plan Inc. are just a few of the companies who sell pet insurance plans.

As pets become more like family members, many owners consider how they transport their pets. Pet Airways is an airline designed for pets; the company flies pets to nine major cities and intends to expand its service. Pets flying Pet Airways have access to pet lounges at airports, regular "potty breaks," pet attendants, and first-class cabin accommodations. The company also offers the Pet Airways pet tracker, which allows pet owners to monitor a pet's flight in real time online. Rescue groups and shelters also use the service to transport dogs and cats. This service is more expensive than flying people, but owners think it is worth the expense to know that their animals are being treated well. The pet products and services market is growing rapidly and provides an opportunity for marketers.[1]

Both online and traditional marketers go to great lengths to understand their customers' needs and gain a better grasp of customers' **buying behavior**: the decision processes and actions of people involved in buying and using products. **Consumer buying behavior** refers to the buying behavior of ultimate consumers—those who purchase products for personal or household use and not for business purposes. Marketers attempt to understand buying behavior for several reasons. First, customers' overall opinions and attitudes toward a firm's products have a great impact on the firm's success. Second, as we saw in Chapter 1, the marketing concept stresses that a firm should create a marketing mix that satisfies customers. To find out what satisfies buyers, marketers must examine the main influences on what, where, when, and how consumers buy. Third, by gaining a deeper understanding of the factors that affect buying behavior, marketers are in a better position to predict how consumers will respond to marketing strategies.

Understanding buyer behavior requires more than simply examining the buying decision process. Consumption is a key element that continues after the purchase takes place. The consumption process will determine how much value is created from the purchase. In fact, consumption represents the process by which products are transformed into value. Sometimes, this process takes a long time. The full utility of many products and services is often not realized at once, and consumers' decisions to purchase such products are often based on calculations of future enjoyment.[2] The marketer who understands buying and consumption will be able to respond to customer needs and develop long-term relationships that are mutually beneficial to the consumer and the firm. Understanding buyer behavior and consumption patterns can help firms improve relationships with buyers. Public policy officials can also help to improve regulatory systems through gaining an understanding of buyer behavior.

We begin this chapter by examining the major stages of the consumer buying decision process, beginning with problem recognition, information search, and evaluation of alternatives and proceeding through purchase and postpurchase evaluation. Next, we examine situational influences—surroundings, time, purchase reason, and buyer's mood and condition—that affect purchasing decisions. We go on to consider psychological influences on purchasing decisions: perception, motives, learning, attitudes, personality and self-concept, and lifestyles. We follow this with an examination of how a customer's level of involvement with a product affects the type of problem solving they employ and by discussing the types of consumer problem solving processes. Next, we discuss social influences that affect buying behavior, including roles, family, reference groups and opinion leaders, social classes, and culture and subcultures. We conclude with a discussion of consumer misbehavior.

Consumer Buying Decision Process

The **consumer buying decision process**, shown in Figure 7.1, includes five stages: problem recognition, information search, evaluation of alternatives, purchase, and postpurchase evaluation. Before we examine each stage, consider these important points. First, the actual act of purchasing is just one stage in the process and usually not the first stage. Second, even though we indicate that a purchase occurs, not all decision processes lead to a purchase; individuals may end the process at any stage. Finally, not all consumer decisions include all five stages. People who are engaged in extended problem solving usually go through all stages of this decision process, whereas those who are engaged in limited problem solving and routinized response behavior may omit some stages.

Problem Recognition

Problem recognition occurs when a buyer becomes aware of a difference between a desired state and an actual condition. Consider a female student who owns an older, out-of-date calculator, and she learns that a newer calculator is going to be necessary to run software required for class. She recognizes that a difference exists between the desired state—having a programmable calculator—and her actual condition. She therefore decides to buy a new calculator.

buying behavior The decision processes and actions of people involved in buying and using products

consumer buying behavior The decision processes and purchasing activities of people who purchase products for personal or household use and not for business purposes

consumer buying decision process A five-stage purchase decision process that includes problem recognition, information search, evaluation of alternatives, purchase, and postpurchase evaluation

internal search An information search in which buyers search their memories for information about products that might solve their problem

external search An information search in which buyers seek information from sources other than their memories

FIGURE 7.1 Consumer Buying Decision Process and Possible Influences on the Process

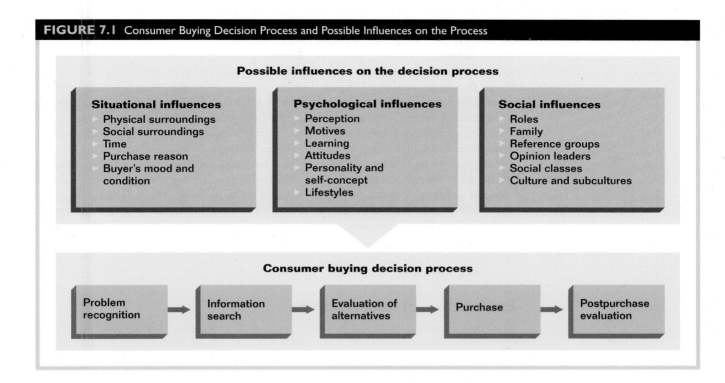

Possible influences on the decision process

Situational influences
- Physical surroundings
- Social surroundings
- Time
- Purchase reason
- Buyer's mood and condition

Psychological influences
- Perception
- Motives
- Learning
- Attitudes
- Personality and self-concept
- Lifestyles

Social influences
- Roles
- Family
- Reference groups
- Opinion leaders
- Social classes
- Culture and subcultures

Consumer buying decision process

Problem recognition → Information search → Evaluation of alternatives → Purchase → Postpurchase evaluation

Problem Recognition
In this advertisement, L'Oréal tries to stimulate problem recognition regarding the possible effects of fatigue on a man's face.

The speed of consumer problem recognition can be quite rapid or rather slow. Sometimes a person has a problem or need but is unaware of it. Marketers use sales personnel, advertising, and packaging to help trigger recognition of such needs or problems. For example, a university bookstore may advertise programmable calculators in the school newspaper at the beginning of the term. Students who see the advertisement may recognize that they need these calculators for their course work.

Information Search

After recognizing the problem or need, a buyer (if continuing the decision process) searches for product information that will help resolve the problem or satisfy the need. To reference the example given earlier, after recognizing her need for a new calculator, the student may search for information about different types and brands of calculators. She acquires information over time from her surroundings. However, the information's impact depends on how she interprets it.

An information search has two aspects. In an **internal search**, buyers search their memories for information about products that might solve their problem. If they cannot retrieve enough information from memory to make a decision, they seek additional information from outside sources in an **external search**. The external search may focus on communication with friends or relatives, comparison of available brands and prices, marketer-dominated sources, and/or public sources. An individual's personal contacts—friends, relatives, and coworkers—often are influential sources of information because the person trusts and respects them. However, research suggests that consumers may overestimate friends' knowledge about products and their ability to evaluate them. Using marketer-dominated sources of information, such as salespeople, advertising, websites, package labeling, and in-store demonstrations and displays, typically requires little effort on the consumer's part. Indeed, the Internet has become a major information source during the consumer buying decision process, especially for product and pricing information. Buyers also obtain information from independent sources—for instance, government reports, news presentations, publications such as *Consumer Reports,* and reports from product-testing organizations. Consumers frequently view information from these sources as highly credible because of their factual and unbiased nature.

Repetition, a technique well-known to advertisers, increases consumers' learning of information. When they see or hear an advertising message for the first time, recipients may not grasp all its important details, but they learn more details as the message is repeated. Nevertheless, even when commercials are initially effective, repetition eventually may cause wear-out, meaning consumers pay less attention to the commercial and respond to it less favorably than they did at first. Information can be presented verbally, numerically, or visually. Marketers pay great attention to the visual components of their advertising materials.

Evaluation of Alternatives

A successful information search within a product category yields a group of brands that a buyer views as possible alternatives. This group of brands is sometimes called a **consideration set** (also called an *evoked set*). For example, a consideration set of computers might include desktop, laptop, and notebook computers from Dell, Acer, and HP. Research suggests that consumers assign a greater value to a brand they have heard of than to one they have not—even when they do not know anything else about the brand. Thus, when attempting to choose between two airlines for an emergency trip, most consumers will choose the one they have heard of over an unfamiliar name.

To assess the products in a consideration set, the buyer uses **evaluative criteria**: objective characteristics (such as the size) and subjective characteristics (such as style) that are important to him or her. Consider that one buyer may want a large display, whereas another may want a computer with a large amount of memory. The buyer also assigns a certain level of importance to each criterion: some features and characteristics carry more weight than others. The buyer rates and eventually ranks brands in the consideration set using the preceding criteria. The evaluation stage may yield no brand the buyer is willing to purchase. In that case, a further information search may be necessary.

Marketers may influence consumers' evaluations by *framing* the alternatives—that is, describing the alternatives and their attributes in a certain manner. Framing can make a characteristic seem more important to a consumer and facilitate its recall from memory. For example, by stressing a car's superior comfort and safety features over those of a competitor's, a carmaker can direct consumers' attention toward these points of superiority. Framing probably influences the decision processes of inexperienced buyers more than those of experienced ones. If the evaluation of alternatives yields one or more brands that the consumer is willing to buy, he or she is ready to move on to the next stage of the decision process: the purchase.

Purchase

In the purchase stage, the consumer chooses the product or brand to be bought. Selection is based on the outcome of the evaluation stage and on other dimensions. Product availability may influence which brand is purchased. For instance, if the brand that ranked highest in evaluation is unavailable, the buyer may purchase the brand that ranked second. If a consumer wants a pair of black Nikes and cannot find them in his size, he may buy a pair of black Reeboks.

During this stage, buyers also pick the seller from which they will buy the product. The choice of seller may affect final product selection and therefore the terms of sale, which, if negotiable, are determined at this stage. Other issues, such as price, delivery,

consideration set A group of brands within a product category that a buyer views as alternatives for possible purchase

evaluative criteria Objective and subjective product characteristics that are important to a buyer

warranties, maintenance agreements, installation, and credit arrangements, are also settled. Finally, the actual purchase takes place during this stage, unless the consumer decides to terminate the buying decision process.

Postpurchase Evaluation

After the purchase, the buyer begins evaluating the product to ascertain if its actual performance meets expected levels. Many criteria used in evaluating alternatives are applied again during post-purchase evaluation. The outcome of this stage is either satisfaction or dissatisfaction, which influences whether the consumer complains, communicates with other possible buyers, and repurchases the brand or product.

Shortly after purchase of an expensive product, evaluation may result in **cognitive dissonance**, doubts in the buyer's mind about whether purchasing the product was the right decision. For example, after buying the iPhone 4 and hearing that some purchasers had experienced dropped signals due to an antennae defect, the consumer might start having concerns about his or her own phone's reception. Cognitive dissonance is most likely to arise when a person has recently bought an expensive, high-involvement product that lacks some of the desirable features of competing brands. A buyer who is experiencing cognitive dissonance may attempt to return the product or seek positive information about it to justify choosing it. Marketers sometimes attempt to reduce cognitive dissonance by having salespeople telephone or e-mail recent purchasers to make sure they are satisfied with their new purchases. At times, recent buyers are sent results of studies showing that other consumers are very satisfied with the brand.

As Figure 7.1 shows, three major categories of influences are believed to affect the consumer buying decision process: situational, psychological, and social. In the remainder of this chapter, we focus on these influences. Although we discuss each major influence separately, their effects on the consumer decision process are interrelated.

Marketers employ a number of marketing research techniques to better understand their customers' buying decision processes and factors that influence those buying decision processes. Both conventional and unconventional marketing research methods are used.

cognitive dissonance A buyer's doubts shortly after a purchase about whether the decision was the right one

situational influences Influences that result from circumstances, time, and location that affect the consumer buying decision process

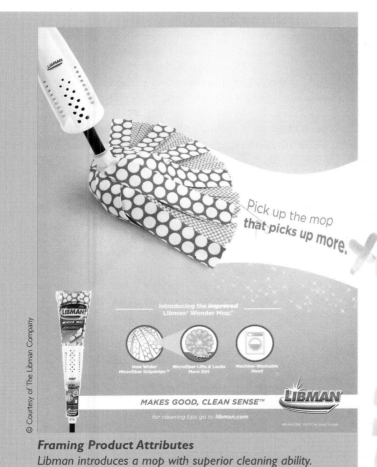

© Courtesy of The Libman Company

Pick up the mop that picks up more.

Framing Product Attributes
Libman introduces a mop with superior cleaning ability.

Situational Influences on the Buying Decision Process

Situational influences result from circumstances, time, and location that affect the consumer buying decision process. Imagine buying an automobile tire after noticing, while washing your car, that the current tire is badly worn; this is a different experience from buying a tire right after a blowout on the highway spoils your vacation. Situational factors can influence the buyer during any stage of the consumer buying decision process and may cause the individual to shorten, lengthen, or terminate the process. Situational factors can be classified into five categories: physical surroundings, social surroundings, time perspective, reason for purchase, and the buyer's momentary mood and condition.[3]

Physical surroundings include location, store atmosphere, aromas, sounds, lighting, weather, and other factors in the physical environment in which the decision process occurs. Research suggests that retail store chains should design their store environments to make browsing as easy as possible to increase shoppers' willingness to choose and eventually make purchases.[4] Marketers at banks, department stores, and specialty stores go to considerable effort and expense to create physical settings that are conducive to making purchase decisions. Most restaurant chains, such as Olive Garden and Chili's, invest heavily in facilities, often building from the ground up, to provide special surroundings that enhance customers' dining experiences. In some settings, dimensions such as weather, traffic sounds, and odors are clearly beyond the marketers' control; instead, marketers must try to make customers more comfortable. General climatic conditions, for example, may influence a customer's decision to buy a specific type of vehicle (such as an SUV) and certain accessories (such as four-wheel drive). Current weather conditions, depending on whether they are favorable or unfavorable, may be either encouraging or discouraging to consumers when they are deciding whether to go shopping to seek out specific products.

Social surroundings include characteristics and interactions of others who are present during a purchase decision, such as friends, relatives, salespeople, and other customers. Buyers may feel pressured to behave in a certain way because they are in a public place such as a restaurant, store, or sports arena. Thoughts about who will be around when the product is used or consumed are another dimension of the social setting. An overcrowded store or an argument between a customer and a salesperson may cause consumers to leave the store.

The time dimension, too, influences the buying decision process in several ways, such as the amount of time required to become knowledgeable about a product, to search for it, and to buy and use it. For instance, more men are buying diamond engagement rings online partly to make an informed decision at their own convenience. An online jeweler like Blue Nile features a comfortable, anonymous, easy-to-use website to help men educate themselves about diamonds and then select a unique combination from its large inventory of diamonds and settings.[5] Time plays a major role in that the buyer considers the possible frequency of product use, the length of time required to use the product, and the length of the overall product life. Other time dimensions that influence purchases include time of day, day of the week or month, seasons, and holidays. The amount of time pressure a consumer is under affects how much time is devoted to purchase decisions. A customer under severe time constraints is likely to either make a quick purchase decision or delay a decision.

The purchase reason raises the questions of what exactly the product purchase should accomplish and for whom. Generally, consumers purchase an item for their own use, for household use, or as a gift. For example, people who are buying a gift may buy a different product from one they would buy for themselves. If you own a Mont Blanc pen, for example, it is unlikely that you bought it for yourself.

The buyer's momentary moods (such as anger, anxiety, or contentment) or momentary conditions (fatigue, illness, or the possession of cash) may have a bearing on the consumer buying decision process. These moods or conditions immediately precede the current situation and are not chronic. Any of these moods or conditions can affect a person's ability and desire to search for information, receive information, or seek and evaluate alternatives. Research suggests that sad buyers are more inclined to take risks, whereas happy buyers are more likely to be risk averse when making buying decisions. They can also significantly influence a consumer's post-purchase evaluation.

Psychological Influences on the Buying Decision Process

psychological influences
Factors that in part determine people's general behavior, thus influencing their behavior as consumers

Psychological influences partly determine people's general behavior and thus influence their behavior as consumers. Primary psychological influences on consumer behavior are perception, motives, learning, attitudes, personality and self-concept, and lifestyles.

Fish or Fowl?
Do you see fish or birds?

Even though these psychological factors operate internally, they are very much affected by social forces outside the individual.

Perception

Different people perceive the same thing at the same time in different ways. When you first look at the illustration on the left, do you see fish or birds? Similarly, an individual may perceive the same item in a number of ways at different times. **Perception** is the process of selecting, organizing, and interpreting information inputs to produce meaning. **Information inputs** are sensations received through sight, taste, hearing, smell, and touch. When we hear an advertisement, see a friend, smell food cooking at a nearby restaurant, or touch a product, we receive information inputs. Perception is a complicated thing. For instance, research has shown that advertisements for food items that appeal to multiple senses at once are more effective than ones that focus on taste alone.[6] Marketers are increasingly taking a multisensory approach. They sometimes even use scent to help attract consumers who may be in the problem recognition or information search stages of the buying decision process. Some Westin Hotels, for example, use a fragrance that blends green tea, geranium, green ivy, black cedar, and freesia to evoke a sense of serenity and tranquility in their lobbies, and Sony uses an orange-vanilla-cedarwood scent in some Sony Style stores to make women shoppers feel more comfortable.[7]

As the definition indicates, perception is a three-step process. Although we receive numerous pieces of information at once, only a few reach our awareness. We select some inputs and ignore others because we cannot be conscious of all inputs at one time. This process is called **selective exposure** because an individual selects which inputs will reach awareness. If you are concentrating on this paragraph, you probably are not aware that cars outside are making noise, that the room light is on, that a song is playing on your MP3 player, or that you are touching this page. Even though you receive these inputs, they do not reach your awareness until they are pointed out.

An individual's current set of needs affects selective exposure. Information inputs that relate to one's strongest needs at a given time are more likely to be selected to reach awareness. It is not by random chance that many fast-food commercials are aired near mealtimes. Customers are more likely to tune in to these advertisements at these times.

The selective nature of perception may result not only in selective exposure but also in two other conditions: selective distortion and selective retention. **Selective distortion** is changing or twisting received information; it occurs when a person receives information inconsistent with personal feelings or beliefs, and he or she selectively interprets the information. Selective distortion describes the tendency for people to reject information that is inconsistent with their beliefs, even when presented with information to the contrary. Selective distortion can both help and hurt marketers. For example, a consumer may become loyal to a brand and remain loyal even when confronted with evidence that another brand performs better. Selective distortion can also lessen the effect of the advertisement on the individual substantially. In **selective retention**, a person remembers information inputs that support personal feelings and beliefs and forgets inputs that do not. After hearing a sales presentation and leaving a store, for

perception The process of selecting, organizing, and interpreting information inputs to produce meaning

information inputs Sensations received through sight, taste, hearing, smell, and touch

selective exposure The process by which some inputs are selected to reach awareness and others are not

selective distortion An individual's changing or twisting of information that is inconsistent with personal feelings or beliefs

selective retention Remembering information inputs that support personal feelings and beliefs and forgetting inputs that do not

example, a customer may forget many selling points if they contradict personal beliefs or preconceived notions.

The second step in the process of perception is perceptual organization. Information inputs that reach awareness are not received in an organized form. To produce meaning, an individual must mentally organize and integrate new information with what is already stored in memory. People use several methods to organize. One method, called *closure,* occurs when a person mentally fills in missing elements in a pattern or statement. In an attempt to draw attention to its brand, an advertiser will capitalize on closure by using incomplete images, sounds, or statements in its advertisements.

Interpretation, the third step in the perceptual process, is the assignment of meaning to what has been organized. A person bases interpretation on what he or she expects or what is familiar. For this reason, a manufacturer who changes a product or its package faces a major problem: when people are looking for the old, familiar product or package, they may not recognize the new one. Consider PepsiCo, who pulled the plug on a package redesign for its Tropicana juices after consumer outrage over the new look affected sales.[8] Consumers were happy with the look of the old containers and felt it was too difficult to distinguish between different types of juice with the new container design. Unless a product or package change is accompanied by a promotional program that makes people aware of the change, an organization may suffer a sales decline, like that of Tropicana's.

Although marketers cannot control buyers' perceptions, they often try to influence them through information. Several problems may arise from such attempts, however. First, a consumer's perceptual process may operate so that a seller's information never reaches that person. For example, a buyer may block out a salesperson's presentation. Second, a buyer may receive a seller's information but perceive it differently than was intended, as occurs in selective distortion. For instance, when a toothpaste producer advertises that "35 percent of the people who use this toothpaste have fewer cavities," a customer might infer that 65 percent of users have more cavities. Third, a buyer who perceives information inputs to be inconsistent with prior beliefs is likely to forget the information quickly, as is the case with selective retention.

Motives

A **motive** is an internal energizing force that directs a person's activities toward satisfying needs or achieving goals. Buyers' actions are affected by a set of motives rather than by just one motive. At a single point in time, some of a person's motives are stronger than others. For example, a person's motives for having a cup of coffee are much stronger right after waking up than just before going to bed. Motives also affect the direction and intensity of behavior. Some motives may help an individual achieve his or her goals, whereas others create barriers to goal achievement. Research indicates that for consumers who are trying to avoid impulsive eating behaviors, self-distraction, substitution, and reframing the tempting food item in a less attractive manner are all motivational strategies that can be used to correct inappropriate impulsive behaviors.[9]

Abraham Maslow, an American psychologist, conceived a theory of motivation based on a hierarchy of needs. According to Maslow, humans seek to satisfy five levels of needs, from most important to least important, as shown in Figure 7.2. This sequence is known as **Maslow's hierarchy of needs.** Once needs at one level are met, humans seek to fulfill needs at the next level up in the hierarchy.

At the most basic level are *physiological needs,* requirements for survival such as food, water, sex, clothing, and shelter, which people try to satisfy first. Food and beverage marketers often appeal to physiological needs. Marketers of whitening toothpastes such as Rembrant® sometimes promote their brands based on sex appeal.

At the next level are *safety needs,* which include security and freedom from physical and emotional pain and suffering. Life insurance, automobile air bags, carbon monoxide

motive An internal energizing force that directs a person's behavior toward satisfying needs or achieving goals

Maslow's hierarchy of needs The five levels of needs that humans seek to satisfy, from most to least important

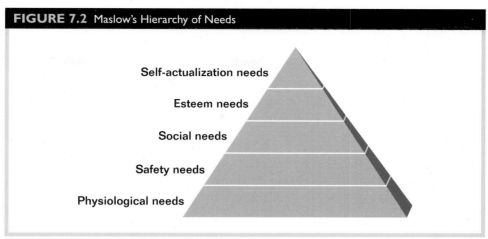

FIGURE 7.2 Maslow's Hierarchy of Needs

Self-actualization needs

Esteem needs

Social needs

Safety needs

Physiological needs

Maslow believed that people seek to fulfill five categories of needs.

patronage motives Motives that influence where a person purchases products on a regular basis

detectors, vitamins, and decay-fighting toothpastes are products that consumers purchase to meet safety needs.

Next are *social needs:* the human requirements for love and affection and a sense of belonging. Advertisements frequently appeal to social needs. Ads for cosmetics and other beauty products, jewelry, and even cars often suggest that purchasing these products will bring love. Certain types of trendy clothing, such as Abercrombie jeans, Nike athletic shoes, or T-shirts imprinted with logos or slogans, appeal to the customer's need to belong.

At the level of *esteem needs,* people require respect and recognition from others as well as self-esteem, a sense of one's own worth. Owning a Lexus automobile, having a beauty makeover, or flying first class can satisfy esteem needs. Many consumers are more willing to purchase products, even if they cost more, from firms that have a reputation for making charitable contributions. Part of this may be motivated by a desire by consumers to be perceived as caring about socially responsible causes.

At the top of the hierarchy are *self-actualization needs.* These refer to people's need to grow and develop and to become all they are capable of becoming. Some products that satisfy these needs include fitness center memberships, education, self-improvement workshops, and skiing lessons. In its recruiting advertisements, the U.S. Army told potential enlistees to "be all that you can be in the Army," a message that implies that people can reach their full potential by enlisting in the U.S. Army.

Motives that influence where a person purchases products on a regular basis are called **patronage motives.** A buyer may shop at a specific store because of such patronage motives as price, service, location, product variety, or friendliness of salespeople. To capitalize on patronage motives, marketers try to determine why regular customers patronize a particular store and to emphasize these characteristics in the store's marketing mix.

Motives
Motives relate to an energizing force that orients a person's activities toward satisfying a personal goal, such as whiter teeth.

Sustainable Marketing
Consumers Choose Organic Foods

Thanks to the growth of the "green movement," many consumers know it's more eco-friendly to purchase organic food. The movement toward organic food took off in the 1960s and 1970s as people responded to the harm caused to the environment and human health by conventional chemicals and fertilizers. In the 1990s and 2000s, people reawakened to the desire to go organic, and the popularity of organic foods has grown once again. In addition to avoiding harsh chemicals and fertilizers on their plants, organic farmers must adhere to certain standards regarding the treatment of animals raised for food. The ways in which organic foods are produced reduces each food's carbon footprint, which can be reduced still further if the food is sold locally. With so many benefits, you may wonder why not everyone goes organic. Until recently, much of the resistance to buying organic food had to do with price. Because of the additional costs associated with organic farming, organic food is more expensive than conventional food.

Recently, a number of stores launched their own private-label organic brands in response to the price issue. This trend continued through the most recent recession. As demand for high-cost organic products diminished, more stores responded with less expensive private-label brands. What makes private label organics more affordable? Essentially, the stores cut out the middlemen and avoid incurring that cost. This move toward private label organics may both retain existing cost-conscious organic customers and attract new customers.

J.D. Power and Associates released its Private Label Industry Report, revealing that quality organic private labels have positively influenced overall customer opinion of store brands. Although price is a huge draw, consumers first responded to the quality and taste of these brands. According to the report, the top private-label organic brands came from Safeway, Trader Joe's, and Whole Foods. As awareness grows and people become more concerned about the foods they are consuming, more consumers are going organic. The private-label response by retailers reveals that this trend is becoming more mainstream.[a]

Learning

Learning refers to changes in a person's thought processes and behavior caused by information and experience. Consequences of behavior strongly influence the learning process. Behaviors that result in satisfying consequences tend to be repeated. For example, a consumer who buys a Snickers candy bar and enjoys the taste is more likely to buy a Snickers again. In fact, the individual will probably continue to purchase that brand until it no longer provides satisfaction. When outcomes of the behavior are no longer satisfying, the person may switch brands or stop eating candy bars altogether.

When making purchasing decisions, buyers process information. Individuals' abilities in this regard differ. The type of information inexperienced buyers use may differ from the type used by experienced shoppers who are familiar with the product and purchase situation. Thus, two potential purchasers of an antique desk may use different types of information in making their purchase decisions. The inexperienced buyer may judge the desk's value by price, whereas the more experienced buyer may seek information about the manufacturer, period, and place of origin to judge the desk's quality and value. Consumers who lack experience may seek information from others when making a purchase and even take along an informed "purchase pal." More experienced buyers have greater self-confidence and more knowledge about the product and can recognize which product features are reliable cues to product quality.

learning Changes in an individual's thought processes and behavior caused by information and experience

Marketers help customers learn about their products by helping them gain experience with them. Free samples, sometimes coupled with coupons, can successfully encourage trial and reduce purchase risk. For instance, because some consumers may be wary of exotic menu items, restaurants sometimes offer free samples. In-store demonstrations foster knowledge of product uses. A software producer may use point-of-sale product demonstrations to introduce a new product. Test drives give potential new-car purchasers some experience with the automobile's features.

Consumers also learn by experiencing products indirectly through information from salespeople, advertisements, websites, friends, and relatives. Through sales personnel and advertisements, marketers offer information before (and sometimes after) purchases to influence what consumers learn and to create more favorable attitudes toward the product. However, their efforts are seldom fully successful. Marketers encounter problems in attracting and holding consumers' attention, providing consumers with important information for making purchase decisions and convincing them to try the product.

Attitudes

An **attitude** is an individual's enduring evaluation of feelings about and behavioral tendencies toward an object or idea. The objects toward which we have attitudes may be tangible or intangible, living or nonliving. For example, we have attitudes toward sex, religion, politics, and music, just as we do toward cars, football, and breakfast cereals. Although attitudes can change over time, they generally tend to remain stable and do not vary much in the short term. However, all of a person's attitudes do not have equal impact at any one time; some are stronger than others. Individuals acquire attitudes through experience and interaction with other people.

An attitude consists of three major components: cognitive, affective, and behavioral. The cognitive component is the person's knowledge and information about the object or idea. The affective component comprises the individual's feelings and emotions toward the object or idea. Emotions involve both psychological and biological elements. They relate to feelings and can create visceral responses related to behavior. Love, hate, and anger are emotions that can influence behavior. For some people, certain brands, such as Apple Computers, Starbucks, or their favorite sports franchise, elicit an emotional response. Firms that create an emotional experience or connection establish a positive brand image and will contribute to customer affinity and loyalty. This means it is important for marketers to generate authentic, genuine messages that consumers can relate to emotionally.[10] The behavioral component manifests itself in the person's actions regarding the object or idea. Changes in one of these components may or may not alter the other components. Thus, a consumer may become more knowledgeable about a specific brand without changing the affective or behavioral components of his or her attitude toward that brand.

Consumer attitudes toward a company and its products greatly influence success or failure of the firm's marketing strategy. When consumers have strong negative attitudes toward one or more aspects of a firm's marketing practices, they may not only stop using its products but also urge relatives and friends to do likewise.

Because attitudes play an important part in determining consumer behavior, marketers should measure consumer attitudes toward prices, package designs, brand names, advertisements, salespeople, repair services, store locations, features of existing or proposed products, and social responsibility efforts. Seeking to understand attitudes has resulted in two major academic models: the attitude toward the object (the Fishbein model) and the behavioral intentions model (also known as the Theory of Reasoned Action). These models provide an understanding of the role of attitudes in decision making.

The attitude toward the object model can be used to understand, and possibly predict, a consumer's attitude. The three elements of this model include beliefs about product attributes, the strength of belief, and the evaluation of the belief. These elements

attitude An individual's enduring evaluation of feelings about and behavioral tendencies toward an object or idea combine to form what is called the overall attitude toward the object.[11] The behavioral intentions model, rather than focusing on attributes, focuses on intentions to act or purchase. This model considers consumer perceptions of what other people, such as peers, believe is the best choice among a set of alternatives. This model also focuses on attitudes toward the buying behavior, not toward the object. The subjective norm component is important in recognizing that individuals live in an inherently social environment and are influenced by what others think and believe. Consider attitudes toward personal appearance (such as what clothes people wear, hairstyles, or body modifications such as piercings or tattoos). Consumers will take into account what others will think of their decisions. Many people are motivated to comply with what others hold to be an acceptable norm and stay in close communication through traditional word-of-mouth communications, media, and online social networking.

Several methods help marketers gauge consumer attitudes. One of the simplest ways is to question people directly. The Internet and social networking sites have become valuable tools for marketers seeking information on consumer attitudes. Using sites like Facebook, companies can ask consumers directly for feedback and reviews of their products. Marketers also evaluate attitudes through attitude scales. An **attitude scale** usually consists of a series of adjectives, phrases, or sentences about an object. Respondents indicate the intensity of their feelings toward the object by reacting to the adjectives, phrases, or sentences in a certain way. For example, a marketer who is measuring people's attitudes toward shopping might ask respondents to indicate the extent to which they agree or disagree with a number of statements, such as "shopping is more fun than watching television." By using an attitude scale, a marketing research company was able to identify and classify six major types of clothing purchasers. The scale was based on such attributes as demographics, media use, and purchase behavior.

When marketers determine that a significant number of consumers have negative attitudes toward an aspect of a marketing mix, they may try to change those attitudes to make them more favorable. This task is generally lengthy, expensive, and difficult, and may require extensive promotional efforts. For instance, Walmart, after years of negative publicity over how it treated its workers, its unsustainable supply chain, and its negative impacts on the environment, made a concerted effort to change consumers' perceptions. The retail giant altered its slogan to "Save Money. Live Better." It also began to stock more local and organic food and announced that it is undertaking an ambitious plan to track the carbon footprint of every product in its store. Although expensive, the moves have helped Walmart make gradual inroads with consumer groups that previously shunned the chain. To alter consumers' responses so that more of them buy a given brand, a firm might launch an information-focused campaign to change the cognitive component of a consumer's attitude or a persuasive (emotional) campaign to influence the affective component. Distributing free samples might help change the behavioral component. Both business and nonbusiness organizations try to change people's attitudes about many things, from health and safety to prices and product features.

Personality and Self-Concept

Personality is a set of internal traits and distinct behavioral tendencies that result in consistent patterns of behavior in certain situations. An individual's personality arises from hereditary characteristics and personal experiences that make the person unique. Personalities typically are described as having one or more characteristics, such as compulsiveness, ambition, gregariousness, dogmatism, authoritarianism, introversion, extroversion, and competitiveness. Marketing researchers look for relationships between such characteristics and buying behavior. Even though a few links between several personality traits and buyer behavior have been determined, results of many studies have been inconclusive. The weak association between personality and buying behavior may be the result of unreliable measures rather than a lack of a relationship. A number of marketers are convinced

attitude scale A means of measuring consumer attitudes by gauging the intensity of individuals' reactions to adjectives, phrases, or sentences about an object

personality A set of internal traits and distinct behavioral tendencies that result in consistent patterns of behavior in certain situations

that consumers' personalities do influence types and brands of products purchased. For example, the type of clothing, jewelry, or automobile a person buys may reflect one or more personality characteristics. The VALS™ program is one consumer framework, based on individual personality differences, that is successful. (See Lifestyles section.)

At times, marketers aim advertising at certain types of personalities. For instance, ads for certain cigarette brands are directed toward specific personality types. Marketers focus on positively valued personality characteristics, such as security consciousness, sociability, independence, or competitiveness, rather than on negatively valued ones, such as insensitivity or timidity.

A person's self-concept is closely linked to personality. **Self-concept** (sometimes called *self-image*) is a perception or view of oneself. Individuals develop and alter their self-concepts based on an interaction between psychological and social dimensions. Research shows that buyers purchase products that reflect and enhance their self-concepts and that purchase decisions are important to the development and maintenance of a stable self-concept. For example, consumers who feel insecure about their self-concept may purchase products that help them bolster the image of themselves that they would like to project.[12] Consumers' self-concepts may influence whether they buy a product in a specific product category and may affect brand selection as well as where they buy. Consider Timothy S. Leatherman, who named his specialty pocketknife the Pocket Survival Tool. He did so to attract the attention of outdoor survivalists. The ploy worked; it turns out that many people envisioned themselves needing such a tool in their pockets. It didn't take long for sales to grow beyond expectations.[13]

self-concept A perception or view of oneself

lifestyle An individual's pattern of living expressed through activities, interests, and opinions

Lifestyles
KYMCO promotes specific types of lifestyles in its advertisements.

Add yourself to the riders of the road.

And the non-conformists of the world.

"Its big machine power sold me."
Kevin & Laura Beckett
Charlotte, NC

The new KYMCO Xciting 500Ri. Its 500cc DOHC, fuel-injected power and CVT automatic transmission gives you the power to breakaway from the norm. The Xciting 500Ri comes with dual-disc front brakes plus a rear disc for maxi braking power. Our Step-through design makes it easy to jump on and go. Go to MyKymco.com and tell us about your latest getaway.

KYMCO
Choose Your Own Path.

Lifestyles

As we saw in Chapter 6, many marketers attempt to segment markets by lifestyle. A **lifestyle** is an individual's pattern of living expressed through activities, interests, and opinions. Lifestyle patterns include the ways people spend time, the extent of their interaction with others, and their general outlook on life and living. People partially determine their own lifestyles, but the pattern is also affected by personality and by demographic factors such as age, education, income, and social class. Lifestyles are measured through a lengthy series of questions.

Lifestyles have a strong impact on many aspects of the consumer buying decision process, from problem recognition to postpurchase evaluation. Lifestyles influence consumers' product needs, brand preferences, types of media used, and how and where they shop.

One of the most popular frameworks for exploring consumer lifestyles is a survey from SRI Consulting Business Intelligence. The company's VALS Program uses a short questionnaire to help classify consumers into eight basic groups: Innovators, Thinkers, Achievers, Experiencers, Believers, Strivers, Makers, and Survivors (see Figure 7.3). The segmentation is based on psychological characteristics that are correlated with purchase behavior and four key demographics. This VALS questionnaire is then attached to larger surveys that focus on particular products, services, leisure activities, or media preferences to learn about the lifestyles of the eight groups.[14] VALS is a framework that links personality with consumers' lifestyles.

FIGURE 7.3 VALS™ Types

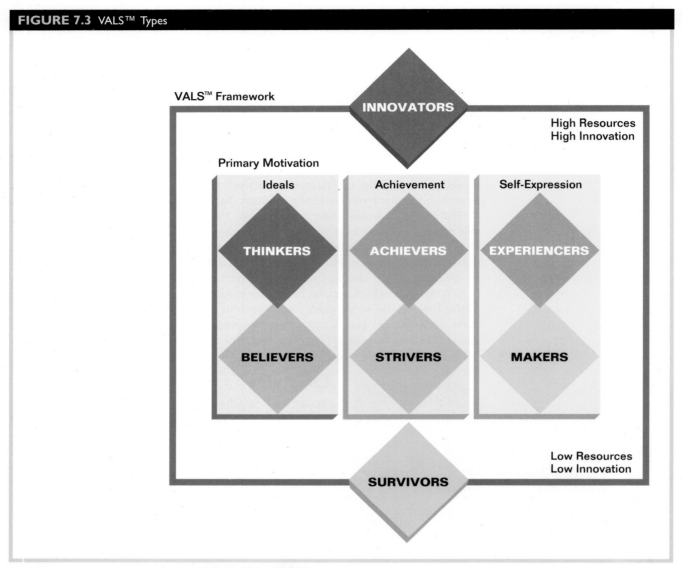

Source: VALS™ Program. SRI Consulting Business Intelligence (SRIC-BI), www.sric-bi.com/VALS/types.shtml. Reprinted with permission.

Level of Involvement and Consumer Problem-Solving Processes

To acquire products that satisfy their current and future needs, consumers must engage in problem solving. People engage in different types of problem-solving processes depending on the nature of the products involved. The amount of effort, both mental and physical, that buyers expend in solving problems also varies considerably. A major determinant of the type of problem-solving process employed depends on the customer's **level of involvement**: the degree of interest in a product and the importance the individual places on that product. High-involvement products tend to be those that are visible to others (such as clothing, furniture, or automobiles) and are expensive. High-importance issues, such as health care, are also associated with high levels of involvement. Low-involvement products tend to be less expensive and have less associated social risk, such as many grocery items. A person's interest in a product or product category that is ongoing and long term is referred to as *enduring involvement*. For instance, a consumer who is interested in technology might always have the most advanced electronic devices,

level of involvement An individual's degree of interest in a product and the importance of the product for that person

Marketing in Transition
Using Colors to Impact Consumers

Pantone LLC is a leader in products, services, and technologies related to color. Lawrence Herbert founded the company in 1963 when he created a system for identifying, matching, and communicating colors within the graphic arts community. Pantone has since extended its reach to the digital technology, fashion, home, plastics, architecture and contract interiors, and paint industries. Over time, Pantone colors have become the standard language through which designers in these industries communicate.

Each year, Pantone produces much anticipated color guides. It also labels one color the color of the year: 2010's color of the year was turquoise—a color evoking thoughts of soothing tropical water and escape from everyday trouble while restoring well-being. To determine the color of the year, executive director Liatrice Eiseman travels the globe observing different products and designs, noting colors that appear frequently, and researching the meanings behind the colors. Turquoise, in many cultures, is a protective color; it is also thought to represent compassion, healing, truth, and faith. In a time troubled by job loss, financial constriction, and fear, turquoise and all it represents seemed to be the perfect choice.

Pantone's color selections guide many industries. This year, it expanded into the bridal industry by working with The Dessy Group (a leading manufacturer of bridal apparel) to create the PANTONE WEDDING™ color guide for brides and wedding planners. According to Pantone, companies

looking to market products should pay particular attention to color and the moods colors evoke. Eiseman uses the color brown as an example of how the meaning of a particular color can change over time. For years, people thought brown was lackluster and uninteresting until Starbucks made coffee exciting and sophisticated and the film *Chocolat* made chocolate sexy. Suddenly, seeing the color brown inspired a new set of thoughts and ideas. By paying attention to colors, marketers can tap into consumer psychology to create positive emotional responses to their products.[b]

read electronics magazines, and work in a related field. However, most consumers have an enduring involvement with only a very few activities or items. In contrast, *situational involvement* is temporary and dynamic, and it results from a particular set of circumstances, such as the need to buy a new car after being involved in an accident. For a short time period, the consumer will visit car dealerships, visit a car company's website, or even purchase automotive-related magazines or books. However, once the car purchase is made, the consumer's interest and involvement taper off. Consumer involvement may be attached to product categories (such as sports), loyalty to a specific brand, interest in a specific advertisement (e.g., a funny commercial) or a medium (such as a particular television show), or to certain decisions and behaviors (e.g., a love of shopping). On the other hand, a consumer may find a particular advertisement entertaining but still not get involved with the brand advertised because of loyalty to another brand. Involvement level, as well as other factors, affects a person's selection of one of three types of consumer problem solving: routinized response behavior, limited problem solving, or extended problem solving (Table 7.1).

routinized response behavior A consumer problem-solving process used when buying frequently purchased, low-cost items that require very little search-and-decision effort

A consumer uses **routinized response behavior** when buying frequently purchased, low-cost items that require very little search-and-decision effort. When buying such items, a consumer may prefer a particular brand but is familiar with several brands in the product class and views more than one as acceptable. Typically, low-involvement products are bought through routinized response behavior—that is, almost automatically. For example, most buyers spend little time or effort selecting soft drinks or cereals.

TABLE 7.1 Consumer Decision Making

	Routinized Response	Limited	Extended
Product cost	Low	Low to moderate	High
Search effort	Little	Little to moderate	Extensive
Time spent	Short	Short to medium	Lengthy
Brand preference	More than one is acceptable, although one may be preferred	Several	Varies; usually many

Buyers engage in **limited problem solving** when they buy products occasionally or when they need to obtain information about an unfamiliar brand in a familiar product category. This type of problem solving requires a moderate amount of time for information gathering and deliberation. For instance, if Procter & Gamble introduces an improved Tide laundry detergent, interested buyers will seek additional information about the new product, perhaps by asking a friend who has used it, watching a commercial about it, or visiting the company's website, before making a trial purchase.

The most complex type of problem solving, **extended problem solving**, occurs when purchasing unfamiliar, expensive, or infrequently bought products—for instance, a car, home, or college education. The buyer uses many criteria to evaluate alternative brands or choices and spends much time seeking information and deciding on the purchase. Extended problem solving is frequently used for purchasing high-involvement products.

Purchase of a particular product does not always elicit the same type of problem-solving process. In some instances, we engage in extended problem solving the first time we buy a certain product but find that limited problem solving suffices when we buy it again. If a routinely purchased, formerly satisfying brand no longer satisfies us, we may use limited or extended problem solving to switch to a new brand. Thus, if we notice that the brand of pain reliever we normally buy is no longer working well, we may seek out a different brand through limited problem solving. Most consumers occasionally make purchases solely on impulse and not on the basis of any of these three problem-solving processes. **Impulse buying** involves no conscious planning but results from a powerful urge to buy something immediately.

Social Influences on the Buying Decision Process

Forces that other people exert on buying behavior are called **social influences**. As Figure 7.1 shows, they are grouped into five major areas: roles, family, reference groups and opinion leaders, social classes, and culture and subcultures.

Roles

All of us occupy positions within groups, organizations, and institutions. As part of each position, we all play one or more **roles**, which are sets of actions and activities a person in a particular position is supposed to perform based on expectations of both the individual and surrounding persons. Because people occupy numerous positions, they have many roles. For example, a man may perform the roles of son, husband, father, employee or employer, church member, civic organization member, and student in an evening college class. Thus, multiple sets of expectations are placed on each person's behavior.

An individual's roles influence both general behavior and buying behavior. The demands of a person's many roles may be diverse and even inconsistent. Consider the

limited problem solving A consumer problem-solving process used when purchasing products occasionally or needing information about an unfamiliar brand in a familiar product category

extended problem solving A consumer problem-solving process employed when purchasing unfamiliar, expensive, or infrequently bought products

impulse buying An unplanned buying behavior resulting from a powerful urge to buy something immediately

social influences The forces other people exert on one's buying behavior

roles Actions and activities that a person in a particular position is supposed to perform based on expectations of the individual and surrounding persons

various types of clothes that you buy and wear depending on whether you are going to class, to work, to a party, or to the gym. You and others involved in these settings have expectations about what is acceptable clothing for these events. Thus, the expectations of those around us affect our purchases of clothing and many other products.

Family Influences

Family influences have a direct impact on the consumer buying decision process. Parents teach children how to cope with a variety of problems, including those dealing with purchase decisions. **Consumer socialization** is the process through which a person acquires the knowledge and skills to function as a consumer. Often children gain this knowledge and set of skills by observing parents and older siblings in purchase situations, as well as through their own purchase experiences. Children observe brand preferences and buying practices in their families and, as adults, retain some of these brand preferences and buying practices as they establish and raise their own families. Buying decisions made by a family are a combination of group and individual decision making.

The extent to which family members take part in family decision making varies among families and product categories. Traditionally, family decision-making processes have been grouped into four categories: autonomic, husband dominant, wife dominant, and syncratic, as shown in Table 7.2. Although female roles continue to change, women still make buying decisions related to most household items, including health-care products, laundry supplies, paper products, and foods. Indeed, research indicates that women are the primary decision makers for 75 percent of all consumer buying decisions.[15] Spouses participate jointly in the purchase of a variety of products, especially durable goods.

The family life-cycle stage affects individual and joint needs of family members. For example, consider how the car needs of recently married "twenty-somethings" differ from those of the same couple when they are "forty-somethings" with a 13-year-old daughter and a 17-year-old son. Family life-cycle changes can affect which family members are involved in purchase decisions and the types of products purchased. Children make many purchase decisions and influence numerous household purchase decisions.

When two or more family members participate in a purchase, their roles may dictate that each is responsible for performing certain purchase-related tasks, such as initiating the idea, gathering information, determining if the product is affordable, deciding whether to buy the product, or selecting the specific brand. The specific purchase tasks performed depend on the types of products being considered, the kind of family purchase decision process typically employed, and the amount of influence children have in the decision process. Thus, different family members may play different roles in the family buying process.

Within a household, an individual may perform one or more roles related to making buying decisions. The gatekeeper is the household member who collects and

consumer socialization The process through which a person acquires the knowledge and skills to function as a consumer

Table 7.2 Types of Family Decision Making

Decision-Making Type	Decision Maker	Types of Products
Husband dominant	Male head of household	Lawn mowers, hardware and tools, stereos, automobile parts
Wife dominant	Female head of household	Children's clothing, women's clothing, groceries, household furnishings
Autonomic	Equally likely to be made by the husband or wife, but not by both	Men's clothing, luggage, toys and games, sporting equipment, cameras
Syncratic	Made jointly by husband and wife	Vacations, TVs, living room furniture, carpets, financial planning services, family cars

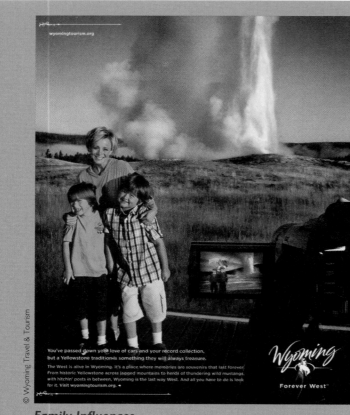

© Wyoming Travel & Tourism

Family Influences
Vacations, such as this family trip to Wyoming, are highly influenced by parents' needs as well as children's desires.

controls information. This may include price and quality comparisons, locations of sellers, and assessment of which brand best suits the family's needs. For example, if a family is planning a summer vacation, the gatekeeper might compare prices for hotels and airfare. The influencer is a family member who expresses his or her opinions and tries to influence buying decisions. In the vacation example, an influencer might be a child who wants to go to Disney World or a teenager who wants only to go snowboarding. The decider is a member who makes the buying choice. This role switches based on the type and expense of the product being purchased. In the case of a vacation, the decider will more likely be the adults, who use a combination of information, influences, and their own preferences. The buyer is a member who actually makes the purchase. After the family has decided to go to Disney World, the buyer will make all of the actual travel purchases. The user is a household member who consumes or uses the product. In this Disney World example, all members of the family would be users.

Reference Groups

A **reference group** is a group that a person identifies with so strongly that he or she adopts the values, attitudes, and behavior of group members. Reference groups can be large or small. Most people have several reference groups, such as families, work-related groups, fraternities or sororities, civic clubs, professional organizations, or church-related groups.

In general, there are three major types of reference groups: membership, aspirational, and disassociative. A membership reference group is one to which an individual actually belongs; the individual identifies with group members strongly enough to take on the values, attitudes, and behaviors of people in that group. An aspirational reference group is a group to which a person aspires to belong; the individual desires to be like those group members. A group that a person does not wish to be associated with is a disassociative or negative reference group; the individual does not want to take on the values, attitudes, and behavior of group members.

A reference group may serve as an individual's point of comparison and source of information. A customer's behavior may change to be more in line with actions and beliefs of group members. For instance, a person may stop buying one brand of shirts and switch to another based on reference group members' advice. An individual may also seek information from the reference group about other factors regarding a prospective purchase, such as where to buy a certain product.

The extent to which a reference group affects a purchase decision depends on the product's conspicuousness and on the individual's susceptibility to reference group influence. Generally, the more conspicuous a product, the more likely that reference groups will influence the purchase decision. A product's conspicuousness is determined by whether others can see it and whether it can attract attention. Reference groups can affect whether a person does or does not buy a product at all, buys a type of product within a product category, or buys a specific brand. One way that reference groups may influence behavior is by ridiculing people who violate group norms; research has identified this practice among adolescents who admonish, haze, or even shun peers who deviate from group norms.[16]

reference group A group that a person identifies with so strongly that he or she adopts the values, attitudes, and behavior of group members

A marketer sometimes tries to use reference group influence in advertisements by suggesting that people in a specific group buy a product and are highly satisfied with it. In this type of appeal, the advertiser hopes that many people will accept the suggested group as a reference group and buy (or react more favorably to) the product. Whether this kind of advertising succeeds depends on three factors: how effectively the advertisement communicates the message, the type of product, and the individual's susceptibility to reference group influence.

Opinion Leaders

An **opinion leader** is a member of an informal group who provides information about a specific topic, like software, to other group members who seek that information. He or she is in a position or has knowledge or expertise that makes him or her a credible source of information about a few topics. Opinion leaders are easily accessible, and they are viewed by other group members as being well informed about a particular topic. Opinion leaders are not the foremost authority on all topics, but because such individuals know they are opinion leaders, they feel a responsibility to remain informed about a topic and thus seek out advertisements, manufacturers' brochures, salespeople, and other sources of information. Opinion leaders have a strong influence on the behavior of others in their group, particularly relating to product adoption and purchases. They are often highly confident and active socially.[17]

An opinion leader is likely to be most influential when consumers have high product involvement but low product knowledge, when they share the opinion leader's values and attitudes, and when the product details are numerous or complicated. Possible opinion leaders and topics are shown in Table 7.3.

Social Classes

In all societies, people rank others into higher or lower positions of respect. This ranking process, called social stratification, results in social classes. A **social class** is an open aggregate of people with similar social rank. A class is referred to as *open* because people can move into and out of it. Criteria for grouping people into classes vary from one society to another. In the United States, we take into account many factors, including occupation, education, income, wealth, race, ethnic group, and possessions. A person who is ranking someone does not necessarily apply all of a society's criteria. Sometimes, too, the role of income tends to be overemphasized in social class determination. Although income does help determine social class, the other factors also play a role. Within social classes, both incomes and spending habits differ significantly among members.

Analyses of social class in the United States commonly divide people into three to seven categories. Social scientist Richard P. Coleman suggests that for purposes of consumer analysis the population is divided into the three major status groups shown in Table 7.4. However, he cautions marketers that considerable diversity exists in people's life situations within each status group.

opinion leader A member of an informal group who provides information about a specific topic to other group members

social class An open group of individuals with similar social rank

TABLE 7.3 Examples of Opinion Leaders and Topics

Opinion Leader	Possible Topics
Local religious leader	Charities to support, political ideas, lifestyle choices
Sorority president	Clothing and shoe purchases, hair styles, nail and hair salons
"Movie buff" friend	Movies to see in theater or to rent, DVDs to buy, television programs to watch
Family doctor	Prescription drugs, vitamins, health products
"Techie" acquaintance	Computer and other electronics purchases, software purchases, Internet service choices, video game purchases

TABLE 7.4 Social Class Behavioral Traits and Purchasing Characteristics

Class (Percent of Population)	Behavioral Traits	Buying Characteristics
UPPER AMERICANS		
Upper-upper (0.5)	Social elite Of aristocratic, prominent families Inherited their position in society	Children attend private preparatory schools and best colleges Do not consume ostentatiously Spend money on private clubs, various causes, and the arts
Lower-upper (3.8)	Newer social elite Successful professionals earning very high incomes Earned their position in society	Purchase material symbols of their status, such as large, suburban houses and expensive automobiles Provide a substantial market for luxury product offerings Visit museums and attend live theater Spend money on skiing, golf, swimming, and tennis
Upper-middle (13.8)	Career-oriented, professional degree holders Demand educational attainment of their children	Provide a substantial market for quality product offerings Family lifestyle characterized as gracious yet careful Spend money on movies, gardening, and photography
MIDDLE AMERICANS		
Middle class (32.8)	"Typical" Americans Work conscientiously and adhere to culturally defined standards Average-pay white-collar workers Attend church and obey the law Often very involved in children's school and sports activities	Greatly value living in a respected neighborhood and keep their homes well furnished Generally price sensitive Adopt conventional consumption tastes and consult category experts Spend on family-oriented, physical activities, such as fishing, camping, boating, and hunting
Working class (32.3)	Average-pay blue-collar workers Live a routine life with unchanging day-to-day activities Hold jobs that entail manual labor and moderate skills Some are union members Socially not involved in civic or church activities; limit social interaction to close neighbors and relatives	Reside in small houses or apartments in depressed areas Impulsive as consumers yet display high loyalty to national brands Seek best bargains Enjoy leisure activities like local travel and recreational parks
LOWER AMERICANS		
Upper-lower (9.5)	Low-income individuals who generally fail to rise above this class Reject middle-class morality	Living standard is just above poverty Seek pleasure whenever possible, especially through impulse purchases Frequently purchase on credit
Lower-lower (7.3)	Some are on welfare and may be homeless Poverty stricken Some have strong religious beliefs Some are unemployed In spite of their problems, often good-hearted toward others May be forced to live in less desirable neighborhoods	Spend on products needed for survival Able to convert discarded goods into usable items

Source: Roger D. Blackwell, Paul W. Miniard, and James F. Engel, *Consumer Behavior*, 10th ed. (Mason, OH: South-western, 2005); "The Continuing Significance of Social Class Marketing," *Journal of Consumer Research* 10 (Dec. 1983): 265–280; Eugene Sivadas, George Mathew, and David J. Curry," A Preliminary Examination of the Continued Significance of Social Class in Marketing," *Journal of Consumer Marketing* 14, no. 6 (1997): 463–469.

Entrepreneurial Marketing
Some Can Face It—Some Can't

Are you one of the millions of people who can't go a day—or an hour—without checking Facebook? Facebook was started just a few years ago as an online directory for Harvard students. Two weeks after the site went live, more than 4,000 members had posted their profiles. Within a few months, Facebook was a full-blown social phenomenon that connected young people all over the globe.

A recent study shows a staggering jump in the number of 35- to 54-year-old users—doubling roughly every two months. And users 55 and over are increasing almost as fast. The result? Teens are looking for new places to hang out where they won't be running into Granny and her "25 random things about me."[c]

To some degree, individuals within social classes develop and assume common behavioral patterns. They may have similar attitudes, values, language patterns, and possessions. Social class influences many aspects of people's lives. Because people have the most frequent interaction with people from within their own social class, most people are more likely to be influenced by others within their own class than by those in other classes. For example, it affects their chances of having children and their children's chances of surviving infancy. It influences their childhood training, choice of religion, financial planning decisions, access to higher education, selection of occupation, and leisure time activities. Because social class has a bearing on so many aspects of a person's life, it also affects buying decisions.

Social class influences people's spending, saving, and credit practices. It determines to some extent the type, quality, and quantity of products a person buys and uses. For instance, it affects purchases of clothing, foods, financial and health-care services, travel, recreation, entertainment, and home furnishings. The behaviors of people in one class can influence consumers in others. Most common is the "trickle-down" effect in which members of lower classes attempt to emulate members of higher social classes, such as purchasing expensive automobiles, homes, appliances, and other status symbols. For example, couture fashions designed for the upper class influence the clothing sold in department stores frequented by the middle class, which eventually influences the working class who shop at discount clothing stores. Less often, status float will occur, when a product that is traditionally associated with a lower class gains status and usage among upper classes. Blue jeans, for example, were originally worn exclusively by the working class. Youth of the 1950s began wearing them as a symbol of rebellion against their parents. By the 1970s and 1980s, jeans had also been adopted by upper-class youth when they began to acquire designer labels. Today, blue jeans are acceptable attire for all social classes and cost anywhere from a few dollars to thousands of dollars, depending on the brand.

Social class also affects an individual's shopping patterns and types of stores patronized. In some instances, marketers attempt to focus on certain social classes through store location and interior design, product design and features, pricing strategies, personal sales efforts, and advertising. Many companies focus on the middle and working classes because they account for such a large portion of the population. Outside the United States, the middle class is growing in India, China, Mexico, and other countries, making these consumers increasingly desirable to marketers as well. Some firms target different classes with different products. For example, luxury brands BMW and Mercedes-Benz have both released more moderately priced vehicles ($20,000 to $40,000) to target middle-class consumers, although it usually targets upper-class customers with more expensive vehicles ($80,000 plus).[18]

Culture and Subcultures

culture The accumulation of values, knowledge, beliefs, customs, objects, and concepts that a society uses to cope with its environment and passes on to future generations

Culture is the accumulation of values, knowledge, beliefs, customs, objects, and concepts that a society uses to cope with its environment and passes on to future generations. Examples of objects are foods, furniture, buildings, clothing, and tools. Concepts include education, welfare, and laws. Culture also includes core values and the degree of acceptability of a wide range of behaviors in a specific society. For example, in U.S. culture, customers as well as businesspeople are expected to behave ethically.

Culture influences buying behavior because it permeates our daily lives. Our culture determines what we wear and eat and where we reside and travel. Society's interest in the healthfulness of food affects food companies' approaches to developing and promoting their products. Culture also influences how we buy and use products and our satisfaction from them. In the U.S. culture, makers of furniture, cars, and clothing strive to understand how people's color preferences are changing.

Because culture determines product purchases and uses to some degree, cultural changes affect product development, promotion, distribution, and pricing. Food marketers, for example, have made a multitude of changes in their marketing efforts. Thirty years ago, most U.S. families ate at least two meals a day together, and the mother spent four to six hours a day preparing those meals. Today, the majority of women work outside the home before they reach retirement age, and average family incomes have risen considerably. These shifts, along with scarcity of time, have resulted in dramatic changes in the national per capita consumption of certain food products, such as take-out foods, frozen dinners, and shelf-stable foods.

When U.S. marketers sell products in other countries, they realize the tremendous impact those cultures have on product purchases and use. Global marketers find that people in other regions of the world have different attitudes, values, and needs, which call for different methods of doing business as well as different types of marketing mixes. Some international marketers fail because they do not or cannot adjust to cultural differences.

A culture consists of various subcultures. A **subculture** is a group of individuals whose characteristics, values, and behavioral patterns are similar within the group and different from those of people in the surrounding culture. Subcultural boundaries are usually based on geographic designations and demographic characteristics, such as age, religion, race, and ethnicity. U.S. culture is marked by many different subcultures. Among them are West Coast, teenage, Asian American, and college students. Within subcultures, greater similarities exist in people's attitudes, values, and actions than within the broader culture. For example, teenage girls in the United States are 84 percent more likely to consume iced coffee than other Americans.[19] Relative to other subcultures, individuals in one subculture may have stronger preferences for specific types of clothing, furniture, or foods. Research has shown that subcultures can play a significant role in how people respond to advertisements, particularly when pressured to make a snap judgment. It is important to understand that a person can be a member of more than one subculture and that the behavioral patterns and values attributed to specific subcultures do not necessarily apply to all group members.

The percentage of the U.S. population consisting of ethnic and racial subcultures is expected to grow. (See the Snapshot for an idea of how U.S. demographics have changed over time.) By 2050, about one-half of the U.S. population will be members of racial and ethnic minorities. The U.S. Census Bureau reports that the three largest and fastest-growing ethnic U.S. subcultures are African Americans, Hispanics, and Asians.[20] Forty-seven percent of children under the age of five in the United States are minorities, as are 43 percent of people under 20.[21] The population

subculture A group of individuals whose characteristics, values, and behavioral patterns are similar within the group and different from those of people in the surrounding culture

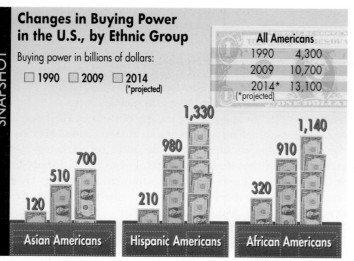

SNAPSHOT

Changes in Buying Power in the U.S., by Ethnic Group

Buying power in billions of dollars:

☐ 1990 ☐ 2009 ☐ 2014 (*projected)

All Americans	
1990	4,300
2009	10,700
2014* (*projected)	13,100

	Asian Americans	Hispanic Americans	African Americans
1990	120	210	320
2009	510	980	910
2014	700	1,330	1,140

Source: Jeffrey M. Humphreys, "The Multicultural Economy 2009," *Georgia Business and Economic Conditions* 69, www.terry.uga.edu/selig/docs/GBEC0903q.pdf (accessed September 2, 2010).

growth of these subcultures interests marketers. Businesses recognize that to succeed, their marketing strategies will have to take into account the values, needs, interests, shopping patterns, and buying habits of various subcultures.

AFRICAN AMERICAN SUBCULTURE

In the United States, the African American subculture represents 12.3 percent of the population.[22] Like all subcultures, African American consumers possess distinct buying patterns. For example, African American consumers spend much of their money on depreciable products such as clothing, entertainment, food, and more.[23] The combined buying power of African American consumers is projected to reach $1.24 trillion by 2013.[24]

With the election of the first African American president, many companies are renewing their focus on the African American community. Coca-Cola has launched a series of campaigns aimed specifically at African American mothers and teenagers, stating that they are the decision makers and the trend setters in their demographic. Allstate, the insurance company, places a hefty emphasis on multicultural advertising. It runs the Beyond February program—a 365-day-a-year promise to support and grow the African American community.[25]

HISPANIC SUBCULTURE

Hispanics represent 15.1 percent of the U.S. population, and their buying power is expected to reach $1.4 trillion by 2013.[26] Hispanic buying power increased 94.3 percent between 2000 and 2008 and is expected to increase another 45.8 percent by 2013.[27] This development makes this subculture a powerful and attractive consumer group for marketers. When considering the buying behavior of Hispanics, marketers must keep in mind that this subculture is really composed of many diverse cultures coming from a huge geographic region that encompasses nearly two dozen nationalities, including Cuban, Mexican, Puerto Rican, Caribbean, Spanish, and Dominican. Each has its own history and unique culture that affect consumer preferences and buying behavior. They should also recognize that the terms *Hispanic* and *Latino* refer to an ethnic category rather than a racial distinction. Because of the group's growth and purchasing power, understanding the Hispanic subculture is critical to marketers. Like African American consumers, Hispanics spend more of their income on housing, groceries, telephone services, and children's apparel and shoes. But they also spend more on men's apparel and appliances, while they spend less than average on health care, entertainment, and education.[28]

To attract this powerful subculture, marketers are developing products and creating advertising and promotions with Hispanic values and preferences in mind. For example, Target focused 2009's year-long Dream in Color campaign on Hispanics, honoring Hispanic celebrities and community leaders.[29] Insurance company State Farm found success with the Hispanic market when it launched its "Ahí Estoy" campaign. Honing in on the Hispanic culture's love of music, the company sponsored a Hispanic music band that has gathered a following and improved State Farm's reputation in the Hispanic community.[30]

Image courtesy of The Advertising Archives

Subcultures
Kelly Osbourne is a member of a subculture that has similar values and behavior patterns that differ from the surrounding culture.

ASIAN AMERICAN SUBCULTURE

The term *Asian American* includes people from more than 15 ethnic groups, including Filipinos, Chinese, Japanese, Asian Indians, Koreans, and Vietnamese, and this group represents 4.4 percent of the U.S. population. The individual language, religion, and value system of each group influences its members' purchasing decisions. Some traits of this subculture, however, carry across ethnic divisions, including an emphasis on hard work, strong family ties, and a high value placed on education.[31] Asian Americans wield $509 billion in buying power, a number expected to increase 47 percent by 2013.[32]

Marketers are targeting the diverse Asian American market in many ways. Walmart stores have established a multicultural marketing department and new Asian American strategies, among other moves. Walmart launched a back-to-school microsite in both English and Vietnamese. The site was positioned as a back-to-school resource for study and clothing tips, school supplies, and other suggestions.[33]

Consumer Misbehavior

consumer misbehavior
Behavior that violates generally accepted norms of a particular society.

Approaching the topic of inappropriate consumer behavior requires some caution because of varying attitudes and cultural definitions of what comprises misbehavior. However, there is general agreement that some conduct, such as shoplifting or purchasing illegal drugs, falls under the category of activities that are not accepted by established norms. Therefore, we will define **consumer misbehavior** as simply behavior that violates generally accepted norms of a particular society. Shoplifting is one of the most obvious misconduct areas, with organized retail crime (where people are paid to shoplift certain goods from retail stores) on the rise. Experts estimate that organized retail crime alone costs businesses between $10 billion and $30 billion annually.[34] Consumer motivation for shoplifting include the low risk of being caught, a desire to be accepted by a group of peers (particularly among young people), and the excitement associated with the activity.

Consumer fraud includes purposeful actions to take advantage of and/or damage others. Fraudulently obtaining credit cards, bank accounts, or false insurance claims fall into this category. Some consumers engage in identity theft, which is a serious and growing legal problem. Another example of consumer fraud would be purchasing a dress for a special event, wearing it once, and then returning it. To combat such behavior, Best Buy implemented a restocking fee to deal

---

Responsible Marketing?
Banks in Credit Trouble

CRITICAL THINKING

ISSUE: *Should banks be allowed to solicit applications for credit cards on college campuses?*

From the moment college students step on campus, they are bombarded by credit card companies who offer them airline miles and free T-shirts if they apply for a credit card. The average student racks up more than $1,500 in credit card debt by the end of his or her freshman year. Many activists stress that the major banks are poaching a vulnerable market of teens who are unlikely to be able to pay their balance on time. They believe it is unethical for credit card companies to be on campus. Other activists aim to educate students on how to effectively manage their credit rather than discouraging them from having a card at all.

Many credit card companies are accused of using overly complex billing systems and fee assessment. In a recent study, a usability consultant for the Government Accountability Office (GAO) found that many disclosures in customer solicitation materials and card-member agreements were too complicated for many consumers to understand. Some of the more confusing issues included rate increases after a late payment and the different rates used for different types of purchases. Critics argue that it is expecting too much for college students to really know what they are getting into when they swipe that card. Should credit card companies be allowed on college campuses? Are they taking advantage of a vulnerable market, or are they simply offering a service to new customers?[d]

TABLE 7.5 Motivations for Unethical or Illegal Misbehavior

• Justification/rationalization	• The thrill of getting away with it
• Economic reasons	• There is little risk of getting caught
• It is accepted by peers	• People think they are smarter than others

Source: Kevin J. Shanahan and Michael J. Hyman, "Motivators and Enablers of SCOURing: A Study of Online Piracy in the US and UK," *Journal of Business Research 63*, September–October 2010, pp. 1095–1102 (accessed September 2, 2010).

with consumers who purchased electronics, such as computers or televisions, used them for a short time, and then returned them. Pirating computer software, video games, or music is illegal and costs the electronics and entertainment industries an estimated $53 billion annually.[35] The influence of peers has been found to be a major factor in the decision to illegally pirate music.[36] The recording industry uses this information to craft messages to emphasize why pirating music may not be acceptable. Understanding motivations for pirating can be helpful in developing a plan to combat the issue. (See Table 7.5)

Yet another area of concern with consumer misbehavior is abusive consumers. Rude customers engage in verbal or physical abuse, can be uncooperative, and may even break policies. Airlines remove abusive consumers, as they represent a threat to employees and other passengers. Belligerently drunk customers, especially in environments like bars and restaurants, have to be removed in order to protect others. Understanding psychological and social reasons for consumer misconduct can be helpful in preventing or responding to the problem. For example, pirating and counterfeiting is a major problem globally. The U.S. Chamber of Commerce estimates that, globally, counterfeiting and pirating goods (such as clothing, electronics, medicine, music, toys, and even cars) is a $650 billion a year industry.[37]

summary

1. To recognize the stages of the consumer buying decision process

The consumer buying decision process includes five stages: problem recognition, information search, evaluation of alternatives, purchase, and postpurchase evaluation. Not all decision processes culminate in a purchase, nor do all consumer decisions include all five stages. Problem recognition occurs when buyers become aware of a difference between a desired state and an actual condition. After recognizing the problem or need, buyers search for information about products to help resolve the problem or satisfy the need. In the internal search, buyers search their memories for information about products that might solve the problem. If they cannot retrieve from memory enough information for a decision, they seek additional information through an external search. A successful search yields a group of brands, called a consideration set, which a buyer views as possible alternatives. To evaluate the products in the consideration set, the buyer establishes certain criteria by which to compare, rate, and rank different products. Marketers can influence consumers' evaluations by framing alternatives.

In the purchase stage, consumers select products or brands on the basis of results from the evaluation stage and on other dimensions. Buyers also choose the seller from whom they will buy the product. After the purchase, buyers evaluate the product to determine if its actual performance meets expected levels. Shortly after the purchase of an expensive product, for example, the postpurchase evaluation may result in cognitive dissonance, dissatisfaction brought on by the consumer's doubts as to whether he or she should have bought the product in the first place or would have been better off buying another desirable brand.

2. To explore how situational influences may affect the consumer buying decision process

Three major categories of influences affect the consumer buying decision process: situational, psychological, and social. Situational influences are external circumstances or conditions existing when a consumer makes a purchase decision. Situational influences include surroundings, time, reason for purchase, and the buyer's mood and condition.

3. To understand the psychological influences that may affect the consumer buying decision process

Psychological influences partly determine people's general behavior, thus influencing their behavior as consumers. The primary psychological influences on consumer behavior are perception, motives, learning, attitudes, personality and self-concept, and lifestyles. Perception is the process of selecting, organizing, and interpreting information inputs (sensations received through sight, taste, hearing, smell, and touch) to produce meaning. The three steps in the perceptual process are selection, organization, and interpretation. Individuals have numerous perceptions of packages, products, brands, and organizations that affect their buying decision processes. A motive is an internal energizing force that orients a person's activities toward satisfying needs or achieving goals. Learning refers to changes in a person's thought processes and behavior caused by information and experience. Marketers try to shape what consumers learn to influence what they buy. An attitude is an individual's enduring evaluation, feelings, and behavioral tendencies toward an object or idea and consists of three major components: cognitive, affective, and behavioral. Personality is the set of traits and behaviors that make a person unique. Self-concept, closely linked to personality, is one's perception or view of oneself. Researchers have found that buyers purchase products that reflect and enhance their self-concepts. Lifestyle is an individual's pattern of living expressed through activities, interests, and opinions. Lifestyles influence consumers' needs, brand preferences, and how and where they shop.

4. To understand consumers' level of involvement with a product and describe the types of consumer problem-solving processes

Buying behavior consists of the decision processes and acts of people involved in buying and using products. Consumer buying behavior is the buying behavior of ultimate consumers.

An individual's level of involvement—the importance and intensity of interest in a product in a particular situation—affects the type of problem-solving process used. Enduring involvement is an ongoing interest in a product class because of personal relevance, whereas situational involvement is a temporary interest that stems from the particular circumstance or environment in which buyers find themselves. There are three kinds of consumer problem solving: routinized response behavior, limited problem solving, and extended problem solving. Consumers rely on routinized response behavior when buying frequently purchased, low-cost items requiring little search-and-decision effort. Limited problem solving is used for products purchased occasionally or when buyers need to acquire information about an unfamiliar brand in a familiar product category. Consumers engage in extended problem solving when purchasing an unfamiliar, expensive, or infrequently bought product. Purchase of a certain product does not always elicit the same type of decision making. Impulse buying is not a consciously planned buying behavior but involves a powerful urge to buy something immediately.

5. To examine the social influences that may affect the consumer buying decision process

Social influences are forces that other people exert on buying behavior. They include roles, family, reference groups and opinion leaders, electronic networks, social class, and culture and subcultures. Everyone occupies positions within groups, organizations, and institutions, and each position has a role, a set of actions and activities that a person in a particular position is supposed to perform based on expectations of both the individual and surrounding persons. In a family, children learn from parents and older siblings how to make decisions, such as purchase decisions. Consumer socialization is the process through which a person acquires the knowledge and skills to function as a consumer. The consumer socialization process is partially accomplished through family influences. A reference group is a group that a person identifies with so strongly that he or she adopts the values, attitudes, and behavior of group members. The three major types of reference groups are membership, aspirational, and disassociative. An opinion leader is a member of an informal group who provides information about a specific topic to other group members. Consumers may turn to the Internet—especially blogs, wikis, and social networks—for information to aid them in buying decisions. A social class is an open group of individuals with similar social rank. Social class influences people's spending, saving, and credit practices. Culture is the accumulation of values, knowledge, beliefs, customs, objects, and concepts that a society uses to cope with its environment and passes on to future generations. A culture is made up of subcultures, groups of individuals whose characteristic values and behavior patterns are similar but different from those of the surrounding culture. U.S. marketers focus on three major ethnic subcultures: African American, Hispanic, and Asian American.

Go to www.cengagebrain.com for resources to help you master the content in this chapter as well as materials that will expand your marketing knowledge!

important terms

buying behavior, 192
consumer buying behavior, 192
consumer buying decision process, 192
internal search, 192
external search, 192
consideration set, 194
evaluative criteria, 194
cognitive dissonance, 195
situational influences, 195

psychological influences, 196
perception, 197
information inputs, 197
selective exposure, 197
selective distortion, 197
selective retention, 197
motive, 198
Maslow's hierarchy of needs, 198
patronage motives, 199
learning, 200

attitude, 201
attitude scale, 202
personality, 202
self-concept, 203
lifestyle, 203
level of involvement, 204
routinized response behavior, 205
limited problem solving, 206
extended problem solving, 206

impulse buying, 206
social influences, 206
roles, 206
consumer socialization, 207
reference group, 208
opinion leader, 209
social class, 209
culture, 211
subculture, 212
consumer misbehavior, 214

discussion and review questions

1. How does a consumer's level of involvement affect his or her choice of problem-solving process?
2. Name the types of consumer problem-solving processes. List some products you have bought using each type. Have you ever bought a product on impulse? If so, describe the circumstances.
3. What are the major stages in the consumer buying decision process? Are all these stages used in all consumer purchase decisions? Why or why not?
4. What are the categories of situational factors that influence consumer buying behavior? Explain how each of these factors influences buyers' decisions.
5. What is selective exposure? Why do people engage in it?
6. How do marketers attempt to shape consumers' learning?
7. Why are marketers concerned about consumer attitudes?
8. In what ways do lifestyles affect the consumer buying decision process?

9. How do roles affect a person's buying behavior? Provide examples.
10. What are family influences, and how do they affect buying behavior?
11. What are reference groups? How do they influence buying behavior? Name some of your own reference groups.
12. How does an opinion leader influence the buying decision process of reference group members?
13. How might consumer behavior be influenced by digital networks?
14. In what ways does social class affect a person's purchase decisions?
15. What is culture? How does it affect a person's buying behavior?
16. Describe the subcultures to which you belong. Identify buying behavior that is unique to one of your subcultures.

application questions

CRITICAL THINKING

1. Consumers use one of three problem-solving processes when purchasing goods or services: routinized response behavior, limited problem solving, or extended problem solving. Describe three buying experiences you have had (one for each type of problem solving), and identify which problem-solving type you used. Discuss why that particular process was appropriate.

2. The consumer buying process consists of five stages: problem recognition, information search, evaluation of alternatives, purchase, and post-purchase evaluation. Not every buying decision goes through all five stages, and the process does not necessarily conclude in a purchase. Interview a classmate about the last purchase he or she made. Report the stages used and those skipped, if any.

3. Attitudes toward products or companies often affect consumer behavior. The three components of an attitude are cognitive, affective, and behavioral. Briefly describe how a beer company might alter the cognitive and affective components of consumer attitudes toward beer products and toward the company.

4. An individual's roles influence that person's buying behavior. Identify two of your roles, and give an example of how they have influenced your buying decisions.

5. Select five brands of toothpaste and explain how the appeals used in advertising these brands relate to Maslow's hierarchy of needs.

internet exercise

Amazon.com

Some mass-market e-commerce sites, such as **Amazon.com**, have extended the concept of customization to their customer base. **Amazon.com** has created an affinity group by drawing on certain users' likes and dislikes to make product recommendations to other users. Check out this pioneering online retailer at **www.amazon.com**.

1. What might motivate some consumers to read a "Top Selling" list?

2. Is the consumer's level of involvement with an online book purchase likely to be high or low?

3. Discuss the consumer buying decision process as it relates to a decision to purchase from **Amazon.com**.

developing your marketing plan

CRITICAL THINKING

Understanding the process that an individual consumer goes through when purchasing a product is essential for developing marketing strategy. Knowledge about the potential customer's buying behavior will become the basis for many of the decisions in the specific marketing plan. Using the information from this chapter, you should be able to determine the following:

1. What type of problem solving are your customers likely to use when purchasing your product (see Table 7.1)?

2. Determine the evaluative criteria that your target market(s) would use when choosing between alternative brands.

3. Using Table 7.2, what types of family decision making, if any, would your target market(s) use?

4. Identify the reference groups or subcultures that may influence your target market's product selection.

The information obtained from these questions should assist you in developing various aspects of your marketing plan found in the *Interactive Marketing Plan* exercise at **www.cengagebrain.com**.

VIDEO CASE 7.1

Click to Get Away with Travelocity

CRITICAL THINKING

When Travelocity began in 1996, it was one of the first Internet travel websites offering airline and hotel reservations, cruises, vacation packages, and car rentals. Today, Travelocity offers consumers a choice of more than 70,000 hotels, 50 car rental companies, 6,000 travel packages, and flights on dozens of airlines worldwide. Its total travel bookings exceed more than $7 billion annually.

Although it helped pioneer the online travel business, Travelocity faces intense competition from Expedia, Orbitz, and other popular travel websites. That's why its marketers decided several years ago to make the company stand out by standing behind travelers every step of the way. The result is the unique Travelocity Guarantee. First, Travelocity guarantees its low price. If, within 24 hours, consumers find a lower price for travel than the one they booked through Travelocity, the company will refund the difference and add a $50 credit toward future travel. Second, Travelocity allows customers to change passenger names, flight dates, and flight times without paying extra if they make the change within 24 hours of booking their travel. Third, Travelocity pledges to alert customers in advance to any issues that might negatively affect their travel arrangements, such as hotel construction, and work with its trusted partners to fix the problem by switching hotels or making other changes. Fourth, if something goes wrong during a customer's travels, Travelocity will work with its partners to make things right. For example, if a customer books a hotel with a swimming pool but finds that the swimming pool is closed on arrival, Travelocity will, at its own expense, find a comparable or better-quality hotel and move the customer there. Once, the company made a mistake and sold $0 tickets to Fiji and, despite the cost, stood by its guarantee and honored the price. Travelocity maintains a 24-hour hotline open seven days a week to ensure that customers get what they want.

The Travelocity Guarantee allays the concerns of customers who may be worried about booking online. The company has promoted the guarantee with a "Roaming Gnome: Enforcer of the Travelocity Guarantee" advertising campaign. The distinctive Roaming Gnome humanized the brand, embodied the joy of travel, and symbolized seeing

the world with new eyes. The advertising campaign created a tremendous buzz about Travelocity and boosted revenues by 37 percent. Based on customer reaction to the campaign, Travelocity opened an online store to sell mugs, magnets, tote bags, and other items featuring the Roaming Gnome, who even has his own page on Facebook.

Over time, Travelocity has acquired a number of travel sites to broaden its offerings. When it purchased Site59, for example, Travelocity solidified its position as a major player in the last-minute travel business. Now customers who feel the urge to travel can get special deals by booking no more than 14 days before they want to leave. The savings are even bigger when customers book a vacation package just a few days in advance. To find out about special deals to favorite destinations, customers simply subscribe to Travelocity's Easy Escapes e-mail newsletter.

Travelocity regularly tests its website for ease of use. It has seven testers clicking all over its website to determine what customers might find confusing and how to make the site faster and more convenient. One lesson Travelocity learned was that customers don't always remember their passwords. To counteract this problem, Travelocity changed the system so that customers could reenter an address or e-mail address and use those details to access their personal profile rather than relying on a password. Thanks to this change, revenues quickly rose by 10 percent. Watch for more changes ahead as Travelocity finds new ways to satisfy its customers and new places for its Gnome to visit.[38]

QUESTIONS FOR DISCUSSION

1. How does the Travelocity Guarantee give Travelocity a competitive advantage in various stages of the consumer buying decision process?
2. What is Travelocity doing to influence consumer perceptions of and attitudes toward its product offerings?
3. What are the major situational influences that affect Travelocity customers' buying decisions? Explain.

© AP Images/PRNewsFoto/Travelocity / © Comstock Images/Getty Images

CASE 7.2

Iams Understands People Who Love Pets

Any company that wants to retain current customers and attract new ones must be aware of trends and be able to adapt to the changing needs of their customers. Iams, the successful retailer of Iams and Eukanuba pet products, is a good example of a company making the most of understanding consumer behavior to successfully grow their business. Iams recognizes the importance of psychological and social influences in pet food purchasing.

Today, many pet owners treat their pets as family members and want to provide their pets with high-quality products. Procter & Gamble (P&G) and Iams, picking up on this trend, market premium pet products mirroring products purchased and used by humans. For example, Iams ProActive Health™ formulas include PreBiotics, good bacteria that promote healthy digestion. The company also has a Healthy Naturals™ line that includes ingredients such as Atlantic salmon and contains no artificial colors, flavors, or preservatives. The popularity of these products indicates that consumers are developing a higher level of involvement when shopping for pet food. As an additional member of the family, pets are entitled to the same quality and nutrition as other family members. Fresh Pet, in partnership with Tyson, provides refrigerated pet foods for dogs and cats.

At one time, Iams focused primarily on pet nutrition. Now the company has expanded to products aimed at making pet owners happy by fulfilling their requests for fancy pet treats, sauces, and other items that allow them to spoil their pets. The

company has made this shift as a result of surveying its customers. For example, customers were concerned about feeding cats in multi-cat households in which one cat might be overweight while another was not. As a result, the company created a Multi-Cat formula with ingredients aimed at reducing fat in heavy cats while still providing protein for lean cats. The company's Savory Sauce™ formulas for dogs are bottled just like human barbecue sauces or marinades. The sauces are fortified with vitamins, minerals, and antioxidants, are low in calories and fat, and come in flavors such as Pot Roast or Country Style Chicken. Premium products like these reflect the changes in consumer attitudes toward their pets and their pets' food. Consumers like to reflect their lifestyle through activities and interests, including their relationship and investment in their pet.

Iams also partners with *Dog Fancy®* and *Cat Fancy®* magazines to offer free online classes to pet owners at Dog College and Cat College. The curriculum includes courses on physiology, natural nutrition, communication, genetics, environmental science, health science, and art history. Participants learn more about caring for their pets, can enter to win pet food, and even print a Dog College "bark-alaureate" diploma. Dog College and Cat College offer Iams the unique opportunity to educate pet owners and have an impact on several stages of the buying decision process. A person's self concept is closely linked to their personality, values, and associated buying behavior.

Realizing the importance of consumers' relationships with their pets, Iams is expanding its business into the

© Gregg Cerenzio/Shutterstock.com / © John Wang/Photodisc/Getty Images veterinary industry. The company works with Veterinary Pet Insurance Co. to provide pet health insurance. Iams is also branching out into MRI (magnetic resonance imaging) machines, in partnership with ProScan. Iams Pet Imaging Centers in select cities allow doctors to investigate health problems in pets without resorting to exploratory surgery. By offering a wide variety of healthy products, Iams is clearly paying attention to the needs of pet owners and making it possible for them to create healthy lifestyles for their pets.[39]

QUESTIONS FOR DISCUSSION

1. What are some of the psychological influences that are most important to Iams in understanding their buyers?

2. Speculate on the buying behavior of a person that treats their pet(s) the same as other family members.

3. Why have pet supply purchases been relatively unaffected by the economic downturn of 2008–2010?

Chapter 8

Business Markets and Buying Behavior

OBJECTIVES

1. To be able to distinguish among the various types of business markets

2. To identify the major characteristics of business customers and transactions

3. To understand several attributes of demand for business products

4. To become familiar with the major components of a buying center

5. To understand the stages of the business buying decision process and the factors that affect this process

6. To describe industrial classification systems and explain how they can be used to identify and analyze business markets

Google Ad(d)s Up to $24 Billion Annually

The Internet was still young when Google launched its search engine in 1998. The company's mission: "To organize the world's information and make it universally accessible and useful." Despite fierce competition from established online businesses such as Yahoo!, Google has built its brand into a household name by giving away its search services and introducing a steady stream of innovative web-based applications.

Today, Google dominates the online search industry and rings up $24 billion in annual sales. Most of its revenue is generated from the sale of advertising displayed alongside search results, You Tube videos, and 148 other Google websites. The company follows a "mobile first" strategy to capitalize on global growth in cell phone usage, tailoring display ads specifically for viewing on phone screens. For business advertisers, the benefit is the ability to reach out to customers anytime, anywhere that people use any electronic device to access Google.

Understanding demand has helped Google do a better job of marketing to businesses. The company's researchers not only monitor global and local search trends, they analyze a virtual mountain of data about searchers' behavior. This allows them to predict how, when, and how often searchers will use particular words and phrases in the future. As a result, Google's salespeople can show advertisers how to target audiences more precisely.

Google auctions off ad space adjacent to each search word and phrase, letting competition among business customers determine the exact price paid. Just as important, Google's researchers are always crunching the numbers to improve the match between the ad message and the audience. If business customers aren't reaching the right audience, they won't bid for Google's ad space.

Not long ago, Google announced it would build super-fast Internet access systems in several U.S. cities to publicize the benefits of high-speed broadband networks. Businesses that buy ads next to search results will benefit as Google finds new ways to make searching more efficient, more effective, and more profitable.[1]

Serving business markets effectively requires understanding those markets. Marketers at Google go to considerable lengths to understand their customers so they can provide better products and develop and maintain long-term customer relationships. Like consumer marketers, business marketers are concerned about satisfying their customers.

In this chapter, we look at business markets and business buying decision processes. We first discuss various kinds of business markets and the types of buyers that comprise those markets. Next, we explore several dimensions of business buying, such as characteristics of transactions, attributes and concerns of buyers, methods of buying, and distinctive features of demand for products sold to business purchasers. We then examine how business buying decisions are made and who makes the purchases. Finally, we consider how business markets are analyzed.

Business Markets

As defined in Chapter 6, a **business market** (also called a *business-to-business market* or *B2B market*) consists of individuals, organizations, or groups that purchase a specific kind of product for one of three purposes: resale, direct use in producing other products, or use in general daily operations. Marketing to businesses employs the same concepts as marketing to ultimate consumers, such as defining target markets, understanding buying behavior, and developing effective marketing mixes, but we devote a complete chapter to business marketing because there are structural and behavioral differences in business markets. A company that markets to another company must understand how its product will affect other firms in the marketing channel, such as resellers and other manufacturers. Business products can also be technically complex, and the market often consists of sophisticated buyers.

Because the business market consists of relatively smaller customer populations, a segment of the market could be as small as a few customers.[2] The market for railway equipment in the United States, for example, is limited to a few major carriers. On the other hand, a business product can be a commodity, such as corn or a bolt or screw, but the quantity purchased and the buying methods differ significantly from the consumer market. Business marketing is often based on long-term mutually profitable relationships across members of the marketing channel. Networks of suppliers and customers recognize the importance of building strong alliances based on cooperation, trust, and collaboration.[3] Manufacturers may even co-develop new products, with business customers sharing marketing research, production, scheduling, inventory management, and information systems. Although business marketing can be based on collaborative long-term buyer-seller relationships, there are also transactions based on timely exchanges of basic products at highly competitive market prices. For most business marketers, the goal is understanding customer needs and providing a value-added exchange that shifts from attracting customers to keeping customers and developing relationships.

The four categories of business markets are producer, reseller, government, and institutional. In the remainder of this section, we discuss each of these types of markets.

Producer Markets

Individuals and business organizations that purchase products for the purpose of making a profit by using them to produce other products or using them in their operations are classified as **producer markets**. Producer markets include buyers of raw materials, as well as purchasers of semifinished and finished items, used to produce other products. For instance, manufacturers buy raw materials and component parts for direct use in product production. Grocery stores and supermarkets are part of producer markets for numerous support products such as paper and plastic bags, shelves, counters, and scanners. Farmers are part of producer markets for farm machinery, fertilizer, seed, and livestock. Producer markets include a broad array of industries ranging from

business market Individuals, organizations, or groups that purchase a specific kind of product for resale, direct use in producing other products, or use in general daily operations

producer markets Individuals and business organizations that purchase products to make profits by using them to produce other products or using them in their operations

agriculture, forestry, fisheries, and mining to construction, transportation, communications, and utilities. As Table 8.1 indicates, the number of business establishments in national producer markets is enormous.

Manufacturers are geographically concentrated. More than half are located in just seven states: New York, California, Pennsylvania, Illinois, Ohio, New Jersey, and Michigan. This concentration sometimes enables businesses that sell to producer markets to serve them more efficiently. Within certain states, production in a specific industry may account for a sizable proportion of that industry's total production.

Reseller Markets

Reseller markets consist of intermediaries, such as wholesalers and retailers, which buy finished goods and resell them for a profit. Aside from making minor alterations, resellers do not change the physical characteristics of the products they handle. Except for items producers sell directly to consumers, all products sold to consumer markets are first sold to reseller markets.

Wholesalers purchase products for resale to retailers, other wholesalers, producers, governments, and institutions. Arrow Electronics, for example, buys computer chips and other electronics components and resells them to producers of subsystems for cell phones, computers, and automobiles. Of the 429,952 wholesalers in the United States, a large number are located in New York, California, Illinois, Texas, Ohio, Pennsylvania, New Jersey, and Florida.[4] Although some products are sold directly to end users, many manufacturers sell their products to wholesalers, which in turn sell the products to other firms in the distribution system. Thus, wholesalers are very important in helping producers get products to customers. Professional buyers and buying committees make wholesalers' initial purchase decisions. Reordering is often automated.

Retailers purchase products and resell them to final consumers. There are approximately 1.1 million retailers in the United States, employing almost 16 million people and generating nearly $4 trillion in annual sales.[5] Half of the top ten largest retail companies in the world are based in the United States. These retailers include Walmart, Home Depot, The Kroger Co., Target, and Costco.[6] Some retailers—Home Depot, PetSmart, and Staples, for example—carry a large number of items. Supermarkets may handle as many as 50,000 different products. In small, individually owned retail stores, owners

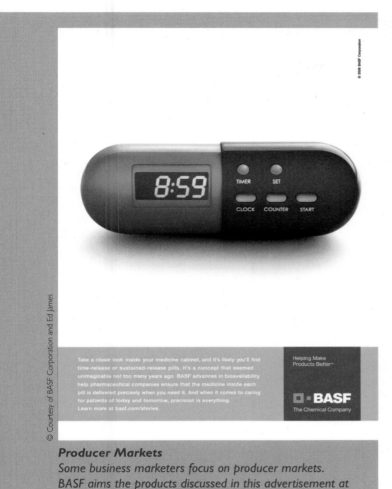

Take a closer look inside your medicine cabinet, and it's likely you'll find time-release or sustained-release pills. It's a concept that seemed unimaginable not too many years ago. BASF advances in bioavailability help pharmaceutical companies ensure that the medicine inside each pill is delivered precisely when you need it. And when it comes to caring for patients of today and tomorrow, precision is everything. Learn more at basf.com/stories

Helping Make Products Better™

□ ■ BASF
The Chemical Company

Producer Markets
Some business marketers focus on producer markets. BASF aims the products discussed in this advertisement at manufacturers of pharmaceutical products.

reseller markets
Intermediaries that buy finished goods and resell them for a profit

TABLE 8.1 Number of Establishments in Industry Groups

Industry	Number of Establishments
Forestry, fishing, hunting, and agriculture	23,600
Mining	26,200
Construction	802,300
Manufacturing	331,100
Transportation, warehousing, and utilities	232,300
Finance, insurance, and real estate	876,400

Source: U.S. Bureau of the Census, *Statistical Abstract of the United States, 2010* (www.census.gov/prod/2009pubs/10statab/business.pdf), Table 743.

Responsible Marketing?
For Mattel, Did Outsourcing Mean Out of Control?

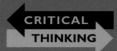 CRITICAL THINKING

ISSUE: Who should be held responsible?

Over the last decade, many U.S. manufacturers have joined the widely publicized trend of outsourcing to foreign countries for cheaper products to cut their costs, particularly in China. Many of the products made in China have an acceptable quality level, but some products do not and may even be unsafe. Can the country to which work is outsourced influence the consumers' ultimate purchasing decision?

During the summer of 2007, Mattel Toys had to recall nearly 1 million toys because the products were covered in paint that contained lead, a potential health hazard. Once the news hit the media, Mattel had to make countless public relations moves to try and maintain consumer confidence in its products. The products were made in factories in China, and public opinion regarding Chinese products has become rather shaky after several product recalls.

When manufacturing is outsourced to producers in another country, who should take responsibility? Should the Chinese take responsibility, or should the U.S. government share some of the blame? How much is the cost of losing a good reputation worth to companies that want to cut costs through outsourcing? Can the cost of a tarnished reputation more than offset the cost savings associated with outsourcing production?[a]

or managers make purchasing decisions. In chain stores, a central office buyer or buying committee frequently decides whether a product will be made available for selection by store managers. For most products, however, local managers make the actual buying decisions for a particular store.

When making purchase decisions, resellers consider several factors. They evaluate the level of demand for a product to determine in what quantity and at what prices the product can be resold. Retailers assess the amount of space required to handle a product relative to its potential profit, sometimes on the basis of sales per square foot of selling area. Because customers often depend on resellers to have products available when needed, resellers typically appraise a supplier's ability to provide adequate quantities when and where wanted. Resellers also take into account the ease of placing orders and the availability of technical assistance and training programs from producers. When resellers consider buying a product not previously carried, they try to determine whether the product competes with or complements products they currently handle. These types of concerns distinguish reseller markets from other markets.

Government Markets

government markets
Federal, state, county, or local governments that buy goods and services to support their internal operations and provide products to their constituencies

Federal, state, county, and local governments make up **government markets**. These markets spend billions of dollars annually for a variety of goods and services, ranging from office supplies and health care services to vehicles, heavy equipment, and weapons, to support their internal operations and provide citizens with such products as highways, education, water, energy, and national defense. The federal government spends more than $570 billion annually on national defense alone. Government expenditures annually account for about 21 percent of the U.S. gross domestic product.[7] Besides the federal government, there are 50 state governments, 3,033 county governments, and 86,443 local governments.[8] The amount spent by federal, state, and local units during the last 30 years has increased rapidly because the total number of government units, and the services they provide have both increased. Costs of providing these services have also risen.

Government contracts are awarded to firms of all sizes and across a wide variety of industries. One example is Nashville-based Film House, a firm that specializes in TV commercials and film production. For more than 10 years, Film House has been granted government contracts to produce TV and radio spot announcements for the American Forces Radio and Television Service.[9] Although it is common to hear of large corporations being awarded government contracts, in fact businesses of all sizes market to government agencies.

Because government agencies spend public funds to buy the products needed to provide services, they are accountable to the public. This accountability explains their relatively complex set of buying procedures. Some firms do not even try to sell to government buyers because they want to avoid the tangle of red tape. However, many marketers have learned to deal efficiently with government procedures and do not find them to be a stumbling block. For certain products, such as defense-related items, the government may be the only customer. The U.S. Government Printing Office publishes and distributes several documents that explain buying procedures and describe the types of products various federal agencies purchase.

Governments make purchases through bids or negotiated contracts. Although companies may be reluctant to approach government markets because of the complicated bidding process, once they understand the rules of this process, some firms routinely penetrate government markets. To make a sale under the bid system, firms must apply and be approved for placement on a list of qualified bidders. When a government unit wants to buy, it sends out a detailed description of the products to qualified bidders. Businesses that want to sell such products submit bids. The government unit is usually required to accept the lowest bid.

When buying nonstandard or highly complex products, a government unit often uses a negotiated contract. Under this procedure, the government unit selects only a few firms and then negotiates specifications and terms; it eventually awards the contract to one of the negotiating firms. Most large defense-related contracts, once held by such companies as McDonnell Douglas and General Dynamics, traditionally were negotiated in this fashion. However, as the number and size of such contracts have declined, these companies have had to strengthen their marketing efforts and look to other markets. Although government markets can impose intimidating requirements, they can also be very lucrative.

Institutional Markets

Organizations with charitable, educational, community, or other nonbusiness goals constitute **institutional markets**. Members of institutional markets include churches, some hospitals, fraternities and sororities, charitable organizations, and private colleges. Institutions purchase millions of dollars' worth of products annually to provide goods, services, and ideas to congregations, students, patients, and others. Because institutions often have different goals and fewer resources than other types of organizations, marketers may use special marketing efforts to serve them. For example, Hussey Seating in Maine sells stadium seating to schools, colleges, churches, and other institutions, as well as to sports arenas around the world. The family-owned business shows its support for institutional customers through assistance with school funding and reduced-cost construction of local economic development projects.

Dimensions of Marketing to Business Customers

Now that we have considered different types of business customers, we look at several dimensions of marketing to them, including transaction characteristics, attributes of business customers and some of their primary concerns, buying methods, major types of purchases, and the characteristics of demand for business products (see Figure 8.1).

Characteristics of Transactions with Business Customers

Transactions between businesses differ from consumer sales in several ways. Orders by business customers tend to be much larger than individual consumer sales. Consider that Fiji's Air Pacific placed an order for three Boeing 787-9 Dreamliner passenger jet aircrafts at an estimated cost of $580 million. Combined with a recent order of five Dreamliner aircrafts, Air Pacific's total Boeing order amounts to $1.5 billion, the largest transaction ever undertaken by a Fijian company. Suppliers often must sell products in

institutional markets
Organizations with charitable, educational, community, or other nonbusiness goals

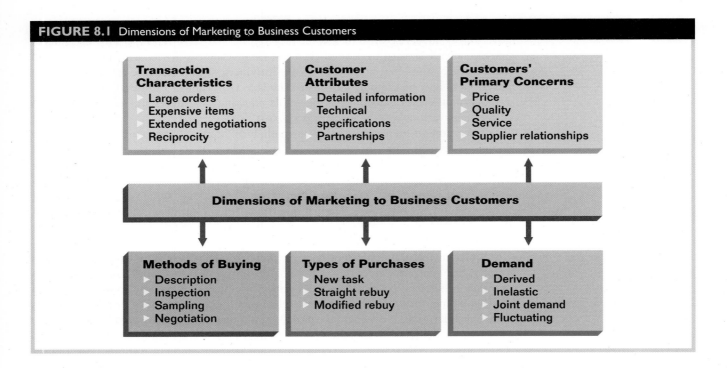

FIGURE 8.1 Dimensions of Marketing to Business Customers

Transaction Characteristics
- Large orders
- Expensive items
- Extended negotiations
- Reciprocity

Customer Attributes
- Detailed information
- Technical specifications
- Partnerships

Customers' Primary Concerns
- Price
- Quality
- Service
- Supplier relationships

Dimensions of Marketing to Business Customers

Methods of Buying
- Description
- Inspection
- Sampling
- Negotiation

Types of Purchases
- New task
- Straight rebuy
- Modified rebuy

Demand
- Derived
- Inelastic
- Joint demand
- Fluctuating

large quantities to make profits; consequently they prefer not to sell to customers who place small orders. For example, Airborne Express competes successfully against FedEx and UPS by providing low-cost overnight delivery services primarily to businesses that buy such services in high volume.

Some business purchases involve expensive items, such as computer systems. Other products, such as raw materials and component items, are used continuously in production, and their supply may need frequent replenishing. The contract regarding terms of sale of these items is likely to be a long-term agreement.

Discussions and negotiations associated with business purchases can require considerable marketing time and selling effort. Purchasing decisions are often made by committee, orders are frequently large and expensive, and products may be custom built. Several people or departments in the purchasing organization are often involved. For example, one department expresses a need for a product, a second department develops the specifications, a third stipulates maximum expenditures, and a fourth places the order.

One practice unique to business markets is **reciprocity**, an arrangement in which two organizations agree to buy from each other. Reciprocal agreements that threaten competition are illegal. The Federal Trade Commission and the Justice Department take actions to stop anticompetitive reciprocal practices. Nonetheless, a certain amount of reciprocal activity occurs among small businesses and, to a lesser extent, among larger companies. Because reciprocity influences purchasing agents to deal only with certain suppliers, it can lower morale among agents and lead to less than optimal purchases.

Attributes of Business Customers

Business customers differ from consumers in their purchasing behavior because they are better informed about the products they purchase. They typically demand detailed information about a product's functional features and technical specifications to ensure that it meets their needs. Personal goals, however, may also influence business buying behavior. Most purchasing agents seek the psychological satisfaction that comes with organizational advancement and financial rewards. Agents who consistently exhibit rational business buying behavior are likely to attain these personal goals because they help their firms achieve organizational objectives. Today many suppliers and their customers build and maintain mutually beneficial relationships, sometimes called *partnerships*.

reciprocity An arrangement unique to business marketing in which two organizations agree to buy from each other

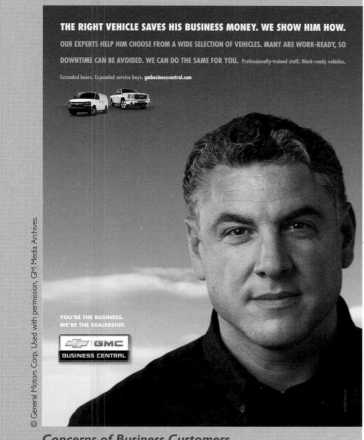

THE RIGHT VEHICLE SAVES HIS BUSINESS MONEY. WE SHOW HIM HOW.

OUR EXPERTS HELP HIM CHOOSE FROM A WIDE SELECTION OF VEHICLES. MANY ARE WORK-READY, SO DOWNTIME CAN BE AVOIDED. WE CAN DO THE SAME FOR YOU. Professionally-trained staff. Work-ready vehicles.

Extended hours. Expanded service bays. gmbusinesscentral.com

YOU'RE THE BUSINESS.
WE'RE THE DEALERSHIP.

GMC
BUSINESS CENTRAL

Concerns of Business Customers
Business customers are concerned about numerous factors, including cost and getting the right product that works effectively.

Researchers find that even in a partnership between a small vendor and a large corporate buyer, a strong partnership exists because high levels of interpersonal trust can lead to higher levels of commitment to the partnership by both organizations.[10]

Primary Concerns of Business Customers

When making purchasing decisions, business customers take into account a variety of factors. Among their chief considerations are price, product quality, service, and supplier relationships. Obviously, price matters greatly to business customers because it influences operating costs and costs of goods sold, which in turn affect selling price, profit margin, and ultimately the ability to compete. When purchasing major equipment, a business customer views price as the amount of investment necessary to obtain a certain level of return or savings. A business customer is likely to compare the price of a product with the benefits the product will yield to the organization, often over a period of years.

Most business customers try to achieve and maintain a specific level of quality in the products they buy. To achieve this goal, most firms establish standards (usually stated as a percentage of defects allowed) for these products and buy them on the basis of a set of expressed characteristics, commonly called *specifications*. A customer evaluates the quality of the products being considered to determine whether they meet specifications. If a product fails to meet specifications or malfunctions for the ultimate consumer, the customer may drop that product's supplier and switch to a different one. On the other hand, customers are ordinarily cautious about buying products that exceed specifications because such products often cost more, thus increasing the organization's overall costs. Specifications are designed to meet a customer's wants, and anything that does not contribute to meeting those wants may be considered wasteful.

Business buyers value service. Services offered by suppliers directly and indirectly influence customers' costs, sales, and profits. In some instances, the mix of customer services is the major means by which marketers gain a competitive advantage. Procter & Gamble, for example, provided Wendy's International with customized videos and laminated guides to show Wendy's employees how to use its industrial cleaning supplies to clean every part of each restaurant. Typical services customers desire are market information, inventory maintenance, on-time delivery, and repair services. Business buyers are likely to need technical product information, data regarding demand, information about general economic conditions, or supply and delivery information. Maintaining adequate inventory is critical because it helps make products accessible when a customer needs them and reduces the customer's inventory requirements and costs. Because business customers are usually responsible for ensuring that products are on hand and ready for use when needed, on-time delivery is crucial. Furthermore, reliable, on-time delivery saves business customers money because it enables them to carry less inventory. Purchasers of machinery are especially concerned about obtaining repair services and replacement parts quickly because inoperable equipment is costly. Caterpillar Inc., manufacturer of earth-moving, construction, and materials-handling machinery, has built an international reputation, as well as a competitive advantage, by providing prompt service and replacement parts for its products around the world.[11]

Quality of service is a critical issue because customer expectations about service have broadened. Using traditional service quality standards based only on traditional manufacturing and accounting systems is not enough. Communication channels that allow customers to ask questions, voice complaints, submit orders, and trace shipments are indispensable components of service. Marketers should strive for uniformity of service, simplicity, truthfulness, and accuracy. They should also develop customer service objectives and monitor customer service programs. Firms can monitor service by formally surveying customers or informally calling on customers and asking questions about the service they receive. Expending the time and effort to ensure that customers are happy can greatly benefit marketers by increasing customer retention.

Finally, business customers are concerned about the costs of developing and maintaining relationships with their suppliers. By developing relationships and building trust with a particular supplier, buyers can reduce their search efforts and uncertainty about monetary prices. Research also demonstrates that satisfaction and perceived product quality in B2B relationships foster loyalty and future purchase intentions. Business customers have to keep in mind the overall fit of a purchase, including its potential to reduce inventory and carrying costs, as well as to increase inventory turnover and ability to move the right products to the right place at the right time.

Methods of Business Buying

Although no two business buyers do their jobs the same way, most use one or more of the following purchase methods: *description, inspection, sampling,* and *negotiation.* When products are standardized according to certain characteristics (such as size, shape, weight, and color) and graded using such standards, a business buyer may be able to purchase simply by describing or specifying quantity, grade, and other attributes. Agricultural products often fall into this category. Sometimes buyers specify a particular brand or its equivalent when describing the desired product. Purchases on the basis of description are especially common between a buyer and seller with an ongoing relationship built on trust.

Sustainable Marketing
Can We Help Kids by Day and Kill Trees by Night?

Manufacturers, resellers, government agencies, and institutions expect their business purchases to help (or at least not hurt) their bottom lines. When economic times are tough, budgets get even tighter. Green products often carry a higher upfront cost than traditional products. So are business customers looking to go green these days?

The answer, in a word, is "yes." For one thing, businesses are successful only when they meet the needs of their customers. Now that eco-conscious consumers are actively seeking out green products, resellers such as Home Depot are responding to the higher demand by buying and stocking such items. This, in turn, builds demand for materials and components that come from renewable sources or include recycled content.

Just as important, many business customers have socially responsible reasons for buying green. Christel House, a not-for-profit organization that operates learning centers for children in poor communities, is buying printed materials that are environmentally-friendly. "We can't help kids by day and kill trees by night," says a development associate.

Finally, business customers understand that buying green will, over time, save money as well as the planet. Darden Restaurants, which owns Red Lobster and Olive Garden, recently bought 24,000 energy-efficient light bulbs for its 1,800 U.S. restaurants. Because the bulbs require 80 percent less electricity than incandescent bulbs, Darden saves big on its energy bills while giving sustainability a big boost.[b]

Certain products, such as industrial equipment, used vehicles, and buildings, have unique characteristics and may vary with regard to condition. For example, a particular used truck may have a bad transmission. Consequently, business buyers of such products must base purchase decisions on inspection.

Sampling entails taking a specimen of the product from the lot and evaluating it on the assumption that its characteristics represent the entire lot. This method is appropriate when the product is homogeneous—for instance, grain—and examining the entire lot is not physically or economically feasible.

Some purchases by businesses are based on negotiated contracts. In certain instances, buyers describe exactly what they need and ask sellers to submit bids. They then negotiate with the suppliers that submit the most attractive bids. This approach may be used when acquiring commercial vehicles, for example. In other cases, the buyer may be unable to identify specifically what is to be purchased and can provide only a general description, as might be the case for a piece of custom-made equipment. A buyer and seller might negotiate a contract that specifies a base price and provides for the payment of additional costs and fees. These contracts are most commonly used for onetime projects such as buildings, capital equipment, and special projects.

Types of Business Purchases

Most business purchases are one of three types: new-task, straight rebuy, or modified rebuy purchase. Each type is subject to different influences and thus requires business marketers to modify their selling approaches appropriately.[12] For a **new-task purchase**, an organization makes an initial purchase of an item to be used to perform a new job or solve a new problem. A new-task purchase may require development of product specifications, vendor specifications, and procedures for future purchases of that product. To make the initial purchase, the business buyer usually needs much information. New-task purchases are important to suppliers because if business buyers are satisfied with the products, suppliers may be able to sell buyers large quantities of them for many years.

A **straight rebuy purchase** occurs when buyers purchase the same products routinely under approximately the same terms of sale. Buyers require little information for these routine purchase decisions and tend to use familiar suppliers that have provided satisfactory service and products in the past. These marketers try to set up automatic reordering systems to make reordering easy and convenient for business buyers. A supplier may even monitor the business buyer's inventories and indicate to the buyer what should be ordered and when.

For a **modified rebuy purchase**, a new-task purchase is changed the second or third time it is ordered, or requirements associated with a straight rebuy purchase are modified. A business buyer might seek faster delivery, lower prices, or a different quality level of product specifications. A modified rebuy situation may cause regular suppliers to become more competitive to keep the account since other suppliers could obtain the business. When a firm changes the terms of a service contract, such as for telecommunication services, it has made a modified purchase.

Demand for Business Products

Unlike consumer demand, demand for business products (also called *industrial demand*) can be characterized as (1) derived, (2) inelastic, (3) joint, or (4) fluctuating.

new-task purchase An organization's initial purchase of an item to be used to perform a new job or solve a new problem

straight rebuy purchase A routine purchase of the same products under approximately the same terms of sale by a business buyer

modified rebuy purchase A new-task purchase that is changed on subsequent orders or when the requirements of a straight rebuy purchase are modified

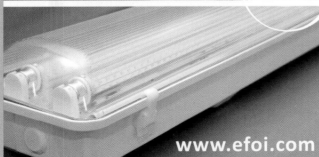

© AP Images/PRNewsFoto/Energy Focus, Inc.

Types of Business Purchases
When purchasing this type of equipment, business buyers are likely to use rebuy or modified rebuy.

DERIVED DEMAND

Because business customers, especially producers, buy products for direct or indirect use in the production of goods and services to satisfy consumers' needs, the demand for business products derives from the demand for consumer products; it is therefore called **derived demand**. In the long run, no demand for business products is totally unrelated to the demand for consumer products. The derived nature of demand is usually multilevel. Business marketers at different levels are affected by a change in consumer demand for a particular product. For instance, consumers have become concerned with health and good nutrition and, as a result, are purchasing more products with less fat, cholesterol, and sodium. When consumers reduced their purchases of high-fat foods, a change occurred in the demand for products marketed by food processors, equipment manufacturers, and uppliers of raw materials associated with these products. Change in consumer demand for a product affects demand for all firms involved in the production of that product.

INELASTIC DEMAND

With **inelastic demand**, a price increase or decrease will not significantly alter demand for a business product. Because some business products contain a number of parts, price increases that affect only one or two parts may yield only a slightly higher per-unit production cost. When a sizable price increase for a component represents a large proportion of the product's cost, demand may become more elastic because the price increase in the component causes the price at the consumer level to rise sharply. For example, if aircraft engine manufacturers substantially increase the price of engines, forcing Boeing to raise the prices of the aircraft it manufactures, the demand for airliners may become more elastic as airlines reconsider whether they can afford to buy new aircraft. An increase in the price of windshields, however, is unlikely to greatly affect either the price of or the demand for airliners.

Inelasticity applies only to industry demand for business products, not to the demand an individual firm faces. Suppose a spark plug producer increases the price of spark plugs sold to small-engine manufacturers, but its competitors continue to maintain lower prices. The spark plug company will probably experience reduced unit sales because most small-engine producers will switch to lower-priced brands. A specific firm is vulnerable to elastic demand, even if industry demand for a specific business product is inelastic.

JOINT DEMAND

Demand for certain business products, especially raw materials and components, is subject to joint demand. **Joint demand** occurs when two or more items are used in combination to produce a product. Consider a firm that manufactures axes. The firm will need the same number of ax handles as it does ax blades; these two products thus are demanded jointly. If a shortage of ax handles exists, the producer buys fewer ax blades. Understanding the effects of joint demand is particularly important for a marketer that sells multiple jointly demanded items. Such a marketer realizes that when a customer begins purchasing one of the jointly demanded items, a good opportunity exists to sell related products.

FLUCTUATING DEMAND

Because the demand for business products is derived from consumer demand, it may fluctuate enormously. In general, when particular consumer products are in high demand, their producers buy large quantities of raw materials and

derived demand Demand for business products that stems from demand for consumer products

inelastic demand Demand that is not significantly altered by a price increase or decrease

joint demand Demand involving the use of two or more items in combination to produce a product

© Hewlett Packard Company

Derived Demand
Intel attempts to generate derived demand by promoting that its products are inside the computers made by companies like HP. The sale of computers made by HP and other companies generates demand for Intel products.

Steelcase Wants to Keep Business Customers Healthy

Steelcase received its first patent in 1914 for a steel wastebasket, marketed as a solution to the common business problem of straw wastebaskets catching on fire. Today they are finding solutions to help businesses create office environments that enhance efficiency. Knowing that employee health is a growing concern, Steelcase's marketing experts worked with a doctor at Mayo Clinic to develop a line of office furniture that helps office workers get (or stay) in shape. The Walkstation consists of an adjustable desk and computer workstation attached to a treadmill (matching chair is optional)! Steelcase's CEO asks one key question over and over again of his marketing experts: "What's the user insight that led to this product?"[c]

components to ensure meeting long-run production requirements. In addition, these producers may expand production capacity, which entails acquiring new equipment and machinery, more workers, and more raw materials and component parts. Conversely, a decline in demand for certain consumer goods significantly reduces demand for business products used to produce those goods. For example, Nucor, America's largest steel maker, has experienced smaller product losses compared to other steel makers during the recession when demand for its products decreased. Because its electric furnaces can be turned on and off quicker, the company wastes less energy by turning the furnaces off when demand fluctuates, and they are not in use.[13]

Marketers of business products may notice changes in demand when customers alter inventory policies, perhaps because of expectations about future demand. For example, if several dishwasher manufacturers that buy timers from one producer increase their inventory of timers from a two-week to a one-month supply, the timer producer will have a significant, immediate increase in demand.

Sometimes, price changes lead to surprising temporary changes in demand. A price increase for a business product may initially cause business customers to buy more of the item because they expect the price to rise further. Similarly, demand for a business product may decrease significantly following a price cut because buyers are waiting for further price reductions. Fluctuations in demand can be substantial in industries in which prices change frequently.

Virtual Trade Shows: Everything But the Jet Lag and Freebies

In every industry, trade shows bring business buyers and suppliers together for a few days of face-to-face meetings and product demonstrations. During a show, buyers visit suppliers' booths in search of goods and services to solve business problems or for use in business operations. Meanwhile, suppliers have new opportunities to learn about business buyers' challenges and purchasing plans.

Increasingly, however, trade shows are going virtual. Instead of paying to travel to a show and walking down aisle after aisle to see all the suppliers, buyers can log on from any home or office computer, mouse around the interactive exhibitors' hall, and attend online seminars or product demonstrations. Such shows are cost-effective for suppliers as well, because they eliminate travel expenses and because the digital materials used to "build" virtual booths can be reused in show after show.

Sony Electronics uses virtual trade shows to introduce its professional broadcasting equipment to buyers for television stations, movie studios, and video production companies. To personalize the experience, Sony representatives and show attendees upload photos of themselves, which appear on screen as they "chat" about products. IBM often conducts virtual trade

shows and product demonstrations in Second Life, a virtual world where attendees and exhibitors interact as avatars.

To promote their participation in virtual trade shows, many B2B marketers link their booths to social media sites such as LinkedIn, Facebook, and YouTube. Before, during, and after a show, buyers are encouraged to access marketing messages, watch product videos, and click to contact suppliers when they're ready to buy.[d]

Business Buying Decisions

Business (organizational) buying behavior refers to the purchase behavior of producers, government units, institutions, and resellers. Although several factors that affect consumer buying behavior (discussed in the previous chapter) also influence business buying behavior, a number of factors are unique to the latter. In this section, we first analyze the buying center to learn who participates in business purchase decisions. Then we focus on the stages of the buying decision process and the factors that affect it.

The Buying Center

Relatively few business purchase decisions are made by just one person; often they are made through a buying center. The **buying center** is the group of people within the organization who make business purchase decisions. They include users, influencers, buyers, deciders, and gatekeepers.[14] One person may perform several roles. These participants share some goals and risks associated with their decisions.

Users are the organizational members who actually use the product being acquired. They frequently initiate the purchase process and/or generate purchase specifications. After the purchase, they evaluate product performance relative to the specifications.

Influencers are often technical personnel, such as engineers, who help develop the specifications and evaluate alternative products. Technical personnel are especially important influencers when the products being considered involve new, advanced technology.

Buyers select suppliers and negotiate terms of purchase. They may also become involved in developing specifications. Buyers are sometimes called purchasing agents or purchasing managers. Their choices of vendors and products, especially for new-task purchases, are heavily influenced by people occupying other roles in the buying center. For straight rebuy purchases, the buyer plays a major role in vendor selection and negotiations.

Deciders actually choose the products. Although buyers may be deciders, it is not unusual for different people to occupy these roles. For routinely purchased items, buyers are commonly deciders. However, a buyer may not be authorized to make purchases that exceed a certain dollar limit, in which case higher-level management personnel are deciders.

Finally, gatekeepers, such as secretaries and technical personnel, control the flow of information to and among people who occupy other roles in the buying center. Buyers who deal directly with vendors also may be gatekeepers because they can control information flows. The flow of information from a supplier's sales representatives to users and influencers is often controlled by personnel in the purchasing department.

The number and structure of an organization's buying centers are affected by the organization's size and market position, the volume and types of products being purchased, and the firm's overall managerial philosophy regarding exactly who should be involved in purchase decisions. The size of a buying center is influenced by the stage of the buying decision process and by the type of purchase. The size of the buying center likely would be larger for a new-task purchase than for a straight rebuy. Varying goals among members of a buying center can have both positive and negative effects on the purchasing process.

A marketer attempting to sell to a business customer should determine who is in the buying center, the types of decisions each individual makes, and which individuals are most influential in the decision process. Because in some instances many people make up the buying center, marketers cannot feasibly contact all participants. Instead, they must be certain to contact a few of the most influential.

Stages of the Business Buying Decision Process

Like consumers, businesses follow a buying decision process. This process is summarized in the lower portion of Figure 8.2. In the first stage, one or more individuals recognize that a problem or need exists. Problem recognition may arise under a variety of circumstances—for instance, when machines malfunction or a firm modifies an existing product or introduces a new one. Individuals in the buying center, such as

business (organizational) buying behavior The purchase behavior of producers, government units, institutions, and resellers

buying center The people within an organization who make business purchase decisions

value analysis An evaluation of each component of a potential purchase

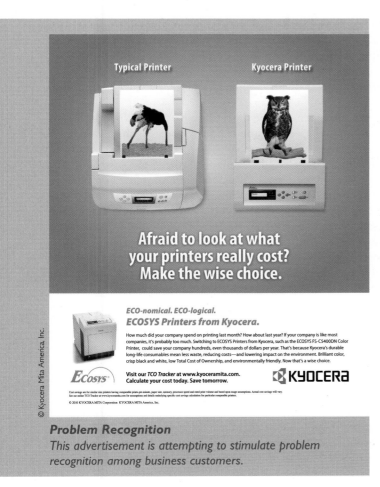

ECO-nomical. ECO-logical.
ECOSYS Printers from Kyocera.

Problem Recognition
This advertisement is attempting to stimulate problem recognition among business customers.

users, influencers, or buyers, may be involved in problem recognition, but it may be stimulated by external sources, such as sales representatives or advertisements.

The second stage of the process, development of product specifications, requires that buying center participants assess the problem or need and determine what is necessary to resolve or satisfy it. During this stage, users and influencers, such as engineers, often provide information and advice for developing product specifications. By assessing and describing needs, the organization should be able to establish product specifications.

Searching for and evaluating potential products and suppliers is the third stage in the decision process. Search activities may involve looking in company files and trade directories; contacting suppliers for information; soliciting proposals from known vendors; and examining websites, catalogs, and trade publications. To facilitate a vendor search, some organizations, such as Walmart, advertise their desire to build partnerships with specific types of vendors, such as those owned by women or by minorities. During this stage, some organizations engage in **value analysis**, an evaluation of each component of a potential purchase. Value analysis examines quality, design, materials, and possibly item reduction or deletion to acquire the product in the most cost-effective way. Some vendors may be deemed unacceptable because they are not large enough to supply needed quantities; others may be excluded because of poor delivery and service records. Sometimes the product is not available from any existing vendor and the buyer must find a company known for its

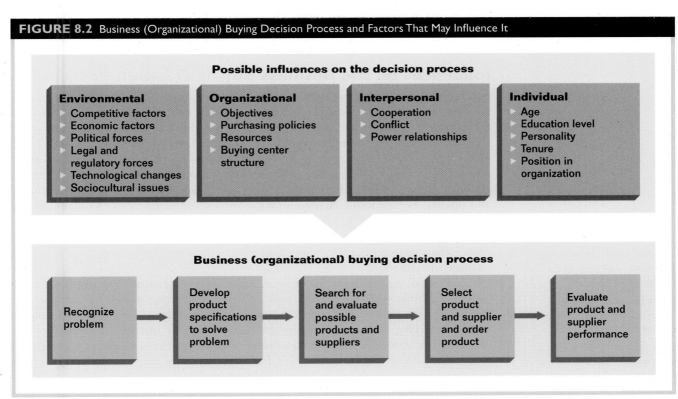

FIGURE 8.2 Business (Organizational) Buying Decision Process and Factors That May Influence It

innovation, such as 3M, to design and make it. Products are evaluated to make sure they meet or exceed product specifications developed in the second stage. Usually suppliers are judged according to multiple criteria. A number of firms employ **vendor analysis**, a formal, systematic evaluation of current and potential vendors, focusing on such characteristics as price, product quality, delivery service, product availability, and overall reliability.

Results of deliberations and assessments in the third stage are used during the fourth stage to select the product to be purchased and the supplier from which to buy it. In some cases, the buyer selects and uses several suppliers, a process known as **multiple sourcing**. At times, only one supplier is selected, a situation called **sole sourcing**. For instance, Barrick, a company based out of Japan, used a multiple sourcing approach to ensure its needs for tires for upcoming projects could be met despite the tire shortages the world was experiencing.[15] Firms with federal government contracts are required to have several sources for an item. Sole sourcing has traditionally been discouraged except when a product is available from only one company. Sole sourcing is much more common today, however, partly because such an arrangement means better communications between buyer and supplier, stability and higher profits for suppliers, and often lower prices for buyers. However, many organizations still prefer multiple sourcing because this approach lessens the possibility of disruption caused by strikes, shortages, or bankruptcies. The actual product is ordered in this fourth stage, and specific details regarding terms, credit arrangements, delivery dates and methods, and technical assistance are finalized.

During the fifth stage, the product's performance is evaluated by comparing it with specifications. Sometimes the product meets the specifications, but its performance fails to adequately solve the problem or satisfy the need recognized in the first stage. In that case, product specifications must be adjusted. The supplier's performance is also evaluated during this stage. If supplier performance is inadequate, the business purchaser seeks corrective action from the supplier or searches for a new one. Results of the evaluation become feedback for the other stages in future business purchase decisions.

This business buying decision process is used in its entirety primarily for new-task purchases. Several stages, but not necessarily all, are used for modified rebuy and straight rebuy situations.

Influences on the Business Buying Decision Process

Figure 8.2 also lists four major categories of factors that influence business buying decisions: environmental, organizational, interpersonal, and individual. Environmental factors include competitive and economic factors, political forces, legal and regulatory forces, technological changes, and sociocultural issues. These factors generate considerable uncertainty for an organization, which can make individuals in the buying center apprehensive about certain types of purchases. Changes in one or more environmental forces can create new purchasing opportunities and threats. For example, changes in competition and technology can make buying decisions difficult for products such as software, computers, and telecommunications equipment. On the other hand, many business marketers believe the Internet can reduce their customer service costs and allow firms to improve relationships with business customers.[16]

Organizational factors that influence the buying decision process include the company's objectives, purchasing policies, and resources, as well as the size and composition of its buying center. An organization may have certain buying policies to which buying center participants must conform. For instance, a firm's policies may mandate unusually long- or short-term contracts, perhaps longer or shorter than most sellers desire. An organization's financial resources may require special credit arrangements. Any of these conditions could affect purchase decisions.

vendor analysis A formal, systematic evaluation of current and potential vendors

multiple sourcing An organization's decision to use several suppliers

sole sourcing An organization's decision to use only one supplier

Business Markets Can Help Their Small-Business Customers during Tough Economic Times

During the recession, I took actions like having enough cash and reducing staff benefits.

46%   54%

My customers remained loyal during the recession.

Source: Huntington Bank survey of 200 small-business owners.

Interpersonal factors are the relationships among people in the buying center. Trust among all members of collaborative partnerships is crucial, particularly in purchases involving customized products.[17] The use of power and the level of conflict among buying center participants influence business buying decisions. Certain individuals in the buying center may be better communicators and more persuasive than others. Often these interpersonal dynamics are hidden, making them difficult for marketers to assess.

Individual factors are personal characteristics of participants in the buying center, such as age, education level, personality, and tenure and position in the organization. Consider a 55-year-old manager who has been in the organization for 25 years. This manager may affect decisions made by the buying center differently than a 30-year-old person employed only two years. How influential these factors are depends on the buying situation; the type of product being purchased; and whether the purchase is new-task, modified rebuy, or straight rebuy. Negotiating styles of people vary within an organization and from one organization to another. To be effective, marketers must know customers well enough to be aware of these individual factors and their potential effects on purchase decisions.

Using Industrial Classification Systems

Marketers have access to a considerable amount of information about potential business customers, since much of this information is available through government and industry publications and websites. Marketers use this information to identify potential business customers and to estimate their purchase potential.

Identifying Potential Business Customers

Much information about business customers is based on industrial classification systems. In the United States, marketers traditionally have relied on the *Standard Industrial Classification (SIC) system,* which the federal government developed to classify selected economic characteristics of industrial, commercial, financial, and service organizations. However, the SIC system has been replaced by a new industry classification system called the **North American Industry Classification System (NAICS).** NAICS is a single industry classification system used by the United States, Canada, and Mexico to generate comparable statistics among the three partners of the North American Free Trade Agreement (NAFTA). The NAICS classification is based on the types of production activities performed. NAICS is similar to the International Standard Industrial Classification (ISIC) system used in Europe and many other parts of the world. Whereas the SIC system divided industrial activity into 10 divisions, NAICS divides it into 20 sectors. NAICS contains 1,170 industry classifications, compared with 1,004 in the SIC system. NAICS is more comprehensive and up-to-date, and it provides considerably more information about service industries and high-tech products.[18] Table 8.2 shows some NAICS codes for Apple Inc. and AT&T Inc. Over the next few years, all three NAFTA countries will convert from previously used industrial classification systems to NAICS.

Industrial classification systems are ready-made tools that enable marketers to categorize organizations into groups based mainly on the types of goods and services

North American Industry Classification System (NAICS) An industry classification system that generates comparable statistics among the United States, Canada, and Mexico

TABLE 8.2 Examples of NAICS Classification

NAICS Hierarchy for AT&T, Inc.		NAICS Hierarchy for Apple, Inc.	
Sector 51	Information	Sector 31–33	Manufacturing
Subsector 517	Telecommunications	Subsector 334	Computer and Electronic Manufacturing
Industry Group 5171	Wired Telecommunication Carriers	Industry Group 3341	Computer and Peripheral Equipment Manufacturing
Industry Group 5172	Wireless Telecommunications Carriers		
Industry 51711	Wired Telecommunication Carriers	Industry 33411	Computer and Peripheral Equipment Manufacturing
Industry 51721	Wireless Telecommunications Carriers		
Industry 517110	Wired Telecommunication Carriers	U.S. Industry 334111	Electronic Computer Manufacturing
Industry 517210	Wireless Telecommunications Carriers		

Source: NAICS Association, www.census.gov/eos/www/naics/index.html (accessed April 7, 2010).

provided. Although an industrial classification system is a vehicle for segmentation, it is most appropriately used in conjunction with other types of data to determine exactly how many and which customers a marketer can reach.

Input–output analysis works well in conjunction with an industrial classification system. This type of analysis is based on the assumption that the output, or sales, of one industry are the input, or purchases, of other industries. **Input–output data** identify what types of industries purchase the products of a particular industry. A major source of national input–output data is the *Survey of Current Business,* published by the Office of Business Economics, U.S. Department of Commerce. After learning which industries purchase the major portion of an industry's output, the next step is to find the industrial classification numbers for those industries. Because firms are grouped differently in input–output tables and industrial classification systems, ascertaining industrial classification numbers can be difficult. However, the Office of Business Economics provides some limited conversion tables with input–output data. These tables can help marketers assign classification numbers to industry categories used in input–output analysis.

After determining the classification numbers of industries that buy the firm's output, a marketer is in a position to ascertain the number of organizations that are potential buyers. Government sources, such as the *Census of Business,* the *Census of Manufacturers,* and *County Business Patterns,* report the number of establishments, the value of industry shipments, the number of employees, the percentage of imports and exports, and industry growth rates within classifications. Commercial sources also provide information about organizations categorized by industrial classifications.

A marketer can take several approaches to determine the identities and locations of organizations in specific groups. One approach is to use state directories or commercial industrial directories, such as *Standard & Poor's Register* and Dun &

input–output data
Information that identifies what types of industries purchase the products of a particular industry

Bradstreet's *Million Dollar Directory*. These sources contain such information about a firm as its name, industrial classification, address, phone number, and annual sales. By referring to one or more of these sources, marketers isolate business customers with industrial classification numbers, determine their locations, and develop lists of potential customers by desired geographic area. A more expedient, although more expensive, approach is to use a commercial data service. Dun & Bradstreet, for example, can provide a list of organizations that fall into a particular industrial classification group. For each company on the list, Dun & Bradstreet gives the name, location, sales volume, number of employees, type of products handled, names of chief executives, and other pertinent information. Either method can effectively identify and locate a group of potential customers. However, a marketer probably cannot pursue all organizations on the list. Because some companies have greater purchasing potential than others, marketers must determine which customer or customer group to pursue.

Estimating Purchase Potential

To estimate the purchase potential of business customers or groups of customers, a marketer must find a relationship between the size of potential customers' purchases and a variable available in industrial classification data, such as the number of employees. For example, a paint manufacturer might attempt to determine the average number of gallons purchased by a specific type of potential customer relative to the number of employees. A marketer with no previous experience in this market segment will probably have to survey a random sample of potential customers to establish a relationship between purchase sizes and numbers of employees. Once this relationship is established, it can be applied to customer groups to estimate their potential purchases. After deriving these estimates, the marketer is in a position to select the customer groups with the most sales and profit potential.

Despite their usefulness, industrial classification data pose several problems. First, a few industries do not have specific designations. Second, because a transfer of products from one establishment to another is counted as a part of total shipments, double counting may occur when products are shipped between two establishments within the same firm. Third, because the Census Bureau is prohibited from providing data that identify specific business organizations, some data, such as value of total shipments, may be understated. Finally, because government agencies provide industrial classification data, a significant lag usually exists between data-collection time and the time the information is released.

summary

1. To be able to distinguish among the various types of business markets

Business (B2B) markets consist of individuals, organizations, and groups that purchase a specific kind of product for resale, direct use in producing other products, or use in day-to-day operations. Producer markets include those individuals and business organizations that purchase products for the purpose of making a profit by using them to produce other products or as part of their operations. Intermediaries that buy finished products and resell them to make a profit are classified as reseller markets. Government markets consist of federal, state, county, and local governments, which spend billions of dollars annually for goods and services to support internal operations and to provide citizens with needed services. Organizations with charitable, educational, community, or other nonprofit goals constitute institutional markets.

2. To identify the major characteristics of business customers and transactions

Transactions that involve business customers differ from consumer transactions in several ways. Such transactions tend to be larger, and negotiations occur less frequently, though they are often lengthy. They frequently involve more than one person or department in the purchasing organization. They may also involve reciprocity, an arrangement in which two organizations agree to buy from each other. Business customers are usually better informed than ultimate consumers and more likely to seek information about a product's features and technical specifications.

When purchasing products, business customers are particularly concerned about quality, service, price, and supplier relationships. Quality is important because it directly affects the quality of products the buyer's firm produces. To achieve an exact level of quality, organizations often buy products on the basis of a set of expressed characteristics, called specifications. Because services have such a direct influence on a firm's costs, sales, and profits, factors such as market information, on-time delivery, and availability of parts are crucial to a business buyer. Although business customers do not depend solely on price to decide which products to buy, price is of primary concern because it directly influences profitability.

Business buyers use several purchasing methods, including description, inspection, sampling, and negotiation. Most organizational purchases are new-task, straight rebuy, or modified rebuy. In a new-task purchase, an organization makes an initial purchase of items to be used to perform new jobs or solve new problems. In a modified rebuy purchase, a new-task purchase is changed the second or third time it is ordered or requirements associated with a straight rebuy purchase are modified. A straight rebuy purchase occurs when a buyer purchases the same products routinely under approximately the same terms of sale.

3. To understand several attributes of demand for business products

Industrial demand differs from consumer demand along several dimensions. Industrial demand derives from demand for consumer products. At the industry level, industrial demand is inelastic. If an industrial item's price changes, product demand will not change as much proportionally. Some industrial products are subject to joint demand, which occurs when two or more items are used in combination to make a product. Finally, because organizational demand derives from consumer demand, the demand for business products can fluctuate widely.

4. To become familiar with the major components of a buying center

Business (or organizational) buying behavior refers to the purchase behavior of producers, resellers, government units, and institutions. Business purchase decisions are made through a buying center, the group of people involved in making such purchase decisions. Users are those in the organization who actually use the product. Influencers help develop specifications and evaluate alternative products for possible use. Buyers select suppliers and negotiate purchase terms. Deciders choose the products. Gatekeepers control the flow of information to and among individuals occupying other roles in the buying center.

5. To understand the stages of the business buying decision process and the factors that affect this process

The stages of the business buying decision process are problem recognition, development of product specifications to solve problems, search for and evaluation of products and suppliers, selection and ordering of the most appropriate product, and evaluation of the product's and supplier's performance.

Four categories of factors influence business buying decisions: environmental, organizational, interpersonal, and individual. Environmental factors include competitive forces, economic conditions, political forces, laws and regulations, technological changes, and sociocultural factors. Business factors include the company's objectives, purchasing policies, and resources, as well as the size and composition of its buying center. Interpersonal factors are the relationships among people in the buying center. Individual factors are personal characteristics of members of the buying center, such as age, education level, personality, and tenure and position in the organization.

6. To describe industrial classification systems and explain how they can be used to identify and analyze business markets

Business marketers have a considerable amount of information available for use in planning marketing strategies. Much of this information is based on an industrial classification system, which categorizes businesses into major industry groups, industry subgroups, and detailed industry categories. An industrial classification system—like the North American Industry Classification System (NAICS) used by the United States, Canada, and Mexico—provides marketers with information needed to identify business customer groups. It can best be used for this purpose in conjunction with other information, such as input–output data. After identifying target industries, a marketer can obtain the names and locations of potential customers by using government and commercial data sources. Marketers then must estimate potential purchases of business customers by finding a relationship between a potential customer's purchases and a variable available in industrial classification data.

Go to www.cengagebrain.com for resources to help you master the content in this chapter as well as materials that will expand your marketing knowledge!

important terms

business market, 224

producer markets, 224

reseller markets, 225

government markets, 226

institutional markets, 227

reciprocity, 228

new-task purchase, 231

straight rebuy purchase, 231

modified rebuy purchase, 231

derived demand, 232

inelastic demand, 232

joint demand, 232

business (organizational) buying behavior, 234

buying center, 234

value analysis, 234

vendor analysis, 236

multiple sourcing, 236

sole sourcing, 236

North American Industry Classification System (NAICS), 237

input–output data, 238

discussion and review questions

1. Identify, describe, and give examples of the four major types of business markets.
2. Why might business customers generally be considered more rational in their purchasing behavior than ultimate consumers?
3. What are the primary concerns of business customers?
4. List several characteristics that differentiate transactions involving business customers from consumer transactions.
5. What are the commonly used methods of business buying?
6. Why do buyers involved in straight rebuy purchases require less information than those making new-task purchases?

7. How does demand for business products differ from consumer demand?
8. What are the major components of a firm's buying center?
9. Identify the stages of the business buying decision process. How is this decision process used when making straight rebuys?
10. How do environmental, business, interpersonal, and individual factors affect business purchases?
11. What function does an industrial classification system help marketers perform?
12. List some sources that a business marketer can use to determine the names and addresses of potential customers.

application questions

CRITICAL THINKING

1. Identify organizations in your area that fit each business market category: producer, reseller, government, and institutional. Explain your classifications.

2. Indicate the method of buying (description, inspection, sampling, or negotiation) an organization would be most likely to use when purchasing each of the following items. Defend your selections.
   a. A building for the home office of a light bulb manufacturer
   b. Wool for a clothing manufacturer
   c. An Alaskan cruise for a company retreat, assuming a regular travel agency is used
   d. One-inch nails for a building contractor

3. Purchases by businesses may be described as new-task, modified rebuy, or straight rebuy. Categorize the following purchase decisions and explain your choices.
   a. Bob has purchased toothpicks from Smith Restaurant Supply for 25 years and recently placed an order for yellow toothpicks rather than the usual white ones.

   b. Jill's investment company has been purchasing envelopes from AAA Office Supply for a year and now needs to purchase boxes to mail year-end portfolio summaries to clients. Jill calls AAA to purchase these boxes.
   c. Reliance Insurance has been supplying its salespeople with small personal computers to assist in their sales efforts. The company recently agreed to begin supplying them with faster, more sophisticated computers.

4. Identifying qualified customers is important to the survival of any organization. NAICS provides helpful information about many different businesses. Find the NAICS manual at the library or online at **www.naics.com** and identify the NAICS code for the following items.
   a. Chocolate candy bars
   b. Automobile tires
   c. Men's running shoes

internet exercise

Boeing

Boeing is the world's leading aerospace corporation and largest manufacturer of commercial and military aircraft.

Visit the company at **www.boeing.com**.

1. At what types of business markets are Boeing's products targeted?

2. How does Boeing address some of the concerns of business customers?

3. What environmental factors do you think affect demand for Boeing products?

developing your marketing plan

CRITICAL THINKING

When developing a marketing strategy for business customers, it is essential to understand the process the business goes through when making a buying decision. Knowledge of business buying behavior is important when developing several aspects of the marketing plan. To assist you in relating the information in this chapter to the creation of a marketing plan for business customers, consider the following issues:

1. What are the primary concerns of business customers? Could any of these concerns be addressed with strengths of your company?

2. Determine the type of business purchase your customer will likely be using when purchasing your product. How would this impact the level of information required by the business when moving through the buying decision process?

3. Discuss the different types of demand that the business customer will experience when purchasing your product.

The information obtained from these questions should assist you in developing various aspects of your marketing plan found in the *Interactive Marketing Plan* exercise at **www. cengagebrain.com**.

VIDEO CASE 8.1

Numi Tea Pours It on with Resellers

Tea, one of the oldest beverages in the world, is a growth industry these days. Served hot or cold, brewed in bags or using loose leaves, tea accounts for $10 billion in U.S. sales every year. Although the business is dominated by corporate giants such as Lipton, companies with unique tea products can compete quite effectively by connecting with key resellers.

Numi Tea of Oakland, California, is riding the wave of tea popularity in just this way. Founded in 1999 by the brother-and-sister team Ahmed and Reem Rahim, Numi markets only organic full-leaf teas. Many of its teas are Fair Trade certified, which means the growers in India, China, and South Africa are paid more than the usual market rate for their leaves. For environmental sustainability, Numi's gift boxes and store displays are made from fast-growing bamboo.

Numi's product offerings include tea bags, tea leaf mixtures, herbal teas, and accessories such as teapots and filters. One of its most unusual products is flowering tea. When a hand-sewn bundle of these black, white, or green tea leaves is dropped into boiling water, it releases its fragrant flavor as it expands into a pretty blossom shape. In addition, Numi runs a Tea Garden in downtown Oakland, furnished with eco-friendly materials and featuring Numi's organic teas plus an assortment of cheeses, fruits, and bakery items.

How did Numi bring its sales to a multimillion-dollar boil so quickly? From the start, the Rahims recognized that their company's growth depended on building long-term relationships with good wholesalers, retailers, and restaurants. Numi needed to educate resellers (and help them educate their customers) about the advantages of Numi's tea products. To do this, it created training materials for reseller employees and a series of informational tea cards for resellers to give to customers. It also developed colorful product highlight cards and displays for store shelves and restaurant tables, plus eye-catching posters and banners showcasing the brand.

Service is another important element of Numi's marketing strategy. The company has a brand ambassador who visits restaurants, wholesalers, and retailers to introduce new products and promotions, discuss point-of-purchase displays, conduct product demonstrations, and identify new sales opportunities. It also sends out newsletters and e-mails with product and promotion updates.

Rather than using a "one-size-fits-all" approach, Numi adapts its service to the differing needs of its various resellers. For instance, to help upscale restaurants make a good impression on their patrons, Numi provides handsome bamboo tea chests and boxes in which to present tea choices at table-side. Numi also makes glossy presentation folders in which luxury hotels can leave Numi tea bags in guest rooms as a special amenity. In addition, it helps its hotel and restaurant customers create custom menus and inserts that describe Numi's special teas in more detail.

For the convenience of its resellers, Numi offers a number of ordering options. Depending on the size of their order and where they are located, retailers can buy through a local wholesaler, Numi's website, or the wholesaler WorldPantry.com. To make it easy for consumers to find Numi retailers in the United States and Canada, the company's website includes a store locator function.

Careful attention to reseller relationships has helped Numi increase annual revenues beyond $13 million. No wonder it was recently named one of the fast-growing inner-city companies in America. More growth is ahead as the company expands distribution by intensifying its marketing to gourmet grocery stores, quality restaurants, and upscale hotels across North America.[19]

QUESTIONS FOR DISCUSSION

1. What important concerns might retailers and wholesalers have when making decisions about buying from Numi?
2. During vendor analysis, how much weight do you think a buyer for a high-end restaurant is likely to give Numi's service capabilities? Why?
3. How might local wholesalers react to the policy of allowing retailers to order directly from Numi's website?

CASE 8.2

Bombardier Serves Multiple Business Markets

CRITICAL THINKING

Bombardier is all about trains and planes. Founded by Joseph-Armand Bombardier in 1942, the company originally marketed snowmobiles for transportation through the wintry terrain of Canada's Quebec province. Among its earliest products were snowmobiles for delivering mail, shuttling students to and from schools, and moving commercial freight shipments. The company also served consumer markets through its Ski-Doo, a pioneer of the personal snowmobile industry, and its Sea-Doo, a pioneer of the personal water-craft industry.

Today, however, Bombardier's primary markets are governments and businesses that purchase aerospace and railroad-related products. For example, Bombardier markets its narrow-body jet-liners to commercial airlines. Republic Airways recently signed a $3 billion deal to buy 40 of the company's medium-range jets, with an option to buy another 40 in the future. To seal such sales, Bombardier emphasizes fuel efficiency, low operating costs, and other bottom-line benefits that airlines seek when buying new planes. Competition for orders is especially intense as the global economy recovers from recession and airlines plan ahead to replace the oldest models in their aging fleets. Depending on their needs, airlines may look at aircraft made by Airbus, Boeing, Embraer, Mitsubishi, or other competitors, not just at Bombardier's products. The exact configuration of each jet is customized airline by airline, which means every order represents a major investment of time, energy, and negotiation for buyer and seller alike.

Bombardier also markets corporate jets, under the brand names of Learjet, Challenger, and Global, to big businesses that fly executives from state to state, across the country, or halfway around the world. Because different businesses have different needs, Bombardier listens carefully to learn where and when the aircraft will be used. Business customers that don't need a jet standing by every day may be good prospects for other Bombardier offerings. If they anticipate using a jet for 50 or more flight hours per year, they can become part-owners of a plane through Bombardier's Flexjet program. If they occasionally need a private plane for specific trips, they may prefer Bombardier's Skyjet charter program.

Both commercial airlines and corporate buyers expect a high level of customer service when they purchase a new jet.

To meet their needs, Bombardier operates round-the-clock customer response centers staffed by specialists who understand each product inside and out, from engineering and technical systems to parts and supplies. When customers call, the company is ready to help get their planes back in the air as quickly as possible.

Government markets are the focus of Bombardier's rail transportation division. During the 1970s, with a global oil crisis hurting sales of gasoline-powered vehicles such as snowmobiles, Bombardier diversified by winning a large and lucrative contract to make subway trains for its headquarters city of Montreal. This paved the way for marketing to other municipalities who were expanding or modernizing their mass-transit systems. Now the company markets all manner of train and railway equipment, including passenger cars, high-speed locomotives, mass-transit systems, signal and control mechanisms, and railway-related maintenance and services.

Rail transportation is booming these days as countries and urban centers upgrade their infrastructures. Although no two government buyers have exactly the same requirements, Bombardier knows that quality, reliability, safety, and price are always major concerns in such purchases. Therefore, to compete with General Electric, Siemens, and other rivals, the company showcases its manufacturing expertise and points with pride to its many satisfied customers worldwide. Sustainability is an increasingly important factor for government buyers as well. "Everybody accepts that rail transportation is an eco-friendly way to move people in large cities," says Bombardier's CEO. As a result, Bombardier's marketing communicates that the firm's new energy-efficient, low-emission rail products have been designed with the environment in mind.

Knowing that business and government customers care about the reputation of their vendors, Bombardier requires all employees, managers, suppliers, and agents to follow its strict code of ethics and business conduct. Its social-responsibility initiatives include programs to reduce waste, conserve water and energy, and obtain electricity from renewable power sources. From its current level of $19 billion in annual sales and a workforce of 66,000 employees on five continents, Bombardier is poised for even better performance as its business marketing takes off.[20]

QUESTIONS FOR DISCUSSION

1. How does derived demand apply to the demand for commercial jets purchased by airlines? What are the implications for Bombardier's marketing efforts?

2. When an airline wants to order new jets to replace older jets in its fleet, do you think it would approach the decision as a new-task purchase, a straight rebuy, or a modified rebuy purchase? Explain. Also, which methods of business buying are Bombardier's customers most likely to use? Why?

3. In which stage of the business buying decision process is Bombardier's reputation likely to have the most influence on a government that is considering the purchase of new subway cars?

Chapter 9
Reaching Global Markets

OBJECTIVES

1. To understand the nature of global marketing strategy

2. To analyze the environmental forces that affect international marketing efforts

3. To understand several important international trade agreements

4. To identify methods of international market entry

5. To examine various forms of global organizational structures

6. To examine the use of the marketing mix internationally

Harley Rides into India

Hitting the open road on a Harley has been an American dream since 1903, and now consumers in India can share the dream as well. Harley-Davidson has been interested in entering the Indian market for several years, but government restrictions and high tariffs held it back. In 2007, a deal involving the United States and India changed Indian emissions restrictions and opened the door for Harley's entry.

In 2010, Harley began selling 12 models in India, the least expensive priced at $15,000 (almost twice what U.S. customers pay). Although India is the second-largest motorcycle market worldwide, most Indians favor cheaper motorcycles and scooters priced under $1,000. However, because of India's growing economy, expanding middle class, and new highway construction, Harley is not worried about selling to Indian consumers. The company was also drawn to India's rapidly growing luxury market.

Harley's CEO, Keith Wandell, says the company is committed to making its entrance into India a long-term success. Harley imports its bikes into India fully assembled, avoiding the need for factories and other overhead. The company must pay high tariffs (roughly 90 percent) as well as Indian taxes. Harley also needs to pay special attention to strategic planning, taking into account the social, cultural, economic, political, and ethical forces within India. Harley is optimistic about its possibilities in India, and many Indian consumers are looking forward to owning Harley bikes.[1]

Technological advances and rapidly changing political and economic conditions are making it easier than ever for companies to market their products overseas as well as at home. With most of the world's population and two-thirds of total purchasing power outside the United States, international markets represent tremendous opportunities for growth. Accessing these markets can promote innovation, while intensifying global competition can spur companies to market better, less expensive products. MTV provides a potential viewing audience of more than 1.2 billion people through MTV's global network of 65 channels reaching 641 million households around the world. In terms of the interactive community and audience, MTV offers more than 200 digital media entities throughout the world.[2]

In deference to the increasingly global nature of marketing, we devote this chapter to the unique features of global markets and international marketing. We begin by considering the nature of global marketing strategy and the environmental forces that create opportunities and threats for international marketers. Next, we consider several regional trade alliances, markets, and agreements. Then we examine the modes of entry into international marketing and companies' degree of involvement in it, as well as some of the structures that can be used to organize multinational enterprises. Finally, we examine how firms may alter their marketing mixes when engaging in international marketing efforts. All of these factors must be considered in any marketing plan that includes an international component.

The Nature of Global Marketing Strategy

International marketing involves developing and performing marketing activities across national boundaries. For instance, Walmart has more than 2 million employees and operates more than 7,800 stores in 16 countries, including the United States, Brazil, and China; Starbucks serves tens of millions of customers a week at more than 16,000 shops in 50 countries.[3] American icon Jack Daniels now sells more cases of whiskey abroad than it does in its own backyard.[4]

international marketing
Developing and performing marketing activities across national boundaries

Firms are finding that international markets provide tremendous opportunities for growth. To encourage international growth, many countries offer significant practical assistance and valuable benchmarking research that will help their domestic firms become more competitive globally. One example is the benchmarking of best international practices that is conducted by the network of CIBERs—Centers for International Business Education and Research—at leading business schools in the United States. These 31 CIBERs are funded by the U.S. government to help U.S. firms become more competitive globally.[5] A major element of the assistance that these governmental organizations can provide for firms (especially small and medium-sized firms) is knowledge of the internationalization process of firms.

Traditionally, most companies—such as McDonald's and KFC—have entered the global marketplace incrementally as they gained knowledge about various markets and opportunities. Beginning in the 1990s, however, some firms—such as eBay, Google, and Logitech—were founded with the knowledge and resources to expedite their commitment and investment in the global marketplace. These "born globals"—typically small technology-based firms earning as much as 70 percent of their sales outside the domestic home market—export their products almost immediately after being established in market niches in which they compete with larger, more established firms.[6] Whether a firm adopts the traditional approach, the born global approach, or an approach that merges attributes of

Courtesy of Suzanna Bainbridge

International Marketing
As part of an extensive international marketing program, McDonald's releases Spanish-language advertisements.

both approaches to market products and services, international marketing strategy is a critical element of a firm's global operations. Today, global competition in most industries is intense and becoming increasingly fierce with the addition of newly emerging markets and firms.

Environmental Forces in Global Markets

Firms that enter international markets often find that they must make significant adjustments in their marketing strategies. The environmental forces that affect foreign markets may differ dramatically from those that affect domestic markets. It took McDonald's 14 years of intense negotiations before it was able to open its restaurants in Russia, but the past 20 years of operating restaurants in 60 Russian cities has been an enormous success. The first location in Russia was the Pushkin Square location, which remains the single busiest McDonald's in the world. When McDonald's entered Russia, the Soviet Union was falling apart, the economy was failing, and political tensions were high; despite all of this, McDonald's Russian restaurants were successful. Because of this past success, McDonald's is planning to spend an additional $135 million on restaurant expansion.[7] Thus, a successful international marketing strategy requires a careful environmental analysis. Conducting research to understand the needs and desires of international customers is crucial to global marketing success. Many firms have demonstrated that such efforts can generate tremendous financial rewards, increase market share, and heighten customer awareness of their products around the world. In this section, we explore how differences in the sociocultural; economic; political, legal, and regulatory; social and ethical; competitive; and technological forces in other countries can profoundly affect marketing activities.

Sociocultural Forces

Cultural and social differences among nations can have significant effects on marketing activities. Because marketing activities are primarily social in purpose, they are influenced by beliefs and values regarding family, religion, education, health, and recreation. By identifying major sociocultural deviations among countries, marketers lay groundwork for an effective adaptation of marketing strategy. In India, for instance, three-quarters of McDonald's menu was created to appeal to Indian tastes, including many vegetarian items, and it does not include pork or beef products at all. In Italy, where the quality of ingredients is very important, McDonald's created the McItaly burger. It features all locally grown ingredients such as Asiago cheese and artichokes. In spite of protests, the country's agricultural minister endorsed the concept because it will mean millions in increased revenues for struggling Italian farmers.[8]

Local preferences, tastes, and idioms can all prove complicated for international marketers. Although football is a popular sport in the United States and a major opportunity for many television advertisers, soccer is the most popular televised sport in Europe and Latin America. And, of course, marketing communications often must be translated into other languages. Sometimes, the true meaning of translated messages can be misinterpreted or lost. Consider some translations that went awry in foreign markets: KFC's long-running slogan "Finger lickin' good" was translated into Spanish as "Eat your fingers off," and Coors' "Turn it loose" campaign was translated into Spanish as "Drink Coors and get diarrhea."[9]

It can be difficult to transfer marketing symbols, trademarks, logos, and even products to international markets, especially if these are associated with objects that have profound religious or cultural significance in a particular culture. Gerber began marketing their baby food products in Africa and made minimal changes to the traditional packaging, showing the Gerber baby on the label. When baby food sales fell way below expectations, the company did some investigation and learned that because the literacy rate is low in many parts of Africa, it is customary to put a picture of what is in the container on the package. Many consumers were not buying the product because they thought Gerber was selling baby meat. Cultural differences may also affect marketing negotiations and decision-making behavior. Although U.S. and Taiwanese sales agents are equally sensitive to customer interests, research suggests that the Taiwanese are more sensitive to the interests of their companies and competitors and less attuned to the interests of colleagues. Identifying such differences in work-related values of employees across different nationalities helps companies design more effective sales management practices. Cultural differences in the emphasis placed on personal relationships, status, and decision-making styles have been known to complicate dealings between Americans and businesspeople from other countries. In many parts of Asia, a gift may be considered a necessary introduction before negotiation, whereas in the United States or Canada, a gift may be misconstrued as an illegal bribe.

Buyers' perceptions of other countries can influence product adoption and use. Multiple research studies have found that consumer preferences for products depend on both the country of origin and the product category of competing products.[10] When people are unfamiliar with products from another country, their perceptions of the country as a whole may affect their attitude toward the product and influence whether they will buy it. If a country has a reputation for producing quality products and therefore has a positive image in consumers' minds, marketers of products from that country will want to make the country of origin well known. For example, a generally favorable image of Western computer technology has fueled sales of U.S.-made Dell, Apple, and Microsoft computers and software in Japan. On the other hand, marketers may want to dissociate themselves from a particular country in order to build a brand's reputation as truly global or because a country does not have a good reputation for quality. Because China has had issues with product safety in the past, companies that produce toys or medicines, for example, may not want to advertise that their products are made in China. The extent to which a product's brand image and country of origin influence purchases is subject to considerable variation based on national culture characteristics.

When products are introduced from one nation into another, acceptance is far more likely if similarities exist between the two cultures. In fact, many similar cultural characteristics exist across countries. For international marketers, cultural differences have implications for product development, advertising, packaging, and pricing. When the original Mini automobile was introduced in England in 1959, its dimensions were 10 feet in length, 4 feet in width, and 4 feet in height. Although BMW was reluctant to export the car to the United States, they gave it a try in 2002 and were surprised that Americans who drove SUVs, trucks, and mini-vans were very interested in the Mini. The United States now represents the largest market for Minis. In light of its surprising success and its desire to grow market share for the Mini in the United States, BMW is introducing the Countryman, a larger version of the Mini with comparable handling that will appeal to a potentially broader American audience.[11]

Cultural Differences

A U.K. ad to encourage the Queen to end the use of bear skin in the Queen's Guards' caps highlights how advocacy issues may be different from culture to culture.

Sustainable Marketing
China Is Going Green

China may have been slow on the environmental uptake, but it's now making up for lost time. As the largest producer worldwide of greenhouse gases, the country has a tough job ahead of it. To assist with this challenge, China recently established the Ministry of Environmental Protection. The government officials' goals are to clean up China's air and water and to establish the country as an alternative energy powerhouse.

In a short amount of time, China has implemented a wide variety of green initiatives. The country imposed tighter fuel efficiency standards than the United States, redesigned its coal plants for better filtration, suspended industrial development along its rivers, and launched a renewable energy program. In addition, China heavily fines CEOs responsible for dumping waste, requires utilities to purchase energy from renewable sources, has focused its car industry on electric and hybrid vehicles, sells carbon credits to fund renewable energy plants, and is working on perfecting clean coal technology.

However, some of China's green initiatives have met with criticism. The UN has accused China of accepting carbon credit funding for alternative energy programs that it would have implemented with or without carbon credit funding. This violates

the carbon credit sales requirements of the Kyoto Protocol, which are designed to assist countries otherwise unable to create alternative energy resources. Regardless, China is moving toward environmental stewardship. China has a difficult battle to fight, but with environmental concern growing daily, there is hope of progress.[a]

Economic Forces

Global marketers need to understand the international trade system, particularly the economic stability of individual nations, as well as trade barriers that may stifle marketing efforts. Economic differences among nations—differences in standards of living, credit, buying power, income distribution, national resources, exchange rates, and the like—dictate many of the adjustments firms must make in marketing internationally.

Instability is one of the guaranteed constants in the global business environment. The United States and the European Union are more stable economically than many other regions of the world. However, even these economies have downturns in regular cycles, one of which occurred in 2008–2009 during the worst global recession since the 1930s. A number of other countries, including Korea, Russia, Singapore, and Thailand, have all experienced economic problems such as depressions, high unemployment, corporate bankruptcies, instability in currency markets, trade imbalances, and financial systems that need major reforms. Even more stable developing countries, such as Mexico and Brazil, tend to have greater fluctuations in their business cycles than the United States does. Economic instability can disrupt the markets for U.S. products in places that otherwise might be excellent marketing opportunities. On the other hand, competition from the sustained economic growth of countries such as China and India can disrupt markets for U.S. products.

In terms of the value of all products produced by a nation, the United States has the largest gross domestic product in the world, more than $14 trillion in 2009.[12] **Gross domestic product (GDP)** is an overall measure of a nation's economic standing; it is the market value of a nation's total output of goods and services for a given period. However, it does not take into account the concept of GDP in relation to population (GDP per capita). The United States has a GDP per capita of $46,900. Switzerland

gross domestic product (GDP) The market value of a nation's total output of goods and services for a given period; an overall measure of economic standing

TABLE 9.1 Comparative Analysis of Selected Countries

Country	Population (in Millions)	GDP (U.S.$ in Billions)	Exports (U.S.$ in Billions)	Imports (U.S.$ in Billions)	Internet Users (in Millions)	Cell Phones (in Millions)	Broadcast Television Stations
Brazil	198.74	2,024	158.9	136	65	150.64	138
Canada	33.49	1,287	298.5	305.2	25	21.45	148
China	1,340	8,767	1,194	921.5	298	634	3,240
Honduras	7.8	33.14	5.25	7.57	.66	6.21	11
India	1,170	3,548	155	232.3	81	427.3	562
Japan	127.08	4,141	516.3	490.6	90.9	110.4	211
Jordan	6.34	33.06	6.99	12.31	1.5	5.314	22
Kenya	39	63.52	4.48	9.03	3.4	16.234	8
Mexico	111.21	1,473	223.6	234.6	23.3	75.3	236
Russia	140.04	2,103	295.6	196.8	45.3	187.5	7,306
South Africa	49.05	488.6	67.93	70.24	4.2	45	556
Switzerland	7.6	316.1	190.1	177.2	5.7	8.78	106
Turkey	71.81	861	111.1	134.2	24.5	65.82	251
Thailand	65.91	535.8	136.6	106.4	16.1	62	111
U.S.	307.21	14,260	994.7	1,445	231	270	2,218

Source: The CIA, *The World Fact Book*, www.cia.gov/library/publications/the-world-factbook/geos/us.html (accessed February 24, 2010).

is roughly 230 times smaller than the United States—a little larger than the state of Maryland—but its population density is six times greater than that of the United States. Although Switzerland's GDP is about one-forty-sixth the size of the United States' GDP, its GDP per capita is only a little lower. Even Canada, which is comparable in size to the United States, has a lower GDP and GDP per capita.[13] Table 9.1 provides a comparative economic analysis of 15 countries, including the United States. Knowledge about per capita income, credit, and the distribution of income provides general insights into market potential.

Opportunities for international trade are not limited to countries with the highest incomes. Some nations are progressing at a much faster rate than they were a few years ago, and these countries—especially in Latin America, Africa, eastern Europe, and the Middle East—have great market potential. Consider the market potential for mobile value-added service businesses, which is growing rapidly in rural areas. In India, for example, dominant cellular companies such as Reliance Communications Ltd. and Tata Teleservices are adding services that are useful for farmers, such as using cell phones to control water pumps for crops. These nonvoice cellular services are growing and are estimated to account for 25 percent of revenues in the next five years.[14] Marketers must, however, understand the political and legal environments before they can convert buying power of customers in these countries into actual demand for specific products.

Political, Legal, and Regulatory Forces

The political, legal, and regulatory forces of the environment are closely intertwined in the United States. To a large degree, the same is true in many countries internationally. Typically, legislation is enacted, legal decisions are interpreted, and regulatory agencies are operated by elected or appointed officials. A country's legal and regulatory infrastructure is a direct reflection of the political climate in the country. In some countries, this political climate is determined by the people via elections, whereas in other countries leaders are appointed or have assumed leadership based on certain powers. Although laws and regulations have direct effects on a firm's operations in a country, political forces are indirect and often not clearly known in all countries. For example, although China has opened to international investment in recent years, other countries are required to work with the Chinese government in order to enter and establish operations. This has been a highly political process since the advent of Communist rule.

The political climate in a country or region, political officials in a country, and political officials in charge of trade agreements directly affect the legislation and regulations (or lack thereof). Within industries, elected or appointed officials of influential industry associations also set the tone for the regulatory environment that guides operations in a particular industry. Consider the American Marketing Association, which has one of the largest professional associations for marketers with 30,000 members worldwide in every area of marketing. It has established a statement of ethics, called Ethical Norms and Values for Marketers, that guide the marketing profession in the United States.[15]

A nation's political system, laws, regulatory bodies, special-interest groups, and courts all have a great impact on international marketing. A government's policies toward public and private enterprise, consumers, and foreign firms influence marketing across national boundaries. Some countries have established import barriers, such as tariffs. An **import tariff** is any duty levied by a nation on goods bought outside its borders and brought into the country. Because they raise the prices of foreign goods, tariffs impede free trade between nations. Tariffs are usually designed either to raise revenue for a country or to protect domestic products. In the United States, tariff revenues account for less than 2 percent of total federal revenues, down from about 50 percent of total federal revenues in the early 1900s.[16]

Nontariff trade restrictions include quotas and embargoes. A **quota** is a limit on the amount of goods an importing country will accept for certain product categories in a specific period of time. The United States maintains tariff-rate quotas on imported raw cane sugar, refined and specialty sugar, and sugar-containing products. The goal is to allow countries to export specific products to the United States at a relatively low tariff but acknowledges higher tariffs above predetermined quantities.[17] An **embargo** is a government's suspension of trade in a particular product or with a given country. Embargoes are generally directed at specific goods or countries and are established for political, health, or religious reasons. Products that were created in the United States or by U.S. companies or those containing more than 20 percent of U.S.-manufactured parts cannot be sold to Cuba.[18] Laws regarding pricing policies may also serve as trade barriers. For example, the European Union has stronger antitrust laws than the United States. Being found guilty of anticompetitive behavior has cost companies like Intel billions of dollars. Because some companies do not have the resources to comply with more stringent laws, this can act as a barrier to trade.

Exchange controls, government restrictions on the amount of a particular currency that can be bought or sold, may also limit international trade. They can force businesspeople to buy and sell foreign products through a central agency, such as a central bank. On the other hand, to promote international trade, some countries have joined to form free trade zones, multinational economic communities that eliminate tariffs and other trade barriers. Such regional trade alliances are discussed later in the chapter. Foreign currency exchange rates also affect the prices marketers can charge in foreign markets. Fluctuations in the international monetary market can change the prices charged across national boundaries on a daily basis. Thus, these fluctuations must be considered in any international marketing strategy.

Countries may limit imports to maintain a favorable balance of trade. The **balance of trade** is the difference in value between a nation's exports and its imports. When a nation exports more products than it imports, a favorable balance of trade exists because money is flowing into the country. The United States has a negative balance of trade for goods and services of $380 billion.[19] A negative balance of trade is considered harmful because it means U.S. dollars are supporting foreign economies at the expense of U.S. companies and workers. At the same time, U.S. citizens benefit from the assortment of imported products and their typically lower prices.

---

import tariff A duty levied by a nation on goods bought outside its borders and brought into the country

quota A limit on the amount of goods an importing country will accept for certain product categories in a specific period of time

embargo A government's suspension of trade in a particular product or with a given country

exchange controls Government restrictions on the amount of a particular currency that can be bought or sold

balance of trade The difference in value between a nation's exports and its imports

Many nontariff barriers, such as quotas and minimum price levels set on imports, port-of-entry taxes, and stringent health and safety requirements, still make it difficult for U.S. companies to export their products. For instance, the collectivistic nature of Japanese culture and the high-context nature of Japanese communication make some types of direct marketing messages less effective and may predispose many Japanese to support greater regulation of direct marketing practices.[20] A government's attitude toward importers has a direct impact on the economic feasibility of exporting to that country.

Ethical and Social Responsibility Forces

Differences in national standards are illustrated by what the Mexicans call *la mordida:* "the bite." The use of payoffs and bribes is deeply entrenched in many governments. Because U.S. trade and corporate policy, as well as U.S. law, prohibits direct involvement in payoffs and bribes, U.S. companies may have a hard time competing with foreign firms that engage in these practices. Some U.S. businesses that refuse to make payoffs are forced to hire local consultants, public relations firms, or advertising agencies, which results in indirect payoffs. The ultimate decision about whether to give small tips or gifts where they are customary must be based on a company's code of ethics. However, under the Foreign Corrupt Practices Act of 1977, it is illegal for U.S. firms to attempt to make large payments or bribes to influence policy decisions of foreign governments. Nevertheless, facilitating payments, or small payments to support the performance of standard tasks, are often acceptable. The Foreign Corrupt Practices Act also subjects all publicly held U.S. corporations to rigorous internal controls and record-keeping requirements for their overseas operations. Many other countries have also outlawed bribery.

Differences in ethical standards can also affect marketing efforts. In China and Vietnam, for example, standards regarding intellectual property differ dramatically from those in the United States, creating potential conflicts for marketers of computer software, music, and books. Pirated consumer goods, according to the U.S. Department of Commerce, cost $650 billion annually.[21] See Table 9.2 for the most counterfeited objects. In China, luxury handbag manufacturer

Responsible Marketing?

Would You Like Paper . . . or Paper? The Worldwide Debate on Paper versus Plastic Bags

ISSUE: Should plastic bags be banned globally?

What started in London as a Parliamentary bill to ban free plastic bags among retailers has sweeping implications throughout the world. The capital of Bangladesh was an innovator in 2002 when it banned plastic bags, but the world market has been slow to follow—until now. San Francisco has banned plastic bags, Ireland is now charging a nationwide tax of 15 cents on all supermarket shopping bags, and Australia and China are planning a similar program. Whole Foods, the United States' leading natural and organic supermarket, ended its use of plastic bags on Earth Day 2008. Whole Foods estimates this move will keep 150 million new plastic grocery bags out of the environment each year. Annual usage of plastic bags worldwide is estimated to be between 500 billion and 1 trillion.

Why are disposable plastic bags under fire? First, they do not disintegrate for more than 1,000 years, contributing to our landfill crisis, "rivaling the cockroach for indestructibility." The bags also contribute to a throwaway mentality, not a recycling one. The bags pose a serious threat to wildlife, particularly birds, turtles, and other sea creatures. According to the World Wildlife Fund, nearly 200 different species of sea life die after consuming plastic bags they thought were food. Plastic bags make up 10 percent of all debris on U.S. coastlines.

With the plastic bag industry facing scrutiny and abandonment, new technologies are coming into play to manufacture environmentally friendly plastic bags. Symphony Environmental Technologies in the United Kingdom has produced an additive that makes plastic bags break down in only two years. Diamant Film produces a plastic that biodegrades into nothing but carbon dioxide, water, and biomass. Should retailers continue to use plastic bags if they can be produced in an eco-friendly way?[b]

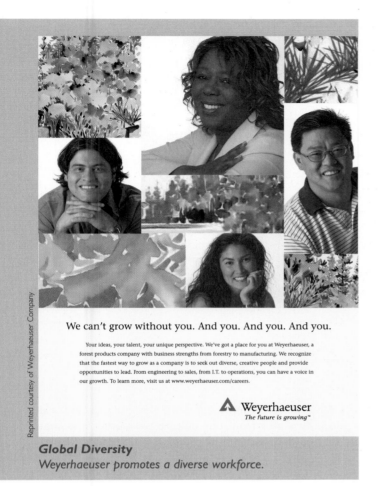

We can't grow without you. And you. And you. And you.

Your ideas, your talent, your unique perspective. We've got a place for you at Weyerhaeuser, a forest products company with business strengths from forestry to manufacturing. We recognize that the fastest way to grow as a company is to seek out diverse, creative people and provide opportunities to lead. From engineering to sales, from I.T. to operations, you can have a voice in our growth. To learn more, visit us at www.weyerhaeuser.com/careers.

Weyerhaeuser
The future is growing

Reprinted courtesy of Weyerhaeuser Company

Global Diversity
Weyerhaeuser promotes a diverse workforce.

Louis Vuitton (LV) pursued a store selling knockoffs of their purses. The store admitted to selling counterfeit LV goods to Canadian singer Celine Dion. The store was ordered to pay more than $73,000 in compensation to LV over trademark infringement. In the Shanghai court system, this was the maximum compensation that could be awarded to LV.[22] Unfortunately, not all companies have had as much luck as Louis Vuitton in combating counterfeit products. The enormous amount of counterfeit products available worldwide, the time it takes to track them down, and legal barriers in certain countries make the pursuit of counterfeiters challenging for many companies.

When marketers do business abroad, they sometimes perceive that other business cultures have different modes of operation. This uneasiness is especially pronounced for marketers who have not traveled extensively or interacted much with foreigners in business or social settings. For example, a perception exists among many in the United States that U.S. firms are often different from those in other countries. This implied perspective of "us" versus "them" is also common in other countries. Table 9.3 indicates the countries that businesspeople, risk analysts, and the general public perceived as the most and least corrupt. In business, the idea that "we" differ from "them" is called the self-reference criterion (SRC). The SRC is the unconscious reference to one's own cultural values, experiences, and knowledge. When confronted with a situation, we react on the basis of knowledge we have accumulated over a lifetime, which is usually grounded in our culture of origin. Our reactions are based on meanings, values, and symbols that relate to our culture but may not have the same relevance to people of other cultures.

However, many businesspeople adopt the principle of "When in Rome, do as the Romans do." These businesspeople adapt to the cultural practices of the country they are in and use the host country's cultural practices as the rationalization for sometimes straying from their own ethical values when doing business internationally. For instance, by defending the payment of bribes or "greasing the wheels of business" and other

TABLE 9.2 Most Frequently Counterfeited Goods

1. Brand-name clothing
2. Electronics
3. Handbags and luxury accessories
4. Medicine
5. CDs, DVDs, and video games
6. Automotive parts
7. Toys
8. Cosmetics and personal hygiene products
9. Cigarettes
10. Food and beverages

Source: "Counterfeit Culture," *CBC News*, www.cbc.ca/news/interactives/map-counterfeit-goods (accessed March 15, 2010).

TABLE 9.3 Perceptions of the Least and Most Corrupt Countries

Least Corrupt	Most Corrupt
1. New Zealand	1. Somalia
2. Denmark	2. Afghanistan
3. Singapore	3. Myanmar
4. Sweden	4. Sudan
5. Switzerland	5. Iraq
6. Finland	6. Chad
7. Netherlands	7. Uzbekistan
8. Australia	8. Turkmenistan
9. Canada	9. Iran
10. Iceland	10. Haiti
11. Norway	11. Guinea
12. Hong Kong	12. Equatorial Guinea
13. Luxembourg	13. Burundi

* The United States is perceived as the 19th least-corrupt nation.

Source: "Transparency International Corruption Perceptions Index 2009," Transparency International, www.transparency.org/policy_research/surveys_indices/cpi/2009/cpi_2009_table (accessed March 1, 2010).

questionable practices in this fashion, some businesspeople are resorting to **cultural relativism**—the concept that morality varies from one culture to another and that business practices are therefore differentially defined as right or wrong by particular cultures.

Because of differences in cultural and ethical standards, many companies work both individually and collectively to establish ethics programs and standards for international business conduct. Levi Strauss's code of ethics, for example, bars the firm from manufacturing in countries where workers are known to be abused. Starbucks's global code of ethics strives to protect agricultural workers who harvest coffee beans. Many other firms, including Texas Instruments, Coca-Cola, Du Pont, Hewlett-Packard, Levi Strauss & Company, Texaco, and Walmart, endorse following responsible business practices internationally. These companies support a globally based resource system called Business for Social Responsibility (BSR). BSR tracks emerging issues and trends, provides information on corporate leadership and best practices, conducts educational workshops and training, and assists organizations in developing practical business ethics tools. It addresses such issues as community investment, corporate social responsibility, the environment, governance, and accountability. BSR has also established formal partnerships with other organizations that focus on corporate responsibility in Brazil, Israel, the United Kingdom, Chile, and Panama.[23]

Competitive Forces

Competition is often viewed as a staple of the global marketplace. Customers thrive on the choices offered by competition, and firms constantly seek opportunities to outmaneuver their competition to gain customers' loyalty. Firms typically identify their competition when they establish target markets worldwide. Customers who are seeking alternative solutions to their product needs find the firms that can solve those needs. However, the increasingly interconnected international marketplace and advances in technology have resulted in competitive forces that are unique to the international marketplace.

cultural relativism The concept that morality varies from one culture to another and that business practices are therefore differentially defined as right or wrong by particular cultures

Think "INSIDE" The Box

These days, it seems that everyone is telling you to "think outside the box". When it comes to clutch replacement, that's just not good advice. Many clutch marketers mix and match parts from various sources, a practice that creates quality and installation problems. The parts may bolt up, but can fail prematurely, resulting in a comeback for you. When you install a LuK RepSet, you get the same flawless performance as the original equipment parts.

Designed and engineered to work together. Why risk your time and reputation with anything else?

Trust the quality of LuK
Trust the yellow box

www.lukclutch.com

Certified to ISO 9001:2008 without Design

5370 Wegman Drive, Valley City, OH 44280
800 274 5001 • www.lukclutch.com

© AP Images/PRNewsFoto/Schaeffler Group USA Inc.

Competitive Forces
Luk focuses on the quality of its products and the trust you can place in the brand name to create a competitive advantage.

Beyond the types of competition (i.e., brand, product, generic, and total budget competition) and types of competitive structures (i.e., monopoly, oligopoly, monopolistic competition, and pure competition), which are discussed in Chapter 3, firms that operate internationally must do the following:

- Be aware of the competitive forces in the countries they target.
- Identify the interdependence of countries and the global competitors in those markets.
- Be mindful of a new breed of customers: the global customer.

Each country has unique competitive aspects—often founded in the other environmental forces (i.e., sociocultural, technological, political, legal, regulatory, and economic forces)—that are often independent of the competitors in that market. The most globally competitive countries are listed in Table 9.4. Although competitors drive competition, nations establish the infrastructure and the rules for the types of competition that can take place. For example, Microsoft's almost monopolistic dominance in many countries' markets led the United Nations' European Commission to a long-standing legal battle over the firm's marketing and competitive practices related to its bundling of a media player with its Windows computer operating system. Microsoft ultimately lost the battle as well as an appeal to the Court of First Instance and paid fines and penalties of nearly $2.4 billion.[24] Like the United States, other countries allow some monopoly structures to exist. Consider Sweden; their alcohol sales are made through the governmental store Systembolaget, which is legally supported by the Swedish Alcohol Retail Monopoly. According to Systembolaget, the Swedish Alcohol Retail Monopoly exists for one reason: "to minimize alcohol-related problems by selling alcohol in a responsible way."[25]

TABLE 9.4 Ranking of the Most Competitive Countries in the World

1. Switzerland	11. Hong Kong SAR
2. United States	12. Taiwan, China
3. Singapore	13. United Kingdom
4. Sweden	14. Norway
5. Denmark	15. Australia
6. Finland	16. France
7. Germany	17. Austria
8. Japan	18. Belgium
9. Canada	19. Korea, Rep.
10. Netherlands	20. New Zealand

Source: Porter/Sala-i-Martin/Shwab, *The Global Competitiveness Report 2009–2010*, World Economic Forum (Palgrave Macmillan), www.weforum.org/en/initiatives/gcp/Global%20Competitiveness%20Report/index.htm (accessed March 1, 2010).

A new breed of customer—the global customer—has changed the landscape of international competition drastically. In the past, firms simply produced goods or services and provided local markets with information about the features and uses of their goods and services. Customers seldom had opportunities to compare products from competitors, know details about the competing products' features, and compare other options beyond the local (country or region) markets. Now, however, not only do customers who travel the globe expect to be able to buy the same product in most of the world's more than 200 countries, but they also expect that the product they buy in their local store in Miami will have the same features as similar products sold in London or even in Beijing. If either the quality of the product or the product's features are more advanced in an international market, customers will soon demand that their local markets offer the same product at the same or lower prices.

Technological Forces

Advances in technology have made international marketing much easier. Interactive web systems, instant messaging, and podcast downloads (along with the traditional vehicles of voice mail, e-mail, fax, and cell phones) make international marketing activities more affordable and convenient. Internet use has accelerated dramatically within the United States and abroad. In Japan, 90.9 million have Internet access, and more than 45 million Russians, 81 million Indians, and 298 million Chinese are logging on to the Internet (see Table 9.1).[26]

In many developing countries that lack the level of technological infrastructure found in the United States and Japan, marketers are beginning to capitalize on opportunities to leapfrog existing technology. For example, cellular and wireless phone technology is reaching many countries at a more affordable rate than traditional hard-wired telephone systems. Consequently, opportunities for growth in the cell phone market remain strong in Southeast Asia, Africa, and the Middle East. One opportunity created by the rapid growth in cell phone service contracts in China is the *shouji jiayouzhan,* or "cell phone gas station," which allows consumers to recharge their phone, camera, and PDA batteries quickly and cheaply, and they can watch commercials during the 10-minute charging session.[27]

Staying Ahead of the Competition
AT&T's extensive global network provides a competitive advantage.

Regional Trade Alliances, Markets, and Agreements

Although many more firms are beginning to view the world as one huge marketplace, various regional trade alliances and specific markets affect companies engaging in international marketing; some create opportunities, and others impose constraints. In fact, while trade agreements in various forms have been around for centuries, the last century can be classified as the trade agreement period in the world's international development. Today, there are nearly 200 trade agreements around the world compared with only a select handful in the early 1960s. In this section, we examine several of the more critical regional trade alliances, markets, and changing conditions affecting markets. These include the North American Free Trade Agreement, European Union, Common Market of the Southern Cone, Asia-Pacific Economic Cooperation, and World Trade Organization.

The North American Free Trade Agreement (NAFTA)

The **North American Free Trade Agreement (NAFTA)**, implemented in 1994, effectively merged Canada, Mexico, and the United States into one market of nearly 444 million consumers. NAFTA eliminated virtually all tariffs on goods produced and traded among Canada, Mexico, and the United States to create a free trade area. The estimated annual output for this trade alliance is more than $14 trillion.[28]

NAFTA makes it easier for U.S. businesses to invest in Mexico and Canada; provides protection for intellectual property (of special interest to high-technology and entertainment industries); expands trade by requiring equal treatment of U.S. firms in both countries; and simplifies country-of-origin rules, hindering Japan's use of Mexico as a staging ground for further penetration into U.S. markets. Although most tariffs on products coming to the United States were lifted, duties on more sensitive products, such as household glassware, footwear, and some fruits and vegetables, were phased out over a 15-year period.

Canada's more than 33 million consumers are relatively affluent, with a per capita GDP of $38,400. Trade between the United States and Canada totals approximately $430 billion.[29] Currently, exports to Canada support approximately 1.5 million U.S. jobs. In fact, Canada is the single largest trading partner of the United States.

With a per capita GDP of $13,500, Mexico's 112 million consumers are less affluent than Canadian consumers. However, they bought more than $129 billion worth of U.S. products last year.[30] Many U.S. companies, including Hewlett-Packard, IBM, and General Motors, have taken advantage of Mexico's low labor costs and close proximity to the United States to set up production facilities, sometimes called *maquiladoras.* Production at the *maquiladoras,* especially in the automotive, electronics, and apparel industries, has grown rapidly as companies as diverse as Ford, John Deere, Motorola, Sara Lee, Kimberly-Clark, and VF Corporation set up facilities in north-central Mexican states. U.S. companies in Mexico will invest $2.5 billion this year and produce 30 percent of the jobs in Mexico.[31] Although Mexico experienced financial instability throughout the 1990s and is experiencing another bout of instability because of drug cartel violence, privatization of some government-owned firms and other measures instituted by the Mexican government and businesses, along with a booming U.S. economy, have helped Mexico's economy. Moreover, increasing trade between the United States and Canada constitutes a strong base of support for the ultimate success of NAFTA.

Mexico's membership in NAFTA links the United States and Canada with other Latin American countries, providing additional opportunities to integrate trade among all the nations in the Western Hemisphere. Indeed, efforts to create a free trade agreement among the 34 nations of North and South America are under way. A related trade agreement—the *Dominican Republic–Central American Free Trade Agreement (CAFTA-DR)*—among Costa Rica, the Dominican Republic, El Salvador, Guatemala, Honduras, Nicaragua,

North American Free Trade Agreement (NAFTA) An alliance that merges Canada, Mexico, and the United States into a single market

and the United States has also been ratified in all those countries except Costa Rica. U.S. exports more than $26 billion to the CAFTA-DR countries annually.[32]

Despite its benefits, NAFTA has been controversial, and disputes continue to arise over its implementation. ExxonMobil, for example, filed a lawsuit against the Canadian government for damages resulting from Canada's imposition of new costs on offshore petroleum projects, which the company believes violates the provisions of NAFTA.[33] Although many Americans feared the agreement would erase jobs in the United States, Mexicans have been disappointed that it failed to create more jobs. Although NAFTA has been controversial, it has become a positive factor for U.S. firms that want to engage in international marketing. Because licensing requirements have been relaxed under the pact, smaller businesses that previously could not afford to invest in Mexico and Canada will be able to do business in those markets without having to locate there. NAFTA's long phase-in period provides ample time for adjustment for those firms affected by reduced tariffs on imports. Furthermore, increased competition should lead to a more efficient market, and the long-term prospects of including most Western Hemisphere countries in the alliance promise additional opportunities for U.S. marketers.

The European Union (EU)

The **European Union (EU)**, sometimes also referred to as the *European Community* or *Common Market,* was established in 1958 to promote trade among its members, which initially included Belgium, France, Italy, West Germany, Luxembourg, and the Netherlands. In 1991, East and West Germany united, and by 2010, the EU included the United Kingdom, Spain, Denmark, Greece, Portugal, Ireland, Austria, Finland, Sweden, Cyprus, Poland, Hungary, the Czech Republic, Slovenia, Estonia, Latvia, Lithuania, Slovakia, Malta, Romania, and Bulgaria. Croatia, the Former Yugoslav Republic of Macedonia, and Turkey are candidate countries that hope to join the European Union in the near future.[34]

The European Union consists of nearly half a billion consumers and has a combined GDP of more than $14 trillion.[35] The EU is a relatively diverse set of democratic European countries. It is not a state that is intended to replace existing country states, nor is it

European Union (EU) An alliance that promotes trade among its member countries in Europe

European Union
An EU meeting held in Madrid.

© Javier Soriano/AFP/Getty Images

an organization for international cooperation. Instead, its member states have common institutions to which they delegate some of their sovereignty to allow specific matters of joint interest to be decided at the European level. The primary goals of the EU are to establish European citizenship; ensure freedom, security, and justice; promote economic and social progress; and assert Europe's role in world trade.[36] To facilitate free trade among members, the EU is working toward standardizing business regulations and requirements, import duties, and value-added taxes; eliminating customs checks; and creating a standardized currency for use by all members. Many European nations (Austria, Belgium, Finland, France, Germany, Ireland, Italy, Luxembourg, the Netherlands, Portugal, and Spain) are linked to a common currency, the *euro,* but several EU members have rejected the euro in their countries (e.g., Denmark, Sweden, and the United Kingdom). Although the common currency may necessitate that marketers modify their pricing strategies and subjects them to increased competition, it also frees companies that sell products among European countries from the complexities of exchange rates. The long-term goals are to eliminate all trade barriers within the EU, improve the economic efficiency of the EU nations, and stimulate economic growth, thus making the union's economy more competitive in global markets, particularly against Japan and other Pacific Rim nations and North America.

As the EU nations attempt to function as one large market, consumers in the EU may become more homogeneous in their needs and wants. Marketers should be aware, however, that cultural differences among the nations may require modifications in the marketing mix for customers in each nation. Differences in tastes and preferences in these diverse markets are significant for international marketers. But there is evidence that such differences may be diminishing, especially within the younger population that includes teenagers and young professionals. Gathering information about these distinct tastes and preferences is likely to remain a very important factor in developing marketing mixes that satisfy the needs of European customers.

The Common Market of the Southern Cone (MERCOSUR)

The **Common Market of the Southern Cone (MERCOSUR)** was established in 1991 under the Treaty of Asunción to unite Argentina, Brazil, Paraguay, and Uruguay as a free trade alliance. Venezuela joined in 2006. Currently, Bolivia, Chile, Colombia, Ecuador, and Peru are associate members. The alliance represents two-thirds of South America's population and has a combined GDP of more than $2.4 trillion, making it the fourth-largest trading bloc behind NAFTA and the EU. Like NAFTA, MERCOSUR promotes "the free circulation of goods, services, and production factors among the countries" and establishes a common external tariff and commercial policy.[37]

The Asia-Pacific Economic Cooperation (APEC)

The **Asia-Pacific Economic Cooperation (APEC)**, established in 1989, promotes open trade and economic and technical cooperation among member nations, which initially included Australia, Brunei Darussalam, Canada, Indonesia, Japan, Korea, Malaysia, New Zealand, the Philippines, Singapore, Thailand, and the United States. Since then the alliance has grown to include China, Hong Kong, Taiwan, Mexico, Papua New Guinea, Chile, Peru, Russia, and Vietnam. The 21-member alliance represents approximately 41 percent of the world's population, 54 percent of world GDP, and nearly 44 percent of global trade. APEC differs from other international trade alliances in its commitment to facilitating business and its practice of allowing the business/private sector to participate in a wide range of APEC activities.[38]

Companies of the APEC have become increasingly competitive and sophisticated in global business in the last few decades. Moreover, the markets of the APEC offer tremendous opportunities to marketers who understand them. In fact, the APEC region has consistently been one of the most economically dynamic parts of the world. In its first decade, the APEC countries generated almost 70 percent of worldwide economic growth, and the APEC region consistently outperformed the rest of the world.[39]

Common Market of the Southern Cone (MERCOSUR) An alliance that promotes the free circulation of goods, services, and production factors, and has a common external tariff and commercial policy among member nations in South America

Asia-Pacific Economic Cooperation (APEC) An alliance that promotes open trade and economic and technical cooperation among member nations throughout the world

Japanese firms in particular have made tremendous inroads on world markets for automobiles, motorcycles, watches, cameras, and audio and video equipment. Products from Sony, Sanyo, Toyota, Mitsubishi, Canon, Suzuki, and Toshiba are sold all over the world and have set standards of quality by which other products are often judged. Sony is often viewed as the benchmark of the global company. Despite the high volume of trade between the United States and Japan, the two economies are less integrated than the U.S. economy is with Canada and the European Union. If Japan imported goods at the same rate as other major nations, the United States would sell billions of dollars more each year to Japan.

The most important emerging economic power is China, which has become one of the most productive manufacturing nations. China, which is now the United States' second-largest trading partner, has initiated economic reforms to stimulate its economy by privatizing many industries, restructuring its banking system, and increasing public spending on infrastructure. China is a manufacturing powerhouse with an economy growing at a rate of nearly 11 percent in early 2010 compared to a low of 6.2 percent in early 2009.[40] Many foreign companies, including Nike and Adidas, have factories in China to take advantage of its low labor costs, and China has become a major global producer in virtually every product category. The potential of China's consumer market is so vast that it is almost impossible to measure, but doing business in China also entails many risks. Political and economic instability—especially inflation, corruption, and erratic policy shifts—have undercut marketers' efforts to stake a claim in what could become the world's largest market. Moreover, piracy is a major issue, and protecting a brand name in China is difficult. Because copying is a tradition in China, and laws that protect copyrights and intellectual property are weak and minimally enforced, the country is flooded with counterfeit videos, movies, compact discs, computer software, furniture, and clothing.

Pacific Rim regions such as South Korea, Thailand, Singapore, Taiwan, and Hong Kong are also major manufacturing and financial centers. Even before Korean brand names such as Samsung, Daewoo, and Hyundai became household words, these products prospered under U.S. company labels, including GE, GTE, RCA, and JCPenney. Singapore boasts huge global markets for rubber goods and pharmaceuticals. Hong Kong is still a strong commercial center after being transferred to Chinese control. Vietnam is one of Asia's fastest-growing markets for U.S. businesses, but Taiwan, given its stability and high educational attainment, has the most promising future of all the Pacific Rim nations as a strong local economy and low import barriers draw increasing imports. The markets of APEC offer tremendous opportunities to marketers who understand them. For instance, YUM! Brands, the number-two fast-food chain after McDonald's, opened its first KFC fast-food restaurant in China in 1987 and has since opened more than 3,000 KFC and Pizza Hut outlets in China, as well as a new concept store called East Dawning, which serves Chinese fast food. China accounts for about 16 percent of the company's profits.[41]

World Trade Organization (WTO) An entity that promotes free trade among member nations by eliminating trade barriers and educating individuals, companies, and governments about trade rules around the world

General Agreement on Tariffs and Trade (GATT) An agreement among nations to reduce worldwide tariffs and increase international trade

The World Trade Organization (WTO)

The **World Trade Organization (WTO)** is a global trade association that promotes free trade among 153 member nations. The WTO is the successor to the **General Agreement on Tariffs and Trade (GATT)**, which was originally

Entrepreneurial Marketing
Entrepreneurs Take on Chinese Piracy: The Story of BraBaby

Even inexpensive household products face competitive challenges in global markets. Robert and Laura Engel, founders of Angel Sales Inc., invented the "BraBaby," a plastic device used for laundering bras that preserves and extends their wear. They realized their product was being copied and made available throughout the world without their permission, partnership, licensing, or compensation. The Engels spent nearly $125,000 registering, patenting, and copyrighting the trademark in the United States, European communities, Australia, New Zealand, Taiwan, Hong Kong, and China, and yet pirates paid no attention to these measures. The Engels learned a valuable lesson about the challenges inherent in developing and marketing a successful product. Inventing the product is the beginning of the battle in global markets with intellectual property standards that are not enforced or culturally accepted.[c]

signed by 23 nations in 1947 to provide a forum for tariff negotiations and a place where international trade problems could be discussed and resolved. Rounds of GATT negotiations reduced trade barriers for most products and established rules to guide international commerce, such as rules to prevent **dumping**, the selling of products at unfairly low prices.

The WTO came into being in 1995 as a result of the Uruguay Round (1988–1994) of GATT negotiations. Broadly, WTO is the main worldwide organization that deals with the rules of trade between nations; its main function is to ensure that trade flows as smoothly, predictably, and freely as possible between nations. In 2009, 153 nations were members of the WTO.[42]

Fulfilling the purpose of the WTO requires eliminating trade barriers; educating individuals, companies, and governments about trade rules around the world; and assuring global markets that no sudden changes of policy will occur. At the heart of the WTO are agreements that provide legal ground rules for international commerce and trade policy. Based in Geneva, Switzerland, the WTO also serves as a forum for dispute resolution.[43] For example, the WTO authorized Brazil to set annual penalties against the United States for failure to comply with competitive practices by giving billions of dollars in subsidies to American cotton growers.[44]

Modes of Entry into International Markets

Marketers enter international markets and continue to engage in marketing activities at several levels of international involvement. Traditionally, firms have adopted one of four different modes of entering an international market; each successive "stage" represents different degrees of international involvement.

- Stage 1: No regular export activities
- Stage 2: Export via independent representatives (agents)
- Stage 3: Establishment of one or more sales subsidiaries internationally
- Stage 4: Establishment of international production/manufacturing facilities[45]

As Figure 9.1 shows, companies' international involvement today covers a wide spectrum, from purely domestic marketing to global marketing. Domestic marketing involves marketing strategies aimed at markets within the home country; at the other extreme, global marketing entails developing marketing strategies for the entire world (or at least more than one major region of the world). Many firms with an international presence start out as small companies serving local and regional domestic markets and expand to national markets before considering opportunities in foreign markets (the born global firm, described earlier, is one exception to this internationalization process). Limited exporting may occur even if a firm makes little or no effort to obtain foreign sales. Foreign buyers may seek out the company and/or its products, or a distributor may discover the firm's products and export them. The level of commitment to international marketing is a major variable in global marketing strategies. In this section, we examine importing and exporting, trading companies, licensing and franchising, contract manufacturing, joint ventures, direct ownership, and some of the other approaches to international involvement.

Importing and Exporting

Importing and exporting require the least amount of effort and commitment of resources. **Importing** is the purchase of products from a foreign source. **Exporting**, the sale of products to foreign markets, enables firms of all sizes to participate in global business. A firm may find an exporting intermediary to take over most marketing functions associated with marketing to other countries. This approach entails minimal effort

dumping Selling products at unfairly low prices

importing The purchase of products from a foreign source

exporting The sale of products to foreign markets

FIGURE 9.1 Levels of Involvement in Global Marketing

Globalized marketing
Marketing strategies are developed for the entire world
(or more than one major region), with the focus on the
similarities across regions and country markets.

Regional marketing
Marketing strategies are developed for each major region, with
the countries in the region being marketed to in the same way
based on similarities across the region's country markets.

Multinational marketing
International markets are a consideration in the marketing
strategy, with customization for the country markets based on
critical differences across regions and country markets.

Limited exporting
The firm develops no international marketing strategies, but
international distributors, foreign firms, or selected
customers purchase some of its products.

Domestic marketing
All marketing strategies focus on the market
in the country of origin.

and cost. Modifications in packaging, labeling, style, or color may be the major expenses in adapting a product for the foreign market.

Export agents bring together buyers and sellers from different countries and collect a commission for arranging sales. Export houses and export merchants purchase products from different companies and then sell them abroad. They are specialists at understanding customers' needs in global markets. Using exporting intermediaries involves limited risk because no foreign direct investment is required.

Buyers from foreign companies and governments provide a direct method of exporting and eliminate the need for an intermediary. These buyers encourage international exchange by contacting overseas firms about their needs and the opportunities available in exporting to them. Indeed, research suggests that many small firms tend to rely heavily on such native contacts, especially in developed markets, and remain production oriented rather than marketing oriented in their approach to international marketing.[46] Domestic firms that want to export with minimal effort and investment should seek out export intermediaries. Once a company becomes involved in exporting, it usually develops more knowledge of the country and becomes more confident in its competitiveness.[47]

Trading Companies

trading company A
company that links buyers and
sellers in different countries

Marketers sometimes employ a **trading company**, which links buyers and sellers in different countries but is not involved in manufacturing and does not own assets related to manufacturing. Trading companies buy products in one country at the lowest price consistent with quality and sell them to buyers in another country. For instance, SCiNet World Trade System offers a 24-hour-per-day online world trade system that connects 17 million companies in 245 countries, offering more than 50 million products and services. The SCiNet system offers online payments and handles customs, tariffs, and inspections of goods for their clients.[48] A trading company acts like a wholesaler, taking on much of the responsibility of finding markets while facilitating all marketing aspects of a transaction. An important function of trading companies is taking title to products and performing all the activities necessary to move the products to the targeted foreign country. For instance, large grain-trading companies that operate out-of-home offices in both the United States and overseas control a major portion of world trade of basic food commodities. These trading companies sell homogeneous agricultural commodities that can be stored and moved rapidly in response to market conditions.

Trading companies reduce risk for firms that want to get involved in international marketing. A trading company provides producers with information about products that meet quality and price expectations in domestic and international markets. Additional services a trading company may provide include consulting, marketing research, advertising, insurance, product research and design, legal assistance, warehousing, and foreign exchange.

Licensing and Franchising

When potential markets are found across national boundaries, and when production, technical assistance, or marketing know-how is required, **licensing** is an alternative to direct investment. The licensee (the owner of the foreign operation) pays commissions or royalties on sales or supplies used in manufacturing. The licensee may also pay an initial down payment or fee when the licensing agreement is signed. Exchanges of management techniques or technical assistance are primary reasons for licensing agreements. Yoplait, for example, is a French yogurt that is licensed for production in the United States; the Yoplait brand tries to maintain a French image. Similarly, sports organizations such as the International Olympic Committee (IOC), which is responsible for the Olympic Games, typically concentrate on organizing their sporting events while licensing the merchandise and other products that are sold.

Licensing is an attractive alternative when resources are unavailable for direct investment or when the core competencies of the firm or organization are not related to the product being sold (such as in the case of Olympics merchandise). Licensing can also be a viable alternative when the political stability of a foreign country is in doubt. In addition, licensing is especially advantageous for small manufacturers wanting to launch a well-known brand internationally. For example, Questor Corporation owns the Spalding name but does not produce a single golf club or tennis ball itself; all Spalding sporting products are licensed worldwide.

Franchising is a form of licensing in which a company (the franchiser) grants a franchisee the right to market its product, using its name, logo, methods of operation, advertising, products, and other elements associated with the franchiser's business, in return for a financial commitment and an agreement to conduct business in accordance with the franchiser's standard of operations. This arrangement allows franchisers to minimize the risks of international marketing in four ways: (1) the franchiser does not have to put up a large capital investment; (2) the franchiser's revenue stream is fairly consistent because franchisees pay a fixed fee and royalties; (3) the franchiser retains control of its name and increases global penetration of its product; and (4) franchise agreements ensure a certain standard of behavior from franchisees, which protects the franchise name.[49] Subway, McDonald's, and 7-Eleven are among the "top 10" franchises in the world; other well-known franchisers with international visibility include Hampton Inn, H&R Block, and Supercuts (refer to the Snapshot).

licensing An alternative to direct investment that requires a licensee to pay commissions or royalties on sales or supplies used in manufacturing

franchising A form of licensing in which a franchiser, in exchange for a financial commitment, grants a franchisee the right to market its product in accordance with the franchiser's standards

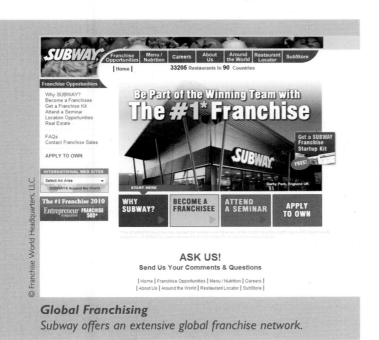

Global Franchising
Subway offers an extensive global franchise network.

© Franchise World Headquarters, LLC

contract manufacturing The practice of hiring a foreign firm to produce a designated volume of the domestic firm's product or a component of it to specification; the final product carries the domestic firm's name

outsourcing The practice of contracting noncore operations with an organization that specializes in that operation

offshoring The practice of moving a business process that was done domestically at the local factory to a foreign country, regardless of whether the production accomplished in the foreign country is performed by the local company (e.g., in a wholly owned subsidiary) or a third party (e.g., subcontractor)

offshore outsourcing The practice of contracting with an organization to perform some or all business functions in a country other than the country in which the product or service will be sold

joint venture A partnership between a domestic firm and a foreign firm or government

Contract Manufacturing

Contract manufacturing occurs when a company hires a foreign firm to produce a designated volume of the firm's product (or a component of a product) to specification and the final product carries the domestic firm's name. The Gap, for example, relies on contract manufacturing for some of its apparel; Reebok uses Korean contract manufacturers to produce many of its athletic shoes. Marketing may be handled by the contract manufacturer or by the contracting company.

Three specific forms of contract manufacturing have become popular in the last decade: outsourcing, offshoring, and offshore outsourcing. **Outsourcing** is defined as the contracting of noncore operations or jobs from internal production within a business to an external entity that specializes in that operation. For example, outsourcing certain elements of a firm's operations to China and Mexico has become popular. The majority of all footwear is now produced in China, regardless of the brand name on the shoe you wear. Services can also be outsourced. Vodafone and France-telecom owned Orange, mobile telecommunications companies in Britain, outsource the management of their networks to Ericsson and Nokia, in an effort to improve margins and cost efficiencies as well as to focus more on innovation.[50] **Offshoring** is defined as moving a business process that was done domestically at the local factory to a foreign country, regardless of whether the production accomplished in the foreign country is performed by the local company (e.g., in a wholly owned subsidiary) or a third party (e.g., subcontractor). Typically, the production is moved to reap the advantages of lower cost of operations in the foreign location. **Offshore outsourcing** is the practice of contracting with an organization to perform some or all business functions in a country other than the country in which the product or service will be sold.

Joint Ventures

In international marketing, a **joint venture** is a partnership between a domestic firm and a foreign firm or government. Joint ventures are especially popular in industries that require large investments, such as natural resources extraction or automobile manufacturing. Control of the joint venture may be split equally, or one party may control decision making. Joint ventures are often a political necessity because of nationalism and government restrictions on foreign ownership. In spite of an unpredictable political environment under democratically elected socialist president Hugo Chávez, many nations are eager to form joint ventures with Venezuelan national oil companies in order to gain access to Venezuela's petroleum resources. Russian and Belarusian oil companies have both joined up with Petroleos de Venezuela.[51] However, the Chávez regime has been hostile to some direct foreign investment from capitalist countries, particularly that of U.S. companies. Joint ventures may also occur when acquisition or internal development is not feasible or when the risks and constraints leave no other alternative. They also provide legitimacy in the eyes of the host country's citizens. Local partners have firsthand knowledge of the economic and sociopolitical environment and the workings of available distribution networks, and they may have privileged access to local resources (raw materials, labor management, and so on). However, joint venture relationships require trust throughout the relationship to provide a foreign partner with a ready means of implementing its own marketing strategy. Joint ventures are assuming greater global importance because of cost advantages and the number of inexperienced firms that are entering foreign markets. They may be the result of a trade-off between a firm's desire for completely unambiguous control of an enterprise and its quest for additional resources.

Strategic alliances are partnerships formed to create competitive advantage on a worldwide basis. They are very similar to joint ventures, but while joint ventures are defined in scope, strategic alliances are typically represented by an agreement to work together (which can ultimately mean more involvement than a joint venture). In an international strategic alliance, the firms in the alliance may have been traditional rivals competing for the same market. They may also be competing in certain markets while working together in other markets where it is beneficial for both parties. One such collaboration is the Sky Team Alliance—involving KLM, Aeromexico, Air France, Alitalia, CSA Czech Airlines, Delta, Korean Air, Kenya Airways, and China Southern Airlines—which is designed to improve customer service among the nine firms. Ascent Solar, a company that makes solar panels, formed a strategic alliance with Indian firm Kirloskar Integrated Technologies Limited. The alliance benefits both companies, because Kirloskar will integrate Ascent Solar's technologies into its products, and Ascent Solar gains a foothold in the fast-growing Indian market.[52] Whereas joint ventures are formed to create a new identity, partners in strategic alliances often retain their distinct identities, with each partner bringing a core competency to the union.

The success rate of international alliances could be higher if a better fit between the companies existed. A strategic alliance should focus on a joint market opportunity from which all partners can benefit. In the automobile, computer, and airline industries, strategic alliances are becoming the predominant means of competing internationally. Competition in these industries is so fierce and the costs of competing on a global basis are so high that few firms have all the resources needed to do it alone. Firms that lack the internal resources essential for international success may seek to collaborate with other companies. A shared mode of leadership among partner corporations combines joint abilities and allows collaboration from a distance. Focusing on customer value and implementing innovative ways to compete create a winning strategy.

Direct Ownership

Once a company makes a long-term commitment to marketing in a foreign country that has a promising market as well as a suitable political and economic environment, **direct ownership** of a foreign subsidiary or division is a possibility. Most foreign investment covers only manufacturing equipment or personnel because the expenses of developing a separate foreign distribution system can be tremendous. The opening of retail stores in Europe, Canada, or Mexico can require a staggering financial investment in facilities, research, and management.

The term **multinational enterprise**, sometimes called *multinational corporation*, refers to a firm that has operations or subsidiaries in many countries. Often the parent company is based in one country and carries on production, management, and marketing activities in other countries. The firm's subsidiaries may be autonomous so they can respond to the needs of individual international markets, or they may be part of a global network that is led by the headquarters' operations.

At the same time, a wholly owned foreign subsidiary may be allowed to operate independently of the parent company to give its management more freedom to adjust to the local environment. Cooperative arrangements are developed to assist in marketing efforts, production, and management. A wholly owned foreign subsidiary may export products to the home country, its market may serve as a test market for the firm's global products, or it may be a component of the firm's globalization efforts. Some U.S. automobile manufacturers, for example, import cars built by their foreign subsidiaries. A foreign subsidiary offers important tax, tariff, and other operating advantages. Table 9.5 lists the 10 largest global corporations.

strategic alliance A partnership that is formed to create a competitive advantage on a worldwide basis

direct ownership A situation in which a company owns subsidiaries or other facilities overseas

multinational enterprise A firm that has operations or subsidiaries in many countries

TABLE 9.5 The 10 Largest Global Corporations

Rank	Company	Country	Industry	Revenue (in Millions)
1	Royal Dutch Shell	Netherlands	Petroleum refining	$458,361
2	ExxonMobil	U.S.	Petroleum refining	$442,851
3	Walmart Stores	U.S.	General merchandiser	$405,607
4	BP	Britain	Petroleum refining	$367,053
5	Chevron	U.S.	Petroleum refining	$263,159
6	Total	France	Petroleum refining	$234,674
7	ConocoPhillips	U.S.	Petroleum refining	$230,764
8	ING Group	Netherlands	Banks: commercial and savings	$226,577
9	Sinopec	China	Petroleum refining	$207,814
10	Toyota Motor	Japan	Motor vehicles and parts	$204,352

Source: "Global 500: 2009," *Fortune*, http://money.cnn.com/magazines/fortune/global500/2009/snapshots/6388.html (accessed March 1, 2010).

One of the greatest advantages of a multinational enterprise is the cross-cultural approach. A subsidiary usually operates under foreign management so it can develop a local identity. In particular, the firm (i.e., seller) is often expected to adapt, if needed, to the buyer's culture. Interestingly, the cultural values of customers in the younger age group (30 years and younger) is becoming increasingly similar around the world. Today, a 20-year-old in Russia is increasingly similar in mindset to a 20-year-old in China and a 20-year-old in the United States, especially with regard to their tastes in music, clothes, and cosmetics. This makes marketing goods and services to the younger population easier today than it was only a generation ago. Nevertheless, there is still great danger involved in having a wholly owned subsidiary in some parts of the world due to political uncertainty, terrorism threats, and economic instability.

Global Organizational Structures

Firms develop their international marketing strategies and manage their marketing mixes (i.e., product, distribution, promotion, and price) by developing and maintaining an organizational structure that best leverages their resources and core competencies. This organizational structure is defined as the way a firm divides its operations into separate functions and/or value-adding units and coordinates its activities. Most firms undergo a step-by-step development in their internationalization efforts of the firm's people, processes, functions, culture, and structure. The pyramid in Figure 9.2 symbolizes how deeply rooted the international operations and values are in the firm, with the base of the pyramid—structure—being the most difficult to change (especially in the short term). Three basic structures of international organizations exist: export departments, international divisions, and internationally integrated structures (e.g., product division structures, geographic area structures, and matrix structures). The existing structure of the firm, or the structure that the firm chooses to adopt, has implications for international marketing strategy.

Export Departments

For most firms, the early stages of international development are often informal and not fully planned. During this early stage, sales opportunities in the global marketplace motivate a company to engage internationally. For instance, born global firms make exporting a primary objective from their inceptions. For most firms, however, very

FIGURE 9.2 Organizational Architecture

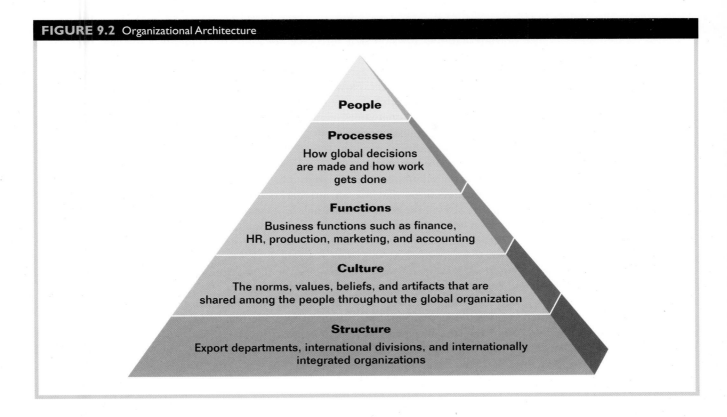

People

Processes
How global decisions
are made and how work
gets done

Functions
Business functions such as finance,
HR, production, marketing, and accounting

Culture
The norms, values, beliefs, and artifacts that are
shared among the people throughout the global organization

Structure
Export departments, international divisions, and internationally
integrated organizations

minimal, if any, organizational adjustments take place to accommodate international sales. Foreign sales are typically so small that many firms cannot justify allocating structural or other resources to the internationalization effort in the infancy of internationalization. Exporting, licensing, and using trading companies are preferred modes of international market entry for firms with an export department structure.

Some firms develop an export department as a subunit of the marketing department, whereas others organize it as a department that structurally coexists at an equal level with the other functional units. Clipsal, an Australian maker of more than 20,000 different lines of electrical accessories, is Australia's number-one brand of electrical accessories. The company has achieved international success led by its high-quality products and operations of its export department, which offers global support in many areas of its business. A strong sense of culture and teamwork has helped the brand to maintain its strong global position for many years.[53]

Another unique case of developing a successful export operation early after its inception is the born global firm of Logitech International. Founded in 1981, Logitech is a Swiss company that designs personal computer peripherals that enable people to effectively work, play, and communicate in the digital world. Its products include a wide variety of electronics accessories such as headsets, key boards, and remote controls.

As demand for a firm's goods and services grows or its commitments increase due to its internationalization efforts, it develops an international structure. Many firms evolve from using their export department structure to forming an international division.

International Divisions

A company's international division centralizes all of the responsibility for international operations (and in many cases, all international activities also become centralized in the international division). The typical international division concentrates human resources (i.e., international expertise) into one unit and serves as the central point for all information flow related to international operations (e.g., international market opportunities, international research and development). At the same time, firms with an international division structure take advantage of economies of scale by keeping manufacturing and related functions within the domestic divisions. Firms may develop international divisions at a relatively early stage, as well as a mature stage, of their international development. However, an increasing number of firms are recognizing the importance of going global early on. As such, these firms use exporting, licensing and franchising, trading companies, contract manufacturing, and joint ventures as possible modes of international market entry.

This international division structure illustrates the importance of coordination and cooperation among domestic and international operations. Frequent interaction and strategic planning meetings are required to make this structure work effectively. In particular, firms that use an international division structure are often organized domestically on the basis of functions or product divisions, whereas the international division is organized on the basis of geography. This means that coordination and strategic alignment across domestic divisions and the international division are critical to success. At the same time, lack of coordination between domestic and international operations is commonly the most significant flaw in the international division structure.

An example of a firm that has used the international division structure to achieve worldwide success is Abbott Laboratories, a $30 billion diversified health-care company that develops products and services that span prevention and diagnosis to treatment and cures. As international sales grew in the late 1960s, the firm added an international division to its structure. This international division structure has benefits and drawbacks for Abbott, as it does for other firms that use it.[54]

Some argue that to offset the natural "isolation" that may result between domestic and international operations in this structure, the international division structure should be used only when a company (1) intends to market only a small assortment of goods or services internationally and (2) when foreign sales account for only a small portion of total sales. When the product assortment increases or the percentage of foreign sales becomes significant, an internationally integrated structure may be more appropriate.

Internationally Integrated Structures

A number of different internationally integrated structures have been developed and implemented by firms in their quest to achieve global success. The three most common structures are the product division structure, the geographic area structure, and the global matrix structure. Firms with these varied structures have multiple choices for international market entry similar to international divisions (e.g., exporting, licensing and franchising, trading companies, contract manufacturing, and joint ventures). However, firms that have internationally integrated structures are the most likely to engage in direct ownership activities internationally.

The product division structure is the form used by the majority of multinational enterprises. This structure lends itself well to firms that are diversified, often driven by their current domestic operations. Each division is a self-contained entity with responsibility for its own operations, whether it is based on a country or regional structure. However, the worldwide headquarters maintains the overall responsibility for the strategic direction of the firm, whereas the product division is in charge of implementation. Procter & Gamble has a long-standing tradition of operating as a product division structure, with leading brands such as Pampers, Tide, Ariel, Always, Pantene, Bounty, Folgers, Pringles, Charmin, Downy, Crest, and Olay.

The geographic area structure lends itself well to firms with a low degree of diversification. Under this domestically influenced functional structure, the world is divided into logical geographical areas based on the firms' operations and the customers' characteristics. Accenture, a global management consulting firm, operates worldwide largely based on a geographic area structure. Each area tends to be relatively self-contained, and integration across areas is typically via the worldwide or the regional headquarters. This structure facilitates local responsiveness, but it is not ideal for reducing global costs and transferring core knowledge across the firm's geographic units. A key issue in geographic area structures, as in almost all multinational corporations, is the need to become more regionally and globally integrated.

The global matrix structure was designed to achieve both global integration and local responsiveness. Asea Brown Boveri (ABB), a Swedish-Swiss engineering multinational, is the best-known firm to implement a global matrix structure. ABB is an international leader in power and automation technologies that enable customers to improve their performance while lowering environmental impact. Global matrix structures theoretically facilitate a simultaneous focus on realizing local responsiveness, cost efficiencies, and knowledge transfers. However, few firms can operate a global matrix well, since the structure is based on, for example, product and geographic divisions simultaneously (or a combination of any two traditional structures). This means that employees belong to two divisions and often report to two managers throughout the hierarchies of the firm. An effectively implemented global matrix structure has the benefit of being global in scope while also being nimble and responsive locally. However, a poorly implemented global matrix structure results in added bureaucracy and indecisiveness in leadership and implementation.

Marketing in Transition
Kit-Kat Shifts to Fair Trade

Fair trade promotes equal, fair, and sustainable trade partnerships and aims to combat poverty by helping individuals in developing countries to compete in the global market. Many organizations support fair trade and certify fair trade products. The most well-known is the World Fair Trade Organization (WFTO), which represents more than 350 organizations committed to fair trade. However, according to the WFTO, advocating fair trade is not enough; in order for it to succeed, there must be a demand for fair trade products. This is where mainstream brands can help.

Nestlé is one mainstream brand becoming more involved in fair trade. In the past, Nestlé faced criticism for its business practices in the developing world. In order to improve its reputation, Nestlé searched for ways to establish itself as a socially responsible company and decided to focus on its use of cocoa beans. The company announced its Cocoa Plan, an investment program designed to address economic and social issues in cocoa farming communities. Through its Cocoa Plan, Nestlé provides cocoa farmers with fair compensation for their cocoa beans, additional training, and disease-resistant cocoa plants. The company uses only fair trade cocoa and sugar in its Kit-Kat bars sold in the United Kingdom and Ireland. Nestlé also agreed to fight child labor and to provide better health care to cocoa suppliers.

Critics of Nestlé accuse the company of using fair trade merely to generate good publicity. Whether or not this is true, the company's Kit-Kat bar is the second most popular chocolate bar

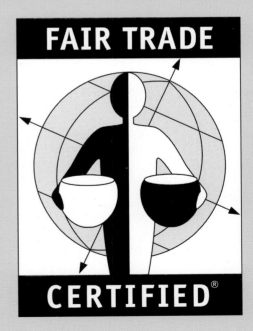

in the UK. Nestlé needs to purchase large amounts of fair trade cocoa, which will have a huge impact on the market. Nestlé's transition into fair trade may help motivate other companies to pursue fair trade—possibly supplying the demand that the WFTO says the fair trade movement so desperately needs.[d]

Customization versus Globalization of International Marketing Mixes

Like domestic marketers, international marketers develop marketing strategies to serve specific target markets. Traditionally international marketing strategies have customized marketing mixes according to cultural, regional, and national differences. Table 9.6 provides a sample of international issues related to product, distribution, promotion, and price. For example, many soap and detergent manufacturers adapt their products to local water conditions, equipment, and washing habits. Colgate-Palmolive even devised an inexpensive plastic hand-powered washing machine for use in households that have no electricity in less-developed countries. Coca-Cola markets distinct versions of its soft drinks for the tastes of different regions of the world;

TABLE 9.6 Marketing Mix Issues Internationally

	Sample International Issues
Product Element	
Core Product	Is there a commonality of the customer's needs across countries? What will the product be used for and in what context?
Product Adoption	How is awareness created for the product in the various country markets? How and where is the product typically bought?
Managing Products	How are truly new products managed in the country markets vis-à-vis existing products or products that have been modified slightly?
Branding	Is the brand accepted widely around the world? Does the home country help or hurt the brand perception of the consumer?
Distribution Element	
Marketing Channels	What is the role of the channel intermediaries internationally? Where is value created beyond the domestic borders of the firm?
Physical Distribution	Is the movement of products the most efficient from the home country to the foreign market or to a regional warehouse?
Retail Stores	What is the availability of different types of retail stores in the various country markets?
Retailing Strategy	Where do customers typically shop in the targeted countries—downtown, in suburbs, or in malls?
Promotion Element	
Advertising	Some countries' customers prefer firm-specific advertising instead of product-specific advertising. How does this affect advertising?
Public Relations	How is public relations used to manage the stakeholders' interests internationally? Are the stakeholders' interests different worldwide?
Personal Selling	What product types require personal selling internationally? Does it differ from how those products are sold domestically?
Sales Promotion	Is coupon usage a widespread activity in the targeted international markets? What other forms of sales promotion should be used?
Pricing Element	
Core Price	Is price a critical component of the value equation of the product in the targeted country markets?
Analysis of Demand	Is the demand curve similar internationally as it is domestically? Will a change in price drastically change demand?
Demand, Cost, and Profit Relationships	What are the fixed and variable costs when marketing the product internationally? Are they similar to the domestic setting?
Determination of Price	How do the pricing strategy, environmental forces, business practices, and cultural values affect price?

Globalization
Coca-Cola customizes its products in many markets, such as China.

© Imaginechina via AP Images

it also customizes promotion to feature local people, humor, and sports teams in its advertising. Realizing that both similarities and differences exist across countries is a critical first step to developing the appropriate marketing strategy effort targeted to particular international markets. Today, many firms strive to build their marketing strategies around similarities that exist instead of customizing around differences.

For many firms, **globalization** of marketing is the goal; it involves developing marketing strategies as though the entire world (or its major regions) were a single entity: a globalized firm markets standardized products in the same way everywhere. Nike and Adidas shoes, for example, are standardized worldwide. Other examples of globalized products include electronic communications equipment, Western-style clothing, movies, soft drinks, rock and alternative music, cosmetics, and toothpaste. Sony televisions, Starbucks coffee, and many products sold at Walmart all post year-to-year gains in the world market.

For many years, organizations have attempted to globalize their marketing mixes as much as possible by employing standardized products, promotion campaigns, prices, and distribution channels for all markets. The economic and competitive payoffs for globalized marketing strategies are certainly great. Brand name, product characteristics, packaging, and labeling are among the easiest marketing mix variables to standardize; media allocation, retail outlets, and price may be more difficult. In the end, the degree of similarity among the various environmental and market conditions determines the feasibility and degree of globalization. A successful globalization strategy often depends on the extent to which a firm is able to implement the idea of "think globally, act locally."[55] Even take-out food lends itself to globalization: McDonald's, KFC, and Taco Bell restaurants satisfy hungry customers in both hemispheres, although menus may be altered slightly to satisfy local tastes. When Dunkin' Donuts entered the Chinese market, it served coffee, tea, donuts, and bagels, just as it does in the United States, but in China, the donut case also includes items like green tea and honeydew melon donuts and mochi rings, which are similar to donuts but are made with rice flour.[56]

International marketing demands some strategic planning if a firm is to incorporate foreign sales into its overall marketing strategy. International marketing activities often require customized marketing mixes to achieve the firm's goals. Globalization requires a total commitment to the world, regions, or multinational areas as an integral part of the firm's markets; world or regional markets become as important as domestic ones. Regardless of the extent to which a firm chooses to globalize its marketing strategy, extensive environmental analysis and marketing research are necessary to understand the needs and desires of the target market(s) and successfully implement the chosen marketing strategy. A global presence does not automatically result in a global competitive advantage. However, a global presence generates five opportunities for creating value: (1) to adapt to local market differences, (2) to exploit economies of global scale, (3) to exploit economies of global scope, (4) to mine optimal locations for activities and resources, and (5) to maximize the transfer of knowledge across locations.[57] To exploit these opportunities, marketers need to conduct marketing research and work within the constraints of the international environment and regional trade alliances, markets, and agreements.

globalization The development of marketing strategies that treat the entire world (or its major regions) as a single entity

summary

1. To understand the nature of global marketing strategy

International marketing involves developing and performing marketing activities across national boundaries. International markets can provide tremendous opportunities for growth and renewed opportunity for the firm.

2. To analyze the environmental forces that affect international marketing efforts

A detailed analysis of the environment is essential before a company enters an international market. Environmental aspects of special importance include sociocultural; economic, political, legal, and regulatory; social and ethical; competitive; and technological forces. Because marketing activities are primarily social in purpose, they are influenced by beliefs and values regarding family, religion, education, health, and recreation. Cultural differences may affect marketing negotiations, decision-making behavior, and product adoption and use. A nation's economic stability and trade barriers can affect marketing efforts. Significant trade barriers include import tariffs, quotas, embargoes, and exchange controls. Gross domestic product (GDP) and GDP per capita are common measures of a nation's economic standing. Political and legal forces include a nation's political system, laws, regulatory bodies, special-interest groups, and courts. In the area of ethics, cultural relativism is the concept that morality varies from one culture to another and that business practices are therefore differentially defined as right or wrong by particular cultures. In addition to considering the types of competition and the types of competitive structures that exist in other countries, marketers also need to consider the competitive forces at work and recognize the importance of the global customer who is well informed about product choices from around the world. Advances in technology have greatly facilitated international marketing.

3. To understand several important international trade agreements

Various regional trade alliances and specific markets create both opportunities and constraints for companies engaged in international marketing. These include the North American Free Trade Agreement, European Union, Common Market of the Southern Cone, Asia-Pacific Economic Cooperation, and World Trade Organization.

4. To identify methods of international market entry

There are several ways to enter international marketing. Importing (the purchase of products from a foreign source) and exporting (the sale of products to foreign markets) are the easiest and most flexible methods. Marketers may employ a trading company, which links buyers and sellers in different countries but is not involved in manufacturing and does not own assets related to manufacturing. Licensing and franchising are arrangements whereby one firm pays fees to another for the use of its name, expertise, and supplies. Contract manufacturing occurs when a company hires a foreign firm to produce a designated volume of the domestic firm's product to specification, and the final product carries the domestic firm's name. Joint ventures are partnerships between a domestic firm and a foreign firm or government. Strategic alliances are partnerships formed to create competitive advantage on a worldwide basis. Finally, a firm can build its own marketing or production facilities overseas. When companies have direct ownership of facilities in many countries, they may be considered multinational enterprises.

5. To examine various forms of global organizational structures

Firms develop their international marketing strategies and manage their marketing mixes by developing and maintaining an organizational structure that best leverages their resources and core competencies. Three basic structures of international organizations include export departments, international divisions, and internationally integrated structures (e.g., product division structures, geographic area structures, and matrix structures).

6. To examine the use of the marketing mix internationally

Although most firms adjust their marketing mixes for differences in target markets, some firms standardize their marketing efforts worldwide. Traditional full-scale international marketing involvement is based on products customized according to cultural, regional, and national differences. Globalization, however, involves developing marketing strategies as if the entire world (or regions of it) were a single entity; a globalized firm markets standardized products in the same way everywhere. International marketing demands some strategic planning if a firm is to incorporate foreign sales into its overall marketing strategy.

Go to www.cengagebrain.com for resources to help you master the content in this chapter as well as materials that will expand your marketing knowledge!

important terms

international marketing, 248

gross domestic product (GDP), 251

import tariff, 253

quota, 253

embargo, 253

exchange controls, 253

balance of trade, 253

cultural relativism, 256

North American Free Trade Agreement (NAFTA), 259

European Union (EU), 260

Common Market of the Southern Cone (MERCOSUR), 261

Asia-Pacific Economic Cooperation (APEC), 261

World Trade Organization (WTO), 262

General Agreement on Tariffs and Trade (GATT), 262

dumping, 263

importing, 263

exporting, 263

trading company, 264

licensing, 265

franchising, 265

contract manufacturing, 266

outsourcing, 266

offshoring, 266

offshore outsourcing, 266

joint venture, 266

strategic alliance, 267

direct ownership, 267

multinational enterprise, 267

globalization, 273

discussion and review questions

1. How does international marketing differ from domestic marketing?
2. What factors must marketers consider as they decide whether to engage in international marketing?
3. Why are the largest industrial corporations in the United States so committed to international marketing?
4. Why do you think this chapter focuses on an analysis of the international marketing environment?
5. If you were asked to provide a small tip (or bribe) to have a document approved in a foreign nation where this practice is customary, what would you do?
6. How will NAFTA affect marketing opportunities for U.S. products in North America (the United States, Mexico, and Canada)?

7. What should marketers consider as they decide whether to license or enter into a joint venture in a foreign nation?
8. Discuss the impact of strategic alliances on international marketing strategies.
9. Contrast globalization with customization of marketing strategies. Is one practice better than the other?
10. What are some of the product issues that you need to consider when marketing luxury automobiles in Australia, Brazil, Singapore, South Africa, and Sweden?

application questions

1. To successfully implement marketing strategies in the international marketplace, a marketer must understand the complexities of the global marketing environment. Which environmental forces (sociocultural, economic, political/legal/regulatory, ethical, competitive, or technological) might a marketer need to consider when marketing the following products in the international marketplace, and why?

a. Barbie dolls
b. Beer
c. Financial services
d. Television sets

2. Many firms, including Procter & Gamble, FedEx, and Occidental Petroleum, wish to do business in eastern Europe and in the countries that were once part of the former Soviet Union. What events could occur that would

make marketing in these countries more difficult? What events might make it easier?

3. This chapter discusses various organizational approaches to international marketing. Which would be the best arrangements for international marketing of the following products, and why?

a. Construction equipment
b. Cosmetics
c. Automobiles

4. Procter & Gamble has made a substantial commitment to foreign markets, especially in Latin America. Its actions may be described as a "globalization of marketing." Describe how a shoe manufacturer (e.g., Wolverine World Wide) would go from domestic marketing to limited exporting, to international marketing, and finally to a globalization of marketing. Give examples of some activities that might be involved in this process.

internet exercise

FTD

Founded in 1910 as Florists' Telegraph Delivery, FTD was the first company to offer a "flowers-by-wire" service. FTD does not deliver flowers itself, but it depends on local florists to do it. In 1994, FTD expanded its toll-free telephone-ordering service by establishing a website. Visit the site at **www.ftd.com**, and answer the following:

1. Click on "International." Select a country to which you would like to send flowers. Summarize the

delivery and pricing information that would apply to that country.

2. Determine the cost of sending fresh-cut seasonal flowers to Germany.

3. What are the benefits of this global distribution system for sending flowers worldwide? What other consumer products could be distributed globally through the Internet?

developing your marketing plan

When formulating marketing strategy, one of the issues a company must consider is whether or not to pursue international markets. Although international markets present increased marketing opportunities, they also require more complex decisions when formulating marketing plans. To assist you in relating the information in this chapter to the development of your marketing plan, focus on the following:

1. Review the environmental analysis that was completed in Chapter 3. Extend the analysis for each of the seven factors to include global markets.

2. Using Figure 9.1 as a guide, determine the degree of international involvement that is appropriate for your product and your company.

3. Discuss the concepts of customization and globalization for your product when moving to international markets. Refer to Table 9.5 for guidance in your discussion.

The information obtained from these questions should assist you in developing various aspects of your marketing plan found in the *Interactive Marketing Plan* exercise at **www.cengagebrain.com**.

VIDEO CASE 9.1

Lonely Planet Provides Guidance to Global Explorer

CRITICAL THINKING

Lonely Planet has been global since before it was even a company—in its audience, its scope, and its foundation. The now ubiquitous guidebook brand got its start in 1973 when Brit Tony Wheeler and his wife, Maureen, holed up in Australia to write a pamphlet on their experiences traveling in Asia. The couple met in their native Britain, found that they shared a love of adventure, and got married soon thereafter. For their honeymoon, they chose to make a trip that no one at the time believed was possible—a journey from Britain across Europe and Asia via land all the way to Australia. They made it, but by that time they were stuck in Australia with 27 cents between the two of them. Tony made the best of the situation by writing the 94-page *Across Asia on the Cheap,* which sold 8,500 copies. From this suitably adventurous start, Lonely Planet ballooned into one of the powerhouses of the growing guidebook and phrasebook industry, with around 500 titles on 118 countries. Lonely Planet now represents one-quarter of all English-language guidebooks sold in the world and has annual revenues in excess of $75 million.

The company has offices in London and Oakland, California, with its headquarters in Melbourne. It employs 500 office staff and around 300 on-the-road contributors. Thanks to these contributors from dozens of different countries, the company has a global scope and a global perspective, which helps the company successfully market worldwide. The huge variety of languages, cultures, and interests across their consumer base makes marketing and developing a coherent brand image difficult. To cope with these hurdles, Lonely Planet works on maintaining a balance between consistency in branding and customizing marketing to suit specific target markets.

In 2007, the Wheelers finally relinquished control of the company when they sold it to BBC Worldwide, which is the commercial branch of the British Broadcasting Company. The addition of the BBC's extensive network of distribution channels has helped Lonely Planet to market itself more successfully and to branch into complementary business areas such as Lonely Planet Images, Lonely Planet Television,

Lonely Planet Foreign Rights Team, Lonely Planet Business Solutions unit, and Lonely Planet Foundation (which contributes 5 percent of all profits to international charities and has established a carbon offset program for printing and the travels of all employees). From the start, one of the fundamental tenets of the Lonely Planet brand has been that travel can truly change the world and make it a better place. Through the Lonely Planet Foundation, the Wheelers have tried to make profound differences in the places they visit. Their far-reaching message is being heard loud and clear, as evidenced by the more than 5 million unique visitors clicking on lonelyplanet.com each month.

This marketing strategy of selective customization combined with relentless fact checking and updating, along with a focus on hiring the best and most knowledgeable travel writers, has earned Lonely Planet a reputation for quality. Lonely Planet books are not only popular; they are considered by many to be the definitive guidebooks. In fact, Jay Garner, the first American administrator in Iraq, considers Lonely Planet such an authority on global travel that he used the book *Lonely Planet Iraq* to develop a list of historical sites worth saving. Another nod to the success of the brand is the fact that in Asia, imitation Lonely Planet guidebooks are now sold alongside imitation Gucci and Chanel handbags and Rolex watches.

No matter what criticisms people may have of Lonely Planet, this single guidebook brand has been responsible for the soaring popularity of adventure tourism worldwide. Because of Lonely Planet, there are surf camps in El Salvador, foreign-owned luxury resorts in Nicaragua, and remote villages in the heights of the Himalayas with economies based around tourism—monuments to the success of their marketing strategy.

Lonely Planet continues its trek toward boundless success, due largely to the organization's clear vision of its target market. The Lonely Planet traveler is willing to embrace foreign food and culture, but still wants to do it comfortably and cheaply, if possible. The company reaches its market through smart marketing and promotion strategies that balance a recognizable brand with customization to accommodate local tastes. Lonely Planet has never forgotten that there really is no such thing as global—that the world consists of thousands of different local populations. And Lonely Planet, by knowing clearly who comprises its market and by smart marketing strategies, has grown from a pamphlet written in a cheap hostel to a huge global brand loved by millions of travelers the world over.[58]

QUESTIONS FOR DISCUSSION

1. Why is Lonely Planet a global success?
2. How has Lonely Planet been able to provide and market guidebooks that are useful across languages and cultures?
3. How could Lonely Planet guidebooks help marketers to develop effective marketing strategies in targeted foreign markets?

CASE 9.2

Nokia Leads with Global Strategy

CRITICAL THINKING

Think "cool, trendy cell phone maker," and companies like Apple or BlackBerry producer Research in Motion (RIM) may come to mind. Yet in terms of global market share, Apple and RIM hold about 0.9 and 1.9 percent, respectively. Conversely, their less trend-setting competitor Nokia holds a whopping 40 percent of the market. The reason has to do with the different target markets of the companies. Apple and RIM cater to a more elite, smaller portion of the market. For instance, the iPhone ranges from $99 to $299 while the BlackBerry Storm costs about $279.99. Many people around the world cannot afford such high-priced products. Nokia, however, caters to a much broader set of consumers. Its phones range from $10 to $700, which allows Nokia to reach many more customers in emerging economies and elsewhere. Advances in technology have provided developing countries the opportunity to catch up with developed countries in communication. Therefore, opportunities for growth in the cell phone market remain especially strong in Southeast Asia, Africa, and the Middle East.

Developing nations lack infrastructure for land lines and, as a result, are turning to cell phones to leapfrog ahead technologically. For people in emerging markets, the mobile phone is the primary way of accessing the Internet. The greatest growth areas for mobile companies are countries such as Indonesia, Egypt, and Russia. Nokia has developed less expensive smartphones to target these emerging markets. The Nokia C3 handset has full keyboards for instant messaging, a 2-megapixel camera, and access to e-mails for about $120. Nokia has sold 83 million phones with global positioning systems and expects these phones to increase in sales rapidly. In order to be successful, Nokia has to understand the political, legal, and regulatory forces that relate to a specific country. The political climate in the region can influence how Nokia enters the market and develops a marketing strategy.

The Telecommunication Union estimates that 4 billion people are cell phone subscribers, most in developing countries. About 20 percent of these subscribers are expected to be high-performance phone browsers by 2013. The popularity of mobile phones has encouraged the building of towers, power stations, and other types of wireless technology infrastructure. Nokia's low-cost innovations have resulted in marketing efforts in the entire mobile communications industry. Nokia's innovations even include a free music downloading service in China, as well as in 30 other nations. Although Nokia is the largest handset company in China, and the world's largest mobile company by number of subscribers, it faces increasing competition from smartphones such as Apple's iPhone and Android-based phones. China is a complex market because it has a tradition of failing to protect copyrights and intellectual property. There is always a danger of counterfeit handsets entering the local market.

The secret to its success is its understanding of global marketing. Nokia extensively researches both its current and potential customers, looking into their cultures and needs. By identifying major sociocultural deviations among companies, Nokia lays the groundwork for an effective adaptation for marketing strategy. Cultural differences also affect marketing negotiations with channel members and consumer decision-making behavior. By understanding these differences, Nokia can then create programs to meet those needs. For instance, its program Life Tools allows customers in India to spend $1.30 per month to receive information on daily crop prices or weather updates—coveted information for consumers whose livelihood depends on farming. Nokia funds ten research labs throughout the world to help it learn more about its global consumers.

As a result, Nokia has become an expert on efficiency, cost management, and top-notch distribution. Apple and RIM may be responsible for changing the cell phone experience for higher-end elite smartphone users, but Nokia is responsible for allowing people in hard-to-reach areas throughout the world to access cellular service.[59]

QUESTIONS FOR DISCUSSION

1. What are the environmental forces that influence Nokia's marketing strategy in various countries?
2. Compare Nokia's marketing strategy for global success with the marketing strategy of Apple Research in Motion (RIM).
3. What has given Nokia its global competitive advantage in the cell phone market?

Chapter 10

E-Marketing, Digital Media, and Social Networking

OBJECTIVES

1. To define *digital media* and *electronic marketing* and recognize their increasing importance in strategic planning

2. To understand the characteristics of digital media and electronic marketing—addressability, interactivity, accessibility, connectivity, control—and how they differentiate from traditional marketing activities

3. To identify and understand the role of digital media in a marketing strategy and how each type of digital media can be used as an effective marketing tool

4. To understand and identify how digital media affects the marketing mix and marketing research techniques

5. To identify legal and ethical considerations in digital media and electronic marketing

NASCAR Turns to Social Media to Attract a Larger Crowd

NASCAR (the National Association for Stock Car Auto Racing) was founded in 1947 by Bill France Jr. as a sanctioning body for stock car racing. The first official NASCAR race was held in 1948, less than a week after its founding. In the early 1970s, a time when television coverage of sports exploded, corporations began marketing by sponsoring events and drivers. Today, NASCAR is the United States' most popular spectator sport and second most popular television sport.

Whether or not you watch NASCAR, you have likely seen the cars and jumpsuits covered in advertisements. For years, sponsors have relayed their messages via this and other conventional media. In 2009, the organization also announced a three-year deal to run ads in movie theaters. All of this has worked out well—statistics show that NASCAR fans patronize its sponsor companies.

NASCAR and its sponsors are also looking toward the future. As part of a step forward, they have begun using online social media to launch campaigns and interact with consumers. NASCAR.com is a popular site that features links to sponsors via Facebook, Twitter, and YouTube. Sprint, one of NASCAR's cup sponsors, created Facebook and Twitter Miss Sprint Cup accounts, which have around 80,000 fans. The Miss Sprint Cup representatives travel the NASCAR circuit and post updates to their pages. NASCAR fans tune in to Miss Sprint Cup's posts for information on favorite drivers and images from races. Extending the strategy a step further, NASCAR recently reviewed independent NASCAR fan sites and awarded journalistic status to some. These fan bloggers were then given access to media resources, special events, and press boxes at racetracks.

NASCAR's successful entrance into the world of digital marketing has already earned it recognition. For instance, Forrester Research named NASCAR its 2009 Groundswell Award winner for business-to-consumer listening based on the handling of its NASCAR Fan Council, an online community founded to learn more about its fans.[1]

Since the 1990s, the Internet and information technology have dramatically changed the marketing environment and the strategies that are necessary for marketing success. Digital media have created exciting opportunities for companies to target specific markets more effectively, develop new marketing strategies, and gather more information about customers than was possible in the past. Using digital media channels, marketers are better able to analyze and address consumer needs.

One of the defining characteristics of information technology in the 21st century is accelerating change. New systems and applications advance so rapidly that a chapter on this topic has to strain to incorporate the possibilities of the future. For example, the social networking site Friendster was the market leader from its launch in 2003 until MySpace usurped it in 2006. Then Facebook emerged; since 2008, it has been even more popular than its predecessors. As another example, when Google first arrived on the scene in 1998, a number of search engines were fighting for dominance, including WebCrawler, Lycos, Magellan, Infoseek, and Excite. Google, with its fast, easy-to-use format, soon became the number-one search engine. Today Google provides additional competition to many industries, including advertising, newspaper, mobile phone, and book publishing. In addition, Google poses a threat to the large and growing online social networking industry. The environment for marketing is changing rapidly based on these factors as well as unknown future developments within information technology.

In this chapter, we focus on digital marketing strategies, particularly new communication channels such as social networks, and discuss how consumers are changing their information searches and consumption behaviors to fit with these emerging technologies and trends. Most importantly, we analyze how marketers can use new media to their advantage to better connect with consumers, gather more information about their target markets, and convert this information into successful marketing strategies.

digital media Electronic media that function using digital codes; when we refer to digital media, we are referring to media available via computers, cellular phones, smartphones, and other digital devices that have been released in recent years

digital marketing Uses all digital media, including the Internet and mobile and interactive channels, to develop communication and exchanges with customers

electronic marketing (e-marketing) The strategic process of distributing, promoting, pricing products, and discovering the desires of customers using digital media and digital marketing

Growth and Benefits of E-Marketing

Before we move on, we must first provide a definition of digital media. **Digital media** are electronic media that function using digital codes—when we refer to digital media, we are referring to media available via computers, cellular phones, smartphones, and other digital devices that have been released in recent years. A number of terms have been coined to describe marketing activities on the Internet. **Digital marketing** uses all digital media, including the Internet and mobile and interactive channels, to develop communication and exchanges with customers. In this chapter, we focus on how the Internet relates to all aspects of marketing, including strategic planning. Thus, we use the term **electronic marketing**, or **e-marketing**, to refer to the strategic process of distributing, promoting, pricing products, and discovering the desires of customers using digital media and digital marketing. Our definition of e-marketing goes beyond the Internet and also includes mobile phones, banner ads, digital outdoor marketing, and social networks.

The phenomenal growth of the Internet has provided unprecedented opportunities for marketers to forge interactive relationships with consumers. As the Internet and digital communication technologies have advanced, they have made it possible to target markets more precisely and reach markets that were previously inaccessible. Because of its ability to enhance the exchange of information between the marketer and the customer, the Internet has become an important component of firms' marketing strategies. As the world of digital media continues to develop, Internet marketing has been integrated into strategies that include

Digital Marketing
Telescope assists marketers with their digital marketing strategies.

all digital media, including television advertising and other mobile and interactive media that do not use the Internet (advertising media are discussed in detail in Chapter 19). In fact, marketers are using the term *digital marketing* as a catch-all for capturing all digital channels for reaching customers. This area is changing and evolving quickly, and the digital world is still in an early stage of integration into marketing strategy.[2]

One of the most important benefits of e-marketing is the ability of marketers and customers to share information. Through websites, social networks, and other digital media, consumers can learn about everything they consume and use in life. These media provide feedback mechanisms through which customers can ask questions, voice complaints, indicate preferences, and otherwise communicate about their needs and desires. The Internet has changed the way marketers communicate and develop relationships not only with their customers but also with their employees and suppliers. Many companies use not just e-mail and mobile phones but also social networking, wikis, video sharing, podcasts, blogs, videoconferencing, and other technologies to coordinate activities and communicate with employees. Twitter, considered both a social network and micro blog, illustrates how these digital technologies are combined to create new communication opportunities.

Nielsen Marketing Research finds that consumers spend more time on social networking sites than e-mail, and the gap is growing. The most avid online social networkers are Australians, followed by British, Italians, and residents of the United States. In 2009, the average American spent more than twice as much time surfing social networking sites than two years earlier.[3] Because of the way they facilitate communications while significantly reducing their costs, these new information technologies represent a tremendous opportunity for any industry or activity that depends on the flow of information.

For many businesses, engaging in digital and online marketing activities is essential to attain and retain a competitive edge. Increasingly, small businesses can use digital media to develop strategies to reach new markets and access inexpensive communication channels. In addition, large companies like Walmart utilize online catalogs and company websites to supplement their brick-and-mortar stores. At the other end of the spectrum, companies like Amazon.com, which lack physical stores and sell products solely online, are emerging to challenge traditional brick-and-mortar businesses. Social networking sites such as Facebook are advancing e-marketing by providing features such as developing their own currency to purchase products, send gifts, and engage in the entire shopping experience.[4] Finally, some corporate websites provide feedback mechanisms through which customers can ask questions, voice complaints, indicate preferences, and otherwise communicate about their needs and desires.

Characteristics of E-Marketing

One of the biggest mistakes a marketer can make when engaging in digital marketing is to treat it like a traditional marketing channel. Digital media offer a whole new dimension to marketing that marketers must consider when concocting their companies' marketing strategies. Some of the characteristics that distinguish online media from traditional marketing include addressability, interactivity, accessibility, connectivity, and control.

Addressability

Digital media technology makes it possible for visitors on a website to identify themselves and provide information about their product needs and wants before making a purchase. The ability of a marketer to identify customers before they make a purchase is called **addressability**. Many websites encourage visitors to register to maximize their use of the site or to gain access to premium areas. Social networks are also enhancing addressability. A **social network** is defined as "a web-based meeting

addressability The ability of a marketer to identify customers before they make a purchase

social network Web-based meeting place for friends, family, coworkers, and peers that allow users to create a profile and connect with other users for purposes that range from getting acquainted, to keeping in touch, to building a work-related network

place for friends, family, co-workers and peers that allows users to create a profile and connect with other users for the purposes that range from getting acquainted, to keeping in touch, to building a work related network."[5] Addressability on social networks is achieved through their ability to provide a meeting ground for individuals and groups with similar interests and consumption patterns. On social networks, members register varying degrees of personal information; many users also post more information such as likes and dislikes, hobbies, and photographs. By becoming "friends" with other consumers on these social networks, companies are able to gain more access to consumer preferences.

An addressable channel means the marketer knows who the customer is and can specifically address that person, rather than using a more generic appeal, as occurs in traditional personal interactions. From the standpoint of integrated marking communications, this creates the opportunity for customization of promotions. Addressability provides the opportunity for the implementation of relationship marketing. In addition, there are the possibilities of valuing the customer with financial metrics, developing new promotions, and increasing the seller's share of the customer's purchase.

The service dimension of products can be enhanced through e-marketing using digital media. Firms can cut costs and involve the customer in the production or operations activities that provide service. Addressability greatly facilitates relationship marketing because it enables customer engagement to create product innovation. Marketers get to know their customers, hear their desires, adapt products to meet those desires, and thereby turn customers into brand advocates. Hyundai took advantage of the most recent recession by creating a Customer Assurance Program. The program helped to bolster vehicle sales in an uncertain economic climate by allowing buyers to walk away from a purchased vehicle in times of financial distress. After implementing the program, Hyundai saw sales increase by 14 percent.[6] Hyundai Assurance utilizes the Internet because consumers who wish to take advantage of this program must apply online. The company also has a Facebook page with games and other interactive features that allow potential customers to develop a relationship with Hyundai.

Addressability represents the ultimate expression of the marketing concept. Armed with knowledge about individual customers gleaned from the Web, particularly online social networking sites, marketers can tailor marketing mixes more precisely to target customers with narrow interests. Although the most famous social networks like MySpace and Facebook address a wide range of Internet users, niche social networks exist that address specific demographics in the population. One example is Snowago, a social network that allows skiers and snowboarders to connect with one another and get updates about more than 700 resorts. Another is Tennisopolis, which allows tennis enthusiasts to follow tennis news, track events, and find partners in their area. Addressability enables marketers to track website visits and online buying activity, which makes it easier for them to accumulate data and target individual customers to enhance future marketing efforts. Netflix uses addressability to store data about what movies customers have watched and their movie ratings, enabling the company to make recommendations the next time the customer visits the site.

Courtesy of Susan Van Etten

Characteristics of E-Marketing
Biore encourages consumers to visit its website and take the "2 Week Challenge" to appreciate the benefits of using its skin products.

Interactivity

Another distinguishing characteristic of social networks is **interactivity**, which allows customers to express their needs and wants directly to the firm in response to its marketing communications. Traditional marketing usually involves one-way forms of communication. The marketer contacts the customer through an advertising message, and if the customer has questions or concerns, he or she contacts company representatives by phone or via other feedback mechanisms. This sometimes lengthy process requires companies to employ service representatives and/or call centers to interact with customers, and customers often experience a waiting period of some duration from between the time they issue the request to when they receive an answer. (Think of how often you are put on hold when you contact an organization by phone.) Too much waiting can result in customer dissatisfaction.

Another problem with traditional modes of advertising is when consumers see marketing messages as an intrusion on their time. For instance, receiving a sales call during dinner or placing commercials in movie previews at theaters are often viewed as annoying. This makes it harder for businesses to create marketing messages that will attract viewers' attention.

As an alternative to traditional marketing, interactivity focuses on the kinds of digital media that can make interpersonal connections possible. By utilizing appropriate digital media, companies can facilitate interactivity and enable a conversation with the customer. Features like interactive links on websites, for example, allow Internet users to view marketing messages at their own pace, which is different from the more "intrusive" advertisements like television commercials or sales calls. Thus, digital communication can help advertising move away from being an intrusion to developing relationships through greater interaction between business and consumer.

Digital media like blogs and some social networks allow marketers to interact with prospective customers in real time (or a close approximation of it). The one-sided communication common to traditional marketing channels is being replaced with interactive conversations between customer and marketer. Interactivity provides the advantages of a virtual sales representative, with broader market coverage at lower costs.

Interactivity helps marketers maintain high-quality relationships with existing customers by shaping customer expectations and perceptions. Additionally, digital media has created a myriad of relationships. Where traditionally a relationship existed between a company and a consumer, the Internet now allows consumers to form relationships with one another as well—through online chats, blogs, and electronic word of mouth.[7] By providing information, ideas, and a context for interacting with other customers, interactive marketers can enhance customers' interest in and involvement with their products.

Accessibility

An extraordinary amount of information is available on the Internet, and users can access this information with a few simple clicks. The ability to obtain digital information is referred to as **accessibility**. Because customers can access in-depth information about competing products, prices, reviews, and so forth, they are much better informed about a firm's products and their relative value than ever before.

Mobile devices such as smartphones, mobile computing devices, and PDAs allow customers to leave their desktop and access digital networks from anywhere. Thanks to the popularity of smartphones and PDAs, one of the fastest-growing areas in mobile technology is the creation of applications (known as *apps*) that help consumers to access more information about businesses. The paint manufacturer Benjamin Moore & Co. has an iPhone app that allows users to match colors in photographs with shades in Benjamin Moore's 3,300-hue color system.[8] The most important feature of apps is the convenience and cost savings they offer to the consumer. Certain apps, for instance, allow consumers to scan a product's barcode and then compare it with the prices of identical products in other stores.

interactivity Allows customers to express their needs and wants directly to the firm in response to its marketing communications

accessibility The ability to obtain digital information

To remain competitive, companies are beginning to use mobile marketing to offer additional incentives to consumers, with some success. The automotive services company Jiffy Lube, for instance, used coupons offered over mobile devices for one of its franchises. The company estimated that 50 percent of the new customers that came to that franchise did so as a result of its mobile marketing.[9] Another app that benefits both consumers and retailers is the mobile app known as Yowza!!, which uses the GPS devices in cell phones to locate consumers and send them coupons from retailers in that area.[10] Imagine walking by a Starbucks and immediately having a coupon for a mocha latte appear on your cell phone. Mobile apps are now making this possible, introducing a whole new layer to digital marketing.

Accessibility does not only refer to the consumer's ability to obtain information. A firm can also use accessibility to its advantage. Many companies are adopting a digital media philosophy of "open innovation." Firms can go to sites such as GeniusRocket.com or Innocentive.com to request ideas for new products. For example, rather than go to an advertising agency, some firms have posted online offerings of $1,000 for a winning logo design. One firm offered $10,000 for innovative ways to communicate male grooming ideas to target markets.[11]

Digital media requires Internet marketers to be creative. Hewlett-Packard Co., for instance, has conducted research to find new ways to adapt its website so that customers can access it through mobile devices like cell phones. Marketers must be increasingly diligent and innovative to attract Internet users, requiring a level of creativity that extends beyond traditional marketing media.

Connectivity

Connectivity is one of the key contributions of social networking, connecting customers with marketers as well as with other customers. It involves the use of digital networks to provide linkages between information providers and users. Connectivity has been made easier by Facebook, the world's largest online social network, and other global sites such as MySpace, LinkedIn, and Twitter. Many countries have their own much smaller social networking sites as well. Orkut is a Google-owned service that has gained popularity in India and Brazil. In China, QQ is the major social networking site; some of its counterparts are Skyrocket in France, VKONTAKTE in Russia, and Cy-World in South Korea. Muxlim targets the world's Muslims, and researchGATE connects scientists and researchers. Being a 21st-century phenomenon and therefore a fairly new development in marketing, the social networking industry has grown by leaps and bounds. One estimate by E-marketer suggests that more than 6 million people worldwide will use their cell phones to engage in social networking by 2013.[12]

One reason that marketers are drawn to social networks is the size and diversity of the audience. The Facebook audience is larger than the audience of any television network that has ever existed in history, and Facebook attracts users from all over the world. Using Facebook and other online social networking sites, marketers can more easily target communication to specific markets based on age, gender, interest, and lifestyle than they can using more traditional marketing media. Consumers can connect and express their interests to one another, and marketers can use social networking sites to gather information, advertise, and develop various types of interactive dialogues.[13]

Control

Control refers to customers' abilities to regulate the information that they view and the rate and sequence of their exposure to that information. The Internet is sometimes referred to as a *pull* medium because users determine which websites they are going to view; the marketer has only limited ability to control the content to which users are exposed, and in what sequence. Digital media like blogs and social networks have endowed users with even greater power because they can more easily associate themselves with certain groups and can actively rate products and services. Marketers may fear that their power is being undermined by digital media because they blur the line between

connectivity Use of digital networks to provide linkages between information providers and users

control Customers' abilities to regulate the information they view and the rate and sequence of their exposure to that information

Control
Bissell promotes the effectiveness of its vacuum cleaners through a pet photo contest. The company promotes the contest through a mix of traditional and digital media.

marketer and consumer. Digital media certainly require marketers to approach their jobs in very different ways than traditional marketing.[14]

Enterprise 2.0 is a term coined to describe firms' efforts to use cutting-edge technology associated with social networks and blogs to assist in workplace connections. It involves software modifications to contribute to traditional software platforms used by large companies. Companies like the telecom firm Alcatel Lucent have designed their own internal social networks for in-house networking. Alcatel found that knowledge workers spend 6 to 10 hours per week hunting for information. By using the company's own social network, employees can find data faster. Internal social networks are a great way to capture knowledge and identify experts on different subjects within an organization.[15]

Other companies are using this increased power of the consumer to their advantage. While negative ratings and reviews are damaging to a company, positive customer feedback is free publicity that often helps the company more than corporate messages do. Because consumer-generated content appears more authentic than corporate messages, it can go far in increasing a company's credibility. Many firms, such as PepsiCo, launch digital marketing campaigns with a social responsibility angle in order to help bolster their reputations. PepsiCo's Pepsi sought to engage consumers and make them feel closer to its products by utilizing community outreach online. Its Pepsi Refresh Project calls for consumer ideas for socially responsible initiatives—on which other consumers can vote to determine which idea Pepsi will fund.[16]

Companies are also beginning to tap into consumers' knowledge and expertise in order to profit. In 2009, Frito-Lay (a PepsiCo company) used a consumer-generated video featuring its Doritos tortilla chips product to win the Ad Meter contest for the Super Bowl. By taking a chance on two unknown amateur filmmakers, Frito-Lay was able to harness their talent into an extremely profitable publicity campaign.[17] The company sought to repeat the feat in 2010 with a slew of new amateur ads. Frito-Lay promised $5 million to winners if they could take the top three Ad Meter spots, but they fell short when the number-two place went to a Doritos ad.[18] Marketers who invest in and experiment with new digital media are transforming the threat to corporate power into an opportunity to send authentic consumer-generated messages to a broad audience.

Types of Consumer-Generated Marketing and Digital Media

While e-marketing has generated exciting opportunities for producers of products to interact with consumers, it is essential to recognize that digital media are more consumer-driven than traditional media. Consumer-generated material is having a profound effect on marketing. As the Internet becomes more accessible worldwide, consumers are creating and reading consumer-generated content like never before. Social networks and advances in software technology, such as Enterprise 2.0, provide an environment for marketers to utilize consumer-generated digital media.

Two major trends have caused consumer-generated information to gain importance:

1. The increased tendency of consumers to publish their own thoughts, opinions, reviews, and product discussions through blogs or digital media.
2. Consumers' tendencies to trust other consumers over corporations. Consumers often rely on the recommendations of friends, family, and fellow consumers when making purchasing decisions.

By understanding where online users are likely to express their thoughts and opinions, marketers can use these forums to interact with consumers, address problems, and promote their companies. Types of digital media in which Internet users are likely to participate include social networking sites, blogs, wikis, video-sharing sites, podcasts, virtual reality sites, mobile applications, and more.

Social Networks

Social networks have evolved quickly in a short period of time (see Table 10.1 for the launch dates of major social networking sites). The precursors to today's social networks began in the 1970s with bulletin board systems. These systems allowed users to log on and interact with one another. The first modern social network was SixDegrees. com, launched in 1997. This system permitted users to create a profile and connect with friends—the core attributes of today's social networks.[19] Although Six Degrees was later shut down due to lack of interest and adoption by Internet users, the seed

Marketing in Transition
Facebook Can Be a Marketer's Best Friend

Founded in 2004, Facebook was initially created just to connect students at Harvard and other Ivy League universities; it soon expanded to include family, friends, and coworkers. Since being opened to the general public, it has grown to support more than 500 million users worldwide. Although it still serves its original purpose, Facebook has acquired diverse new roles as well, even changing how people use the Internet. When conducting research, many people now seek recommendations from social media friends before conducting other kinds of searches. Facebook users share more than 5 billion pieces of Web content each week.

Marketing strategists say businesses now must worry about how to connect to consumers via social media. One of the ways is to create a fan page, of which Facebook has billions. The average user becomes a fan of four pages each month. Fan pages use widgets, which help companies keep track of information on who is becoming a fan of their page. Businesses can use widgets to learn about and track their customers in order to better understand and serve them. These pages are inexpensive and easy to produce, making them accessible to all businesses.

Businesses must tread carefully, however. Generally, Facebook users do not want to feel as if they are being subjected to sales pitches. In order to make fans feel connected to a company without making them feel like they are being pressured to buy something against their will, companies must dedicate time to responding to fan posts and providing relevant information. Problems aside, fan pages and other uses of widgets are a cheap

way for companies to advertise their goods and services while also garnering information about consumers. Art Meets Commerce—a marketing firm commissioned to promote Broadway and Off-Broadway shows—has used Facebook with great success, as it is the company's number-one source of ticket sales. Given the popularity of fan pages and the low cost commitment, Facebook may be the future of advertising for some firms.[a]

TABLE 10.1 Launch Dates of Major Social Network Sites

Before 2000	Six Degrees.com, Asian Avenue, LiveJournal, Black Planet
2000	LunarStorm (SNS Relaunch), MiGente, Six Degrees Closes
2001	Cyworld, Ryze
2002	Fotolog, Friendster, Skyblog
2003	Coachsurfing, LinkedIn, MySpace, Tribe.net, Open BC/Xing, Last.FM, Hi5
2004	Orkut, Dogster, Flickr, Piczo, Mixi, Facebook (Harvard-only), Multiply, aSmallWorld, Dodgeball, Care2 (SNS Relaunch), Catster, Hyves
2005	Yahoo! 360, YouTube, Xanga (SNS relaunch), Cyworld (China), Bebo (SNS relaunch), Facebook (high school networks), Ning, Asian Avenue, BlackPlanet (relaunch)
2006	QQ (relaunch), Facebook (corporate networks), Windows Live Spaces, Cyworld (U.S.), Twitter, MyChurch, Facebook (everyone)
2007	Badoo (relaunched), Mom Bloggers Club, Hulu, FriendFeed
2008	Kaixin001, Greenwala
2009	MyBlackberry, MySears, MyKmart
2010	Google Buzz

Sources: Jennifer James, "About Us," Mom Bloggers Club, www.mombloggersclub.com/notes/About_Us (accessed June 1, 2010); "About Us," Greenwala, www.greenwala.com/greenwala/about_us (accessed June 1, 2010); Mark Bresseel, "The History of Social Media in a Blink," http://mbresseel.spaces.live.com/Blog/cns%2133234018BF280C82%21345. entry (accessed October 3, 2010).

was planted and social networks were here to stay.[20] Other social networks followed, including LiveJournal, Friendster, and Hi5.[21] Each wave of social network has become increasingly sophisticated. Today's social networks—Facebook, MySpace, LinkedIn, and Twitter being among the most popular—offer a multitude of consumer benefits, including musical downloads, apps, forums, and more.

As the number of social network users increases, interactive marketers are finding new opportunities to reach out to consumers in new target markets. MyYearBook is a social networking site that offers teenagers a forum in which to write on particular subjects important to teens, including sensitive topics facing today's younger generation. Its popularity with teenagers is rising; the site's traffic has increased 36 percent annually, with most users coming from the United States. For advertisers, this particular site is an opportunity to reach out to teens and young adults, a demographic that is difficult to reach with traditional marketing. Advertisers from Nikon and Paramount Pictures have both made deals to advertise through the site.[22] Other social networking sites also offer ways for marketers to advertise on their sites. More information on how marketers use social networks is provided in later sections of this chapter.

Internet users join social networks for many reasons, from chatting with friends to professional networking. In 2009, an estimated two-thirds of consumers in the United States had visited social networks or blogs.[23]

Social networks are not just for Americans; they have become very popular in other countries as well, as mentioned earlier in this chapter. One in three South Korean and one in five Japanese Internet users participate in social networks.[24] As social networks evolve, both marketers and the owners of social networking sites are realizing the incredible opportunities such networks offer—an influx of advertising dollars for social networking owners and a large reach for the advertiser. As a result, marketers have begun investigating and experimenting with promotion on social networks.

FACEBOOK

In April 2008, the social networking site Facebook surpassed MySpace in its number of members, becoming the most popular social networking site in the world.[25] Nearly one-third of all Internet users have visited the site.[26] Internet users create Facebook profiles and then search the network for people with whom to connect. Users must be a "friend" of the person whose profile they are trying to view before they can see personal information. Facebook has a cleaner, more family-friendly image that appeals to a larger demographic than MySpace. It markets to parents and grandparents as well as to teenagers.[27] In fact, the fastest-growing group on Facebook is that of women 55 and over.[28]

For this reason, many marketers are turning to Facebook to market products, interact with consumers, and take advantage of free publicity. It is possible for consumers to become "fans" of major companies like Procter & Gamble (P&G) by clicking on the "Become a Fan" icon on its Facebook page. Companies are also using Facebook to generate excitement about new products. BMW, for instance, generated enthusiasm for its BMW-1 Series by sponsoring a Facebook contest where users could create their own drawings of a BMW-1 car and share their work with others. This contest created excitement for the product, a sense of personal involvement, and greater recognition of the brand.[29]

Social networking sites are also useful for small businesses. Hansen Cakes in Beverly Hills uses interactive marketing on a social networking outlet to drum up more business. One of their cake decorators provides updates on her current projects and offers free cake samples to Facebook users. By using Facebook, companies are better able to engage in relationship marketing or the creation of relationships that mutually benefit the marketing business and the customer. Other products that have utilized relationship marketing to help consumers feel more connected to products are Pepsi and Procter & Gamble's heartburn medication, Prilosec OTC. Prilosec responded to falling market share by embracing new digital media. In order to make consumers feel more connected and loyal to the product, the company began micro-sponsoring causes and companies important to its consumers. Prilosec declared itself the "official sponsor of everything" and aimed to strike 1,000 deals worth $1,000 each. The brand largely relied on word-of-mouth publicity via social networking sites to spread the word about its unique campaign.[30]

MYSPACE

MySpace is a social networking site that offers users the chance to create a profile and connect with other MySpace members across the world. It is similar to Facebook but was released earlier. Like Facebook, MySpace allows users to watch videos, listen to and promote music, instant message friends, write on various topics (called forums), network with friends/colleagues, play games, and more. Since 2006, MySpace has been accessible in a variety of languages, including Swedish, Chinese, Spanish, Portuguese, and Turkish. Alternative versions also exist depending on the location of the user. MySpace receives approximately 59 million monthly viewers.[31] MySpace has experienced difficulties competing with Facebook, in part because of its reputation as more of a dating networking site than one for keeping in touch with friends or making job connections.

Nevertheless, MySpace retains a loyal following who prefer its layout and interface to other online social networking sites. Businesses have come up with unique ways to interact with consumers through MySpace. Burger King created a fictional profile for its mascot, The King, on MySpace to appeal to the 18- to-34 age group. Financial institutions like American Express and Citigroup have also created MySpace pages to better connect with their customers who are MySpace users. By allowing consumers to become friends, businesses can provide updates to everyone in their network and permit users to post comments. Marketers should be warned, however, that not all comments from users will be positive. MySpace is home to hundreds of profiles specifically created to boycott certain businesses. Yet if marketers are willing to take the risk and address negative feedback, using MySpace can be an effective and creative way to generate customer loyalty and interest.

LINKEDIN

LinkedIn is a social networking site geared toward professionals. Users can network with professionals from all over the world. According to the LinkedIn website, the

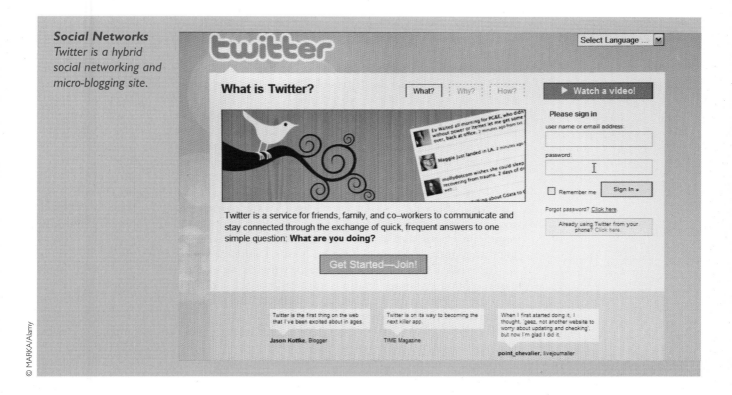

Social Networks
Twitter is a hybrid social networking and micro-blogging site.

network had more than 55 million members in 2010, including executives from all *Fortune* 500 companies. LinkedIn is the fifth largest social networking site, with several million monthly visitors.[32]

A LinkedIn profile resembles a résumé. It contains information on past and current job experiences, qualifications, goals, and educational background. Like all social networking sites, LinkedIn allows users to locate and connect with other LinkedIn members and join groups, which in this case are predominantly professional organizations. Perhaps most beneficial, LinkedIn facilitates job searches and allows companies to search the network for potential employees with the necessary skills. Microsoft, Target, eBay, and Netflix have all used the LinkedIn network to recruit for new employees.[33]

Although a professional networking site like LinkedIn seems more like a recruiting site rather than a marketing tool, companies use LinkedIn to familiarize users with their businesses. For instance, in addition to listing job openings, the discount retailer Target uses its LinkedIn page to offer stock information, a link to the company website, some background on the business, and links to news updates on company activities and products. Similarly, Procter & Gamble has a LinkedIn page that allows users to locate professionals, research careers, and get updates on the company. Smart marketers can thereby use LinkedIn to reach professionals not only for recruiting purposes but also to spread information and interest in the company.

TWITTER

Twitter is a hybrid mix of a social networking site and a micro-blogging site that asks viewers one simple question: "What's happening?" Users can post answers of up to 140 characters, which are then available for their "followers" to read. It sounds simple enough, but its effects on digital media have been immense. Twitter emerged at a brainstorming session at the podcasting company Odeo. Odeo member Jack Dorsey proposed the idea of sharing online messages with friends without having to go through the more lengthy process of making blog entries. Essentially, he wanted to explore a prototype that would use SMS (text messaging) as a form of online communication. The podcasting elements were eventually removed from the company, leaving behind only the social networking parts.

Twitter was officially born in 2006, and it became available to the public in 2007. Twitter quickly progressed from novelty to social networking staple, attracting 6 million monthly viewers.[34] About 11 percent of Internet users have used a micro-blogging site like Twitter.[35]

The thrill of Twitter is that users get to tell the world about their daily lives in short messages, known as "tweets." These tweets can range from the mundane, such as "I'm eating a sandwich," to the highly significant. For instance, President Obama used Twitter to announce "We just made history" when he won the 2008 presidential election. Twitter has allowed people to report information fast—even scooping major news networks on important topics, like the 2008 Mumbai shootings when those in the area used Twitter to provide details on the incident almost immediately.[36]

A limitation of 140 characters may not seem like enough for companies to send an effective message, but some have become experts at micro-blogging. The restaurant Tupelo in Cambridge, Massachusetts, used Twitter to give updates before it even opened, covering topics from what would be on the menu to updates on health inspections. The restaurant claims that at least half the customers present on the restaurant's opening night were there as a result of the business's Twitter activity.[37]

Like other social networking sites, Twitter is also being used to build or, in some cases, rebuild customer relationships. Perhaps the most notable example are banks, which used Twitter to reach out to consumers and restore consumer trust in financial institutions after the Wall Street financial crisis of 2008. In addition to using MySpace, Wells Fargo and Bank of America have begun tweeting about their companies' services and customer benefits as well as using Twitter to address customer concerns quickly.[38]

Finally, companies are using Twitter to gain a competitive advantage. Microsoft's search engine Bing developed a partnership with Twitter in which Bing sorts through the millions of tweets, arranging them by relevance and the popularity of the person tweeting. By doing a Bing-Twitter search, Twitter fans get the most important tweets in real time. Not to be outdone, Google created its own deal with Twitter shortly afterward.[39] The race is on for companies who want to use Twitter to get an edge over the competition.

blogs Web-based journals (short for "weblogs") in which writers editorialize and interact with other Internet users

Responsible Marketing?

Yelp Provides Customer Reviews, But Does It Also Hurt Businesses?

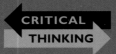
CRITICAL THINKING

ISSUE: Does Yelp manipulate consumer reviews to make some businesses look bad, or is it providing a great service by directing consumers toward the best local businesses?

If you want recommendations on a business, Yelp, Inc. may be your answer. As of 2010, the site had over 10 million reviews. It started when co-founder Jeremy Stoppleman went online to find recommendations for a good local doctor. His search was fruitless, leading him to create a site that would offer a better service to consumers. In many ways, Yelp is changing the consumer-business relationship by putting more power into consumers' hands. It supports itself by selling advertising to the businesses it covers. However, some companies that choose not to advertise accuse Yelp of purposely removing positive reviews of their companies and posting negative reviews. They have filed class-action lawsuits against Yelp. Yelp says this confusion may stem from its filtering process. To keep reviews authentic, Yelp filters content that looks like spam along with reviews that look like they were written by people with a hidden agenda. Whatever the case, consumers searching for reliable businesses continue flocking to Yelp for recommendations.[b]

Blogs and Wikis

Today's marketers must recognize the impact of consumer-generated material like blogs and wikis, as their significance to online consumers has increased a great deal. **Blogs** (short for "weblogs") are web-based journals in which writers can editorialize and interact with other Internet users. Two-thirds of Internet users read blogs, and more than half of bloggers say that they blog about topics and brands about which they feel strongly.[40] The blogging phenomenon is not limited to North America. In South Korea, for example, blogging is even more popular. More than two-thirds of the online population in South Korea creates blogs or similar material.[41]

Blogs give consumers power, sometimes more than companies would like. Whether or not the blog's content is factually accurate, bloggers can post whatever opinions they like about a company or its products. When a Korean Dunkin' Donuts worker created a blog alleging that a company factory had unsanitary conditions, the company forced him to remove the blog. However, readers had already created copies of the blog, and they spread it across the Internet after the original's removal.[42] The company was not able to thwart the power of the Internet user. In other cases, a positive review of a product or service posted on a popular blog can result in large increases in sales. Thus, blogs can represent a potent threat to corporations or an opportunity for them.

Blogs have major advantages as well. Rather than trying to eliminate blogs that cast their companies in a negative light, some businesses are using such blogs to answer consumer concerns or defend their corporate reputations. Many major corporations have created their own blogs or encourage employees to blog about the company. Boeing operates a corporate blog to highlight company news and to post correspondence from Boeing enthusiasts from all over the world.[43] As blogging changes the face of media, companies like Boeing are using them to build enthusiasm for their products and create relationships with consumers.

A **wiki** is a type of software that creates an interface that enables users to add or edit the content of some types of websites. One of the best-known wikis is Wikipedia.com, an online encyclopedia which exists in dozens of languages—from English, Spanish, and Chinese to Finnish, Croatian, and Thai. Wikipedia has more than 3 million articles in English alone, covering nearly every subject imaginable. Wikipedia is consistently one of the top 10 most popular sites on the Web. Because Wikipedia can be edited and read by anyone, it is easy for online consumers to correct inaccuracies in content.[44] Wikipedia is expanded, updated, and edited by a large team of volunteer contributors who are overseen by 1,500 administrators. For the most part, only information that is verifiable through another source is considered appropriate. Access to some entries, however, is restricted because of increased risk for vandalism. Because of its open format, Wikipedia has suffered from some high-profile instances of vandalism in which incorrect information was disseminated. Such problems have historically been detected and corrected quickly. Like all digital media, wikis have advantages and disadvantages for companies. Wikis on controversial companies like Walmart and Nike often contain negative publicity about the company, such as worker rights violations. However, some companies have begun to use wikis as internal tools for teams working on a project requiring lots of documentation (for example, a book project with lots of collaborators may use an internal wiki to help make the process more efficient).[45] Additionally, monitoring wikis provides companies with a better idea of how consumers feel about the company brand.

There is too much at stake financially for marketers to ignore blogs and wikis. Despite this fact, statistics show that less than one-fifth of Fortune 500 companies have a blog.[46] Marketers who want to form better customer relationships and promote their company's products must not underestimate the power of these two tools as new media outlets.

Photo Sharing

Flickr is owned by Yahoo! and is the most popular photo sharing site on the Internet. It allows users to upload and share their photos and short videos with the world. Other popular photo sharing sites are SmugMug and Webshots. A Flickr user can upload images, edit them, classify the images, create photo albums, and share photos or videos with friends without having to e-mail bulky image files or send photos through the mail. Flickr is so popular that the site experiences thousands of new image uploads every minute. Most users have free accounts that allow them to upload two videos and 100 MB of photos per month, but for around $25 a year, users can open an unlimited Pro account.[47] Photo sharing represents an opportunity for companies to market themselves visually by displaying snapshots of company events, company staff, and/or company products. Companies can direct viewers to their photostreams (their sets of photographs) by marking their pictures with the appropriate keywords, or tags.[48] Tags are essential for marketing on Flickr as they help direct traffic to the corporate photostreams.

wiki Type of software that creates an interface that enables users to add or edit the content of some types of websites

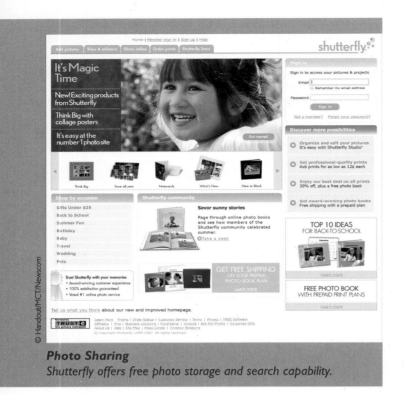

Photo Sharing
Shutterfly offers free photo storage and search capability.

Many businesses with pictures on Flickr have a link connecting their Flickr photostreams to their corporate websites.[49] General Motors, for example, uses Flickr not only to showcase its cars and important events but also to provide links that connect users to GM's blog and to *The Lab,* GM's "interactive research community," where the company test markets designs and project ideas on consumers.[50] In addition to the White House's stream of photos by official White House photographers, President Obama has his own Flickr photostream, which he used to post images that related directly to the health-care bill he signed into law in March 2010.[51]

Picasa Web Albums is a Google photo-sharing site that developed out of Google's photo-editing program, called Picasa. The program has grown rapidly and is growing in popularity, because it provides more features than Flickr and some of the other major photo-sharing websites. Picasa Web Albums is free to users; it generates revenues through ads shown on the site. If users want to use more than 1 GB of storage space, they can rent additional space up to 16 TBs.

As one web marketer puts it, companies that use photo sharing "add a personal touch to their businesses."[52] Although it is too early to gauge the effects of marketing through photo-sharing sites, more and more marketers will likely use the site as an inexpensive way to reach their audience.

Video Sharing

Video-sharing sites allow virtually anybody to upload videos, from professional marketers at *Fortune* 500 corporations to the average Internet user. The most popular video-sharing site on the Internet is YouTube, with users uploading 20 hours of video each minute.[53] YouTube is the king of video-sharing websites, but Video.Yahoo.com and Metacafe.com also attract millions of visitors, giving companies the opportunity to upload ads and informational videos about their products. There are hundreds of smaller video-sharing sites on the Internet, available in dozens of languages. A few videos become viral at any given time, and although many of these gain popularity because they embarrass the subject in some way, others reach viral status because people find them entertaining. (Viral marketing will be discussed in more detail in Chapter 18.) For instance, IBM created a series of six videos called "The Art of the Sale," which presents three attributes of the company's mainframe computer in a humorous format reminiscent of episodes of the TV sitcom *The Office.* Though some wrote off the video as an excessively forced attempt at humorous marketing, the video received nearly 300,000 hits on YouTube.[54]

A new trend in video marketing is the use of amateur filmmakers. Businesses have begun to realize that they can use consumer-generated content, which saves companies a lot of money because they do not have to hire advertising firms to develop professional advertising campaigns. After an initially disappointing advertising campaign for its Flip video cameras, Cisco Systems launched 10-second television and web clips of both celebrities and ordinary consumers using the Flip camera to record aspects of their daily lives. Consumers enjoyed the opportunity to showcase their talent. Submissions included videos ranging from a baby with spaghetti dangling from her mouth to singer Lenny Kravitz brushing his teeth—all filmed with the Flip camera.[55] Marketers believe consumer videos appear more authentic and create enthusiasm for the product among consumer participants.

Google is so confident in the future of video-sharing sites that it purchased YouTube for $1.65 billion in 2006.[56] If Google is correct in its predictions, then online videos clips—both corporate-sponsored and consumer-generated—are likely to revolutionize the marketing industry.

Podcasting

Podcasting, traditionally used for music and radio broadcasts, is also an important digital marketing tool. **Podcasts** are audio or video files that can be downloaded from the Internet with a subscription that automatically delivers new content to listening devices or personal computers. Podcasts offer the benefit of convenience, giving users the ability to listen to or view content when and where they choose.

Podcasts are rapidly gaining in popularity. A survey estimates that by 2013, 37.6 million Americans will be downloading podcasts on a monthly basis. The fact that the majority of current podcast users are between 18 and 29 years of age makes podcasts a key tool for businesses marketing to this demographic.[57] One business that uses podcasting is the Student Loan Network, which offers a free weekly Financial Aid Podcast to college-age students that gives advice on affordable college education, credit cards, and other financial subjects important to young people. Listeners also have the added benefit of making comments and offering feedback to the podcaster on the material presented in the podcasts.[58] This allows listeners to actively weigh in on how helpful the podcasts are and provides the creators of the podcasts with feedback on how to improve them in the future.

As podcasting continues to catch on, radio and television networks like CBC Radio, NPR, MSNBC, and PBS are creating podcasts of their shows to profit from this growing trend. Through podcasting, many companies hope to create brand awareness, promote their products, and encourage customer loyalty.

Virtual Realities

Second Life is perhaps the most popular of all virtual worlds, which are computer-based online simulated environments that can involve thousands of participants. Other virtual worlds are Everquest, Sim City, and the role-playing game World of Warcraft. Such virtual worlds can be classified as social networks with a twist. Virtual realities are virtual, user-created, three-dimensional worlds that have their own economies and currencies, lands, and residents that come in every shape and size. Internet users who participate in virtual realities like Second Life choose a fictional persona called an avatar. Residents of Second Life connect with other users, communicate with one another, purchase goods with virtual Linden dollars (which are convertible to real dollars on a floating exchange rate of around 250 Linden dollars per $1), and can even own virtual businesses. For entertainment purposes, residents can shop, attend concerts, or travel to virtual environments—all while spending real money.

Whereas the businesses in Second Life are virtual ones, real-world marketers and organizations have been eager to capitalize on Second Life's popularity. Second Life allows businesses to reach consumers in a way that is creative and fun. For instance, in an effort to connect with consumers and build brand loyalty, car companies like Toyota and General Motors began selling virtual cars to Second Life residents.[59] Other businesses are looking toward Second Life to familiarize consumers with their products and services. In 2006, Sun Microsystems Chief Researcher John Gage held a Second Life press conference in which his avatar announced the opening of a Sun Microsystems facility in Second Life, complete with video kiosks to show recent Sun Microsystems projects and innovations.[60]

Companies are also using virtual realities to encourage residents to participate in company activities. For instance, CNN created a virtual news hub in Second Life and began encouraging residents to submit stories that occur in this virtual world.[61] Companies embarking into Second Life are not only creating brand loyalty by connecting

podcast Audio or video file that can be downloaded from the Internet with a subscription that automatically delivers new content to listening devices or personal computers; podcasts offer the benefit of convenience, giving users the ability to listen to or view content when and where they choose

Virtual Realities
Manpower alters its headquarters in Second Life.

with Second Life residents, they are using consumer knowledge and money to profit the companies—virtually and in real-time. Although the presence of real-world companies in virtual worlds is still in the experimental stages, virtual worlds like Second Life offer a creative and novel way for marketers to interact with consumers.

Changing Digital Media Behaviors of Consumers

Since the beginning of e-marketing, businesses have witnessed a range of changes in consumer behavior. Today, with a click of a button, consumers expect to be able to gain access to a vast amount of information on companies, products, and issues that can aid them in their purchasing decisions. Deal websites have emerged that now allow online shoppers to find the best deals, giving retailers a run for their money. E-marketers like Amazon.com, eBay, and Netflix have taken market share away from brick-and-mortar bookstores and movie rental stores. Companies are working to provide creative incentives to consumers and market to them in completely new ways in order to compete.

With the onset of social networking sites and digital media like blogs, consumers are able to connect with each other like never before. Through these connections, consumers are able to share information and experiences without company interference, allowing consumers to get more of the "real story" on a product or company. In many ways, some of the power of the professional marketer to control and dispense information has been placed in the hands of the consumer. Today, blogs, wikis, podcasts, ratings, and the like have the capability to publicize, praise, or challenge the company. However, as the Snapshot shows, most companies in the United States do not routinely monitor consumers' postings to online social networking sites. In many cases, this represents a missed opportunity to gather information.

However, the changing social behavior of consumers does not have to be a sign of doom to marketers who choose to harness the power of the consumer and Internet technology. While consumers can use digital media to access more information, marketers can also use the same sites to get information on the consumer—often more information than could be garnered through traditional marketing venues. They can examine how consumers are using the Internet to target better marketing messages to their audience. Marketers increasingly use consumer-generated content to aid in their own marketing efforts, even going so far as to incorporate Internet bloggers in their publicity campaigns. Finally, marketers are also beginning to use the Internet to track the success of their Internet marketing campaigns, creating an entirely new way of gathering marketing research.

Online Consumer Behavior

As Internet technology evolves, digital media marketers must constantly adapt to new technologies and changing consumer patterns. Unfortunately, with so many new technologies emerging, the attrition rate for digital media channels is very high, with some dying off each year as new ones emerge. Social networks are no exception: the earliest social networks like Six Degrees were dropped when they failed to catch on with the general public. Friendster, though still active, was quickly surpassed by MySpace and Facebook. As time passes, digital media are becoming more sophisticated so as to reach consumers in more effective ways. Those that are not able to adapt and change eventually fail.

Mastering digital media presents a daunting task for marketers, particularly those used to more traditional means of marketing. For this reason, it is essential that marketers focus on the changing social behaviors of consumers and how they interact with digital media. Social networking and new digital technologies, as their adoption becomes more widespread, are changing how consumers gather and use information. Consumers have access to more information than ever before, and the Internet is enabling the average consumer to get involved in the marketing process.

Forrester Research, a technology and market research company, emphasizes the importance of understanding these changing relationships in the online media world. By grouping online consumers into different segments based on how they utilize digital online media, marketers can garner a better understanding of the online market and how best to proceed.[62]

The Social Technographics Profile developed by Forrester Research groups the online community into six segments according to how they interact with new digital media. It is important to note that these segments overlap; many online consumers may belong to multiple segments simultaneously. Table 10.2 provides a description of these six different groups. *Creators* are those consumers who create their own media outlets, such as blogs, podcasts, consumer-generated videos, and wikis.[63] Creators are becoming increasingly important to online marketers as a conduit for addressing consumers directly. These types of consumer-generated media are becoming a major part of companies' public relations strategies. For instance, many marketers are pitching new products or stories to professional reporters and bloggers. Bloggers who post this information can reach

Does Your Company Audit and Monitor Postings to Social Networking Sites?

36% Yes
64% No

Source: PricewaterhouseCoopers, The Global State of Information Security Survey 2010 (survey of 7,200 managerial positions).

TABLE 10.2 Social Technographics

Creators	• Publish a blog • Publish personal web pages • Upload original video • Upload original audio/music • Write articles or stories and post them
Critics	• Post ratings/reviews of products or services • Comment on someone else's blog • Contribute to online forums • Contribute to/edit articles in a wiki
Collectors	• Use RSS feeds • Add tags to web pages or photos • "Vote" for websites online
Joiners	• Maintain profile on a social networking site • Visit social networking sites
Spectators	• Read blogs • Watch video from other users • Listen to podcasts • Read online forums • Read customer ratings/reviews
Inactives	• None of the activities

Source: Charlene Li and Josh Bernoff. *Groundswell* (Boston: Harvard Business Press, 2008), p. 43.

online consumers as well as reporters in the mainstream media, who often read blogs for story ideas.[64]

The Technographics profile calls its second group of Internet users *Critics*. Critics are people who comment on blogs or post ratings and reviews. If you've ever posted a product review or rated a movie, you have engaged in this activity. Critics need to be an important component in a company's digital marketing strategy, because the majority of online shoppers read ratings and reviews to aid in their purchasing decisions. As mentioned before, consumer-generated content like ratings and reviews are viewed as more credible than corporate messages. Hence, marketers should carefully monitor what consumers are saying about their products and address consumer concerns that may affect their corporate reputation.

Collectors are perhaps the most newly recognized group of the six. Collectors gather information and organize content generated by Critics and Creators. The growing popularity of this segment is leading to the creation of social networking sites like Digg, del.icio.us, and RSS feeds. Want to know the top 10 stories according to online consumers? Collectors gather this type of information and post their findings to social networking sites like Digg, where users vote on the sites they like the best. Collectors usually constitute a smaller part of the online population than the other groups; however, they can still have a significant impact on marketing activities.[65] Because collectors are active members in the online community, a company story or site that catches the eye of a collector is likely to be posted and discussed on collector sites and made available to other online users looking for information.

Another Technographic segment, known as *Joiners*, is growing dramatically. Anyone who becomes a member of MySpace, Twitter, Facebook, or other social networking sites is a Joiner.[66] It is not unusual for consumers to be members of several social networking sites at once. Joiners join these sites to connect and network with other users, but, as previously discussed, marketers can take significant advantage of these sites to connect with consumers and form customer relationships.

The last two segments are classified as *Spectators* and *Inactives*. Inactives are online users who do not participate in any digital online media, but as more and more people begin to use computers as a resource, this number is dwindling. Spectators are the

Technographics
Websites like Facebook create social experiences for Joiners.

largest group in most countries, and it is not hard to see why. Spectators are those consumers who read what other consumers produce but do not produce any content themselves.

Marketers who want to capitalize on social and digital media marketing will need to consider what portion of online consumers are creating, rating, collecting, joining, or simply reading online materials. As with traditional marketing efforts, marketers need to know the best ways to reach their target market. In markets where Spectators make up the majority of the online population, companies should post their own corporate messages through blogs and websites promoting their organizations. In a population of Joiners, companies could try to connect with their target audience by creating profile pages and inviting consumers to post their thoughts; as we discussed earlier, Procter & Gamble and Pepsi are doing this through their Prilosec "official sponsor of everything" and Pepsi Refresh Project, respectively. In areas where a significant portion of the online community consists of Creators, marketers should continually monitor what other consumers are saying and incorporate bloggers into their public relations strategies. Companies must exercise care, however, when challenging the power of the blogger or consumer. The Korean Dunkin' Donuts scenario cited earlier in this chapter is a prime example of what happens when a company tries to use its influence to stifle online criticism and gets hit with a backlash. The power of the consumer in the online world should not be underestimated by the online marketer. By knowing how to segment the online population, marketers can better tailor their online messages to their target markets.

E-Marketing Strategy

Although the Internet has yet to take off in many countries due to a lack of infrastructure, basic Internet literacy is increasingly common. More than one-fourth of the world's population uses the Internet, and this number is growing at a high rate. In North America, approximately three-fourths of the population has Internet access.[67] These trends display a growing need for businesses to use the Internet to reach an increasingly web-savvy population. As more and more shoppers go online for purchases, the power of traditional brick-and-mortar businesses is lessening. Online retailers like Amazon.com are challenging more traditional retailers like Barnes & Noble or Kmart, and even small businesses are finding ways to reach customers and grab share away from established competitors.

This makes it essential for businesses, small and large alike, to learn how to effectively use new digital media. Most businesses are finding it necessary to use digital marketing to grab or maintain market share. When Amazon.com first became popular as an online bookstore in the 1990s, the brick-and-mortar bookseller chain Barnes & Noble quickly made online shopping possible through its website, but did not abandon its physical stores. This "brick-and-clicks" model is now standard for businesses from neighborhood family-owned restaurants to national chain retailers. In the process, companies that use digital media and social networking marketing well can receive the added benefit of streamlining their organizations and offering entirely new benefits and convenience to consumers. The following sections will examine how businesses are effectively using these digital media forums to create effective marketing strategies on the web.

Product Considerations

As with traditional marketing, marketers must anticipate consumer needs and preferences and then tailor their products to meet these needs. The same is true with

It likes the sun as much as you do.

amazonkindle

The Lost Symbol

CHAPTER 1

The Otis elevator climbing the south pillar of the Eiffel Tower was overflowing with tourists. Inside the cramped lift, an austere businessman in a pressed suit gazed down at the boy beside him. "You look pale, son. You should have stayed on the ground."

"I'm okay . . ." the boy answered, struggling to control his anxiety. "I'll get out on the next level." I can't breathe.

The man leaned closer. "I thought by now you would have gotten over this." He brushed the child's cheek affectionately.

The boy felt ashamed to disappoint his father, but he could barely hear through the ringing in his ears. I can't breathe. I've got to get out of this box!

Easy to read in bright sunlight.

Thin and lightweight, only 10.2 ounces.

Holds up to 1,500 books.

amazonkindle
amazon.com/kindle

Distribution

The Kindle e-book reader is a direct channel for the distribution of books and magazines.

marketing products using digital media. Digital media provide an opportunity to add a service dimension to traditional products and to create new products that could only be accessible on the Internet. The applications available on the iPad, for instance, provide examples of products that are only available in the digital world. The ability to access product information for any product can have a major impact on buyer decision making. However, with larger companies now launching their own extensive marketing campaigns and with the constant sophistication of digital technology, many businesses are finding it necessary to continually upgrade their product offerings to meet consumer needs. As has been discussed throughout this chapter, the Internet represents a large resource to marketers for learning more about consumer wants and needs.

Some companies now utilize online advertising campaigns and contests to help develop better products. Netflix, the online movie rental-by-mail service, offers a much wider array of movies and games than what is available at the average movie rental store, plus a number of convenience features: no late fees, a two-week free trial service, quick delivery times, and online video streaming of some movies. Netflix also prides itself on its recommendation engine that recommends movies for users based on their previous rental history and how they rate movies they have seen. In an effort to stay ahead of the competition and to keep consumers satisfied, Netflix awarded a consumer team $1 million for an algorithm the company will use to improve its product recommendations by 10 percent. The Internet can make it much easier to anticipate consumer needs. However, the fierce competition makes quality product and service offerings more important than ever.

Distribution Considerations

The role of distribution is to make products available at the right time, at the right place, in the right quantities. Digital marketing can be viewed as a new distribution channel that helps businesses increase efficiency. The ability to process orders electronically and increase the speed of communications via the Internet reduces inefficiencies, costs, and redundancies while increasing speed throughout the marketing channel. Shipping times and costs have become an important consideration in attracting consumers, prompting many companies to offer consumers low shipping costs or next-day delivery. Walmart, for example, is attempting to take market share away from e-marketers like Amazon. com by decreasing its delivery time and by creating a "site-to-store" system, whereby consumers get free shipping if they pick up their purchases at a Walmart store of their choice. This offer has the increased benefit of getting the customer into the store where he or she might make "add-on purchases." Walmart has even tested a new distribution concept to complement store pickups: a drive-through window that allows customers to pick up the products they ordered through Walmart's website. Through even more sophisticated distribution systems, Walmart hopes to overtake other e-marketers and become the biggest online merchant.[68]

Distribution involves a push–pull dynamic: the firm that provides a product will push to get that product in front of the consumer, while at the same time connectivity aids those channel members that desire to find each other—the pull side of the dynamic. For example, an iPhone application can help consumers find the closest

Starbucks, McDonald's, or KFC. On the other hand, a blog or Twitter feed can help a marketer communicate the availability of products and how and when they can be purchased. This process can help push products through the marketing channel to consumers or enable customers to pull products through the marketing channel. Hasbro, manufacturer of Monopoly, provided an interesting mix of digital and hard-copy product when it launched a multiplayer online game, Monopoly City Streets, to promote a new offline board game called Monopoly City. More than 5 million users participated in games of Monopoly City Streets over a period of three months.[69] In addition to playing these online games, they were able to purchase the new offline game through the website.

Promotion Considerations

The majority of this chapter has discussed ways that marketers use digital media and social networking sites to promote products, from creating profiles on social networking sites to connecting with consumers (P&G) to using Twitter to build customer relationships (banks) to taking advantage of virtual worlds like Second Life to increase consumer interest (Sun Microsystems). Social networking sites also allow marketers to approach promotion in entirely new, creative ways. For instance, Samsung used the Internet to help publicize the launch of its ST 1000 digital camera. The company partnered with the SchonBrunn Zoo in Vienna for the promotion. The zoo equipped a resident orangutan with the camera and then uploaded the images she took to a Facebook page in order to demonstrate how easy it is to use the camera. The campaign was deemed a great success, with the Facebook page receiving more than 200,000 hits, and the company was granted a CLIO award for excellence in advertising.[70]

These digital promotions all attempt to increase brand awareness and market to consumers. As a result of online promotion, consumers are more informed, reading consumer-generated content before making purchasing decisions and increasingly shopping at Internet stores. Consumer consumption patterns are changing radically, and marketers must adapt their promotional efforts to meet these new patterns. These trends are not just limited to the developed world. Businesses around the world are tapping into digital media like online auction sites to increase company sales. This represents a revolutionary shift in countries like China, where online shopping had not been widely adopted by consumers. This is quickly changing as businesses realize the benefits of marketing online. One of the first Chinese companies to adopt Internet selling was Taobao, an auction site for consumers that also features sections for Chinese brands and retailers. Taobao has been enormously successful, with the majority of online sales in China going through its site.[71] The changing consumer trends in China demonstrate that the shift to digital media promotion is well under way.

Almost any traditional promotional event can be enhanced or replaced by digital media. Pepsi symbolizes the shift from traditional advertising to digital media. In 2010, Pepsi withdrew from Super Bowl advertising for the first time in more than 20 years to concentrate on digital advertising and public relations. Banks are using blogs, podcasts, and Twitter to post rates and financial products and to answer financial questions.[72] Even direct selling representatives from firms such as Avon or Amway are gathering their consumers on Facebook to discuss products, much like socializing around the kitchen table or engaging in a focus group.

Pricing Considerations

Pricing relates to perceptions of value and is the most flexible element of the marketing mix. Digital online media marketing facilitates both price and nonprice competition because the accessibility characteristic of Internet marketing gives consumers access to more information about costs and prices. As consumers become more informed about their options, the demand for low-priced products has grown, leading to the creation of deal sites like BizRate.com, NexTag.com, PriceGrabber.com, and Shopzilla.com, where consumers can directly compare prices. Travel sites like Expedia.com, Kayak.com, and FareCompare.com provide consumers with a wealth of information, from flights to hotels, allowing them to compare benefits and prices. Several marketers are also offering buying incentives like online coupons or free samples to generate consumer demand for their product offerings.

Digital connections can help the customer find the price of the product available from various competitors in an instant. Websites provide price information, and mobile applications can help the customer find the lowest price. Customers can even bargain with retailers in the store by using a smartphone to show the lowest price available during a transaction. While this new access to price information benefits the consumer, it also places new pressures on the seller to be competitive and to differentiate products so that customers focus on attributes and benefits other than price. For the business that wants to compete on price, digital marketing provides unlimited opportunities.

Using Digital Media in Marketing Research

Marketing research and information systems can use digital media and social networking sites to gather useful information for marketing decisions. Sites such as Twitter, Facebook, MySpace, and LinkedIn can be a good substitute for focus groups. Online surveys can serve as an alternative to mail, telephone, or personal interviews.

Crowdsourcing refers to the way digital media can be used to outsource tasks to a large group of people. In the case of digital marketing, crowdsourcing is often used to obtain the opinions or needs of the crowd (or potential markets). Communities of interested consumers join crowdsourcing sites like threadless.com, which designs T-shirts, or crowdspring.com, which creates logos, print, and web designs. On crowdspring.com, participants can submit a project that needs to be designed, and it is shared with more than 64,000 designers or writers who can choose whether to work on the project. Project submitters name the prices they are willing to pay, along with a small fee and commission that the site charges. On threadless.com, participants can submit and score T-shirt designs. Designs with the highest votes are printed and then sold. There are even sites that crowdsource entire advertising campaigns. For example, victorandspoils.com uses digital technology to bring together creative people worldwide into their "creative department." Companies that require marketing or advertising campaigns have the advantage of engaging the services of people from across the world to work on their projects.[73]

While large companies are paying millions of dollars for creative ideas, innovative competitors are offering creative services at bargain prices. For example, crowdspring.com was designed for small businesses that could not pay the high fees charged by traditional agencies. Harnessing consumers' creativity also provides a cost-effective way to come up with new ideas: mobile phone brand LG paid out more than $80,000 in awards to gather ideas on what the mobile phone should look like in 2, 5 or 10 years, and the Italian pasta brand Barilla used crowdspring.com to post an assignment for interested individuals who wanted to try their hand at designing a new pasta product— at a cost far less than paying for banner ads on websites.[74]

There is no end to the opportunities for companies to gain information and insights from consumers that can be used in developing new products and marketing strategies. When Rupert Barksfield developed the Multi-Pet Feeder as a solution to pet feeding-time frenzy (where one greedy pet eats the other pet's food), he paid $99 to post his concept, along with some of his drawings, at quirky.com. There, 30,000 people passed judgment on his idea.[75]

Procter & Gamble views social networking as an important marketing research tool that allows the company to venture into consumers' lives and the environments where

crowdsourcing Refers to the way digital media can be used to outsource tasks to a large group of people

they are spending their time. For instance, P&G develops Facebook fan pages for each of its brands. The Pringles fan page has more than 2 million global fans. The company also views Twitter as a valuable marketing research tool; its Twitter page enables consumers to ask questions that can help product marketing teams understand consumers' interest in their products and address issues that need to be resolved.[76]

Twitter and Facebook are putting small businesses on the same level as Starbucks and Dell when it comes to gathering information. By spending time on Twitter, employees at Cordaround.com, a small American clothing company, learned that many people are using their bicycles to get to work. In response, the firm produced a new line of clothing called "Bike to Work Pants," featuring built-in reflective material that makes it safer to ride after dark.[77]

It is also important for organizations to harness all of their internal information, and internal social networks can be helpful for that. Danone, a global food group based in France, has an internal social network system to connect employees spread across more than 100 countries. This network provides knowledge sharing and internal communications about products, customers, and market opportunities.

Consumer feedback is an important aspect of the digital media equation. One of the oldest forms of digital media is the forum, where participants post responses and converse on certain topics. Discussion forums are very popular with the online population. While some communities are more involved in online debates than others, about one-fifth of Americans participate in discussion forums, which can range from product discussions to comments on movies. Ratings and reviews have become even more popular, with 25 percent of the U.S. online population reading these types of consumer-generated feedback.[78] Retailers that use e-marketing, such as Amazon, Netflix, and Priceline, are capitalizing on these ratings and reviews by allowing consumers to post comments on their sites concerning books, movies, hotels, and more. Today, it is estimated that over three-fourths of online shoppers read ratings and reviews before making purchasing decisions.[79]

These simple forms of consumer-generated content present both challenges and opportunities for marketing. Positive reviews act as reputation enhancers, while negative reviews can damage a company's reputation. At the same time, these digital media forums allow marketers to closely monitor what their customers are saying. In the case of negative feedback, marketers can communicate with consumers to address problems or complaints much more easily than with traditional marketing channels. Yet despite the ease and obvious importance of online feedback, one study conducted by Chief Marketing Officer Council revealed that less than one-fifth of marketing chiefs continually monitor their message boards for consumer feedback.[80]

It should be clear by now that digital media marketing offers a range of benefits and opportunities for businesses. However, as with all marketing activities, launching a promotional campaign is never enough. The business must also be able to monitor marketing performance. To evaluate whether an online promotional campaign was successful, marketers should ask themselves the following questions:

- *Did the online promotional campaign generate more business for the company?* This requires the marketing researcher to compare sales before and after the campaign was launched. (Note that a question may arise as to how long a campaign should have to generate results; just because sales do not increase overnight does not mean the campaign was a failure.)
- *Did the campaign create more interest in the company?* For instance, if a web advertisement contained a link to the company's website, the researcher could monitor the website to see whether web traffic increased after the launch of the campaign. The more the advertisement attracts the interest of Internet users, the more likely they are to remember the company in the future.
- *Is this increase in demand significant?* The company should set a goal concerning how much it wants demand to increase. This will help the company to decide whether investing in a large-scale digital marketing effort is worth its resources.

■   *Are there any extraneous variables that could account for an increase in sales?* Just because sales or web traffic increased after the launch of a digital online media campaign does not mean the campaign was successful if there were other reasons why demand could have increased (e.g., other types of promotional campaigns, major discounts, or seasons of the year like Christmas).

By launching a baseline, comparing revenue from before and after the digital media program was launched, measuring the number of net new customers and transactions, and carefully analyzing the data, the marketing researcher can sufficiently measure the success of its digital media marketing promotion.[81] For those who do not want to take the time to perform this research, software companies are developing programs to make the process easier. For instance, software firm Live Oak helps companies that market on social networking sites to track which social networking sites drive the most traffic to the company's website.

Measurement systems for digital media marketing received a boost during the recession that began in 2008. As money became tighter, many organizations realized they could save on advertising dollars by utilizing digital media marketing. This prompted the creation of measurement systems to make sure the company's marketing dollars were being used effectively. Chrysler's digital marketing agency, Organic, is one such organization. In its transition to digital media marketing, Organic created a forecasting model to determine how much Chrysler would need to spend on digital media advertising in order to meet sales targets; it also assessed the effectiveness of the online advertising message. By using models to determine which web activities affect end sales, Chrysler was able to refine its messages and predict sales more accurately.[82] As more and more companies begin to market through digital media, digital media measurement systems are likely to become more common.

Ethical and Legal Issues

How marketers use technology to gather information—both online and offline—raises numerous legal and ethical issues. The popularity and widespread use of the Internet grew so quickly in the 1990s that global regulatory systems were unable to keep pace, although today there are an increasing number of laws in place to protect businesses and consumers (see Table 10.3). Among the issues of concern are personal privacy, fraud, and misappropriation of copyrighted intellectual property.

Privacy

One of the most significant privacy issues involves the use of personal information that companies collect from website visitors in their efforts to foster long-term relationships with customers. Some people fear the collection of personal information from website users may violate users' privacy, especially when it is done without their knowledge. Another concern is that hackers may break into websites and steal users' personal information, enabling them to commit identity theft. This has become a legitimate concern for both consumers and organizations. In 2009, security researcher The Ponemon Institute and e-mail and data encryption security software developer PGP Corp. conducted a joint study that concluded that security and data breaches cost organizations more than $6 million each time they occurred. These costs result from a variety of factors, including reductions in worker productivity, legal expenses, the time it takes to investigate and upgrade security systems, detection costs, reputation management, the recovery of lost data, and the time it takes to change information (such as PIN numbers, credit cards, etc.). Many of these breaches occur at banks, universities, and other businesses that contain sensitive consumer information.[83] This requires organizations to implement increased security measures to prevent database theft.

Sustainable Marketing
Social Networks Advance Sustainability

It seems natural that online marketing would be more sustainable than other media outlets. It saves paper; it also reduces greenhouse gas emissions by eliminating the consumption involved in maintaining a brick-and-mortar store and delivering and stocking merchandise on store shelves. Doing away with paper-oriented banking transactions alone can save 6.6 pounds of paper, 4.5 gallons of gasoline, 63 gallons of wastewater, and 171 pounds of greenhouse gas emissions annually per household. Although it still takes energy to power up your computer, imagine the impact businesses can have by reducing wasted paper and transportation-related pollution through utilizing social networking sites to conduct marketing activities. Additionally, social networks can be a great place for companies to establish their green reputation, gather information about customers, and even discover new markets.

Care2.com is one such social network. This large green social network has nearly 13 million members. The site features four basic categories: causes and news, healthy and green living, take action, and community and fun. With or without becoming a member, a visitor may sign petitions on a wide variety of topics such as animal rights, global warming, food and water safety, and more. Another green site, Treehugger. com, supported 3,200,000 visitors per month in 2009. The site aims to help people maintain their lifestyles while making an environmental difference.

Care2.com is supported by advertising. While the company certainly supports advertisers that are eco-friendly, it also allows companies supporting and working toward sustainability to advertise. This means that Care2.com is open to companies that may not be eco-friendly now but have initiatives in place for the future. Treehugger.com is also supported by advertising, offering advertisers a wide variety of ad choices. The same applies to greenwala.com, a site that enables visitors to participate in contests that sponsor the site and its partners, purchase green items, and view advertising. All of these sites are heavily involved in promoting both their messages and their revenue streams, although each site uses a slightly different technique. For all things green, and to avoid that paper trail, these are sites worth visiting.[c]

Due to consumer concerns over privacy, the Federal Trade Commission (FTC) is considering developing regulations that would better protect consumer privacy by limiting the amount of consumer information that businesses can gather online. While consumers may welcome such added protections, web advertisers, who use consumer information to better target advertisements to online consumers, see it as a threat. In response to impending legislation, many web advertisers attempt self-regulation in order to stay ahead of the game. Companies create rules to govern how consumer information is collected and used online, even though these rules do not carry the force of law. Trade groups such as the American Association of Advertising Agencies, Association of National Advertisers, Direct Marketing Association, and Interactive Advertising Bureau are trying to implement new policies that give consumers more control over how their online information will be used by companies. One proposal being considered is to feature icons on company web pages that provide information on how the online information will be gathered and used. This will give consumers a choice to opt out of having their information gathered.[84] The hope among online marketers is that widespread adoption of these policies could prevent regulation that would make it more difficult to advertise online effectively.

TABLE 10.3 A Timeline of Internet-Related Policy

1986	Electronic Communications Privacy Act	Developed by the government to extend laws on wiretaps to electronic transmissions
1996	Digital Millenium Copyright Act	Refined copyright laws to protect digital versions of copyrighted materials, including music and movies
1998	European Union Directive	Requires companies to explain how the personal information they collect will be used and to obtain the individual's permission
1999	Anti-Cyber Squatting Consumer Protection Act	Makes it illegal to register others' trademarks as domain names in order to profit from the sale or transfer of the domain name, tarnish the trademark owner's reputation, or mislead consumers
1999	Uniform Electronic Transactions Act	Sets guidelines for electronic transactions, including the retention of records, electronic contracts, and electronic signatures
2000	Children's Online Privacy and Protection Act (COPPA)	Regulates the collection of personally identifiable information (name, address, e-mail address, hobbies, interests, or information collected through cookies) online from children under age 13
2004	Controlling the Assault of Non-Solicited Pornography and Marketing Act (CAN-SPAM)	Bans fraudulent or deceptive unsolicited commercial e-mail and requires senders to provide information on how recipients can opt out of receiving additional messages

Sources: "Federal Statutes Relevant in the Information Sharing Environment (ISE)," Justice Information Sharing: U.S. Department of Justice, Office of Justice Programs, February 27, 2009, www.it.ojp.gov/default.aspx?area=privacy&page=1285- (accessed February 18, 2010); REPORT TO CONGRESS: The Anticybersquatting Consumer Protection Act of 1999, section 3006 concerning the abusive registration of domain names, www.uspto.gov/web/offices/dcom/olia/tmcybpiracy/repcongress.pdf (accessed February 18, 2010).

Online Fraud

Online fraud includes any attempt to conduct dishonest activities online. Online fraud includes, among other things, attempts to deceive consumers into releasing personal information. It is becoming a major source of frustration with social networking sites. Cybercriminals are discovering entirely new ways to use sites like Facebook and Twitter to carry out fraudulent activities. For instance, it has become common for cybercriminals to create profiles under a company's name. These fraudulent profiles are often created to either damage the company's reputation (this is particularly common with larger, more controversial companies) or as a way to lure that company's customers into releasing personal information that the cybercriminal can then use for monetary gain. Another tactic some fraudsters have used is to copy a blog entry from a reputable company and then repost the entry with a link that connects the user to their own sites, where they attempt to sell the user goods (under the reputable company's name) or collect personal information from the consumer. For instance, a fraudster may repost a blog written by a professional sports organization with a fraudulent link that connects users to a site that sells unlicensed sporting goods. Perhaps the most disturbing is the practice of using social networking sites to pose as charitable institutions. During the Haitian earthquake disaster of 2010, fraudsters set up fake accounts to scam Facebook users into donating money that was used for the fraudsters' own financial gain.[85] The Better Business Bureau worked with the FBI to compile and release a list of suspected scams seeking to benefit from the Haiti disaster. A similar problem arose after the tsunami in Indonesia.

Organizations and social networking sites alike are developing ways to combat fraudulent activity on new digital media sites. For instance, Twitter is discussing ways to act as a middleman for companies, for a fee, where it will investigate the different profiles on its site to determine their authenticity—in the process weeding out any fake profiles.[86] Other organizations, known as brand-protection firms, monitor social networks for fraudulent accounts. Whenever these sites are found, the organizations notify their clients

online fraud Any attempt to conduct fraudulent activities online, including deceiving consumers into releasing personal information

about the fraud and help them to remove the fraudulent account.[87] However, the best protection for consumers is to be careful when divulging information online. Privacy advocates advise that the best way to stay out of trouble is to avoid giving out personal information, such as social security number or credit card information, unless the site is definitely legitimate.

Intellectual Property

The Internet has also created issues associated with intellectual property, the copyrighted or trademarked ideas and creative materials developed to solve problems, carry out applications, and educate and entertain others. Each year, intellectual property losses in the United States total billions of dollars stemming from the illegal copying of computer programs, movies, compact discs, and books. This has become a particular problem for social networking sites that use consumer-generated materials. YouTube, for example, often faces lawsuits over whether it has infringed on other company's copyrights. In one case, Viacom Inc. sued YouTube's owner Google, claiming that the site violated its copyrights by airing Viacom videos without permission. Although YouTube is responsible for the video content it shows on its sites, with millions of users uploading content to YouTube, it can be hard for Google to monitor and remove all the videos that may contain copyrighted materials.

The software industry is particularly hard-hit when it comes to the pirating of materials and illegal filesharing. The Business Software Alliance estimates that the global computer software industry loses over $53 billion a year to illegal theft.[88] Consumers view illegal downloading in different ways, depending on the motivation for the behavior. If the motivation is primarily utilitarian, or for personal gain, then the act is viewed as less ethically acceptable than if it is for a hedonistic reason, meaning just for fun.[89] Consumers rationalize pirating software, video games, and music for a number of reasons. First, many consumers feel that they just don't have the money to pay for what they want. Second, because their friends engage in piracy and swap digital content, they feel influenced to engage in this activity. Third, for some, the attraction is the thrill of getting away with it and the slim risk of consequences. Fourth, to some extent, there are people who think they are smarter than others; engaging in piracy allows them to show how tech savvy they are.[90]

As digital media continues to evolve, more legal and ethical issues will certainly arise. As a result, marketers and all other users of digital media should make an effort to learn and abide by ethical practices to ensure that they get the most out of the resources available in this growing medium. Doing so will allow marketers to maximize the tremendous opportunities digital media has to offer.

© 3M Corporation

Ethical and Legal Issues in Digital Media
3M Privacy Filters help protect personal and confidential information while consumers work on computers in open areas.

summary

1. To define *digital media* and *electronic marketing* and recognize their increasing importance in strategic planning

Digital media are electronic media that function using digital codes—when we refer to digital media, we are referring to media available via computers, cellular phones, smartphones, and other digital devices that have been released in recent years. Digital marketing uses all digital media, including the Internet and mobile and interactive channels, to develop communication and exchanges with customers. Electronic marketing (e-marketing) refers to the strategic process of distributing, promoting, pricing products, and discovering the desires of customers using digital media and digital marketing. E-marketing goes beyond the Internet and also includes mobile phones, banner ads, digital outdoor marketing, and social networks.

2. To understand the characteristics of digital media and electronic marketing—addressability, interactivity, accessibility, connectivity, control—and how they differentiate from traditional marketing activities

One of the biggest mistakes a marketer can make when engaging in digital marketing is to treat it like a traditional marketing channel. Digital media offer a whole new dimension to marketing that marketers must consider when concocting their companies' marketing strategies. Some of the characteristics that distinguish online media from traditional marketing include addressability, interactivity, accessibility, connectivity, and control.

- The ability of a marketer to identify customers before they make a purchase is called addressability. Many websites encourage visitors to register to maximize their use of the site or to gain access to premium areas. Armed with knowledge about individual customers gleaned from the Web, particularly online social networking sites, marketers can tailor marketing mixes more precisely to target customers with narrow interests.
- Interactivity allows customers to express their needs and wants directly to the firm in response to its marketing communications. Interactivity focuses on digital media that can make interpersonal connections possible. Therefore, the selection of appropriate digital media facilitates interactivity that can enable a conversation between the firm and the customer. Digital media like blogs and some social networks

allow marketers to interact with prospective customers in real time (or a close approximation of it).
- The ability to obtain information is referred to as accessibility. Because customers can access in-depth information about competing products, prices, reviews, and so forth, they are much better informed about a firm's products and their relative value than ever before. Accessibility does not only refer to the consumer's ability to obtain information. It can also be viewed from a firm's perspective. Many companies are adopting a digital media philosophy of "open innovation."
- Connectivity is one of the key contributions of social networking, connecting customers with marketers as well as with other customers. Connectivity has been made easier by Facebook, the world's largest online social network, and other global sites such as MySpace, LinkedIn, and Twitter. Many countries have their own, much smaller social networking sites as well.
- Control refers to customers' ability to regulate the information they view and the rate and sequence of their exposure to that information. The Internet is sometimes referred to as a *pull* medium because users determine which websites they are going to view; the marketer has only limited ability to control the content to which users are exposed and in what sequence. Digital media like blogs and social networks have endowed users with even greater power because they can more easily associate themselves with certain groups and can actively rate products and services.

3. To identify and understand the role of digital media in a marketing strategy and how each type of digital media can be used as an effective marketing tool

Digital media in marketing is advancing at a rapid rate. The self-sustaining nature of digital technology means that current advances act as a catalyst to spur even faster development. As faster digital transmissions evolve, marketing applications are emerging that offer an opportunity for companies to reach consumers in entirely new ways.

As a result, e-marketing is moving from a niche strategy to becoming a core consideration in the marketing mix. At the same time, digital technologies are largely changing the dynamic between marketer and consumer. Consumers use mobile applications to do everything from playing games to booking airline and hotel reservations. The menu of digital media alternatives continues to grow, requiring marketers to make informed decisions about strategic approaches.

4. To understand and identify how digital media affects the marketing mix and marketing research techniques

The reasons for a digital marketing strategy are many. The low costs of many digital media channels can provide major savings in promotional budgets. Laptops, smartphones, mobile broadband, webcams, and other digital technologies can provide low-cost internal communication as well as external connections with customers. Digital marketing is allowing companies to connect with market segments that are harder to reach with traditional media. Despite the challenges involved in such a strategy, digital marketing is opening up new avenues in the relationship between businesses and consumers.

Because digital tools, strategies, tactics, and channels are not static, marketers must prepare to learn new ways to reach customers. There is still a need to balance traditional media with new digital media. Developing skills to manage the appropriate mix of traditional and digital media is important for success. Assuming that everything has changed to digital can be a mistake in reaching some market segments. Collaboration across the organization is necessary to make digital decisions that break down the walls between products and customers. Customers should be engaged to help this bond evolve. Finally, marketers must find ways to address the challenges that come with digital marketing, such as formulating ways to evaluate the effectiveness of a digital marketing campaign. The implementation of an effective digital marketing strategy will help businesses reap the rewards that digital technologies have to offer.

5. To identify legal and ethical considerations in digital media and electronic marketing

How marketers use technology to gather information—both online and offline—has raised numerous legal and ethical issues.

- Privacy is one of the most significant issues, involving the use of personal information that companies collect from website visitors in their efforts to foster long-term relationships with customers. Some people fear that the collection of personal information from website users may violate users' privacy, especially when it is done without their knowledge. Another concern is that hackers may break into websites and steal users' personal information, enabling them to commit identity theft.
- Online fraud includes any attempt to conduct dishonest activities online. Online fraud includes, among other things, attempts to deceive consumers into releasing personal information. It is becoming a major source of frustration with social networking sites. Cybercriminals are discovering entirely new ways to use sites like Facebook and Twitter to carry out fraudulent activities. Organizations and social networking sites alike are developing ways to combat fraudulent activity on new digital media sites.
- The Internet has also created issues associated with intellectual property, the copyrighted or trademarked ideas and creative materials developed to solve problems, carry out applications, and educate and entertain others. Each year intellectual property losses in the United States total billions of dollars stemming from the illegal copying of computer programs, movies, compact discs, and books. The software industry is particularly hard-hit when it comes to pirating material and illegal filesharing.

Go to www.cengagebrain.com for resources to help you master the content in this chapter as well as materials that will expand your marketing knowledge!

important terms

digital media, 282

digital marketing, 282

electronic marketing
(e-marketing), 282

addressability, 283

social network, 283

interactivity, 285

accessibility, 285

connectivity, 286

control, 286

blogs, 292

wiki, 293

podcast, 295

crowdsourcing, 302

online fraud, 306

discussion and review questions

1. How does addressability differentiate e-marketing from the traditional marketing environment? How do marketers use social networks to achieve addressability?

2. Define *interactivity* and explain its significance. How can marketers exploit this characteristic to improve relations with customers?

3. Explain the distinction between *push* and *pull* media. What is the significance of control in terms of using websites to market products?

4. Why are social networks becoming an increasingly important marketing tool? Find an example on the Web in which a company has improved the effectiveness of its marketing strategy by using social networks.

5. How has new media changed consumer behavior? What are the opportunities and challenges that face marketers with this in mind?

6. Describe the different technographic segments. How can marketers use this segmentation in their strategies?

7. How can marketers exploit the characteristics of the Internet to improve the product element of their marketing mixes?

8. How do the characteristics of e-marketing affect the promotion element of the marketing mix?

9. How has digital media changed the marketing research industry? Give examples of the opportunities and challenges presented to marketers in light of these changes.

10. Name and describe the major ethical and legal issues that have developed in response to the Internet. How should policymakers address these issues?

application questions

1. Amazon.com is one of the Web's most recognizable marketers. Visit the company's website at **www.amazon.com** and describe how the company adds value to its customers' buying experiences.

2. Social networking has become a popular method of communication not only for individuals but for businesses as well. Visit the various social networking sites, such as Facebook.com and Twitter.com, and identify how companies are utilizing each of these sites in their marketing strategies.

3. Some products are better suited than others to electronic marketing activity. For example, Art.com specializes in selling art prints via its online store. The ability to display a variety of prints in many different categories gives customers a convenient and efficient way to

search for art. On the other hand, General Electric has a website displaying its appliances, but customers must visit a retailer to purchase them. Visit **www.art.com** and **www.geappliances.com** and compare how each firm uses the electronic environment of the Internet to enhance its marketing efforts.

4. Visit the information technology company website **www.covisint.com** and evaluate the nature of the business customers attracted. Who is the target audience for this business marketing site? Describe the types of firms currently doing business through this exchange. What other types of organizations might be attracted? Is it appropriate to sell any banner advertising on a site such as this? What other industries might benefit from developing similar e-marketing exchange hubs?

internet exercise

Victors & Spoils

To learn more about the world's first creative ad agency built on crowdsourcing principles, including an opportunity to engage the world's most talented creatives, look at the Victors & Spoils site at **http://victorsandspoils.com/.**

1. How can Victors & Spoils be used to outsource advertising campaigns through co-creation and mass collaboration?

2. Victors & Spoils and crowdsourcing is built on the foundation that good ideas should come from anywhere. Is it possible that this new approach will eliminate traditional ad agencies and creative departments?

3. If you want to engage in activities related to what would be found in the creative department of an advertising agency, how can Victors & Spoils help you launch your career?

developing your marketing plan

CRITICAL THINKING When developing a marketing strategy using new digital media, a marketer must be aware of the strengths and weaknesses of these new media. Digital media are relatively new to the field of marketing and have different pros and cons relative to traditional media sources. Different products and target markets may be more or less suited for different digital media outlets.

© Comstock Images/Getty Images

1. Review the key concepts of addressability, interactivity, accessibility, connectivity, and control, and explain how they relate to new digital media. Think about how a marketing strategy focused on new digital media differs from a marketing campaign reliant on traditional media sources.

2. No matter what marketing media are used, determining the correct marketing mix for your company is always important. Think about how digital media might affect the marketing mix.

3. Discuss different digital media and the pros and cons of using each as part of your marketing plan.

The information obtained from these questions should assist you in developing various aspects of your marketing plan found in the *Interactive Marketing Plan* at **www.cengagebrain.com.**

VIDEO CASE 10.1

RogueSheep's Postage App: The Postcard of the Future

CRITICAL THINKING

That 25-cent postcard in the gift shop may soon become a thing of the past. RogueSheep's postage application is giving the traditional postcard a run for its money, as it allows users to send a digital postcard to their family members quickly and efficiently. RogueSheep is a software development and consulting company based in Seattle. Co-founders Christopher Parrish, Daniel Guenther, Matt Joss, and Jeff Argast founded RogueSheep as an Adobe Development shop. The company specializes in graphics and publishing software while acting as a consultant to clients with their software development projects.

By far the company's most newsworthy product is its mobile app "Postage," iPhone's first postcard application. The idea for Postage came from a business conference when Parrish's business partner wanted to send a postcard back to his wife. The founders of RogueSheep thought this would make a great iPhone app, and development of this app began.

For $4.99, iPhone users can purchase the app, choose from more than 60 postcard designs, customize the design by inserting their own photos, and send the postcard to their friends or relatives. What takes a few days by regular mail can now take only seconds. Connectivity based on digital communication keeps people connected in an instant. Social networking sites provide a way that consumers can connect and express their feelings, emotions, and opinions. In the case of the RogueSheep Postage app, it provides better and more personalized connections than a traditional postcard.

RogueSheep has become a major success in the software design world, winning Apple's 2009 Design Award and *Macworld*'s 2009 Mac Gems Award for best e-mail app. Much of its success likely comes from the great care that RogueSheep puts into its Postage designs. Each postcard in the app is created by the application designer, and designs are continually added to give customers a range of options to choose from. Additionally, RogueSheep has broken into the social networking world by creating ways that users can share their customized postcards with friends and followers on Facebook and Twitter. Now that social networking is more popular for personal communication than email, RogueSheep's app is perfect for social networks.

To create awareness of the product, RogueSheep uses a combination of digital and traditional media. By using social networking sites like Twitter and Facebook, RogueSheep encourages users to become fans or followers and share information about RogueSheep with others. RogueSheep also uses web advertising and traditional magazines like *Macworld* as promotional tools. Finally, RogueSheep encourages trials of its Postage app by giving out promotional codes through Twitter to enable free trials of its product. RogueSheep's Postage app could also be utilized for businesses that send postcards to remind customers about their products or special events. This application could potentially be customized to be a less expensive, more impactful business-to-the-consumer promotional postcard.

As more and more people become familiar with iPhone apps, RogueSheep must constantly adapt its products to anticipate and meet customer needs. In addition to its new update to allow for Facebook sharing, RogueSheep is also offering new product apps such as SnoGlobe—which allows users to turn their iPhone into a snow globe with falling flakes that move as the iPhone moves—and Holiday ~ Postage for seasonal postcards. By creating a new, efficient way to meet a consumer need, Rogue Sheep's Postage app may supplant printed materials to become the future of postcards. The business applications of sending RogueSheep postcards are unlimited. It can be just another form of digital marketing. RogueSheep's postage application, like all digital marketing activities, should be integrated into a marketing strategy that relates to the target market's ability and interest in digital communication.[91]

QUESTIONS FOR DISCUSSION

1. How do you think businesses could effectively use RogueSheep postcards in their communications program?

2. Is it possible for RogueSheep to advance its digital postcards to those who do not have access to iPhone apps?

3. What are the advantages of the RogueSheep digital postcard over traditional postcards?

CASE 10.2

Twitter Emerges as a Digital Marketing Tool

CRITICAL THINKING

Businesses big and small are discovering tweeting in order to inform the world about their companies. By asking the question "What's happening?", Twitter allows users to tell their followers about moments in their daily lives. Based out of a South Park, San Francisco warehouse, Twitter was founded by Biz Stone and Evan Williams. It started as a podcasting company but quickly morphed into its current social networking form. People use Twitter for everything from "I'm catching some zzz's in class," to President Obama's "We just made history" on election night, to a San Francisco writer tweeting that his house was being broken into. On Facebook, users are able to communicate directly only if the users have agreed to be "friends." On Twitter, anyone can sign up to follow any public tweets available. For instance, actor Ashton Kutcher has more than 4 million followers.

> **Keep up with Dell on Twitter!**
> Breaking news · 24/7 updates · Deals and discounts
> Follow us, tweet us, and retweet us to all your friends. We'll see you on Twitter!

Many marketers have been quick to jump on the Twitter bandwagon, finding it to be an effective communications tool for attracting consumers. For example, Bradsdeals.com, a site that identifies online shopping deals, started posting company updates on Twitter. Bakeries are even tweeting to tell customers when fresh cookies are available. Cake decorator Hansen's Cakes in Beverly Hills posts a simple message or an update on Twitter to encourage online "friends" and "followers" to get excited about its products. Aaron Chronister saw his status update on Twitter about his barbecue club and bacon recipe get media attention on CNN and the *New York Times*, which resulted in a book deal with Simon & Schuster. The bottom line is that a Twitter post can tell others what you are up to in your business. These posts can then be forwarded to others to create a buzz.

"Follow me on Twitter" signs are appearing on the doors and windows of small businesses around the globe. One survey by a mobile phone company in the UK found 17 percent of small businesses were using Twitter. According to the 2010 Social Media Marketing Industry Report, which surveyed 1,898 small businesses, a whopping 88 percent indicated that they tweet, while 87 percent use Facebook, 78 percent use LinkedIn, and 70 percent use blogs. While some of these businesses are attracting new customers, many are saving money by cutting out other forms of promotion. Kogi BBQ in Los Angeles, which uses vans to cater Korean food, has incorporated Twitter as part of its core promotional strategy. The company has more than 50,000 followers on Twitter and uses the service to tell customers where their mobile Korean food vans can be found each day. An advertising agency, Razurfish, found that 44 percent of heavy Twitter users are looking for exclusive deals that firms offer only to users.

Another interesting way to fully utilize the value of Twitter is by using TweetDeck, a free software that enables users to search up to 10 terms simultaneously. For example, Lorien Gabel, the CEO of Pingg, an online invitation company, uses Twitter in this way to track what consumers are saying about his company and his competitors. This is an invaluable way for companies to gather feedback in an unobtrusive manner, increase customer satisfaction, and stay in touch with their competitors.

Twitter introduced advertising to generate sales from marketers eager to reach its audience. The site is carrying promoted tweets from advertisers including Best Buy and Starbucks. Eventually, social networking sites want to make money from the millions of people who interact with each other online. The promoted tweets allow Twitter to capitalize on the millions of people who go to their site.

Of course, with the success of Twitter comes criticism as well. Some feel that many Twitter users post mundane details of their lives just to kill time. Yet these complaints have not dulled Twitter's success. With two-thirds of online users visiting Twitter, the craze is continuing at full force.[92]

QUESTIONS FOR DISCUSSION

1. Why is Twitter appealing to companies?
2. How could Twitter be used as a tool to strengthen customer relationships and to gather consumer feedback?
3. What are some of the drawbacks of using Twitter as a marketing tool?

McDonald's Marketing Serves Up Global and Local Profits

Serving 52 million people in 32,000 locations worldwide may be a tall order, but it's just an ordinary day for McDonald's. McDonald's has increased annual revenues to more than $22 billion by smart marketing and understanding what, when, where, why, and how customers want to eat. Facing intense competition from traditional fast-food rivals like Burger King and KFC, and casual dining chains like Panera, McDonald's never stops looking for new ways to reinforce customer loyalty and build profits.

What's in Store?

One key to McDonald's success is its menu of core items that are inextricably linked to the McDonald's brand and other items that are adapted to regional tastes. In Moscow, consumers have made Fresh McMuffin sausage sandwiches a top-selling morning item. In Argentina, the Ranchero hamburger sandwich, with a special salsa sauce, is a particular customer favorite. In France, the Croque McDo is McDonald's version of the popular croque monsieur hot ham-and-cheese sandwich.

Although McDonald's built its reputation on burgers and fries, its marketers recognize that many consumers have become more health conscious. That's why McDonald's has developed lighter fast-food fare for adults and children alike, including new salads, wrap sandwiches, and apple slices. The company now posts nutrition information online for consumers and changed its cooking oil so that all fried items have 0 grams of trans fats per serving.

Ready for Customers Early, Late, and on the Go

Another way McDonald's has increased sales and profits is by opening stores early to serve the breakfast crowd and keeping selected stores open until midnight or later. Some of its units operate drive-through service 24 hours a day. In China, where McDonald's has more than 1,100 outlets, late-night hours are popular and have helped the company significantly increase revenues. Also, McDonald's sees drive-through lanes as an important competitive element in China, where car ownership is growing fast and competitors like KFC have few drive-through locations. Now half of the new stores McDonald's opens in China are equipped for drive-through operations. Under an agreement with state-owned Sinopec, McDonald's is adding drive-through outlets at Sinopec gas stations all around China.

Dealing with the Dollar Menu

To appeal to its customers who have very tight budgets, McDonald's offers a Dollar Menu. The idea is to "bring in consumers who are looking for ways to stretch their wallets," explains the company's president. In fact, the Dollar Menu items account for more than 10 percent of overall sales in U.S. restaurants.

However, with food prices rising and other costs inching upward, some McDonald's franchisees complain that they are earning low profit margins on Dollar Menu items. Under the terms of their franchise agreements with McDonald's, franchisees are free to charge more (or less) than the corporation's official Dollar Menu price. Therefore, some stores in high-cost markets charge $1.29 or $1.39 for the Double Cheeseburger that in other areas sell for $1.

Rising costs are a problem for McDonald's international stores as well. In countries like Russia, for example, McDonald's boosts menu prices multiple times in a year to cope with inflation that drives up the costs of food. The company increases the price of less-expensive menu items by about half the inflation rate but increases the price of premium menu items by more than the inflation rate because, according to one executive, "We still have a huge amount of people who are price sensitive." Despite the price hikes, the McDonald's in Moscow's Pushkin Square remains the busiest McDonald's on the planet, with 26 cash registers and seating for 900.

Social Responsibility on the Menu

Ronald McDonald is one of the world's most recognizable brand mascots. Not only does he appear in McDonald's marketing communications, but he also headlines the company's Ronald McDonald House Charities, which provide accommodations for families while their critically ill children are treated in hospitals far from home. The nonprofit group, now more than three decades old, operates houses in 52 nations. Local McDonald's outlets support neighborhood charities and community causes as well.

Prodded in part by animal activists, the company has established animal-handling standards for its meat suppliers. It's also going green by using paper and cardboard packaging made from recycled materials. To showcase its charitable and environmental activities, the company issues a yearly corporate responsibility report and publicizes achievements such as raising millions of dollars on World Children's Day.

However, not all of McDonald's community activities are well received. For instance, McDonald's restaurants in Seminole County, Florida, arranged to give Happy Meals to local elementary school students as rewards for good grades and attendance. But some parents and child advocates raised concerns when students brought home report card jackets with a picture of Ronald McDonald on them. "It's a terribly troubling trend because it really, clearly links doing well in school with getting a Happy Meal," the head of the Campaign for a Commercial-Free Childhood told the *New York Times*.

Blogging about Beef

McDonald's has a strong presence on the Internet, with a corporate website, product and nutrition websites, and individual websites geared to each country where it does business. To generate grassroots word-of-mouth communications about food and service quality, it has enlisted six Mom's Quality Correspondents to go behind the scenes at headquarters, suppliers' facilities, and individual McDonald's stores. The moms are free to look around, ask questions, videotape what they see, and then blog about their experiences, including video snippets.

These bloggers can say whatever they like because, says a McDonald's marketing official, "if moms were out there speaking to their communities and online communities unedited, it would get us far more credibility than just posting an article or doing website copy." For example, after the moms traveled to a McDonald's beef supplier in Oklahoma City, one wrote on the blog, "Hey, moms across America—it is really 100% beef!"

McDonald's also maintains a corporate social responsibility blog where its managers post informal notes about issues such as environmental programs, healthy lifestyles, and responsible purchasing. When consumers post comments in response to these blogs, the resulting dialogue helps McDonald's to better understand public sentiment surrounding such issues and to plan appropriate actions and communications.

Selling the Arch Card

Although McDonald's has sold gift certificates for many years, it now has a corporate sales division that targets businesses that want to give small incentives to employees or customers. The incentive program that McDonald's offers is its Arch Card, a prepaid gift card issued in the amount of $5, $10, $25, or $50. Businesses can buy up to 25 Arch Cards through local McDonald's outlets. The corporate sales division handles bulk purchases and gives business customers a discount if they buy $10,000 worth of Arch Cards. After recipients spend the initial gift amount, they can pay to reload up to $110 on each card. The next time they visit a McDonald's restaurant, they'll be ready to grab and go with just a swipe of plastic.[93]

QUESTIONS FOR DISCUSSION

1. What role do opinion leaders play in McDonald's marketing?

2. How is McDonald's using marketing to spark learning and positive attitudes toward its brand and offerings?

3. Why would McDonald's select businesses as a target market for its Arch Cards?

4. What environmental forces have created challenges for McDonald's in global markets? What forces have created opportunities in global markets?

Product Decisions

We are now prepared to analyze the decisions and activities associated with developing and maintaining effective marketing mixes. In Parts Five through Eight, we focus on the major components of the marketing mix: product, distribution, promotion, and price. **PART FIVE** explores the product component of the marketing mix. **CHAPTER 11** introduces basic concepts and relationships that must be understood to make effective product decisions. **CHAPTER 12** analyzes a variety of dimensions regarding product management, including line extensions and product modification, new-product development, and product deletions. **CHAPTER 13** explores the nature, importance, and characteristics of services. **CHAPTER 14** discusses branding, packaging, and labeling.

Economic forces

Competitive forces

Political forces

Product

Price   Customer   Distribution

Promotion

Sociocultural forces

Legal and regulatory forces

Technological forces

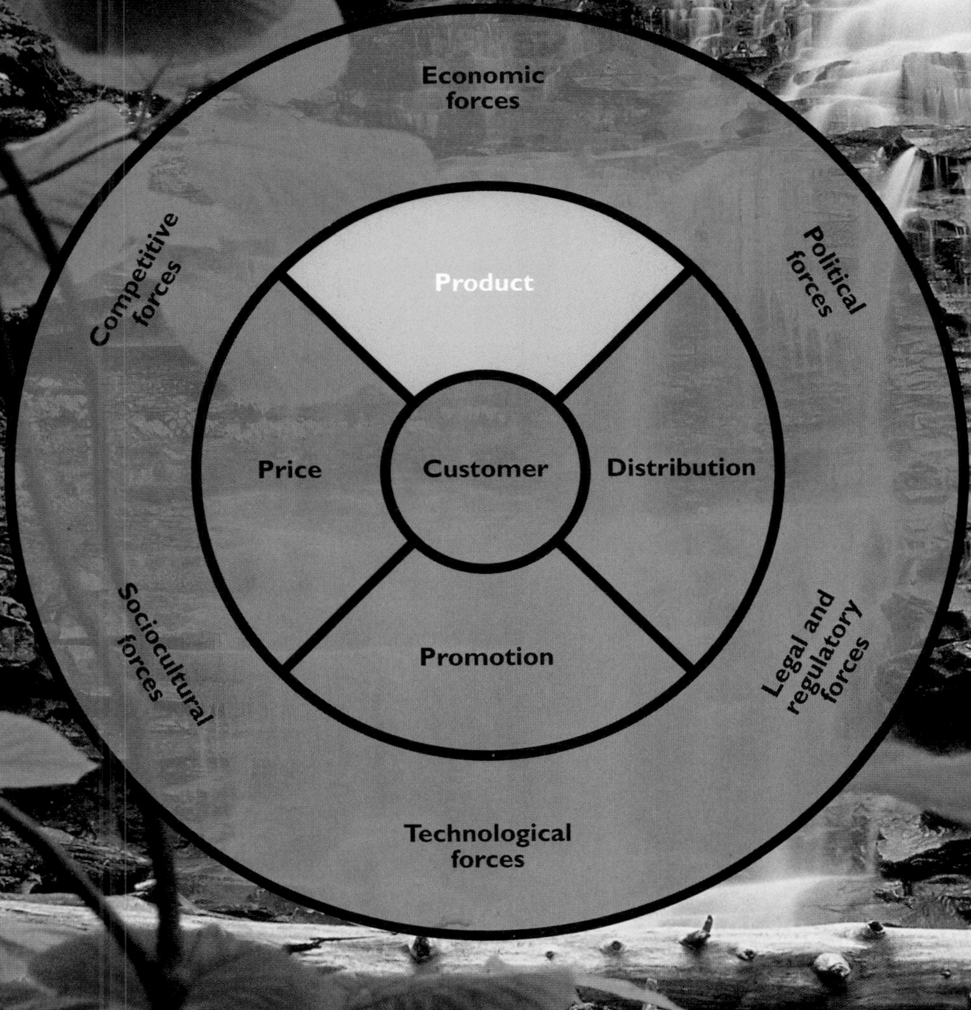

© Comstock Images/Getty Images

Chapter 11

Product Concepts

OBJECTIVES

1. To understand the concept of a product

2. To explain how to classify products

3. To examine the concepts of product item, product line, and product mix and understand how they are connected

4. To understand the product life cycle and its impact on marketing strategies

5. To describe the product adoption process

6. To understand why some products fail and some succeed

Taurus Strives for Greatness Again

Ford Motor Company's Taurus was first introduced in 1986. Customers responded positively to its streamlined design, an oddity at the time, but a style that was soon adopted by many competitors. Taurus rapidly moved from introduction to growth stage, topping the sales charts in the early 1990s and pulling Ford out of a major profit slump. Ten years after its debut, Ford released the Taurus 2.0, which flopped. The attempt to reinvent the brand signaled the decline of the Taurus; in 2004, Ford halted its production.

Four years later, Ford reintroduced the Taurus with lackluster results. Some analysts claim that the company simply wanted to keep the name alive until it had a Taurus worth promoting. Ford tried again in 2010 with yet another new model of the Taurus. This update resembled the original Taurus in name only. Rather than producing another mid-size car, Ford has made its new Taurus into a full-size sedan—a curious move considering that the full-size sedan market is considerably smaller than that for mid-size cars. With four models and prices ranging from $25,170 to $37,170, the 2010 Taurus resembles its competition (such as the Toyota Avalon) in many ways.

What may set it apart are the bells and whistles available as add-ons, although these can drive the cost to above $38,000. The Taurus product options have both pros and cons. On the pro side, the add-ons can turn the car into something truly exciting and high-tech. On the con side, once you drive the price up, you're butting heads with luxury vehicles such as the BMW and Mercedes. For the consumer, it then becomes an issue of choosing brand or features.

In general, reviews suggest that the 2010 Taurus is a huge improvement over its predecessors. It offers a more complete package and better performance. However, some say the car still needs work and feel it is priced too high. Ford, on the other hand, believes that it finally has a winner and is looking to the 2010 Taurus (along with its 2011 Fiesta) to once again carry it out of a slump. Can Ford succeed this time and experience a profitable growth cycle on the way to maturity?[1]

The product is a key variable in the marketing mix. Products, such as the cars manufactured and sold by Ford Motors, are typically a firm's most important asset. If a company's products do not meet customers' desires and needs, the firm will fail unless it is willing to make adjustments. Developing successful products like the original Taurus, and carrying out strategic moves like the decisions to discontinue and reintroduce the brand, requires highly sophisticated knowledge of fundamental marketing and product concepts.

In this chapter, we first define *product* and discuss how buyers view products. Next, we examine the concepts of product line and product mix. We then explore the stages of the product life cycle and the effect of each life cycle stage on marketing strategies. Then we outline the product adoption process. Finally, we discuss the factors that contribute to a product's failure or success.

What Is a Product?

As defined in Chapter 1, a *product* is a good, a service, or an idea received in an exchange. It can be either tangible or intangible and includes functional, social, and psychological utilities or benefits. It also includes supporting services, such as installation, guarantees, product information, and promises of repair or maintenance. Thus, the four-year/50,000-mile warranty that covers most new automobiles is part of the product itself. A **good** is a tangible physical entity, such as an iPad or a Quiznos sandwich. A **service**, in contrast, is intangible; it is the result of the application of human and mechanical efforts to people or objects. Examples of services include a performance by Lady Gaga, an online travel agency booking, a medical examination, child day care, real estate services, and martial arts lessons. (Chapter 14 provides a detailed discussion of services.) An **idea** is a concept, philosophy, image, or issue. Ideas provide the psychological stimulation that aids in solving problems or adjusting to the environment. For example, MADD (Mothers Against Drunk Driving) promotes safe consumption of alcoholic beverages and stricter enforcement of laws against drunk driving.

It is helpful to think of a total product offering as having a combination of three interdependent elements: the core product itself, its supplemental features, and its symbolic or experiential value (Figure 11.1). Consider that some people buy new tires for their basic utility (e.g., Sears's Guardsman III), whereas some look for safety (e.g., Michelin) and others buy on the basis of brand name or exemplary performance (e.g., Pirelli).

The core product consists of a product's fundamental utility or main benefit. Broadband Internet services, for instance, offer speedy Internet access, but some buyers want additional features such as wireless connectivity anywhere they go. The core product usually addresses a fundamental need of the consumer. When you buy bottled water, you can buy name brands such as Dasani and Aquafina or more exclusive brands like Fiji, Voss, or Evian. Regardless of price, each alternative will quench your thirst. Retailers such as Target and Walmart specialize in offering core products (store brands and generics) of a generally acceptable quality level at competitive prices. Hotels such as Clarion and the Hampton Inn specialize in providing quality services at affordable prices.

A product's supplemental features provide added value or attributes in addition to its core utility or

good A tangible physical entity

service An intangible result of the application of human and mechanical efforts to people or objects

idea A concept, philosophy, image, or issue

What Is a Product?
Mummies of the World presents the largest collection of mummies and related artifacts, representing a service.

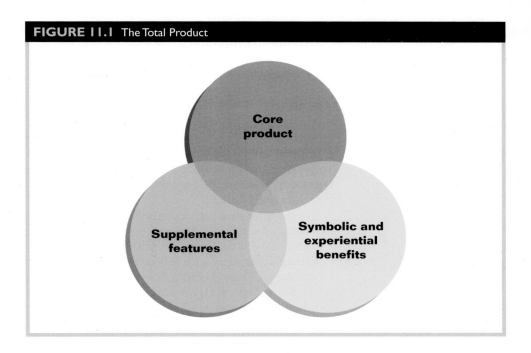

FIGURE 11.1 The Total Product

Core product

Supplemental features

Symbolic and experiential benefits

benefit. Supplemental products can also provide installation, delivery, training, and financing. These supplemental attributes are not required to make the core product function effectively, but they help differentiate one product brand from another. In the U.S. Hotel Chain Survey by *Business Travel News* magazine, Ritz-Carlton Hotels topped the survey's deluxe tier segment by changing their approach to food; they now offer a differentiated dining experience through partnerships with well-known chefs such as Wolfgang Puck. In addition, Ritz-Carlton offers unprecedented group travel arrangements by providing free nights and free Internet usage.[2] These supplemental features add real value to the core product of overnight hotel stays.

Finally, customers also receive benefits based on their experiences with the product. In addition, many products have symbolic meaning for buyers. For some consumers, the simple act of shopping gives symbolic value and improves their attitudes. Some stores capitalize on this value by striving to create a special experience for customers. You can buy stuffed toys at many retailers, but at Build-A-Bear, you can choose the type of animal, stuff it yourself, give it a heart, and create a name complete with a birth certificate, as well as give the toy a bath and clothe and accessorize it. The atmosphere and décor of a retail store, the variety and depth of product choices, the customer support, and even the sounds and smells all contribute to the experiential element. When you check into a Hotel Monaco, not only do you get a great room with down comforters, bed toppers, and pillows, but you can also "check out" a fish as your companion during your stay. Many customers credit the Hotel Monaco with providing a differentiated, enjoyable stay and become loyal customers. In addition, Hotel Monacos offer complementary wine happy hours to allow guests to socialize in their lobby. These symbolic and experiential features are all part of the Hotel Monaco total product.

Thus, when buyers purchase a product, they are really buying the benefits and satisfaction they think the product will provide. A Rolex or Patek Philippe watch is purchased to make a statement of success, not just for telling time. Services in particular are purchased on the basis of expectations. Expectations, suggested by images, promises, and symbols, as well as processes and delivery, help consumers make judgments about tangible and intangible products. Products are formed by the activities and processes that help satisfy expectations. Starbucks did not invent the coffee shop, but it did make high-quality coffee beverages readily available around the world with standardized service and in stylish, comfortable stores. Often symbols and cues are used to make intangible products more tangible, or real, to the consumer. Allstate Insurance Company, for example, uses giant hands to symbolize security, strength, and friendliness, whereas Travelers Insurance uses an umbrella to signify protection.

Classifying Products

Products fall into one of two general categories. Products that are purchased to satisfy personal and family needs are **consumer products**. Products bought to use in a firm's operations, to resell, or to make other products are **business products**. Consumers buy products to satisfy their personal wants, whereas business buyers seek to satisfy the goals of their organizations.

The same item can be classified as both a consumer product and a business product. When a person buys a 100-watt light bulb for lighting a home closet, it is classified as a consumer product. However, when an organization purchases a 100-watt light bulb for lighting a reception area, it is considered a business product because it is used in daily operations. Thus, the buyer's intent—or the ultimate use of the product—determines whether an item is classified as a consumer or business product. In addition, the sizes of business product purchases are often very large as they are used to accommodate an office, manufacturing facility, or warehouse.

Product classifications are important because classes of products are aimed at particular target markets; this targeting in turn affects distribution, promotion, and pricing decisions.

consumer products Products purchased to satisfy personal and family needs

business products Products bought to use in a firm's operations, to resell, or to make other products

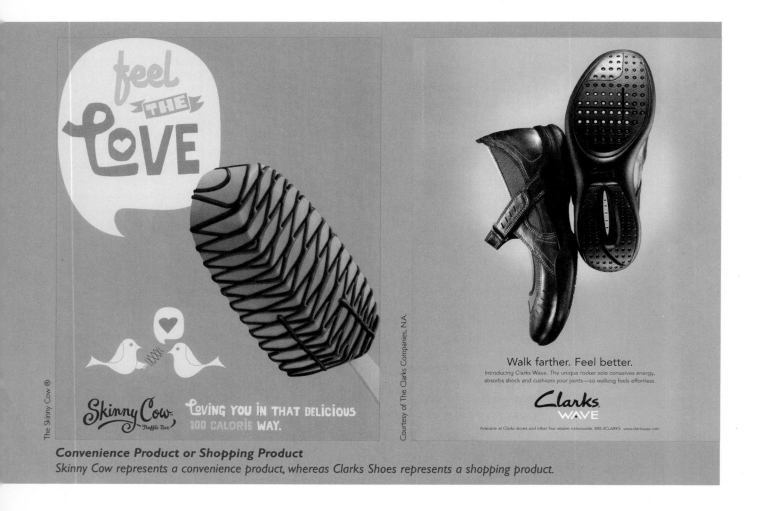

Convenience Product or Shopping Product
Skinny Cow represents a convenience product, whereas Clarks Shoes represents a shopping product.

Furthermore, appropriate marketing strategies vary among the classes of consumer and business products. In short, how a product is classified can affect the entire marketing mix. In this section, we examine the characteristics of consumer and business products and explore the marketing activities associated with some of these products.

Consumer Products

The most widely accepted approach to classifying consumer products is based on characteristics of consumer buying behavior. It divides products into four categories: convenience, shopping, specialty, and unsought products. However, not all buyers behave in the same way when purchasing a specific type of product. Thus, a single product can fit into several categories. To minimize this problem, marketers think in terms of how buyers *generally* behave when purchasing a specific item. In addition, they recognize that the "correct" classification can be determined only by considering a particular firm's intended target market. Examining the four traditional categories of consumer products can provide further insight.

CONVENIENCE PRODUCTS

Convenience products are relatively inexpensive, frequently purchased items for which buyers exert only minimal purchasing effort. They range from bread, soft drinks, and chewing gum to gasoline and newspapers. The buyer spends little time planning the purchase or comparing available brands or sellers. Today, time has become one of our most precious assets, and many consumers therefore buy products at the closest location to preserve time for other activities. Even a buyer who prefers a specific brand will often willingly choose a substitute if the preferred brand is not readily available.

Classifying a product as a convenience product has several implications for a firm's marketing strategy. A convenience product is normally marketed through many retail outlets. Examples of typical outlets include 7-Eleven, ExxonMobil, and Starbucks. Starbucks coffee is available in airports, hotels, and grocery stores, and many of the Starbucks company-owned stores now have drive-through lanes to ensure that customers can get coffee whenever or wherever the desire strikes.[3] Because sellers experience high inventory turnover, per-unit gross margins can be relatively low. Producers of convenience products, such as Altoid mints, expect little promotional effort at the retail level and thus must provide it themselves with advertising and sales promotion. Packaging is also an important element of the marketing mix for convenience products. The package may have to sell the product because many convenience items are available only on a self-service basis at the retail level.

SHOPPING PRODUCTS

Shopping products are items for which buyers are willing to expend considerable effort in planning and making the purchase. Buyers spend much time comparing stores and brands with respect to prices, product features, qualities, services, and perhaps warranties. Shoppers may compare products at a number of outlets such as Best Buy, Amazon. com, Lowe's, or Home Depot. Appliances, bicycles, furniture, stereos, cameras, and shoes exemplify shopping products. These products are expected to last a fairly long time and thus are purchased less frequently than convenience items. Although shopping products are more expensive than convenience products, few buyers of shopping products are particularly brand loyal. As an example, most consumers are not brand loyal for home appliances and decorations. If they were, they would be unwilling to shop and compare among brands. Even when they are brand loyal, they may still spend considerable time comparing the features of different models

convenience products Relatively inexpensive, frequently purchased items for which buyers exert minimal purchasing effort

shopping products Items for which buyers are willing to expend considerable effort in planning and making purchases

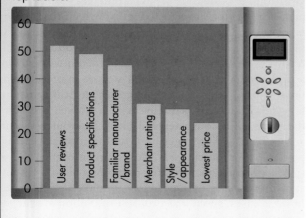

SNAPSHOT

What Is the Most Important Factor in Your Purchase of a Major Home or Kitchen Appliance Online?

Top factors:

of a brand. A consumer who is looking for a new LG washing machine may explore the company's website to compare the features of different washers before visiting a store and talking to a salesperson. (See the Snapshot for different factors that consumers consider when making home appliance purchases.) Regardless of the number of brands of interest, buyers may also consult buying guides such as *Consumer Reports* or visit consumer information websites such as **www.epinions.com** to view others' opinions or ratings of brands and models before they are ready to make an actual purchase.

To market a shopping product effectively, a marketer considers several key issues. Shopping products require fewer retail outlets than convenience products. Because shopping products are purchased less frequently, inventory turnover is lower, and marketing channel members expect to receive higher gross margins. Although large sums of money may be required to advertise shopping products, an even larger percentage of resources are likely to be used for personal selling. The producer and the marketing channel members usually expect some cooperation from one another with respect to providing parts and repair services and performing promotional activities. In certain situations, both shopping products and convenience products may be marketed in the same location. Both Target and Walmart carry shopping products such as televisions, computers, and cameras as well as groceries and other convenience products.

SPECIALTY PRODUCTS

specialty products Items with unique characteristics that buyers are willing to expend considerable effort to obtain

unsought products Products purchased to solve a sudden problem, products of which customers are unaware, and products that people do not necessarily think of buying

Specialty products possess one or more unique characteristics, and generally buyers are willing to expend considerable effort to obtain them. Buyers actually plan the purchase of a specialty product; they know exactly what they want and will not accept a substitute. Examples of specialty products include a Mont Blanc pen and a one-of-a-kind piece of baseball memorabilia, such as a ball signed by Babe Ruth. When searching for specialty products, buyers do not compare alternatives; they are concerned primarily with finding an outlet that has the preselected product available. Racing fans interested in a high-status way to commemorate attending the Indy 500 doubtless found the specially designed Tag Heuer Indy 500 wristwatch very attractive.

The fact that an item is a specialty product can affect a firm's marketing efforts in several ways. Specialty products are often distributed through a limited number of retail outlets. Like shopping products, they are purchased infrequently, causing lower inventory turnover and thus requiring relatively high gross margins.

UNSOUGHT PRODUCTS

Unsought products are products purchased when a sudden problem must be solved, products of which customers are unaware, and products that people do not necessarily think of purchasing. Emergency medical services and automobile repairs are examples of products needed quickly to solve a problem. A consumer who is sick or injured has little time to plan to go to an emergency medical center or a hospital. Likewise, in the event of a broken fan belt on the highway, a consumer will likely seek out the nearest auto repair facility to get back on the road as quickly as possible. Computer users must purchase antivirus and spyware detection software to protect their computers even though they may not want to make such purchases. In these cases, speed and problem resolution are far more important than price, in addition to other features buyers might consider if they had more time for decision making. Companies like ServiceMaster, which markets emergency services such as disaster recovery and plumbing repair, are making the purchases of these unsought products more

CapriPlus Collection   ◆ ROBERTO COIN

Specialty Products
Roberto Coin's jewelry represents a specialty product.

Sustainable Marketing
Honeywell Focuses on Green—Earning Money and Saving the Planet

Novar—a division of *Fortune* 100 technology and manufacturing company Honeywell International—is a global leader in energy management solutions that is trying to be highly profitable and sustainable at the same time. Novar has the goal of helping businesses create sustainability strategies and become more profitable. Through Novar and its other businesses, Honeywell is capitalizing on stakeholder concerns about global warming and the rising costs of power.

Novar currently assists more than 40,000 retail businesses. Case in point: the company advised Staples stores to utilize its Smart Meters. The Smart Meter energy solution includes Smart Meter systems, software, and live assessments. Among its many capabilities, the Smart Meter can identify store electronics running after a store is closed—thereby notifying someone to turn them off, reducing energy costs. Staples also uses Novar's "employee lighting program," which automatically adjusts the use of lighting based on need. Smart Meters have saved Staples 15 percent on its energy expenses compared to before it adopted the system. Novar has helped other clients save anywhere from $10,000 to beyond $100,000 per store. Assistance ranges from providing equipment to fully managing a company's site(s).

Although initial costs for Novar's solutions are high, Staples managed to recoup the investment in two years. The recession that began in 2008 had an impact on Novar's success, but the strength of its business positions sustained future growth. Novar's approach

is appealing because it delivers measurable results. While switching to alternative energy sources and other eco-friendly measures are great, simply managing your energy usage more carefully and trimming where possible can yield a faster and therefore more obvious financial return. Novar's CEO, Dean Lindstrom, says businesses can see an immediate return on investment of 20 to 40 percent and achieve 100 percent return quickly. What Novar offers is the marriage between efficient energy savings and profitability.[a]

bearable by building trust with consumers through recognizable brands (ServiceMaster Clean and Rescue Rooter) and superior functional performance.

Business Products

Business products are usually purchased on the basis of an organization's goals and objectives. Generally the functional aspects of the product are more important than the psychological rewards sometimes associated with consumer products. Business products can be classified into seven categories according to their characteristics and intended uses: installations, accessory equipment, raw materials, component parts, process materials, MRO supplies, and business services.

INSTALLATIONS

Installations include facilities, such as office buildings, factories, and warehouses, as well as major pieces of equipment that are nonportable, such as production lines and very large machines. Major equipment is normally used for production purposes. Some major equipment is custom made to perform specific functions for a particular organization; other items are standardized and perform similar tasks for many types of firms. Normally installations are expensive and intended to be used for a considerable length of time. Because they are so expensive and typically involve a long-term investment of capital, purchase decisions are often made by high-level management. Marketers of installations frequently must provide a variety of services, including training, repairs, maintenance assistance, and even financial assistance.

installations Facilities and nonportable major equipment

Introducing a corporate stimulus package that eliminates the package.

The new Xerox ColorQube™ multifunction printer uses unique cartridge-free Solid Ink technology, which is non-toxic, mess-free and reduces waste by 90%. Better yet, you can also save up to 62% on color prints. The ultimate win-win. What's more, this high-performance line of MFPs can handle the busiest of workloads without compromising image quality. Finally, good news for both business and the environment.

1-800-ASK-XEROX
FinallyColorIsLess.com

Ready For Real Business **xerox**

© Xerox Corporation

Business Products
Xerox offers many business products and support services.

ACCESSORY EQUIPMENT

Accessory equipment does not become a part of the final physical product but is used in production or office activities. Examples include file cabinets, fractional-horsepower motors, calculators, and tools. Compared with major equipment, accessory items are usually much cheaper, purchased routinely with less negotiation, and treated as expense items rather than capital items because they are not expected to last as long. Accessory products are standardized items that can be used in several aspects of a firm's operations. More outlets are required for distributing accessory equipment than for installations, but sellers do not have to provide the numerous services expected of installations marketers.

RAW MATERIALS

Raw materials are the basic natural materials that actually become part of a physical product. They include minerals, chemicals, agricultural products, and materials from forests and oceans. They are usually bought and sold according to grades and specifications, and in relatively large quantities. Corn, for example, is a raw material that is found in many different products, including food, beverages (as corn syrup), and even fuel (ethanol).

COMPONENT PARTS

Component parts become part of the physical product and are either finished items ready for assembly or products that need little processing before assembly. Although they become part of a larger product, component parts often can be easily identified and distinguished. Spark plugs, tires, clocks, brakes, and switches are all component parts of an automobile. German-based Robert Bosch GmbH, the world's largest auto parts maker, supplies 30 percent of the 46 million antilock brakes installed in vehicles worldwide.[4] Buyers purchase such items according to their own specifications or industry standards. They expect the parts to be of specified quality and delivered on time so that production is not slowed or stopped. Producers that are primarily assemblers, such as most lawn mower and computer manufacturers, depend heavily on suppliers of component parts.

PROCESS MATERIALS

Process materials are used directly in the production of other products. Unlike component parts, however, process materials are not readily identifiable. A salad dressing manufacturer may include vinegar in its salad dressing; the vinegar is a process material because it is included in the salad dressing but is not identifiable. As with component parts, process materials are purchased according to industry standards or the purchaser's specifications.

MRO SUPPLIES

MRO supplies are maintenance, repair, and operating items that facilitate production and operations but do not become part of the finished product. Paper, pencils, oils, cleaning agents, and paints are in this category. Although you might be familiar with Tide, Downy, and Febreze as consumer products, to restaurants and hotels, they are MRO supplies required to wash dishes and launder sheets and towels. Procter & Gamble is increasingly targeting business customers in the $3.5 billion market for janitorial and housekeeping products.[5] MRO supplies are commonly sold through numerous outlets and are purchased routinely. To ensure supplies are available when needed, buyers often deal with more than one seller.

BUSINESS SERVICES

Business services are the intangible products that many organizations use in their operations. They include financial, legal, market research, information technology, and

accessory equipment Equipment that does not become part of the final physical product but is used in production or office activities

raw materials Basic natural materials that become part of a physical product

component parts Items that become part of the physical product and are either finished items ready for assembly or items that need little processing before assembly

process materials Materials that are used directly in the production of other products but are not readily identifiable

MRO supplies Maintenance, repair, and operating items that facilitate production and operations but do not become part of the finished product

Blendtec Asks, "Will It Blend?"

Millions of people have viewed Blendtec's videos on YouTube to find out whether the firm's home blenders can reduce the unlikeliest of objects—some marbles, a dozen glow sticks, an iPod—to dust and smoke. Based in Orem, Utah, Blendtec originally targeted restaurants, bars, and other businesses that require high-powered blenders to make sauces, soups, smoothies, and other specialties. Its success in that market set the stage for the decision to grow even faster by expanding into consumer products.

After Blendtec's webmaster posted the videos on the company-owned willitblend.com and on YouTube, they were picked up by other popular websites. By the end of the year, Blendtec's consumer sales had risen by 43 percent. Says George Wright, the director of marketing for Blendtec, "The blender used in restaurants for your smoothie is available for the home now, too, and the word is out among consumers."[b]

janitorial services. Firms must decide whether to provide their own services internally or obtain them from outside the organization. This decision depends on the costs associated with each alternative and how frequently the services are needed. As an example, IBM focuses on services that help companies with business processes and management systems and with integrating advanced technology into their operations.

Product Line and Product Mix

Marketers must understand the relationships among all the products of their organization to coordinate the marketing of the total group of products. The following concepts help describe the relationships among an organization's products.

A **product item** is a specific version of a product that can be designated as a distinct offering among an organization's products. An Abercrombie and Fitch polo shirt represents a product item. A **product line** is a group of closely related product items that are considered to be a unit because of marketing, technical, or end-use considerations. SunnyRidge Farm Inc., which is a berry farm as well as a distributor and a marketer for berry farms throughout the Americas, launched a new line of organic blueberries with anticipated sales of 5 million pounds in the first year. Within SunnyRidge's organic blueberry line, different product items relate to packaging, branding, and modifications in the original product.[6] The exact boundaries of a product line (although sometimes blurred) are usually indicated by the use of descriptive terms such as "frozen dessert product line" or "shampoo product line." Specific product items in a product line, such as different dessert flavors or shampoos for oily and dry hair, usually reflect the desires of different target markets or the different needs of consumers. Thus, to develop the optimal product line, marketers must understand buyers' goals. Firms with high market share are likely to expand their product lines aggressively, as are marketers with relatively high prices or limited product lines.[7] This pattern can be seen in the personal computer industry, where companies are likely to expand their product lines when industry barriers are low or perceived market opportunities exist.

A **product mix** is the composite, or total, group of products that an organization makes available to customers. Procter & Gamble's product mix comprises all the health-care, beauty-care, laundry and cleaning, food and beverage, paper, cosmetic, and fragrance products that the firm manufactures. The **width of product mix** is measured by the number of product lines a company offers. General Electric offers multiple product lines, including consumer products such as housewares, health-care products such as molecular imaging, and commercial engines for the military.[8] The **depth of product mix** is the average number of different products offered in each product line. Figure 11.2 shows the width and depth of a part of Procter & Gamble's product mix. Procter & Gamble is known for using distinctive branding, packaging, and consumer advertising to promote individual items in its detergent product line. Tide, Bold, Gain, Cheer, and Era—all Procter & Gamble detergents—share the same distribution channels and similar manufacturing facilities, but each is promoted as a distinctive product, adding depth to the product line.

business services Intangible products that many organizations use in their operations

product item A specific version of a product that can be designated as a distinct offering among a firm's products

product line A group of closely related product items viewed as a unit because of marketing, technical, or end-use considerations

product mix The composite, or total, group of products that an organization makes available to customers

width of product mix The number of product lines a company offers

depth of product mix The average number of different products offered in each product line

FIGURE 11.2 The Concepts of Product Mix Width and Depth Applied to U.S. Procter & Gamble Products

Laundry detergents	Toothpastes	Bar soaps	Deodorants	Shampoos	Tissue/Towel
Ivory Snow 1930	Gleem 1952	Ivory 1879	Old Spice 1948	Pantene 1947	Charmin 1928
Dreft 1933	Crest 1955	Camay 1926	Secret 1956	Head & Shoulders 1961	Puffs 1960
Tide 1946		Zest 1952	Sure 1972	Vidal Sassoon 1974	Bounty 1965
Cheer 1950		Safeguard 1963		Pert Plus 1979	
Bold 1965		Oil of Olay 1993		Ivory 1983	
Gain 1966				Infusium 23 1986	
Era 1972				Physique 2000	
Febreze Clean Wash 2000				Herbal Essence 2001	

Depth

Width

Product Life Cycles and Marketing Strategies

Just as biological cycles progress from birth through growth and decline, so do product life cycles. As Figure 11.3 shows, a **product life cycle** has four major stages: introduction, growth, maturity, and decline. As a product moves through its life cycle, the strategies that relate to competition, promotion, distribution, pricing, and market information must be periodically evaluated and possibly changed. Astute marketing managers use the life-cycle concept to make sure the introduction, alteration, and termination of a product are timed and executed properly. By understanding the typical life-cycle pattern, marketers are better able to maintain profitable products and drop unprofitable ones.

Introduction

The **introduction stage** of the product life cycle begins at a product's first appearance in the market, when sales start at zero and profits are negative. Profits are below zero because initial revenues are low, and the company generally must cover large expenses for promotion and distribution. Notice in Figure 11.3 how sales should move upward from zero, and profits should also move upward from a position in which they are negative because of high expenses in developing new products.

Developing and introducing a new product can mean an outlay of millions. Cadbury Schweppes spent two years and millions of dollars to develop Trident Splash, a sugar-free gum with a candy shell and a liquid center, which it markets to adults for 99 cents a package.[9] And although the importance of new products is significant, the risk of new-product failure is quite high, depending on the industry. Consider the development of frozen vegetables. Clarence Birdseye invented the "quick-freeze machine" that created a new product, "frozen vegetables," in 1920. A completely new product, the frozen vegetables could not be distributed or sold until Birds Eye developed super-insulated railcars for transportation and retail freezer cases for display. Today, Birds Eye still has 27 percent of the $2.8 billion frozen vegetable market.[10]

Because of high risks and costs, few product introductions represent revolutionary inventions. More typically, product introductions involve a new variety of packaged convenience food, a new model of automobile, or a new fashion in clothing rather than a major product innovation. The more market-oriented the firm, the more likely it will be to launch innovative, new-to-the-market products.[11]

Potential buyers must be made aware of the new product's features, uses, and advantages. Efforts to highlight a new product's value can create a foundation for building brand loyalty and customer relationships.[12] Two difficulties may arise at this point. First,

product life cycle The progression of a product through four stages: introduction, growth, maturity, and decline

introduction stage The initial stage of a product's life cycle; its first appearance in the marketplace when sales start at zero and profits are negative

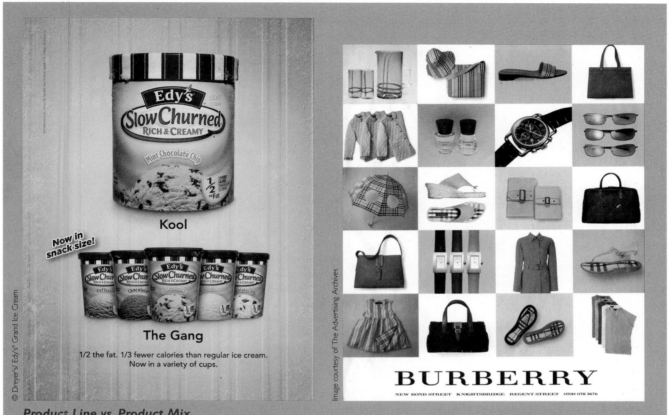

Product Line vs. Product Mix
Edy's Ice Cream represents a product line with a wide variety of flavors. Burberry produces several product lines, including shoes, watches, and sunglasses.

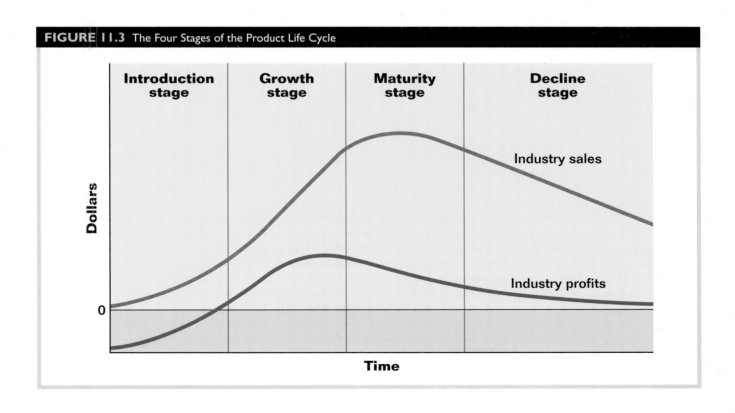

FIGURE 11.3 The Four Stages of the Product Life Cycle

Marketing in Transition
A Love/Hate Relationship with the World of Digital Books

Digital books are quickly gaining in popularity, although many consumers remain wary of the product. The digital reader is currently in the growth stage as increasing numbers of customers adopt the technology. Competition in the e-reader market is thus increasing rapidly.

Currently, the two main contenders are Amazon's Kindle and Sony's e-reader, although other companies are also developing digital readers in an effort to dominate e-book sales (for example, the Barnes & Noble/Plastic Logic collaboration). Book access makes this a complicated product. Barnes & Noble currently offers the largest selection—at 700,000 titles—but it is unavailable to Kindle owners, who can only download texts from the Amazon catalog.

Another competitor is Google, which controls a gigantic digital library, including many public domain titles. However, releasing books into the digital world opens up questions of intellectual property. For instance, Google has been repeatedly sued over its plans to create digital versions of many copyrighted books, including those that have gone out of print. Critics fear that if court decisions ultimately allow Google to proceed, Google will have a virtual monopoly on e-books.

The age of digital books also offers marketers new opportunities. Simon & Schuster, Berrett-Koehler, and other publishing companies are using digital text sites such as Scribd to post excerpts of books with the hope of attracting readers to

purchase the full texts. Many textbook companies and academic presses have made digital textbooks a viable alternative to traditional texts. The publishing company Hearst Group is set to release Skiff, a service selling digital newspapers and magazines from the company's product line. Public domain texts and unpublished works are available on sites such as Scribd, Feedbook, and Google. As digital reading grows in popularity, many media companies are getting involved. Nevertheless, despite new opportunities, questions over pricing, access, and intellectual property persist.[c]

sellers may lack the resources, technological knowledge, and marketing know-how to launch the product successfully. Firms without large budgets can still attract attention by giving away free samples, as Essence of Vali did with its aromatherapy products. Another small-budget tactic is to gain visibility through media appearances. Dave Dettman, a.k.a. Dr. Gadget, specializes in promoting new products on television news and talk programs. Companies such as Sony, Disney, Warner Brothers, and others have hired Dr. Gadget to help with the introduction of new products.[13] Second, the initial product price may have to be high to recoup expensive marketing research or development costs. Given these difficulties, it is not surprising that many products never get beyond the introduction stage.

Most new products start off slowly and seldom generate enough sales to bring immediate profits. Less than 10 percent of new products succeed in the marketplace, and 90 percent of successes come from a handful of companies.[14] Dell Computers' customization processes explain why it has secured such a large share of the computer industry.[15] As buyers learn about the new product, marketers should be alert for product weaknesses and make corrections quickly to prevent the product's early demise. Marketing strategy should be designed to attract the segment that is most interested in the product and has the fewest objections. As the sales curve moves upward and the break-even point is reached, the growth stage begins.

Growth

growth stage The product life-cycle stage when sales rise rapidly, profits reach a peak, and then they start to decline

During the **growth stage**, sales rise rapidly, profits reach a peak, and then they start to decline (see Figure 11.3). The growth stage is critical to a product's survival because competitive reactions to the product's success during this period will affect the product's

Digital Rights Management: Changing the Convenience Levels When Shopping for Music

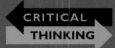

ISSUE: Is digital rights management (DRM) technology violating fair use rights in the entertainment industry?

Digital rights management, or DRM, refers to a number of ways to restrict the free use and transfer of digital content. With piracy becoming a big problem in media distribution by cutting into profits and sales, companies have started using DRM technologies in their media to limit the ability of users to copy and distribute the data.

Critics of DRM argue that the use of digital technology should be unrestricted and that shifting the control of sharing to producers could ultimately hurt creative expression and damage consumer rights. Advocates for civil liberties make the case that while most music is protected by copyright, consumers have some flexibility under fair use clauses. However, DRM technologies make no concessions for fair use; thus, they restrict the legal use of content.

The digital media platform iTunes is making millions of dollars a day in sales, while the overall music industry's numbers are declining. Most DRM-protected media purchased outside of iTunes are not technically compatible with the highly used iPod (which dominates more than 70 percent of the MP3 player market), so users are forced to find ways around purchasing and sharing DRM-protected media to get music on their MP3 players. Steve Jobs, Apple's CEO, has said he would like the music companies to sell their music without DRM. "DRM restrictions only hurt people purchasing music legally, and … DRM only encourages users to obtain music illegally," he explains.

Does DRM help or hurt the music industry's interests? Are there other avenues the music companies can take besides using DRM to protect their digital media from being pirated? Do you think DRM violates the fair use of digital content?[d]

life expectancy. When Splenda, a sugar substitute, was introduced, sales rose quickly as consumers switched from other low-calorie sweeteners. Sales rose even more quickly when restaurants such as McDonald's and Starbucks began offering Splenda in single-serving packets.[16]

Profits begin to decline late in the growth stage as more competitors enter the market, driving prices down and creating the need for heavy promotional expenses. At this point, a typical marketing strategy encourages strong brand loyalty and competes with aggressive emulators of the product. During the growth stage, the organization tries to strengthen its market share and develop a competitive niche by emphasizing the product's benefits. Marketers should also analyze competing brands' product positions relative to their own brands and take corrective actions. Aggressive pricing, including price cuts, is also typical during this stage.

As sales increase, management must support the momentum by adjusting the marketing strategy. The goal is to establish and fortify the product's market position by encouraging brand loyalty. To achieve greater market penetration, segmentation may have to be used more intensely. This would require developing product variations—a deeper product mix—to satisfy the needs of people in several different market segments. Apple, for example, introduced more variations on its wildly popular iPod MP3 player, including the affordable iPod shuffle, the smaller iPod nano, the iPod touch with a touchscreen interface, and the iPad, all of which helped expand Apple's market penetration in the competitive MP3 player industry.

Gaps in geographic market coverage should be filled during the growth period. As a product gains market acceptance, new distribution outlets usually become easier to obtain. Marketers sometimes move from an exclusive or a selective exposure to a more intensive network of dealers to achieve greater market penetration. Marketers must also make sure the physical distribution system is running efficiently so that customers' orders are processed accurately and delivered on time.

Promotion expenditures may be slightly lower than during the introductory stage but are still quite substantial. As sales increase, promotion costs should drop as a percentage of total sales. A falling ratio between promotion expenditures and sales should contribute significantly to increased profits. The advertising messages should stress brand benefits. Coupons and samples may be used to increase market share.

After recovering development costs, a business may be able to lower prices. As sales volume increases, efficiencies in production can result in lower costs. These savings may be passed on to buyers, as in the case of flat-screen televisions; when they were initially introduced, the price was $5,000 or more. As demand soared, manufacturers of both LCD and plasma technologies were able to take advantage of economies of scale to reduce production costs and lower prices to less than $1,000 within several years. If demand remains strong and there are few competitive threats, prices tend to remain stable. If price cuts are feasible, they can help a brand gain market share and discourage new competitors from entering the market.

Maturity

During the **maturity stage**, the sales curve peaks and starts to decline and profits continue to fall (see Figure 11.3). This stage is characterized by intense competition because many brands are now in the market. Competitors emphasize improvements and differences in their versions of the product. As a result, during the maturity stage, stronger companies tend to squeeze out their weaker competitors or consumers begin to lose interest in the product.

During the maturity phase, the producers who remain in the market are likely to change their promotional and distribution efforts. Advertising and dealer-oriented promotions are typical during this stage of the product life cycle. Marketers must also take into account that as the product matures, buyers' knowledge of it reaches a high level. Consumers of the product are no longer inexperienced generalists; instead they are experienced specialists. Marketers of mature products sometimes expand distribution into global markets.

Often the products have to be adapted to more precisely fit the differing needs of customers. Consider Tide Basic, a product released by Procter & Gamble to appeal to money-conscious consumers during the most recent recession. Tide Basic was a stripped-down version of the company's Tide product that cost 20 percent less. It was meant to appeal to consumers who needed to save money but still wanted the same basic benefits that Tide had to offer. P&G started out by testing it in certain markets: it initially introduced the new product into only 100 stores in the South so it could carefully measure its success before introducing the product on a wider scale.[17]

maturity stage The stage of a product's life cycle when the sales curve peaks and starts to decline, and profits continue to fall

Because many products are in the maturity stage of their life cycles, marketers must know how to deal with these products and be prepared to adjust their marketing strategies. As Table 11.1 shows, there are many approaches to altering marketing strategies during the maturity stage. As noted in the table, to increase the sales of mature products, marketers may suggest new uses for them. Arm & Hammer, through

TABLE 11.1 Selected Approaches for Managing Products in the Maturity Stage

Approach	Examples
Develop new-product uses	Knox gelatin used as a plant food Arm & Hammer baking soda marketed as a refrigerator and cat litter deodorant as well as co-branded in toothpastes Cheez Whiz promoted as a microwavable cheese sauce
Increase product usage among current users	Multiple packaging used for products in which a larger supply at the point of consumption actually increases consumption (such as for soft drinks with the "cube" or beer)
Increase number of users	Global markets or small niches in domestic markets pursued
Add product features	Traditional SUVs slowly replaced by crossover vehicles Satellite radio and MP3 systems in automobiles
Change package sizes	Single-serving sizes introduced Travel-size packages of personal-care products introduced Concentrated versions of cleaning products in smaller packages
Increase product quality	Life of light bulbs increased Reliability and durability of U.S.-made automobiles increased
Change nonproduct marketing mix variables—promotion, price, distribution	Focus of Dr Pepper advertisements shifted from teenagers to people ages 18 to 54 A package of dishwasher detergent containing one-third more product offered for the same price Computer hardware marketed through mail-order outlets

refrigerator freshening and partnerships with toothpaste manufacturers, has boosted demand for its baking soda with this method.

As customers become more experienced and knowledgeable about products during the maturity stage (particularly about business products), the benefits they seek may change as well, necessitating product modifications. Consider that traditional truck-based sport utility vehicles, such as the Ford Explorer and GMC Tahoe, have reached maturity and their sales are beginning to decline. Facing rising gasoline costs, consumers seem more interested in "crossovers": car-based utility vehicles like the Chevrolet Equinox, Honda CR-V, Audi Q5, and Volvo XC60. Automakers responded to this interest with more models and features. With their improved ride, handling, and fuel economy, crossovers are in a rapid sales growth stage at the expense of traditional SUVs.[18]

Three general objectives can be pursued during the maturity stage:

1. *Generate cash flow.* This is essential for recouping the initial investment and generating excess cash to support new products.
2. *Maintain share of market.* Companies with marginal market share must decide whether they have a reasonable chance to improve their position or whether they should drop out.
3. *Increase share of customer.* Whereas *market share* refers to the percentage of total customers a firm holds, *share of customer* relates to the percentage of each customer's needs that the firm is meeting. For example, many banks have added new services (brokerage, financial planning, auto leasing, etc.) to gain more of each customer's financial services business. Likewise, many supermarkets are seeking to increase share of customer by adding services such as restaurants, movie rentals, banking, and dry cleaning to provide one-stop shopping for their customers' household needs.[19]

During the maturity stage, marketers actively encourage dealers to support the product. Dealers may be offered promotional assistance in lowering their inventory costs. In general, marketers go to great lengths to serve dealers and provide incentives for selling their brands.

Maintaining market share during the maturity stage requires moderate, and sometimes large, promotion expenditures. Advertising messages focus on differentiating a brand from the field of competitors, and sales promotion efforts are aimed at both consumers and resellers.

A greater mixture of pricing strategies is used during the maturity stage. Strong price competition is likely and may ignite price wars. Firms also compete in ways other than price, such as through product quality or service. In addition, marketers develop price flexibility to differentiate offerings in product lines. Markdowns and price incentives are common. Prices may have to be increased, however, if distribution and production costs rise.

Even something as simple as packaging can be used to revitalize a product. In a Harris interactive panel, three-fourths of respondents replied they would be willing to pay more money for certain packaging attributes. Some of the more important attributes cited included reusability, "staying fresh longer," and "made in the United States."[20]

Decline

During the **decline stage**, sales fall rapidly (refer to Figure 11.3). When this happens, the marketer considers pruning items from the product line to eliminate those that are no longer earning a profit. The marketer may also cut promotion efforts, eliminate marginal distributors, and finally plan to phase out the product. This can be seen in the decline in demand for most bottled beverages, which has been continuing for several years as consumers turn away from higher-calorie carbonated beverages. Experts predict that soft-drink sales will continue to fall at least 1.5 percent each year for the next 5 to 10 years. This shift in consumer preferences are already changing the way companies produce and market bottled beverages.[21]

decline stage The stage of a product's life cycle when sales fall rapidly

An organization can justify maintaining a product only as long as the product contributes to profits or enhances the overall effectiveness of a product mix. Kodak, after spending $1 billion over eight years to develop its Advantix photography system, pulled the plug after sales declined by 75 percent.[22]

In the decline stage, marketers must determine whether to eliminate the product or try to reposition it to extend its life. Usually a declining product has lost its distinctiveness because similar competing products have been introduced. Competition engenders increased substitution and brand switching as buyers become insensitive to minor product differences. For these reasons, marketers do little to change a product's style, design, or other attributes during its decline. New technology or social trends, product substitutes, or environmental considerations may also indicate that the time has come to delete the product. Consider the incandescent light bulb. As consumers switch to "greener" compact fluorescent bulbs and LED lighting—increasingly prompted by government bans on incandescent bulbs—manufacturers are beginning to implement plans to phase them out of their product mixes.

During a product's decline, outlets with strong sales volumes are maintained and unprofitable outlets are weeded out. An entire marketing channel may be eliminated if it does not contribute adequately to profits. An outlet that was not previously used, such as a factory outlet or Internet retailer, is sometimes used to liquidate remaining inventory of an obsolete product. As sales decline, the product becomes more inaccessible, but loyal buyers seek out dealers who still carry it.

Spending on promotion efforts is usually reduced considerably. Advertising of special offers may slow the rate of decline. Sales promotions, such as coupons and premiums, may temporarily recapture buyers' attention. As the product continues to decline, the marketing manager has two options during the decline stage: attempt to postpone the decline or accept its inevitability. Many firms lack the resources to renew a product's demand and are forced to consider harvesting or divesting the product or the strategic business unit (SBU). The *harvesting* approach employs a gradual reduction in marketing expenditures and a less resource-intensive marketing mix. A company adopting the *divesting* approach withdraws all marketing support from the declining product or SBU. It may continue to sell the product until losses are sustained, or it may arrange for another firm to acquire the product. Procter & Gamble's Sure deodorant had been around since the 1970s, but sharply declining sales in 2006 led the company to sell the well-known brand to Innovative Brands LLC, which had earlier purchased P&G's Pert shampoo brand.[23]

Because most businesses have a product mix that consists of multiple products, a firm's destiny is rarely tied to one product. A composite of life-cycle patterns forms when various products in the mix are at different cycle stages: as one product is declining, other products are in the introduction, growth, or maturity stage. Marketers must deal with the dual problem of prolonging the lives of existing products and introducing new products to meet organizational sales goals. Figure 11.4 shows products at different stages of the product life cycle.

FIGURE 11.4 Products at Different Stages of Life Cycle

Introduction
- 3D televisions
- Internet-streamed movies
- Touchscreen tablets

Growth
- DVRs
- E-book readers
- Netbook computers

Maturity
- Flat-panel televisions
- Internet movie rentals
- Laptop computers

Decline
- Retail-store movie rentals
- Gas SUVs
- DVD players

The Product Adoption Process

Acceptance of new products—especially new-to-the-world products—usually doesn't happen overnight. In fact, it can take a very long time. People are sometimes cautious or even skeptical about adopting new products, as indicated by some of the remarks quoted in Table 11.2. Customers who eventually accept a new product do so through an adoption process. The stages of the **product adoption process** are as follows:

1. *Awareness.* The buyer becomes aware of the product.
2. *Interest.* The buyer seeks information and is receptive to learning about the product.
3. *Evaluation.* The buyer considers the product's benefits and decides whether to try it.
4. *Trial.* The buyer examines, tests, or tries the product to determine if it meets his or her needs.
5. *Adoption.* The buyer purchases the product and can be expected to use it again whenever the need for this general type of product arises.[24]

In the first stage, when individuals become aware that the product exists, they have little information about it and are not concerned about obtaining more. Consumers enter the interest stage when they are motivated to get information about the product's features, uses, advantages, disadvantages, price, or location. During the evaluation stage, individuals consider whether the product will satisfy certain criteria that are crucial to meeting their particular needs. In the trial stage, they use or experience the product for the first time, possibly by purchasing a small quantity, taking advantage of free samples, or borrowing the product from someone. Supermarkets, for instance, frequently offer special promotions to encourage consumers to taste new food products. During this stage, potential adopters determine the usefulness of the product under the specific conditions for which they need it.

Individuals move into the adoption stage by choosing a specific product when they need a product of that general type. However, entering the adoption process does not mean the person will eventually adopt the new product. Rejection may occur at any stage, including the adoption stage. Both product adoption and product rejection can be temporary or permanent. This adoption model has several implications when launching a new product. First, the company must promote the product to create widespread

product adoption process
The five-stage process of buyer acceptance of a product: awareness, interest, evaluation, trial, and adoption

TABLE 11.2 Most New Ideas Have Their Skeptics

"I think there is a world market for maybe five computers." —Thomas Watson, chairman of IBM, 1943
"This 'telephone' has too many shortcomings to be seriously considered as a means of communication. The device is inherently of no value to us." —Western Union internal memo, 1876
"The wireless music box has no imaginable commercial value. Who would pay for a message sent to nobody in particular?" —David Sarnoff's associates in response to his urgings for investment in the radio in the 1920s
"The concept is interesting and well-formed, but in order to earn better than a 'C,' the idea must be feasible." —A Yale University Management professor in response to Fred Smith's paper proposing reliable overnight delivery service (Smith went on to found Federal Express Corporation)
"Who the hell wants to hear actors talk?" (on the future of the movie industry after silent films) —H. M. Warner, Warner Brothers, 1927
"A cookie store is a bad idea. Besides, the market research reports say America likes crispy cookies, not soft and chewy cookies like you make." —Banker's response to Debbie Fields's idea of starting Mrs. Fields' Cookies
"We don't like their sound, and guitar music is on the way out." —Decca Recording Company rejecting the Beatles, 1962

FIGURE 11.5 Distribution of Product Adopter Categories

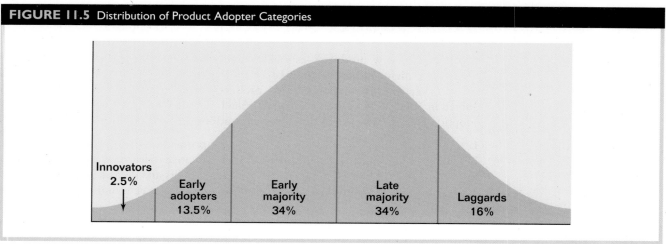

awareness of its existence and its benefits. Samples or simulated trials should be arranged to help buyers make initial purchase decisions. At the same time, marketers should emphasize quality control and provide solid guarantees to reinforce buyer opinion during the evaluation stage. Finally, production and physical distribution must be linked to patterns of adoption and repeat purchases.

When an organization introduces a new product, people do not begin the adoption process at the same time, nor do they move through the process at the same speed. Of those who eventually adopt the product, some enter the adoption process rather quickly, whereas others start considerably later. For most products, there is also a group of nonadopters who never begin the process. For business marketers, success in managing production innovation, diffusion, and adoption requires great adaptability and significant effort in understanding customers.[25]

Depending on the length of time it takes them to adopt a new product, consumers fall into one of five major adopter categories: innovators, early adopters, early majority, late majority, and laggards.[26] Figure 11.5 illustrates each adopter category and the percentage of total adopters it typically represents. **Innovators** are the first to adopt a new product; they enjoy trying new products and tend to be venturesome. **Early adopters** choose new products carefully and are viewed as "the people to check with" by those in the remaining adopter categories. People in the **early majority** adopt a new product just prior to the average person; they are deliberate and cautious in trying new products. Individuals in the **late majority** are quite skeptical of new products but eventually adopt them because of economic necessity or social pressure. **Laggards**, the last to adopt a new product, are oriented toward the past. They are suspicious of new products, and when they finally adopt the innovation, it may already have been replaced by a new product.

innovators First adopters of new products

early adopters People who adopt new products early, choose new products carefully, and are viewed as "the people to check with" by later adopters

early majority Individuals who adopt a new product just prior to the average person

late majority Skeptics who adopt new products when they feel it is necessary

laggards The last adopters, who distrust new products

Why Some Products Fail and Others Succeed

Thousands of new products are introduced annually, and many fail. Statistical bureaus, consulting firms, and trade publications estimate that one out of every three new products fails each year; others report an annual new-product failure rate as high as 80 to 90 percent. The annual cost of product failures to U.S. firms can reach $100 billion.

© AP Images/PRNewsFoto/Pepsi-Cola North America Beverages

Why Some Products Fail and Others Succeed
Pepsi Throwback, with its retro positioning, was a successful new product for the company.

Failure and success rates vary from organization to organization, but consumer products fail more often than business products in general.

Being one of the first brands launched in a product category is no guarantee of success; however, the Apple's iPod is a good example of success. It is the most popular digital music player, occupying more than 70 percent of the music player market. Since its launch in 2001, more than 225 million iPods have been sold, 1.8 billion apps downloaded, and more than 8.5 billion songs purchased. Its App Store also has more than 21,000 games. To maintain its high growth, Apple has also introduced the iTunes 9, the iPod Classic, iPod Touch, and the iPad.[27] Table 11.3 shows examples of recent product successes and failures.

Products fail for many reasons. One of the most common reasons is the company's failure to match product offerings to customer needs. When products do not offer value and lack the features customers want, they fail in the marketplace. Coca-Cola's C2 and PepsiCo's Pepsi Edge, both targeted at low-carbohydrate dieters with their midrange calorie count, ultimately garnered just 1 percent share of the market together because low-carb dieters generally avoid products with any refined sugar.[28] Ineffective or inconsistent branding has also been blamed for product failures. Examples of products that failed because they didn't convey the right message or image include Gerber Singles (gourmet food for adults packaged in baby food jars), Microsoft's Bob (a "social interface" cartoon character that many users perceived as juvenile), and Gillette's For Oily Hair Only shampoo (whose name gave an unappealing mental image, for although many people have oily hair, few are proud of it).[29] Other reasons cited for new-product failure include technical or design problems, poor timing, overestimation of market size, ineffective promotion, and insufficient distribution.

When examining the problem of product failure, it is important to distinguish the degree of failure. Absolute failure occurs when an organization loses money on a new product because it is unable to recover development, production, and marketing costs. This product usually is deleted from the product mix. Relative product failure occurs when a product returns a profit but does not meet a company's profit or market

TABLE 11.3 Product Successes and Failures

Successes	Failures
Smith Kline Beecham Nicoderm CQ	R. J. Reynolds Premier smokeless cigarettes
Palm PDAs	Apple Lisa personal computer
Coca-Cola Dasani water	Heinz Ketchup Salsa
Starbucks coffee shops	Nestlé Panache coffee
Procter & Gamble Pantene shampoos	Gillette For Oily Hair Only shampoo
Tide High Efficiency laundry detergent	Dryel home dry cleaning kits
Procter & Gamble Swiffer mop and dusting cloths	S. C. Johnson Allercare aerosol spray, carpet powder, and dust mite powder
Bacardi Breezers	Bud and Michelob Dry beer

share objectives. If a company repositions or improves a relative product failure, that product may become a successful member of the product line. On the other hand, some products experience relative product failure after years of success. Gramophone records, for example, were the main medium for music for most of the 20th century. However, they experienced relative product failure in the 1980s, when the record was supplanted by cassettes and compact discs. Despite its past popularity, the gramophone record is little more than an antique today.

In contrast to this gloomy picture of product failures, some new products are very successful. In order to compete more effectively against coffee chains like Starbucks, McDonald's introduced its first American McCafé in Chicago in 2001. In 2007, the company introduced iced coffee to its menu and began testing its new line of espresso-based beverages. However, it was not until 2009 that McDonald's implemented nationwide commercialization of its McCafés. Its launch was McDonald's largest in 30 years.[30]

Perhaps the most important ingredient for success is the product's ability to provide a significant and perceivable benefit to a sizable number of customers. New products with an observable advantage over similar available products, such as more features, ease of operation, or improved technology, have a greater chance to succeed. Sometimes a product is simply in touch with consumers' feelings and taste. Consider the Whoopie Pie, a Maine product similar to the Moon Pie sold in the South. Critical to launching a product that will achieve market success is effective planning and management. Companies that follow a systematic, customer-focused plan for new-product development, such as Procter & Gamble and 3M, are well-positioned to launch successful products.

summary

1. To understand the concept of a product

A product is a good, a service, or an idea received in an exchange. It can be either tangible or intangible; either way, it includes functional, social, and psychological utilities or benefits. When consumers purchase a product, they are buying the benefits and satisfaction they think the product will provide.

2. To explain how to classify products

Products can be classified on the basis of the buyer's intentions. Consumer products are those purchased to satisfy personal and family needs. Business products are purchased for use in a firm's operations, to resell, or to make other products. Consumer products can be subdivided into convenience, shopping, specialty, and unsought products. Business products can be classified as installations, accessory equipment, raw materials, component parts, process materials, MRO supplies, or business services.

3. To examine the concepts of product item, product line, and product mix and understand how they are connected

A product item is a specific version of a product that can be designated as a distinct offering among an organization's

products. A product line is a group of closely related product items that are viewed as a unit because of marketing, technical, or end-use considerations. The product mix is the composite, or total, group of products that an organization makes available to customers. The width of the product mix is measured by the number of product lines the company offers. The depth of the product mix is the average number of different products offered in each product line.

4. To understand the product life cycle and its impact on marketing strategies

The product life cycle describes how product items in an industry move through four stages: introduction, growth, maturity, and decline. The life-cycle concept is used to ensure that the introduction, alteration, and termination of a product are timed and executed properly. The sales curve is at zero at introduction, rises at an increasing rate during growth, peaks at maturity, and then declines. Profits peak toward the end of the growth stage of the product life cycle. The life expectancy of a product is based on buyers' wants, the availability of competing products, and other environmental conditions. Most businesses have a composite of life-cycle patterns for various products. It is important to manage existing products and develop new ones to keep the overall sales performance at a desired level.

5. To describe the product adoption process

When customers accept a new product, they usually do so through a five-stage adoption process. The first stage is awareness, when buyers become aware that a product exists. Interest, the second stage, occurs when buyers seek information about the product. In the third stage, evaluation, buyers consider the product's benefits and decide whether to try it. The fourth stage is trial, when buyers examine, test, or try the product to determine if it meets their needs. The last stage is adoption, when buyers actually purchase the product and use it whenever a need for this general type of product arises.

6. To understand why some products fail and some succeed

Of the thousands of new products introduced every year, many fail. Absolute failure occurs when an organization loses money on a new product. Absolute failures are usually removed from the product mix. Relative failure occurs when a product returns a profit but fails to meet a company's objectives. Reasons for product failure include failure to match product offerings to customer needs, poor timing, and ineffective or inconsistent branding. New products that succeed provide significant and observable benefits to customers. Products that have perceivable advantages over similar products also have a better chance to succeed. Effective marketing planning and product management are important factors in a new product's chances of success.

Go to www.cengagebrain.com for resources to help you master the content in this chapter as well as materials that will expand your marketing knowledge!

important terms

good, 320

service, 320

idea, 320

consumer
  products, 322

business products, 322

convenience
  products, 323

shopping products, 323

specialty products, 324

unsought products, 324

installations, 325

accessory
  equipment, 326

raw materials, 326

component parts, 326

process materials, 326

MRO supplies, 326

business services, 327

product item, 327

product line, 327

product mix, 327

width of product
  mix, 327

depth of product
  mix, 327

product life cycle, 328

introduction
  stage, 328

growth stage, 330

maturity stage, 332

decline stage, 333

product adoption
  process, 335

innovators, 336

early adopters, 336

early majority, 336

late majority, 336

laggards, 336

discussion and review questions

1. List the tangible and intangible attributes of a pair of Nike athletic shoes. Compare its benefits with those of an intangible product such as hairstyling in a salon.

2. A product has been referred to as a "psychological bundle of satisfaction." Is this a good definition of a product? Why or why not?

3. Is a personal computer sold at a retail store a consumer product or a business product? Defend your answer.

4. How do convenience products and shopping products differ? What are the distinguishing characteristics of each type of product?

5. In the category of business products, how do component parts differ from process materials?

6. How does an organization's product mix relate to its development of a product line? When should an enterprise add depth to its product lines rather than width to its product mix?

7. How do industry profits change as a product moves through the four stages of its life cycle?

8. What is the relationship between the concepts of product mix and product life cycle?

9. What are the stages in the product adoption process, and how do they affect the commercialization phase?

10. What are the five major adopter categories describing the length of time required for a consumer to adopt a new product, and what are the characteristics of each?

11. In what ways does the marketing strategy for a mature product differ from the marketing strategy for a growth product?

12. What are the major reasons for new-product failure?

application questions

1. Choose a familiar clothing store. Describe its product mix, including its depth and width. Evaluate the mix and make suggestions to the owner.

2. Tabasco pepper sauce is a product that has entered the maturity stage of the product life cycle. Name products that would fit into each of the four stages: introduction, growth, maturity, and decline. Describe each product and explain why it fits in that stage.

3. Generally buyers go through a product adoption process before becoming loyal customers. Describe your experience in adopting a product you now use consistently. Did you go through all the stages of the process?

4. Identify and describe a friend or family member who fits into each of the following adopter categories. How would you use this information if you were product manager for a fashion-oriented, medium-priced clothing retailer such as J.Crew or JCPenney?
   a. Innovator
   b. Early adopter
   c. Early majority
   d. Late majority
   e. Laggard

internet exercise

Goodyear Tire & Rubber Company

In addition to providing information about the company's products, Goodyear's website helps consumers find the exact products they want and will even direct them to the nearest Goodyear retailer. Visit the Goodyear site at **www.goodyear. com**.

1. How does Goodyear use its website to communicate information about the quality of its tires?

2. How does Goodyear's website demonstrate product design and features?

3. Based on what you learned at the website, describe what Goodyear has done to position its tires.

developing your marketing plan

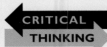

Identifying the needs of consumer groups and developing products that satisfy those needs are essential when creating a marketing strategy. Successful product development begins with a clear understanding of fundamental product concepts. The product concept is the basis on which many of the marketing plan decisions are made. When relating the information in this chapter to the development of your marketing plan, consider the following:

1. Using Figure 11.2 as a guide, create a matrix of the current product mix for your company.

2. Discuss how the profitability of your product will change as it moves through each of the phases of the product life cycle.

3. Create a brief profile of the type of consumer who is likely to represent each of the product adopter categories for your product.

4. Discuss the factors that could contribute to the failure of your product. How will you define product failure?

The information obtained from these questions should assist you in developing various aspects of your marketing plan found in the *Interactive Marketing Plan* at **www.cengagebrain.com.**

VIDEO CASE 11.1

Artistry Meets Affordability with Blu Dot Furniture

The phrase "not cheap, but affordable" summarizes the pricing strategy of Blu Dot, a Minneapolis-based furniture maker. Blu Dot prides itself on selling artistically modern, high-quality furniture at prices that it feels are more affordable for consumers. Blu Dot's pricing decisions stem from the personal experiences of co-founders John Christakos, Maurice Blanks, and Charles Lazor. When furnishing their first apartments, the three men quickly realized that the furniture they wanted was beyond their price range. They saw a market need for quality furniture that was affordable. With a background in architecture and art, the men felt they could use innova-

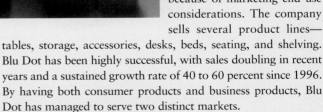

tion, simple manufacturing processes, and off-the-shelf materials to fill this need. In 1997, Blu Dot was born.

Today, Blu Dot products can be found in boutiques nationwide, with products available to order online as well. For consumer products, Blu Dot can be considered more of a shopping product than a specialty product. Blu Dot differentiates its products through quality and affordable furniture with more of a

modern design appeal. The founders of Blu Dot have designed their furniture using inspiration from the modernism art movement, which includes artists such as Michel Duchamp and Donald Judd. Trade discounts are offered to store buyers, interior designers, architects, exporters, and corporate gift buyers. This market represents the business products that are usually purchased due to the functional aspects of the product more than the fashion or psychological involvement with the product. Business products are considered accessory equipment that does not become a part of the final product and assists with office activities. By having different product lines, Blu Dot is able to market a closely related group of product items because of marketing end use considerations. The company sells several product lines—tables, storage, accessories, desks, beds, seating, and shelving. Blu Dot has been highly successful, with sales doubling in recent years and a sustained growth rate of 40 to 60 percent since 1996. By having both consumer products and business products, Blu Dot has managed to serve two distinct markets.

However, the challenges Blu Dot encounters have not diminished with its success. Blu Dot still struggles with keeping affordability at the lower end of the spectrum and craftsmanship at the high end. When pricing products, the designers add up their fixed and variable costs plus the markup needed to allow the business to function. Creative pricing strategies are often employed to make the appropriate margins. For example, when selling a set of coffee tables, one table may have a higher markup while another one has a slightly lower markup in order to appeal to the price-conscious consumer and create profit. Blu Dot recognizes that they have to think of the total product offering as having a combination of three interdependent elements: the core product itself, its supplemental features, and its symbolic or experiential value. While some customers focus on the artistic aspects of the product, other consumers are more concerned with value. Therefore, Blu Dot must synchronize its marketing mix to make product and price consistent.

The designers have also found ways to keep costs lower through innovative and efficient uses of materials, processes, and distribution methods. For instance, Blu Dot contracts with suppliers that make industrial products due to the more efficient technologies and processes used. Blu Dot furniture is

designed to be able to ship easily, cutting down on distribution costs. Additionally, the designers use simple manufacturing processes and straightforward materials to create what they term "a by-product of the process." Add aesthetics into the equation, and the designers have significant challenges indeed.

Despite these difficulties, the designers thrive on their ability to blend manufacturing and art to create high-end furniture at more affordable prices than their competitors. For those with a flair for modern, affordable furnishings, Blu Dot offers a range of products to suit your artistic palate.[31]

QUESTIONS FOR DISCUSSION

1. What are the different challenges for Blu Dot in selling consumer products versus business products?
2. Do you think that the product life cycle would be an important marketing concept in developing and managing Blu Dot products?
3. Describe the product mix and the importance of different product lines in Blu Dot's marketing strategy.

CASE 11.2

Dell Develops New Products as Customer Needs Change

CRITICAL THINKING

Dell, based in Round Rock, Texas, originally made its name selling personal computers directly to customers through its website, catalogs, and phone orders. Over the years, it has expanded into related product lines while battling aggressive rivals such as Hewlett-Packard and Apple. A few years ago, Dell decided to enter the lucrative $100 billion world of consumer electronics, hoping to derive an ever-larger portion of revenues and profits from a wider mix of products for use beyond the home office.

With a long history of marketing technology-based products, Dell has become a well-known U.S. brand. Management saw the brand as a strength and set out to exploit it by marketing new flat-screen televisions, tiny digital music players, and other non-

computer products. "We've come out of nowhere to be the number three consumer brand in the United States in less than five years, while Coca-Cola has been doing it for 100 years," said Dell's general manager of consumer business for the United States. "We're not in this to be number three. Number one is the only target around here."

Despite considerable research and marketing investment, Dell's consumer electronics strategy did not succeed. In fact, it wasn't long before the company reversed course, pulling back from diversification to refocus on its core computer expertise. What happened? First, Dell launched its consumer electronics items just as major technological developments were roiling the industry and changing how consumers buy and use such products. Dell's affordable handheld

© AP Images/PRNewsFoto/Cellular South / © John Wang/Photodisc/Getty Images computers initially touched off a flurry of customer interest and then sparked a price war with Hewlett-Packard as the two fought for market share. However, when Apple, Nokia, and others began marketing new-generation cell phones with built-in computer capabilities and multiple entertainment functions, customers found those offerings more appealing than the kind of stand-alone handhelds that Dell offered.

Second, Dell was caught in the crossfire of intense competition. At the start of its consumer electronics initiative, the company introduced the Dell Digital Jukebox and the Dell Music Store, putting it on a competitive collision course with Apple's popular iPods and iTunes store. In the end, Apple had so much momentum that Dell discontinued its own brand of music players and has been reselling products made by Samsung and other manufacturers. This allows Dell to satisfy customer demand for certain consumer electronics items but without the expense of researching, developing, manufacturing, and marketing the products under the Dell name.

Although Dell is not looking to pioneer revolutionary new lines for early adopters, today the company is expanding into proven markets by introducing products that align with consumer demand. For instance, Dell formed a mobile device division to create products such as mobile phones and other portable devices. After two years of research, Dell entered into an agreement with AT&T to carry its Mini 3 Smart Phone that uses Google's Android software. Since the inception of the first smartphone in 1992 by IBM, smartphones became commonplace during the 2000s and have proven to be a source of lucrative growth. By remaining innovative in

its product designs, Dell continues to be a major player in the computer industry. Moving away from its traditional policy of only selling directly to customers, Dell began distributing its brand of computers, monitors, printers, and accessories through Walmart, Staples office supply stores, and other retailers around the world.

The company is also shining up its brand by improving customer service, an especially important step as PC sales grow more slowly throughout the industry and competitors dig in to defend market share. Dell's relentless cost cutting hurt its ability to handle technical questions and complaints, which in turn hurt customer satisfaction scores. Dell is rebuilding relationships by increasing its service budget and encouraging customers to have their say. "By listening to our customers, that is actually the most perfect form of marketing you could have," says Dell's chief marketing officer.[32]

QUESTIONS FOR DISCUSSION

1. Why would Dell not pioneer revolutionary new products for innovators and early adopters the way its competitor Apple does?

2. In what stage of the product life cycle do personal computers appear to be? How does this explain Dell's attempt to expand into consumer electronics?

3. How far can Dell widen its product mix without hurting the company's credibility? For example, what might be the impact of new products such as Dell motorcycles or Dell frozen pastries?

Chapter 12

Developing and Managing Products

OBJECTIVES

1. To understand how companies manage existing products through line extensions and product modifications

2. To describe how businesses develop a product idea into a commercial product

3. To understand the importance of product differentiation and the elements that differentiate one product from another

4. To examine how product deletion is used to improve product mixes

5. To describe organizational structures used for managing products

Bendable Concrete: New Marketing Opportunity

Victor Li, a professor of civil and environmental engineering at the University of Michigan, is something of a concrete expert. He knows that concrete's major flaw is its tendency to crack. Li has developed a flexible concrete (known as engineered cement composite—ECC). Special fibers allow ECC to bend rather than break, making it 500 times less likely to crack and almost 50 percent lighter. ECC has been used in Japanese skyscrapers to help make them more resilient during earthquakes. Li has also developed a self-healing concrete. While cracks in traditional concrete quickly spread and cause problems, both bendable and self-healing concretes will only develop hairline cracks. In the self-healing version, the cracks merely require water and carbon dioxide to fix.

Li's self-healing concrete may be a tremendous asset for the United States infrastructure. The American Society of Civil Engineers believes that the country is facing a possible infrastructure disaster as bridges and roads age and become brittle. The need for bridge construction/reconstruction is overwhelming. Li's goal is to ensure that it's done properly and made to last. The self-healing concrete also brings environmental benefits—it is lighter, uses less energy, and will not need to be replaced as frequently, creating a smaller carbon footprint. The question remains: Can Li's self-healing concrete be fabricated for mass production? Li feels that the product needs further testing to ensure quality prior to commercialization. In addition, the cost of Li's concrete is triple that of traditional concrete; however, the savings in repairs will pay off in the long run.

Although Li's inventions take some time to come to the market, he continues to develop innovative products. He is currently developing a self-healing concrete that communicates when repairs are necessary; he has financial backing from numerous organizations, including the Michigan Department of Transportation.[1]

To compete effectively and achieve their goals, organizations must be able to adjust their products' features in response to changes in customers' needs. To provide products that satisfy target markets and achieve the firm's objectives, a marketer must develop, alter, and maintain an effective product mix. An organization's product mix may require adjustment for a variety of reasons. Because customers' attitudes and product preferences change over time, their desire for certain products may wane. Coca-Cola, for example, has seen sales of its traditional carbonated beverages decline as consumers seek alternatives to corn syrup and artificial sweeteners, since consumers have increasingly negative opinions of both. Thus, the company partnered with Cargill to create TRUVIA, a sweetener derived from the Stevia plant. The resulting product is low in calories and has initially been marketed to active teens and young adults.[2] Coke also introduced NESTEA Red Tea Pomegranate Passion Fruit (red tea is a touted source of antioxidants) and Odwalla Reduced Calorie Quenchers (sweetened with TRUVIA and organic evaporated cane juice). In some cases, a company needs to alter its product mix for competitive reasons. A marketer may have to delete a product from the mix because a competitor dominates the market for that product. Similarly, a firm may have to introduce a new product or modify an existing one to compete more effectively. A marketer may expand the firm's product mix to take advantage of excess marketing and production capacity.

In this chapter, we examine several ways to improve an organization's product mix. First, we discuss managing existing products through effective line extension and product modification. Next, we examine the stages of new-product development, including idea generation, screening, concept testing, business analysis, product development, test marketing, and commercialization. Then we look at how companies differentiate their products in the marketplace through quality, design, and support services. Next, we examine the importance of deleting weak products and the methods companies use to eliminate them. Finally, we look at the organizational structures used to manage products.

Managing Existing Products

A company can benefit by capitalizing on its existing products. By assessing the composition of the current product mix, a marketer can identify weaknesses and gaps. This analysis can then lead to improvement of the product mix through line extension and product modification.

Line Extensions

A **line extension** is the development of a product that is closely related to one or more products in the existing product line but designed specifically to meet somewhat different customer needs. For example, the 2011 Porsche Cayenne S Hybrid V-1 can drive short distances using electric power but at high speeds can switch to gas and match the power of a V-8 engine. This product extension of the Cayenne model provides an added benefit of fuel economy without compromising the performance that is a hallmark of the brand.

Many of the so-called new products introduced each year are in fact line extensions. Line extensions are more common than new products because they are a less-expensive, lower-risk alternative for increasing sales. A line extension may focus on a different market segment or be an attempt to increase sales within the same market segment by more precisely satisfying the needs of people in that segment. SunnyRidge Farm, for example, recently extended its successful line of produce by launching a line of organic blueberry products.[3] Line extensions are also used to take market share from competitors. For instance, the Ford Fusion Hybrid is a product line extension that was designed to compete directly with the Toyota Prius. However, one side effect of employing a line extension is that it may result in a more negative evaluation of the core product. To

line extension Development of a product that is closely related to existing products in the line but is designed specifically to meet different customer needs

Line Extensions

Multi-grain Pringles is a line extension of traditional Pringles.

avoid this concern, Coke Zero, which is a line extension, is targeted at young males as a sugar-free alternative to Coca Cola Classic, without the stigma of drinking a diet beverage. Coke emphasizes the appeal of a product that tastes like the original, but without the calories and sugar.

Product Modifications

Product modification means changing one or more characteristics of a product. A product modification differs from a line extension in that the original product does not remain in the line. For example, U.S. automakers use product modifications annually when they create new models of the same brand. Once the new models are introduced, the manufacturers stop producing last year's model. Like line extensions, product modifications entail less risk than developing new products.

Product modification can indeed improve a firm's product mix but only under certain conditions. First, the product must be modifiable. Second, customers must be able to perceive that a modification has been made. Third, the modification should make the product more consistent with customers' desires so it provides greater satisfaction. One drawback to modifying a successful product is that the consumer who had experience with the original version of the product may view a modified version as a riskier purchase. There are three major ways to modify products: quality, functional, and aesthetic modifications.

QUALITY MODIFICATIONS

Quality modifications are changes relating to a product's dependability and durability. The changes usually are executed by altering the materials or the production process. For instance, for a service, such as a sporting event or air travel, quality modifications may involve enhancing the emotional experience that makes the consumer passionate and loyal to the brand.

Reducing a product's quality may allow an organization to lower its price and direct the item at a different target market. In contrast, increasing the quality of a product may give a firm an advantage over competing brands. Higher quality may enable a company to charge a higher price by creating customer loyalty and lowering customer sensitivity to price. However, higher quality may require the use of more expensive components and processes, thus forcing the organization to cut costs in other areas. Some firms, such as Caterpillar, are finding ways to increase quality while reducing costs.

FUNCTIONAL MODIFICATIONS

Changes that affect a product's versatility, effectiveness, convenience, or safety are called **functional modifications**; they usually require redesign of the product. Product categories that have undergone considerable functional modification include office and farm equipment, appliances, cleaning products, and telecommunications services. For example, Sub-Zero modified its refrigerators with dual compressors. This feature allows for independent climate control of different compartments in the unit. The functional benefit is fresher food.

Functional modifications can make a product useful to more people and thus enlarge its market. Research in Motion, for example, created the slide down key pad in an effort to blur the line between touchscreen and key pad.[4] Companies can place a product in a favorable competitive position by providing benefits that competing brands do not offer.

product modifications
Changes in one or more characteristics of a product

quality modifications
Changes relating to a product's dependability and durability

functional modifications
Changes affecting a product's versatility, effectiveness, convenience, or safety

Product Modification
Procter & Gamble's Swiffer is often modified to accommodate different functional uses.

They can also help an organization achieve and maintain a progressive image. Finally, functional modifications are sometimes made in response to product shortcomings and assist in reducing the possibility of product liability lawsuits.

AESTHETIC MODIFICATIONS

Aesthetic modifications change the sensory appeal of a product by altering its taste, texture, sound, smell, or appearance. A buyer making a purchase decision is swayed by how a product looks, smells, tastes, feels, or sounds. Thus, an aesthetic modification may strongly affect purchases. The fashion industry relies heavily on aesthetic modifications from season to season. For example, Prada clothing, handbags, and perfumes are leaders in the haute couture industry. In order to maintain its reputation for the utmost level of quality and style, the company performs aesthetic modifications on its products regularly. This ensures that Prada maintains its reputation for cutting-edge design and quality. In addition, aesthetic modifications attempt to minimize the amount of illegal product counterfeiting that occurs through constant change in design and quality.

Aesthetic modifications can help a firm differentiate its product from competing brands and thus gain a sizable market share. The major drawback in using aesthetic modifications is that consumers determine their value subjectively. Although a firm may strive to improve the product's sensory appeal, some customers may actually find the modified product less attractive.

Developing New Products

A firm develops new products as a means of enhancing its product mix and adding depth to a product line. However, developing and introducing new products is frequently expensive and risky. For instance, Microsoft's Vista operating system launched to lackluster reviews and abundant problems, causing many PC users to refuse to upgrade from Microsoft's XP. Microsoft responded to the negative reviews by creating Windows 7, which was formulated as a replacement to Vista. As we discussed in the previous chapter, new-product failures occur frequently and can create major financial problems for organizations, sometimes even causing them to go out of business. Failure to introduce new products is also risky. General Motors lost market share and entered bankruptcy due, in part, to failing to innovate and stay in touch with what competitors were producing and what consumers wanted.[5]

The term *new product* can have more than one meaning. A genuinely new product offers innovative benefits. For example, Spanx (a line of popular slimming undergarments for women known for its popularity on the red carpet) recently launched a line of slimming undershirts for men. Although they look like T-shirts, they are said to slim the torso and make wearers look more physically fit.[6] However, products that are different and distinctly better are often viewed as new. For instance, Palm introduced its Pre smartphone in 2009. After a less-than-stellar debut of Pre, the company released Pre Plus. The new and improved model offers a feature that may well draw users—the Mobile HotSpot, a capability allowing Pre Plus users to share their Internet connections with up to five other devices.[7] Some product innovations of the past 30 years include Post-it Notes, cell phones, personal computers, PDAs, digital music players, satellite radio, and digital video recorders. Thus, a new product can be an innovative product that has never been sold by any organization, such as the digital camera was when introduced for the first time. A radically new product involves a complex developmental

aesthetic modifications
Changes relating to the sensory appeal of a product

process, including an extensive business analysis to determine the potential for success. Sometimes the business analysis does not accurately depict consumer demand for the product. Satellite radio has struggled to find a strong market, and both XM and Sirius failed to have adequate market share for the two direct competitors. Therefore, Sirius acquired XM in order to find a profitable market share.

A new product can also be a product that a given firm has not marketed previously, although similar products have been available from other companies, such as Crayola School Glue. Companies such as Eddie Bauer, best known for rugged outdoor apparel, have extended their image with the introduction of a new line of baby products, which includes diaper bags and car seats. Finally, a product can be viewed as new when it is brought to one or more markets from another market. For example, when Daimler brought its Smart Car to the United States, it was viewed as a new product, although the Smart had been out in Europe for years.[8]

Before a product is introduced, it goes through the seven phases of the **new-product development process** shown in Figure 12.1: (1) idea generation, (2) screening, (3) concept testing, (4) business analysis, (5) product development, (6) test marketing, and (7) commercialization. A product may be dropped (and many are) at any stage of development. In this section, we look at the process through which products are developed, from idea inception to fully commercialized product.

Idea Generation

Businesses and other organizations seek product ideas that will help them achieve their objectives. This activity is **idea generation**. The fact that only a few ideas are good enough to be commercially successful underscores the challenge of the task.

Although some organizations get their ideas almost by chance, firms that try to manage their product mixes effectively usually develop systematic approaches for generating new-product ideas. Indeed, in organizations there is a relationship between the amount of market information gathered and the number of ideas generated by work groups. At the heart of innovation is a purposeful, focused effort to identify new ways to serve a market.

New-product ideas can come from several sources. They may stem from internal sources: marketing managers, researchers, sales personnel, engineers, or other organizational personnel. Brainstorming and incentives or rewards for good ideas are typical intra-firm devices for stimulating development of ideas. For example, the idea for 3M Post-it adhesive-backed notes came from an employee. As a church choir member, he used slips of paper to mark songs in his hymnal. Because the pieces of paper kept falling out, he suggested developing an adhesive-backed note.

In the restaurant industry, ideas may come from franchisees. At McDonald's, for example, franchise owners invented the Big Mac and the Egg McMuffin. Today, new McDonald's product ideas often come from corporate chef Dan Coudreaut, who developed the fast-food giant's new snack wrap.[9] New-product ideas may also arise from sources outside the firm, such as customers, competitors, advertising agencies, management consultants, and private research organizations. Procter & Gamble gets 35 percent of its ideas from inventors and outside consultants.[10] Consultants are often used as sources for stimulating new-product ideas. For example, Fahrenheit 212 serves as an "idea factory" that provides ready-to-go product ideas, including market potential analysis for major *Fortune* 500 firms including Campbell's, Best Buy, Citibank, Coca-Cola, Samsung,

new-product development process A seven-phase process for introducing products: idea generation, screening, concept testing, business analysis, product development, test marketing, and commercialization

idea generation Seeking product ideas to achieve organizational objectives

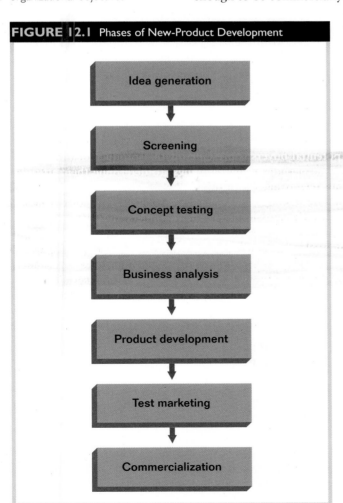

FIGURE 12.1 Phases of New-Product Development

- Idea generation
- Screening
- Concept testing
- Business analysis
- Product development
- Test marketing
- Commercialization

"Crazy" Former Comic Laughs All the Way to the Bank—Thanks to Spanx!

When amateur stand-up comic Sara Blakely wanted footless control-top pantyhose for a smooth line under tight-fitting pants, she cut the feet off of her pantyhose to get what she wanted. She realized that other women were probably seeking solutions to the same problem, so she quickly went online to start the lengthy process of patenting her innovative idea.

When she tried to find a manufacturer for her prototype product, she was repeatedly turned down because the idea "made no sense, and would never sell." Finally, one manufacturer called her back and offered to work with her. What made him change his mind? He had two daughters and they didn't think the idea was crazy at all. Spanx now has annual sales in excess of $150 million.[a]

Adidas, and P&G, to name a few.[11] When outsourcing new-product development activities to outside organizations, the best results are achieved from spelling out the specific tasks with detailed contractual specifications. Asking customers what they want from products and organizations has helped many firms become successful and remain competitive. Today, marketers are using online social networking sites such as quirky.com and crowdspring.com to communicate with customers and to gather new product ideas.

Screening

In the process of **screening**, the ideas with the greatest potential are selected for further review. During screening, product ideas are analyzed to determine whether they match the organization's objectives and resources. If a product idea results in a product similar to the firm's existing offerings, marketers must assess the degree to which the new product could cannibalize the sales of current products. The company's overall abilities to produce and market the product are also analyzed. Keeping the product idea in focus and on track by understanding consumer needs and wants is the key to success. Other aspects of an idea to be weighed are the nature and wants of buyers and possible environmental changes. At times, a checklist of new-product requirements is used when making screening decisions. This practice encourages evaluators to be systematic and thus reduces the chances of overlooking some pertinent fact. Most new-product ideas are rejected during the screening phase.

Concept Testing

To evaluate ideas properly, it may be necessary to test product concepts. In **concept testing**, a small sample of potential buyers is presented with a product idea through a written or oral description (and perhaps a few drawings) to determine their attitudes and initial buying intentions regarding the product. For a single product idea, an organization can test one or several concepts of the same product. Concept testing is a low-cost procedure that allows a company to determine customers' initial reactions to a product idea before it invests considerable resources in research and development. Input from online communities may also be beneficial in the product development process. The results of concept testing can help product development personnel better understand which product attributes and benefits are most important to potential customers.

Figure 12.2 shows a concept test for a proposed tick and flea control product. Notice that the concept is briefly described and then a series of questions is presented. The questions vary considerably depending on the type of product being tested. Typical questions include the following: In general, do you find this proposed product attractive? Which benefits are especially attractive to you? Which features are of little or no interest to you? Do you feel that this proposed product would work better for you than the product you currently use? Compared with your current product, what are the primary advantages of the proposed product? If this product were available at an appropriate price, would you buy it? How often would you buy this product? How could this proposed product be improved?

Business Analysis

During the **business analysis** stage, the product idea is evaluated to determine its potential contribution to the firm's sales, costs, and profits. In the course of a business analysis, evaluators ask a variety of questions: Does the product fit in with the organization's existing

screening Selecting the ideas with the greatest potential for further review

concept testing Seeking a sample of potential buyers' responses to a product idea

business analysis Evaluating the potential impact of a product idea on the firm's sales, costs, and profits

FIGURE 12.2 Concept Test for a Tick and Flea Control Product

Product description

An insecticide company is considering the development and introduction of a new tick and flea control product for pets. This product would consist of insecticide and a liquid-dispensing brush for applying the insecticide to dogs and cats. The insecticide is in a cartridge that is installed in the handle of the brush. The insecticide is dispensed through the tips of the bristles when they touch the pet's skin (which is where most ticks and fleas are found). The actual dispensing works very much like a felt-tip pen. Only a small amount of insecticide actually is dispensed on the pet because of this unique dispensing feature. Thus, the amount of insecticide that is placed on your pet is minimal compared to conventional methods of applying a tick and flea control product. One application of insecticide will keep your pet free from ticks and fleas for 14 days.

Please answer the following questions:

1. In general, how do you feel about using this type of product on your pet?

2. What are the major advantages of this product compared with the existing product that you are currently using to control ticks and fleas on your pet?

3. What characteristics of this product do you especially like?

4. What suggestions do you have for improving this product?

5. If it is available at an appropriate price, how likely are you to buy this product?

        Very likely   Semi-likely   Not likely

6. Assuming that a single purchase would provide 30 applications for an average-size dog or 48 applications for an average-size cat, approximately how much would you pay for this product?

product mix? Is demand strong enough to justify entering the market, and will this demand endure? What types of environmental and competitive changes can be expected, and how will these changes affect the product's future sales, costs, and profits? Are the organization's research, development, engineering, and production capabilities adequate to develop the product? If new facilities must be constructed, how quickly can they be built, and how much will they cost? Is the necessary financing for development and commercialization on hand or obtainable at terms consistent with a favorable return on investment?

In the business analysis stage, firms seek market information. The results of customer surveys, along with secondary data, supply the specifics needed to estimate potential sales, costs, and profits.

For many products in this stage (when they are still just product ideas), forecasting sales accurately is difficult. This is especially true for innovative and completely new products. Organizations sometimes employ break-even analysis to determine how many units they would have to sell to begin making a profit. At times an organization also uses payback analysis, in which marketers compute the time period required to recover the funds that would be invested in developing the new product. Because break-even and payback analyses are based on estimates, they are usually viewed as useful but not particularly precise during this stage.

Product Development

product development
Determining if producing a product is technically feasible and cost effective

Product development is the phase in which the organization determines if it is technically feasible to produce the product and if it can be produced at costs low enough to make the final price reasonable. To test its acceptability, the idea or concept is converted into

Marketing in Transition
Try Out Your Dream Guitar

It is not uncommon for musicians to pay a great deal of money for their instruments. However, many artists do not have a lot of money for things like guitars. Guitar Affair, launched by Jim Basara in 2007, is a company that encourages musicians to sample guitars without the financial commitments. Guitar Affair allows you to rent its high-end guitars on a daily or weekly basis in order to give you a chance to try out multiple instruments before committing, or to use one for an out-of-town gig. For a $50 one-time membership fee, you gain access to the complete inventory of guitars. Selections include the Eric Clapton Signature Stratocaster, Fenders, Gibsons, and Beltonas, among others. The guitars are shipped via UPS in custom-made cases bearing prepaid return shipping labels. If a customer decides he or she cannot part with a selection, Guitar Affair does allow for the purchase of its guitars.

Inc. magazine asked industry experts how they might advise Guitar Affair. In a nutshell, analysts agree that the company's main challenge lies in attracting its tiny target market (guitar enthusiasts with cash to spare). Among the suggestions were to get famous musicians on board and have them promote the service, provide quality service while keeping costs low, and focus on an online marketing strategy. Jim Basara has heeded some of their advice. He has worked to develop an online marketing strategy that includes posting to online

musician and music forums. Basara addresses individual inquiries from his target market, proving that he is serious about developing quality customer relationships and providing through service. A visit to the company's MySpace page, which includes customer comments, indicates that his target market is taking notice of the company. So, whether you are in the mood to shop around or try out the guitar of your dreams, Guitar Affair may fit the bill.[b]

a prototype, or working model. The prototype should reveal tangible and intangible attributes associated with the product in consumers' minds. The product's design, mechanical features, and intangible aspects must be linked to wants in the marketplace. Through marketing research and concept testing, product attributes important to buyers are identified. These characteristics must be communicated to customers through the design of the product. GreenTech Automotive, for example, has developed a series of hybrid prototypes meant to appeal to consumers looking for efficient hybrid vehicles.

After a prototype is developed, its overall functioning must be tested. Its performance, safety, convenience, and other functional qualities are tested both in a laboratory and in the field. Functional testing should be rigorous and lengthy enough to test the product thoroughly. Manufacturing issues that come to light at this stage may require adjustments. When Nintendo and Opera Software partnered on the Wii, Nintendo engineers had to come up with many prototypes before the two companies could agree on a final version.

A crucial question that arises during product development is how much quality to build into the product. For example, a major dimension of quality is durability. Higher quality often calls for better materials and more expensive processing, which increase production costs and, ultimately, the product's price. In determining the specific level of quality, a marketer must ascertain approximately what price the target market views as acceptable. In addition, a marketer usually tries to set a quality level consistent with that of the firm's other products. Obviously the quality of competing brands is also a consideration.

The development phase of a new product is frequently lengthy and expensive; thus, a relatively small number of product ideas are put into development. If the product appears sufficiently successful during this stage to merit test marketing, marketers begin to make decisions regarding branding, packaging, labeling, pricing, and promotion for use in the test marketing stage.

Test Marketing

Test marketing is a limited introduction of a product in geographic areas chosen to represent the intended market. Taco Bell, for example, conducted a market test of a breakfast menu in 13 of its Texas locations.[12] The aim of test marketing is to determine the extent to which potential customers will buy the product. It is not an extension of the development stage but a sample launching of the entire marketing mix. Test marketing should be conducted only after the product has gone through development and initial plans have been made regarding the other marketing mix variables. Companies use test marketing to lessen the risk of product failure. The dangers of introducing an untested product include undercutting already profitable products and, should the new product fail, loss of credibility with distributors and customers.

Test marketing provides several benefits. It lets marketers expose a product in a natural marketing environment to measure its sales performance. The company can strive to identify weaknesses in the product or in other parts of the marketing mix. A product weakness discovered after a nationwide introduction can be expensive to correct. Moreover, if consumers' early reactions are negative, marketers may be unable to persuade consumers to try the product again. Thus, making adjustments after test marketing can be crucial to the success of a new product. On the other hand, test marketing results may be positive enough to warrant accelerating the product's introduction. Test marketing also allows marketers to experiment with variations in advertising, pricing, and packaging in different test areas and to measure the extent of brand awareness, brand switching, and repeat purchases resulting from these alterations in the marketing mix.

Selection of appropriate test areas is very important because the validity of test marketing results depends heavily on selecting test sites that provide accurate representation of the intended target market. Table 12.1 lists some of the most popular test market cities. The criteria used for choosing test market cities depend on the product's attributes, the target market's characteristics, and the firm's objectives and resources.

© AP Images/PRNewsFoto/Kiehl's Since 1851

Example of a New Product
Kiehl's Photo-Age Corrector line of skin care products is an example of a new product line.

test marketing A limited introduction of a product in geographic areas chosen to represent the intended market

TABLE 12.1 Popular Test Markets in the United States

Rank	City
1	Albany, NY
2	Rochester, NY
3	Greensboro, NC
4	Birmingham, AL
5	Syracuse, NY
6	Charlotte, NC
7	Nashville, TN
8	Eugene, OR
9	Wichita, KS
10	Richmond, VA

Source: "Which American City Provides the Best Consumer Test Market?" *Business Wire*, May 24, 2004.

Test marketing is not without risks. It is expensive, and competitors may try to interfere. A competitor may attempt to "jam" the test program by increasing its own advertising or promotions, lowering prices, and offering special incentives, all to combat recognition and purchase of the new brand or product. Such competitor-thwarting tactics can invalidate test results. Sometimes, too, competitors copy the product in the testing stage and rush to introduce a similar product. This is the time to conduct research to identify issues that might drive potential customers to market-leading competitors instead. It is therefore desirable to move to the commercialization phase as soon as possible after successful testing. On the other hand, some firms have been known to heavily promote new products long before they are ready for the market to discourage competitors from developing similar new products.

Because of these risks, many companies use alternative methods to measure customer preferences. One such method is simulated test marketing. Typically consumers at shopping centers are asked to view an advertisement for a new product and are given a free sample to take home. These consumers are subsequently interviewed over the phone or through online panels and asked to rate the product. The major advantages of simulated test marketing are greater speed, lower costs, and tighter security, which reduce the flow of information to competitors and reduce jamming. Gillette's Personal Care Division, for example, spends less than $200,000 for a simulated test that lasts three to five months. A live test market costs Gillette $2 million, counting promotion and distribution, and takes one to two years to complete. Several marketing research firms, such as ACNielsen Company, offer test marketing services to provide independent assessment of proposed products.

Clearly not all products that are test-marketed are launched. At times, problems discovered during test marketing cannot be resolved. Procter & Gamble, for example, test-marketed a new plastic wrap product called Impress in Grand Junction, Colorado, but decided not to launch the brand nationally based on the results of test marketing.

Commercialization

During the **commercialization** phase, plans for full-scale manufacturing and marketing must be refined and finalized and budgets for the project prepared. Early in the commercialization phase, marketing management analyzes the results of test marketing to find out what changes in the marketing mix are needed before introducing the product. The results of test marketing may tell marketers to change one or more of the product's physical attributes, modify the distribution plans to include more retail outlets, alter promotional efforts, or change the product's price. However, as more and more changes are made based on test marketing findings, the test marketing projections may become less valid.

During the early part of this stage, marketers must not only gear up for larger-scale production but also make decisions about warranties, repairs, and replacement parts. The type of warranty a firm provides can be a critical issue for buyers, especially for expensive, technically complex goods such as appliances or frequently used items such as mattresses. Tempur-Pedic mattresses offer a 90-day, no-risk, in-home trial of their innovative mattresses. If after 90 days, the customer is not satisfied, the retailer will pick up the mattress for a modest return fee. Maytag also provides a money-back guarantee on its refrigerators. Establishing an effective system for providing repair services and replacement parts is necessary to maintain favorable customer relationships. Although the producer may furnish these services directly to buyers, it is more common for the producer to provide such services through regional service centers. Regardless of how services are provided, it is important to customers that they be performed quickly and correctly.

The product enters the market during the commercialization phase. When introducing a product, a firm may spend enormous sums for advertising, personal selling, and other types of promotion, as well

commercialization Refining and finalizing plans and budgets for full-scale manufacturing and marketing of a product

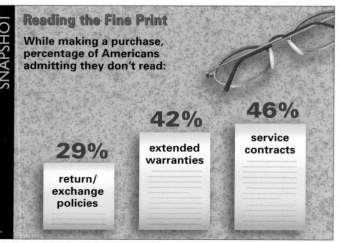

SNAPSHOT

Reading the Fine Print

While making a purchase, percentage of Americans admitting they don't read:

29% return/exchange policies

42% extended warranties

46% service contracts

Source: Kelton Research survey for the Better Business Bureau.

as for more manufacturing facilities and equipment. Such expenditures may not be recovered for several years. Smaller firms may find this process difficult, but even so they may use press releases, blogs, podcasts, and other tools to capture quick feedback as well as to promote the new product. Another low-cost promotional tool is product reviews in newspapers and magazines, which can be especially helpful when they are positive and target the same customers.

Usually products are not launched nationwide overnight but are introduced through a process called a *roll-out*. With a roll-out, a product is introduced in stages, starting in one set of geographic areas and gradually expanding into adjacent areas. It may take several years to market the product nationally. Sometimes the test cities are used as initial marketing areas, and the introduction of the product becomes a natural extension of test marketing. A product test-marketed in Sacramento, Fort Collins, Abilene, Springfield, and Jacksonville, as the map in Figure 12.3 shows, could be introduced first in those cities. After the stage 1 introduction is complete, stage 2 could include market coverage of the states where the test cities are located. In stage 3, marketing efforts might be extended into adjacent states. All remaining states would then be covered in stage 4.

Gradual product introductions do not always occur state by state; other geographic combinations, such as groups of counties that overlap across state borders, are sometimes used. Products destined for multinational markets may also be rolled out one country or region at a time. For instance, Sky Zone (a company marketing locations filled with giant trampolines on which people can pay to play dodge ball, take fitness classes, or simply jump around for $9 per hour) first opened in Las Vegas, Nevada. After realizing success there, the company tested in St. Louis and Sacramento. It plans to unveil locations in Houston, Boston, Chicago, Columbus, and Los Angeles as well.[13] Gradual product introduction is desirable for several reasons. First, it reduces the risks of introducing a new product. If the product fails, the firm will experience smaller losses if it introduced the item in only a few geographic areas than if it marketed the product nationally. Second, a company cannot introduce a product nationwide overnight because a system of wholesalers and retailers to distribute the product cannot be established so quickly; developing a distribution network may take considerable time. Third, if the product is successful, the number of units needed to satisfy nationwide demand

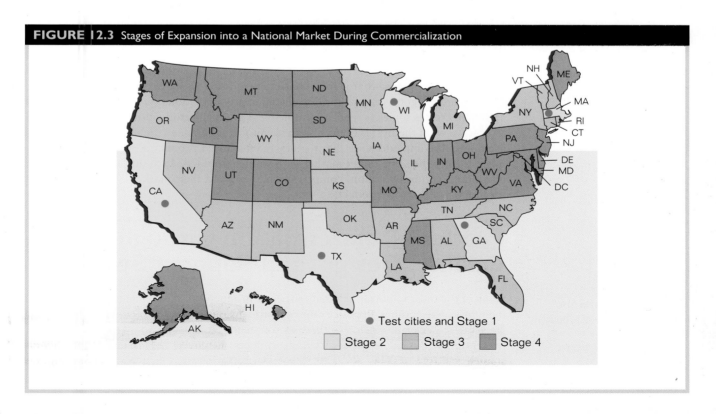

FIGURE 12.3 Stages of Expansion into a National Market During Commercialization

Sustainable Marketing
Frito Lay Investigates Biodegradable Chip Bags

Frito Lay created SunChips in 1991 as a healthier alternative to potato chips. As consumer concern for the environment has increased over the years, Frito-Lay decided to make SunChips better for the environment as well. One of its eight manufacturing plants is solar-powered, and SunChips bags are now made of plant-based materials and are biodegradable. The SunChips division of Frito Lay is also interested in helping communities. It donated $1 million toward the rebuilding of Greensburg, Kansas, after it was completely destroyed in a 2007 tornado. It has also partnered with *National Geographic* to launch the Green Effect project—a competition awarding grants for ideas on how to green up homes, communities, and more.

In order to publicize its green efforts, Frito Lay has turned to YouTube, Twitter, and *People* magazine. Viewers online can find videos of the SunChips bags biodegrading, and marketers placed samples of the new bags in *People* magazines along with instructions on how to turn the bags into compost. Frito Lay has taken advantage of the fact that its health-conscious target market is also generally concerned about the environment. Frito Lay has gone beyond using the green initiative as a marketing ploy. The company must meet rigid standards in order to call its new bag compostable—an expense many

companies would not take on. In part, Frito Lay's shift in focus has been prompted by increasing competition for healthy snack market share. Frito Lay working the environmental angle will create a competitive advantage for SunChips. The results thus far have been positive. SunChips has received an Effie Award for green production and solar power and an Ogilvy Award for its green campaign.[c]

for it may be too large for the firm to produce in a short time. Finally, it allows for fine-tuning of the marketing mix to better satisfy target customers. Procter & Gamble, for example, originally conceived of Febreze deodorizer as a fabric-care product, but over time, the company's view of the highly successful brand evolved into an air-freshening line because that is how consumers indicated they were using it.[14]

Despite the good reasons for introducing a product gradually, marketers realize this approach creates some competitive problems. A gradual introduction allows competitors to observe what the firm is doing and to monitor results just as the firm's own marketers are doing. If competitors see that the newly introduced product is successful, they may quickly enter the same target market with similar products. In addition, as a product is introduced region by region, competitors may expand their marketing efforts to offset promotion of the new product.

Product Differentiation through Quality, Design, and Support Services

product differentiation
Creating and designing products so that customers perceive them as different from competing products

Some of the most important characteristics of products are the elements that distinguish them from one another. **Product differentiation** is the process of creating and designing products so customers perceive them as different from competing products. Customer perception is critical in differentiating products. Perceived differences might include quality, features, styling, price, or image. A crucial element used to differentiate one product from another is the brand, discussed in the next chapter. In this section, we examine three aspects of product differentiation that companies must consider when creating and offering products for sale: product quality, product design and features, and product support services. These aspects involve the company's attempt to create real differences among products.

Product Quality

Quality refers to the overall characteristics of a product that allow it to perform as expected in satisfying customer needs. The words *as expected* are very important to this definition because quality usually means different things to different customers. For some, durability signifies quality. Among the most durable products on the market today is the Craftsman line of tools at Sears; indeed, Sears provides a lifetime guarantee on the durability of its tools. Similarly in the household market, Cutco provides a lifetime warranty on their high-quality line of knives and cutlery. For other consumers, a product's ease of use may indicate quality.

The concept of quality also varies between consumer and business markets. Consumers consider high-quality products to be reliable, durable, and easy to maintain. For business markets, technical suitability, ease of repair, and company reputation are important characteristics. Unlike consumers, most organizations place far less emphasis on price than on product quality.

One important dimension of quality is **level of quality**: the amount of quality a product possesses. The concept is a relative one; that is, the quality level of one product is difficult to describe unless it is compared with that of other products. The American Customer Satisfaction Index, compiled by the National Quality Research Center at the University of Michigan, ranks customer satisfaction among a wide variety of businesses. Dissatisfied customers may curtail their overall spending, which could stifle economic growth. In the full-service restaurant category, The Olive Garden received the highest satisfaction score, and Chili's was fourth.[15]

A second important dimension is consistency. **Consistency of quality** refers to the degree to which a product has the same level of quality over time. Consistency means giving consumers the quality they expect every time they purchase the product. Like level of quality, consistency is a relative concept; however, it implies a quality comparison within the same brand over time. For example, if FedEx delivers more than 99 percent of overnight packages on time, its service has a consistent quality.

The consistency of product quality can also be compared across competing products. It is at this stage that consistency becomes critical to a company's success. Companies that can provide quality on a consistent basis have a major competitive advantage over rivals. FedEx, for example, is viewed as more consistent in delivery schedules than the U.S. Postal Service, which has earned FedEx a higher consumer satisfaction rating for express deliveries.[16] In simple terms, no company has ever succeeded by creating and marketing low-quality products. Many companies have taken major steps, such as implementing total quality management (TQM), to improve the quality of their products.

By and large, higher product quality means marketers will charge a higher price for the product. This fact forces marketers to consider quality carefully in their product-planning efforts. Not all customers want or can afford the highest-quality products available. Thus, some companies offer products with moderate quality.

Product Design and Features

Product design refers to how a product is conceived, planned, and produced. Design is a very complex topic because it involves the total sum of all the product's physical characteristics. Many companies are known for the outstanding designs of their products: Sony for personal electronics, Hewlett-Packard for printers, Apple for computers and music players, and JanSport for backpacks. Good design is one of the best competitive advantages any brand can possess.

quality The overall characteristics of a product that allow it to perform as expected in satisfying customer needs

level of quality The amount of quality a product possesses

consistency of quality The degree to which a product has the same level of quality over time

product design How a product is conceived, planned, and produced

Fan blades 'chop' the airflow, causing buffeting. The new Dyson fan works differently. An annular jet accelerates the surrounding air and amplifies it fifteen times. There are no blades to chop the air so the airflow is smooth – it cools without the unpleasant buffeting.

dyson air multiplier
No blades. No buffeting.
Learn more at www.dyson.com

© Dyson

Product Quality
Dyson provides high-quality products known for exceptional design and production.

One component of design is **styling**, or the physical appearance of the product. The style of a product is one design feature that can allow certain products to sell very rapidly. Good design, however, means more than just appearance; it also involves a product's functioning and usefulness. For instance, a pair of jeans may look great, but if they fall apart after three washes, clearly the design was poor. Most consumers seek out products that both look good and function well.

Product features are specific design characteristics that allow a product to perform certain tasks. By adding or subtracting features, a company can differentiate its products from those of the competition. Chrysler promotes its line of minivans as having more features related to passenger and pet safety—Stow 'n Go seating and storage, rearview conversation mirrors, rear back-up cameras, and Blind-spot Monitoring and Rear Cross Path advanced safety systems—than any other minivan.[17] Product features can also be used to differentiate products within the same company. For example, Nike offers both a walking shoe and a run-walk shoe for specific consumer needs as well as technology that can link to your iPod to track your distance traveled and calories burned. In these cases, the company's products are sold with a wide range of features, from low-priced "base" or "stripped-down" versions to high-priced, prestigious "feature-packed" ones. The automotive industry regularly sells products with a wide range of features. In general, the more features a product has, the higher its price and, often, the higher its perceived quality.

For a brand to have a sustainable competitive advantage, marketers must determine the product designs and features that customers desire. Information from marketing research efforts and from databases can help in assessing customers' product design and feature preferences. Being able to meet customers' desires for product design and features at prices they can afford is crucial to a product's long-term success. Marketers must be careful not to misrepresent or overpromise regarding product features or product performance.

Product Support Services

Many companies differentiate their product offerings by providing support services. Usually referred to as **customer services**, these services include any human or mechanical efforts or activities a company provides that add value to a product. Examples of customer services include delivery and installation, financing arrangements, customer training, warranties and guarantees, repairs,

Responsible Marketing?
Airborne's Lofty Advertising

CRITICAL
THINKING

ISSUE: Can drug companies get away with false advertising?

Recently, the makers of the herbal supplement Airborne agreed to pay a $23.3 million class-action lawsuit over claims of false advertising. The company first claimed that their product could ward off colds. Airborne later backed off and changed its campaign to claim the product helped "boost your immune system." In fact, Airborne had no evidence to support either claim. Although Airborne has agreed to refund the purchase price to consumers, they will not admit to false advertising.

Even though the class-action lawsuit was successful, Airborne is still available over the counter to anyone who wants to buy it. Ten years of advertising, although promoting false claims, still reside in the minds of many uninformed consumers who want to stay healthy this cold and flu season. In essence, Airborne has settled its lawsuit involving the false claims, but the public opinion on the product is still up in the air.

Should Airborne be forced to produce corrective advertising? If Airborne cannot prove to its customers that its product is beneficial, should it even be allowed on the shelves? Could the tests that show Airborne to be ineffective be wrong?[d]

Product Support Services
Best Buy attracts customers to its stores with the promise of service support provided by the Geek Squad.

© Newscom

layaway plans, convenient hours of operation, adequate parking, and information through toll-free numbers and websites. For example, Zappos, an online shoe retailer, has earned a reputation for excellent customer service, in part due to its 24-hour service and free, fast returns.

Whether as a major or minor part of the total product offering, all marketers of goods sell customer services. Providing good customer service may be the only way a company can differentiate its products when all products in a market have essentially the same quality, design, and features. This is especially true in the computer industry. When buying a laptop computer, for example, consumers shop more for fast delivery, technical support, warranties, and price than for product quality and design, as witnessed by the high volume of "off-the-shelf," noncustomized, sometimes lagging in technology, discount laptops sold at Best Buy, Costco, Walmart, Target, etc. Through research, a company can discover the types of services customers want and need. For example, some customers are more interested in financing, whereas others are more concerned with installation and training. The level of customer service a company provides can profoundly affect customer satisfaction. Add-on features can enhance a product in the eyes of the consumer. Consumers often infer a higher level of quality from the mere availability of add-on services.[18]

styling The physical appearance of a product

product features Specific design characteristics that allow a product to perform certain tasks

customer services Human or mechanical efforts or activities that add value to a product

product deletion Eliminating a product from the product mix when it no longer satisfies a sufficient number of customers

Product Deletion

Generally a product cannot satisfy target market customers and contribute to the achievement of the organization's overall goals indefinitely. **Product deletion** is the process of eliminating a product from the product mix, usually because it no longer satisfies a sufficient number of customers. Condé Nast, for example, discontinued its iconic *Gourmet* magazine due to reduced advertising support as recession-hampered consumers turn to quick, accessible, and affordable cooking options.[19] A declining product reduces an organization's profitability and drains resources that could be used to modify other products or develop new ones. A marginal product may require shorter production runs, which can increase per-unit production costs. Finally, when a dying product completely loses favor with customers, the negative feelings may transfer to some of the company's other products.

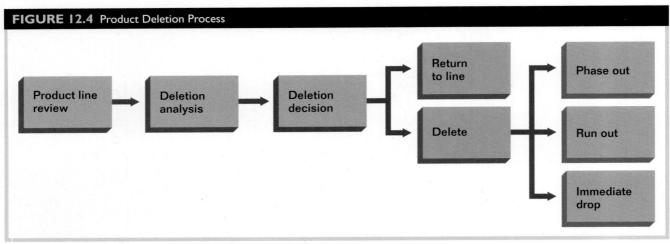

FIGURE 12.4 Product Deletion Process

Source: Martin L. Bell. *Marketing: Concepts and Strategy*, 3rd ed., p. 267; Copyright © 1979, Houghton Mifflin Company. Reprinted by permission of Mrs. Martin L. Bell.

Most organizations find it difficult to delete a product. A decision to drop a product may be opposed by managers and other employees who believe the product is necessary to the product mix. Salespeople who still have some loyal customers are especially upset when a product is dropped. In such cases, companies may spend considerable resources and effort to change a slipping product's marketing mix to improve its sales and thus avoid having to eliminate it. Products constantly undergo reformulation and redesign to fortify their fit in the product line and avoid deletion.

Some organizations delete products only after the products have become heavy financial burdens. A better approach is some form of systematic review in which each product is evaluated periodically to determine its impact on the overall effectiveness of the firm's product mix. Such a review should analyze the product's contribution to the firm's sales for a given period, as well as estimate future sales, costs, and profits associated with the product. It should also gauge the value of making changes in the marketing strategy to improve the product's performance. A systematic review allows an organization to improve product performance and ascertain when to delete products. General Motors decided to delete the Hummer, Saturn, and Pontiac brands in order to lower costs, improve reputation, and become more profitable.

Basically, a product can be deleted in three ways: phase it out, run it out, or drop it immediately (see Figure 12.4). A *phase-out* allows the product to decline without a change in the marketing strategy; no attempt is made to give the product new life. A *run-out* exploits any strengths left in the product. Intensifying marketing efforts in core markets or eliminating some marketing expenditures, such as advertising, may cause a sudden jump in profits. This approach is commonly taken for technologically obsolete products, such as older models of computers and calculators. Often the price is reduced to generate a sales spurt. The third alternative, an *immediate drop* of an unprofitable product, is the best strategy when losses are too great to prolong the product's life.

Organizing to Develop and Manage Products

After reviewing the concepts of product line and mix and life cycles, it should be obvious that managing products is a complex task. Often the traditional functional form of an organization, in which managers specialize in such business functions as advertising, sales, and distribution, does not fit a company's needs. In this case, management must find an organizational approach that accomplishes the tasks necessary to develop and manage products. Alternatives to functional organization include the product or brand manager approach, the market manager approach, and the venture team approach.

A **product manager** is responsible for a product, a product line, or several distinct products that make up an interrelated group within a multiproduct organization. A **brand manager** is responsible for a single brand. Kraft, for example, has one brand manager for Nabisco Oreos, its number-one selling cookie, and one for Oscar Mayer Lunchables. Both product and brand managers operate cross-functionally to coordinate the activities, information, and strategies involved in marketing an assigned product. Product managers and brand managers plan marketing activities to achieve objectives by coordinating a mix of distribution, promotion (especially sales promotion and advertising), and price. They must consider packaging and branding decisions and work closely with personnel in research and development, engineering, and production. Marketing research helps product managers understand consumers and find target markets. Because luxury brands such as BMW and Porsche can have their brand image reduced by association with their producers' other mass-market brands, brand managers must balance their brands' independent image with associated brands of the firm. The product or brand manager approach to organization is used by many large, multiple-product companies.

A **market manager** is responsible for managing the marketing activities that serve a particular group of customers. This organizational approach is particularly effective when a firm engages in different types of marketing activities to provide products to diverse customer groups. A company might have one market manager for business markets and another for consumer markets. Markets also could be divided by geographic region. For example, the Jack-in-the-Box fast-food chain offers different menu items in New Mexico than it does in Oregon. Because Hindus believe cows are sacred, and India has a large vegetarian population, McDonald's offers lamb and vegetarian options in lieu of beef burgers at its restaurants in India. The chains recognize that different markets have different preferences. These broad market categories might be broken down into more limited market responsibilities.

A **venture team** creates entirely new products that may be aimed at new markets. Unlike a product or market manager, a venture team is responsible for all aspects of developing a product: research and development, production and engineering, finance and accounting, and marketing. Venture team members are brought together from different functional areas of the organization. In working outside established divisions, venture teams have greater flexibility to apply inventive approaches to develop new products that can take advantage of opportunities in highly segmented markets. Companies are increasingly using such cross-functional teams for product development in an effort to boost product quality. Quality may be positively related to information integration within the team, customers' influence on the product development process, and a quality orientation within the firm. When a new product has demonstrated commercial potential, team members may return to their functional areas, or they may join a new or existing division to manage the product.

product manager The person within an organization who is responsible for a product, a product line, or several distinct products that make up a group

brand manager The person responsible for a single brand

market manager The person responsible for managing the marketing activities that serve a particular group of customers

venture team A cross-functional group that creates entirely new products that may be aimed at new markets

summary

1. To understand how companies manage existing products through line extensions and product modifications

Organizations must be able to adjust their product mixes to compete effectively and achieve their goals. A product mix can be improved through line extension and product modification. A line extension is the development of a product closely related to one or more products in the existing line but designed specifically to meet different customer needs. Product modification is the changing of one or more characteristics of a product. This approach can be effective when the product is modifiable, when customers can perceive the change, and when customers want the modification. Quality modifications relate to a product's dependability and durability. Functional modifications affect a product's versatility, effectiveness, convenience, or safety. Aesthetic modifications change the sensory appeal of a product.

2. To describe how businesses develop a product idea into a commercial product

Before a product is introduced, it goes through a seven-phase new-product development process. In the idea generation phase, new-product ideas may come from internal or external sources. In the process of screening, ideas are evaluated to determine whether they are consistent with the firm's overall objectives and resources. Concept testing, the third phase, involves having a small sample of potential customers review a brief description of the product idea to determine their initial perceptions of the proposed product and their early buying intentions. During the business analysis stage, the product idea is evaluated to determine its potential contribution to the firm's sales, costs, and profits. In the product development stage, the organization determines if it is technically feasible to produce the product and if it can be produced at a cost low enough to make the final price reasonable. Test marketing is a limited introduction of a product in areas chosen to represent the intended market. Finally, in the commercialization phase, full-scale production of the product begins and a complete marketing strategy is developed.

3. To understand the importance of product differentiation and the elements that differentiate one product from another

Product differentiation is the process of creating and designing products so that customers perceive them as different from competing products. Product quality, product design and features, and product support services are three aspects of product differentiation that companies consider when creating and marketing products. Product quality includes the overall characteristics of a product that allow it to perform as expected in satisfying customer needs. The level of quality is the amount of quality a product possesses. Consistency of quality is the degree to which a product has the same level of quality over time. Product design refers to how a product is conceived, planned, and produced. Components of product design include styling (the physical appearance of the product) and product features (the specific design characteristics that allow a product to perform certain tasks). Companies often differentiate their products by providing support services, usually called customer services. Customer services are human or mechanical efforts or activities that add value to a product.

4. To examine how product deletion is used to improve product mixes

Product deletion is the process of eliminating a product that no longer satisfies a sufficient number of customers. Although a firm's personnel may oppose product deletion, weak products are unprofitable, consume too much time and effort, may require shorter production runs, and can create an unfavorable impression of the firm's other products. A product mix should be systematically reviewed to determine when to delete products. Products to be deleted can be phased out, run out, or dropped immediately.

5. To describe organizational structures used for managing products

Often the traditional functional form of organization does not lend itself to the complex task of developing and managing products. Alternative organizational forms include the product or brand manager approach, the market manager approach, and the venture team approach. A product manager is responsible for a product, a product line, or several distinct products that make up an interrelated group within a multiproduct organization. A brand manager is responsible for a single brand. A market manager is responsible for managing the marketing activities that serve a particular group or class of customers. A venture team is sometimes used to create entirely new products that may be aimed at new markets.

Go to www.cengagebrain.com for resources to help you master the content in this chapter as well as materials that will expand your marketing knowledge!

important terms

line extension, 346

product
    modifications, 347

quality
    modifications, 347

functional
    modifications, 347

aesthetic
    modifications, 348

new-product
    development
    process, 349

idea generation, 349

screening, 350

concept testing, 350

business analysis, 350

product
    development, 351

test marketing, 353

commercialization, 354

product
    differentiation, 356

quality, 357

level of quality, 357

consistency of
    quality, 357

product design, 357

styling, 359

product features, 359

customer services, 359

product deletion, 359

product manager, 361

brand manager, 361

market manager, 361

venture team, 361

discussion and review questions

1. What is a line extension, and how does it differ from a product modification? 346 - 347
2. Compare and contrast the three major approaches to modifying a product. 347-348
3. Identify and briefly explain the seven major phases of the new-product development process.
4. Do small companies that manufacture just a few products need to be concerned about developing and managing products? Why or why not?
5. Why is product development a cross-functional activity—involving finance, engineering, manufacturing, and other functional areas—within an organization? 351
6. What is the major purpose of concept testing, and how is it accomplished? 350
7. What are the benefits and disadvantages of test marketing? 354

8. Why can the process of commercialization take a considerable amount of time?
9. What is product differentiation, and how can it be achieved? 356
10. Explain how the term *quality* has been used to differentiate products in the automobile industry in recent years. What are some makes and models of automobiles that come to mind when you hear the terms *high quality* and *poor quality*?
11. What types of problems does a weak product cause in a product mix? Describe the most effective approach for avoiding such problems.
12. What type of organization might use a venture team to develop new products? What are the advantages and disadvantages of such a team?

application questions

1. When developing a new product, a company often test-markets the proposed product in a specific area or location. Suppose you wish to test-market your new, revolutionary SuperWax car wax, which requires only one application for a lifetime finish. Where and how would you test-market your new product?

2. A product manager may make quality, functional, or aesthetic modifications when modifying a product. Identify a familiar product that recently was modified, categorize

the modification (quality, functional, or aesthetic), and describe how you would have modified it differently.

3. Phasing out a product from the product mix often is difficult for an organization. Visit a retail store in your area, and ask the manager what products he or she has had to discontinue in the recent past. Find out what factors influenced the decision to delete the product and who was involved in the decision. Ask the manager to identify any products that should be but have not been deleted, and try to ascertain the reason.

internet exercise

Merck & Company

Merck, a leading global pharmaceutical company, develops, manufactures, and markets a broad range of health-care products. In addition, the firm's Merck-Medco Managed Care Division manages pharmacy benefits for more than 40 million Americans. The company has established a website to serve as an educational and informational resource for Internet users around the world. To learn more about the company and its research, visit its award-winning site at **www.merck.com**.

1. What products has Merck developed and introduced recently?

2. What role does research play in Merck's success? How does research facilitate new-product development at Merck?

3. Find Merck's mission statement. Is Merck's focus on research consistent with the firm's mission and values?

developing your marketing plan

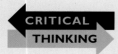

A company's marketing strategy may be revised to include new products as it considers its SWOT analysis and the impact of environmental factors on its product mix. When developing a marketing plan, the company must decide whether new products are to be added to the product mix or if existing ones should be modified. The information in this chapter will assist you in the creation of your marketing plan as you consider the following:

1. Identify whether your product will be a modification of an existing one in your product mix or the development of a new product.

2. If the product is an extension of one in your current product mix, determine the type(s) of modifications that will be performed.

3. Using Figure 12.1 as a guide, discuss how your product idea would move through the stages of new-product development. Examine the idea, using the tests and analyses included in the new-product development process.

4. Discuss how the management of this product will fit into your current organizational structure.

The information obtained from these questions should assist you in developing various aspects of your marketing plan found in the *Interactive Marketing Plan* exercise at **www. cengagebrain.com.**

VIDEO CASE 12.1

Harley-Davidson: More Than Just a Motorcycle

CRITICAL THINKING

Harley-Davidson's customers can spot each other instantly by the iconic black, white, and orange logo on their motorcycles, clothing, and saddlebags. More than a century after the first Harley-Davidson motorcycle hit the road, the company's annual worldwide sales total more than $4 billion. Harley-Davidson dominates the U.S. motorcycle market, and sales are also strong in Japan and Europe. Its annual output of 200,000 motorcycles covers 35 models in seven product lines (Sportster, Dyna, Softail, VRSC, Touring, Trike, and CVO). An important part of the Harley-Davidson product is customer services. Harley dealerships help differentiate its product with customer training, warranties, guarantees, repairs, and accessories. Harley dealerships become social centers for customers to interact and have fun.

Although Harley-Davidson teetered on the brink of bankruptcy in the 1980s, it roared back by limiting production to focus on a consistently high level of quality. Like other automobile and motorcycle manufacturers, the company is facing decreased sales due to the slow economy, but Harley-Davidson hopes to revitalize the company with its new products. The new motorcycles combine the brand's image of freedom and individuality with styling, performance, and features that appeal to younger buyers and women buyers. To attract first-time buyers as well as experienced riders trading up to better bikes, Harley-Davidson prices its motorcycles starting at $6,999 and offers financing and insurance. Each model's price depends on its specific combination of features and styling.

Buyers can also order limited-edition motorcycles custom built with distinctive paint designs and accessories. Customers see their bikes as a way of expressing their individuality. However, Harley-Davidson selects only a small number of orders annually for custom-built bikes. Not surprisingly, these custom products are in high demand. The product modifications that go into custom bikes are almost like new models of the same brand, but they represent a one-time production run.

To encourage the next generation of biking enthusiasts to learn to drive a motorcycle and then buy the Harley-Davidson bike of their dreams, many of the company's dealers offer the Rider's Edge driving course. Since 2000, when the course was first offered, more than 150,000 people have graduated and earned a motorcycle license. The Rider's Edge also helps experienced riders hone their driving skills and learn special techniques for riding in groups.

Group riding is such an important part of the overall product experience that the company founded the Harley Owners Group (HOG) to foster a sense of community among its customers. Today, more than 1 million HOG members enjoy benefits such as access to dozens of exclusive group rides, a special customer service hotline, and a members-only website. They also receive two magazines: *Hog Tales*, with articles about members and member events, and *Enthusiast*, with articles about Harley-Davidson's goods and services. In addition, customers can use the Harley-Davidson website to plan travel, book hotels, rent bikes, or ship their bikes for their next riding adventure.

Knowing that customers are passionate about motorcycles and about Harley-Davidson in particular, the company arranges tours at four of its factories in Wisconsin, Pennsylvania, and Missouri. It opened the Harley-Davidson Museum in Milwaukee, Wisconsin, home of its headquarters, with 130,000 square feet of exhibits. Many of the exhibits feature products from Harley-Davidson's past, including a sample of the bikes, boats, golf carts, and snowmobiles that the company once manufactured. Museum-goers can get a taste of the Harley experience by climbing onto one of the company's current bikes for a virtual ride through beautiful country scenery projected on a big screen.

The museum also looks ahead by highlighting Harley-Davidson's latest technology, its newest engines, and the inner workings of its new-product development process. One exhibit shows how a new motorcycle starts life as a sketch, is transformed into a clay model, becomes a testable prototype, and ultimately enters full production. "In creating this museum, we wanted to make sure that it told an evolving story," says the museum director. "We have a rich heritage, but we also have an exciting future."[20]

QUESTIONS FOR DISCUSSION

1. Why would Harley-Davidson put as much emphasis on consistency of quality as it does on level of quality?

2. How does Harley-Davidson use customer services to differentiate its motorcycle products?

3. What role do you think the Harley-Davidson Museum might play in influencing how consumers perceive the company and its products?

CASE 12.2

Pepsi Sales Bubble with Limited-Edition Soft Drinks

CRITICAL THINKING

Cucumber, berry, and cinnamon soft drinks may come and go in Japan, but colas are seemingly forever—at least in Pepsi's product lineup. The company and its local partner, Suntory, are using limited-edition soft drinks to boost market share in the $30 billion Japanese beverage market and keep sales bubbling despite a cola war with rival Coca-Cola and fierce competition for space on store shelves.

No new product is a sure thing, but the Japanese market is particularly challenging. Of the 1,500 beverages launched there every year, only the tiniest percentage survives the introductory period. Why? First, because Japanese convenience stores are small, they make room only for products that sell quickly. New drinks that don't gain a following soon after they're introduced are pulled from store shelves in a hurry and replaced by the next new thing. Second, despite intense brand loyalty, many Japanese consumers crave novelty and go out of their way to hunt down limited-edition products made for specific seasons, regions, or reasons. Nestlé has been effective in using a limited-edition strategy to drive sales of seasonal treats like soy sauce–flavored Kit Kat chocolate bars. Similarly, the Japanese division of Mars has attracted customers by offering limited-edition M&M candies linked to the local release of major Hollywood movies.

When Pepsi and Suntory set out to tap this widespread interest in variety by marketing limited-edition soft drinks, they started with berry-flavored Pepsi Blue. In the United States, Pepsi Blue remained on the market for two years. In Japan, however, the entire production run of 1.7 million bot-

tles sold out within a few weeks. That experience led Pepsi and Suntory to plan the short-and-sweet life of Pepsi Red, Carnival, and other limited-edition soft drinks based on Pepsi drinks that are available in other countries.

Now the two companies were ready to plan for the development and introduction of a blockbuster limited-edition summer soft drink. After testing 60 possibilities, they chose a cucumber-melon flavor, created samples, and asked for feedback from focus-group participants. The positive reaction prompted Pepsi and Suntory to produce 4.8 million bottles of Ice Cucumber soft drink.

As with the previous limited-edition soft drinks, the entire production run sold out within a few weeks, fueled largely by word of mouth and YouTube clips showing fans gulping down bottle after bottle. But even though demand remained high, both scarcity and seasonality added to the appeal, which is why the partners decided not to produce more Ice Cucumber. "We didn't want it on the market past the summer," a Suntory marketer said at the time. "The value of Ice Cucumber is that it's gone already."

In contrast to the Japanese market, the U.S. market does not respond in the same way to unique flavors in beverages. For example, Jones Soda, a specialty soda brand, introduces limited-edition soda beverages like their annual holiday pack, which includes Turkey & Gravy, Wild Herb Stuffing, Pumpkin Pie, and Brussels Sprout flavors. The free publicity that Jones received from manufacturing these limited-edition flavored sodas was significant. The appeal is in the value as a collector's item, due to their novelty, rather than a beverage to guzzle down before the last one is purchased, as in the case of the Azuki-flavored Pepsi beverage introduced in Japan.

Given the competitive environment, the pressure from retailers to make new products perform, the speed with which consumer tastes change, and the cost of launching a new soft drink, Pepsi and Suntory are being careful not to overuse their limited-edition strategy. To make each new product stand out, they plan no more than four limited-edition introductions a year. If all goes according to plan, consumers will be primed for the introduction of the next new taste treat and will recognize that they have to buy quickly before that flavor disappears.[21]

QUESTIONS FOR DISCUSSION

1. Pepsi and Suntory cap their limited-edition soft drink introductions at four per year. What effect is this cap likely to have on the new-product development process?

2. How important is product quality when a limited-edition soft drink like Ice Cucumber sells out in a matter of weeks?

3. What criteria would you suggest that Pepsi and Suntory use when screening ideas for new limited-edition soft drinks

Chapter 13

Services Marketing

OBJECTIVES

1. To understand the growth and importance of services

2. To identify the characteristics of services that differentiate them from goods

3. To describe how the characteristics of services influence the development of marketing mixes for services

4. To understand the importance of service quality and explain how to deliver exceptional service quality

5. To explore the nature of nonprofit marketing

Tell Us What You Really Think!

What do customers *really* think of your services? Although reports by professional reviewers can be a major factor in choosing restaurants, hotels, and other services, consumers and business customers also seek personal recommendations from friends and colleagues. Now the whole world can read what everyday customers have to say about services—the compliments as well as the complaints—by checking popular review sites such as Angie's List, Yelp, and Zagat.

Zagat (www.zagat.com) is among the oldest and best-established reviewing services in the business. Founded in 1979, Zagat publishes yearly reviews and ratings of restaurants, hotels, resorts, movies, and retailers in 100 countries, based on input from 350,000 consumers worldwide. At first, the Zagat Survey was available in print only. Today, customers can check out reviews online, through GPS devices, via cell phone, and on Amazon.com's Kindle e-book reader.

Yelp (www.yelp.com) was founded in 2004 to help customers find good service providers. Now the website attracts 29 million visitors monthly to browse its 9 million consumer reviews of restaurants, beauty salons, stores, and other services. Yelp profits by selling online advertising space to firms that want to catch the eye of customers who visit the site to research their service purchases.

Angie's List (www.angieslist.com) is a members-only review site featuring more than 1 million comments about local services. No anonymous reviews are allowed, which enhances the site's credibility. And when customers write about a negative experience with a service, Angie's List invites the firm to add its own comments so members get both sides of the story.

As valuable as review sites are for customers seeking services, they also help marketers understand public perceptions of their services and identify areas for improvement. Julian Wright, who owns a restaurant in Tempe, Arizona, reads every Yelp comment about his business and says that "the reviews help us get better faster."[1]

The products offered by these organizations—namely, customer evaluations of service providers—are service products rather than tangible goods. This chapter explores concepts that apply specifically to products that are services. The organizations that market service products include for-profit firms, such as those offering financial, personal, and professional services, and nonprofit organizations, such as educational institutions, churches, charities, and governments.

We begin this chapter with a focus on the growing importance of service industries in our economy. We then address the unique characteristics of services. Next, we deal with the challenges these characteristics pose in developing and managing marketing mixes for services. We then discuss customers' judgment of service quality and the importance of delivering high-quality services. Finally, we define nonprofit marketing and examine the development of nonprofit marketing strategies.

The Growth and Importance of Services

All products, whether goods, services, or ideas, are intangible to some extent. We previously defined a service as an intangible product that involves a deed, a performance, or an effort that cannot be physically possessed.[2] Services are usually provided through the application of human and/or mechanical efforts that are directed at people or objects. For example, a service such as education involves the efforts of service providers (teachers) that are directed at people (students), whereas janitorial and interior decorating services direct their efforts at objects. Services can also involve the use of mechanical efforts directed at people (air transportation) or objects (freight transportation). A wide variety of services, such as health care and landscaping, involve both human and mechanical efforts. Although many services entail the use of tangibles such as tools and machinery, the primary difference between a service and a good is that a service is dominated by the intangible portion of the total product.

Services as products should not be confused with the related topic of customer services. Customer service involves any human, mechanical, or electronic activity that

The Importance of Services
The marketing of services can be challenging because services are intangible products, as opposed to goods, which are physical and tangible products.

© image100/Photolibrary

adds value to the product. Although the core product may be a good or electronic, complementary services help create the total product, and although customer service is a part of the marketing of goods, service marketers also provide customer services. For instance, many service companies offer guarantees to their customers in an effort to increase value. Hampton Inn, a national chain of mid-price hotels, gives its guests a free night if they are not 100 percent satisfied with their stay (less than one-half of 1 percent of Hampton customers ask for a refund). In some cases, a 100 percent satisfaction guarantee or similar service commitment may motivate employees to provide high-quality service, not because failure to do so leads to personal penalties but because they are proud to be part of an organization that is so committed to good service.

The increasing importance of services in the U.S. economy has led many people to call the United States the world's first service economy. In most developed countries, including Germany, Japan, Australia, and Canada, services account for about 70 percent of the gross domestic product (GDP). More than one-half of new businesses are service businesses, and service employment is expected to continue to grow. These industries have absorbed much of the influx of women and minorities into the workforce. In the United States, some customer-contact jobs, especially at call centers, have been outsourced—into the homes of U.S. workers, especially women. Several companies, including Carnival Cruise Lines, JetBlue, and Hilton Hotels, now use "homesourcing" to fill thousands of customer service jobs in U.S. homes that were once contracted to foreign countries.[3]

One major catalyst in the growth of consumer services has been long-term economic growth (slowed only by a few recessions) in the United States, which has led to increased interest in financial services, travel, entertainment, and personal care. Lifestyle changes have similarly encouraged expansion of the service sector. The need for child care, domestic services, online dating services, and other time-saving services has increased, and many consumers want to avoid such tasks as meal preparation, house cleaning, yard maintenance, and tax preparation. Consequently, franchise service operations such as Subway, Merry Maids, Jiffy Lube, ChemLawn, and H&R Block have experienced rapid growth. Also, because Americans have become more health, fitness, and recreation oriented, the demand for exercise and recreational facilities has escalated. In terms of demographics, the U.S. population is growing older, a fact that has spurred tremendous expansion of health-care services. Finally, the increasing number and complexity of high-tech goods have spurred demand for support services. Indeed, the services sector has been enhanced by dramatic changes in information technology. Consider service companies such as Google, eBay, and Amazon.com, which use technology to provide services to challenge and change traditional ways of conducting business.

Business services have prospered as well. Business services include support and maintenance, consulting, installation, equipment leasing, marketing research, advertising, temporary office personnel, and janitorial services. Expenditures for business services have risen even faster than expenditures for consumer services. The growth in business services has been attributed to the increasingly complex, specialized, and competitive business environment. IBM, for example, has shifted from a focus on computer hardware to consulting services and software applications. During the recent economic downturn when numerous service providers were struggling, the demand for online dating services surged. Match.com saw its best fourth quarter in seven years, the traffic to SpeedDate. com went up 60 percent, and the number of members on PerfectMatch.com saw a 30 percent increase in January.[4]

One way to view services is from a theater framework with production elements such as actors, audience, a setting, and a performance. The actors (service workers) create a performance (service) for the audience (customers) in a setting (service environment) where the performance unfolds. Costumes (uniforms), props (devices, music, machines), and the setting (face-to-face or indirect through telephone or Internet) help complete the theatrical metaphor.[5] At Disney World, for example, all employees wear costumes, there is an entertainment setting, and most service contact with employees involves playing roles and engaging in planned skits. But the theatrical components are also visible in a Subway fast-food restaurant or on an airline flight. In addition, a performance involves a "script," a chronologically ordered representation of the steps that comprise the service performance from the customer's perspective.[6] Even sports events such as football, basketball, and hockey have sequences of events and rules that standardize the performance, even if the outcome depends on the performance itself.

Characteristics of Services

The issues associated with marketing service products differ somewhat from those associated with marketing goods. To understand these differences, we need to look at the distinguishing characteristics of services. Services have six basic characteristics: intangibility, inseparability of production and consumption, perishability, heterogeneity, client-based relationships, and customer contact.[7]

Intangibility

As already noted, the major characteristic that distinguishes a service from a good is intangibility. **Intangibility** means a service is not physical and therefore cannot be perceived by the senses. For example, it is impossible to touch the education that students derive from attending classes; the intangible benefit is becoming more knowledgeable. In addition, services cannot be physically possessed. Students obviously cannot physically possess knowledge as they can an iPod or a car. There is a direct relationship between the level of intangibility and consumers' use of brands as a cue to the nature and quality of the service.[8]

Figure 13.1 depicts a tangibility continuum from pure goods (tangible) to pure services (intangible). Pure goods, if they exist at all, are rare because practically all marketers of goods also provide customer services. Even a tangible product such as sugar must be delivered to the store, priced, and placed on a shelf before a customer can purchase it. Intangible, service-dominant products such as education or health care are clearly service products. But what about products near the center of the continuum? Is a restaurant such as Chili's a goods marketer or a service marketer? Services like airline

intangibility The characteristic that a service is not physical and cannot be perceived by the senses

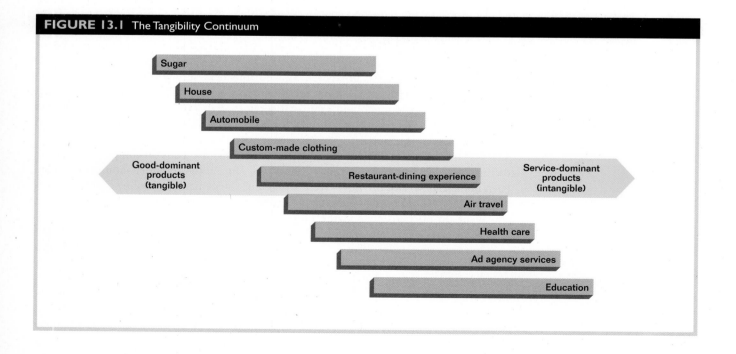

FIGURE 13.1 The Tangibility Continuum

Sugar

House

Automobile

Custom-made clothing

Good-dominant products (tangible)   Restaurant-dining experience   Service-dominant products (intangible)

Air travel

Health care

Ad agency services

Education

flights have something tangible to offer, such as seats and drinks. An Internet search engine such as Google or a news site such as CNN or MSNBC is service-dominant. Knowing where the product lies on the continuum is important in creating marketing strategies for service-dominant products.

Inseparability of Production and Consumption

Another important characteristic of services that creates challenges for marketers is **inseparability**, which refers to the fact that the production of a service cannot be separated from its consumption by customers. For instance, air passenger service is produced and consumed simultaneously—that is, services are often produced, sold, and consumed at the same time. In goods marketing, a customer can purchase a good, take it home, and store it until ready to use it. The manufacturer of the good may never see an actual customer. Customers, however, often must be present at the production of a service (such as investment consulting or surgery) and cannot take the service home. Indeed, both the service provider and the customer must work together to provide and receive the service's full value.[9] Because of inseparability, customers not only want a specific type of service but expect it to be provided in a specific way by a specific individual. For example, the production and consumption of a medical exam occur simultaneously, and the patient knows in advance who the physician is and generally understands how the exam will be conducted. Inseparability implies a shared responsibility between the customer and service provider. As a result, training programs for employees should stress the customer's role in the service experience to elevate their perceptions of shared responsibility and positive feelings.[10]

Perishability

Services are characterized by **perishability** in that the unused service capacity of one time period cannot be stored for future use. For instance, empty seats on an airline flight today cannot be stored and sold to passengers at a later date. Other examples of service perishability include unsold basketball tickets, unscheduled dentists'

inseparability The quality of being produced and consumed at the same time

perishability The inability of unused service capacity to be stored for future use

Inseparability Receiving a massage is characterized by inseparability. Production and consumption occur simultaneously.

© Phil Date/Shutterstock.com

appointment times, and empty hotel rooms. Although some goods, such as meat, milk, and produce, are perishable, goods generally are less perishable than services. If a pair of jeans has been sitting on a department store shelf for a week, someone can still buy them the next day. Goods marketers can handle the supply-demand problem through production scheduling and inventory techniques. Service marketers do not have the same advantage and face several hurdles in trying to balance supply and demand. They can, however, plan for demand that fluctuates according to day of the week, time of day, or season.

Heterogeneity

Services delivered by people are susceptible to **heterogeneity**, or variation in quality. Quality of manufactured goods is easier to control with standardized procedures, and mistakes are easier to isolate and correct. Because of the nature of human behavior, however, it is very difficult for service providers to maintain a consistent quality of service delivery. This variation in quality can occur from one organization to another, one service person to another within the same service facility, and one service facility to another within the same organization. For example, one bank may provide more convenient hours and charge fewer fees than the one next door, or the retail clerks in one bookstore may be more knowledgeable and therefore more helpful than those in another bookstore owned by the same chain. In addition, the service a single employee provides can vary from customer to customer, day to day, or even hour to hour. Although many service problems are one-time events that cannot be predicted or controlled ahead of time, training and establishment of standard procedures can help increase consistency and reliability. Because research suggests that service employees with greater sensitivity toward people of different countries and cultures are more attentive and have better interpersonal skills, job satisfaction, and social satisfaction, training that improves cultural sensitivity should improve consistency of service quality in cross-cultural environments.[11]

Heterogeneity usually increases as the degree of labor intensiveness increases. Many services, such as auto repair, education, and hairstyling, rely heavily on human labor. Other services, such as telecommunications, health clubs, grocery delivery, and public transportation, are more equipment intensive. People-based services are often prone to fluctuations in quality from one time period to the next. For instance, the fact that a hairstylist gives a customer a good haircut today does not guarantee that customer a haircut of equal quality from the same hairstylist at a later date or even a later hour. A morning customer may receive a better haircut than an end-of-the-day customer from the same stylist. Equipment-based services suffer from this problem to a lesser degree than people-based services. For instance, automated teller machines have reduced inconsistency in the quality of teller services at banks, and bar-code scanning has improved the accuracy of service at checkout counters in grocery stores.

Client-Based Relationships

The success of many services depends on creating and maintaining **client-based relationships:** interactions that result in satisfied customers who use a service repeatedly over time.[12] In fact, some service providers, such as lawyers, accountants, and financial advisers, call their customers *clients* and often develop and maintain close, long-term relationships with them. For such service providers, it is not enough to attract customers. They are successful only to the degree to which they can maintain a group of clients who use their services on an ongoing basis. For example, an accountant may serve a family in his or her area for decades. If the members of this family like the quality of the accountant's services, they are likely to recommend the accountant to other families. If several families repeat this positive word-of-mouth communication, the accountant will likely acquire a long list of satisfied clients before long. Social media have made it easier for customers to share information about

heterogeneity Variation in quality

client-based relationships Interactions that result in satisfied customers who use a service repeatedly over time

service companies. People may ask friends from online communities like Facebook or reference service rating sites like Angie's List and ServiceMagic. Indeed, researchers have found that word-of-mouth communication plays a key role in services, particularly for consumers with innovative personalities.[13] Word-of-mouth is a key factor in creating and maintaining client-based relationships. To ensure that it actually occurs, the service provider must take steps to build trust, demonstrate customer commitment, and satisfy customers so well that they become very loyal to the provider and unlikely to switch to competitors.

Customer Contact

Not all services require a high degree of customer contact, but many do. **Customer contact** refers to the level of interaction between the service provider and the customer necessary to deliver the service. High-contact services include health care, real estate, and legal and spa services. Examples of low-contact services are tax preparation, auto repair, travel reservations, and dry cleaning. Some service-oriented businesses are reducing their level of customer contact through technology. Note that high-contact services generally involve actions directed toward people, who must be present during production. A hairstylist's customer, for example, must be present during the styling process. Because the customer must be present, the process of production may be just as important as its final outcome. Although it is sometimes possible for the service provider to go to the customer, high-contact services typically require that the customer go to the production facility. Thus, the physical appearance of the facility may be a major component of the customer's overall evaluation of the service. Even in low-contact service situations, the appearance of the facility is important because the customer likely will need to be present to initiate and finalize the service transaction. Consider customers of auto-repair services. They bring in the vehicle and describe its symptoms, but often do not remain during the repair process.

Employees of high-contact service providers are a crucial ingredient in creating satisfied customers. A fundamental precept of customer contact is that satisfied employees

customer contact The level of interaction between provider and customer needed to deliver the service

Level of Customer Contact
There is a high level of customer contact associated with medical services.

lead to satisfied customers. In fact, employee satisfaction is the single most important factor in providing high-service quality. Thus, to minimize the problems customer contact can create, service organizations must take steps to understand and meet the needs of employees by adequately training them, empowering them to make more decisions, and rewarding them for customer-oriented behavior.[14] The giant electronics and appliance retailer, Best Buy, which is known for providing knowledgeable customer service with technology and consumer electronics, completely revamped its training program last year. The company has created a wiki site that allows employees to share information and provides employees with several learning mediums to choose from, which include paper-based, e-learning, audio training, and videos.[15]

Developing and Managing Marketing Mixes for Services

The characteristics of services discussed in the previous section create a number of challenges for service marketers (see Table 13.1). These challenges are especially evident in the development and management of marketing mixes for services. Although such mixes contain the four major marketing-mix variables—product, distribution, promotion, and price—the characteristics of services require that marketers consider additional issues.

Development of Services

A service offered by an organization generally is a package, or bundle, of services consisting of a core service and one or more supplementary services. A core service is the basic service experience or commodity that a customer expects to receive. A supplementary service is a supportive one related to the core service and is used

TABLE 13.1 Service Characteristics and Marketing Challenges

Service Characteristics	Resulting Marketing Challenges
Intangibility	Difficult for customer to evaluate. Customer does not take physical possession. Difficult to advertise and display. Difficult to set and justify prices. Service process is usually not protectable by patents.
Inseparability of production and consumption	Service provider cannot mass produce services. Customer must participate in production. Other consumers affect service outcomes. Services are difficult to distribute.
Perishability	Services cannot be stored. Balancing supply and demand is very difficult. Unused capacity is lost forever. Demand may be very time sensitive.
Heterogeneity	Service quality is difficult to control. Service delivery is difficult to standardize.
Client-based relationships	Success depends on satisfying and keeping customers over the long term. Generating repeat business is challenging. Relationship marketing becomes critical.
Customer contact	Service providers are critical to delivery. Requires high levels of service employee training and motivation. Changing a high-contact service into a low-contact service to achieve lower costs is difficult to achieve without reducing customer satisfaction.

Sources: K. Douglas Hoffman and John E. G. Bateson, *Services Marketing: Concepts, Strategies, and Cases,* 3rd ed. (Cincinnati: Thomson/South-Western, 2006); Valarie A. Zeithaml, A. Parasuraman, and Leonard L. Berry, *Delivering Quality Service: Balancing Customer Perceptions and Expectations* (New York: Free Press, 1990); Leonard L. Berry and A. Parasuraman, *Marketing Services: Competing through Quality* (New York: Free Press, 1991), p. 5.

to differentiate the service bundle from competitors'. For example, when a student attends a tutoring session for a class, the core service is the tutoring. Bundled with the core service might be access to outlines with additional information, handouts with practice questions, or online service like an email address or chat room for questions outside the designated tutoring time.

As discussed earlier, heterogeneity results in variability in service quality and makes it difficult to standardize service delivery. However, heterogeneity provides one advantage to service marketers: it allows them to customize their services to match the specific needs of individual customers. Customization plays a key role in providing competitive advantage for the service provider. Being able to personalize the service to fit the exact needs of the customer accommodates individual needs, wants, or desires.[16] Subway, for example, tries to let each customer participate in developing his or her own customized sandwich. IBM determines a business's needs and then develops information technology services to provide a customized application. Health care is an example of an extremely customized service; the services provided differ from one patient to the next.

Such customized services can be expensive for both provider and customer, and some service marketers therefore face a dilemma: how to provide service at an acceptable level of quality in an efficient and economic manner and still satisfy individual customer needs. To cope with this problem, some service marketers offer standardized packages. For instance, a spa may provide a number of treatments such as hair styling, facials, and massages for one price. When service bundles are standardized, the specific actions and activities of the service provider usually are highly specified. Automobile quick-lube providers frequently offer a service bundle for a single price; the specific work to be done on a customer's car is spelled out in detail. Various other equipment-based services are also often standardized into packages. For instance, cable television providers frequently offer several packages, such as "Basic," "Standard," and "Premier."

The characteristic of intangibility makes it difficult for customers to evaluate a service prior to purchase. A customer who is shopping for a pair of jeans can try them on before buying them, but how does she or he evaluate legal advice before receiving the service? Intangibility requires service marketers such as attorneys to market promises to customers. The customer is forced to place some degree of trust in the service provider to perform the service in a manner that meets or exceeds those promises. Service marketers must guard against making promises that raise customer expectations beyond what they can provide.

To cope with the problem of intangibility, marketers employ tangible cues, such as well-groomed, professional-appearing contact personnel and clean, attractive physical facilities, to help assure customers about the quality of the service. Most service providers uniform at least some of their high-contact employees. Uniforms help make the service experience more tangible and serve as physical evidence to signal quality, create consistency, and send cues to suggest a desired image.[17] Consider the professionalism, experience, and competence conveyed by an airline pilot's uniform. Life insurance companies sometimes try to make the quality of their policies more tangible by printing them on premium-quality paper and enclosing them in leather sheaths. Because customers often rely on brand names as an indicator of product quality, service marketers at organizations whose names are the same as their service brand names should strive to build a strong national image for their companies. For example, American Express, McDonald's, eBay, American Life, and America Online try to maintain strong, positive national company images because these names are the brand names of the services they provide.

The inseparability of production and consumption and the level of customer contact also influence the development and management of services. The fact that customers take part in the production of a service means other customers can affect the outcome of the service. For instance, if a nonsmoker dines in a restaurant without a no-smoking section, the overall quality of service experienced by the nonsmoking customer declines. For this reason, many restaurants have no-smoking sections, and some prohibit smoking anywhere on their premises. Service marketers can reduce these problems by encouraging customers to share the responsibility of maintaining an environment that allows all participants to receive the intended benefits of the service.

Distribution of Services

Marketers deliver services in a variety of ways. In some instances, customers go to a service provider's facility. For instance, most health-care, dry-cleaning, and spa services are delivered at the provider's facilities. Some services are provided at the customer's home or business. Lawn care, air conditioning and heating repair, and carpet cleaning are examples. Other services are delivered primarily at "arm's length," meaning no face-to-face contact occurs between the customer and the service provider. A number of equipment-based services are delivered at arm's length, including electric, online, cable television, and telephone services. Providing high-quality customer service at arm's length can be costly but essential in keeping customers satisfied and maintaining market share. For example, many airlines, although trying to cut costs, are also increasing spending on overhauling their websites to make them more user-friendly and thus serve customers better.

Marketing channels for services are usually short and direct, meaning the producer delivers the service directly to the end user. Some services, however, use intermediaries. For example, travel agents facilitate the delivery of airline services, independent insurance agents participate in the marketing of a variety of insurance policies, and financial planners market investment services.

Sustainable Marketing
Is That Meal Certifiably Green?

Sustainability is one of today's hottest trends in dining out. As service businesses, restaurants of all sizes can take action to protect the environment while also differentiating themselves and attracting the growing segment of eco-conscious customers. Serving organic foods and buying locally to avoid the pollution problems of transporting products over long distances are only two of the ways that restaurants across the country are going green.

Although many restaurants are making changes on their own, others are seeking ideas and certification from groups such as the Green Restaurant Association (GRA), which provides specific guidelines and sets standards for sustainability. GRA assesses a restaurant's operations in seven areas: waste reduction and recycling, use of energy, use of sustainable furnishings and building materials, water conservation, use of sustainable foods, use of disposable materials, and use of potentially polluting products.

For example, to achieve GRA certification, Boston's Taranta Restaurant replaced the wax candles on each table with solar-powered candles, switched to biodegradable packaging for take-home meals, and converted its delivery truck to run on used cooking oil. Rathbun's Blue Plate Kitchen in Dallas not only cooks with organic foods, it has also installed solar panels to generate some of its electricity and redecorated with eco-friendly fabrics and carpeting.

The Thrive Café in Savannah, Georgia, composts scraps, recycles egg and produce crates, recycles rain water, and uses environmentally safe cleaning products. Communicating its green

certification complements the café's marketing, as the owner explains, "It says something to customers that we've made this commitment."[a]

Distribution of Services

Services can be distributed through physical facilities, such as FedEx Kinko's, or online, through sites like Travelocity.

Service marketers are less concerned with warehousing and transportation than are goods marketers. They are, however, very concerned about inventory management, especially balancing supply and demand for services. The service characteristics of inseparability and level of customer contact contribute to the challenges of demand management. In some instances, service marketers use appointments and reservations as approaches for scheduling delivery of services. Health-care providers, attorneys, accountants, auto mechanics, and restaurants often use appointments or reservations to plan and pace delivery of their services. DayJet, a new air-taxi service for businesspeople, uses sophisticated computer systems, software, and mathematical algorithms to develop efficient routes and schedules for its custom flights, which carry a maximum of three passengers.[18] To increase the supply of a service, marketers use multiple service sites and also increase the number of contact service providers at each site. National and regional eye-care and hair-care services are examples.

To make delivery more accessible to customers and increase the supply of a service, as well as reduce labor costs, some service providers have replaced some contact personnel with equipment. In other words, they have changed a high-contact service into a low-contact one. The banking industry is an example. By installing ATMs, banks have increased production capacity and reduced customer contact. In addition, a number of automated banking services are now available by telephone 24 hours a day. ATMs and online banking have helped lower costs by reducing the need for customer service representatives. Changing the delivery of services from man-powered to automated has created some problems, however. Some customers complain that automated services are less personal. When designing service delivery, marketers must pay attention to the degree of personalization customers desire.

Promotion of Services

The intangibility of services results in several promotion-related challenges to service marketers. Because it may not be possible to depict the actual performance of a service in an advertisement or display it in a store, explaining a service to customers can be a difficult task. Promotion of services typically includes tangible cues that symbolize the service. Consider Trans America, which uses its pyramid-shaped building to symbolize strength, security, and reliability. These are important features associated with insurance and other financial services. Similarly, the cupped hands Allstate uses in its ads symbolize personalized service and trustworthy, caring representatives. Although these symbols have nothing to do with the actual services, they make it much easier for customers to understand the intangible attributes associated with insurance services. To make a service more tangible, advertisements for services often show pictures of facilities, equipment, and service personnel. Marketers may also promote their services as a tangible expression of consumers' lifestyles. Ameriprise, for example, featured *Easy Rider* actor Dennis Hopper in commercials for retirement financial services targeted at baby boomers nearing retirement age. The company chose Hopper for his "great antihero hero image" to provide an emotional appeal for baby boomers who may not desire a conventional retirement on the golf course.[19]

Compared with goods marketers, service providers are more likely to promote price, guarantees, performance documentation, availability, and training and certification of contact personnel. For example, it is common to promote degrees and certifications earned by trainers as a way to ensure customers that the trainers will help them reach their fitness goals.[20] When preparing advertisements, service marketers are careful to use concrete, specific language to help make services more tangible in customers' minds. Bear Stearns, for example, advertises that it was voted "America's most admired securities company." Service companies are also careful not to promise too much regarding their services so that customer expectations do not rise to unattainable levels.

Through their actions, service contact personnel can be directly or indirectly involved in the personal selling of services. Personal selling is often important because personal influence can help the customer visualize the benefits of a given service. Because service contact personnel may engage in personal selling, some companies invest heavily in training. Best Buy, for example, spends 5 percent of its payroll on employee training. On a salesperson's first day on the job, he or she gets a four-hour classroom session that covers topics like how to fit into the company's sales force and the basics for providing customer satisfaction.[21]

As noted earlier, intangibility makes experiencing a service prior to purchase difficult, if not impossible in some cases. A car can be test-driven, a snack food can be sampled in a supermarket, and a new brand of bar soap can be mailed to customers as a free sample. Some services also can be offered on a trial basis at little or no risk to the customer, but a number of services cannot be sampled before purchase. Promotional programs that encourage trial use of insurance, health care, or auto repair are difficult to design because, even after purchase of such services, assessing their quality may require a considerable length of time. For instance, an individual may purchase auto insurance from the same provider for 10 years before filing a claim, but the quality of the coverage is based primarily on how the customer is treated and protected when a claim is made.

Because of the heterogeneity and intangibility of services, word-of-mouth communication is particularly important in service promotion. What other people say about a service provider can have a tremendous impact on whether an individual decides to use that provider. Some service marketers attempt to stimulate

Entrepreneurial Marketing
What a Circus!

When Guy Laliberté founded Cirque du Soleil in 1984, his goal was to reinvent the circus. Starting with a handful of street performers, today he employs thousands of performers, choreographers, artists, trainers, and planners who concurrently stage 19 distinctly different shows each year. Cirque's scouts travel the world searching for talent to fill the roles for each show. Cast members receive months of training to fine-tune every aspect of their performance before taking the stage.

Meanwhile, Cirque's marketing experts consider the image they want to project as they plan their marketing mix, including print ads and merchandise. These tangible elements help convey Cirque's innovative approach to the circus concept and hint at the memorable experiences that await audience members at every performance.[b]

positive word-of-mouth communication by asking satisfied customers to tell their friends and associates about the service and may even provide incentives to the current or new customers. Banfield, The Pet Hospital, has locations inside several PetSmart stores and places referral certificates inside every patient room. These certificates allow first-time clients to receive a free office visit and physical exam for their pet.[22]

Pricing of Services

Services should be priced with consumer price sensitivity, the nature of the transaction, and its costs in mind.[23] Prices for services can be established on several different bases. The prices of pest control services, dry cleaning, carpet cleaning, and health consultations are usually based on the performance of specific tasks. Other service prices are based on time. For example, attorneys, consultants, counselors, piano teachers, and plumbers often charge by the hour or day.

Some services use demand-based pricing. When demand for a service is high, the price is also high; when demand for a service is low, so is the price. The perishability of services means that when demand is low, the unused capacity cannot be stored and therefore is lost forever. Every empty seat on an airline flight or in a movie theater represents lost revenue. Some services are very time sensitive in that a significant number of customers desire the service at a particular time. This point in time is called *peak demand*. A provider of time-sensitive services brings in most of its revenue during peak demand. For an airline, peak demand is usually early and late in the day; for cruise lines, peak demand occurs in the winter for Caribbean cruises and in the summer for Alaskan cruises. Customers can receive better deals on services by purchasing during nonpeak times. The new travel search by Microsoft's Bing allows travelers looking to book a flight to view the cheapest dates to fly to their destination. This service allows travelers with flexibility in scheduling to save money on their flight.[24] Providers of time-sensitive services often use demand-based pricing to manage the problem of balancing supply and demand. They charge top prices during peak demand and lower prices during off-peak demand to encourage more customers to use the service. This is why the price of a matinee movie is often half the price of the same movie shown at night. Major airlines maintain sophisticated databases to help them adjust ticket prices to fill as many seats as possible on every flight. On a single day, each airline makes thousands of fare changes to maximize the use of its seating capacity and thus maximize its revenues. To accomplish this objective, many airlines have to overbook flights and discount fares. However, research suggests that overbooking as a revenue management tool can cause dissatisfied customers to take their business elsewhere in the future, and customers who are "bumped up" or upgraded as a result of the overbooking may not exhibit particularly positive responses to the upgrade.[25]

When services are offered to customers in a bundle, marketers must decide whether to offer the services at one price, price them separately, or use a combination of the two methods. For instance, some hotels offer a package of services at one price, whereas others charge separately for the room, phone service, breakfast, and even in-room safes. Some service providers offer a one-price option for a specific bundle of services and make add-on bundles available at additional charges. For example, a number of cable television companies offer a standard package of channels for one price and offer add-on channel packages for additional charges. Telephone services, such as call waiting and caller ID, are frequently bundled and sold as a package for one price.

Because of the intangible nature of services, customers sometimes rely heavily on price as an indicator of quality. If customers perceive the available services in a service category as being similar in quality, and if the quality of such services is difficult to judge even after these services are purchased, customers may seek out the lowest-priced provider. For example, many customers seek auto insurance providers with the lowest rates. If the quality of different service providers is likely to vary, customers may rely heavily on the price-quality association. For instance, if you have to have an appendectomy, will

Bundled or A La Carte Pricing: Would You Fly on Airlines That Charge for Restroom Use?

78% No

19% Yes, if cheap

3% Yes, regardless

Source: TripAdvisor.com survey of 5,357 travelers.

you choose the surgeon who charges an average price of $1,500 or the surgeon who will take your appendix out for $399?

For certain types of services, market conditions may limit how much can be charged for a specific service, especially if the services in this category are perceived as generic in nature. For example, the prices charged by a self-serve laundromat are likely to be limited by the going price for laundromat services in a given community. Also, state and local government regulations may reduce price flexibility. Such regulations may substantially control the prices charged for auto insurance, utilities, cable television service, and even housing rentals.

Service Quality

Delivery of high-quality services is one of the most important and difficult tasks any service organization faces. Because of their characteristics, services are very difficult to evaluate. Hence customers must look closely at service quality when comparing services. **Service quality** is defined as customers' perceptions of how well a service meets or exceeds their expectations.[26] A survey by Customer Care Alliance and Arizona State University found that 70 percent of consumers that responded had experienced "customer rage," indicating they were "extremely" or "very" upset about a negative service experience. More than 33 percent indicated they had raised their voices, and 3 percent admitted to using profanity when interacting with customer service representatives. Although 75 percent of respondents wanted an explanation of why the problem occurred, only 18 percent got an explanation, and only 25 percent heard "I'm sorry" from a customer service representative.[27] Note that customers, not the organization, evaluate service quality. This distinction is critical because it forces service marketers to examine quality from the customer's viewpoint. Thus, it is important for service organizations to determine what customers expect and then develop service products that meet or exceed those expectations. Research has identified a direct relationship among consumers' personality orientation, their emotional characteristics, and their self-reported satisfaction with the service experience.[28]

Customer Evaluation of Service Quality

service quality Customers' perceptions of how well a service meets or exceeds their expectations

search qualities Tangible attributes that can be judged before the purchase of a product

experience qualities Attributes that can be assessed only during purchase and consumption of a service

credence qualities Attributes that customers may be unable to evaluate even after purchasing and consuming a service

The biggest obstacle for customers in evaluating service quality is the intangible nature of the service. How can customers evaluate something they cannot see, feel, taste, smell, or hear? Evaluation of a good is much easier because all goods possess **search qualities**, tangible attributes such as color, style, size, feel, or fit that can be evaluated prior to purchase. Trying on a new coat and taking a car for a test drive are examples of how customers evaluate search qualities. Services, on the other hand, have very few search qualities; instead, they abound in experience and credence qualities. **Experience qualities** are attributes, such as taste, satisfaction, or pleasure, that can be assessed only during the purchase and consumption of a service.[29] Restaurants and vacations are examples of services high in experience qualities. **Credence qualities** are attributes that customers may be unable to evaluate even after the purchase and consumption of the service. Examples of services high in credence qualities are surgical operations, automobile repairs, and legal representation. Most consumers lack the knowledge or skills to evaluate the quality of these types of services. Consequently they must place a great deal of faith in the integrity and competence of the service provider. In hopes of

Quality of Service
This ad communicates about the quality of service provided by Jax Desmond Worldwide, provider of protection services for executives.

having more control over their legal fate, as well as being able to better evaluate their legal services, many customers are turning to Lawyers.com. On this site, visitors can find easy to understand information about several areas of law, discussion forums for a variety of legal topics, videos, and more.[30]

Despite the difficulties in evaluating quality, service quality may be the only way customers can choose one service over another. For this reason, service marketers live or die by understanding how consumers judge service quality. Table 13.2 defines five dimensions consumers use when evaluating service quality: tangibles, reliability, responsiveness, assurance, and empathy. Note that all of these dimensions have links to employee performance. Of the five, reliability is the most important in determining customer evaluations of service quality.[31]

Service marketers pay a great deal of attention to the tangibles of service quality. For example, at FreshDirect, an online grocery delivery service in the New York City area, every grocery item is scanned at least three times before it is loaded into a truck for delivery to reduce the potential for mistakes.[32] Tangible elements, such as the appearance of facilities and employees, are often the only aspects of a service that can be viewed before purchase and consumption. Therefore, service marketers must ensure that these tangible elements are consistent with the overall image of the service.

Except for the tangibles dimension, the criteria customers use to judge service quality are intangible. For

TABLE 13.2 Dimensions of Service Quality

Dimension	Evaluation Criteria	Examples
Tangibles: Physical evidence of the service	Appearance of physical facilities Appearance of service personnel Tools or equipment used to provide the service	A clean and professional-looking doctor's office A clean and neatly attired repairperson The freshness of food in a restaurant The equipment used in a medical exam
Reliability: Consistency and dependability in performing the service	Accuracy of billing or recordkeeping Performing services when promised	An accurate bank statement A confirmed hotel reservation An airline flight departing and arriving on time
Responsiveness: Willingness or readiness of employees to provide the service	Returning customer phone calls Providing prompt service Handling urgent requests	A server refilling a customer's cup of tea without being asked An ambulance arriving within three minutes
Assurance: Knowledge/competence of employees and ability to convey trust and confidence	Knowledge and skills of employees Company name and reputation Personal characteristics of employees	A highly trained financial adviser A known and respected service provider A doctor's bedside manner
Empathy: Caring and individual attention provided by employees	Listening to customer needs Caring about customers' interests Providing personalized attention	A store employee listening to and trying to understand a customer's complaint A nurse counseling a heart patient

Sources: Adapted from Leonard L. Berry and A. Parasuraman, *Marketing Services: Competing through Quality* (New York: Free Press, 1991); Valarie A. Zeithaml, A. Parasuraman, and Leonard L. Berry, *Delivering Quality Service: Balancing Customer Perceptions and Expectations* (New York: Free Press, 1990); A. Parasuraman, Leonard L. Berry, and Valarie A. Zeithaml, "An Empirical Examination of Relationships in an Extended Service Quality Model," *Marketing Science Institute Working Paper Series*, Report no. 90–112 (Cambridge, MA: Marketing Science Institute, 1990), p. 29.

instance, how does a customer judge reliability? Because dimensions such as reliability cannot be examined with the senses, customers must rely on other ways of judging service. One of the most important factors in customer judgments of service quality is service expectations. Service expectations are influenced by past experiences with the service, word-of-mouth communication from other customers, and the service company's own advertising. For instance, customers are usually eager to try a new restaurant, especially when friends recommend it. These same customers may have also seen advertisements placed by the restaurant. As a result, they have an idea of what to expect when they visit the restaurant for the first time. When they finally dine there, the quality they experience will change the expectations they have for their next visit. That is why providing consistently high service quality is important. If the quality of a restaurant, or of any service, begins to deteriorate, customers will alter their own expectations and change their word-of-mouth communication to others accordingly.

Delivering Exceptional Service Quality

Providing high-quality service on a consistent basis is very difficult. All consumers have experienced examples of poor service: late flight departures and arrivals, inattentive restaurant servers, rude bank employees, long lines. Obviously it is impossible for a service organization to ensure exceptional service quality 100 percent of the time. However, an organization can take many steps to increase the likelihood of providing high-quality service. First, though, the service company must consider the four factors that affect service quality: (1) analysis of customer expectations, (2) service quality specifications, (3) employee performance, and (4) management of service expectations (see Figure 13.2).[33]

ANALYSIS OF CUSTOMER EXPECTATIONS

Providers need to understand customer expectations when designing a service to meet or exceed those expectations. Only then can they deliver good service. Customers usually have two levels of expectations: desired and acceptable. The desired level of expectations is what the customer really wants. If this level of expectations is provided, the customer will be very satisfied. The acceptable level of expectations is what the customer views as adequate. The difference between these two levels of expectations is called the customer's *zone of tolerance*.[34]

FIGURE 13.2 Service Quality Model

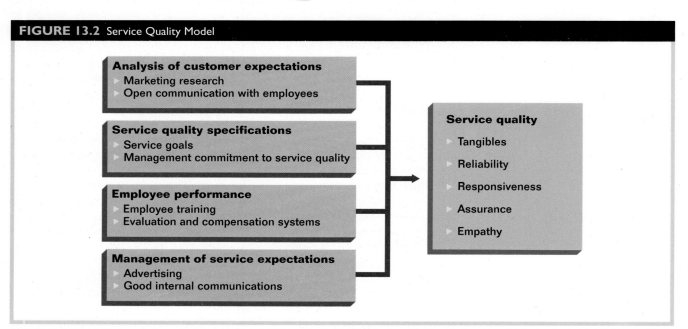

Source: Adapted from A. Parasuraman, Leonard L. Berry, and Valarie A. Zeithaml, "An Empirical Examination of Relationships in an Extended Service Quality Model," *Marketing Science Institute Working Paper Series*, Report no. 90–112, 1990. Reprinted by permission of Marketing Science Institute, and the authors.

Service companies sometimes use marketing research, such as surveys and focus groups, to discover customer needs and expectations. For instance, the All England Lawn Tennis and Croquet Club faces many challenges in hosting the annual Wimbledon Lawn Tennis Championships every year. The club surveys attendees during the event, and executives examine the data immediately after each year's event to identify areas that require improvement. Those areas then become a planning focus for the next year's event. The feedback and painstaking planning help the club maintain Wimbledon's reputation as a genteel sporting event.[35] Other service marketers, especially restaurants, use comment cards on which customers can complain or provide suggestions. Still another approach is to ask employees. Because customer contact employees interact daily with customers, they are in good positions to know what customers want from the company. Service managers should regularly interact with their employees by asking their opinions on the best way to serve customers.

SERVICE QUALITY SPECIFICATIONS

Once an organization understands its customers' needs, it must establish goals to help ensure good service delivery. These goals, or service specifications, are typically set in terms of employee or machine performance. For example, a bank may require its employees to conform to a dress code. Likewise, the bank may require that all incoming phone calls be answered by the third ring. Specifications such as these can be very important in providing quality service as long as they are tied to the needs expressed by customers.

Perhaps the most critical aspect of service quality specifications is managers' commitment to service quality. Service managers who are committed to quality become role models for all employees in the organization. Such commitment motivates customer contact employees to comply with service specifications. It is crucial that all managers within the organization embrace this commitment, especially frontline managers, who are much closer to customers than higher-level managers.

EMPLOYEE PERFORMANCE

Once an organization sets service quality standards and managers are committed to them, the firm must find ways to ensure that customer contact employees perform their jobs well. Contact employees in most service industries (bank tellers, flight attendants, servers, sales clerks, etc.) are often the least-trained and lowest-paid members of the organization. Service organizations must realize that contact employees are the most important link to the customer, and thus their performance is critical to customer perceptions of service quality. The way to ensure that employees perform well is to train them effectively so they understand how to do their jobs. Providing information about customers, service specifications, and the organization itself during the training promotes this understanding.

The evaluation and compensation system the organization uses also plays a part in employee performance. Many service employees are evaluated and rewarded on the basis of output measures, such as sales volume (automobile salespeople) or a low error rate (bank tellers). But systems using output measures overlook other major aspects of job performance, including friendliness, teamwork, effort, and customer satisfaction. These customer-oriented measures of performance may be a better basis for evaluation and reward. In fact, a number of service marketers use customer satisfaction ratings to determine a portion of service employee compensation.

MANAGEMENT OF SERVICE EXPECTATIONS

Because expectations are so significant in customer evaluations of service quality, service companies recognize they must set realistic expectations about the service they can provide. They can set these expectations through advertising and good internal communication. In their advertisements, service companies make promises about the

Responsible Marketing?
Cell Phone Companies' Customer Service Temporarily Out of Order

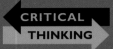

CRITICAL THINKING

ISSUE: Does the quality of customer service affect consumer trust and selection of cell phone service providers?

The Better Business Bureau (BBB) recently commissioned a survey that focuses on consumer trust of businesses. Cell phone companies ranked as one of the least-trusted industries in the United States. The survey results showed that 26 percent of consumers said that customer service is a core component of trust in companies. On the other side of the coin, 30 percent of consumers said that high charges and fees, like those used by cellular phone service providers, are the largest factors in creating distrust in companies.

It's no secret that many cell phone companies don't always make their customers happy. In 2005 and 2006, cellular telephone companies ranked highest in the total number of complaints received by the Better Business Bureau. Steven Cole, president and CEO of the BBB, stated, "Earning consumers' trust isn't simply the result of good ethics or even low prices.... If they don't provide quality customer service and deliver on promises, they won't be trusted." Interestingly, the number of cell phone users continues to rise. Do the cell phone service providers' long-term contracts (12 to 24 months) lead to inferior customer service? Does the lack of service translate into a general distrust in cell phone service companies?[c]

kind of service they will deliver. As already noted, a service company is forced to make promises because the intangibility of services prevents the organization from showing the benefits in the advertisement. However, the advertiser should not promise more than it can deliver. Doing so will likely mean disappointed customers.

To deliver on promises made, a company needs to have thorough internal communication among its departments, especially management, advertising, and store operations. Assume, for example, that a restaurant's radio advertisements guarantee service within five minutes, or the meal is free. If top management or the advertising department fails to inform store operations about the five-minute guarantee, the restaurant will very likely fail to meet its customers' service expectations. Even though customers might appreciate a free meal, the restaurant will lose some credibility as well as revenue.

As mentioned earlier, word-of-mouth communication from other customers also shapes customer expectations. However, service companies cannot manage this "advertising" directly. The best way to ensure positive word-of-mouth communication is to provide exceptional service quality. It has been estimated that customers tell four times as many people about bad service as they do about good service.

Nonprofit Marketing

nonprofit marketing
Marketing activities conducted to achieve some goal other than ordinary business goals such as profit, market share, or return on investment

Nonprofit marketing refers to marketing activities that are conducted by individuals and organizations to achieve some goal other than ordinary business goals such as profit, market share, or return on investment. Nonprofit marketing is divided into two categories: nonprofit-organization marketing and social marketing. Nonprofit-organization marketing is the use of marketing concepts and techniques by organizations whose goals do not include making profits. Social marketing promotes social causes, such as AIDS research and recycling.

Most of the previously discussed concepts and approaches to service products also apply to nonprofit organizations. Indeed, many nonprofit organizations provide mainly service products. In this section, we examine the concept of nonprofit marketing to determine how it differs from marketing activities in for-profit business organizations. We also explore the marketing objectives of nonprofit organizations and the development of their product strategies.

How Is Nonprofit Marketing Different?

Many nonprofit organizations strive for effective marketing activities. Charitable organizations and supporters of social causes are major nonprofit marketers in this country. Political parties, unions, religious sects, and fraternal organizations also perform marketing activities, but they are not considered businesses. Whereas the chief beneficiary of a business enterprise is whoever owns or holds stock in it, in theory the only beneficiaries of a nonprofit organization are its clients, its members, or the public at large. The American Museum of Natural History, for example, is a nonprofit service organization.

Nonprofit organizations have greater opportunities for creativity than most for-profit business organizations, but trustees or board members of nonprofit organizations are likely to have difficulty judging the performance of the trained professionals they oversee. It is harder for administrators to evaluate the performance of professors or social workers than it is for sales managers to evaluate the performance of salespeople in a for-profit organization.

Another way nonprofit marketing differs from for-profit marketing is that nonprofit marketing is sometimes quite controversial. Nonprofit organizations such as Greenpeace, the National Rifle Association, and the National Organization for Women spend lavishly on lobbying efforts to persuade Congress, the White House, and even the courts to support their interests, in part because not all of society agrees with their aims. However, marketing as a field of study does not attempt to state what an organization's goals should be or to debate the issue of nonprofit versus for-profit business goals. Marketing tries only to provide a body of knowledge and concepts to help further an organization's goals. Individuals must decide whether they approve or disapprove of a particular organization's goal orientation. Most marketers would agree that profit and consumer satisfaction are appropriate goals for business enterprises but would probably disagree considerably about the goals of a controversial nonprofit organization.

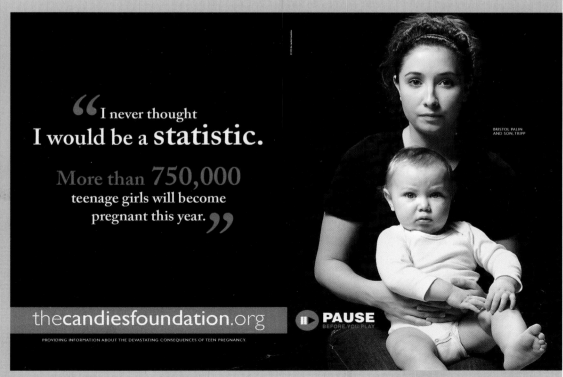

Marketing in Nonprofit Organizations Some nonprofit marketers use advertising to explain their objectives and to seek support.

Nonprofit Marketing Objectives

The basic aim of nonprofit organizations is to obtain a desired response from a target market. The response could be a change in values, a financial contribution, the donation of services, or some other type of exchange. For example, the primary objective of the nonprofit organization Declare Yourself is to register 300,000 18- to 25-year-olds to vote in the next presidential election. To help achieve its goal, the organization is using a website, celebrities who appeal to young people, mobile and Internet technologies, and viral videos.[36] Nonprofit marketing objectives are shaped by the nature of the exchange and the goals of the organization. These objectives should state the rationale for the organization's existence. An organization that defines its marketing objective as providing a product can be left without a purpose if the product becomes obsolete. However, servicing and adapting to the perceived needs and wants of a target public, or market, enhances an organization's chance to survive and achieve its goals.

Developing Nonprofit Marketing Strategies

Nonprofit organizations develop marketing strategies by defining and analyzing a target market and creating and maintaining a total marketing mix that appeals to that market.

TARGET MARKETS

We must revise the concept of target markets slightly to apply it to nonprofit organizations. Whereas a business seeks out target groups that are potential purchasers of its product, a nonprofit organization may attempt to serve many diverse groups. For our purposes, a **target public** is a collective of individuals who have an interest in or a concern about an organization, a product, or a social cause. The terms *target market* and *target public* are difficult to distinguish from many nonproduct or social cause profit organizations. The target public of the Partnership for a Drug Free America consists of parents, adults, and concerned teenagers. However, the target market for the organization's advertisements consists of potential and current drug users. When an organization is concerned about changing values or obtaining a response from the public, it views the public as a market.[37]

In nonprofit marketing, direct consumers of the product are called **client publics** and indirect consumers are called **general publics**.[38] For example, the client public for a university is its student body, and its general public includes parents, alumni, and trustees. The client public usually receives most of the attention when an organization develops a marketing strategy.

DEVELOPING MARKETING MIXES

A marketing-mix strategy limits alternatives and directs marketing activities toward achieving organizational goals. The strategy should include a blueprint for making decisions about product, distribution, promotion, and price. These decision variables should be blended to serve the target market.

In developing the product, nonprofit organizations usually deal with ideas and services. Problems may evolve when an organization fails to define what it is providing. What product, for example, does the Peace Corps provide? Its services include vocational training, health services, nutritional assistance, and community development. It also markets the ideas of international cooperation and the implementation of U.S. foreign policy. The product of the Peace Corps is more difficult to define than the average business product. As indicated in the first part of this chapter, services are intangible and therefore need special marketing efforts. The marketing of ideas and concepts is likewise more abstract than the marketing of tangibles, and much effort is required to present benefits.

Distribution decisions in nonprofit organizations relate to how ideas and services will be made available to clients. If the product is an idea, selecting the right media to communicate the idea will facilitate distribution. By nature, services consist of assistance,

target public A collective of individuals who have an interest in or concern about an organization, product, or social cause

client publics Direct consumers of a product of a nonprofit organization

general publics Indirect consumers of a product of a nonprofit organization

Marketing in Transition
Nonprofits Find It Pays to Have Online Fans and Followers

Tweeting for charity? Yes, many charities and nonprofit groups now use social media such as Twitter, Facebook, YouTube, and Flickr to keep their target audiences informed about activities and, just as important, to encourage donations. Habitat for Humanity has more than 40,000 Facebook fans and 6,000 Twitter followers, as well as designated pages on YouTube and Flickr for sharing user-generated videos and photos. The Boy Scouts of America has 5,600 Twitter followers and 57,000 Facebook fans, plus its own channel on YouTube.

By one estimate, nonprofit marketers that harness the power of social media can improve their fundraising performance by as much as 40 percent. Project Medishare, a nonprofit that has been helping to improve medical services in Haiti since 1994, recently began using Facebook and Twitter to stay in touch with donors. After incorporating social media into its year-end fundraising campaign, the nonprofit saw its audience response triple, which translated into thousands of additional dollars in donations.

Social media are also important marketing tools for influencing attitudes about, and behavior toward, social causes. The New

Hampshire Society for the Prevention of Cruelty to Animals maintains two Facebook pages to promote pet adoption, for example, as well as to generate donations. Not only is Facebook more cost-effective than printing and mailing a newsletter, it provides more timely updates for the target audience and reinforces other marketing-mix activities.[d]

convenience, and availability. Availability is thus part of the total service. Making a product like health services available calls for knowledge of such retailing concepts as site location analysis.

Developing a channel of distribution to coordinate and facilitate the flow of nonprofit products to clients is a necessary task, but in a nonprofit setting, the traditional concept of the marketing channel may need to be revised. The independent wholesalers available to a business enterprise do not exist in most nonprofit situations. Instead, a very short channel—nonprofit organization to client—is the norm because production and consumption of ideas and services are often simultaneous.

Making promotional decisions may be the first sign that a nonprofit organization is performing marketing activities. Nonprofit organizations use advertising and publicity to communicate with clients and the public. The March of Dimes, for example, launched a promotional campaign using television, radio, and print advertising in the form of public-service announcements to raise awareness of its public health programs for expectant mothers.[39] Direct mail remains the primary means of fundraising for social services, such as those provided by the Red Cross and Special Olympics. However, last year, about 30 percent of these types of organizations reported that they reduced use of direct mail.[40] Environmentally focused organizations face a unique challenge in promotional materials: how to communicate using environmentally friendly products such as recycled paper and environmentally sensitive inks. The Nature Conservancy, for example, uses paper products that have been certified by the Forest Stewardship Council as having come from well-managed forests.[41] Increasingly, nonprofits are using the Internet to reach fundraising and promotional goals through e-mail, websites, and software that permits accepting online gifts. In fact, 73 percent of nonprofits plan to increase the use of e-mail marketing and 70 percent plan to increase the use of social media this year. These increases come as many organizations start to limit the use of print advertisements and direct mail.[42] A new medium nonprofits are using to raise money quickly is mobile marketing. After the recent earthquake in Haiti, the Red Cross encouraged citizens to donate money to the fund by simply sending a text message.[43]

Many nonprofit organizations also use personal selling, although they may call it by another name. Churches and charities rely on personal selling when they send volunteers to recruit new members or request donations. The U.S. Army uses personal selling when its recruiting officers attempt to persuade men and women to enlist. Special events to obtain funds, communicate ideas, or provide services are also effective promotional activities. Amnesty International, for example, has held worldwide concert tours featuring well-known musical artists to raise funds and increase public awareness of political prisoners around the world.

Although product and promotional techniques may require only slight modification when applied to nonprofit organizations, pricing is generally quite different, and decision making is more complex. The different pricing concepts the nonprofit organization faces include pricing in user and donor markets. Two types of monetary pricing exist: *fixed* and *variable*. There may be a fixed fee for users, or the price may vary depending on the user's ability to pay. When a donation-seeking organization will accept a contribution of any size, it is using variable pricing.

The broadest definition of price (valuation) must be used to develop nonprofit marketing strategies. Financial price, an exact dollar value, may or may not be charged for a nonprofit product. Economists recognize the giving up of alternatives as a cost. **Opportunity cost** is the value of the benefit given up by selecting one alternative over another. According to this traditional economic view of price, if a nonprofit organization persuades someone to donate time to a cause or to change his or her behavior, the alternatives given up are a cost to (or a price paid by) the individual. Volunteers who answer phones for a university counseling service or a suicide hotline, for example, give up the time they could spend studying or doing other things as well as the income they might earn from working at a for-profit business organization.

For other nonprofit organizations, financial price is an important part of the marketing mix. Nonprofit organizations today are raising money by increasing the prices of their services or are starting to charge for services if they have not done so before. They are using marketing research to determine what kinds of products people will pay for. Pricing strategies of nonprofit organizations often stress public and client welfare over equalization of costs and revenues. If additional funds are needed to cover costs, the organization may solicit donations, contributions, or grants.

opportunity cost The value of the benefit given up by choosing one alternative over another

summary

1. To understand the growth and importance of services

Services are intangible products that involve deeds, performances, or efforts that cannot be physically possessed. They are the result of applying human or mechanical efforts to people or objects. Services are a growing part of the U.S. economy. They have six fundamental characteristics: intangibility, inseparability of production and consumption, perishability, heterogeneity, client-based relationships, and customer contact.

2. To identify the characteristics of services that differentiate them from goods

Intangibility means that a service cannot be seen, touched, tasted, or smelled. Inseparability refers to the fact that the production of a service cannot be separated from its consumption by customers. Perishability means unused service capacity of one time period cannot be stored for future use. Heterogeneity is variation in service quality. Client-based relationships are interactions with customers that lead to the repeated use of a service over time.

Customer contact is the interaction between providers and customers needed to deliver a service.

3. To describe how the characteristics of services influence the development of marketing mixes for services

Core services are the basic service experiences customers expect; supplementary services are those that relate to and support core services. Because of the characteristics of services, service marketers face several challenges in developing and managing marketing mixes. To address the problem of intangibility, marketers use cues that help assure customers about the quality of their services. The development and management of service products are also influenced by the service characteristics of inseparability and level of customer contact. Some services require that customers come to the service provider's facility; others are delivered with no face-to-face contact. Marketing channels for services are usually short and direct, but some services employ intermediaries. Service marketers are less concerned with warehousing and transportation than are goods marketers, but inventory management and balancing supply and demand for services are important issues. The intangibility of services poses several promotion-related challenges. Advertisements with tangible cues that symbolize the service and depict facilities, equipment, and personnel help address these challenges. Service providers are likely to promote price, guarantees, performance documentation, availability, and training and certification of contact personnel. Through their actions, service personnel can be involved directly or indirectly in the personal selling of services.

Intangibility makes it difficult to experience a service before purchasing it. Heterogeneity and intangibility make word-of-mouth communication an important means of promotion. The prices of services are based on task performance, time required, or demand. Perishability creates difficulties in balancing supply and demand because unused capacity cannot be stored. The point in time when a significant number of customers desire a service is called peak demand; demand-based pricing results in higher prices charged for services during peak demand. When services are offered in a bundle, marketers must decide whether to offer them at one price, price them separately, or use a combination of the two methods. Because services are intangible, customers may rely on price as a sign of quality. For some services, market conditions may dictate the price; for others, state and local government regulations may limit price flexibility.

4. To understand the importance of service quality and explain how to deliver exceptional service quality

Service quality is customers' perception of how well a service meets or exceeds their expectations. Although one of the most important aspects of service marketing, service quality is very difficult for customers to evaluate because the nature of services renders benefits impossible to assess before actual purchase and consumption. These benefits include experience qualities, such as taste, satisfaction, or pleasure, and credence qualities, which customers may be unable to evaluate even after consumption. When competing services are very similar, service quality may be the only way for customers to distinguish among them. Service marketers can increase the quality of their services by following the four-step process of understanding customer expectations, setting service specifications, ensuring good employee performance, and managing customers' service expectations.

5. To explore the nature of nonprofit marketing

Nonprofit marketing is marketing aimed at nonbusiness goals, including social causes. It uses most of the same concepts and approaches that apply to business situations. Whereas the chief beneficiary of a business enterprise is whoever owns or holds stock in it, the beneficiary of a nonprofit enterprise should be its clients, its members, or its public at large. The goals of a nonprofit organization reflect its unique philosophy or mission. Some nonprofit organizations have very controversial goals, but many organizations exist to further generally accepted social causes.

The marketing objective of nonprofit organizations is to obtain a desired response from a target market. Developing a nonprofit marketing strategy consists of defining and analyzing a target market and creating and maintaining a marketing mix. In nonprofit marketing, the product is usually an idea or a service. Distribution is aimed at the communication of ideas and the delivery of services. The result is a very short marketing channel. Promotion is very important to nonprofit marketing. Nonprofit organizations use advertising, publicity, and personal selling to communicate with clients and the public. Direct mail remains the primary means of fundraising for social services, but some nonprofits use the Internet for fundraising and promotional activities. Price is more difficult to define in nonprofit marketing because of opportunity costs and the difficulty of quantifying the values exchanged.

Go to www.cengagebrain.com for resources to help you master the content in this chapter as well as materials that will expand your marketing knowledge!

important terms

intangibility, 372
inseparability, 373
perishability, 373
heterogeneity, 374

client-based
    relationships, 374
customer contact, 375
service quality, 382
search qualities, 382

experience qualities, 382
credence qualities, 382
nonprofit
    marketing, 386
target public, 388

client publics, 388
general publics, 388
opportunity cost, 390

discussion and review questions

1. How important are services in the U.S. economy?
2. Identify and discuss the major characteristics of services.
3. For each marketing mix element, which service characteristics are most likely to have an impact? Explain.
4. What is service quality? Why do customers find it difficult to judge service quality?
5. Identify and discuss the five components of service quality. How do customers evaluate these components?
6. What is the significance of tangibles in service marketing?
7. How do search, experience, and credence qualities affect the way customers view and evaluate services?

8. What steps should a service company take to provide exceptional service quality?
9. How does nonprofit marketing differ from marketing in for-profit organizations?
10. What are the differences among clients, publics, and customers? What is the difference between a target public and target market?
11. Discuss the development of a marketing strategy for a university. What marketing decisions must be made as the strategy is developed?

application questions

CRITICAL THINKING

1. Imagine you are the owner of a new service business. What is your service? Be creative. What are some of the most important considerations in developing the service, training salespeople, and communicating about your service to potential customers?
2. As discussed in this chapter, the characteristics of services affect the development of marketing mixes for services. Choose a specific service and explain how each marketing mix element could be affected by these service characteristics.

3. In advertising services, a company must often use symbols to represent the offered product. Identify three service organizations you have seen in outdoor, television, or magazine advertising. What symbols do these organizations use to represent their services? What message do the symbols convey to potential customers?
4. Delivering consistently high-quality service is difficult for service marketers. Describe an instance when you received high-quality service and an instance when you experienced low-quality service. What contributed to your perception of high quality? Of low quality?

internet exercise

Matchmaker.com

The Internet abounds with dating sites, but few offer as much information about their members as Matchmaker.com. Matchmaker profiles are gleaned from a survey of about 60 question and essay responses. Check out the site at **www. matchmaker.com**.

1. Classify Matchmaker.com's product in terms of its position on the service continuum.

2. How does Matchmaker.com enhance customer service and foster better client-based relationships through its Internet marketing efforts?

3. Discuss the degree to which experience and credence qualities exist in the services offered by Matchmaker.com and other dating websites.

developing your marketing plan

CRITICAL THINKING

Products that are services rather than tangible goods present unique challenges to companies when they formulate marketing strategy. A clear comprehension of the concepts that apply specifically to service products is essential when developing the marketing plan. These concepts will form the basis for decisions in several plan areas. To assist you in relating the information in this chapter to the development of your marketing plan for a service product, focus on the following:

1. Using Figure 13.1, determine your product's degree of tangibility. If your product lies close to the tangible end of the continuum, then you may proceed to the questions in the next chapter. If your product is more intangible, then continue with this chapter's issues.

2. Discuss your product with regard to the six service characteristics. To what degree does it possess the qualities that make up each of these characteristics?

3. Using Table 13.1 as a guide, discuss the marketing challenges you are likely to experience.

4. Determine the search, experience, and credence qualities that customers are likely to use when evaluating your service product.

5. Consider how your service product relates to each of the dimensions of service quality. Using Table 13.2 as a guide, develop the evaluation criteria and examples that are appropriate for your product.

The information obtained from these questions should assist you in developing various aspects of your marketing plan found in the *Interactive Marketing Plan* exercise at **www. cengagebrain.com**.

© Comstock Images/Getty Images

VIDEO CASE 13.1

Service Flies High at Southwest Airlines

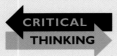

CRITICAL THINKING

Southwest Airlines has risen to the top of the airline industry by making top-quality customer service and no-frills prices its highest priorities. Founded in 1971 as a regional airline flying three planes between Dallas, Houston, and San Antonio, Southwest has grown into a major national carrier with 35,000 employees nationwide and $10 billion in annual revenue. Its stock symbol is LUV, which also sums up the airline's service attitude toward customers.

From the start, Southwest set its airfares low and its service standards high. The airline sees every flight as an opportunity to reinforce its reputation for friendly, attentive service in the sky and on the ground. In recognition of Southwest's financial and service successes, *Fortune* magazine regularly ranks it among the top 20 most admired U.S. companies.

Maintaining a consistently high level of customer service is an ongoing challenge as Southwest adds new destinations and expands its flight schedule year after year. Southwest starts by carefully screening job applicants in order

to hire people who enjoy customer interaction, have good communication skills, and can work cooperatively with colleagues. The airline provides extensive training and allows customer contact personnel to take the initiative by resolving complaints and service problems on the spot. Southwest employees, especially those who deal directly with customers, are required to look and behave professionally. They're also encouraged to add a bit of fun to the flying experience, a key element that differentiates Southwest from competitors. For instance, some crew members coax smiles from seat-belted passengers by leading toilet paper games or enlivening routine announcements with gentle humor. Delivering service with a smile shows that Southwest genuinely cares about its customers.

Just as important, Southwest keeps the service spirit alive through a culture committee at headquarters and similar committees in each of its airport and maintenance facilities across the country. These committees celebrate the achievements of employees who provide outstanding service. They also plan customer and employee appreciation events around the country, such as surprising incoming flight passengers and crew members with cookies and milk.

Thanks in part to its service spirit, Southwest has remained at cruising altitude for decades, despite some

periods of turbulence. When the price of jet fuel reached sky-high levels not long ago, many large carriers cut back on flights, parked planes, and withdrew from certain destinations to save money. Southwest was in a stronger position. Because of smart negotiating, Southwest had its fuel costs under control and actually gained market share while competitors were shrinking their schedules and tightening their belts.

To offset higher fuel costs and lower demand, other airlines have been unbundling services and tacking on extra fees for checking baggage and other services that used to be bundled with the ticket price. Southwest has avoided adding fee after fee after fee, even during difficult economic periods. The airline does charge for some services, such as allowing passengers to jump to the front of the line at boarding time, because seats are not reserved on its flights. But instead of fee-heavy pricing, Southwest prefers to offer bundles that flyers value.

One example is its "bags fly free" campaign, which promotes the airline's policy of charging nothing for each passenger's first two items of checked luggage. Another is its "Business Select" airfare, which bundles priority boarding, a free drink, and extra frequent-flyer points at a slightly higher price. If a Business Select customer is unable to make the flight as scheduled, he or she can apply the airfare toward the cost of a future Southwest flight at any time in the next year, a feature that makes this bundle appealing to businesspeople.

Southwest Airlines has navigated all kinds of business challenges to continue its remarkable record of reporting an annual profit for more than 35 years in a row. Although running an airline is serious business, Southwest's spirited approach to service keeps customers smiling—and keeps them coming back for more LUV.[44]

QUESTIONS FOR DISCUSSION

1. As a high-contact service provider, how does Southwest Airlines ensure that its employees satisfy customers?

2. What experience qualities might weigh most heavily in customers' evaluations of the services delivered by Southwest Airlines? What are the implications for the airline's services marketing efforts?

3. What is Southwest Airlines doing to manage customers' service expectations?

CASE 13.2

Marketing In-store Medical Services: Flu Shots in Aisle 6

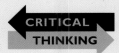

CRITICAL THINKING

Millions of people with minor ailments or urgent medical needs are trying out in-store clinics located inside drug chains, discount stores, and supermarkets. Across the United States, more than 1,000 stores now contain walk-in clinics, and the number is growing. Hundreds of CVS drug stores contain MinuteClinics, and hundreds of Walgreen drug stores contain Take Care clinics. Both Walmart and Target have clinics in selected stores, as do regional grocery chains such as Kroger and United Supermarkets.

In most in-store clinics, consumers meet with a nurse practitioner or a physician's assistant who is trained to treat earaches, sprained ankles, sinus infections, and similar complaints. (Depending on state and local regulations, doctors provide overall medical supervision but may not have to be on-site at every clinic.) If needed, staff members can issue prescriptions that customers can fill immediately at the store's pharmacy. They are also ready to administer vaccinations against tetanus, influenza, and other illnesses, and provide physical checkups before youngsters go to camp or join a sports team.

The two main keys to successfully marketing in-store medical services are convenience and price. The clinics promote their convenient location inside local stores and emphasize that no appointment is necessary. Most in-store clinics offer day, evening, and weekend hours to accommodate consumers' busy schedules. Rarely do consumers have to wait more than a few minutes when they stop by to get a flu shot or have a sore throat treated. Having the pharmacy located in the next aisle is particularly convenient for consumers who walk out of the clinic with a prescription to fill.

The clinics are also handy alternatives when the family doctor's office is closed, too far away, or unable to see a patient right away. Some consumers, especially those without health insurance, may not even have family doctors. "We know that each demographic group has unique problems," observes the CEO of Take Care Health Systems, which operates clinics inside Walgreen stores. "More-affluent patients can't get in to see their doctors, while less-affluent patients often don't have doctors."

Price is another positive. The price for treatment at in-store clinics is generally far lower than at a doctor's office, let alone in the emergency room. Although most of the clinics accept popular health insurance plans as partial or full payment for services, consumers who lack insurance are price-sensitive because they must cover the costs themselves. Price is therefore an important

element for marketing in-store medical services. Describing MinuteClinic's appeal, a CVS spokesperson notes: "High-quality care and lower costs combine to offer real relief to consumers struggling with the steadily increasing costs of health care."

One characteristic of services delivered in an in-store clinic is a little different from conventional medical services. Clinic staff members don't have the opportunity to develop close relationships with the people they treat, because consumers are only occasional visitors, coming in when they have an unexpected illness or know it's time for a flu shot. In contrast, family physicians can and do get to know their patients very well over the course of many visits. "When a child comes in for something minor, we use that time to talk about other things," says a pediatrician in Rochester. "All of that gets missed at the retail clinic."

For their part, the clinics aren't marketing themselves as replacements for regular medical care. Still, MinuteClinic is aware that one-third of its customers do not have a family doctor. Its chief nursing officer is ready to help with that need, too: "That's why we keep a list of local doctors who are taking new patients at each location," she says. "We want people to establish a relationship with a primary care doctor."

Recent changes to U.S. legislation affecting the health-care industry, including provisions for expanding access to health insurance, are affecting the marketing of in-store clinics as well. Walgreens is preparing for higher demand by opening new Take Care clinics in more stores and considering whether to offer a wider range of medical services. Take Care and Walgreens jointly market the in-store clinics in Walgreens' ad campaigns and on the chain's website. In addition, Take Care uses its website plus television, radio, and direct mail to tell consumers about the features and benefits of its services. Attention, shoppers: Easy access to medical treatment is only one aisle away.[45]

QUESTIONS FOR DISCUSSION

1. Which of the six basics characteristics of services are likely to have the most influence on the way in-store clinics are marketed?

2. Do you think consumers would use search qualities, experience qualities, or credence qualities to evaluate the in-store medical services? Explain your answer.

3. How do you suggest that in-store clinics such as MinuteClinic and Take Care manage the service expectations of consumers seeking medical attention?

Chapter 14

Branding and Packaging

OBJECTIVES

1. To explain the value of branding
2. To understand brand loyalty
3. To analyze the major components of brand equity
4. To recognize the types of brands and their benefits
5. To understand how to select and protect brands
6. To examine three types of branding strategies
7. To understand co-branding and brand licensing
8. To describe the major packaging functions and design considerations and how packaging is used in marketing strategies
9. To examine the functions of labeling and describe some legal issues pertaining to labeling

Why Did You Call It Yahoo!?

When Jerry Yang and David Filo set up their first website in 1994, they had no idea that the second name they chose would quickly become one of the Internet's best-known brands. The two Stanford University Ph.D. candidates had been mousing around online, adding site after site to what soon became a long list of favorite links. Only by grouping these links into categories and subcategories could Yang and Filo bring order to their ever-growing collection of links. They shared these categories with friends via a site they originally called "Jerry and David's Guide to the World Wide Web." Then they changed the name to a much simpler and catchier word followed by exuberant punctuation: Yahoo!.

Although Yahoo! is said to stand for "Yet Another Hierarchical Officious Oracle," Filo and Yang insist they chose it for its dictionary meaning of "rude, unsophisticated, uncouth." The exclamation point—which emphasizes the fun of the experience—was in place when Yahoo! was incorporated in early 1995. By mid-1996, the fledgling dot-com company had gone public and launched its first ad campaign, built around the irreverent yodeled tagline "Do You Yahoo!?"

These days, Yahoo! continues to serve a large and loyal global user base, despite serious competition from Google, the leader in online search, as well as from fast-growing social media sites such as Facebook. To reinforce the Yahoo! brand and what it stands for, the company has brought back a new form of its famous yodel in a $100 million advertising campaign. The focal point is "You!," in line with the Yahoo! vision: "To be the center of people's online lives." The company offers multiple ways to access the Internet and customize Yahoo! to suit individual needs and preferences. "Our brand strategy shows our commitment to delivering personally relevant online experiences," explains the chief marketing officer.[1]

Brands, components of brands, packages, and labels are all part of a product's tangible features, the verbal and physical cues that help customers identify the products they want and influence their choices when they are unsure. As such, branding and packaging play an important role in marketing strategy. A successful brand like Yahoo! is distinct and memorable; without one, a firm could not differentiate its products, and shoppers' choices would essentially be arbitrary. A good package design is cost-effective, safe, environmentally responsible, and valuable as a promotional tool.

In this chapter, we first discuss branding, its value to customers and marketers, brand loyalty, and brand equity. Next, we examine the various types of brands. We then consider how companies choose and protect brands, the various branding strategies employed, co-branding, and brand licensing. We look at packaging's critical role as part of the product. Next, we explore the functions of packaging, issues to consider in packaging design, how the package can be a major element in marketing strategy, and packaging criticisms. Finally, we discuss the functions of labeling and relevant legal issues.

Branding

Marketers must make many decisions about products, including choices about brands, brand names, brand marks, trademarks, and trade names. A **brand** is a name, term, design, symbol, or any other feature that identifies one marketer's product as distinct from those of other marketers. A brand may identify a single item, a family of items, or all of a seller's items.[2] Some have defined a brand as not just the physical good, name, color, logo, or ad campaign but everything associated with the product, including its symbolism and experiences.[3] For instance, Hearts on Fire has branded a particular hearts and arrows cut for its diamonds, which maximizes their brilliance and fire—and allows Hearts on Fire diamonds to command a 15 to 20 percent premium over traditional diamonds.[4] A **brand name** is the part of a brand that can be spoken—including letters, words, and numbers—such as 7Up. A brand name is often a product's only distinguishing characteristic. Without the brand name, a firm could not differentiate its products. To consumers, a brand name is as fundamental as the product itself. Indeed, many brand names have become synonymous with the product, such as Scotch Tape and Xerox copiers. Through promotional activities, the owners of these brand names try to protect them from being used as generic names for tape and photocopiers, respectively.

The element of a brand that is not made up of words—often a symbol or design—is a **brand mark**. Examples of brand marks include McDonald's golden arches, Nike's "swoosh," and the stylized silhouette of Apple's iPod. A **trademark** is a legal designation indicating that the owner has exclusive use of a brand or a part of a brand, and others are prohibited by law from using it. To protect a brand name or brand mark in the United States, an organization must register it as a trademark with the U.S. Patent and Trademark Office. Recently, the Patent and Trademark Office registered almost 195,000 new trademarks in a single year.[5] Finally, a **trade name** is the full legal name of an organization, such as Ford Motor Company, rather than the name of a specific product.

Value of Branding

Both buyers and sellers benefit from branding. Brands help customers identify specific products that they do and do not like, which in turn facilitates the purchase of items that satisfy their needs and reduces the time required to purchase the product. Without brands, product selection would be quite random because buyers would have no assurance they were purchasing what they preferred. The purchase of certain brands can be a form of self-expression. For instance, clothing brand names are important to many consumers; names such as Tommy Hilfiger, Polo, Champion, Guess, and Nike give manufacturers an advantage in the marketplace. A brand also helps buyers evaluate the quality of

brand A name, term, design, symbol, or other feature that identifies one marketer's product as distinct from those of other marketers

brand name The part of a brand that can be spoken, including letters, words, and numbers

brand mark The part of a brand that is not made up of words, such as a symbol or design

trademark A legal designation of exclusive use of a brand

trade name The full legal name of an organization

Brand Mark
The Nike "swoosh" is a well-known example of a brand mark.

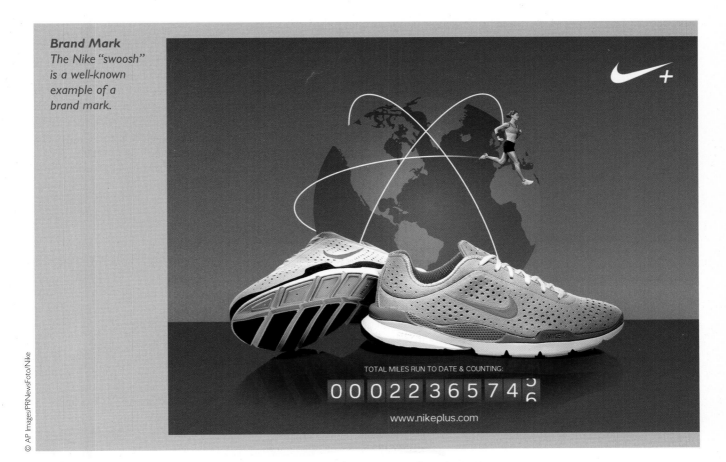

products, especially when they are unable to judge a product's characteristics; that is, a brand may symbolize a certain quality level to a customer, and in turn the person lets that perception of quality represent the quality of the item. A brand helps reduce a buyer's perceived risk of purchase. Customers want to purchase brands they trust, even if it is a private label brand like Walmart's Great Value brand, which recently underwent a re-branding effort and product improvement process while keeping costs down.[6] In addition, a psychological reward may come from owning a brand that symbolizes status. The Mercedes-Benz brand in the United States is an example.

Sellers benefit from branding because each company's brand identifies its products, which makes repeat purchasing easier for customers. Branding helps a firm to introduce a new product that carries the name of one or more of its existing products because buyers are already familiar with those brands. It also facilitates promotional efforts because the promotion of each branded product indirectly promotes all other similarly branded products. Branding also fosters brand loyalty. To the extent that buyers become loyal to a specific brand, the company's market share for that product achieves a certain level of stability, allowing the firm to use its resources more efficiently. Once a firm develops some degree of customer loyalty for a brand, it can maintain a fairly consistent price rather than continually cutting the price to attract customers. A brand is as much of an asset as the company's building or machinery. When marketers increase their brand's value, they also raise the total asset value of the organization. Companies often spend significant resources to boost their brands' value. (We discuss brand value in more detail later in this chapter.) At times, marketers must decide whether to change a brand name. This is a difficult decision because the value in the existing brand name must be given up to gain the potential to build a higher value in a new brand name.

There is a cultural dimension to branding. Most brand experiences are individual, and each consumer confers his or her own social meaning onto brands. A brand's appeal is largely at an emotional level based on its symbolic image and key associations.[7] For some brands, such as Harley-Davidson, Google, and Apple, this can result in an almost cult-like following. These brands often develop a community of loyal customers that communicate through get-togethers, online forums, blogs, podcasts, and other means. These brands may even help consumers develop their identities and self-concepts and serve as forms of self-expression. In fact, the term *cultural branding* has been used to explain how a brand conveys a powerful myth that consumers find useful in cementing their identities.[8] It is also important to recognize that because a brand exists independently in the consumer's mind, it is not directly controlled by the marketer. Every aspect of a brand is subject to a consumer's emotional involvement, interpretation, and memory. By understanding how branding influences purchases, marketers can facilitate customer loyalty.

Brand Loyalty

As we just noted, creating and maintaining customer loyalty toward a brand are two of the benefits of branding. **Brand loyalty** is a customer's favorable attitude toward a specific brand. If brand loyalty is strong enough, customers may consistently purchase this brand when they need a product in that product category. Although brand loyalty may not result in a customer purchasing a specific brand all the time, the brand is at least viewed as a potentially viable choice in the variety of brands being considered for purchase. Development of brand loyalty in a customer reduces his or her risks and shortens the time spent buying the product. However, the degree of brand loyalty for products varies from one product category to another. For example, it is challenging to develop brand loyalty for most products because customers can usually judge a product's quality and do not need to refer to a brand as an indicator of quality. Brand loyalty also varies by country. Customers in France, Germany, and the United Kingdom tend to be less brand loyal than U.S. customers.

Three degrees of brand loyalty exist: recognition, preference, and insistence. **Brand recognition** occurs when a customer is aware that the brand exists and views it as an alternative purchase if the preferred brand is unavailable or if the other available brands are unfamiliar. This is the mildest form of brand loyalty. The term *loyalty* clearly is used very loosely here. One of the initial objectives when introducing a new brand is to create widespread awareness of the brand to generate brand recognition.

Brand preference is a stronger degree of brand loyalty: a customer definitely prefers one brand over competitive offerings and will purchase this brand if available. However, if the brand is not available, the customer will accept a substitute brand rather than expending additional effort finding and purchasing the preferred brand. A marketer is likely to be able to compete effectively in a market when a number of customers have developed brand preference for its specific brand. In an attempt to increase preference for the Charmin brand of toilet paper, the company has created Charmin Restrooms. The Charmin Restrooms contain 20 free and clean stalls at Times Square in NYC available to the public during the holiday season. Besides being one of the few public restrooms in the city, the facility also provides a variety of family friendly activities. The company hopes customers will remember this great experience and purchase Charmin brand toilet paper.[9]

When **brand insistence** occurs, a customer strongly prefers a specific brand, will accept no substitute, and is willing to spend a great deal of time and effort to acquire that brand. If a brand-insistent customer goes to a store and finds the brand unavailable, he or she will seek the brand elsewhere rather than purchase a substitute brand. Brand insistence can also apply to service products such as Hilton Hotels or sports teams such as the Chicago Bears or the Dallas Cowboys. Brand insistence is the strongest degree of brand loyalty—a brander's dream. However, it is the least-common type of brand loyalty. Customers vary considerably regarding the product categories for which they may be brand insistent. Can you think of products for which you are brand insistent? Perhaps it's a brand of deodorant, soft drink, jeans, or even pet food (if your pet is brand insistent).

Building brand loyalty is a major challenge for many marketers. Brand loyalty in general seems to be declining, partly because of marketers' increased reliance on sales, coupons, and other short-term promotions, and partly because of the sometimes

brand loyalty A customer's favorable attitude toward a specific brand

brand recognition The degree of brand loyalty in which a customer is aware that a brand exists and views the brand as an alternative purchase if their preferred brand is unavailable

brand preference The degree of brand loyalty in which a customer prefers one brand over competitive offerings

brand insistence The degree of brand loyalty in which a customer strongly prefers a specific brand and will accept no substitute

Brand Insistence

Some consumers are brand insistent about their deodorant. When they find just the right brand that works with their body chemistry, they keep buying the same brand.

brand equity The marketing and financial value associated with a brand's strength in a market

overwhelming array of similar new products from which customers can choose. Thus, it is an extremely important issue. The creation of brand loyalty significantly contributes to an organization's ability to achieve a sustainable competitive advantage.

Brand Equity

A well-managed brand is an asset to an organization. The value of this asset is often referred to as brand equity. **Brand equity** is the marketing and financial value associated with a brand's strength in a market. Besides the actual proprietary brand assets, such as patents and trademarks, four major elements underlie brand equity: brand-name awareness, brand loyalty, perceived brand quality, and brand associations (see Figure 14.1).[10]

Recognition of a brand leads to brand familiarity, which in turn results in a level of comfort with the brand. A familiar brand is more likely to be selected than an unfamiliar brand because the familiar brand is often viewed as more reliable and of more acceptable quality. The familiar brand is likely to be in a customer's consideration set, whereas the unfamiliar brand is not.

Brand loyalty is an important component of brand equity because it reduces a brand's vulnerability to competitors' actions. Brand loyalty allows an organization to keep its existing customers and avoid spending an enormous amount of resources gaining new ones. Loyal customers provide brand visibility and reassurance to potential new customers. Because customers expect their brands to be available when and where they shop, retailers strive to carry the brands known for their strong customer following.

Customers associate a particular brand with a certain level of overall quality. A brand name may be used as a substitute for judgment of quality. In many cases, customers can't actually judge the quality of the product for themselves and instead must rely on the brand as a quality indicator. For instance, Toyota was able to survive as a company, despite the massive recalls that affected several million vehicles, because of its historically high perceived brand quality. Even though the recalls were a

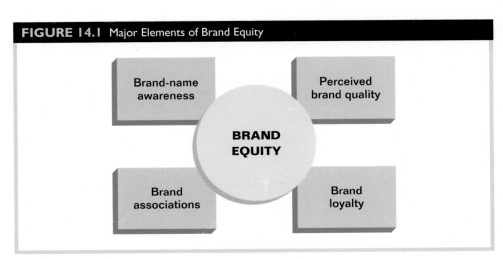

FIGURE 14.1 Major Elements of Brand Equity

Brand-name awareness

Perceived brand quality

BRAND EQUITY

Brand associations

Brand loyalty

Source: Adapted with the permission of The Free Press, a division of Simon & Schuster Adult Publishing Group, from *Managing Brand Equity: Capitalizing on the Value of a Brand Name* by David A. Aaker. Copyright © 1991 by David A. Aaker. All rights reserved.

Top Three Computer Brands, Each with Strong Brand Equity

Dell 50%

Hewlett-Packard/Compaq 39%

Apple 11%

Source: Nielsen (based on percentage of ownership).

huge mark against the brand, the company's loyalists and previously perceived high brand quality enabled it to survive.[11] Perceived high brand quality helps support a premium price, allowing a marketer to avoid severe price competition. Also, favorable perceived brand quality can ease the introduction of brand extensions, since the high regard for the brand will likely translate into high regard for the related products.

The set of associations linked to a brand is another key component of brand equity. At times, a marketer works to connect a particular lifestyle or, in some instances, a certain personality type with a specific brand. For example, customers associate Michelin tires with protecting family members; a De Beers diamond with a loving, long-lasting relationship ("A Diamond Is Forever"); and Dr Pepper with a unique taste. These types of brand associations contribute significantly to the brand's equity. Brand associations are sometimes facilitated by using trade characters, such as the Jolly Green Giant, the Pillsbury Dough Boy, and the Monster.com Monster. Placing these trade characters in advertisements and on packages helps consumers link the ads and packages to the brands.

Although difficult to measure, brand equity represents the value of a brand to an organization. An organization may buy a brand from another company at a premium price because outright brand purchase may be less expensive and less risky than creating and developing a brand from scratch. Consider Coca-Cola, which decided that it would be a better business decision to buy an established brand—Glaceau—than to create a new brand of its own. Glaceau, which included the Vitaminwater and Smartwater brands, was acquired to strengthen Coca-Cola's water and energy drink product line.[12] Brand equity helps give a brand the power to capture and maintain a consistent market share, which provides stability to the organization's sales volume.

Table 14.1 lists the 10 global brands with the greatest economic value, as compiled by Interbrand, a consulting firm. Interbrand's top 100 brands account for nearly 30 percent of the market value of the firms that own them. Any company that owns a brand listed in Table 14.1 would agree that the economic value of that brand is likely to be the greatest single asset the organization possesses. A brand's overall economic value rises and falls with the brand's profitability, brand awareness, brand loyalty, and perceived brand quality and with the strength of positive brand associations.

TABLE 14.1 The World's Most Valuable Brands

Brand	Brand Value (In Millions of Dollars)
Coca-Cola	$68,734
IBM	60,211
Microsoft	56,647
GE	47,777
Nokia	34,864
McDonald's	32,275
Google	31,980
Toyota	31,330
Intel	30,636
Disney	28,447

Source: www.interbrand.com/best_global_brands.aspx (accessed April 9, 2010).

My job is saving you money.

I love my job.

Get a FREE rate quote today.

1-800-947-AUTO

© GEICO

Government Employees Insurance Co. • GEICO General Insurance Co. • GEICO Indemnity Co. • GEICO Casualty Co. These companies are subsidiaries of Berkshire Hathaway Inc. GEICO auto insurance is not available in Mass. GEICO, Washington, DC 20076 © 2006 GEICO

Courtesy of GEICO

Stimulating Brand Associations
Geico uses the gecko as a trade character to stimulate favorable brand associations.

Types of Brands

Brands come in three categories: manufacturer, private distributor, and generic. **Manufacturer brands** are initiated by producers and ensure that producers are identified with their products at the point of purchase—for example, Green Giant, Compaq Computer, and Levi's jeans. A manufacturer brand usually requires a producer to become involved in distribution, promotion, and, to some extent, pricing decisions. Brand loyalty is encouraged by promotion, quality control, and guarantees; it is a valuable asset to a manufacturer. The producer tries to stimulate demand for the product, which tends to encourage sellers and resellers to make the product available.

Private distributor brands (also called *private brands, store brands,* or *dealer brands*) are initiated and owned by resellers—that is, wholesalers or retailers. The major characteristic of private brands is that the manufacturers are not identified on the products. Retailers and wholesalers use private distributor brands to develop more efficient promotion, generate higher gross margins, and change store image. Despite the many strong national brands available to consumers, the top-selling consumer brand on this continent is Walmart's private label brand, Great Value.[13] Private distributor brands give retailers or wholesalers freedom to purchase products of a specified quality at the lowest cost without disclosing the identities of the manufacturers. Wholesaler brands include IGA (Independent Grocers' Alliance) and Topmost (General Grocer). Familiar retailer brand names include Sears's Kenmore and JCPenney's Arizona. Many successful private brands are distributed nationally. Kenmore appliances are as well known as most manufacturer brands. Sometimes retailers with successful private distributor brands start manufacturing their own products to gain more control over product costs, quality, and design in the hope of increasing profits. Sales of private labels now account for one out of every four product items sold in supermarkets, drugstores, and mass merchandisers, totaling some $88 billion of retail business.[14] Supermarket private brands are popular globally, too.

Competition between manufacturer brands and private distributor brands (sometimes called "the battle of the brands") is ongoing. To compete against manufacturer brands, retailers have tried to strengthen consumer confidence in private brands. Results of a recent study on consumer perceptions of private and manufacturer brands appear in Figure 14.2. For manufacturers, developing multiple manufacturer brands and distribution systems has been an effective means of combating the increased competition from private brands. By developing a new brand name, a producer can adjust various elements of its marketing mix to appeal to a different target market.

The growth of private brands has been steady. One reason for this is that retailers advertise the manufacturer brands, which brings customers to their stores, but sell the private brands, especially to price-sensitive customers. To compete against private brands, some manufacturer brand makers have stopped increasing prices or even have cut their prices, which has narrowed the price gap—the major advantage of buying a private brand. Traditionally private brands have appeared in packaging that directly imitates the packaging of competing manufacturers' brands without significant legal ramifications. However, the legal risks of using look-alike packaging are increasing for private branders.

manufacturer brand A brand initiated by producers to ensure that producers are identified with their products at the point of purchase

private distributor brand A brand initiated and owned by a reseller

Marketing in Transition
Who's Behind That Brand?

Have you heard of Great Value? It's the best-selling grocery brand in the United States. Yet if you go looking for Great Value products, the only place you'll find them is at Walmart. Why? Because Great Value is a *private distributor brand,* used on products designed for and distributed exclusively through a single reseller's network (in this case, Walmart).

Private distributor brands, which are priced lower than manufacturers' brands, are extremely profitable for many retailers—and they're not just for penny-pinching shoppers anymore. Walmart, Stop & Shop, Staples, and Macy's are just a few of the retailers using such brands to target both price- and quality-conscious customers. In recent years, Walmart has introduced dozens of unique products under its Great Value brand, including fat-free caramel swirl ice cream and pepperoni pizza with focaccia crust. "The national brands are not designing items [exclusively] for the Walmart customer," says a senior vice president. "We are."

The Stop & Shop supermarket chain is taking its private distributor brands upscale, with organic products marketed under its Nature's Promise brand and specialty foods marketed under its Simply Enjoy brand. Staples, the office supply retailer, offers only private distributor brands in some product categories, such as shredders.

Now that sales of such brands are increasing faster than sales of manufacturers' brands, companies such as Campbell Soup and Procter & Gamble are fighting back. They're reassessing customers' needs, testing new products, and emphasizing the extra value they provide. Next time you pluck a product from the store shelf, take a moment to consider: Who's behind that brand?[a]

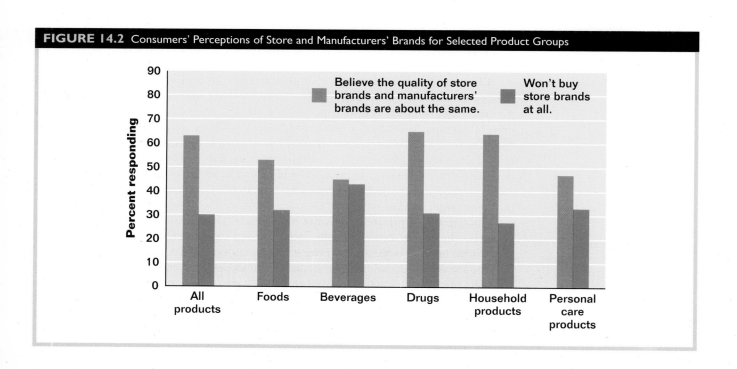

FIGURE 14.2 Consumers' Perceptions of Store and Manufacturers' Brands for Selected Product Groups

Legend: Believe the quality of store brands and manufacturers' brands are about the same. | Won't buy store brands at all.

Y-axis: Percent responding (0–90)

X-axis categories: All products, Foods, Beverages, Drugs, Household products, Personal care products

Private Brand
Sears has initiated and developed many private branded products. Craftsman is a private brand that Sears uses for tools.

Some private distributor brands are produced by companies that specialize in making only private distributor brands; others are made by producers of manufacturer brands. At times, producers of both types of brands find it difficult to ignore the opportunities that arise from producing private distributor brands. If a producer decides not to produce a private brand for a reseller, a competitor probably will. Moreover, the production of private distributor brands allows the producer to use excess capacity during periods when its own brands are at nonpeak production. The ultimate decision of whether to produce a private or a manufacturer brand depends on a company's resources, production capabilities, and goals.

Some marketers of traditionally branded products have embarked on a policy of not branding, often called *generic branding*. **Generic brands** indicate only the product category (such as aluminum foil) and do not include the company name or other identifying terms. Generic brands are usually sold at lower prices than comparable branded items. Although at one time generic brands may have represented as much as 10 percent of all retail grocery sales, today they account for less than half of 1 percent.

Selecting a Brand Name

Marketers consider a number of factors when selecting a brand name. First, the name should be easy for customers (including foreign buyers, if the firm intends to market its products in other countries) to say, spell, and recall. Short, one-syllable names, such as Cheer, often satisfy this requirement. Second, the brand name should indicate the product's major benefits and, if possible, suggest in a positive way the product's uses and special characteristics; negative or offensive references should be avoided. For example, the brand names of such household cleaning products as Ajax dishwashing liquid, Vanish toilet bowl cleaner, Formula 409 multipurpose cleaner, Cascade dishwasher detergent, and Wisk laundry detergent connote strength and effectiveness. Research suggests that consumers are more likely to recall and to evaluate favorably names that convey positive attributes or benefits.[15] Third, to set it apart from competing brands, the brand should be distinctive. AT&T, for example, renamed its Cingular Wireless service AT&T so all the company's products would have the same brand name.[16] If a marketer intends to use a brand for a product line, that brand must be compatible with all products in the line. Finally, a brand should be designed so that it can be used and recognized in all types of media. Finding the right brand name has become a challenging task because many obvious product names have already been used.

How are brand names devised? Brand names can be created from single or multiple words—for example, Bic or Dodge Nitro. Letters and numbers are used to create such brands as Volvo's S60 sedan or RIM's BlackBerry 8100. Words, numbers, and letters are combined to yield brand names such as Motorola's RAZR V3 phone or BMW's Z4 Roadster. To avoid terms that have negative connotations, marketers sometimes use fabricated words that have absolutely no meaning when created—for example, Kodak and Exxon. Occasionally a brand is simply brought out of storage and used as is or modified. Firms often maintain banks of registered brands, some of which may have been used in the past. Cadillac, for example, has a bank of approximately 360 registered trademarks. The LaSalle brand, used in the 1920s and 1930s, could be called up for a new Cadillac model in the future. Possible brand names sometimes are tested in focus groups or other settings to assess customers' reactions.

generic brand A brand indicating only the product category

Who actually creates brand names? Brand names can be created internally by the organization. At Del Monte, a team of executives brainstormed 27 ideas for new cat food offerings with names like "pate," "souffle," and "crème brulee."[17] Sometimes a name is suggested by individuals who are close to the product's development. Some organizations have committees that participate in brand name creation and approval. Large companies that introduce numerous new products annually are likely to have a department that develops brand names. At times, outside consultants and companies that specialize in brand-name development are used.

Although most of the important branding considerations apply to both goods and services, branding a service has some additional dimensions. The service brand is usually the same as the company name. Financial companies, such as Fidelity Investments and Charles Schwab Discount Brokerage, have established strong brand recognition. These companies have used their names to create an image of value and friendly, timely, responsible, accurate, and knowledgeable customer assistance. Service providers (such as United Airlines) are perceived by customers as having one brand name, even though they offer multiple products (first class, business class, and coach). Because the service brand name and company name are so closely interrelated, a service brand name must be flexible enough to encompass a variety of current services, as well as new ones the company may offer in the future. Geographical references such as *western* and descriptive terms such as *trucking* limit the scope of possible associations with the brand name. Because Southwest Airlines now flies to many parts of the country, its name has become too limited in its scope of associations. *Humana,* with its connotations of kindness and compassion, is flexible enough to encompass all services that a hospital, insurance plan, or health-care facility offers. Frequently a service marketer employs a symbol along with its brand name to make the brand distinctive and communicate a certain image.

Protecting a Brand

A marketer should also design a brand so that it can be protected easily through registration. A series of court decisions has created a broad hierarchy of protection based on brand type. From most protectable to least protectable, these brand types are fanciful (Exxon), arbitrary (Dr Pepper), suggestive (Spray 'n Wash), descriptive (Minute Rice), and generic (aluminum foil). Generic brands are not protectable. Surnames and descriptive, geographic, or functional names are difficult to protect.[18] Because of their designs, some brands can be legally infringed on more easily than others. Although registration protects trademarks domestically for 10 years, and trademarks can be renewed indefinitely, a firm should develop a system for ensuring that its trademarks are renewed as needed.

To protect its exclusive rights to a brand, a company must ensure that the brand is not likely to be considered an infringement on any brand already registered with the U.S. Patent and Trademark Office. This task may be complex because infringement is determined by the courts, which base their decisions on whether a brand causes consumers to be confused, mistaken, or deceived about the source of the product. McDonald's is one company that aggressively protects its trademarks against infringement;

Entrepreneurial Marketing
Why Spanx?

It all started when founder Sara Blakely wanted to wear control-top pantyhose for a smooth line under tight-fitting pants while leaving her feet bare for open-toed shoes. Not able to find the right hosiery or undergarment, she resorted to cutting the feet off ordinary pantyhose. Blakely then realized an opportunity, and she began the lengthy process of patenting her innovation and finding a manufacturer willing to create a prototype.

Now she needed a brand name to embody the confident, spunky attitude she wanted her product to project. As a former stand-up comic, Blakely knew that words with the letter "k" tend to make people laugh. She initially chose "Spanks," but at the last minute, she substituted "Spanx," after hearing that made-up words are more appealing than real words for brand names and are more easily trademarked. This last-minute change to the brand name added just the right touch of personality to get Spanx off on the right foot for fast growth. Today, Spanx brand products achieve annual sales in excess of $350 million.[b]

it has brought charges against a number of companies with *Mc* names because it fears that the use of that prefix will give consumers the impression that these companies are associated with or owned by McDonald's. Auto Shack changed its name to AutoZone when faced with legal action from Tandy Corporation, owner of Radio Shack. Tandy maintained that it owned the name *Shack*. After research showed that virtually every auto supply store in the country used *auto* in its name, *zone* was deemed the best word to pair with *auto*.

A marketer should guard against allowing a brand name to become a generic term used to refer to a general product category. Generic terms cannot be protected as exclusive brand names. For instance, *aspirin, escalator,* and *shredded wheat*—all brand names at one time—eventually were declared generic terms that refer to product classes. Thus, they could no longer be protected. To keep a brand name from becoming a generic term, the firm should spell the name with a capital letter and use it as an adjective to modify the name of the general product class, as in Kool-Aid Brand Soft Drink Mix.[19] Including the word *brand* just after the brand name is also helpful. An organization can deal with this problem directly by advertising that its brand is a trademark and should not be used generically. The firm can also indicate that the brand is a registered trademark by using the symbol ®.

In the interest of strengthening trademark protection, Congress enacted the Trademark Law Revision Act in 1988, the only major federal trademark legislation since the Lanham Act of 1946. The purpose of this more recent legislation is to increase the value of the federal registration system for U.S. firms relative to foreign competitors and to better protect the public from counterfeiting, confusion, and deception.

A U.S. firm that tries to protect a brand in a foreign country frequently encounters problems. In many countries, brand registration is not possible; the first firm to use a brand in such a country automatically has the rights to it. In some instances, U.S. companies actually have had to buy their own brand rights from a firm in a foreign country because the foreign firm was the first user in that country.

Marketers that are trying to protect their brands must also contend with brand counterfeiting. In the United States, for instance, one can purchase counterfeit General Motors parts, Cartier watches, Louis Vuitton handbags, Walt Disney character dolls, Warner Bros. clothing, Mont Blanc pens, and a host of other products illegally marketed by manufacturers that do not own the brands. Annual losses caused by counterfeit products are estimated at between $250 billion and $350 billion. Many counterfeit products are manufactured overseas—in Turkey, China, Thailand, Italy, and Colombia, for example—but some are counterfeited in the United States. Counterfeit products are often hard to distinguish from the real brands. Products most likely to be counterfeited are well-known brands that appeal to a mass market and products whose physical materials are inexpensive relative to the products' prices. Microsoft estimates that its revenues would double if counterfeiting of its brand-name products were eliminated. Some $40 billion a year is lost in the computer software business because of counterfeit and pirated products. Brand fraud results not only in lost revenue for the brand's owner; it also results in a low-quality product for customers, distorts competition, affects investment levels, reduces tax revenues and legitimate employment, creates safety risks, and affects international relations. It also likely affects customers' perceptions of the brand due to the counterfeit product's inferior quality.

Branding Strategies

Before establishing branding strategies, a firm must decide whether to brand its products at all. If a company's product is homogeneous and similar to competitors' products, it may be difficult to brand. Raw materials such as coal, sand, and farm produce are hard to brand because of the homogeneity and physical characteristics of such products.

If a firm chooses to brand its products, it may opt for one or more of the following branding strategies: individual, family, or brand extension branding. **Individual branding** is a strategy in which each product is given a different name. Sara Lee uses individual branding among its many divisions, which include Hanes underwear, L'eggs pantyhose,

individual branding A branding strategy in which each product is given a different name

Protecting a Brand
Companies try to protect their brands by using certain phrases and symbols in their advertisements. Note the term "brand" after Ziploc, and the use of the ® symbol.

Champion sportswear, Jimmy Dean, Bali, Ball Park, and other vastly diverse brands. A major advantage of individual branding is that if an organization introduces a poor product, the negative images associated with it do not contaminate the company's other products. An individual branding strategy may also facilitate market segmentation when a firm wishes to enter many segments of the same market. Separate, unrelated names can be used and each brand aimed at a specific segment.

In **family branding**, all of a firm's products are branded with the same name or part of the name, such as Kellogg's Frosted Flakes, Kellogg's Rice Krispies, and Kellogg's Corn Flakes. In some cases, a company's name is combined with other words to brand items. Arm & Hammer uses its name on all its products, along with a generic description of the item, such as Arm & Hammer Heavy Duty Detergent, Arm & Hammer Pure Baking Soda, and Arm & Hammer Carpet Deodorizer. Unlike individual branding, family branding means that the promotion of one item with the family brand promotes the firm's other products. Other major companies that use family branding include Mitsubishi, Kodak, and Fisher-Price.

A **brand extension** occurs when a firm uses one of its existing brands to brand a new product in a different product category. For example, Bic, the maker of disposable pens, employed a brand extension when it introduced Bic disposable razors and Bic lighters. A brand extension should not be confused with a line extension, which involves using an existing brand on a new product in the same product category, such as new flavors or sizes. For instance, when the maker of Tylenol, McNeil Consumer Products, introduced Extra Strength Tylenol P.M., the new product was a line extension because it was in the same category. Researchers have found that there may be an opportunity to charge a premium price relative to comparable products when extending a strong brand into a new-product category because of consumers' perceptions of lower risk associated with a known brand name.[20]

Marketers share a common concern that if a brand is extended too many times or extended too far outside its original product category, the brand can be significantly

family branding Branding all of a firm's products with the same name or part of the name

brand extension An organization uses one of its existing brands to brand a new product in a different product category

weakened. For example, Miller Brewing Company has extended its brand to Miller Lite, Genuine Draft, MGD 64, Chill, High Life, Icehouse, Milwaukee's Best, and Red Dog, but so many extensions may confuse customers and encourage them to engage in considerable brand switching.[21] For instance, Kellogg's extended its brand name to a line of hip-hop street clothing that was later named one of the worst brand extensions that year.[22] Research has found that a line extension into premium categories can be an effective strategy to revitalize a brand, but the line extension needs to be closely linked to the core brand.[23] Other research, however, suggests that diluting a brand by extending it into dissimilar product categories could have the potential to suppress consumer consideration and choice for the original brand.[24]

An organization is not limited to a single branding strategy. A company that uses primarily individual branding for many of its products may also use brand extensions. Branding strategy is influenced by the number of products and product lines the company produces, the characteristics of its target markets, the number and types of competing products available, and the size of the firm's resources.

Co-Branding

Co-branding is the use of two or more brands on one product. Marketers employ co-branding to capitalize on the brand equity of multiple brands. It is popular in a number of processed food categories and in the credit card industry. The brands used for co-branding can be owned by the same company. For example, Kraft's Lunchables product teams the Kraft cheese brand with Oscar Mayer lunchmeats, another Kraft-owned brand. The brands may also be owned by different companies. Credit card companies such as American Express, Visa, and MasterCard, for instance, team up with other brands such as General Motors, AT&T, and many airlines to co-brand and jointly promote their products.

Effective co-branding capitalizes on the trust and confidence customers have in the brands involved. The brands should not lose their identities, and it should be clear to customers which brand is the main brand. For instance, it is fairly obvious that Kellogg owns the brand and is the main brander of Kellogg's Healthy Choice Cereal (the Healthy Choice brand is owned by ConAgra). It is important for marketers to understand that when a co-branded product is unsuccessful, both brands are implicated in the product failure. To gain customer acceptance, the brands involved must represent a complementary fit in the minds of buyers. Trying to link a brand like Harley-Davidson with a brand like Healthy Choice will not achieve co-branding objectives because customers are not likely to perceive these brands as compatible.

Co-branding can help an organization differentiate its products from those of competitors. For example, T-Mobile, a cell phone provider, teamed up with Eric Clapton to create the myTouch 3G Fender Limited Edition cell phone priced just under $180 with the signing of a two-year contract.[25] By using the product development skills of a co-branding partner, an organization can create a distinctive product. Co-branding can also allow the partners to take advantage of each other's distribution capabilities.

Although co-branding has been used for a number of years, it began to grow in popularity in the 1980s when Monsanto aggressively promoted its NutraSweet product as an ingredient in such well-known brands as Diet Coke. Later, a rival sweetener, Splenda, was co-branded with Diet Coke, Starbucks, and many other brands. Intel, too, has capitalized on ingredient co-branding through its "Intel Inside" program. The effectiveness of ingredient co-branding relies heavily on continued promotional efforts by the ingredient's producer.

co-branding Using two or more brands on one product

brand licensing An agreement whereby a company permits another organization to use its brand on other products for a licensing fee

Brand Licensing

A popular branding strategy involves **brand licensing**, an agreement in which a company permits another organization to use its brand on other products for a licensing fee. Royalties may be as low as 2 percent of wholesale revenues, or higher than 10 percent. The licensee is responsible for all manufacturing, selling, and advertising functions, and bears the costs if the licensed product fails. Not long ago only a few firms licensed their

Co-Branding
Lunchables is a co-branded item consisting of Oscar Mayer and Kraft products.

corporate trademarks, but today licensing is a multi-billion-dollar business. The top U.S. licensing company is Walt Disney Company. The NFL, the NCAA, NASCAR, and Major League Baseball are all leaders in the retail sales of licensed products.

The advantages of licensing range from extra revenues and low-cost or free publicity to new images and trademark protection. For instance, Coca-Cola has licensed its trademark for use on glassware, radios, trucks, and clothing in the hope of protecting its trademark. However, brand licensing has drawbacks. The major disadvantages are a lack of manufacturing control, which could hurt the company's name, and bombarding consumers with too many unrelated products bearing the same name. Licensing arrangements can also fail because of poor timing, inappropriate distribution channels, or mismatching of product and name.

Packaging

Packaging involves the development of a container and a graphic design for a product. A package can be a vital part of a product, making it more versatile, safer, and easier to use. Like a brand name, a package can influence customers' attitudes toward a product and thus affect their purchase decisions. For example, several producers of jellies, sauces, and ketchups have packaged their products in squeezable containers to make use and storage more convenient, and some paint manufacturers have introduced easy-to-open and -pour paint cans. Package characteristics help shape buyers' impressions of a product at the time of purchase or during use. In this section, we examine the main functions of packaging and consider several major packaging decisions.

Packaging Functions

Effective packaging involves more than simply putting products in containers and covering them with wrappers. First, packaging materials serve the basic purpose of protecting the product and maintaining its functional form. Fluids such as milk, orange juice, and hair spray need packages that preserve and protect them. The packaging should prevent damage that could affect the product's usefulness and thus lead to higher costs. Because product tampering has become a problem, several packaging techniques have been developed to counter this danger. Some packages are also designed to deter shoplifting.

Another function of packaging is to offer convenience to consumers. Consider small aseptic packages—individual-size boxes or plastic bags that contain liquids and do not require refrigeration. This packaging appeals strongly to children and young adults with active lifestyles. The size or shape of a package may relate to the product's storage, convenience of use, or replacement rate. Small, single-serving cans of vegetables, for instance, may prevent waste and make storage easier.

A third function of packaging is to promote a product by communicating its features, uses, benefits, and image. Sometimes a reusable package is developed to make the product more desirable. For example, the Cool Whip package doubles as a food storage container.

Finally, packaging can be used to communicate symbolically the quality or premium nature of a product. It can also evoke an emotional response.

Major Packaging Considerations

In developing packages, marketers must take many factors into account. Obviously one major consideration is cost. Although a variety of packaging materials, processes, and designs are available, costs vary greatly. In recent years, buyers have shown a willingness to pay more for improved packaging, but there are limits. Marketers should conduct research to determine exactly how much customers are willing to pay for effective and efficient package designs.

As already mentioned, developing tamper-resistant packaging is very important for certain products. Although no package is tamperproof, marketers can develop packages that are difficult to contaminate. At a minimum, all packaging must comply with the Food and Drug Administration's packaging regulations. However, packaging should also make any product tampering evident to resellers and consumers. Although effective tamper-resistant packaging may be expensive to develop, when balanced against the costs of lost sales, loss of consumer confidence and company reputation, and potentially expensive product liability lawsuits, the costs of ensuring consumer safety are minimal.

Marketers should also consider how much consistency is desirable among an organization's package designs. No consistency may be the best policy, especially if a firm's products are unrelated or aimed at vastly different target markets. To promote an overall company image, a firm may decide that all packages should be similar or include one major element of the design. This approach is called **family packaging**. Sometimes it is used only for lines of products, such as Campbell's soups, Weight Watchers' foods, and Planter's nuts.

A package's promotional role is an important consideration. Through verbal and nonverbal symbols, the package can inform potential buyers about the product's content, features, uses, advantages, and hazards. A firm can create desirable images and associations by its choice of color, design, shape, and texture. Many cosmetics manufacturers, for example, design their packages to create impressions of richness, luxury, and exclusivity. A package performs a promotional function when it is designed to be safer or more convenient to use if such characteristics help stimulate demand.

To develop a package that has a definite promotional value, a designer must consider size, shape, texture, color, and graphics. Beyond the obvious limitation that the package must be large enough to hold the product, a package can be designed to appear taller or shorter. Light-colored packaging may make a package appear larger, whereas darker colors may minimize the perceived size.

Colors on packages are often chosen to attract attention, and color can positively influence customers' emotions. People associate specific colors with certain feelings and experiences. Here are some examples:

- Blue is soothing; it is also associated with wealth, trust, and security.
- Gray is associated with strength, exclusivity, and success.

family packaging Using similar packaging for all of a firm's products or packaging that has one common design element

Responsible Marketing?

Does Campbell's Own the Red and White Package?

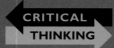

ISSUE: Should a retailer be allowed to design its private branded package to look like the leading manufacturers' brand?

Discount stores, supermarkets, and drugstores like CVS and Walgreens sometimes design the packages for their private brands to look very similar to packaging used for leading manufacturers' brands. At times, a retailer will place its "look-alike" private brand right next to the leading manufacturers' brand on the shelf. The retailer may defend this type of action on the basis that the colors and color combinations used to package the leading manufacturers' brand are actually used by consumers to identify the product category. For instance, a number of private branded soups are packaged in red and white because the color combination identifies the canned soup product category, even though a leading manufacturer's brand, Campbell's, popularized red and white as the major color combination for packaging soup. The producer of the manufacturers' brand accuses the retailers' private brand package design of infringing on its brand. Also, some critics of this practice indicate that it leads to consumer confusion regarding the source of the product.

Is the leading manufacturer's brand affected by the presence of a private brand that is packaged to look like the leading brand? If so, in what ways are consumers confused by this practice on the part of retailers that engage in this type of private branding practice? Is it fair for a retailer to use a "look-alike" package design for its private brand?

- Orange often signifies low cost.
- Red connotes excitement and stimulation.
- Purple is associated with dignity and stateliness.
- Yellow connotes cheerfulness and joy.
- Black is associated with being strong and masterful.[26]

When opting for color on packaging, marketers must judge whether a particular color will evoke positive or negative feelings when linked to a specific product. Rarely, for example, do processors package meat or bread in green materials because customers may associate green with mold. Marketers must also determine whether a specific target market will respond favorably or unfavorably to a particular color. Cosmetics for women are more likely to be sold in pastel packaging than are personal-care products for men. Packages designed to appeal to children often use primary colors and bold designs. A relatively recent trend in packaging is colorless packages. Clear products and packaging connote a pure, natural product.

Packaging must also meet the needs of resellers. Wholesalers and retailers consider whether a package facilitates transportation, storage, and handling. Concentrated versions of laundry detergents and fabric softeners, for example, enable retailers to offer more product diversity within the existing shelf space. Resellers may refuse to carry certain products if their packages are cumbersome.

A final consideration is whether to develop packages that are environmentally responsible. Nearly one-half of all garbage consists of discarded plastic packaging, such as polystyrene containers, plastic soft-drink bottles, and carryout bags. Plastic packaging material does not biodegrade, and paper requires the destruction of valuable forests. Consequently, many companies have changed to environmentally sensitive packaging; they are also recycling more materials. Last year, Naked Juice became the first beverage with national distribution to produce its packaging completely from recycled plastic.[27] H. J. Heinz is looking for alternatives to its plastic ketchup squeeze bottles. Other companies are also searching for alternatives to environmentally harmful packaging. In some instances, however, customers have objected to such switches because the newer environmentally responsible packaging may be less effective or more inconvenient. Therefore, marketers must carefully balance society's desire to preserve the environment against customers' desire for convenience.

Packaging and Marketing Strategies

Packaging can be a major component of a marketing strategy. A new cap or closure, a better box or wrapper, or a more convenient container may give a product a competitive advantage. The right type of package for a new product can help it gain market recognition very quickly. Sunsweet Growers, for example, had this in mind when it

Sustainable Marketing
Packaging Undergoes Green-sizing

According to the U.S. Environmental Protection Agency, packaging accounts for 25 percent of the waste that winds up in landfills. That's why, in the world of sustainable packaging, less is more. The trend is toward downsizing packages—without reducing the amount of product inside—to reduce the volume of material that gets discarded.

AT&T, for example, is requiring cell-phone manufacturers to make their outside packages slimmer and use less cardboard and plastic inside. Such seemingly small changes in packaging can make a big difference to the environment. Nokia's two-year drive to downsize its cell phone packaging slashed its use of paper-based materials by 100,000 tons worldwide, saving a lot of trees. Because more of the small packages could be packed into each truck, Nokia needed 12,000 fewer trucks to transport its phones in those two years, saving energy while reducing emissions.

Sometimes greener packaging is so subtle that consumers don't notice the difference. The chief environmental officer for corporate packaging at global cosmetics giant Estée Lauder points to the company's use of "lightweighting," making a bottle or jar lighter without changing its basic shape or size. PepsiCo has cut the amount of plastic in its Eco-Fina water bottles by 50 percent, and Nestlé is redesigning its water bottles to incorporate a higher percentage of recycled plastic.[c]

Other marketers are experimenting with packages made from eco-friendly materials, like the biodegradable corn-resin cosmetics jars used by Cover FX and the plant-based plastic bottles used by Coca-Cola. Recycling is yet another road to sustainable packaging. Origins and other beauty marketers now encourage customers to return empty bottles and jars to their stores and, in exchange, receive free samples of new products.

introduced New Ones dried prunes, targeted at consumers who wanted healthier snacks. Sold in transparent canisters containing 20 individually wrapped pitted prune snacks that look rather like candy, the package protects the product and makes it portable enough for the lunchbox or desk.[28] In the case of existing brands, marketers should reevaluate packages periodically. Marketers should view packaging as a major strategic tool, especially for consumer convenience products. For instance, in the food industry, jumbo and large package sizes for such products as hot dogs, pizzas, English muffins, frozen dinners, and biscuits have been very successful. When considering the strategic uses of packaging, marketers must also analyze the cost of packaging and package changes. Table 14.2 lists the biggest packaging spenders. In this section, we examine several ways to use packaging strategically.

ALTERING THE PACKAGE

At times, a marketer changes a package because the existing design is no longer in style, especially when compared with the packaging of competitive products. Arm & Hammer

TABLE 14.2 Companies That Spend the Most on Packaging

Anheuser-Busch	Kraft General Foods
Campbell Soup	Kraft USA
Coca-Cola	Miller Brewing
General Mills	PepsiCo
Procter & Gamble	

Altering the Package
Eclipse gum employs innovative packaging to make the product more attractive and easier to use.

now markets a refillable plastic shaker for its baking soda. Quaker Oats hired a package design company to redesign its Rice-A-Roni package to give the product the appearance of having evolved with the times while retaining its traditional taste appeal. Rice-A-Roni had been experiencing a lag in sales because of increased competition. An overhaul of the product packaging to a refreshing and more up-to-date look was credited with a 20 percent increase in sales over the previous year. Similarly, Del Monte introduced a contemporary look for its tomato products and experienced a double-digit gain in the first year.

A package may be redesigned because new product features need to be highlighted or because new packaging materials have become available. An organization may decide to change a product's packaging to reposition the product or to make the product safer or more convenient to use. Oscar Mayer introduced sliced bacon in a redesigned "Stay-Fresh Reclosable Tray" to address consumer complaints that traditional bacon packaging is sometimes messy and can't be sealed to ensure freshness through multiple servings. Developed in cooperation with packaging company Bemis Co., the new package represents the most significant change in bacon packaging since the 1920s.[29]

SECONDARY-USE PACKAGING

A secondary-use package can be reused for purposes other than its initial function. For example, a margarine container can be reused to store leftovers, and a jelly container can serve as a drinking glass. Customers often view secondary-use packaging as adding value to products, in which case its use should stimulate unit sales.

CATEGORY-CONSISTENT PACKAGING

With category-consistent packaging, the product is packaged in line with the packaging practices associated with a particular product category. Some product categories—for example, mayonnaise, mustard, ketchup, and peanut butter—have traditional package shapes. Other product categories are characterized by recognizable color combinations, such as red and white for soup and red, white, and blue for Ritz-like crackers. When an organization introduces a brand in one of these product categories, marketers will often use traditional package shapes and color combinations to ensure that customers will recognize the new product as being in that specific product category.

INNOVATIVE PACKAGING

Sometimes a marketer employs a unique cap, design, applicator, or other feature to make a product distinctive. Such packaging can be effective when the innovation makes the product safer or easier to use, or provides better protection for the product. Healthy Choice, for example, created an innovative package for its new Healthy Choice Fresh Mixers. Consumers are able to store their meal without a refrigerator or freezer as well as cook their meal in the container and strain water with the lid.[30] In some instances, marketers use innovative or unique packages that are inconsistent with traditional packaging practices to make the brand stand out from competitors. To distinguish their products, marketers in the beverage industry have long used innovative shapes and packaging materials. Unusual packaging sometimes requires expending considerable resources, not only on package design but also on making customers aware of the unique package and its benefit. Research suggests that uniquely shaped packages that attract attention are more likely to be perceived as containing a higher volume of product.[31]

MULTIPLE PACKAGING

Rather than packaging a single unit of a product, marketers sometimes use twin packs, tri-packs, six-packs, or other forms of multiple packaging. For certain types of products, multiple packaging may increase demand because it increases the amount of the product available at the point of consumption (e.g., in one's house). It may also increase consumer acceptance of the product by encouraging the buyer to try the product several times. Multiple packaging can make products easier to handle and store, as in the case of six-packs for soft drinks; it can also facilitate special price offers, such as two-for-one sales. However, multiple packaging does not work for all types of products. One would not use additional table salt, for example, simply because an extra box is in the pantry.

HANDLING-IMPROVED PACKAGING

A product's packaging may be changed to make it easier to handle in the distribution channel—for example, by changing the outer carton or using special bundling, shrink-wrapping, or pallets. In some cases, the shape of the package is changed. An ice cream producer, for instance, may change from a cylindrical package to a rectangular one to facilitate handling. In addition, at the retail level, the ice cream producer may be able to get more shelf facings with a rectangular package than with a round one. Outer containers for products are sometimes changed so they will proceed more easily through automated warehousing systems.

Criticisms of Packaging

The last several decades have brought a number of improvements in packaging. However, some packaging problems still need to be resolved. Some packages suffer from functional problems in that they simply do not work well. The packaging for flour and sugar is, at best, poor. Both grocers and consumers are very much aware that these packages leak and tear easily. Can anyone open and close a bag of flour without spilling at least a little bit? Certain packages, such as refrigerated biscuit cans, milk cartons with fold-out spouts, and potato chip bags, are frequently difficult to open. The traditional shapes of packages for products such as ketchup and salad dressing make the product inconvenient to use. Have you ever wondered when tapping on a ketchup bottle why the producer didn't put the ketchup in a mayonnaise jar?

Although many steps have been taken to make packaging safer, critics still focus on the safety issues. Containers with sharp edges and breakable glass bottles are sometimes viewed as a threat to safety. Certain types of plastic packaging and aerosol containers represent possible health hazards.

At times, packaging is viewed as deceptive. Package shape, graphic design, and certain colors may be used to make a product appear larger than it actually is. The inconsistent use of certain size designations, such as giant, economy, family, king, and super, can lead to customer confusion.

Finally, although customers in the United States traditionally prefer attractive, effective, convenient packaging, the cost of such packaging is high.

Labeling

Labeling is very closely interrelated with packaging and is used for identification, promotional, informational, and legal purposes. Labels can be small or large relative to the size of the product and carry varying amounts of information. The sticker on a Chiquita banana, for example, is quite small and displays only the brand name of the fruit and perhaps a stock-keeping unit number. A label can be part of the package itself or a separate feature attached to the package. The label on a can of Coke is actually part of the can, whereas the label on a two-liter bottle of Coke is separate and can be removed. Information presented on a label may include the brand name and mark, the registered trademark symbol, package size and content, product features, nutritional information, potential presence of allergens, type and style of the product, number of servings, care instructions, directions for use and safety precautions, the name and address of the manufacturer, expiration dates, seals of approval, and other facts.

For many products, the label includes a **universal product code (UPC)**, a series of electronically readable lines identifying the product and providing inventory and pricing information for producers and resellers. The UPC is electronically read at the retail checkout counter.

Labels can facilitate the identification of a product by displaying the brand name in combination with a unique graphic design. For instance, Heinz ketchup is easy to identify on a supermarket shelf because the brand name is easy to read and the label has a distinctive crown-like shape. By drawing attention to products and their benefits, labels can strengthen an organization's promotional efforts. Labels may contain such promotional messages as the offer of a discount or a larger package size at the same price, or information about a new or improved product feature.

A number of federal laws and regulations specify information that must be included on the labels of certain products. Garments must be labeled with the name of the manufacturer, country of manufacture, fabric content, and cleaning instructions. Labels on nonedible items such as shampoos and detergents must include both safety precautions and directions for use. In 1966, Congress passed the Fair Packaging and Labeling Act, one of the most comprehensive pieces of labeling and packaging legislation. This law focuses on mandatory labeling requirements, voluntary adoption of packaging standards by firms within industries, and the provision of power to the Federal Trade Commission and the Food and Drug Administration to establish and enforce packaging regulations. A product that has come under fire recently is the printer cartridge. Consumers are pushing for more disclosure on labels about the amount of ink in each cartridge. Currently, it is difficult for consumers to compare offerings and prices without knowing the amount of ink contained in each cartridge. Companies have responded by saying ink does not fall under the Fair Packaging and Labeling Act. This dispute is currently under review.[32]

The Nutrition Labeling Act of 1990 requires the FDA to review food labeling and packaging, focusing on nutrition content, label format, ingredient labeling, food descriptions, and health messages. This act regulates much of the labeling on more than 250,000 products made by some 17,000 U.S. companies. Any food product for which

labeling Providing identifying, promotional, or other information on package labels

universal product code (UPC) A series of electronically readable lines identifying a product and containing inventory and pricing information

"Made-in..." Labels
The country of origin affects customers' perceptions of the product.

© Feng Yu/Alamy

a nutritional claim is made must have nutrition labeling that follows a standard format. Food product labels must state the number of servings per container, serving size, number of calories per serving, number of calories derived from fat, number of carbohydrates, and amounts of specific nutrients such as vitamins. In addition, new nutritional labeling requirements focus on the amounts of trans-fatty acids in food products. Although consumers have responded favorably to this type of information on labels, evidence as to whether they actually use it has been mixed. One study reported that 80 percent of American consumers claim to read food labels, yet 44 percent admitted to buying a product even when the information on the label indicated that it was less than healthy.[33]

Despite legislation to make labels as accurate and informative as possible, questionable labeling practices persist. The Center for Science in the Public Interest questions the practice of naming a product "Strawberry Frozen Yogurt Bars" when it contains strawberry flavoring but no strawberries, or of calling a breakfast cereal "lightly sweetened" when sugar makes up 22 percent of its ingredients. Many labels on vegetable oils say "no cholesterol," but many of these oils contain saturated fats that can raise cholesterol levels. The Food and Drug Administration amended its regulations to forbid producers of vegetable oil from making "no cholesterol" claims on their labels.

Another area of concern is "green labeling." Consumers who are committed to making environmentally responsible or natural purchasing decisions are sometimes fooled by labels that claim a product is environmentally friendly or organic. The U.S. Public Interest Research Group accused several manufacturers of "greenwashing" customers: using misleading claims to sell products by playing on customers' concern for the environment. For example, some manufacturers put a recycling symbol on labels for products made of polyvinyl chloride plastic, which cannot be recycled in the vast majority of U.S. communities.

Of concern to many manufacturers are the Federal Trade Commission's guidelines regarding "Made in U.S.A." labels, a growing problem due to the increasingly global nature of manufacturing. The FTC requires that "all or virtually all" of a product's components be made in the United States if the label says "Made in U.S.A." Although the FTC recently considered changing its guidelines to read "substantially all," it rejected this idea and maintains the "all or virtually all" standard. In light of this decision, the FTC ordered New Balance to stop using the "Made in U.S.A." claim on its athletic-shoe labels because some components (rubber soles) are made in China. The "Made in U.S.A." labeling issue has not been totally resolved. The FTC criteria for using "Made in U.S.A." are likely to be challenged and subsequently changed.[34] Table 14.3 provides insight into just how important the "Made in U.S.A." label can be for both Americans and western Europeans. It includes assessments of both quality and value for U.S.A.-, Japanese-, Korean-, and Chinese-origin labels.

TABLE 14.3 Perceived Quality and Value of Products Based on Country of Origin*

	"Made in U.S.A."		"Made in Japan"		"Made in Korea"		"Made in China"	
	Value	Quality	Value	Quality	Value	Quality	Value	Quality
U.S. adults	4.0	4.2	3.2	3.2	2.6	2.4	2.8	2.4
Western Europeans	3.3	3.4	3.5	3.5	2.8	2.4	2.9	2.4

*On a scale of 1 (low) to 5 (high).

Source: "American Demographics 2006 Consumer Perception Survey," *Advertising Age*, January 2, 2006, p. 9. Data by Synovate.

summary

1. To explain the value of branding

A brand is a name, term, design, symbol, or any other feature that identifies one seller's good or service and distinguishes it from those of other sellers. A brand name is the part of a brand that can be spoken. A brand mark is the element not made up of words. A trademark is a legal designation indicating that the owner has exclusive use of the brand or part of the brand and others are prohibited by law from using it. A trade name is the legal name of an organization. Branding helps buyers identify and evaluate products, helps sellers facilitate product introduction and repeat purchasing, and fosters brand loyalty.

2. To understand brand loyalty

Brand loyalty is a customer's favorable attitude toward a specific brand. If brand loyalty is strong enough, customers may consistently purchase a particular brand when they need a product in this product category. The three degrees of brand loyalty are brand recognition, brand preference, and brand insistence. Brand recognition occurs when a customer is aware that the brand exists and views it as an alternative purchase if the preferred brand is unavailable. With brand preference, a customer prefers one brand over competing brands and will purchase it if available. Brand insistence occurs when a customer will accept no substitute.

3. To analyze the major components of brand equity

Brand equity is the marketing and financial value associated with a brand's strength. It represents the value of a brand to an organization. The four major elements underlying brand equity include brand-name awareness, brand loyalty, perceived brand quality, and brand associations.

4. To recognize the types of brands and their benefits

A manufacturer brand, initiated by the producer, ensures that the firm is associated with its products at the point of purchase. A private distributor brand is initiated and owned by a reseller, sometimes taking on the name of the store or distributor. Manufacturers combat growing competition from private distributor brands by developing multiple brands. A generic brand indicates only the product category and does not include the company name or other identifying terms.

5. To understand how to select and protect brands

When selecting a brand name, a marketer should choose one that is easy to say, spell, and recall and that alludes to the product's uses, benefits, or special characteristics. Brand names can be devised from words, letters, numbers, nonsense words, or a combination of these. Brand names are created inside an organization by individuals, committees, or branding departments and by outside consultants. Services as well as products are branded, often with the company name and an accompanying symbol that makes the brand distinctive or conveys a desired image.

Producers protect ownership of their brands through registration with the U.S. Patent and Trademark Office. A company must make certain the brand name it selects does not infringe on an already registered brand by confusing or deceiving consumers about the source of the product. In most foreign countries, brand registration is on a first-come, first-serve basis, making protection more difficult. Brand counterfeiting is becoming increasingly common and can undermine consumers' confidence in a brand.

6. To examine three types of branding strategies

Companies brand their products in several ways. Individual branding designates a unique name for each of a company's products, family branding identifies all of a firm's products with a single name, and brand extension branding applies an existing name to a new product in a different product category.

7. To understand co-branding and brand licensing

Co-branding is the use of two or more brands on one product. Effective co-branding profits from the trust and confidence customers have in the brands involved. Finally, through a licensing agreement and for a licensing fee, a firm may permit another organization to use its brand on other products. Brand licensing enables producers to earn extra revenue, receive low-cost or free publicity, and protect their trademarks.

8. To describe the major packaging functions and design considerations and how packaging is used in marketing strategies

Packaging involves development of a container and a graphic design for a product. Effective packaging offers protection, economy, safety, and convenience. It can influence a customer's purchase decision by promoting features, uses, benefits, and image. When developing a package, marketers must consider the value to the customer of efficient and effective packaging, offset by the price the customer is willing to pay. Other considerations include making the package tamper resistant, whether to use multiple packaging and family packaging, how to design the package as an effective promotional tool, how best to accommodate resellers, and whether to develop environmentally responsible packaging. Firms choose particular colors, designs, shapes, and textures to create desirable images and associations. Packaging can be an important part of an overall marketing strategy and can be used to target certain market segments. Modifications in packaging can revive a mature product and extend its product life cycle. Producers alter packages to convey new features or to make them safer or more convenient. If a package has a secondary use, the product's value to the consumer may increase. Category-consistent packaging makes products more easily recognizable to consumers.

Innovative packaging enhances a product's distinctiveness. Consumers may criticize packaging that does not work well, poses health or safety problems, is deceptive in some way, or is not biodegradable or recyclable.

> **9. To examine the functions of labeling and describe some legal issues pertaining to labeling**

Labeling is closely interrelated with packaging and is used for identification, promotional, informational, and legal purposes. The labels of many products include a universal product code, a series of electronically readable lines identifying a product and containing inventory and pricing information. Various federal laws and regulations require that certain products be labeled or marked with warnings, instructions, nutritional information, manufacturer's identification, and the like. Despite legislation, questionable labeling practices persist, including misleading information about fat content and cholesterol, freshness, and "greenness" of packaging.

Go to www.cengagebrain.com for resources to help you master the content in this chapter as well as materials that will expand your marketing knowledge!

important terms

brand, 398
brand name, 398
brand mark, 398
trademark, 398
trade name, 398
brand loyalty, 400

brand recognition, 400
brand preference, 400
brand insistence, 400
brand equity, 401
manufacturer brand, 403

private distributor brand, 403
generic brand, 405
individual branding, 407
family branding, 408
brand extension, 408

co-branding, 409
brand licensing, 409
family packaging, 411
labeling, 416
universal product code (UPC), 416

discussion and review questions

1. What is the difference between a brand and a brand name? Compare and contrast a brand mark and a trademark.
2. How does branding benefit consumers and marketers?
3. What are the three major degrees of brand loyalty?
4. What is brand equity? Identify and explain the major elements of brand equity.
5. Compare and contrast manufacturer brands, private distributor brands, and generic brands.
6. Identify the factors a marketer should consider in selecting a brand name.
7. The brand name Xerox is sometimes used generically to refer to photocopiers, and Kleenex is used to refer to facial tissues. How can the manufacturers protect their brand names, and why would they want to do so?

8. What is co-branding? What major issues should be considered when using co-branding?
9. What are the major advantages and disadvantages of brand licensing?
10. Describe the functions a package can perform. Which function is most important? Why?
11. What are the main factors a marketer should consider when developing a package?
12. In what ways can packaging be used as a strategic tool?
13. What are the major criticisms of packaging?
14. What are the major functions of labeling?
15. In what ways do regulations and legislation affect labeling?

application questions

1. Identify two brands for which you are brand insistent. How did you begin using these brands? Why do you no longer use other brands?
2. Honda introduced an SUV called Element, a name that suggests freedom and comfort in any environment. Invent a brand name for a line of luxury sports cars that also would appeal to an international market. Suggest a name that implies quality, luxury, and value.
3. When a firm decides to brand its products, it may choose one of several strategies. Name one company that uses each of the following strategies. How does each strategy help the company?
   a. Individual branding
   b. Family branding
   c. Brand extension

4. For each of the following product categories, choose an existing brand. Then, for each selected brand, suggest a co-brand and explain why the co-brand would be effective.
   a. Cookies
   b. Pizza
   c. Chips
   d. A sports drink
5. Packaging provides product protection; customer convenience; and promotion of image, key features, and benefits. Identify a product that uses packaging in each of these ways, and evaluate the effectiveness of the package for that function.
6. Identify a package that you believe is inferior. Explain why you think the package is inferior, and discuss your recommendations for improving it.

internet exercise

Pillsbury

Like other marketers of consumer products, Pillsbury has set up a website to inform and entertain consumers. Catering to the appeal of its most popular product spokesperson, Pillsbury has given its Dough Boy his own site. Visit him at **www.doughboy.com**.

1. What branding strategy does Pillsbury seem to be using with regard to the products it presents on this site?
2. How does this Pillsbury website promote brand loyalty?
3. What degree of consistency exists in Pillsbury's packaging of its products displayed on the website?

developing your marketing plan

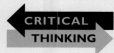

CRITICAL THINKING The selection and protection of the appropriate brand name is an important part of formulating a marketing strategy. A clear understanding of how branding and packaging decisions influence a customer's choice of products is essential when developing the marketing plan. The brand name and its packaging will influence several other marketing plan decisions. Relating to the information provided in this chapter, focus on the following issues:

1. Discuss the level of brand equity your company's products currently have in the marketplace. How will brand equity affect your branding strategy?
2. Which type of branding strategy is most appropriate for your new-product idea?

3. Do any strategic opportunities exist from co-branding your new product with existing brands in your company's product mix or with other company's brands? You may want to refer to your SWOT analysis in Chapter 2.
4. Discuss the style, color, and labeling options for your product. Consider your target market's needs and your branding strategy in this discussion.

The information obtained from these questions should assist you in developing various aspects of your marketing plan found in the *Interactive Marketing Plan* exercise at **www.cengagebrain.com**.

© Comstock Images/Getty Images

VIDEO CASE 14.1

New Belgium Brews Up Strong Brand Equity

CRITICAL THINKING

The idea for New Belgium Brewing Company began with a bicycling trip through Belgium, where some of the world's finest ales have been brewed for centuries. As Jeff Lebesch, a U.S. electrical engineer, cruised around on a fat-tired mountain bike, he wondered if he could produce such high-quality ales in his home state of Colorado. After returning home, Lebesch began to experiment in his Fort Collins basement. When his home-brewed experiments earned rave reviews from friends, Lebesch and his wife, Kim Jordan, opened the New Belgium Brewing (NBB) in 1991. They named their first brew Fat Tire Amber Ale in honor of Lebesch's biking adventure.

Although the overall craft-brewing industry has done well in recent years, with sales growing steadily even during the recent economic downturn, NBB has done even better. Today, NBB is a successful $100 million company that markets 567,000 barrels of ales and pilsners every year. The entrepreneurial company has steadily expanded its distribution throughout the western United States, partnering with regional breweries to produce and sell its fresh-brewed beers in local communities farther and farther from its Colorado headquarters.

The standard product line includes Sunshine Wheat, Blue Paddle Pilsner, Abbey Ale, and 1554 Black Ale, as well as the firm's best-seller, the original Fat Tire Amber Ale. NBB also markets seasonal beers, such as Frambozen, released at Thanksgiving and Christmas, and Hoptober, sold during the early fall. The firm occasionally offers one-time-only brews—such as LaFolie, a wood-aged beer—that are sold only until the batch runs out.

To reinforce the firm's commitment to old-fashioned brewing quality, NBB's packaging and labels evoke a touch of nostalgia. The Fat Tire label, for example, features an old-style cruiser bike with wide tires, a padded seat, and a basket hanging from the handlebars. All the label and packaging designs were created by the same watercolor artist, Jeff Lebesch's next-door neighbor.

NBB prices its beers to reflect high quality and set the products apart from those of more widely available brands such as Coors and Budweiser. This pricing strategy conveys the message that the products are special but also keeps them competitive with other microbrews, such as Pete's Wicked Ale and Sierra Nevada. To demonstrate its appreciation for its retailers and business partners, NBB does not sell beer to consumers on-site at the brewhouse for less than the retailers charge.

Since its founding, NBB's most effective promotion has been via word-of-mouth communication by customers devoted to the brand. The company initially avoided mass advertising, relying instead on small-scale, local promotions, such as print advertisements in alternative magazines, participation in local festivals, and sponsorship of alternative sports events. Through event sponsorships, such as the Tour de Fat, NBB has raised thousands of dollars for various environmental, social, and cycling nonprofit organizations. The company is also a member of 1% for the Planet, donating 1 percent of its annual sales revenue to environmental-protection groups around the world.

With expanding distribution, however, the brewery recognized a need to connect more effectively with a far-flung customer base. NBB's top management consulted with Dr. David Holt, an Oxford professor and branding expert. After studying the fast-growing company, Holt, together with NBB's marketing director, drafted a 70-page "manifesto" describing the brand's attributes, character, cultural relevancy, and promise. In particular, Holt identified an ethos of pursuing creative activities simply for the joy of doing them well and in harmony with the natural environment.

With the brand defined, NBB went in search of an advertising agency to help communicate that brand identity; it soon found Amalgamated, a young, independent New York advertising agency. Amalgamated created a $10 million advertising campaign that targets high-end beer drinkers, men ages 25 to 44, and highlights the brewery's image as being down to earth. The grainy ads focus on a man rebuilding a cruiser bike out of used parts and then riding it along pastoral country roads. The product appears in just five seconds of each ad between the tag lines "Follow Your Folly ... Ours Is Beer." The ads helped position the growing brand as whimsical, thoughtful, and reflective. In addition to advertising, the company promotes its brand by sponsoring bicycle tours and engaging customers and employees in online conversations via social media such as Twitter, Facebook, and blogs.

NBB's mission is: "To operate a profitable brewery which makes our love and talent manifest." From top-quality brewing to a strong belief in giving back to the local and global community, the company reinforces the positive qualities that make its brand so successful every day.[35]

QUESTIONS FOR DISCUSSION

1. What has New Belgium Brewing done to increase brand recognition and brand preference?
2. How is New Belgium Brewing using packaging to support its brand image?
3. Assess New Belgium's brand equity in terms of awareness, quality, associations, and loyalty.

CASE 14.2

Will the "G" Branding Initiatives for Gatorade Work?

CRITICAL THINKING

Gatorade, which single-handedly pioneered the sports drink category more than 45 years ago, is making "G" the centerpiece of its branding efforts. Invented by researchers at the University of Florida, the original Gatorade formula was developed to help players on the college football team avoid dehydration. Other schools took notice of the Gators' performance and soon began ordering batches of Gatorade for their athletes. One by one, Gatorade attracted the interest of professional football teams, and in 1983, it was named the National Football League's official sports drink. That year, Gatorade was acquired by Quaker Oats and, in 2001, Quaker was, in turn, purchased by PepsiCo.

Throughout its history, Gatorade has remained the leader in sports drinks. However, in recent years, changes in customer behavior and increased competition have combined to take a toll on sales. First, increasingly health-conscious customers are seeking out low-calorie, low-sodium beverages instead of traditional sports drinks. Second, PepsiCo's main rival, Coca-Cola, has been powering up its marketing of Powerade sports drinks and winning over customers. As a result, Gatorade's annual sales were stalled at around $5 billion, and its market share had fallen to 75 percent, while Powerade's market share shot up to 24 percent.

Now Gatorade's marketers are fighting for higher sales with new branding initiatives for specific target markets and redesigned packaging to grab customers' attention. Both the Gatorade brand name and the lightning bolt brand mark have been fine-tuned to emphasize the G and the thunderbolt while downplaying the rest of the name. The goal is to make the combination instantly recognizable as representing Gatorade, in much the same way that the Nike swoosh has become the iconic representation of that brand.

Gatorade is also introducing a series of G sports drinks targeting the specific needs of athletes. This is a change for Gatorade, which had for several years broadened its targeting

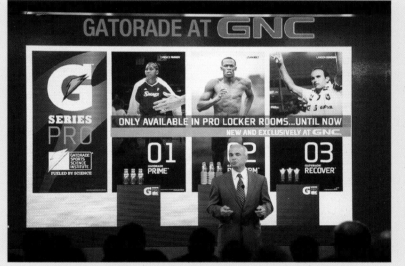

and positioned the brand as a thirst-quencher for a cross-section of consumers, not just athletes. Now the brand, under its revamped G branding, is going back to its sports roots with the G Series line of drink products for casual and serious athletes at a variety of experience levels.

Gatorade Prime 01 contains vitamins and other nutrients to help athletes "start strong." Gatorade Perform 02 products include the original green Gatorade beverage for rehydration during exertion plus a low-calorie drink, branded as G2. In addition, mix-your-own powdered versions of both Perform drinks are available. Gatorade Recover 03 is a special drink developed to replenish energy and help muscles recover after any sports activity. The Elite Series of Gatorade drinks for athletes, more widely available than in the past, offers special formulations featuring protein, carbohydrates, and other nutritional enhancements.

Thanks to a new distribution arrangement, G Series Pro—once sold to professional athletes in gyms and locker rooms—can now be purchased at 5,500 GNC stores. "This line alone, reaching a new target audience, is going to be a killer," comments GNC's CEO. "We have consumers who are extremely passionate about what they [drink]." In another new deal, Gatorade is marketing its G Natural and G2 Natural low-calorie drinks through Whole Foods Market, which specializes in natural and organic foods.

Along with fine-tuning the brand and individual products, Gatorade is fine-tuning its packaging and labeling. For years, all bottles featured the full "Gatorade" brand name bisected by the brand's stylized orange lightning bolt. Today, the G has taken center stage on container labels, with a small bolt within the G and a bolder bolt as the backdrop for the product name. Overall, the G Series packaging unifies the product line while allowing each item enough distinctive touches (such as different bottle shapes) to help customers quickly find the particular product they want on crowded store shelves. The sophisticated new packaging also sets this line apart from the traditional Gatorade green-and-orange look, visually reinforcing the innovativeness of the G Series.

Gatorade's advertising and promotional efforts, including a YouTube channel and Facebook fan page, carry through the focus on athleticism. Sports stars such as Serena Williams and Derek Jeter are featured, along with behind-the-scenes interviews with athletes getting ready for major sporting events. However, with Coca-Cola putting a big push behind its Powerade products, will Gatorade's target market embrace the big G idea and gulp down enough G Series drinks to increase the brand's market share?[36]

QUESTIONS FOR DISCUSSION

1. What are the marketing advantages and disadvantages of emphasizing "G" as the primary element in the Gatorade brand?

2. As Gatorade sharpens its marketing focus on athletes, should it vary its packaging for different distribution channels or different sports? Explain your answer.

3. For competitive reasons, do you think Gatorade should consider co-branding to build on the equity of another major brand name as it seeks higher sales? Why or why not?

Digital Photo Products Put Shutterfly in the Profit Zone

Picture this: Just ten years ago, digital cameras were high-end products owned only by tech-savvy photo buffs, and most consumers who surfed the Internet used slow dial-up connections. The idea of uploading digital images to order prints from a web-based company was new even to people who enjoyed speedy broadband connections. Yet when Shutterfly started offering photo-printing services on the Internet late in 1999, it was entering a market that was already teeming with competition. Today, digital photography has moved into the mainstream, and Shutterfly has become a major force in the online photo-printing industry, introducing dozens of new products every year for consumers to embellish with their favorite photos.

Keeping Quality in Focus

Early on, Shutterfly, which is based in Redwood City, California, offered free prints to induce customers to try its photo-printing services, a technique used by many competitors, then and now. In all, Shutterfly gave away more than 80 percent of its prints during its first six months,

part of a plan to showcase Shutterfly's high-quality printing. The company invested in special printing equipment at the outset so it would have full control over quality rather than outsourcing some or all of its orders to an outside photo-processing firm. Shutterfly's goal was to ensure that the customer photos it printed would always come out clear, crisp, and colorful. Its site also included photo-enhancement functions so customers could add special borders, eliminate the red-eye effect, and make other improvements before ordering prints.

Another way Shutterfly distinguished itself was by inviting consumers to upload and store their photos on its website without charge. Unlike some competitors, Shutterfly promised never to delete any photos, no matter how many had been uploaded or how long they had been stored—a feature highly valued by the company's fast-growing customer base. Photo sharing was also a key fea-

ture: Shutterfly made it easy for customers to let friends and family members view and order their photos online.

Staying Ahead of the Shakeout

To stay ahead of competitors, Shutterfly introduced a never-ending parade of new products for photo personalization, from calendars and cards to mugs and magnets. Meanwhile, intense competition and a prolonged price war resulted in an industry shakeout that drove many smaller firms out of business. Some of the stronger firms were acquired by big corporations. Kodak bought Ofoto and rebranded the business as the Kodak Gallery; Hewlett-Packard bought Snapfish and kept the site's catchy brand. Shutterfly survived all of this industry turmoil and, by continuing to build on its high-quality reputation, became profitable in 2003.

In 2005, the CEO broadened the company's mission. Thinking about the lifestyle aspects of how consumers take, use, and share photos, he launched what he called "a next-generation personal publishing platform that would enable our customers to be more creative." In preparation, Shutterfly surveyed its customers to learn more about their needs and preferences. It also invested heavily in additional production capacity, buying sophisticated industrial printers that can each turn out 20,000 photos per hour.

Shutterfly sought to escape the print price war by diversifying its product mix beyond standard prints. Adding higher-margin items such as customizable T-shirts, jewelry boxes, and tote bags helped the firm to expand its appeal and gave current customers more reasons to log on, upload new photos, and buy from Shutterfly again and again. The company also negotiated to license well-known characters such as Clifford the Big Red Dog, SpongeBob SquarePants, and other Nickelodeon characters for use on personalized photo greeting cards, photo albums, and other products.

Digital Imaging Goes Mainstream

By now, millions of U.S. consumers have made the transition from film-based cameras to digital cameras. Many cell phones are equipped with digital cameras, as well, which only adds to the market potential. So many people are busy snapping so many photos, but Shutterfly's analysis revealed that women accounted for 70 percent of its customer base. Why? "Women often are the people who take on the role of family historian or chief memory officer," the CEO explains. Not only are women taking photos (or taking charge of photos taken by other family members), but they are making key decisions about which photos to print, which printing service to use, and what kinds of prints and personalized products to buy. For this reason, much of Shutterfly's promotion budget is devoted to media that reach women.

The biggest surge in buying occurs in the last three months of the year. On the day after Halloween, for instance, Shutterfly's site is inundated by 3 million photos of costumed kids of all ages. On that day alone, customers order a total of 1.2 million prints—and the holiday rush is just beginning. "From Halloween, it is straight on to Thanksgiving, holiday cards, and calendars," the CEO says, "and our lab is running 24 hours a day, seven days a week."

The Shutterfly of Tomorrow

To date, Shutterfly has sold millions of prints and personalized products and is storing at least 1 billion images for its customers. Sales have increased to nearly $250 million,

but profits still depend largely on the all-important year-end holiday season. The company's reputation for quality and responsive service has helped it maintain an enviably high customer-retention rate. It has one production facility in the east and another in the west so customers can receive their orders quickly, regardless of location.

More innovations are ahead as Shutterfly's marketers act on their insights about the strong emotions that photos evoke. "People have an intrinsic desire for social expression: to capture and share their experiences, to relive special moments, and to communicate their memories," the CEO notes. A Shutterfly senior vice president adds, "Prints are great, and that is one way to tell a story. But there is another way—books, collages, and other products. You will see a lot more of that. That's the area where we are proud to have put up the flag and to be a leader."[37]

QUESTIONS FOR DISCUSSION

1. What is Shutterfly doing to manage the marketing challenges of heterogeneity?

2. How has Shutterfly used marketing to draw customers through the product adoption process?

3. What has Shutterfly done to add supplemental features as well as symbolic and experiential benefits to its offerings?

4. Why would Shutterfly negotiate to license Nickelodeon characters for personalized photo products?

Part 6

Distribution Decisions

Developing products that satisfy customers is important, but it is not enough to guarantee successful marketing strategies. Products must also be available in adequate quantities in accessible locations at the times when customers desire them. **PART 6** deals with the distribution of products and the marketing channels and institutions that help to make products available. **CHAPTER 15** discusses supply-chain management, marketing channels, and the decisions and activities associated with the physical distribution of products, such as order processing, materials handling, warehousing, inventory management, and transportation. **CHAPTER 16** explores retailing and wholesaling, including types of retailers and wholesalers, direct marketing and selling, and strategic retailing issues.

Economic forces

Competitive forces

Political forces

Product

Price   Customer   Distribution

Sociocultural forces

Legal and regulatory forces

Promotion

Technological forces

Chapter 15

Marketing Channels and Supply-Chain Management

OBJECTIVES

1. To describe the foundations of supply-chain management

2. To explore the role and significance of marketing channels and supply chains

3. To identify types of marketing channels

4. To understand factors that influence marketing channel selection

5. To identify the intensity of market coverage

6. To examine strategic issues in marketing channels, including leadership, cooperation, and conflict

7. To examine physical distribution as a part of supply-chain management

8. To explore legal issues in channel management

Coca-Cola Seeks More Control over Distribution Channels

Can Coca-Cola double its global revenue to $200 billion by 2020? That's one major goal of the Atlanta-based beverage company's long-term "Vision 2020" plan for super-charging future growth. Another goal is to be selling 3 billion servings of its soft drinks every day by 2020, counting purchases in stores, restaurants, vending machines, and every other outlet where its beverages are available.

To achieve these ambitious targets and compete with both local brands and multinational rivals such as PepsiCo, Coca-Cola is working with bottlers, distributors, and retail accounts to get its 500-plus beverage brands to customers worldwide. More than 75 percent of its revenue comes from non-U.S. sales, which is why the company is expanding distribution in international markets and making its brands more visible to customers when and where they want to buy.

For example, Coca-Cola has its eye on the fast-growing market in India, where ready-to-drink beverages are becoming more popular. Getting its products into more stores, restaurants, bakeries, and other outlets is only the beginning. The company arranges for branded cooling units to be prominently positioned where customers can see and reach them. It also provides colorful signs to build demand at the point of purchase.

In China, Coca-Cola's bright red vending machines are commonplace in urban centers, one reason that the nation's average annual per capita consumption of its beverages has reached 28 bottles. In Jiangxi Province, however, per capita consumption is just seven bottles per year. To support higher sales, Coca-Cola has a joint venture to build new production facilities, open more warehouses, expand the delivery fleet, and computerize routes for higher efficiency. It is following a similar strategy in several other provinces.

Recently, the company purchased the North American operations of Coca-Cola Enterprises, its largest bottler and distributor. The purchase streamlines the distribution network in Coca-Cola's home market and cuts costs as well. Now the company can deal directly with its retail accounts—an important consideration because ten large retailers account for 40 percent of Coca-Cola's North American sales volume.[1]

Decisions like those made by Coca-Cola relate to the **distribution** component of the marketing mix, which focuses on the decisions and activities involved in making products available to customers when and where they want to purchase them. Choosing which channels of distribution to use is a major decision in the development of marketing strategies.

In this chapter, we focus on marketing channels and supply-chain management. First, we explore the concept of the supply chain and its various activities. Second, we elaborate on marketing channels and the need for intermediaries and then analyze the primary functions they perform. Next, we outline the types and characteristics of marketing channels, discuss how they are selected, and explore how marketers determine the appropriate intensity of market coverage for a product. We examine the strategic channel issues of leadership, cooperation, and conflict. We also look at the role of physical distribution within the supply chain, including its objectives and basic functions. Finally, we look at several legal issues that affect channel management.

Foundations of the Supply Chain

An important function of distribution is the joint effort of all involved organizations to be part of creating an effective **supply chain**, which refers to all the activities associated with the flow and transformation of products from raw materials through to the end customer. This results in a total distribution system that involves firms that are both "upstream" in the supply chain (e.g., suppliers) and "downstream" (e.g., wholesalers, retailers) to serve customers and generate competitive advantage. Historically, marketing focused on only certain downstream activities of supply chains, but today marketing professionals are recognizing that important marketplace advantages can be secured by effectively integrating important activities in the supply chain. These include operations, logistics, sourcing, and marketing channels. Integrating these activities requires marketing managers to work with their counterparts in operations management, logistics management, and supply management.[2] **Operations management** is the total set of managerial activities used by an organization to transform resource inputs into products.[3] **Logistics management** involves planning, implementing, and controlling the efficient and effective flow and storage of products and information from the point of origin to consumption to meet customers' needs and wants. **Supply management** (e.g., purchasing, procurement, sourcing) in its broadest form refers to the processes that enable the progress of value from raw material to final customer and back to redesign and final disposition.

Supply-chain management is therefore a set of approaches used to integrate the functions of operations management, logistics management, supply management, and marketing channel management so products are produced and distributed in the right quantities, to the right locations, and at the right time. It includes activities such as manufacturing, research, sales, advertising, shipping, and most of all, cooperating and understanding of tradeoffs throughout the whole chain to achieve optimal levels of efficiency and service. The key tasks involved in supply-chain management are outlined in Table 15.1. Supply-chain management also includes suppliers of raw materials and other components to make goods and services, logistics and transportation firms, communication firms, and other firms that indirectly take part in marketing exchanges. Thus, the supply chain includes all entities that facilitate product distribution and benefit from cooperative efforts. Consider that Intel, the computer chip maker, spends $3 billion to build a new semiconductor facility, and it loses $1 million a day if an assembly line goes down due to system failures or part shortages. Consequently, Intel requires its equipment suppliers to respond to failures within 15 minutes.[4] Worldwide spending on supply-chain management systems is more than $25 billion.[5]

Technology has improved supply-chain management capabilities on a global basis. Information technology in particular has created an almost seamless distribution process for matching inventory needs to manufacturer requirements in the upstream portion of the supply chain and to customers' requirements in the downstream portion of the chain. With integrated information sharing among chain members, costs can be reduced, service

---

distribution The decisions and activities that make products available to customers when and where they want to purchase them

supply chain All the activities associated with the flow and transformation of products from raw materials through to the end customer

operations management The total set of managerial activities used by an organization to transform resource inputs into products

logistics management Planning, implementing, and controlling the efficient and effective flow and storage of products and information from the point of origin to consumption to meet customers' needs and wants

supply management In its broadest form, refers to the processes that enable the progress of value from raw material to final customer and back to redesign and final disposition

supply-chain management A set of approaches used to integrate the functions of operations management, logistics management, supply management, and marketing channel management so products are produced and distributed in the right quantities, to the right locations, and at the right time

Technology Facilitates Supply-Chain Management
BAX Global provides services and technology to facilitate supply-chain management for business customers.

can be improved, and increased value can be provided to the end customer. Indeed, information is crucial in operating supply chains efficiently and effectively.

As demand for innovative goods and services has escalated in recent years, marketers have had to increase their flexibility and responsiveness to develop new products and modify existing ones to meet the ever-changing needs of customers. Suppliers now provide material and service inputs to meet customer needs in the upstream portion of the supply chain. Customers are increasingly a knowledge source in developing the right product in the downstream portion of the supply chain. This means that the entire supply chain is critically important in ensuring that customers get the products when, where, and how they want them. Consider the challenge Nike faces with NIKEiD, the company's custom product line that includes shoes, clothing and equipment. Each product is designed by the customer and must be specially made to their specifications. The product is then transported across the ocean and by land to their home. While Nike does charge a fee for the custom order, ensuring the company's supply chain is flexible enough to handle these orders requires a large investment of time and money.

Firms must therefore be involved in the management of their own supply chains in partnership with the network of upstream and downstream organizations in the supply chain. Upstream firms provide direct or indirect input to make the product. Downstream firms are responsible for delivery of the product and after-market services to the end customers. The management of the upstream and downstream in the supply-chain activities is what is involved in managing supply chains.

Effective supply-chain management is closely linked to a market orientation. All functional areas of business (marketing, management, production, finance, and information systems) are involved in executing a customer orientation and supply-chain management. Both of these activities overlap with operations management, logistics management, and supply management. If a firm has established a marketing strategy based on continuous customer-focused leadership, then supply-chain management will be driven by cooperation and strategic coordination to ensure customer satisfaction. Managers should recognize that supply-chain management is critical to fulfilling customer requirements and requires coordination with all areas of the business. This logical association between market orientation and supply-chain management should lead to increased firm performance.[6]

Table 15.1 Key Tasks in Supply-Chain Management

Marketing Activities	Sample Activities
Operations management	Organizational and systemwide coordination of operations and partnerships to meet customers' product needs
Supply management	Sourcing of necessary resources, products, and services from suppliers to support all supply-chain members
Logistics management	All activities designed to move the product through the marketing channel to the end user, including warehousing and inventory management
Channel management	All activities related to selling, service, and the development of long-term customer relationships

The Role of Marketing Channels in Supply Chains

A **marketing channel** (also called a *channel of distribution* or *distribution channel*) is a group of individuals and organizations that direct the flow of products from producers to customers within the supply chain. The major role of marketing channels—in concert with operations management, logistics management, and supply management—is to make products available at the right time at the right place in the right quantities. Providing customer satisfaction should be the driving force behind marketing channel decisions. Buyers' needs and behavior are therefore important concerns of channel members.

Some marketing channels are direct, meaning that the product goes directly from the producer to the customer. For instance, when a customer orders food online from Omaha Steaks (**www.omahasteaks.com**), the product is sent from the manufacturer to the customer. Most channels, however, have one or more **marketing intermediaries** that link producers to other intermediaries or to ultimate consumers through contractual arrangements or through the purchase and reselling of products. Marketing intermediaries perform the activities described in Table 15.2. They also play key roles in customer relationship management, not only through their distribution activities but also by maintaining databases and information systems to help all members of the marketing channel maintain effective customer relationships. For example, eBay serves as a marketing intermediary between Internet sellers and buyers. eBay not only provides a forum for these exchanges but also helps facilitate relationships among eBay channel members and eases payment issues through its PayPal subsidiary.

Wholesalers and retailers are examples of intermediaries. Wholesalers buy and resell products to other wholesalers, retailers, and industrial customers. Retailers purchase products and resell them to the end consumers. Consider your local supermarket, which probably purchased the Tylenol or Advil on its shelves from a wholesaler. The wholesaler purchased that pain medicine, along with other over-the-counter and prescription drugs, from manufacturers such as McNeil Consumer Labs and Whitehall-Robins. Chapter 16 discusses the functions of wholesalers and retailers in marketing channels in greater detail.

Supply chains start with the customer and require the cooperation of channel members to satisfy customer requirements. All members should focus on cooperation to reduce the costs of all channel members and thereby improve profits. For example, some customers seek products that are more environmentally friendly. In response to this as well as a request from Walmart to reduce costs, P&G began producing concentrated detergents. By reducing the weight and size of its products, the company was able to reduce its footprint on the world while also saving money on its packaging, transportation and storage costs.[7] When the buyer, the seller, marketing intermediaries, and facilitating agencies

marketing channel A group of individuals and organizations that direct the flow of products from producers to customers within the supply chain

marketing intermediaries Middlemen that link producers to other intermediaries or ultimate consumers through contractual arrangements or through the purchase and resale of products

Table 15.2 Marketing Channel Activities Performed by Intermediaries

Marketing Activities	Sample Activities
Marketing information	Analyze sales data and other information in databases and information systems. Perform or commission marketing research.
Marketing management	Establish strategic and tactical plans for developing customer relationships and organizational productivity.
Facilitating exchanges	Choose product assortments that match the needs of customers. Cooperate with channel members to develop partnerships.
Promotion	Set promotional objectives. Coordinate advertising, personal selling, sales promotion, publicity, and packaging.
Price	Establish pricing policies and terms of sales.
Physical distribution	Manage transportation, warehousing, materials handling, inventory control, and communication.

work together, the cooperative relationship results in compromise and adjustments that meet customers' needs regarding delivery, scheduling, packaging, or other requirements.

Each supply-chain member requires information from other channel members. For instance, suppliers need order and forecast information from the manufacturer; they also may need availability information from their own suppliers. Customer relationship management (CRM) systems exploit the information from supply-chain partners' information systems to help all channel members make marketing strategy decisions that develop and sustain desirable customer relationships. Thus, managing relationships with supply-chain partners is crucial to satisfying customers. CRM is gaining popularity, with companies such as Hewlett-Packard and Amazon.com spending large sums of money on implementation and support for data mining and CRM analytical applications.

The Significance of Marketing Channels

Although marketing channel decisions do not have to precede other marketing decisions, they are a powerful influence on the rest of the marketing mix (i.e., product, promotion, and pricing). Channel decisions are critical because they determine a product's market presence and buyers' accessibility to the product. Without effective marketing channel operations, even the best goods and services will not be successful. Consider that small businesses are more likely to purchase computers from chain specialty stores such as Best Buy and Office Depot, putting computer companies without distribution through these outlets at a disadvantage. In fact, even Dell—which pioneered the direct-sales model in the computer industry—is now selling its computers at Best Buy. The option of buying Dell systems directly from Dell or in retail stores such as Best Buy means that customers can purchase what they need when and where they want while also allowing customers to "test drive" a computer system of their choice.

Marketing channel decisions have additional strategic significance because they generally entail long-term commitments among a variety of firms (e.g., suppliers, logistics providers, and operations firms). It is usually easier to change prices or promotional strategies than to change marketing channels. Marketing channels also serve many functions, including creating utility and facilitating exchange efficiencies. Although some of these functions may be performed by a single channel member, most functions are accomplished through both independent and joint efforts of channel members.

MARKETING CHANNELS CREATE UTILITY

Marketing channels create four types of utility: time, place, possession, and form. *Time utility* is having products available when the customer wants them. Services like Movies On Demand allow customers to watch a movie whenever they want, unlike most video stores that are not open 24 hours. *Place utility* is created by making products available in locations where customers wish to purchase them. For example, a bowling alley that has a vending machine with socks allows customers who did not bring socks to purchase a pair without leaving the facility. *Possession utility* means that the customer has access to the product to use or to store for future use. Possession utility can occur through ownership or through arrangements that give the customer the right to use the product, such as a lease or rental agreement. Channel members sometimes create *form utility* by assembling, preparing, or otherwise refining the product to suit individual customer needs.

MARKETING CHANNELS FACILITATE EXCHANGE EFFICIENCIES

Marketing intermediaries can reduce the costs of exchanges by performing certain services or functions efficiently. Even if producers and buyers are located in the same city, there are costs associated with exchanges. As Figure 15.1 shows, when four buyers seek products from four producers, 16 transactions are possible. If one intermediary serves both producers and buyers, the number of transactions can be reduced to eight. Intermediaries are specialists in facilitating exchanges. They provide valuable assistance because of their access to and control over important resources used in the proper functioning of marketing channels.

Figure 15.1 Efficiency in Exchanges Provided by an Intermediary

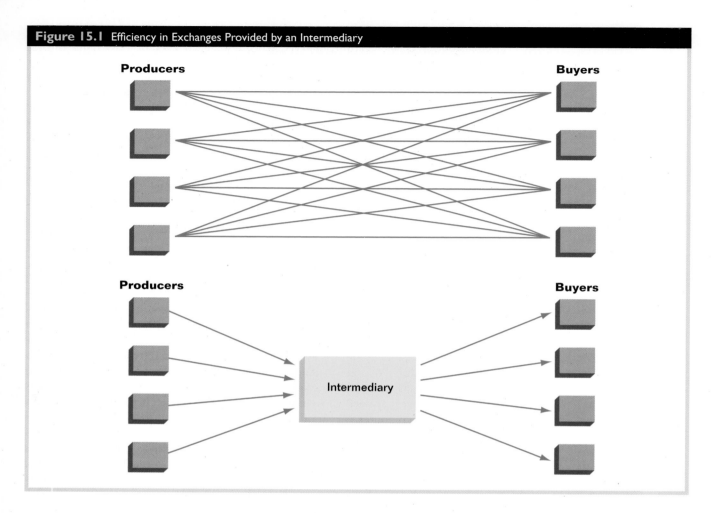

Nevertheless, the press, consumers, public officials, and even other marketers freely criticize intermediaries, especially wholesalers. Critics accuse wholesalers of being inefficient and parasitic. Buyers often wish to make the distribution channel as short as possible, assuming the fewer the intermediaries, the lower the price will be.

Critics who suggest that eliminating wholesalers would lower customer prices fail to recognize that this would not eliminate the need for the services the wholesalers provide. Although wholesalers can be eliminated, their functions cannot. Other channel members would have to perform those functions, and customers still would have to pay for them. In addition, all producers would have to deal directly with retailers or customers, meaning that every producer would have to keep voluminous records and hire enough personnel to deal with a multitude of customers. Customers might end up paying a great deal more for products because prices would reflect the costs of less-efficient channel members.

Because suggestions to eliminate wholesalers come from both ends of the marketing channel, wholesalers must be careful to perform only those marketing activities that are truly desired. To survive, they must be more efficient and more customer-focused than other marketing institutions. Indeed, research suggests that lower wholesale prices may result in higher sales volume when combined with low retailing costs at discount firms such as Walmart.[8]

Types of Marketing Channels

Because marketing channels that are appropriate for one product may be less suitable for others, many different distribution paths have been developed. The various marketing channels can be classified generally as channels for consumer products and channels for business products.

CHANNELS FOR CONSUMER PRODUCTS

Figure 15.2 illustrates several channels used in the distribution of consumer products. Channel A depicts the direct movement of products from producer to consumers. For instance, the legal advice given by attorneys moves through channel A. Producers that sell products directly from their factories to end users use direct marketing channels, as do companies that sell their own products via the Internet, such as Omaha Steaks. Direct marketing via the Internet has become a critically important part of some companies' distribution strategies, often as a complement to their products being sold in traditional retail stores. Faced with the strategic choice of going directly to the customer or using intermediaries, a firm must evaluate the benefits of going direct versus the transaction costs involved in using intermediaries.

Channel B, which moves goods from the producer to a retailer and then to customers, is a frequent choice of large retailers because it allows them to buy in quantity from manufacturers. Retailers such as Kmart and Walmart sell clothing, stereos, and many other items purchased directly from producers. New automobiles and new college textbooks are also sold through this type of marketing channel. Primarily nonstore retailers, such as L.L. Bean and J. Crew, also use this type of channel.

Channel C represents a long-standing distribution channel, especially for consumer products. It takes goods from the producer to a wholesaler, then to a retailer, and finally to consumers. It is a practical option for producers that sell to hundreds of thousands of customers through thousands of retailers. Consider the number of retailers marketing Wrigley's chewing gum. It would be extremely difficult, if not impossible, for Wrigley to deal directly with each retailer that sells its brand of gum. Manufacturers of tobacco products, some home appliances, hardware, and many convenience goods sell their products to wholesalers, which then sell to retailers, which in turn do business with individual consumers.

Channel D, through which goods pass from producer to agents to wholesalers to retailers and then to consumers, is used frequently for products intended for mass distribution, such as processed foods. For example, to place its cracker line in specific retail outlets, a food processor may hire an agent (or a food broker) to sell the crackers

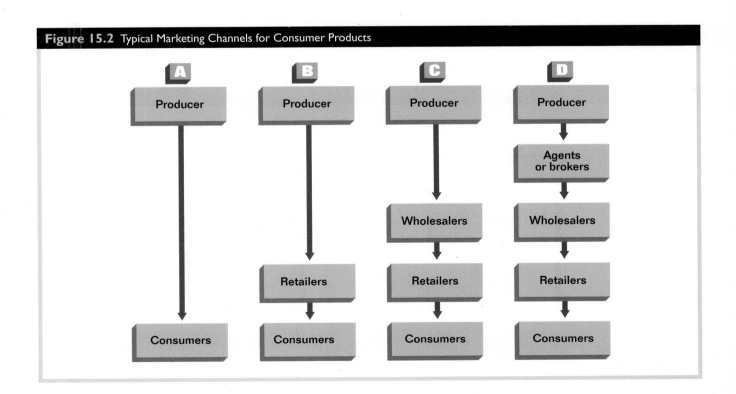

Figure 15.2 Typical Marketing Channels for Consumer Products

to wholesalers. Wholesalers then sell the crackers to supermarkets, vending machine operators, and other retail outlets.

Contrary to popular opinion, a long channel may be the most efficient distribution channel for some consumer goods. When several channel intermediaries perform specialized functions, costs may be lower than when one channel member tries to perform them all. In essence, this logic is similar to outsourcing part of the production to firms in low-cost countries. For the marketing channel, it means that firms that specialize in certain elements of producing a product or moving it through the channel are more effective and efficient at performing specialized tasks than the manufacturer. This results in cost efficiencies and added value to customers.

CHANNELS FOR BUSINESS PRODUCTS

Figure 15.3 shows four of the most common channels for business products. As with consumer products, manufacturers of business products sometimes work with more than one level of wholesalers.

Channel E illustrates the direct channel for business products. In contrast to consumer goods, more than half of all business products, especially expensive equipment, are sold through direct channels. Business customers prefer to communicate directly with producers, especially when expensive or technically complex products are involved. For instance, buyers prefer to purchase expensive and highly complex SQL server computers directly from Dell. Similarly, Intel has established direct marketing channels for selling its microprocessor chips to computer manufacturers. In these circumstances, a customer wants the technical assistance and personal assurances that only a producer can provide.

In channel F, an industrial distributor facilitates exchanges between the producer and the customer. An **industrial distributor** is an independent business that takes title to products and carries inventories. Industrial distributors usually sell standardized items such as maintenance supplies, production tools, and small operating equipment. Some industrial distributors carry a wide variety of product lines. W.W. Grainger, for example, sells more than $6 billion worth of power and hand tools, pumps, janitorial supplies, and many other products to producer, government, and institutional markets around the world.[9] Other industrial distributors specialize in one or a small number of lines. Industrial distributors are carrying an increasing percentage of business products. Overall, these distributors can be most effectively used when a product has broad market appeal, is easily stocked and serviced, is sold in small quantities, and is needed on demand to avoid high losses.

industrial distributor An independent business organization that takes title to industrial products and carries inventories

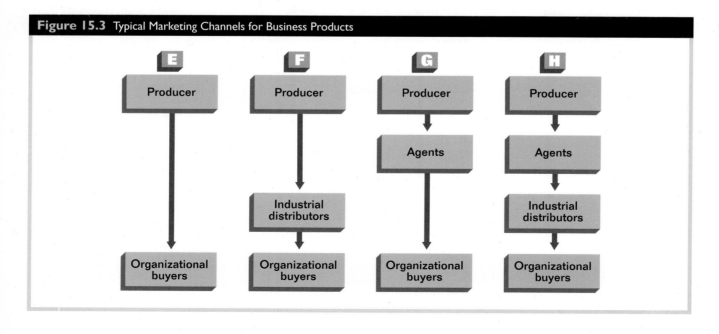

Figure 15.3 Typical Marketing Channels for Business Products

Industrial distributors offer sellers several advantages. They can perform the needed selling activities in local markets at a relatively low cost to a manufacturer and reduce a producer's financial burden by providing customers with credit services. Also, because industrial distributors usually maintain close relationships with their customers, they are aware of local needs and can pass on market information to producers. By holding adequate inventories in their local markets, industrial distributors reduce producers' capital requirements.

Using industrial distributors has several disadvantages, however. Industrial distributors may be difficult to control since they are independent firms. Because they often stock competing brands, a producer cannot depend on them to sell its brand aggressively. Furthermore, since industrial distributors maintain inventories, they incur numerous expenses; consequently, they are less likely to handle bulky or slow-selling items or items that need specialized facilities or extraordinary selling efforts. In some cases, industrial distributors lack the technical knowledge necessary to sell and service certain products.

The third channel for business products, channel G, employs a *manufacturers' agent,* an independent businessperson who sells complementary products of several producers in assigned territories and is compensated through commissions. Unlike an industrial distributor, a manufacturers' agent does not acquire title to the products and usually does not take possession. Acting as a salesperson on behalf of the producers, a manufacturers' agent has little or no latitude in negotiating prices or sales terms.

Using manufacturers' agents can benefit an organizational marketer. These agents usually possess considerable technical and market information and have an established set of customers. For an organizational seller with highly seasonal demand, a manufacturers' agent can be an asset because the seller does not have to support a year-round sales force. The fact that manufacturers' agents are typically paid on a commission basis may also be an economical alternative for a firm that has highly limited resources and cannot afford a full-time sales force.

The use of manufacturers' agents is not problem-free. Even though straight commissions may be more financially viable, the seller may have little control over manufacturers' agents. Because of the compensation method, manufacturers' agents generally prefer to concentrate on their larger accounts. They are often reluctant to spend time following up sales, putting forth special selling efforts, or providing sellers with market information when such activities reduce the amount of productive selling time. Because they rarely maintain inventories, manufacturers' agents have a limited ability to provide customers with parts or repair services quickly.

Finally, channel H includes both a manufacturers' agent and an industrial distributor. This channel may be appropriate when the producer wishes to cover a large geographic area but maintains no sales force due to highly seasonal demand or because it cannot afford a sales force. This type of channel can also be useful for a business marketer that wants to enter a new geographic market without expanding its existing sales force.

MULTIPLE MARKETING CHANNELS AND CHANNEL ALLIANCES

To reach diverse target markets, manufacturers may use several marketing channels simultaneously, with each channel involving a different group of intermediaries. In particular, a manufacturer often uses multiple channels when the same product is directed to both consumers and business customers. For example, when Del Monte markets ketchup for household use, the product is sold to supermarkets through grocery wholesalers or, in some cases, directly to retailers, whereas ketchup being sold to restaurants or institutions follows a different distribution channel.

In some instances, a producer may prefer **dual distribution**, the use of two or more marketing channels to distribute the same products to the same target market. For instance, Kellogg sells its cereals directly to large retail grocery chains (channel B) and to food wholesalers that, in turn, sell the cereals to retailers (channel C). Another example of dual distribution is a firm that sells products through retail outlets and its own mail-order catalog or website. P&G plans to expand its distribution strategy, which currently

dual distribution The use of two or more marketing channels to distribute the same products to the same target market

Using Multiple Marketing Channels
Dunkin' Donuts coffee products are available at company stores and in select grocery stores.

includes selling to wholesalers and retailers, to the Internet. Later this year, the company will open an eStore where customers can purchase all of their favorite P&G brands, including Tide, Pampers, and Pantene, directly from the company online.[10]

Dual distribution, however, can cause dissatisfaction among wholesalers and smaller retailers when they must compete with large retail grocery chains that make direct purchases from manufacturers such as Kellogg. Another example is State Farm Insurance, which has decided to maintain its "old" business model of using agents as the primary vehicle for customer interaction, potentially losing sales to other insurance companies by not offering insurance policies online as others, such as Progressive, do.

A **strategic channel alliance** exists when the products of one organization are distributed through the marketing channels of another. The products of the two firms are often similar with respect to target markets or uses, but they are not direct competitors. A brand of bottled water might be distributed through a marketing channel for soft drinks, or a domestic cereal producer might form a strategic channel alliance with a European food processor. Such alliances can provide benefits for both the organization that owns the marketing channel and the company whose brand is being distributed through the channel.

Selecting Marketing Channels

Selecting appropriate marketing channels is important. Although the process varies across organizations, channel selection decisions usually are significantly affected by one or more of the following factors: customer characteristics, product attributes, type of organization, competition, marketing environmental forces, and characteristics of intermediaries (see Figure 15.4).

CUSTOMER CHARACTERISTICS

Marketing managers must consider the characteristics of target-market members in channel selection. As we have already seen, the channels that are appropriate for consumers are different from those for business customers. A different marketing channel will be required for business customers purchasing carpet for commercial buildings compared with consumers purchasing carpet for their homes. Business customers often prefer to deal directly with producers (or very knowledgeable channel intermediaries such as industrial distributors), especially for highly technical or expensive products such as mainframe computers, jet airplanes, and large mining machines. Moreover, business customers are more likely to buy complex products that require strict specifications and technical assistance or to buy in considerable quantities.

Consumers, on the other hand, generally buy limited quantities of a product, purchase from retailers, and often do not mind limited customer service. Additionally, when customers are concentrated in a small geographic area, a more direct channel may be ideal, but when many customers are spread across an entire state or nation, distribution through multiple intermediaries is likely to be more efficient.

PRODUCT ATTRIBUTES

The attributes of the product can have a strong influence on the choice of marketing channels. Marketers of complex and expensive products such as automobiles likely will employ short channels, as will marketers of perishable products such as dairy and

strategic channel alliance An agreement whereby the products of one organization are distributed through the marketing channels of another

Figure 15.4 Selecting Marketing Channels

produce. Less-expensive, more standardized products such as soft drinks and canned goods can employ longer channels with many intermediaries. In addition, channel decisions may be affected by a product's sturdiness: fragile products that require special handling are more likely to be distributed through shorter channels to minimize the risk of damage. Firms that desire to convey an exclusive image for their products may wish to limit the number of outlets available.

TYPE OF ORGANIZATION

Clearly, the characteristics of the organization will have a great impact on the distribution channels chosen. Owing to their sheer size, larger firms may be better able to negotiate better deals with vendors or other channel members. Compared with small firms, they may be in a better position to have more distribution centers, which may reduce delivery times to customers. A smaller regional company that uses regional or local channel members may be in a position to better serve customers in that region compared with a larger, less-flexible organization. Compared with smaller organizations, large companies can use an extensive product mix as a competitive tool. Smaller firms may not have the resources to develop their own sales force, ship their products long distances, store or own products, or extend credit. In such cases, they may have to include other channel members that have the resources to provide these services to customers efficiently and cost effectively.

COMPETITION

Competition is another important factor for supply-chain managers to consider. The success or failure of a competitor's marketing channel may encourage or dissuade an organization from considering a similar approach. A firm also may be forced to adopt a similar strategy to remain competitive. In a highly competitive market, it is important for a company to keep its costs low so it can offer lower prices than its competitors if necessary.

Responsible Marketing?
Duke Power Tries to Come Clean

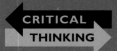
CRITICAL THINKING

ISSUE: Reducing carbons or greenwashing?

Duke Power is the third-largest corporate emitter of carbon dioxide (after American Electric Power and Southern Companies) in the United States. Many utility companies are good examples of vertically integrated supply chains and marketing channels because they produce energy and also deliver it to final customers. Therefore, utility companies have the potential to improve their environmental impacts through all levels of the marketing channel. Charlotte, North Carolina–based Duke Power is facing the possibility that they may have to start paying for CO_2 emissions if government regulators put a tax on greenhouse gases. Therefore, Duke is proactively going green with 500,000 solar panels on rooftops in a five-state territory. The utility is also installing a $1 billion communication network to optimize the flow of electricity through the grid. Duke built low-cost coal plants in the 1960s and 1970s when cheap, secure power supplies were the main concern. With current concerns about global warming, the firm has to reduce some of the 100,000 tons of CO_2 (27 million tons of carbon) in its supply chain. The firm is looking to nuclear plants and a Save-A-Watt program to encourage customers to use less energy. The company believes that conservation is the best and cheapest zero-emission power plant. Duke claims that not even plastering wind turbines all across the outer banks of North Carolina would produce enough electricity for the growing needs of customers in the Carolinas.

Yet Duke still has its hands full defending its emissions-reduction plan to environmentalists such as the Southern Alliance for Clean Energy. Environmentalists are concerned that the company is merely greenwashing, or "creating a positive association with environmental issues for an unsustainable product, service, or practice." Critics also raise questions about Duke's Save-A-Watt program, which is designed as an alternative revenue stream for the company. Duke will earn money for the power customers save by proportionately raising rates for the power they use. Even while preaching conservation as a solution, Duke plans to invest $23 billion in the next five years to build new coal and gas plants.[a]

ENVIRONMENTAL FORCES

Environmental forces also can play a role in channel selection. Adverse economic conditions might force an organization to use a low-cost channel, even though customer satisfaction is reduced. In contrast, a booming economy might allow a company to choose a channel that previously had been too costly to consider. The introduction of new technology might cause an organization to add or modify its channel strategy. For instance, as the Internet became a powerful marketing communication tool, many companies were forced to go online to remain competitive. Government regulations also can affect channel selection. As new labor and environmental regulations are passed, an organization may be forced to modify its existing distribution channel structure. Firms may choose to make the changes before regulations are passed to appear compliant or to avoid legal issues. Governmental regulations also can include trade agreements with other countries that complicate the supply chain.

CHARACTERISTICS OF INTERMEDIARIES

When an organization believes that a current intermediary is not promoting the organization's products adequately, it may reconsider its channel choices. In these instances, the company may choose another channel member to handle its products, or it may choose to eliminate intermediaries altogether and perform the eliminated intermediaries' functions itself. Alternatively, an existing intermediary may not offer an appropriate mix of services, forcing an organization to switch to another intermediary.

Intensity of Market Coverage

In addition to deciding which marketing channels to use to distribute a product, marketers must determine the intensity of coverage that a product should get—that is, the number and kinds of outlets in which it will be sold. This decision depends on the characteristics of the product and the target market. To achieve the desired intensity of market coverage, distribution must correspond to behavior patterns of buyers. In Chapter 10, we divided consumer products into four

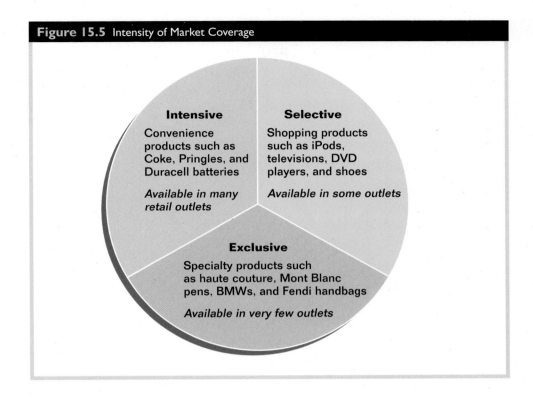

Figure 15.5 Intensity of Market Coverage

Intensive
Convenience products such as Coke, Pringles, and Duracell batteries

Available in many retail outlets

Selective
Shopping products such as iPods, televisions, DVD players, and shoes

Available in some outlets

Exclusive
Specialty products such as haute couture, Mont Blanc pens, BMWs, and Fendi handbags

Available in very few outlets

categories—convenience products, shopping products, specialty products, and unsought products—according to how consumers make purchases. In considering products for purchase, consumers take into account replacement rate, product adjustment (services), duration of consumption, time required to find the product, and similar factors.[11] These variables directly affect the intensity of market coverage. As shown in Figure 15.5, the three major levels of market coverage are intensive, selective, and exclusive distribution.

Intensive Distribution

Intensive distribution uses all available outlets for distributing a product. Intensive distribution is appropriate for most convenience products such as bread, chewing gum, soft drinks, and newspapers. Convenience products have a high replacement rate, require almost no service, and are often bought based on price cues. To meet these demands, intensive distribution is necessary, and multiple channels may be used to sell through all possible outlets. For example, soft drinks, snacks, laundry detergent, and pain relievers are available at convenience stores, service stations, supermarkets, discount stores, and other types of retailers. To consumers, availability means a store is located nearby, and minimum time is necessary to search for the product at the store. This ensures that consumers are provided with the greatest speed in obtaining the product, the quality they have come to expect of a certain convenience product, the flexibility to buy the product wherever it is convenient to them, and the lowest cost possible.

Sales may have a direct relationship to product availability. The successful sale of convenience products such as bread and milk at service stations or gasoline at convenience grocery stores illustrates that the availability of these products is more important than the nature of the outlet. Companies such as Procter & Gamble that produce consumer packaged items rely on intensive distribution for many of their products (e.g., soaps, detergents, food and juice products, and personal-care products) because consumers want ready availability.

intensive distribution Using all available outlets to distribute a product

Image courtesy of The Advertising Archives

© GEOX S.p.A.

...like a second skin.

Comparing Intensive and Selective Distribution
Gum is typically distributed through intensive distribution, whereas shoes, like Geox, are usually distributed through selective distribution.

Selective Distribution

Selective distribution uses only some available outlets in an area to distribute a product. Selective distribution is appropriate for shopping products; durable goods such as televisions, stereos, and home computers usually fall into this category. These products are more expensive than convenience goods, and consumers are willing to spend more time visiting several retail outlets to compare prices, designs, styles, and other features.

Selective distribution is desirable when a special effort, such as customer service from a channel member, is important to customers. Shopping products require differentiation at the point of purchase. To motivate retailers to provide adequate presale service, selective distribution and company-owned stores are often used. Many business products are sold on a selective basis to maintain control over the products—for example, in cases where dealers must offer services to buyers such as instructions about how to apply herbicides safely or the option to have the dealer apply the herbicide. Other examples include the launch of Apple's iPhone, distributed in AT&T and Apple retail stores in the United States, and perfumes distributed through large department and specialty perfume stores. The majority of perfumes and colognes use selective distribution in order to maintain a particular image. For example, eBay was recently fined by a Parisian court for selling certain brands of perfume on its website that include Christian Dior, Givenchy, and Kenzo. These companies are trying to protect their brand's image by only selling through select retail outlets.[12]

Exclusive Distribution

selective distribution Using only some available outlets in an area to distribute a product

exclusive distribution Using a single outlet in a fairly large geographic area to distribute a product

Exclusive distribution uses only one outlet in a relatively large geographic area. Exclusive distribution is suitable for products purchased infrequently, consumed over a long period of time, or requiring service or information to fit them to buyers' needs. It is also used for expensive, high-quality products, such as Porsche, BMW, and other luxury automobiles. It is not appropriate for convenience products and many shopping products.

Exclusive distribution is often used as an incentive to sellers when only a limited market is available for products. Consider Patek Philippe watches that may sell for $10,000 or more. These watches, like luxury automobiles, are available in only a few select locations. A producer using exclusive distribution generally expects dealers to carry a complete inventory, send personnel for sales and service training, participate in promotional programs, and provide excellent customer service. Some products are appropriate for exclusive distribution when first introduced, but as competitors enter the market and the product moves through its life cycle, other types of market coverage and distribution channels often become necessary. A problem that can arise with exclusive distribution (and selective distribution) is that unauthorized resellers acquire and sell products, violating the agreement between a manufacturer and its exclusive authorized dealers. This has been a problem for Rolex, a manufacturer of luxury watches.

Strategic Issues in Marketing Channels

To fulfill the potential of effective supply-chain management and to ensure customer satisfaction, marketing channels require a strategic focus on certain competitive priorities and the development of channel leadership, cooperation, and the management of channel conflict. They may also require consolidation of marketing channels through channel integration.

Competitive Priorities in Marketing Channels

Much evidence exists that supply chains can provide a competitive advantage for many marketers. As mentioned earlier, effective supply-chain management has been linked to a marketing orientation. Because supply-chain decisions cut across all functional areas of the business, it is a competitive priority. Building the most effective and efficient supply chain can sustain a business in a variety of competitive environments.

It is estimated that a significant supply-chain problem can reduce a firm's market value by more than 10 percent. Deloitte has reported that just 7 percent of companies today are managing their supply chains effectively; however, these companies are 73 percent more profitable than other firms. Many well-known firms, including Amazon. com, Dell, FedEx, Toyota, and Walmart, owe much of their success to outmaneuvering rivals with unique supply-chain capabilities.

If supply-chain activities are not integrated, functions exist without coordination. As supply chains integrate functions, the reward is efficiency and effectiveness as well as a holistic view of the supply chain. Goal-driven supply chains, by direction of their firms, focus on the "competitive priorities" of speed, quality, cost, or flexibility as the performance objective. For example, before Domino's got into legal trouble for its 30-minute-or-free promise for pizza deliveries, speed was its main concern. The quality, cost, and the variety of toppings on the pizza were secondary to the time it took to get a hot pizza delivered to the customer's door. Other companies (e.g., Rolls Royce) focus on different competitive priorities, such as delivering top-notch quality products, where neither cost nor speed is an issue. Rolls Royce, however, still stresses certain flexibility in the product customization. Walmart is the poster example of stressing low cost, often at the "cost" of speed, quality, and flexibility. Yet, some firms thrive on being flexible. For instance, L.L. Bean provides almost endless flexibility, particularly in return policies. However, very few L.L. Bean stores exist, so customers may receive products at a slower speed than they do from other competitors. Cost is higher than the industry average, but their products are usually of high quality.

Channel Leadership, Cooperation, and Conflict

Each channel member performs a different role in the distribution system and agrees (implicitly or explicitly) to accept certain rights, responsibilities, rewards, and sanctions for nonconformity. Moreover, each channel member holds certain expectations of other channel members. Retailers, for instance, expect wholesalers to maintain adequate inventories and deliver goods on time. Wholesalers expect retailers to honor payment agreements and keep them informed of inventory needs.

Channel partnerships facilitate effective supply-chain management when partners agree on objectives, policies, and procedures for physical distribution efforts associated with the supplier's products. Such partnerships eliminate redundancies and reassign tasks for maximum systemwide efficiency.

One of the best-known partnerships is that between Walmart and Procter & Gamble. Procter & Gamble locates some of its staff near Walmart's purchasing department in Bentonville, Arkansas, to establish and maintain the supply chain. Sharing information through a cooperative information system, P&G monitors Walmart's inventory and additional data to determine production and distribution plans for its products. The results are increased efficiency, decreased inventory costs, and greater satisfaction for the customers of both companies. In this section, we discuss channel member behavior, including leadership, cooperation, and conflict, that marketers must understand to make effective channel decisions.

channel captain The dominant leader of a marketing channel or a supply channel

channel power The ability of one channel member to influence another member's goal achievement

CHANNEL LEADERSHIP

Many marketing channel decisions are determined by give-and-take among channel partners, with the idea that the overall channel ultimately will benefit. Some marketing channels, however, are organized and controlled by a single leader, or **channel captain** (also called *channel leader*). The channel captain may be a producer, wholesaler, or retailer. Channel captains may establish channel policies and coordinate development of the marketing mix. Walmart, for example, dominates the supply chain for its retail stores by virtue of the magnitude of its resources (especially information management) and strong, nationwide customer base. To attain desired objectives, the captain must possess **channel power**, the ability to influence another channel member's goal achievement. The member that becomes the channel captain will accept the responsibilities and exercise the power associated with this role.

When a manufacturer's large-scale production efficiency demands that it increase sales volume, the manufacturer may exercise power by giving channel members financing, business advice, ordering assistance, advertising services, sales and service training, and support materials. For example, U.S. automakers provide these services to retail automobile dealerships. However, these manufacturers also place numerous requirements on their retail dealerships with respect to sales volume, sales and service training, and customer satisfaction.

Retailers may also function as channel captains. With the rise in power of national chain stores and private-brand merchandise, many large retailers such as Walmart are taking a leadership role in the channel. Small retailers too may assume leadership roles when they gain strong customer loyalty in local or regional markets. These retailers control many brands and sometimes replace uncooperative producers. Increasingly, leading retailers are concentrating their buying power with fewer suppliers and, in the process, improving their marketing effectiveness and efficiency. Long-term commitments enable retailers to place smaller and more frequent orders as needed rather than waiting for large-volume discounts or placing huge orders and assuming the risks associated with carrying a larger inventory.

Channel Leadership
Dell provides channel leadership in the distribution of its products.

Marketing in Transition
Can Independent Retailers Survive?

Can independent stores survive the shift in channel power toward retail giants? Big retailers such as Macy's and Kroger buy in such massive quantities and have such marketing muscle that it's hard for independents to compete. Independents can't match the low prices and advertising onslaught of a national discounter or category killer. Yet resourceful independents are thriving by differentiating themselves in ways that customers value.

Personalized service is a major point of differentiation at Kilgore Trout, an independent menswear store in Cleveland. Founder Wally Naymon says he's always hearing complaints about the poor service at large stores. "People can't get waited on or they can't get the help they need," he explains. "That's the reason we exist." As "an alternative to the price wars," Naymon focuses on educating customers about quality and the coming trends in fashion: "We'll show [a customer] something he can wear for the next ten years, not something he wore for the last ten." Kilgore Trout views customers as people with individual needs and fashion interests, not as transactions to be tallied. According to the founder, the big stores have "the passion for numbers, we've got the passion for relationships."

Selection is the differentiator at Ben's Supercenter, a family-owned store in Brown City, Michigan. Although Ben's started out

as a small grocery store, it has grown into a 72,000-square-foot superstore filled with everything from groceries and grills to meats and medicines. Practicing "extreme retailing," Ben's has a 27,000-square-foot lumberyard, sells wood-burning stoves, carries five types of trailers, and contains both a bank and print shop. The result is one-stop shopping convenience unmatched in the area. "We want to do everything our competitors won't do," Ben's president says.[b]

Wholesalers assume channel leadership roles as well, although they were more powerful decades ago, when many manufacturers and retailers were smaller, underfinanced, and widely scattered. Today wholesaler leaders may form voluntary chains with several retailers, which they supply with bulk buying or management services; these chains may also market their own brands. In return, the retailers shift most of their purchasing to the wholesaler leader. The Independent Grocers' Alliance (IGA) is one of the best-known wholesaler leaders in the United States. IGA's power is based on its expertise in advertising, pricing, and purchasing knowledge that it makes available to independent business owners. Other wholesaler leaders help retailers with store layouts, accounting, and inventory control.

CHANNEL COOPERATION

Channel cooperation is vital if each member is to gain something from other members. Cooperation enables retailers, wholesalers, suppliers, and logistics providers to speed up inventory replenishment, improve customer service, and cut the costs of bringing products to the consumer.[13] Without cooperation, neither overall channel goals nor individual member goals can be realized. All channel members must recognize that the success of one firm in the channel depends in part on other member firms. Thus, marketing channel members should make a coordinated effort to satisfy market requirements. Channel cooperation leads to greater trust among channel members and improves the overall functioning of the channel. It also leads to more satisfying relationships among channel members.

There are several ways to improve channel cooperation. If a marketing channel is viewed as a unified supply chain competing with other systems, individual members will be less likely to take actions that create disadvantages for other members. Similarly, channel members should agree to direct efforts toward common objectives so channel roles can be structured for maximum marketing effectiveness, which in turn can help members achieve individual objectives. A critical component in cooperation is a precise definition of each channel member's tasks. This provides a basis for reviewing the intermediaries' performance and helps reduce conflicts because each channel member knows exactly what is expected of it.

CHANNEL CONFLICT

Although all channel members work toward the same general goal—distributing products profitably and efficiently—members sometimes may disagree about the best methods for attaining this goal. However, if self-interest creates misunderstanding about role expectations, the end result is frustration and conflict for the whole channel. For individual organizations to function together, each channel member must clearly communicate and understand the role expectations. Communication difficulties are a potential form of channel conflict because ineffective communication leads to frustration, misunderstandings, and ill-coordinated strategies, jeopardizing further coordination.

The increased use of multiple channels of distribution, driven partly by new technology, has increased the potential for conflict between manufacturers and intermediaries. For instance, Hewlett-Packard makes products available directly to consumers through its website, thereby competing directly with existing distributors and retailers, such as Best Buy. Channel conflicts also arise when intermediaries overemphasize competing products or diversify into product lines traditionally handled by other intermediaries. Sometimes conflict develops because producers strive to increase efficiency by circumventing intermediaries. Such conflict is occurring in marketing channels for computer software. A number of software-only stores are establishing direct relationships with software producers, bypassing wholesale distributors altogether.

Channel Conflict
Textbook publishers, which traditionally have marketed college textbooks through campus bookstores and now sell textbooks through their own websites, may be experiencing channel conflict.

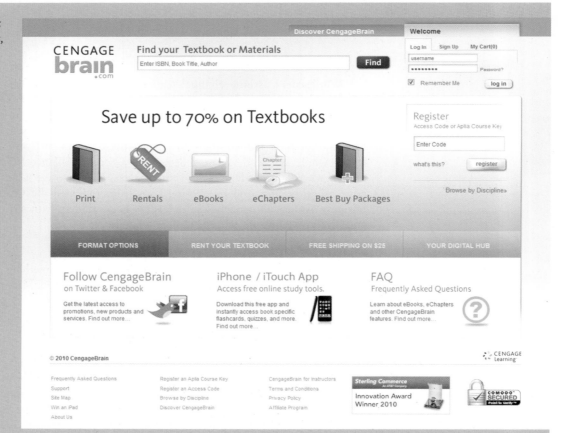

When a producer that has traditionally used franchised dealers broadens its retailer base to include other types of retail outlets, considerable conflict can arise. When Goodyear intensified its market coverage by allowing Sears and Discount Tire to market Goodyear tires, its action antagonized 2,500 independent Goodyear dealers.

Although there is no single method for resolving conflict, partnerships can be reestablished if two conditions are met. First, the role of each channel member must be specified. To minimize misunderstanding, all members must be able to expect unambiguous, agreed-on performance levels from one another. Second, members of channel partnerships must institute certain measures of channel coordination, which requires leadership and benevolent exercise of control. To prevent channel conflict from arising, producers or other channel members may provide competing resellers with different brands, allocate markets among resellers, define policies for direct sales to avoid potential conflict over large accounts, negotiate territorial issues among regional distributors, and provide recognition to certain resellers for their importance in distributing to others.

Channel Integration

Channel members can either combine and control most activities or pass them on to another channel member. Channel functions may be transferred between intermediaries and to producers and even to customers. However, a channel member cannot eliminate supply-chain functions; unless buyers themselves perform the functions, they must pay for the labor and resources needed to perform them.

Various channel stages may be combined under the management of a channel captain either horizontally or vertically. Such integration may stabilize supply, reduce costs, and increase coordination of channel members.

VERTICAL CHANNEL INTEGRATION

Vertical channel integration combines two or more stages of the channel under one management. This may occur when one member of a marketing channel purchases the operations of another member or simply performs the functions of another member, eliminating the need for that intermediary. PepsiCo, for example, recently purchased PepsiAmericas and The Pepsi Bottling Group, both of which own and operate local bottling and distribution organizations. Although the purchase may trigger antitrust concerns, it represents a new strategy among beverage manufacturers to better control the distribution and marketing of all of their drink products, not just sodas, as consumers increasingly buy other beverages, such as energy drinks, juices, and flavored waters.[14]

Unlike conventional channel systems, participants in vertical channel integration coordinate efforts to reach a desired target market. In this more progressive approach to distribution, channel members regard other members as extensions of their own operations. Vertically integrated channels are often more effective against competition because of increased bargaining power and the sharing of information and responsibilities. At one end of a vertically integrated channel, a manufacturer might provide advertising and training assistance, and the retailer at the other end might buy the manufacturer's products in large quantities and actively promote them.

Integration has been successfully institutionalized in marketing channels called **vertical marketing systems (VMSs)**, in which a single channel member coordinates or manages channel activities to achieve efficient, low-cost distribution aimed at satisfying target market customers. Vertical integration brings most or all stages of the marketing channel under common control or ownership. The Limited, a retail clothing chain, uses a wholly owned subsidiary, Mast Industries, as its primary supply source. Radio Shack operates as a VMS, encompassing both wholesale and retail functions. Because efforts of individual channel members are combined in a VMS, marketing activities can be coordinated for maximum effectiveness and economy without duplication of services. VMSs are competitive, accounting for a share of retail sales in consumer goods.

Most vertical marketing systems take one of three forms: corporate, administered, or contractual. A *corporate VMS* combines all stages of the marketing channel, from

vertical channel integration Combining two or more stages of the marketing channel under one management

vertical marketing systems (VMSs) A marketing channel managed by a single channel member to achieve efficient, low-cost distribution aimed at satisfying target market customers

producers to consumers, under a single owner. For example, The Limited established a corporate VMS that operates corporate-owned production facilities and retail stores. Supermarket chains that own food-processing plants and large retailers that purchase wholesaling and production facilities are other examples of corporate VMSs.

In an *administered VMS*, channel members are independent, but a high level of interorganizational management is achieved through informal coordination. Members of an administered VMS, for example, may adopt uniform accounting and ordering procedures and cooperate in promotional activities for the benefit of all partners. Although individual channel members maintain autonomy, as in conventional marketing channels, one channel member (such as a producer or large retailer) dominates the administered VMS so that distribution decisions take the whole system into account. Because of its size and power, Intel exercises a strong influence over distributors and manufacturers in its marketing channels, as do Kellogg (cereal) and Magnavox (televisions and other electronic products).

Under a *contractual VMS*, the most popular type of vertical marketing system, channel members are linked by legal agreements spelling out each member's rights and obligations. Franchise organizations, such as McDonald's and KFC, are contractual VMSs. Other contractual VMSs include wholesaler-sponsored groups, such as IGA (Independent Grocers' Alliance) stores, in which independent retailers band together under the contractual leadership of a wholesaler. Retailer-sponsored cooperatives, which own and operate their own wholesalers, are a third type of contractual VMS.

HORIZONTAL CHANNEL INTEGRATION

Combining organizations at the same level of operation under one management constitutes **horizontal channel integration**. An organization may integrate horizontally by merging with other organizations at the same level in the marketing channel. The owner of a dry-cleaning firm, for example, might buy and combine several other existing dry-cleaning establishments. Horizontal integration may enable a firm to generate sufficient sales revenue to integrate vertically as well.

Although horizontal integration permits efficiencies and economies of scale in purchasing, marketing research, advertising, and specialized personnel, it is not always the most effective method of improving distribution. Problems of size often follow, resulting in decreased flexibility, difficulties in coordination, and the need for additional marketing research and large-scale planning. Unless distribution functions for the various units can be performed more efficiently under unified management than under the previously separate managements, horizontal integration will neither reduce costs nor improve the competitive position of the integrating firm.

Physical Distribution in Supply-Chain Management

Physical distribution, also known as *logistics*, refers to the activities used to move products from producers to consumers and other end users. Physical distribution systems must meet the needs of both the supply chain and customers. Distribution activities are thus an important part of supply-chain planning and require the cooperation of all partners.

Within the marketing channel, physical distribution activities may be performed by a producer, a wholesaler, or a retailer, or they may be outsourced. In the context of distribution, **outsourcing** is the contracting of physical distribution tasks to third parties. Most physical distribution activities can be outsourced to third-party firms that have special expertise in areas such as warehousing, transportation, inventory management, and information technology. Perot Systems, a company recently acquired by Dell, provides business processing outsourcing (BPO) services to several agencies of the federal government, including U.S. Citizenship and Immigration Services. Perot

horizontal channel integration Combining organizations at the same level of operation under one management

physical distribution Activities used to move products from producers to consumers and other end users

outsourcing The contracting of physical distribution tasks to third parties

Systems helps this agency process citizenship and immigration applications more efficiently, maintain records and files, and schedule interviews and oath ceremonies.[15]

Cooperative relationships with third-party organizations, such as trucking companies, warehouses, and data-service providers, can help to reduce marketing channel costs and boost service and customer satisfaction for all supply-chain partners. When choosing companies through which to outsource, marketers must be cautious and use efficient firms that help the outsourcing company provide excellent customer service. They also need to recognize the importance of logistics functions such as warehousing and information technology in reducing physical distribution costs associated with outsourcing.[16]

Planning an efficient physical distribution system is crucial to developing an effective marketing strategy because it can decrease costs and increase customer satisfaction. Speed of delivery, flexibility, and quality of service are often as important to customers as costs. Companies that have the right goods, in the right place, at the right time, in the right quantity, and with the right support services are able to sell more than competitors that do not. Even when the demand for products is unpredictable, suppliers must be able to respond quickly to inventory needs. In such cases, physical distribution costs may be a minor consideration when compared with service, dependability, and timeliness.

Customer relationship management systems exploit the information from supply-chain partners' database systems to help logistics managers identify and root out inefficiencies in the supply chain for the benefit of all marketing channel members—from the producer to the ultimate consumer. Indeed, technology is playing a larger and larger role in physical distribution within marketing channels. It has transformed physical distribution by facilitating just-in-time delivery, precise inventory visibility, and instant shipment tracking capabilities, which help companies to avoid expensive mistakes, reduce costs, and even generate revenues. Information technology brings visibility to the supply chain by allowing all marketing channel members to see precisely where an item is within the supply chain at any time.[17]

Although physical distribution managers try to minimize the costs associated with order processing, inventory management, materials handling, warehousing, and transportation, decreasing the costs in one area often raises them in another. Figure 15.6 shows the percentage of total costs that physical distribution functions

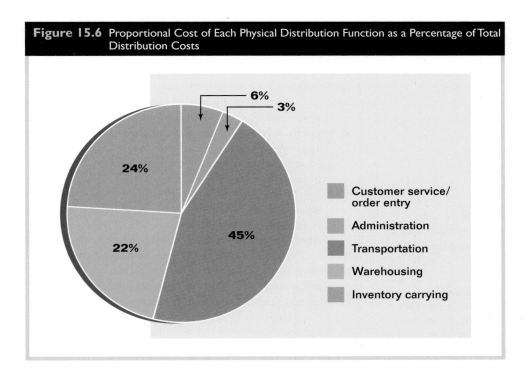

Figure 15.6 Proportional Cost of Each Physical Distribution Function as a Percentage of Total Distribution Costs

6%
3%
24%
22%
45%

Customer service/order entry
Administration
Transportation
Warehousing
Inventory carrying

represent. A total-cost approach to physical distribution enables managers to view physical distribution as a system rather than a collection of unrelated activities. This approach shifts the emphasis from lowering the separate costs of individual activities to minimizing overall distribution costs.

Physical distribution managers must be sensitive to the issue of cost tradeoffs. Higher costs in one functional area of a distribution system may be necessary to achieve lower costs in another. Trade-offs are strategic decisions to combine (and recombine) resources for greatest cost-effectiveness. When distribution managers regard the system as a network of integrated functions, trade-offs become useful tools in implementing a unified, cost-effective distribution strategy.

Another important goal of physical distribution involves **cycle time**, the time needed to complete a process. For instance, reducing cycle time while maintaining or reducing costs and/or maintaining or increasing customer service is a winning combination in supply chains and ultimately leads to greater end-customer satisfaction. Footwear manufacturers, for example, are looking for ways to reduce cycle times, delivering new products to retailers faster. Because the majority of footwear sold in the United States comes from China, products must be shipped to a port and then distributed across the country. To limit a portion of the ground transportation, some companies are starting to use a two-point distribution strategy instead of just one U.S. entry point. Products are transported to the East and West coasts, placing them closer to distribution centers and customers.[18]

In the rest of this section, we take a closer look at a variety of physical distribution activities, including order processing, inventory management, materials handling, warehousing, and transportation.

Order Processing

Order processing is the receipt and transmission of sales order information. Although management sometimes overlooks the importance of these activities, efficient order processing facilitates product flow. Computerized order processing provides a database for all supply-chain members to increase their productivity. When carried out quickly and accurately, order processing contributes to customer satisfaction, decreased costs and cycle time, and increased profits.

Order processing entails three main tasks: order entry, order handling, and order delivery. Order entry begins when customers or salespeople place purchase orders via telephone, snail mail, e-mail, or website. Electronic ordering is less time-consuming than a manual, paper-based ordering system and reduces costs. In some companies, sales representatives receive and enter orders personally and also handle complaints, prepare progress reports, and forward sales order information.

Order handling involves several tasks. Once an order is entered, it is transmitted to a warehouse, where product availability is verified, and to the credit department, where prices, terms, and the customer's credit rating are checked. If the credit department approves the purchase, warehouse personnel (sometimes assisted by automated equipment) pick and assemble the order. If the requested product is not in stock, a production order is sent to the factory, or the customer is offered a substitute.

When the order has been assembled and packed for shipment, the warehouse schedules delivery with an appropriate carrier. If the customer pays for rush service, overnight delivery by FedEx, UPS, DHL, or another overnight carrier is used. The customer is sent an invoice, inventory records are adjusted, and the order is delivered.

Whether a company uses a manual or an electronic order-processing system depends on which method provides the greater speed and accuracy within cost limits. Manual processing suffices for small-volume orders and is more flexible in certain situations. Most companies, however, use **electronic data interchange (EDI)**, which uses computer technology to integrate order processing with production, inventory, accounting, and transportation. Within the supply chain, EDI functions as an information system that links marketing channel members and outsourcing firms together. It reduces paperwork for all members of the supply chain and allows them to share information on invoices,

cycle time The time needed to complete a process

order processing The receipt and transmission of sales order information

electronic data interchange (EDI) A computerized means of integrating order processing with production, inventory, accounting, and transportation

orders, payments, inquiries, and scheduling. Consequently, many companies have pushed their suppliers toward EDI to reduce distribution costs and cycle times.

Inventory Management

Inventory management involves developing and maintaining adequate assortments of products to meet customers' needs. It is a key component of any effective physical distribution system. Inventory decisions have a major impact on physical distribution costs and the level of customer service provided. When too few products are carried in inventory, the result is *stockouts*, or shortages of products that, in turn, can result in brand switching, lower sales, and loss of customers. When too many products (or too many slow-moving products) are carried, costs increase, as do risks of product obsolescence, pilferage, and damage. The objective of inventory management is to minimize inventory costs while maintaining an adequate supply of goods to satisfy customers. To achieve this objective, marketers focus on two major issues: when to order and how much to order.

To determine when to order, a marketer calculates the *reorder point*: the inventory level that signals the need to place a new order. To calculate the reorder point, the marketer must know the order lead time, the usage rate, and the amount of safety stock required. The *order lead time* refers to the average time lapse between placing the order and receiving it. The *usage rate* is the rate at which a product's inventory is used or sold during a specific time period. *Safety stock* is the amount of extra inventory a firm keeps to guard against stockouts resulting from above-average usage rates and/or longer-than-expected lead times. The reorder point can be calculated using the following formula:

$$\text{reorder point} = (\text{order lead time} \times \text{usage rate}) + \text{safety stock}$$

Thus, if order lead time is 10 days, usage rate is 3 units per day, and safety stock is 20 units, the reorder point is 50 units.

Efficient inventory management with accurate reorder points is crucial for firms that use a **just-in-time (JIT)** approach, in which supplies arrive just as they are needed for use in production or for resale. When using JIT, companies maintain low inventory levels and purchase products and materials in small quantities whenever they need them. Usually there is no safety stock, and suppliers are expected to provide consistently high-quality products. JIT inventory management requires a high level of coordination between producers and suppliers, but it eliminates waste and reduces inventory costs significantly. This approach has been used successfully by many well-known firms, including Chrysler, Harley-Davidson, and Dell Computer, to reduce costs and boost customer satisfaction. When a JIT approach is used in a supply chain, suppliers often move close to their customers.

Materials Handling

Materials handling, the physical handling of tangible goods, supplies, and resources, is an important factor in warehouse operations, as well as in transportation from points of production to points of consumption. Efficient procedures and techniques for materials handling minimize inventory management costs, reduce the number of times a good is handled, improve customer service, and increase customer satisfaction. Systems for packaging, labeling, loading, and movement must be coordinated to maximize cost reduction and customer satisfaction.

A growing number of firms are turning to radio waves to track materials tagged with radio frequency ID (RFID) through every phase of handling. Daisy Brand, for example, is using RFID to track its dairy products throughout the supply chain, which helps the firm recognize when a retailer has run out of product and needs to be replenished. The firm is also using data analyzed from its RFID program to help identify high-volume shopping times and manage promotions and new-product introductions.[19]

Product characteristics often determine handling. For example, the characteristics of bulk liquids and gases determine how they can be moved and stored. Internal packaging is also an important consideration in materials handling; goods must be packaged correctly

inventory management Developing and maintaining adequate assortments of products to meet customers' needs

just-in-time (JIT) An inventory-management approach in which supplies arrive just when needed for production or resale

materials handling Physical handling of tangible goods, supplies, and resources to prevent damage or breakage during handling and transportation. Most companies employ packaging consultants during the product design process to help them decide which packaging materials and methods will result in the most efficient handling.

Unit loading and containerization are two common methods used in materials handling. With *unit loading,* one or more boxes are placed on a pallet or skid; these units then can be loaded efficiently by mechanical means such as forklifts, trucks, or conveyer systems. *Containerization* is the consolidation of many items into a single, large container that is sealed at its point of origin and opened at its destination. Containers are usually 8 feet wide, 8 feet high, and 10 to 40 feet long. They can be conveniently stacked and shipped via train, barge, or ship. Once containers reach their destinations, wheel assemblies can be added to make them suitable for ground transportation. Because individual items are not handled in transit, containerization greatly increases efficiency and security in shipping.

Warehousing

Warehousing, the design and operation of facilities for storing and moving goods, is another important physical distribution function. Warehousing provides time utility by enabling firms to compensate for dissimilar production and consumption rates. When mass production creates a greater stock of goods than can be sold immediately, companies may warehouse the surplus until customers are ready to buy. Warehousing also helps to stabilize prices and the availability of seasonal items.

The choice of warehouse facilities is an important strategic consideration. The right type of warehouse allows a company to reduce transportation and inventory costs or improve service to customers. The wrong type of warehouse may drain company resources. Beyond deciding how many facilities to operate and where to locate them, a company must determine which type of warehouse is most appropriate. Warehouses fall into two general categories: private and public. In many cases, a combination of private and public facilities provides the most flexible warehousing approach.

warehousing The design and operation of facilities for storing and moving goods

Warehousing and Inventory Management Warehousing and inventory management efforts are expensive and are important elements in providing customer satisfaction.

© Marcin Balcerzak/Shutterstock.com

Sustainable Marketing
Green Practices in Physical Distribution

Warehousing and transportation are two key areas for supply-chain sustainability as more marketers adopt green practices in physical distribution. In particular, marketers are embracing eco-friendly physical distribution by taking steps to conserve natural resources, reduce waste and pollution, improve energy efficiency, and tap alternative power sources.

Patagonia, which markets outdoor clothing and gear, had the environment in mind when it recently expanded its high-volume distribution center in Reno, Nevada, which handles more than 7 million pieces of merchandise every year. The newly enlarged center features carpeting fashioned from recycled materials and wooden fixtures made from lumber logged in sustainably managed forests. It's also highly energy efficient, including state-of-the-art conveyor equipment, heating systems, and lighting systems that require far less power to operate than the previous systems.

Hall's Warehouse, a family-owned warehousing complex in New Jersey, now uses rooftop solar panels to generate some of the power for its cold-storage facilities. In addition, the facility is equipped with eco-friendly lights that automatically turn on and off, depending on which areas of the warehouse are actually in use at any given time.

Transportation is getting greener, thanks to technology and the movement away from traditional gasoline power. FedEx, for

example, has both hybrid and all-electric trucks making deliveries in U.S. and European markets. Coca-Cola, Frito-Lay, and other major marketers are beginning to replace their conventional delivery trucks with electric and hybrid trucks. And Ryder Trucking, like a growing number of transportation companies, uses computerized routing to save fuel and guide drivers quickly and conveniently to their delivery destinations.[c]

Companies operate **private warehouses** for shipping and storing their own products. A firm usually leases or purchases a private warehouse when its warehousing needs in a given geographic market are substantial and stable enough to warrant a long-term commitment to a fixed facility. Private warehouses are also appropriate for firms that require special handling and storage and that want control of warehouse design and operation. Retailers such as Sears and Radio Shack find it economical to integrate private warehousing with purchasing and distribution for their retail outlets. When sales volumes are fairly stable, ownership and control of a private warehouse may provide benefits such as property appreciation. Private warehouses, however, face fixed costs such as insurance, taxes, maintenance, and debt expense. They also limit flexibility when firms wish to move inventories to more strategic locations. Many private warehouses are being eliminated by direct links between producers and customers, reduced cycle times, and outsourcing to public warehouses.

Public warehouses lease storage space and related physical distribution facilities to other companies. They sometimes provide distribution services such as receiving, unloading, inspecting, and reshipping products; filling orders; providing financing; displaying products; and coordinating shipments. Distribution Unlimited Inc., for example, offers a wide range of such services through its three facilities in New York, which contain more than 7.5 million total square feet of warehouse space.[20]

Public warehouses are especially useful to firms that have seasonal production or low-volume storage needs, have inventories that must be maintained in many locations, are testing or entering new markets, or own private warehouses but occasionally require additional storage space. Public warehouses also serve as collection points during product-recall programs. Whereas private warehouses have fixed costs, public

private warehouses
Company-operated facilities for storing and shipping products

public warehouses Storage space and related physical distribution facilities that can be leased by companies

warehouses offer variable (and often lower) costs because users rent space and purchase warehousing services only as needed.

Many public warehouses furnish security for products that are used as collateral for loans, a service provided at either the warehouse or the site of the owner's inventory. *Field public warehouses* are established by public warehouses at the owner's inventory location. The warehouser becomes custodian of the products and issues a receipt that can be used as collateral for a loan. Public warehouses also provide *bonded storage,* a warehousing arrangement in which imported or taxable products are not released until the products' owners pay U.S. customs duties, taxes, or other fees. Bonded warehouses enable firms to defer tax payments on such items until they are delivered to customers.

Distribution centers are large facilities used for receiving, warehousing, and redistributing products to stores or customers. Distribution centers are specially designed for rapid flow of products. They are usually one-story buildings (to eliminate elevators) with access to transportation networks such as major highways and/or railway lines. Many distribution centers are highly automated, with computer-directed robots, forklifts, and hoists that collect and move products to loading docks. American Eagle Outfitters, for example, operates three distribution centers to serve the needs of more than 1,100 American Eagle Outfitters, aerie, and 77kids stores in the United States, Canada, and the Middle East. The American Eagle Outfitters and aerie brands market apparel to 15- to 25-year-old market, while the new 77kids brand markets apparel to 2- to 12-year-olds. Efficiency and creativity in distribution operations help the firm to keep up with a high volume of merchandise moving through the centers and to stay on top of busy holiday seasons.[21] Although some public warehouses offer such specialized services, most distribution centers are privately owned. They serve customers in regional markets and, in some cases, function as consolidation points for a company's branch warehouses.

Transportation

distribution centers Large, centralized warehouses that focus on moving rather than storing goods

transportation The movement of products from where they are made to intermediaries and end users

Transportation, the movement of products from where they are made to intermediaries and end users, is the most expensive physical distribution function. Today, approximately 10 percent of a company's total expenses are freight charges.[22] Because product availability and timely deliveries depend on transportation functions, transportation decisions directly affect customer service. A firm may even build its distribution and marketing strategy around a unique transportation system if that system can ensure on-time deliveries and thereby give the firm a competitive edge. Companies may build their own transportation fleets (private carriers) or outsource the transportation function to a common or contract carrier.

TRANSPORTATION MODES

The basic transportation modes for moving physical goods are railroads, trucks, waterways, airways, and pipelines. Each has distinct advantages. Many companies adopt physical handling procedures that facilitate the use of two or more modes in combination. Table 15.3 shows the percentage of intercity freight carried by each transportation mode.

Railroads such as Union Pacific and Canadian National carry heavy, bulky freight that must be shipped long distances over land. Railroads commonly haul minerals, sand, lumber, chemicals, and farm products, as well as low-value manufactured goods and automobiles. However, transporting chemicals via railroads can be dangerous in an accident. Currently, Clorox is changing the way it manufactures its product, eliminating chlorine gas, to make the product safer to transport via rail.[23] They are especially efficient for transporting full carloads, which can be shipped at lower rates than smaller quantities because they require less handling. Many companies locate factories or warehouses near rail lines for convenient loading and unloading.

SNAPSHOT

Theft by the Truckload
Top five products most often stolen in truck cargo thefts
Product Category (%)

27.1	Electronics
16.8	Building and Industrial Materials
16.3	Food and Drinks
9.8	Home and Garden
8.2	Apparel

Source: "The Cargo Theft Threat," *Inbound Logistics,* January 2010, p. 242.

Table 15.3 Characteristics and Ratings of Transportation Modes by Selection Criteria

Selection Criteria	Railroads	Trucks	Pipelines	Waterways	Airplanes
Cost	Moderate	High	Low	Very low	Very high
Speed	Average	Fast	Slow	Very slow	Very fast
Dependability	Average	High	High	Average	High
Load flexibility	High	Average	Very low	Very high	Low
Accessibility	High	Very high	Very limited	Limited	Average
Frequency	Low	High	Very high	Very low	Average
Percentage of truck miles transported	39.4	28.6	19.6	12.0	0.3
Products carried	Coal, grain, lumber, paper and pulp products, chemicals	Clothing, computers, books, groceries and produce, livestock	Oil, processed coal, natural gas	Chemicals, bauxite, grain, motor vehicles, agricultural implements	Flowers, food (highly perishable), technical instruments, emergency parts and equipment, overnight mail

Source: U.S. Bureau of Transportation Statistics, National Transportation Statistics (Washington, DC: U.S. Government Printing Office), September 2009, www.bts.gov/publications/national_transportation_statistics/html/table_01_46b.html.

Trucks provide the most flexible schedules and routes of all major transportation modes in the United States because they can go almost anywhere. Because trucks have a unique ability to move goods directly from factory or warehouse to customer, they are often used in conjunction with other forms of transport that cannot provide door-to-door deliveries. Trucks are more expensive and somewhat more vulnerable to bad weather than trains. They are also subject to size and weight restrictions on the products they carry. Trucks are sometimes criticized for high levels of loss and damage to freight and for delays caused by the rehandling of small shipments.

Waterways are the cheapest method of shipping heavy, low-value, nonperishable goods such as ore, coal, grain, and petroleum products. Water carriers offer considerable capacity. Powered by tugboats and towboats, barges that travel along intracoastal canals, inland rivers, and navigation systems can haul at least ten times the weight of one rail car, and oceangoing vessels can haul thousands of containers. More than 95 percent of international cargo is transported by water. However, many markets are inaccessible by water transportation unless supplemented by rail or truck. Droughts and floods also may create difficulties for users of inland waterway transportation. Nevertheless, the extreme fuel efficiency of water transportation and the continuing globalization of marketing likely will increase its use in the future.

Air transportation is the fastest but most expensive form of shipping. It is used most often for perishable goods; for high-value, low-bulk items; and for products that require quick delivery over long distances, such as emergency shipments. Some air carriers transport combinations of passengers, freight, and mail. Despite its expense, air transit can reduce warehousing and packaging costs and losses from theft and damage, thus helping to lower total costs (but truck transportation needed for pickup and final delivery adds to cost and transit time). Although air transport accounts for less than 1 percent of total ton-miles carried, its importance as a mode of transportation is growing. In fact, the success of many businesses is now based on the availability of overnight air delivery service provided by organizations such as UPS, FedEx, DHL, RPS Air, and the U.S. Postal Service. Amazon.com, for example, ships many of the products that are ordered online via UPS within one day.

Pipelines, the most automated transportation mode, usually belong to the shipper and carry the shipper's products. Most pipelines carry petroleum products or chemicals. The Trans-Alaska Pipeline, owned and operated by a consortium of oil companies that includes ExxonMobil and BP-Amoco, transports crude oil from remote oil-drilling sites

Entrepreneurial Marketing
French Fries Go Back to the Future—
By Rail!

Efficient physical distribution—minimizing costs and increasing value—is crucial to marketing strategy.

Back when Martin-Brower Company trucked all their frozen potato products for 600 McDonald's restaurants around Virginia, they faced skyrocketing transportation costs. They decided to go back to the future and make all of their incoming frozen fries ride the rails. Many thought it couldn't be done, because few railroads offered refrigerated service. But through cooperation with Cryo-Trans, builder of refrigerated rail cars, they created a solution that even included tracking capabilities to make inventory visible during the entire shipping process. The Martin-Brower Company was able to slash transportation costs, decrease congestion at loading docks, and reduce their carbon footprint.[d]

in central Alaska to shipping terminals on the coast. Slurry pipelines carry pulverized coal, grain, or wood chips suspended in water. Pipelines move products slowly but continuously and at relatively low cost. They are dependable and minimize the problems of product damage and theft. However, contents are subject to as much as 1 percent shrinkage, usually from evaporation. Pipelines also have been a concern to environmentalists, who fear installation and leaks could harm plants and animals.

CHOOSING TRANSPORTATION MODES

Logistics managers select a transportation mode based on the combination of cost, speed, dependability, load flexibility, accessibility, and frequency that is most appropriate for their products and generates the desired level of customer service. Table 15.3 shows relative ratings of each transportation mode by these selection criteria.

Marketers compare alternative transportation modes to determine whether the benefits from a more expensive mode are worth the higher costs. Companies such as Iron Data can assist marketers in analyzing various transportation options. This Internet firm's software provides corporate users with several services, including the ability to view information about the speed and cost of different transportation modes, print labels, order shipping, and then track shipments online.[24]

Intermodal Transportation
Containers facilitate intermodal transportation because they can be transported by ships, trains, and trucks.

COORDINATING TRANSPORTATION

To take advantage of the benefits offered by various transportation modes and compensate for deficiencies, marketers often combine and coordinate two or more modes. In recent years, **intermodal transportation**, as this integrated approach is sometimes called, has become easier because of new developments within the transportation industry. Several kinds of intermodal shipping are available. All combine the flexibility of trucking with the low cost or speed of other forms of transport. Containerization facilitates intermodal transportation by consolidating shipments into sealed containers for transport by *piggyback* (shipping that uses both truck trailers and railway flatcars), *fishyback* (truck trailers and water carriers), and *birdyback* (truck trailers and air carriers). As transportation costs have increased, intermodal shipping has gained popularity. To transport its floor cleaners to retail locations, Electrolux relies on several modes of transportation, which include water, rail, and truck carriers. The majority of products are shipped from Asia to ports in the United States, transported to the distribution center in El Paso, Texas, via rail and finally to destinations via trucks.[25]

Specialized outsource agencies provide other forms of transport coordination. Known as **freight forwarders**, these firms combine shipments from several organizations into efficient lot sizes. Small loads (less than 500 pounds) are much more expensive to ship than full carloads or truckloads, which frequently require consolidation. Freight forwarders take small loads from various marketers, buy transport space from carriers, and arrange for goods to be delivered to buyers. For instance, L'Oreal USA uses freight forwarders for shipments that are less-than-truckload, weighing less than 20,000 pounds.[26] Freight forwarders' profits come from the margin between the higher, less-than-carload rates they charge each marketer and the lower carload rates they themselves pay. Because large shipments require less handling, use of freight forwarders can speed delivery. Freight forwarders also can determine the most efficient carriers and routes and are useful for shipping goods to foreign markets. Currently, Boeing and Damco, a Danish logistics company, are using each other's expertise, in manufacturing and freight forwarding, to improve global supply chain management by creating industrial and technological logistics tools.[27] Some companies prefer to outsource their shipping to freight forwarders because the latter provide door-to-door service.

Another transportation innovation is the development of **megacarriers**, freight transportation companies that offer several shipment methods, including rail, truck, and air service. CSX, for example, has trains, barges, container ships, trucks, and pipelines, thus offering a multitude of transportation services. In addition, air carriers have increased their ground-transportation services. As they expand the range of transportation alternatives, carriers also put greater stress on customer service.

Legal Issues in Channel Management

The numerous federal, state, and local laws governing channel management are based on the general principle that the public is best served by protecting competition and free trade. Under the authority of such federal legislation as the Sherman Antitrust Act and the Federal Trade Commission Act, courts and regulatory agencies determine under what circumstances channel management practices violate this underlying principle and must be restricted. Although channel managers are not expected to be legal experts, they should be aware that attempts to control distribution functions may have legal repercussions. The following practices are among those frequently subject to legal restraint.

Dual Distribution

Earlier we noted that some companies may use dual distribution by using two or more marketing channels to distribute the same products to the same target market. Hewlett-Packard, for example, sells computers directly to consumers through a toll-free telephone line and a website, as well as through electronics retailers such as Best Buy. Courts do not consider this practice illegal when it promotes competition. A manufacturer can

intermodal transportation
Two or more transportation modes used in combination

freight forwarders
Organizations that consolidate shipments from several firms into efficient lot sizes

megacarriers Freight transportation firms that provide several modes of shipment

also legally open its own retail outlets. But the courts view as a threat to competition a manufacturer that uses company-owned outlets to dominate or drive out of business independent retailers or distributors that handle its products. In such cases, dual distribution violates the law. To avoid this interpretation, producers should use outlet prices that do not severely undercut independent retailers' prices.

Restricted Sales Territories

To tighten control over distribution of its products, a manufacturer may try to prohibit intermediaries from selling its products outside designated sales territories. Intermediaries themselves often favor this practice because it gives them exclusive territories, allowing them to avoid competition for the producer's brands within these territories. In recent years, the courts have adopted conflicting positions in regard to restricted sales territories. Although the courts have deemed restricted sales territories a restraint of trade among intermediaries handling the same brands (except for small or newly established companies), they have also held that exclusive territories can actually promote competition among dealers handling different brands. At present, the producer's intent in establishing restricted territories and the overall effect of doing so on the market must be evaluated for each individual case.

Tying Agreements

When a supplier (usually a manufacturer or franchiser) furnishes a product to a channel member with the stipulation that the channel member must purchase other products as well, a **tying agreement** exists. Suppliers may institute tying agreements to move weaker products along with more popular items, or a franchiser may tie purchase of equipment and supplies to the sale of franchises, justifying the policy as necessary for quality control and protection of the franchiser's reputation.

A related practice is *full-line forcing,* in which a supplier requires that channel members purchase the supplier's entire line to obtain any of the supplier's products. Manufacturers sometimes use full-line forcing to ensure that intermediaries accept new products and that a suitable range of products is available to customers.

The courts accept tying agreements when the supplier alone can provide products of a certain quality, when the intermediary is free to carry competing products as well, and when a company has just entered the market. Most other tying agreements are considered illegal.

Exclusive Dealing

When a manufacturer forbids an intermediary to carry products of competing manufacturers, the arrangement is called **exclusive dealing**. Manufacturers receive considerable market protection in an exclusive-dealing arrangement and may cut off shipments to intermediaries that violate the agreement.

The legality of an exclusive-dealing contract is generally determined by applying three tests. If the exclusive dealing blocks competitors from as much as 15 percent of the market, the sales volume is large, and the producer is considerably larger than the retailer, the arrangement is considered anticompetitive. If dealers and customers in a given market have access to similar products or if the exclusive-dealing contract strengthens an otherwise weak competitor, the arrangement is allowed.

Refusal to Deal

For more than 75 years, the courts have held that producers have the right to choose channel members with which they will do business (and the right to reject others). Within existing distribution channels, however, suppliers may not legally refuse to deal with wholesalers or dealers merely because these wholesalers or dealers resist policies that are anticompetitive or in restraint of trade. Suppliers are further prohibited from organizing some channel members in refusal-to-deal actions against other members that choose not to comply with illegal policies.

tying agreement An agreement in which a supplier furnishes a product to a channel member with the stipulation that the channel member must purchase other products as well

exclusive dealing A situation in which a manufacturer forbids an intermediary to carry products of competing manufacturers

summary

1. To describe the foundations of supply-chain management

The distribution component of the marketing mix focuses on the decisions and activities involved in making products available to customers when and where they want to purchase them. An important function of distribution is the joint effort of all involved organizations to be part of creating an effective supply chain, which refers to all the activities associated with the flow and transformation of products from raw materials through to the end customer. Operations management is the total set of managerial activities used by an organization to transform resource inputs into products. Logistics management involves planning, implementation, and controlling the efficient and effective flow and storage of goods, services, and information from the point of origin to consumption in order to meet customers' needs and wants. Supply management in its broadest form refers to the processes that enable the progress of value from raw material to final customer and back to redesign and final disposition. Supply-chain management therefore refers to a set of approaches used to integrate the functions of operations management, logistics management, supply management, and marketing channel management so that products and services are produced and distributed in the right quantities, to the right locations, and at the right time. The supply chain includes all entities—shippers and other firms that facilitate distribution, as well as producers, wholesalers, and retailers—that distribute products and benefit from cooperative efforts.

2. To explore the role and significance of marketing channels and supply chains

A marketing channel, or channel of distribution, is a group of individuals and organizations that direct the flow of products from producers to customers. The major role of marketing channels is to make products available at the right time, at the right place, and in the right amounts. In most channels of distribution, producers and consumers are linked by marketing intermediaries. The two major types of intermediaries are retailers, which purchase products and resell them to ultimate consumers, and wholesalers, which buy and resell products to other wholesalers, retailers, and business customers.

Marketing channels serve many functions. They create time, place, and possession utilities by making products available when and where customers want them and providing customers with access to product use through sale or rental. Marketing intermediaries facilitate exchange efficiencies, often reducing the costs of exchanges by performing certain services and functions. Although some critics suggest eliminating wholesalers, the functions of the intermediaries in the marketing channel must be performed. As such, eliminating one or more intermediaries results in other organizations in the channel having to do more. Because intermediaries serve both producers and buyers, they reduce the total number of transactions that otherwise would be needed to move products from producer to the end customer.

3. To identify types of marketing channels

Channels of distribution are broadly classified as channels for consumer products and channels for business products. Within these two broad categories, different channels are used for different products. Although consumer goods can move directly from producer to consumers, consumer channels that include wholesalers and retailers are usually more economical and knowledge-efficient. Distribution of business products differs from that of consumer products in the types of channels used. A direct distribution channel is common in business marketing. Also used are channels containing industrial distributors, manufacturers' agents, and a combination of agents and distributors. Most producers have multiple or dual channels so the distribution system can be adjusted for various target markets.

4. To understand factors that influence marketing channel selection

Selecting an appropriate marketing channel is a crucial decision for supply-chain managers. To determine which channel is most appropriate, managers must think about customer characteristics, the type of organization, product attributes, competition, environmental forces, and the availability and characteristics of intermediaries. Careful consideration of these factors will assist a supply-chain manager in selecting the correct channel.

5. To identify the intensity of market coverage

A marketing channel is managed such that products receive appropriate market coverage. In choosing intensive distribution, producers strive to make a product available to all possible dealers. In selective distribution, only some outlets in an area are chosen to distribute a product. Exclusive distribution usually gives a single dealer rights to sell a product in a large geographic area.

6. To examine strategic issues in marketing channels, including leadership, cooperation, and conflict

Each channel member performs a different role in the system and agrees to accept certain rights, responsibilities, rewards, and sanctions for nonconformance. Although many marketing channels are determined by consensus, some are organized and controlled by a single leader, or channel captain. A channel captain may be a producer, wholesaler, or retailer. A marketing channel functions most effectively when members cooperate; when they deviate from their roles, channel conflict can arise.

Integration of marketing channels brings various activities under one channel member's management. Vertical integration combines two or more stages of the channel under one management. The vertical marketing system (VMS) is managed centrally for the mutual benefit of all channel members. Vertical marketing systems may be corporate, administered, or contractual. Horizontal integration combines institutions at the same level of channel operation under a single management.

7. To examine physical distribution as a part of supply-chain management

Physical distribution, or logistics, refers to the activities used to move products from producers to customers and other end users. These activities include order processing, inventory management, materials handling, warehousing, and transportation. An efficient physical distribution system is an important component of an overall marketing strategy because it can decrease costs and increase customer satisfaction. Within the marketing channel, physical distribution activities are often performed by a wholesaler, but they may also be performed by a producer or retailer or outsourced to a third party. Efficient physical

distribution systems can decrease costs and transit time while increasing customer service.

Order processing is the receipt and transmission of sales order information. It consists of three main tasks—order entry, order handling, and order delivery—that may be done manually but are more often handled through electronic data interchange systems. Inventory management involves developing and maintaining adequate assortments of products to meet customers' needs. Logistics managers must strive to find the optimal level of inventory to satisfy customer needs while keeping costs down. Materials handling, the physical handling of products, is a crucial element in warehousing and transporting products. Warehousing involves the design and operation of facilities for storing and moving goods; such facilities may be privately owned or public. Transportation, the movement of products from where they are made to where they are purchased and used, is the most expensive physical distribution function. The basic modes of transporting goods include railroads, trucks, waterways, airways, and pipelines.

8. To explore legal issues in channel management

Federal, state, and local laws regulate channel management to protect competition and free trade. Courts may prohibit or permit a practice depending on whether it violates this underlying principle. Procompetitive legislation applies to distribution practices. Channel management practices frequently subject to legal restraint include dual distribution, restricted sales territories, tying agreements, exclusive dealing, and refusal to deal. When these practices strengthen weak competitors or increase competition among dealers, they may be permitted; in most other cases, when competition may be weakened considerably, they are deemed illegal.

Go to www.cengagebrain.com for resources to help you master the content in this chapter as well as materials that will expand your marketing knowledge!

important terms

distribution, 430

supply chain, 430

operations
  management, 430

logistics
  management, 430

supply management, 430

supply-chain
  management, 430

marketing channel, 432

marketing
  intermediaries, 432

industrial
  distributor, 436

dual distribution, 437

strategic channel
  alliance, 438

intensive distribution, 441

selective
  distribution, 442

exclusive
  distribution, 442

channel captain, 444

channel power, 444

vertical channel
  integration, 447

vertical marketing
  systems (VMSs), 447

horizontal channel
  integration, 448

physical
  distribution, 448

outsourcing, 448

cycle time, 450

order processing, 450

electronic data
  interchange (EDI), 450

inventory
  management, 451

just-in-time (JIT), 451

materials handling, 451

warehousing, 452

private
  warehouses, 453

public
  warehouses, 453

distribution
  centers, 454

transportation, 454

intermodal
  transportation, 457

freight
  forwarders, 457

megacarriers, 457

tying agreement, 458

exclusive dealing, 458

discussion and review questions

1. Define supply-chain management. Why is it important?
2. Describe the major functions of marketing channels. Why are these functions better accomplished through combined efforts of channel members?
3. List several reasons consumers often blame intermediaries for distribution inefficiencies.
4. Compare and contrast the four major types of marketing channels for consumer products. Through which type of channel is each of the following products most likely to be distributed?
   a. New automobiles
   b. Saltine crackers
   c. Cut-your-own Christmas trees
   d. New textbooks
   e. Sofas
   f. Soft drinks
5. Outline the four most common channels for business products. Describe the products or situations that lead marketers to choose each channel.
6. Describe an industrial distributor. What types of products are marketed through an industrial distributor?
7. Under what conditions is a producer most likely to use more than one marketing channel?

8. Identify and describe the factors that may influence marketing channel selection decisions.
9. Explain the differences among intensive, selective, and exclusive methods of distribution.
10. "Channel cooperation requires that members support the overall channel goals to achieve individual goals." Comment on this statement.
11. Explain the major characteristics of each of the three types of vertical marketing systems (VMSs): corporate, administered, and contractual.
12. Discuss the cost and service tradeoffs involved in developing a physical distribution system.
13. What are the main tasks involved in order processing?
14. Explain the tradeoffs that inventory managers face when they reorder products or supplies. How is the reorder point computed?
15. Explain the major differences between private and public warehouses. How do they differ from a distribution center?
16. Compare and contrast the five major transportation modes in terms of cost, speed, and dependability.
17. Under what conditions are tying agreements, exclusive dealing, and dual distribution judged illegal?

application questions

CRITICAL THINKING

1. *Supply-chain management* involves long-term partnerships among channel members that are working together to reduce inefficiencies, costs, and redundancies and to develop innovative approaches to satisfy customers. Select one of the following companies and explain how supply-chain management could increase marketing productivity.

a. Dell
b. FedEx
c. Nike
d. Taco Bell

2. Marketers can select from three major levels of marketing coverage when determining the number and kinds of outlets in which to sell a product: intensive, selective, or exclusive distribution. Characteristics of the product and its target market determine the intensity of coverage a product should receive. Indicate the intensity level best suited for the following products, and explain why it is appropriate.

a. Personal computers
b. Deodorant
c. Canon digital cameras
d. Nike athletic shoes

3. Describe the decision process you might go through if you were attempting to determine the most appropriate distribution channel for one of the following:

a. Shotguns for hunters
b. Women's lingerie
c. Telephone systems for small businesses
d. Toy trucks for 2-year-olds

4. Assume that you are responsible for the physical distribution of computers at a web-based company. What would you do to ensure product availability, timely delivery, and quality service for your customers?

internet exercise

FedEx

Many companies lack their own distribution systems. Firms in this situation may rely on the services provided by companies such as FedEx to handle their distribution. Learn more about the services provided by FedEx at **www.fedex.com.**

1. What tools does FedEx provide to make the shipping process easier?

2. Other than shipping products, what other services does FedEx provide?

3. Is there information on the FedEx website that would help a potential FedEx customer to evaluate FedEx regarding some of the selection criteria shown in Table 15.3?

developing your **marketing plan**

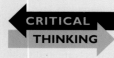

CRITICAL THINKING

One of the key components in a successful marketing strategy is the plan for getting the products to your customer. To make the best decisions about where, when, and how your products will be made available to the customer, you need to know more about how these distribution decisions relate to other marketing mix elements in your marketing plan. To assist you in relating the information in this chapter to your marketing plan, consider the following issues:

1. Marketing intermediaries perform many activities. Using Table 15.2 as a guide, discuss the types of activities where a channel member could provide needed assistance.

2. Using Figure 15.2 (or 15.3 if your product is a business product), determine which of the channel distribution paths is most appropriate for your product. Given the nature of your product, could it be distributed through more than one of these paths?

3. Determine the level of distribution intensity that is appropriate for your product. Consider the characteristics of your target market(s), the product attributes, and environmental factors in your deliberation.

4. Discuss the physical functions that will be required for distributing your product, focusing on materials handling, warehousing, and transportation.

The information obtained from these questions should assist you in developing various aspects of your marketing plan found in the *Interactive Marketing Plan* exercise at **www. cengagebrain.com.**

Netflix's Distribution Goes Beyond Disks

CRITICAL THINKING

Founded in 1997, Netflix was originally nothing more than an online version of a traditional video rental store. Customers could visit the Netflix website and choose movies to rent by mail. Each DVD rental cost $4, along with a $2 shipping fee, plus late fees, if applicable. However, with bricks-and-mortar video rental stores booming, Netflix quickly figured out that it needed a more compelling competitive advantage to attract a large and loyal customer base.

Instead of charging for individual DVDs, Netflix instituted a monthly subscription plan, charging customers based on the number of movies they want to have at home. Monthly packages range from one-at-a-time to four-at-a-time DVD rentals—no late fees, ever. Members create a list of movies they would like to see in order of preference, and Netflix delivers them. As soon as a customer returns a DVD in Netflix's prepaid envelope, the company sends the next one on the list.

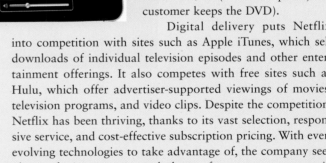

As Netflix's cost-efficient subscription model became more popular, it expanded its film and television show collection and now offers more independent and foreign films, documentaries, and television shows than anyone else. It also added a "Play Instantly" feature, allowing subscribers to download movies from the Netflix website. Customers enjoy being able to click and watch a movie right away—and Netflix saves on shipping fees, not to mention lightening its physical distribution load.

To keep up with the high volume of rentals by mail, Netflix employees check in and mail out more than 600 DVDs every hour. Netflix maintains 58 distribution centers around the country. As a result, DVDs typically arrive one day after they're shipped to customers. Netflix knows that speed is critical because customers want to make the most of their subscriptions. The faster DVDs arrive, the faster they can be viewed and dropped in the mailbox, to be checked in by the nearest Netflix distribution center. Then the next DVD on the list is mailed, and the cycle begins again.

Today, Netflix invites subscribers to stream rented movies electronically through a variety of devices, including Microsoft's Xbox 360, Sony's PS3, Nintendo's Wii, selected Blu-ray DVD players, and web-enabled televisions from several manufacturers. Although a growing number of customers are opting for these digital rental options, the majority still prefer Netflix's original rent-by-mail offering. Within a few years, however, digital delivery could become the company's mainstay.

Now Netflix has grown into a major power in the movie rental business, ringing up $1.6 billion in revenue every year and serving more than 12 million customers. During the past decade, it's adapted to an ever-changing competitive landscape. Blockbuster, whose superstores once dominated the industry, has been struggling financially and closing outlets. Even the mighty Walmart tried to compete with Netflix at one time, but it ultimately decided to exit the DVD rental business. Regional video rental chains and independent stores are disappearing, partly because of economic pressures and partly because of changing technology and customer behavior.

Meanwhile, Redbox is the rising star of in-person DVD rentals. Its 22,000 gleaming red vending machines are seemingly everywhere, in supermarkets, convenience stores, and other high-traffic retail outlets, inviting impulse rentals. Customers can see, at a glance, which movies are available for rent and swipe a credit or debit card to pay the wallet-pleasing rental fee of $1 per day. If they wish, customers can reserve specific movies online or via iPhone before heading out to the nearest Redbox kiosk to pick them up. Unlike Netflix, which lets customers keep DVDs for days or even weeks without paying additional fees, Redbox charges $1 per day for every rental, up to a maximum of $25 (at which point, the customer keeps the DVD).

Digital delivery puts Netflix into competition with sites such as Apple iTunes, which sell downloads of individual television episodes and other entertainment offerings. It also competes with free sites such as Hulu, which offer advertiser-supported viewings of movies, television programs, and video clips. Despite the competition, Netflix has been thriving, thanks to its vast selection, responsive service, and cost-effective subscription pricing. With ever-evolving technologies to take advantage of, the company sees plenty of room to grow and plenty of new customers to win over.[28]

QUESTIONS FOR DISCUSSION

1. How is Netflix using physical distribution for competitive advantage?

2. How have product attributes and customer characteristics changed the competitive landscape for distribution in the movie rental industry?

3. Can Netflix be considered a channel captain? Explain your answer.

CASE 15.2

Dell Direct and Not-So-Direct

CRITICAL THINKING

When Michael Dell started his Texas-based computer business in 1984, he chose a distribution strategy that was radically different from that of other computer marketers. Instead of selling through wholesalers and retailers, the company dealt directly with customers. This kept costs low and allowed Dell to cater to customers' needs by building each computer to order. Using a direct channel also minimized inventory costs and reduced the risk that parts and products would become obsolete even before customers placed their orders, a constant concern in high-tech industries.

By 1997, Dell's website alone was responsible for $1 million a day in sales. Relying on the strength of its online sales, catalogs, and phone orders, Dell expanded beyond the United States and added new products for four target markets: consumers, large corporations, small businesses, and government agencies. Meanwhile, Apple, Hewlett-Packard, and other competitors were reaching out to many of the same segments with a combination of direct and indirect channels. Apple Stores, for example, proved to be major customer magnets and gave a significant boost to sales of Macintosh computers and other Apple electronics. Hewlett-Packard forged strong ties with value-added resellers (VARs), intermediaries that assemble systems of computers, servers, and other products customized to meet the special needs of business buyers.

Although Dell tested retail distribution on a number of occasions, it never let the experiments go on too long. In the 1990s, it tried selling PCs through a few big U.S. retail chains, but soon discontinued the arrangement because the profit margins weren't as healthy as in the direct channel. Later, it opened a series of branded retail kiosks in major U.S. markets to display its products and answer customers' questions. Unlike stores, however, the kiosks didn't actually sell anything: Customers could only place orders for future delivery. Dell ultimately closed the kiosks down.

By 2007, with competitors coming on strong, Dell was ready to rethink its worldwide channel strategy. As convenient as online shopping was for many U.S. computer buyers, it was much less popular in many other countries. To gain market share domestically and internationally, Dell would have to follow consumers into stores, malls, and downtown shopping districts. The company began selling a few models through Walmart's U.S. stores, Carphone Warehouse's U.K. stores, Bic Camera's Japanese stores, and Gome's Chinese stores. In addition, it opened Dell stores in Moscow, Budapest, and other world capitals.

By 2010, sales through retailers had gained enough momentum that Dell sought out other retail deals. In another channel change, it began selling through VAR partners that serve small- and medium-sized businesses and lined up wholesalers to distribute its products in Europe, Latin America, and elsewhere. When Dell introduced a new line of smartphones, it needed a new channel arrangement to reach buyers. Therefore, it arranged for cell phone carriers such as AT&T to sell the new models to their customers.

As successful as Dell has been in revamping its indirect channels, selling directly to customers remains a top priority. Dell invites orders around the clock through Web pages tailored to the needs of each target market. It also maintains an online outlet store to sell discontinued and refurbished products. It mails millions of catalogs and direct-mail pieces every year. And its sales force calls on government officials and big businesses that buy in volume. Dell's website notes, with pride, that the 10 largest U.S. corporations and five largest U.S. commercial banks "run on Dell."

Moreover, the company is a pioneer in stimulating exchanges with customers through social media. Dell has 139,000 fans on Facebook, for example, and regularly posts offers that drive customers to its various websites. It's become a pioneer in selling directly to customers via the microblog site Twitter. In less than three years, it generated $6.5 million in revenue from sales transactions that originated on Twitter. That may be a tiny sliver of Dell's $53 billion in annual revenue, but it demonstrates the company's flexibility in adapting to shifts in customer behavior and environmental forces, such as technological advances.

With market share and profit-margin challenges still facing the company, and global demand just picking up steam after a long, difficult recession, watch for Dell to make more channel adjustments in the coming years.[29]

QUESTIONS FOR DISCUSSION

1. Is Dell using intensive, selective, or exclusive distribution for its market coverage? Why is this appropriate for Dell's products and target markets?

2. How does Dell's preference for direct channels affect its decisions about physical distribution?

3. What issues in channel conflict might arise from Dell's current distribution arrangements?

Chapter 16

Retailing, Direct Marketing, and Wholesaling

OBJECTIVES

1. To understand the purpose and function of retailers in the marketing channel
2. To identify the major types of retailers
3. To explore strategic issues in retailing
4. To recognize the various forms of direct marketing and selling
5. To examine franchising and its benefits and weaknesses
6. To understand the nature and functions of wholesaling
7. To understand how wholesalers are classified

Best Buy's Best Retailing Practices

From low prices and huge product mix to personal shopping assistance and product trouble-shooters, the electronics retailer Best Buy makes it easy for customers to feel they're getting... well, the best buy. The Minnesota-based company was founded in 1966 as a music retailer but changed its name to Best Buy in 1983 when it opened its first supersized store, stocked with thousands of consumer electronics items.

Today, Best Buy rings up $50 billion in annual revenue through stores in North America, Europe, and China, as well as through its busy website. The company's global workforce of 180,000 includes 24,000 members of the Geek Squad, a competitive advantage because its high-tech experts make house calls to install and repair products.

Although rival Circuit City went bankrupt a few years ago, Best Buy still faces competition from Walmart and Costco, both of which see growth in electronics. To compete more effectively, Best Buy has researched its customers' needs and behavior and segmented the market into five core groups: young gadget enthusiasts, busy mothers looking for kids' electronics, fathers shopping for lifestyle electronics, affluent professionals interested in home entertainment, and small-business owners.

Based on this analysis, Best Buy has adapted its retail activities to better serve its targeted segments. For example, it opened up store layouts to encourage easy browsing between departments (important for non-tech-savvy shoppers) and set up displays of cutting-edge products (making gadget fans happy). It also designated employees to help consumers and businesspeople seeking "solutions," rather than individual products. These personal shopping assistants know store stock very well and can bring together a group of products to fit each customer's specifications and budget.

Finally, Best Buy has been introducing a wider selection of private-brand products under names such as Geek Squad and Dynex. These brands are available nowhere else, another way to demonstrate that Best Buy does its best for customers.[1]

Retailers such as Best Buy are the most visible and accessible marketing channel members to consumers. They are an important link in the marketing channel because they are both marketers for and customers of producers and wholesalers. They perform many supply-chain functions, such as buying, selling, grading, risk taking, and developing and maintaining information databases about customers. Retailers are in a strategic position to develop relationships with consumers and partnerships with producers and intermediaries in the marketing channel.

In this chapter, we examine the nature of retailing, direct marketing, and wholesaling, and their importance in supplying consumers with goods and services. First, we explore the major types of retail stores and consider strategic issues in retailing: location, retail positioning, store image, and category management. Next, we discuss direct marketing, including catalog marketing, response marketing, telemarketing, television home shopping, and online retailing. We also explore direct selling and vending. Then we look at franchising, a retailing form that continues to grow in popularity. Finally, we examine the importance of wholesalers in marketing channels, including their functions and classifications.

Retailing

Retailing includes all transactions in which the buyer intends to consume the product through personal, family, or household use. Buyers in retail transactions are therefore the ultimate consumers. A **retailer** is an organization that purchases products for the purpose of reselling them to ultimate consumers. Although most retailers' sales are made directly to the consumer, nonretail transactions occur occasionally when retailers sell products to other businesses.

Retailing often takes place in stores or service establishments, but it also occurs through direct selling, direct marketing, and vending machines. Given the purchasing pattern trends of the last decade, there is a clear expectation that consumers will increasingly buy their goods and services online. Online shoppers prefer shopping on the Internet to avoid crowds, find lower prices, avoid the inconvenience of having to travel to stores, and have a wider selection of products. This trend is evident when looking at sales from Black Friday, the Friday after Thanksgiving when most retailers drastically mark down products to jump-start the holiday shopping season. It is common to find customers camping outside of retail stores in order to take advantage of the huge discounts. This trend may be dwindling as many consumers decide to sleep in and take advantage of the price reductions from their computer at home. Last year, online sales were up 11 percent on Black Friday.[2]

Retailing is important to the national U.S. economy. Approximately 1.1 million retailers operate in the United States.[3] This number has remained relatively constant for the past 25 years, but sales volume has increased more than fourfold. Most personal income is spent in retail stores, and nearly one of every five people employed in the United States works in a retail operation.[4]

Retailers add value for customers by providing services and assisting in making product selections. They can enhance the value of products by making buyers' shopping experiences more convenient, as in online shopping. Through their locations, retailers can facilitate comparison shopping; for example, car dealerships often cluster in the same general vicinity, as do furniture stores. Product value is also enhanced when retailers offer services, such as technical advice, delivery, credit, and repair. Finally, retail sales personnel can demonstrate to customers how products can satisfy their needs or solve problems.

The value added by retailers is significant for both producers and end consumers. Retailers are the critical link between producers and end consumers because they provide the environment in which exchanges with ultimate consumers occur. Ultimate consumers benefit through retailers' performance of marketing functions that result in the availability of broader arrays of products that can satisfy the needs of consumers.

retailing All transactions in which the buyer intends to consume the product through personal, family, or household use

retailer An organization that purchases products for the purpose of reselling them to ultimate consumers

Responsible Marketing?
Starbucks Tries to Serve All Stakeholders

ISSUE: Is Starbucks doing enough to be socially responsible?

Starbucks is the largest coffee house chain in the world, with more than 15,000 stores. Starbucks claims that "life happens over coffee" and has attempted to create a coffee culture that inspires customers to create a dialogue and discuss important concerns of the day. For instance, the company listened to customers and moved from whole to 2 percent milk and eliminated ingredients that contain trans fats. Starbucks does much to support responsible and sustainable coffee purchasing and supports long-term relationships with coffee farmers. The company gives back to communities, supports diversity in hiring, and donates to community causes. Employee volunteerism is supported, and health care is provided for both full- and part-time employees. All employees receive stock options called Bean Stock. Annual reports use 100 percent recycled fibers, and certified renewable energy is used in their production to reduce cost and minimize the environmental footprint.

On the other hand, Starbucks has been accused of unfair competitive tactics in buying out small independent coffee retailers and saturating markets in its aggressive expansion. There is a concern that Starbucks dictates a pop culture of diminishing creativity and diversity and that they promote high-calorie coffee drinks that can contribute to obesity. Although less than 10 percent of the coffee that Starbucks purchases is fair trade certified, Starbucks is the largest purchaser of fair trade coffee in North America. Starbucks promotes recycling, but its cups are made with only 10 percent recycled material. Starbucks was the first to use recycled material in direct contact with food, and a higher content is not allowed by the FDA. The company does use recycled material in cardboard cup sleeves, napkins, and cardboard carriers.[a]

Retailers play a major role in creating time, place, and possession utility and, in some cases, form utility.

Leading retailers such as Walmart, Home Depot, Macy's, Staples, and Best Buy offer consumers a place to browse and compare merchandise to find just what they need. However, such traditional retailing is being challenged by direct marketing channels that provide home shopping through catalogs, television, and the Internet. "Brick-and-mortar" retailers are responding to this change in the retail environment in various ways. Walmart, for example, has established a website for online shopping and joined forces with fast-food giants McDonald's and KFC to attract consumers and offer them the added convenience of eating where they shop.

New store formats and advances in information technology are making the retail environment highly dynamic and competitive. Instant-messaging technology is enabling online retailers to converse in real time with customers so they do not click away to another site. Consider Lands' End: at the Lands' End website, shoppers can click to chat, via keyboard, directly with a customer service representative about sizes, colors, or other product details. The key to success in retailing is to have a strong customer focus with a retail strategy that provides the level of service, product quality, and innovation that consumers desire.

Partnerships among noncompeting retailers and other marketing channel members are providing new opportunities for retailers. For example, airports are leasing space to retailers such as McDonald's, Sunglass Hut, and The Body Shop. Kroger and Nordstrom have developed joint co-branded credit cards that offer rebates to customers at participating stores.

Retailers are also finding global opportunities. For example, both McDonald's and The Gap Inc. are now opening more international stores than domestic ones, a trend that is likely to continue for the foreseeable future. Starbucks has opened hundreds of stores in Japan and Southeast Asia. Increasingly, retailers from abroad, such as IKEA, are opening stores in the United States.

Major Types of Retail Stores

Many types of retail stores exist. One way to classify them is by the breadth of products they offer. Two general categories include general-merchandise retailers and specialty retailers.

General-Merchandise Retailers

A retail establishment that offers a variety of product lines that are stocked in considerable depth is referred to as a **general-merchandise retailer**. The types of product offerings, mixes of customer services, and operating styles of retailers in this category vary considerably. The primary types of general-merchandise retailers are department stores, discount stores, convenience stores, supermarkets, superstores, hypermarkets, warehouse clubs, and warehouse showrooms (see Table 16.1).

DEPARTMENT STORES

Department stores are large retail organizations characterized by wide product mixes and staffs of at least 25 people. To facilitate marketing efforts and internal management in these stores, related product lines are organized into separate departments, such as cosmetics, housewares, apparel, home furnishings, and appliances, to facilitate marketing and internal management. Often, each department functions as a self-contained business, and buyers for individual departments are fairly autonomous.

Department stores are distinctly service-oriented. Their total product may include credit, delivery, personal assistance, merchandise returns, and a pleasant atmosphere. Although some so-called department stores are actually large, departmentalized specialty stores, most department stores are shopping stores. Consumers can compare price, quality, and service at one store with those at competing stores. Along with large discount stores, department stores are often considered retailing leaders in a community and are found in most places with populations of more than 50,000.

Typical department stores, such as Macy's, Sears, JCPenney, Dillard's, and Neiman Marcus, obtain a large proportion of sales from apparel, accessories, and cosmetics. Other products these stores carry include gift items, luggage, electronics, home accessories, and sports equipment. Some department stores offer such services as automobile insurance, hair care, income tax preparation, and travel and optical services. In some cases, space for these specialized services is leased out, with proprietors managing their own operations and paying rent to the store.

DISCOUNT STORES

In recent years, department stores have been losing sales to discount stores, especially Walmart and Target. **Discount stores** are self-service general-merchandise

general-merchandise retailer A retail establishment that offers a variety of product lines that are stocked in considerable depth

department stores Large retail organizations characterized by a wide product mix and organized into separate departments to facilitate marketing efforts and internal management

discount stores Self-service, general-merchandise stores that offer brand name and private brand products at low prices

TABLE 16.1 General-Merchandise Retailers

Type of Retailer	Description	Examples
Department store	Large organization offering a wide product mix and organized into separate departments	Macy's, Sears, JCPenney
Discount store	Self-service, general-merchandise store offering brand name and private brand products at low prices	Walmart, Target, Kmart
Convenience store	Small self-service store offering narrow product assortment in convenient locations	7-Eleven
Supermarket	Self-service store offering complete line of food products and some nonfood products	Kroger, Albertson's, Winn-Dixie
Superstore	Giant outlet offering all food and nonfood products found in supermarkets, as well as most routinely purchased products	Walmart Supercenters
Hypermarket	Combination supermarket and discount store; larger than a superstore	Carrefour
Warehouse club	Large-scale, members-only establishments combining cash-and-carry wholesaling with discount retailing	Sam's Club, Costco
Warehouse showroom	Facility in a large, low-cost building with large on-premises inventories and minimal service	IKEA

Department Stores
Department stores like Nordstrom offer a wide variety of product lines.

outlets that regularly offer brand name and private brand products at low prices. Discounters accept lower margins than conventional retailers in exchange for high sales volume. To keep inventory turnover high, they carry a wide but carefully selected assortment of products, from appliances to housewares to clothing. Major discount establishments also offer food products, toys, automotive services, garden supplies, and sports equipment.

Walmart and Target are the two largest discount stores. Walmart has grown to 7,270 stores worldwide and brings in nearly $450 billion in sales annually.[5] Some discounters, such as Meijer Inc., are regional organizations. Most of them operate in large (50,000 to 80,000 square feet), no-frills facilities. Discount stores usually offer everyday low prices rather than relying on sales events.

Discount retailing developed on a large scale in the early 1950s, when postwar production began catching up with consumer demand for appliances, home furnishings, and other hard goods. Discount stores were often cash-only operations in warehouse districts, offering goods at savings of 20 to 30 percent over conventional retailers. Facing increased competition from department stores and other discount stores, some discounters have improved store services, atmosphere, and location, raising prices and sometimes blurring the distinction between discount store and department store. Even Walmart is investing in its stores in hopes of retaining the more affluent customers who began shopping at Walmart during the recent recession. The goal is to remodel all of the stores to make them more inviting and reduce the clutter by reducing the number of items sold. Even though the company has seen increases in sales, it laid off 800 staff members at the Bentonville, Arkansas worldwide headquarters to keep costs low for the company and the consumer, which is the company's main strategy.[6]

CONVENIENCE STORES

convenience store A small self-service store that is open long hours and carries a narrow assortment of products, usually convenience items

A **convenience store** is a small self-service store that is open long hours and carries a narrow assortment of products, usually convenience items such as soft drinks and other beverages, snacks, newspapers, tobacco, and gasoline, as well as services such as automatic teller machines. The primary product offered by the "corner store" is convenience.

According to the National Association of Convenience Stores, there are 144,541 convenience stores in the United States with 1.5 million employees. They are typically less than 5,000 square feet; open 24 hours a day, 7 days a week; and stock about 500 items. In addition to many national chains, there are many family-owned independent convenience stores in operation. The convenience store concept was developed in 1927 when Southland Ice in Dallas began stocking milk, eggs, and other products for customers who wanted to replenish their "ice boxes."[7]

SUPERMARKETS

Supermarkets are large self-service stores that carry a complete line of food products, as well as some nonfood products such as cosmetics and nonprescription drugs. Supermarkets are arranged in departments for maximum efficiency in stocking and handling products but have central checkout facilities. They offer lower prices than smaller neighborhood grocery stores, usually provide free parking, and also may cash checks.

Today, consumers make more than three-quarters of all grocery purchases in supermarkets. Even so, supermarkets' total share of the food market is declining because consumers now have widely varying food preferences and buying habits, and in many communities, shoppers can choose from several convenience stores, discount stores, and specialty food stores, as well as a wide variety of restaurants. Walmart, for example, expects to generate in its "supermarket-type" stores more revenue than the top three U.S. supermarket chains—Kroger, Albertson's, and Safeway—combined.

SUPERSTORES

Superstores, which originated in Europe, are giant retail outlets that carry not only food and nonfood products that are ordinarily found in supermarkets but also routinely purchased consumer products. Besides a complete food line, superstores sell housewares, hardware, small appliances, clothing, personal-care products, garden products, and tires—about four times as many items as supermarkets. Services available at superstores include dry cleaning, automotive repair, check cashing, bill paying, and snack bars.

Superstores combine features of discount stores and supermarkets. Examples include Walmart Supercenters, some Kroger stores, and Super Kmart Centers. Target also continues to launch superstores. While Target is known more for its affordable fashions and home accessories than its grocery offerings, Super Target plans to increase grocery offerings in its stores.[8]

To cut handling and inventory costs, superstores use sophisticated operating techniques and often have tall shelving that displays entire assortments of products. Superstores can have an area of as much as 200,000 square feet (compared with 20,000 square feet in traditional supermarkets). Sales volume is two to three times that of supermarkets, partly because locations near good transportation networks help generate the in-store traffic needed for profitability.

HYPERMARKETS

Hypermarkets combine supermarket and discount store shopping in one location. Larger than superstores, they range from 225,000 to 325,000 square feet and offer 45,000 to 60,000 different types of low-priced products. They commonly allocate 40 to 50 percent of their space to grocery products and the remainder to general merchandise, including athletic shoes, designer jeans, and other apparel; refrigerators, televisions, and other appliances; housewares; cameras; toys; jewelry; hardware; and automotive supplies. Many lease space to noncompeting businesses such as banks, optical shops, and fast-food restaurants. All hypermarkets focus on low prices and vast selections.

Although Kmart, Walmart, and Carrefour (a French retailer) have operated hypermarkets in the United States, most of these stores were unsuccessful and closed. Such stores may be too big for time-constrained U.S. shoppers. However, hypermarkets are more successful in Europe, South America, and Mexico, and more recently in the Middle East and India.

supermarkets Large, self-service stores that carry a complete line of food products, along with some nonfood products

superstores Giant retail outlets that carry food and nonfood products found in supermarkets, as well as most routinely purchased consumer products

hypermarkets Stores that combine supermarket and discount store shopping in one location

WAREHOUSE CLUBS

Warehouse clubs, a rapidly growing form of mass merchandising, are large-scale, members-only selling operations that combine cash-and-carry wholesaling with discount retailing. Sometimes called *buying clubs,* warehouse clubs offer the same types of products as discount stores but in a limited range of sizes and styles. Whereas most discount stores carry around 40,000 items, a warehouse club handles only 3,500 to 5,000 products, usually acknowledged brand leaders. Sam's Club stores, for example, stock about 4,000 items, with 1,400 available most of the time and the rest being one-time buys. Costco leads the warehouse club industry with sales of $71.4 billion. Sam's Club is second with nearly $47 billion in store sales. A third company, BJ's Wholesale Club, which operates in the Northeast and Florida, has a much smaller market.[9] All these establishments offer a broad product mix, including food, beverages, books, appliances, housewares, automotive parts, hardware, and furniture.

To keep prices lower than those of supermarkets and discount stores, warehouse clubs provide few services. They generally do not advertise, except through direct mail. Their facilities, often located in industrial areas, have concrete floors and aisles wide enough for forklifts. Merchandise is stacked on pallets or displayed on pipe racks. Customers must transport purchases themselves. Warehouse clubs appeal to many price-conscious consumers and small retailers unable to obtain wholesaling services from large distributors. The average warehouse club shopper has more education, a higher income, and a larger household than the average supermarket shopper.

WAREHOUSE SHOWROOMS

Warehouse showrooms are retail facilities with five basic characteristics: large, low-cost buildings; warehouse materials-handling technology; vertical merchandise displays; large on-premises inventories; and minimal services. IKEA, a Swedish company, sells furniture, household goods, and kitchen accessories in warehouse showrooms and through catalogs around the world, including China and Russia. These high-volume, low-overhead operations stress fewer personnel and services. Lower costs are possible

warehouse clubs Large-scale, members-only establishments that combine features of cash-and-carry wholesaling with discount retailing

warehouse showrooms Retail facilities in large, low-cost buildings with large on-premises inventories and minimal services

Warehouse Club
Costco is a warehouse club that markets many product lines. Most of Costco's product lines have limited depth.

Will You Pay More for a Luxury Item at a Brand Store Than at a Discount Store?

$$$

YES 59%

NO 41%

Source: Accenture Consumer Luxury survey of 1,002 adults, February 18, 2010.

because some marketing functions have been shifted to consumers, who must transport, finance, and perhaps store larger quantities of products. Most consumers carry away purchases in the manufacturer's carton, although stores will deliver for a fee.

Specialty Retailers

In contrast to general-merchandise retailers with their broad product mixes, specialty retailers emphasize narrow and deep assortments. Despite their name, specialty retailers do not sell specialty items (except when specialty goods complement the overall product mix). Instead, they offer substantial assortments in a few product lines. We examine three types of specialty retailers: traditional specialty retailers, category killers, and off-price retailers.

TRADITIONAL SPECIALTY RETAILERS

Traditional specialty retailers are stores that carry a narrow product mix with deep product lines. Sometimes called *limited-line retailers*, they may be referred to as *single-line retailers* if they carry unusual depth in one main product category. Specialty retailers commonly sell such shopping products as apparel, jewelry, sporting goods, fabrics, computers, and pet supplies. The Limited, Radio Shack, Hickory Farms, The Gap, and Foot Locker are examples of retailers offering limited product lines but great depth within those lines.

Although the number of chain specialty stores is increasing, many specialty stores are independently owned. Florists, bakery shops, coffee shops, pet stores, and bookstores are among the small, independent specialty retailers that appeal to local target markets, although these stores can be owned and managed by large corporations. Even if this kind of retailer adds a few supporting product lines, the store may still be classified as a specialty store.

Because they are usually small, specialty stores may have high costs in proportion to sales, and satisfying customers may require carrying some products with low turnover rates. However, these stores sometimes obtain lower prices from suppliers by purchasing limited lines of merchandise in large quantities. Successful specialty stores understand their customer types and know what products to carry, thus reducing the risk of unsold merchandise. Specialty stores usually offer better selections and more sales expertise than department stores, their main competitors. By capitalizing on fashion, service, personnel, atmosphere, and location, specialty retailers position themselves strategically to attract customers in specific market segments. Specialty stores may even become exclusive dealers in their markets for certain products. Through specialty stores, small-business owners provide unique services to match consumers' varied desires. For consumers dissatisfied with the impersonal nature of large retailers, the close, personal contact offered by a small specialty store can be a welcome change.

traditional specialty retailers Stores that carry a narrow product mix with deep product lines

Entrepreneurial Marketing
Tara's Organic Ice Cream: A Growing Niche Business

When Santa Fe artist Tara Esperanza's friends gave her a home ice cream maker, they had no idea how it would inspire her creativity and entrepreneurial spirit. Tara experimented with unique flavors such as lemongrass, lavender, and garam masala, which friends willingly tasted, and told her, "You should sell this!" Tara did and became New Mexico's Emerging Entrepreneur of the Year, selling organic ice cream in Santa Fe. Good distribution is necessary for success, so she also started selling her product to retailers and online.

Tara emphasizes environmentally friendly business practices. In addition to using all organic ingredients, her new shop in Berkeley, California (where she moved to be closer to her source of organic dairy products), serves ice cream in compostable containers with spoons made from potato starch.[b]

CATEGORY KILLERS

Over the last 20 years, a new breed of specialty retailer, the category killer, has evolved. A **category killer** is a very large specialty store that concentrates on a major product category and competes on the basis of low prices and enormous product availability. These stores are referred to as category killers because they expand rapidly and gain sizable market shares, taking business away from smaller, high-cost retail outlets. Examples of category killers include Home Depot and Lowe's (home improvement chains); Staples, Office Depot, and OfficeMax (office-supply chains); Borders and Barnes & Noble (booksellers); Petco and PetSmart (pet-supply chains); and Best Buy (consumer electronics).

OFF-PRICE RETAILERS

Off-price retailers are stores that buy manufacturers' seconds, overruns, returns, and off-season production runs at below-wholesale prices for resale to consumers at deep discounts. Unlike true discount stores, which pay regular wholesale prices for goods and usually carry second-line brand names, off-price retailers offer limited lines of national-brand and designer merchandise, usually clothing, shoes, or housewares. The number of off-price retailers such as T.J. Maxx, Marshalls, Stein Mart, and Burlington Coat Factory has grown since the mid-1980s.

Off-price stores charge 20 to 50 percent less than department stores for comparable merchandise but offer few customer services. They often feature community dressing rooms and central checkout counters. Some of these stores do not take returns or allow exchanges. Off-price stores may or may not sell goods with the original labels intact. They turn over their inventory 9 to 12 times a year, three times as often as traditional specialty stores. They compete with department stores for the same customers: price-conscious customers who are knowledgeable about brand names.

To ensure a regular flow of merchandise into their stores, off-price retailers establish long-term relationships with suppliers that can provide large quantities of goods at reduced prices. Manufacturers may approach retailers with samples, discontinued products, or items that have not sold well. Also, retailers may seek out manufacturers,

category killer A very large specialty store that concentrates on a major product category and competes on the basis of low prices and product availability

off-price retailers Stores that buy manufacturers' seconds, overruns, returns, and off-season merchandise for resale to consumers at deep discounts

Traditional Specialty Store and an Off-Price Specialty Store
Victoria's Secret is a traditional specialty store. T.J. Maxx is an example of an off-price specialty retailer.

offering to pay cash for goods produced during the manufacturers' off-season. Although manufacturers benefit from such arrangements, they also risk alienating their specialty and department store customers. Department stores tolerate off-price stores as long as they do not advertise brand names, limit merchandise to lower-quality items, and are located away from the department stores. When off-price retailers obtain large stocks of in-season, top-quality merchandise, tension builds between department stores and manufacturers.

Strategic Issues in Retailing

Whereas most business purchases are based on economic planning and necessity, consumer purchases may result from social and psychological influences. Because consumers shop for various reasons—to search for specific items, escape boredom, or learn about something new—retailers must do more than simply fill space with merchandise. They must make desired products available, create stimulating shopping environments, and develop marketing strategies that increase store patronage. In this section, we discuss how store location, retail positioning, store image, and category management are used strategically by retailers.

Location of Retail Stores

"Location, location, location" is a common saying among retailers (as well as realtors) because of its critical importance to success. At the same time, the retail location is the least flexible of the strategic retailing issues but is one of the most important

Marketing in Transition
Want to Go to the Mall? Not All Retailers Do

Formerly major hubs of retail activity, regional and superregional shopping centers are now having a tough time. In the aftermath of the recession, high unemployment and tight credit conditions have prompted consumers to slow down spending. When they do buy, many seek bargains at discount stores or superstores, as well as online, but not at the mall. Brand-conscious consumers are traveling to outlet centers in search of great buys.

Changes in the retail industry are also affecting large shopping centers. Consolidation among department stores has resulted in fewer anchor stores and, in some cases, empty buildings where now-defunct stores such as Filene's once served their customers. Specialty store chains, looking to cut expenses, are closing under-performing mall units, and struggling independents are moving to smaller centers or downtown as they try to stay alive.

These trends leave the traditional mall in a tight spot. In the boom years, developers vied to build the biggest, best shopping center. Today, the United States has about 1,400 enclosed shopping centers competing with each other and with other retail locations. Some of the oldest were bypassed by newer highway construction and now stand mostly empty as stores and shoppers flock to more convenient locations.

To bring back the crowds, malls are courting financially strong local stores and offering events such as film festivals, concerts, and classes. Mall of America has a regular schedule of activities, including weddings on its indoor roller coaster, to attract visitors. "Consumers are on a spending diet, but diets don't last forever," says the vice president of marketing. "We certainly don't want them to go adjust their spending, but we are happy to see them buy anything they can afford."[c]

because location dictates the limited geographic trading area from which a store draws its customers. Retailers consider various factors when evaluating potential locations, including location of the firm's target market within the trading area, kinds of products being sold, availability of public transportation, customer characteristics, and competitors' locations.

In choosing a location, a retailer evaluates the relative ease of movement to and from the site, including factors such as pedestrian and vehicular traffic, parking, and transportation. Retailers also evaluate the characteristics of the site itself: types of stores in the area; size, shape, and visibility of the lot or building under consideration; and rental, leasing, or ownership terms. Retailers look for compatibility with nearby retailers because stores that complement one another draw more customers for everyone.

Many retailers choose to locate in downtown central business districts, whereas others prefer sites within various types of shopping centers. Some retailers, including Toys"R"Us, Walmart, Home Depot, and many fast-food restaurants, opt for freestanding structures that are not connected to other buildings, but many chain stores are found in planned shopping centers and malls. JCPenney is transitioning away from malls to freestanding structures, allowing the retailer to be closer to its customers and reduce rent.[10] Sometimes, retailers choose to locate in less orthodox settings. McDonald's, for example, has opened several stores inside hospitals, whereas Subway has franchise locations inside churches, laundromats, and hospitals.[11]

There are several types of shopping centers including neighborhood, community, regional, superregional, lifestyle, power, and outlet centers (Table 16.2).

Neighborhood shopping centers usually consist of several small convenience and specialty stores, such as small grocery stores, gas stations, and fast-food restaurants. Many of these retailers consider their target markets to be consumers who live within two to three miles of their stores, or 10 minutes' driving time. Because most purchases are based on convenience or personal contact, there is usually little coordination of selling efforts within a neighborhood shopping center. Generally, product mixes consist of essential products, and depth of the product lines is limited.

neighborhood shopping centers Shopping centers usually consisting of several small convenience and specialty stores

TABLE 16.2 Types and Characteristics of Shopping Centers

Type	Concept	Open or Enclosed?	Acreage	Number of Anchors	Radius of Primary Trade Area (Miles)
Neighborhood center	Convenience	Open	3–15	1 or more	3
Community center	General merchandise, convenience	Open	10–40	2 or more	3–6
Regional center	General merchandise, fashion	Enclosed	40–100	2 or more	5–15
Superregional center	More variety than regional center	Enclosed	60–120	3 or more	5–25
Lifestyle center	Upscale specialty, dining, and entertainment, usually national chains	Open	10–40	0–2	8–12
Power center	Category-dominant anchors, a few smaller businesses	Open	25–80	3 or more	5–10
Outlet center	Manufacturers' outlet stores	Open	10–50	N/A	25–75

Source: ICSC Shopping Center Definitions, www.icsc.org/srch/lib/2009_S-C_classification_May09.pdf (accessed: April 9, 2010).

Community shopping centers include one or two department stores and some specialty stores, as well as convenience stores. They draw consumers looking for shopping and specialty products not available in neighborhood shopping centers. Because these centers serve larger geographic areas, consumers must drive longer distances to community shopping centers than to neighborhood centers. Community shopping centers are planned and coordinated to attract shoppers. Special events, such as art exhibits, automobile shows, and sidewalk sales, stimulate traffic. Managers of community shopping centers look for tenants that complement the centers' total assortment of products. Such centers have wide product mixes and deep product lines.

Regional shopping centers usually have the largest department stores, widest product mixes, and deepest product lines of all shopping centers. Many shopping malls are regional shopping centers, although some are community shopping centers. With 150,000 or more consumers in their target market, regional shopping centers must have well-coordinated management and marketing activities. Target markets may include consumers traveling from a distance to find products and prices not available in their hometowns. Because of the expense of leasing space in regional shopping centers, tenants are more likely to be national chains than small, independent stores. Large centers usually advertise, have special events, furnish transportation to some consumer groups, maintain their own security forces, and carefully select the mix of stores. The largest of these centers, sometimes called **superregional shopping centers**, have the widest and deepest product mixes and attract customers from many miles away. Superregional centers often have special attractions beyond stores, such as skating rinks, amusement centers, or upscale restaurants. Mall of America, in the Minneapolis area, is the largest shopping mall in the United States with 520 stores, including Nordstrom and Bloomingdale's, and 50 restaurants. The shopping center also includes a walk-through aquarium, museum, theme parks, a 14-screen movie theater, hotels, and many special events.[12]

With traditional mall sales declining, some shopping center developers are looking to new formats that differ significantly from traditional shopping centers. A **lifestyle shopping center** is typically an open-air shopping center that features upscale specialty, dining, and entertainment stores, usually owned by national chains. They are often located near affluent neighborhoods and may have fountains, benches, and other amenities that encourage "casual browsing." Indeed, architectural design is an important aspect of these "minicities," which may include urban streets or parks and is intended to encourage consumer loyalty by creating a sense of place. Some lifestyle centers are designed to resemble traditional "Main Street" shopping centers or may have a central theme evidenced by architecture.[13] An example of a lifestyle center is the Mount Pleasant Towne Centre in South Carolina. This outdoor shopping center has large chain stores ranging from Banana Republic and JoS. A. Bank Clothiers to Edward Jones Investments and GameStop, as well as a few local stores like Sweet Julep's Candy & Gifts. Visitors can also find a Mt. Pleasant Police Substation and several restaurants in the shopping center.[14]

Some shopping center developers are bypassing the traditional department store anchor and combining off-price stores and small stores with category killers in **power shopping center** formats. These centers may be anchored by stores such as The Gap, Toys"R"Us, PetSmart, and Home Depot. The number of power shopping centers is growing, resulting in a variety of formats vying for the same retail dollar.

Factory outlet malls feature discount and factory outlet stores carrying traditional manufacturer brands, such as Quicksilver, Liz Claiborne, Reebok, and Le Creuset. Some outlet centers feature upscale products. Manufacturers own these stores and make a special effort to avoid conflict with traditional retailers of their products. Manufacturers claim their stores are in noncompetitive locations; indeed, most factory outlet centers are located outside metropolitan areas. Not all factory outlets stock closeouts and irregulars, but most avoid comparison with discount houses. Factory outlet centers attract value-conscious customers seeking quality and major brand names. They operate in much the same way as regional shopping centers, but usually draw customers, some of whom may be tourists, from a larger shopping radius. Promotional activity is at the heart of these shopping centers. Craft and antique shows, contests, and special events attract a great deal of traffic.

community shopping centers Shopping centers with one or two department stores, some specialty stores, and convenience stores

regional shopping center A type of shopping center with the largest department stores, widest product mixes, and deepest product lines of all shopping centers

superregional shopping center A type of shopping center with the widest and deepest product mixes that attracts customers from many miles away

lifestyle shopping center A type of shopping center that is typically open air and features upscale specialty, dining, and entertainment stores

power shopping center A type of shopping center that combines off-price stores with category killers

Retail Positioning

The large variety of shopping centers and the expansion of product offerings by traditional stores have intensified retailing competition. Retail positioning is therefore an important consideration. **Retail positioning** involves identifying an unserved or underserved market segment and serving it through a strategy that distinguishes the retailer from others in the minds of those customers. For example, Payless ShoeSource, a specialty store chain, has built a reputation for providing a wide variety of low-price shoes in a warehouse-like environment. The retailer is attempting to reposition itself as a purveyor of stylish and trendy shoes with a wider price range (going as high as $60) by expanding its merchandise mix and sprucing up its 4,500 stores. Targeting more women who are as interested in fashion as in low prices, Payless has even opened a New York design office to focus on original styles and has introduced a line of shoes designed by Laura Poretzky.[15] In recent years, a number of discount and specialty store chains have positioned themselves to appeal to time- and cash-strapped consumers with convenient locations and layouts as well as low prices. This strategy has helped them gain market share at the expense of large department stores.

Store Image

To attract customers, a retail store must project an image—a functional and psychological picture in the consumer's mind—that appeals to its target market. Store environment, merchandise quality, and service quality are key determinants of store image.

Atmospherics, the physical elements in a store's design that appeal to consumers' emotions and encourage buying, help to create an image and position a retailer. Barnes & Noble, for example, uses murals of authors and framed pictures of classic book covers to convey a literary image. Studies show that retailers can use different elements—music, color, and complexity of layout and merchandise presentation—to influence customer arousal based on their shopping motivation. Supermarkets, for example, should use cooler colors and simple layout and presentations because their customers tend to be task-motivated, whereas specialty retailers may be able to use more complex layouts and brighter colors to stimulate their more recreationally motivated customers.[16]

retail positioning Identifying an unserved or underserved market segment and serving it through a strategy that distinguishes the retailer from others in the minds of consumers in that segment

atmospherics The physical elements in a store's design that appeal to consumers' emotions and encourage buying

Atmospherics
Atmospherics in a restaurant, such as The Cheesecake Factory, can have very positive effects on the customer experience.

© Craig Ruttle/MCT/Newscom

Exterior atmospheric elements include the appearance of the storefront, display windows, store entrances, and degree of traffic congestion. Exterior atmospherics are particularly important to new customers, who tend to judge an unfamiliar store by its outside appearance and may not enter if they feel intimidated by the building or inconvenienced by the parking lot.

Interior atmospheric elements include aesthetic considerations such as lighting, wall and floor coverings, dressing facilities, and store fixtures. Interior sensory elements contribute significantly to atmosphere. Caesar's Palace, the hotel and casino in Las Vegas, provides a truly memorable experience for its customers by incorporating items to reflect the hotel theme, ancient Rome. The hotel and casino has marble floors, ancient Roman statues and fountain recreations including the Statue of David and Trevi Fountain, as well as sky-painted ceilings in the Forum Shops and white walls with plenty of columns. By providing customers with a truly authentic experience, the company hopes visitors will spend more at the casino, stores, restaurants, and bars.[17] Color can attract shoppers to a retail display. Many fast-food restaurants use bright colors, such as red and yellow, because these have been shown to make customers feel hungrier and eat faster, which increases turnover. Sound is another important sensory component of atmosphere and may range from silence to subdued background music. Pottery Barn, for example, plays 1950s cocktail bar music, whereas JCPenney varies the music in its stores—even within departments—based on local demographics.[18] Many retailers employ scent, especially food aromas, to attract customers. Research suggests that consumer evaluations of a product are affected by scent, but only when the scent employed is congruent with the product.[19]

category management
A retail strategy of managing groups of similar, often substitutable products produced by different manufacturers

Category Management

Category management is a retail strategy of managing groups of similar, often substitutable products produced by different manufacturers. For instance, supermarkets such as Safeway use category management to determine space for products such as

Sustainable Marketing
Retailers Tap Green Power

Renewable energy—from the sun, the wind, and the ground—is giving a growing number of retailers the power to go green and serve their customers in earth-friendly ways. In the long run, the stores reduce their dependence on traditional energy sources and cut their power costs. They also show customers how much they care about the environment. The result is a greener image as well as a greener planet.

Hannaford Supermarkets plans for green power when it opens new stores. Its newest store in Augusta, Maine, is topped by the largest array of solar panels in the state. The building employs geothermal energy to help heat and cool the store interior and makes the most of natural sunlight for lighting in the aisles and in backroom locations.

Kohl's Department Stores buys energy from renewable sources to power all of its stores. Dozens of its stores meet up to half of their electrical needs through solar power generated on-site. Its distribution center in San Bernadino, California, has more than 6,200 solar panels and produces one megawatt of power. "We recognize the importance of encouraging environmentally smart energy practices," says a Kohl's executive, "and we aim to set a positive example in how we operate our buildings and run our business."

Multinational retailers such as Walmart and IKEA are already taking steps to switch from conventional power sources to renewable sources for all their stores, warehouses, and offices. Wherever you shop, watch for signs of green power coming your way.[d]

cosmetics, cereals, and soups. An assortment of merchandise is both customer and strategically driven to improve performance. Category management developed in the food industry because supermarkets were concerned about highly competitive behavior among manufacturers.

Category management is a move toward a collaborative supply-chain initiative to enhance customer value. Successful category management requires the acquisition, analysis, and sharing of sales and consumer information between the retailer and manufacturer. Walmart, for example, has developed strong supplier relationships with manufacturers such as Procter & Gamble. The development of information about demand, consumer behavior, and optimal allocations of products should be available from one source. Firms such as SAS provide software to manage data associated with each step of the category management decision cycle. The key is cooperative interaction between the manufacturers of category products and the retailer to create maximum success for all parties in the supply chain.

Direct Marketing and Direct Selling

Although retailers are the most visible members of the supply chain, many products are sold outside the confines of a retail store. Direct selling and direct marketing account for an increasing percentage of product sales. Products also may be sold in automatic vending machines, but these account for less than 2 percent of all retail sales.

Direct Marketing

Direct marketing is the use of the telephone, Internet, and nonpersonal media to communicate product and organizational information to customers, who can then purchase products via mail, telephone, or the Internet. Direct marketing is one type of nonstore retailing. Sales through direct marketing activities amount to $1.8 trillion per year.[20] In the auto industry alone, $77.8 billion in sales stemmed from the $8 billion spent on direct marketing campaigns in a recent year.[21] **Nonstore retailing** is the selling of products outside the confines of a retail facility. This form of retailing accounts for an increasing percentage of total sales. Direct marketing can occur through catalog marketing, direct-response marketing, telemarketing, television home shopping, and online retailing.

CATALOG MARKETING

In **catalog marketing**, an organization provides a catalog from which customers make selections and place orders by mail, telephone, or the Internet. Catalog marketing began in 1872, when Montgomery Ward issued its first catalog to rural families. Today there are more than 7,000 catalog marketing companies in the United States, as well as several retail stores, such as Chico's, that engage in catalog marketing. Some organizations offer a broad array of products through a sizeable catalog. Spiegel, for example, offers a variety of products spread over multiple product lines. JCPenney historically has used a similar approach. However, JCPenney recently revamped its catalog strategy at the end of last year, doing away with "The Big Book," a 1,000-page catalog and replacing it with smaller specialty catalogs.[22] Catalog companies such as Lands' End, Pottery Barn, and J. Crew offer considerable depth in just a few major lines of products. Still other catalog companies specialize in only a few products within a single line. Some catalog retailers—for instance, Cabela's and Crate & Barrel—have stores in major metropolitan areas.

The advantages of catalog retailing include efficiency and convenience for customers. The retailer benefits by being able to locate in remote, low-cost areas; save on expensive store fixtures; and reduce both personal selling and store operating expenses. On the other hand, catalog retailing is inflexible, provides limited service, and is most effective for a selected set of products.

direct marketing The use of the telephone, Internet, and nonpersonal media to introduce products to customers, who can then purchase them via mail, telephone, or the Internet

nonstore retailing The selling of products outside the confines of a retail facility

catalog marketing A type of marketing in which an organization provides a catalog from which customers make selections and place orders by mail, telephone, or the Internet

DIRECT-RESPONSE MARKETING

Direct-response marketing occurs when a retailer advertises a product and makes it available through mail or telephone orders. Generally, customers use a credit card, but other forms of payment may be permitted. Examples of direct-response marketing include a television commercial offering exercise machines, cosmetics or household cleaning products available through a toll-free number, and a newspaper or magazine advertisement for a series of children's books available by filling out the form in the ad or calling a toll-free number. One of the most successful direct-response initiatives in the past few years was for the Snuggie. This product was first introduced on late night TV, and then made its way into retail outlets like Bed Bath & Beyond, Walgreens, and eventually into pet stores like PetSmart when the Snuggie for dogs was created. The company sold 5 million Snuggies its first year and expects to sell 20 million this year.[23] Direct-response marketing is also conducted by sending letters, samples, brochures, or booklets to prospects on a mailing list and asking that they order the advertised products by mail or telephone. In general, products must be priced above $20 to justify the advertising and distribution costs associated with direct-response marketing.

TELEMARKETING

A number of organizations use the telephone to strengthen the effectiveness of traditional marketing methods. **Telemarketing** is the performance of marketing-related activities by telephone. Some organizations use a prescreened list of prospective clients. Telemarketing can help to generate sales leads, improve customer service, speed up payments on past-due accounts, raise funds for nonprofit organizations, and gather marketing data.

Currently, the laws and regulations regarding telemarketing, although in a state of flux, are becoming more restrictive. In 2003, Congress implemented a national do-not-call registry for consumers who do not wish to receive telemarketing calls. So far, more than 191 million phone numbers in the United States have been listed on the registry. The national registry is enforced by the Federal Trade Commission and the Federal Communications Commission, and companies are subject to a fine of up to $16,000 for each call made to a consumer listed on the national do-not-call registry. Since the registry went into effect, the two federal agencies have collected $21 million in penalties and $12 million in restitution from violators.[24] Certain exceptions apply to do-not-call lists. A company still can use telemarketing to communicate with existing customers. In addition, charitable, political, and telephone survey organizations are not restricted by the national registry.

TELEVISION HOME SHOPPING

Television home shopping presents products to television viewers, encouraging them to order through toll-free numbers and pay with credit cards. The Home Shopping Network in Florida originated and popularized this format. The most popular products sold through television home shopping are jewelry (40 percent of total sales), clothing, housewares, and electronics. Home shopping channels have grown so rapidly in recent years that more than 60 percent of U.S. households have access to home shopping programs. Home Shopping Network and QVC are two of the largest home shopping networks. Approximately 60 percent of home shopping sales revenues come from repeat purchasers.

The television home shopping format offers several benefits. Products can be demonstrated easily, and an adequate amount of time can be spent showing the product so viewers are well informed. The length of time a product is shown depends not only on the time required for doing demonstrations but also on whether the product is selling. Once the calls peak and begin to decline, a new product is shown. Other benefits are that customers can shop at their convenience and from the comfort of their homes.

direct-response marketing A type of marketing in which a retailer advertises a product and makes it available through mail or telephone orders

telemarketing The performance of marketing-related activities by telephone

television home shopping A form of selling in which products are presented to television viewers, who can buy them by calling a toll-free number and paying with a credit card

ONLINE RETAILING

Online retailing makes products available to buyers through computer connections. The phenomenal growth of Internet use and online information services such as AOL has created new retailing opportunities. Many retailers have set up websites to disseminate information about their companies and products. Although many retailers with websites use them primarily to promote products, a number of companies, including Barnes & Noble, REI, Lands' End, and OfficeMax, sell goods online. However, the number of companies selling online and in stores is growing dramatically as consumers demand multiple channels to obtain the goods and services they desire.

Consumers can purchase hard-to-find items, such as Pez candy dispensers and Elvis memorabilia, on eBay. They can buy upscale items for their dogs at SitStay.com, a Web retailer specializing in high-end dog supplies that carries a carefully screened selection of 1,500 products. Banks and brokerage firms have established websites to give customers direct access to manage their accounts and enable them to trade online. Forrester Research projects that online retail sales in the United States will climb to nearly $250 billion by 2014, up from $155 billion in 2009.[25] With advances in computer technology continuing and consumers ever more pressed for time, online retailing will continue to escalate.

Although online retailing represents a major retailing venue, security remains an issue. In a recent survey conducted by the Business Software Alliance, about 75 percent of Internet users expressed concerns about shopping online. The major issues are identity theft and credit card theft.

Direct Selling

Direct selling is the marketing of products to ultimate consumers through face-to-face sales presentations at home or in the workplace. Traditionally called *door-to-door selling*, direct selling in the United States began with peddlers more than a century ago and has since grown into a sizable industry of several hundred firms. Although direct sellers historically used a cold-canvass, door-to-door approach for finding prospects, many

online retailing Retailing that makes products available to buyers through computer connections

direct selling Marketing products to ultimate consumers through face-to-face sales presentations at home or in the workplace

Online Retailing
Amazon is an online retailer of numerous products.

companies today, such as Kirby, Amway, Mary Kay, and Avon, use other approaches. They initially identify customers through the mail, telephone, Internet, or shopping-mall intercepts and then set up appointments.

Although the majority of direct selling takes place on an individual, or person-to-person, basis, it sometimes also includes the use of a group, or "party," plan. With a party plan, a consumer acts as a host and invites friends and associates to view merchandise in a group setting, where a salesperson demonstrates products. The congenial party atmosphere helps to overcome customers' reluctance and encourages them to buy. Tupperware and Mary Kay were the pioneers of this selling technique, paving the way for companies such as Pampered Chef to grow from a basement business into a corporation that brings in more than $500 million in revenues annually.[26]

Direct selling has both benefits and limitations. It gives the marketer an opportunity to demonstrate the product in an environment—usually customers' homes—where it most likely would be used. The door-to-door seller can give the customer personal attention, and the product can be presented to the customer at a convenient time and location. Personal attention to the customer is the foundation on which some direct sellers, such as Mary Kay, have built their businesses. Because commissions for salespeople are so high, ranging from 30 to 50 percent of the sales price, and great effort is required to isolate promising prospects, overall costs of direct selling make it the most expensive form of retailing. Furthermore, some customers view direct selling negatively, owing to unscrupulous and fraudulent practices used by some direct sellers in the past. Some communities even have local ordinances that control or, in some cases, prohibit direct selling. Despite these negative views held by some individuals, direct selling is still alive and well, bringing in revenues of $30 billion a year.[27]

Automatic Vending

Automatic vending is the use of machines to dispense products. It accounts for less than 2 percent of all retail sales. Video game machines provide an entertainment service, and most banks offer automatic teller machines (ATMs), which dispense cash and perform other services.

Automatic vending is one of the most impersonal forms of retailing. Small, standardized, routinely purchased products (e.g., chewing gum, candy, newspapers, soft drinks, coffee) can be sold in machines because consumers usually buy them at the nearest available location. Redbox vending machines have started a new trend in vending: DVD rentals. These machines allow customers to rent DVDs at a time that is convenient for them, without a membership and from their choice of over 15,400 locations.[28] Machines in areas of heavy foot traffic provide efficient and continuous service to consumers. Such high-volume areas may have more diverse product availability—for example, hot and cold sandwiches, and even upscale merchandise. ZoomSystems, for example, operates vending machines that market iPod cell phones in airports and Macy's department stores. Some new airport vending machines dispense digital cameras and designer cosmetics—and they accept credit cards.[29]

Because vending machines need only a small amount of space and no sales personnel, this retailing method has some advantages over stores. The advantages are partly offset, however, by the high costs of equipment and frequent servicing and repairs.

automatic vending The use of machines to dispense products

franchising An arrangement in which a supplier (franchiser) grants a dealer (franchisee) the right to sell products in exchange for some type of consideration

Franchising

Franchising is an arrangement in which a supplier, or franchiser, grants a dealer, or franchisee, the right to sell products in exchange for some type of consideration. The franchiser may receive some percentage of total sales in exchange for furnishing equipment, buildings, management know-how, and marketing assistance to the franchisee. The franchisee supplies labor and capital, operates the franchised business, and agrees to abide by the provisions of the franchise agreement. Table 16.3 lists the leading U.S. franchises, types of products, and startup costs.

Because of changes in the international marketplace, shifting employment options in the United States, the expanding U.S. service economy, and corporate interest in

TABLE 16.3 Top U.S. Franchisers and Their Startup Costs

Rank	Franchise and Description	Number of Franchise Outlets Worldwide	Startup Costs
1	**Subway** Submarine sandwiches and salads	33,188	$84,300–$258,300
2	**McDonald's** Hamburgers, chicken, salads	26,209	$1,057,200–$1,885,000
3	**7-Eleven** Convenience store	37,039	$30,800–$604,500
4	**Hampton Hotels** Mid-priced hotels	1,753	$3,716,000–$13,148,800
5	**Supercuts** Hair salon	1,035	$112,550–$243,200
6	**H&R Block** Tax preparation and electronic filing	4,572	$34,438–$110,033
7	**Dunkin' Donuts** Coffee, doughnuts, baked goods	9,235	$358,200–$1,980,300
8	**Jani-King** Commercial cleaning	12,260	$13,150–$93,150
9	**Servpro** Insurance/disaster restoration and cleaning	1,526	$127,300–$174,700
10	**Ampm** Convenience store and gas station	3,177	$1,786,929–$7,596,688
11	**Jan-Pro Franchising Intl, Inc.** Commercial cleaning	11,248	$3,145–$50,405
12	**Kumon Math & Reading Centers** Supplemental education	25,169	$36,538–$145,250
13	**Stratus Building Solutions** Commercial cleaning	3,519	$3,450–$57,750
14	**Miracle-Ear Inc.** Hearing instruments	1,301	$122,500–$570,000
15	**Pizza Hut** Pizza, pasta, wings	11,213	$302,000–$2,149,000
16	**Hardee's** Burgers, chicken, biscuits	1,428	$1,182,000–$1,583,500
17	**Denny's** Full-service family restaurant	1,374	$1,125,609–$2,396,419
18	**Jazzercise Inc.** Dance fitness classes	8,009	$2,980–$75,500
19	**Matco Tools** Mechanics' tools and service equipment	1,439	$79,926–$188,556
20	**The UPS Store / Mail Boxes Etc.** Postal, business, and communications services	4,741	$150,984–$337,946

Source: "2010 Franchise 500 Rankings," *Entrepreneur*, www.entrepreneur.com/franchises/rankings/franchise500-115608/2010,.html (accessed November 30, 2010).

more joint-venture activity, franchising is increasing rapidly. There are more than 883,000 franchised small businesses in over 100 industries. Franchised businesses produce an estimated $845 billion in output per year and employ nearly 10 million people.[30]

Major Types of Retail Franchises

Retail franchise arrangements fall into three general categories. In one arrangement, a manufacturer authorizes a number of retail stores to sell a certain brand name item. This franchise arrangement, one of the oldest forms, is common in sales of cars and trucks, farm equipment, shoes, paint, earth-moving equipment, and petroleum. In the second type of retail franchise, a producer licenses distributors to sell a given product to retailers. This arrangement is common in the soft-drink industry. Most national manufacturers of soft-drink syrups, including Coca-Cola, Dr Pepper, and PepsiCo, grant franchises to bottlers, which in turn serve retailers. In the third type of retail franchise, a franchiser supplies brand names, techniques, or other services instead of complete products. The franchiser may provide certain production and distribution services, but its primary role in the arrangement is careful development and control of marketing strategies. This approach to franchising is very common today and is used by such organizations as Holiday Inn, AAMCO, McDonald's, Dairy Queen, KFC, and H&R Block.

Advantages and Disadvantages of Franchising

Franchising offers several advantages to both the franchisee and the franchiser. It enables a franchisee to start a business with limited capital and benefit from the business experience of others. Moreover, nationally advertised franchises, such as ServiceMaster and Burger King, are often assured of customers as soon as they open. If business problems arise, the franchisee can obtain guidance and advice from the franchiser at little or no cost. Franchised outlets are generally more successful than independently owned businesses. Fewer than 10 percent of franchised retail businesses fail during the first two years of operation, compared to approximately 50 percent of independent retail businesses. Also, the franchisee receives materials to use in local advertising and can benefit from national promotional campaigns sponsored by the franchiser.

Through franchise arrangements, the franchiser gains fast and selective product distribution without incurring the high cost of constructing and operating its own outlets. The franchiser therefore has more capital for expanding production and advertising. It can also ensure, through the franchise agreement, that outlets are maintained and operated according to its own standards. Some franchisers, however, permit their franchisees to modify their menus, hours, or other operating elements to better match their target market's needs. For instance, Wings Over, a buffalo-style chicken wing franchise, has permitted menu variations to match local tastes and allowed some franchisees located near colleges and universities to open at 4 p.m. and close at 3 a.m.[31] The franchiser benefits from the fact that the franchisee, being a sole proprietor in most cases, is likely to be very highly motivated to succeed. Success of the franchise means more sales, which translate into higher income for the franchiser.

© Alan Gallery/Alamy

Franchising
Subway is a franchise. A Subway store is owned and managed by the franchisee.

Franchise arrangements also have several drawbacks. The franchiser can dictate many aspects of the business: decor, menu, design of employees' uniforms, types of signs, hours of operation, and numerous details of business operations. In addition, franchisees must pay to use the franchiser's name, products, and assistance. Usually there is a one-time franchise fee and continuing royalty and advertising fees, often collected as a percentage of sales. For example, Subway requires franchisees to come up with $80,000 to $260,000 in startup costs. Franchisees often must work very hard, putting in 10- to 12-hour days six or seven days a week. In some cases, franchise agreements are not uniform; one franchisee may pay more than another for the same services. Finally, the franchiser gives up a certain amount of control when entering into a franchise agreement. Consequently, individual establishments may not be operated exactly according to the franchiser's standards.

Wholesaling

wholesaling Transactions in which products are bought for resale, for making other products, or for general business operations

wholesaler An individual or organization that sells products that are bought for resale, for making other products, or for general business operations

Wholesaling refers to all transactions in which products are bought for resale, for making other products, or for general business operations. It does not include exchanges with ultimate consumers. A **wholesaler** is an individual or organization that sells products that are bought for resale, making other products, or general business operations. In other words, wholesalers buy products and resell them to reseller, government, and institutional users. For instance, Sysco, the nation's number-one food-service distributor, supplies restaurants, hotels, schools, industrial caterers, and hospitals with everything from frozen and fresh food and paper products to medical and cleaning supplies. There are more than 430,000 wholesaling establishments in the United States, and more than half of all products sold in this country pass through these firms.[32]

Table 16.4 lists the major activities wholesalers perform, but individual wholesalers may perform more or fewer functions than those in the table. Distribution of all goods requires wholesaling activities whether or not a wholesaling firm is involved. Wholesaling activities are not limited to goods; service companies, such as financial institutions, also use active wholesale networks. For example, some banks buy loans in bulk from other financial institutions in addition to making loans to their own retail customers.

TABLE 16.4 Major Wholesaling Functions

Supply-chain management	Creating long-term partnerships among channel members
Promotion	Providing a sales force, advertising, sales promotion, and publicity
Warehousing, shipping, and product handling	Receiving, storing, and stock keeping Packaging Shipping outgoing orders Materials handling Arranging and making local and long-distance shipments
Inventory control and data processing	Processing orders Controlling physical inventory Recording transactions Tracking sales data for financial analysis
Risk taking	Assuming responsibility for theft, product obsolescence, and excess inventories
Financing and budgeting	Extending credit Borrowing Making capital investments Forecasting cash flow
Marketing research and information systems	Providing information about markets Conducting research studies Managing computer networks to facilitate exchanges and relationships

Wholesalers may engage in many supply-chain management activities, including warehousing, shipping and product handling, inventory control, information system management and data processing, risk taking, financing, budgeting, and even marketing research and promotion. Regardless of whether there is a wholesaling firm involved in the supply chain, all product distribution requires the performance of these activities. In addition to bearing the primary responsibility for the physical distribution of products from manufacturers to retailers, wholesalers may establish information systems that help producers and retailers better manage the supply chain from producer to customer. Many wholesalers are using information technology and the Internet to allow their employees, customers, and suppliers to share information between intermediaries and facilitating agencies such as trucking companies and warehouse firms. Other firms are making their databases and marketing information systems available to their supply-chain partners to facilitate order processing, shipping, and product development and to share information about changing market conditions and customer desires. As a result, some wholesalers play a key role in supply-chain management decisions.

Services Provided by Wholesalers

Wholesalers provide essential services to both producers and retailers. By initiating sales contacts with a producer and selling diverse products to retailers, wholesalers serve as an extension of the producer's sales force. Wholesalers also provide financial assistance. They often pay for transporting goods; reduce a producer's warehousing expenses and inventory investment by holding goods in inventory; extend credit and assume losses from buyers who turn out to be poor credit risks; and, when they buy a producer's entire output and pay promptly or in cash, are a source of working capital. Wholesalers also serve as conduits for information within the marketing channel, keeping producers up-to-date on market developments and passing along the manufacturers' promotional plans to other intermediaries. Using wholesalers therefore gives producers a distinct advantage because the specialized services wholesalers perform allow producers to concentrate on developing and manufacturing products that match customers' needs and wants.

Wholesalers support retailers by assisting with marketing strategy, especially the distribution component. Wholesalers also help retailers select inventory. They are often specialists on market conditions and experts at negotiating final purchases. In industries in which obtaining supplies is important, skilled buying is indispensable. For instance, Atlanta-based Genuine Parts Company (GPC), the nation's top automotive parts wholesaler, has more than 80 years of experience in the auto parts business, which helps it serve its customers effectively. GPC supplies more than 300,000 replacement parts (from about 150 different suppliers) to about 1,000 NAPA Auto Parts stores.[33] Effective wholesalers make an effort to understand the businesses of their customers. They can reduce a retailer's burden of looking for and coordinating supply sources. If the wholesaler purchases for several different buyers, expenses can be shared by all customers. Furthermore, whereas a manufacturer's salesperson offers retailers only a few products at a time, independent wholesalers always have a wide range of products available. Thus, through partnerships, wholesalers and retailers can forge successful relationships for the benefit of customers.

The distinction between services performed by wholesalers and those provided by other businesses has blurred in recent years. Changes in the competitive nature of business, especially the growth of strong retail chains like Walmart, Home Depot, and Best Buy, are changing supply-chain relationships. In many product categories, such as electronics, furniture, and even food products, retailers have discovered that they can deal directly with producers, performing wholesaling activities themselves at a lower cost. An increasing number of retailers are relying on computer technology to expedite ordering, delivery, and handling of goods. Technology is thus allowing retailers to take over many wholesaling functions. However, when a wholesaler is eliminated from a marketing channel, wholesaling activities still have to be performed by a member of the supply chain, whether a producer, retailer, or facilitating agency. These wholesaling activities are critical components of supply-chain management.

Types of Wholesalers

Wholesalers are classified according to several criteria. Whether a wholesaler is independently owned or owned by a producer influences how it is classified. Wholesalers also can be grouped according to whether they take title to (own) the products they handle. The range of services provided is another criterion used for classification. Finally, wholesalers are classified according to the breadth and depth of their product lines. Using these criteria, we discuss three general types of wholesaling establishments: merchant wholesalers, agents and brokers, and manufacturers' sales branches and offices.

MERCHANT WHOLESALERS

Merchant wholesalers are independently owned businesses that take title to goods, assume risks associated with ownership, and generally buy and resell products to other wholesalers, business customers, or retailers. A producer is likely to rely on merchant wholesalers when selling directly to customers would be economically unfeasible. Merchant wholesalers are also useful for providing market coverage, making sales contacts, storing inventory, handling orders, collecting market information, and furnishing customer support. Some merchant wholesalers are even involved in packaging and developing private brands to help retail customers be competitive. Merchant wholesalers go by various names, including *wholesaler, jobber, distributor, assembler, exporter,* and *importer.* They fall into one of two broad categories: full service and limited service (see Figure 16.1).

Full-Service Wholesalers **Full-service wholesalers** perform the widest possible range of wholesaling functions. Customers rely on them for product availability, suitable assortments, breaking large quantities into smaller ones,

---

merchant wholesalers
Independently owned businesses that take title to goods, assume ownership risks, and buy and resell products to other wholesalers, business customers, or retailers

full-service wholesalers
Merchant wholesalers that perform the widest range of wholesaling functions

---

FIGURE 16.1 Types of Merchant Wholesalers

Merchant wholesalers
Take title, assume risk, and buy and resell products to other wholesalers, to retailers, or to other business customers

Full-service wholesalers
▸ General merchandise
▸ Limited line
▸ Specialty line

Limited-service wholesalers
▸ Cash-and-carry
▸ Truck
▸ Drop shipper
▸ Mail order

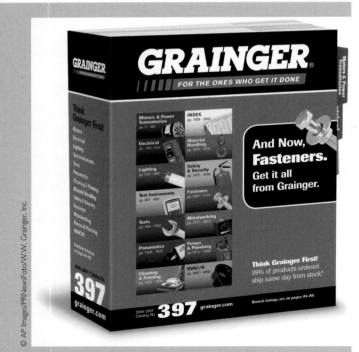

Merchant Wholesalers
Grainger is a full-service, limited-line wholesaler of electrical equipment and supplies.

financial assistance, and technical advice and service. Universal Corporation, the world's largest buyer and processor of leaf tobacco, is an example of a full-service wholesaler. Based in Richmond, Virginia, the firm buys, processes, resells, and ships tobacco and provides financing for its customers, which include cigarette manufacturers such as Philip Morris (which accounts for a significant portion of Universal's sales). Universal is also involved in sales of lumber, building products, and other agricultural products and has operations in 35 countries.[34] Full-service wholesalers handle either consumer or business products and provide numerous marketing services to their customers. Many large grocery wholesalers help retailers with store design, site selection, personnel training, financing, merchandising, advertising, coupon redemption, and scanning. Although full-service wholesalers often earn higher gross margins than other wholesalers, their operating expenses are also higher because they perform a wider range of functions.

Full-service wholesalers are categorized as general-merchandise, limited-line, and specialty-line wholesalers. **General-merchandise wholesalers** carry a wide product mix but offer limited depth within product lines. They deal in products such as drugs, nonperishable foods, cosmetics, detergents, and tobacco. **Limited-line wholesalers** carry only a few product lines, such as groceries, lighting fixtures, or oil-well-drilling equipment, but offer an extensive assortment of products within those lines. Bergen Brunswig Corporation, for example, is a limited-line wholesaler of pharmaceuticals and health and beauty aids.

General-line wholesalers provide a range of services similar to those of general-merchandise wholesalers. **Specialty-line wholesalers** offer the narrowest range of products, usually a single product line or a few items within a product line. Red River Commodities, Inc., for example, is the leading importer (specialty-line wholesaler) of nuts, seeds, and dried fruits in the United States.[35] **Rack jobbers** are full-service, specialty-line wholesalers that own and maintain display racks in supermarkets, drugstores, and discount and variety stores. They set up displays, mark merchandise, stock shelves, and keep billing and inventory records; retailers need furnish only space. Rack jobbers specialize in nonfood items with high profit margins, such as health and beauty aids, books, magazines, hosiery, and greeting cards.

Limited-Service Wholesalers **Limited-service wholesalers** provide fewer marketing services than do full-service wholesalers and specialize in just a few functions. Producers perform the remaining functions or pass them on to customers or other intermediaries. Limited-service wholesalers take title to merchandise but often do not deliver merchandise, grant credit, provide marketing information, store inventory, or plan ahead for customers' future needs. Because they offer restricted services, limited-service wholesalers are compensated with lower rates and have smaller profit margins than full-service wholesalers. The decision about whether to use a limited-service or a full-service wholesaler depends on the structure of the marketing channel and the need to manage the supply chain to provide competitive advantage. Although certain types of limited-service wholesalers are few in number, they are important in the distribution of products such as specialty foods, perishable items, construction materials, and coal.

Table 16.5 summarizes the services provided by four typical limited-service wholesalers: cash-and-carry wholesalers, truck wholesalers, drop shippers, and mail-

general-merchandise wholesalers Full-service wholesalers with a wide product mix but limited depth within product lines

limited-line wholesalers Full-service wholesalers that carry only a few product lines but many products within those lines

specialty-line wholesalers Full-service wholesalers that carry only a single product line or a few items within a product line

rack jobbers Full-service, specialty-line wholesalers that own and maintain display racks in stores

limited-service wholesalers Merchant wholesalers that provide some services and specialize in a few functions

TABLE 16.5 Services That Limited-Service Wholesalers Provide

	Cash-and-Carry	Truck	Drop Shipper	Mail Order
Physical possession of merchandise	Yes	Yes	No	Yes
Personal sales calls on customers	No	Yes	No	No
Information about market conditions	No	Some	Yes	Yes
Advice to customers	No	Some	Yes	No
Stocking and maintenance of merchandise in customers' stores	No	No	No	No
Credit to customers	No	No	Yes	Some
Delivery of merchandise to customers	No	Yes	No	No

order wholesalers. **Cash-and-carry wholesalers** are intermediaries whose customers—usually small businesses—pay cash and furnish transportation. Cash-and-carry wholesalers usually handle a limited line of products with a high turnover rate, such as groceries, building materials, and electrical or office supplies. Many small retailers whose accounts are refused by other wholesalers survive because of cash-and-carry wholesalers. **Truck wholesalers,** sometimes called *truck jobbers,* transport a limited line of products directly to customers for on-the-spot inspection and selection. They are often small operators who own and drive their own trucks. They usually have regular routes, calling on retailers and other institutions to determine their needs. **Drop shippers,** also known as *desk jobbers,* take title to products and negotiate sales but never take actual possession of products. They forward orders from retailers, business buyers, or other wholesalers to manufacturers and arrange for carload shipments of items to be delivered directly from producers to these customers. They assume responsibility for products during the entire transaction, including the costs of any unsold goods. **Mail-order wholesalers** use catalogs instead of sales forces to sell products to retail and business buyers. Wholesale mail-order houses generally feature cosmetics, specialty foods, sporting goods, office supplies, and automotive parts. Mail-order wholesaling enables buyers to choose and order particular catalog items for delivery through United Parcel Service, the U.S. Postal Service, or other carriers. This is a convenient and effective method of selling small items to customers in remote areas that other wholesalers might find unprofitable to serve. The Internet has provided an opportunity for mail-order wholesalers to sell products over their own websites and have the products shipped by the manufacturers.

AGENTS AND BROKERS

Agents and brokers negotiate purchases and expedite sales but do not take title to products (see Figure 16.2). Sometimes called *functional middlemen,* they perform a limited number of services in exchange for a commission, which generally is based on the product's selling price. **Agents** represent either buyers or sellers on a permanent basis, whereas **brokers** are intermediaries that buyers or sellers employ temporarily.

Although agents and brokers perform even fewer functions than limited-service wholesalers, they are usually specialists in particular products or types of customers and can provide valuable sales expertise. They know their markets well and often form long-lasting associations with customers. Agents and brokers enable manufacturers to expand sales when resources are limited, benefit from the services of a trained sales force, and hold down personal selling costs. Table 16.6 summarizes the services provided by agents and brokers.

Manufacturers' agents, which account for more than half of all agent wholesalers, are independent intermediaries that represent two or more sellers and usually offer customers complete product lines. They sell and take orders year-round, much as a

cash-and-carry wholesalers Limited-service wholesalers whose customers pay cash and furnish transportation

truck wholesalers Limited-service wholesalers that transport products directly to customers for inspection and selection

drop shippers Limited-service wholesalers that take title to goods and negotiate sales but never actually take possession of products

mail-order wholesalers Limited-service wholesalers that sell products through catalogs

agents Intermediaries that represent either buyers or sellers on a permanent basis

brokers Intermediaries that bring buyers and sellers together temporarily

manufacturers' agents Independent intermediaries that represent two or more sellers and usually offers customers complete product lines

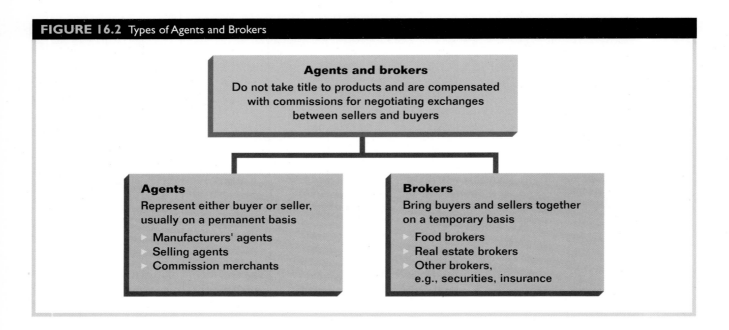

FIGURE 16.2 Types of Agents and Brokers

Agents and brokers

Do not take title to products and are compensated with commissions for negotiating exchanges between sellers and buyers

Agents

Represent either buyer or seller, usually on a permanent basis

▸ Manufacturers' agents
▸ Selling agents
▸ Commission merchants

Brokers

Bring buyers and sellers together on a temporary basis

▸ Food brokers
▸ Real estate brokers
▸ Other brokers,
   e.g., securities, insurance

manufacturer's sales force does. Restricted to a particular territory, a manufacturer's agent handles noncompeting and complementary products. The relationship between the agent and the manufacturer is governed by written contracts that outline territories, selling price, order handling, and terms of sale relating to delivery, service, and warranties. Manufacturers' agents have little or no control over producers' pricing and marketing policies. They do not extend credit and may be unable to provide technical advice. Manufacturers' agents are commonly used in sales of apparel, machinery and equipment, steel, furniture, automotive products, electrical goods, and certain food items.

Selling agents market either all of a specified product line or a manufacturer's entire output. They perform every wholesaling activity except taking title to products. Selling agents usually assume the sales function for several producers simultaneously and are used often in place of marketing departments. In fact, selling agents are used most often by small producers or by manufacturers that have difficulty maintaining a marketing department because of seasonal production or other factors. In contrast to manufacturers' agents, selling agents generally have no territorial limits and have complete authority over prices, promotion, and distribution. To avoid conflicts of interest, selling agents represent noncompeting product lines. They play a key role in advertising, marketing research, and credit policies of the sellers they represent, at times even advising on product development and packaging.

selling agents Intermediaries that market a whole product line or a manufacturer's entire output

TABLE 16.6 Services That Agents and Brokers Provide

	Manufacturers' Agents	Selling Agents	Commission Merchants	Brokers
Physical possession of merchandise	Some	Some	Yes	No
Long-term relationship with buyers or sellers	Yes	Yes	Yes	No
Representation of competing product lines	No	No	Yes	Yes
Limited geographic territory	Yes	No	No	No
Credit to customers	No	Yes	Some	No
Delivery of merchandise to customers	Some	Yes	Yes	No

Commission merchants receive goods on consignment from local sellers and negotiate sales in large, central markets. Sometimes called *factor merchants,* these agents have broad powers regarding prices and terms of sale. They specialize in obtaining the best price possible under market conditions. Most often found in agricultural marketing, commission merchants take possession of truckloads of commodities, arrange for necessary grading or storage, and transport the commodities to auction or markets where they are sold. When sales are completed, the agents deduct commission and the expense of making the sale and then turn over profits to the producer. Commission merchants also offer planning assistance and sometimes extend credit but usually do not provide promotional support.

A broker's primary purpose is to bring buyers and sellers together. Thus brokers perform fewer functions than other intermediaries. They are not involved in financing or physical possession, have no authority to set prices, and assume almost no risks. Instead, they offer customers specialized knowledge of a particular commodity and a network of established contacts. Brokers are especially useful to sellers of certain types of products, such as supermarket products and real estate. Food brokers, for example, sell food and general merchandise to retailer-owned and merchant wholesalers, grocery chains, food processors, and business buyers.

MANUFACTURERS' SALES BRANCHES AND OFFICES

Sometimes called *manufacturers' wholesalers,* manufacturers' sales branches and offices resemble merchant wholesalers' operations. **Sales branches** are manufacturer-owned intermediaries that sell products and provide support services to the manufacturer's sales force. Situated away from the manufacturing plant, they are usually located where large customers are concentrated and demand is high. They offer credit, deliver goods, give promotional assistance, and furnish other services. Customers include retailers, business buyers, and other wholesalers. Manufacturers of electrical supplies, such as Westinghouse Electric, and of plumbing supplies, such as American Standard, often have branch operations. They are also common in the lumber and automotive parts industries.

Sales offices are manufacturer-owned operations that provide services normally associated with agents. Like sales branches, they are located away from manufacturing plants, but unlike sales branches, they carry no inventory. A manufacturer's sales office (or branch) may sell products that enhance the manufacturer's own product line.

Manufacturers may set up these branches or offices to reach their customers more effectively by performing wholesaling functions themselves. A manufacturer also may set up such a facility when specialized wholesaling services are not available through existing intermediaries. A manufacturer's performance of wholesaling and physical distribution activities through its sales branch or office may strengthen supply-chain efficiency. In some situations, though, a manufacturer may bypass its sales office or branches entirely—for example, if the producer decides to serve large retailer customers directly.

commission merchants Agents that receive goods on consignment from local sellers and negotiate sales in large, central markets

sales branches Manufacturer-owned intermediaries that sell products and provide support services to the manufacturer's sales force

sales offices Manufacturer-owned operations that provide services normally associated with agents

summary

Retailing includes all transactions in which buyers intend to consume products through personal, family, or household use. Retailers, organizations that sell products primarily to ultimate consumers, are important links in the marketing channel because they are both marketers for and customers of wholesalers and producers. Retailers add value, provide services, and assist in making product selections.

2. To identify the major types of retailers

Retail stores can be classified according to the breadth of products offered. Two broad categories are general-merchandise retailers and specialty retailers. The primary types of general-merchandise retailers include department stores, discount stores, supermarkets, superstores, hypermarkets, warehouse clubs, and warehouse and catalog showrooms. Department stores are large retail organizations employing at least 25 people and characterized by wide product mixes of considerable depth for most product lines. Their products are organized into separate departments that function like self-contained businesses. Discount stores are self-service, low-price, general-merchandise outlets. A convenience store is a small self-service store that is open long hours and carries a narrow assortment of products, usually convenience items. Supermarkets are large, self-service food stores that also carry some nonfood products. Superstores are giant retail outlets that carry all the products found in supermarkets as well as most consumer products purchased on a routine basis. Hypermarkets offer supermarket and discount store shopping at one location. Warehouse clubs are large-scale, members-only discount operations. Warehouse and catalog showrooms are low-cost operations characterized by warehouse methods of materials handling and display, large inventories, and minimal services.

Specialty retailers offer substantial assortments in a few product lines. They include traditional specialty retailers, which carry narrow product mixes with deep product lines; off-price retailers, which sell brand name manufacturers' seconds and production overruns at deep discounts; and category killers, large specialty stores that concentrate on a major product category and compete on the basis of low prices and enormous product availability.

3. To explore strategic issues in retailing

To increase sales and store patronage, retailers must consider strategic issues. Location determines the trading area from which a store draws its customers and should be evaluated carefully. When evaluating potential sites, retailers take into account a variety of factors, including the location of the firm's target market within the trading area, kinds of products sold, availability of public transportation, customer characteristics, and competitors' locations. Retailers can choose among several types of locations, including freestanding structures, traditional business districts, or shopping centers. The major types of shopping centers are neighborhood shopping centers, community shopping centers, regional shopping centers, superregional shopping centers, lifestyle shopping centers, power shopping centers, and outlet shopping centers.

Retail positioning involves identifying an unserved or underserved market segment and serving it through a strategy that distinguishes the retailer from others in those customers' minds. Store image, which various customers perceive differently, derives not only from atmospherics but also from location, products offered, customer services, prices, promotion, and the store's overall reputation. Atmospherics refers to the physical elements of a store's design that can be adjusted to appeal to consumers' emotions and thus induce them to buy. Category management is a retail strategy of managing groups of similar, often substitutable products produced by different manufacturers.

4. To recognize the various forms of direct marketing and selling

Direct marketing is the use of the telephone, Internet, and nonpersonal media to communicate product and organizational information to customers, who can then purchase products via mail, telephone, or the Internet. Direct marketing is a type of nonstore retailing, the selling of goods or services outside the confines of a retail facility. Forms of direct marketing include catalog marketing, direct-response marketing, telemarketing, television home shopping, and online retailing. Two other types of nonstore retailing are direct selling and automatic vending. Direct selling is the marketing of products to ultimate consumers through face-to-face sales presentations at home or in the workplace. Automatic vending is the use of machines to dispense products.

5. To examine franchising and its benefits and weaknesses

Franchising is an arrangement in which a supplier grants a dealer the right to sell products in exchange for some type of consideration. Retail franchises are of three general types. A manufacturer may authorize a number of retail stores to sell a certain brand name item; a producer may license distributors to sell a given product to retailers; or a franchiser may supply brand names, techniques, or other services instead of a complete product. Franchise arrangements have a number of advantages and disadvantages over traditional business forms, and their use is increasing.

6. To understand the nature and functions of wholesaling

Wholesaling consists of all transactions in which products are bought for resale, making other products, or general business operations. Wholesalers are individuals or organizations that facilitate and expedite exchanges that are primarily wholesale transactions. For producers, wholesalers are a source of financial assistance and information; by performing specialized accumulation and allocation functions, they allow producers to concentrate on manufacturing products. Wholesalers provide retailers with buying expertise, wide product lines, efficient distribution, and warehousing and storage.

7. To understand how wholesalers are classified

Merchant wholesalers are independently owned businesses that take title to goods and assume ownership risks. They are either full-service wholesalers, offering the widest possible range of wholesaling functions, or limited-service wholesalers, providing only some marketing services and specializing in a few functions. Full-service merchant wholesalers include general-merchandise wholesalers, which offer a wide but relatively shallow product mix; limited-line wholesalers, which offer extensive assortments within a few product lines; specialty-line wholesalers, which carry only a single product line or a few items within a line; and rack jobbers, which own and service display racks in supermarkets and other stores. Limited-service merchant wholesalers include cash-and-carry wholesalers, which sell to small businesses, require payment in cash, and do not deliver; truck wholesalers, which sell a limited line of products from their own trucks directly to customers; drop shippers, which own goods and negotiate sales but never take possession of products; and mail-order wholesalers, which sell to retail and business buyers through direct-mail catalogs.

Agents and brokers, sometimes called functional middlemen, negotiate purchases and expedite sales in exchange for a commission, but they do not take title to products. Usually specializing in certain products, they can provide valuable sales expertise. Whereas agents represent buyers or sellers on a permanent basis, brokers are intermediaries that buyers and sellers employ on a temporary basis to negotiate exchanges. Manufacturers' agents offer customers the complete product lines of two or more sellers. Selling agents market a complete product line or a producer's entire output and perform every wholesaling function except taking title to products. Commission merchants are agents that receive goods on consignment from local sellers and negotiate sales in large, central markets. Manufacturers' sales branches and offices are owned by manufacturers. Sales branches sell products and provide support services for the manufacturer's sales force in a given location. Sales offices carry no inventory and function much as agents do.

Go to www.cengagebrain.com for resources to help you master the content in this chapter as well as materials that will expand your marketing knowledge!

important terms

retailing, 468

retailer, 468

general-merchandise retailer, 470

department stores, 470

discount stores, 470

convenience store, 471

supermarkets, 472

superstores, 472

hypermarkets, 472

warehouse clubs, 473

warehouse showrooms, 473

traditional specialty retailers, 474

category killer, 475

off-price retailers, 475

neighborhood shopping centers, 477

community shopping centers, 478

regional shopping center, 478

superregional shopping center, 478

lifestyle shopping center, 478

power shopping center, 478

retail positioning, 479

atmospherics, 479

category management, 480

direct marketing, 481

nonstore retailing, 481

catalog marketing, 481

direct-response marketing, 482

telemarketing, 482

television home shopping, 482

online retailing, 483

direct selling, 483

automatic vending, 484

franchising, 484

wholesaling, 487

wholesaler, 487

merchant wholesalers, 489

full-service wholesalers, 489

general-merchandise wholesalers, 490

limited-line wholesalers, 490

specialty-line wholesalers, 490

rack jobbers, 490

limited-service wholesalers, 490

cash-and-carry wholesalers, 491

truck wholesalers, 491

drop shippers, 491

mail-order wholesalers, 491

agents, 491

brokers, 491

manufacturers' agents, 491

selling agents, 492

commission merchants, 493

sales branches, 493

sales offices, 493

discussion and review questions

1. What value is added to a product by retailers? What value is added by retailers for producers and ultimate consumers?

2. What are the major differences between discount stores and department stores?

3. In what ways are traditional specialty stores and off-price retailers similar? How do they differ?

4. What major issues should be considered when determining a retail site location?

5. Describe the three major types of traditional shopping centers. Give an example of each type in your area.

6. Discuss the major factors that help to determine a retail store's image. How does atmosphere add value to products sold in a store?

7. How is door-to-door selling a form of retailing? Some consumers believe that direct-response orders bypass the retailer. Is this true?

8. If you were opening a retail business, would you prefer to open an independent store or own a store under a franchise arrangement? Explain your preference.

9. What services do wholesalers provide to producers and retailers?

10. What is the difference between a full-service merchant wholesaler and a limited-service merchant wholesaler?

11. Drop shippers take title to products but do not accept physical possession of them, whereas commission merchants take physical possession of products but do not accept title. Defend the logic of classifying drop shippers as merchant wholesalers and commission merchants as agents.

12. Why are manufacturers' sales offices and branches classified as wholesalers? Which independent wholesalers are replaced by manufacturers' sales branches? By sales offices?

have extended product lines, including a revised design meant to appeal to young consumers and features like custom bike shops with around-the-clock technicians. Highlighting bike offerings is a strategy that is paying off in times when people are searching for cheap means of transportation.

These days, the company is still opening new stores, but it's also moving out of shopping centers as older leases come up for renewal. It now prefers 15,000-square-foot free-standing stores located in lifestyle shopping centers or urban centers, ideally in or near areas where people enjoy outdoor activities. The recession hurt the entire retail industry, and EMS was no exception, so it has been keeping a close eye on expenses as the economy improves. The retailer is also boosting profit margins by stocking more private-branded

products. Given EMS's renewed focus on core customers, and its most recent decisions about choosing retail locations, the company is poised to climb even higher in the coming years.[36]

QUESTIONS FOR DISCUSSION

1. What changes occurred at EMS that caused the company to lose its unique retail position?
2. Evaluate the CEO's decision to take the company back to its roots.
3. Why would EMS prefer to open in a lifestyle shopping center rather than a regional shopping center? Do you agree with this retail location decision? Explain your answer.

CASE 16.2

Tesco Freshens Up Fresh and Easy's Retail Strategy

Tesco, the U.K. supermarket giant, is hardly a newcomer to international retailing. It's the world's third-largest retailer (behind Walmart and Carrefour) and has nearly a century of experience in its home country. The retailer embarked on a new era of global expansion in 1995 when it opened its first stores in Hungary. Within a few years, Tesco had stores throughout eastern Europe and in Thailand and South Korea. It has continued adding to its retail empire with new stores in China, Malaysia, and Japan, as well as plans for stores in India.

By the time Tesco ventured across the Atlantic in 2007, its marketing experts had studied the U.S. retail industry for some time. They saw 4,000-square-foot convenience stores at the small end of the store spectrum. In the middle, supermarkets offered a larger assortment of foods and household items in stores of 35,000 square feet or more. At the top end, 200,000-square-foot superstores offered even more varieties of food and

© Chris Ratcliffe/Bloomberg via Getty Images / © John Wang/Photodisc/Getty Images

non-food products. Between these conventional store sizes, Tesco's experts identified an opportunity. "There is a gap between 4,000-square-foot stores and 35,000-square-foot-plus [stores]," explained Tesco's store design and planning director. "In Europe, that gap is filled by discount stores, but in the U.S., this segment is under-served."

Tesco set out to fill the gap with a chain of Fresh and Easy neighborhood grocery stores, stocked with high-quality fruits and vegetables, fresh meats, prepared meals under the store brand, and household staples carrying manufacturers' brands. Instead of fancy atmospherics, elaborate displays, and expensive shopper-reward programs, the stores would be simple, self-service, and easy to navigate for in-and-out convenience. The idea was to keep overhead costs down and pass the savings along to customers in the form of low everyday prices.

Originally, Tesco planned to open as many as 1,000 stores in the first five years. It scouted locations in California, Arizona, and Nevada and built a 1.4 million-square-foot distribution center capable of supporting an extensive store network. Even though Tesco operated everything from convenience stores to superstores in other countries, it was creating an entirely new retail brand from scratch and investing $2 billion to make it work. As part of its marketing research, the company built a prototype store inside a California warehouse to test potential shopper reaction. Only then did it finalize the retail design and begin opening stores.

However, Fresh and Easy's early results didn't live up to its parent's expectations. With rising unemployment and a deepening recession, consumers were cutting back on spending, even for food and other basics. Competition was another factor. Between supermarkets such as Ralph's and Vons, natural-food grocers like Trader Joe's and Whole Foods, and convenience stores such as 7-Eleven, the competitive environment was extremely challenging. Still, Tesco's management believed in Fresh and Easy's retail positioning and saw long-term profit potential in making its mark in the U.S. market.

One year into its U.S. expansion, Tesco slowed the rate of new-store openings as it fine-tuned Fresh and Easy's positioning. "After customers found the stores a little sterile, we warmed up the look, adding more graphics," says an official. "Family budgets being under pressure, we introduced more promotions and value packs." In addition, the chain installed higher shelving to increase the number of items available on the selling floor.

With these changes in place, Fresh and Easy launched its first-ever ad campaign to reinforce the message of fresh foods at low prices and used public relations to spotlight its support of its local communities and environmentally friendly operations. It connected with consumers through videos on YouTube, photos on Flickr, blog posts, and Twitter tweets. The retailer also made a special effort to reach out to Hispanic consumers with a Spanish-language website and Spanish-language advertising. Store by store, it adapted the merchandise mix to include more of the foods and brands favored by Hispanic shoppers in each neighborhood.

Three years after Tesco started Fresh and Easy, its 150 U.S. stores were enjoying higher traffic and higher revenue. The economy was improving, the chain had shifted its new-store schedule into high gear, and customer feedback was positive. Profits, however, remained elusive. Looking ahead, can Fresh and Easy capture the hearts and wallets of enough U.S. shoppers to assure its long-term financial success?[37]

QUESTIONS FOR DISCUSSION

1. What type of store is Fresh and Easy? Knowing that Fresh and Easy falls into this classification of retailers, what does that tell us about Fresh and Easy's marketing efforts?

2. Based on Fresh and Easy's retail positioning and marketing situation, what types of locations should it seek out as it expands its store network?

3. A few grocery retailers offer online shopping for customers' convenience. Should Fresh and Easy offer online shopping? Explain.

GameStop Plays to Win

The Super Mario Bros. and Iron Man games fly off the shelves when GameStop pulls out all the stops in its video game marketing. Based in Grapevine, Texas, GameStop rings up $9 billion in annual sales as a specialty retailer of new and used video game hardware and software. Its 6,450 stores in 17 countries stock popular video game consoles and accessories from Sony, Microsoft, and Nintendo, plus thousands of games. Each 1,400-square-foot store is packed with an ever-changing merchandise assortment, some items purchased new from manufacturers or distributors and some taken as trade-ins from customers.

Founded in 1996, GameStop went through several names and mergers as it refined its retailing model and kicked off an aggressive expansion strategy that continues today, with the opening of 400 new stores every year. Its network of brick-and-mortar stores is complemented by an e-commerce site where customers can click to browse inventory, buy games and gear to be shipped to their homes, download free or paid games, and register for online game tournaments.

Highly Seasonal, Highly Competitive

GameStop's business is both highly seasonal and highly competitive. Approximately 40 percent of its sales are made during the last three months of the year. In the United States, it must contend with the marketing muscle of giant discounters such as Walmart and Target, toy stores like Toys"R"Us, and national electronics chains such as Best Buy, as well as specialty stores, catalog merchants, and online retailers of all sizes. Outside the United States, GameStop also competes with multinational hypermarket retailers like Carrefour.

The company targets three customer segments: enthusiasts, casual gamers, and seasonal gift givers. In addition, some customers are value-oriented and prefer to buy used products, including older consoles and games that are no longer available as new items.

Used Games for Sale

One of GameStop's competitive advantages is its trade-in policy. Customers can bring in their games, consoles, and accessories and receive a store credit toward the purchase of other merchandise. Trade-ins must be in working condition and must include the original box and the instruction manual. GameStop's refurbishment centers in North America, Australia, and Europe test all trade-ins, fix defects when necessary, repackage the products, and ship them to stores for retail sale. Not only do trade-ins stimulate store traffic, sales of used products result in a higher gross margin than sales of new products. Used games account for about one-fourth of GameStop's revenue and as much as 45 percent of its profits.

The profit potential in used games has drawn competition for GameStop. Best Buy and Walmart briefly tested the sale of used games, partnering with an outside company, but then ended their experiments. Now the convenience store chain 7-Eleven has entered this market, selling used games through a partnership with the wholesaler Game Trading Technologies. Toys"R"Us also offers some used games and consoles and invites trade-ins, in person and by mail. Amazon.com allows game trade-ins by mail and serves as a virtual storefront for used video games sold by consumers and businesses, in addition to retailing new games and consoles.

The Right Merchandise in the Right Location

GameStop chooses store locations based on a number of factors, including demographic trends, visibility to pedestrians and vehicular traffic, and parking availability. It prefers to put stores in power shopping centers and malls that draw a high volume of customers. It also checks out the competitive situation in each area before making a final decision. Store atmospherics are designed to appeal to game players, and include equipment where customers can sample games and watch videos of game clips before making a purchase.

Over the years, GameStop has developed a sophisticated information system for analyzing historic trends in store sales so it can project future demand for current and new products. This is especially important for satisfying the needs of enthusiasts, who may buy elsewhere if GameStop doesn't have the latest game or console in stock immediately after its release. To help predict demand, GameStop invites customers to preorder new items for pick up at their local stores on or after the release date. It also tracks customer requests and monitors media coverage in advance of new product introductions. During a busy period of new-game introductions, GameStop may have more than 1,000 new games in stock and ready for purchase. Because new games and equipment can make older products obsolete, GameStop has negotiated deals with its primary suppliers to allow returns in such instances.

Thanks to its marketing information system, GameStop knows exactly which products sell in each of its stores and what inventory is available in its distribution centers. The system automatically reorders merchandise as it sells and schedules twice-weekly shipments to replenish stock, so store shelves are never empty. On the other hand, daily analysis of inventory positions and frequent restocking allows GameStop to tailor the merchandise mix for each store while avoiding the expense of carrying too much safety stock in each store.

For high efficiency, GameStop supplies replenishment stock to U.S. stores from its 400,000-square-foot distribution center in Grapevine, Texas. Its 260,000-square-foot center in Louisville, Kentucky, is dedicated to receiving, sorting, and shipping hot new games and consoles to its stores nationwide. The company uses centrally located distribution centers to restock stores in other countries.

The Digital Dilemma

Despite GameStop's considerable investment in brick-and-mortar retailing, it sees great value in maintaining a strong online retailing presence. Game enthusiasts tend to be heavy Internet users, and GameStop wants to be where they like to be. Its website has a feature of interest to all of the targeted segments: a "wish list"

where enthusiasts and casual gamers can itemize the products they would most like to receive (from gift-givers). GameStop also offers a weekly e-newsletter with exclusive discounts and advance notice of sales, tournaments, midnight openings for new releases, and other events.

Game consoles are increasingly Internet-ready and many players already play games on their personal computers, so digital game downloads are a must for GameStop. Its e-commerce site sells downloadable versions of popular episodes of *Grand Theft Auto* and other games. The site also offers hundreds of free games, some downloadable and some that play in the user's web browser, including GameStop's own free online game, *Legends of Zork*.

Digital downloads pose a dilemma. GameStop's executives have been monitoring the situation in the music industry, where downloads have cut into retailers' sales of actual CDs. However, digital music files are relatively small, compared with digital game files. This means buyers would have to have a very speedy broadband Internet connection to get a game downloaded in a reasonable length of time. For now, GameStop is concentrating on retailing disc-based games through store and online retailing. "We simply don't believe there's enough capacity and speed to create a full download game business in the short term," says the chief operating officer.[38]

QUESTIONS FOR DISCUSSION

1. What role does physical distribution play in GameStop's retailing strategy?
2. Why would video game marketers such as Sony prefer dual distribution? What does this mean for GameStop's marketing efforts?
3. How does GameStop create time, place, possession, and form utility for customers who want to buy used video games?
4. Do you think GameStop should market used video games via vending machines placed on college campuses? Why or why not?

Part 7

Promotion Decisions

PART SEVEN focuses on communication with target market members and, at times, other groups. A specific marketing mix cannot satisfy people in a particular target market unless they are aware of the product and know where to find it. Some promotion decisions relate to a specific marketing mix; others are geared toward promoting the entire organization. **CHAPTER 17** discusses integrated marketing communications. It describes the communication process and the major promotional methods that can be included in promotion mixes. **CHAPTER 18** analyzes the major steps in developing an advertising campaign. It also explains what public relations is and how it can be used. **CHAPTER 19** deals with personal selling and the role it can play in a firm's promotional efforts. This chapter also explores the general characteristics of sales promotion and describes sales promotion techniques.

Economic forces

Competitive forces

Political forces

Product

Price · Customer · Distribution

Promotion

Sociocultural forces

Legal and regulatory forces

Technological forces

Chapter 17

Integrated Marketing Communications

OBJECTIVES

1. To describe the nature of integrated marketing communications
2. To examine the process of communication
3. To understand the role and objectives of promotion
4. To explore the elements of the promotion mix
5. To examine the selection of promotion mix elements
6. To understand word-of-mouth communication and how it affects promotion
7. To understand product placement promotions
8. To examine criticisms and defenses of promotion

La Música to the Ears: State Farm Reaches the Hispanic Population with a Band

Data collected by the University of Georgia indicates that Hispanics may be spending $1.4 trillion by 2013. This is causing businesses to take notice of an often under-served demographic. And "like a good neighbor, State Farm is there." State Farm is actively seeking to connect with the Hispanic market. Prior to its recent marketing pushes, State Farm ranked low among Hispanics, with many saying that the company did not understand them or their culture. This is changing. To connect, State Farm first developed the slogan "Ahi Estoy (I'm there)" and capitalized on the Hispanic love of music by running an ad featuring an imaginary regional Mexican band composed of real-life struggling musicians.

Working with ad agency Alma DDB (an agency specializing in Hispanic advertising) and Fire Advertisement, the collaborators decided State Farm ought to launch a real band using the performers from the commercial. For this campaign to succeed, the band had to create quality music, gain fans, and resonate with its audience. Most important for State Farm was that the band be intimately connected to the company without becoming a blatant advertising mouthpiece. Instead of State Farm advertising itself through the band, the musicians now credit the company as a critical component of their success. A general survey indicates that about one-third of Hispanics listening to the band's music are aware of State Farm's connection, while concert surveys indicate that the band's fans have a positive connection to State Farm. The band has performed on television, gone on tour, and appeared in its own reality show on Telemundo.

Through it all, State Farm is there—albeit in a subtle way. By honoring Hispanic culture through connections based on values, State Farm is exploring little-known advertising territory. The short-term benefits for the company are few, but the company hopes that State Farm will become the go-to insurance company for Hispanics. What State Farm and its ad agencies have created is a prime example of integrated marketing communication because, via the band, State Farm is able to communicate a consistent message to its Hispanic market. *Advertising Age* recently awarded State Farm the bronze Hispanic Creative Advertising Award. The company's unique approach may be the start of a new trend in marketing.[1]

STATE FARM

Auto

Life Fire

INSURANCE

®

Organizations such as State Farm employ a variety of promotional methods to communicate with their target markets. Providing information to customers and other stakeholders is vital to initiating and developing long-term relationships with them.

This chapter looks at the general dimensions of promotion. First, we discuss the nature of integrated marketing communications. Next, we analyze the meaning and process of communication. We then define and examine the role of promotion and explore some of the reasons promotion is used. Then we consider major promotional methods and the factors that influence marketers' decisions to use particular methods. Next, we explain the positive and negative effects of personal and electronic word-of-mouth communication. Finally, we examine criticisms and defenses of promotion.

The Nature of Integrated Marketing Communications

Integrated marketing communications refer to the coordination of promotion and other marketing efforts to ensure maximum informational and persuasive impact on customers. Coordinating multiple marketing tools to produce this synergistic effect requires a marketer to employ a broad perspective. A major goal of integrated marketing communications is to send a consistent message to customers. For a number of years, Major League Baseball has been struggling with image issues due to steroid scandals and other controversies. To create a more family-friendly image, when the San Diego Padres constructed their new stadium, they partnered with Petco by selling the nationally recognized company naming rights to the stadium. The team also illustrates its dedication to its fans by issuing an e-newsletter in addition to traditional advertising and promotions. The Padres also maintain an online fan forum, which includes a special link for children, and offers a wide variety of mobile apps.[2]

integrated marketing communications
Coordination of promotion and other marketing efforts for maximum informational and persuasive impact

Because various units both inside and outside most companies have traditionally planned and implemented promotional efforts, customers have not always received consistent messages. Integrated marketing communications allow an organization to coordinate and manage its promotional efforts to transmit consistent messages. Integrated marketing communications also enable synchronization of promotion elements and can improve the efficiency and effectiveness of promotion budgets. Thus, this approach fosters not only long-term customer relationships but also the efficient use of promotional resources.

The concept of integrated marketing communications has been increasingly accepted for several reasons. Mass media advertising, a very popular promotional method in the past, is used less frequently today because of its high cost and lower effectiveness in reaching some target markets. Marketers can now take advantage of more precisely targeted promotional tools, such as cable TV, direct mail, the Internet, special-interest magazines, DVDs, cell phones, and even iPods. Database marketing is also allowing marketers to more precisely target individual customers. Until recently, suppliers of marketing communications were specialists. Advertising agencies provided advertising campaigns, sales promotion companies provided sales promotion activities and materials, and public relations organizations engaged in publicity efforts. Today, a number of promotion-related companies provide one-stop shopping for the client seeking advertising, sales promotion, and public

Integrated Marketing Communication
Small Steps utilizes integrated marketing communication to create awareness of its environmentally sensitive paper products.

relations, thus reducing coordination problems for the sponsoring company. Because the overall cost of marketing communications has risen significantly, upper management demands systematic evaluations of communication efforts and a reasonable return on investment.

The specific communication vehicles employed and the precision with which they are used are changing as both information technology and customer interests become increasingly dynamic. For example, companies can run short advertisements during broadcasts of TV shows and other videos that users can watch on their cell phones. Some companies are even creating their own branded content to exploit the many vehicles through which consumers obtain information. For instance, Ford partners with *American Idol* to create a series of commercials featuring top *American Idol* contestants and various Ford vehicles. These commercials play during *American Idol* on Fox and on the *American Idol* website.[3] Apple also partners with *American Idol* by offering current contestant performances for downloading at its popular iTunes store.[4]

Today marketers and customers have almost unlimited access to data about each other. Integrating and customizing marketing communications while protecting customer privacy has become a major challenge. Through digital media, companies can provide product information and services that are coordinated with traditional promotional activities. In fact, gathering information about goods and services is one of the main reasons people use the Internet. College students in particular say they are influenced by Internet ads when buying online or just researching product purchases. The sharing of information and use of technology to facilitate communication between buyers and sellers are essential for successful customer relationship management.

Promotion and the Communication Process

Communication is essentially the transmission of information. For communication to take place, both the sender and receiver of information must share some common ground. They must have a common understanding of the symbols, words, and pictures used to transmit information. An individual transmitting the following message may believe he or she is communicating with you:

在工廠吾人製造化粧品，在商店吾人銷售希望。

However, communication has not taken place if you don't understand the language in which the message is written. Thus, we define **communication** as a sharing of meaning. Implicit in this definition is the notion of transmission of information because sharing necessitates transmission.

As Figure 17.1 shows, communication begins with a source. A **source** is a person, group, or organization with a meaning it attempts to share with an audience. A source could be a salesperson wishing to communicate a sales message or an organization wanting to send a message to thousands of customers through an advertisement. Developing a strategy can enhance the effectiveness of the source's communication. For example, a strategy in which a salesperson attempts to influence a customer's decision by eliminating competitive products from consideration has been found to be effective. A **receiver** is the individual, group, or organization that decodes a coded message, and an *audience* is two or more receivers.

To transmit meaning, a source must convert the meaning into a series of signs or symbols representing ideas or concepts. This is called the **coding process**, or *encoding*. When coding meaning into a message, the source must consider certain characteristics of the receiver or audience. To share meaning, the source should use signs or symbols familiar to the receiver or audience. Research has shown that persuasive messages

communication A sharing of meaning through the transmission of information

source A person, group, or organization with a meaning it tries to share with a receiver or an audience

receiver The individual, group, or organization that decodes a coded message

coding process Converting meaning into a series of signs or symbols

Figure 17.1 The Communication Process

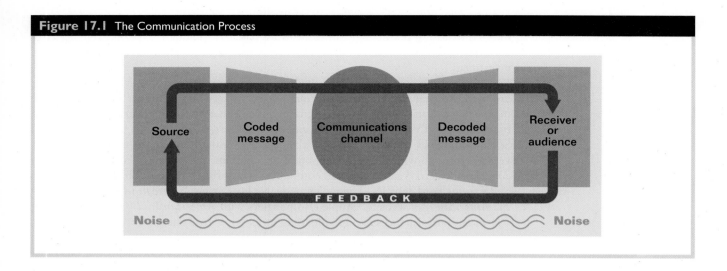

| Source | Coded message | Communications channel | Decoded message | Receiver or audience |

FEEDBACK

Noise   Noise

from a source are more effective when the appeal matches an individual's personality.[5] Marketers that understand this realize the importance of knowing their target market and ensuring that an advertisement or promotion uses language the target market understands and depicts behaviors acceptable within the culture. For instance, Pepsodent toothpaste was sold in Southeast Asia, promoting its teeth whitening capability. The product did not sell well because local natives chew betel nuts to blacken their teeth, which is considered more attractive than light teeth. Another example involves a U.S. telephone company whose ad campaign failed to reach Latinos with a commercial that showed a wife telling her husband to call friends and explain that they would be arriving late for dinner. First, in general, Latino women do not dictate their husband's behavior. Also, it is not customary in Latino cultures to call if you are going to be late for dinner. United Airlines also struggled with a promotion introducing new service to Hong Kong. White carnations were handed to passengers when boarding their flight; the advertisers did not realize that, in Chinese culture, white flowers are related to bad luck or even death. United quickly changed the promotion so that the passengers were given red carnations.[6]

When coding a meaning, a source needs to use signs or symbols that the receiver or audience uses to refer to the concepts the source intends to convey. Instead of technical jargon, explanatory language that helps consumers understand the message is more likely to result in positive attitudes and purchase intentions. Marketers try to avoid signs or symbols that may have several meanings for an audience. For example, *soda* as a general term for soft drinks may not work well in national advertisements. Although in some parts of the United States the word means "soft drink," in other regions it may connote bicarbonate of soda, an ice cream drink, or something one mixes with Scotch whiskey.

To share a coded meaning with the receiver or audience, a source selects and uses a **communications channel**, the medium of transmission that carries the coded message from the source to the receiver or audience. Transmission media include ink on paper, air wave vibrations produced by vocal cords, chalk marks on a chalkboard, and electronically produced vibrations of air waves (in radio and television signals, for example). Table 17.1 summarizes the leading communications channels from which people obtain information and news.

When a source chooses an inappropriate communication channel, several problems may arise. The coded message may reach some receivers, but possibly the wrong receivers. For example, dieters who adopt the Atkins low-carbohydrate diet are more likely to focus on communications that relate to their food concerns, such as "Eat Meat Not Wheat" T-shirts and fast-food chain advertisements that communicate

communications channel
The medium of transmission that carries the coded message from the source to the receiver

Table 17.1 Where People Get Their News and Information

On a Typical Day:
78 percent of Americans say they get news from a local TV station
73 percent say they get news from a national network, such as CBS, or a cable TV station, such as CNN or FoxNews
61 percent say they get some kind of news online
54 percent say they listen to a radio news program at home or in the car
50 percent say they read news in a local newspaper
17 percent say they read news in a national newspaper, such as the *New York Times* or *USA Today*

Source: Kristen Purcell, Lee Rainie, Amy Mitchell, Tom Rosenstiel, Kenny Olmstead, "Understanding the Participatory News Consumer," Pew Internet & American Life Project, March 1, 2010, http://pewinternet.org/Reports/2010/Online-News .aspx?r=1 (accessed March 3, 2010).

information about the carbohydrate content of menu items. An advertiser that wants to reach this group would need to take this information into account when choosing an appropriate communications channel. At the same time, however, these advertisements can easily be adopted by the wrong types of receivers—those who want an excuse to eat all the meats and fatty foods they want without guilt, which is not the purpose of the Atkins diet. Thus, finding the right messages that target the right receivers can be a challenging process.

Coded messages may also reach intended receivers in incomplete form because the intensity of the transmission is weak. For instance, radio and broadcast television signals are received effectively only over a limited range, which varies according to climactic conditions. Members of the target audience living on the fringe of the broadcast area may receive a weak signal; others well within the broadcast area may also receive an incomplete message if, for example, they listen to the radio while driving or studying.

In the **decoding process**, signs or symbols are converted into concepts and ideas. Seldom does a receiver decode exactly the same meaning the source coded. When the result of decoding differs from what was coded, noise exists. **Noise** is anything that reduces the clarity and accuracy of the communication; it has many sources and may affect any or all parts of the communication process. Noise sometimes arises within the communications channel itself. Radio static, poor or slow Internet connections, and laryngitis are sources of noise. Noise also occurs when a source uses signs or symbols that are unfamiliar to the receiver or have a meaning different from the one intended. Noise may also originate in the receiver; a receiver may be unaware of a coded message when perceptual processes block it out.

The receiver's response to a decoded message is **feedback** to the source. The source usually expects and normally receives feedback, although perhaps not immediately. During feedback, the receiver or audience is the source of a message directed toward the original source, which then becomes a receiver. Feedback is coded, sent through a communications channel, and decoded by the receiver, the source of the original communication. Thus, communication is a circular process, as indicated in Figure 17.1.

During face-to-face communication, such as personal selling and product sampling, verbal and nonverbal feedback can be immediate. Instant feedback lets communicators adjust messages quickly to improve the effectiveness of their communications. For example, when a salesperson realizes through feedback that a customer does not understand a sales presentation, the salesperson adapts the presentation to make it more meaningful to the customer. This is why face-to-face communication is the most adaptive and flexible, especially compared to digital, web-based, or telephone communications. In interpersonal communication, feedback occurs through talking, touching, smiling, nodding, eye movements, and other body movements and postures.

decoding process
Converting signs or symbols into concepts and ideas

noise Anything that reduces a communication's clarity and accuracy

feedback The receiver's response to a decoded message

When mass communication such as advertising is used, feedback is often slow and difficult to recognize. Also, it may be several years before the effects of this promotion will be known. Feedback does exist for mass communication in the form of measures of changes in sales volume or in consumers' attitudes and awareness levels.

Each communication channel has a limit on the volume of information it can handle effectively. This limit, called **channel capacity**, is determined by the least efficient component of the communication process. Consider communications that depend on speech. An individual source can speak only so fast, and there is a limit to how much an individual receiver can take in aurally. Beyond that point, additional messages cannot be decoded; thus, meaning cannot be shared. Although a radio announcer can read several hundred words a minute, a one-minute advertising message should not exceed 150 words, because most announcers cannot articulate words into understandable messages at a rate beyond 150 words per minute.

channel capacity The limit on the volume of information a communication channel can handle effectively

promotion Communication to build and maintain relationships by informing and persuading one or more audiences

The Role and Objectives of Promotion

Promotion is communication that builds and maintains favorable relationships by informing and persuading one or more audiences to view an organization positively and to accept its products. Toward this end, many organizations spend considerable resources on promotion to build and enhance relationships with current and potential customers and other stakeholders. For example, 60 companies advertising in Super Bowl XLIV spent between $2 and $3 million per 30 second ad to influence consumers' purchase behavior.[7] Marketers also indirectly facilitate favorable relationships by focusing information about company activities and products on interest groups (such as environmental and consumer groups), current and potential investors, regulatory agencies, and society in general. For instance, some organizations promote responsible use of products criticized by society such as tobacco, alcohol, and violent movies. Companies sometimes promote programs that help selected groups. Yoplait, for instance, supported the Susan G. Komen Breast Cancer Research Foundation with its "Save Lids to Save Lives" campaign, which contributed 10 cents to the charity for every pink yogurt lid sent in by consumers, resulting in more than $25 million in donations.[8] Such cause-related marketing, as we discussed in Chapter 4, links the purchase of products to philanthropic efforts for one or more causes. By contributing to causes that its target markets support, cause-related marketing can help marketers boost sales and generate goodwill.

For maximum benefit from promotional efforts, marketers strive for proper planning, implementation, coordination, and control of communications. Effective management of integrated marketing communications is based on information about and feedback from customers and the marketing environment, often obtained from an organization's marketing information system (see Figure 17.2). How successfully marketers use promotion to maintain positive relationships depends to some extent on the quantity and quality of information the organization receives. Because customers derive information and opinions from many different sources, integrated marketing

Objectives of Promotion
The producer of Ethos Water uses this advertisement to increase brand awareness and make consumers aware of its program to make clean water available in several developing countries.

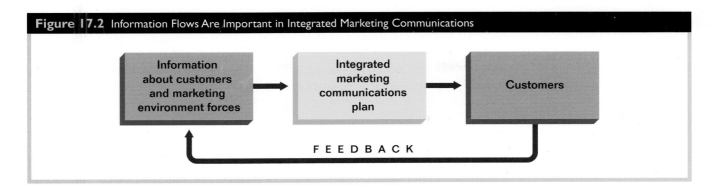

Figure 17.2 Information Flows Are Important in Integrated Marketing Communications

communications planning also takes into account informal methods of communication such as word of mouth and independent information sources on the Internet. Because promotion is communication that can be managed, we now analyze what communication is and how the communication process works.

Promotional objectives vary considerably from one organization to another and within organizations over time. Large firms with multiple promotional programs operating simultaneously may have quite varied promotional objectives. For the purpose of analysis, we focus on the eight promotional objectives shown in Table 17.2. Although the list is not exhaustive, one or more of these objectives underlie many promotional programs.

Create Awareness

A considerable amount of promotion efforts focus on creating awareness. For an organization that is introducing a new product or a line extension, making customers aware of the product is crucial to initiating the product adoption process. A marketer that has invested heavily in product development strives to create product awareness quickly to generate revenues to offset the high costs of product development and introduction. To make customers aware of its new Lunchables sub sandwiches, Kraft's Oscar Mayer division partnered with Animal Planet and its popular TV host, Jeff Corwin. The partnership involves a contest for children through which they can enter to win a trip to Boston to meet Corwin and tour a local zoo.[9]

Creating awareness is important for existing products, too. Promotional efforts may aim to increase awareness of brands, product features, image-related issues (such as organizational size or socially responsive behavior), or operational characteristics (such as store hours, locations, and credit availability). Some promotional programs are unsuccessful because marketers fail to generate awareness of critical issues among a significant portion of target market members. During the height of the global financial crisis, Hyundai made a bold advertising move by stating that if you lost your job, you could return your Hyundai. While other dealer promotions offered 0 percent financing, big sales, and various promotional tactics, Hyundai's guarantee and understanding of consumer concerns resonated and generated an authentic sense of "shared suffering" or "camaraderie."[10]

Table 17.2 Possible Objectives of Promotion

Create awareness	Retain loyal customers
Stimulate demand	Facilitate reseller support
Encourage product trial	Combat competitive promotional efforts
Identify prospects	Reduce sales fluctuations

Stimulate Demand

When an organization is the first to introduce an innovative product, it tries to stimulate **primary demand**—demand for a product category rather than for a specific brand of product—through **pioneer promotion**. Pioneer promotion informs potential customers about the product: what it is, what it does, how it can be used, and where it can be purchased. Because pioneer promotion is used in the introductory stage of the product life cycle, meaning there are no competing brands, it neither emphasizes brand names nor compares brands. When Apple introduced the iPad, it envisioned that this product would be different than desktop computers and notebooks and that it would be used in and around the home for easy access of news, e-mail, entertainment, and a broad diversity of service options. The goal was to promote the iPad as a new product, not as a replacement to a product you might already have.[11]

To build **selective demand**, demand for a specific brand, a marketer employs promotional efforts that point out the strengths and benefits of a specific brand. Building selective demand also requires singling out attributes important to potential buyers. Selective demand can be stimulated by differentiating the product from competing brands in the minds of potential buyers. Selective demand can also be stimulated by increasing the number of product uses and promoting them through advertising campaigns, as well as through price discounts, free samples, coupons, consumer contests and games, and sweepstakes. For example, Nike creates awareness for its "Reuse a Shoe" recycling program on its website and within its stores. After shoes are returned for recycling, Nike breaks them into three components: (1) rubber soles are turned into running tracks, (2) foam midsoles turn into the springy surface for tennis courts, and (3) fabric uppers become padding for basketball courts. Since 1990, Nike has recycled more than 25 million pairs of shoes. Nike's commitment to environmental issues can stimulate selective demand for athletic shoes.[12] Promotions for large package sizes or multiple-product packages are directed at increasing consumption, which in turn can stimulate demand. In addition, selective demand can be stimulated by encouraging existing customers to use more of the product.

primary demand Demand for a product category rather than for a specific brand

pioneer promotion Promotion that informs consumers about a new product

selective demand Demand for a specific brand

Stimulating Demand
Apple stimulates primary demand for its iPad through advertising and promotion.

Encourage Product Trial

When attempting to move customers through the product adoption process, a marketer may successfully create awareness and interest, but customers may stall during the evaluation stage. In this case, certain types of promotion—such as free samples; coupons; test drives; or limited free-use offers, contests, and games—are employed to encourage product trial. For instance, many software companies offer free 30-day trials of their software. Whether a marketer's product is the first in a new product category, a new brand in an existing category, or simply an existing brand seeking customers, trial-inducing promotional efforts aim to make product trial convenient and low risk for potential customers.

Identify Prospects

Certain types of promotional efforts aim to identify customers who are interested in the firm's product and are most likely to buy it. A marketer may use a magazine advertisement with a direct-response information form, requesting the reader to complete and mail in the form to receive additional information. Some advertisements have toll-free numbers to facilitate direct customer response. Customers who fill out information blanks or call the organization usually have higher interest in the product, which makes them likely sales prospects. The organization can respond with phone calls, follow-up letters, or personal contact by salespeople.

Retain Loyal Customers

Clearly, maintaining long-term customer relationships is a major goal of most marketers. Such relationships are quite valuable. Promotional efforts directed at customer retention can help an organization control its costs because the costs of retaining customers are usually considerably lower than those of acquiring new ones. Frequent-user programs, such as those sponsored by airlines, car rental agencies, and hotels, aim to reward loyal customers and encourage them to remain loyal. Regal Entertainment, for example, introduced the Regal Crown Club. Membership entitles consumers to earn points that can be used for free movies, popcorn, or beverages at a Regal Cinema.[13] Some organizations employ special offers that only their existing customers can use. To retain loyal customers, marketers not only advertise loyalty programs but also use reinforcement advertising, which assures current users they have made the right brand choice and tells them how to get the most satisfaction from the product.

Facilitate Reseller Support

Reseller support is a two-way street: producers generally want to provide support to resellers to maintain sound working relationships, and in turn they expect resellers to support their products. When a manufacturer advertises a product to consumers, resellers should view this promotion as a form of strong manufacturer support. In some instances, a producer agrees to pay a certain proportion of retailers' advertising expenses for promoting its products. When a manufacturer is introducing a new consumer brand in a highly competitive product category, it may be difficult to persuade supermarket managers to carry this brand. However, if the manufacturer promotes the new brand with free samples and coupon distribution in the retailer's area, a supermarket manager views these actions as strong support and is much more likely to handle the product. To encourage wholesalers and retailers to increase their inventories of its products, a manufacturer may provide them with special offers and buying allowances. In certain industries, a producer's salesperson may provide support to a wholesaler by working with the wholesaler's customers (retailers) in the presentation and promotion of the products. Strong relationships with resellers are important to a firm's ability to maintain a sustainable competitive advantage. The use of various promotional methods can help an organization achieve this goal.

Combat Competitive Promotional Efforts

At times, a marketer's objective in using promotion is to offset or lessen the effect of a competitor's promotional or marketing programs. This type of promotional activity does not necessarily increase the organization's sales or market share, but it may prevent a sales or market share loss. A combative promotional objective is used most often by firms in extremely competitive consumer markets, such as the fast-food and automobile industries. When airlines introduced fees to customers for checking in their bags, Southwest Airlines began heavy promotion of their "bags fly free" campaign. Southwest does not charge for the first or second bag checked, while competitors charge up to $120 round trip for checking two bags. While Southwest has a competitive pricing advantage, it is not unusual for competitors to respond with a counter-pricing strategy or even match a competitor's pricing.

Reduce Sales Fluctuations

Demand for many products varies from one month to another because of such factors as climate, holidays, and seasons. A business, however, cannot operate at peak efficiency when sales fluctuate rapidly. Changes in sales volume translate into changes in production, inventory levels, personnel needs, and financial resources. When promotional techniques reduce fluctuations by generating sales during slow periods, a firm can use its resources more efficiently.

Promotional techniques are often designed to stimulate sales during sales slumps. For example, advertisements promoting price reduction of lawn-care equipment can increase sales during fall and winter months. During peak periods, a marketer may refrain from advertising to prevent stimulating sales to the point where the firm cannot handle all of the demand. On occasion, a company advertises that customers can be better served by coming in on certain days. A pizza outlet, for example, might distribute coupons that are valid only Monday through Thursday because on Friday through Sunday the restaurant is extremely busy.

To achieve the major objectives of promotion discussed here, companies must develop appropriate promotional programs. In the next section, we consider the basic components of such programs: the promotion mix elements.

The Promotion Mix

Several promotional methods can be used to communicate with individuals, groups, and organizations. When an organization combines specific methods to manage the integrated marketing communications for a particular product, that combination constitutes the promotion mix for that product. The four possible elements of a **promotion mix** are advertising, personal selling, public relations, and sales promotion (see Figure 17.3). For some products, firms use all four elements; for others, they use only two or three. In this section, we provide an overview of each promotion mix element; they are covered in greater detail in the next two chapters.

Advertising

promotion mix A combination of promotional methods used to promote a specific product

Advertising is a paid nonpersonal communication about an organization and its products transmitted to a target audience through mass media, including television, radio, the Internet, newspapers, magazines, video games, direct mail, outdoor displays, and signs on mass transit vehicles. Advertising is changing as consumers' mass media consumption habits are changing. Companies are striving to maximize their presence

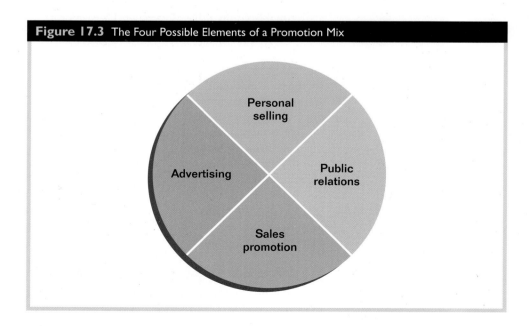

Figure 17.3 The Four Possible Elements of a Promotion Mix

Advertising Aimed at Prevention
This ad focuses on one of the many health risks associated with secondhand smoke.

and impact through digital media; ads are being designed that cater to smaller, more personalized audiences; and traditional media such as newspapers are in a decline due to a drop in readership. Individuals and organizations use advertising to promote goods, services, ideas, issues, and people. Being highly flexible, advertising can reach an extremely large target audience or focus on a small, precisely defined segment. For instance, Burger King's advertising focuses on a large audience of potential fast-food customers, ranging from children to adults, whereas advertising for Gulfstream jets aims at a much smaller and more specialized target market.

Advertising offers several benefits. It is extremely cost-efficient when it reaches a vast number of people at a low cost per person. For example, the cost of a four-color, full-page advertisement in the national edition of *Time* magazine costs $287,440. With a circulation of more than 287,000, this makes the cost of reaching roughly a thousand subscribers $85.00.[14] Advertising also lets the source repeat the message several times. Subway credits its promotional and advertising success to a catchy theme and heavy repetition of its "$5.00 footlong" sub sandwich campaign. Furthermore, advertising a product a certain way can add to the product's value, and the visibility an organization gains from advertising can enhance its image. For instance, research suggests that incorporating touchable elements that generate a positive sensory feedback in mail and print advertising can be a positive persuasive tool.[15] At times, a firm tries to enhance its own or its product's image by including celebrity endorsers in advertisements. For example, during the 2010 Grammy Awards, celebrity endorsements were up 150 percent with celebrities such as Drew Barrymore and the Black Eyed Peas promoting products for various companies.[16]

Advertising has disadvantages as well. Even though the cost per person reached may be low, the absolute dollar outlay can be extremely high, especially for commercials during popular television shows. High costs can limit, and sometimes preclude, use of advertising in a promotion mix. Moreover, advertising rarely provides rapid feedback. Measuring its effect on sales is difficult, and it is ordinarily less persuasive than personal selling. In most instances, the time available to communicate a message to customers is limited to seconds, because people look at a print advertisement for only a few seconds, and most broadcast commercials are 30 seconds or less. Of course, the use of infomercials can increase exposure time for viewers.

Personal Selling

Personal selling is a paid personal communication that seeks to inform customers and persuade them to purchase products in an exchange situation. The phrase *purchase products* is interpreted broadly to encompass acceptance of ideas and issues. Telemarketing, described in Chapter 16 as direct marketing over the telephone, relies heavily on personal selling. However, negative consumer attitudes and legislation restricting telemarketing have lessened its effectiveness as a personal selling technique.

Personal selling has both advantages and limitations when compared with advertising. Advertising is general communication aimed at a relatively large target audience, whereas personal selling involves more specific communication directed at one or several individuals. Reaching one person through personal selling costs considerably more than through advertising, but personal selling efforts often have greater impact

Sustainable Marketing
Advertising Agencies Go Green

Ad agencies are embracing green marketing as they seek to reduce their environmental impact. Several tools have been invented to help in this endeavor. One example is Clear Sky Digital Media, a free carbon offset calculator for online advertising campaigns. Developed by ad engagement agency IMC[2], Jon Koomy of Stanford University, and Cody Taylor of ICF International, the simple online tool estimates the total cost of carbon credits based on the energy required to support an online campaign. For many marketers, Clear Sky Digital Media's calculator is the first step in recognizing the environmental impact of digital media and ultimately in reducing carbon emissions.

Some marketing companies also offer environmentally friendly promotional services. Advertising agency Union Green works exclusively with green vendors and provides "totally green" print, television, and digital advertising. Union Green also created ratings system called EcoMark that allows companies to label their promotions as eco-friendly.

In addition to providing green services, Union Green operates as a green company. Most of the company's work is virtual, eliminating the need for their employees to commute to work. The company stores most of its photographs and documents as digital files, reducing their paper waste. Union Green uses only 100 percent recycled paper and environmentally friendly printing processes.

The Lab, a productions studio based in Chelsea, New York, participates in several eco-friendly programs. The company recycles computers, ink cartridges, and other industrial products using specially designed Technotrash Cans supplied by GreenDisk. GreenDisk sorts the materials and ensures that intellectual property is destroyed. The Lab also donates $2 for each proof that it creates to the Arbor Day Foundation. In its first year, the program funded 25,000 new trees, which generated 182 tons of clean air.[a]

---

on customers. Personal selling also provides immediate feedback, allowing marketers to adjust their messages to improve communication. It helps them determine and respond to customers' information needs.

When a salesperson and a customer meet face to face, they use several types of interpersonal communication. The predominant communication form is language, both spoken and written. A salesperson and customer frequently use **kinesic communication**, or communication through the movement of head, eyes, arms, hands, legs, or torso. Winking, head nodding, hand gestures, and arm motions are forms of kinesic communication. A good salesperson often can evaluate a prospect's interest in a product or presentation by noting eye contact and head nodding. **Proxemic communication**, a less obvious form of communication used in personal selling situations, occurs when either person varies the physical distance separating them. When a customer backs away from a salesperson, for example, he or she may be displaying a lack of interest in the product or expressing dislike for the salesperson. Touching, or **tactile communication**, is also a form of communication, although less popular in the United States than in many other countries. Handshaking is a common form of tactile communication both in the United States and elsewhere.

Public Relations

Although many promotional activities focus on a firm's customers, other stakeholders—suppliers, employees, stockholders, the media, educators, potential investors,

kinesic communication
Communicating through the movement of head, eyes, arms, hands, legs, or torso

proxemic communication
Communicating by varying the physical distance in face-to-face interactions

tactile communication
Communicating through touching

government officials, and society in general—are important to an organization as well. To communicate with customers and stakeholders, a company employs public relations. Public relations is a broad set of communication efforts used to create and maintain favorable relationships between an organization and its stakeholders. Maintaining a positive relationship with one or more stakeholders can affect a firm's current sales and profits, as well as its long-term survival.

Public relations uses a variety of tools, including annual reports, brochures, event sponsorship, and sponsorship of socially responsible programs aimed at protecting the environment or helping disadvantaged individuals. The goal of public relations is to create and enhance a position image of the organization. Increasingly, marketers are going directly to consumers with their public relations efforts to bypass the traditional media intermediary (newspapers, magazines, and television). Companies like Best Buy have been creating content on YouTube with the goal of bringing viewers into the "geek world" as well as providing tutorial videos on electronics-related issues.[17]

Other tools arise from the use of publicity, which is a component of public relations. Publicity is nonpersonal communication in news-story form about an organization or its products, or both, transmitted through a mass medium at no charge. A few examples of publicity-based public relations tools are news releases, press conferences, and feature articles. To generate publicity, companies sometimes give away products to celebrities in the hope that the celebrity will be seen and photographed with the product, and those photos will stimulate awareness and product trial among their fans. Gift bags for celebrities attending the 82nd Academy Awards included $91,000 worth of trinkets, including a $45,000 safari trip, a $14,500 stay at the Monte Carlo Beach Hotel, as well as other products and services from marketers who hope these celebrities will use their properties, products, or services. There is one problem, though: with the change in tax laws, if you use these gifts, you have to pay taxes on them. Therefore, many celebrities are donating their "swag bags" to charity and getting a tax break in the process, not resulting in the celebrity end use and affiliation that marketers would ultimately like.[18] Ordinarily, public relations efforts are planned and implemented to be consistent with and support other elements of the promotion mix. Public relations efforts may be the responsibility of an individual or of a department within the organization, or the organization may hire an independent public relations agency.

Unpleasant situations and negative events, such as product tampering or an environmental disaster, may generate unfavorable public relations for an organization.

Responsible Marketing?

Using Guerilla Marketing to Create Buzz: To Regulate or Not to Regulate?

ISSUE: Companies are using more invasive forms of sales promotion. Should marketers be more heavily regulated in this area?

Marketers are getting more aggressive in their promotion tactics. Many marketers use "guerilla" and buzz marketing activities to penetrate the clutter and reach consumers. Two companies were perhaps too aggressive in their promotion tactics. The Cartoon Network dropped electronic advertisements for its then upcoming movie *Aqua Teen Hunger Force* in several major markets across the country. Turner Broadcasting Systems never anticipated the response they received in Boston. The devices were dropped from the air and fell on highways, bridges, subway stations, and the Charles River. Witnesses thought Boston was experiencing some sort of terrorist attack. Police and fire squads were mobilized, traffic was disrupted, and general panic ensued. Turner Broadcasting apologized for the misunderstanding and paid $1 million to reimburse federal, state, and local agencies for the cost of the increased mobilization to thwart an alleged terrorism plot and an additional $1 million in goodwill funds for emergency response agencies.

Around this same time, Dr Pepper was promoting a national contest with a top prize of $1 million. It had created a sales promotion where participants could listen for clues and try to find coins that were hidden in cities all over the country. In Boston, a Dr Pepper coin was hidden in the Old Granary Burial Ground cemetery, where Paul Revere and many historic figures are buried. Contestants were told to bring implements to the cemetery to dig up the coin. Needless to say, the outcry was immediate and deafening.

Do you think that marketers should have to receive approval from cities or counties before engaging in these types of tactics to create buzz or publicity? What might be the effect on marketers of such a regulation?[b]

Table 17.3 Product Categories with the Greatest Distribution of Coupons

Product Category	Number of Coupons Issued (in Millions)
1. Combination/personal	13.3
2. Pet food and treats	13.2
3. Household cleaning products	11.5
4. Snacks	11.0
5. Rug/room deodorizer	8.8
6. Vitamins	8.7
7. Cough/cold/sinus/allergy	8.1
8. Hair care	7.5
9. Shaving cream/razor	6.2
10. Antiperspirant/deodorant	6.2

Source: "FSI Coupon Activity Increased 8.0 Percent to More Than 272 Billion Coupons Dropped during 2009," *Marx Promo Intelligence,* January 6, 2010, www.tnsmi-marx.com/news/01062010.htm (accessed March 3, 2010).

For instance, Goldman Sachs has received tremendous negative publicity regarding its excessive compensation packages and its involvement in the global recession. In response, Goldman sought public relations assistance and labeled negative publicity as a new risk factor.[19] Goldman Sachs Group was sued by shareholders for wasting their assets when it paid more than $16 billion to employees in the first three quarters of 2009.[20] To minimize the damaging effects of unfavorable coverage, effective marketers have policies and procedures in place to help manage any public relations problems.

Public relations should not be viewed as a set of tools to be used only during crises. To get the most from public relations, an organization should have someone responsible for public relations either internally or externally and should have an ongoing public relations program.

Sales Promotion

Sales promotion is an activity or material that acts as a direct inducement, offering added value or incentive for the product to resellers, salespeople, or consumers. Examples include free samples, games, rebates, sweepstakes, contests, premiums, and coupons. Old Navy, for example, conducted a supermodelquin search, offering the winner $100,000 and a modelquin (an Old Navy mannequin) cast in his or her image. The company promoted the sweepstakes on its website, in stores, on television, and in print ads.[21] *Sales promotion* should not be confused with *promotion;* sales promotion is just one part of the comprehensive area of promotion. Marketers spend more on sales promotion than on advertising, and sales promotion appears to be a faster-growing area than advertising. Coupons are especially important; Table 17.3 shows the product categories with the greatest distribution of coupons.

Generally, when companies employ advertising or personal selling, they depend on these activities continuously or cyclically. However, a marketer's use of sales promotion tends to be irregular. Many products

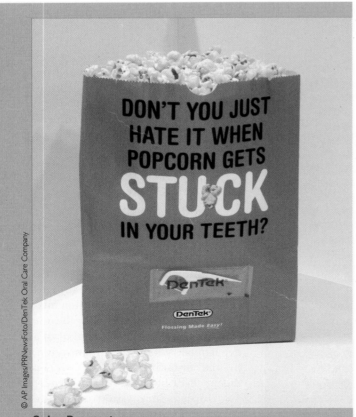

Sales Promotion
DenTek is using this giveaway promotion to encourage trial of its floss pick.

© AP Images/PRNewsFoto/DenTek Oral Care Company

are seasonal. A company such as Toro may offer more sales promotions in August than in the peak selling season of April or May, when more people buy tractors, lawn mowers, and other gardening equipment. Marketers frequently rely on sales promotion to improve the effectiveness of other promotion mix elements, especially advertising and personal selling. Nearly two-thirds of consumers make lists before going shopping, and 51 percent indicate that coupons have a significant effect on their purchasing behavior.[22]

An effective promotion mix requires the right combination of components. To see how such a mix is created, we now examine the factors and conditions affecting the selection of promotional methods that an organization uses for a particular product.

Selecting Promotion Mix Elements

Marketers vary the composition of promotion mixes for many reasons. Although a promotion mix can include all four elements, frequently a marketer selects fewer than four. Many firms that market multiple product lines use several promotion mixes simultaneously.

Promotional Resources, Objectives, and Policies

The size of an organization's promotional budget affects the number and relative intensity of promotional methods included in a promotion mix. If a company's promotional budget is extremely limited, the firm is likely to rely on personal selling because it is easier to measure a salesperson's contribution to sales than to measure the sales effectiveness of advertising. Businesses must have sizable promotional budgets to use regional or national advertising. Procter & Gamble, for example, spends $1,941 million a year on advertising in the United States.[23] Organizations with extensive promotional resources generally include more elements in their promotion mixes, but having more promotional dollars to spend does not necessarily mean using more promotional methods. Researchers have found that resources spent on promotion activities have a positive influence on shareholder value.

An organization's promotional objectives and policies also influence the types of promotion selected. If a company's objective is to create mass awareness of a new convenience good, such as a breakfast cereal, its promotion mix probably leans heavily toward advertising, sales promotion, and possibly public relations. If a company hopes to educate consumers about the features of a durable good, such as a home appliance, its promotion mix may combine a moderate amount of advertising, possibly some sales promotion designed to attract customers to retail stores, and a great deal of personal selling because this method is an efficient way to inform customers about such products. If a firm's objective is to produce immediate sales of nondurable services, the promotion mix will probably stress advertising and sales promotion. For example, dry cleaners and carpet-cleaning firms are more likely to use advertising with a coupon or discount rather than personal selling.

Characteristics of the Target Market

Size, geographic distribution, and demographic characteristics of an organization's target market help dictate the methods to include in a product's promotion mix. To some degree, market size determines composition of the mix. If the size is limited, the promotion mix will probably emphasize personal selling, which can be very effective for reaching small numbers of people. Organizations selling to industrial markets and firms marketing products through only a few wholesalers frequently make personal selling the major component of their promotion mixes. When a product's market consists of millions of customers, organizations rely on advertising and sales promotion because these methods reach masses of people at a low cost per person.

Geographic distribution of a firm's customers also affects the choice of promotional methods. Personal selling is more feasible if a company's customers are concentrated in a small area than if they are dispersed across a vast region. When the company's customers are numerous and dispersed, advertising may be more practical.

Distribution of a target market's demographic characteristics, such as age, income, or education, may affect the types of promotional techniques a marketer selects, as well as the messages and images employed. According to the U.S. Census Bureau, so-called traditional families—those composed of married couples with children—account for fewer than one-quarter of all U.S. households.[24] To reach the more than three-quarters of households consisting of single parents, unmarried couples, singles, and "empty nesters" (whose children have left home), more companies are modifying the images used in their promotions.

Characteristics of the Product

Generally, promotion mixes for business products concentrate on personal selling, whereas advertising plays a major role in promoting consumer goods. This generalization should be treated cautiously, however. Marketers of business products use some advertising to promote products. Advertisements for computers, road-building equipment, and aircrafts are fairly common, and some sales promotion is also used occasionally to promote business products. Personal selling is used extensively for consumer durables, such as home appliances, automobiles, and houses, whereas consumer convenience items are promoted mainly through advertising and sales promotion. Public relations appears in promotion mixes for both business and consumer products.

Marketers of highly seasonal products often emphasize advertising, and sometimes sales promotion as well, because off-season sales generally will not support an extensive year-round sales force. Although most toy producers have sales forces to sell to resellers, many of these companies depend chiefly on advertising to promote their products.

A product's price also influences the composition of the promotion mix. High-priced products call for personal selling because consumers associate greater risk with the purchase of such products and usually want information from a salesperson. For low-priced convenience items, marketers use advertising rather than personal selling. Research suggests that consumers visiting a store specifically to purchase a product on sale are more likely to have read flyers and to have purchased other sale-priced products than consumers visiting the same store for other reasons.[25]

Another consideration in creating an effective promotion mix is the stage of the product life cycle. During the introduction stage, much advertising may be necessary for both business and consumer products to make potential users aware of them. Sharp introduced Quattron technology through a significant advertising campaign for its AQUOS LCD televisions, which educated consumers on the benefits of adding yellow to the color filter in addition to the RGB filters of red, yellow, and green. The benefits to consumers included exceptionally high quality pictures and reduced energy consumption.[26] For many products, personal selling and sales promotion are also helpful in this stage. In the growth and maturity stages, consumer services require heavy emphasis on advertising, whereas business products often call for a concentration of personal selling and some sales promotion. In the decline stage, marketers usually decrease all promotional activities, especially advertising.

Intensity of market coverage is still another factor affecting the composition of the promotion mix. When products are marketed through intensive distribution, firms depend strongly on advertising and sales promotion. Many convenience products like lotions, cereals, and coffee are promoted through samples, coupons, and money refunds. When marketers choose selective distribution, promotion mixes vary considerably. Items handled through exclusive distribution, such as expensive watches, furs, and high-quality furniture, typically require a significant amount of personal selling.

A product's use also affects the combination of promotional methods. Manufacturers of highly personal products, such as laxatives, nonprescription contraceptives, and feminine hygiene products, depend on advertising because many customers do not want to talk with salespeople about these products.

Costs and Availability of Promotional Methods

Costs of promotional methods are major factors to analyze when developing a promotion mix. National advertising and sales promotion require large expenditures. However, if these efforts succeed in reaching extremely large audiences, the cost per individual reached may be quite small, possibly a few pennies. Some forms of advertising are relatively inexpensive. Many small, local businesses advertise products through local newspapers, magazines, radio and television stations, outdoor displays, search engine result ads, and signs on mass transit vehicles.

Another consideration that marketers explore when formulating a promotion mix is availability of promotional techniques. Despite the tremendous number of media vehicles in the United States, a firm may find that no available advertising medium effectively reaches a certain target market. The problem of media availability becomes more pronounced when marketers advertise in foreign countries. Some media, such as television, simply may not be available, or advertising on television may be illegal. In addition, regulations or standards for media content may be restrictive in varying global outlets. For instance, European fashion magazines are increasingly either mandating that "real women" be used in ads (not unrealistically proportioned models) and/or that when an ad has been altered to change a person's physical appearance, this change must be noted on the ad.[27] In some countries, advertisers are forbidden to make brand comparisons on television. Other promotional methods also have limitations. For instance, a firm may wish to increase its sales force but is unable to find qualified personnel.

Product Characteristics
Inexpensive, frequently purchased convenience products usually require the manufacturers to include significant levels of advertising in their promotion mixes.

Push and Pull Channel Policies

Another element that marketers consider when planning a promotion mix is whether to use a push policy or a pull policy. With a **push policy**, the producer promotes the product only to the next institution down the marketing channel. In a marketing channel with wholesalers and retailers, the producer promotes to the wholesaler because, in this case, the wholesaler is the channel member just below the producer (see Figure 17.4). Each channel member in turn promotes to the next channel member. A push policy normally stresses personal selling. Sometimes sales promotion and advertising are used in conjunction with personal selling to push the products down through the channel.

As Figure 17.4 shows, a firm that uses a **pull policy** promotes directly to consumers to develop strong consumer demand for its products. It does so primarily through advertising and sales promotion. Because consumers are persuaded to seek the products in retail stores, retailers in turn go to wholesalers or the producers to buy the products. This policy is intended to pull the goods down through the channel by creating demand at the consumer level. Consumers are told that if the stores don't have it, ask them to get it.

Push and pull policies are not mutually exclusive. At times, an organization uses both simultaneously.

push policy Promoting a product only to the next institution down the marketing channel

pull policy Promoting a product directly to consumers to develop strong consumer demand that pulls products through the marketing channel

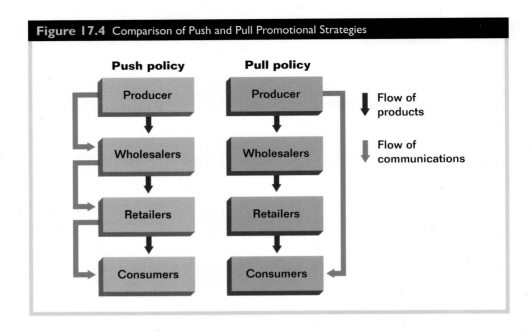

Figure 17.4 Comparison of Push and Pull Promotional Strategies

The Growing Importance of Word-of-Mouth Communications

When making decisions about the composition of promotion mixes, marketers should recognize that commercial messages, whether from advertising, personal selling, sales promotion, or public relations, are limited in the extent to which they can inform and persuade customers and move them closer to making purchases. Depending on the type of customers and the products involved, buyers to some extent rely on word-of-mouth communication from personal sources such as family members and friends. **Word-of-mouth communication** is personal, informal exchanges of communication that customers share with one another about products, brands, and companies. Most customers are likely to be influenced by friends and family members when they make purchases. Word-of-mouth communication is very important when people are selecting restaurants and entertainment along with automotive, medical, legal, banking, and personal services such as hair care. Research has identified a link between word-of-mouth communication and new-customer acquisition when there is customer involvement and satisfaction.[28] Effective marketers who understand the importance of word-of-mouth communication attempt to identify opinion leaders and encourage them to try their products in the hope that they will spread favorable publicity about them. Apple Computer, for example, has long relied on its nearly cult consumer following to spread by word of mouth their satisfaction with Apple products such as PowerBooks, iPods, iPhones, and iPads.

In addition, customers are increasingly going online for information and opinions about goods and services as well as about the companies. Electronic word of mouth is communicating about products through websites, blogs, e-mail, social networks, or online forums. Users can go to a number of consumer-oriented websites, such as epinions.com and consumerreview.com. At these sites, they can learn about other consumers' feelings toward and experiences with specific products; some sites even encourage consumers to rate products they have tried. Users can also search within product categories and compare consumers' viewpoints on various brands and models. Not surprisingly, research has identified credibility as the most important attribute of

word-of-mouth communication Personal informal exchanges of communication that customers share with one another about products, brands, and companies

a ratings website and found reducing risk and saving search effort to be the primary motives for using such sites.[29] Buyers can peruse Internet-based newsgroups, forums, and blogs to find word-of-mouth information. A consumer looking for a new cell phone service, for example, might inquire in forums about other participants' experiences and level of satisfaction to gain more information before making a purchase decision. A recent Nielsen Global Online Consumer Survey found that 90 percent of consumers trust recommendations they get from their friends, while 70 percent trust consumer comments posted online.[30]

Electronic word of mouth is particularly important to consumers staying abreast of trends. Hundreds of blogs (such as TechCrunch, Perez Hilton, and Tree Hugger) play an essential role in propagating electronic word-of-mouth communications about everything from gossip to politics to consumer goods. They provide consumers with information on trends, reviews of products, and other information on what is new, exciting, and fashionable for consumers. These sites have become so influential in introducing consumers to new products and shaping their views about them that marketers are increasingly monitoring them to identify new trends; some firms have even attempted to influence users' votes on their favorite items. Marketers increasingly must court bloggers,

Marketing in Transition
Hulu.com Gives Advertisers Viewers When and How They Want Them

Free movies and television shows used to only be available on network television stations. Now they seem to be everywhere, including on Hulu.com. Founded in 2007, Hulu provides TV and movie viewers with access to content from almost 200 media companies. Content is free and legal, thanks to Hulu's advertising agreements and the permission it solicits to distribute all content. The site is also designed to direct users to resources offering content not found on Hulu. With a mission to provide viewers with content when and how they want it, the site has been popular with viewers and advertisers. Hulu is already profitable, generating more than $200 million in the last year, and is set to become even more so in the future.

As communication via the Internet grows, advertising is transitioning from traditional television to online media viewing. Hulu, functioning thanks to advertising, is a major player in this change. It took some convincing, but advertisers eventually saw the appeal of Hulu. Because Hulu limits advertising to one advertiser per show/film, ads are repeated, meaning viewers will see them more than once while they watch a show. Users can also make choices about how they view the ads and vote on the ads they see. This gives companies valuable feedback. An added benefit is word-of-mouth promotion and viral marketing—as users view shows/films, they can share them with friends via word of mouth, e-mail, and social networking sites, thereby spreading the ads as they share. Many traditional television viewers use TiVo or a DVR (digital video recorder) to skip commercials altogether or use commercial breaks to head to the restroom or grab a snack. On Hulu, viewers are far more likely to actually watch the commercial breaks because they are short and viewers cannot fast forward through or skip them. Advertising has increased with Hulu's growth, and, for the time being, users are tolerating the ad breaks.

Networks, movies, and television shows benefit from Hulu as well. For example, *The Simpsons* has been a hit on 20th Century Fox for almost 20 years, but traditional television viewers are dwindling. However, *The Simpsons* has experienced a second life through on-demand views on Hulu. *PCWorld* recently noted that ad rates for the show on Hulu are $20 to $40 per thousand viewers higher than they are for prime time television. Some speculate that free services like Hulu may not remain free for long, but, for the time-being, Hulu gives no indication that it will change its model. It is profitable and popular as is.[c]

Entrepreneurial Marketing
Comic Book Marketing Creates Buzz

Andrew Sinkov got into comic books as an adult and is now in charge of marketing for CoreStreet, a Cambridge, Massachusetts, security software company that markets PIVMAN™, a handheld computer system for emergency workers. Not the most exciting technology product, the PIVMAN™ required a creative communications strategy to build good buzz or word-of-mouth hype about the product. So, he hired an artist to draw a 12-page comic book that explained technical information about the product and included characters for educational training. In fact, CoreStreet's popular comic book is generating potential buyers at twice the rate of other marketing materials. The company was able to land part of a security contract with the city of Los Angeles as well as attract many other customers through comic book buzz.[d]

© Theo Wargo/WireImage/Getty Images

Viral Marketing
The use of celebrities in advertising and promotion can help generate awareness and buzz.

who wield growing influence over consumer perception of companies, products, and services.

Buzz marketing is an attempt to incite publicity and public excitement surrounding a product through a creative event. For instance, when the Barbie doll turned 50, Mattel went all out by launching a Barbie fashion show as part of New York's Fashion Week. Heidi Klum and other celebrities attended a party at Barbie's Malibu mansion.[31]

Buzz marketing works best as a part of an integrated marketing communication program that also uses advertising, personal selling, sales promotion, and publicity. However, marketers should also take care that buzz marketing campaigns do not violate any laws or have the potential to be misconstrued and cause undue alarm. Columbia Pictures, for example, created a false website entitled Institute for Human Continuity to help advertise its end-of-the-world movie *2012*. The site alluded to 25 years worth of threats toward humans and scared a number of people who then contacted NASA to see what could be done. NASA had to launch its own site to counteract the false site's information.[32]

Viral marketing is a strategy to get consumers to share a marketer's message, often through e-mail or online video, in a way that spreads dramatically and quickly. The Australian Government used viral marketing to attract a caretaker/video blogger for islands in the Great Barrier Reef. Although originally announced on Reuters, the government then used a host of social media sites to attract attention. The contest site attracted more than 34,000 applicants and generated more than $70 million in publicity dollars.[33] [It is important to realize, however, that it is the public that determines whether something is interesting enough to "go viral."]

Word of mouth, no matter how it is transmitted, is not effective in all product categories. It seems to be most effective for new-to-market and more expensive products. Despite the obvious benefits of positive word of mouth, marketers must also recognize the potential dangers of negative word of mouth. This is particularly important in dealing with online platforms that can reach more people and encourage consumers to "gang up" on a company or product. For example, the second largest national music downloading site, eMusic, has long been known and loved for its commitment to independent music, artists, and labels. When the company decided to welcome mainstream Sony BMG's catalog into the mix, loyal users were irate and freely shared their feelings on eMusic's message boards. When the company also discretely announced price hikes, users became more furious. Many users left or threatened to leave for another site. Although CEO Danny Stein knew the company would face backlash, he did not expect the level of anger felt by many users. The company hasn't yet recovered from the results of its choices, but it has learned a great deal from the experience in terms of the need for transparency and open communication with your customers.[34]

Product Placement

A growing technique for reaching consumers is the selective placement of products within the context of television programs viewed by the target market. **Product placement** is a form of advertising that strategically locates products or product promotions within entertainment media to reach the product's target markets. When Volvo was looking for a movie placement to promote their XC60 Crossover, it became the vehicle of Edward Cullen in *Twilight: New Moon*. Volvo ran significant integrated marketing communication to connect the popular film character to their vehicle, including a website, whatdrivesedward.com, which offered chances to win promotional items. In addition, Volvo used Facebook, Twitter, YouTube, and Flickr to spread promotional messages about its products.[35] Such product placement has become more important due to the increasing fragmentation of television viewers who have ever-expanding viewing options and technology that can screen advertisements (e.g., digital video recorders such as TiVo). Researchers have found that 60 to 80 percent of digital video recorder users skip over the commercials when they replay programming.[36]

In-program product placements have been successful in reaching consumers as they are being entertained rather than in the competitive commercial break time periods. In one season of the *Celebrity Apprentice*, contestants were asked to create a store front for Kodak. When products become the center of a program such as the *Apprentice* series, viewers gain greater insights into the products, benefits, and target market. For example, viewers were invited to interact with the show by submitting their favorite "Kodak Moment" from an episode. Winners were selected weekly from this online contest.[37] Reality programming in particular has been a natural fit for product placements because

buzz marketing An attempt to incite publicity and public excitement surrounding a product through a creative event

viral marketing A strategy to get consumers to share a marketer's message, often through e-mail or online videos, in a way that spreads dramatically and quickly

product placement The strategic location of products or product promotions within entertainment media content to reach the product's target market

Product Placement Coca-Cola cups and products on *American Idol* are an example of product placement.

Consumers Report They Have "Some Degree of Trust" in the Following Forms of Promotion

- Editorial content — 69%
- Brand websites — 70%
- Consumer opinions posted online — 70%
- Recommendations from known people — 90%

(Scale: 0, 20, 40, 60, 80, 100)

Source: Nielsen Wire, "Global Advertising: Consumers Trust Real Friends and Virtual Strangers the Most," July 7, 2009, http://blog.nielsen.com/nielsenwire/consumer/(accessed March 3, 2010).

of the close interchange between the participants and the product (e.g., Sears and *Extreme Makeover Home Edition*; Levi's, Burger King, Marquis Jet, Dove and *The Apprentice*; Coca-Cola and *American Idol*). For instance, at the top of its 2010 season, *Biggest Loser* managed to feature Subway, 24 Hour Fitness, Extra gum, and Ziploc.[38]

Product placement is not limited to U.S. television shows. The European Parliament greenlighted limited use of product placement, albeit only during certain types of programs and only if consumers were informed at the beginning of the segment that companies had paid to have their products displayed. In general, the notion of product placement has not been favorably viewed in Europe and has been particularly controversial in the United Kingdom. However, British viewers have already been exposed to product placement within shows that have been imported from the United States, including *Desperate Housewives, The OC,* and *American Idol.*[39]

Criticisms and Defenses of Promotion

Even though promotional activities can help customers make informed purchasing decisions, social scientists, consumer groups, government agencies, and members of society in general have long criticized promotion. There are two main reasons for such criticism: promotion does have flaws, and it is a highly visible business activity that pervades our daily lives. Although complaints about too much promotional activity are almost universal, a number of more specific criticisms have been lodged. In this section, we discuss some of the criticisms and defenses of promotion.

Is Promotion Deceptive?

One common criticism of promotion is that it is deceptive and unethical. During the 19th and early 20th centuries, much promotion was blatantly deceptive. Although no longer widespread, some deceptive promotion still occurs. AT&T dropped a lawsuit against Verizon whereby Verizon indicated that its 3G coverage was superior to that of AT&T. There was speculation that AT&T was doubtful that it could win the lawsuit and was concerned that the suit provided more promotion for the differential advantage of Verizon over AT&T.[40] Many industries suffer from claims of deception from time to time. One industry that is seemingly constantly bombarded with truthfulness claims is the diet products and exercise equipment industry. Some promotions are unintentionally deceiving; for instance, when advertising to children, it is easy to mislead them because they are more naive than adults and less able to separate fantasy from reality. A promotion may also mislead some receivers because words can have diverse meanings for different people. However, not all promotion should be condemned because a small portion is flawed. Laws, government regulation, and industry self-regulation have helped decrease deceptive promotion.

Does Promotion Increase Prices?

Promotion is also criticized for raising prices, but in fact it often tends to lower them. The ultimate purpose of promotion is to stimulate demand. If it does, the business should be able to produce and market products in larger quantities and thus reduce per-unit production and marketing costs, which can result in lower prices. For example, as demand for flat-screen TVs and MP3 players has increased, their prices have dropped.

When promotion fails to stimulate demand, the price of the promoted product increases because promotion costs must be added to other costs. Promotion also helps keep prices lower by facilitating price competition. When firms advertise prices, their prices tend to remain lower than when they are not promoting prices. Gasoline pricing illustrates how promotion fosters price competition. Service stations with the highest prices seldom have highly visible price signs.

Does Promotion Create Needs?

Some critics of promotion claim that it manipulates consumers by persuading them to buy products they do not need, hence creating "artificial" needs. In his theory of motivation, Abraham Maslow (discussed in Chapter 7) indicates that an individual tries to satisfy five levels of needs: physiological needs, such as hunger, thirst, and sex; safety needs; needs for love and affection; needs for self-esteem and respect from others; and self-actualization needs, or the need to realize one's potential. When needs are viewed in this context, it is difficult to demonstrate that promotion creates them. If there were no promotional activities, people would still have needs for food, water, sex, safety, love, affection, self-esteem, respect from others, and self-actualization.

Although promotion may not create needs, it does capitalize on them (which may be why some critics believe promotion creates needs). Many marketers base their appeals on these needs. For instance, several mouthwash, toothpaste, and perfume advertisements associate these products with needs for love, affection, and respect. These advertisers rely on human needs in their messages, but they do not create the needs.

Does Promotion Encourage Materialism?

Another frequent criticism of promotion is that it leads to materialism. The purpose of promoting goods is to persuade people to buy them; thus, if promotion works, consumers will want to buy more and more things. Marketers assert that values are instilled in the home and that promotion does not change people into materialistic consumers. However, the behavior of today's children and teenagers contradicts this view; many insist on high-priced, brand name apparel such as Gucci, Coach, and Ralph Lauren.

Does Promotion Help Customers without Costing Too Much?

Every year, firms spend billions of dollars for promotion. The question is whether promotion helps customers enough to be worth the cost. Consumers do benefit because promotion informs them about product uses, features, advantages, prices, and locations where they can buy the products. Consumers thus gain more knowledge about available products and can make more intelligent buying decisions. Promotion also informs consumers about services—for instance, health care, educational programs, and day care—as well as about important social, political, and health-related issues. For example, several organizations, such as the California Department of Health Services, inform people about the health hazards associated with tobacco use.

Should Potentially Harmful Products Be Promoted?

Finally, some critics of promotion, including consumer groups and government officials, suggest that certain products should not be promoted at all. Primary targets are products associated with violence and other possibly unhealthy activities, such as handguns, alcohol, and tobacco. Cigarette advertisements, for example, promote smoking, a behavior proven to be harmful and even deadly. Tobacco companies, which spend billions on promotion, have countered criticism of their advertising by pointing out that advertisements for red meat and coffee are not censured even though these products may also cause health problems. Those who defend such promotion assert that as long as it is legal to sell a product, promoting that product should be allowed.

summary

1. To describe the nature of integrated marketing communications

Integrated marketing communications is the coordination of promotion and other marketing efforts to ensure maximum informational and persuasive impact on customers.

2. To examine the process of communication

Communication is a sharing of meaning. The communication process involves several steps. First, the source translates meaning into code, a process known as coding or encoding. The source should employ signs or symbols familiar to the receiver or audience. The coded message is sent through a communications channel to the receiver or audience. The receiver or audience then decodes the message and usually supplies feedback to the source. When the decoded message differs from the encoded one, a condition called noise exists.

3. To understand the role and objectives of promotion

Promotion is communication to build and maintain relationships by informing and persuading one or more audiences. Although promotional objectives vary from one organization to another and within organizations over time, eight primary objectives underlie many promotional programs. Promotion aims to create awareness of a new product, a new brand, or an existing product; to stimulate primary and selective demand; to encourage product trial through the use of free samples, coupons, limited free-use offers, contests, and games; to identify prospects; to retain loyal customers; to facilitate reseller support; to combat competitive promotional efforts; and to reduce sales fluctuations.

4. To explore the elements of the promotion mix

The promotion mix for a product may include four major promotional methods: advertising, personal selling, public relations, and sales promotion. Advertising is paid nonpersonal communication about an organization and its products transmitted to a target audience through a mass medium. Personal selling is paid personal communication that attempts to inform customers and persuade them to purchase products in an exchange situation. Public relations is a broad set of communication efforts used to create and maintain favorable relationships between an organization and its stakeholders. Sales promotion is an activity or material that acts as a direct inducement, offering added value or incentive for the product, to resellers, salespeople, or consumers.

5. To examine the selection of promotion mix elements

The promotional methods used in a product's promotion mix are determined by the organization's promotional resources, objectives, and policies; characteristics of the target market; characteristics of the product; and cost and availability of promotional methods. Marketers also consider whether to use a push policy or a pull policy. With a push policy, the producer promotes the product only to the next institution down the marketing channel. Normally, a push policy stresses personal selling. Firms that use a pull policy promote directly to consumers, with the intention of developing strong consumer demand for the products. Once consumers are persuaded to seek the products in retail stores, retailers go to wholesalers or the producer to buy the products.

6. To understand word-of-mouth communication and how it affects promotion

Most customers are likely to be influenced by friends and family members when making purchases. Word-of-mouth communication is personal, informal exchanges of communication that customers share with one another about products, brands, and companies. Customers may also choose to go online to find electronic word of mouth about products or companies. Buzz marketing is an attempt to incite publicity and public excitement surrounding a product through a creative event. Viral marketing is a strategy to get consumers to share a marketer's message, often through e-mail or online videos, in a way that spreads dramatically and quickly.

7. To understand product placement promotions

Product placement is the strategic location of products or product promotions within television program content to reach the product's target market. In-program product placements have been successful in reaching consumers as they are being entertained rather than in the competitive commercial break time periods.

8. To examine criticisms and defenses of promotion

Promotional activities can help consumers make informed purchasing decisions, but they have also evoked many criticisms. Promotion has been accused of deception. Although some deceiving or misleading promotions do exist, laws, government regulation, and industry self-regulation minimize deceptive promotion. Promotion has been blamed for increasing prices, but it usually tends to lower them. When demand is high, production and marketing costs decrease, which can result in lower prices. Moreover, promotion helps keep prices lower by facilitating

price competition. Other criticisms of promotional activity are that it manipulates consumers into buying products they do not need, that it leads to a more materialistic society, and that consumers do not benefit sufficiently from promotional activity to justify its high cost. Finally, some critics of promotion suggest that potentially harmful products, especially those associated with violence, sex, and unhealthy activities, should not be promoted at all.

Go to **www.cengagebrain.com** for resources to help you master the content in this chapter as well as materials that will expand your marketing knowledge!

important terms

integrated marketing communications, 506	decoding process, 509	selective demand, 512	push policy, 521
communication, 507	noise, 509	promotion mix, 514	pull policy, 521
source, 507	feedback, 509	kinesic communication, 516	word-of-mouth communication, 522
receiver, 507	channel capacity, 510	proxemic communication, 516	buzz marketing, 525
coding process, 507	promotion, 510		viral marketing, 525
communications channel, 508	primary demand, 512	tactile communication, 516	product placement, 525
	pioneer promotion, 512		

discussion and review questions

1. What does the term *integrated marketing communications* mean?

2. Define *communication* and describe the communication process. Is it possible to communicate without using all the elements in the communication process? If so, which elements can be omitted?

3. Identify several causes of noise. How can a source reduce noise?

4. What is the major task of promotion? Do firms ever use promotion to accomplish this task and fail? If so, give several examples.

5. Describe the possible objectives of promotion and discuss the circumstances under which each objective might be used.

6. Identify and briefly describe the four promotional methods an organization can use in its promotion mix.

7. What forms of interpersonal communication besides language can be used in personal selling?

8. How do target market characteristics determine which promotional methods to include in a promotion mix?

Assume a company is planning to promote a cereal to both adults and children. Along what major dimensions would these two promotional efforts have to differ from each other?

9. How can a product's characteristics affect the composition of its promotion mix?

10. Evaluate the following statement: "Appropriate advertising media are always available if a company can afford them."

11. Explain the difference between a pull policy and a push policy. Under what conditions should each policy be used?

12. In which ways can word-of-mouth communication influence the effectiveness of a promotion mix for a product?

13. Which criticisms of promotion do you believe are the most valid? Why?

14. Should organizations be allowed to promote offensive, violent, sexual, or unhealthy products that can be legally sold and purchased? Support your answer.

application questions

CRITICAL THINKING

1. The overall objective of promotion is to stimulate demand for a product. Through television advertising, the American Dairy Association promotes the benefits of drinking milk, a campaign that aims to stimulate primary demand. Advertisements for a specific brand of milk focus on stimulating selective demand. Identify two television commercials, one aimed at stimulating primary demand and one aimed at stimulating selective demand. Describe each commercial and discuss how each attempts to achieve its objective.

2. Developing a promotion mix is contingent on many factors, including the type of product and the product's attributes. Which of the four promotional methods—advertising, personal selling, public relations, or sales promotion—would you emphasize if you were developing the promotion mix for the following products? Explain your answers.

a. Washing machine
b. Cereal
c. Halloween candy
d. Compact disc

3. Suppose marketers at Falcon International Corporation have come to you for recommendations on how to promote their products. They want to develop a comprehensive promotional campaign and have a generous budget with which to implement their plans. What questions would you ask them, and what would you suggest they consider before developing a promotional program?

4. Marketers must consider whether to use a push or a pull policy when deciding on a promotion mix (see Figure 17.4). Identify a product for which marketers should use each policy and a third product that might best be promoted using a mix of the two policies. Explain your answers.

internet exercise

MySpace

MySpace is not just for friends. It is also a unique promotional platform for musical artists, especially unsigned and independent artists. By creating a MySpace page, musicians can share their songs, post important dates, or even blog. MySpace music pages are different from record company websites because they feel more personal. Artists also take advantage of MySpace's viral nature by allowing other MySpace members to post their pictures, songs, and music videos on their own MySpace profile pages. Visit the website at **http://music.myspace.com,** and look for your favorite artist or discover a new one.

1. Who is the target market for members?
2. What is being promoted to these individuals?
3. What are the promotional objectives of this website?
4. Is word-of-mouth communication occurring at this website? Explain.

developing your marketing plan

CRITICAL THINKING

A vital component of a successful marketing strategy is the company's plan for communication to its stakeholders. One segment of the communication plan is included in the marketing mix as the promotional element. A clear understanding of the role that promotion plays, as well as the various methods of promotion, is important in developing the promotional plan. The following questions should assist you in relating the information in this chapter to several decisions in your marketing plan.

1. Review the communication process in Figure 17.1. Identify the various players in the communication process for promotion of your product.

2. What are your objectives for promotion? Use Table 17.2 as a guide in answering this question.

3. Which of the four elements of the promotional mix are most appropriate for accomplishing your objectives? Discuss the advantages and disadvantages of each.

4. What role should word-of-mouth communications, buzz marketing, or product placement play in your promotional plan?

The information obtained from these questions should assist you in developing various aspects of your marketing plan found in the *Interactive Marketing Plan* exercise at **www.cengagebrain.com.**

VIDEO CASE 17.1

The Toledo Mud Hens Make Marketing Fun

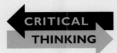

CRITICAL THINKING

Since their dismal beginnings in 1896 when they played near a swamp (earning the name Mud Hens in honor of the coots inhabiting the marshy land), the Triple-A Toledo Mud Hens have become one of the most successful minor league baseball teams in the country, and their games some of the best attended. How did they leverage their climb from such a murky start? In a word: marketing. With their two slogans, "Toledo's Family Fun Park" and "Experience the Joy of Mudville," the Mud Hens harness the twin themes of family and history. These days, the Mud Hens are the Triple-A affiliate of the major league team the Detroit Tigers. Because the Tigers do all of the hiring and firing of players, trainers, and medical staff, the Mud Hens' home office can focus all of its energy on improving the image and profitability of the Mud Hens enterprise.

The Mud Hens do not have the star power of the major league teams (aside from their popular bird mascots, Muddy and Muddonna), so marketers must seek another way to promote the games. They advertise the games as wholesome, affordable family fun—an alternative to bowling or going to the movies. People of all ages can come to the games and socialize, while watching potential up-and-coming baseball stars develop into mature athletes. Because there is no star paraphernalia to sell, most of the marketing attention is paid to promoting Mud Hens merchandise, like T-shirts and hats, and food and beverage sales. In fact, the team has been the league leader in ballpark merchandise sales since 2000. The on-premise Swampshop offers dozens of styles of T-shirts and baseball caps in all sizes. Truly avid fans can shop online from anywhere in the world. As fans wear the merchandise, it creates good word-of-mouth advertising and buzz about the team.

The league's continued sales and revenue growth stand in contrast to an overall downturn in attendance and purchases at minor league baseball games. This statistic attests to the strength of the Mud Hens' marketing strategy. They market directly to advance ticket buyers in order to target those people who are apt to buy tickets early, buy in quantity, and spend cash at the games. Other marketing channels include radio, television, print media, and even Facebook. The Mud Hens enjoy an especially close relationship with local newspapers,

where a prominent story about the team is almost guaranteed whenever the Mud Hens have a home game.

Even in the midst of a recession, the Toldeo Mud Hens managed to boost revenues by incorporating a new network to integrate its e-mail platform with other applications. This ability allows the Mud Hens to target segments of its customer base with tailored messages. For example, in 2009, three of the Mud Hen suite rentals were available, without any obvious takers. By using the new system to identify customers who had clicked on the online suite rental links in the past six months, the Mud Hens sent e-mails to 50 to 60 specific people to inform them about the rentals' vacancies. All three suites were rented that same day. By integrating this new system into its marketing communications strategy, the Mud Hens are able to coordinate promotional and marketing efforts to have maximum impact on customers.

In addition to its successful marketing strategies, the Mud Hens have become an integral part of the community—through direct marketing and regular media coverage, but also through charitable endeavors. Because the marketing focus is so much on family fun, community, and socializing, the organization does its best to give back to the community that so avidly supports them. The organization engages in educational and community outreach through various programs such as Muddy's Knothole Club, which provides tickets to underprivileged kids; regular fundraisers and auctions; and donations to local charities. Even pro-bono activities such as these can be part of a well-managed, integrated marketing communications strategy because they increase goodwill toward the organization and encourage people to attend games.[41]

QUESTIONS FOR DISCUSSION

1. How do the Toledo Mud Hens use integrated marketing communications to promote their enterprise?
2. How do the Mud Hens identify and market to their target audience?
3. Suggest how the Mud Hens can gain publicity in order to maintain and increase attendance.

CASE 17.2

At Southwest Airlines, "We Love Your Bags"

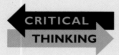

CRITICAL THINKING

Although Southwest Airlines started small, today it is one of the largest airlines in the country, flying to 69 cities on more than 3,200 flights a day. The Texas-based company prides itself on its sense of humor and down-home attitude, which has been developed and advanced over the years through advertising, promotions, and public relations programs. Its national advertising campaigns ("You are now free to move about the country" and "We Love Your Bags") are success stories. This is the airline that once paid an Elvis impersonator to serenade customers at the Manchester, New Hampshire, airport to celebrate its addition of flights to Las Vegas; the airline that paints some of its fleet in state colors, with its recent addition of Florida One decorated with colors and symbols from the Florida flag. Southwest's vision is to be a low-budget airline that enables its customers to have fun flying.

The corporate culture owes a lot to the outgoing personality of the airline's co-founder, Herb Kelleher. But humor also serves as a way to make cheap travel more palatable. The Southwest Way that employees are encouraged to adopt includes displaying a Warrior Spirit, a Servant's Heart, and a Fun-LUVing attitude. It is typical for Southwest flight crews to joke with the passengers. These tactics build worldwide customer allegiance. The airline also tries to engage its customers in dialogue with its Nuts About Southwest blog and its social media presence on sites such as Facebook, LinkedIn, and Twitter.

Southwest's "Ding" promotion is a terrific example of its use of integrated marketing communication. Customers can download software from the airline's website, and when Southwest offers a low fare it notifies them with a "ding" sound—the same "ding" you hear when airline captains turn off the seatbelt sign; the same "ding" that precedes Southwest's well-known tagline, "You are now free to move about the

country." Southwest also caters to pet-LUVing customers through its P.A.W.S. program, which allows passengers with small pets to take their pets into the airline cabin (in a carrier) for $75 each way.

Southwest's recent campaign "Grab Your Bag. It's On!" emphasizes Southwest's bags-fly-free policy. Southwest Airlines allows passengers to check two bags free per customer, while most other airlines charge $15 to $25 each for checked bags (the prices go up as the amount of bags increases). Baggage fees for airlines generated about $2 billion for the first nine months of 2009, but at the cost of customer satisfaction with airlines. Many passengers are avoiding checking their luggage and are instead opting to take carry-on baggage. However, more carry-on baggage has been problematic as well, occasionally resulting in flight attendants becoming injured when removing heavy carry-on bags from the overhead bins. As a result, Spirit Airlines will become the first airline to charge for carry-on bags.

Southwest is capitalizing on customer discontent over bagging fees by integrating it with the recession. CEO Gary C. Kelly stated that "it's time to kick the recession to the curb with 'Grab Your Bag. It's On!'" Southwest is positioning itself as an airline that wants to save consumers money in difficult time periods. This is made even more apparent in Southwest commercials that criticize competing airlines, asking, "Why do they hate your bags?" And, of course, Southwest Airlines instilled its customary humor in its commercials as well. One of the "It's On!" commercials featured Southwest Airlines rampers proclaiming how much they love bags and waving goodbye to bags as the plane takes off. In 2010, Southwest announced plans to launch new ads that will carry on the bags-fly-free campaign but will also expand the ads to include even more of the positive experiences Southwest provides for its customers.

These fun campaigns are creative, but do they work? More importantly, are the revenues that Southwest forgoes from its two-bags-fly-free policy justified by an increased market share? Southwest seems to think so. In 2009, the airline recorded a record full-load factor of 76 percent and an increase of $1 billion in market share. These positive results are thought to have come at least in part from the "Grab Your Bag. It's On!" campaign. Through effective integrated marketing, Southwest has been able to launch successful campaigns, gain market share, and thrive even during the most recent recession.[42]

QUESTIONS FOR DISCUSSION

1. Describe the various promotion elements that Southwest Airlines uses in its integrated marketing communications.

2. How does the engaging and entertaining performance of Southwest flight crews contribute to promotion activities?

3. How has Southwest Airlines positioned its advertising by focusing on simple concepts such as "We Love Your Bags" and "Grab Your Bag. It's On!"?

Chapter 18

Advertising and Public Relations

OBJECTIVES

1. To describe the nature and types of advertising
2. To explore the major steps in developing an advertising campaign
3. To identify who is responsible for developing advertising campaigns
4. To examine the tools used in public relations
5. To analyze how public relations is used and evaluated

Is 3-D the Future?

Three-dimensional, or 3-D, advertising is becoming more popular in movie theaters, especially before high-profile films like *Avatar* and *Up*. 3-D advertisements catch the attention of audiences before major 3-D films.

But is 3-D advertising ready for television? In 2009, only 1 million of America's 115 million television viewing households were equipped to view 3-D, according to the Consumer Electronics Association. However, experts predict that Americans will buy 4.3 million 3-D compatible televisions in 2010 and that 3-D TVs will represent 25 percent of all television sales by 2013. Furthermore, television companies are starting to embrace 3-D. Cable programmers ESPN and The Discovery Channel both plan to launch 3-D channels in 2010 and 2011.

However, many marketers are skeptical about the future of 3-D. 3-D technology is expensive for home viewers. A 3-D compatible television may cost more than $2,000. 3-D televisions also require viewers to wear goofy glasses. Furthermore, producing a 3-D commercial is expensive. Screenvision, a cinema-media company, charges $20,000 to $70,000 to convert a traditional commercial into 3-D. The Air Force spent more than $1 million creating a 3-D commercial. Until 3-D technology catches up with the needs of home consumers and becomes less expensive, it may appear only in theaters.[1]

Both large organizations and small companies use conventional and online promotional efforts such as advertising to change their corporate images, launch new products, or promote current brands. In this chapter, we explore several dimensions of advertising and public relations. First, we focus on the nature and types of advertising. Next, we examine the major steps in developing an advertising campaign and describe who is responsible for developing such campaigns. We then discuss the nature of public relations and how it is used. We examine various public relations tools and ways to evaluate the effectiveness of public relations. Finally, we focus on how companies deal with unfavorable public relations.

The Nature and Types of Advertising

Advertising permeates our daily lives. At times, we view it positively; at other times, we avoid it. Some advertising informs, persuades, or entertains us; some bores, annoys, or even offends us.

As mentioned in Chapter 17, **advertising** is a paid form of nonpersonal communication that is transmitted to a target audience through mass media, such as television, radio, the Internet, newspapers, magazines, direct mail, outdoor displays, and signs on mass transit vehicles. Spending more than $1 billion a year in advertising, McDonald's has successfully branded and advertised their products. In one study of children 3 to 5 years old, food packaged in a McDonald's wrapper was perceived as better tasting even when the food in the plain wrapper was the same food. Effective advertising can influence purchase behavior throughout a lifetime, as McDonald's hopes to do in effectively communicating its message to children.[2] Organizations use advertising to reach a variety of audiences ranging from small, specific groups, such as stamp collectors in Idaho, to extremely large groups, such as all athletic-shoe purchasers in the United States.

When asked to name major advertisers, most people immediately mention business organizations. However, many nonbusiness organizations—including governments, churches, universities, and charitable organizations—employ advertising to communicate with stakeholders. The U.S. government was the 31st largest advertiser in the nation, spending more than $1,195.6 million in advertising to advise and influence the behavior of its citizens. Although this chapter analyzes advertising in the context of business organizations, much of the following material applies to all types of organizations. For example, the state of Texas is utilizing an advertising campaign to attract vacationers to the state. Tourism is important to the Texas economy, creating 544,000 jobs and $60.6 billion in industry revenue.[3]

Advertising is used to promote goods, services, ideas, images, issues, people, and anything else advertisers want to publicize or foster. Depending on what is being promoted, advertising can be classified as institutional or product advertising. **Institutional advertising** promotes organizational images, ideas, and political issues. It can be used to create or maintain an organizational image. Institutional advertisements may deal with broad image issues, such as organizational strength or the friendliness of employees. They may also aim to create a more favorable view of the organization in the eyes of noncustomer groups such as shareholders, consumer advocacy groups, potential shareholders, or the general public. When a company promotes its position on a public issue—for instance, a tax increase, abortion, gun control, or international trade coalitions—institutional advertising is referred to as **advocacy advertising**. Such advertising may be used to promote socially approved behavior such as recycling or moderation in consuming alcoholic beverages. Philip Morris, for example, has run television advertisements encouraging parents to talk to their children about not smoking. Research has identified a number of themes that advertisers like Philip Morris can use to increase the effectiveness of antismoking messages for adolescents.[4] This type of advertising not only has social benefits but also helps build an organization's image.

Product advertising promotes the uses, features, and benefits of products. There are two types of product advertising: pioneer and competitive. **Pioneer advertising**

advertising Paid nonpersonal communication about an organization and its products transmitted to a target audience through mass media

institutional advertising Advertising that promotes organizational images, ideas, and political issues

advocacy advertising Advertising that promotes a company's position on a public issue

product advertising Advertising that promotes the uses, features, and benefits of products

pioneer advertising Advertising that tries to stimulate demand for a product category rather than a specific brand by informing potential buyers about the product

Advocacy Advertising
Ben & Jerry's Ice Cream advocates environmental conservation in its new-product offerings.

Image courtesy of The Advertising Archives

focuses on stimulating demand for a product category (rather than a specific brand) by informing potential customers about the product's features, uses, and benefits. This type of advertising is employed when the product is in the introductory stage of the product life cycle, exemplified in the launch of the General Motors' Volt in the new electric car category. **Competitive advertising** attempts to stimulate demand for a specific brand by promoting the brand's features, uses, and advantages, sometimes through indirect or direct comparisons with competing brands. Advertising effects on sales must reflect competitors' advertising activities. The type of competitive environment will determine the most effective industry approach.

To make direct product comparisons, marketers use a form of competitive advertising called **comparative advertising**, which compares the sponsored brand with one or more identified competing brands on the basis of one or more product characteristics. Advil PM, for example, used comparative advertising to promote the effectiveness of its over-the-counter sleeping pill as compared to Tylenol PM. Often the brands that are promoted through comparative advertisements have low market shares and are compared with competitors that have the highest market shares in the product category. Product categories that commonly use comparative advertising include soft drinks, toothpaste, pain relievers, foods, tires, automobiles, and detergents. Under the provisions of the 1988 Trademark Law Revision Act, marketers using comparative advertisements in the United States must not misrepresent the qualities or characteristics of competing products. Other countries may have laws that are stricter or less strict with regard to comparative advertising.

Other forms of competitive advertising include reminder and reinforcement advertising. **Reminder advertising** tells customers that an established brand is still around and still offers certain characteristics, uses, and advantages. Clorox, for example, reminds customers about its many advantages and uses. **Reinforcement advertising** assures current users that they have made the right brand choice and tells them how to get the most satisfaction from that brand. Insurance companies like State Farm suggest that customers check with their agent to ensure they have the right kind of coverage to protect against risks.

competitive advertising
Tries to stimulate demand for a specific brand by promoting its features, uses, and advantages relative to competing brands

comparative advertising
Compares the sponsored brand with one or more identified brands on the basis of one or more product characteristics

reminder advertising
Advertising used to remind consumers about an established brand's uses, characteristics, and benefits

reinforcement advertising
Advertising that assures users they chose the right brand and tells them how to get the most satisfaction from it

advertising campaign The creation and execution of a series of advertisements to communicate with a particular target audience

Developing an Advertising Campaign

An **advertising campaign** involves designing a series of advertisements and placing them in various advertising media to reach a particular target audience. As Figure 18.1 shows, the major steps in creating an advertising campaign are (1) identifying and analyzing the target audience, (2) defining the advertising objectives, (3) creating the advertising platform, (4) determining the advertising appropriation, (5) developing the media plan, (6) creating the advertising message, (7) executing the campaign, and (8) evaluating advertising effectiveness. The number of steps and the exact order in which they are carried out may vary according to the organization's resources, the nature of its product, and the type of target audience to be reached. Nevertheless, these general guidelines for developing an advertising campaign are appropriate for all types of organizations.

Figure 18.1 General Steps in Developing and Implementing an Advertising Campaign

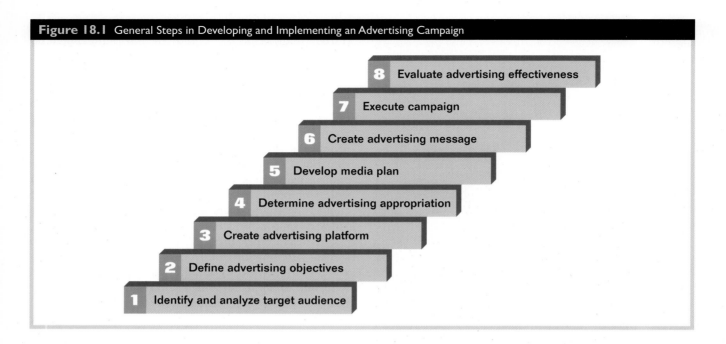

8 Evaluate advertising effectiveness

7 Execute campaign

6 Create advertising message

5 Develop media plan

4 Determine advertising appropriation

3 Create advertising platform

2 Define advertising objectives

1 Identify and analyze target audience

Identifying and Analyzing the Target Audience

The **target audience** is the group of people at whom advertisements are aimed. Advertisements for Barbie cereal are targeted toward young girls who play with Barbie dolls, whereas those for Special K cereal are directed at health-conscious adults. Identifying and analyzing the target audience are critical processes; the information yielded helps determine other steps in developing the campaign. The target audience may include everyone in the firm's target market. Marketers may, however, direct a campaign at only a portion of the target market. For instance, American Airlines is targeting the Latino population with a multimedia campaign aired on Spanish-language TV-networks Telemundo and Univision to create awareness of the benefits of the American Airlines AAdvantage frequent flyer program.[5]

Advertisers research and analyze advertising targets to establish an information base for a campaign. Information commonly needed includes location and geographic distribution of the target group; the distribution of demographic factors, such as age, income, race, gender, and education; lifestyle information; and consumer attitudes regarding purchase and use of both the advertiser's products and competing products. The exact kinds of information an organization finds useful depend on the type of product being advertised, the characteristics of the target audience, and the type and amount of competition. Generally, the more an advertiser knows about the target audience, the more likely the firm is to develop an effective advertising campaign. When the advertising target is not precisely identified and properly analyzed, the campaign may fail, as illustrated in the boxed feature.

Defining the Advertising Objectives

The advertiser's next step is to determine what the firm hopes to accomplish with the campaign. Because advertising objectives guide campaign development, advertisers should define objectives carefully. Advertising objectives should be stated clearly, precisely, and in measurable terms. Precision and measurability allow advertisers to evaluate advertising success at the end of the campaign in terms of whether objectives have been met. To provide precision and measurability, advertising objectives should contain benchmarks and indicate how far the advertiser wishes to move from these

target audience The group of people at whom advertisements are aimed

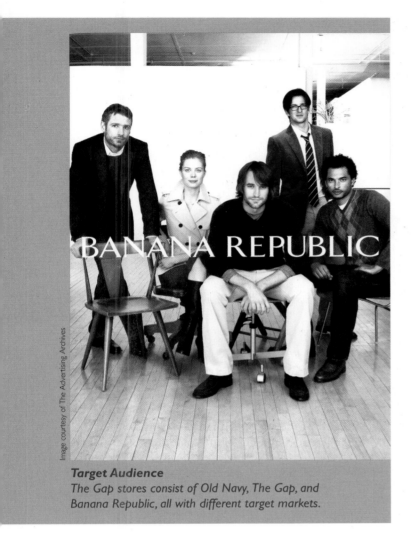

Target Audience
The Gap stores consist of Old Navy, The Gap, and Banana Republic, all with different target markets.

Image courtesy of The Advertising Archives

standards. If the goal is to increase sales, the advertiser should state the current sales level (the benchmark) and the amount of sales increase sought through advertising. An advertising objective should also specify a time frame so that advertisers know exactly how long they have to accomplish the objective. An advertiser with average monthly sales of $450,000 (the benchmark) might set the following objective: "Our primary advertising objective is to increase average monthly sales from $450,000 to $540,000 within 12 months."

If an advertiser defines objectives on the basis of sales, the objectives focus on increasing absolute dollar sales or unit sales, increasing sales by a certain percentage, or increasing the firm's market share. Even though an advertiser's long-run goal is to increase sales, not all campaigns are designed to produce immediate sales. Some campaigns aim to increase product or brand awareness, make consumers' attitudes more favorable, heighten consumers' knowledge of product features, or create awareness of positive, healthy consumer behavior like not drinking. If the goal is to increase product awareness, the objectives are stated in terms of communication. A specific communication objective might be to increase product feature awareness from 0 to 40 percent in the target audience by the end of six months.

Creating the Advertising Platform

Before launching a political campaign, party leaders develop a political platform stating major issues that are the basis of the campaign. Like a political platform, an **advertising platform** consists of the basic issues or selling points that an advertiser wishes to include in the advertising campaign. For instance, GEICO consistently includes a key selling point in its insurance ads: "15 minutes can save you 15 percent or more on your car insurance." A single advertisement in an advertising campaign may contain one or several issues from the platform. Although the platform sets forth the basic issues, it does not indicate how to present them.

An advertising platform should consist of issues important to customers. One of the best ways to determine those issues is to survey customers about what they consider most important in the selection and use of the product involved. Selling features must not only be important to customers, they should also be strongly competitive features of the advertised brand. For instance, E*Trade capitalizes upon its positioning of "liberation and value." E*Trade is a competitively priced investment tool that offers easily accessible and usable investor features. Customer research validates the value proposition's use in E*Trade advertising.[6] Although research is the most effective method for determining what issues to include in an advertising platform, it is expensive. Therefore, an advertising platform is most commonly based on opinions of personnel within the firm and of individuals in the advertising agency, if an agency is used. This trial-and-error approach generally leads to some successes and some failures.

Because the advertising platform is a base on which to build the advertising message, marketers should analyze this stage carefully. A campaign can be perfect in terms of selection and analysis of its target audience, statement of its objectives, media strategy, and the form of its message. But the campaign will ultimately fail if the advertisements communicate information that consumers do not deem important when selecting and using the product.

advertising platform Basic issues or selling points to be included in an advertising campaign

Advertising Platform

An advertising platform contains multiple issues or selling points. Usually, all of the platform issues are not included in one ad. What platform issues are in this ad?

Determining the Advertising Appropriation

The **advertising appropriation** is the total amount of money a marketer allocates for advertising for a specific time period. To increase consumer response rates to the 2010 Census, the U.S. government budgeted $340 million on promotional campaigns, of which $140 million was for paid television advertising.[7] It is difficult to determine how much to spend on advertising for a specific period because the potential effects of advertising are so difficult to measure precisely. However, data from previous U.S. Census periods underscore the importance of advertising. To reduce costs, the U.S. Census Bureau began mailing census forms to citizens in 1970. That same year, the response rate was 78 percent. In 1980, the number of returned forms was 75 percent, with a significant fall off in 1990 to 65 percent. In 2000, to assist in reversing the falling response rate, the Census Bureau started to advertise. The advertising effort resulted in a 67 percent response rate. Was the investment in advertising worth the money? It is estimated that each 1 percent increase in response rate on the Census saves the U.S. government $85 million.[8]

Many factors affect a firm's decision about how much to appropriate for advertising. Geographic size of the market and the distribution of buyers within the market have a great bearing on this decision. Both the type of product advertised and the firm's sales volume relative to competitors' sales volumes also play roles in determining what proportion of revenue to spend on advertising. Advertising appropriations for business products are usually quite small relative to product sales, whereas consumer convenience items, such as soft drinks, soaps, and cosmetics, generally have large advertising expenditures relative to sales. Table 18.1 shows the top 10 advertisers for 2008 and 2009.

Of the many techniques used to determine the advertising appropriation, one of the most logical is the **objective-and-task approach**. Using this approach, marketers determine the objectives a campaign is to achieve and then attempt to list the tasks required to accomplish them. The costs of the tasks are calculated and added to arrive at the total appropriation. This approach has one main problem: marketers sometimes have trouble accurately estimating the level of effort needed to attain certain objectives. A coffee marketer, for example, may find it extremely difficult to determine how much of an increase in national television advertising is needed to raise a brand's market share from 8 to 10 percent.

advertising appropriation The advertising budget for a specific time period

objective-and-task approach Budgeting for an advertising campaign by first determining its objectives and then calculating the cost of all the tasks needed to attain them

Table 18.1 Top 10 Advertisers: January–September 2009 versus January–September 2008[1]

Rank	Company	Jan–Sep 2009 (Millions)	Jan–Sep 2008 (Millions)	Percent Change
1.	Procter & Gamble Co.	$ 1,941.1	$ 2,307.6	−15.9%
2.	Verizon Communications Inc.	1,692.1	1,796.0	−5.8%
3.	General Motors Corp.	1,352.6	1,599.9	−15.5%
4.	AT&T Inc.	1,339.4	1,426.5	−6.1%
5.	Johnson & Johnson	1,037.0	1,050.5	−1.3%
6.	News Corp.	947.8	1,046.5	−9.4%
7.	Sprint Nextel Corp.	912.8	603.9	51.1%
8.	Pfizer Inc.	896.6	801.0	11.9%
9.	Time Warner Inc.	874.5	979.6	−10.7%
10.	General Electric Co.	763.6	876.8	−12.9%
	Total[2]	**$11,757.6**	**$12,488.3**	**−5.9%**

[1]Figures do not include FSI, House Ads, or PSA activity.

[2]The sum of the individual companies may differ from the total shown due to rounding.

Source: TNS Media Intelligence, "TNS Media Intelligence Reports U.S. Advertising Expenditures Declined 14.7 Percent in First Nine Months of 2009," December 8, 2009, www.tns-mi.com/news/2009-Ad-Spending-Q3.htm (accessed March 3, 2010).

In the more widely used **percent-of-sales approach**, marketers simply multiply the firm's past sales, plus a factor for planned sales growth or decline, by a standard percentage based on both what the firm traditionally spends on advertising and the industry average. This approach, too, has a major flaw: it is based on the incorrect assumption that sales create advertising rather than the reverse. A marketer using this approach during declining sales will reduce the amount spent on advertising, but such a reduction may further diminish sales. Though illogical, this technique has been favored because it is easy to use.

Another way to determine advertising appropriation is the **competition-matching approach**. Marketers following this approach try to match their major competitors' appropriations in absolute dollars or to allocate the same percentage of sales for advertising that their competitors do. Although a marketer should be aware of what competitors spend on advertising, this technique should not be used alone because the firm's competitors probably have different advertising objectives and different resources available for advertising. Many companies and advertising agencies review competitive spending on a quarterly basis, comparing competitors' dollar expenditures on print, radio, and television with their own spending levels. Competitive tracking of this nature occurs at both the national and regional levels.

At times, marketers use the **arbitrary approach**, which usually means a high-level executive in the firm states how much to spend on advertising for a certain period. The arbitrary approach often leads to underspending or overspending. Although hardly a scientific budgeting technique, it is expedient.

Deciding how large the advertising appropriation should be is critical. If the appropriation is set too low, the campaign cannot achieve its full potential. When too much money is appropriated, overspending results, and financial resources are wasted.

Developing the Media Plan

As Figure 18.2 shows, advertisers spend tremendous amounts on advertising media. These amounts have grown rapidly during the past two decades. To derive maximum results from media expenditures, marketers must develop effective media plans. A **media plan** sets forth the exact media vehicles to be used (specific magazines, television stations, newspapers, and so forth) and the dates and times the advertisements will

percent-of-sales approach Budgeting for an advertising campaign by multiplying the firm's past and expected sales by a standard percentage

competition-matching approach Determining an advertising budget by trying to match competitors' advertising outlays

arbitrary approach Budgeting for an advertising campaign as specified by a high-level executive in the firm

media plan A plan that specifies the media vehicles to be used and the schedule for running advertisements

Figure 18.2 Advertising Spending by Media Category: 1985, 2007, and 2010

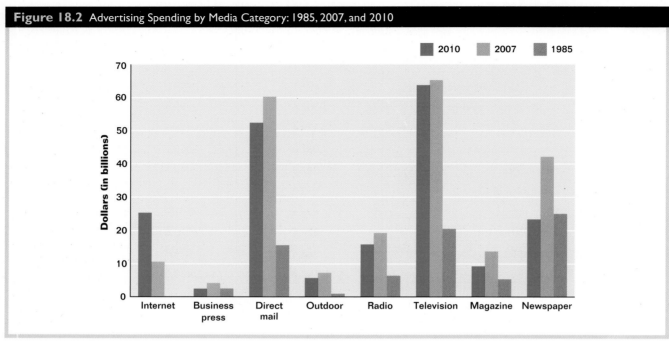

Sources: "Total U.S. Advertising Spending by Medium ($ in millions), Advertising Age, October 27, 2009 www.businessinsider.com/us-advertising-spending-by-medium-2009-10 (accessed March 29, 2010).

appear. The plan determines how many people in the target audience will be exposed to the message. Table 18.2 illustrates how marketers allocate their advertising to digital media methods. The method also determines, to some degree, the effects of the message on those specific target markets. Media planning is a complex task requiring thorough analysis of the target audience. Sophisticated computer models have been developed to attempt to maximize the effectiveness of media plans.

To formulate a media plan, the planners select the media for the campaign and prepare a time schedule for each medium. The media planner's primary goal is to reach the largest number of people in the advertising target that the budget will allow. A secondary goal is to achieve the appropriate message reach and frequency for the target audience while staying within budget. *Reach* refers to the percentage of consumers in the target audience actually exposed to a particular advertisement in a stated period. *Frequency* is the number of times these targeted consumers are exposed to the advertisement.

Media planners begin with broad decisions but eventually make very specific ones. They first decide which kinds of media to use: radio, television, the Internet,

Table 18.2 Digital Advertising Methods (in Millions of U.S. Dollars)

	2009	2010	2011	2012	2013	2014	CAGR
Mobile marketing	$ 391	$ 561	$ 748	$ 950	$,131	$ 1,274	27%
Social media	716	935	1,217	1,649	2,254	3,113	34%
Email marketing	1,248	1,355	1,504	1,676	1,867	2,081	11%
Display advertising	7,829	8,395	9,846	11,732	14,339	16,900	17%
Search marketing	15,393	17,765	20,763	24,299	27,786	31,588	15%
Total	**$25,577**	**$29,012**	**$34,077**	**$40,306**	**$47,378**	**$54,956**	**17%**
Percentage of all advertising spend	12%	13%	15%	17%	19%	21%	

Source: Forrester's Interactive Advertising Models, April 2009 and October 2008 (United States only).

newspapers, magazines, direct mail, outdoor displays, or signs on mass transit vehicles. Digital marketing in particular is growing, with companies allocating 12 percent of advertising spending to digital outlets, and it is projected to grow to 21 percent in five years. For example, social media advertising accounts for $716 million of advertising spending, and it is projected to grow to $3 billion by 2014. Media planners assess different formats and approaches to determine which are most effective. Some media plans are highly focused and use just one medium. The media plans of manufacturers of consumer packaged goods, however, can be quite complex and dynamic.

Media planners take many factors into account when devising a media plan. They analyze location and demographic characteristics of consumers in the target audience because people's tastes in media differ according to demographic groups and locations. There are radio stations especially for teenagers, magazines for men ages 18 to 34, and television cable channels aimed at women in various age groups. Media planners also consider the sizes and types of audiences that specific media reach. For instance, *Glamour* magazine reaches relatively affluent women who are interested in fashion. Approximately 75 percent of their readership have a household income of more than $75,000 with a median age of 35. Many marketers of cosmetics, clothing, and fashion items would consider this an attractive demographic.[9] Declining broadcast television ratings and newspaper and magazine readership have led many companies to explore alternative media, including not only cable television and Internet advertising but also ads on cell phones and product placements in video games. Several data services collect and periodically provide information about circulations and audiences of various media.

The content of the message sometimes affects media choice. Print media can be used more effectively than broadcast media to present complex issues or numerous details in single advertisements. If an advertiser wants to promote beautiful colors, patterns, or textures, media offering high-quality color reproduction, such as magazines or television, should be used instead of newspapers. For example, food can be effectively promoted in full-color magazine advertisements but far less effectively in black and white.

The cost of media is an important but troublesome consideration. Planners try to obtain the best coverage possible for each dollar spent. However, there is no accurate way to compare the cost and impact of a television commercial with the cost and impact

Media Plan
Kia uses an extensive print and broadcast media plan for its vehicles, such as the Sorento.

Table 18.3 Advantages and Disadvantages of Major Media Classes

Medium	Advantages	Disadvantages
Newspapers	Reaches large audience; purchased to be read; geographic flexibility; short lead time; frequent publication; favorable for cooperative advertising; merchandising services	Not selective for socioeconomic groups or target market; short life; limited reproduction capabilities; large advertising volume limits exposure to any one advertisement
Magazines	Demographic selectivity; good reproduction; long life; prestige; geographic selectivity when regional issues are available; read in leisurely manner	High costs; 30–90-day average lead time; high level of competition; limited reach; communicates less frequently
Direct mail	Little wasted circulation; highly selective; circulation controlled by advertiser; few distractions; personal; stimulates actions; use of novelty; relatively easy to measure performance; hidden from competitors	Very expensive; lacks editorial content to attract readers; often thrown away unread as junk mail; criticized as invasion of privacy; consumers must choose to read the ad
Radio	Reaches 95 percent of consumers; highly mobile and flexible; very low relative costs; ad can be changed quickly; high level of geographic and demographic selectivity; encourages use of imagination	Lacks visual imagery; short life of message; listeners' attention limited because of other activities; market fragmentation; difficult buying procedures; limited media and audience research
Television	Reaches large audiences; high frequency available; dual impact of audio and video; highly visible; high prestige; geographic and demographic selectivity; difficult to ignore	Very expensive; highly perishable message; size of audience not guaranteed; amount of prime time limited; lack of selectivity in target market
Internet	Immediate response; potential to reach a precisely targeted audience; ability to track customers and build databases; highly interactive medium	Costs of precise targeting are high; inappropriate ad placement; effects difficult to measure; concerns about security and privacy
Yellow Pages	Wide availability; action and product category oriented; low relative costs; ad frequency and longevity; nonintrusive	Market fragmentation; extremely localized; slow updating; lack of creativity; long lead times; requires large space to be noticed
Outdoor	Allows for frequent repetition; low cost; message can be placed close to point of sale; geographic selectivity; operable 24 hours a day; high creativity and effectiveness	Message must be short and simple; no demographic selectivity; seldom attracts readers' full attention; criticized as traffic hazard and blight on countryside; much wasted coverage; limited capabilities

Sources: William F. Arens, *Contemporary Advertising* (Burr Ridge, IL: Irwin/McGraw-Hill, 2007); George E. Belch and Michael Belch, *Advertising and Promotion* (Burr Ridge, IL: Irwin/McGraw-Hill, 2006).

cost comparison indicator
A means of comparing the costs of advertising vehicles in a specific medium in relation to the number of people reached

of a newspaper advertisement. A **cost comparison indicator** lets an advertiser compare the costs of several vehicles within a specific medium (such as two magazines) in relation to the number of people each vehicle reaches. The *cost per thousand impressions (CPM)* is the cost comparison indicator for magazines; it shows the cost of exposing 1,000 people to a one-page advertisement.

Figure 18.2 shows that the extent to which each medium is used varies, as well as how they have varied since 1985. For instance, the proportion of total advertising dollars spent on television has risen since 1985 and surpassed that spent on newspapers. Media are selected by weighing the various advantages and disadvantages of each (see Table 18.3).

Like media selection decisions, media scheduling decisions are affected by numerous factors, such as target audience characteristics, product attributes, product seasonality, customer media behavior, and size of the advertising budget. There are three general types of media schedules: continuous, flighting, and pulsing. When a *continuous* schedule is used, advertising runs at a constant level with little variation throughout the campaign period. McDonald's is an example of a company that uses a continuous schedule. With a *flighting* schedule, advertisements run for set periods of time, alternating with periods in which no ads run. For example, an advertising campaign might have an ad run for two weeks, then suspend it for two weeks, and then run it again for two weeks. Companies such as Hallmark, John Deere, and Ray-Ban use a flighting schedule. A *pulsing* schedule combines continuous and flighting schedules: during the entire campaign, a certain portion of advertising runs continuously, and during specific time periods of the campaign, additional advertising is used to intensify the level of communication with the target audience.

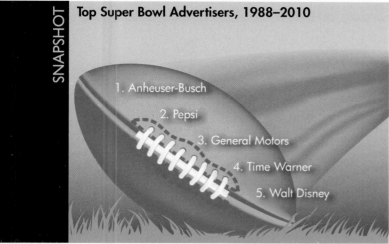

SNAPSHOT

Top Super Bowl Advertisers, 1988–2010

1. Anheuser-Busch
2. Pepsi
3. General Motors
4. Time Warner
5. Walt Disney

Source: TNS Media Intelligence.

Creating the Advertising Message

The basic content and form of an advertising message are a function of several factors. A product's features, uses, and benefits affect the content of the message. Characteristics of the people in the target audience—gender, age, education, race, income, occupation, lifestyle, and other attributes—influence both content and form. For instance, gender affects how people respond to advertising claims that use hedging words such as *may* and *probably* and pledging words such as *definitely* and *absolutely*. Researchers have found that women respond negatively to both types of claims, but pledging claims have little effect on men.[10] When Procter & Gamble promotes Crest toothpaste to children, the company emphasizes daily brushing and cavity control. When marketing Crest to adults, P&G stresses tartar and plaque control as well as whitening. To communicate effectively, advertisers use words, symbols, and illustrations that are meaningful, familiar, and appealing to people in the target audience.

An advertising campaign's objectives and platform also affect the content and form of its messages. If a firm's advertising objectives involve large sales increases, the message may include hard-hitting, high-impact language and symbols. When campaign objectives aim to increase brand awareness, the message may use much repetition of the brand name and words and illustrations associated with it. Thus, the advertising platform is the foundation on which campaign messages are built.

Choice of media obviously influences the content and form of the message. Effective outdoor displays and short broadcast spot announcements require concise, simple messages. Magazine and newspaper advertisements can include considerable detail and long explanations. Because several kinds of media offer geographic selectivity, a precise message can be tailored to a particular geographic section of the target audience. Some magazine publishers produce **regional issues**, in which advertisements and editorial content of copies appearing in one geographic area differ from those appearing in other areas. As Figure 18.3 shows, *Time* magazine publishes eight regional issues. A company advertising in *Time* might decide to use one message in the New England region and another in the rest of the nation. A company may also choose to advertise in only one region. Such geographic selectivity lets a firm use the same message in different regions at different times.

COPY

Copy is the verbal portion of an advertisement and may include headlines, subheadlines, body copy, and signature. Not all advertising contains all of these copy elements. Even handwritten notes on direct-mail advertising that say, "Try this. It works!" seem to increase requests for free samples.[11] The headline is critical because often it is the only part of the copy that people read. It should attract readers' attention and create enough interest to make them want to read the body copy. The subheadline, if there is one, links the headline to the body copy and sometimes serves to explain the headline.

Body copy for most advertisements consists of an introductory statement or paragraph, several explanatory paragraphs, and a closing paragraph. Some copywriters have adopted guidelines for developing body copy systematically: (1) identify a specific desire or problem, (2) recommend the product as the best way to satisfy that desire or solve that problem, (3) state product benefits and indicate why the product is best for the buyer's particular situation, (4) substantiate advertising claims, and (5) ask the buyer to take action. When substantiating claims, it is important to present the substantiation in a credible manner. The proof of claims should help strengthen both the image of the product and company integrity. Typeface selection can help advertisers create a desired impression using fonts that are engaging, reassuring, or very prominent.[12]

regional issues Versions of a magazine that differ across geographic regions

copy The verbal portion of advertisements

Figure 18.3 Geographic Divisions for Time Regional Issues

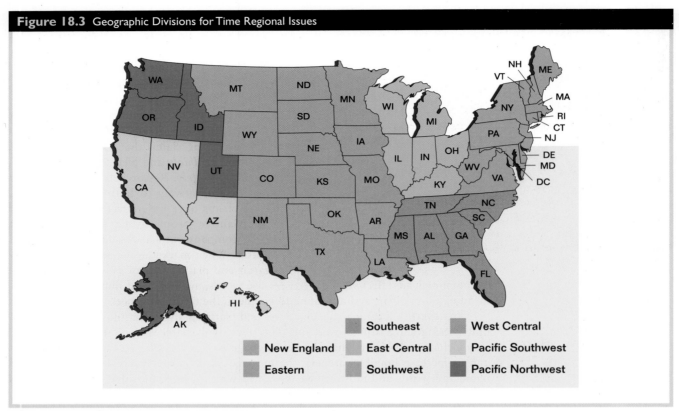

Source: *Time* Magazine. © 2006 Time Inc. Reprinted by permission.

The signature identifies the advertisement's sponsor. It may contain several elements, including the firm's trademark, logo, name, and address. The signature should be attractive, legible, distinctive, and easy to identify in a variety of sizes.

Because radio listeners often are not fully "tuned in" mentally to what they're hearing on the radio, radio copy should be informal and conversational to attract listeners' attention. Radio messages are highly perishable and should consist of short, familiar terms, which increase their impact. The length should not require a rate of speech exceeding approximately two and one-half words per second.

In television copy, the audio material must not overpower the visual material, and vice versa. However, a television message should make optimal use of its visual portion, which can be very effective for product demonstrations. Copy for a television commercial is sometimes initially written in parallel script form. Video is described in the left column and audio in the right. When the parallel script is approved, the copywriter and artist combine copy with visual material by using a **storyboard**, which depicts a series of miniature television screens showing the sequence of major scenes in the commercial. Beneath each screen is a description of the audio portion to be used with that video segment. Technical personnel use the storyboard as a blueprint when producing the commercial.

ARTWORK

Artwork consists of an advertisement's illustrations and layout. **Illustrations** are often photographs but can also be drawings, graphs, charts, and tables. Illustrations are used to draw attention, encourage audiences to read or listen to the copy, communicate an idea quickly, or communicate ideas that are difficult to express. Illustrations can be more important in capturing attention than text or brand elements, independent of size.[13] They are especially important because consumers tend to recall the visual portions of advertisements better than the verbal portions. Advertisers use a variety of illustration techniques. They may show the product alone, in a setting, or in use, or show the results

storyboard A blueprint that combines copy and visual material to show the sequence of major scenes in a commercial

artwork An advertisement's illustrations and layout

illustrations Photos, drawings, graphs, charts, and tables used to spark audience interest in an advertisement

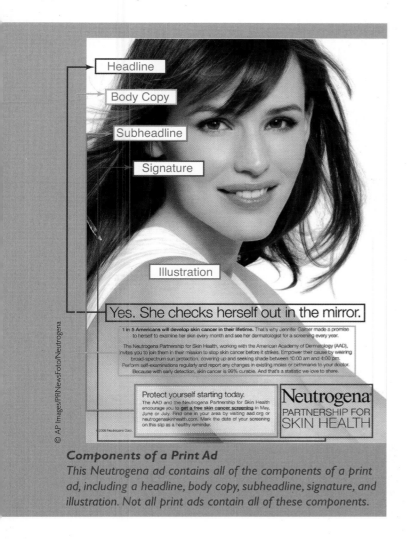

Headline

Body Copy

Subheadline

Signature

Illustration

Yes. She checks herself out in the mirror.

1 in 5 Americans will develop skin cancer in their lifetime. That's why Jennifer Garner made a promise to herself to examine her skin every month and see her dermatologist for a screening every year.

The Neutrogena Partnership for Skin Health, working with the American Academy of Dermatology (AAD), invites you to join them in their mission to stop skin cancer before it strikes. Empower their cause by wearing broad-spectrum sun protection, covering up and seeking shade between 10:00 am and 4:00 pm. Perform self-examinations regularly and report any changes in existing moles or birthmarks to your doctor. Because with early detection, skin cancer is 99% curable. And that's a statistic we love to share.

Protect yourself starting today.
The AAD and the Neutrogena Partnership for Skin Health encourage you to get a free skin cancer screening in May, June or July. Find one in your area by visiting aad.org or neutrogenaskinhealth.com. Mark the date of your screening on this slip as a healthy reminder.

Neutrogena
PARTNERSHIP FOR
SKIN HEALTH

© AP Images/PRNewsFoto/Neutrogena

Components of a Print Ad
This Neutrogena ad contains all of the components of a print ad, including a headline, body copy, subheadline, signature, and illustration. Not all print ads contain all of these components.

of the product's use. Illustrations can also take the form of comparisons, contrasts, diagrams, and testimonials.

The **layout** of an advertisement is the physical arrangement of the illustration and the copy (headline, subheadline, body copy, and signature). These elements can be arranged in many ways. The final layout is the result of several stages of layout preparation. As it moves through these stages, the layout promotes an exchange of ideas among people developing the advertising campaign and provides instructions for production personnel.

Executing the Campaign

Execution of an advertising campaign requires extensive planning and coordination because many tasks must be completed on time and several people and firms are involved. Production companies, research organizations, media firms, printers, and commercial artists are just a few of the people and firms contributing to a campaign.

Implementation requires detailed schedules to ensure that various phases of the work are done on time. Advertising management personnel must evaluate the quality of the work and take corrective action when necessary. Wendy's, for example, pulled the plug on its "That's Right" promotion campaign after it failed to generate sales. The short-lived campaign, which featured characters wearing pigtailed red-haired wigs (like the chain's mascot) declared, "I deserve a hot juicy burger," and attracted attention as well as controversy. The company has launched a more positive food-focused campaign with the tag line "You Know When It's Real."[14] In some instances, changes are made during the campaign so it meets objectives more effectively. Sometimes, one firm develops a campaign and another executes it.

Evaluating Advertising Effectiveness

A variety of ways exist to test the effectiveness of advertising. They include measuring achievement of advertising objectives; assessing effectiveness of copy, illustrations, or layouts; and evaluating certain media.

Advertising can be evaluated before, during, and after the campaign. An evaluation performed before the campaign begins is called a **pretest**. A pretest usually attempts to evaluate the effectiveness of one or more elements of the message. To pretest advertisements, marketers sometimes use a **consumer jury**, a panel of existing or potential buyers of the advertised product. Jurors judge one or several dimensions of two or more advertisements. Such tests are based on the belief that consumers are more likely than advertising experts to know what influences them. Companies can also solicit the assistance of marketing research firms such as Information Resources Inc. (IRI) to help assess ads.

To measure advertising effectiveness during a campaign, marketers usually rely on "inquiries." In a campaign's initial stages, an advertiser may use several advertisements simultaneously, each containing a coupon, form, toll-free phone number, or website through which potential customers can request information. The advertiser records the number of inquiries returned from each type of advertisement. If an advertiser receives 78,528 inquiries from advertisement A, 37,072 from advertisement B, and 47,932 from advertisement C, advertisement A is judged superior to advertisements B and C. Internet advertisers can also assess how many people "clicked" on an ad to obtain more product information. The outdoor advertising industry has created a system called "Eyes On"

layout The physical arrangement of an advertisement's illustration and copy

pretest Evaluation of advertisements performed before a campaign begins

consumer jury A panel of a product's existing or potential buyers who pretest ads

to determine the audiences likely to see an ad, with demographic and ethnographic data included. Previous measurement systems used Daily Effective Circulation that essentially evolved around traffic counts, not on interested audiences.[15]

Evaluation of advertising effectiveness after the campaign is called a **posttest**. Advertising objectives often determine what kind of posttest is appropriate. If the objectives focus on communication—to increase awareness of product features or brands or to create more favorable customer attitudes—the posttest should measure changes in these dimensions. Advertisers sometimes use consumer surveys or experiments to evaluate a campaign based on communication objectives. These methods are costly, however. In posttests, generalizations can be made about why advertising is failing or why media vehicles are not delivering the desired results. Table 18.4 shows some of the beliefs about why digital advertising is failing to deliver to audiences and create the response rates that advertisers hope for.[16]

For campaign objectives stated in terms of sales, advertisers should determine the change in sales or market share attributable to the campaign. For example, after a tourism campaign by the state of Utah—with the slogan "Utah: Life Elevated"—tourist spending in the state increased by 6.2 percent to more than $7 billion.[17] However, changes in sales or market share brought about by advertising cannot be measured precisely; many factors independent of advertisements affect a firm's sales and market share. Competitors' actions, regulatory actions, and changes in economic conditions, consumer preferences, and weather are only a few factors that might enhance or diminish a company's sales or market share. By using data about past and current sales and advertising expenditures, advertisers can make gross estimates of the effects of a campaign on sales or market share.

Because it is difficult to determine the direct effects of advertising on sales, many advertisers evaluate print advertisements according to how well consumers can remember them. The marketers of HeadOn, an analgesic, used endless repetition to help consumers recall their product and gain rapid sales growth, from $1.9 million to $6.5 million in just one year. Researchers have found that ads that play on the theme of social desirability are more memorable when viewed in the presence of other people.[18]

Posttest methods based on memory include recognition and recall tests. Such tests are usually performed by research organizations through surveys. In a **recognition test**, respondents are shown the actual advertisement and asked whether they recognize it. If they do, the interviewer asks additional questions to determine how much of the advertisement each respondent read. When recall is evaluated, respondents are not shown the actual advertisement but instead are asked about what they have seen or heard recently. For Internet advertising, research suggests that the longer a person is exposed to a website containing a banner advertisement, the more likely he or she is to recall the ad.[19]

Recall can be measured through either unaided or aided recall methods. In an **unaided recall test**, respondents identify advertisements they have seen recently but are not shown

posttest Evaluation of advertising effectiveness after the campaign

recognition test A posttest in which respondents are shown the actual ad and are asked if they recognize it

unaided recall test A posttest in which respondents are asked to identify advertisements they have seen recently but are not given any recall clues

Table 18.4 Digital Advertising's Shortcomings

1. Overly detail-focused.
2. Too long to reach the point.
3. Message is unclear.
4. Boring or very unattractive design that fails to catch audience's attention.
5. Use of Flash technology for the sake of Flash—not for effectively reaching the target audience.
6. Often visually hard to decipher or read.
7. Short on noting key benefits.
8. Focused Internet users are often angered by promotional messages that do not deliver immediate messages of interest.

Source: Adapted from Philip W. Sawyer, "Why Most Digital Ads Still Fail to Work," *Advertising Age*, January 27, 2010, http://adage.com/digitalnext/post?article_id=141751 (accessed April 9, 2010).

SAVE **$1**⁰⁰

on any **TWO** packages of
Keebler® Club® Crackers
(9 oz. or Larger, Any Flavor, Mix or Match)

MANUFACTURER COUPON
EXPIRES NOVEMBER 30, 2009

CONSUMER: LIMIT ONE COUPON PER
PURCHASE OF PRODUCT INDICATED.
VOID WHERE TAXED, RESTRICTED OR
PROHIBITED. CONSUMER MUST PAY
SALES TAX. DEALER: We will reimburse
you face value of this coupon plus 5.0¢
handling if in accordance with Keebler
coupon redemption terms. Copies
available upon request. Mail properly
redeemed coupons to: Keebler P.O. Box
880274, El Paso, TX 88588-0274
Cash value 1/20 of 5.0¢
K.™, © 2009 Kellogg NA Co. 62027361

Visit snackpicks.com for more ways to save.

Taste a little richer. **Feel a little richer.**

A cracker that melts in your mouth? **Now that's rich.**

CLUB
ORIGINAL   CRACKERS

Courtesy of Susan Van Etten

Evaluating Ad Effectiveness
*Evaluating the effectiveness of advertising is made easier if
there is a measurement of success, such as coupon redemption.*

any clues to help them remember. A similar procedure is used with an **aided recall test,** but respondents are shown a list of products, brands, company names, or trademarks to jog their memories. Schering-Plough, maker of products such as Claritin, Dr. Scholl's, Coppertone, and other pharmaceutical and packaged goods, is increasing its use of digital out-of-home advertising. Claritin's digital, out-of-home advertising produced increased purchase intent among 26 percent of those surveyed, with 73 percent of allergy sufferers reporting increased purchase intent. The unaided ad recall was 9 percent, and the aided ad recall was 38 percent. Results such as these show promise for increasing the variety and location of advertising.[20] Several research organizations, such as Daniel Starch, provide research services that test recognition and recall of advertisements.

The major justification for using recognition and recall methods is that people are more likely to buy a product if they can remember an advertisement about it than if they cannot. However, recalling an advertisement does not necessarily lead to buying the product or brand advertised. Researchers also use a sophisticated technique called *single-source data* to help evaluate advertisements. With this technique, individuals' behaviors are tracked from television sets to checkout counters. Monitors are placed in preselected homes, and microcomputers record when the television set is on and which station is being viewed. At the supermarket checkout, the individual in the sample household presents an identification card. Checkers then record the purchases by scanner, and data are sent to the research facility. Some single-source data companies provide sample households with scanning equipment for use at home to record purchases after returning from shopping trips. Single-source data supplies information that links exposure to advertisements with purchase behavior.

Who Develops the Advertising Campaign?

An advertising campaign may be handled by an individual, a few people within a firm, a firm's own advertising department, or an advertising agency.

In very small firms, one or two individuals are responsible for advertising (and for many other activities as well). Usually, these individuals depend heavily on personnel at local newspapers and broadcast stations for copywriting, artwork, and advice about scheduling media.

In certain large businesses, especially large retail organizations, advertising departments create and implement advertising campaigns. Depending on the size of the advertising program, an advertising department may consist of a few multiskilled individuals or a sizable number of specialists, including copywriters, artists, media buyers, and technical production coordinators. Advertising departments sometimes obtain the services of independent research organizations and hire freelance specialists when a particular project requires it.

Many firms employ an advertising agency to develop advertising campaigns. Kraft Foods, for example, contracted with McGarry Bowen to create an advertising campaign

aided recall test A posttest that asks respondents to identify recent ads and provides clues to jog their memories

Table 18.5 Leading International Media Agencies by Revenue

International Media Agencies	Estimated Billings
OMD Worldwide	$32.0 billion
Starcom Mediavest	$30.3 billion
ZenithOptimedia	$28.1 billion
Mindshare	$27.9 billion
Carat	$27.3 billion

Source: "Leading Media Agency Brands in 2008 by Estimated Billings," *Adbrands.net*, www.adbrands.net/agencies_index_media.htm (accessed July 30, 2010).

to distinguish its Miracle Whip brand from mayonnaise brands. The campaign is expected to cost $15.3 million.[21] When an organization uses an advertising agency, the firm and the agency usually develop the advertising campaign jointly. How much each participates in the campaign's total development depends on the working relationship between the firm and the agency. Ordinarily, a firm relies on the agency for copywriting, artwork, technical production, and formulation of the media plan.

Advertising agencies assist businesses in several ways. An agency, especially a large one, can supply the services of highly skilled specialists—not only copywriters, artists, and production coordinators but also media experts, researchers, and legal advisers. Agency personnel often have broad advertising experience and are usually more objective than a firm's employees about the organization's products.

Because an agency traditionally receives most of its compensation from a 15 percent commission paid by the media from which it makes purchases, firms can obtain some agency services at low or moderate costs. If an agency contracts for $400,000 of television time for a firm, it receives a commission of $60,000 from the television station. Although the traditional compensation method for agencies is changing and now includes other factors, media commissions still offset some costs of using an agency. Table 18.5 lists some of the leading U.S. ad agencies. Like advertising, public relations can be a vital element in a promotion mix. We turn to this topic next.

Public Relations

Public relations is a broad set of communication efforts used to create and maintain favorable relationships between an organization and its stakeholders. An organization communicates with various stakeholders, both internal and external, and public relations efforts can be directed toward any and all of them. A firm's stakeholders can include customers, suppliers, employees, shareholders, the media, educators, potential investors, government officials, and society in general. In light of a gas pedal recall in 2010, Toyota engaged in a massive advertising and public relations campaign to help rebuild trust among stakeholders in its products, brand name, and dealers. The company issued press releases, ran television ads to remind stakeholders of the heritage of the brand, and attempted to reassure consumers through company spokespersons. This promotional campaign resulted in an 89 percent awareness of the recall, and around 50 percent of those aware were "much less likely" or "somewhat less likely" to buy a Toyota.[22] While making stakeholders aware of the recall may have hurt Toyota's sales in the short run, it developed a foundation for open communication and trust in the long run. Table 18.6 lists some of the top public relations campaigns in the past 10 years.

Public relations can be used to promote people, places, ideas, activities, and even countries. It is often used by nonprofit organizations to achieve their goals. Public relations focuses on enhancing the image of the total organization. Assessing public attitudes and creating a favorable image are no less important than direct promotion of the organization's products. Because the public's attitudes toward a firm are likely to affect the sales of its products, it is very important for firms to maintain positive public perceptions. In addition, employee morale is strengthened if the public perceives the firm

public relations
Communication efforts used to create and maintain favorable relations between an organization and its stakeholders

Table 18.6 Top Five Public Relations Campaigns of the Decade

	PR Agency	Client (Company or Nonprofit Organization Paying for the Campaign)	Title of PR Campaign
1.	Ogilvy Public Relations	The National Heart, Lung, and Blood Institute	Red Dress Campaign
2.	Patrice Tanaka and Company	Liz Claiborne	Women's Work (cause-related marketing campaign)
3.	MGA Communications	Shell Oil Company, US Army, and the National Wildlife Agency	Rocky Mountain Arsenal clean-up and wildlife preserve campaign
4.	Fleishman-Hillard	Telco Companies	Hurricane Katrina Aid for the Displaced
5.	Ketchum	Frito-Lay	User-Generated Commercials—Doritos Crashes the Super Bowl

Source: "Holmes Reports Top 5 Advertising Campaigns of the Decade," www.designtaxi.com/news.php?id=30160 (accessed April 9, 2009).

positively.[23] Although public relations can make people aware of a company's products, brands, or activities, it can also create specific company images, such as innovativeness or dependability. Companies like Green Mountain Coffee Roasters, Patagonia, Sustainable Harvest, and Honest Tea have reputations for being socially responsible not only because they engage in socially responsible behavior but because their actions are reported through news stories and other public relations efforts. By getting the media to report on a firm's accomplishments, public relations helps the company maintain positive public visibility. Some firms use public relations for a single purpose; others use it for several purposes.

Public Relations Tools

Companies use a variety of public relations tools to convey messages and create images. Public relations professionals prepare written materials and use digital media to deliver brochures, newsletters, company magazines, news releases, blogs, and annual reports that reach and influence their various stakeholders. Procter & Gamble, for example, created a social networking website called Capessa, where women—who are major consumers of P&G products—can discuss issues like health, work, weight loss, pregnancy, and personal problems. The website changed URLs and identity in 2009 and captured the stories of women and their real life challenges (realwomenrealadvice.wordpress.com/about/). Although no longer collecting new information, the website remains a static resource and artifact of P&G's original website.[24]

Public relations personnel also create corporate identity materials, such as logos, business cards, stationery, and signs, which make firms immediately recognizable. Speeches are another public relations tool. Because what a company executive says publicly at meetings or to the media can affect the organization's image, the speech must convey the desired message clearly. Event sponsorship, in which a company pays for part or all of a special event, like a benefit concert or a tennis tournament, is another public relations tool. Examples are Coca-Cola's sponsorship of the FIFA World Cup and Special Olympics. Sponsoring special events can be an

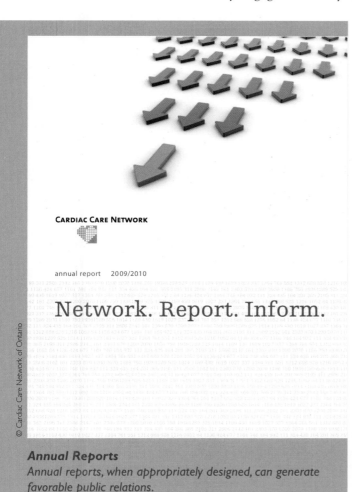

CARDIAC CARE NETWORK

annual report   2009/2010

Network. Report. Inform.

© Cardiac Care Network of Ontario

Annual Reports
Annual reports, when appropriately designed, can generate favorable public relations.

Entrepreneurial Marketing
Womankind: An Advertising Agency for Women

Because experts estimate that most purchasing power in the United States is in women's hands, a man named Jerry Judge decided to create an advertising company for women. Called Womankind, the company provides marketing services to companies targeting women. Judge employs female freelancers and assembles groups of small businesswomen, mothers, and activists to function as a focus group and communicate via a website and in informal communication, like phone conversations. Judge's venture has already attracted attention from marketers like Proctor & Gamble. The company has also created a research project called Womantuition. The function is to measure the difference between men and women when they view ads. Womankind provides an opportunity for marketers to send the right message to women.[a]

publicity A new story type of communication about an organization and/or its products transmitted through a mass medium at no charge

effective means of increasing company or brand recognition with relatively minimal investment. Event sponsorship can gain companies considerable amounts of free media coverage. An organization tries to ensure that its product and the sponsored event target a similar audience and that the two are easily associated in customers' minds. Many companies set up foundations to assist in their charitable giving. When Bill Daniels, the founder of Cablevision, died in 2000, he set up a fund supported with $1,000,000 to provide financial support for many causes, including business ethics. Bill Daniels believed that ethics were integral to business success, especially in the cable industry. The Daniels Fund is actively supporting business ethics education in Colorado, New Mexico, Utah, and Wyoming. Public relations personnel also organize unique events to "create news" about the company. These may include grand openings with celebrities, prizes, hot-air balloon rides, and other attractions that appeal to a firm's public.

Publicity is a part of public relations. **Publicity** is communication in news story form about the organization, its products, or both, transmitted through a mass medium at no charge. For instance, after Apple chairman Steve Jobs announced that the company

Marketing in Transition
Viral Expansion: The Good and the Bad

Viral expansion may sound like something to avoid, but it's actually sought by marketers who want to promote products and services. Often called "going viral," viral expansion occurs on sites like Facebook, Twitter, and YouTube. As more users share information on social media sites, digital information can spread across the Internet, rapidly generating publicity for very little cost to the company itself.

Although creating publicity via digital word of mouth may sound like a good idea, viral expansion does have some problems. Businesses cannot control what people write about the advertisements, promotions, and other information once it is released into the World Wide Web. For example, if a movie studio's trailer receives thousands upon thousands of views along with several negative comments, it could create negative publicity and hurt the film before it even debuts. Companies also have to be careful not to pitch too many hard sales. Social media users aren't interested in being sold to directly. For this reason, businesses must walk a fine line between garnering and retaining interest and creating sales pitches.

Despite the risks, many businesses benefit from viral expansion through social media. In fact, some need it. Los Angeles-based Kogi Korean BBQ relies on social media. The company runs four food carts and changes the carts' locations on a regular basis.

Kogi uses Twitter to communicate cart locations to followers (currently 50,000 and counting). This kind of flexibility allows Kogi to change a cart's location at the last minute if the original spot does not yield much business. In one year, the company's business has increased tremendously. By paying attention to consumers and understanding the risks of social media marketing, companies can use viral expansion to their advantage.[b]

Press Release
An example of a press release.

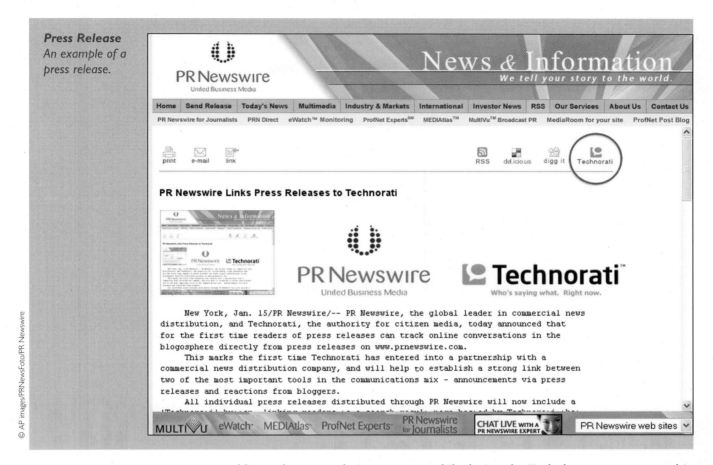

would introduce a revolutionary new mobile device, the iPad, the story was covered in newspapers and television news shows throughout the world for months afterward. Although public relations has a larger, more comprehensive communication function than publicity, publicity is a very important aspect of public relations. Publicity can be used to provide information about goods or services; to announce expansions, acquisitions, research, or new-product launches; or to enhance a company's image.

The most common publicity-based public relations tool is the **news release**, sometimes called a *press release*, which is usually a single page of typewritten copy containing fewer than 300 words and describing a company event or product. A news release gives the firm's or agency's name, address, phone number, and contact person. Automakers and other manufacturers sometimes use news releases when introducing new products or making significant announcements. Dozens of organizations, including Nike, Starbucks, and clean energy companies, are partnering to create awareness of the economic benefits of national climate and energy legislation. According to the alliance, up to 1.7 million new jobs could be created nationally, while GDP could be boosted by $39 to $111 billion.[25] As Table 18.7 shows, news releases tackle a multitude of specific issues. A **feature article** is a manuscript of up to 3,000 words prepared for a specific publication. A **captioned photograph** is a photograph with a brief description explaining its contents. Captioned photographs are effective for illustrating new or improved products with highly visible features.

There are several other kinds of publicity-based public relations tools. A **press conference** is a meeting called to announce major news events. Media personnel are invited to a press conference and are usually supplied with written materials and photographs. Letters to the editor and editorials are sometimes prepared and sent to newspapers and magazines. Videos and audiotapes may be distributed to broadcast stations in the hope that they will be aired.

Publicity-based public relations tools offer several advantages, including credibility, news value, significant word-of-mouth communications, and a perception of media endorsement. The public may consider news coverage more truthful and credible than

news release A short piece of copy publicizing an event or a product

feature article A manuscript of up to 3,000 words prepared for a specific publication

captioned photograph A photograph with a brief description of its contents

press conference A meeting used to announce major news events

Table 18.7 Possible Issues for Publicity Releases

Changes in marketing personnel	Packaging changes
Support of a social cause	New products
Improved warranties	New slogan
Reports on industry conditions	Research developments
New uses for established products	Company's history and development
Product endorsements	Employment, production, and sales records
Quality awards	Award of contracts
Company name changes	Opening of new markets
Interviews with company officials	Improvements in financial position
Improved distribution policies	Opening of an exhibit
International business efforts	History of a brand
Athletic event sponsorship	Winners of company contests
Visits by celebrities	Logo changes
Reports on new discoveries	Speeches of top management
Innovative marketing activities	Merit awards
Economic forecasts	Anniversary of inventions

Sustainable Marketing
Sustainable Organization Beats Recession

Water filtration company Brita has achieved something many companies should envy—market share growth during a recession. Brita, owned by Clorox Co., attributes its success to its eco-friendly efforts. Eco-friendly advocates have urged people to adopt reusable water bottles and filtered water instead of purchasing bottled water, which uses energy and creates wasteful packaging. In addition, reports indicate that bottled water has little regulation, making bottled water potentially more dangerous than tap water. Brita's marketing vice president, Suzanne Sengelmann, saw an opportunity and positioned Brita as the perfect solution to these issues.

Brita joined forces with popular reusable bottle maker Nalgene to create the Filter for Good Campaign. At FilterforGood.com, customers can locate eco-friendly water products and learn how they can have a positive ecological impact. Organizations such as The Surfrider Foundation and Climate Ride and musical groups U2 and Lady Antebellum promote Brita's and Nalgene's products on their sites and through their events.

A good portion of Brita's growth depends on connecting with individuals concerned with the water situation. To reach them, Sengelmann places Brita in locations in which people are focused on water, such as gyms. The company also uses traditional advertising channels like television and print. Brita also benefits from the help of an outside public relations agency, an internal PR division, and a strong brand team. All of these components have come together to create a powerful message to consumers.[c]

an advertisement because the media are not paid to provide the information. In addition, stories regarding a new-product introduction or a new environmentally responsible company policy, for example, are handled as news items and are likely to receive notice. Finally, the cost of publicity is low compared with the cost of advertising.[26]

Publicity-based public relations tools have some limitations. Media personnel must judge company messages to be newsworthy if the messages are to be published or broadcast at all. Consequently, messages must be timely, interesting, accurate, and in the public interest. It may take a great deal of time and effort to convince media personnel of the news value of publicity releases, and many communications fail to qualify. Although public relations personnel usually encourage the media to air publicity releases at certain times, they control neither the content nor the timing of the communication. Media personnel alter length and content of publicity releases to fit publishers' or broadcasters' requirements and may even delete the parts of messages that company personnel view as most important. Furthermore, media personnel use publicity releases in time slots or positions most convenient for them. Thus, messages sometimes appear in locations or at times that may not reach the firm's target audiences. Although these limitations can be frustrating, properly managed publicity-based public relations tools offer an organization substantial benefits.

Evaluating Public Relations Effectiveness

Because of the potential benefits of good public relations, it is essential that organizations evaluate the effectiveness of their public relations campaigns. Research can be conducted to determine how well a firm is communicating its messages or image to its target audiences. *Environmental monitoring* identifies changes in public opinion affecting an organization. A *public relations audit* is used to assess an organization's image among the public or to evaluate the effect of a specific public relations program. A *communications audit* may include a content analysis of messages, a readability study, or a readership survey. If an organization wants to measure the extent to which stakeholders view it as being socially responsible, it can conduct a *social audit*.

One approach to measuring the effectiveness of publicity-based public relations is to count the number of exposures in the media. To determine which releases are published in print media and how often, an organization can hire a clipping service, a firm that clips and sends news releases to client companies. To measure the effectiveness of television coverage, a firm can enclose a card with its publicity releases requesting that the television station record its name and the dates when the news item is broadcast (although station personnel do not always comply). Some television and radio tracking services exist, but they are quite costly.

Counting the number of media exposures does not reveal how many people have actually read or heard the company's message or what they thought about the message afterward. However, measuring changes in product awareness, knowledge, and attitudes resulting from the publicity campaign helps yield this information. To assess these changes, companies must measure these levels before and after public relations campaigns. Although precise measures are difficult to obtain, a firm's marketers should attempt to assess the impact of public relations efforts on the organization's sales. For example, critics' reviews of films can affect the films' box office performance. Interestingly, negative reviews (publicity) harm revenue more than positive reviews help revenue in the early weeks of a film's release.[27]

Dealing with Unfavorable Public Relations

Thus far, we have discussed public relations as a planned element of the promotion mix. However, companies may have to deal with unexpected and unfavorable publicity resulting from an unsafe product, an accident resulting from product use, controversial actions of employees, or some other negative event or situation. For example, an airline that experiences a plane crash faces a very tragic and distressing situation. Charges of anticompetitive behavior against Microsoft have raised public concern and generated unfavorable public relations for that organization. The public's image of The Body

Shop as a socially responsible company diminished considerably when it was reported that the company's actions were less socially responsible than its promotion promised. Many companies have experienced unfavorable publicity connected to contamination issues, such as salmonella in peanut butter, lead in toys, and industrial compounds in pet foods. Unfavorable coverage can have quick and dramatic effects. The global financial crisis has caused a trust breach for many companies, perhaps the greatest damage in the financial services industry. Goldman Sachs has been accused of providing very large bonuses at a time of financial uncertainty, generating significant negative publicity. A new risk area noted in Goldman Sachs' annual report was "negative publicity," along with economic conditions, market volatility, and uncertainty regarding regulation[28] As it did with Toyota, negative events that generate public relations can wipe out a company's favorable image and destroy positive customer attitudes established through years of expensive advertising campaigns and other promotional efforts. Moreover, today's mass media, including online services and the Internet, disseminate information faster than ever before, and bad news generally receives considerable media attention.

To protect its image, an organization needs to prevent unfavorable public relations or at least lessen its effect if it occurs. First and foremost, the organization should try to prevent negative incidents and events through safety programs, inspections, and effective quality control procedures. Experts insist that sending consistent brand messages and images throughout all communications at all times can help a brand maintain its strength even during a crisis.[29] However, because negative events can befall even the most cautious firms, an organization should have plans in place to handle them when they do occur. Firms need to establish policies and procedures for reducing the adverse impact of news coverage of a crisis or controversy. In most cases, organizations should expedite news coverage of negative events rather than try to discourage or block them. If news coverage is suppressed, rumors and other misinformation may replace facts.

An unfavorable event can easily balloon into serious problems or public issues and become very damaging. By being forthright with the press and public and taking prompt action, a firm may be able to convince the public of its honest attempts to deal with the situation, and news personnel may be more willing to help explain complex issues to the public. Dealing effectively with a negative event allows an organization to lessen, if not eliminate, the unfavorable impact on its image. Consider that after news reports about JetBlue leaving passengers stranded on runways for hours, the company offered the passengers full refunds and vouchers for free flights in the future. It also ran apologetic ads and issued press releases to communicate with affected stakeholders. JetBlue founder and CEO David Neeleman, who said he was "humiliated and mortified" by the incident, immediately implemented plans to add and train staff to remedy communications and operations issues that contributed to the crisis. He also pledged to enact a customer bill of rights that would penalize the airline and reward passengers should such a fiasco happen again.[30] Experts generally advise companies that are dealing with negative publicity to respond quickly and honestly to the situation and to keep the lines of communication with all stakeholders open.

summary

1. To describe the nature and types of advertising

Advertising is a paid form of nonpersonal communication transmitted to consumers through mass media, such as television, radio, the Internet, newspapers, magazines, direct mail, outdoor displays, and signs on mass transit vehicles. Both business and nonbusiness organizations use advertising. Institutional advertising promotes organizational images, ideas, and political issues. When a company promotes its position on a public issue like taxation, institutional advertising is referred to as advocacy advertising. Product advertising promotes uses, features, and benefits of products. The two types of product advertising are pioneer advertising, which focuses on stimulating demand for a product category rather than a specific brand, and competitive advertising, which attempts to stimulate demand for a specific brand by indicating the brand's features, uses, and advantages. To make direct product comparisons, marketers use comparative advertising, which compares two or more brands. Two other forms of competitive advertising are reminder advertising, which reminds customers about an established brand's uses, characteristics, and benefits, and reinforcement advertising, which assures current users they have made the right brand choice.

2. To explore the major steps in developing an advertising campaign

Although marketers may vary in how they develop advertising campaigns, they should follow a general pattern. First, they must identify and analyze the target audience, the group of people at whom advertisements are aimed. Second, they should establish what they want the campaign to accomplish by defining advertising objectives. Objectives should be clear, precise, and presented in measurable terms. Third, marketers must create the advertising platform, which contains basic issues to be presented in the campaign. Advertising platforms should consist of issues important to consumers. Fourth, advertisers must decide how much money to spend on the campaign; they arrive at this decision through the objective-and-task approach, percent-of-sales approach, competition-matching approach, or arbitrary approach.

Advertisers must then develop a media plan by selecting and scheduling media to use in the campaign. Some factors affecting the media plan are location and demographic characteristics of the target audience, content of the message, and cost of the various media. The basic content and form of the advertising message are affected by product features, uses, and benefits; characteristics of the people in the target audience; the campaign's objectives and platform; and the choice of media. Advertisers use copy and artwork to create the message. The execution of an advertising campaign requires extensive planning and coordination.

Finally, advertisers must devise one or more methods for evaluating advertisement effectiveness. Pretests are evaluations performed before the campaign begins; posttests are conducted after the campaign. Two types of posttests are a recognition test, in which respondents are shown the actual advertisement and asked whether they recognize it, and a recall test. In aided recall tests, respondents are shown a list of products, brands, company names, or trademarks to jog their memories. In unaided tests, no clues are given.

3. To identify who is responsible for developing advertising campaigns

Advertising campaigns can be developed by personnel within the firm or in conjunction with advertising agencies. A campaign created by the firm's personnel may be developed by one or more individuals or by an advertising department within the firm. Use of an advertising agency may be advantageous because an agency provides highly skilled, objective specialists with broad experience in advertising at low to moderate costs to the firm.

4. To examine the tools used in public relations

Public relations is a broad set of communication efforts used to create and maintain favorable relationships between an organization and its stakeholders. Public relations can be used to promote people, places, ideas, activities, and countries, and to create and maintain a positive company image. Some firms use public relations for a single purpose; others use it for several purposes. Public relations tools include written materials, such as brochures, newsletters, and annual reports; corporate identity materials, like business cards and signs; speeches; event sponsorships; and special events. Publicity is communication in news story form about an organization, its products, or both, transmitted through a mass medium at no charge. Publicity-based public relations tools consist of news releases, feature articles, captioned photographs, and press conferences. Problems that organizations confront in using publicity-based public relations include reluctance of media personnel to print or air releases and lack of control over timing and content of messages.

5. To analyze how public relations is used and evaluated

To evaluate the effectiveness of their public relations programs, companies conduct research to determine how well their messages are reaching their audiences. Environmental monitoring, public relations audits, and counting the number of media exposures are all means of evaluating public relations effectiveness. Organizations should avoid negative public relations by taking steps to prevent negative events that result in unfavorable publicity. To diminish the impact of unfavorable public relations, organizations should institute policies and procedures for dealing with news personnel and the public when negative events occur.

Go to www.cengagebrain.com for resources to help you master the content in this chapter as well as materials that will expand your marketing knowledge!

important terms

advertising, 536

institutional
    advertising, 536

advocacy
    advertising, 536

product
    advertising, 536

pioneer advertising, 536

competitive
    advertising, 537

comparative
    advertising, 537

reminder
    advertising, 537

reinforcement
    advertising, 537

advertising
    campaign, 537

target audience, 538

advertising platform, 539

advertising
    appropriation, 540

objective-and-task
    approach, 540

percent-of-sales
    approach, 541

competition-matching
    approach, 541

arbitrary approach, 541

media plan, 541

cost comparison
    indicator, 544

regional issues, 545

copy, 545

storyboard, 546

artwork, 546

illustrations, 546

layout, 547

pretest, 547

consumer jury, 547

posttest, 548

recognition
    test, 548

unaided recall
    test, 548

aided recall test, 549

public relations, 550

publicity, 552

news release, 553

feature article, 553

captioned
    photograph, 553

press
    conference, 553

discussion and review questions

1. What is the difference between institutional and product advertising?

2. What is the difference between competitive advertising and comparative advertising?

3. What are the major steps in creating an advertising campaign?

4. What is a target audience? How does a marketer analyze the target audience after identifying it?

5. Why is it necessary to define advertising objectives?

6. What is an advertising platform, and how is it used?

7. What factors affect the size of an advertising budget? What techniques are used to determine an advertising budget?

8. Describe the steps in developing a media plan.

9. What is the function of copy in an advertising message?

10. Discuss several ways to posttest the effectiveness of advertising.

11. What role does an advertising agency play in developing an advertising campaign?

12. What is public relations? Whom can an organization reach through public relations?

13. How do organizations use public relations tools? Give several examples you have observed recently.

14. Explain the problems and limitations associated with publicity-based public relations.

15. In what ways is the effectiveness of public relations evaluated?

16. What are some sources of negative public relations? How should an organization deal with unfavorable public relations?

application questions

CRITICAL THINKING

1. An organization must define its objectives carefully when developing an advertising campaign. Which of the following advertising objectives would be most useful for a company, and why?

a. The organization will spend $1 million to move from second in market share to market leader.

b. The organization wants to increase sales from $1.2 million to $1.5 million this year to gain the lead in market share.

c. The advertising objective is to gain as much market share as possible within the next 12 months.

d. The advertising objective is to increase sales by 15 percent.

2. Copy, the verbal portion of advertising, is used to move readers through a persuasive sequence called AIDA: attention, interest, desire, and action. To achieve this, some copywriters have adopted guidelines for developing advertising copy. Select a print ad and identify how it (a) identifies a specific problem, (b) recommends the product as the best solution to the problem, (c) states the product's advantages and benefits, (d) substantiates the ad's claims, and (e) asks the reader to take action.

3. Advertisers use several types of publicity mechanisms. Look through some recent newspapers and magazines or use an Internet search engine and identify a news release, a feature article, or a captioned photograph used to publicize a product. Describe the type of product.

4. Negative public relations can harm an organization's marketing efforts if not dealt with properly. Identify a company that was recently the target of negative public relations. Describe the situation and discuss the company's response. What did marketers at this company do well? What, if anything, would you recommend that they change about their response?

internet exercise

LEGO Company

LEGO Company has been making toys since 1932 and has become one of the most recognized brand names in the toy industry. With the company motto "Only the best is good enough," it is no surprise that LEGO has developed an exciting and interactive website. See how the company promotes LEGO products and encourages consumer involvement with the brand by visiting **www.lego.com**.

1. Which type of advertising is LEGO using on its website?
2. What target audience is LEGO attempting to reach through its website?
3. Identify the advertising objectives LEGO is attempting to achieve through its website.

developing your marketing plan

CRITICAL THINKING Determining the message that advertising is to communicate to the customer is an important part of developing a marketing strategy. A sound understanding of the various types of advertising and different forms of media is essential in selecting the appropriate methods for communicating the message. These decisions form a critical segment of the marketing plan. To assist you in relating the information in this chapter to the development of your marketing plan, consider the following issues:

1. What class and type of advertising would be most appropriate for your product?
2. Discuss the different methods for determining the advertising appropriation.

3. Using Table 18.3 as a guide, evaluate the different types of media and determine which would be most effective in meeting your promotional objectives (from Chapter 17).
4. What methods would you use to evaluate the effectiveness of your advertising campaign?
5. Review Table 18.7 and discuss possible uses for publicity in your promotional plan.

The information obtained from these questions should assist you in developing various aspects of your marketing plan found in the *Interactive Marketing Plan* exercise at **www.cengagebrain.com**.

VIDEO CASE 18.1

Vans Leverages Athletes in Its Advertising Platform

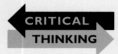

For most people, surfing and skateboarding come to mind immediately when they think of southern California culture. For 40 years, Vans has embodied the California lifestyle and remains one of the preeminent skater-shoe companies. Founded in Los Angeles in 1966 by Paul Van Doren, his brother Steve, and Belgian investor Serge D'Elia, Vans quickly became a staple in southern California. Starting with a few versions of the traditional lace-up deck shoe sold out of a factory, the style of shoe became popular almost immediately. Vans rapidly increased its level of popularity by customizing shoes in all kinds of different fabrics and designs. The Van Dorens secured their local customized shoe business by selling plaid shoes to Catholic schools and sneakers with school colors to high school athletes. But when the checkered slip-on was donned by Sean Penn and his surfer buddies in the film *Fast Times at Ridgemont High,* skaters all over the country were demanding their own pairs of Vans. The shoes went from local wear to an iconic symbol in just a few years.

Contrary to many corporate success stories, the Vans company never spent much money on advertising. Paul Van Doren knew that he offered a superior product, and he relied on word of mouth to popularize the high-quality, extremely durable shoes. The most marketing Van Doren did at first was to have his children canvas their neighborhood with flyers. At all early Vans stores, signs encouraged customers to "tell a friend about Vans." For years, Van Doren focused mostly on the manufacturing aspect of the company so that, even with a minimal amount of advertising, popularity grew because Vans were, quite simply, quality shoes. It wasn't until the late 1980s and early 1990s, when manufacturing was taken overseas, that Vans turned its attention to marketing.

One of Vans's earliest forays into promotion came about by chance. As skateboarders began to discover Vans shoes, the company responded by creating styles more amenable to skating. With their skater following growing, Vans paid some top skaters a few hundred dollars apiece to wear their shoes at skating events. In 1989, Vans produced its first signature skateboarding shoe, the Steve Caballero shoe. Since then, Vans has partnered with numerous athletes like Geoff Rowley, who has the best-selling signature Vans shoe to date, and Johnny

Layton. As skateboarding culture has continued to flourish over the decades, Vans's connection to the scene has remained strong.

Vans's two-man marketing and promotional team focuses on spreading interest in Vans by doing its best to remain plugged into the youth culture and by fueling teenage interest in Vans products. To this end, the company advertises through print, online, TV, and sporting and music events. Currently, the key to Vans's marketing strategy is developing advertising partnerships with athletes, artists, and media outlets. People immersed in this culture want to own Vans products. Vans is not just a shoe; it is a lifestyle.

Young extreme-sports athletes, like skaters and surfers, remain Vans's most important customer base. In 1995, Vans hosted its first Triple Crown event. The Triple Crown spotlights skateboarding, surfing, snowboarding, BMX, FMX, and wakeboarding. Tony Hawk won the skateboarding competition that first year and has since become a household name. Also in 1995, Vans launched its first annual Warped Tour, blending skating with music through concerts and competitions. These types of events allow Vans to build brand recognition, cement its integral place in the skating lifestyle, and connect with customers via giveaways and promotions, such as designing custom shoes.

In addition to events, Vans connects with its audience through magazine advertisements, television, and the Internet, especially in an effort to attract young female consumers, who represent a growing part of the Vans consumer base. In the past, the company has partnered with magazines like *Teen Vogue* and *CosmoGirl* to reach the female demographic. In addition, the company works with some of television's action-sports networks and hosts a weekly show, *Vans Off the Wall Hour,* on FSN. Although it is more than 40 years old, Vans still connects with youth culture as well as ever—and shows no signs of slowing down.[31]

QUESTIONS FOR DISCUSSION

1. Evaluate Vans's early word-of-mouth marketing strategy.
2. Why were the early Vans advertising activities related to skateboard shoes so successful?
3. How does Vans continue to capture its target market?

CASE 18.2

Toyota Uses Advertising to Restore Trust

For decades, Toyota set the standard for quality and reliability. Known worldwide for its commitment to quality production, Toyota created the "Toyota Way," a manufacturing philosophy that emphasized continuous progress and reduced waste. Among the important principles of the Toyota Way are long-term planning, working to find and solve problems, and creating a corporate culture that encourages improvement. Thanks to the success of the Toyota Way, Toyota became the top automobile manufacturer in the world in 2008.

However, Toyota's success was cut short by a desire to grow rapidly at the expense of quality. In 2009 and 2010, Toyota issued a series of recalls on several of their popular models because of safety problems with accelerators, brakes, and power steering. The recalls affected more than 8 million vehicles across five continents. Following the announcement of the recalls, Toyota engineers and mechanics began to search for solutions to the problems and started the process of repairing millions of cars. The company also temporarily suspended production in the United States while it researched the causes of the problems. Many critics accused the company of acting too slowly to recall the defective cars and of trying to push the problem under the rug. Because of the negative press, Toyota sales declined significantly. Toyota president Akio Toyoda admitted, "We so aggressively pursued numbers that we were unable to keep up with training staff to oversee quality." Toyoda also recognized that Toyota was slow to act on reports of problems provided by consumers.

Toyota was fined $16.4 million for allegedly hiding safety defects from consumers. This came after their reputation was already tarnished by a seemingly endless number of recalls on various car models. Toward the end of the various safety recalls related to sudden acceleration, the 2010 Lexus GX460 was declared unsafe to buy by *Consumer Reports*. Toyota became the target for late-night television jokes and seemed to constantly be in the news regarding yet another recall. This negative publicity damaged the reputation and goodwill that Toyota had developed over many years.

In the wake of massive recalls, Toyota had to adjust its advertising strategy. The world's largest car maker pulled its national advertising campaign that promoted its cars for dependability, safety, and reliability. Toyota, which had long been the leader in automotive quality, had to scramble to figure out how to handle a growing public relations crisis resulting from recalls and even a halt in sales. All experts agreed that Toyota had

to move quickly in an attempt to restore trust and deal with a crisis resulting from millions of recalled vehicles. A series of ads were developed to deal directly with the crisis and admit that the company had strayed from keeping its eye on quality while its sales had been growing rapidly. A number of low-key ads dealt directly with the issue and promised to regain consumer's trust.

Initially, Toyota tried to tackle the recall problem by addressing individual nations or sales territories. The company thought it could deal with the issue in different ways in different markets. The company forgot that social networking sites quickly highlight product-related problems through global digital media. As the largest global auto manufacturer, Toyota faced a global problem and found that it could not control information in different territories. Toyota violated the first rule of crisis management by not responding quickly, but when the company did respond, it took out full-page ads in major newspapers and produced feel-good television spots featuring dealers, mechanics, and owners. The company offered no-interest loans, discount leases, and a complementary two-year maintenance program to get buyers back.

In addition to repairing its vehicles, Toyota had to repair its reputation. Shortly after the recalls, Toyota established a global quality committee and promised to appoint chief quality officers for each of its regions. Toyota is also in the process of designing new safety systems and inspection processes for its vehicles. All future models will include a new brake-override system designed to activate the brakes in the event that both the brake and accelerator pedals are pushed down. Additionally, Toyota will have a third party test its electronic acceleration system. Ultimately, it will take more than committees, promises, and programs to rebuild Toyota. In order to regain its reputation and eventually innovate, Toyota will have to return to the Toyota Way.[32]

QUESTIONS FOR DISCUSSION

1. How can a company like Toyota use advertising to overcome negative publicity associated with a product quality issue?

2. Why did Toyota have to pull advertising for its cars' dependability, safety, and reliability during a time when it was getting so much public attention for safety recalls related to sudden acceleration?

3. What can Toyota do going forward to gain positive publicity and restore its image?

Chapter 19

Personal Selling and Sales Promotion

OBJECTIVES

1. To understand the major purposes of personal selling
2. To describe the basic steps in the personal selling process
3. To identify the types of sales force personnel
4. To recognize new types of personal selling
5. To understand sales management decisions and activities
6. To explain what sales promotion activities are and how they are used
7. To explore specific consumer sales promotion methods
8. To explore trade sales promotion methods

IBM's Celebrity Salesman

In Vivek Gupta's opinion, making a sale is similar to a courtship. In India's fast-growing telecom industry, Gupta has made the courtship of the customer an art form. Ever since he started working for IBM, Gupta has become one of its top salesmen. His 17 years in the telecom industry has given him the expertise to form relationships with some of India's biggest telecom companies. Among his many sales victories, Gupta has secured for IBM a five-year contract with Vodafone, India's fourth-largest cellular phone company. At first, the prospects of a contract with Vodafone were not very good.

Even though Vodafone explicitly told Gupta that the company never intended to do business with IBM, Gupta managed to convince Vodafone to transfer much of its information technology–related responsibilities to IBM. The secret to Gupta's sales success is his strategy. He works on studying his customers to discover their underlying needs, or what he terms the customer's "pain points." During this study period, Gupta familiarizes himself with the company so well that he often knows more about it than its employees do. Once he understands what his customers want, he finds the best way for IBM to meet those needs. He has also become adept at recognizing key signals his prospects give off. When first meeting with Vodafone, Gupta could tell when his prospects were losing interest. This is where his courtship analogy came in. "Look, this customer is not prepared for marriage, he is prepared for courtship, so let's spend some time on courtship," he told his sales team. Eventually, Gupta was able to sell Vodafone a $600 million contract. With millions of dollars of sales under his belt and opportunities to expand his sales globally, Gupta is the epitome of a successful, committed salesperson.[1]

For many organizations, targeting customers with appropriate personal selling techniques and messages can play a major role in maintaining long-term, satisfying customer relationships, which in turn contribute to company success. Marketing strategy development should involve the sales organization during all stages of development and implementation. Top managers need extensive feedback from the sales force. Managers should strive to make information transparent and should jointly analyze sales data. Sales managers should communicate marketing strategy in a language with which salespeople feel comfortable.[2] As we saw in Chapter 17, personal selling and sales promotion are two possible elements in a promotion mix. Personal selling is sometimes a company's sole promotional tool, and it is becoming increasingly professional and sophisticated, with sales personnel acting more as consultants, advisers, and sometimes as partners.

In this chapter, we focus on personal selling and sales promotion. We first consider the purposes of personal selling and then examine its basic steps. Next, we look at types of salespeople and how they are selected. After taking a look at several new types of personal selling, we discuss major sales force management decisions, including setting objectives for the sales force and determining its size; recruiting, selecting, training, compensating, and motivating salespeople; managing sales territories; and controlling and evaluating sales force performance. Then we examine several characteristics of sales promotion, reasons for using sales promotion, and sales promotion methods available for use in a promotion mix.

personal selling Paid personal communication that attempts to inform customers and persuade them to buy products in an exchange situation

The Nature of Personal Selling

Courtesy of Trend Micro Incorporated

LAST YEAR ALONE CYBERCRIMINALS STOLE OVER $40 MILLION FROM SMALL BUSINESS BANK ACCOUNTS.*

"You don't want to spend years building your business just so a hacker can retire early."

Jamz Yaneza
Threat Research Manager
Trend Micro

Like any good predator, cybercriminals go for the easy kill, and small businesses are a prime target. Using malicious software called *bots* hackers break into computers, steal banking pass codes, and drain cash from small business accounts before anyone notices. Many victims actually have an Internet security solution in place at the time of attack, but it just isn't good enough. Trend Micro's Worry-Free™ Business Security is different. It provides all-in-one protection that stops attacks like these before they reach you. You just set it and forget it. We do the rest.

Think your current Internet security is good enough? Think again.
Try our free Threat Protection Toolkit and see what's getting through.
trendmicro.com/threatprotection

TREND MICRO
Securing Your Web World

Nature of Personal Selling
Trend Micro uses personal selling for products that help small banks avoid cybercrimes.

Personal selling is paid personal communication that attempts to inform customers and persuade them to purchase products in an exchange situation. For example, a Hewlett-Packard (HP) salesperson describing the benefits of the company's servers, PCs, and printers to a small-business customer is engaging in personal selling. Likewise, a volunteer manning a petition-signing booth for a social or political cause uses personal selling to inform passersby about the issues and to persuade them to change their views or become involved. Personal selling gives marketers the greatest freedom to adjust a message to satisfy customers' information needs. It is the most precise of all promotion methods, enabling marketers to focus on the most promising sales prospects. Other promotion mix elements are aimed at groups of people, some of whom may not be prospective customers. However, personal selling is generally the most expensive element in the promotion mix. The average cost of a sales call is more than $400.[3]

Millions of people, including increasing numbers of women, earn their living through personal selling. Sales careers can offer high income, a great deal of freedom, a high level of training, and a high degree of job satisfaction. Although the public may harbor negative perceptions of personal selling, unfavorable stereotypes of salespeople are changing thanks to the efforts of major corporations, professional sales associations, and academic institutions. Researchers have found that personal selling will continue to gain respect as professional sales associations develop and enforce ethical codes of conduct.[4] The Snapshot illustrates some of the top ethical issues to consider when developing an ethics program and building a sales force.

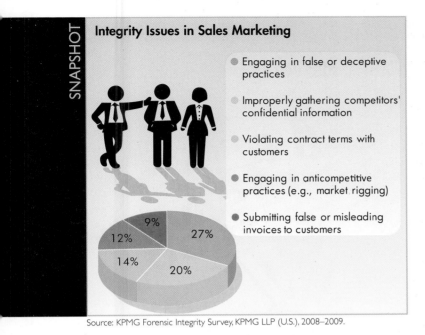

Integrity Issues in Sales Marketing

- Engaging in false or deceptive practices
- Improperly gathering competitors' confidential information
- Violating contract terms with customers
- Engaging in anticompetitive practices (e.g., market rigging)
- Submitting false or misleading invoices to customers

27%
20%
14%
12%
9%

Source: KPMG Forensic Integrity Survey, KPMG LLP (U.S.), 2008–2009.

Personal selling goals vary from one firm to another. However, they usually involve finding prospects, determining their needs, persuading prospects to buy, following up on the sale, and keeping customers satisfied. Identifying potential buyers interested in the organization's products is critical. Because most potential buyers seek information before making purchases, salespeople can ascertain prospects' informational needs and then provide relevant information. To do so, sales personnel must be well-trained regarding both their products and the selling process in general.

Salespeople must be aware of their competitors. They must monitor the development of new products and keep abreast of competitors' sales efforts in their sales territories, how often and when the competition calls on their accounts, and what the competition is saying about their product in relation to its own. Salespeople must emphasize the benefits their products provide, especially when competitors' products do not offer those specific benefits.

To be successful, personal selling needs to utilize information technology that can enhance communication with customers. Using websites to manage orders and product information, track inventory, and train salespeople can save companies time and money. Twitter is a relatively new tool that can be used to post product information and updates, obtain prospects, recruit new salespeople, and communicate with salespeople. Facebook is another valuable tool that can supplement and support face-to-face contacts. On Facebook, salespeople can carry on conversations very similar to traditional face-to-face social networks. Mobile technology and applications provide salespeople with opportunities to offer service and connect with customers. Customer relationship management (CRM) technology enables improved service, marketing and sales processes, and contact and data management and analysis. CRM can help facilitate the delivery of valuable customer experiences and provide the metrics to measure progress and sales successes.[5]

Few businesses survive solely on profits from one-time customers. For long-run survival, most marketers depend on repeat sales and thus need to keep their customers satisfied. In addition, satisfied customers provide favorable word of mouth and other electronic communications, thereby attracting new customers. Although the whole organization is responsible for achieving customer satisfaction, much of the burden falls on salespeople because they are almost always closer to customers than anyone else in the company and often provide buyers with information and service after the sale. Indeed, research shows that a firm's market orientation has a positive influence on salespeople's attitudes, commitment, and influence on customer purchasing intentions.[6] Such contact gives salespeople an opportunity to generate additional sales and offers them a good vantage point for evaluating the strengths and weaknesses of the company's products and other marketing mix components. Their observations help develop and maintain a marketing mix that better satisfies both the firm and its customers.

Elements of the Personal Selling Process

The specific activities involved in the selling process vary among salespeople, selling situations, and cultures. No two salespeople use exactly the same selling methods. Nonetheless, many salespeople move through a general selling process. This process

Marketing in Transition
Coupons Go High Tech

Is coupon clipping a thing of the past? Not just yet. Coupon use grew in 2009 for the first time in 17 years. The use of digital coupons increased by about 170 percent. These days, consumers use about 1 percent of paper coupons and about 13 percent of digital coupons, making digital the clear winner.

Recognizing this new trend, companies are embracing the consumer's love for all things digital by offering coupons online or through mobile devices. For instance, Kroger Co. launched a text message coupon service. With a click, customers can receive coupons linked to their Kroger bonus cards. Giant, another grocery chain, has incorporated scanning devices similar to those used for bridal or baby registries. The devices register deals for customers based on purchasing habits. Shoppers themselves are utilizing sites like coupon.com and retailmenot.com, which catalogs coupons from popular retailers. Homegrown blogs about how to make the most of digital coupons are also emerging all over the Internet.

By offering coupons, companies hope to draw in new customers, encourage repeat purchases, and introduce new products or changes to existing products. Companies also use coupons to learn about consumer purchasing behavior, such as identifying target markets for products. During the most recent recession, coupons became more important than ever as consumers sought to stretch their budgets. With the advent of digital coupons, businesses also began drawing an entirely new audience—the younger market segment. Today's coupons are no

longer the sole domain of the traditional coupon-clipper. They are also enticing the younger generations who are looking to save money and are comfortable with digital technologies like mobile apps. With an overall fiscal year savings of $317 billion, coupon clipping is far from dead—it's merely changed with the times.[a]

consists of seven steps, outlined in Figure 19.1: prospecting, preapproach, approach, making the presentation, overcoming objections, closing the sale, and following up.

Prospecting

Developing a database of potential customers is called **prospecting**. Salespeople seek names of prospects from company sales records, trade shows, commercial databases, newspaper announcements (of marriages, births, deaths, and so on), public records, telephone directories, trade association directories, and many other sources. Sales personnel also use responses to traditional and online advertisements that encourage interested persons to send in information request forms. Seminars and meetings, targeted at particular types of clients, such as attorneys or accountants, may also produce leads.

Most salespeople prefer to use referrals—recommendations from current customers—to find prospects. For example, salespeople for Cutco Cutlery, which sells high-quality knives and kitchen cutlery, first make sales calls to their friends and families and then use referrals from them to seek out new prospects. Obtaining referrals requires that the salesperson have a good relationship with the current customer and therefore must have performed well before asking the customer for help. As might be

prospecting Developing a database of potential customers

FIGURE 19.1 General Steps in the Personal Selling Process

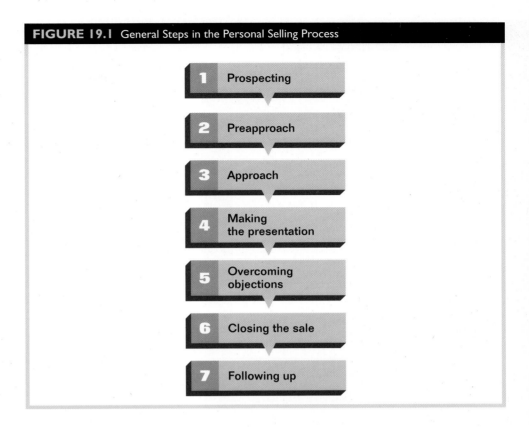

expected, a customer's trust in and satisfaction with a salesperson influences his or her willingness to provide referrals. Research shows that one referral is as valuable as 12 cold calls.[7] Also, 80 percent of clients are willing to give referrals, but only 20 percent are ever asked. Among the advantages of using referrals are more highly qualified sales leads, greater sales rates, and larger initial transactions. Some companies even award discounts off future purchases to customers who refer new prospects to their salespeople. Consistent activity is critical to successful prospecting. Salespeople must actively search the customer base for qualified prospects that fit the target market profile. After developing the prospect list, a salesperson evaluates whether each prospect is able, willing, and authorized to buy the product. Based on this evaluation, prospects are ranked according to desirability or potential.

Preapproach

Before contacting acceptable prospects, a salesperson finds and analyzes information about each prospect's specific product needs, current use of brands, feelings about available brands, and personal characteristics. In short, salespeople need to know what potential buyers and decision makers consider most important and why they need a specific product. The most successful salespeople are thorough in their *preapproach*, which involves identifying key decision makers, reviewing account histories and problems, contacting other clients for information, assessing credit histories and problems, preparing sales presentations, identifying product needs, and obtaining relevant literature. Marketers are increasingly using information technology and customer relationship management systems to comb through databases and thus identify their most profitable products and customers. CRM systems can also help sales departments manage leads, track customers, forecast sales, and assess performance. A salesperson with a lot of information about a prospect is better equipped to develop a presentation that precisely communicates with that prospect.

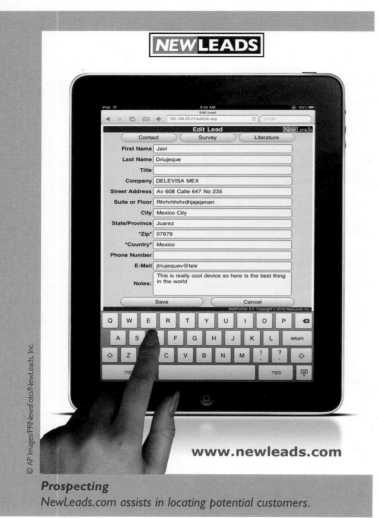

Prospecting
NewLeads.com assists in locating potential customers.

Approach

The **approach**—the manner in which a salesperson contacts a potential customer—is a critical step in the sales process. In more than 80 percent of initial sales calls, the purpose is to gather information about the buyer's needs and objectives. Creating a favorable impression and building rapport with prospective clients are important tasks in the approach because the prospect's first impressions of the salesperson are usually lasting ones. During the initial visit, the salesperson strives to develop a relationship rather than just push a product. Indeed, coming across as a "salesperson" may not be the best approach because some people are put off by strong selling tactics. The salesperson may have to call on a prospect several times before the product is considered. The approach must be designed to deliver value to targeted customers. If the sales approach is inappropriate, the salesperson's efforts are likely to have poor results.

One type of approach is based on referrals, as discussed in the section on prospecting. The salesperson who uses the "cold canvass" approach calls on potential customers without prior consent. Repeat contact is another common approach: when making the contact, the salesperson mentions a previous meeting. The exact type of approach depends on the salesperson's preferences, the product being sold, the firm's resources, and the prospect's characteristics.

Making the Presentation

During the sales presentation, the salesperson must attract and hold the prospect's attention, stimulate interest, and spark a desire for the product. Researchers have found that salespeople who carefully monitor the selling situation and adapt their presentations to meet the needs of prospects are associated with effective sales performance.[8] Salespeople should match their influencing tactics—such as information exchange, recommendations, threats, promises, ingratiation, and inspirational appeals—to their prospects. Different types of buyers respond to different tactics, but most respond well to information exchange and recommendations, and virtually no prospects respond to threats.[9] The salesperson should have the prospect touch, hold, or use the product. If possible, the salesperson should demonstrate the product or invite the prospect to use it. Automobile salespeople, for example, typically invite potential buyers to test-drive the vehicle that interests them. Audiovisual equipment and software may also enhance the presentation.

During the presentation, the salesperson must not only talk, but also listen. Nonverbal modes of communication are especially beneficial in building trust during the presentation.[10] The sales presentation gives the salesperson the greatest opportunity to determine the prospect's specific needs by listening to questions and comments and observing responses. Even though the salesperson plans the presentation in advance, she or he must be able to adjust the message to meet the prospect's informational needs. Research demonstrates that adapting the message in response to the customer's needs generally enhances performance, particularly in new-task or modified rebuy purchase situations.[11]

approach The manner in which a salesperson contacts a potential customer

Overcoming Objections

An effective salesperson usually seeks out a prospect's objections in order to address them. If they are not apparent, the salesperson cannot deal with them, and the prospect may not buy. One of the best ways to overcome objections is to anticipate and counter them before the prospect raises them. However, this approach can be risky because the salesperson may mention objections that the prospect would not have raised. If possible, the salesperson should handle objections as they arise. They can also be addressed at the end of the presentation.

Closing the Sale

Closing is the stage in the personal selling process when the salesperson asks the prospect to buy the product. During the presentation, the salesperson may use a *trial close* by asking questions that assume the prospect will buy. The salesperson might ask the potential customer about financial terms, desired colors or sizes, or delivery arrangements. Reactions to such questions usually indicate how close the prospect is to buying. Properly asked questions may allow prospects to uncover their own problems and identify solutions themselves. One questioning approach uses broad questions *(what, how, why)* to probe or gather information and focused questions *(who, when, where)* to clarify and close the sale. A trial close allows prospects to indicate indirectly that they will buy the product without having to say those sometimes difficult words: "I'll take it."

A salesperson should try to close at several points during the presentation because the prospect may be ready to buy. An attempt to close the sale may result in objections. Thus, closing can uncover hidden objections, which the salesperson can then address. One closing strategy involves asking the potential customer to place a low-risk, trial order.

Following Up

After a successful closing, the salesperson must follow up the sale. In the follow-up stage, the salesperson determines whether the order was delivered on time and installed properly, if installation was required. He or she should contact the customer to learn if any problems or questions regarding the product have arisen. The follow-up stage is also used to determine customers' future product needs.

Types of Salespeople

To develop a sales force, a marketing manager decides what kind of salesperson will sell the firm's products most effectively. Most business organizations use several different kinds of sales personnel. Based on the functions performed, salespeople can be classified into three groups: order getters, order takers, and support personnel. One salesperson can, and often does, perform all three functions.

closing The stage in the personal selling process when the salesperson asks the prospect to buy the product

order getter A salesperson who sells to new customers and increases sales to current customers

Order Getters

To obtain orders, a salesperson informs prospects and persuades them to buy the product. The responsibility of the **order getter** is to increase sales by selling to new customers and increasing sales to present customers. This task is sometimes called *creative selling*. It requires that salespeople recognize potential buyers' needs and give them necessary information. Order getting is frequently divided into two categories: current-customer sales and new-business sales.

CURRENT-CUSTOMER SALES

Sales personnel who concentrate on current customers call on people and organizations that have purchased products from the firm before. These salespeople seek more sales from existing customers by following up previous sales. Current customers can also be sources of leads for new prospects.

NEW-BUSINESS SALES

Business organizations depend to some degree on sales to new customers. New-business sales personnel locate prospects and convert them into buyers. Salespeople help generate new business in many organizations, but even more so in organizations that sell real estate, insurance, appliances, automobiles, and business-to-business supplies and services. These organizations depend in large part on new-customer sales.

Order Takers

Taking orders is a repetitive task salespeople perform to perpetuate long-lasting, satisfying customer relationships. **Order takers** primarily seek repeat sales, generating the bulk of many firms' total sales. One of their major objectives is to be certain that customers have sufficient product quantities where and when needed. Most order takers handle orders for standardized products that are purchased routinely and do not require extensive sales efforts. The role of order takers is changing, however, as the position moves more toward one that identifies and solves problems to better meet the needs of customers. There are two groups of order takers: inside order takers and field order takers.

INSIDE ORDER TAKERS

In many businesses, inside order takers, who work in sales offices, receive orders by mail, telephone, and the Internet. Certain producers, wholesalers, and retailers have sales personnel who sell from within the firm rather than in the field. Some inside order takers communicate with customers face to face; retail salespeople, for example, are classified as inside order takers. As more orders are placed electronically, the role of the inside order taker continues to change.

FIELD ORDER TAKERS

Salespeople who travel to customers are outside, or field, order takers. Often, customers and field order takers develop interdependent relationships. The buyer relies on the salesperson to take orders periodically (and sometimes to deliver them), and the salesperson counts on the buyer to purchase a certain quantity of products periodically. Use of small computers has improved the field order taker's inventory and order-tracking capabilities.

Support Personnel

Support personnel facilitate selling but usually are not involved solely with making sales. They engage primarily in marketing industrial products, locating prospects, educating customers, building goodwill, and providing service after the sale. There are many kinds of sales support personnel; the three most common are missionary, trade, and technical salespeople.

MISSIONARY SALESPEOPLE

Missionary salespeople, usually employed by manufacturers, assist the producer's customers in selling to their own customers. Missionary salespeople may call on retailers to inform and persuade them to buy the manufacturer's products. When they succeed, retailers purchase products from wholesalers, which are the producer's customers. Manufacturers of medical supplies and pharmaceuticals often use missionary salespeople, called *detail reps*, to promote their products to physicians, hospitals, and pharmacists.

order takers Salespeople who primarily seek repeat sales

support personnel Sales staff members who facilitate selling but usually are not involved solely with making sales

missionary salespeople Support salespeople, usually employed by a manufacturer, who assist the producer's customers in selling to their own customers

trade salespeople
Salespeople involved mainly in helping a producer's customers promote a product

technical salespeople
Support salespeople who give technical assistance to a firm's current customers

team selling The use of a team of experts from all functional areas of a firm, led by a salesperson, to conduct the personal selling process

relationship selling The building of mutually beneficial long-term associations with a customer through regular communications over prolonged periods of time

TRADE SALESPEOPLE

Trade salespeople are not strictly support personnel because they usually take orders as well. However, they direct much effort toward helping customers—especially retail stores—promote the product. They are likely to restock shelves, obtain more shelf space, set up displays, provide in-store demonstrations, and distribute samples to store customers. Food producers and processors commonly employ trade salespeople.

TECHNICAL SALESPEOPLE

Technical salespeople give technical assistance to the organization's current customers, advising them on product characteristics and applications, system designs, and installation procedures. Because this job is often highly technical, the salesperson usually has formal training in one of the physical sciences or in engineering. Technical sales personnel often sell technical industrial products, such as computers, heavy equipment, and steel.

When hiring sales personnel, marketers seldom restrict themselves to a single category, because most firms require different types of salespeople. Several factors dictate how many of each type a particular company should have. Product use, characteristics, complexity, and price influence the kind of sales personnel used, as do the number and characteristics of customers. The types of marketing channels and the intensity and type of advertising also affect the composition of a sales force.

Team Selling
At times, sales representatives work in teams to provide detailed sales presentations. Sales team members may specialize in product knowledge, technical support, and applications.

Selected Types of Selling

Personal selling has become an increasingly complex process due in large part to rapid technological innovation. Most importantly, the focus of personal selling is shifting from selling a specific product to building long-term relationships with customers by finding solutions to their needs, problems, and challenges. As a result, the roles of salespeople are changing. Among the newer philosophies for personal selling are team selling and relationship selling.

Team Selling

Many products, particularly expensive high-tech business products, have become so complex that a single salesperson can no longer be expert in every aspect of the product and purchase process. **Team selling**, which involves the salesperson joining with people from the firm's financial, engineering, and other functional areas, is appropriate for such products. The salesperson takes the lead in the personal selling process, but other members of the team bring their unique skills, knowledge, and resources to the process to help customers find solutions to their own business challenges. Selling teams may be created to address a particular short-term situation or they may be formal, ongoing teams. Team selling is advantageous in situations calling for detailed knowledge of new, complex, and dynamic technologies like jet aircraft and medical equipment. It can be difficult, however, for highly competitive salespersons to adapt to a team selling environment.

Relationship Selling

Relationship selling, also known as consultative selling, involves building mutually beneficial long-term associations with a customer through regular communications over prolonged periods of time. Like team selling, it is especially used in business-to-business marketing. Relationship selling involves finding solutions to customers' needs by listening to them, gaining a detailed understanding of their organizations, understanding and caring about their needs and challenges, and providing support after the sale. Relationship selling efforts can be enhanced through sales automation technology tools that enhance interactive communication.[12] New applications for customer relationship management are also being provided through companies like Salesforce.com, which offers a cloud-computing model to help companies keep track of the customer life cycle without having to install any software (applications are downloaded). Social networks are being utilized in sales, adding new layers to the selling process. Salesforce CRM, for instance, now allows users to connect with their customers in real-time through such networks as Twitter and Facebook. Sales force automation, which involves utilizing information technology to automatically track all stages of the sales process (a part of customer relationship management) has been found to increase salesperson professionalism and responsiveness, customer interaction frequency, and customer relationship quality.[13]

Managing the Sales Force

The sales force is directly responsible for generating one of an organization's primary inputs: sales revenue. Without adequate sales revenue, businesses cannot survive. In addition, a firm's reputation is often determined by the ethical conduct of its sales force. Indeed, a positive ethical climate, one component of corporate culture, has been linked with decreased role stress and turnover intention and improved job attitudes and job performance in sales.[14] Research has demonstrated that a negative ethical climate will trigger higher-performing salespeople to leave a company at a higher rate than those in a company perceived to be ethical.[15] The morale and ultimately the success of a firm's sales force depend in large part on adequate compensation, room for advancement, sufficient training, and management support—all key areas of sales management. Salespeople who are not satisfied with these elements may leave. Evaluating the input of salespeople is an important part of sales force management because of its strong bearing on a firm's success. Table 19.1 provides recommendations on how to attract and retain a top-quality sales force.

TABLE 19.1 Suggestions for Attracting and Retaining a Top Sales Force

Training and Development	• On-the-job training • Individual instruction • Seminars • On-site classroom instruction
Compensation	• Make sure pay mix isn't too risky (high commission, low base) for sales role • Mix base salary with commission, bonus, or both • Base bonuses/commission on reaching sales goals rather than on individual sales dollars • Maintain competitive benefits and expense reimbursement practices
Work/Life Autonomy	• Offer flexible hours • Consider telecommuting/work-at-home options
Product Quality and Service	• Ensure products and services meet customer needs • Provide the appropriate service after the sale

Source: "Attracting & Retaining a Top Sales Force," Where Great Workplaces Start, http://greatworkplace.wordpress.com/2010/02/10/attracting-retaining-a-top-sales-force/ (accessed April 6, 2010).

We explore eight general areas of sales management: establishing sales force objectives, determining sales force size, recruiting and selecting salespeople, training sales personnel, compensating salespeople, motivating salespeople, managing sales territories, and controlling and evaluating sales force performance.

Establishing Sales Force Objectives

To manage a sales force effectively, sales managers must develop sales objectives. Sales objectives tell salespeople what they are expected to accomplish during a specified time period. They give the sales force direction and purpose, and serve as standards for evaluating and controlling the performance of sales personnel. Sales objectives should be stated in precise, measurable terms, specify the time period and geographic areas involved, and be achievable.

Sales objectives are usually developed for both the total sales force and individual salespeople. Objectives for the entire force are normally stated in terms of sales volume, market share, or profit. Volume objectives refer to dollar or unit sales. For example, the objective for an electric drill producer's sales force might be to sell $18 million worth of drills, or 600,000 drills annually. When sales goals are stated in terms of market share, they usually call for an increase in the proportion of the firm's sales relative to the total number of products sold by all businesses in that industry. When sales objectives are based on profit, they are generally stated in terms of dollar amounts or return on investment.

Sales objectives, or quotas, for individual salespeople are commonly stated in terms of dollar or unit sales volume. Other bases used for individual sales objectives include average order size, average number of calls per time period, and ratio of orders to calls.

Determining Sales Force Size

Sales force size is important because it influences the company's ability to generate sales and profits. Moreover, size of the sales force affects the compensation methods used, salespeople's morale, and overall sales force management. Sales force size must be adjusted periodically because a firm's marketing plans change along with markets and forces in the marketing environment. One danger in cutting back the size of the sales force to increase profits is that the sales organization may lose strength and resiliency, preventing it from rebounding when growth occurs or better market conditions prevail.

Several analytical methods can help determine optimal sales force size. One method involves determining how many sales calls per year are necessary for the organization to serve customers effectively and then dividing this total by the average number of sales calls a salesperson makes annually. A second method is based on marginal analysis, in which additional salespeople are added to the sales force until the cost of an additional salesperson equals the additional sales generated by that person. Although marketing managers may use one or several analytical methods, they normally temper decisions with subjective judgments.

Recruiting and Selecting Salespeople

To create and maintain an effective sales force, sales managers must recruit the right type of salespeople. In **recruiting**, the sales manager develops a list of qualified applicants for sales positions. Effective recruiting efforts are a vital part of implementing the strategic sales force plan and can help assure successful organizational performance. Costs of hiring and training a salesperson are soaring, reaching more than $60,000 in some industries. Thus, recruiting errors are expensive.

To ensure that the recruiting process results in a pool of qualified applicants, a sales manager establishes a set of qualifications before beginning to recruit. Although marketers have tried for years to identify a set of traits characterizing effective salespeople, no set of generally accepted characteristics exists yet. Experts agree that good salespeople exhibit optimism, flexibility, self-motivation, good time

recruiting Developing a list of qualified applicants for sales positions management skills, empathy, and the ability to network and maintain long-term customer relationships. Today, companies are increasingly seeking applicants capable of employing relationship-building and consultative approaches as well as the ability to work effectively in team selling efforts.

Sales managers must determine what set of traits best fits their companies' particular sales tasks. Two activities help establish this set of required attributes. First, the sales manager should prepare a job description listing specific tasks salespeople are to perform. Second, the manager should analyze characteristics of the firm's successful salespeople, as well as those of ineffective sales personnel. From the job description and analysis of traits, the sales manager should be able to develop a set of specific requirements and be aware of potential weaknesses that could lead to failure.

A sales manager generally recruits applicants from several sources: departments within the firm, other firms, employment agencies, educational institutions, respondents to advertisements, websites (like Monster.com), and individuals recommended by current employees. The specific sources depend on the type of salesperson required and the manager's experiences and successes with particular recruiting tactics.

The process of recruiting and selecting salespeople varies considerably from one company to another. Companies intent on reducing sales force turnover are likely to have strict recruiting and selection procedures. Sales management should design a selection procedure that satisfies the company's specific needs. Some organizations use the specialized services of other companies to hire sales personnel. The process should include steps that yield the information required to make accurate selection decisions. However, because each step incurs a certain amount of expense, there should be no more steps than necessary. Stages of the selection process should be sequenced so that the more expensive steps, such as a physical examination, occur near the end. Fewer people will then move through higher-cost stages.

Recruitment should not be sporadic; it should be a continuous activity aimed at reaching the best applicants. The selection process should systematically and effectively match applicants' characteristics and needs with the requirements of specific selling tasks. Finally, the selection process should ensure that new sales personnel are available where and when needed.

Training Sales Personnel

Many organizations have formal training programs; others depend on informal, on-the-job training. Some systematic training programs are quite extensive, whereas others are rather short and rudimentary. Whether the training program is complex or simple, developers must consider what to teach, whom to train, and how to train them.

A sales training program can concentrate on the company, its products, or selling methods. Training programs often cover all three. Such programs can be aimed at newly hired salespeople, experienced salespeople, or both. Training for experienced company salespeople usually emphasizes product information or the use of new technology, although salespeople must also be informed about new selling techniques and changes in company plans, policies, and procedures. Sales managers should use ethics training to institutionalize an ethical climate, improve employee satisfaction, and help prevent misconduct. IBM's Health Care and Life Sciences Group, for example, constantly educates its sales force concerning changing trends and effective ways to reach clients. The vice president of IBM's Eastern Regional Solution Sales runs two weeks of extensive sales force training each year, part of which is used to familiarize the sales representatives with new products and services as well as current customer concerns.[16] Ordinarily, new sales personnel require comprehensive training, whereas experienced personnel need both refresher courses on established products and training regarding new-product information and technology changes.

Sales training may be done in the field, at educational institutions, in company facilities, and/or online using web-based technology. For example, Platinum Guild International USA used web-based technologies to launch its first online sales training program as an interactive module that retail jewelers could utilize to learn about the

Recruiting and Selecting Salespeople *Potential sales force employees can be recruited through a variety of sources, including job fairs.*

platinum industry.[17] For many companies, online training saves time and money and helps salespeople learn about new products quickly. Some firms train new employees before assigning them to a specific sales position. Others put them into the field immediately, providing formal training only after they have gained some experience. Training programs for new personnel can be as short as several days or as long as three years; some are even longer. Sales training for experienced personnel is often scheduled when sales activities are not too demanding. Because experienced salespeople usually need periodic retraining, a firm's sales management must determine the frequency, sequencing, and duration of these efforts.

Sales managers, as well as other salespeople, often engage in sales training, whether daily on the job or periodically during sales meetings. Salespeople sometimes receive training from technical specialists within their own organizations. In addition, a number of outside companies specialize in providing sales training programs. Materials for sales training programs range from videos, texts, online materials, manuals, and cases to programmed learning devices and digital media. Lectures, demonstrations, simulation exercises, role-plays, and on-the-job training can all be effective training methods. Self-directed learning to supplement traditional sales training has the potential to improve sales performance. The choice of methods and materials for a particular sales training program depends on type and number of trainees, program content and complexity, length and location, size of the training budget, number of trainers, and a trainer's expertise.

Compensating Salespeople

To develop and maintain a highly productive sales force, an organization must formulate and administer a compensation plan that attracts, motivates, and retains the most effective individuals. The plan should give sales management the desired level of control and provide sales personnel with acceptable levels of income, freedom, and incentive. It should be flexible, equitable, easy to administer, and easy to understand. Good compensation programs facilitate and encourage proper treatment of customers. Obviously, it is quite difficult to incorporate all of these requirements into a single program. Figure 19.2 shows the average salaries for sales representatives.

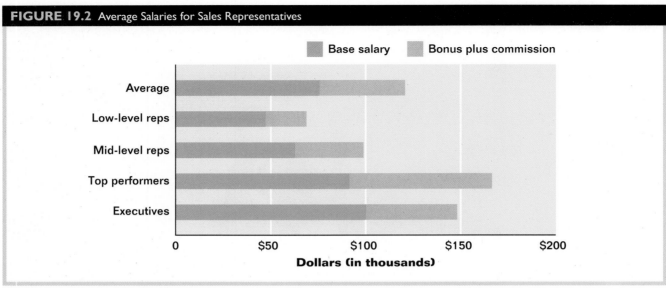

FIGURE 19.2 Average Salaries for Sales Representatives

Source: Joseph Kornik, "What's It All Worth?" *Sales and Marketing Management*, May 2007, p. 29.

Developers of compensation programs must determine the general level of compensation required and the most desirable method of calculating it. In analyzing the required compensation plan, sales management must ascertain a salesperson's value to the company on the basis of the tasks and responsibilities associated with the sales position. Sales managers may consider a number of factors, including salaries of other types of personnel in the firm, competitors' compensation plans, costs of sales force turnover, and nonsalary selling expenses. The average low-level salesperson earns about $71,000 annually (including commissions and bonuses), whereas a high-level, high-performing salesperson can make hundreds of thousands a year.

Sales compensation programs usually reimburse salespeople for selling expenses, provide some fringe benefits, and deliver the required compensation level. To achieve this, a firm may use one or more of three basic compensation methods: straight salary, straight commission, or a combination of the two. Table 19.2 lists the major characteristics, advantages, and disadvantages of each method. In a **straight salary compensation plan**, salespeople are paid a specified amount per time period, regardless of selling effort. This sum remains the same until they receive a pay increase or decrease. Although this method is easy to administer and affords salespeople financial security, it provides little incentive for them to boost selling efforts. In a **straight commission compensation plan**, salespeople's compensation is determined solely by sales for a given period. A commission may be based on a single percentage of sales or on a sliding scale involving several sales levels and percentage rates (e.g., sales under $500,000 a quarter would receive a smaller commission than sales over $500,000 each quarter). Although this method motivates sales personnel to escalate their selling efforts, it offers them little financial security, and it can be difficult for sales managers to maintain control over the sales force. Many new salespeople indicate a reluctance to accept the risks associated with straight commission. However, more experienced salespeople know this option can provide the greatest income potential. For these reasons, many firms offer a **combination compensation plan** in which salespeople receive a fixed salary plus a commission based on sales volume. Some combination programs require that a salesperson exceed a certain sales level before earning a commission; others offer commissions for any level of sales.

When selecting a compensation method, sales management weighs the advantages and disadvantages listed in the table. Researchers have found that higher commissions are the most preferred reward, followed by pay increases.[18] For example, the Container Store, which markets do-it-yourself organizing and storage products, prefers to pay its

straight salary compensation plan Paying salespeople a specific amount per time period, regardless of selling effort

straight commission compensation plan Paying salespeople according to the amount of their sales in a given time period

combination compensation plan Paying salespeople a fixed salary plus a commission based on sales volume

TABLE 19.2 Characteristics of Sales Force Compensation Methods

Compensation Method	Use (%)*	When Especially Useful	Advantages	Disadvantages
Straight salary	17.5	Compensating new salespeople; firm moves into new sales territories that require developmental work; sales requiring lengthy presale and post-sale services	Gives salespeople security; gives sales managers control over salespeople; easy to administer; yields more predictable selling expenses	Provides no incentive; necessitates closer supervision of salespeople; during sales declines, selling expenses remain constant
Straight commission	14.0	Highly aggressive selling is required; nonselling tasks are minimized; company uses contractors and part-timers	Provides maximum amount of incentive; by increasing commission rate, sales managers can encourage salespeople to sell certain items; selling expenses relate directly to sales resources	Salespeople have little financial security; sales managers have minimum control over sales force; may cause salespeople to give inadequate service to smaller accounts; selling costs less predictable
Combination	68.5	Sales territories have relatively similar sales potential; firm wishes to provide incentive but still control sales force activities	Provides certain level of financial security; provides some incentive; can move sales force efforts in profitable direction	Selling expenses less predictable; may be difficult to administer

*The figures are computed from *Dartnell's 30th Sales Force Compensation Survey,* Dartnell Corporation, Chicago, 1999.

Source: Charles Futrell, *Sales Management* (Ft. Worth: Dryden Press), 2001, pp. 307–316.

sales staff salaries that are 50 to 100 percent higher than those offered by rivals instead of basing pay on commission plans.[19] During the recent economic downturn, sales fell for the first time in 30 years. Instead of laying off the sales staff, the Container Store froze salaries for everyone in the company and introduced sales contests as a way to motivate staff.[20]

Motivating Salespeople

Although financial compensation is an important incentive, additional programs are necessary for motivating sales personnel. A sales manager should develop a systematic approach for motivating salespeople to be productive. Effective sales force motivation is achieved through an organized set of activities performed continuously by the company's sales management.

Sales personnel, like other people, join organizations to satisfy personal needs and achieve personal goals. Sales managers must identify those needs and goals and strive to create an organizational climate that allows each salesperson to fulfill them. Enjoyable working conditions, power and authority, job security, and opportunity to excel are effective motivators, as are company efforts to make sales jobs more productive and efficient. At the Container Store, for example, sales personnel receive 241 hours of training about the company's products every year so they can help customers solve organizational and storage problems.[21] Research has shown that a strong corporate culture leads to higher levels of job satisfaction and organizational commitment and lower levels of job stress.[22] Sales contests and other incentive programs can also be effective motivators. These can motivate salespeople to increase sales or add new accounts, promote special items, achieve greater volume per sales call, and cover territories more thoroughly. However, companies need to understand salespersons' preferences when designing contests in order to make them effective in increasing sales. Some companies find such contests powerful tools for motivating sales personnel to achieve company goals. Managers should be careful to craft sales contests that support a strong customer orientation as well as motivate salespeople. In smaller firms lacking the resources for a formal incentive program, a simple but public "thank-you" and the recognition from management at a sales meeting, along with a small-denomination gift card, can be very rewarding.

Motivating Salespeople
Vacations and other incentives can be utilized to motivate salespeople to achieve their goals.

Properly designed incentive programs pay for themselves many times over, and sales managers are relying on incentives more than ever. Recognition programs that acknowledge outstanding performance with symbolic awards, such as plaques, can be very effective when carried out in a peer setting. The most common incentive offered by companies is cash, followed by gift cards and travel.[23] Travel reward programs can confer a high-profile honor, provide a unique experience that makes recipients feel special, and build camaraderie among award-winning salespeople. However, some recipients of travel awards may feel they already travel too much on the job. Cash rewards are easy to administer, are always appreciated by recipients, and appeal to all demographic groups. However, cash has no visible "trophy" value and provides few "bragging rights." The benefits of awarding merchandise are that the items have visible trophy value. In addition, recipients who are allowed to select the merchandise experience a sense of control, and merchandise awards can help build momentum for the sales force. The disadvantages of using merchandise are that employees may have lower perceived value of the merchandise, and the company may experience greater administrative problems. Some companies outsource their incentive programs to companies that specialize in the creation and management of such programs.

Managing Sales Territories

The effectiveness of a sales force that must travel to customers is somewhat influenced by management's decisions regarding sales territories. When deciding on territories, sales managers must consider size, geographic shape, routing, and scheduling.

CREATING SALES TERRITORIES

Several factors enter into the design of a sales territory's size and geographic shape. First, sales managers must construct territories that allow sales potential to be measured. Sales territories often consist of several geographic units, such as census tracts, cities, counties, or states, for which market data are obtainable. Sales managers usually try to create territories with similar sales potential, or requiring about the same amount of work. If territories have equal sales potential, they will almost always be unequal in geographic size. Salespeople with larger territories have to work longer and harder to generate a certain sales volume. Conversely, if sales territories requiring equal amounts of work are created, sales potential for those territories will often vary. Think about the effort required to sell in New York and Connecticut versus the sales effort required in a larger, less populated area like Montana and Wyoming. If sales personnel are partially or fully compensated through commissions, they will have unequal income potential. Many sales managers try to balance territorial workloads and earning potential by using differential commission rates. At times, sales managers use commercial programs to help them balance sales territories. Although a sales manager seeks equity when developing and maintaining sales territories, some inequities always prevail. A territory's size and geographical shape should also help the sales force provide the best possible customer coverage and should minimize selling costs. Customer density and distribution are important factors.

ROUTING AND SCHEDULING SALESPEOPLE

The geographic size and shape of a sales territory are the most important factors affecting the routing and scheduling of sales calls. Next in importance is the number and distribution of customers within the territory, followed by sales call frequency and duration. Those in charge of routing and scheduling must consider the sequence in which customers are called on, specific roads or transportation schedules to be used, number of calls to be made in a given period, and time of day the calls will occur. In some firms, salespeople plan their own routes and schedules with little or no assistance from the sales manager. In others, the sales manager maintains significant responsibility. No matter who plans the routing and scheduling, the major goals should be to minimize salespeople's nonselling time (time spent traveling and waiting) and maximize their selling time. The goal in planning should try to achieve these goals so that a salesperson's travel and lodging costs are held to a minimum.

Controlling and Evaluating Sales Force Performance

To control and evaluate sales force performance properly, sales management needs information. A sales manager cannot observe the field sales force daily and thus relies on salespeople's call reports, customer feedback, contracts, and invoices. Call reports identify the customers called on and present detailed information about interactions with those clients. Sales personnel often must file work schedules indicating where they plan to be during specific time periods. Data about a salesperson's interactions with customers and prospects can be included in the company's customer relationship management system. This information provides insights about the salesperson's performance.

Dimensions used to measure a salesperson's performance are determined largely by sales objectives, normally set by the sales manager. If an individual's sales objective is stated in terms of sales volume, that person should be evaluated on the basis of sales volume generated. Even if a salesperson is assigned a major objective, he or she is ordinarily expected to achieve several related objectives as well. Thus, salespeople are often judged along several dimensions. Sales managers evaluate many performance indicators, including average number of calls per day, average sales per customer, actual sales relative to sales potential, number of new-customer orders, average cost per call, and average gross profit per customer.

To evaluate a salesperson, a sales manager may compare one or more of these dimensions with predetermined performance standards. However, sales managers commonly compare a salesperson's performance with that of other employees operating under similar selling conditions, or the salesperson's current performance with past performance. Sometimes management judges factors that have less direct bearing on sales performance, such as personal appearance, product knowledge, and ethical standards. One concern is the tendency to reprimand top sellers less severely than poor performers for engaging in unethical selling practices.

After evaluating salespeople, sales managers take any needed corrective action to improve sales force performance. They may adjust performance standards, provide additional training, or try other motivational methods. Corrective action may demand comprehensive changes in the sales force.

The Nature of Sales Promotion

sales promotion An activity and/or material intended to induce resellers or salespeople to sell a product or consumers to buy it

Sales promotion is an activity or material, or both, that acts as a direct inducement, offering added value or incentive for the product, to resellers, salespeople, or consumers. It encompasses all promotional activities and materials other than personal selling, advertising, and public relations. Wendy's, for example, has used an online reverse auction to attract consumers to three value sandwiches that sell for 99 cents each. The auction sold various high-end items, including an Xbox 360 console and game chair, to bidders for 99 cents each. The auction was promoted virally online and aimed to reach out to consumers in the 18 to 24 age range.[24] In competitive markets, where products are very similar, sales promotion provides additional inducements that encourage product trial and purchase.

Sustainable Marketing
Avon Empowers Women Environmentally

Avon, the world's largest direct seller, is taking its theme of woman empowerment to a whole new level in its creation of a "global women's environmental movement." Avon recently launched the environmental initiative Hello Green Tomorrow in 65 countries with an aim to replenish South America's rainforests. Helping in its endeavor is Avon's 6.2 million sales representatives, who will promote green education worldwide.

Its message to consumers is simple: donate as little as $1 to plant a tree. Determined to lead by example, Avon started off by donating $1 million to the Nature Conservancy. This money will be used to plant 1 million trees in the Atlantic Rainforest in South America. Avon hopes its efforts will begin the steps to restore the 93 percent of South American rainforest that has been depleted.

Avon is also encouraging its suppliers to be sustainable through its Avon Paper Promise. The company plans to be 100 percent supplied by recycled or certified paper products within the next decade (certification indicates that the wood came from responsibly managed forests). Although these requirements may put some pressure on suppliers, Avon intends to aid suppliers in obtaining paper products in a sustainable manner. Avon has also

begun replacing paper order forms with online forms and phone orders. In 2009, 75 percent of Avon order forms in America were placed online.

Due to Avon's efforts in sustainability, the company was ranked number 25 in *Newsweek*'s green list of the top 500 companies. Avon appears dedicated to saving the environment one dollar at a time.[b]

Marketers often use sales promotion to facilitate personal selling, advertising, or both. Companies also employ advertising and personal selling to support sales promotion activities. For example, marketers frequently use advertising to promote contests, free samples, and premiums. The most effective sales promotion efforts are highly interrelated with other promotional activities. Decisions regarding sales promotion often affect advertising and personal selling decisions, and vice versa.

Sales promotion can increase sales by providing extra purchasing incentives. Many opportunities exist to motivate consumers, resellers, and salespeople to take desired actions. Some kinds of sales promotion are designed specifically to stimulate resellers' demand and effectiveness, some are directed at increasing consumer demand, and some focus on both consumers and resellers. Regardless of the purpose, marketers must ensure that sales promotion objectives are consistent with the organization's overall objectives, as well as with its marketing and promotion objectives.

When deciding which sales promotion methods to use, marketers must consider several factors, particularly product characteristics (price, size, weight, costs, durability, uses, features, and hazards) and target market characteristics (age, gender, income, location, density, usage rate, and shopping patterns). How products are distributed and the number and types of resellers may determine the type of method used. The competitive and legal environment may also influence the choice.

The use of sales promotion has increased dramatically over the past 30 years, primarily at the expense of advertising. This shift in how promotional dollars are used has occurred for several reasons. Heightened concerns about value have made customers more responsive to promotional offers, especially price discounts and point-of-purchase displays. Thanks to their size and access to checkout scanner data, retailers have gained considerable power in the supply chain and are demanding greater promotional efforts from manufacturers to boost retail profits. Declines in brand loyalty have produced an environment in which sales promotions aimed at persuading customers to switch brands are more effective. Finally, the stronger emphasis placed on improving short-term performance results calls for greater use of sales promotion methods that yield quick (although perhaps short-lived) sales increases.[25]

In the remainder of this chapter, we examine several consumer and trade sales promotion methods, including what they entail and what goals they can help marketers achieve.

Consumer Sales Promotion Methods

Consumer sales promotion methods encourage or stimulate consumers to patronize specific retail stores or try particular products. Consumer sales promotion methods initiated by retailers often aim to attract customers to specific locations, whereas those used by manufacturers generally introduce new products or promote established brands. In this section, we discuss coupons, cents-off offers, money refunds and rebates, frequent-user incentives, point-of-purchase displays, demonstrations, free samples, premiums, consumer contests and games, and consumer sweepstakes.

COUPONS

Coupons reduce a product's price and aim to prompt customers to try new or established products, increase sales volume quickly, attract repeat purchasers, or introduce new package sizes or features. Savings are deducted from the purchase price. Coupons are the most widely used consumer sales promotion technique. Consumer packaged goods manufacturers distributed about 311 billion coupons in 2009, saving consumers an estimated $3.5 billion. About 89 percent of consumers use coupons.[26] Table 19.3 outlines the top 10 most popular coupon categories.

For best results, coupons should be easily recognized and state the offer clearly. The nature of the product (seasonal demand for it, life-cycle stage, and frequency of purchase) is the prime consideration in setting up a coupon promotion. Paper coupons are distributed on and inside packages, through freestanding inserts, in print advertising, on the back of cash register receipts, and through direct mail. Electronic coupons are distributed online, via in-store kiosks, through shelf dispensers in stores, and at checkout counters.[27] As shown in Figure 19.3, young people are more accepting of online coupons than older age groups. When deciding on the distribution method for coupons, marketers should consider strategies

consumer sales promotion methods Sales promotion techniques that encourage consumers to patronize specific stores or try particular products

coupons Written price reductions used to encourage consumers to buy a specific product

---

Responsible Marketing?

Saving with Internet Coupons

ISSUE: Are online coupons good for everyone?

Sales promotions that use coupons can stimulate consumer purchases. The real advantage of using coupons is developing loyalty repeat purchases. The Internet has aided this process by providing an opportunity to obtain coupons and information that will allow discounts. As a result, the search for coupons and retailers who will accept them has evolved into a science for some people. Entire websites are devoted to the distribution of coupons and coupon codes, giving the consumer the ammunition he or she needs to get the lowest price on a product.

Internet sites such as Reesycakes.com post apparel discount codes that consumers can use to buy reduced-price merchandise. Shopstyle.com provides the opportunity to locate all the sites carrying the same item. A shopper can visit Reesycakes.com to match retailer coupons to desired merchandise that was located on Shopstyle.com. Once the information is acquired, the consumer can contact the retailer of choice to use the coupon. The game continues, and many wonder why retailers permit some consumers to bargain and search for discounts while other dedicated customers are paying full price. The answer is the nature of the highly competitive retail market. The bottom line is that a retailer can develop consumer loyalty by offering online coupons, and repeat sales support sales growth. It is much cheaper for a retailer to sell an item over the Internet than to have consumers phoning in and inquiring about discounts and coupon acceptability. The result is that consumers are paying different prices for the same product.[c]

TABLE 19.3 Top 10 Coupon Categories, 2009

1.	Cereal
2.	Sweet snacks
3.	Yogurt
4.	Refrigerated dough
5.	Salty snacks
6.	Dessert items
7.	Nutritional snacks
8.	Dinners/entrees
9.	Cookies
10.	Spreads

Source: "Cereal Retains No. 1 Position as Top Coupon Category in August According to Coupons.com," *BusinessWire,* September 16, 2009, www.businesswire.com/portal/site/home/permalink/ ?ndmViewId=news_view&newsId=20090916005834&newsLang=en (accessed July 30, 2010).

and objectives, redemption rates, availability, circulation, and exclusivity. The coupon distribution and redemption arena has become very competitive. To avoid losing customers, many grocery stores will redeem any coupons offered by competitors. Also, to draw customers to their stores, grocers double and sometimes even triple the value of customers' coupons.

Coupons offer several advantages. Print advertisements with coupons are often more effective at generating brand awareness than are print ads without coupons. Generally, the larger the coupon's cash offer, the better the recognition generated. Coupons reward present product users, win back former users, and encourage purchases in larger quantities. Because they are returned, coupons also help a manufacturer determine whether it reached the intended target market. The advantages of using electronic coupons over paper coupons include lower cost per redemption, greater targeting ability, improved data-gathering capabilities, and greater experimentation capabilities to determine optimal face values and expiration cycles.[28]

Drawbacks of coupon use include fraud and misredemption, which can be expensive for manufacturers. Coupon fraud—including counterfeit Internet coupons

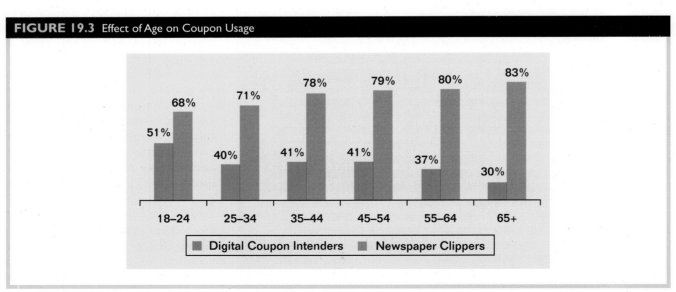

FIGURE 19.3 Effect of Age on Coupon Usage

Source: Katy Bachman, "Younger Consumers Prefer Online Coupons," *Brand Week,* April 2, 2009, www.brandweek.com/bw/content_display/news-and-features/ shopper-marketing/e3i73a607e8e83226da705b8c06515229c4 (accessed April 6, 2010).

Coupons
Daisy stimulates sales for its products through the use of coupons.

as well as coupons cashed in under false retailer names—costs manufacturers at least $300 million a year.[29] Another disadvantage, according to some experts, is that coupons are losing their value; because so many manufacturers offer them, consumers have learned not to buy without some incentive, whether that pertains to a coupon, a rebate, or a refund. Furthermore, brand loyalty among heavy coupon users has diminished, and many consumers redeem coupons only for products they normally buy. It is believed that about three-fourths of coupons are redeemed by people already using the brand on the coupon. Thus, coupons have questionable success as an incentive for consumers to try a new brand or product. An additional problem with coupons is that stores often do not have enough of the coupon item in stock. This situation generates ill will toward both the store and the product.

CENTS-OFF OFFERS

With **cents-off offers**, buyers pay a certain amount less than the regular price shown on the label or package. Like coupons, this method can serve as a strong incentive for trying new or unfamiliar products and is commonly used in product introductions. It can stimulate product sales or multiple purchases, yield short-lived sales increases, and promote products during off-seasons. It is an easy method to control and is often used for specific purposes. If used on an ongoing basis, however, cents-off offers reduce the price for customers who would buy at the regular price and may also cheapen a product's image. In addition, the method often requires special handling by retailers who are responsible for giving the discount at the point of sale.

MONEY REFUNDS

With **money refunds**, consumers submit proof of purchase and are mailed a specific amount of money. Usually, manufacturers demand multiple product purchases before consumers qualify for money refunds. Marketers employ money refunds as an alternative to coupons to stimulate sales. Money refunds, used primarily to promote trial use of a product, are relatively low in cost. However, they sometimes generate a low response rate, and thus have limited impact on sales.

REBATES

cents-off offer A promotion that allows buyers to pay less than the regular price to encourage purchase

money refund A sales promotion technique that offers consumers a specified amount of money when they mail in a proof of purchase, usually for multiple product purchases

rebate A sales promotion technique in which a consumer receives a specified amount of money for making a single product purchase

With **rebates**, the consumer is sent a specified amount of money for making a single product purchase. Rebates are generally given on more expensive products than money refunds and are used to encourage customers. Marketers also use rebates to reinforce brand loyalty, provide promotion buzz for salespeople, and advertise the product. On larger items, such as cars, rebates are often given at the point of sale. Most rebates, however, especially on smaller items, are given after the sale, usually through a mail-in process.

One problem with money refunds and rebates is that many people perceive the redemption process as too complicated. Only about 40 percent of individuals who purchase rebated products actually apply for the rebates.[30] Because of this, many marketers allow customers to apply for a rebate online, which eliminates the need for forms that may confuse customers and frustrate retailers. Consumers may also have negative perceptions of manufacturers' reasons for offering rebates. They may believe the products are untested or have not sold well. If these perceptions are not changed, rebate offers may actually degrade product image and desirability.

Frequent-User Incentives
Airlines and hotels, like Carlson Hotels, are major providers of frequent-user incentive programs.

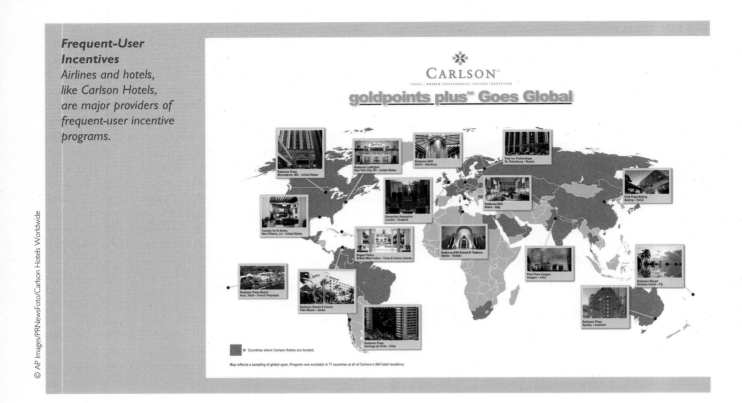

FREQUENT-USER INCENTIVES

Greeting cards aren't the only products offered by Hallmark. To reward loyal customers, the company offers the Hallmark Gold Crown Card, which allows frequent greeting card buyers to accrue points that are redeemable for merchandise and discounts.[31] Many firms develop incentive programs to reward customers who engage in repeat (frequent) purchases. For example, most major airlines offer frequent-flyer programs that reward customers who have flown a specified number of miles with free tickets for additional travel. Frequent-user incentives foster customer loyalty to a specific company or group of cooperating companies. They are favored by service businesses such as airlines, auto rental agencies, hotels, and local coffee shops. Indeed, research shows that 93 percent of consumers with household incomes above $100,000 participate in frequent-user programs, whereas only 58 percent of shoppers with incomes below $50,000 participate.[32] Frequent-user programs not only reward loyal customers but also generate data that can contribute significant information about customers that helps marketers foster desirable customer relationships.

POINT-OF-PURCHASE MATERIALS AND DEMONSTRATIONS

Point-of-purchase (POP) materials include outdoor signs, window displays, counter pieces, display racks, and self-service cartons. Innovations in POP displays include sniff-teasers, which give off a product's aroma in the store as consumers walk within a radius of four feet, and computerized interactive displays. These items, often supplied by producers, attract attention, inform customers, and encourage retailers to carry particular products. A retailer is likely to use point-of-purchase materials if they are attractive, informative, well-constructed, and in harmony with the store's image.

Demonstrations are excellent attention-getters. Manufacturers offer them temporarily to encourage trial use and purchase of a product or to show how a product works. Because labor costs can be extremely high, demonstrations are not used widely. They can be highly effective for promoting certain types of products, such as appliances, cosmetics, and cleaning supplies. Even automobiles can be demonstrated, not only by a salesperson but also by the prospective buyer during a test drive. Cosmetics marketers,

point-of-purchase (POP) materials Signs, window displays, display racks, and similar devices used to attract customers

demonstration A sales promotion method a manufacturer uses temporarily to encourage trial use and purchase of a product or to show how a product works

such as Estée Lauder and Clinique, sometimes offer potential customers "makeovers" to demonstrate product benefits and proper application.

FREE SAMPLES

Marketers use **free samples** to stimulate trial of a product, increase sales volume in the early stages of a product's life cycle, and obtain desirable distribution. Coca-Cola, for example, often gives out free samples of products like Vitamin Water at business conventions, concerts, and sporting events. Sampling is the most expensive sales promotion method because production and distribution—at local events, by mail or door-to-door delivery, online, in stores, and on packages—entail high costs. However, it can also be one of the most effective sales promotion methods: a survey by the Promotion Marketing Association's Product Sampling Council found that 92 percent of respondents said they would buy a new product that they had sampled and liked. Nonetheless, sampling's expense remains a key reason why it is not used more often.[33]

Many consumers prefer to get their samples by mail. Other consumers like to sample new food products at supermarkets or try samples of new recipes featuring foods they already like. In designing a free sample, marketers should consider factors like seasonal demand for the product, market characteristics, and prior advertising. Free samples usually are inappropriate for slow-turnover products. Despite high costs, use of sampling is increasing. In a given year, almost three-fourths of consumer product companies may use sampling. Distribution of free samples through websites like StartSampling.com and FreeSamples.com is growing.

PREMIUMS

Premiums are items offered free or at a minimal cost as a bonus for purchasing a product. Like the prize in the Cracker Jack box, premiums are used to attract competitors' customers, introduce different sizes of established products, add variety to other promotional efforts, and stimulate consumer loyalty. Creativity is essential when using premiums; to stand out and achieve a significant number of redemptions, the premium must match both the target audience and the brand's image. Premiums must also be easily recognizable and desirable. Premiums are placed on or inside packages and can also be distributed by retailers or through the mail. Examples include a service station giving a free carwash with a fill-up, a free shaving cream with the purchase of a razor, and a free plastic storage box with the purchase of Kraft Cheese Singles.

CONSUMER CONTESTS

In **consumer contests**, individuals compete for prizes based on their analytical or creative skills. This method can be used to generate retail traffic and frequency of exposure to promotional messages. Contestants are usually more highly involved in consumer contests than in games or sweepstakes, even though total participation may be lower. Contests may also be used in conjunction with other sales promotional methods, such as coupons. For example, Coca-Cola invited amateur filmmakers to submit films for its Coca-Cola Refreshing Filmmaker's Award with a grand prize of $10,000 and the chance to have their film featured on movie screens across the country.[34]

CONSUMER GAMES

In **consumer games**, individuals compete for prizes based primarily on chance—often by collecting game pieces like bottle caps or a sticker on a carton of French fries. Because collecting multiple pieces may be necessary to win or increase an individual's chances of winning, the game stimulates repeated business. Development and management of consumer games is often outsourced to an independent public relations firm, which can help marketers navigate federal and state laws that regulate games. Although games may stimulate sales temporarily, there is no evidence to suggest that they affect a company's long-term sales.

Marketers considering games should exercise care. Problems or errors may anger customers and could result in a lawsuit. McDonald's' wildly popular Monopoly game promotion, in which customers collect Monopoly real estate pieces on drink and

free sample A sample of a product given out to encourage trial and purchase

premium An item offered free or at a minimal cost as a bonus for purchasing a product

consumer contests Sales promotion methods in which individuals compete for prizes based on their analytical or creative skills

consumer games Sales promotion methods in which individuals compete for prizes based primarily on chance

French fry packages, has been tarnished by both fraud and lawsuits. After six successful years, McDonald's was forced to end the annual promotion when a crime ring, including employees of the promotional firm running the game, were convicted of stealing millions of dollars in winning game pieces. McDonald's later reintroduced the Monopoly game with heightened security. However, the Monopoly promotion is once again under scrutiny as it is the focus of a class-action lawsuit filed by Burger King franchisees, who claim their customers were lured away by the false promises of McDonald's game. The claim did not hold up in court, however, and was later dismissed.[35]

SWEEPSTAKES

Entrants in a **consumer sweepstakes** submit their names for inclusion in a drawing for prizes. Advil pain reliever created the "Live Life to the Fullest" sweepstakes, with a chance to win a grand prize of $25,000 and a trip for two to see a live taping of the Ellen DeGeneres show in Los Angeles. Sweepstakes are employed more often than consumer contests and tend to attract a greater number of participants. However, contestants are usually more involved in consumer contests and games than in sweepstakes, even though total participation may be lower. Contests, games, and sweepstakes may be used in conjunction with other sales promotion methods like coupons.

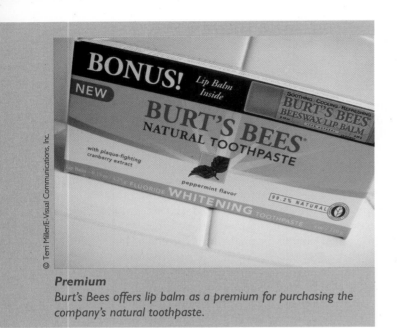

Premium
Burt's Bees offers lip balm as a premium for purchasing the company's natural toothpaste.

Trade Sales Promotion Methods

To encourage resellers, especially retailers, to carry their products and promote them effectively, producers use trade sales promotion methods. **Trade sales promotion methods** attempt to persuade wholesalers and retailers to carry a producer's products and market them more aggressively. Marketers use trade sales methods for many reasons, including countering the effect of lower-priced store brands, passing along a discount to a price-sensitive market segment, boosting brand exposure among target consumers, or providing additional incentives to move excess inventory or counteract competitors. These methods include buying allowances, buy-back allowances, scan-back allowances, merchandise allowances, cooperative advertising, dealer listings, free merchandise, dealer loaders, premium or push money, and sales contests.

TRADE ALLOWANCES

Many manufacturers offer trade allowances to encourage resellers to carry a product or stock more of it. One such trade allowance is a **buying allowance**, a temporary price reduction offered to resellers for purchasing specified quantities of a product. A soap producer, for example, might give retailers $1 for each case of soap purchased. Such offers provide an incentive for resellers to handle new products, achieve temporary price reductions, or stimulate purchase of items in larger-than-normal quantities. The buying allowance, which takes the form of money, yields profits to resellers and is simple and straightforward. There are no restrictions on how resellers use the money, which increases the method's effectiveness. One drawback of buying allowances is that customers may buy "forward"—that is, buy large amounts that keep them supplied for many months. Another problem is that competitors may match (or beat) the reduced price, which can lower profits for all sellers.

A **buy-back allowance** is a sum of money that a producer gives to a reseller for each unit the reseller buys after an initial promotional deal is over. This method is a secondary incentive in which the total amount of money resellers receive is proportional to their purchases during an initial consumer promotion, such as a coupon offer. Buy-back allowances foster cooperation during an initial sales promotion effort and stimulate repurchase afterward. The main disadvantage of this method is expense.

consumer sweepstakes A sales promotion in which entrants submit their names for inclusion in a drawing for prizes

trade sales promotion methods Methods intended to persuade wholesalers and retailers to carry a producer's products and market them aggressively

buying allowance A temporary price reduction to resellers for purchasing specified quantities of a product

buy-back allowance A sum of money given to a reseller for each unit bought after an initial promotion deal is over

A **scan-back allowance** is a manufacturer's reward to retailers based on the number of pieces moved through the retailers' scanners during a specific time period. To participate in scan-back programs, retailers are usually expected to pass along savings to consumers through special pricing. Scan-backs are becoming widely used by manufacturers because they link trade spending directly to product movement at the retail level.

A **merchandise allowance** is a manufacturer's agreement to pay resellers certain amounts of money for providing promotional efforts like advertising or point of-purchase displays. This method is best suited to high-volume, high-profit, easily handled products. A drawback is that some retailers perform activities at a minimally acceptable level simply to obtain allowances. Before paying retailers, manufacturers usually verify their performance. Manufacturers hope that retailers' additional promotional efforts will yield substantial sales increases.

COOPERATIVE ADVERTISING AND DEALER LISTINGS

Cooperative advertising is an arrangement in which a manufacturer agrees to pay a certain amount of a retailer's media costs for advertising the manufacturer's products. The amount allowed is usually based on the quantities purchased. As with merchandise allowances, a retailer must show proof that advertisements did appear before the manufacturer pays the agreed-on portion of the advertising costs. These payments give retailers additional funds for advertising. Some retailers exploit cooperative-advertising agreements by crowding too many products into one advertisement. Not all available cooperative-advertising dollars are used. Some retailers cannot afford to advertise, while others can afford it but do not want to advertise. A large proportion of all cooperative-advertising dollars is spent on newspaper advertisements.

Dealer listings are advertisements promoting a product and identifying participating retailers that sell the product. Dealer listings can influence retailers to carry the product, build traffic at the retail level, and encourage consumers to buy the product at participating dealers.

FREE MERCHANDISE AND GIFTS

Manufacturers sometimes offer **free merchandise** to resellers that purchase a stated quantity of products. Occasionally, free merchandise is used as payment for allowances provided through other sales promotion methods. To avoid handling and bookkeeping problems, the "free" merchandise usually takes the form of a reduced invoice.

A **dealer loader** is a gift to a retailer that purchases a specified quantity of merchandise. Dealer loaders are often used to obtain special display efforts from retailers by offering essential display parts as premiums. For example, a manufacturer might design a display that includes a sterling silver tray as a major component and give the tray to the retailer. Marketers use dealer loaders to obtain new distributors and push larger quantities of goods.

PREMIUM MONEY

Premium money (push money) is additional compensation offered by the manufacturer to salespeople as an incentive to push a line of goods. This method is appropriate when personal selling is an important part of the marketing effort; it is not effective for promoting products sold through self-service. Premium money often helps a manufacturer obtain a commitment from the sales force, but it can be very expensive.

SALES CONTEST

A **sales contest** is designed to motivate distributors, retailers, and sales personnel by recognizing outstanding achievements. To be effective, this method must be equitable for all individuals involved. One advantage is that it can achieve participation at all distribution levels. Positive effects may be temporary, however, and prizes are usually expensive.

scan-back allowance A manufacturer's reward to retailers based on the number of pieces scanned

merchandise allowance A manufacturer's agreement to pay resellers certain amounts of money for providing special promotional efforts, such as setting up and maintaining a display

cooperative advertising An arrangement in which a manufacturer agrees to pay a certain amount of a retailer's media costs for advertising the manufacturer's products

dealer listing An advertisement that promotes a product and identifies the names of participating retailers that sell the product

free merchandise A manufacturer's reward given to resellers that purchase a stated quantity of products

dealer loader A gift, often part of a display, given to a retailer that purchases a specified quantity of merchandise

premium money (push money) Extra compensation to salespeople for pushing a line of goods

sales contest A sales promotion method used to motivate distributors, retailers, and sales personnel through recognition of outstanding achievements

summary

I. To understand the major purposes of personal selling

Personal selling is the process of informing customers and persuading them to purchase products through paid personal communication in an exchange situation. The three general purposes of personal selling are finding prospects, persuading them to buy, and keeping customers satisfied.

2. To describe the basic steps in the personal selling process

Many salespeople, either consciously or unconsciously, move through a general selling process as they sell products. In prospecting, the salesperson develops a database of potential customers. Before contacting prospects, the salesperson conducts a preapproach that involves finding and analyzing information about prospects and their needs. The approach is the manner in which the salesperson contacts potential customers. During the sales presentation, the salesperson must attract and hold the prospect's attention to stimulate interest and desire for the product. If possible, the salesperson should handle objections as they arise. During the closing, the salesperson asks the prospect to buy the product or products. After a successful closing, the salesperson must follow up the sale.

3. To identify the types of sales force personnel

In developing a sales force, marketing managers consider which types of salespeople will sell the firm's products most effectively. The three classifications of salespeople are order getters, order takers, and support personnel. Order getters inform both current customers and new prospects and persuade them to buy. Order takers seek repeat sales and fall into two categories: inside order takers and field order takers. Sales support personnel facilitate selling, but their duties usually extend beyond making sales.

4. To recognize new types of personal selling

The three types of support personnel are missionary, trade, and technical salespeople. The roles of salespeople are changing, resulting in an increased focus on team selling and relationship selling. Team selling involves the salesperson joining with people from the firm's financial, engineering, and other functional areas. Relationship selling involves building mutually beneficial long-term associations with a customer through regular communications over prolonged periods of time.

5. To understand sales management decisions and activities

Sales force management is an important determinant of a firm's success because the sales force is directly responsible for generating the organization's sales revenue. Major decision areas and activities are establishing sales force objectives; determining sales force size; recruiting, selecting, training, compensating, and motivating salespeople; managing sales territories; and controlling and evaluating sales force performance.

Sales objectives should be stated in precise, measurable terms and specify the time period and geographic areas involved. The size of the sales force must be adjusted occasionally because a firm's marketing plans change along with markets and forces in the marketing environment.

Recruiting and selecting salespeople involve attracting and choosing the right type of salesperson to maintain an effective sales force. When developing a training program, managers must consider a variety of dimensions, such as who should be trained, what should be taught, and how training should occur. Compensation of salespeople involves formulating and administering a compensation plan that attracts, motivates, and retains the right types of salespeople. Motivated salespeople should translate into high productivity. Managing sales territories focuses on such factors as size, shape, routing, and scheduling. To control and evaluate sales force performance, sales managers use information obtained through salespeople's call reports, customer feedback, and invoices.

6. To explain what sales promotion activities are and how they are used

Sales promotion is an activity or a material (or both) that acts as a direct inducement, offering added value or incentive for the product to resellers, salespeople, or consumers. Marketers use sales promotion to identify and attract new customers, introduce new products, and increase reseller inventories.

7. To explore specific consumer sales promotion methods

Sales promotion techniques fall into two general categories: consumer and trade. Consumer sales promotion methods encourage consumers to patronize specific stores or try a particular product. These sales promotion methods include coupons; cents-off offers; money refunds and rebates; frequent-user incentives; point-of-purchase displays; demonstrations; free samples and premiums; and consumer contests, games, and sweepstakes.

8. To explore trade sales promotion methods

Trade sales promotion techniques can motivate resellers to handle a manufacturer's products and market them aggressively. These sales promotion techniques include buying allowances, buy-back allowances, scan-back allowances, merchandise allowances, cooperative advertising, dealer listings, free merchandise, dealer loaders, premium (or push) money, and sales contests.

Go to www.cengagebrain.com for resources to help you master the content in this chapter as well as materials that will expand your marketing knowledge!

important terms

personal selling, 564

prospecting, 566

approach, 568

closing, 569

order getter, 569

order takers, 570

support personnel, 570

missionary
salespeople, 570

trade salespeople, 571

technical
salespeople, 571

team selling, 571

relationship selling, 571

recruiting, 573

straight salary
compensation
plan, 576

straight commission
compensation
plan, 576

combination
compensation
plan, 576

sales promotion, 579

consumer sales
promotion
methods, 581

coupons, 581

cents-off offer, 583

money refund, 583

rebate, 583

point-of-purchase
(POP) materials, 584

demonstration, 584

free sample, 585

premium, 585

consumer contests, 585

consumer games, 585

consumer
sweepstakes, 586

trade sales promotion
methods, 586

buying allowance, 586

buy-back allowance, 586

scan-back
allowance, 587

merchandise
allowance, 587

cooperative
advertising, 587

dealer listing, 587

free merchandise, 587

dealer loader, 587

premium money
(push money), 587

sales contest, 587

discussion and review questions

1. What is personal selling? How does personal selling differ from other types of promotional activities?
2. What are the primary purposes of personal selling?
3. Identify the elements of the personal selling process. Must a salesperson include all these elements when selling a product to a customer? Why or why not?
4. How does a salesperson find and evaluate prospects? Do you consider any of these methods to be ethically questionable? Explain.
5. Are order getters more aggressive or creative than order takers? Why or why not?
6. Why are team selling and relationship selling becoming more prevalent?
7. Identify several characteristics of effective sales objectives.
8. How should a sales manager establish criteria for selecting sales personnel? What do you think are the general characteristics of a good salesperson?
9. What major issues or questions should management consider when developing a training program for the sales force?
10. Explain the major advantages and disadvantages of the three basic methods of compensating salespeople. In general, which method would you prefer? Why?
11. What major factors should be taken into account when designing the size and shape of a sales territory?

12. How does a sales manager, who cannot be with each salesperson in the field on a daily basis, control the performance of sales personnel?

13. What is sales promotion? Why is it used?

14. For each of the following, identify and describe three techniques and give several examples: (a) consumer sales promotion methods and (b) trade sales promotion methods.

15. What types of sales promotion methods have you observed recently? Comment on their effectiveness.

application questions

1. Briefly describe an experience you have had with a salesperson at a clothing store or an automobile dealership. Describe the steps the salesperson used. Did the salesperson skip any steps? What did the salesperson do well? Not so well? Would you describe the salesperson as an order getter, an order taker, or a support salesperson? Why? Did the salesperson perform more than one of these functions?

2. Leap Athletic Shoe Inc., a newly formed company, is in the process of developing a sales strategy. Market researchers have determined that sales management should segment the market into five regional territories. The sales potential for the North region is $1.2 million; for the West region, $1 million; for the Central region, $1.3 million; for the South Central region, $1.1 million; and for the Southeast region, $1 million. The firm wishes to maintain some control over the training and sales processes because of the unique features of its new product line, but Leap marketers realize that the salespeople need to be fairly aggressive in their efforts to break into these markets. They would like to provide the incentive needed for the extra selling effort. What type of sales force compensation method would you recommend to Leap? Why?

3. Consumer sales promotions aim to increase sales of a particular retail store or product. Identify a familiar type of retail store or product. Recommend at least three sales promotion methods that could effectively promote the store or product. Explain why you would use these methods.

4. Producers use trade sales promotions to encourage resellers to promote their products more effectively. Identify which method or methods of sales promotion a producer might use in the following situations, and explain why the method would be appropriate.
   a. A golf ball manufacturer wants to encourage retailers to add a new type of golf ball to current product offerings.
   b. A life insurance company wants to increase sales of its universal life products, which have been lagging recently (the company has little control over sales activities).
   c. A light bulb manufacturer with an overproduction of 100-watt bulbs wants to encourage its grocery store chain resellers to increase their bulb inventories.

internet exercise

TerrAlign

TerrAlign offers consulting services and software products designed to help a firm maximize control and deployment of its field sales representatives.

1. Identify three features of TerrAlign software that are likely to benefit salespeople.

2. Identify three features of TerrAlign software that are likely to benefit sales managers.

3. Why might field sales professionals object to the use of software from TerrAlign?

developing your marketing plan

When developing its marketing strategy, a company must consider the different forms of communication that are necessary to reach a variety of customers. Several types of promotion may be required. Knowledge of the advantages and disadvantages of each promotional element is necessary when developing the marketing plan. Consider the information in this chapter when evaluating your promotional mix:

1. Review the various types of salespeople described in this chapter. Given your promotional objectives (from Chapter 17), do any of these types of salespeople have a place in your promotional plan?

2. Identify the resellers in your distribution channel. Discuss the role that trade sales promotions to these resellers could play in the development of your promotional plan.

3. Evaluate each type of consumer sales promotion as it relates to accomplishing your promotional objectives.

The information obtained from these questions should assist you in developing various aspects of your marketing plan found in the *Interactive Marketing Plan* exercise at **www.cengagebrain.com.**

Murray's Cheese Achieves Success through Personal Selling

For Murray's Cheese, personal selling is the driving force behind its success. The business has retail sales of $2,500 per square foot and a growth rate of 15 to 20 percent per year at its main store in Greenwich Village, New York. It also recently established a partnership with the supermarket giant Kroger to bring Murray's customer-friendly environment to select Kroger supermarkets. Murray's views personal selling as a core competency that sets itself apart from the competition. The key is to inform customers and persuade them to purchase products in a store environment. Murray's sales representatives understand the importance of a quick presentation, overcoming objectives, and closing the sale. Because Murray's wants its customers to be repeat buyers, there is an attempt to listen to customers, gain an understanding of their interests, and try to find the right product to satisfy their needs.

Murray's Cheese began in 1940 as a wholesale butter and egg shop owned by Jewish Spanish Civil War Veteran Murray Greenberg. When the current president Rob Kaufelt purchased the shop in 1991, the store was little more than a local hole-in-the-wall. Kaufelt and his staff made the decision to focus on

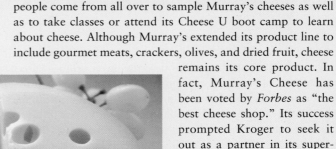

high-quality gourmet cheeses from around the world. Today, people come from all over to sample Murray's cheeses as well as to take classes or attend its Cheese U boot camp to learn about cheese. Although Murray's extended its product line to include gourmet meats, crackers, olives, and dried fruit, cheese remains its core product. In fact, Murray's Cheese has been voted by *Forbes* as "the best cheese shop." Its success prompted Kroger to seek it out as a partner in its supermarkets. Murray's Cheese shops can now be found in different Kroger supermarkets throughout the country.

The cost that Murray's Cheese spent on advertising to become so successful: zero dollars. Instead of advertising, the company relies on in-store salespersons providing customer service and creating positive word-of-mouth communication to promote and secure its reputation. When training its cheesemongers, the company recruits those who are passionate about both cheese and people. The company sets qualifications before beginning to recruit and identifies a set of traits characterizing effective salespeople to become cheesemongers. All customers who enter Murray's Greenwich Village store get to taste free samples of cheese before they buy it. This sampling creates an image of Murray's Cheese as a customer-friendly company. Customer relationships are so integral to Murray's that its cheesemongers taste the cheese with the customers. In this way, Murray's in-store sales force educates themselves about the cheeses they are selling and creates a valuable experience where the customer feels appreciated. By establishing this unique experience, Murray's often succeeds in getting customers to purchase more products at once and make repeat purchases.

This positive customer environment is what Murray's Cheese hopes to bring to Kroger's. Those Kroger employees who sell Murray's cheeses undergo extensive training beforehand. Murray's even created a 300-page cheese service guide for these recruits. Kroger customers seem to appreciate the more attentive customer service they receive in these Murray-branded shops. In a pilot program where three Murray's Cheese shops replaced Kroger cheese departments, sales increased 50 to 100 percent. It was such a success that, under the new partnership, Murray's Cheese will open 50 Murray's shops in Kroger supermarkets within three years.

Personal selling does not always have to be about traveling throughout sales territories, calling on prospects. Murray's in-store cheesemongers make and close sales doing what they do best: educating customers and sharing the gourmet cheese experience. With Kroger's success at promotion and Murray's strengths in personal selling, it looks to be a win-win situation for both partners. Murray's motivated cheesemongers help to satisfy the needs of their customers and achieve personal goals.[36]

QUESTIONS FOR DISCUSSION

1. How would you explain the sales presentation that is most effective for selling Murray's cheese products?
2. How would you apply the concept of relationship selling to building long-term customers at Murray's Cheese?
3. Do you think that Murray's Cheese salespeople need extensive motivation and training?

CASE 19.2

Direct Selling in China Booms in the 21st Century

What activities come to mind when you think of the words "evil," "cultish," and "superstitious"? In China, the government has used these words to describe direct selling. Direct selling, to the benefit of consumers, involves marketing products through face-to-face sales presentations at home or in the workplace. This method of selling has been linked to door-to-door selling through a cold-canvass approach for finding prospects. In countries like China, direct selling is associated with network selling and the fact that prospects are often found through relatives, friends, and neighbors. While direct selling is often criticized by the government as being a questionable activity, consumers in China respect direct selling and are aware that direct sales companies' products are often among the highest quality products available to consumers.

The Chinese government's negative attitude toward direct selling is the result of prior abuses through illegal pyramid schemes, which led to riots. Pyramid schemes occur when money is exchanged for recruiting other people into the scheme. Leaders of successful schemes make the most money, while those who fail to recruit others lose out. Multilevel marketing, on the other hand, is a very legitimate activity; it is not designed to exploit others, and support is given to sell products directly to consumers.

In 2006, direct selling was once again allowed in China under the provision that pyramid schemes and multilevel

selling was forbidden. In fact, multilevel selling and pyramid sales in China can result in serious fines and even criminal prosecution. Although some people in China still hold negative views toward direct selling, for many women, direct selling has gone from "evil" to "empowering." Today, direct selling is flourishing in China, offering women a way to earn income and maintain enough flexibility to perform domestic responsibilities.

In countries where women are not usually able to start their own businesses, direct selling offers advancement opportunities and training. Additionally, despite the worldwide recession, items like cosmetics and Tupperware remain in high demand, enabling direct selling companies to flourish. Direct selling has become an $8 billion industry in China. In China, Avon has become a leading seller of beauty and related products. Avon sets up retail stores and provides the products to salespeople to sell directly to consumers on the streets and in their neighborhoods. Although Amway is known for being a multilevel marketer in the United States, it sells its products through the same system. The success of both of these companies has been incredible. For example, China is now Amway's largest market (even greater than in the United States), and its Artistry cosmetics and Nutrilite vitamins are market leaders.

Some people do not view direct selling personal sales reps as legitimate or authentic salespeople. But many of the basic approaches to personal selling are used by sales representatives from companies like Amway and Avon. The salespeople have to be involved in the personal selling process of prospecting, preapproach, approach, making the presentation, overcoming objections, and closing the sale. There are sales managers who have to recruit, train, and motivate the company's sales representatives. Many direct sales representatives develop long-term associations with the customers through regular communications over prolonged periods of time. Besides direct personal relationships and contacts, many of the sales reps are using social networking to simulate communication that would otherwise occur face-to-face. The importance of this method of selling can be seen with global sales results of more than $8.4 billion for Amway and more than $11 billion for Avon.

However, despite the growing popularity of direct selling in China, the career does have its downsides. Although some direct sellers have become wealthy, many do not earn any more income than they would have as a cashier or clerk. Some Chinese officials still regard direct selling with suspicion since a common tactic of con artists is to pose as direct sellers. Therefore, China implemented laws limiting the ways direct selling companies could compensate their sales force and banned teachers, doctors, and civil servants from becoming direct sellers.

Taking all of that into account, many direct sellers find the benefits outweigh the costs. Not only is direct selling flexible, it also helps women earn income in uncertain financial times when family members are out of work. Even women who do not earn much money in sales appreciate the flexibility and corporate culture. They look forward to the promise of future rewards with the company. Direct selling companies are also benefiting, with Amway predicting at least a 10 percent gain in 2010 Chinese sales. Although direct selling may be taken for granted in America, it is gaining an eager fan base among women in China.[37]

QUESTIONS FOR DISCUSSION

1. Why are direct selling personal sales representatives legitimate or authentic salespeople?

2. Why do you think direct selling is even more successful in China than the United States?

3. What are the social and economic benefits of the sales opportunities that are provided to women in developing countries?

Indy Racing League (IRL) Focuses on Integrated Marketing Communications

For the first 17 years of its existence, CART dominated auto racing in the United States. Open-wheel racing, involving cars whose wheels are located outside the body of the car rather than underneath the body or fenders as found on street cars, enjoyed greater notoriety than other forms of racing—including stock-car racing like NASCAR. However, not everyone associated with open-wheel racing in the United States welcomed the success enjoyed by CART. One person with major concerns about the direction of CART was Tony George, president of the Indianapolis Motor Speedway and founder of the Indianapolis 500.

In 1994, George announced that he was creating a new open-wheel league that would compete with CART, beginning in 1996. The Indy Racing League (IRL) was divisive to open-wheel racing in the United States, as team owners were forced to decide whether to remain with CART or move to the new IRL. Only IRL members would be allowed to race in the Indianapolis 500—the world's largest spectator sport and the premiere open-wheeled racing competition. CART teams responded by planning their own event on the same day as the Indianapolis 500. The real challenge for the new IRL was developing an integrated marketing communications program to ensure maximum informational and persuasive impact on potential fans (customers). The rift between CART and the IRL resulted in both parties being unable to use the terms "IndyCar" and "Indy car." This loss of the Indy Car brand name created a challenge for promoting the new league.

A 2001 ESPN Sports Poll survey found that 56 percent of American auto racing fans said stock car racing was their favorite type of racing, with open-wheel racing

third at 9 percent. The diminished appeal of open-wheel racing contributed to additional problems with sponsor relationships. Three major partners left CART, including two partners (Honda and Toyota) that provided engines and technical support to CART and its teams. During the same time, the IRL struggled to find corporate partners as a weakened economy and a fragmented market for open-wheel racing made both the IRL and CART less attractive to sponsors.

The IRL experienced ups and downs in the years following the split. Interest in IRL as measured by television ratings took a noticeable dip between 2002 and 2004, with 25 percent fewer viewers tuning in during 2004 than just two years earlier. More recently, some sponsors pulled out, including talk-show host David Letterman. Furthermore, Tony George resigned his top positions with the IRL and the Indianapolis Motor Speedway (IMS) in July 2009. He was a proponent of using profits from IMS to support operations of the IRL, funneling an estimated hundreds of millions of dollars over the years to sustain the IRL.

In response to declining interest in IRL, marketing initiatives were taken to reverse the trend by recognizing the various promotional tools available. For instance, the league dedicated a marketing staff in 2001 to their operations. In 2005, the IRL launched a new ad campaign that targeted 18- to 34-year-old males. The campaign was part of a broader strategy to expand the association of IRL beyond a sport for middle-aged Midwestern males to a younger market. IRL has created profiles on social networking sites like Facebook and Twitter to further target this market.

In support of this effort, two developments can be noted. First, IRL has followed a trend observed in NASCAR and has involved several celebrities in the sport through team ownership. Among the celebrities involved with IRL teams are NBA star Carmelo Anthony, former NFL quarterback Jim Harbaugh, and actor Patrick Dempsey. Another celebrity involved with the IRL is rock star Gene Simmons. He is a partner in Simmons Abramson Marketing, who was hired to help the IRL devise new marketing strategies. The firm's entertainment marketing savvy is being tapped to help the IRL connect with fans on an emotional level through its drivers, whom Simmons referred to as "rock stars in rocket ships."

Second, driver personalities began to give the IRL some visibility. The emergence of Danica Patrick as a star in the IRL has broadened the appeal of the league and assists in efforts to reach young males. Patrick was a 23-year-old IRL rookie in 2005 who finished fourth in the Indianapolis 500. The combination of the novelty of a female driver, her captivating looks, provocative advertising (particularly her Go Daddy ads), and personality made her the darling of American sports in 2005. Patrick's effect on the IRL was very noticeable; the IRL reported gains in event attendance, merchandise sales, website traffic, and television ratings during Patrick's rookie season. Patrick has drawn the interest of many companies that have hired her as a product endorser, including Motorola, Boost Mobile, and XM Radio. In addition, she has appeared in photo shoots in *FHM* and the 2008 and 2009 *Sports Illustrated* swimsuit issues. Other drivers such as Helio Castroneves and Marco Andretti, who have gained notoriety in Indy racing, also increased awareness of the IRL.

Driver personalities are critical to the promotion and communication process. Most of the drivers endorse their respective sponsors and end up in television advertising promoting the product. This is often done while showing the driver in an Indy Racing Car, also promoting the league. Drivers to some extent engage in personal selling by interacting with fans, signing autographs, and making personal appearances. Public relations for the drivers is important in television talk show appearances and various other word-of-mouth communication that is created when spectators start discussing the drivers. It is even possible for drivers to appear in television programs as a type of product placement, promoting themselves, the Indy League, and the IRL.

The Future

Another development for the IndyCar Series is a new television broadcast partner. ABC has televised the Indianapolis 500 for 45 years, and IRL will continue that relationship, but most of the other races on the IndyCar Series schedule (at least 13 per season) will be televised by VERSUS, a cable channel that replaced ESPN as IRL's broadcast partner. While VERSUS has a smaller audience than ESPN, it covers fewer sports and plans to give the IndyCar Series more coverage than ESPN did when it owned the broadcast rights. In addition, VERSUS signed a 10-year contract with the IRL.

Perhaps the biggest development for IRL in recent years is its acquisition of a title sponsorship. A title sponsorship is the use of a corporate brand name to be associated with all communication about the league. Due to the decline in its popularity, the IRL lacked a title sponsor for many years. In 2009, the clothing provider Izod decided to become the official title sponsor of the IRL for the next six years. This sponsorship is likely to be very beneficial for the IRL, particularly as it came at a time when many sponsors for NASCAR and the IRL were pulling out due to the recession.

Auto racing is the fastest-growing spectator sport in the United States. Unfortunately, the disagreement among top leadership in open-wheel racing divided the sport, leading to a period of decline in open-wheel racing, while other forms of auto racing have grown. Therefore, the new IRL must strengthen its standing in the American motorsports market. The support of major celebrities like Patrick Dempsey and the popularity of drivers like Danica Patrick have boosted the ratings of the IRL, but not enough to overtake NASCAR. With the two major open-wheel leagues unified once more, the IRL must begin the task of reconnecting with former fans and building connections with a new audience.[38]

QUESTIONS FOR DISCUSSION

1. How does the Indy Racing League utilize the various components of integrated marketing communication?
2. How do driver appearances on television and public events contribute to promoting the Indy Racing League?
3. What is the link between sponsorships of cars and drivers by corporations and promotion of the IRL?

Part 8

Pricing Decisions

To provide a satisfying marketing mix, an organization must set a price that is acceptable to target market members. Pricing decisions can have numerous effects on other parts of the marketing mix. For example, price can influence how customers perceive the product, what types of marketing institutions are used to distribute the product, and how the product is promoted. **CHAPTER 20** discusses the importance of price and looks at some characteristics of price and nonprice competition. It explores fundamental concepts such as demand, elasticity, marginal analysis, and break-even analysis. The chapter then examines the major factors that affect marketers' pricing decisions. **CHAPTER 21** discusses six major stages in the process marketers use to establish prices.

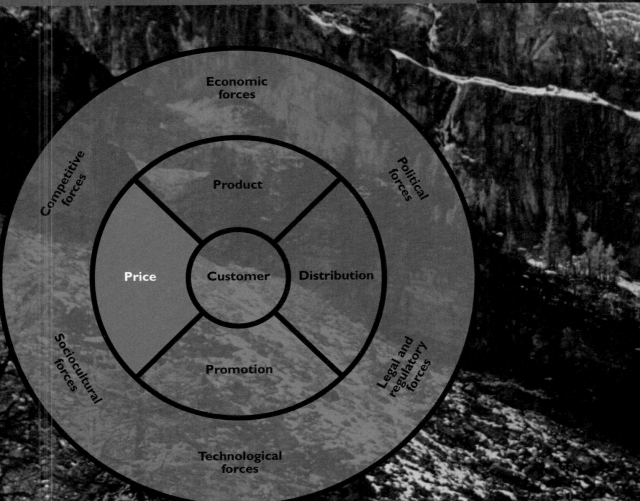

Chapter 20

Pricing Concepts

OBJECTIVES

1. To understand the nature and importance of price

2. To identify the characteristics of price and nonprice competition

3. To explore demand curves and price elasticity of demand

4. To examine the relationships among demand, costs, and profits

5. To describe key factors that may influence marketers' pricing decisions

6. To consider issues affecting the pricing of products for business markets

Does Freemium Pricing Pay?

For companies that market online offerings, one of the hottest trends in pricing is *freemium*. The idea is to let customers download or access stripped-down, sample, or limited versions of an online product for free. Then customers who want or need more can pay to upgrade to full-featured versions.

Some companies that rely on freemium pricing generate part of their revenue from the sale of advertising. The more visitors they can attract with their free basic offer, the more money they can charge advertisers for posting messages to reach that audience. EverNote, a company that makes downloadable software for collecting, storing, and searching "notes" on computers, smartphones, or the Web, has 1.5 million freemium users. That's a sizable audience for advertisers. Yet most of EverNote's revenue comes from the 30,000 customers who choose to pay $5 per month for more storage space, additional security features, and no advertising.

Spotify, a digital music streaming service, markets both an ad-supported free version and an ad-free premium subscription. Of its 7 million users, more than 250,000 have opted to pay for the premium experience, which allows them to listen to music without commercial interruptions. The premium version is also higher quality and includes access to new songs and other extras for music fans.

Newspapers are eyeing freemium pricing as a way to wring more profit from their websites. The *Wall Street Journal* site, for example, has more than 2 million paid subscribers. Anyone can read the site's headlines, but only paid subscribers can click to read every article in full. Although the *Wall Street Journal*'s success has prompted other newspapers and magazines to test online subscriptions, attracting paying customers is tricky because so much news and information is available all over the Web for free. Can freemium pricing lead to long-term profits?[1]

The right price can mean the difference between success and failure for a marketer. It can influence potential buyers' perceptions of and response to a product and it can determine whether a firm achieves profitability. Additionally, the right price can help boost demand for a new product and potentially discourage competitors from entering the market.

In this chapter, we focus first on the nature of price and its importance to marketers. We then consider some characteristics of price and nonprice competition. Next, we discuss several pricing-related concepts such as demand, elasticity, and break-even analysis. Then we examine in some detail the numerous factors that can influence pricing decisions. Finally, we discuss selected issues related to pricing products for business markets.

The Nature of Price

The purpose of marketing is to facilitate satisfying exchange relationships between buyer and seller. **Price** is the value paid for a product in a marketing exchange. Many factors may influence the assessment of value, including time constraints, price levels, perceived quality, and motivations to use available information about prices.[2] In most marketing situations, the price is apparent to both buyer and seller. However, price does not always take the form of money paid. In fact, **barter**, the trading of products, is the oldest form of exchange. Money may or may not be involved. Barter among businesses accounts for about $12 billion in annual U.S. sales.[3] Certain websites help facilitate B2B bartering.

Buyers' interest in price stems from their expectations about the usefulness of a product or the satisfaction they may derive from it. Because consumers have limited resources, they must allocate those resources to obtain the products they most desire. They must decide whether the utility gained in an exchange is worth the buying power sacrificed. Almost anything of value—ideas, services, rights, and goods—can be assessed by a price. In our society, financial price is the measurement of value commonly used in exchanges.

Terms Used to Describe Price

Value can be expressed in different terms for different marketing situations. For instance, students pay *tuition* for a college education. Automobile insurance companies charge a *premium* for protection from the cost of injuries or repairs stemming from an automobile accident. An officer who stops you for speeding writes a ticket that requires you to pay a *fine*, and the lawyer you hire to defend you in traffic court charges a *fee*. Airlines and taxi cabs charge a *fare*. A *toll* is charged for the use of bridges or toll roads. *Rent* is paid for the use of equipment or an apartment. A *commission* is remitted to a broker for the sale of real estate. *Dues* are paid for membership in a club or group. A *deposit* is made to hold or lay away merchandise. *Tips* help pay food servers for their services. *Interest* is charged for a loan, and *taxes* are paid for government services. Although price may be expressed in a variety of ways, its purpose is to quantify and express the value of the items in a marketing exchange.

The Importance of Price to Marketers

As pointed out in Chapter 11, developing a product may be a lengthy process. It takes time to plan promotion and to communicate benefits. Distribution usually requires a long-term commitment to dealers that will handle the product. Often, price is the only thing a marketer can change quickly to respond to changes in demand or to actions of competitors. Under certain circumstances, however, the price variable may be relatively inflexible.

Price is a key element in the marketing mix because it relates directly to the generation of total revenue. The following equation is an important one for the entire organization:

$$\text{profit} = \text{total revenue} - \text{total costs}$$
$$\text{profit} = (\text{price} \times \text{quantity sold}) - \text{total costs}$$

price The value paid for a product in a marketing exchange

barter The trading of products

Price affects an organization's profits in several ways because it is a key component of the profit equation and can be a major determinant of quantities sold. For instance, price is a top priority for Hewlett-Packard in gaining market share and improving financial performance.[4] Furthermore, total costs are influenced by quantities sold.

Because price has a psychological impact on customers, marketers can use it symbolically. By pricing high, they can emphasize the quality of a product and try to increase the prestige associated with its ownership. By lowering a price, marketers can emphasize a bargain and attract customers who go out of their way to save a small amount of money. Thus, as this chapter details, price can have strong effects on a firm's sales and profitability.

Price and Nonprice Competition

The competitive environment strongly influences the marketing mix decisions associated with a product. Pricing decisions are often made according to the price or nonprice competitive situation in a particular market. Price competition exists when consumers have difficulty distinguishing competitive offerings and marketers emphasize low prices. Nonprice competition involves a focus on marketing mix elements other than price.

Price Competition

price competition
Emphasizing price as an issue and matching or beating competitors' prices

When engaging in **price competition**, a marketer emphasizes price as an issue and matches or beats competitors' prices. To compete effectively on a price basis, a firm

Price and Nonprice Competition
Mattress manufacturers often engage in price competition. Ghirardelli, like most other premium chocolate brands, engages in nonprice competition.

should be the low-cost seller of the product. If all firms producing the same product charge the same price for it, the firm with the lowest costs is the most profitable. Firms that stress low price as a key marketing mix element tend to market standardized products. A seller competing on price may change prices frequently, or at least must be willing and able to do so. For example, when increasing numbers of coffee sellers entered the market, competition increased. Starbucks Corp. needed to counter the widespread perception that it was the home of the $4 cup of coffee, especially during the economic downturn. In order to compete with McDonald's inexpensive coffee, Starbucks cut its coffee prices and started selling discounted breakfast foods for $3.95, including coffee.[5] Whenever competitors change their prices, the company usually responds quickly and aggressively.

Price competition gives marketers flexibility. They can alter prices to account for changes in their costs or respond to changes in demand for the product. If competitors try to gain market share by cutting prices, a company competing on a price basis can react quickly to such efforts. However, a major drawback of price competition is that competitors have the flexibility to adjust prices too. If they quickly match or beat a company's price cuts, a price war may ensue. For instance, Sony recently introduced a less expensive version of its Playstation 3, Microsoft reduced the price of its console, Xbox 360, and Nintendo slashed the price of the Wii. As companies fight for a greater share of the video game industry, consumers continue to see falling prices.[6] Chronic price wars such as this one can substantially weaken organizations.

Nonprice Competition

Nonprice competition occurs when a seller decides not to focus on price and instead emphasizes distinctive product features, service, product quality, promotion, packaging, or other factors to distinguish its product from competing brands. Thus, nonprice competition allows a company to increase its brand's unit sales through means other than changing the brand's price. Mars, for example, markets not only Snickers and M&Ms, but also has an upscale candy line called ethel's chocolates. With the tagline "no mystery middles," ethel's chocolates competes on the basis of taste, attractive appearance, and hip packaging, and thus has little need to engage in price competition.[7] A major advantage of nonprice competition is that a firm can build customer loyalty toward its brand. If customers prefer a brand because of nonprice factors, they may not be easily lured away by competing firms and brands. In contrast, when price is the primary reason customers buy a particular brand, a competitor is often able to attract those customers through price cuts.

Nonprice competition is effective only under certain conditions. A company must be able to distinguish its brand through unique product features, higher product quality, effective promotion, distinctive packaging, or excellent customer service. Apple is known for producing products that demand a premium price because of the capabilities and service that come with its products. One writer went as far as to say that Linux will not be able to compete with the Apple iPad because it lacks the "magic" that Apple products have. It is difficult to define and therefore imitate Apple's magic; it is a combination of several qualities including the appearance of its products, ease of use, and product integration.[8] Buyers not only must be able to perceive these distinguishing characteristics but must also view them as important. The distinguishing features that set a particular brand apart from competitors should be difficult, if not impossible, for competitors to imitate. Finally, the firm must extensively promote the brand's distinguishing characteristics to establish its superiority and set it apart from competitors in the minds of buyers.

Even a marketer that is competing on a nonprice basis cannot ignore competitors' prices. This organization must be aware of them and sometimes be prepared to price its brand near or slightly above competing brands. Therefore, price remains a crucial marketing mix component even in environments that call for nonprice competition.

nonprice competition
Emphasizing factors other than price to distinguish a product from competing brands

Analysis of Demand

Determining the demand for a product is the responsibility of marketing managers, who are aided in this task by marketing researchers and forecasters. Marketing research and forecasting techniques yield estimates of sales potential, or the quantity of a product that could be sold during a specific period. These estimates are helpful in establishing the relationship between a product's price and the quantity demanded.

The Demand Curve

For most products, the quantity demanded goes up as the price goes down, and the quantity demanded goes down as the price goes up. For example, after Nintendo's research indicated there were about 50 million people in the United States on the verge of becoming gamers, the company reduced the price of its console by $50 in order to increase demand for its Wii console.[9] Thus, an inverse relationship exists between price and quantity demanded. As long as the marketing environment and buyers' needs, ability (purchasing power), willingness, and authority to buy remain stable, this fundamental inverse relationship holds.

Figure 20.1 illustrates the effect of one variable, price, on the quantity demanded. The classic **demand curve** ($D1$) is a graph of the quantity of products expected to be sold at various prices if other factors remain constant.[10] It illustrates that, as price falls, quantity demanded usually rises. Demand depends on other factors in the marketing mix, including product quality, promotion, and distribution. An improvement in any of these factors may

demand curve A graph of the quantity of products expected to be sold at various prices if other factors remain constant

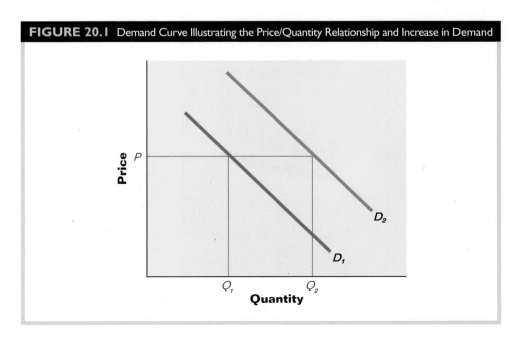

FIGURE 20.1 Demand Curve Illustrating the Price/Quantity Relationship and Increase in Demand

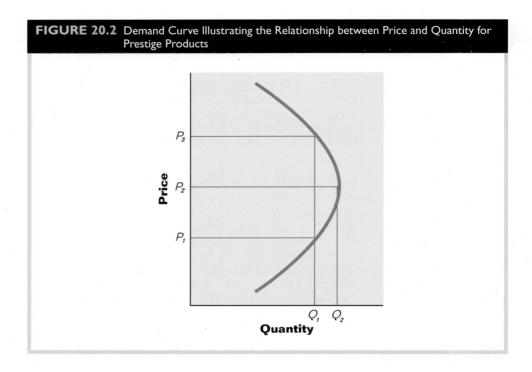

FIGURE 20.2 Demand Curve Illustrating the Relationship between Price and Quantity for Prestige Products

Prestige Demand

Many cosmetic products have a prestige-based demand curve.

cause a shift to, say, demand curve *D*2. In such a case, an increased quantity (*Q*2) will be sold at the same price (*P*).

Many types of demand exist, and not all conform to the classic demand curve shown in Figure 20.1. Prestige products, such as selected perfumes and jewelry, tend to sell better at high prices than at low ones. These products are desirable partly because their expense makes buyers feel elite. If the price fell drastically and many people owned these products, they would lose some of their appeal. The demand curve in Figure 20.2 shows the relationship between price and quantity demanded for prestige products. Quantity demanded is greater, not less, at higher prices. For a certain price range—from *P*1 to *P*2—the quantity demanded (*Q*1) goes up to *Q*2. After a certain point, however, raising the price backfires: if the price goes too high, the quantity demanded goes down. The figure shows that if price is raised from *P*2 to *P*3, quantity demanded goes back down from *Q*2 to *Q*1.

Demand Fluctuations

Changes in buyers' needs, variations in the effectiveness of other marketing mix variables, the presence of substitutes, and dynamic environmental factors can influence demand. Restaurants and utility companies experience large fluctuations in demand daily. Toy manufacturers, fireworks suppliers, and air-conditioning and heating contractors also face demand fluctuations because of the seasonal nature of their products. The demand for broadband services, beef, and flat-screen TVs has changed over the last few years. In some cases, demand fluctuations are predictable. It is no surprise to restaurants and utility company managers that demand fluctuates. However, changes in demand for other products may be less predictable, leading to problems for some companies. Other organizations anticipate demand fluctuations and develop new products and prices to meet consumers' changing needs.

Assessing Price Elasticity of Demand

Up to this point, we have seen how marketers identify the target market's evaluation of price and its ability to purchase and how they examine demand to learn whether price is related inversely or directly to quantity. The next step is to assess price elasticity of demand. **Price elasticity of demand** provides a measure of the sensitivity of demand to changes in price. It is formally defined as the percentage change in quantity demanded relative to a given percentage change in price (see Figure 20.3).[11] The percentage change in quantity demanded caused by a percentage change in price is much greater for elastic demand than for inelastic demand. For a product like electricity, demand is relatively inelastic: when its price increases, say, from $P1$ to $P2$, quantity demanded goes down only a little, from $Q1$ to $Q2$. For products like recreational vehicles, demand is relatively elastic: when price rises sharply, from $P1$ to $P2$, quantity demanded goes down a great deal, from $Q1$ to $Q2$.

If marketers can determine the price elasticity of demand, setting a price is much easier. By analyzing total revenues as prices change, marketers can determine whether a product is price elastic. Total revenue is price times quantity; thus, 10,000 rolls of wallpaper sold in one year at a price of $10 per roll equals $100,000 of total revenue. If demand is *elastic,* a change in price causes an opposite change in total revenue: an increase in price will decrease total revenue, and a decrease in price will increase total revenue. *Inelastic* demand results in a change in the same direction as total revenue: an increase in price will increase total revenue, and a decrease in price will decrease total revenue. Demand for gasoline, for example, is relatively inelastic—even when prices well exceed $3 per gallon—because people must still drive to work, run errands, shop, and engage in other behaviors that require fuel for their vehicles. Although higher gasoline prices have forced more consumers to change some behaviors in an effort to reduce the amount of gasoline they use, most have cut spending in other areas instead because they require a certain level of fuel for weekly activities like commuting.[12] The following formula determines the price elasticity of demand:

price elasticity of demand
A measure of the sensitivity of demand to changes in price

$$\text{price elasticity of demand} = \frac{(\text{\% change in quantity demand})}{(\text{\% change in price})}$$

FIGURE 20.3 Elasticity of Demand

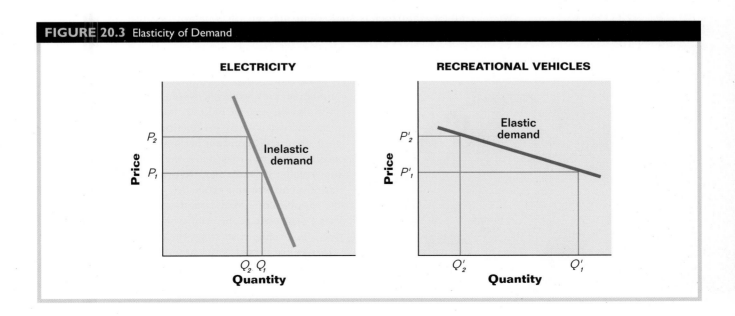

For instance, if demand falls by 8 percent when a seller raises the price by 2 percent, the price elasticity of demand is -4 (the negative sign indicating the inverse relationship between price and demand). If demand falls by 2 percent when price is increased by 4 percent, elasticity is $-\frac{1}{2}$. The less elastic the demand, the more beneficial it is for the seller to raise the price. Products without readily available substitutes and for which consumers have strong needs (e.g., electricity or appendectomies) usually have inelastic demand. Marketers cannot base prices solely on elasticity considerations. They must also examine the costs associated with different sales volumes and evaluate what happens to profits.

Demand, Cost, and Profit Relationships

The analysis of demand, cost, and profit is important because customers are becoming less tolerant of price increases, forcing manufacturers to find new ways to control costs. In the past, many customers desired premium brands and were willing to pay extra for those products. Today, customers pass up certain brand names if they can pay less without sacrificing quality. To stay in business, a company must set prices that not only cover its costs but also meet customers' expectations. In this section, we explore two approaches to understanding demand, cost, and profit relationships: marginal analysis and break-even analysis.

Marginal Analysis

Marginal analysis examines what happens to a firm's costs and revenues when production (or sales volume) changes by one unit. Both production costs and revenues must be evaluated. To determine the costs of production, it is necessary to distinguish among several types of costs. **Fixed costs** do not vary with changes in the number of units produced or sold. For example, a wallpaper manufacturer's cost of renting a factory does not change because production increases from one to two shifts a day or because twice as much wallpaper is sold. Rent may go up, but not because the factory has doubled production or revenue. **Average fixed cost** is the fixed cost per unit produced and is calculated by dividing fixed costs by the number of units produced.

Variable costs vary directly with changes in the number of units produced or sold. The wages for a second shift and the cost of twice as much wallpaper are extra costs incurred when production is doubled. Variable costs are usually constant per unit; that is, twice as many workers and twice as much material produce twice as many rolls of wallpaper. **Average variable cost**, the variable cost per unit produced, is calculated by dividing the variable costs by the number of units produced.

Total cost is the sum of average fixed costs and average variable costs times the quantity produced. The **average total cost** is the sum of the average fixed cost and the average variable cost. **Marginal cost (MC)** is the extra cost a firm incurs when it produces one more unit of a product.

Elasticity of Demand
The demand for electricity is inelastic.

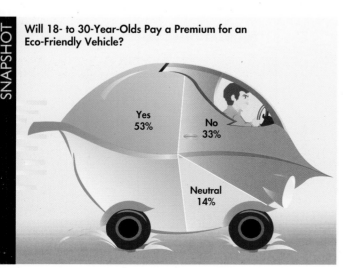

SNAPSHOT

Will 18- to 30-Year-Olds Pay a Premium for an Eco-Friendly Vehicle?

Yes 53%

No 33%

Neutral 14%

Source: Deloitte LLP and Michigan State University survey of 1,100 millennial generation consumers.

TABLE 20.1 Costs and Their Relationships

1 Quantity	2 Fixed Cost	3 Average Fixed Cost (2) ÷ (1)	4 Average Variable Cost	5 Average Total Cost (3) + (4)	6 Total Cost (5) × (1)	Marginal Cost
1	$40	$40.00	$20.00	$60.00	$60	
						$10
2	40	20.00	15.00	35.00	70	
						2
3	40	13.33	10.67	24.00	72	
						18
4	40	10.00	12.50	22.50	90	
						20
5	40	8.00	14.00	22.00	110	
						30
6	40	6.67	16.67	23.33	140	
						40
7	40	5.71	20.00	25.71	180	

fixed costs Costs that do not vary with changes in the number of units produced or sold

average fixed cost The fixed cost per unit produced

variable costs Costs that vary directly with changes in the number of units produced or sold

average variable cost The variable cost per unit produced

total cost The sum of average fixed and average variable costs times the quantity produced

average total cost The sum of the average fixed cost and the average variable cost

marginal cost (MC) The extra cost incurred by producing one more unit of a product

marginal revenue (MR) The change in total revenue resulting from the sale of an additional unit of a product

Table 20.1 illustrates various costs and their relationships. Notice that average fixed cost declines as output increases. Average variable cost follows a U shape, as does average total cost. Because average total cost continues to fall after average variable cost begins to rise, its lowest point is at a higher level of output than that of average variable cost. Average total cost is lowest at five units at a cost of $22.00, whereas average variable cost is lowest at three units at a cost of $10.67. As Figure 20.4 shows, marginal cost equals average total cost at the latter's lowest level. In Table 20.1, this occurs between five and six units of production. Average total cost decreases as long as marginal cost is less than average total cost and increases when marginal cost rises above average total cost.

Marginal revenue (MR) is the change in total revenue that occurs when a firm sells an additional unit of a product. Figure 20.5 depicts marginal revenue and a demand curve. Most firms in the United States face downward-sloping demand curves for their products; in other words, they must lower their prices to sell additional units. This situation means that each additional unit of product sold provides the firm with less revenue than the previous unit sold. MR then becomes less-than-average revenue, as Figure 20.5 shows. Eventually, MR reaches zero, and the sale of additional units actually hurts the firm.

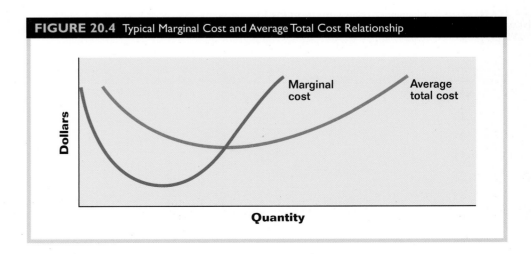

FIGURE 20.4 Typical Marginal Cost and Average Total Cost Relationship

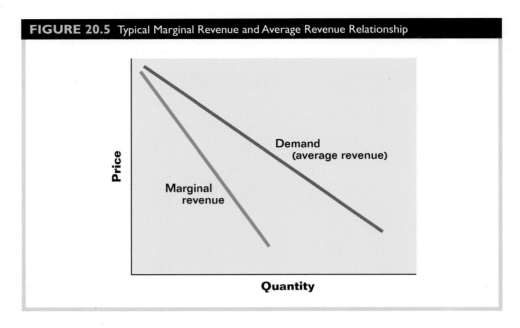

FIGURE 20.5 Typical Marginal Revenue and Average Revenue Relationship

However, before the firm can determine whether a unit makes a profit, it must know its cost, as well as its revenue, because profit equals revenue minus cost. If MR is a unit's addition to revenue and MC is a unit's addition to cost, MR minus MC tells us whether the unit is profitable. Table 20.2 illustrates the relationships among price, quantity sold, total revenue, marginal revenue, marginal cost, and total cost. It indicates where maximum profits are possible at various combinations of price and cost. Notice that the total cost and the marginal cost figures in Table 20.2 are calculated and appear in Table 20.1.

Profit is the highest where MC = MR. In Table 20.2, note that at a quantity of four units, profit is the highest and MR − MC = 0. The best price is $33, and the profit is $42. Up to this point, the additional revenue generated from an extra unit sold exceeds the additional cost of producing it. Beyond this point, the additional cost of producing another unit exceeds the additional revenue generated, and profits decrease. If the price were based on minimum average total cost—$22 (Table 20.1)—it would result in a lower profit of $40 (Table 20.2) for five units priced at $30 versus a profit of $42 for four units priced at $33.

Graphically combining Figures 20.4 and 20.5 into Figure 20.6 shows that any unit for which MR exceeds MC adds to a firm's profits, and any unit for which MC exceeds MR subtracts from profits. The firm should produce at the point where MR equals MC, because this is the most profitable level of production.

This discussion of marginal analysis may give the false impression that pricing can be highly precise. If revenue (demand) and cost (supply) remained constant, prices could

TABLE 20.2 Marginal Analysis Method for Determining the Most Profitable Price

1 Price	2 Quantity Sold	3 Total Revenue (1) × (2)	4 Marginal Revenue	5 Marginal Cost	6 Total Cost	7 Profit (3) − (6)
$57	1	$57	$57	$60	$60	$−3
50	2	100	43	10	70	30
38	3	114	14	2	72	42
33*	**4**	**132**	**18**	**18**	**90**	**42**
30	5	150	18	20	110	40
27	6	162	12	30	140	22
25	7	175	13	40	180	−5

*Boldface indicates the best price-profit combination

FIGURE 20.6 Combining the Marginal Cost and Marginal Revenue Concepts for Optimal Profit

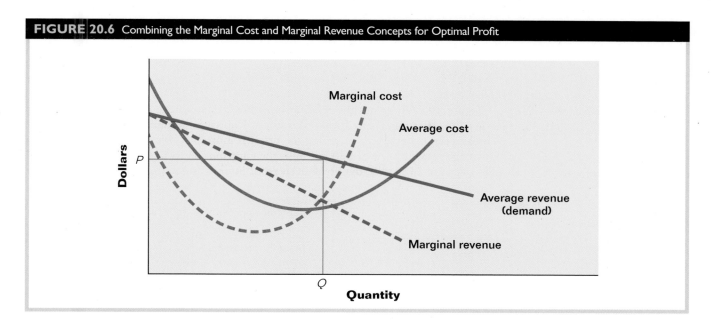

be set for maximum profits. In practice, however, cost and revenue change frequently. The competitive tactics of other firms or government action can quickly undermine a company's expectations of revenue. Thus, marginal analysis is only a model from which to work. It offers little help in pricing new products before costs and revenues are established. On the other hand, in setting prices of existing products, especially in competitive situations, most marketers can benefit by understanding the relationship between marginal cost and marginal revenue.

Sustainable Marketing
Will Buyers Pay More for Green Products?

Green products are often priced higher than their conventional counterparts, due to special materials, innovative manufacturing processes, or separate handling procedures that raise marketers' costs. But will buyers pay more for green products? The short answer is: It depends.

Surveys show that a core segment of consumers will pay higher prices for green products, especially foods, beverages, and personal-care products. There are limits, however. Walmart, one of the biggest marketers to move green products into the mainstream, recognizes that even a small price difference between green and conventional products can be a barrier. "When you ask [consumers] to pay more for a green product, you're also asking them to cut something else out of their life," says Walmart's chairman.

At the same time, he observes that parents at all income levels have been willing to pay slightly higher prices for organic children's foods. Sales figures bear this out. Before the downturn, growth in sales of natural and organic foods and beverages had been skyrocketing at double-digit levels. Once the recession began, however, sales growth continued, but at a slower pace, because consumers felt under pressure and were pinching their pennies.

Meanwhile, as more marketers make the move to eco-friendly goods and services and demand increases, competition

and economies of scale are bringing costs closer to those of conventional products. Procter & Gamble, for example, is using promotional pricing to capture market share for its growing portfolio of green household products. Over time, marketers will be able to lower the prices of green products and attract more buyers as the pricing gap between green and nongreen products narrows.[b]

Break-Even Analysis

The point at which the costs of producing a product equal the revenue made from selling the product is the **break-even point**. If a wallpaper manufacturer has total annual costs of $100,000 and sells $100,000 worth of wallpaper in the same year, the company has broken even.

Figure 20.7 illustrates the relationships among costs, revenue, profits, and losses involved in determining the break-even point. Knowing the number of units necessary to break even is important in setting the price. If a product priced at $100 per unit has an average variable cost of $60 per unit, the contribution to fixed costs is $40. If total fixed costs are $120,000, the break-even point in units is determined as follows:

$$\text{break-even point} = \frac{\text{fixed costs}}{\text{per-unit contribution to fixed costs}}$$
$$= \frac{\text{fixed costs}}{\text{price} - \text{variable costs}}$$
$$= \frac{\$120,000}{\$40}$$
$$= 3,000 \text{ units}$$

To calculate the break-even point in terms of dollar sales volume, the seller multiplies the break-even point in units by the price per unit. In the preceding example, the break-even point in terms of dollar sales volume is 3,000 (units) times $100, or $300,000.

To use break-even analysis effectively, a marketer should determine the break-even point for each of several alternative prices. This determination allows the marketer to compare the effects on total revenue, total costs, and the break-even point for each price under consideration. Although this comparative analysis may not tell the marketer exactly what price to charge, it will identify highly undesirable price alternatives that should definitely be avoided.

Break-even analysis is simple and straightforward. It does assume, however, that the quantity demanded is basically fixed (inelastic) and that the major task in setting prices is to recover costs. It focuses more on how to break even than on how to achieve a pricing objective, such as percentage of market share or return on investment. Nonetheless, marketing managers can use this concept to determine whether a product will achieve at least a break-even volume.

break-even point The point at which the costs of producing a product equal the revenue made from selling the product

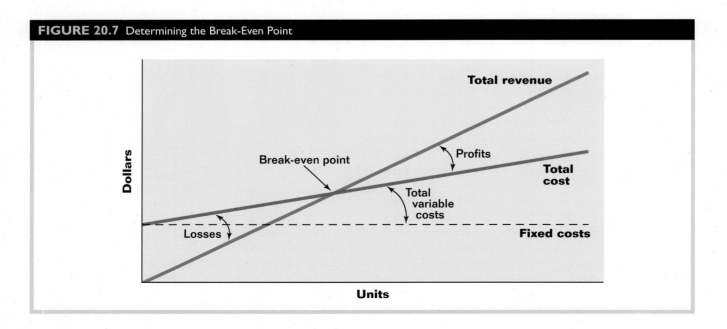

FIGURE 20.7 Determining the Break-Even Point

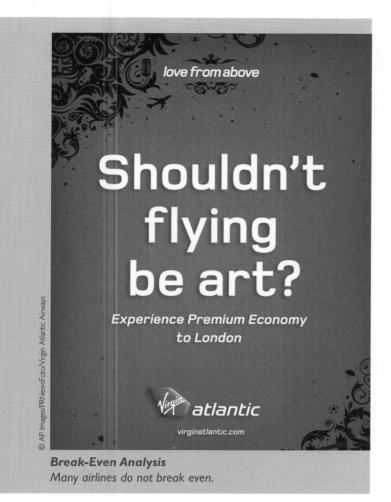

Break-Even Analysis
Many airlines do not break even.

Factors That Affect Pricing Decisions

Pricing decisions can be complex because of the number of factors to consider. Frequently, there is considerable uncertainty about the reactions to price among buyers, channel members, and competitors. Price is also an important consideration in marketing planning, market analysis, and sales forecasting. It is a major issue when assessing a brand's position relative to competing brands. Most factors that affect pricing decisions can be grouped into one of the eight categories shown in Figure 20.8. In this section, we explore how each of these groups of factors enters into price decision making.

Organizational and Marketing Objectives

Marketers should set prices that are consistent with the organization's goals and mission. For example, a retailer trying to position itself as value-oriented may wish to set prices that are quite reasonable relative to product quality. In this case, a marketer would not want to set premium prices on products but would strive to price products in line with this overall organizational goal.

Pricing decisions should also be compatible with the firm's marketing objectives. For instance, suppose one of a producer's marketing objectives is a 12 percent increase in unit sales by the end of the following year. Assuming buyers are price-sensitive, increasing the price or setting a price above the average market price would not be in line with this objective.

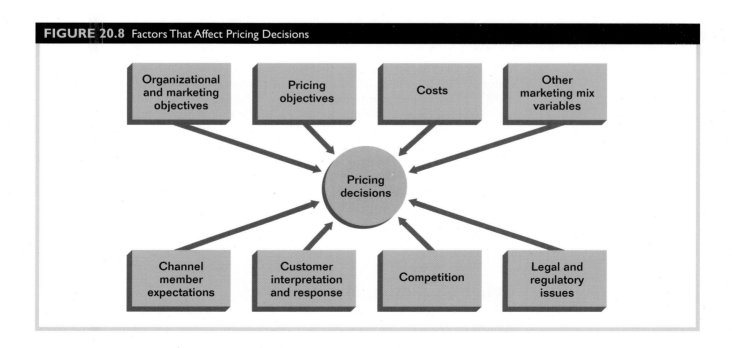

FIGURE 20.8 Factors That Affect Pricing Decisions

Responsible Marketing?
Credit Limits

CRITICAL THINKING

Issue: Are credit card companies playing fair?

Some credit card companies lobby Congress for less regulation and for regulation that is more favorable to credit card issuers. Have regulatory changes led to questionable practices by some companies? Credit card companies can increase credit card interest rates even though the card holder has paid at least the minimum payments on time and has not been charged penalty payments. Credit card companies sometimes change a holder's billing cycle, which reduces the number of days between receiving the bill and the due date, hoping that the card holder does not notice the new due date and makes a "late payment" that results in both a late fee and a finance charge. Last year, a majority of all credit card holders in the United States paid at least one late fee. Credit card companies can also add penalties, such as for a late payment, which puts the balance on the card over the credit limit and incurs an over-the-limit fee.

Is it fair for a credit card company to shorten the billing cycle without notice and charge a late fee if the card holder fails to pay "on time"? Why should a credit card company be allowed to charge an over-the-limit penalty when the account is over its limit due to charges made only by the credit card company? Should a credit card company be permitted to increase a card holder's interest rate when the customer has paid according to the original contract?[c]

Types of Pricing Objectives

The types of pricing objectives a marketer uses obviously have considerable bearing on the determination of prices. For instance, an organization that uses pricing to increase its market share would likely set the brand's price below those of competing brands of similar quality to attract competitors' customers. A marketer sometimes uses temporary price reductions in the hope of gaining market share. If a business needs to raise cash quickly, it will likely use temporary price reductions, such as sales, rebates, and special discounts. We examine pricing objectives in more detail in the next chapter.

Costs

Clearly, costs must be an issue when establishing price. A firm may temporarily sell products below cost to match competition, generate cash flow, or even increase market share, but in the long run, it cannot survive by selling its products below cost. Even a firm that has a high-volume business cannot survive if each item is sold slightly below its cost. A marketer should be careful to analyze all costs so they can be included in the total cost associated with a product.

To maintain market share and revenue in an increasingly price-sensitive market, many marketers have concentrated on reducing costs. Sony, for example, was able to remain in business during the recession by eliminating more than 20,000 jobs, closing 20 percent of its plants, and redesigning its supply chain to cut costs by more than $3 billion. The company also reduced the production costs of its televisions, digital cameras, and video game consoles.[13]

Labor-saving technologies, a focus on quality, and efficient manufacturing processes have brought productivity gains that translate into reduced costs and lower prices for customers. In an industry ravaged by labor concerns and monetary losses, Southwest Airlines has managed to stay one step ahead of its larger rivals. Southwest is the low-fare leader on more of the top 100 routes in the United States than the three largest airlines—American, Delta, and United. One reason for the Texas-based airline's success is its ability to control costs. Southwest's per-seat mile costs are somewhat lower than those of its "big three" rivals. However, Southwest now faces competition from other low-cost airlines like JetBlue.

Besides considering the costs associated with a particular product, marketers must take into account the costs the product shares with others in the product line. Products often share some costs, particularly the costs of research and development, production, and distribution. Most marketers view a product's cost as a minimum, or floor, below which the product cannot be priced.

Other Marketing Mix Variables

All marketing mix variables are highly interrelated. Pricing decisions can influence evaluations and activities associated with product, distribution, and promotion variables. A product's price frequently affects the demand for that item. A high price, for instance, may result in low unit sales, which in turn may lead to higher production costs per unit. Conversely, lower per-unit production costs may result from a low price. For many products, buyers associate better product quality with a high price and poorer product quality with a low price. This perceived price–quality relationship influences customers' overall image of products or brands. For example, some individuals view Apple computers as higher quality than other brands' computers and are willing to pay a higher price. Individuals who associate quality with a high price are likely to purchase products with well-established and recognizable brand names.[14]

The price of a product is linked to several dimensions of its distribution. Premium-priced products, Bentley or Rolls-Royce automobiles, for example, are often marketed through selective or exclusive distribution; lower-priced products in the same product category may be sold through intensive distribution. For instance, Cross pens are distributed through selective distribution and Bic pens through intensive distribution. Moreover, an increase in physical distribution costs, such as shipping, may have to be passed on to customers. When fuel prices increase significantly, some distribution companies pass on these additional costs through surcharges or higher prices. When setting a price, the profit margins of marketing channel members, such as wholesalers and retailers, must also be considered. Channel members must be adequately compensated for the functions they perform.

Price may determine how a product is promoted. Bargain prices are often included in advertisements. Premium prices are less likely to be advertised, though they are sometimes included in advertisements for upscale items like luxury cars or fine jewelry. Higher-priced products are more likely than lower-priced ones to require personal selling. Furthermore, the price structure can affect a salesperson's relationship with customers. A complex pricing structure takes longer to explain to customers, is more likely to confuse potential buyers, and may cause misunderstandings that result in long-term customer dissatisfaction. For example, the pricing structures of many airlines are complex and frequently confuse ticket sales agents and travelers alike.

Channel Member Expectations

When making price decisions, a producer must consider what members of the distribution channel expect. A channel member certainly expects to receive a profit for the functions it performs. The amount of profit expected depends on what the intermediary could make if it were handling a competing product instead. Also, the amount of time and the resources required to carry the product influence intermediaries' expectations.

Channel members often expect producers to give discounts for large orders and prompt payment. At times, resellers expect producers to provide several support activities, such as sales training, service training, repair advisory service, cooperative advertising, sales promotions, and perhaps a program for returning unsold merchandise to the producer. These support activities clearly have associated costs that a producer must consider when determining prices.

Customers' Interpretation and Response

When making pricing decisions, marketers should address a vital question: How will our customers interpret our prices and respond to them? *Interpretation* in this context refers to what the price means or what it communicates to customers. Does the price mean "high quality" or "low quality," or "great deal," "fair price," or "rip-off"? Customer *response* refers to whether the price will move customers closer to purchase of the product and the degree to which the price enhances their satisfaction with the purchase experience and with the product after purchase.

Customers' interpretation of and response to a price are to some degree determined by their assessment of value, or what they receive compared with what they give up to make the purchase. In evaluating what they receive, customers consider product attributes, benefits, advantages, disadvantages, the probability of using the product, and possibly the status associated with the product. In assessing the cost of the product, customers likely will consider its price, the amount of time and effort required to obtain it, and perhaps the resources required to maintain it after purchase.

At times, customers interpret a higher price as higher product quality. They are especially likely to make this price–quality association when they cannot judge the quality of the product themselves. This is not always the case, however; whether price is equated with quality depends on the types of customers and products involved. Obviously marketers that rely on customers making a price–quality association and that provide moderate- or low-quality products at high prices will be unable to build long-term customer relationships.

When interpreting and responding to prices, how do customers determine if the price is too high, too low, or about right? In general, they compare prices with internal or external reference prices. An **internal reference price** is a price developed in the buyer's mind through experience with the product. It reflects a belief that a product should cost approximately a certain amount. To arrive at an internal reference price, consumers may consider one or more values, including what they think the product "ought" to cost, the price usually charged for it, the last price they paid, the highest and lowest amounts they would be willing to pay, the price of the brand they usually buy, the average price of similar products, the expected future price, and the typical discounted price.[15] Research has found that less-confident consumers tend to have higher internal reference prices than consumers with greater confidence, and frequent buyers—perhaps because of their experience and confidence—are more likely to judge high prices unfairly.[16] As consumers, our experiences have given each of us internal reference prices for a number of products. For instance, most of us have a reasonable idea of how much to pay for a six-pack of soft drinks, a loaf of bread, or a cup of coffee. For the product categories with which we have less experience, we rely more heavily on external reference prices. An **external reference price** is a comparison price provided by others, such as retailers or manufacturers. When culinary retailer Williams-Sonoma, for example, wanted to improve the sales of its bread maker priced at $250, the company added another bread maker to the selection priced 50 percent higher. For consumers unfamiliar with the product category, it provided a reference point. Sales of the original $250 bread maker increased after the addition.[17] Customers' perceptions of prices are also influenced by their expectations about future price increases, what they paid for the product recently, and what they would like to pay for the product. Other factors affecting customers' perceptions of whether the price is right include time or financial constraints, the costs associated with searching for lower-priced products, and expectations that products will go on sale.

Buyers' perceptions of a product relative to competing products may allow the firm to set a price that differs significantly from rivals' prices. If the product is deemed superior to most of the competition, a premium price may be feasible. However, even products with superior quality can be overpriced. Strong brand loyalty sometimes provides the opportunity to charge a premium price. On the other hand, if buyers view a product less than favorably (though not extremely negatively), a lower price may generate sales.

In the context of price, buyers can be characterized according to their degree of value consciousness, price consciousness, and prestige sensitivity. Marketers that understand these characteristics are better able to set pricing objectives and policies. **Value-conscious** consumers are concerned about both price and quality of a product.[18] During recessions, customers become more value and price conscious and tend to limit discretionary spending. Lululemon Athletics Inc., a yoga apparel and accessories retailer, realized

internal reference price
A price developed in the buyer's mind through experience with the product

external reference price
A comparison price provided by others

value conscious Concerned about price and quality of a product

External Reference Price
Advertisements, like this one, provide information that customers use to establish or change their reference prices.

this when the company was facing drastic declines in sales during the recent economic slump. Because customers were cutting back on their personal trainers, Lululemon began offering more free yoga classes. By focusing on value, the company increased net revenue by 17 percent the first three quarters of that year.[19] These value-conscious consumers may perceive value as quality per unit of price or as not only economic savings but also the additional gains expected from one product over a competitor's brand. The first view is appropriate for commodities such as bottled water, bananas, and gasoline. If a value-conscious consumer perceives the quality of gasoline to be the same for Exxon and Shell, he or she will go to the station with the lower price. For consumers looking not just for economic value but additional gains they expect from one brand over another, a product differentiation value could be associated with benefits and features that are believed to be unique.[20] For example, a BMW may be considered to be better than a Cadillac.

Price-conscious individuals strive to pay low prices. They want the lowest prices and would respond to Walmart's claim that "we sell for less." To further capitalize on this, Walmart emphasizes the amount of money its customers can save and added 80 new products that carry the Great Value brand.[21]

Prestige-sensitive buyers focus on purchasing products that signify prominence and status. For instance, Coty Inc., a major producer of fragrances and beauty products for prestige-sensitive buyers, recently partnered with the Home Shopping Network (HSN) to offer select Coty products. One such product is the Lancaster 365 Cellular Elixer, an advanced anti-aging product from Coty Prestige's Lancaster brand, which costs $95 for a 1.7 fluid ounce bottle.[22]

Some consumers vary in their degree of value, price, and prestige consciousness. In some market segments, consumers "trade up" to higher-status products in categories such as automobiles, home appliances, restaurants, and even pet food, yet remain price conscious regarding cleaning and grocery products. This trend has benefited marketers like Starbucks, Sub-Zero, BMW, Whole Foods, and PETCO, which can charge premium prices for high-quality, prestige products.

price conscious Striving to pay low prices

prestige sensitive Drawn to products that signify prominence and status

Marketing in Transition
Groupon's Group Deals Bring in Business

Promotional pricing meets social media—that's the appeal of Groupon, a site that e-mails one big deal every day to members in more than 50 U.S. cities. One day, the deal might be 50 percent off the price of a restaurant meal. The next, it might be 55 percent off custom-tailored men's shirts. However, the deal is only valid if a certain number of members buy. That's where the social media angle comes into play: Members use Twitter, Facebook, and blogs to talk up deals so they can reach the required minimum.

Many marketers use Groupon to attract new customers. The rental car firm Zipcar, for example, gained 1,500 new members in six months through Groupon. "The viral nature of [Groupon's] community plays to our strength as a word-of-mouth brand," says Zipcar's vice president of marketing. When Vitality Unlimited Spa in St. Louis offered a $68 massage at the promotional price of $30, it attracted 600 new customers. Just as important, 70 percent of the Groupon members who bought into the deal returned a second time.

Does this kind of promotional pricing pay off? Although response can stimulate strong demand, marketers must be prepared for the costs. Not long ago, Hannah's Bretzel, an organic sandwich shop in Chicago, offered a two-for-one deal

through Groupon. Within hours, 3,400 customers had clicked to buy. Even after paying Groupon's commission, the sandwich shop enjoyed a $15,000 revenue boost. Considering the extra labor and food costs, Hannah's Bretzel figures it broke even, and the deal was a good way to reach thousands of new customers.[d]

Competition

A marketer needs to know competitors' prices so it can adjust its own prices accordingly. This does not mean a company will necessarily match competitors' prices; it may set its price above or below theirs. However, for some organizations (such as airlines), matching competitors' prices is an important strategy for survival.

When adjusting prices, a marketer must assess how competitors will respond. Will competitors change their prices and, if so, will they raise or lower them? In Chapter 3, we described several types of competitive market structures. The structure that characterizes the industry to which a firm belongs affects the flexibility of price setting. For example, because of reduced pricing regulation, firms in the telecommunications industry have moved from a monopolistic market structure to an oligopolistic one, which has resulted in significant price competition.

When an organization operates as a monopoly and is unregulated, it can set whatever prices the market will bear. However, the company may not price the product at the highest-possible level to avoid government regulation or penetrate a market by using a lower price. If the monopoly is regulated, it normally has less pricing flexibility; the regulatory body lets it set prices that generate a reasonable but not excessive return. A government-owned monopoly may price products below cost to make them accessible to people who otherwise could not afford them. Transit systems, for example, sometimes operate this way. However, government-owned monopolies sometimes charge higher prices to control demand. In some states with state-owned liquor stores, the price of liquor is higher than in states where liquor stores are not owned by a government body.

The automotive and airline industries exemplify oligopolies, in which only a few sellers operate and barriers to competitive entry are high. Companies in such industries can raise their prices in the hope that competitors will do the same. When an organization cuts its price to gain a competitive edge, other companies are likely to follow suit. Thus, very little advantage is gained through price cuts in an oligopolistic market structure.

A market structure characterized by monopolistic competition has numerous sellers with product offerings that are differentiated by physical characteristics, features, quality, and brand images. The distinguishing characteristics of its product may allow a company

Impact of Market Structure
The camera industry is an example of an oligopoly.

© AP Images/Paul Sakuma

to set a different price than its competitors. However, firms in a monopolistic competitive market structure are likely to practice nonprice competition, discussed earlier in this chapter.

Under conditions of perfect competition, many sellers exist. Buyers view all sellers' products as the same. All firms sell their products at the going market price, and buyers will not pay more than that. This type of market structure, then, gives a marketer no flexibility in setting prices. Farming, as an industry, has some characteristics of perfect competition. Farmers sell their products at the going market price. At times, for example, corn, soybean, and wheat growers have had bumper crops and been forced to sell them at depressed market prices.

Legal and Regulatory Issues

As discussed in Chapter 3, legal and regulatory issues influence pricing decisions. To curb inflation, the federal government can invoke price controls, freeze prices at certain levels, or determine the rates at which firms may increase prices. In some states and many other countries, regulatory agencies set prices on such products as insurance, dairy products, and liquor. Many regulations and laws affect pricing decisions and activities in the United States. The Sherman Antitrust Act prohibits conspiracies to control prices, and in interpreting the act, courts have ruled that price fixing among firms in an industry is illegal. Marketers must refrain from fixing prices by developing independent pricing policies and setting prices in ways that do not even hint at collusion. Recently, the Justice Department began investigating AT&T and Verizon for possible violations of the Sherman Antitrust Act. The actions in question are the exclusive contracts signed between the wireless providers and popular cellular phones, including the iPhone and RIM's BlackBerry Bold. The current administration hopes to crack down on monopolies and cartels in this industry as well as health care and energy.[23] Both the Federal Trade Commission Act and the Wheeler-Lea Act prohibit deceptive pricing. Some other nations and trade agreements have similar prohibitions. The European Commission, for example, is investigating allegations of price fixing in the global candy industry, asking numerous candy makers, including U.S.-based Hershey and Mars, to provide it with information on their pricing practices.[24] In establishing prices, marketers must guard against deceiving customers.

The Robinson-Patman Act has had a particularly strong impact on pricing decisions. For various reasons, marketers may wish to sell the same type of product at different prices. Provisions in the Robinson-Patman Act, as well as those in the Clayton Act, limit the use of such price differentials. **Price discrimination**, the practice of employing price differentials that tend to injure competition by giving one or more buyers a competitive advantage over other buyers, is prohibited by law. Currently, the biggest U.S. oil company, ExxonMobil Corp., is facing a lawsuit from some of its operators in New Jersey. Exxon apparently divides stations into zones and charges different rates to each zone for gasoline as well as delivers gasoline on a schedule that saves Exxon money while costing the operator more. Operators cite the Robinson-Patman Act as one of the laws violated by their supplier.[25] However, not all price differentials are discriminatory. A marketer can use price differentials if they do not hinder competition, result from differences in the costs of selling or transportation to various customers, or arise because the firm has had to cut its price to a particular buyer to meet competitors' prices. Airlines, for example, may charge different customers different prices for the same flights based on the availability of seats at the time of purchase. As a result, flyers sitting in adjacent seats may have paid vastly different fares because one passenger booked weeks ahead, whereas the other booked on the spur of the moment a few days before when only a few seats were still available.

Pricing for Business Markets

Business markets consist of individuals and organizations that purchase products for resale, use in their own operations, or producing other products. Establishing prices for this category of buyers sometimes differs from setting prices for consumers. Differences in the size of purchases, geographic factors, and transportation considerations require

price discrimination
Employing price differentials that injure competition by giving one or more buyers a competitive advantage

sellers to adjust prices. In this section, we discuss several issues unique to the pricing of business products, including discounts, geographic pricing, and transfer pricing.

Price Discounting

Producers commonly provide intermediaries with discounts, or reductions, from list prices. Although many types of discounts exist, they usually fall into one of five categories: trade, quantity, cash, seasonal, and allowance. Table 20.3 summarizes some reasons to use each type of discount and provides examples. Such discounts can be a significant factor in a marketing strategy.

TRADE DISCOUNTS

A reduction off the list price given by a producer to an intermediary for performing certain functions is called a **trade (functional) discount**. A trade discount is usually stated in terms of a percentage or series of percentages off the list price. Intermediaries are given trade discounts as compensation for performing various functions, such as selling, transporting, storing, final processing, and perhaps providing credit services. Although certain trade discounts are often a standard practice within an industry, discounts vary considerably among industries. It is important that a manufacturer provide a trade discount large enough to offset the intermediary's costs, plus a reasonable profit, to entice the reseller to carry the product.

QUANTITY DISCOUNTS

Deductions from list price that reflect the economies of purchasing in large quantities are called **quantity discounts**. Quantity discounts are used in many industries and pass on to the buyer cost savings gained through economies of scale.

Quantity discounts can be either cumulative or noncumulative. **Cumulative discounts** are quantity discounts aggregated over a stated time period. Purchases totaling $10,000 in a three-month period, for example, might entitle the buyer to a 5 percent, or $500, rebate. Such discounts are intended to reflect economies in selling and to encourage the buyer to purchase from one seller. **Noncumulative discounts** are one-time reductions in prices based on the number of units purchased, the dollar value of the order, or the product mix purchased. Like cumulative discounts, these discounts should reflect some economies in selling or trade functions.

CASH DISCOUNTS

A **cash discount**, or price reduction, is given to a buyer for prompt payment or cash payment. Accounts receivable are an expense and a collection problem for many

---

trade (functional) discount A reduction off the list price a producer gives to an intermediary for performing certain functions

quantity discounts Deductions from the list price for purchasing in large quantities

cumulative discounts Quantity discounts aggregated over a stated time period

noncumulative discounts Onetime price reductions based on the number of units purchased, the dollar value of the order, or the product mix purchased

cash discounts Price reductions given to buyers for prompt payment or cash payment

seasonal discount A price reduction given to buyers for purchasing goods or services out of season

allowance A concession in price to achieve a desired goal

TABLE 20.3 Discounts Used for Business Markets

Type	Reasons for Use	Examples
Trade	To attract and keep effective resellers by compensating them for performing certain functions, such as transportation, warehousing, selling, and providing credit	A college bookstore pays about (functional) one-third less for a new textbook than the retail price a student pays.
Quantity	To encourage customers to buy large quantities when making purchases and, in the case of cumulative discounts, to encourage customer loyalty	Large department store chains purchase some women's apparel at lower prices than do individually owned specialty stores.
Cash	To reduce expenses associated with accounts receivable and collection by encouraging prompt payment of accounts	Numerous companies serving business markets allow a 2 percent discount if an account is paid within 10 days.
Seasonal	To allow a marketer to use resources more efficiently by stimulating sales during off-peak periods	Florida hotels provide companies holding national and regional sales meetings with deeply discounted accommodations during the summer months.
Allowance	In the case of a trade-in allowance, to assist the buyer in making the purchase and potentially earning a profit on the resale of used equipment; in the case of a promotional allowance, to ensure that dealers participate in advertising and sales support programs	A farm equipment dealer takes a farmer's used tractor as a trade-in on a new one. Nabisco pays a promotional allowance to a supermarket for setting up and maintaining a large, end-of-aisle display for a two-week period.

geographic pricing Reductions for transportation and other costs related to the physical distance between buyer and seller

F.O.B. factory The price of merchandise at the factory before shipment

F.O.B. destination A price indicating the producer is absorbing shipping costs

uniform geographic pricing Charging all customers the same price, regardless of geographic location

zone pricing Pricing based on transportation costs within major geographic zones

base-point pricing Geographic pricing that combines factory price and freight charges from the base point nearest the buyer

organizations. A policy to encourage prompt payment is a popular practice and sometimes a major concern in setting prices.

Discounts are based on cash payments or cash paid within a stated time. For instance, "2/10 net 30" means that a 2 percent discount will be allowed if the account is paid within 10 days. If the buyer does not make payment within the 10-day period, the entire balance is due within 30 days without a discount. If the account is not paid within 30 days, interest may be charged.

SEASONAL DISCOUNTS

A price reduction to buyers that purchase goods or services out of season is a **seasonal discount**. These discounts let the seller maintain steadier production during the year. For example, automobile rental agencies offer seasonal discounts in winter and early spring to encourage firms to use automobiles during the slow months of the automobile rental business.

ALLOWANCES

Another type of reduction from the list price is an **allowance**, a concession in price to achieve a desired goal. Trade-in allowances, for example, are price reductions granted for turning in a used item when purchasing a new one. Allowances help make the buyer better able to make the new purchase. This type of discount is popular in the aircraft industry. Another example is a promotional allowance, a price reduction granted to dealers for participating in advertising and sales support programs intended to increase sales of a particular item.

Geographic Pricing

Geographic pricing involves reductions for transportation costs or other costs associated with the physical distance between buyer and seller. Prices may be quoted as F.O.B. (free-on-board) factory or destination. An **F.O.B. factory** price indicates the price of the merchandise at the factory, before it is loaded onto the carrier, and thus excludes transportation costs. The buyer must pay for shipping. An **F.O.B. destination** price means the producer absorbs the costs of shipping the merchandise to the customer. This policy may be used to attract distant customers. Although F.O.B. pricing is an easy way to price products, it is sometimes difficult to administer, especially when a firm has a wide product mix or when customers are widely dispersed. Because customers will want to know about the most economical method of shipping, the seller must be informed about shipping rates.

To avoid the problems involved in charging different prices to each customer, **uniform geographic pricing**, sometimes called *postage-stamp pricing*, may be used. The same price is charged to all customers regardless of geographic location, and the price is based on average shipping costs for all customers. Paper products and office equipment are often priced on a uniform basis.

Zone pricing sets uniform prices for each of several major geographic zones; as the transportation costs across zones increase, so do the prices. For instance, a Florida manufacturer's prices may be higher for buyers on the Pacific Coast and in Canada than for buyers in Georgia.

Base-point pricing is a geographic pricing policy that includes the price at the factory, plus freight charges from the base point nearest the buyer. This approach to pricing has virtually been abandoned because of its questionable legal status. The policy resulted in all buyers paying freight

Pricing for Business Markets
Network Solutions offers computer-based marketing services to small businesses. These services include website design tools, real-person customer service, personalized e-mail, and online sales and marketing tools, starting at $24.95 per month.

charges from one location, such as Detroit or Pittsburgh, regardless of where the product was manufactured.

When the seller absorbs all or part of the actual freight costs, **freight absorption pricing** is being used. The seller might choose this method because it wishes to do business with a particular customer or to get more business; more business will cause the average cost to fall and counterbalance the extra freight cost. This strategy is used to improve market penetration and retain a hold in an increasingly competitive market.

Transfer Pricing

Transfer pricing occurs when one unit in an organization sells a product to another unit. The price is determined by one of the following methods:

- *Actual full cost:* calculated by dividing all fixed and variable expenses for a period into the number of units produced
- *Standard full cost:* calculated based on what it would cost to produce the goods at full plant capacity
- *Cost plus investment:* calculated as full cost plus the cost of a portion of the selling unit's assets used for internal needs
- *Market-based cost:* calculated at the market price less a small discount to reflect the lack of sales effort and other expenses

The choice of transfer pricing method depends on the company's management strategy and the nature of the units' interaction. An organization must also ensure that transfer pricing is fair to all units involved in the transactions.

freight absorption pricing Absorption of all or part of actual freight costs by the seller

transfer pricing Prices charged in sales between an organization's units

summary

1. To understand the nature and importance of price

Price is the value paid for a product in a marketing exchange. Barter, the trading of products, is the oldest form of exchange. Price is a key element in the marketing mix because it relates directly to generation of total revenue. The profit factor can be determined mathematically by multiplying price by quantity sold to get total revenue and then subtracting total costs. Price is the only variable in the marketing mix that can be adjusted quickly and easily to respond to changes in the external environment.

2. To identify the characteristics of price and nonprice competition

A product offering can compete on either a price or a nonprice basis. Price competition emphasizes price as the product differential. Prices fluctuate frequently, and price competition among sellers is aggressive. Nonprice competition emphasizes product differentiation through distinctive features, service, product quality, or other factors. Establishing brand loyalty by using nonprice competition works best when the product can be physically differentiated and the customer can recognize these differences.

3. To explore demand curves and price elasticity of demand

An organization must determine the demand for its product. The classic demand curve is a graph of the quantity of products expected to be sold at various prices if other factors hold constant. It illustrates that, as price falls, the quantity demanded usually increases. However, for prestige products, there is a direct positive relationship between price and quantity demanded: demand increases as price increases. Next, price elasticity of demand, the percentage change in quantity demanded relative to a given percentage change in price, must be determined. If demand is elastic, a change in price causes an opposite change in total revenue. Inelastic demand results in a parallel change in total revenue when a product's price is changed.

4. To examine the relationships among demand, costs, and profits

Analysis of demand, cost, and profit relationships can be accomplished through marginal analysis or break-even analysis. Marginal analysis examines what happens to a firm's costs and revenues when production (or sales volume) is changed by one unit. Marginal analysis combines the demand curve with the firm's costs to develop a price that yields maximum profit. Fixed costs do not vary with changes in the number of units produced or sold; average fixed cost is the fixed cost per unit produced. Variable costs vary directly with changes in the number of units produced or sold. Average variable cost is the variable cost per unit produced. Total cost is the sum of average fixed cost and average variable cost times the quantity produced. The optimal price is the point at which marginal cost (the cost associated with producing one more unit of the product) equals marginal revenue (the change in total revenue that occurs when one additional unit of the product is sold). Marginal analysis is only a model; it offers little help in pricing new products before costs and revenues are established.

Break-even analysis, determining the number of units that must be sold to break even, is important in setting price. The point at which the costs of production equal the revenue from selling the product is the break-even point. To use break-even analysis effectively, a marketer should determine the break-even point for each of several alternative prices. This makes it possible to compare the effects on total revenue, total costs, and the break-even point for each price under consideration. However, this approach assumes the quantity demanded is basically fixed and the major task is to set prices to recover costs.

5. To describe key factors that may influence marketers' pricing decisions

Eight factors enter into price decision making: organizational and marketing objectives, pricing objectives, costs, other marketing mix variables, channel member expectations, customer interpretation and response, competition, and legal and regulatory issues. When setting prices, marketers should make decisions consistent with the organization's goals and mission. Pricing objectives heavily influence price-setting decisions. Most marketers view a product's cost as the floor below which a product cannot be priced. Because of the interrelationship among the marketing mix variables, price can affect product, promotion, and distribution decisions. The revenue channel members expect for their functions must also be considered when making price decisions.

Buyers' perceptions of price vary. Some consumer segments are sensitive to price, but others may not be.

Thus, before determining price, a marketer needs to be aware of its importance to the target market. Knowledge of the prices charged for competing brands is essential to allow the firm to adjust its prices relative to competitors'. Government regulations and legislation also influence pricing decisions. Several laws aim to enhance competition in the marketplace by outlawing price fixing and deceptive pricing. Legislation also restricts price differentials that can injure competition. Moreover, the government can invoke price controls to curb inflation.

6. To consider issues affecting the pricing of products for business markets

Unlike consumers, business buyers purchase products for resale, for use in their own operations, or for producing other products. When adjusting prices, business sellers consider the size of the purchase, geographic factors, and transportation requirements. Producers commonly provide discounts off list prices to intermediaries. The categories of discounts include trade, quantity, cash, seasonal, and allowance. A trade discount is a price reduction for performing such functions as storing, transporting, final processing, or providing credit services. If an intermediary purchases in large enough quantities, the producer gives a quantity discount, which can be either cumulative or noncumulative. A cash discount is a price reduction for prompt payment or payment in cash. Buyers who purchase goods or services out of season may be granted a seasonal discount. An allowance, such as a trade-in allowance, is a concession in price to achieve a desired goal.

Geographic pricing involves reductions for transportation costs or other costs associated with the physical distance between buyer and seller. With an F.O.B. factory price, the buyer pays for shipping from the factory. An F.O.B. destination price means the producer pays for shipping; this is the easiest way to price products, but it is difficult to administer. When the seller charges a fixed average cost for transportation, it is using uniform geographic pricing. Zone prices are uniform within major geographic zones; they increase by zone as transportation costs increase. With base-point pricing, prices are adjusted for shipping expenses incurred by the seller from the base point nearest the buyer. Freight absorption pricing occurs when a seller absorbs all or part of the freight costs.

Go to www.cengagebrain.com for resources to help you master the content in this chapter as well as materials that will expand your marketing knowledge!

important terms

price, 600	average variable cost, 607	value conscious, 614	seasonal discount, 618
barter, 600	total cost, 607	price conscious, 615	allowance, 618
price competition, 601	average total cost, 607	prestige sensitive, 615	geographic pricing, 619
nonprice competition, 602	marginal cost (MC), 607	price discrimination, 617	F.O.B. factory, 619
demand curve, 603	marginal revenue (MR), 607	trade (functional) discount, 618	F.O.B. destination, 619
price elasticity of demand, 605	break-even point, 610	quantity discounts, 618	uniform geographic pricing, 619
fixed costs, 607	internal reference price, 614	cumulative discounts, 618	zone pricing, 619
average fixed cost, 607	external reference price, 614	noncumulative discounts, 618	base-point pricing, 619
variable costs, 607		cash discounts, 618	freight absorption pricing, 620
			transfer pricing, 620

discussion and review questions

1. Why are pricing decisions important to an organization?
2. Compare and contrast price and nonprice competition. Describe the conditions under which each form works best.
3. Why do most demand curves demonstrate an inverse relationship between price and quantity?
4. List the characteristics of products that have inelastic demand, and give several examples of such products.
5. Explain why optimal profits should occur when marginal cost equals marginal revenue.
6. Chambers Company has just gathered estimates for conducting a break-even analysis for a new product. Variable costs are $7 a unit. The additional plant will cost $48,000. The new product will be charged $18,000 a year for its share of general overhead. Advertising expenditures will be $80,000, and $55,000 will be spent on distribution. If the product sells for $12, what is the break-even point in units? What is the break-even point in dollar sales volume?
7. In what ways do other marketing mix variables affect pricing decisions?
8. What types of expectations may channel members have about producers' prices? How might these expectations affect pricing decisions?
9. How do legal and regulatory forces influence pricing decisions?
10. Compare and contrast a trade discount and a quantity discount.
11. What is the reason for using the term *F.O.B.*?
12. What are the major methods used for transfer pricing?

application questions

1. Price competition is intense in the fast-food, air travel, and personal computer industries. Discuss a recent situation in which companies had to meet or beat a rival's price in a price-competitive industry. Did you benefit from this situation? Did it change your perception of the companies and/or their products?
2. Customers' interpretations and responses regarding a product and its price are an important influence on marketers' pricing decisions. Perceptions of price are affected by the degree to which a customer is value conscious, price conscious, or prestige sensitive. Discuss how value consciousness, price consciousness, and prestige sensitivity influence the buying decision process for the following products:
   a. A new house
   b. Weekly groceries for a family of five
   c. An airline ticket
   d. A soft drink from a vending machine

internet exercise

AutoSite

AutoSite offers car buyers a free, comprehensive website to find the invoice prices for almost all car models. The browser can also access a listing of all the latest new-car rebates and incentives. Visit this site at **www.autosite.com.**

1. Find the lowest-priced Lexus available today, and examine its features. Which Lexus dealer is closest to you?

2. If you wanted to purchase this Lexus, what are the lowest monthly payments you could make over the longest time period?

3. Is this free site more credible than a "pay" site? Why or why not?

developing your marketing plan

CRITICAL THINKING

The appropriate pricing of a product is an important factor in developing a successful marketing strategy. The price contributes to the profitability of the product and can deter competition from entering the market. A clear understanding of pricing concepts is essential in developing strategy and the marketing plan. Consider the information in this chapter when focusing on the following issues:

1. Does your company currently compete based on price or nonprice factors? Should your new product continue with this approach?

2. Discuss the level of elasticity of demand for your product. Is additional information needed for you to determine its elasticity?

3. At various price points, calculate the break-even point for sales of your product.

4. Using Figure 20.8 as a guide, discuss the various factors that affect the pricing of your product.

The information obtained from these questions should assist you in developing various aspects of your marketing plan found in the *Interactive Marketing Plan* exercise at **www.cengagebrain.com.**

VIDEO CASE 20.1

Washburn Guitars Tunes Up Pricing Decisions

CRITICAL THINKING

Chicago-based Washburn Guitars has been making guitars, banjos, and mandolins for every kind of music and every kind of budget since 1883. Whether they play blues or bluegrass, heavy metal or hard rock, musicians and music students buy Washburn instruments for their sound quality, solid craftsmanship, and good looks. Professionals especially appreciate the way Washburn guitars stand up to the wear and tear of lengthy concert tours.

Washburn offers six product lines: electric guitars, acoustic guitars, bass guitars, bluegrass instruments, classical guitars, and travel guitars. More than two dozen of its guitars are designated as "Signature" models designed by well-known musicians, such as Dan Donegan of Disturbed, Scott Ian of Anthrax, Joe Trohman of Fall Out Boy, Nick Catanese of

Black Label Society, Paul Stanley of Kiss, Nuno Bettencourt of Extreme, and Greg Tribbett of Mudvayne. These names add luster to the Washburn brand and enhance the perceived value of the specially designed Signature models.

In setting the manufacturer's suggested retail price for each product, the company has established four broad price points. At the low end, products that sell for $349 or less are entry level. Products that sell for $350 to $999 are intermediate level, and products that sell for $1,000 to $3,000 are professional level. At the high end, products that sell for more than $3,000 are collectors' level. At every level, Washburn promises that each of its instruments "represents the finest quality at the best possible price."

The guitars made in Washburn's U.S. factory are priced at $2,259 and up, reflecting the high cost of handcrafting. These guitars are perceived to be high quality and are therefore in high demand among professional musicians. In fact, Washburn has a six- to nine-month backlog of orders for its U.S.-made guitars. Its highest-priced guitars—the few Signature models that sell for $5,000 or more—not only influence customers' perceptions of Washburn quality, they also attract attention and get people talking about the brand.

Apart from the high-end models, Washburn's instruments are machine-manufactured outside the United States. This keeps both fixed and variable costs lower than in the U.S. factories. Although Washburn's variable costs go down as its manufacturing volume rises, the company has found that changing equipment to make different models takes time and adds to its costs.

Washburn sells its instruments through independent retailers in the United States, Canada, and several dozen countries worldwide. These stores receive quantity discounts for large orders and expect to earn a certain profit margin based on a percentage of the manufacturer's suggested retail price for each product. Although the stores now face intense price competition from online-only retailers that have lower fixed costs, Washburn insists that its authorized retailers not offer discounts below certain minimum prices. Stores that price Washburn products lower than the company's minimum

receive a warning, and if they don't change their prices, they are removed from the list of authorized retailers and receive no more shipments.

Washburn's advertising campaigns include magazine and television commercials spotlighting the star quality of the performers and the particular Washburn guitars they prefer, without mentioning prices. Recent campaigns included podcasts that showed Washburn's skilled employees carefully crafting Signature guitars for Nick Catanese and other musicians. Washburn has a strong online presence, including a virtual catalog and a MySpace page with a company blog and information about selected products and the performers who use them. Even after more than 125 years in the music business, Washburn still keeps its marketing—including its pricing—as fresh as the newest number-one hit song.[26]

QUESTIONS FOR DISCUSSION

1. Is Washburn using price or nonprice competition? Explain your answer.
2. What effect do you think a manufacturer's suggested retail price is likely to have on customers who buy Washburn guitars from a local music store?
3. Which factors shown in Figure 20.8 are likely to have a major impact on pricing decisions at Washburn?

CASE 20.2

Order Just About Anything from Amazon at a Reasonable Price

Online retail pioneer Amazon.com has built a profitable $24.5 billion business by paying close attention to pricing details. Founded as a web-based bookstore with discount prices, Amazon has since expanded into dozens of product categories and countries. The company never stops investing in technology to upgrade its sites, systems, and offerings. Although hefty high-tech costs are a drag on profit margins, they are essential to Amazon's strategy of attracting customers and keeping them loyal by making the shopping experience easy, fast, and fun.

One hallmark of Amazon's pricing is its long-running offer of free shipping for orders of $25 or more. Because

shoppers know they are saving money, they are more inclined to keep spending even after they reach the $25 order threshold to qualify for free shipping. Free shipping has helped Amazon build sales over the years, but it has also added to the company's costs and cut into profits. In the wake of Amazon's success with free shipping, L.L. Bean and others have tested free shipping with no minimum purchase requirement during some holiday periods. But making free shipping pay off is tricky, notes a marketing executive at L.L. Bean: "It is expensive to do, and it is easy to lose a lot of money doing it."

Amazon is earning significant profits from serving as an online storefront for other marketers (and consumers) to sell their products. Every time a customer buys something from a seller participating in the Amazon Marketplace, Amazon collects a fee. The margins are especially attractive in this fast-growing part of the business because Amazon does not pay to buy or store any inventory, and the cost of posting items for others is extremely low now that the electronic storefront is up and running.

All-digital products like electronic books, music, movies, and games are lucrative because they entail no inventory or shipping costs. This is why Amazon is moving aggressively into digital content and related products. Its popular Kindle, first introduced in 2007, is an e-book reader that wirelessly connects to the Internet so customers can download an electronic book, newspaper, or magazine in seconds. Initially, Amazon priced the Kindle higher than the Sony Reader, its main competitor at the time. Despite the high price, demand outstripped supply for a time, and Amazon struggled to increase output. As Barnes & Noble and others began offering their own e-book readers, Amazon lowered the price and poured on the promotion to keep up the Kindle's sales momentum.

The Kindle also created a controversy over e-book pricing. When Amazon first launched the Kindle, it priced most best-selling e-books at only $9.99 each, with a few priced even lower. Publishers fumed, because the hard-cover price of these books was considerably higher. The situation changed in early 2010, as Apple prepared to debut its iPad tablet computer. Apple was trumpeting the iPad's capabilities as an e-book reader and making deals with publishers to carry downloadable digital content. Under pressure from the publishers and faced with a new level of competition from Apple's much-anticipated device, Amazon took a step back from its digital discounting. It listened to the publishers and raised the retail price of many digital best-sellers by a few dollars but retained the $9.99 price for selected e-books.

Today, Kindle customers can buy and instantly download more than 450,000 books. "Our vision is to have every book that has ever been in print available in less than 60 seconds," says Amazon founder Jeff Bezos. The Kindle has become Amazon's best-selling product and dramatically increased sales of electronic books, magazines, and similar products. In fact, when Amazon offers the same book in printed and digital format, it sells 6 digital downloads for every 10 physical units. Multiply the savings in shipping costs alone, and it's easy to see why Amazon has put so much emphasis on electronic delivery of books and other content.

Looking ahead, Amazon will be paying close attention to the pricing of rival gadgets and the way digital content is being priced. Although it's now the undisputed leader in electronic book sales, that market share is likely to erode little by little as more customers are offered the opportunity to buy and download more books from additional sources.[27]

QUESTIONS FOR DISCUSSION

1. Are Amazon's shipping costs variable or fixed? How is the company's profitability likely to be affected if customers do not buy more than $25 worth each time they shop?

2. Why would publishers be so concerned about the difference in price between a hard-cover best-seller and the digital version? Explain your answer in terms of this chapter's pricing concepts.

3. Do you think Amazon should be concerned about losing market share in e-book retailing? What are the implications for its pricing decisions?

Chapter 21

Setting Prices

OBJECTIVES

1. To describe the six major stages of the process used to establish prices

2. To explore issues related to developing pricing objectives

3. To understand the importance of identifying the target market's evaluation of price

4. To examine how marketers analyze competitors' prices

5. To describe the bases used for setting prices

6. To explain the different types of pricing strategies

Talk Is Not Always Cheap

From very high to very low, Nokia has a cell phone handset priced to fit wallets in every market. Headquartered in Finland, the company is the global leader in cell phones and rings up $58 billion in sales every year. Nokia's strategy of marketing a full range of products, priced appropriately for each target market, has helped the company cope with intense competition from strong rivals like Samsung, Motorola, Research in Motion (maker of BlackBerry), and Apple.

At the top of the pricing range, Nokia's status-symbol Vertu phones carry price tags starting at $5,000. Vertu phones are made of titanium, stainless steel, gold, or platinum, and many are decorated with diamonds and other super-luxury touches. Special-edition versions can sell for more than $325,000. Even the ringtone is distinctive, another sign that Vertu is not just another cell phone.

At the low end of the pricing range are basic phones geared to first-time buyers in developing countries. The company sells millions of inexpensive cell phones in China and India, which are by far its two highest-volume markets. In those countries, it is also profiting from increased demand for its mid-priced smartphones that allow users to check e-mail, send and receive text messages, browse the Web, participate in social media, download music, and play games.

For business customers, Nokia has introduced full-keyboard, multifunction smartphones that can access corporate e-mail systems. Thanks to its economies of scale, Nokia can keep costs low and set affordable prices to encourage switching from BlackBerry smartphones, a favorite among corporate users. Looking ahead, Nokia continues to research the communication needs and priorities of consumers and businesspeople, with an eye toward fine-tuning its pricing strategy and achieving its worldwide profit and market-share objectives.[1]

FIGURE 21.1 Stages for Establishing Prices

1. Development of pricing objectives
2. Assessment of target market's evaluation of price
3. Evaluation of competitors' prices
4. Selection of a basis for pricing
5. Selection of a pricing strategy
6. Determination of a specific price

Because price has such a profound impact on a firm's success, finding the right pricing strategy is crucial. Marketers at Nokia are able to set very competitive prices because the costs of raw materials are low. Selecting a pricing strategy is one of the fundamental components of the process of setting prices.

In this chapter, we examine six stages of a process that marketers can use when setting prices. Figure 21.1 illustrates these stages. Stage 1 is the development of a pricing objective that is compatible with the organization's overall marketing objectives. Stage 2 entails assessing the target market's evaluation of price. Stage 3 involves evaluating competitors' prices, which helps determine the role of price in the marketing strategy. Stage 4 requires choosing a basis for setting prices. Stage 5 is the selection of a pricing strategy, or the guidelines for using price in the marketing mix. Stage 6, determining the final price, depends on environmental forces and marketers' understanding and use of a systematic approach to establishing prices. These stages are not rigid steps that all marketers must follow; rather, they are guidelines that provide a logical sequence for establishing prices.

Development of Pricing Objectives

The first step in setting prices is developing **pricing objectives**—goals that describe what a firm wants to achieve through pricing. Developing pricing objectives is an important task because pricing objectives form the basis for decisions for other stages of the pricing process. Thus, pricing objectives must be stated explicitly, and the statement should include the time frame for accomplishing them.

Marketers must ensure that pricing objectives are consistent with the firm's marketing and overall objectives because pricing objectives influence decisions in many functional areas, including finance, accounting, and production. A marketer can use both short- and long-term pricing objectives and can employ one or multiple pricing objectives. For instance, a firm may wish to increase market share by 18 percent over the next three years, achieve a 15 percent return on investment, and promote an image of quality in the marketplace.

In this section, we examine some of the pricing objectives companies might set for themselves. Table 21.1 shows the major pricing objectives and typical actions associated with them.

pricing objectives Goals that describe what a firm wants to achieve through pricing

TABLE 21.1 Pricing Objectives and Typical Actions Taken to Achieve Them

Objective	Possible Action
Survival	Adjust price levels so the firm can increase sales volume to match organizational expenses
Profit	Identify price and cost levels that allow the firm to maximize profit
Return on investment	Identify price levels that enable the firm to yield targeted ROI
Market share	Adjust price levels so the firm can maintain or increase sales relative to competitors' sales
Cash flow	Set price levels to encourage rapid sales
Status quo	Identify price levels that help stabilize demand and sales
Product quality	Set prices to recover research and development expenditures and establish a high-quality image

Survival

Survival is one of the most fundamental pricing objectives. Most organizations will tolerate setbacks, such as short-run losses and internal upheaval, if necessary for survival. Even Abercrombie & Fitch had to resort to price reductions on its luxury priced clothing to stay in business during the recent economic downturn. Last year, A&F's first quarter result was a loss of close to $27 million compared to the previous year's income of just over $62 million. This drastic difference forced the retailer to adjust prices to better compliment customer's smaller budgets.[2] Because price is a flexible variable, it is sometimes used to keep a company afloat by increasing sales volume to levels that match expenses.

Cash Flow Pricing Objective
The pricing objective for this retailer is cash flow.

© Terri Miller/ E-Visual Communications, Inc.

Profit

Although a business may claim that its objective is to maximize profits for its owners, the objective of profit maximization is rarely operational because its achievement is difficult to measure. Because of this difficulty, profit objectives tend to be set at levels that the owners and top-level decision makers view as satisfactory. Specific profit objectives may be stated in terms of either actual dollar amounts or a percentage of sales revenues.

Return on Investment

Pricing to attain a specified rate of return on the company's investment is a profit-related pricing objective. Most pricing objectives based on return on investment (ROI) are achieved by trial and error because not all cost and revenue data needed to project the return on investment are available when setting prices. General Motors, for example, uses ROI pricing objectives. Many pharmaceutical companies also use ROI pricing objectives because of their great investment in research and development.

Market Share

Many firms establish pricing objectives to maintain or increase market share, a product's sales in relation to total industry sales. To maintain its significant share of the hybrid market, Toyota, for example, intends to slash the price of its next-generation hybrid.[3] Many firms recognize

Product Quality
This ad for Dyson vacuum cleaners focuses on the high quality of Dyson's premium products.

that high relative market shares often translate into higher profits. The Profit Impact of Market Strategies (PIMS) studies, conducted over the past 30 years, have shown that both market share and product quality heavily influence profitability. Thus, marketers often use an increase in market share as a primary pricing objective.

Maintaining or increasing market share need not depend on growth in industry sales. Remember that an organization can increase its market share even if sales for the total industry are flat or decreasing. On the other hand, a firm's sales volume may increase while its market share decreases if the overall market is growing.

Cash Flow

Some companies set prices so they can recover cash as quickly as possible. Financial managers understandably seek to quickly recover capital spent to develop products. This objective may have the support of a marketing manager who anticipates a short product life cycle. Although it may be acceptable in some situations, the use of cash flow and recovery as an objective oversimplifies the contribution of price to profits. If this pricing objective results in high prices, competitors with lower prices may gain a large share of the market.

Status Quo

In some cases, an organization is in a favorable position and, desiring nothing more, may set an objective of status quo. Status quo objectives can focus on several dimensions, such as maintaining a certain market share, meeting (but not beating) competitors' prices, achieving price stability, and maintaining a favorable public image. A status quo pricing objective can reduce a firm's risks by helping to stabilize demand for its products. The use of status quo pricing objectives sometimes minimizes pricing as a competitive tool, leading to a climate of nonprice competition in an industry. Professionals such as accountants and attorneys often operate in such an environment.

Product Quality

A company may have the objective of leading its industry in product quality. This goal normally dictates a high price to cover the costs of achieving high product quality and, in some instances, the costs of research and development. For example, Bentley Motors uses premium prices to help signal the quality of its hand-made cars, which can range in cost from $182,800 to more than $334,990, depending on accessories and options.[4] As previously mentioned, the PIMS studies have shown that both product quality and market share are good indicators of profitability. The products and brands that customers perceive to be of high quality are more likely to survive in a competitive marketplace. High quality usually enables a marketer to charge higher prices for the product.

Assessment of the Target Market's Evaluation of Price

After developing pricing objectives, marketers next must assess the target market's evaluation of price. Despite the general assumption that price is a major issue for buyers, the importance of price depends on the type of product, the type of target market, and

TABLE 21.2 Examples of Perceptions of Product Value

Basic, Cost-Effective Product	Expensive, Time-Saving Product
1 head romaine lettuce, $1.99	1 bag EarthGreens organic romaine hearts, $3.99
1 sandwich with Welch's jelly, Jif peanut butter, white bread, 46¢	1 Smucker's Uncrustables ready-made peanut butter and jelly sandwich, 82¢
24 oz. Clorox Liquid Bleach, roll of Viva paper towels, $2.69	1 package Clorox Disinfecting Wipes, $3.49

Source: "Stop Getting Eaten Alive by Grocery Bills," *Money*, January 2006, p. 34.

the purchase situation. For instance, buyers are probably more sensitive to gasoline prices than luggage prices. With respect to the type of target market, adults may have to pay more than children for certain products. The purchase situation also affects the buyer's view of price. Most moviegoers would never pay in other situations the prices charged for soft drinks, popcorn, and candy at movie concession stands. By assessing the target market's evaluation of price, a marketer is in a better position to know how much emphasis to put on price in the overall marketing strategy. Information about the target market's price evaluation may also help a marketer determine how far above the competition the firm can set its prices.

Because some consumers today are seeking less-expensive products and shopping more selectively, some manufacturers and retailers are focusing on the value of their products. Value combines a product's price and quality attributes, which customers use to differentiate among competing brands. According to an IRI poll, 56 percent of consumers said they would not spend as much eating out last year. Despite this trend, Steak 'n Shake actually saw a 3 percent gain in sales when the company changed its marketing strategy to focus on value. The company's marketing highlighted its food's flavor as well as its four meals under $4.[5] Consumers are looking for good deals on products that provide better value for their money. They may also view products that have highly desirable attributes, such as organic content or time-saving features, as having great value. Consumers are increasingly willing to pay a higher price for food that is convenient and time saving, as illustrated in Table 21.2. Companies that offer both low prices and high quality, like Target and Best Buy, have altered consumers' expectations about how much quality they must sacrifice for low prices.[6] Understanding the importance of a product to customers, as well as their expectations about quality and value, helps marketers correctly assess the target market's evaluation of price.

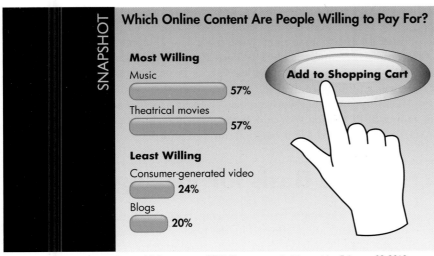

SNAPSHOT

Which Online Content Are People Willing to Pay For?

Add to Shopping Cart

Most Willing

Music 57%

Theatrical movies 57%

Least Willing

Consumer-generated video 24%

Blogs 20%

Source: Nielsen survey of 27,548 consumers in 54 countries, February 23, 2010.

Evaluation of Competitors' Prices

In most cases, marketers are in a better position to establish prices when they know the prices charged for competing brands, the third step in establishing prices. Discovering competitors' prices may be a regular function of marketing research. Some grocery and department stores, for example, have full-time comparative shoppers who systematically collect data on prices.

Marketing in Transition
Pricing Virtual Products

A tractor priced at $3.33 and fish food priced at $4.89—welcome to the world of virtual products, where buyers pay real money to receive digital representations of real-world items that appear only on computer and cell phone screens. What began as a tiny trickle of sales has become a rushing river as consumers buy virtual products to gain a performance edge in online games, give virtual products as gifts, or impress others in social media settings. Yearly sales of virtual products have reached the $1 billion mark and are growing so quickly that the total market will soon top $3.5 billion.

According to one survey, 20 percent of U.S. consumers have already had the experience of paying for virtual products. The price is so low that even consumers who are casual players will be tempted to buy a FarmVille tractor while they're playing the game on Facebook. Paying for extras such as a tractor speeds up the game and allows players to keep up with their "neighbors" (Facebook friends who also play FarmVille).

Zynga, the marketer of FarmVille, FishVille, and other free online games, facilitates purchases by accepting credit cards, PayPal, and Facebook Credits in exchange for purchases. It also raises money for charity by selling limited-edition virtual products. Not long ago, Zynga set a special price for virtual fish to raise money for Water.org, a nonprofit group that provides safe drinking water in developing nations. In just five days, Zynga sold 70,000 virtual fish and raised $13,000 in donations for Water.org.[a]

Companies may also purchase price lists, sometimes weekly, from syndicated marketing research services.

Uncovering competitors' prices is not always easy, especially in producer and reseller markets. Competitors' price lists are often closely guarded. Even if a marketer has access to competitors' price lists, those lists may not reflect the actual prices at which competitive products are sold because those prices may be established through negotiation.

Knowing the prices of competing brands can be very important for a marketer. Competitors' prices and the marketing mix variables they emphasize partly determine how important price will be to customers. A marketer in an industry in which price competition prevails needs competitive price information to ensure its prices are the same as, or lower than, competitors' prices. In some instances, an organization's prices are designed to be slightly above competitors' prices to give its products an exclusive image. In contrast, another company may use price as a competitive tool and price its products below those of competitors. The Ford Fusion hybrid sedan, for example, is priced about $3,000 less than the top-selling Toyota Prius. Although the Prius delivers nearly 10 miles per gallon more than the Fusion, Ford's vehicle offers a more spacious interior; considerably more horsepower; eco-friendly cloth seats; and several new features, including BLIS, a blind spot monitoring system, and Cross Traffic Alert, which checks for traffic when the vehicle is backing out of a parking spot or driveway.[7]

Selection of a Basis for Pricing

The fourth step involves selecting a basis for pricing: cost, demand, and/or competition. The selection of the basis to use is affected by the type of product, the market structure of the industry, the brand's market share position relative to competing brands, and customer characteristics. Although we discuss each basis separately in this section, an organization generally considers two or all three of these dimensions, even if one is the primary basis on which it determines prices. For example, if a company is using cost as a basis for setting prices, marketers in that firm are also aware of and concerned about competitors' prices. If a company is using demand as a basis for pricing, those making pricing decisions still must consider costs and competitors' prices. Indeed, cost is a factor in every pricing decision because it establishes a price minimum below which the firm will not be able to recoup its production and other costs; demand likewise sets an effective price maximum above which customers are unlikely to buy the product. Fairchild Semiconductor uses software to assess all three dimensions, as well as buying behavior, manufacturing capacity, inventories, and product life cycles, in setting prices for more than 44,000 products.[8]

Cost-Based Pricing

With **cost-based pricing**, a dollar amount or percentage is added to the cost of the product. This approach thus involves calculations of desired profit margins. Cost-based pricing does not necessarily take into account the economic aspects of supply and demand, nor must it relate to just one pricing strategy or pricing objective. Cost-based pricing is straightforward and easy to implement. Two common forms of cost-based pricing are cost-plus and markup pricing.

COST-PLUS PRICING

With **cost-plus pricing**, the seller's costs are determined (usually during a project or after a project is completed), and then a specified dollar amount or percentage of the cost is added to the seller's cost to establish the price. When production costs are difficult to predict, cost-plus pricing is appropriate. Projects involving custom-made equipment and commercial construction are often priced using this technique. The government frequently uses such cost-based pricing in granting defense contracts. One pitfall for the buyer is that the seller may increase costs to establish a larger profit base. Furthermore, some costs, such as overhead, may be difficult to determine. In periods of rapid inflation, cost-plus pricing is popular, especially when the producer must use raw materials that are fluctuating in price. In industries in which cost-plus pricing is common and sellers have similar costs, price competition may not be especially intense.

MARKUP PRICING

With **markup pricing**, commonly used by retailers, a product's price is derived by adding a predetermined percentage of the cost, called *markup*, to the cost of the product. For instance, Costco, a warehouse club, has a very low average markup of 11 percent, while most supermarkets are in the mid-20s range.[9] One markup that might shock you is the average markup for popcorn in movie theaters, which is about 1,300 percent. Popcorn is not expensive, but consumers are willing to pay the markup to enhance their movie experience by enjoying warm buttery popcorn at the theater.[10] Although the percentage markup in a retail store varies from one category of goods to another—35 percent of cost for hardware items and 100 percent of cost for greeting cards, for example—the same percentage is often used to determine the prices on items within a single product category, and the percentage markup may be largely standardized across an industry at the retail level. Using a rigid percentage markup for a specific product category reduces pricing to a routine task that can be performed quickly.

Markup can be stated as a percentage of the cost or as a percentage of the selling price. The following example illustrates how percentage markups are determined and points out the differences in the two methods. Assume a retailer purchases a can of tuna at 45 cents, adds 15 cents to the cost, and then prices the tuna at 60 cents. Here are the figures:

cost-based pricing Adding a dollar amount or percentage to the cost of the product

cost-plus pricing Adding a specified dollar amount or percentage to the seller's cost

markup pricing Adding to the cost of the product a predetermined percentage of that cost

$$\text{markup as percentage of cost} = \text{markup/cost}$$
$$= 15/45$$
$$= 33.3\%$$
$$\text{markup as percentage of selling price} = \text{markup/selling price}$$
$$= 15/60$$
$$= 25.0\%$$

Obviously, when discussing a percentage markup, it is important to know whether the markup is based on cost or selling price.

Markups normally reflect expectations about operating costs, risks, and stock turnovers. Wholesalers and manufacturers often suggest standard retail markups that are considered profitable. To the extent that retailers use similar markups for the same product category, price competition is reduced. In addition, using rigid markups is convenient and is the major reason retailers, which face numerous pricing decisions, favor this method.

Demand-Based Pricing

Marketers sometimes base prices on the level of demand for the product. When **demand-based pricing** is used, customers pay a higher price when demand for the product is strong and a lower price when demand is weak. For example, hotels that otherwise attract numerous travelers often offer reduced rates during lower-demand periods. Some telephone companies, such as Sprint and AT&T, also use demand-based pricing by charging peak and off-peak rates or offering free cell phone minutes during off-peak times. While demand-based pricing is a common practice with cell phone minutes,

demand-based pricing
Pricing based on the level of demand for the product

Sustainable Marketing
Going Green, Saving Green

Going green is not just a great way to save the planet, it's a great way to control costs and save money—which, in turn, can help marketers maintain competitive prices. Every time Starbucks and Peet's Coffee & Tea pour coffee into a refillable mug brought in by a customer, they're reducing waste and saving water. They also save the cost of providing a disposable cup or washing a mug—and they pass the savings along in the form of a 10-cent discount to mug-toting customers.

Going green can lower costs for many marketers. Allstate, for example, saves a lot of trees when customers agree to receive their insurance bills by e-mail and have their premiums electronically deducted from their bank accounts instead of mailing checks to pay. The company also saves the time and effort of printing and mailing bills and processing payments. That's why Allstate can give customers who go paperless a discount of up to 5 percent on auto insurance.

The department store JCPenney saves millions of dollars every year simply by recycling the 176 million plastic clothing hangers used in its stores. When trucks deliver merchandise to its 1,000 U.S. stores and distribution centers, the company makes the most of the return trip by filling the empty trucks with recyclables,

packaging, and other nonmerchandise. These green initiatives save resources and money, savings that the department store can put to use when it sets prices.[b]

Demand-Based Pricing
Cruise lines often engage in demand-based pricing. When demand for a specific cruise is high, the price will be higher; when the demand for a specific cruise is low, the price of that cruise will be lower.

airplane seats, and hotel rooms, some concerts and road shows have also implemented demand-based pricing for ticket sales. Once a show sells a certain number of tickets, the price per ticket increases. This allows companies to adjust ticket prices accordingly, improving profit for popular shows.[11]

To use this pricing basis, a marketer must be able to estimate the amounts of a product consumers will demand at different prices. The marketer then chooses the price that generates the highest total revenue. Obviously, the effectiveness of demand-based pricing depends on the marketer's ability to estimate demand accurately. Compared with cost-based pricing, demand-based pricing places a firm in a better position to reach higher profit levels, assuming buyers value the product at levels sufficiently above the product's cost.

Competition-Based Pricing

With **competition-based pricing**, an organization considers costs to be secondary to competitors' prices. The importance of this method increases when competing products are relatively homogeneous and the organization is serving markets in which price is a key purchase consideration. A firm that uses competition-based pricing may choose to price below competitors' prices, above competitors' prices, or at the same level. Airlines use competition-based pricing, often charging identical fares on the same routes. Online travel services such as Orbitz, Expedia, and Priceline. com have also employed competition-based pricing. If you want to sell your home without the aid of a realtor, how do you determine the value of your home and thus a competitive asking price? One way is to turn to websites that offer estimates of your home's value based on its size and the sale of comparable homes in the area. While you may think your home is worth as much as a castle, if you set the asking price too high above comparable homes for sale, buyers will likely choose one with a lower price.

Although not all introductory marketing texts have exactly the same price, they do have similar prices. The price the bookstore paid to the publishing company for

competition-based pricing
Pricing influenced primarily by competitors' prices

this textbook was determined on the basis of competitors' prices. Competition-based pricing can help a firm achieve the pricing objective of increasing sales or market share. Competition-based pricing may necessitate frequent price adjustments. For instance, for many competitive airline routes, fares are adjusted often.

Selection of a Pricing Strategy

After choosing a basis for pricing, the next step is to select a pricing strategy, an approach or a course of action designed to achieve pricing and marketing objectives. Generally, pricing strategies help marketers solve the practical problems of establishing prices. Table 21.3 lists the most common pricing strategies, which we discuss in this section.

Differential Pricing

An important issue in pricing decisions is whether to use a single price or different prices for the same product. Using a single price has several benefits. A primary advantage is simplicity. A single price is easily understood by both employees and customers, and because many salespeople and customers dislike having to negotiate a price, it reduces the chance of an adversarial relationship developing between marketer and customer. The use of a single price does create some challenges, however. If the single price is too high, some potential customers may be unable to afford the product. If it is too low, the organization loses revenue from those customers who would have paid more had the price been higher.

Differential pricing means charging different prices to different buyers for the same quality and quantity of product. As a student, you might be familiar with differential pricing for your tuition. Some colleges charge a higher tuition for certain majors, such as business, engineering, and medicine. These higher fees are called differential tuition.[12] For differential pricing to be effective, the market must consist of multiple segments with different price sensitivities, and the method should be used in a way that avoids confusing or antagonizing customers. Customers who are paying the lower prices should not be able to resell the product to the individuals and organizations that are paying the

differential pricing Charging different prices to different buyers for the same quality and quantity of product

TABLE 21.3 Common Pricing Strategies

Differential Pricing	Psychological Pricing
Negotiated pricing	Reference pricing
Secondary-market pricing	Bundle pricing
Periodic discounting	Multiple-unit pricing
Random discounting	Everyday low prices
	Odd-even pricing
New-Product Pricing	Customary pricing
Price skimming	Prestige pricing
Penetration pricing	
	Professional Pricing
Product-Line Pricing	
Captive pricing	**Promotional Pricing**
Premium pricing	Price leaders
Bait pricing	Special-event pricing
Price lining	Comparison discounting

higher prices, unless that is the seller's intention. Differential pricing can occur in several ways, including negotiated pricing, secondary-market discounting, periodic discounting, and random discounting.

NEGOTIATED PRICING

Negotiated pricing occurs when the final price is established through bargaining between seller and customer. If you buy a house, for example, you are likely to negotiate the final price with the seller. Negotiated pricing occurs in a number of industries and at all levels of distribution. Cutler-Hammer/Eaton streamlined its contract-negotiations process for more than 90,000 products by reducing quote response times and implementing automatic acceptance of offers.[13] Even when there is a predetermined stated price or a price list, manufacturers, wholesalers, and retailers may negotiate to establish the final sales price. Consumers commonly negotiate prices for houses, cars, and used equipment.

SECONDARY-MARKET PRICING

Secondary-market pricing means setting one price for the primary target market and a different price for another market. Often the price charged in the secondary market is lower. However, when the costs of serving a secondary market are higher than normal, secondary-market customers may have to pay a higher price. Examples of secondary markets include a geographically isolated domestic market, a market in a foreign country, and a segment willing to purchase a product during off-peak times. For example, some restaurants offer special "early-bird" prices during the early evening hours, movie theaters offer senior citizen and afternoon matinee discounts, and some textbooks and pharmaceutical products are sold for considerably less in certain foreign countries than in the United States. Secondary markets give an organization an opportunity to use excess capacity and stabilize the allocation of resources.

negotiated pricing
Establishing a final price through bargaining between seller and customer

secondary-market pricing
Setting one price for the primary target market and a different price for another market

periodic discounting
Temporary reduction of prices on a patterned or systematic basis

PERIODIC DISCOUNTING

Periodic discounting is the temporary reduction of prices on a patterned or systematic basis. Most retailers, for example, have annual holiday sales. Some women's apparel stores have two seasonal sales each year: a winter sale in the last two weeks of January and a summer sale in the first two weeks of July. Automobile dealers regularly discount prices on current models in the fall, when the next year's models are introduced. Most grocers, like Safeway, rely on periodic discounts to lure customers into its stores. However, the company is currently moving away from this strategy to an everyday low price strategy in order to effectively compete.[14] From the marketer's point of view, a major problem with periodic discounting is that because the discounts follow a pattern, customers can predict when the reductions will occur and may delay their purchases until they can take advantage of the lower prices. Research suggests that placing a time limit on periodic discounts does not

Responsible Marketing?
Nonstop Pricing

ISSUE: Should airlines be allowed to charge different customers different prices for the same level of service?

If you were to survey passengers on a specific flight and ask them how much they paid for their tickets, how many different prices would you get? Airlines use demand-based pricing, which means that different passengers pay different prices. Because they must fill every seat on the plane, the airlines use discount fares and overbooking. They would lose considerable revenue and be unable to make a profit if they offered discounted fares to all passengers. Instead, they provide a few discounted seats at several points prior to the flight to fill seats on the plane. They also hold a few expensive seats close to departure time for travelers who need to make last-minute travel changes and are willing to pay higher fares.

Should airlines be allowed to charge different prices to different customers for the same class of service? Is it fair for a passenger who booked several weeks in advance to pay a higher fare than a customer who bought a ticket only a few days in advance? Would it be more fair if an airline charged the same coach fare to all passengers, even if the average ticket price were somewhat higher than the current average ticket price?

Random Discounting
This advertisement promotes a jewelry sale based upon random discounting.

directly affect consumers' perceptions of the products' value or their search and purchase behavior.

RANDOM DISCOUNTING

To alleviate the problem of customers knowing when discounting will occur, some organizations employ **random discounting**; that is, they temporarily reduce their prices on an unsystematic basis. When price reductions of a product occur randomly, current users of that brand are likely unable to predict when the reductions will occur and thus will not delay their purchases. However, in the automobile industry, with its increasing reliance on sales, rebates, and incentives such as 0 percent financing, random discounting has become nearly continuous discounting, and some analysts have warned that automakers will find it increasingly difficult to cease the generous incentives that consumers have come to expect. Marketers also use random discounting to attract new customers. For instance, Lever Brothers may temporarily reduce the price of one of its bar soaps in the hope of attracting new customers.

Whether they use periodic discounting or random discounting, retailers often employ tensile pricing when putting products on sale. *Tensile pricing* refers to a broad statement about price reductions as opposed to detailing specific price discounts. Examples of tensile pricing would be statements such as "20 to 50 percent off," "up to 75 percent off," and "save 10 percent or more." Generally, using and advertising the tensile price that mentions only the maximum reduction (such as "up to 50 percent off") generates the highest customer response.[15]

New-Product Pricing

Setting the base price for a new product is a necessary part of formulating a marketing strategy. The base price is easily adjusted (in the absence of government price controls), and its establishment is one of the most fundamental decisions in the marketing mix. The base price can be set high to recover development costs quickly or provide a reference point for developing discount prices for different market segments. When a marketer sets base prices, it also considers how quickly competitors will enter the market, whether they will mount a strong campaign on entry, and what effect their entry will have on the development of primary demand. Two strategies used in new-product pricing are price skimming and penetration pricing.

PRICE SKIMMING

Price skimming means charging the highest possible price that buyers who most desire the product will pay. This approach provides the most flexible introductory base price. Demand tends to be inelastic in the introductory stage of the product life cycle.

Price skimming can provide several benefits, especially when a product is in the introductory stage of its life cycle. A skimming policy can generate much-needed initial cash flows to help offset sizable development costs. Price skimming protects the marketer from problems that arise when the price is set too low to cover costs. When a firm introduces a product, its production capacity may be limited. A skimming price can help keep demand consistent with the firm's production capabilities. The use of a skimming price may attract competition into an industry because the high price makes that type of business appear quite lucrative. New-product prices should be based on both the value to the customer and competitive products.

random discounting
Temporary reduction of prices on an unsystematic basis

price skimming Charging the highest possible price that buyers who most desire the product will pay

Entrepreneurial Marketing
TerraCycle Turns Trash into Cash

Back in 2001, two Princeton University students founded TerraCycle, selling organic plant food made from worm castings. Their latest product line includes tote bags, umbrellas, and shower curtains made from recycled trash.

TerraCycle's raw materials come from thousands of local "brigades"—recycling programs who receive postage-paid collection bags from sponsors, like Stonyfield Farm and Coca-Cola, in which to send bundles of used containers to TerraCycle. Their products are made from trash, so their raw material prices aren't going up. As a result, TerraCycle can set highly competitive prices for its products and build profits while helping the environment. Annual sales are headed past $15 million as the company expands its recycling brigades, designs new products, and gears up to turn more trash into cash.[c]

PENETRATION PRICING

With **penetration pricing**, prices are set below those of competing brands to penetrate a market and gain a large market share quickly. This approach is less flexible for a marketer than price skimming because it is more difficult to raise a penetration price than to lower or discount a skimming price. It is not unusual for a firm to use a penetration price after having skimmed the market with a higher price.

Penetration pricing can be especially beneficial when a marketer suspects that competitors could enter the market easily. If penetration pricing allows the marketer to gain a large market share quickly, competitors may be discouraged from entering the market. In addition, because the lower per-unit penetration price results in lower per-unit profit, the market may not appear to be especially lucrative to potential new entrants.

Product-Line Pricing

Rather than considering products on an item-by-item basis when determining pricing strategies, some marketers employ product-line pricing. **Product-line pricing** means establishing and adjusting the prices of multiple products within a product line. When marketers use product-line pricing, their goal is to maximize profits for an entire product line rather than focusing on the profitability of an individual product. Product-line pricing can lend marketers flexibility in price setting. For example, marketers can set prices so that one product is quite profitable while another increases market share due to having a lower price than competing products.

Before setting prices for a product line, marketers evaluate the relationship among the products in the line. When products in a line are complementary, sales increases in one item raise demand for other items. For instance, desktop printers and toner cartridges are complementary products. When products in a line function as substitutes for one another, buyers of one product in the line are unlikely to purchase one of the other products in the same line. In this case, marketers must be sensitive to how a price change for one of the brands may affect the demand not only for that brand but also for the substitute brands. For instance, if decision makers at Procter & Gamble were considering a price change for Tide detergent, they would be concerned about how the price change might influence sales of Cheer, Bold, and Gain.

When marketers employ product-line pricing, they have several strategies from which to choose. These include captive pricing, premium pricing, bait pricing, and price lining.

CAPTIVE PRICING

With **captive pricing**, the basic product in a product line is priced low, whereas items required to operate or enhance it are priced higher. Printer companies have used this pricing strategy: providing relatively low-cost, low-margin printers and selling ink cartridges to generate significant profits. Kodak, however, is promoting a printer that goes against the captive pricing strategy used by the majority in the market. Kodak has introduced a slightly more expensive printer that uses ink cartridges that are priced cheaper than the competition.[16]

penetration pricing Setting prices below those of competing brands to penetrate a market and gain a significant market share quickly

product-line pricing Establishing and adjusting prices of multiple products within a product line

captive pricing Pricing the basic product in a product line low, while pricing related items higher

Change the way you ink.

Introducing NextLife™ Ink by Dell™

- Save up to 20% compared to branded ink cartridges¹
- Rated EXCELLENT in reliability and prints up to 20% more pages²

Find ink for your brand-name printer at **dell.com/nextlife**.

DELL.COM/NEXTLIFE | 1-877-INK2YOU

next life ink
by **DELL**™

¹ Based on pricing data from staples.com, bestbuy.com and dell.com as of December 2009. ² Based on an independent report commissioned by Dell from Buyers Laboratory Inc. in October 2009.

Captive Pricing

Products that require component replacement on a regular basis, such as razors and printers, may be relatively inexpensive, but the replacement components are premium priced. This type of pricing is referred to as captive pricing.

PREMIUM PRICING

Premium pricing is often used when a product line contains several versions of the same product; the highest-quality products or those with the most versatility are given the highest prices. Chevrolet, for example, prices its fastest, most powerful Corvette ZR1 at more than $107,000. The company expects its premium-priced Corvette, with its hand-built 620-horsepower V8 engine, to compete with the performance of a Ferrari.[17] Other products in the line are priced to appeal to price-sensitive shoppers or to buyers who seek product-specific features.

Marketers that use a premium strategy often realize a significant portion of their profits from premium-priced products. Examples of product categories that commonly use premium pricing are small kitchen appliances, beer, ice cream, and cable television service.

BAIT PRICING

To attract customers, marketers may put a low price on one item in the product line with the intention of selling a higher-priced item in the line; this strategy is known as **bait pricing**. For example, a computer retailer might advertise its lowest-priced computer model, hoping that when customers come to the store they will purchase a higher-priced one. This strategy can facilitate sales of a line's higher-priced products. As long as a retailer has sufficient quantities of the advertised low-priced model available for sale, this strategy is considered acceptable. In contrast, *bait and switch* is an activity in which retailers have no intention of selling the bait product; they use the low price merely to entice customers into the store to sell them higher-priced products. Bait and switch is considered unethical, and in some states it is illegal.

PRICE LINING

When an organization sets a limited number of prices for selected groups or lines of merchandise, it is using **price lining**. A retailer may have various styles and brands of similar-quality men's shirts that sell for $15 and another line of higher-quality shirts that sell for $22. Microsoft set different prices for different versions of its Windows 7 operating system depending on features: the barebones Windows 7 Home Premium for $120, Windows 7 Professional for $200, and the feature-packed Windows 7 Ultimate for $220.[18] Price lining simplifies customers' decision making by holding constant one key variable in the final selection of style and brand within a line.

The basic assumption in price lining is that the demand for various groups or sets of products is inelastic. If the prices are attractive, customers will concentrate their purchases without responding to slight changes in price. Thus, a women's dress shop that carries dresses priced at $85, $55, and $35 may not attract many more sales with a drop to, say, $83, $53, and $33. The "space" between the price of $85 and $55, however, can stir changes in consumer response. With price lining, the demand curve looks like a series of steps, as shown in Figure 21.2.

Another type of price lining is subscription services. Cable or satellite TV subscribers choose different packages or groupings of channels with different prices. Likewise, subscribers to subscription DVD rental services like Netflix can choose a membership price based on the number of DVDs they want to receive at one time.

premium pricing Pricing the highest-quality or most versatile products higher than other models in the product line

bait pricing Pricing an item in a product line low with the intention of selling a higher-priced item in the line

price lining Setting a limited number of prices for selected groups or lines of merchandise

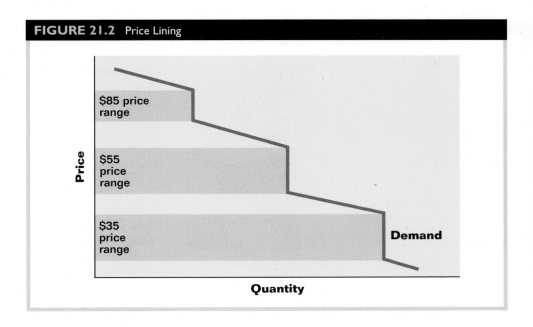

FIGURE 21.2 Price Lining

Psychological Pricing

Learning the price of a product is not always a pleasant experience for customers. It is sometimes surprising (as at a movie concession stand) and sometimes downright horrifying; most of us have experienced some sort of "sticker shock." Researchers have found that consumers are likely to have negative reactions to incomplete or unclear pricing information, especially when it is conveyed through misleading communications.[19] **Psychological pricing** attempts to influence a customer's perception of price to make a product's price more attractive. In this section, we consider several forms of psychological pricing: reference pricing, bundle pricing, multiple-unit pricing, everyday low prices (EDLP), odd-even pricing, customary pricing, and prestige pricing.

REFERENCE PRICING

Reference pricing means pricing a product at a moderate level and displaying it next to a more expensive model or brand in the hope that the customer will use the higher price as an external reference price (i.e., a comparison price). Because of the comparison, the customer is expected to view the moderate price favorably. Reference pricing is based on the "isolation effect," meaning an alternative is less attractive when viewed by itself than when compared with other alternatives. When you go to Best Buy to buy a DVD player, a moderately priced DVD player may appear especially attractive because it offers most of the important attributes of the more expensive alternatives on display and at a lower price.

BUNDLE PRICING

Bundle pricing is packaging together two or more products, usually complementary ones, to be sold at a single price. Many fast-food restaurants, for example, offer combination meals at a price that is lower than the combined prices of each item priced separately. Most telephone and cable television providers bundle local telephone service, broadband Internet access, and digital cable or satellite television for one monthly fee. To attract customers, the single bundled price is usually considerably less than the sum of the prices of the individual products. This is true for what Microsoft calls "The Xbox 360 Game of the Year Bundle," which includes the Xbox 360 Elite along with two popular video games. Basically, consumers are paying for the top Microsoft console and getting the two video games free of charge.[20] The opportunity to buy the bundled combination

psychological pricing Pricing that attempts to influence a customer's perception of price to make a product's price more attractive

reference pricing Pricing a product at a moderate level and displaying it next to a more expensive model or brand

bundle pricing Packaging together two or more complementary products and selling them at a single price

SPECIAL & CHEESY BREAD

$19⁹⁹

One Large Special (Round or Square)
Cheese, Pepperoni, Ham, Mushrooms, Green Pepper, Onions & Bacon
Small Order of Cheesy Bread With Sauce
& 2 Liter Pepsi Product

Bundle Pricing
*This offer for a large pizza, an order of cheesy bread, and a
2 liter Pepsi for $19.99 is an example of bundle pricing.*

of products in a single transaction may be of value to the customer as well. Marketing research models suggest that marketers can develop heterogeneous bundles of products with optimal prices for different market segments.[21] Bundle pricing facilitates customer satisfaction and, when slow-moving products are bundled with those with a higher turnover, can help stimulate sales and increase revenues. It may also help foster customer loyalty and improve customer retention. Selling products as a package rather than individually may also result in cost savings. Bundle pricing is commonly used for banking and travel services, computers, and automobiles with option packages.

MULTIPLE-UNIT PRICING

Multiple-unit pricing occurs when two or more identical products are packaged together and sold at a single price. This normally results in a lower per-unit price than the price regularly charged. Multiple-unit pricing is commonly used for twin-packs of potato chips, 4-packs of light bulbs, and 6- and 12-packs of soft drinks. Customers benefit from the cost saving and convenience this pricing strategy affords. A company may use multiple-unit pricing to attract new customers to its brands and, in some instances, to increase consumption of them. When customers buy in larger quantities, their consumption of the product may increase. For instance, multiple-unit pricing may encourage a customer to buy larger quantities of snacks, which are likely to be consumed in higher volume at the point of consumption simply because they are available. However, this is not true for all products. For instance, greater availability at the point of consumption of light bulbs, bar soap, and table salt is not likely to increase usage.

Discount stores and especially warehouse clubs, like Sam's Club and Costco, are major users of multiple-unit pricing. For certain products in these stores, customers receive significant per-unit price reductions when they buy packages containing multiple units of the same product, such as an eight-pack of canned tuna fish.

EVERYDAY LOW PRICES (EDLP)

To reduce or eliminate the use of frequent short-term price reductions, some organizations use an approach referred to as **everyday low prices (EDLP)**. With EDLP, a marketer sets a low price for its products on a consistent basis rather than setting higher prices and frequently discounting them. Everyday low prices, though not deeply discounted, are set far enough below competitors' prices to make customers feel confident they are receiving a fair price. EDLP is employed by retailers like Walmart and manufacturers like Procter & Gamble. Indeed, Walmart, which has already trademarked the phrase "Always Low Prices. Always," sought to trademark the acronym EDLP because of its extensive use of the practice. However, vociferous opposition from the National Grocers Association and SuperValu, a supermarket chain, as well as other firms ultimately led Walmart to withdraw its trademark application.[22] A company that uses EDLP benefits from reduced losses from frequent markdowns, greater stability in sales, and decreased promotional costs.

One of the major problems with EDLP is that customers can respond to it in several different ways. Over the last several years, many marketers have inadvertently "trained" customers to expect and seek out deeply discounted prices. In some product categories, such as apparel, finding the deepest discount has become almost a national consumer sport. Thus, failure to provide deep discounts can be a problem for certain marketers. In some instances, customers simply do not believe everyday low prices are what marketers claim they are but are instead a marketing gimmick.

multiple-unit pricing
Packaging together two or more identical products and selling them at a single price

everyday low prices (EDLP)
Pricing products low on a consistent basis

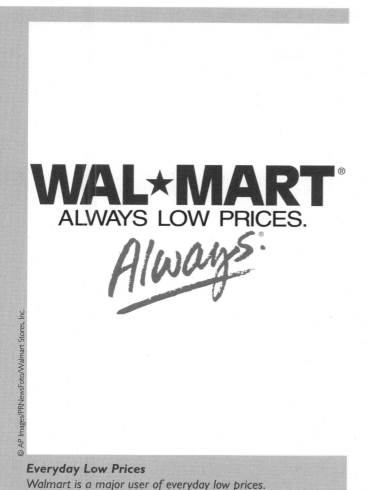

Everyday Low Prices
Walmart is a major user of everyday low prices.

ODD-EVEN PRICING

Through **odd-even pricing**—ending the price with certain numbers—marketers try to influence buyers' perceptions of the price or the product. Odd pricing assumes more of a product will be sold at $99.95 than at $100. Theoretically, customers will think, or at least tell friends, that the product is a bargain—not $100, but $99 and change. Also, customers will supposedly think the store could have charged $100 but instead cut the price to the last cent, to $99.95. Some claim, too, that certain types of customers are more attracted by odd prices than by even ones. Researchers have found that women are more likely to respond to odd-ending prices than men are.[23] However, research on the effect of odd-even prices has demonstrated conflicting results; one recent study found that odd prices that end in 5 or 9 failed to trigger the threshold of consumer response.[24] Nonetheless, odd prices are far more common today than even prices.

Even prices are often used to give a product an exclusive or upscale image. An even price supposedly will influence a customer to view the product as being a high-quality, premium brand. A shirt maker, for example, may print on a premium shirt package a suggested retail price of $42.00 instead of $41.95; the even price of the shirt is used to enhance its upscale image.

CUSTOMARY PRICING

With **customary pricing**, certain goods are priced primarily on the basis of tradition. Recent economic uncertainties have made most prices fluctuate fairly widely, but the classic example of the customary, or traditional, price is the price of a candy bar. For years, a candy bar cost 5 cents. A new candy bar would have had to be something very special to sell for more than a nickel. This price was so sacred that rather than change it, manufacturers increased or decreased the size of the candy bar itself as chocolate prices fluctuated. Today, of course, the nickel candy bar has disappeared. However, most candy bars still sell at a consistent, but obviously higher, price. Thus, customary pricing remains the standard for this market.

PRESTIGE PRICING

With **prestige pricing**, prices are set at an artificially high level to convey prestige or a quality image. Prestige pricing is used especially when buyers associate a higher price with higher quality. Pharmacists report that some consumers complain when a prescription does not cost enough; apparently some consumers associate a drug's price with its potency. Research confirms that many consumers believe a more expensive medicine works better than a less costly one.[25]

Typical product categories in which selected products are prestige priced include perfumes, liquor, jewelry, and cars. Although appliances have not traditionally been prestige priced, upscale appliances have appeared in recent years to capitalize on the willingness of some consumer segments to "trade up" for high-quality products. These consumers do not mind paying extra for a Subzero refrigerator, a Viking commercial range, or a Whirlpool Duet washer and dryer because these products offer high quality as well as a level of prestige. If these producers lowered their prices dramatically, the new prices would be inconsistent with the perceived high-quality images of their products. From golf clubs to handbags, prestige products are selling at record levels. Consider some of the prestige products shown in Table 21.4 that were selected as the best by *Smart Money* magazine.

odd-even pricing Ending the price with certain numbers to influence buyers' perceptions of the price or product

customary pricing Pricing on the basis of tradition

prestige pricing Setting prices at an artificially high level to convey prestige or a quality image

TABLE 21.4 Sample Prestige Product Prices

Mail-order beef	Neiman's Ranch Grass-Fed Prime Filet	$63/pound
Plasma TVs	Panasonic TH-50PZ750U 50"	$3,499
Winter adventures	Week at Lake Placid Lodge's Owl's Head Cabin	$4,480/couple
Champagne	House of Salon's Salon Le Mesnil 1996	$350

Source: Kristen Bellstrom, "The Best of Everything," *Smart Money*, November 13, 2007, www.smartmoney.com.

Professional Pricing

Professional pricing is used by people who have great skill or experience in a particular field. Professionals often believe their fees (prices) should not relate directly to the time and effort spent in specific cases; rather, a standard fee is charged regardless of the problems involved in performing the job. Some doctors' and lawyers' fees are prime examples, such as $75 for an office visit, $2,000 for an appendectomy, and $995 for a divorce. Other professionals set prices in other ways. Like other marketers, professionals have costs associated with facilities, labor, insurance, equipment, and supplies. Certainly, costs are considered when setting professional prices.

The concept of professional pricing carries the idea that professionals have an ethical responsibility not to overcharge customers. In some situations, a seller can charge customers a high price and continue to sell many units of the product. Medicine offers several examples. If a person with diabetes requires one insulin treatment per day to survive, she or he will probably buy that treatment whether its price is $1 or $10. In fact, the patient will probably purchase the treatment even if the price rose. In these situations, sellers could charge exorbitant fees. Drug companies claim that despite their positions of strength in this regard, they charge ethical prices rather than what the market will bear.

Promotional Pricing

As an ingredient in the marketing mix, price is often coordinated with promotion. The two variables are sometimes so closely interrelated that the pricing policy is promotion-oriented. Types of promotional pricing include price leaders, special-event pricing, and comparison discounting.

PRICE LEADERS

Sometimes, a firm prices a few products below the usual markup, near cost, or below cost, which results in prices known as **price leaders**. This type of pricing is used most often in supermarkets and restaurants to attract customers by giving them especially low prices on a few items. Management hopes that sales of regularly priced products will more than offset the reduced revenues from the price leaders.

SPECIAL-EVENT PRICING

To increase sales volume, many organizations coordinate price with advertising or sales promotions for seasonal or special situations. **Special-event pricing** involves advertised sales or price cutting linked to a holiday, a season, or an event. If the pricing objective is survival, special sales events may be designed to generate the necessary operating capital. Special-event pricing entails coordination of production, scheduling, storage, and physical distribution. Whenever a sales lag occurs, special-event pricing is an alternative that marketers should consider.

COMPARISON DISCOUNTING

Comparison discounting sets the price of a product at a specific level and simultaneously compares it with a higher price. The higher price may be the product's previous price, the price of a competing brand, the product's price at another retail outlet, or a manufacturer's

professional pricing Fees set by people with great skill or experience in a particular field

price leaders A product priced below the usual markup, near cost, or below cost

special-event pricing Advertised sales or price cutting linked to a holiday, a season, or an event

comparison discounting Setting a price at a specific level and comparing it with a higher price

Price Leaders
Price leaders are commonly used in the retail grocery industry.

suggested retail price. Customers may find comparative discounting informative, and it can have a significant impact on their purchases. However, overuse of comparison pricing may reduce customers' internal reference prices, meaning they no longer believe the higher price is the regular or normal price.[26]

Because this pricing strategy has occasionally led to deceptive pricing practices, the Federal Trade Commission has established guidelines for comparison discounting. If the higher price against which the comparison is made is the price formerly charged for the product, the seller must have made the previous price available to customers for a reasonable period of time. If the seller presents the higher price as the one charged by other retailers in the same trade area, it must be able to demonstrate that this claim is true. When the seller presents the higher price as the manufacturer's suggested retail price, the higher price must be similar to the price at which a reasonable proportion of the product was sold. Some manufacturers' suggested retail prices are so high that very few products are actually sold at those prices. In such cases, comparison discounting would be deceptive. An example of deceptive comparison discounting occurred when a major retailer put 93 percent of its power tools on sale, with discounts ranging from 10 to 40 percent. The retailer's frequent price reductions meant the tools sold at sale prices most of the year. Thus, comparisons with regular prices were deemed to be deceptive.

Determination of a Specific Price

A pricing strategy will yield a certain price, the final step in the process. However, this price may need refinement to make it consistent with circumstances as well as pricing practices in a particular market or industry. Pricing strategies should help in setting a final price. If they are to do so, marketers must establish pricing objectives; have considerable knowledge about target market customers; and determine demand, price elasticity, costs, and competitive factors. Also, the way pricing is used in the marketing mix will affect the final price.

In the absence of government price controls, pricing remains a flexible and convenient way to adjust the marketing mix. In many situations, prices can be adjusted quickly—over a few days or even in minutes. Such flexibility is unique to this component of the marketing mix.

summary

The six stages in the process of setting prices are (1) developing pricing objectives, (2) assessing the target market's evaluation of price, (3) evaluating competitors' prices, (4) choosing a basis for pricing, (5) selecting a pricing strategy, and (6) determining a specific price.

Setting pricing objectives is critical because pricing objectives form a foundation on which the decisions of subsequent stages are based. Organizations may use numerous pricing objectives, including short-term and long-term ones, and different objectives for different products and market segments. Pricing objectives are overall goals that describe the role of price in a firm's long-range plans. There are several major types of pricing objectives. The most fundamental pricing objective is the organization's survival. Price usually can be easily adjusted to increase sales volume or combat competition to help the organization stay alive. Profit objectives, which are usually stated in terms of sales dollar volume or percentage change, are normally set at a satisfactory level rather than at a level designed to maximize profits. A sales growth objective focuses on increasing the profit base by raising sales volume. Pricing for return on investment (ROI) has a specified profit as its objective. A pricing objective to maintain or increase market share links market position to success. Other types of pricing objectives include cash flow, status quo, and product quality.

Assessing the target market's evaluation of price tells the marketer how much emphasis to place on price and may help determine how far above the competition the firm can set its prices. Understanding how important a product is to customers relative to other products, as well as customers' expectations of quality, helps marketers correctly assess the target market's evaluation of price.

A marketer needs to be aware of the prices charged for competing brands. This allows the firm to keep its prices in line with competitors' prices when nonprice competition is used. If a company uses price as a competitive tool, it can price its brand below competing brands.

The three major dimensions on which prices can be based are cost, demand, and competition. When using cost-based pricing, the firm determines price by adding a dollar amount or percentage to the cost of the product. Two common cost-based pricing methods are cost-plus and markup pricing. Demand-based pricing is based on the level of demand for the product. To use this method, a marketer must be able to estimate the amounts of a product buyers will demand at different prices. Demand-based pricing results in a high price when demand for a product is strong and a low price when demand is weak. In the case of competition-based pricing, costs and revenues are secondary to competitors' prices.

A pricing strategy is an approach or a course of action designed to achieve pricing and marketing objectives. Pricing strategies help marketers solve the practical problems of establishing prices. The most common pricing strategies are differential pricing, new-product pricing, product-line pricing, psychological pricing, professional pricing, and promotional pricing.

When marketers employ differential pricing, they charge different buyers different prices for the same quality and quantity of products. Negotiated pricing, secondary-market discounting, periodic discounting, and random discounting are forms of differential pricing. With negotiated pricing, the final price is established through bargaining between seller and customer. Secondary-market pricing involves setting one price for the primary target market and a different price for another market; often the price charged in the secondary market is lower. Marketers employ periodic discounting when they temporarily lower their prices on a patterned or systematic basis; the reason for the reduction may be a seasonal change, a model-year change, or a holiday. Random discounting occurs on an unsystematic basis.

Two strategies used in new-product pricing are price skimming and penetration pricing. With price skimming, the organization charges the highest price that buyers who most desire the product will pay. A penetration price is a low price designed to penetrate a market and gain a significant market share quickly.

Product-line pricing establishes and adjusts the prices of multiple products within a product line. This strategy includes captive pricing, in which the marketer prices the basic product in a product line low and prices related items higher; premium pricing, in which prices on higher-quality or more versatile products are set higher than those on other models in the product line; bait pricing, in which the marketer tries to attract customers by pricing an item in the product line low with the intention of selling a higher-priced item in the line; and price lining, in which the organization sets a limited number of prices for selected groups or lines of merchandise. Organizations that employ price lining assume the demand for various groups of products is inelastic.

Psychological pricing attempts to influence customers' perceptions of price to make a product's price more attractive. With reference pricing, marketers price a product at a moderate level and position it next to a more expensive model or brand. Bundle pricing is packaging together two or more complementary products and selling them at a single price. With multiple-unit pricing, two or more identical products are packaged together and sold at a single price. To reduce or eliminate use of frequent short-term price reductions, some organizations employ everyday low pricing (EDLP), setting a low price for products on a consistent basis. When employing odd-even pricing, marketers try to influence buyers' perceptions of the price or the product by ending the price with certain numbers. Customary pricing is based on traditional prices. With prestige pricing, prices are set at an artificially high level to convey prestige or a quality image.

Professional pricing is used by people who have great skill or experience in a particular field, therefore allowing them to set the price. This concept carries the idea that professionals have an ethical responsibility not to overcharge customers. As an ingredient in the marketing mix, price is often coordinated with promotion. The two variables are sometimes so closely interrelated that the pricing policy is promotion-oriented. Promotional pricing includes price leaders, special-event pricing, and comparison discounting.

Price leaders are products priced below the usual markup, near cost, or below cost. Special-event pricing involves advertised sales or price cutting linked to a holiday, season, or event. Marketers that use a comparison discounting strategy price a product at a specific level and compare it with a higher price.

Once a price is determined by using one or more pricing strategies, it needs to be refined to a final price consistent with the pricing practices in a particular market or industry.

Go to www.cengagebrain.com for resources to help you master the content in this chapter as well as materials that will expand your marketing knowledge!

important terms

pricing objectives, 628

cost-based
  pricing, 633

cost-plus pricing, 633

markup pricing, 633

demand-based
  pricing, 634

competition-based
  pricing, 635

differential pricing, 636

negotiated pricing, 637

secondary-market
  pricing, 637

periodic
  discounting, 637

random
  discounting, 638

price skimming, 638

penetration
  pricing, 639

product-line
  pricing, 639

captive pricing, 639

premium pricing, 640

bait pricing, 640

price lining, 640

psychological
  pricing, 641

reference
  pricing, 641

bundle pricing, 641

multiple-unit
  pricing, 642

everyday low prices
  (EDLP), 642

odd-even pricing, 643

customary pricing, 643

prestige pricing, 643

professional pricing, 644

price leaders, 644

special-event
  pricing, 644

comparison
  discounting, 644

discussion and review questions

1. Identify the six stages in the process of establishing prices.
2. How does a return on an investment pricing objective differ from an objective of increasing market share?
3. Why must marketing objectives and pricing objectives be considered when making pricing decisions?
4. Why should a marketer be aware of competitors' prices?
5. What are the benefits of cost-based pricing?
6. Under what conditions is cost-plus pricing most appropriate?
7. A retailer purchases a can of soup for 24 cents and sells it for 36 cents. Calculate the markup as a percentage of cost and as a percentage of selling price.
8. What is differential pricing? In what ways can it be achieved?
9. For what types of products would price skimming be most appropriate? For what types of products would penetration pricing be more effective?
10. Describe bundle pricing and give three examples using different industries.
11. What are the advantages and disadvantages of using everyday low prices?
12. Why do customers associate price with quality? When should prestige pricing be used?
13. Are price leaders a realistic approach to pricing? Explain your answer.

application questions

CRITICAL THINKING

1. Price skimming and penetration pricing are strategies that are commonly used to set the base price of a new product. Which strategy is more appropriate for the following products? Explain.
   a. Short airline flights between cities in Florida
   b. A high-definition DVD player
   c. A backpack or book bag with a lifetime warranty
   d. Season tickets for a newly franchised NBA basketball team
2. Price lining is used to set a limited number of prices for selected lines of merchandise. Visit a few local retail stores to find examples of price lining. For what types of products and stores is this practice most common?

For what types of products and stores is price lining not typical or feasible?

3. Professional pricing is used by people who have great skill in a particular field, such as doctors, lawyers, and business consultants. Find examples (advertisements, personal contacts) that reflect a professional pricing policy. How is the price established? Are there any restrictions on the services performed at that price?
4. Organizations often use multiple pricing objectives. Locate an organization that uses several pricing objectives, and discuss how this approach influences the company's marketing mix decisions. Are some objectives oriented toward the short term and others toward the long term? How does the marketing environment influence these objectives?

internet exercise

T-Mobile

T-Mobile has attempted to position itself as a low-cost cellular phone service provider. A person can purchase a calling plan, a cellular phone, and phone accessories at its website. Visit the T-Mobile website at **www.t-mobile.com.**

1. Determine the various nationwide calling rates available in your city.

2. How many different calling plans are available in your area?
3. What type of pricing strategy is T-Mobile using on its rate plans in your area?

developing your marketing plan

CRITICAL THINKING

Setting the right price for a product is a crucial part of marketing strategy. Price helps to establish a product's position in the mind of the consumer and can differentiate a product from its competition. Several decisions in the marketing plan will be affected by the pricing strategy that is selected. To assist you in relating the information in this chapter to the development of your marketing plan, focus on the following:

1. Using Table 21.1 as a guide, discuss each of the seven pricing objectives. Which pricing objectives will you use for your product? Consider the product life cycle, competition, and product positioning for your target market during your discussion.

2. Review the various types of pricing strategies in Table 21.3. Which of these is the most appropriate for your product?

3. Select a basis for pricing your product (cost, demand, and/or competition). How will you know when it is time to revise your pricing strategy?

The information obtained from these questions should assist you in developing various aspects of your marketing plan found in the *Interactive Marketing Plan* exercise at **www.cengagebrain.com**.

VIDEO CASE 21.1

Is Smart Car's Price Smart?

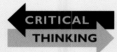
CRITICAL THINKING

Tiny car, tiny price tag, tiny gasoline bill. The Smart Car, made by Daimler's Mercedes Car Group in Hambach, France, first appeared on U.S. roads in 2008, just as prices at the gas pump were hitting record highs week after week. The timing could not have been better. Tired of emptying their wallets every time they filled their gas tanks, many U.S. drivers were thinking about downsizing from a big sport-utility vehicle or pickup truck to a smaller vehicle. But were they ready for a 106-inch-long car that seated only two people? Daimler was ready to find out.

The Smart Car had a good track record in other parts of the world. From 1998 to 2008, Daimler sold more than 900,000 Smart Cars in Europe, the Middle East, Asia, Australia, Mexico, and Canada. The car was cute, nimble, and unconventional—a good size for getting through crowded, narrow city streets and fitting into any tight parking spot. Not only was the purchase price highly affordable, but the excellent fuel efficiency made the car especially popular in countries where gas prices were generally high.

To bring the Smart Car to the United States, Daimler redesigned the body and engineering to meet U.S. safety standards. It added six inches to the car's length and included four air bags, an antilock braking system, a collapsing steering column, and other safety features. It also installed a fuel-saving 71-horsepower engine so that the Smart Car would go about 40 highway miles on a gallon of gasoline.

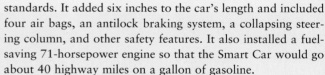

Daimler set the list price of the Smart Fortwo Pure model—the basic version of the two-seater—at $11,590. The list price of the Smart Fortwo Passion Coupe, equipped with more features, was $13,590. The list price of the Smart Fortwo Passion Cabriolet, a convertible with leather seats and additional features, was $16,590. Buyers had the option of ordering extras, like a metallic-paint finish or an alarm system, for an additional fee. Keeping the list price as tiny as the car allowed Daimler to build market share quickly.

Rather than selling Smart Cars through its regular dealer network, Daimler contracted with the Penske Automotive Group to handle distribution and sales. In another unusual move, Daimler set up a website to let buyers reserve the model of their choice and choose from six interior colors and six exterior colors on the car body's removable panels. Three of the exterior colors were offered as part of the purchase price, while the three metallic exterior colors were offered at an extra cost. The $99 reservation fee was applied to the buyer's purchase price once the ordered model became available. By the time Smart Cars arrived in U.S. showrooms, 30,000 people had paid for reservations.

To build customer interest prior to the U.S. launch, Daimler sent a number of Smart Cars on a 50-city U.S. tour. Nearly 50,000 members of the media and prospective car buyers took test drives. Although many reporters couldn't resist poking fun at the tiny car (*USA Today* called it a "breadbox on wheels"), they all noted its high fuel efficiency and low purchase price. Initial demand was so strong that even buyers who had reserved their cars well in advance had to wait months for delivery. A few U.S. customers who didn't want to wait paid as much as $39,000 for European Smart Cars adapted to meet U.S. safety and emissions standards.

Then gasoline prices fell from their record-high levels and the global economy plunged into recession. By 2009, the downturn was so severe that car sales plummeted across the board as U.S. consumers and businesses clamped down on buying. The combination of significantly lower gas prices and a sluggish economy put a serious dent into U.S. sales of the Smart Car. To reignite customer interest, Daimler offered low-interest financing and, for the first time, its U.S. dealers discounted the car's retail price. In 2010, the company also introduced a limited-edition electric Smart Car to appeal to buyers interested in eco-friendly alternatives to traditional gas-driven cars.

Today, Daimler continues to face intense competition in the small-car segment. Looking ahead, what else can it do to accelerate purchases of its stylish Smart Car without depending on constant discounts, rebates, and other price-cutting measures?[27]

QUESTIONS FOR DISCUSSION

1. Why is bundle pricing appropriate for the various models of Smart Cars?
2. How is demand likely to affect dealers' willingness to negotiate prices with Smart Car buyers?
3. Imagine that Daimler is considering whether to sell unpainted Smart Cars and reduce the list price by $1,500. The Smart Car exterior consists of 10 removable panels that can be easily painted. Buyers could paint their own panels, leave the panels unpainted, or pay the dealer an additional fee to personalize their cars by having the panels custom finished in almost any color or design. What are the advantages and disadvantages of this pricing idea?

CASE 21.2

Apple iPhone Pricing Dials Up Customer Demand

Days before the first Apple iPhones went on sale, thousands of buyers lined up outside Apple stores, eager to try the new cell phone's large, user-friendly touch screen and multimedia capabilities. Like Apple's iconic iPod media player, instantly identifiable because of its sleek case and white ear buds, the stylish iPhone became a must-have status symbol for tech-savvy consumers across the United States. However, despite a major promotional campaign, widespread media coverage, many rave reviews, and a fast-growing customer base, the iPhone became the focus of criticism and controversy within two months of its release.

Apple has traditionally set high prices for its new products. One purpose of pricing in this way is to reinforce the brand's high-end positioning and special cachet. Another is to start recouping development costs and build profits from the very start of each product's life. This pricing strategy has worked with the company's Macintosh computers, iPods, and iPads, allowing Apple to increase both revenues and profits year after year.

The iPhone was initially priced at $599, not including the cost of monthly phone service through an exclusive deal with AT&T. Two months later, in a break from its usual pattern, Apple abruptly slashed the iPhone's price by $200. Although electronic products often drop in price over time, they rarely sell for so much less so soon after introduction. This time, Apple had its eye on the year-end holidays, believing that setting a more affordable price during the fall would put the iPhone within reach of a larger number of gift-giving buyers. The company also saw an opportunity to achieve its objective of selling 10 million iPhones worldwide within 18 months of the product's launch (which it did).

Apple's pricing decision provoked angry protests from customers who objected that they had overpaid for a cutting-edge product that was going mainstream more quickly than expected. With Apple on the spot, CEO Steve Jobs quickly conceded that customers had a point. "Our early customers trusted us, and we must live up to that trust with our actions in moments like these," he said in a statement posted on Apple's website. To avoid alienating early buyers, the company offered a $100 Apple store credit to each customer who had purchased an iPhone before the price cut. Although this policy also drew criticism—because the credit had no value except toward the purchase of something from Apple—the pricing controversy lost steam after a few weeks.

Intense competition from multinational rivals like Nokia, Samsung, and Research in Motion (maker of BlackBerry) has been a major influence on smartphone pricing. As Apple launches new iPhone models with more features and more power, it sets prices that are considerably lower than when the product was originally introduced years ago. The lower-priced iPhones have become enormously successful, sparking excitement and prompting long lines at Apple stores worldwide. During one recent three-month period, Apple sold more than 8 million iPhones, thanks to particularly strong demand in Asia and Europe. Just as the iPod attracted many first-time Apple buyers, the iPhone's unique appeal and new, more affordable price tag have brought in new customers and given loyal customers another reason to buy from Apple.

The buzz from the iPhone, the iPad, and other products has also boosted demand for Apple's line of Macintosh computers and allowed the company to gain significant market share in that industry. Higher sales of Apple's entire product mix have also resulted in record-setting company profits and helped the company expand into new markets. Just as important, all these innovations have polished the Apple brand and added to its trend-setting image—which, in turn, allows the company to charge premium prices when it launches new products.[28]

QUESTIONS FOR DISCUSSION

1. What was Apple's primary pricing objective when it introduced the iPhone? What was its primary objective in cutting the product's price just two months after introduction?

2. How much weight does Apple appear to have given to its evaluation of competitive pricing?

3. Do you agree with Apple's decision to switch away from price skimming after the iPhone's introduction? Defend your answer.

Tata's Nano Steers into Low Pricing

How can a car sell for less than $3,000? That's the price Tata Motors set for its Nano, a four-door, four-seat subcompact designed specifically for India and introduced in 2009. With a rear-mounted motor, this tiny car includes absolutely no extras—no radio, no reclining seats. What the Nano does have, however, is an ultra-low price tag. And that is what makes it very attractive to millions of potential buyers in India. Now "someone who never even dreamed of a car finds it within reach," says Tata's CEO.

Racing to develop and market the world's cheapest car has been a challenge, even for a car manufacturer with as much experience as Mumbai-based Tata, which is India's largest automaker. The company began working on the Nano in 2003 with the goal of creating a functional yet eye-pleasing design that would fit buyers' lifestyles and tight

budgets and, at the same time, be profitable to manufacture and sell. The most essential ingredient was keeping costs in line to keep the car ultra-affordable.

Low Price, Low Costs

The first step in developing the Nano was to establish an upper level for the car's price: roughly one lakh (100,000 Indian rupees), the equivalent of less than $3,000. To sell a car at this price, "you have to cut costs on everything—seats, materials, components—the whole package," says a Tata official. That's exactly what Tata did, using expertise gained from its years of marketing trucks, cars, and buses for markets in India, Europe, South America, Southeast Asia, and the Middle East. For instance, Tata sells its Indica compact car for $8,500 in eastern Europe.

The 33-horsepower engine of the Nano may not win any races, but it can get the car to a top speed of about 80 miles per hour. Thanks to low-cost parts and manufacturing, the cost of each engine is only about $700. In contrast, an engine made in the West can cost twice as much. By shaving the cost of each part and component, streamlining assembly methods, and offering only a stripped-down basic model, Tata has been able to achieve its low-price goal.

What's Driving the Market?

India's healthy economy is propelling millions of consumers into the middle class and accelerating demand for affordable transportation. As many as 65 million people currently drive small motor scooters in India, often carrying family members on the back. Some of these drivers will be able to trade up to a new car if the price is right.

In fact, sales of small cars are projected to reach 1 million units by 2016. Small wonder that Tata designed its Nano with four doors to appeal to buyers who often have family members and friends riding along. Finally, India's population skews young, with a median age under 25. If Tata can attract young first-time buyers with a low-priced model and maintain their loyalty as they graduate to higher-priced cars in the years ahead, the company will profit in the long term.

Competition on the Roads of India

Competition is fierce at the low end of the car market. Maruti Suzuki India, which sells small cars starting at about $5,000, is the market leader. With its nationwide service network, high brand recognition, and new production facilities in the works, Maruti Suzuki is a formidable competitor.

Other rivals are also expanding to take advantage of this fast-growing segment of the market. Hyundai India, for instance, is opening a global center for small-car manufacturing and adding manufacturing space. Its Santro sedan, which offers both air conditioning and power steering as standard features, sells for about $6,300. Volkswagen's Skoda division offers the low-priced Fabia model, among others, in India.

Toyota is designing a no-frills car that will sell in India and other emerging nations for under $7,000. In the process, the company expects to develop new technology that will help it cut costs on other vehicles in its global product mix. Honda has a plant in India and is opening a second plant to support its marketing initiatives in the

STRATEGIC CASE 8

area. Meanwhile, U.S. carmakers are looking at how they might enter the market in the near future.

Renault-Nissan, working with Indian motorcycle manufacturer Bajaj, is developing a car to be priced around $3,000. The company knows a lot about low-cost, low-priced cars because, since 2004, it has produced its popular $7,000 Logan four-door sedan in Romania and Russia. Nearly half a million Logans are already on the roads of Europe, and even though Renault-Nissan's two plants are operating at full capacity all day, every day, the firm is still struggling to meet ever-growing demand.

To shave costs, Renault-Nissan limited the number of parts that go into the Logan and avoided expensive electronics. To speed development and eliminate the high costs of building prototypes, the company proceeded from digital design directly to production. This alone saved $40 million and is one reason for the CEO's confidence that Renault-Nissan can succeed in the worldwide ultra-low-price segment. "With the Logan, we have the product and we have the lead," he says.

Environmental and Safety Concerns

As enthusiastic as Tata and other car manufacturers may be about marketing millions of tiny cars with tiny price tags, the car has generated both environmental and safety concerns. Some critics fear that broadening the base of car ownership will only add to the pollution problems in India's largest cities. Where national and local regulations do not require antipollution devices, manufacturers are unlikely to install them because of the added costs.

Safety is an issue because more cars on the road mean more traffic congestion and more opportunity for accidents. Cars made by Tata and its competitors comply with all of India's safety standards, but those standards do not require equipment, such as air bags and antilock brakes. Safety advocates worry that people traveling in the smallest, lightest cars will be more vulnerable to serious injury if involved in a traffic accident. For now, the automakers are moving ahead as they monitor the issues and stay alert for possible changes in government regulations.

Getting in Gear

Buyers have responded to the Nano's low price tag. Tata received more than 200,000 orders during the 12 months after the car's introduction. Because of limited production capabilities, it had to use a lottery system to select the first 100,000 buyers. Recently, Tata opened a second factory that can produce 250,000 Nanos per year, in an effort to keep up with the expected surge in demand as the Indian economy grows and consumers continue to trade up from motorcycles to cars.

Tata has a long history of good marketing management and above-average profitability. Being based in India gives Tata the advantage of being close to its customers and understanding their needs. And Tata's engineers and designers have found creative ways of containing costs to keep the new car ultra-affordable. With increased competition in the superbudget segment, however, Tata will have to get in gear to keep the Nano ahead of the pack.[29]

QUESTIONS FOR DISCUSSION

1. Which factors seem to have the greatest influence on Tata's decision about pricing its Nano? Explain.

2. What appear to be Tata's primary pricing objectives for the Nano?

3. Assess the level of price competition in India's car industry. What are the implications for Tata's marketing?

4. Why must Tata pay close attention to legal and regulatory changes when planning and pricing future models of the Nano?

Between one-fourth and one-third of the civilian workforce in the United States is employed in marketing-related jobs. Although the field offers a multitude of diverse career opportunities, the number of positions in each area varies. For instance, millions of workers are employed in many facets of sales, but relatively few people work in public relations and marketing research.

Many nonbusiness organizations now recognize that they perform marketing activities. For that reason, the number of marketing positions in government agencies, hospitals, charitable and religious groups, educational institutions, and similar organizations is increasing. Today's nonprofit organizations are competitive and better managed, with job growth rates often matching those of private-sector firms.

Some workers outplaced from large corporations are choosing an entrepreneurial path, creating still more new opportunities for first-time job seekers. Even some individuals with secure managerial positions are leaving corporations and heading to smaller companies, toward greater responsibility and autonomy. The traditional career path used to be graduation from college, then a job with a large corporation, and a climb up the ladder to management. This pattern has changed, however. Today, people are more likely to experience a career path of rewarding sideways moves in several organizations rather than sequential steps up a corporate ladder in just one company.

Career Choices Are Major Life Choices

Many people think career planning begins with an up-to-date résumé and a job interview.[1] In reality, it begins long before you prepare your résumé. It starts with *you* and what you want to become. In some ways, you have been preparing for a career ever since you started school. Everything you have experienced during your lifetime you can use as a resource to help you define your career goals. Since you will likely spend more time at work than at any other single place during your lifetime, it makes sense to spend that time doing something you enjoy. Unfortunately, some people just work at a *job* because they need money to survive. Other people choose a *career* because of their interests and talents or a commitment to a particular profession. Whether you are looking for a job or a career, you should examine your priorities.

Personal Factors Influencing Career Choices

Before choosing a career, you need to consider what motivates you and what skills you can offer an employer. The following questions may help you define what you consider important in life:

1. *What types of activities do you enjoy?* Although most people know what they enjoy in a general way, a number of interest inventories exist. By helping you determine specific interests and activities, these inventories can help you land a job that will lead to a satisfying career. In some cases, it may be sufficient just to list the activities you enjoy, along with those you dislike. Watch for patterns that may influence your career choices.

2. *What do you do best?* All jobs and all careers require employees to be able to "do something." It is extremely important to assess what you do best. Be honest

with yourself about your ability to succeed in a specific job. It may help to make a list of your strongest job-related skills. Also, try looking at your skills from an employer's perspective: What can you do that an employer would be willing to pay for?

3. *What kind of education will you need?* The amount of education you need is determined by the type of career you choose. In some careers, it is impossible to get an entry-level position without at least a college degree. Other careers may also require technical or hands-on skills. Generally, additional education increases your potential earning power.

4. *Where do you want to live?* Initially, some college graduates will want to move to a different part of the country before entering the job market, whereas others may prefer to reside close to home, friends, and relatives. In reality, successful job applicants must be willing to go where the jobs are. The location of an entry-level job may be influenced by the type of marketing career selected. For example, some of the largest advertising agencies are in New York, Chicago, and Los Angeles. Likewise, large marketing research organizations are based in metropolitan areas. On the other hand, sales positions and retail management jobs are available in medium-size as well as large cities.

Job Search Activities

When people begin to search for a job, they often first go online or turn to the classified ads in their local newspaper. Those ads are an important source of information about jobs in a particular area, but they are only one source. Many other sources can lead to employment and a satisfying career. Because there is a wealth of information about career planning, you should be selective in both the type and the amount of information you use to guide your job search.

The Internet is a fundamental tool for job hunting today. Almost every major company and most small firms have a website on which they post job openings and accept applications, provide useful information about the company and hiring process, and list contact information of relevant people in the company. In addition, there are many useful third-party sites. There are many websites that publish lists of job openings and descriptions from many different companies and industries, giving job seekers an opportunity to read about a variety of positions and even apply directly for jobs that interest them. Other sites allow users to post reviews about companies they have worked for and read reviews about potential employers.

As you start your job search, you may find the following websites helpful:

CareerBuilder.com: **www.careerbuilder.com**

This site is one of the largest on the Internet, with more than 1 million jobs to view. The site allows a job seeker to find jobs, post résumés, get advice and career resources, and obtain information on career fairs.

Monster Board: **www.monster.com**

Monster.com is one of the largest recruiting sites globally and offers job listings and links to related sites, such as company homepages and sites with information about job fairs.

TheLadders.com: **www.theladders.com**

Typically posting around 35,000 jobs, this recruiting site differentiates itself by only posting jobs with salaries above $100,000. Although a subscription is required to enjoy the full benefits, some basic searches are allowed free of charge.

Federal jobs: **http://usajobs.gov**

If you are interested in working for a government agency, this site lists positions all across the country. You can limit your search to specific states or do a general cross-country search for job openings.

Other web addresses for job seekers include:

www.careers-in-marketing.com

www.marketingjobs.com

www.starthere.com/jobs

www.careermag.com

www.salary.com

In addition to the library and the Internet, the following sources can be of great help when trying to find the "perfect job":

1. *Campus career centers.* Colleges and universities have placement offices staffed by trained personnel specialists. In most cases, these offices serve as clearinghouses for career information. The staff may also be able to guide you in creating a résumé and preparing for a job interview.

2. *Professional sources and networks.* A network is a group of people—friends, relatives, and professionals—who are in a position to exchange information, including information about job openings. According to many job applicants, networking is one of the best sources of career information and job leads. Start with as many people as you can think of to establish your network. (The Internet can be very useful in this regard.) Contact these people and ask specific questions about job opportunities they are aware of. Also, ask each individual to introduce or refer you to someone else who may be able to help you in your job search.

3. *Private employment agencies.* Private employment agencies charge a fee for helping people find jobs. Typical fees can be as high as 15 to 20 percent of an employee's first-year salary. The fee may be paid by the employer or the employee. Like campus placement offices, private employment agencies provide career counseling, help create résumés, and provide preparation for job interviews. Before you use a private employment agency, be sure you understand the terms of any contract or agreement you sign. Above all, make sure you know who is responsible for paying the agency's fee.

4. *State employment agencies.* The local office of your state employment agency is a valuable source of information about job openings in your immediate area. Some job applicants are reluctant to use state agencies because most jobs available through them are for semiskilled or unskilled workers. From a practical standpoint, though, it can't hurt to consult state employment agencies. They will have information about some professional and managerial positions available in your area, and you will not be charged a fee if you obtain a job through one of these agencies.

Many graduates want a job immediately and are discouraged at the thought that an occupational search can take months. But people seeking entry-level jobs should expect their job search to take considerable time. Of course, the state of the economy and whether employers generally are hiring can shorten or extend a job search.

During a job search, you should use the same work habits that effective employees use on the job. Resist the temptation to "take the day off" from job hunting. Instead, make a master list of the activities you want to accomplish each day. If necessary, force yourself to make contacts, do job research, or schedule interviews that might lead to job opportunities. (In fact, many job applicants look at the job hunt as their actual job and "work" full-time at it until they find the job they want.) Above all, realize that an occupational search requires patience and perseverance. According to many successful applicants, perseverance may be the job hunter's most valuable trait.

Planning and Preparation

The key to landing the job you want is planning and preparation—and planning begins with goals. In particular, it is important to determine your *personal* goals, decide on the role your career will play in reaching those goals, and then develop your *career* goals. Once you know where you are going, you can devise a feasible plan for getting there.

The time to begin planning is as early as possible. You must, of course, satisfy the educational requirements for the occupational area you desire. Early planning will give you the opportunity to do so. However, some of the people who will compete with you for the better jobs will also be fully prepared. Can you do more? Company recruiters say the following factors give job candidates a definite advantage.

- *Work experience.* You can get valuable work experience in cooperative work/school programs, during summer vacations, or in part-time jobs during the school year. Experience in your chosen occupational area carries the most weight, but even unrelated work experience is useful.
- *The ability to communicate well.* Verbal and written communication skills are increasingly important in all aspects of business. Yours will be tested in your letters to recruiters, in your résumé, and in interviews. You will use these same communication skills throughout your career.
- *Clear and realistic job and career goals.* Recruiters feel most comfortable with candidates who know where they are headed and why they are applying for a specific job.

Again, starting early will allow you to establish well-defined goals, sharpen your communication skills (through elective courses, if necessary), and obtain solid work experience.

The Résumé

An effective résumé is one of the keys to being considered for a good job. Because your résumé states your qualifications, experiences, education, and career goals, a potential employer can use it to assess your compatibility with the job requirements. The résumé should be accurate and current.

In preparing a résumé, it helps to think of it as an advertisement. Envision yourself as a product and the potential employers as your customer. To interest the customer in buying the product—hiring you—your résumé must communicate information about your qualities and indicate how you can satisfy the customer's needs—that is, how you can help the company achieve its objectives. The information in the résumé should persuade the organization to take a closer look at you by calling you in for an interview.

To be effective, the résumé should be targeted at a specific position, as Figure A.1 shows. This document is only one example of an acceptable résumé. The job target section is specific and leads directly to the applicant's qualifications for the job. The qualifications section details capabilities—what the applicant can do—and also shows that the applicant has an understanding of the job's requirements. Skills and strengths that relate to the specific job should be emphasized. The achievement section ("Experiences" in Figure A.1) indicates success at accomplishing tasks or goals on the job and at school. The work experience section in Figure A.1 includes an unusual listing, which might pique the interviewer's interest: "helped operate relative's blueberry farm in Michigan for three summers." It tends to inspire rather than satisfy curiosity, thus inviting further inquiry.

FIGURE A.1 A Résumé Targeted at a Specific Position

LORRAINE MILLER
2212 WEST WILLOW
PHOENIX, AZ 12345
(416) 862-9169

EDUCATION: BBA Arizona State University, 2010, Marketing, GPA = 3.4 on a 4.0
scale throughout college.

POSITION DESIRED: Product manager with an international firm providing future
career development at the executive level

QUALIFICATIONS:
- Communicates well with individuals to achieve a common goal
- Handles tasks efficiently and in a timely manner
- Understands advertising sales, management, marketing research, packaging, pricing, distribution, and warehousing
- Coordinates many activities at one time
- Receives and carries out assigned tasks or directives
- Writes complete status or research reports

EXPERIENCES:
- Assistant Editor of college paper
- Treasurer of the American Marketing Association (student chapter)
- Internship with 3-Cs Advertising, Berkeley, CA
- Student Assistantship with Dr. Steve Green, Professor of Marketing, Arizona State University
- Solo cross-Canada canoe trek, summer 2003

WORK RECORD:

2009–Present	Blythe and Co. Inc. —Junior Advertising Account Executive
2007–2008	Student Assistant for Dr. Steve Green —Research Assistant
2006–2007	The Men —Retail sales and customer relations
2004–2006	Farmer —Helped operate relative's blueberry farm in Michigan for three summers

---

In some cases, education is more important than unrelated work experience because it indicates the career direction you desire despite the work experience you have acquired thus far.

Another type of résumé is the chronological résumé, which lists work experience and educational history in order by date. This type of résumé is useful for those just entering the job market because it helps highlight education and work experience.

Common suggestions for improving résumés include deleting useless or outdated information, improving organization, using professional printing and typing, listing duties (not accomplishments), maintaining grammatical perfection, and avoiding an overly elaborate or fancy format.[2] Keep in mind that the person who will look at your résumé may have to sift through hundreds of résumés in the course of the day in addition to handling other duties. Consequently, it is important to keep your résumé short (one page is best, never more than two), concise, and neat. Moreover, you want your résumé to be distinctive so it will stand out from all the others.

In addition to having the proper format and content, a résumé should be easy to read. It is best to use only one or two kinds of type and plain, white paper. When sending a résumé to a large company, several copies may be made and distributed. Textured, gray, or colored paper may make a good impression on the first person who sees the résumé, but it will not reproduce well for the others, who will see only a poor copy. You should also proofread your résumé with care. Typos and misspellings will grab attention—the wrong kind.

Along with the résumé itself, always submit a cover letter. In the letter, you can include somewhat more information than in your résumé and convey a message that expresses your interest and enthusiasm about the organization and the job.

The Job Interview

In essence, your résumé and cover letter are an introduction. The deciding factor in the hiring process is the interview (or several interviews) with representatives of the firm. It is through the interview that the firm gets to know you and your qualifications. At the same time, the interview gives you a chance to learn about the firm.

Here again, preparation is the key to success. Research the firm before your first interview. Learn all you can about its products, its subsidiaries, the markets in which it operates, its history, the locations of its facilities, and so on. If possible, obtain and read the firm's most recent annual report. Be prepared to ask questions about the firm and the opportunities it offers. Interviewers welcome such questions. They expect you to be interested enough to spend some time thinking about your potential relationship with their organization.

Also, prepare to respond to questions the interviewer may ask. Table A.1 lists typical interview questions that job applicants often find difficult to answer. But don't expect interviewers to stick to the list given in the table or to the items appearing in your résumé. They will be interested in anything that helps them decide what kind of person and worker you are.

TABLE A.1 Interview Questions Job Applicants Often Find Difficult to Answer

1. Tell me about yourself.
2. What do you know about our organization?
3. What can you do for us? Why should we hire you?
4. What qualifications do you have that make you feel you will be successful in your field?
5. What have you learned from the jobs you've held?
6. What are your special skills, and where did you acquire them?
7. Have you had any special accomplishments in your lifetime that you are particularly proud of?
8. Why did you leave your most recent job?
9. How do you spend your spare time? What are your hobbies?
10. What are your strengths and weaknesses?
11. Discuss five major accomplishments.
12. What kind of boss would you like? Why?
13. If you could spend a day with someone you've known or know of, who would it be?
14. What personality characteristics seem to rub you the wrong way?
15. How do you show your anger? What types of things make you angry?
16. With what type of person do you spend the majority of your time?

Source: Adapted from *The Ultimate Job Hunter's Guidebook*, 5th ed., by Susan D. Greene and Melanie C. L. Martel. Copyright © 2007 by South-Western/Cengage Learning.

Make sure you are on time for your interview and are dressed and groomed in a businesslike manner. Interviewers take note of punctuality and appearance just as they do of other personal qualities. Bring a copy of your résumé, even if you already sent one to the firm. You may also want to bring a copy of your course transcript and letters of recommendation. If you plan to furnish interviewers with the names and addresses of references rather than with letters of recommendation, make sure you have your references' permission to do so.

Consider the interview itself as a two-way conversation rather than a question-and-answer session. Volunteer any information that is relevant to the interviewer's questions. If an important point is skipped in the discussion, don't hesitate to bring it up. Be yourself, but emphasize your strengths. Good eye contact and posture are also important; they should come naturally if you take an active part in the interview. At the conclusion of the interview, thank the recruiter for taking the time to see you.

In most cases, the first interview is used to *screen* applicants, that is, choose those who are best qualified. These applicants are then given a second interview and perhaps a third, usually with one or more department heads. If the job requires relocation to a different area, applicants may be invited there for these later interviews.

After the interviewing process is complete, applicants are told when to expect a hiring decision.

After the Interview

Attention to common courtesy is important as a follow-up to your interview. You should send a brief note of thanks to the interviewer and give it as much care as you did your résumé and cover letter. A short, typewritten letter is preferred to a handwritten note or card, or an e-mail. Avoid not only typos, but also overconfident statements such as "I look forward to helping you make Universal Industries successful over the next decade." Even in the thank-you letter, it is important to show team spirit and professionalism, as well as to convey proper enthusiasm. Everything you say and do reflects on you as a candidate.

After the Hire

Clearly, performing well in a job has always been a crucial factor in keeping a position. In a tight economy and job market, however, a person's attitude, as well as his or her performance, counts greatly. People in their first jobs can commit costly political blunders by being insensitive to their environments. Politics in the business world include how you react to your boss, how you react to your coworkers, and your general demeanor. Here are a few rules to live by.

1. *Don't bypass your boss.* One major blunder an employee can make is to go over the boss's head to resolve a problem. This is especially hazardous in a bureaucratic organization. You should become aware of the generally accepted chain of command and, when problems occur, follow that protocol, beginning with your immediate superior. No boss likes to look incompetent, and making him or her appear so is sure to hamper or even crush your budding career. However, there may be exceptions to this rule in emergency situations. It is wise to discuss with your supervisor what to do in an emergency, before an emergency occurs.[3]

2. *Don't criticize your boss.* Adhering to the old adage "praise in public and criticize in private" will keep you out of the line of retaliatory fire. A more sensible and productive alternative is to present the critical commentary to your boss in a diplomatic way during a private session.

3. *Don't show disloyalty.* If dissatisfied with the position, a new employee may start a fresh job search, within or outside the organization. However, it is not advisable to begin a publicized search within the company for another position unless you have held your current job for some time. Careful attention to the political climate in the organization should help you determine how soon to start a new job campaign

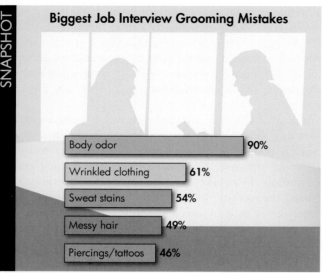

Biggest Job Interview Grooming Mistakes

Body odor	90%
Wrinkled clothing	61%
Sweat stains	54%
Messy hair	49%
Piercings/tattoos	46%

Source: Gillette Career Advantage survey of 500 human resource representatives.

and how public to make it. In any case, it is not a good idea to publicize that you are looking outside the company for a new position.

4. *Don't be a naysayer.* Employees are expected to become part of the organizational team and to work together with others. Behaviors to avoid, especially if you are a new employee, include being critical of others; refusing to support others' projects; always playing devil's advocate; refusing to help others when a crisis occurs; and complaining all the time, even about such matters as the poor quality of the food in the cafeteria, the crowded parking lot, or the temperature in the office.

5. *Learn to correct mistakes appropriately.* No one likes to admit to having made a mistake, but one of the most important political skills you can acquire is minimizing the impact of a blunder. It is usually advantageous to correct the damage as soon as possible to avoid further problems. Some suggestions: be the first to break the bad news to your boss, avoid being defensive, stay poised and don't panic, and have solutions ready for fixing the blunder.[4]

Types of Marketing Careers

In considering marketing as a career, the first step is to evaluate broad categories of career opportunities in the areas of marketing research, sales, industrial buying, public relations, distribution management, product management, advertising, retail management, and direct marketing. Keep in mind that the categories described here are not all-inclusive and that each encompasses hundreds of marketing jobs.

Marketing Research

Clearly, marketing research and information systems are vital aspects of marketing decision making. Marketing researchers survey customers to determine their habits, preferences, and aspirations. The information about buyers and environmental forces that research and information systems provide improves a marketer's ability to understand the dynamics of the marketplace and therefore make effective decisions.

Marketing research firms are usually employed by a client organization such as a provider of goods or services, a nonbusiness organization, a research consulting firm, or an advertising agency. The activities performed include concept testing, product testing, package testing, advertising testing, test market research, and new-product research.

Marketing researchers gather and analyze data relating to specific problems. A researcher may be involved in one or several stages of research depending on the size of the project, the organization of the research unit, and the researcher's experience. Marketing research trainees in large organizations usually perform a considerable amount of clerical work, such as compiling secondary data from the firm's accounting and sales records and from periodicals, government publications, syndicated data services, the Internet, and unpublished sources. A junior analyst may edit and code questionnaires or tabulate survey results. Trainees may also participate in gathering primary data through mail and telephone surveys, personal interviews, and observation. As a marketing researcher gains experience, he or she may become involved in defining problems and developing research questions; designing research procedures; and analyzing, interpreting, and reporting findings. Exceptional personnel may assume responsibility for entire research projects.

Although most employers consider a bachelor's degree sufficient qualification for a marketing research trainee, many specialized positions require a graduate degree in business administration, statistics, or other related fields. Today, trainees are more likely to have a marketing or statistics degree than a liberal arts degree. Courses in statistics, information technology, psychology, sociology, communications, economics, and technical writing are valuable preparation for a career in marketing research.

The Bureau of Labor Statistics indicates that marketing research provides abundant employment opportunities, especially for applicants with graduate training in marketing research, statistics, economics, and the social sciences. Generally, the value of information gathered by marketing information and research systems rises as competition increases, thus expanding opportunities for prospective marketing research personnel.

The major career paths in marketing research are with independent marketing research agencies/data suppliers and marketing research departments in advertising agencies and other businesses. In a company in which marketing research plays a key role, the researcher is often a member of the marketing strategy team. Surveying or interviewing customers is the heart of the marketing research firm's activities. A statistician selects the sample to be surveyed, analysts design the questionnaire and synthesize the gathered data into a final report, data processors tabulate the data, and the research director controls and coordinates all these activities so each project is completed to the client's satisfaction.

Salaries in marketing research depend on the type, size, and location of the firm, as well as the nature of the position. Overall, salaries of marketing researchers have increased slightly during the last few years. However, the specific position within the marketing research field determines the degree of fluctuation.[5] Generally, starting salaries are somewhat higher and promotions somewhat slower than in other occupations requiring similar training. The typical salary for a market analyst is $24,000 to $50,000; a marketing research director can earn $75,000 to $200,000.[6]

Sales

Millions of people earn a living through personal selling. Chapter 21 defines personal selling as paid personal communication that attempts to inform customers and persuade them to purchase products in an exchange situation. Although this definition describes the general nature of sales positions, individual selling jobs vary enormously with respect to the types of businesses and products involved, the educational background and skills required, and the specific activities sales personnel perform. Because the work is so varied, it offers numerous career opportunities for people with a wide range of qualifications, interests, and goals. The two types of career opportunities we discuss relate to business-to-business sales.

SALES POSITIONS IN WHOLESALING

Wholesalers buy products intended for resale, for use in making other products, and for general business operations, and sell them directly to business markets. Wholesalers thus provide services to both retailers and producers. They can help match producers' products to retailers' needs and provide services that save producers time, money, and resources. Some activities a sales representative for a wholesaling firm is likely to perform include planning and negotiating transactions; assisting customers with sales, advertising, sales promotion, and publicity; facilitating transportation and storage; providing customers with inventory control and data processing assistance; establishing prices; and giving customers technical, managerial, and merchandising assistance.

The background needed by wholesale personnel depends on the nature of the product handled. A sales representative for a drug wholesaler, for example, needs extensive technical training and product knowledge, and may have a degree in chemistry, biology, or pharmacology. A wholesaler of standard office supplies, on the other hand, may find it more important that its sales staff be familiar with various brands, suppliers, and prices than have technical knowledge about the products. A person just entering the wholesaling field may begin as a sales trainee or hold a nonselling job that provides experience with inventory, prices, discounts, and the firm's customers. A college graduate usually enters a wholesaler's sales force directly. Competent salespeople also transfer from manufacturer and retail sales positions.

The number of sales positions in wholesaling is expected to grow about as rapidly as the average for all occupations. Earnings for wholesale personnel vary widely because commissions often make up a large proportion of their incomes.

SALES POSITIONS IN MANUFACTURING

A manufacturer's sales personnel sell the firm's products to wholesalers, retailers, and industrial buyers; they thus perform many of the same activities as a wholesaler's representatives. As in wholesaling, educational requirements for a sales position depend largely on the type and complexity of the products and markets. Manufacturers of nontechnical products usually hire college graduates who have a liberal arts or business degree and train them so they become knowledgeable about the firm's products, prices, and customers. Manufacturers of highly technical products generally prefer applicants who have degrees in fields associated with the particular industry and market.

Sales positions in manufacturing are expected to increase at an average rate. Manufacturers' sales personnel are well compensated and earn above-average salaries; most are paid a combination of salary and commission. Commissions vary according to the salesperson's efforts, abilities, and sales territory, as well as the type of products sold. Annual salary and/or commission for sales positions range from $63,511 to $78,348 for a sales manager and $30,000 to $52,000 for a field salesperson. A sales trainee would start at about $35,500 in business sales positions.[7]

Industrial Buying

Industrial buyers, or purchasing agents, are responsible for maintaining an adequate supply of the goods and services an organization requires for its operations. In general, industrial buyers purchase all items needed for direct use in producing other products and for use in day-to-day operations. Industrial buyers in large firms often specialize in purchasing a single, specific class of products—for example, all petroleum-based lubricants. In smaller organizations, buyers may be responsible for many different categories of purchases, including raw materials, component parts, office supplies, and operating services.

An industrial buyer's main job is to select suppliers that offer the best quality, service, and price. When the products to be purchased are standardized, buyers may base their purchasing decisions on suppliers' descriptions of their offerings online and in catalogs and trade journals. Buyers who purchase highly homogeneous products often meet with salespeople to examine samples and observe demonstrations. Sometimes buyers must inspect the actual product before purchasing it; in other cases, they invite suppliers to bid on large orders. Buyers who purchase equipment made to specifications often deal directly with manufacturers. After choosing a supplier and placing an order, an industrial buyer usually must trace the shipment to ensure on-time delivery. Sometimes the buyer is also responsible for receiving and inspecting an order and authorizing payment to the shipper.

Training requirements for a career in industrial buying relate to the needs of the firm and the types of products purchased. A manufacturer of heavy machinery may prefer an applicant who has a background in engineering. A service company, on the other hand, may recruit liberal arts majors. Although not generally required, a college degree is becoming increasingly important for industrial buyers who wish to advance to management positions.

Employment prospects for industrial buyers are expected to increase faster than average. Opportunities will be excellent for individuals with master's degrees in business administration or bachelor's degrees in engineering, science, or business administration. Companies that manufacture heavy equipment, computer equipment, and communications equipment will need buyers with technical backgrounds.

Public Relations

Public relations encompasses a broad set of communication activities designed to create and maintain favorable relationships between an organization and its stakeholders—customers, employees, stockholders, government officials, and society in general. Public relations specialists help clients create the image, issue, or message they wish to present and communicate it to the appropriate audience. According to the Public Relations Society of America, about 120,000 people work in public relations in the United States. Half the billings of the nation's 4,000 public relations agencies and firms come from Chicago and New York. The highest starting salaries are also found there. Communication is basic to all public relations programs. To communicate effectively, public relations practitioners must first gather data about the firm's stakeholders to assess their needs, identify problems, formulate recommendations, implement new plans, and evaluate current activities.

Public relations personnel disseminate large amounts of information to the organization's stakeholders. Written communication is the most versatile tool of public relations; thus, good writing skills are essential. Public relations practitioners must be adept at writing for a variety of media and audiences. It is not unusual for a person in public relations to prepare reports, news releases, speeches, broadcast scripts, technical manuals, employee publications, shareholder reports, and other communications aimed at both organizational personnel and external groups. In addition, a public relations practitioner needs a thorough knowledge of the production techniques used in preparing various communications. Public relations personnel also establish distribution channels for the organization's publicity. They must have a thorough understanding of the various media, their areas of specialization, the characteristics of their target audiences, and their policies regarding publicity. Anyone who hopes to succeed in public relations must develop close working relationships with numerous media personnel to enlist their interest in disseminating clients' communications.

A college education combined with writing or media-related experience is the best preparation for a career in public relations. Most beginners have a college degree in journalism, communications, or public relations, but some employers prefer a business background. Courses in journalism, business administration, marketing, creative writing, psychology, sociology, political science, economics, advertising, English, and public speaking are recommended. Some employers ask applicants to present a portfolio of published articles, scripts written for television or radio programs, slide presentations, and other work samples. Other agencies require written tests that include such tasks as writing sample press releases. Manufacturing firms, public utilities, transportation and insurance companies, and trade and professional associations are the largest employers of public relations personnel. In addition, sizable numbers of public relations personnel work for health-related organizations, government agencies, educational institutions, museums, and religious and service groups.

Although some larger companies provide extensive formal training for new personnel, most new public relations employees learn on the job. Beginners usually perform routine tasks such as maintaining files about company activities and searching secondary data sources for information to be used in publicity materials. More experienced employees write press releases, speeches, and articles, and help plan public relations campaigns.

Employment opportunities in public relations are expected to increase faster than the average for all occupations. One caveat is in order, however: competition for beginning jobs is keen. The prospects are best for applicants who have solid academic preparation and some media experience. Abilities that differentiate candidates, such as an understanding of information technology, are becoming increasingly important. Public relations account executives earn $30,000 to $45,000. Public relations agency managers earn in the $51,460 to $62,874 range.[8]

Distribution Management

A distribution manager arranges for transportation of goods within firms and through marketing channels. Transportation is an essential distribution activity that permits a firm to create time and place utility for its products. It is the distribution manager's job to analyze various transportation modes and select the combination that minimizes cost and transit time while providing acceptable levels of reliability, capability, accessibility, and security.

To accomplish this task, a distribution manager performs many activities. First, the individual must choose one, or a combination of transportation modes, from the five major modes available: railroads, trucks, waterways, airways, and pipelines. The distribution manager must then select the specific routes the goods will travel and the particular carriers to be used, weighing such factors as freight classifications and regulations, freight charges, time schedules, shipment sizes, and loss and damage ratios. In addition, this person may be responsible for preparing shipping documents, tracing shipments, handling loss and damage claims, keeping records of freight rates, and monitoring changes in government regulations and transportation technology.

Distribution management employs relatively few people and is expected to grow about as fast as the average for all occupations in the near future. Manufacturing firms are the largest employers of distribution managers, although some distribution managers work for wholesalers, retail stores, and consulting firms. Salaries of experienced distribution managers vary but generally are much higher than the average for all nonsupervisory personnel. Entry-level positions are diverse, ranging from inventory control and traffic scheduling to operations or distribution management. Inventory management is an area of great opportunity because of increasing global competition. While salaries in the distribution field vary depending on the position and information technology skill requirements, entry salaries start at about $40,000.[9]

Most employers of distribution managers prefer to hire graduates of technical programs or people who have completed courses in transportation, logistics, distribution management, economics, statistics, computer science, management, marketing, and commercial law. A successful distribution manager is adept at handling technical data and is able to interpret and communicate highly technical information.

Product Management

The product manager occupies a staff position and is responsible for the success or failure of a product line. Product managers coordinate most of the activities required to market a product. However, because they hold a staff position, they have relatively little actual authority over marketing personnel. Nevertheless, they take on a large amount of responsibility and typically are paid quite well relative to other marketing employees. Being a product manager can be rewarding both financially and psychologically, but it can also be frustrating because of the disparity between responsibility and authority.

A product manager should have a general knowledge of advertising, transportation modes, inventory control, selling and sales management, sales promotion, marketing research, packaging, pricing, and warehousing. The individual must be knowledgeable enough to communicate effectively with personnel in these functional areas and help assess alternatives when major decisions are being made.

Product managers usually need college training in an area of business administration. A master's degree is helpful, although a person usually does not become a product manager directly out of school. Frequently, several years of selling and sales management experience are prerequisites for a product management position, which is often a major step in the career path of top-level marketing executives. Product managers can earn $60,000 to $120,000, while an assistant product manager starts at about $40,000.[10]

Advertising

Advertising pervades our daily lives. Business and nonbusiness organizations use advertising in many ways and for many reasons. Advertising clearly needs individuals with diverse skills to fill a variety of jobs. Creativity, imagination, artistic talent, and expertise in expression and persuasion are important for copywriters, artists, and account executives. Sales and managerial abilities are vital to the success of advertising managers, media buyers, and production managers. Research directors must have a solid understanding of research techniques and human behavior. A related occupation is an advertising salesperson, who sells newspaper, television, radio, or magazine advertising to advertisers.

Advertising professionals disagree on the most beneficial educational background for a career in advertising. Most employers prefer college graduates. Some employers seek individuals with degrees in advertising, journalism, or business; others prefer graduates with broad liberal arts backgrounds. Still other employers rank relevant work experience above educational background.

"Advertisers look for generalists," says a staff executive of the American Association of Advertising Agencies. "Thus, there are just as many economics or general liberal arts majors as MBAs." Common entry-level positions in an advertising agency are found in the traffic department, account service (account coordinator), or the media department (media assistant). Starting salaries in these positions are often quite low, but to gain experience in the advertising industry, employees must work their way up in the system. Assistant account executives start at $25,000, while a typical account executive earns $30,000 to $50,000. Copywriters earn $30,000 to $50,000 a year.[11]

A variety of organizations employ advertising personnel. Although advertising agencies are perhaps the most visible and glamorous employers, many manufacturing firms, retail stores, banks, utility companies, and professional and trade associations maintain advertising departments. Advertising jobs are also available with television and radio stations, newspapers, and magazines. Other businesses that employ advertising personnel include printers, art studios, letter shops, and package design firms. Specific advertising jobs include advertising manager, account executive, research director, copywriter, media specialist, and production manager. About 59 percent of advertising employees are between 25 and 44 years of age compared to 51 percent of all workers in the U.S. economy.

Retail Management

Although a career in retailing may begin in sales, there is more to retailing than simply selling. Many retail personnel occupy management positions. Besides managing the sales force, they focus on selecting and ordering merchandise, promotional activities, inventory control, customer credit operations, accounting, personnel, and store security.

Organization of retail stores varies. In many large department stores, retail management personnel rarely engage in actual selling to customers; these duties are performed by retail salespeople. Other types of retail organizations may require management personnel to perform selling activities from time to time.

Large retail stores offer a variety of management positions, including assistant buyers, buyers, department managers, section managers, store managers, division managers, regional managers, and vice president of merchandising. The following list describes the general duties of four of these positions; the precise nature of their duties may vary from one retail organization to another.

A section manager coordinates inventory and promotions and interacts with buyers, salespeople, and ultimate consumers. The manager performs merchandising, labor relations, and managerial activities, and usually works more than a 40-hour workweek.

The buyer's task is more focused. This fast-paced occupation involves much travel and pressure, and the need to be open-minded with respect to new, potentially successful items.

The regional manager coordinates the activities of several stores within a given area, usually monitoring and supporting sales, promotions, and general procedures.

The vice president of merchandising has a broad scope of managerial responsibility and reports to the organization's president.

Most retail organizations hire college graduates, put them through management training programs, and then place them directly in management positions. They frequently hire candidates with backgrounds in liberal arts or business administration. Sales positions and retail management positions offer the greatest employment opportunities for marketing students.

Retail management positions can be exciting and challenging. Competent, ambitious individuals often assume a great deal of responsibility very quickly and advance rapidly. However, a retail manager's job is physically demanding and sometimes entails long working hours. In addition, managers employed by large chain stores may be required to move frequently during their early years with the company. Nonetheless, positions in retail management often offer the chance to excel and gain promotion. Growth in retailing, which is expected to accompany the growth in population, is likely to create substantial opportunities during the next ten years. While a trainee may start in the $30,000 to $47,250 range, a store manager can earn from $50,000 to $200,000 depending on the size of the store.[12]

Direct Marketing

One of the more dynamic areas in marketing is direct marketing, in which the seller uses one or more direct media (telephone, online, mail, print, or television) to solicit a response. The telephone is a major vehicle for selling many consumer products. Telemarketing is direct selling to customers using a variety of technological improvements in telecommunications. Direct-mail catalogs appeal to such market segments as working women and people who find going to retail stores difficult or inconvenient. Newspapers and magazines offer great opportunity, particularly in special market segments. *Golf Digest,* for instance, is obviously a good medium for selling golfing equipment. Cable television provides many opportunities for selling directly to consumers. Home shopping channels, for instance, have been very successful. The Internet offers numerous direct marketing opportunities.

The most important asset in direct marketing is experience. Employers often look to other industries to locate experienced professionals. This preference means that if you can get an entry-level position in direct marketing, you will have an advantage in developing a career.

Jobs in direct marketing include buyers, such as department store buyers, who select goods for catalog, telephone, or direct-mail sales. Catalog managers develop marketing strategies for each new catalog that goes into the mail. Research/mail list management involves developing lists of products that will sell in direct marketing and lists of names of consumers who are likely to respond to a direct-mail effort. Order fulfillment managers direct the shipment of products once they are sold. The effectiveness of direct marketing is enhanced by periodic analysis of advertising and communications at all phases of contact with the consumer. Direct marketing involves all aspects of marketing decision making. Most positions in direct marketing involve planning and market analysis. Some direct marketing jobs involve the use of databases that include customer information, sales history, and other tracking data. A database manager might receive a salary of $53,750 to $88,750. A telemarketing director in business-to-business sales could receive a salary of about $35,000.[13]

E-Marketing and Customer Relationship Management

Today, only about 1.5 percent of all retail sales are conducted on the Internet.[14] Currently, approximately one-half of all businesses order online. One characteristic of firms engaged in e-marketing is a renewed focus on relationship marketing by building customer loyalty and retaining customers—in other words, on customer relationship management (CRM). This focus on CRM is possible because of e-marketers' ability to target individual customers. This effort is enhanced over time as the customer invests more time and effort in "teaching" the firms what he or she wants.

Opportunities abound to combine information technology expertise with marketing knowledge. By providing an integrated communication system of websites, fax, telephone, and personal contacts, marketers can personalize customer relationships. Careers exist for individuals who can integrate the Internet as a touch point with customers as part of effective customer relationship management. Many Internet-only companies ("dot-coms") failed because they focused too heavily on brand awareness and did not understand the importance of an integrated marketing strategy.

The use of laptops, cellular phones, e-mail, voice mail, and other devices is necessary to maintain customer relationships and allow purchases on the Internet. A variety of jobs exist for marketers who have integrated technology into their work and job skills. Job titles include e-marketing manager, customer relationship manager, and e-services manager, as well as jobs in dot-coms.

Salaries in this rapidly growing area depend on technical expertise and experience. For example, a CRM customer service manager receives a salary in the $40,000 to $45,000 range. Database administrators earn salaries of approximately $70,500 to $90,000. With five years of experience in e-marketing, individuals responsible for online product offerings can earn from $50,000 to $85,000.

appendix b

Our discussion in this book focuses more on fundamental concepts and decisions in marketing than on financial details. However, marketers must understand the basic components of financial analyses to be able to explain and defend their decisions. In fact, they must be familiar with certain financial analyses to reach good decisions in the first place. To control and evaluate marketing activities, they must understand the income statement and what it says about their organization's operations. They also need to be familiar with performance ratios, which compare current operating results with past results and with results in the industry at large. We examine the income statement and some performance ratios in the first part of this appendix. In the second part, we discuss price calculations as the basis for price adjustments. Marketers are likely to use all these areas of financial analysis at various times to support their decisions and make necessary adjustments in their operations.

The Income Statement

The income, or operating, statement presents the financial results of an organization's operations over a certain period. The statement summarizes revenues earned and expenses incurred by a profit center, whether a department, a brand, a product line, a division, or the entire firm. The income statement presents the firm's net profit or net loss for a month, quarter, or year.

Table B.1 (on page A-18) is a simplified income statement for Stoneham Auto Supplies, a fictitious retail store. The owners, Rose Costa and Nick Schultz, see that net sales of $250,000 are decreased by the cost of goods sold and by other business expenses to yield a net income of $83,000. Of course, these figures are only highlights of the complete income statement, which appears in Table B.2 (on page A-19).

The income statement can be used in several ways to improve the management of a business. First, it enables an owner or a manager to compare actual results with budgets for various parts of the statement. For example, Rose and Nick see that the total amount of merchandise sold (gross sales) is $260,000. Customers returned merchandise or received allowances (price reductions) totaling $10,000. Suppose the budgeted amount was only $9,000. By checking the tickets for sales returns and allowances, the owners can determine why these events occurred and whether the $10,000 figure could be lowered by adjusting the marketing mix.

After subtracting returns and allowances from gross sales, Rose and Nick can determine net sales, the amount the firm has available to pay its expenses. They are pleased with this figure because it is higher than their sales target of $240,000.

A major expense for most companies that sell goods (as opposed to services) is the cost of goods sold. For Stoneham Auto Supplies, it amounts to 18 percent of net sales. Other expenses are treated in various ways by different companies. In our example, they are broken down into standard categories of selling expenses, administrative expenses, and general expenses.

The income statement shows that for Stoneham Auto Supplies, the cost of goods sold was $45,000. This figure was derived in the following way. First, the statement

*We gratefully acknowledge the assistance of Jim L. Grimm, Professor Emeritus, Illinois State University, in writing this appendix.

TABLE B.1 Simplified Income Statement for a Retailer

Stoneham Auto Supplies Income Statement for the Year Ended December 31, 2010	
Net sales	$250,000
Cost of goods sold	45,000
Gross margin	$205,000
Expenses	122,000
Net income	$83,000

shows that merchandise in the amount of $51,000 was purchased during the year. In paying the invoices associated with these inventory additions, purchase (cash) discounts of $4,000 were earned, resulting in net purchases of $47,000. Special requests for selected merchandise throughout the year resulted in $2,000 in freight charges, which increased the net cost of delivered purchases to $49,000. When this amount is added to the beginning inventory of $48,000, the cost of goods available for sale during 2010 totals $97,000. However, the records indicate that the value of inventory at the end of the year was $52,000. Because this amount was not sold, the cost of goods that were sold during the year was $45,000.

Rose and Nick observe that the total value of their inventory increased by 8.3 percent during the year:

$$\frac{\$52,000 - \$48,000}{\$48,000} = \frac{\$4,000}{\$48,000} = \frac{1}{12} = 0.08333, \text{ or } 8.33\%$$

Further analysis is needed to determine whether this increase is desirable or undesirable. (Note that the income statement provides no details concerning the composition of the inventory held on December 31; other records supply this information.) If Nick and Rose determine that inventory on December 31 is excessive, they can implement appropriate marketing action.

Gross margin is the difference between net sales and cost of goods sold. Gross margin reflects the markup on products and is the amount available to pay all other expenses and provide a return to the owners. Stoneham Auto Supplies had a gross margin of $205,000:

Net Sales	$250,000
Cost of Goods Sold	45,000
Gross Margin	205,000

Stoneham's expenses (other than cost of goods sold) during 2010 totaled $122,000. Observe that $53,000, or slightly more than 43 percent of the total, constituted direct selling expenses:

$$\frac{\$53,000 \text{ } selling \text{ expenses}}{\$122,000 \text{ } total \text{ expenses}} = 0.434, \text{ or } 43\%$$

The business employs three salespeople (one full time) and pays competitive wages. The selling expenses are similar to those in the previous year, but Nick and Rose wonder whether more advertising is necessary because the value of inventory increased by more than 8 percent during the year.

The administrative and general expenses are essential for operating the business. A comparison of these expenses with trade statistics for similar businesses indicates that the figures are in line with industry amounts.

Net income, or net profit, is the amount of gross margin remaining after deducting expenses. Stoneham Auto Supplies earned a net profit of $83,000 for the fiscal year ending December 31, 2010. Note that net income on this statement is figured before payment of state and federal income taxes.

TABLE B.2 Income Statement for a Retailer

Stoneham Auto Supplies Income Statement for the Year Ended December 31, 2010			
Gross Sales			$260,000
Less: Sales returns and allowances			10,000
Net Sales			$250,000
Cost of Goods Sold			
Inventory, January 1, 2010 (at cost)		$48,000	
Purchases	$51,000		
Less: Purchase discounts	4,000		
Net purchases	$47,000		
Plus: Freight-in	2,000		
Net cost of delivered purchases		$49,000	
Cost of goods available for sale		$97,000	
Less: Inventory, December 31, 2010		$52,000	
Cost of goods sold			$ 45,000
Gross Margin			$205,000
Expenses			
Selling expenses			
Sales salaries and commissions	$32,000		
Advertising	16,000		
Sales promotions	3,000		
Delivery	2,000		
Total selling expenses		$53,000	
Administrative expenses			
Administrative salaries	$20,000		
Office salaries	20,000		
Office supplies	2,000		
Miscellaneous	1,000		
Total administrative expenses		$43,000	
General expenses			
Rent	$14,000		
Utilities	7,000		
Bad debts	1,000		
Miscellaneous	4,000		
(local taxes, insurance, interest, depreciation)			
Total general expenses		$26,000	
Total expenses			$122,000
Net Income			$ 83,000

TABLE B.3 Cost of Goods Sold for a Manufacturer

ABC Manufacturing Income Statement for the Year Ended December 31, 2010			
Cost of Goods Sold			
Finished Goods Inventory January 1, 2010			**$ 50,000**
Cost of Goods Manufactured			
Work-in-process inventory, January 1, 2010		$ 20,000	
Raw materials inventory, January 1, 2010	$ 40,000		
Net cost of delivered purchases	$240,000		
Cost of goods available for use	$280,000		
Less: Raw materials inventory, December 31, 2010	$ 42,000		
Cost of goods placed in production		$238,000	
Direct labor		32,000	
Manufacturing overhead			
Indirect labor	$ 12,000		
Supervisory salaries	10,000		
Operating supplies	6,000		
Depreciation	12,000		
Utilities	$ 10,000		
Total manufacturing overhead		$ 50,000	
Total manufacturing costs		$320,000	
Total work-in-process		$340,000	
Less: Work-in-process inventory, December 31, 2010		$ 22,000	
Cost of goods manufactured			$318,000
Cost of Goods Available for Sale			**$368,000**
Less: Finished goods inventory, December 31, 2010			48,000
Cost of Goods Sold			**$320,000**

Income statements for intermediaries and for businesses that provide services follow the same general format as that shown for Stoneham Auto Supplies in Table B.2. The income statement for a manufacturer, however, differs somewhat in that the "purchases" portion is replaced by "cost of goods manufactured." Table B.3 shows the entire Cost of Goods Sold section for a manufacturer, including cost of goods manufactured. In other respects, income statements for retailers and manufacturers are similar.

Performance Ratios

Rose and Nick's assessment of how well their business did during fiscal year 2010 can be improved through the use of analytical ratios. Such ratios enable a manager to compare the results for the current year with data from previous years and industry statistics. However, comparisons of the current income statement with income statements and industry statistics from other years are not very meaningful because factors like inflation are not accounted for when comparing dollar amounts. More useful comparisons can be made by converting these figures to a percentage of net sales, as this section shows.

The first analytical ratios we discuss, the operating ratios, are based on the net sales figure from the income statement.

Operating Ratios

Operating ratios express items on the income, or operating, statement as percentages of net sales. The first step is to convert the income statement into percentages of net sales, as illustrated in Table B.4. After making this conversion, the manager looks at several key operating ratios: two profitability ratios (the gross margin ratio and the net income ratio) and the operating expense ratio.

For Stoneham Auto Supplies, these ratios are determined as follows (see Tables B.2 and B.4 for supporting data):

$$\text{gross margin ratio} = \frac{gross\ margin}{net\ sales} = \frac{\$205,000}{\$250,000} = 82\%$$

$$\text{net income ratio} = \frac{net\ income}{net\ sales} = \frac{\$83,000}{\$250,000} = 33.2\%$$

$$\text{operating expense ratio} = \frac{total\ expenses}{net\ sales} = \frac{\$122,000}{\$250,000} = 48.8\%$$

The gross margin ratio indicates the percentage of each sales dollar available to cover operating expenses and achieve profit objectives. The net income ratio indicates the percentage of each sales dollar that is classified as earnings (profit) before payment of income taxes. The operating expense ratio calculates the percentage of each dollar needed to cover operating expenses.

If Nick and Rose believe the operating expense ratio is higher than historical data and industry standards, they can analyze each operating expense ratio in Table B.4 to determine which expenses are too high and then take corrective action. After reviewing several key operating ratios, Nick and Rose, like many managers, will probably want to analyze all the items on the income statement. By doing so, they can determine whether the 8 percent increase in the value of their inventory was necessary.

Inventory Turnover Rate

The inventory turnover rate, or stock-turn rate, is an analytical ratio that can be used to answer the question "Is the inventory level appropriate for this business?" The inventory turnover rate indicates the number of times an inventory is sold (turns over) during one year. To be useful, this figure must be compared with historical turnover rates and industry rates.

The inventory turnover rate is computed (based on cost) as follows:

$$\text{inventory turnover} = \frac{cost\ of\ goods\ sold}{average\ inventory\ at\ cost}$$

Rose and Nick would calculate the turnover rate from Table B.2 as follows:

$$\frac{cost\ of\ goods\ sold}{average\ inventory\ at\ cost} = \frac{\$45,000}{\$50,000} = 0.9$$

Their inventory turnover is less than once per year (0.9 times). Industry averages for competitive firms are 2.8 times. This figure convinces Rose and Nick that their investment in inventory is too large and they need to reduce their inventory.

Return on Investment

Return on investment (ROI) is a ratio that indicates management's efficiency in generating sales and profits from the total amount invested in the firm. For Stoneham Auto Supplies, the ROI is 41.5 percent, which compares well with competing businesses.

TABLE B.4 Income Statement Components as Percentage of Net Sales

Stoneham Auto Supplies Income Statement as a Percentage of Net Sales for the Year Ended December 31, 2010			
			Percentage of Net Sales
Gross Sales			103.8%
Less: Sales returns and allowances			3.8
Net Sales			100.0%
Cost of Goods Sold			
Inventory, January 1, 2010 (at cost)		19.2%	
Purchases	20.4%		
Less: Purchase discounts	1.6		
Net purchases	18.8%		
Plus: Freight-in	0.8		
Net cost of delivered purchases		19.6	
Cost of goods available for sale		38.8%	
Less: Inventory, December 31, 2010 (at cost)		20.8	
Cost of goods sold			18.0
Gross Margin			82.0%
Expenses			
Selling expenses			
Sales salaries and commissions	12.8%		
Advertising	6.4		
Sales promotions	1.2		
Delivery	0.8		
Total selling expenses		21.2%	
Administrative expenses			
Administrative salaries	8.0%		
Office salaries	8.0		
Office supplies	0.8		
Miscellaneous	0.4		
Total administrative expenses		17.2%	
General expenses			
Rent	5.6%		
Utilities	2.8		
Bad debts	0.4		
Miscellaneous	1.6		
Total general expenses		10.4%	
Total expenses			48.8
Net Income			33.2%

We use figures from two different financial statements to arrive at ROI. The income statement, already discussed, gives us net income. The balance sheet, which states the firm's assets and liabilities at a given point in time, provides the figure for total assets (or investment) in the firm.

The basic formula for ROI is

$$ROI = \frac{net\ income}{total\ investment}$$

For Stoneham Auto Supplies, net income is $83,000 (see Table B.2). If total investment (taken from the balance sheet for December 31, 2010) is $200,000, then

$$ROI = \frac{\$83,000}{\$200,000} = 0.415,\ or\ 41.5\%$$

The ROI formula can be expanded to isolate the impact of capital turnover and the operating income ratio separately. Capital turnover is a measure of net sales per dollar of investment; the ratio is figured by dividing net sales by total investment. For Stoneham Auto Supplies,

$$capital\ turnover = \frac{net\ sales}{total\ investment} = \frac{\$250,000}{\$200,000} = 1.25$$

ROI is equal to capital turnover times the net income ratio. The expanded formula for Stoneham Auto Supplies is

$$ROI = \frac{net\ sales}{total\ investment} \times \frac{net\ income}{net\ sales}$$
$$= \frac{\$250,000}{\$200,000} \times \frac{\$83,000}{\$250,000}$$
$$= (1.25)(33.2\%) = 41.5\%$$

Price Calculations

An important step in setting prices is selecting a basis for pricing, as discussed in Chapter 21. The systematic use of markups, markdowns, and various conversion formulas helps in calculating the selling price and evaluating the effects of various prices.

Markups

As discussed in the text, markup is the difference between the selling price and the cost of the item; that is, selling price equals cost plus markup. The markup must cover cost and contribute to profit; thus, markup is similar to gross margin on the income statement.

Markup can be calculated on either cost or selling price as follows:

$$markup\ as\ percentage\ of\ cost = \frac{amount\ added\ to\ cost}{cost} = \frac{dollar\ markup}{cost}$$

$$markup\ as\ percentage\ of\ selling\ price = \frac{amount\ added\ to\ cost}{selling\ price} = \frac{dollar\ markup}{selling\ price}$$

Retailers tend to calculate the markup percentage on selling price.

To review the use of these markup formulas, assume an item costs $10 and the markup is $5:

$$selling\ price = cost + markup$$
$$\$15 = \$10 + \$5$$

Thus,

$$\text{markup percentage on cost} = \frac{\$5}{\$10} = 50\%$$

$$\text{markup percentage on selling price} = \frac{\$5}{\$15} = 33\frac{1}{3}\%$$

It is necessary to know the base (cost or selling price) to use markup pricing effectively. Markup percentage on cost will always exceed markup percentage on price, given the same dollar markup, as long as selling price exceeds cost.

On occasion, we may need to convert markup on cost to markup on selling price, or vice versa. The conversion formulas are as follows:

$$\text{markup percentage on selling price} = \frac{\textit{markup percentage on cost}}{100\% + \textit{markup percentage on cost}}$$

$$\text{markup percentage on cost} = \frac{\textit{markup percentage on selling price}}{100\% - \textit{markup percentage on selling price}}$$

For instance, if the markup percentage on cost is $33\frac{1}{3}$ percent, the markup percentage on selling price is

$$\frac{33\frac{1}{3}\%}{100\% + 33\frac{1}{3}\%} = \frac{33\frac{1}{3}\%}{1.33\frac{1}{3}\%} = 25\%$$

If the markup percentage on selling price is 40 percent, the corresponding percentage on cost is as follows:

$$\frac{40\%}{100\% - 40\%} = \frac{40\%}{60\%} = 66\frac{2}{3}\%$$

Finally, we can show how to determine selling price if we know the cost of the item and the markup percentage on selling price. Assume an item costs $36 and the usual markup percentage on selling price is 40 percent. Remember that selling price equals markup plus cost. Thus, if

$$100\% = 40\% \text{ of selling price} + \text{cost}$$

then,

$$60\% \text{ of selling price} = \text{cost}$$

In our example, cost equals $36. Therefore,

$$0.6X = \$36$$

$$X = \frac{\$36}{0.6}$$

$$\text{selling price} = \$60$$

Alternatively, the markup percentage could be converted to a cost basis as follows:

$$\frac{40\%}{100\% - 40\%} = \frac{40\%}{60\%} = 66\frac{2}{3}\%$$

The selling price would then be computed as follows:

$$\text{selling price} = 66\frac{2}{3}\%(\text{cost}) + \text{cost}$$
$$= 66\frac{2}{3}\%(\$36) + \$36$$
$$= \$24 + \$36 = \$60$$

If you keep in mind the basic formula—selling price equals cost plus markup—you will find these calculations straightforward.

Markdowns

Markdowns are price reductions a retailer makes on merchandise. Markdowns may be useful on items that are damaged, priced too high, or selected for a special sales event.

The income statement does not express markdowns directly because the change in price is made before the sale takes place. Therefore, separate records of markdowns would be needed to evaluate the performance of various buyers and departments.

The markdown ratio (percentage) is calculated as follows:

$$\text{markdown percentage} = \frac{\textit{dollar markdowns}}{\textit{net sales in dollars}}$$

In analyzing their inventory, Nick and Rose discover three special automobile jacks that have gone unsold for several months. They decide to reduce the price of each item from \$25 to \$20. Subsequently, these items are sold. The markdown percentage for these three items is

$$\text{markdown percentage} = \frac{3(\$5)}{3(\$20)} = \frac{\$15}{\$60} = 25\%$$

Net sales, however, include all units of this product sold during the period, not just those marked down. If ten of these items were already sold at \$25 each, in addition to the three items sold at \$20, the overall markdown percentage would be

$$\text{markdown percentage} = \frac{3(\$5)}{10(\$25) + 3(\$20)}$$

$$= \frac{\$15}{\$250 + \$60} = \frac{\$15}{\$310} = 4.8\%$$

Discussion and Review Questions

1. How does a manufacturer's income statement differ from a retailer's income statement?
2. Use the following information to answer parts a, b, and c:

Tea Company

Fiscal Year Ended June 30, 2011	
Net sales	\$500,000
Cost of goods sold	300,000
Net income	50,000
Average inventory at cost	100,000
Total assets (total investment)	200,000

    a. What is the inventory turnover rate for Tea Company? From what sources will the marketing manager determine the significance of the inventory turnover rate?

    b. What is the capital turnover ratio? What is the net income ratio? What is the return on investment (ROI)?

    c. How many dollars of sales did each dollar of investment produce for Tea Company?

3. Product A has a markup percentage on cost of 40 percent. What is the markup percentage on selling price?
4. Product B has a markup percentage on selling price of 30 percent. What is the markup percentage on cost?
5. Product C has a cost of \$60 and a usual markup percentage of 25 percent on selling price. What price should be placed on this item?
6. Apex Appliance Company sells 20 units of product Q for \$100 each and 10 units for \$80 each. What is the markdown percentage for product Q?

appendix c

This sample marketing plan for a hypothetical company illustrates how the marketing planning process described in Chapter 2 might be implemented. If you are asked to create a marketing plan, this model may be a helpful guide, along with the concepts in Chapter 2.

Star Software Inc., Marketing Plan

❶ The Executive Summary, one of the most frequently read components of a marketing plan, is a synopsis of the marketing plan. Although it does not provide detailed information, it does present an overview of the plan so readers can identify key issues pertaining to their roles in the planning and implementation processes. Although this is the first section in a marketing plan, it is usually written last.

❶ I. Executive Summary

Star Software, Inc. is a small, family-owned corporation in the first year of a transition from first-generation to second-generation leadership. Star Software sells custom-made calendar programs and related items to about 400 businesses, which use the software mainly for promotion. As Star's business is highly seasonal, its 18 employees face scheduling challenges, with greatest demand during October, November, and December. In other months, the equipment and staff are sometimes idle. A major challenge facing Star Software is how to increase profits and make better use of its resources during the off-season.

An evaluation of the company's internal strengths and weaknesses and external opportunities and threats served as the foundation for this strategic analysis and marketing plan. The plan focuses on the company's growth strategy, suggesting ways it can build on existing customer relationships, and on the development of new products and/or services targeted to specific customer niches. Since Star Software markets a product used primarily as a promotional tool by its clients, it is currently considered a business-to-business marketer.

❷ The Environmental Analysis presents information regarding the organization's current situation with respect to the marketing environment, the current target market(s), and the firm's current marketing objectives and performance.

❷ II. Environmental Analysis

Founded as a commercial printing company, Star Software, Inc., has evolved into a marketer of high-quality, custom-made calendar software and related business-to-business specialty items. In the mid-1960s, Bob McLemore purchased the company and, through his full-time commitment, turned it into a very successful family-run operation. In the near future, McLemore's 37-year-old son, Jonathan, will take over as Star Software's president and allow the elder McLemore to scale back his involvement.

A. The Marketing Environment

❸ This section of the environmental analysis considers relevant **external environmental forces**, such as competitive, economic, political, legal and regulatory, technological, and sociocultural forces.

❸ 1. *Competitive forces.* The competition in the specialty advertising industry is very strong on a local and regional basis, but somewhat weak nationally. Sales figures for the industry as a whole are difficult to obtain since very little business is conducted on a national scale.

    The competition within the calendar industry is strong in the paper segment and weak in the software-based segment. Currently, paper calendars hold a dominant market share of approximately 65 percent; however, the software-based segment is growing rapidly. The 35 percent market share held by software-based calendars is divided among many different firms. Star Software, which holds 30 percent of the software-based calendar market, is the only company that markets a software-based calendar on a national basis. As software-based calendars become more popular, additional competition is expected to enter the market.

2. *Economic forces.* Nationwide, many companies have reduced their overall promotion budgets as they face the need to cut expenses. However, most of these reductions have occurred in the budgets for mass media advertising (television, magazines, and newspapers). While overall promotion budgets are shrinking, many companies are diverting a larger percentage of their budgets to sales promotion and specialty advertising. This trend is expected to continue as a weak, slow-growth economy forces most companies to focus more on the "value" they receive from their promotion dollars. Specialty advertising, such as can be done with a software-based calendar, provides this value.

3. *Political forces.* There are no expected political influences or events that could affect the operations of Star Software.

4. *Legal and regulatory forces.* In recent years, more attention has been paid to "junk mail." A large percentage of specialty advertising products are distributed by mail, and some of these products are considered "junk." Although this label is attached to the type of products Star Software makes, the problem of junk mail falls on Star's clients and not on the company itself. While legislation may be introduced to curb the tide of advertising delivered through the mail, the fact that more companies are diverting their promotion dollars to specialty advertising indicates that most do not fear the potential for increased legislation.

5. *Technological forces.* A major emerging technological trend involves personal digital assistants (PDAs). A PDA is a handheld device, similar in size to a large calculator, that can store a wide variety of information, including personal notes, addresses, and a calendar. Some PDAs, such as the BlackBerry, can be loaded with a cell phone and walkie-talkie. The user can e-mail and schedule on the electronic calendar. As this trend continues, current software-based calendar products may have to be adapted to match the new technology.

6. *Sociocultural forces.* In today's society, consumers have less time for work or leisure. The hallmarks of today's successful products are convenience and ease of use. In short, if the product does not save time and is not easy to use, consumers will simply ignore it. Software-based calendars fit this consumer need quite well. A software-based calendar also fits in with other societal trends: a move away from paper and hard copies, the need to automate repetitive tasks, and the growing dependence on information technology, for example.

4 The analysis of current target markets assesses demographic, geographic, psychographic, and product usage characteristics of the target markets. It also assesses the current needs of each of the firm's target markets, anticipated changes in those needs, and how well the organization's current products are meeting those needs.

4 B. Target Market(s)

By focusing on commitment to service and quality, Star Software has effectively implemented a niche differentiation strategy in a somewhat diverse marketplace. Its ability to differentiate its product has contributed to superior annual returns. Its target market consists of manufacturers or manufacturing divisions of large corporations that move their products through dealers, distributors, or brokers. Its most profitable product is a software program for a PC-based calendar, which can be tailored to meet client needs by means of artwork, logos, and text. Clients use this calendar software as a promotional tool, providing a disk to their customers as an advertising premium. The calendar software is not produced for resale.

The calendar software began as an ancillary product to Star's commercial printing business. However, due to the proliferation of PCs and the growth in technology, the computer calendar soon became more profitable for Star than its wall and desktop paper calendars. This led to the sale of the commercial printing plant and equipment to employees. Star Software has maintained a long-term relationship with these former employees, who have added capabilities to reproduce computer disks and whose company serves as Star's primary supplier of finished goods. Star's staff focuses on further development and marketing of the software.

C. Current Marketing Objectives and Performance

Star Software's sales representatives call on potential clients and, using a template demonstration disk, help them create a calendar concept. Once the sale has been finalized, Star completes the concept, including design, copywriting, and customization of the demonstration disk. Specifications are then sent to the supplier, located about 1,000 miles away, where the disks are produced. Perhaps what most differentiates Star from its competitors is its high level of service. Disks can be shipped to any location the buyer specifies. Since product development and customization of this type can require significant amounts of time and effort, particularly during the product's first year, Star deliberately pursues a strategy of steady, managed growth. Star Software markets its products on a company-specific basis. It has an annual reorder rate of approximately 90 percent and an average customer-reorder relationship of about eight years. The first year in dealing with a new customer is the most stressful and time-consuming for Star's salespeople and product developers. Subsequent years are faster and significantly more profitable.

A company must set marketing objectives, measure performance against those objectives, and then take corrective action if needed.

The company is currently debt free except for the mortgage on its facility. However, about 80 percent of its accounts receivable are billed during the last three months of the calendar year. Seasonal account billings, along with the added travel of Star's sales staff during the peak season, pose a special challenge to the company. The need for cash to fund operations in the meantime requires the company to borrow significant amounts of money to cover the period until customer billing occurs. Star Software's marketing objectives include increases in both revenues and profits of approximately 10 percent over the previous year. Revenues should exceed $4 million, and profits are expected to reach $1.3 million.

III. SWOT Analysis

5 Strengths are competitive advantages or core competencies that give the organization an advantage in meeting the needs of its customers.

5 ## A. Strengths

1. Star Software's product differentiation strategy is the result of a strong market orientation, commitment to high quality, and customization of products and support services.
2. There is little turnover among employees, who are well compensated and liked by customers. The relatively small staff size promotes camaraderie with coworkers and clients, and fosters communication and quick response to clients' needs.
3. A long-term relationship with the primary supplier has resulted in shared knowledge of the product's requirements, adherence to quality standards, and a common vision throughout the development and production process.
4. The high percentage of reorder business suggests a satisfied customer base, as well as positive word-of-mouth communication, which generates some 30 percent of new business each year.

6 Weaknesses are limitations a firm has in developing or implementing a marketing strategy.

6 ## B. Weaknesses

1. The highly centralized management hierarchy (the McLemores) and the lack of managerial backup may impede creativity and growth. Too few people hold too much knowledge.
2. Despite the successful, long-term relationship with the supplier, single sourcing could make Star Software vulnerable in the event of a natural disaster, strike, or dissolution of the current supplier. Contingency plans for suppliers should be considered.

3. The seasonal nature of the product line creates bottlenecks in productivity and cash flow, places excessive stress on personnel, and strains the facilities.

4. Both the product line and the client base lack diversification. Dependence on current reorder rates could breed complacency, invite competition, or create a false sense of customer satisfaction. The development of a product that would make the software calendar obsolete would probably put Star out of business.

5. While the small size of the staff fosters camaraderie, it also impedes growth and new-business development.

6. Star Software is reactive rather than assertive in its marketing efforts because of its heavy reliance on positive word-of-mouth communication for obtaining new business.

7. Star's current facilities are crowded. There is little room for additional employees or new equipment.

⑦ Opportunities are favorable conditions in the environment that could yield rewards for an organization if acted on properly.

⑦ C. Opportunities

1. Advertising expenditures in the United States exceed $132 billion annually. More than $25 billion of this is spent on direct-mail advertising and another $20 billion on specialty advertising. Star Software's potential for growth is significant in this market.

2. Technological advances have not only freed up time for Americans and brought greater efficiency but have also increased the amount of stress in their fast-paced lives. Personal computers have become commonplace, and personal information managers have gained popularity.

3. As U.S. companies look for ways to develop customer relationships rather than just close sales, reminders of this relationship could come in the form of acceptable premiums or gifts that are useful to the customer.

4. Computer-based calendars are easily distributed nationally and globally. The globalization of business creates an opportunity to establish new client relationships in foreign markets.

⑧ Threats are conditions or barriers that may prevent the organization from reaching its objectives..

⑧ D. Threats

1. Reengineering, right-sizing, and outsourcing trends in management may alter traditional channel relationships with brokers, dealers, and distributors, or eliminate them altogether.

2. Calendars are basically a generic product. The technology, knowledge, and equipment required to produce such an item, even a computer-based one, are minimal. The possible entry of new competitors is a significant threat.

3. Theft of trade secrets and software piracy through unauthorized copying are difficult to control.

4. Specialty advertising through promotional items relies on gadgetry and ideas that are new and different. As a result, product life cycles may be quite short.

5. Single-sourcing can be detrimental or even fatal to a company if the buyer–supplier relationship is damaged or if the supplying company has financial difficulty.

6. Competition from traditional paper calendars and other promotional items is strong.

⑨ During the development of a marketing plan, marketers attempt to match internal strengths to external opportunities. In addition, they try to convert internal weaknesses into strengths and external threats into opportunities.

⑨ E. Matching Strengths to Opportunities/ Converting Weaknesses and Threats

1. The acceptance of technological advances and the desire to control time create a potential need for a computer-based calendar.

2. Star Software has more opportunity for business growth during its peak season than it can presently handle because of resource (human and capital) constraints.

3. Star Software must modify its management hierarchy, empowering its employees through a more decentralized marketing organization.

4. Star Software should discuss future growth strategies with its supplier and develop contingency plans to deal with unforeseen events. Possible satellite facilities in other geographic locations should be explored.
5. Star Software should consider diversifying its product line to satisfy new market niches and develop nonseasonal products.
6. Star Software should consider surveying its current customers and its customers' clients to gain a better understanding of their changing needs and desires.

IV. Marketing Objectives

10 The development of marketing objectives is based on environmental analysis, SWOT analysis, the firm's overall corporate objectives, and the organization's resources. For each objective, this section should answer the question, "What is the specific and measurable outcome and time frame for completing this objective?"

Star Software Inc. is in the business of helping other companies market their products and/or services. Besides formulating a marketing-oriented and customer-focused mission statement, Star Software should establish an objective to achieve cumulative growth in net profit of at least 50 percent over the next five years. At least half of this 50 percent growth should come from new, nonmanufacturing customers and from products that are nonseasonal or that are generally delivered in the off-peak period of the calendar cycle.

To accomplish its marketing objectives, Star Software should develop benchmarks to measure progress. Regular reviews of these objectives will provide feedback and possible corrective actions on a timely basis. The major marketing objective is to gain a better understanding of the needs and satisfaction of current customers. Because Star Software is benefiting from a 90 percent reorder rate, it must be satisfying its current customers. Star could use the knowledge of its successes with current clients to market to new customers. To capitalize on its success with current clients, the company should establish benchmarks to learn how it can improve the products it now offers through knowledge of clients' needs and specific opportunities for new-product offerings. These benchmarks should be determined through marketing research and Star's marketing information system.

Another objective should be to analyze the billing cycle Star now uses to determine if there are ways to bill accounts receivable in a more evenly distributed manner throughout the year. Alternatively, repeat customers might be willing to place orders at off-peak cycles in return for discounts or added customer services.

Star Software should also create new products that can use its current equipment, technology, and knowledge base. It should conduct simple research and analyses of similar products or product lines with an eye toward developing specialty advertising products that are software based but not necessarily calendar related.

V. Marketing Strategies

11 The marketing plan clearly specifies and describes the target market(s) toward which the organization will aim its marketing efforts. The difference between this section and the earlier section covering target markets is that the earlier section deals with present target markets, whereas this section looks at future target markets.

A. Target Market(s)

Target Market 1: Large manufacturers or stand-alone manufacturing divisions of large corporations with extensive broker, dealer, or distributor networks

Example: An agricultural chemical producer, like Dow Chemical, distributes its products to numerous rural "feed and seed" dealers. Customizing calendars with Chicago Board of Trade futures or USDA agricultural report dates would be beneficial to these potential clients.

Target Market 2: Nonmanufacturing, nonindustrial segments of the business-to-business market with extensive customer networks, such as banks, medical services, or financial planners

Example: Various sporting goods manufacturers distribute to specialty shop dealers. Calendars could be customized to the particular sport, such as golf (with PGA, Virginia Slims, or other tour dates), running (with various national marathon dates), or bowling (with national tour dates).

Target Market 3: Direct consumer markets for brands with successful licensing arrangements for consumer products, like Coca-Cola

> Example: Products with major brand recognition and fan club membership, such as Harley-Davidson motorcycles or the Bloomington Gold Corvette Association, could provide additional markets for customized computer calendars. Environmental or political groups represent a nonprofit market. Brands with licensing agreements for consumer products could provide a market for consumer computer calendars in addition to the specialty advertising product, which would be marketed to manufacturers/dealers.

Target Market 4: Industry associations that regularly hold or sponsor trade shows, meetings, conferences, or conventions

> Example: National associations, such as the National Dairy Association or the American Marketing Association, frequently host meetings or annual conventions. Customized calendars could be developed for any of these groups.

(12) Though the marketing mix section in this plan is abbreviated, this component should provide considerable details regarding each element of the marketing mix: product, price, distribution, and promotion.

(12) B. Marketing Mix

1. *Products.* Star Software markets not only calendar software but also the service of specialty advertising to its clients. Star's intangible attributes are its ability to meet or exceed customer expectations consistently, its speed in responding to customers' demands, and its anticipation of new-customer needs. Intangible attributes are difficult for competitors to copy, thereby giving Star Software a competitive advantage.
2. *Price.* Star Software provides a high-quality specialty advertising product customized to its clients' needs. The value of this product and service is reflected in its premium price. Star should be sensitive to the price elasticity of its product and overall consumer demand.
3. *Distribution.* Star Software uses direct marketing. Since its product is compact, lightweight, and nonperishable, it can be shipped from a central location direct to the client via UPS, FedEx, or the U.S. Postal Service. The fact that Star can ship to multiple locations for each customer is an asset in selling its products.
4. *Promotion.* Because 90 percent of Star's customers reorder each year, the bulk of promotional expenditures should focus on new-product offerings through direct-mail advertising and trade journals or specialty publications. Any remaining promotional dollars could be directed to personal selling (in the form of sales performance bonuses) of current and new products.

(13) This section of the marketing plan details how the firm will be organized—by functions, products, regions, or types of customers—to implement its marketing strategies. It also indicates where decision-making authority will rest within the marketing unit.

(13) VI. Marketing Implementation

A. Marketing Organization

Because Star's current and future products require extensive customization to match clients' needs, it is necessary to organize the marketing function by customer groups. This will allow Star to focus its marketing efforts exclusively on the needs and specifications of each target customer segment. Star's marketing efforts will be organized around the following customer groups: (1) manufacturing group; (2) nonmanufacturing, business-to-business group; (3) consumer product licensing group; and (4) industry associations group. Each group will be headed by a sales manager who will report to the marketing director (these positions must be created). Each group will be responsible for marketing Star's products within that customer segment. In addition, each group will have full decision-making authority. This represents a shift from the current, highly centralized management hierarchy. Frontline salespeople will be empowered to make decisions that will better satisfy Star's clients.

These changes in marketing organization will enable Star Software to be more creative and flexible in meeting customers' needs. Likewise, these changes will overcome the current lack of diversification in Star's product lines and client base. Finally, this new marketing organization will give Star a better opportunity to monitor the activities of competitors.

14 This component of the marketing plan outlines the specific activities required to implement the marketing plan, determines who is responsible for performing these activities, and outlines when these activities should be accomplished, based on a specified schedule.

B. Activities, Responsibility, and Timetables for Completion

All implementation activities are to begin at the start of the next fiscal year on April 1. Unless specified, all activities are the responsibility of Star Software's next president, Jonathan McLemore.

- On April 1, create four sales manager positions and the position of marketing director. The marketing director will serve as project leader of a new business analysis team, to be composed of nine employees from a variety of positions within the company.
- By April 15, assign three members of the analysis team to each of the following projects: (1) research potential new-product offerings and clients, (2) analyze the current billing cycle and billing practices, and (3) design a customer survey project. The marketing director is responsible.
- By June 30, the three project groups will report the results of their analyses. The full business analysis team will review all recommendations.
- By July 31, develop a marketing information system to monitor client reorder patterns and customer satisfaction.
- By July 31, implement any changes in billing practices as recommended by the business analysis team.
- By July 31, make initial contact with new potential clients for the current product line. Each sales manager is responsible.
- By August 31, develop a plan for one new-product offering, along with an analysis of its potential customers. The business analysis team is responsible.
- By August 31, finalize a customer satisfaction survey for current clients. In addition, the company will contact those customers who did not reorder this year's product line to discuss their concerns. The marketing director is responsible.
- By December, implement the customer satisfaction survey with a random sample of 20 percent of current clients who reordered this year's product line. The marketing director is responsible.
- By February, implement a new-product offering, advertising to current customers and to a sample of potential clients. The business analysis team is responsible.
- By March, analyze and report the results of all customer satisfaction surveys and evaluate the new-product offering. The marketing director is responsible.
- Reestablish the objectives of the business analysis team for the next fiscal year. The marketing director is responsible.

15 This section details how the results of the marketing plan will be measured and evaluated. The control portion of this section includes the types of actions the firm can take to reduce the differences between the planned and the actual performance.

VII. Evaluation and Control

A. Performance Standards and Financial Controls

A comparison of the financial expenditures with the plan goals will be included in the project report. The following performance standards and financial controls are suggested:

- The total budget for the billing analysis, new-product research, and the customer survey will be equal to 60 percent of the annual promotional budget for the coming year.
- The breakdown of the budget within the project will be a 20 percent allocation to the billing cycle study, a 30 percent allocation to the customer survey and marketing information system development, and a 50 percent allocation to new-business development and new-product implementation.

- Each project team is responsible for reporting all financial expenditures, including personnel salaries and direct expenses, for its segment of the project. A standardized reporting form will be developed and provided by the marketing director.

- The marketing director is responsible for adherence to the project budget and will report overages to the company president on a weekly basis. The marketing director is also responsible for any redirection of budget dollars as required for each project of the business analysis team.

- Any new-product offering will be evaluated on a quarterly basis to determine its profitability. Product development expenses will be distributed over a two-year period, by calendar quarters, and will be compared with gross income generated during the same period.

B. Monitoring Procedures

To analyze the effectiveness of Star Software's marketing plan, it is necessary to compare its actual performance with plan objectives. To facilitate this analysis, monitoring procedures should be developed for the various activities required to bring the marketing plan to fruition. These procedures include, but are not limited to, the following:

- A project management concept will be used to evaluate the implementation of the marketing plan by establishing time requirements, human resource needs, and financial or budgetary expenditures.

- A perpetual comparison of actual and planned activities will be conducted on a monthly basis for the first year and on a quarterly basis after the initial implementation phase. The business analysis team, including the marketing director, will report its comparison of actual and planned outcomes directly to the company president.

- Each project team is responsible for determining what changes must be made in procedures, product focus, or operations as a result of the studies conducted in its area.

glossary

accessibility The ability to obtain digital information

accessory equipment Equipment that does not become part of the final physical product but is used in production or office activities

addressability The ability of a marketer to identify customers before they make a purchase

advertising Paid nonpersonal communication about an organization and its products transmitted to a target audience through mass media

advertising appropriation The advertising budget for a specific time period

advertising campaign The creation and execution of a series of advertisements to communicate with a particular target audience

advertising platform Basic issues or selling points to be included in an advertising campaign

advocacy advertising Advertising that promotes a company's position on a public issue

aesthetic modifications Changes relating to the sensory appeal of a product

agents Intermediaries that represent either buyers or sellers on a permanent basis

aided recall test A posttest that asks respondents to identify recent ads and provides clues to jog their memories

allowance A concession in price to achieve a desired goal

approach The manner in which a salesperson contacts a potential customer

arbitrary approach Budgeting for an advertising campaign as specified by a high-level executive in the firm

artwork An advertisement's illustrations and layout

Asia-Pacific Economic Cooperation (APEC) An alliance that promotes open trade and economic and technical cooperation among member nations throughout the world

atmospherics The physical elements in a store's design that appeal to consumers' emotions and encourage buying

attitude An individual's enduring evaluation of feelings about and behavioral tendencies toward an object or idea

attitude scale A means of measuring consumer attitudes by gauging the intensity of individuals' reactions to adjectives, phrases, or sentences about an object

automatic vending The use of machines to dispense products

average fixed cost The fixed cost per unit produced

average total cost The sum of the average fixed cost and the average variable cost

average variable cost The variable cost per unit produced

bait pricing Pricing an item in a product line low with the intention of selling a higher-priced item in the line

balance of trade The difference in value between a nation's exports and its imports

barter The trading of products

base-point pricing Geographic pricing that combines factory price and freight charges from the base point nearest the buyer

benchmarking Comparing the quality of the company's goods, services, or processes with that of its best-performing competitors

benefit segmentation The division of a market according to benefits that consumers want from the product

Better Business Bureau (BBB) A system of nongovernmental, independent, local regulatory agencies supported by local businesses that helps settle problems between customers and specific business firms

blogs Web-based journals (short for "weblogs") in which writers editorialize and interact with other Internet users

brand A name, term, design, symbol, or other feature that identifies one marketer's product as distinct from those of other marketers

brand competitors Firms that market products with similar features and benefits to the same customers at similar prices

brand equity The marketing and financial value associated with a brand's strength in a market

brand extension An organization uses one of its existing brands to brand a new product in a different product category

brand insistence The degree of brand loyalty in which a customer strongly prefers a specific brand and will accept no substitute

brand licensing An agreement whereby a company permits another organization to use its brand on other products for a licensing fee

brand loyalty A customer's favorable attitude toward a specific brand

brand manager The person responsible for a single brand

brand mark The part of a brand that is not made up of words, such as a symbol or design

brand name The part of a brand that can be spoken, including letters, words, and numbers

brand preference The degree of brand loyalty in which a customer prefers one brand over competitive offerings

brand recognition The degree of brand loyalty in which a customer is aware that a brand exists and views the brand as an alternative purchase if their preferred brand is unavailable

breakdown approach Measuring company sales potential based on a general economic forecast for a specific period and the market potential derived from it

break-even point The point at which the costs of producing a product equal the revenue made from selling the product

brokers Intermediaries that bring buyers and sellers together temporarily

buildup approach Measuring company sales potential by estimating how much of a product a potential buyer in a specific geographic area will purchase in a given period, multiplying the estimate by the number of potential buyers, and adding the totals of all the geographic areas considered

bundle pricing Packaging together two or more complementary products and selling them at a single price

business analysis Evaluating the potential impact of a product idea on the firm's sales, costs, and profits

business cycle A pattern of economic fluctuations that has four stages: prosperity, recession, depression, and recovery

business market Individuals or groups that purchase a specific kind of product for resale, direct use in producing other products, or use in general daily operations

business (organizational) buying behavior The purchase behavior of producers, government units, institutions, and resellers

business products Products bought to use in a firm's operations, to resell, or to make other products

business services Intangible products that many organizations use in their operations

buy-back allowance A sum of money given to a reseller for each unit bought after an initial promotion deal is over

buying allowance A temporary price reduction to resellers for purchasing specified quantities of a product

buying behavior The decision processes and actions of people involved in buying and using products

buying center The people within an organization who make business purchase decisions

buying power Resources, such as money, goods, and services, that can be traded in an exchange

buzz marketing An attempt to incite publicity and public excitement surrounding a product through a creative event

captioned photograph A photograph with a brief description of its contents

captive pricing Pricing the basic product in a product line low, while pricing related items higher

cash-and-carry wholesalers Limited-service wholesalers whose customers pay cash and furnish transportation

cash discounts Price reductions given to buyers for prompt payment or cash payment

catalog marketing A type of marketing in which an organization provides a catalog from which customers make selections and place orders by mail, telephone, or the Internet

category killer A very large specialty store that concentrates on a major product category and competes on the basis of low prices and product availability

category management A retail strategy of managing groups of similar, often substitutable products produced by different manufacturers

cause-related marketing The practice of linking products to a particular social cause on an ongoing or short-term basis

centralized organization A structure in which top-level managers delegate little authority to lower levels

cents-off offer A promotion that allows buyers to pay less than the regular price to encourage purchase

channel capacity The limit on the volume of information a communication channel can handle effectively

channel captain The dominant leader of a marketing channel or a supply channel

channel power The ability of one channel member to influence another member's goal achievement

client-based relationships Interactions that result in satisfied customers who use a service repeatedly over time

client publics Direct consumers of a product of a nonprofit organization

closing The stage in the personal selling process when the salesperson asks the prospect to buy the product

co-branding Using two or more brands on one product

codes of conduct Formalized rules and standards that describe what the company expects of its employees

coding process Converting meaning into a series of signs or symbols

cognitive dissonance A buyer's doubts shortly after a purchase about whether the decision was the right one

combination compensation plan Paying salespeople a fixed salary plus a commission based on sales volume

commercialization Refining and finalizing plans and budgets for full-scale manufacturing and marketing of a product

commission merchants Agents that receive goods on consignment from local sellers and negotiate sales in large, central markets

Common Market of the Southern Cone (MERCOSUR) An alliance that promotes the free circulation of goods, services, and production factors, and has a common external tariff and commercial policy among member nations in South America

communication A sharing of meaning through the transmission of information

communications channel The medium of transmission that carries the coded message from the source to the receiver

community shopping centers Shopping centers with one or two department stores, some specialty stores, and convenience stores

company sales potential The maximum percentage of market potential that an individual firm within an industry can expect to obtain for a specific product

comparative advertising Compares the sponsored brand with one or more identified brands on the basis of one or more product characteristics

comparison discounting Setting a price at a specific level and comparing it with a higher price

competition Other organizations that market products that are similar to or can be substituted for a marketer's products in the same geographic area

competitive advantage The result of a company matching a core competency to opportunities it has discovered in the marketplace

competitive advertising Tries to stimulate demand for a specific brand by promoting its features, uses, and advantages relative to competing brands

competition-based pricing Pricing influenced primarily by competitors' prices

competition-matching approach Determining an advertising budget by trying to match competitors' advertising outlays

component parts Items that become part of the physical product and are either finished items ready for assembly or items that need little processing before assembly

concentrated targeting strategy A market segmentation strategy in which an organization targets a single market segment using one marketing mix

concept testing Seeking a sample of potential buyers' responses to a product idea

conclusive research Research designed to verify insights through objective procedures and to help marketers in making decisions

connectivity Use of digital networks to provide linkages between information providers and users

consideration set A group of brands within a product category that a buyer views as alternatives for possible purchase

consistency of quality The degree to which a product has the same level of quality over time

consumer buying behavior The decision processes and purchasing activities of people who purchase products for personal or household use and not for business purposes

consumer buying decision process A five-stage purchase decision process that includes problem recognition, information search, evaluation of alternatives, purchase, and postpurchase evaluation

consumer contests Sales promotion methods in which individuals compete for prizes based on their analytical or creative skills

consumer games Sales promotion methods in which individuals compete for prizes based primarily on chance

consumer jury A panel of a product's existing or potential buyers who pretest ads

consumer market Purchasers and household members who intend to consume or benefit from the purchased products and do not buy products to make profits

consumer misbehavior Behavior that violates generally accepted norms of a particular society

consumer products Products purchased to satisfy personal and family needs

consumer sales promotion methods Sales promotion techniques that encourage consumers to patronize specific stores or try particular products

consumer socialization The process through which a person acquires the knowledge and skills to function as a consumer

consumer sweepstakes A sales promotion in which entrants submit their names for inclusion in a drawing for prizes

consumerism Organized efforts by individuals, groups, and organizations to protect consumers' rights

contract manufacturing The practice of hiring a foreign firm to produce a designated volume of the domestic firm's product or a component of it to specification; the final product carries the domestic firm's name

control Customers' abilities to regulate the information they view and the rate and sequence of their exposure to that information

convenience products Relatively inexpensive, frequently purchased items for which buyers exert minimal purchasing effort

convenience store A small self-service store that is open long hours and carries a narrow assortment of products, usually convenience items

cooperative advertising An arrangement in which a manufacturer agrees to pay a certain amount of a retailer's media costs for advertising the manufacturer's products

copy The verbal portion of advertisements

core competencies Things a company does extremely well, which sometimes give it an advantage over its competition

corporate strategy A strategy that determines the means for utilizing resources in the various functional areas to reach the organization's goals

cost-based pricing Adding a dollar amount or percentage to the cost of the product

cost comparison indicator A means of comparing the costs of advertising vehicles in a specific medium in relation to the number of people reached

cost-plus pricing Adding a specified dollar amount or percentage to the seller's cost

coupons Written price reductions used to encourage consumers to buy a specific product

credence qualities Attributes that customers may be unable to evaluate even after purchasing and consuming a service

crowdsourcing Refers to the way digital media can be used to outsource tasks to a large group of people

cultural relativism The concept that morality varies from one culture to another and that business practices are therefore differentially defined as right or wrong by particular cultures

culture The accumulation of values, knowledge, beliefs, customs, objects, and concepts that a society uses to cope with its environment and passes on to future generations

cumulative discounts Quantity discounts aggregated over a stated time period

customary pricing Pricing on the basis of tradition

customer advisory boards Small groups of actual customers who serve as sounding boards for new-product ideas and offer insights into their feelings and attitudes toward a firm's products and other elements of its marketing strategy

customer-centric marketing Developing collaborative relationships with customers based on focusing on their individual needs and concerns

customer contact The level of interaction between provider and customer needed to deliver the service

customer forecasting survey A survey of customers regarding the types and quantities of products they intend to buy during a specific period

customer relationship management (CRM) Using information about customers to create marketing strategies that develop and sustain desirable customer relationships

customer services Human or mechanical efforts or activities that add value to a product

customers The purchasers of organizations' products; the focal point of all marketing elements

cycle analysis An analysis of sales figures for a three- to five-year period to ascertain whether sales fluctuate in a consistent, periodic manner

cycle time The time needed to complete a process

database A collection of information arranged for easy access and retrieval

dealer listing An advertisement that promotes a product and identifies the names of participating retailers that sell the product

dealer loader A gift, often part of a display, given to a retailer that purchases a specified quantity of merchandise

decentralized organization A structure in which decision-making authority is delegated as far down the chain of command as possible

decline stage The stage of a product's life cycle when sales fall rapidly

decoding process Converting signs or symbols into concepts and ideas

Delphi technique A procedure in which experts create initial forecasts, submit them to the company for averaging, and then refine the forecasts

demand-based pricing Pricing based on the level of demand for the product

demand curve A graph of the quantity of products expected to be sold at various prices if other factors remain constant

demonstration A sales promotion method a manufacturer uses temporarily to encourage trial use and purchase of a product or to show how a product works

department stores Large retail organizations characterized by a wide product mix and organized into separate departments to facilitate marketing efforts and internal management

depression A stage of the business cycle when unemployment is extremely high, wages are very low, total disposable income is at a minimum, and consumers lack confidence in the economy

depth of product mix The average number of different products offered in each product line

derived demand Demand for business products that stems from demand for consumer products

descriptive research Research conducted to clarify the characteristics of certain phenomena to solve a particular problem

differential pricing Charging different prices to different buyers for the same quality and quantity of product

differentiated targeting strategy A strategy in which an organization targets two or more segments by developing a marketing mix for each segment

digital marketing Uses all digital media, including the Internet and mobile and interactive channels, to develop communication and exchanges with customers

digital media Electronic media that function using digital codes; when we refer to digital media, we are referring to media available via computers, cellular phones, smartphones, and other digital devices that have been released in recent years

direct marketing The use of the telephone, Internet, and nonpersonal media to introduce products to customers, who can then purchase them via mail, telephone, or the Internet

direct ownership A situation in which a company owns subsidiaries or other facilities overseas

direct-response marketing A type of marketing in which a retailer advertises a product and makes it available through mail or telephone orders

direct selling Marketing products to ultimate consumers through face-to-face sales presentations at home or in the workplace

discount stores Self-service, general-merchandise stores that offer brand name and private brand products at low prices

discretionary income Disposable income available for spending and saving after an individual has purchased the basic necessities of food, clothing, and shelter

disposable income After-tax income

distribution The decisions and activities that make products available to customers when and where they want to purchase them

distribution centers Large, centralized warehouses that focus on moving rather than storing goods

drop shippers Limited-service wholesalers that take title to goods and negotiate sales but never actually take possession of products

dual distribution The use of two or more marketing channels to distribute the same products to the same target market

dumping Selling products at unfairly low prices

early adopters People who adopt new products early, choose new products carefully, and are viewed as "the people to check with" by later adopters

early majority Individuals who adopt a new product just prior to the average person

electronic data interchange (EDI) A computerized means of integrating order processing with production, inventory, accounting, and transportation

electronic marketing (e-marketing) The strategic process of distributing, promoting, pricing products, and discovering the desires of customers using digital media and digital marketing

embargo A government's suspension of trade in a particular product or with a given country

empowerment Giving customer-contact employees authority and responsibility to make marketing decisions without seeking approval of their supervisors

environmental analysis The process of assessing and interpreting the information gathered through environmental scanning

environmental scanning The process of collecting information about forces in the marketing environment

ethical issue An identifiable problem, situation, or opportunity requiring a choice among several actions that must be evaluated as right or wrong, ethical or unethical

European Union (EU) An alliance that promotes trade among its member countries in Europe

evaluative criteria Objective and subjective product characteristics that are important to a buyer

everyday low prices (EDLP) Pricing products low on a consistent basis

exchange controls Government restrictions on the amount of a particular currency that can be bought or sold

exchanges The provision or transfer of goods, services, or ideas in return for something of value

exclusive dealing A situation in which a manufacturer forbids an intermediary to carry products of competing manufacturers

exclusive distribution Using a single outlet in a fairly large geographic area to distribute a product

executive judgment A sales forecasting method based on the intuition of one or more executives

experience qualities Attributes that can be assessed only during purchase and consumption of a service

experimental research Research that allows marketers to make causal inferences about relationships

expert forecasting survey Sales forecasts prepared by experts outside the firm, such as economists, management consultants, advertising executives, or college professors

exploratory research Research conducted to gather more information about a problem or to make a tentative hypothesis more specific

exporting The sale of products to foreign markets

extended problem solving A consumer problem-solving process employed when purchasing unfamiliar, expensive, or infrequently bought products

external customers Individuals who patronize a business—the familiar definition of "customers"

external reference price A comparison price provided by others

external search An information search in which buyers seek information from sources other than their memories

family branding Branding all of a firm's products with the same name or part of the name

family packaging Using similar packaging for all of a firm's products or packaging that has one common design element

feature article A manuscript of up to 3,000 words prepared for a specific publication

Federal Trade Commission (FTC) An agency that regulates a variety of business practices and curbs false advertising, misleading pricing, and deceptive packaging and labeling

feedback The receiver's response to a decoded message

fixed costs Costs that do not vary with changes in the number of units produced or sold

F.O.B. destination A price indicating the producer is absorbing shipping costs

F.O.B. factory The price of merchandise at the factory before shipment

focus-group interview An interview that is often conducted informally, without a structured questionnaire, in small groups of 8 to 12 people, to observe interaction when members are exposed to an idea or a concept

franchising A form of licensing in which a franchiser, in exchange for a financial commitment, grants a franchisee the right to market its product in accordance with the franchiser's standards

free merchandise A manufacturer's reward given to resellers that purchase a stated quantity of products

free sample A sample of a product given out to encourage trial and purchase

freight absorption pricing Absorption of all or part of actual freight costs by the seller

freight forwarders Organizations that consolidate shipments from several firms into efficient lot sizes

full-service wholesalers Merchant wholesalers that perform the widest range of wholesaling functions

functional modifications Changes affecting a product's versatility, effectiveness, convenience, or safety

General Agreement on Tariffs and Trade (GATT) An agreement among nations to reduce worldwide tariffs and increase international trade

general-merchandise retailer A retail establishment that offers a variety of product lines that are stocked in considerable depth

general-merchandise wholesalers Full-service wholesalers with a wide product mix but limited depth within product lines

general publics Indirect consumers of a product of a nonprofit organization

generic brand A brand indicating only the product category

generic competitors Firms that provide very different products that solve the same problem or satisfy the same basic customer need

geodemographic segmentation A method of market segmentation that clusters people in zip code areas and smaller neighborhood units based on lifestyle and demographic information

geographic pricing Reductions for transportation and other costs related to the physical distance between buyer and seller

globalization The development of marketing strategies that treat the entire world (or its major regions) as a single entity

good A tangible physical entity

government markets Federal, state, county, or local governments that buy goods and services to support their internal operations and provide products to their constituencies

green marketing A strategic process involving stakeholder assessment to create meaningful long-term relationships with customers while maintaining, supporting, and enhancing the natural environment

gross domestic product (GDP) The market value of a nation's total output of goods and services for a given period; an overall measure of economic standing

growth stage The product life-cycle stage when sales rise rapidly, profits reach a peak, and then they start to decline

heterogeneity Variation in quality

heterogeneous market A market made up of individuals or organizations with diverse needs for products in a specific product class

homogeneous market A market in which a large proportion of customers have similar needs for a product

horizontal channel integration Combining organizations at the same level of operation under one management

hypermarkets Stores that combine supermarket and discount store shopping in one location

hypothesis An informed guess or assumption about a certain problem or set of circumstances

idea A concept, philosophy, image, or issue

idea generation Seeking product ideas to achieve organizational objectives

illustrations Photos, drawings, graphs, charts, and tables used to spark audience interest in an advertisement

import tariff A duty levied by a nation on goods bought outside its borders and brought into the country

importing The purchase of products from a foreign source

impulse buying An unplanned buying behavior resulting from a powerful urge to buy something immediately

income For an individual, the amount of money received through wages, rents, investments, pensions, and subsidy payments for a given period

individual branding A branding strategy in which each product is given a different name

industrial distributor An independent business organization that takes title to industrial products and carries inventories

inelastic demand Demand that is not significantly altered by a price increase or decrease

information inputs Sensations received through sight, taste, hearing, smell, and touch

in-home (door-to-door) interview A personal interview that takes place in the respondent's home

innovators First adopters of new products

input–output data Information that identifies what types of industries purchase the products of a particular industry

inseparability The quality of being produced and consumed at the same time

installations Facilities and nonportable major equipment

institutional advertising Advertising that promotes organizational images, ideas, and political issues

institutional markets Organizations with charitable, educational, community, or other nonbusiness goals

intangibility The characteristic that a service is not physical and cannot be perceived by the senses

integrated marketing communications Coordination of promotion and other marketing efforts for maximum informational and persuasive impact

intended strategy The strategy the organization decides on during the planning phase and wants to use

intensive distribution Using all available outlets to distribute a product

interactivity Allows customers to express their needs and wants directly to the firm in response to its marketing communications

intermodal transportation Two or more transportation modes used in combination

internal customers The company's employees

internal marketing A management philosophy that coordinates internal exchanges between the organization and its employees to achieve successful external exchanges between the organization and its customers

internal reference price A price developed in the buyer's mind through experience with the product

internal search An information search in which buyers search their memories for information about products that might solve their problem

international marketing Developing and performing marketing activities across national boundaries

introduction stage The initial stage of a product's life cycle; its first appearance in the marketplace when sales start at zero and profits are negative

inventory management Developing and maintaining adequate assortments of products to meet customers' needs

joint demand Demand involving the use of two or more items in combination to produce a product

joint venture A partnership between a domestic firm and a foreign firm or government

just-in-time (JIT) An inventory-management approach in which supplies arrive just when needed for production or resale

kinesic communication Communicating through the movement of head, eyes, arms, hands, legs, or torso

labeling Providing identifying, promotional, or other information on package labels

laggards The last adopters, who distrust new products

late majority Skeptics who adopt new products when they feel it is necessary

layout The physical arrangement of an advertisement's illustration and copy

learning Changes in an individual's thought processes and behavior caused by information and experience

level of involvement An individual's degree of interest in a product and the importance of the product for that person

level of quality The amount of quality a product possesses

licensing An alternative to direct investment that requires a licensee to pay commissions or royalties on sales or supplies used in manufacturing

lifestyle An individual's pattern of living expressed through activities, interests, and opinions

lifestyle shopping center A type of shopping center that is typically open air and features upscale specialty, dining, and entertainment stores

limited-line wholesalers Full-service wholesalers that carry only a few product lines but many products within those lines

limited problem solving A consumer problem-solving process used when purchasing products occasionally or needing information about an unfamiliar brand in a familiar product category

limited-service wholesalers Merchant wholesalers that provide some services and specialize in a few functions

line extension Development of a product that is closely related to existing products in the line but is designed specifically to meet different customer needs

logistics management Planning, implementing, and controlling the efficient and effective flow and storage of products and information from the point of origin to consumption to meet customers' needs and wants

mail-order wholesalers Limited-service wholesalers that sell products through catalogs

mail survey A research method in which respondents answer a questionnaire sent through the mail

manufacturer brand A brand initiated by producers to ensure that producers are identified with their products at the point of purchase

manufacturers' agents Independent intermediaries that represent two or more sellers and usually offers customers complete product lines

marginal cost (MC) The extra cost incurred by producing one more unit of a product

marginal revenue (MR) The change in total revenue resulting from the sale of an additional unit of a product

market A group of individuals and/or organizations that have needs for products in a product class and have the ability, willingness, and authority to purchase those products

market density The number of potential customers within a unit of land area

market growth/market share matrix A helpful business tool, based on the philosophy that a product's market growth rate and its market share are important considerations in determining its marketing strategy

market manager The person responsible for managing the marketing activities that serve a particular group of customers

market opportunity A combination of circumstances and timing that permits an organization to take action to reach a particular target market

market orientation An organizationwide commitment to researching and responding to customer needs

market potential The total amount of a product that customers will purchase within a specified period at a specific level of industrywide marketing activity

market segment Individuals, groups, or organizations sharing one or more similar characteristics that cause them to have similar product needs

market segmentation The process of dividing a total market into groups with relatively similar product needs to design a marketing mix that matches those needs

market share The percentage of a market that actually buys a specific product from a particular company

market test Making a product available to buyers in one or more test areas and measuring purchases and consumer responses to marketing efforts

marketing The process of creating, distributing, promoting, and pricing goods, services, and ideas to facilitate satisfying exchange relationships with customers and develop and maintain favorable relationships with stakeholders in a dynamic environment

marketing channel A group of individuals and organizations that direct the flow of products from producers to customers within the supply chain

marketing citizenship The adoption of a strategic focus for fulfilling the economic, legal, ethical, and philanthropic social responsibilities expected by stakeholders

marketing concept A philosophy that an organization should try to provide products that satisfy customers' needs through a coordinated set of activities that also allows the organization to achieve its goals

marketing control process Establishing performance standards, evaluating actual performance by comparing it with established standards, and reducing the differences between desired and actual performance

marketing decision support system (MDSS) Customized computer software that aids marketing managers in decision making

marketing environment The competitive, economic, political, legal and regulatory, technological, and sociocultural forces that surround the customer and affect the marketing mix

marketing ethics Principles and standards that define acceptable marketing conduct as determined by various stakeholders

marketing implementation The process of putting marketing strategies into action

marketing information system (MIS) A framework for managing and structuring information gathered regularly from sources inside and outside the organization

marketing intermediaries Middlemen that link producers to other intermediaries or ultimate consumers through contractual arrangements or through the purchase and resale of products

marketing management The process of planning, organizing, implementing, and controlling marketing activities to facilitate exchanges effectively and efficiently

marketing mix Four marketing elements—product, distribution, promotion, and pricing—that a firm can control to meet the needs of customers within its target markets

marketing objective A statement of what is to be accomplished through marketing activities

marketing plan A written document that specifies the activities to be performed to implement and control the organization's marketing activities

marketing planning The systematic process of assessing marketing opportunities and resources, determining marketing objectives, defining marketing strategies, and establishing guidelines for implementation and control of the marketing program

marketing research The systematic design, collection, interpretation, and reporting of information to help marketers solve specific marketing problems or take advantage of marketing opportunities

marketing strategy A plan of action for identifying and analyzing a target market and developing a marketing mix to meet the needs of that market

markup pricing Adding to the cost of the product a predetermined percentage of that cost

Maslow's hierarchy of needs The five levels of needs that humans seek to satisfy, from most to least important

materials handling Physical handling of tangible goods, supplies, and resources

maturity stage The stage of a product's life cycle when the sales curve peaks and starts to decline, and profits continue to fall

media plan A plan that specifies the media vehicles to be used and the schedule for running advertisements

megacarriers Freight transportation firms that provide several modes of shipment

merchandise allowance A manufacturer's agreement to pay resellers certain amounts of money for providing special promotional efforts, such as setting up and maintaining a display

merchant wholesalers Independently owned businesses that take title to goods, assume ownership risks, and buy and resell products to other wholesalers, business customers, or retailers

micromarketing An approach to market segmentation in which organizations focus precise marketing efforts on very small geographic markets

mission statement A long-term view, or vision, of what the organization wants to become

missionary salespeople Support salespeople, usually employed by a manufacturer, who assist the producer's customers in selling to their own customers

modified rebuy purchase A new-task purchase that is changed on subsequent orders or when the requirements of a straight rebuy purchase are modified

money refund A sales promotion technique that offers consumers a specified amount of money when they mail in a proof of purchase, usually for multiple product purchases

monopolistic competition A competitive structure in which a firm has many potential competitors and tries to develop a marketing strategy to differentiate its product

monopoly A competitive structure in which an organization offers a product that has no close substitutes, making that organization the sole source of supply

motive An internal energizing force that directs a person's behavior toward satisfying needs or achieving goals

MRO supplies Maintenance, repair, and operating items that facilitate production and operations but do not become part of the finished product

multinational enterprise A firm that has operations or subsidiaries in many countries

multiple sourcing An organization's decision to use several suppliers

multiple-unit pricing Packaging together two or more identical products and selling them at a single price

National Advertising Review Board (NARB) A self-regulatory unit that considers challenges to issues raised by the National Advertising Division (an arm of the Council of Better Business Bureaus) about an advertisement

negotiated pricing Establishing a final price through bargaining between seller and customer

neighborhood shopping centers Shopping centers usually consisting of several small convenience and specialty stores

new-product development process A seven-phase process for introducing products: idea generation, screening, concept testing, business analysis, product development, test marketing, and commercialization

new-task purchase An organization's initial purchase of an item to be used to perform a new job or solve a new problem

news release A short piece of copy publicizing an event or a product

noise Anything that reduces a communication's clarity and accuracy

noncumulative discounts Onetime price reductions based on the number of units purchased, the dollar value of the order, or the product mix purchased

nonprice competition Emphasizing factors other than price to distinguish a product from competing brands

nonprobability sampling A sampling technique in which there is no way to calculate the likelihood that a specific element of the population being studied will be chosen

nonprofit marketing Marketing activities conducted to achieve some goal other than ordinary business goals such as profit, market share, or return on investment

nonstore retailing The selling of products outside the confines of a retail facility

North American Free Trade Agreement (NAFTA) An alliance that merges Canada, Mexico, and the United States into a single market

North American Industry Classification System (NAICS) An industry classification system that generates comparable statistics among the United States, Canada, and Mexico

objective-and-task approach Budgeting for an advertising campaign by first determining its objectives and then calculating the cost of all the tasks needed to attain them

odd-even pricing Ending the price with certain numbers to influence buyers' perceptions of the price or product

off-price retailers Stores that buy manufacturers' seconds, overruns, returns, and off-season merchandise for resale to consumers at deep discounts

offshore outsourcing The practice of contracting with an organization to perform some or all business functions in a country other than the country in which the product or service will be sold

offshoring The practice of moving a business process that was done domestically at the local factory to a foreign country, regardless of whether the production accomplished in the foreign country is performed by the local company (e.g., in a wholly owned subsidiary) or a third party (e.g., subcontractor)

oligopoly A competitive structure in which a few sellers control the supply of a large proportion of a product

online fraud Any attempt to conduct fraudulent activities online, including deceiving consumers into releasing personal information

online retailing Retailing that makes products available to buyers through computer connections

online survey A research method in which respondents answer a questionnaire via e-mail or on a website

on-site computer interview A variation of the shopping mall intercept interview in which respondents complete a self-administered questionnaire displayed on a computer monitor

operations management The total set of managerial activities used by an organization to transform resource inputs into products

opinion leader A member of an informal group who provides information about a specific topic to other group members

opportunity cost The value of the benefit given up by choosing one alternative over another

order getter A salesperson who sells to new customers and increases sales to current customers

order processing The receipt and transmission of sales order information

order takers Salespeople who primarily seek repeat sales

organizational (corporate) culture A set of values, beliefs, goals, norms, and rituals that members of an organization share

outsourcing The practice of contracting out a noncore operation to an organization that specializes in that operation

patronage motives Motives that influence where a person purchases products on a regular basis

penetration pricing Setting prices below those of competing brands to penetrate a market and gain a significant market share quickly

percent-of-sales approach Budgeting for an advertising campaign by multiplying the firm's past and expected sales by a standard percentage

perception The process of selecting, organizing, and interpreting information inputs to produce meaning

performance standard An expected level of performance against which actual performance can be compared

periodic discounting Temporary reduction of prices on a patterned or systematic basis

perishability The inability of unused service capacity to be stored for future use

personal interview survey A research method in which participants respond to survey questions face-to-face

personal selling Paid personal communication that attempts to inform customers and persuade them to buy products in an exchange situation

personality A set of internal traits and distinct behavioral tendencies that result in consistent patterns of behavior in certain situations

physical distribution Activities used to move products from producers to consumers and other end users

pioneer advertising Advertising that tries to stimulate demand for a product category rather than a specific brand by informing potential buyers about the product

pioneer promotion Promotion that informs consumers about a new product

podcast Audio or video file that can be downloaded from the Internet with a subscription that automatically delivers new content to listening devices or personal computers; podcasts offer the benefit of convenience, giving users the ability to listen to or view content when and where they choose

point-of-purchase (POP) materials Signs, window displays, display racks, and similar devices used to attract customers

population All the elements, units, or individuals of interest to researchers for a specific study

posttest Evaluation of advertising effectiveness after the campaign

power shopping center A type of shopping center that combines off-price stores with category killers

premium An item offered free or at a minimal cost as a bonus for purchasing a product

premium money (push money) Extra compensation to salespeople for pushing a line of goods

premium pricing Pricing the highest-quality or most versatile products higher than other models in the product line

press conference A meeting used to announce major news events

prestige pricing Setting prices at an artificially high level to convey prestige or a quality image

prestige sensitive Drawn to products that signify prominence and status

pretest Evaluation of advertisements performed before a campaign begins

price The value paid for a product in a marketing exchange

price competition Emphasizing price as an issue and matching or beating competitors' prices

price conscious Striving to pay low prices

price discrimination Employing price differentials that injure competition by giving one or more buyers a competitive advantage

price elasticity of demand A measure of the sensitivity of demand to changes in price

price leaders A product priced below the usual markup, near cost, or below cost

price lining Setting a limited number of prices for selected groups or lines of merchandise

price skimming Charging the highest possible price that buyers who most desire the product will pay

pricing objectives Goals that describe what a firm wants to achieve through pricing

primary data Data observed and recorded or collected directly from respondents

primary demand Demand for a product category rather than for a specific brand

private distributor brand A brand initiated and owned by a reseller

private warehouses Company-operated facilities for storing and shipping products

probability sampling A type of sampling in which every element in the population being studied has a known chance of being selected for study

process materials Materials that are used directly in the production of other products but are not readily identifiable

producer markets Individuals and business organizations that purchase products to make profits by using them to produce other products or using them in their operations

product A good, service, or idea

product adoption process The five-stage process of buyer acceptance of a product: awareness, interest, evaluation, trial, and adoption

product advertising Advertising that promotes the uses, features, and benefits of products

product competitors Firms that compete in the same product class but market products with different features, benefits, and prices

product deletion Eliminating a product from the product mix when it no longer satisfies a sufficient number of customers

product design How a product is conceived, planned, and produced

product development Determining if producing a product is technically feasible and cost effective

product differentiation Creating and designing products so that customers perceive them as different from competing products

product features Specific design characteristics that allow a product to perform certain tasks

product item A specific version of a product that can be designated as a distinct offering among a firm's products

product life cycle The progression of a product through four stages: introduction, growth, maturity, and decline

product line A group of closely related product items viewed as a unit because of marketing, technical, or end-use considerations

product-line pricing Establishing and adjusting prices of multiple products within a product line

product manager The person within an organization who is responsible for a product, a product line, or several distinct products that make up a group

product mix The composite, or total, group of products that an organization makes available to customers

product modifications Changes in one or more characteristics of a product

product placement The strategic location of products or product promotions within entertainment media content to reach the product's target market

product positioning Creating and maintaining a certain concept of a product in customers' minds

professional pricing Fees set by people with great skill or experience in a particular field

promotion Communication to build and maintain relationships by informing and persuading one or more audiences

promotion mix A combination of promotional methods used to promote a specific product

prospecting Developing a database of potential customers

prosperity A stage of the business cycle characterized by low unemployment and relatively high total income, which together ensure high buying power (provided the inflation rate stays low)

proxemic communication Communicating by varying the physical distance in face-to-face interactions

psychological influences Factors that in part determine people's general behavior, thus influencing their behavior as consumers

psychological pricing Pricing that attempts to influence a customer's perception of price to make a product's price more attractive

public relations Communication efforts used to create and maintain favorable relations between an organization and its stakeholders

public warehouses Storage space and related physical distribution facilities that can be leased by companies

publicity A new story type of communication about an organization and/or its products transmitted through a mass medium at no charge

pull policy Promoting a product directly to consumers to develop strong consumer demand that pulls products through the marketing channel

pure competition A market structure characterized by an extremely large number of sellers, none strong enough to significantly influence price or supply

push policy Promoting a product only to the next institution down the marketing channel

quality The overall characteristics of a product that allow it to perform as expected in satisfying customer needs

quality modifications Changes relating to a product's dependability and durability

quantity discounts Deductions from the list price for purchasing in large quantities

quota A limit on the amount of goods an importing country will accept for certain product categories in a specific period of time

quota sampling A nonprobability sampling technique in which researchers divide the population into groups and then arbitrarily choose participants from each group

rack jobbers Full-service, specialty-line wholesalers that own and maintain display racks in stores

random discounting Temporary reduction of prices on an unsystematic basis

random factor analysis An analysis attempting to attribute erratic sales variations to random, nonrecurrent events

random sampling A form of probability sampling in which all units in a population have an equal chance of appearing in the sample, and the various events that can occur have an equal or known chance of taking place

raw materials Basic natural materials that become part of a physical product

realized strategy The strategy that actually takes place

rebate A sales promotion technique in which a consumer receives a specified amount of money for making a single product purchase

receiver The individual, group, or organization that decodes a coded message

recession A stage of the business cycle during which unemployment rises and total buying power declines, stifling both consumer and business spending

reciprocity An arrangement unique to business marketing in which two organizations agree to buy from each other

recognition test A posttest in which respondents are shown the actual ad and are asked if they recognize it

recovery A stage of the business cycle in which the economy moves from recession or depression toward prosperity

recruiting Developing a list of qualified applicants for sales positions

reference group A group that a person identifies with so strongly that he or she adopts the values, attitudes, and behavior of group members

reference pricing Pricing a product at a moderate level and displaying it next to a more expensive model or brand

regional issues Versions of a magazine that differ across geographic regions

regional shopping center A type of shopping center with the largest department stores, widest product mixes, and deepest product lines of all shopping centers

regression analysis A method of predicting sales based on finding a relationship between past sales and one or more independent variables, such as population or income

reinforcement advertising Advertising that assures users they chose the right brand and tells them how to get the most satisfaction from it

relationship marketing Establishing long-term, mutually satisfying buyer-seller relationships

relationship selling The building of mutually beneficial long-term associations with a customer through regular communications over prolonged periods of time

reliability A condition that exists when a research technique produces almost identical results in repeated trials

reminder advertising Advertising used to remind consumers about an established brand's uses, characteristics, and benefits

research design An overall plan for obtaining the information needed to address a research problem or issue

reseller markets Intermediaries that buy finished goods and resell them for a profit

retail positioning Identifying an unserved or underserved market segment and serving it through a strategy that distinguishes the retailer from others in the minds of consumers in that segment

retailer An organization that purchases products for the purpose of reselling them to ultimate consumers

retailing All transactions in which the buyer intends to consume the product through personal, family, or household use

roles Actions and activities that a person in a particular position is supposed to perform based on expectations of the individual and surrounding persons

routinized response behavior A consumer problem-solving process used when buying frequently purchased, low-cost items that require very little search-and-decision effort

sales branches Manufacturer-owned intermediaries that sell products and provide support services to the manufacturer's sales force

sales contest A sales promotion method used to motivate distributors, retailers, and sales personnel through recognition of outstanding achievements

sales force forecasting survey A survey of a firm's sales force regarding anticipated sales in their territories for a specified period

sales forecast The amount of a product a company expects to sell during a specific period at a specified level of marketing activities

sales offices Manufacturer-owned operations that provide services normally associated with agents

sales promotion An activity and/or material intended to induce resellers or salespeople to sell a product or consumers to buy it

sample A limited number of units chosen to represent the characteristics of a total population

sampling The process of selecting representative units from a total population

scan-back allowance A manufacturer's reward to retailers based on the number of pieces scanned

screening Selecting the ideas with the greatest potential for further review

search qualities Tangible attributes that can be judged before the purchase of a product

seasonal analysis An analysis of daily, weekly, or monthly sales figures to evaluate the degree to which seasonal factors influence sales

seasonal discount A price reduction given to buyers for purchasing goods or services out of season

secondary data Data compiled both inside and outside the organization for some purpose other than the current investigation

secondary-market pricing Setting one price for the primary target market and a different price for another market

segmentation variables Characteristics of individuals, groups, or organizations used to divide a market into segments

selective demand Demand for a specific brand

selective distortion An individual's changing or twisting of information that is inconsistent with personal feelings or beliefs

selective distribution Using only some available outlets in an area to distribute a product

selective exposure The process by which some inputs are selected to reach awareness and others are not

selective retention Remembering information inputs that support personal feelings and beliefs and forgetting inputs that do not

self-concept A perception or view of oneself

selling agents Intermediaries that market a whole product line or a manufacturer's entire output

service An intangible result of the application of human and mechanical efforts to people or objects

service quality Customers' perceptions of how well a service meets or exceeds their expectations

shopping mall intercept interview A research method that involves interviewing a percentage of individuals passing by "intercept" points in a mall

shopping products Items for which buyers are willing to expend considerable effort in planning and making purchases

single-source data Information provided by a single marketing research firm

situational influences Influences that result from circumstances, time, and location that affect the consumer buying decision process

social class An open group of individuals with similar social rank

social influences The forces other people exert on one's buying behavior

social network Web-based meeting place for friends, family, coworkers, and peers that allow users to create a profile and connect with other users for the purposes that range from getting acquainted, to keeping in touch, to building a work-related network

social responsibility An organization's obligation to maximize its positive impact and minimize its negative impact on society

sociocultural forces The influences in a society and its culture(s) that change people's attitudes, beliefs, norms, customs, and lifestyles

sole sourcing An organization's decision to use only one supplier

source A person, group, or organization with a meaning it tries to share with a receiver or an audience

special-event pricing Advertised sales or price cutting linked to a holiday, a season, or an event

specialty-line wholesalers Full-service wholesalers that carry only a single product line or a few items within a product line

specialty products Items with unique characteristics that buyers are willing to expend considerable effort to obtain

stakeholders Constituents who have a "stake," or claim, in some aspect of a company's products, operations, markets, industry, and outcomes

statistical interpretation Analysis of what is typical and what deviates from the average

storyboard A blueprint that combines copy and visual material to show the sequence of major scenes in a commercial

straight commission compensation plan Paying salespeople according to the amount of their sales in a given time period

straight rebuy purchase A routine purchase of the same products under approximately the same terms of sale by a business buyer

straight salary compensation plan Paying salespeople a specific amount per time period, regardless of selling effort

strategic alliance A partnership that is formed to create a competitive advantage on a worldwide basis

strategic business unit (SBU) A division, product line, or other profit center within the parent company

strategic channel alliance An agreement whereby the products of one organization are distributed through the marketing channels of another

strategic philanthropy The synergistic use of organizational core competencies and resources to address key stakeholders' interests and achieve both organizational and social benefits

strategic planning The process of establishing an organizational mission and formulating goals, corporate strategy, marketing objectives, marketing strategy, and a marketing plan

strategic windows Temporary periods of optimal fit between the key requirements of a market and the particular capabilities of a company competing in that market

stratified sampling A type of probability sampling in which the population is divided into groups with a common attribute and a random sample is chosen within each group

styling The physical appearance of a product

subculture A group of individuals whose characteristics, values, and behavioral patterns are similar within the group and different from those of people in the surrounding culture

supermarkets Large, self-service stores that carry a complete line of food products, along with some nonfood products

superregional shopping center A type of shopping center with the widest and deepest product mixes that attracts customers from many miles away

superstores Giant retail outlets that carry food and nonfood products found in supermarkets, as well as most routinely purchased consumer products

supply chain All the activities associated with the flow and transformation of products from raw materials through to the end customer

supply-chain management A set of approaches used to integrate the functions of operations management, logistics management, supply management, and marketing channel management so products are produced and distributed in the right quantities, to the right locations, and at the right time

supply management In its broadest form, refers to the processes that enable the progress of value from raw material to final customer and back to redesign and final disposition

support personnel Sales staff members who facilitate selling but usually are not involved solely with making sales

sustainability The potential for the long-term well-being of the natural environment, including all biological entities, as well as the interaction among nature and individuals, organizations, and business strategies

sustainable competitive advantage An advantage that the competition cannot copy

SWOT analysis Assessment of an organization's strengths, weaknesses, opportunities, and threats

tactile communication Communicating through touching

target audience The group of people at whom advertisements are aimed

target market The group of customers on which marketing efforts are focused

target public A collective of individuals who have an interest in or concern about an organization, product, or social cause

team selling The use of a team of experts from all functional areas of a firm, led by a salesperson, to conduct the personal selling process

technical salespeople Support salespeople who give technical assistance to a firm's current customers

technology The application of knowledge and tools to solve problems and perform tasks more efficiently

telemarketing The performance of marketing-related activities by telephone

telephone depth interview An interview that combines the traditional focus group's ability to probe with the confidentiality provided by telephone surveys

telephone survey A research method in which respondents' answers to a questionnaire are recorded by an interviewer on the phone

television home shopping A form of selling in which products are presented to television viewers, who can buy them by calling a toll-free number and paying with a credit card

test marketing A limited introduction of a product in geographic areas chosen to represent the intended market

time series analysis A forecasting method that uses historical sales data to discover patterns in the firm's sales over time and generally involves trend, cycle, seasonal, and random factor analyses

total budget competitors Firms that compete for the limited financial resources of the same customers

total cost The sum of average fixed and average variable costs times the quantity produced

total quality management (TQM) A philosophy that uniform commitment to quality in all areas of the organization will promote a culture that meets customers' perceptions of quality

trade (functional) discount A reduction off the list price a producer gives to an intermediary for performing certain functions

trade name The full legal name of an organization

trade sales promotion methods Methods intended to persuade wholesalers and retailers to carry a producer's products and market them aggressively

trade salespeople Salespeople involved mainly in helping a producer's customers promote a product

trademark A legal designation of exclusive use of a brand

trading company A company that links buyers and sellers in different countries

traditional specialty retailers Stores that carry a narrow product mix with deep product lines

transfer pricing Prices charged in sales between an organization's units

transportation The movement of products from where they are made to intermediaries and end users

trend analysis An analysis that focuses on aggregate sales data over a period of many years to determine general trends in annual sales

truck wholesalers Limited- service wholesalers that transport products directly to customers for inspection and selection

tying agreement An agreement in which a supplier furnishes a product to a channel member with the stipulation that the channel member must purchase other products as well

unaided recall test A posttest in which respondents are asked to identify advertisements they have seen recently but are not given any recall clues

undifferentiated targeting strategy A strategy in which an organization designs a single marketing mix and directs it at the entire market for a particular product

uniform geographic pricing Charging all customers the same price, regardless of geographic location

universal product code (UPC) A series of electronically readable lines identifying a product and containing inventory and pricing information

unsought products Products purchased to solve a sudden problem, products of which customers are unaware, and products that people do not necessarily think of buying

validity A condition that exists when a research method measures what it is supposed to measure

value A customer's subjective assessment of benefits relative to costs in determining the worth of a product

value analysis An evaluation of each component of a potential purchase

value conscious Concerned about price and quality of a product

variable costs Costs that vary directly with changes in the number of units produced or sold

vendor analysis A formal, systematic evaluation of current and potential vendors

venture team A cross-functional group that creates entirely new products that may be aimed at new markets

vertical channel integration Combining two or more stages of the marketing channel under one management

vertical marketing systems (VMSs) A marketing channel managed by a single channel member to achieve efficient, low-cost distribution aimed at satisfying target market customers

viral marketing A strategy to get consumers to share a marketer's message, often through e-mail or online videos, in a way that spreads dramatically and quickly

warehouse clubs Large-scale, members-only establishments that combine features of cash-and-carry wholesaling with discount retailing

warehouse showrooms Retail facilities in large, low-cost buildings with large on-premises inventories and minimal services

warehousing The design and operation of facilities for storing and moving goods

wealth The accumulation of past income, natural resources, and financial resources

wholesaler An individual or organization that sells products that are bought for resale, for making other products, or for general business operations

wholesaling Transactions in which products are bought for resale, for making other products, or for general business operations

width of product mix The number of product lines a company offers

wiki Type of software that creates an interface that enables users to add or edit the content of some types of websites

willingness to spend An inclination to buy because of expected satisfaction from a product, influenced by the ability to buy and numerous psychological and social forces

word-of-mouth communication Personal informal exchanges of communication that customers share with one another about products, brands, and companies

World Trade Organization (WTO) An entity that promotes free trade among member nations by eliminating trade barriers and educating individuals, companies, and governments about trade rules around the world

zone pricing Pricing based on transportation costs within major geographic zones

notes

Chapter 1

1. Sarah Tolkoff, "Vizio Nearly Doubled TV Sales in 2009," *Orange County Business Journal*, February 22, 2010, www.ocbj.com; Steven D. Strauss, "Corner Office: Vizio's William Wang," *Success Magazine*, March 1, 2010, www.successmagazine.com; Beth Snyder Bulik, "Vizio Blu-Ray Player: an America's Hottest Brands Case Study," *Advertising Age*, November 16, 2009, www.adage.com; www.vizio.com; American Marketing Association, Dictionary, www.marketingpower.com (accessed March 1, 2010).

2. "Definition of Marketing," American Marketing Association, www.marketingpower.com/AboutAMA/Pages/DefinitionofMarketing.aspx (accessed July 7, 2010).

3. Michael Lev-Ram, "A Smartphone's BFF: Teens and Tweens," *Business 2.0*, August 24, 2007, www.cnnmoney.com.

4. Nike, http://store.nike.com (accessed March 5, 2010).

5. "Nissan Announces U.S. Pricing on 2010 Cube," *PR Newswire*, January 28, 2010.

6. www.davidbeckham.com (accessed March 1, 2010).

7. Brooks Barnes, "Movie Studios See a Threat in Growth of Redbox," *New York Times*, September 6, 2009.

8. Tim Grierson, "Weezer's 'Ratitude' Gets Off to Slow Sales Start on Billboard Chart," *About.com*, November 12, 2009.

9. "Verizon Wireless Launches 'Don't Text and Drive' Ad Campaign," *Verizon Wireless*, October 23, 2010, http://news.vzw.com.

10. Brad Stone, "Making Sense of New Prices on Apple's iTunes," *New York Times*, April 7, 2009.

11. Michael Liedtke, "Newspaper Circulation May Be Worse Than It Looks," *Seattle Times*, November 22, 2009.

12. Julie Jargon, "Restaurants Look Beyond Chicken Fingers," *Wall Street Journal*, September 1, 2009; Stephanie Clifford, "A Fine Line When Ads and Children Mix," *New York Times*, February 14, 2010.

13. Eugene W. Anderson, Claes Fornell, and Sanal K. Mazvancheryl, "Customer Satisfaction and Shareholder Value," *Journal of Marketing* 68 (October 2004): pp. 172–185.

14. Xeuming Luo and Christian Homburg, "Neglected Outcomes of Customer Satisfaction," *Journal of Marketing* 70 (April 2007).

15. Thomas Rice, "New Fuel-Efficiency Standards Would Choke U.S. Carmakers," *USA Today*, May 28, 2009.

16. Ajay K. Kohli and Bernard J. Jaworski, "Market Orientation: The Construct, Research Propositions, and Managerial Implications," *Journal of Marketing* (April 1990): pp. 1–18.

17. Kwaku Atuahene-Gima, "Resolving the Capability-Rigidity Paradox in New Product Innovation," *Journal of Marketing* 70 (October 2005): pp. 61–83.

18. Gary F. Gebhardt, Gregory S. Carpenter, and John F. Sherry Jr., "Creating a Market Orientation," *Journal of Marketing* 70 (October 2006), www.marketingpower.com.

19. Sunil Gupta, Donald R. Lehmann, and Jennifer Ames Stuart, "Valuing Customers," *Journal of Marketing Research* 41 (February 2004): pp. 7–18.

20. Alan Grant and Leonard Schlesinger, "Realize Your Customers' Full Profit Potential," *Harvard Business Review* (September/October 1995): p. 59; Peter C. Verhoef, "Understanding the Effect of Customer Relationship Management Efforts on Customer Retention and Customer Share Development," *Journal of Marketing* (October 2003): p. 30.

21. Jagdish N. Sheth and Rajendras Sisodia, "More Than Ever Before, Marketing Is Under Fire to Account for What It Spends," *Marketing Manangement* (Fall 2005): pp. 13–14.

22. Stephen L. Vargo and Robert F. Lusch, "Evolving to a New Dominant Logic for Marketing," *Journal of Marketing* 68 (January 2004): pp. 1–17.

23. Paula Andruss, "New OfficeMax Catalog Courts Women Consumers," *Deliver Magazine*, June 29, 2009.

24. Barnes and Noble, www.bn.com; Sears, www.shopyourwayrewards.com (accessed March 1, 2010).

25. Roland T. Rust, Katherine N. Lemon, and Valarie A. Zeithaml, "Return on Marketing: Using Customer Equity to Focus Marketing Strategy," *Journal of Marketing* 68 (January 2004): pp. 109–127.

26. V. Kumar and Morris George, "Measuring and Maximizing Customer Equity: A Critical Analysis," *Journal of the Academy of Marketing Science* 35 (2007): pp. 157–171.

27. Rajneesh Suri, Chiranjeev Kohli, and Kent B. Monroe, "The Effects of Perceived Scarcity on Consumers' Processing of Price Information," *Journal of the Academy of Marketing Science* 35 (2007): pp. 89–100.

28. Natalie Mizik and Robert Jacobson, "Trading Off Between Value Creation and Value Appropriation: The Financial Implications of Shifts in Strategic Emphasis," *Journal of Marketing* (January 2003): pp. 63–76.

29. Emily Bryson York, "Grilled Chicken a Kentucky Fried Fiasco," *Ad Age*, May 11, 2009.

30. American Red Cross, http://amercian.redcross.org (accessed March 14, 2010).

31. "U.S. Charitable Giving Reaches $295.02 Billion in 2006," *Giving USA Foundation, Press Release*, June 25, 2007, www.aafrc.org/press_releases/gusa/20070625.pdf.

32. Kelly Geyskens, Mario Pandlelaere, Sigfried Dewitte, and Luk Warlop, "The Backdoor to Overconsumption: The Effect of Associating 'Low-Fat' Food with Health References," *Journal of Public Policy & Marketing* 26 (Spring 2007): pp. 118–125.

33. Nitasha Tiku, "How to Boost Sales with Mobile Coupons," *Inc.*, December 1, 2009.

34. "Southwest Airlines Fact Sheet," Southwest Airlines, December 31, 2009, www.southwest.com/about_swa/press/factsheet.html.

35. "A Day Made Better: 2009 Fact Sheet," A Day Made Better, October 6, 2009, www.adaymadebetter.com/factsheet.htm.

36. Natalie Zmuda, "Coca-Cola Goes Completely Green at Olympics In Ambitious Eco-Friendly Push, Sponsor Big Red Vows to Produce Zero Waste During Vancouver Games," *Ad Age*, February 1, 2010.

37. Stuart Elliott, "A Clean Break with Staid Detergent Ads," *New York Times*, February 3, 2010, www.nytimes.com/2010/02/03/business/media/03adco.html; Method, www.methodhome.com; Mark Borden, et al., "The World's Most Innovative Companies," *Fast Company*, March 2008, www.fastcompany.com; Sarah Van Schagen, "Fighting Dirty," *Grist*, March 14,

2008, www.grist.org/feature/2008/03/14/index.html?source=rss; Rob Walker, "Consumed: Method," *New York Times,* February 29, 2004, www.nytimes.com.

38. Ladka Bauerova, "Danone Net Climbs 4% as Cheaper Yogurts Boost Sales," *BusinessWeek,* February 11, 2010, www. businessweek.com; Roseanne Harper, "Culture of Growth," *Supermarket News,* February 1, 2010; Donna Berry, "Nutty Ways to Innovate, *Dairy Foods* (January 2010): pp. 70ff; Julian Mellentin, "Put Fibre First and Reap the Benefits," *Dairy Industries International* (January 2010): pp. 16ff; "New Products of the Decade," *Advertising Age,* December 14, 2009, p. 16; www.danone.com.

Feature Notes

a. Rupal Parekh, "Clarins Wonders: Can You Crowdsource a Fragrance?" *Advertising Age,* March 4, 2010, http://adage.com/globalnews/article?article_id=142465; Joe Fernandez, "Doritos Offers Consumers the Chance to Create Its Next TV Ad," *New Media Age,* February 16, 2010, www.nma.co.uk/news/doritos-offers-consumers-the-chance-to-create-its-next-tv-ad/3009998. article; Garrick Schmitt, "Can Creativity Be Crowdsourced?" *Advertising Age,* April 16, 2009, http://adage.com/digitalnext/article?article_id=136019.

b. "Ford, McDonald's, IBM, Abbott, Time Inc. to Share Sustainability Strategies," *Environmental Leader,* www. environmentalleader.com, July 17, 2007 (accessed March 12, 2010); "When Business Tackles Climate Change," Corporate Climate Response Conference, www.greenpowerconferences. com/corporateclimateresponse/index.html (accessed March 12, 2010); "Subscription-Based Sustainability Reporting Database Launches," *Environmental Leader,* March 1, 2007.

c. *Leatherman,* www.leatherman.com (accessed March 10, 2010); Fawn Fitter, "Outdoing the Swiss Army Knife," *Fortune Small Business,* July 25, 2007, http://money.cnn.com/2007/09/27/smbusiness/100123045.fsb/index.htm (accessed March 10, 2010); Shelly Strom, "Leatherman Learns Patent Lesson the Hard Way," *Portland Business Journal,* April 12, 2002, www. bizjournals.com/portland/stories/2002/04/15/focus4.html (accessed March 10, 2010).

d. Katie Ormsby, "'Green' Is the New Black," *Seattle Times,* February 15, 2010, http://seattletimes.nwsource.com/html/businesstechnology/2011085403_greenretail16. html?prmid=related_stories_section; Ariel Schwartz, "Nike Launches GreenXchange for Corporate Idea-Sharing," *Fast Company,* February 2, 2010, www.fastcompany.com/blog/ariel-schwartz/sustainability/nike-launches-greenxchange-corporate-idea-sharing; Dan Tapscott, "Davos: Nike and Partners Launch the GreenXchange," *BusinessWeek,* January 27, 2010, www. businessweek.com/the_thread/techbeat/archives/2010/01/davos_nike_and.html; www.nikereuseashoe.com/; www.adidas.com; www.nike.com.

Chapter 2

1. "Day 64: Latest Oil Disaster Developments," *CNN,* June 22, 2010, http://news.blogs.cnn.com/2010/06/22/day-64-latest-oil-disaster-developments/?iref=allsearch (accessed June 22, 2010); David Leonhardt, "Spillonomics: Underestimating Risk," *New York Times,* May 31, 2010, www.nytimes.com/2010/06/06/magazine/06fob-wwln-t.html (accessed June 22, 2010); Robert Mackey, "Rig Worker Says BP Was Told of Leak in Emergency System Before Explosion," *New York Times,* June 21, 2010, http://thelede.blogs.nytimes.com/2010/06/21/rig-worker-claims-bp-knew-of-leak-in-emergency-system-before-explosion/?scp=5&sq=BP&st=cse (accessed June 22, 2010); O. C. Ferrell

and Jennifer Jackson, "Case 12: BP (Beyond Petroleum) Focuses on Sustainability," pp. 586–593.

2. O. C. Ferrell and Michael Hartline, *Marketing Strategy,* 5th ed. (Mason, OH: South-Western, 2011), p. 10.

3. Christian Homburg, Karley Krohmer, and John P. Workman Jr., "A Strategy Implementation Perspective of Market Orientation," *Journal of Business Research* 57 (2004): pp. 1331–1340.

4. Emily Bryson York, "Nestle, Pepsi and Coke Face Their Waterloo," *Advertising Age,* October 8, 2007, via Care2 Network, www.care2.com/news/member/648204409/503634 (accessed April 5, 2010).

5. Derek F. Abell, "Strategic Windows," *Journal of Marketing* (July 1978): p. 21.

6. "About Fresh and Easy Neighborhood Market," www.freshandeasy.com/Content/pdfs/FreshEasyFactSheet.pdf (accessed March 15, 2010).

7. Catherine Holahan, "Will Less Be More for AOL?" *BusinessWeek Online,* July 31, 2006, www.businessweek.com/technology/content/jul2006/tc20060731_168094.htm (accessed April 5, 2010).

8. Gina Chon, "Chrysler Challenge: Burnish Image," *Wall Street Journal,* August 24, 2007, p. B3.

9. Ibid.

10. Douglas Bowman and Hubert Gatignon, "Determinants of Competitor Response Time to a New Product Introduction," *Journal of Marketing Research* (February 1995): pp. 42–53.

11. "Designed to Grow," 2007 Annual Report, Procter & Gamble, p. 5.

12. "About Us: Social Responsibility," Celestial Seasonings, www.celestialseasonings.com/about/community/social-responsibility.html (accessed April 5, 2010).

13. "Johnson Controls Launches New Brand to Support Focus on Comfort, Safety and Sustainability," *PR Newswire,* October 1, 2007, www.prnewswire.com/news-releases/johnson-controls-launches-new-brand-to-support-focus-on-comfort-safety-and-sustainability-58276407.html (accessed April 5, 2010).

14. Laurence G. Weinzimmer, Edward U. Bond III, Mark B. Houston, and Paul C. Nystrom, "Relating Marketing Expertise on the Top Management Team and Strategic Market Aggressiveness to Financial Performance and Shareholder Value," *Journal of Strategic Marketing* (June 2003): pp. 133–159.

15. "Google Cues Up With YouTube," *USA Today,* October 10, 2006, p. 1A.

16. Thomas Ritter and Hans Georg Gemünden, "The Impact of a Company's Business Strategy on Its Technological Competence, Network Competence and Innovation Success," *Journal of Business Research* 57 (2004): pp. 548–556.

17. "Designed to Grow," Proctor & Gamble's Annual Report, 2007, via www.scribd.com/doc/281864/Procter-Gamble-2007-Annual-Report (accessed March 15, 2010).

18. Stanley F. Slater, G. Tomas M. Hult, and Eric M. Olson, "On the Importance of Matching Strategic Behavior and Target Market Selection to Business Strategy in High-Tech Markets," *Journal of the Academy of Marketing Science* 35 (2007): pp. 5–17.

19. Jean L. Johnson, Ruby Pui-Wan Lee, Amit Saini, and Bianca Grohmann, "Market-Focused Flexibility: Conceptual Advances and an Integrative Model," *Journal of the Academy of Marketing Science* 31 (2003): pp. 74–89.

20. Delahunty, James, "iPod Market Share at 73.8 Percent, 225 Million iPods Sold, More Games for Touch than PSP & NDS: Apple," www.afterdawn.com/news/article.cfm/2009/09/09/ipod_market_share_at_73_8_percent_225_million_ipods_sold_more_games_for_touch_than_psp_nds_apple (accessed April 5, 2010).

21. Robert D. Buzzell, "The PIMS Program of Strategy Research: A Retrospective Appraisal," *Journal of Business Research* 57 (2004): pp. 478–483.

22. Isabelle Maignan, O. C. Ferrell, and Linda Ferrell, "A Stakeholder Model for Implementing Social Responsibility in Marketing," *European Journal of Marketing* 39 (September/October 2005): pp. 956–977.

23. Coca-Cola 2009 Annual Report, www.thecoca-colacompany.com/investors/form_10K_2009.html (accessed April 5, 2010).

24. M. Fry and Michael J. Polonsky, "Examining the Unintended Consequences of Marketing," *Journal of Business Research* 57 (2005): pp. 1303–1306.

25. Maignan, Ferrell, and Ferrell, "A Stakeholder Model for Implementing Social Responsibility in Marketing."

26. G. Tomas M. Hult, David W. Cravens, and Jagdish Sheth, "Competitive Advantage in the Global Marketplace: A Focus on Marketing Strategy," *Journal of Business Research* (January 2001): pp. 1–3.

27. Kwaku Atuahene-Gima and Janet Y. Murray, "Antecedents and Outcomes of Marketing Strategy Comprehensiveness," *Journal of Marketing* 68 (October 2004): pp. 33–46.

28. Christian Homburg, John P. Workman, and Ove Jensen, "Fundamental Changes in Marketing Organization: The Movement Toward a Customer-Focused Organizational Structure," *Journal of the Academy of Marketing Science* (Fall 2000): pp. 459–478.

29. Rajdeep Grewal and Patriya Tansuhaj, "The Chain of Effects from Brand Trust and Brand Affect to Brand Performance: The Role of Brand Loyalty," *Journal of Marketing* (April 2001): pp. 67–80.

30. Steve Watkins, "Marketing Basics: The Four P's Are as Relevant Today as Ever," *Investor's Business Daily,* February 4, 2002, p. A1.

31. Bent Dreyer and Kjell Grønhaug, "Uncertainty, Flexibility, and Sustained Competitive Advantage," *Journal of Business Research* 57 (2004): pp. 484–494.

32. Anuradha Kher, "Time-Share Your Pet," *Business 2.0* (September 2007): p. 27.

33. Hemant C. Sashittal and Avan R. Jassawalla, "Marketing Implementation in Smaller Organizations: Definition, Framework, and Propositional Inventory," *Journal of the Academy of Marketing Science* (Winter 2001): pp. 50–69.

34. O. C. Ferell and Michael Hartline, *Marketing Strategy* (Mason, OH: South-Western Cengage Learning, 2008), p. 257.

35. Maki Shirakai and Kazue Somiya, "Yoshinoya to Add 100 Restaurants as Consumers Seek Budget Meals," *Bloomberg News,* January 15, 2009, www.bloomberg.com/apps/news?pid=20601101&sid=aZPhvBeGwJo0&refer=japan (accessed April 5, 2010).

36. Robert W. Palmatier, Lisa K. Scheer, and Jan-Benedict E. M. Steenkamp, "Customer Loyalty to Whom? Managing the Benefits and Risks of Salesperson-Owned Loyalty," *Journal of Marketing Research* XLIV (May 2007), www.marketingpower.com/AboutAMA/Pages/AMA%20Publications/AMA%20Journals/Journal%20of%20Marketing%20Research/TOCs/summary%20may%2007/CustomerLoyaltyjmrmay07.aspx (accessed April 5, 2010).

37. Chezy Ofir and Itamar Simonson, "The Effect of Stating Expectations on Customer Satisfaction and Shopping Experience," *Journal of Marketing Research* XLIV (February 2007), www.gsb.stanford.edu/facseminars/pdfs/2007_01-31_Simonson_Related_Paper.pdf (accessed April 5, 2010).

38. Kee-hung Lee and T. C. Edwin Cheng, "Effects of Quality Management and Marketing on Organizational Performance," *Journal of Business Research* 58 (2005): pp. 446–456; Wuthichai Sittimalakorn and Susan Hart, "Market Orientation Versus Quality Orientation: Sources of Superior Business Performance," *Journal of Strategic Marketing* 12 (December 2004): pp. 243–253.

39. Philip B. Crosby, *Quality Is Free: The Art of Making Quality Certain* (New York: McGraw-Hill, 1979), pp. 9–10.

40. Piercy, *Market-Led Change.*

41. Douglas W. Vorhies and Neil A. Morgan, "Benchmarking Marketing Capabilities for Sustainable Competitive Advantage," *Journal of Marketing* 69 (January 2005): pp. 80–94.

42. Kenneth W. Thomas and Betty A. Velthouse, "Cognitive Elements of Empowerment: An 'Interpretive' Model of Intrinsic Task Motivation," *Academy of Management Review* (October 1990): pp. 666–681.

43. Rohit Deshpande and Frederick E. Webster Jr., "Organizational Culture and Marketing: Defining the Research Agenda," *Journal of Marketing* (January 1989): pp. 3–15.

44. Eric M. Olson, Stanley F. Slater, and G. Tomas Hult, "The Performance Implications of Fit Among Business Strategy, Marketing Organization Structure, and Strategic Behavior," *Journal of Marketing* 69 (July 2005): pp. 49–65.

45. Bernard J. Jaworski, "Toward a Theory of Marketing Control: Environmental Context, Control Types, and Consequences," *Journal of Marketing* (July 1988): pp. 23–39.

46. "2009 Initial Quality Study," J.D. Power & Associates (accessed March 15, 2010).

47. "Sioux City," White Rock, www.whiterockbeverages.com/SiouxCity.cfm (accessed April 24, 2010), "Drink Boxes," White Rock, www.whiterockbeverages.com/DrinkBoxes.cfm (accessed April 24, 2010); "White Rock Timeline," White Rock, www.whiterockbeverages.com/Timeline.cfm (accessed April 24, 2010); "CREATIVE Beverage Merchandising," Creative Beverage, April/May 2005, www.creativemag.com/cbev505.html (accessed April 24, 2010); *PR Newswire,* "Coca-Cola's Santa Claus: Not the Real Thing!," *PR News Online,* December 15, 2006, www.prnewsonline.com/prnewswire/407.html (accessed April 24, 2010).

48. D. Goldman, June 2, 2009, retrieved October 26, 2009, from *CNN Money:* http://money.cnn.com/2009/06/02/news/companies/auto_sales/index.htm, S. Arvizu. Triple Pundit, April 2009, retrieved October 26, 2009, from www.triplepundit.com/2009/04/electric-cars-for-the-masses-fords-new-strategy; O. Ferrell, W. M. Pride, *Foundations* of *Marketing* 3rd ed. (Boston: Houghton Mifflin, 2009); David Kiley, "One World, One Car, One Name," *BusinessWeek,* March 13, 2008, www.businessweek.com/magazine/content/08_12/b4076063825013.htm (accessed November 1, 2009); Mike Thomas, "Fiesta Is New Ford Small Car," Ford, February 15, 2008, www.ford.com/about-ford/news-announcements/featured-stories/featured-stories-detail/ford-fiesta-geneva (accessed November 1, 2009); Keith Bradsher and Vikas Baja, "Ford Shifts and Gains Ground in Asia," *New York Times,* www.nytimes.com/2010/03/31/business/global/31ford.html (accessed July 8, 2010).

49. Donald L. Barlett, and James B. Steele, "Monsanto's Harvest of Fear," May 5, 2008, *Vanity Fair,* www.vanityfair.com/politics/features/2008/05/monsanto200805 (accessed August 25, 2009); "Biotech Cotton Improving Lives of Farmers, Villages in India," Monsanto, www.monsanto.com/responsibility/sustainable-ag/biotech_cotton_india.asp (accessed March 31, 2009); "Corporate Profile," Monsanto, www.monsanto.com/investors/corporate_profile.asp (accessed March 15, 2009); Lauren Etter and Rebecca Townsend, "Monsanto's Profits Shoot Higher," January 8, 2009; Ellen Gibson, "Monsanto," *BusinessWeek,* December 22, 2008, p. 51; "Growing Hope in Africa," Monsanto, www.monsanto.com/responsibility/our_pledge/stronger_society/growing_self_sufficiency.asp (accessed March 31, 2009); Brian Hindo, "Monsanto: Winning the Ground War," *BusinessWeek,* December 6, 2007, pp.

35–41; Andrew Martin, "Fighting on a Battlefield the Size of a Milk Label," *New York Times,* March 9, 2008, www.nytimes.com/2008/03/09/business/09feed.html?ex=1362805200&en=56197f6ee92b4643&ei=5124&partner=permalink&exprod=permalink (accessed March 2, 2009); "Milk Labeling—Is Monsanto Opposed to Truth in Labeling?," Monsanto, www.monsanto.com/monsanto_today/for_the_record/rbst_milk_labeling.asp (accessed March 2, 2009); "Monsanto & NGO ISAP Launch Project Share—Sustainable Yield Initiative to Improve Farmer Lives," Monsanto, http://monsanto.mediaroom.com/index.php?s=43&item=693 (accessed March 31, 2009); "Monsanto Company—Company Profile, Information, Business Description, History, Background Information on Monsanto Company," www.referenceforbusiness.com/history2/92/Monsanto-Company.html (accessed March 20, 2009); "Monsanto Fund," Monsanto Fund, www.monsantofund.org/asp/About_the_Fund/Main_Menu.as (accessed April 1, 2009); "Monsanto Mania: The Seed of Profits," *iStockAnalyst,* www.istockanalyst.com/article/viewarticle.aspx?articleid=1235584&zoneid=Home (accessed April 12, 2009); Claire Oxborrow, Becky Price, and Peter Riley, "Breaking Free," *Ecologist* 38, no. 9 (November 2008): pp. 35–36; Andrew Pollack, "So What's the Problem with Roundup?" Ecology Center, January 14, 2003, www.ecologycenter.org/factsheets/roundup.html (accessed March 25, 2009); "Produce More," Monsanto (www.monsanto.com/responsibility/sustainable-ag/produce_more.as (accessed April 1, 2009); "Seed Police?" Monsanto, www.monsanto.com/seedpatentprotection/monsanto_seed_police.asp (accessed March 30, 2009); "The Parable of the Sower," *The Economist,* November 21, 2009, pp. 71–73.

Feature Notes

a. ZipCar, www.zipcar.com (accessed March 15, 2010); Joseph Pisani, "Car Sharing Takes Off," *CNBC,* December 4, 2009, www.cnbc.com/id/34257797 (accessed March 15, 2010); Paul Keegan, "The Best in Business," *Fortune,* September 14, 2009, pp. 42–52; Kunur Patel, "Zipcar: An America's Hottest Brands Study Case," *Advertising Age,* November 16, 2009, adage.com/article?article_id=140495 (accessed March 15, 2010); "Zipcar, San Francisco Launch Plug-in Hybrid Pilot Program," *SustainableBusiness.com,* February 19, 2009, www.sustainablebusiness.com/index.cfm/go/news.display/id/17703 (accessed March 15, 2010).

b. Michelle Conlin, "Look Who's Stalking Wal-Mart," *BusinessWeek,* December 7, 2009, pp. 30–33; Ann Zimmerman, "Target Cooks Up Rebound Recipe in Grocery Aisles," *Wall Street Journal,* May 12, 2009, p. B1; Andrew Ross Sorkin, "As It Battles Ackman and Wal-Mart, Target Pushes Basics," *New York Times,* May 27, 2009, http://dealbook.blogs.nytimes.com/2009/05/27/as-it-battles-ackman-and-wal-mart-target-pushes-basics (accessed February 20, 2010); Anthony Zumpano, "Target Changes Strategy, and Possibly Future of Supermarkets," *brandchannel,* January 22, 2010, www.brandchannel.com/home/post/2010/01/22/Target-Changes-Strategy-And-Possibly-Future-of-Supermarkets.aspx (accessed February 20, 2010); Pallari Gogoi, "How Walmart Turned the Tide Against Archrival Target," *Daily Finance,* February 17, 2010, www.dailyfiance.com/story/in-epic-battle-of-discounters-wal-mart-is-winning-ad-war-with-t/19361004 (accessed February 20, 2010); Nicole Maestri, "Wal-Mart, Target Seek Big Returns in Small Store," *Reuters,* February 4, 2010, www.reuters.com/article/idUSTRE6134ZR20100204?type=smallBusinessNews (accessed February 20, 2010); www.target.com (accessed February 21, 2010).

c. "About Crocs," www.crocs.com/company/history/ (accessed March 5, 2009); Diane Anderson, "When Crocs Attack," *Business 2.0,* November 2006, http://money.cnn.com/magazines/business2/business2_archive/2006/11/01/8392028/index.htm (accessed March 5, 2009); YOU by Crocs, www.youbycrocs.com; Crocs SEC Filings, www.crocs.com/company/investor/sec_filings (accessed March 5, 2009).

d. "McDonald's Green Initiatives Different for Individual Markets," *Environmental Leader,* December 23, 2007, www.environmentalleader.com/2007/12/23/mcdonalds-green-initiatives-different-for-individual-markets, (accessed March 17, 2008); "McDonalds Gets A+ for Sustainability Reporting," January 10, 2008, www.mcdonalds.com/corp/values/robert_center_rating.html (accessed March 17, 2008); Nichola Groom, "McDonald's Sees Restaurants as Green Laboratories," *Reuters,* December 20, 2007, www.reuters.com/article/ousiv/idUSN2041601020071220?sp5true (accessed March 24, 2008).

Chapter 3

1. Elizabeth Garone, "A Hole-in-One Idea," *Wall Street Journal,* February 9, 2010, www.wsj.com; "Geox Posts In-Line Earnings After Reorganization," *Reuters,* February 26, 2010, www.reuters.com/article/idUSLDE61P0XD20100226; "Power 100: #76, Mario Polegato, Founder, Chairman; Geox," *Footwear News,* November 2, 2009, pp. 12ff; Pitsinee Jitpleecheep, "Italy's Geox Puts Best Foot Forward in Asia," *Bangkok Post* (Thailand), October 5, 2009, www.bangkokpost.com; www. geoxusa.info.

2. "TrueCar.com Announces Sales Winners and Losers for 2009 Hyundai, Kia and Subaru Only Makes to Experience Growth; Camaro the Most Successful Launch." *PR-Inside.com,* December 2009.

3. Jon Sicher, "Top 10 CSD Results for 2008," *Beverage Digest,* March 30, 2009.

4. O. C. Ferrell and Michael Hartline, *Marketing Strategy* (Mason, OH: South-Western, 2011).

5. Miguel Helft, "Google Introduces Nexus One, Its Rival to the iPhone," *New York Times,* January 5, 2010.

6. Ferrell and Hartline, *Marketing Strategy.*

7. Aron O'Cass and Liem Viet Ngo, "Balancing External Adaptation and Internal Effectiveness: Achieving Better Brand Performance," *Journal of Business Research* 60 (January 2007): pp. 11–20.

8. Eberhard Stickel, "Uncertainty Reduction in a Competitive Environment," *Journal of Business Research* 51 (2001): pp. 169–177.

9. Vanessa Fuhrmans and Kate Linebaugh, "Luxury Car Makers Push Function More Than Flash," *Wall Street Journal,* January 13, 2010.

10. U.S. Bureau of the Census, "Income Poverty, and Health Insurance Coverage in the U.S.: 2008," Press Release, September 10, 2009, www.census.gov (accessed March 12, 2010).

11. Telis Demos, "Does Bling Beat the Market?" *Fortune,* September 17, 2007, p. 77.

12. Jeff Almer, "Is the FDA Inept? Peanut Butter Salmonella Outbreak Sparks Anger, Reforms," *Los Angeles Times,* February 6, 2010.

13. "Clients Lobbying on H.R. 3200," The Center for Responsive Politics, www.opensecrets.org/lobby/billsum.php?id=109547 (accessed March 12, 2010).

14. James Kanter, "Europe Fines Intel $1.45 Billion in Antitrust Case," *New York Times,* May 13, 2009.

15. David Stout, "Senate Passes Bill to Restrict Credit Card Practices," *New York Times,* May 19, 2009.

16. "LifeLock Will Pay $12 Million to Settle Charges by the FTC and 35 States That Identity Theft Prevention and Data Security Claims Were False," Federal Trade Commission, press release, March 9, 2010, www.ftc.gov.

17. Natasha Singer, "A Birth Control Pill That Promised Too Much," New York Times, February 10, 2009.

18. "PhRMA Guiding Principles: Direct to Consumer Advertisements," Pharmaceutical Research and Manufacturers of America, December 2008, www.phrma.org.

19. Jonathan D. Epstein, "BBB Expels Two Contractors over Complaints; Two Collection Agencies Quit," The Buffalo News, October 4, 2007.

20. Todd Wasserman, "Powerade-Gatorade Dispute Goes to FTC," Brandweek, May 4, 2009.

21. "Panel Update," NARB Quarterly 5 (Summer 2007), www.narbreview.org/quarterly/07summer.aspx.

22. Mike Dolan, "Vonage Mobile for iPhone and Blackberry Now Ready for Download," Fierce VoIP, October 5, 2009, www.fiercevoip.com.

23. Bruce Horovitz, "More Takeout Orderers Are All Thumbs," USA Today, January 3, 2008, www.usatoday.com/tech/webguide/internetlife/2008-01-03-text-ordering-food_N.htm.

24. Liz Gannes, "Time Spent Watching Video Jumps 40% in One Year," NewTeeVee, January 5, 2009, http://newteevee.com.

25. Debbie McAlister, Linda Ferrell, and O. C. Ferrell, Business and Society (Mason, OH: South-Western Cengage Learning, 2011), pp. 352–353.

26. Ibid.

27. Vladmir Zwass, "Electronic Commerce: Structures and Issues," International Journal of Electronic Commerce (Fall 2000): pp. 3–23.

28. "Continued CD Sales Declines in 2008, but Music Listening and Digital Downloads Increase," The NPD Group, Press Release, March 17, 2009, www.npd.com/press/releases/press_090317a.html.

29. U.S. Bureau of the Census, Statistical Abstract of the United States, 2010 (Washington DC: Government Printing Office, 2009), p. 15.

30. www.seniorpeoplemeet.com, babyboomerpeoplemeet.com (accessed March 8, 2010).

31. U.S. Bureau of the Census, Statistical Abstract of the United States, 2010, p. 75.

32. Ibid., p. 15.

33. U.S. Bureau of the Census, "Census Bureau Launches 2010 Census Advertising Campaign," January 14, 2010, http://2010.census.gov/news/releases/operations/ad-campaign-release.html.

34. U.S. Bureau of the Census, Statistical Abstract of the United States, 2010, p. 58.

35. U.S. Bureau of the Census, "Projections of the Population by Sex, Race, and Hispanic Origin for the United States: 2010 to 2050," August 14, 2008, www.census.gov/population/www/projections/summarytables.html.

36. "Hispanic Purchasing Power: Projections to 2015," Hispanic Business Inc, May 2008, https://secure.hbinc.com/product/view.asp?id=222.

37. Lauren Bell, "Power Market," DMNews, July 28, 2008, www.dmnews.com.

38. "Parents Grossly Underestimate the Influence Their Children Wield Over In-Store Purchases," Science News, March 17, 2009, www.sciencedaily.com.

39. www.seventhgeneration.com/about (accessed March 10, 2010).

40. Marc Eisen, "Organic Industry Under Strain as 21st Annual Conference Opens," WisBusiness, February 26, 2010, www.wisbusiness.com/index.iml?Article=186912; CROPP Cooperative, www.farmers.coop; Organic Valley, www.organicvalley.coop.

41. Ben Sills, "First Solar's Ahearn, Wal-Mart Protégé, Slashes Stake," BusinessWeek, February 25, 2010, www.businessweek.com/news/2010-02-25/first-solar-s-ahearn-wal-mart-protege-slashes-stake-update2-.html; Poornima Gupta, "U.S. Solar Startup Aims to Match First Solar's Cost," Reuters, February 10, 2010, www.reuters.com/article/idUSN1017639820100211; John Letzing, "First Solar Nabs China Contract to Build World's Largest Field," MarketWatch, September 9, 2009, www.marketwatch.com; "Company Information Overview," First Solar, www.firstsolar.com/company_overview.php; "High-Flying First Solar Takes Aim at Utility."

Feature Notes

a. Mark Milian, "What's A #spon Tweet? It's a Twitter Ad, Silly," Los Angeles Times Technology, February 18, 2010, http://latimesblogs.latimes.com/technology/2010/02/spon-twitter-ad.html; Kayleen Schaefer, "New F.T.C. Rules Have Bloggers and Twitterers Mulling," New York Times, October 14, 2009, www.nytimes.com; Alan Friel, "Navigating FTC's Guidance on Social Media Marketing," November 30, 2009, www.adweek.com.

b. Michael V. Copeland, "The Light Bulb Goes Digital," Fortune, February 8, 2010, pp. 33–38; James Kanter, "Europe's Ban on Old-Style Bulbs Begins, August 31, 2009, http://nytimes.com; John Ewoldt, "Dollars & Sense: On the Lookout for LEDs," Star Tribune (Minneapolis), November 4, 2009, p. 1E.

c. Chaniga Vorasarun, "Clean Machine: James Dyson Got Rich Taking Bags out of Vacuums. Now He Aims to Take Some Bugs out of Public Restrooms," Forbes, March 24, 2008, pp. 98–99; "The Dyson Story: The Airblade Hand Dryer-Clean Home, Clean Hands," www.dyson.com/technology/airblade.asp (accessed March 24, 2010); Steve Hamm, "The Vacuum Man Takes On Wet Hands," BusinessWeek, July 2, 2007, www.businessweek.com/magazine/content/07_27/b4041063.htm?chan5search (accessed March 24, 2010).

d. Anderson Cooper, " A Life Saver Called 'Plumpy'nut'," 60 Minutes, CBS News, October 21, 2007, www.cbsnews.com/stories/2007/10/19/60minutes/main3386661.shtml (accessed March 2, 2009); "WHO Experts Raise Antiquated Nutrition Standards," Doctors without Borders, October 10, 2007, http://doctorswithoutborders.org/news/issue.cfm?id=2396 (accessed March 2, 2009); "Plumpy'nut in the Field," Nutriset, www. nutriset.fr/index.php?option=com_content&task=view&id=41&Itemid=33 (accessed March 2, 2009).

Chapter 4

1. John Hechinger, "FTC Criticizes College-Themed Cans in Anheuser-Busch Marketing Efforts," Wall Street Journal, August 25, 2009, pp. B1, B4; Steve Wieberg and Steve Berkowitz, "Has College Sports Marketing Gone Too Far?" USA Today, April 2, 2009, pp. 1A–2A; Xorje Olivares, "'Fan Can' Beers Come in School Colors of 26 Universities: Invites Binge Drinking?," ABC News, August 28, 2009, http://abcnews.com/Business/anheuser-buschs-bud-light-markets-beer-college-students/story?id=8418866 (accessed January 22, 2010); David Wharton, "Court Ruling in Reggie Bush Case Could Lead to Depositions," Los Angles Times, December 29, 2009, http://articles.latimes.com/2009/dec/29/sports/la-sp-usc-reggie-bush29-2009dec29 (accessed January 22, 2010); William Donovan, "Socially Responsible Investing Blog," About.com, August 23, 2009, http://socialinvesting.about.com/b/2009/08/23/bud-lights-fan-cans-and-social-responsibility.html (accessed January 23, 2010); Annie Thomas, "University Puts Halt to Bud Light 'Fan

Can' Gimmick," *Michigan Daily*, September 6, 2009, www.michigandaily.com/content/university-puts-halt-bud-light-fan-can-gimmick?page=0,1 (accessed January 23, 2010); "NCAA Reportedly Finally Interviews Reggie Bush," *SportingNews*, January 11, 2010, www.sportingnews.com/college-football/article/2010-01-11/ncaa-reportedly-finally-interviews-reggie-bush (accessed January 24, 2010); www.ncaa.org (accessed January 24, 2010).

2. Peter R. Darke and Robin J. B. Ritchie, "The Defensive Consumer: Advertising Deception, Defensive Processing, and Distrust," *Journal of Marketing Research*, 4, no. 1 (February 2007): pp. 114–127.

3. Isabelle Maignan and O. C. Ferrell, "Corporate Social Responsibility and Marketing: An Integrative Framework," *Journal of the Academy of Marketing Science* 32 (January 2004): pp. 3–19.

4. Indra Nooyi, "The Responsible Company," World in 2008 issue, *The Economist*, March 31, 2008, p. 132.

5. Charles Toutant, "GE Unit Ordered to Pay $11.3 Million Over False-Advertising Claims Against Competitor," *Law.com*, April 14, 2009, via www.law.com/jsp/article.jsp?id=1202429880602 (accessed February 4, 2010).

6. "NAFE Announces Top Companies for Female Executives," Avon, March 16, 2009, http://responsibility.avoncompany.com/page-134-NAFE-Announces-Top-Companies-for-Female-Executives (accessed February 5, 2010); "The Avon Breast Cancer Crusade," Avon, www.avoncompany.com/women/avoncrusade/index.html (accessed February 5, 2010).

7. Isabelle Maignan and O. C. Ferrell, "Antecedents and Benefits of Corporate Citizenship: An Investigation of French Businesses," *Journal of Business Research* 51 (2001): pp. 37–51.

8. Debbie Thorne, Linda Ferrell, and O. C. Ferrell, *Business and Society: A Strategic Approach to Social Responsibility*, 4th ed. (Boston: Houghton Mifflin, 2011), pp. 38–40.

9. O. C. Ferrell, "Business Ethics and Customer Stakeholders," *Academy of Management Executive* 18 (May 2004): pp. 126–129.

10. "2007 Corporate Citizenship Report," Pfizer, www.pfizer.com/files/corporate_citizenship/cr_report_2007.pdf (accessed February 10, 2010).

11. Archie Carroll, "The Pyramid of Corporate Social Responsibility: Toward the Moral Management of Organizational Stakeholders," *Business Horizons* (July/August 1991): p. 42.

12. "U.S. Retailers Face $ 191 Billion in Fraud Losses Each Year," *NACS Online*, November 16, 2009, www.nacsonline.com/NACS/News/Daily/Pages/ND1116091.aspx (accessed February 5, 2010); "Common Types of Fraud: Healthcare Fraud and False Claims," Pietragallo Gordon Alfano Bosick & Raspanti, LLP, www.falseclaimsact.com/common_frauds_healthcare.php (accessed February 5, 2010).

13. Reuters, "Intel Pays AMD $1.25 Billion to Settle All Disputes," *Wired*, November 12, 2009, www.wired.com/epicenter/2009/11/intel-pays-amd-125-billion-to-settle-all-disputes/ (accessed January 29, 2010).

14. Todd Cohen, "Corporate Givers Regroup in Recession," *Inside Philanthropy*, October 19, 2009, http://philanthropyjournal.blogspot.com/2009_10_01_archive.html (accessed February 5, 2010).

15. "Haiti Relief: Corporate Donations — See How Much Major Companies Are Donating," *The Huffington Post*, January 20, 2010, www.huffingtonpost.com/2010/01/15/haiti-relief-corporate-do_n_424710.html (accessed February 5, 2010).

16. "Community," Kerbey Lane Café, www.kerbeylanecafe.com/about/community (accessed February 5, 2010).

17. "Save Lids to Save Lives," Yoplait, www.yoplait.com/slsl/# (accessed February 5, 2010).

18. "Consumer Behavior Study Confirms Cause-Related Marketing Can Exponentially Increase Sales," *Cone*, October 1, 2008, www.landchoices.org/contribute/conestudynew.pdf (accessed February 5, 2010)

19. Thorne, Ferrell, and Ferrell, *Business and Society*, p. 335.

20. Jim Witkin, "Despite Recession, Home Depots Keeps on Giving," *Triple Pundit*, February 9, 2010, www.triplepundit.com/2010/02/despite-recession-home-depot-keeps-on-giving/ (accessed February 12, 2010) Habitat for Humanity International and The Home Depot Foundation announce national expansion of "Partners In Sustainable Building," Habitat for Humanity, August 4, 2009, www.habitat.org/newsroom/2009archive/08_04_2009_HFH_Home_Depot_Foundation.aspx (accessed February 5, 2010).

21. Miguel Bustillo, "Wal-Mart to Assign New 'Green' Ratings, *Wall Street Journal*, July 17, 2009, http://online.wsj.com/article/SB124766892562645475.html (accessed February 12, 2010).

22. Amanda Schupak, "An Inconvenient Paint," *Forbes*, March 26, 2007, p. 70.

23. "HP Eco Solutions," Hewlett-Packard, www.hp.com/hpinfo/globalcitizenship/environment/recycling/unwanted-hardware.html (accessed February 5, 2010).

24. "Welcome to Eco Options: Sustainable Forestry," Home Depot, www.homedepot.com/ecooptions/index.html? (accessed February 5, 2010).

25. "Better Banana Project," Chiquita, www.chiquita.com/chiquita/discover/owbetter.asp (accessed February 5, 2010).

26. Paul Hawken and William McDonough, "Seven Steps to Doing Good Business," *Inc.*, (November 1993): pp. 79–90.

27. Jill Gabrielle Klein, N. Craig Smith, and Andrew John, "Why We Boycott: Consumer Motivations for Boycott Participation," *Journal of Marketing* 68 (July 2004): pp. 92–109.

28. Christian Homburg and Andreas Fürst, "How Organizational Complaint Handling Drives Customer Loyalty: An Analysis of the Mechanistic and the Organic Approach," *Journal of Marketing* 69 (July 2005): pp. 95–114.

29. Marc Gunther, "Bet Buy Wants Your Electronic Junk," *Fortune*, December 2009, http://money.cnn.com/2009/11/30/technology/best_buy_recycling.fortune/index.htm (accessed February 12, 2010).

30. "Ecological Initiatives" *Weaver Street Market*, www.weaverstreetmarket.coop/index.php?option=com_content&task=view&id=109&Itemid=212 (accessed February 5, 2010).

31. "Take Charge of Education," Target, https://sites.target.com/site/en/corporate/page.jsp?contentId=PRD03-005174&ref=sr_shorturl_tcoe (accessed February 6, 2010).

32. Kyle Cassidy, "Brewing Change: Why Craft Beer Makers Go Green," *Wend*, June 24, 2009, www.wendmag.com/greenery/2009/06/sustainable-craft-brewing/ (accessed February 9, 2010).

33. "2009 Trust Barometer," Edelman Trust Barometer, www.edelman.com/trust/2009/ (accessed February 6, 2010).

34. "Countrywide Financial: The Subprime Meltdown," in Thorne, Ferrell, Ferrell, *Business & Society*, pp. 512–519.

35. Susan Heavey, "U.S. Joins Lawsuits against J&J over Marketing," *Reuters*, February 19, 2009, www.reuters.com/article/idUSTRE51I7L920090219 (accessed February 8, 2010).

36. Bruce Horowitz, "Unilever Gets All the Trans Fat Out of Its Margarines," *USA Today*, July 27, 2009, www.usatoday.com/money/industries/food/2009-07-26-trans-fat-unilever_N.htm?csp=34 (accessed February 8, 2010); David Zinczenko with Matt Goulding, *Eat This, Not That*, www.smartbalance.com/pr/eat_this_not_that.pdf (accessed February 8, 2010).

37. Tim Barnett and Sean Valentine, "Issue Contingencies and Marketers' Recognition of Ethical Issues, Ethical Judgments and Behavioral Intentions," *Journal of Business Research* 57 (2004): pp. 338–346.

38. Shari R. Veil, and Michael L. Kent, "Issues Management and Inoculation: Tylenol's Responsible Dosing Advertising," *Public Relations Review* 34 (2008): pp. 399–402. Taken from Elsevier website, http://faculty-staff.ou.edu/K/Michael.L.Kent-1/PDFs/Veil_Kent_2008.pdf (accessed July 6, 2010).

39. "PhRMA Guiding Principles Direct to Consumer Advertisements about Prescription Medicines," www.phrma.org/files/attachments/PhRMA%20Guiding%20Principles_Dec%2008_FINAL.pdf (accessed February 12, 2010).

40. David E. Sprott, Kenneth C. Manning, and Anthony D. Miyazaki, "Grocery Price Setting and Quantity Surcharges," *Journal of Marketing* (July 2003): pp. 34–46.

41. Stephen Taub, "SEC Probing Harley Statements," *CFO.com*, July 14, 2005, www.cfo.com/article.cfm/4173321/c_4173841?f=archives&origin=archive.

42. Helena Bottemiller, "China Launches Food Safety Commission," *Food Safety News*, February 11, 2010, www.foodsafetynews.com/2010/02/china-launches-food-safety-commission/ (accessed February 12, 2010).

43. "The Ethics of American Youth: 2008," Josephson Institute Center for Youth Ethics http://charactercounts.org/programs/reportcard/2008/index.html (accessed February 11, 2010).

44. Peggy H. Cunningham and O. C. Ferrell, "The Influence of Role Stress on Unethical Behavior by Personnel Involved in the Marketing Research Process" (working paper, Queens University, Ontario, 2004), p. 35.

45. Joseph W. Weiss, *Business Ethics: A Managerial, Stakeholder Approach* (Belmont, CA: Wadsworth, 1994), p. 13.

46. O. C. Ferrell, Larry G. Gresham, and John Fraedrich, "A Synthesis of Ethical Decision Models for Marketing," *Journal of Macromarketing* (Fall 1989): pp. 58–59.

47. Ethics Resource Center, "The Ethics Resource Center's 2009 *National Business Ethics Survey: Ethics in the Recession*" (Washington, DC: Ethics Resource Center, 2009), p. 9.

48. Barry J. Babin, James S. Boles, and Donald P. Robin, "Representing the Perceived Ethical Work Climate Among Marketing Employees," *Journal of the Academy of Marketing Science* 28 (2000): pp. 345–358.

49. Ferrell, Gresham, and Fraedrich, "A Synthesis of Ethical Decision Models for Marketing."

50. Lawrence B. Chonko and Shelby D. Hunt, "Ethics and Marketing Management: A Retrospective and Prospective Commentary," *Journal of Business Research* 50 (2000): 235–244.

51. Linda K. Trevino and Stuart Youngblood, "Bad Apples in Bad Barrels: A Causal Analysis of Ethical Decision Making Behavior," *Journal of Applied Psychology* 75 (1990): pp. 378–385.

52. Ethics Resource Center, "The Ethics Resource Center's 2009 National Business Ethics Survey," p. 41.

53. Ethics Resource Center, "The Ethics Resource Center's 2007 National Business Ethics Survey," p. ix.

54. Ethics Resource Center, "The Ethics Resource Center's 2009 *National Business Ethics Survey: Ethics in the Recession*" (Washington, DC: Ethics Resource Center, 2009), p. 36.

55. Marjorie Kelly, "Tyco's Ethical Makeover," *Business Ethics* (Summer 2005): pp. 14–19.

56. "Welcome to HCA Ethics and Compliance," HCA Healthcare, http://ec.hcahealthcare.com (accessed January 7, 2008); O. C. Ferrell, John Fraedrich, and Linda Ferrell, *Business Ethics: Ethical Decision Making and Cases*, 6th ed. (Boston: Houghton Mifflin, 2005), pp. 407–424.

57. "Social Responsibility Statement," American Apparel & Footwear Association, www.apparelandfootwear.org/LegislativeTradeNews/SocialResponsibility.asp (accessed February 5, 2010); "About WRAP," WorldwideResponsible Apparel Production, www.wrapapparel.org/modules.php?name=Content&pa=showpage&pid=3 (accessed February 5, 2010).

58. "2009's 100 Most Influential People in Business Ethics," Ethisphere, December 16, 2009, http://ethisphere.com/2009s-100-most-influential-people-in-business-ethics/ (accessed February 8, 2010).

59. David Sarno, Peter Y. Hong, and W.J. Hennigan, "Wells Fargo Fires Executive Accused of Using Bank-Owned Malibu Home," *Los Angeles Times*, September 15, 2009, http://articles.latimes.com/keyword/employee-misconduct (accessed February 8, 2010).

60. Sir Adrian Cadbury, "Ethical Managers Make Their Own Rules," *Harvard Business Review* (September/October 1987): p. 33.

61. Caren Epstein, "Food Companies Marketing Products to People Living with Chronic Disease," *The Fort Colllins Coloradoan*, November 13, 2005, p. E4.

62. Olstad, Scott, "A Brief History of Cigarette Advertising," *Time*, June 15, 2009, www.time.com/time/nation/article/0,8599,1904624,00.html (accessed July 8, 2010); Jon P. Nelson, "Cigarette Advertising Regulation: A Meta-Analysis," originally published in *International Review of Law and Economics* 26 no. 2, (June 2006): pp. 195–226. Downloaded from http://econ.la.psu.edu/papers/Nelson_metaanalysis2.pdf (accessed July 8, 2010).

63. Ferrell, Fraedrich, and Ferrell, *Business Ethics*, pp. 27–30.

64. Marjorie Kelly, "Holy Grail Found: Absolute, Definitive Proof That Responsible Companies Perform Better Financially," *Business Ethics,* Winter 2005, www.business-ethics.com/current_issue/winter_2005_holy_grail_article.html; Xueming Luo and C. B. Bhattacharya, "Corporate Social Responsibility, Customer Satisfaction, and Market Value," *Journal of Marketing* 70 (October 2006), www.marketingpower.com; Isabelle Maignan, O. C. Ferrell, and Linda Ferrell, "A Stakeholder Model for Implementing Social Responsibility in Marketing," *European Journal of Marketing* 39 (September/October 2005): pp. 956–977.

65. "Corporate Citizenship Study," Burson-Marsteller, June 2009, www.burson-marsteller.com/Innovation_and_insights/blogs_and_podcasts/BM_Blog/Documents/Corporate%20Citizenship%20Executive%20Summary.pdf (accessed February 10, 2010), pp. 3, 7.

66. Maignan, Ferrell, and Ferrell, "A Stakeholder Model for Implementing Social Responsibility in Marketing."

67. Ariel Schwartz, "The Putting Lot: An Urban Golf Course in Brooklyn," *Fast Company*, April 15, 2009, www.fastcompany.com/blog/ariel-schwartz/sustainability/putting-lot-urban-golf-course-brooklyn (accessed April 27, 2010); "Answers to Some Frequently Asked Questions about the Putting Lot," Press Release, http://theputtinglot.org/wp-content/uploads/2009/05/Putting-Lot-About.pdf (accessed April 27, 2010); Tim McKeough, "Playful Recycling," *New York Times*, May 27, 2009, www.nytimes.com/2009/05/28/garden/28shop.html?_r=1&ref=garden (accessed April 27, 2010); "The Putting Lot, Mini Golf Collective," *Gothamist*, http://gothamist.com/2009/05/28/the_putting_lot.php (accessed April 27, 2010).

68. "Think Adoption First" program, About PETCO: Petco's Company Information Site, http://about.petco.com/think-adoption-first/ (accessed April 28, 2010); Pet Overpopulation, The Humane Society of the United States, www.humanesociety.org/issues/pet_overpopulation/ (accessed April 28, 2010); Pet Ownership Stats, The American Society for the Prevention of Cruelty to Animals, www.aspca.org/pet-care/pet-ownership-stats.html (accessed April 28, 2010); Industry Statistics & Trends, American pet Products Association, www.americanpetproducts.org/press_industrytrends.asp (accessed April 28, 2010); "Tree of Hope Raises Record $4 million to Help Animals in Need," Press Room, January 6, 2010,

http://about.petco.com/2010/01/tree-of-hope-raises-record-4-million-to-help-animals-in-need/ (accessed April 28, 2010).

69. Francine Kopun, "Earth-friendly Shoes," *Toronto Star,* April 12, 2010, www.thestar.com; "Timberland to Increase Use of Digital through New European Manager Role," *New Media Age,* March 4, 2010, p. 7; "Consumer Spending Shifts Down as Mindset Changes," *Food Institute Report,* January 11, 2010, p. 8; Desda Moss, "The Value of Giving," *HR Magazine* (December 2009): pp. 22ff; "Timberland Partners with Reliance Brands," *Professional Services Close-up,* December 9, 2009; "Timberland Reduces GHG Emissions 36%," *Environmental Leader,* April 8, 2010, www.environmentalleader.com; www.Timberland.com.

Feature Notes

a. www.fifthgroup.com (accessed November 29, 2009); Leslie Kaufman, "Nudging Recycling from Less Waste to None," *New York Times,* October 20, 2009, www.nytimes.com/2009/10/20/science/earth/20trash.html (accessed October 20, 2009); "Fifth Group Restaurant," Glass Packing Institute, www.gpi.org/fifth-group-restaurants.html (accessed November 29, 2009); "Fifth Group Comes in First," *Georgia Green Dining Guide,* May 14, 2009, http://georgiagreendiningguide.com/2009/06/14/hellohellohellohello.aspx (accessed November 29, 2009).

b. "Who Really Pays for CSR Initiatives," *Environmental Leader,* February 15, 2008, www.environmentalleader.com/2008/02/15/who-really-pays-for-csr-initiatives/ (accessed February 12, 2010); "Global Fund," www.theglobalfund.org/en/ (accessed February 12, 2010).

c. Megha Bahree, "Sorghum Beats Corn (Maybe)," *Forbes,* September 7, 2009, pp. 98–99; Ben Wright, "Averting Disaster," *Wall Street Journal,* December 7, 2009, http://online.wsj.com/article/SB126013576440879119.html (accessed December 16, 2009); Richard Harris, "Scientists: Biofuel Laws May Harm Environment," *NPR's Morning Edition,* October 23, 2009, www.npr.org/templates/story.php?storyId=114055974 (accessed February 9, 2010); "Biofuels—New Report Brings Greater Clarity to Burning Issue," United Nations Environment Programme, October 16, 2009, www.unep.org/Documents.Multilingual/Default.asp?DocumentID=599&ArticleID=6347&1=en&+=long (accessed February 9, 2010); "Boeing Joins Abu Dhabi Research in Aviation Biofuels," *UPI.com,* January 19, 2010, www.upi.com/Science_News/Resource-Wars/2010/01/19/Boeing-joins-Abu-Dhabi-research-in-aviation-biofuels/UPI-41721263920400/ (accessed February 10, 2010).

Chapter 5

1. Ellen Byron, "Seeing Store Shelves Through Senior Eyes," *Wall Street Journal,* September 14, 2009, pp. B1–B2; "Seniors and Technology in the United States 2009," *Research and Markets,* www.researchandmarkets.com/reports/996895/seniors_and_technology_in_the_united_states.htm (accessed December 20, 2009); www.us.depend.com (accessed December 20, 2009).

2. "J.D. Power and Associates Reports: For Private Label Grocery Brands, Organic Products Drive Gain in Prestige Among Customers," March 25, 2009, businesscenter.jdpower.com/news/pressrelease.aspx?ID=2009047 (accessed February 2010).

3. Farhad Manjoo, "Can Microsoft's Bing, or Anyone, Seriously Challenge Google?" *Time,* August 31, 2009 (accessed July 16, 2010).

4. Allison Enright, "Surviving 2010," *Marketing News,* February 28, 2010, pp. 30–33.

5. Susan Berfield, "Coach's New Bag," *BusinessWeek,* June 29, 2009, pp. 41–43.

6. Jacquelyn S. Thomas, "A Methodology for Linking Customer Acquisition to Customer Retention," *Journal of Marketing Research* (May 2001): pp. 262–268.

7. Marguerite Reardon, "AT&T Collects iPhone User Complaints about Poor Service," *CNNTech,* December 8, 2009, www.cnn.com/2009/TECH/12/08/cnet.iphone.att.dropped.calls/index.html (accessed March 8, 2010).

8. A. Parasuraman, Dhruv Grewal, and R. Krishnan, *Marketing Research* (Boston: Houghton Mifflin, 2004), p. 63.

9. Ken Manning, O. C. Ferrell, and Linda Ferrell, "Consumer Expectations of Clearance vs. Sale Prices," University of New Mexico, working paper, 2010.

10. Vikas Mittal and Wagner A. Kamakura, "Satisfaction, Repurchase Intent, and Repurchase Behavior: Investigating the Moderating Effects of Customer Characteristics," *Journal of Marketing Research* (February 2001): pp. 131–142.

11. Anjali Cordeiro, "Proctor & Gamble to Test Online Store to Study Buying Habits," *Wall Street Journal,* January 15, 2010, http://online.wsj.com/article/SB10001424052748704363504575003333381682138.html (accessed March 19, 2010).

12. U.S. Census Bureau, American Community Survey, www.census.gov/acs/www/ (accessed March 9, 2010).

13. Aaron Gilchrist, "Census Forms Confusion: 'American Community Survey' Is Legit," *nbc12.com,* January 27, 2010, www.nbc12.com/Global/story.asp?S=11890921 (accessed March 9, 2010).

14. Symphony IRI Group, "About Us," http://symphony iri.com/About/History/tabid/60/Default.aspy (accessed September 10, 2010).

15. David Lieberman, "TiVo to Sell Data on What People Watch, Fast-Forward," *USA Today,* April 20, 2010, www.usatoday.com/tech/news/2009-04-20-tivo-data-new-plan_N.htm (accessed March 19, 2010).

16. Proctor & Gamble 2009 Annual Report, February 24, 2010, p. 3, http://annualreport.pg.com/annualreport2009/index.shtml (accessed March 20, 2010).

17. Warren Davies, "How to Increase Survey Response Rates Using Post-it Notes," *GenerallyThinking.com,* August 3, 2009, http://generallythinking.com/blog/how-to-increase-survey-response-rates-using-post-it-notes/ (accessed March 9, 2010); Randy Garner, "Post-It Note Persuasion: A Sticky Influence," *Journal of Consumer Psychology* 15 (2005): pp. 230–237.

18. Elisabeth A. Sullivan, "A Group Effort," *Marketing News,* February 28, 2010, pp. 23–27.

19. Daniel Gross, "Lies, Damn Lies, and Focus Groups," *Slate,* October 10, 2003, http://slate.msn.com/id/2089677 (accessed March 20, 2010).

20. Piet Levy, "In With the Old, in Spite of the New," *Marketing News,* May 30, 2009, p. 19.

21. Tom Taullli, "Entrepreneur's Journal: Setting Up a Customer Advisory Board that Gets Results," *BloggingStocks,* January 24, 2010, www.bloggingstocks.com/2010/01/24/entrepreneurs-journal-setting-up-a-customer-advisory-board-tha (accessed March 9, 2010).

22. Bas Donkers, Philip Hans Franses, and Peter C. Verhoef, "Selective Sampling for Binary Choice Models," *Journal of Marketing Research* (November 2003): pp. 492–497.

23. Ilan Brat, "The Emotional Quotient of Soup Shopping," *Wall Street Journal,* February 17, 2010, http://online.wsj.com/article/SB10001424052748704804204575069562743700340.html?KEYWORDS=campbell%27s+soup+label (accessed March 19, 2010).

24. Piet Levy, "10 Minutes with…Gregory A. Reid," *Marketing News,* February 28, 2010, p. 34.

25. Eunkyu Lee, Michael Y. Hu, and Rex S. Toh, "Are Consumer Survey Results Distorted? Systematic Impact of Behavioral Frequency and Duration on Survey Response Errors," *Journal of Marketing Research* (February 2000): pp. 125–133.

26. Press release, "BudNet Tracks Beer-Lovers' Buying Habits," Join Together, February 27, 2004, www.jointogether.org/news/headlines/inthenews/2004/budnet-tracks-beer-lovers.html (accessed March 20, 2010).

27. Aaker, V. Kumar, and G. Day, *Marketing Research,* 8th ed. (New York: Wiley & Sons, 2004).

28. Marlus Wübben and Florian von Wangenheim, "Predicting Customer Lifetime Duration and Future Purchase Levels: Simple Heuristics vs. Complex Models," in Jean L. Johnson and John Hulland, eds., *2006: AMA Winter Educators' Conference; Marketing Theory and Applications* 17 (Winter 2006): pp. 83–84.

29. Noah Rubin Brier, John McManus, David Myron, and Christopher Reynolds, "'Zero-In' Heroes," *American Demographics* (October 2004): pp. 36–45.

30. IRI BehaviorScan Testing, http://us.infores.com/portals/0/articlePdfs/IRI_BehaviorScan_0308.pdf (accessed March 9, 2010).

31. Behrooz Noori and Mohammad Hossein Salimi, "A Decision-Support System for Business-to-Business Marketing," *Journal of Business & Industrial Marketing* 20 (2005): pp. 226–236.

32. Spencer E. Ante, "IBM," *BusinessWeek,* November 24, 2003, p. 84.

33. Reprinted with permission of The Marketing Research Association, P.O. Box 230, Rocky Hill, CT 06067–0230, 860–257–4008.

34. "Top 25 Global Research Organizations: The Nielsen Co.," *Marketing News,* August 15, 2007, p. H4.

35. Ogden Publications, www.ogdenpubs.com (accessed April 22, 2010).

36. Look-Look Company Press Kit 2007, www.look-look.com/look/pdfs/presskit.pdf (accessed April 29, 2010); "Team Look-Look," Look-Look.com, www.look-look.com/look/teamll.html (accessed April 29, 2010); "What the Heck Is Team Look-Look and How Do I Sign Up?" TeamLook-Look.com, www.teamlook-look.com/look/whatisteamlooklook (accessed April 29, 2010).

Feature Notes

a. Greenfields Communications, "FreshMinds Research Increases Online Research Community Capabilities," *Market Research World,* September 15, 2009, www.marketresearchworld.net/index.php?option=com_content&task=view&id=2765gItem id=76 (accessed December 21, 2009); www.communispace.com (accessed December 21, 2009); "8 Highlights from ESOMAR'S Online Research 2009 Conference," American Marketing Association, *Marketing Power,* October 29, 2009, www.marketingpower2.com/blog/marketingnews/2009/10/10_highlights_from_esomars_onl.html (accessed December 21, 2009); Jean Halliday, "Mercedes Panel Calls Shots on SLS Ad," *Automotive News,* January 25, 2010, www.autonews.com/apps/pbcs.dll/article?AID=/20100125/RETAIL03/301259991/1286# (accessed January 28, 2010); Jeremiah Owyang, "A Collection of Social Network Stats for 2009," *Web Strategy,* January 11, 2009, www.web-strategist.com/blog/2009/01/11/a-collection-of-social-networks-stats-for-2009 (accessed January 28, 2010).

b. Sarah McBride, "Radio Shows Tune in to Listener Habits," *Wall Street Journal,* September 17, 2009, http://online.wsj.com/article/SB125314774171818133.html (accessed January 23, 2010); www.arbitron.com/portable_people_meters/home.htm (accessed February 21, 2010); "Arbitron Reschedules 4Q Earnings Report," *Associated Press,* January 21, 2010, http://abcnews.go.com/Business/wireStory?id=9626385 (accessed January 23, 2010); Adam Edelman, "Arbitron Shares Rise on Positive People-Meter Views," *Wall Street Journal,* January 6, 2010, http://online.wsj.com/article/BT-CO-20100106-709987.html (accessed January 23, 2010); "How Does Recycling Paper Help Landfills," lovetoknow, *Green Living,* http://greenliving.lovetoknow.com/How_Does_Recycling_Paper_Help_Landfills (accessed February 22, 2010).

c. iModerate, http://imoderate.com (accessed March 23, 2009); Eric Peterson, "Tech Startup of the Month," *ColoradoBiz,* August 2007, www.imoderate.com/cms_images/file_9.pdf (accessed March 23, 2009); Deborah Vence, "10 Minutes With...," *Marketing News,* February 15, 2009.

d. "2007 World's Most Ethical Companies," *Ethisphere,* http://ethisphere.com/2007-worlds-most-ethical-companies (accessed April 10, 2010); "Fortune's Most Admired Companies," www.haygroup.com/ww/Expertise/index.asp?id5906 (accessed April 10, 2010); Cathy Planchard, "'World's Most Ethical Companies' Ranking Issued by *Ethisphere* Magazine," *The Corporate Social Responsibility Newswire,* May 8, 2007, www.csrwire.com/News/8413.html (accessed April 10, 2010).

Chapter 6

1. Mary Jane Credeur and Alan Ohnsman, "Kia Plant Buoys U.S. 'Ambitions' as Toyota Stumbles on Recalls," *BusinessWeek,* February 26, 2010, www.businessweek.com; Ira Siegel, "Chicago Show's Green Debuts," *Chicago Sun Times,* February 19, 2010, http://searchchicago.suntimes.com/autos/news/2059138,debuts21910.article; Steve Minter, "On the Rise—Kia Stresses Value in Tight Times," *IndustryWeek,* February 17, 2010, www.industryweek.com; www.kia.com.

2. "Hybrid Cars," *hybridcars.com,* http://hybridcars.com/compacts-sedans/lexus-ls-660hl-misguided-hybrid.html (accessed February 4, 2010).

3. Jack Neff, Rupal Parekh, "Dove Takes Its New Men's Line to the Super Bowl," *Ad Age,* January 5, 2010.

4. "Canada Just Turned Pink," *Seventeen,* November 3, 2009, www.seventeen.com/fashion/blog/victorias-secret-pink-canada.

5. *FabulousSavings.com,*www.fabuloussavings.com/online/us/nutrisystemads/1/don_shula_for_nutrisystem_silver_age_based_mens_program/ (accessed March 26, 2010).

6. Service Corporation International, www.hoovers.com/company/Service_Corporation_International/rrycri-1.html (accessed March 26, 2010).

7. U.S. Census Bureau, "Age and Sex in the United States: 2008," Table 1, June 2009, www.census.gov.

8. "Disney and Asus Launch Netbook Computer for Kids," Disney, Press Release, June 17, 2009, www.disneyconsumerproducts.com.

9. "Born to Buy," Center for New American Dream, www.newdream.org/kids/borntobuy.php (accessed March 26, 2010).

10. U.S. Census Bureau, *Statistical Abstract of the United States, 2010,* p. 14, www.census.gov (accessed March 26, 2010).

11. David Bohan, "Marketing to Moms: Mom is 'Buyer in Chief,'" *Why Moms Rule,* August 7, 2009, http://whymomsrule.com/2009/08/07/mom-is-%E2%80%9Cbuyer-in-chief%E2%80%9D/.

12. "Barbie Launches a New Line of Black Dolls Called So In Style," Mattel, Press Release, September 29, 2009, http://investor.shareholder.com/mattel/releasedetail.cfm?ReleaseID=412067.

13. "America's Families and Living Arrangements: 2009," *Current Population Reports,* U.S. Census Bureau, www.census.gov/population/www/socdemo/hh-fam/cps2009.html (accessed March 29, 2010).

14. Emily Bryson York, "Taco Bell, Starbucks Trot Out 'Light' Offerings for New Year," *Advertising Age,* December 27, 2007, www.adage.com.

15. Joseph T. Plummer, "The Concept and Application of Life Style Segmentation," *Journal of Marketing* (January 1974): p. 33.

16. SRI Consulting Business Intelligence, "About VALS ™," www.strategicbusinessinsights.com/vals/about.shtml (accessed March 29, 2010).

17. Philip Kotler, *Marketing Management: Analysis, Planning, Implementation, and Control*, 11th ed. (Englewood Cliffs, NJ: Prentice-Hall, 2003), p. 144.

18. Joe Lofaro, "Microsoft's Zune a Worthy iPod Alternative," *Suite101.com*, December 15, 2008, http://mobiletechnology.suite101.com/article.cfm/what_is_a_zune_you_ask_well_its_not_an_ipod.

19. Jason D. O'Grady, "Verizon Droid Ad Attacks iPhone on Features," *ZDNet*, October 19, 2009, http://blogs.zdnet.com/Apple/?p=5055.

20. Lindsey Partos, "Quaker Oats Repositions Brand in Health Focus," *Food&DrinkEurope.com*, March 10, 2009, www.foodanddrinkeurope.com/Products-Marketing/Quaker-Oats-repositions-brand-in-health-focus.

21. Charles W. Chase Jr., "Selecting the Appropriate Forecasting Method," *Journal of Business Forecasting* (Fall 1997): pp. 2, 23, 28–29.

22. Nielsen, http://en-us.nielsen.com/ (accessed March 30, 2010).

23. Noreen O'Leary, "Motorola's Mobile Loyalty Solution Targets Shoppers," *Brandweek*, January 19, 2010, www.brandweek.com.

24. "BRAINy Awards Honor Individuals," *Bicycle Retailer and Industry News*, April 15, 2010, www.bicycleretailer.com/news/newsDetail/3961.html; Francis Lawell, "Raleigh: Cycling to Success?" *Business Review (UK)* (February 2009): pp. 16ff; "Industry Overview 2008," *National Bicycle Dealers Association*, http://nbda.com/articles/industry-overview-2008-pg34.htm; www.raleigh.co.uk/; www.raleighusa.com.

25. Tom Held, "DreamBikes Opens a Store and Opportunities in Milwaukee," *Journal Sentinel*, April 7, 2010, www.jsonline.com; "Trek Announces Title Sponsorship of 2010 Dirt Series," *Mountain Bike Review*, February 3, 2010, http://reviews.mtbr.com/blog/trek-announces-title-sponsorship-of-2010-dirt-series; Joe Vanden Plas, "CIO Leadership: Trek's Brent Leland Cycles through Business-IT Alignment," *Wisconsin Technology Network FusionCIO*, February 24, 2009, http://wistechnology.com/fusioncio/article/5500; *www.trekbikes.com*.

26. Rick Swanborg, "How Marriott Broke Down Customer Data Siloes," *CIO*, November 11, 2009, www.cio.com; "Marriott Partners with AT&T and Cisco for Virtual Meetings," *Hotel Marketing*, January 28, 2010, www.hotelmarketing.com; Dan Butcher, "Marriott Exec Reveals Multichannel Mobile Strategy for SpringHill Suites," *Mobile Marketer*, November 25, 2009, www.mobilemarketer.com; Helen Coster and Laurie Burkitt, "In These Ads, Customers Are the Celebrities," *Forbes*, September 2, 2009, www.forbes.com; www.marriott.com.

Feature Notes

a. Andrew Scott, "Natural Eats, Tasty Profits," *Fairfield County Business Journal* (July 25, 2005): pp. 1+; "Tasty Bite May Raise $12M to Fuel Growth," *The Economic Times* (July 8, 2006); Shivani Vora, "Curry in a Hurry," *Time*, February 12, 2007, p. G10; Tasty Bite, www.tastybite.com (accessed March 30, 2010).

b. Daniel Wolfe, "Channel Surfing," *Bank Technology News*, March 1, 2010, p. 1; Kathy Brister, "Making the Most of Mobile," *US Banker*, March 1, 2010, p. 17; Jennifer Saranow Schultz, "Banking by Text Message," *New York Times Bucks Blog*, February 25, 2010, http://bucks.blog.nytimes.com.

c. Meg Riordan, "Tobacco Company Marketing to Kids," Campaign for Tobacco-Free Kids, www.tobaccofreekids.org/research/factsheets/pdf/0008.pdf, September 22, 2009 (accessed March 30, 2010); "Surgeon General's Report – Reducing Tobacco Use," Centers for Disease Control and Prevention, www.cdc.gov/mmwr/preview/mmwrhtml/rr4916a1.htm, December 22, 2000 (accessed March 30, 2010); "Tobacco Advertising," *Globalink*, http://globalink. org/factsheets/en/advertising.shtml (accessed March 30, 2010).

d. John Vidal, "What It Means to Travel Green," *The Guardian*, February 20, 2010, www.guardian.co.uk; Richard Hammond, "Raising the Game," *Geographical* (January 2010): p. 71; Matthew Clark, "Kurt Holle's Ecolodge Employs Locals While Slowing the Devastation of the Amazon," *Christian Science Monitor*, February 1, 2010, www.csmonitor.com.

Chapter 7

1. Anna Wilde Mathews, "Polly Want an Insurance Policy?" *Wall Street Journal*, December 9, 2009, p. D1, D6; Dan Reed, "For Passengers of New Airline, When the Fur Flies, It's in Style," *USA Today*, June 19, 2009, pp. 1B–2B; http://petairways.com (accessed January 22, 2010); http://press.petinsurance.com (accessed January 22, 2010); www.petsbest.com (accessed January 22, 2010); Industry Statistics & Trends, American Pet Products Association, 2009/2010 National Pet Owners Survey, http://americanpetproducts.org/press_industrytrends.asp (accessed January 27, 2010).

2. Jing Wang, Nathan Novemsky, and Ravi Dhar, "Anticipating Adaptation to Products," *Journal of Consumer Research* 36, no. 2 (June 2009): pp. 149–159.

3. Russell W. Belk, "Situational Variables and Consumer Behavior," *Journal of Consumer Research* (December 1975): pp. 157–164.

4. Nathan Novemsky, Ravi Dhar, Norbert Schwarz, and Itamar Simonson, "Preference Fluency in Choice," *Journal of Marketing Research* 44 (August 2007): pp. 347–356.

5. Blue Nile, Diamond Education, www.bluenile.com/diamond-education?track=head (accessed March 9, 2010).

6. Ryan S. Elder and Ariadna Krishna, "The Effects of Advertising Copy on Sensory Thoughts and Perceived Taste," *Journal of Consumer Research* 36, no. 5 (February 2010): pp. 748–756.

7. Dennis Price, "Retail Sales Strategies: Manipulation or Magic?" dynamicbusiness.com, May 27, 2009, www.dynamicbusiness.com/articles/articles-retail/retail-sales-strategies-manipulation-or-magic3653.html (accessed March 9, 2010).

8. Linda Tischler, "Never Mind! Pepsi Pulls Much-loathed Tropicana Packaging," *Fast Company*, February 23, 2009, www.fastcompany.com/blog/linda-tischler/design-times/never-mind-pepsi-pulls-much-loathed-tropicana-packaging (accessed March 9, 2010).

9. Jaideep and Sengupta Rongrong Zhou, "Understanding Impulsive Eaters' Choice Behaviors: The Motivational Influence of Regulatory Focus," *Journal of Marketing Research* 44 (May 2007): pp. 297–308.

10. Piet Levy, "Express Yourself," *Marketing News*, June 15, 2009, p. 6.

11. Barry J. Babin and Eric G. Harris, *CB2* (Mason, OH: Southwestern Cengage Learning, 2009), p. 126.

12. Aric Rindfleisch, James E. Burroughs, and Nancy Wong, "The Safety of Objects: Materialism, Existential Insecurity, and Brand Connection," *Journal of Consumer Research* 36, no. 1 (June 2009): pp. 1–16.

13. Leatherman, www.leatherman.com (accessed March 11, 2010).

14. Strategic Business Insights, www.strategicbusinessinsights.com/vals/(accessed March 9, 2010).

15. Nancy Gibbs, "What Women Want Now," *Time*, October 14, 2009, www.time.com/time/specials/packages/

article/0,28804,1930277_1930145_1930309-2,00.html (accessed March 9, 2010).

16. David B. Wooten, "From Labeling Possessions to Possessing Labels: Ridicule and Socialization Among Adolescents," *Journal of Consumer Research* 33 (September 2006): p. 188.

17. Babin and Harris, *CB2*, p. 181.

18. Mercedes-Benz USA, Vehicles Menu, www.mbusa.com/mercedes/#/vehiclesMenu (accessed March 10, 2010); BMW North America, All BMWs, www.bmwusa.com/standard/content/allbmws/default.aspx (accessed March 10, 2010).

19. Bruce Horovitz, "Marketers Warm Up to Iced Coffee," *Wall Street Journal,* June 15, 2009, p. B2.

20. "US Population Estimates," Fact Finder, http://factfinder.census.gov/home/saff/main.html?_lang=en (accessed March 26, 2010).

21. Martha Moore, "Gap Between Baby Boomers, Young Minorities Grows," *USA Today,* May 14, 2009, www.usatoday.com/news/nation/census/2009-05-14-census_N.htm (accessed March 26, 2010).

22. U.S. Census Bureau, "ACS Demographic and Housing Estimates: 2006–2008," http://factfinder.census.gov/servlet/ADPTable?_bm=y&-qr_name=ACS_2008_3YR_G00_DP3YR5&-geo_id=01000US&-ds_name=&-_lang=en&-redoLog=false&-format= (accessed March 10, 2010).

23. "The 15th Annual Buying Power of Black America Report," *Target Market News*, www.targetmarketnews.com/publications.htm (accessed March 10, 2010).

24. "African-American Buying Power Rises, per eMarketer," *AdWeek*, March 11, 2009, www.adweek.com/aw/content_display/news/agency/e3i71419f4d58d0cd4ca0c3484537d9982e (accessed March 10, 2010).

25. Bob Barrett, "Allstate Goes All In," *ANA Magazine*, October 2009, www.theadvertisermagazine.com/content/200910-allstate-goes-all-in.php (accessed March 11, 2010).

26. U.S. Census Bureau, "ACS Demographic and Housing Estimates:" 2006–2008; Piet Levy, "La Musica to Their Ears," *Marketing News*, May 15, 2009, pp. 15–16.

27. "Multicultural Marketing," *Marketing News,* April 30, 2009, p. 24.

28. Jeffrey M. Humphreys, "The Multicultural Economy," *Georgia Business and Economic Conditions* 67 (Third Quarter 2007), www.diversityresources.com/rc42e/multicultural_economy.html (accessed March 30, 2010).

29. "Target Celebrates Hispanic Heritage Month with the Launch of the 2009 Dream in Color Campaign," Target Press Release, September 9, 2009, http://pressroom.target.com/pr/news/multicultural/hispanic/hispanic-heritage-month-dream-in-color-campaign.aspx (accessed March 10, 2010).

30. Levy, "La Musica to Their Ears," pp. 15–16.

31. U.S. Census Bureau, "ACS Demographic and Housing Estimates: 2006-2008."

32. "Asian American Lifestyle in the United States in 2009," *Research and Markets*, www.researchandmarkets.com/reports/1194740/asian_american_lifestyle_in_the_united.htm (accessed March 11, 2010).

33. Carol Angrisani, *Supermarket News*, November 10, 2008, pp. 1–7.

34. Bernice Yeung, "Shoplifting, Inc.," *The Crime Report*, March 4, 2010, http://thecrimereport.org/2010/03/04/shoplifting-inc (accessed March 29, 2010).

35. BSA/IDC Global Software Piracy Study 2008, http://global.bsa.org/globalpiracy2008/index.html (accessed March 29, 2010).

36. Aubry Fowler III, Barry J. Babin, and Amy K. Este, "Burning for Fun or Money: Illicit Consumer Behavior in a Contemporary Context," presented at the Academy of Marketing Science annual conference, May 27, 2005, Tampa, FL.

37. "Counterfeit Culture," *CBC News*, www.cbc.ca/news/interactives/map-counterfeit-goods (accessed March 30, 2010).

38. "Travelocity Strengthens Hotel Price Guarantee and Lowers Hotel Fees," *USA Today*, October 27, 2009, content.usatoday.com/communities/hotelcheckin/post/2009/10/620000564/1 (accessed April 22, 2010); "The Travelocity Customer Bill of Rights," Travelocity, http://svc.travelocity.com/about/main/0,,TRAVELOCITY:EN%7CABOUT,00.html (accessed April 22, 2010).

39. "Products," Iams Website, www.iams.com/iams/premium-pet-food.jsp (accessed April 29, 2010); "Iams Healthy Naturals Partners with Dog Fancy(R) to Launch Dog College," Press Release, *PR Newswire*, April 27, 2010, www.prnewswire.com/news-releases/iams-healthy-naturals-partners-with-dog-fancyr-to-launch-dog-college-92188489.html (accessed April 29, 2010); "Pet Health Insurance Helps Care for and Protect Your Pet," Iams, www.iams.com/en-us/pages/Petinsurance.aspx (accessed April 29, 2010); "Iams & ProScan Imaging Partnership: Bringing MR Technology and Expertise to Your Pets," *ProScan*, www.proscan.com/fw/main/IAMS_Pet_Imaging-435.html (accessed April 29, 2010).

Feature Notes

a. Timothy W. Martin, "Organic Foods Get on Private-Label Wagon," *Wall Street Journal*, July 27, 2009, http://online.wsj.com/article/SB124865207118182453.html (accessed March 1, 2010); "J.D. Power and Associates Reports: For Private Label Grocery Brands, Organic Products Drive Gain in Prestige Among Customers," March 25, 2009, http://businesscenter.jdpower.com/news/pressrelease.aspx?ID=2009047 (accessed March 1, 2010); Maureen Callahan, R.D., "How to Buy the Best Organic Foods," *CNNHealth.com*, June 16, 2009, www.cnn.com/2009/HEALTH/06/16/best.organic.produce/index.html (accessed March 1, 2010).

b. Alyssa Abkowitz, "The Color Committee Gets to Work," *Fortune*, October 26, 2009 pp. 34–37; Pantone, www.pantone.com (accessed March 1, 2010).

c. Facebook, www.facebook.com (February 18, 2009); Steven Levy, "Facebook Grows Up," *Newsweek*, August 20, 2007, pp. 41–46; Ellen McGirt, "Hacker, Dropout, CEO," *Fast Company* (May 2007): pp. 74–80; Brad Stone, "In Facebook, Investing in a Theory," *New York Times*, October 4, 2007 C1, C2; "The Aging of Facebook," *iThink Online*, www.targetx.com/ithink/?p=680#more-680 (accessed February 6, 2009).

d. "Arm Teens with Good Credit Skills," *Wall Street Journal*, http://online.wsj.com/article/SB120139461017220029.html, January 27, 2008 (accessed March 31, 2008); "Credit Cards: Increased Complexity in Rates and Fees Heightens Need for More Effective Disclosures to Consumers," Government Accountability Office, January 9, 2006, http://gao.gov/new.items/d06929.pdf, (accessed March 31, 2008).

Chapter 8

1. Daniel Lyons, "Google's Orwell Moment," *Newsweek*, March 1, 2010, p. 20; Douglas MacMillan, "Google's New Billion-Dollar Baby," *BusinessWeek*, February 22, 2010, p. 22; Matt Hamblen, "Google CEO Preaches 'Mobile First,'" *ComputerWorld*, February 17, 2010, www.computerworld.com; Miguel Helft, "Google Set to Showcase Fast Internet," *New York Times*, February 11, 2010, www.nytimes.com; Steven Levy, "Secret of Googlenomics," *Wired*, May 22, 2009, www.wired.com; www.google.com.

2. "STP: Segmentation, Targeting, Positioning," American Marketing Association, www.marketingpower.com (accessed April 7, 2010).

3. Ibid.

4. U.S. Bureau of the Census, *Statistical Abstract of the United States, 2010*, www.census.gov/prod/2009pubs/10statab/domtrade.pdf (Table 1013).

5. Ibid. (Tables 1013, 1017).

6. Barbara Farfan, "World's Largest Retailers—The Biggest and Best Retail Chains in the U.S.," *About.com*, http://retailindustry.about.com/od/famousretailers/a/US_largest_retail_companies.htm (accessed April 7, 2010).

7. U.S. Bureau of the Census, *Statistical Abstract of the United States, 2010*, www.census.gov/prod/2009pubs/10statab/fedgov.pdf (Table 459).

8. Ibid., www.census.gov/prod/2009pubs/10statab/stlocgov.pdf (Table 416).

9. "Film House Wins Two Major Government Contracts," Film House, Press Release, October 8, 2009, www.filmhouse.com/pdf/Military_Contracts_press_release10-8-09.pdf.

10. Das Narayandas and V. Kasturi Rangan, "Building and Sustaining Buyer-Seller Relationships in Mature Industrial Markets," *Journal of Marketing* (July 2004): p. 63.

11. Caterpillar Inc., "Code of Conduct: Value to Customers," www.cat.com/cda/layout?m=209603&x=7 (accessed April 5, 2010).

12. Leonidas C. Leonidou, "Industrial Buyers' Influence Strategies: Buying Situation Differences," *Journal of Business & Industrial Marketing* 20 (January 2005): pp. 33–42.

13. Daniel Lovering, "Nucor Posts 1Q Loss of US$190M on Weak Steel Demand," *The Associated Press*, April 23, 2009, www.canadaeast.com/business/article/645071.

14. Frederick E. Webster Jr., and Yoram Wind, "A General Model for Understanding Organizational Buyer Behavior," *Marketing Management* Winter/Spring 1996 pp. 52–57.

15. Marketwire, "Barrick Signs Innovative 10-year Agreement with Yokohama to Secure Tire Supply," *Sys-Con* Media, January 30, 2008, www.sys-con.com/node/493297.

16. George S. Day and Katrina J. Bens, "Capitalizing on the Internet Opportunity," *Journal of Business & Industrial Marketing* 20 (2005): pp. 160–168.

17. Niklas Myhr and Robert E. Spekman, "Collaborative Supply-Chain Partnerships Built upon Trust and Electronically Mediated Exchange," *Journal of Business & Industrial Marketing* 20 (2005): pp. 179–186.

18. "Development of NAICS," U.S. Census Bureau, www.census.gov/epcd/www/naicsdev.htm (accessed March 30, 2010).

19. "The 25 Fastest-Growing Inner City Companies: Numi Organic Tea," *BusinessWeek*, June 5, 2009, www.businessweek.com; Lisa McLaughlin, "Tea's Got a Brand New Bag," *Time*, March 27, 2008, www.time.com; "Numi Organic Tea," *Beverage Industry* (November 2007): p. 10; "Numi Organic Tea," *Beverage Industry* (June 2007): p. 13; Crystal Detamore-Rodman, "A Perfect Match?" *Entrepreneur* (October 2003): pp. 60+; www.numitea.com.

20. Caroline van Hasselt, "Bombardier's Profit Dips," *Wall Street Journal*, April 1, 2010, www.wsj.com; Scott Deveau, "Bombardier in Finance Deal with China," *Financial Post*, March 31, 2010, www.montrealgazette.com; Andrea Rothman, "Airbus, Boeing Confront Bombardier on Financing Rules," *BusinessWeek*, March 26, 2010, www.businessweek.com; "Start Your Engines; New Competition for Airbus and Boeing," *The Economist*, March 20, 2010, p. 59; Stephen Gandel, "Trains, Planes, and Bombardier," *Time*, March 8, 2010, p. GB8; Caroline van Hasselt and Doug Cameron, "Bombardier Gets $2.1 Billion Order from Republic Airways," *Wall Street Journal*, February 26, 2010, www.wsj.com; www.bombardier.com.

Feature Notes

a. "Lead Paint Prompts Mattel to Recall 967,000 Toys," *New York Times*, http://nytimes.com/2007/08/02/business/02toy.htm

l?ex51343707200&en51f7a6cb6a8627d6e&ei55088&partner5rssnyt&emc5rss, August 2, 2007 (accessed April 9, 2008); "Made in China: Perspectives on the Global Manufacturing Giant," *Inbound Logistics*, http://inboundlogistics.com/articles/features/0308_feature02.shtml, March 1, 2008 (accessed April 9, 2008).

b. Quoted in Bill Esler, "Uptick in Demand for Green Printing," *Graphic Arts Online*, March 17, 2010, www.graphicartsonline.com; Elissa Elan, "How Darden Plans to Go Green," *Nation's Restaurant News*, March 17, 2010, www.nrn.com.

c. Maha Atal, "Sustaining the Dream," *BusinessWeek*, October 15, 2007, p. 60; Kristen Gerencher, "Treadmill Desks Let Employees Feel the Burn," *Boston Globe*, March 26, 2006; Reena Jana, "Exercise More than Just Your Options," *BusinessWeek* October 29, 2007, p. 24; "Making the Tough Call," *Inc.* (November 2007): pp. 36+.

d. Matt Kinsman, "How Virtual Can Bolster a Live Event," *Folio*, March 17, 2010, www.foliomag.com; Melanie Lindner, "How to Tackle a Virtual Trade Show," *Forbes*, July 28, 2009, www.forbes.com; Dean Takahashi, "Sony Electronics Holds a Virtual Trade Show," *Gamesbeat.com*, January 15, 2009, http://games.venturebeat.com/2009/01/15/sony-electronics-holds-a-virtual-trade-show; "Virtual Trade Show Companies," *Inc.*, May 1, 2009, www.inc.com.

Chapter 9

1. Eric Bellman, "Harley to Ride Indian Growth," *Wall Street Journal*, August 28, 2009, pp. B1, B4; Rich Rovito, "Harley Davidson to Enter India Market in 2010," *The Business Journal of Milwaukee*, August 27, 2009, http://milwaukee.bizjournals.com/milwaukee/stories/2009/08/24/daily55.html (accessed March 19, 2010); Rich Rovito, "Harley Bikes Will Be More Expensive in India," *The Business Journal of Milwaukee*, September 4, 2009, http://milwaukee.bizjournals.com/milwaukee/stories/2009/09/07/story6.html?q=harley%20davidson%20enters%20India (accessed March 19, 2010); "Harley-Davidson to Expand into India," press release, August 26, 2009, www.harley-davidson.com (accessed March 19, 2010); Rama Lakshmi, "An American Icon Arrives In India With a Rumble," *The Washington Post*, August 31, 2009, www.washingtonpost.com/wp-dyn/content/article/2009/08/30/AR2009083002250.html (accessed March 19, 2010).

2. "MTV Hits Hollywood with a Double Dose of Movies and Music as the 2010 'MTV Movie Awards' and 'MTV Video Music Awards' Air Live From Los Angeles," February 11, 2010, www.prnewswire.com/news-releases/mtv-hits-hollywood-with-a-double-dose-of-movies-and-music-as-the-2010-mtv-movie-awards-and-mtv-video-music-awards-air-live-from-los-angeles-84125537.html (accessed March 14, 2010).

3. "Company Profile," Starbucks, February 2010, www.starbucks.com/aboutus/Company_Profile.pdf; Wal-Mart.com, Walmart China Factsheet, www.wal-martchina.com/english/walmart/index.htm (accessed March 8, 2010).

4. David Kiley, "Jack's Global Splash," *BusinessWeek*, October 22, 2007, p. 24.

5. "About CIBERs," CIBERweb, http://ciberweb.msu.edu/about.asp (accessed March 23, 2010).

6. Gary A. Knight and S. Tamer Cavusgil, "Innovation, Organizational Capabilities, and the Born-Global Firm," *Journal of International Business Studies* (March 2004): pp. 124–141.

7. Jessica Golloher, "McDonald's Still Thriving in Russia After 20 Years," February 2, 2010, www1.voanews.com/english/news/europe/McDonalds-Still-Thriving-in-Russia-After-20-Years-83327327.html (accessed March 14, 2010).

8. Associated Press, "McItaly Burger Controversial in Home Country," MSNBC, February 8, 2010, www.msnbc.msn.com/id/35301534 (accessed March 23, 2010).

9. Anton Piësch, "Speaking in Tongues," *Inc.* (June 2003): p. 50.

10. Sadrudin A. Ahmed and Alain D'Astous, "Moderating Effects of Nationality on Country-of-Origin Perceptions: English-Speaking Thailand Versus French-Speaking Canada," *Journal of Business Research* 60 (March 2007): pp. 240–248; George Balabanis and Adamantios Diamantopoulos, "Domestic Country Bias, Country-of-Origin Effects, and Consumer Ethnocentrism: A Multidimensional Unfolding Approach," *Journal of the Academy of Marketing Science* (January 2004): pp. 80–95; Harri T. Luomala, "Exploring the Role of Food Origin as a Source of Meanings for Consumers and as a Determinant of Consumers' Actual Food Choices," *Journal of Business Research* 60 (February 2007): pp. 122–129; Durdana Ozretic-Dosen, Vatroslav Skare, and Zoran Krupka, "Assessments of Country of Origin and Brand Cues in Evaluating a Croatian, Western and Eastern European Food Product," *Journal of Business Research* 60 (February 2007): pp. 130–136.

11. William R. Snyder, "Mini's Small Victory," *Wall Street Journal*, March 11, 2010, http://magazine.wsj.com/gatherer/behind-the-brand/small-victory (accessed March 15, 2010).

12. The CIA, *The World Fact Book*, www.cia.gov/library/publications/the-world-factbook/geos/us.html (accessed March 8, 2010).

13. The CIA, *The World Fact Book*; U.S. Bureau of the Census, *Statistical Abstract of the United States, 2008* (Washington, DC: Government Printing Office, 2007), pp. 825–827, 837.

14. Eric Bellman, "Cellphone Entertainment Takes Off in Rural India," *Wall Street Journal*, November 23, 2009, p. B1–B2.

15. Code of Ethics, American Marketing Association, www.marketingpower.com/content435.php (accessed March 8, 2010).

16. "Will the New Congress Shift Gears on Free Trade?" *Wall Street Journal*, November 18–19, 2006, p. A7.

17. "U.S. Trade Representative Announces Fiscal 2010 Tariff-Rate Quota Allocations for Raw Cane Sugar, Refined Specialty Sugar, Sugar Containing Products," October 1, 2009, www.highbeam.com/doc/1P3-1870093731.html (accessed March 15, 2010).

18. "USA: President Obama Should Take the Lead on Lifting Embargo against Cuba," Amnesty International, September 2, 2009, www.amnesty.org/en/for-media/press-releases/usa-president-obama-should-take-lead-lifting-embargo-against-cuba-200909 (accessed March 15, 2010).

19. "U.S. Trade in Goods and Services," U.S. Bureau of the Census, Foreign Trade Statistics, February 10, 2010, www.census.gov/foreign-trade/statistics/historical/gands.pdf (accessed March 8, 2010).

20. Charles R. Taylor, George R. Franke, and Michael L. Maynard, "Attitudes Toward Direct Marketing and Its Regulation: A Comparison of the United States and Japan," *Journal of Public Policy & Marketing* (Fall 2000): pp. 228–237.

21. "Counterfeit Culture," CBC News, www.cbc.ca/news/interactives/map-counterfeit-goods (accessed March 15, 2010).

22. "Fake Goods Come at a High Price," China Intellectual Property Rights Protection Website, www.chinaipr.gov.cn/news/enterprise/285072.shtml (accessed March 15, 2010).

23. Business for Social Responsibility, www.bsr.org (accessed March 8, 2010).

24. Kevin J. O'Brien, "Europe Drops Microsoft Antitrust Case," *New York Times*, December 16, 2009, www.nytimes.com/2009/12/17/business/global/17msft.html?_r=2 (accessed March 8, 2010).

25. "This Is Systembolaget," www.systembolaget.se/Applikationer/Knappar/InEnglish/Swedish_alcohol_re.htm (accessed March 23, 2010).

26. The CIA, *The World Fact Book*, www.cia.gov/library/publications/the-world-factbook/geos/us.html (accessed February 24, 2010).

27. Ting Shi, "A Gas Pump for 300 Million Phones," *Business 2.0* (June 2005) p. 78.

28. "NAFTA," Office of the United States Trade Representative, www.ustr.gov/trade-agreements/free-trade-agreements/north-american-free-trade-agreement-nafta (accessed March 8, 2010), "NAFTA: A Decade of Success," http://ustr.gov/Document_Library/Fact_Sheets/2004/NAFTA_A_Decade_of_Success.html (accessed March 23, 2010).

29. "Trade with Canada: 2009," U.S. Bureau of the Census, www.census.gov/foreign-trade/balance/c1220.html#2009 (accessed March 10, 2010).

30. CIA, *The World Fact Book*; "Trade with Mexico: 2006," U.S. Bureau of the Census, www.census.gov/foreign-trade/balance/c2010.html#2006 (accessed January 28, 2008); U.S. Bureau of the Census, *Statistical Abstract*, p. 802.

31. Maquila Portal, March 12, 2010, www.maquilaportal.com/news (accessed March 15, 2010).

32. "CAFTA-DR (Dominican Republic-Central America FTA)," Office of the United States Trade Representative, www.ustr.gov/trade-agreements/free-trade-agreements/cafta-dr-dominican-republic-central-america-fta (accessed March 18, 2010).

33. "Exxon Mobil Expected to File 40 mln USD NAFTA Suit Against Canada in November," *CNNMoney*, October 16, 2007, www.abcmoney.co.uk/news/162007146139.htm (accessed March 23, 2010).

34. "The History of the European Union," Europa, http://europa.eu/abc/history/index_en.htm (accessed March 10, 2010); "Europe in 12 Lessons," Europa, http://europa.eu/abc/12lessons/lesson_2/index_en.htm (accessed March 3, 2010).

35. The CIA, *The World Factbook*, www.cia.gov/library/publications/the-world-factbook/geos/ee.html (accessed March 15, 2010).

36. "About the European Union," Europa, http://europa.eu/about-eu/index_en.htm (accessed March 10, 2010).

37. "Common Market of the South (MERCOSUR): Agri-Food Regional Profile Statistical Overview," Agriculture and Agrifood Canada, March 2009, www.ats.agr.gc.ca/lat/3947-eng.htm (accessed March 10, 2010); Joanna Klonsky and Stephanie Hanson "Mercosur: South America's Fractious Trade Bloc," Council on Foreign Relations, August 20, 2009, www.cfr.org/publication/12762/mercosur.html (accessed March 18, 2010).

38. "About APEC," Asia-Pacific Economic Cooperation, www.apec.org/apec/about_apec.html (accessed February 25, 2010).

39. Asian Pacific Economic Cooperation, www.apec.org/apec/about_apec/achievements_and_benefits.html (accessed March 10, 2010).

40. "China GDP Growth Rate," *Trading Economics*, www.tradingeconomics.com/Economics/GDP-Growth.aspx?Symbol=CNY (accessed March 15, 2010).

41. Karen Cho, "KFC China's Recipe for Success," *INSEAD Knowledge*, July 1, 2009 http://knowledge.insead.edu/KFCinChina090323.cfm?vid=195; "Yum! China," Yum! Brands www.yum.com/company/china.asp (accessed March 18, 2010).

42. World Trade Organization, www.wto.org/english/theWTO_e/whatis_e/tif_e/org6_e.htm (accessed March 10, 2010).

43. "What Is the WTO?" World Trade Organization, www.wto.org/english/thewto_e/whatis_e/whatis_e.htm (accessed March 10, 2010).

44. "Brazil Slaps Trade Sanctions on U.S. over Cotton Dispute," *BBC News*, March 9, 2010, http://news.bbc.co.uk/2/hi/8556920.stm (accessed March 23, 2010).

45. Jan Johanson and Finn Wiedersheim-Paul, "The Internationalization of the Firm," *Journal of Management*

Studies (October 1975): pp. 305–322; Jan Johanson and Jan-Erik Vahlne, "The Internationalization Process of the Firm—A Model of Knowledge Development and Increasing Foreign Commitments," *Journal of International Business Studies* (Spring/Summer 1977): pp. 23–32; S. Tamer Cavusgil and John R. Nevin, "Internal Determinants of Export Marketing Behavior: An Empirical Investigation," *Journal of Marketing Research* (February 1981): pp. 114–119.

46. Pradeep Tyagi, "Export Behavior of Small Business Firms in Developing Economies: Evidence from the Indian Market," *Marketing Management Journal* (Fall/Winter 2000): pp. 12–20.

47. Berrin Dosoglu-Guner, "How Do Exporters and Non-Exporters View Their 'Country of Origin' Image Abroad?" *Marketing Management Journal* (Fall/Winter 2000): pp. 21–27.

48. SciNet World Trade System, www.scinet-corp.com/associates/index.htm, (accessed March 23, 2010).

49. Farok J. Contractor and Sumit K. Kundu, "Franchising Versus Company-Run Operations: Model Choice in the Global Hotel Sector," *Journal of International Marketing* (November 1997): pp. 28–53.

50. Kerry Capell, "Vodafone and Orange outsource to Ericsson and Nokia," *BusinessWeek*, March 18, 2009 www.businessweek.com/blogs/europeinsight/archives/2009/03/vodafone_and_or.html (accessed March 10, 2010).

51. "Venezuela Approves Oil Joint Venture," *Moscow Times,* March 11, 2010, www.themoscowtimes.com/business/article/venezuela-approves-oil-joint-venture/401372.html (accessed March 23, 2010); "Pdvsa, Belarus Establish Joint Venture to Develop Natural Gas Projects," *El Universal*, March 18, 2010, http://english.eluniversal.com/2010/03/18/en_eco_art_pdvsa,-belarus-estab_18A3607891.shtml (accessed March 23, 2010).

52. Press release, "Ascent Solar Technologies, Inc. Signs Strategic Alliance Agreement With Indian Conglomerate Kirloskar Integrated Technologies Limited, India," *Market Watch*, March 22, 2010, www.marketwatch.com/ (accessed March 23, 2010).

53. "Export Department," Clipsal, www.clipsal.com.au/trade/about_clipsal/worldwide (accessed March 10, 2010)

54. Abbott, www.abbott.com/global/url/content/en_US/10.17:17/general_content/General_Content_00054.htm (accessed March 23, 2010).

55. Deborah Owens, Timothy Wilkinson, and Bruce Keillor, "A Comparison of Product Attributes in a Cross-Cultural/Cross-National Context," *Marketing Management Journal* (Fall/Winter 2000): pp. 1–11.

56. "Dunkin' Donuts Coming to Mainland China," *USA Today,* January 25, 2008, www.usatoday.com/money/world/2008-01-25-dunkin-shanghai_N.htm (accessed March 23, 2010).

57. Anil K. Gupta and Vijay Govindarajan, "Converting Global Presence into Global Competitive Advantage," *Academy of Management Executive* (May 2001): pp. 45–58.

58. "About Lonely Planet: Company History," Lonely Planet, www.lonelyplanet.com/about/company-history (accessed April 27, 2010); "BBC Worldwide Acquires Lonely Planet," Press Release, October 1, 2007, www.lonelyplanet.com/ (accessed April 27, 2010); "Products: WorldGuide," Lonely Planet Corporate Web Site, www.lonelyplanet.biz/product01.htm (accessed April 27, 2010).

59. 1. R. Jai Krishna, "Nokia to Offer Phone Installments in India," *Wall Street Journal*, August 19, 2009, p. B7; Mark Bordon, "iPhone Envy? You Must Be Jöking," *Fast Company* (September 2009): pp. 68–73, 106; Adam Smith, "Nokia Calling," *Time*, August 3, 2009, www.time.com/time/magazine/article/0,9171,1912307,00.html (accessed February 2, 2010); www.wireless.att.com (accessed February 2, 2010); www.verizonwireless.com (accessed February 2, 2010); Associated Press, "Nokia Launches Cheaper Smart Phones," *New York Times*, April 13, 2010; Loretta Chao, "Nokia Launches Free

Music Service in China," *Wall Street Journal*, April 8, 2010, http://online.wsj.com/article/SB10001424052702304830104575171552100434466.html (accessed April 21, 2010); Gustav Sandstrom, "Nokia Redraws Its Mobile Mapping Services," *Wall Street Journal*, January 21, 2010, http://online.wsj.com/article/SB10001424052748703699204575016493222156322.html (accessed April 19, 2010).

Feature Notes

a. Pete Engardio, "Cradle of a Green Revolution," *BusinessWeek*, November 2, 2009, pp. 40–41; Bryan Walsh, "Electric Cars: China's Power Play," *Time*, August 31, 2009, www.time.com/time/printout/0,8816,1917647,00.html (accessed March 18, 2010); Daniel K. Gardner, "Meet China's Green Crusader," *New York Times*, November 1, 2009, www.nytimes.com/2009/02/11/opinion/11iht-edgardner.1.20105872.html (accessed March 18, 2010); Ben Elgin and Bruce Einhorn, "China's Carbon-Credit Hustle," *BusinessWeek*, December 21, 2009, pp. 18–21; "China Gets Greener," *BusinessWeek*, January 11, 2010, p. 7; Adam Aston, "China's Surprising Clout in Cleantech," *BusinessWeek*, November 30, 2009, p. 56.

b. Matthew Knight "Plastic Bags Fly into Environmental Storm," CNN.com, http://edition.cnn.com, November 16, 2007 (accessed March 17, 2008); "Whole Foods Market to Sack Disposable Plastic Grocery Bags," www.wholefoodsmarket.com, January 22, 2008 (accessed March 17, 2008); "Diamant Corporation Furthers National Consumer Awareness Efforts as British Prime Minister Gordon Brown Announces Tougher Measures to Dramatically Reduce the Society's Dependence on Single-Use Plastic Bags," CNNMoney.com, http://money.cnn.com/news, March 25, 2008 (accessed March 25, 2008).

c. BraBaby, www.brababy.com/ (accessed March 30, 2009); Jonathan Cheng, "A Small Firm Takes on Chinese Pirates," *Wall Street Journal,* July 5, 2007, http://online.wsj.com/article/SB118359376477257609.html?mod=djemITP# (accessed March 30, 2009).

d. Deborah Ball, "U.K. KitKats Shift to Fair Trade As Nestlé Burnishes Reputation," *Wall Street Journal,* December 8, 2009, p. B6; "Kit Kat goes Fairtrade in the UK and Ireland," Nestlé, December 7, 2009, www.nestle.com/MediaCenter/NewsandFeatures/AllNewsFeatures/KitKat_Fairtrade_UK_Ireland.htm (accessed March 19, 2010); Harry Wallop, "Nestle's Kit Kat goes Fairtrade," *Telegraph*, December 7, 2009, www.telegraph.co.uk/foodanddrink/foodanddrinknews/6730155/Nestles-Kit-Kat-goes-Fairtrade.html (accessed March 19, 2010); Rebecca Smithers, "Big Break for Fairtrade as Kit Kat Receives Certification," *The Guardian*, December 7, 2009, www.guardian.co.uk/environment/2009/dec/07/fairtrade-kit-kat (accessed March 19, 2010); www.fairtradefederation.org (accessed March 19, 2010); www.eftafairtrade.org (accessed March 19, 2010); www.wfto.com (accessed March 19, 2010).

Chapter 10

1. Matthew Schwartz, "NASCAR: Driving Social Media," *Advertising Age*, November 16, 2009, pp. C3, C13; Sara Page, "NASCAR Digs Up Old Roots in a New Way," WSLS 10, Media General News Service, September 23, 2009, www.2wsls.com/sls/sports/motor_sports/nextel/article/nascar_digs_up_old_roots_in_a_new_way/49154 (accessed January 23, 2010); "NASCAR and Vision Critical Win Award for Listening to Fans Using Online Panel," *Vision Critical*, October 27, 2009, www.visioncritical.com/2009/10/nascar-and-vision-critical-win-award-for-listening-to-fans-using-online-panel (accessed January 23, 2010); www.nascar.com (accessed February 16, 2010); Laurie

Burkitt, "NASCAR Ads, Coming to a Theatre Near You," *Forbes*, October 21, 2009, www.forbes.com/2009/10/21/nascar-screenvision-cmo-network-cinema-ads.html (accessed February 17, 2010).

2. Emily Roley, Pete Stein, and David Tomas, "The State of Digital Marketing," *Marketing News*, March 15, 2010, p. 20–21.

3. "A Special Report on Social Networking," *The Economist*, January 30, 2010, p. 4.

4. Don Fletcher, "Gift Giving on Facebook Gets Real," *Time*, February 15, 2010, www.time.com/time/magazine/article/0,9171,1960260,00.html (accessed February 18, 2010).

5. "2009 Digital Handbook," *Marketing News*, April 30, 2009, p. 13.

6. Samantha Stey, "A Next Step in Online Customer Engagement," *Marketing News*, March 15, 2010, p. 10.

7. "17 Key Differences Between Social Media and Traditional Marketing," *Microgeist*, April 20, 2009, http://microgeist.com (accessed February 18, 2010).

8. Dana Van Den Heuvel, "Digital Dozen," *Marketing News*, March 15, 2010, p.16.

9. Josh Bernoff, "Don't Screw Up Your Mobile Marketing Opportunity," *Marketing News*, October 6, 2009, p. 10.

10. Claire Cain Miller, "Mobile Phones Become Essential Tool for Holiday Shopping," *New York Times*, December 18, 2009, www.nytimes.com/2009/12/18/technology/18mobile.html?_r=1&ref=technology (accessed January 6, 2010).

11. Mya Frazier, "CrowdSourcing" *World Traveler*, February 2010, via http://msp.imirus.com/ (accessed February 18, 2010).

12. "A Special Report on Marketing," p. 3.

13. "A Special Report on Marketing," p. 4.

14. "17 Key Differences Between Social Media and Traditional Marketing."

15. "A Special Report on Marketing," p. 17.

16. Pepsi Refresh Project, www.refresheverything.com (accessed March 25, 2010).

17. Bruce Horovitz, "'Two Nobodies from Nowhere' Craft Winning Super Bowl ad," *USA Today*, February 3, 2009, www.usatoday.com/money/advertising/admeter/2009admeter.htm (accessed January 19, 2010).

18. Bruce Horovitz, "Betty White, Snickers Top Ad Meter," *USA Today*, February 8, 2010, www.usatoday.com/money/advertising/admeter/2010admeter.htm (accessed February 17, 2010).

19. Cameron Chapman, "The History and Evolution of Social Media," WebDesigner Depot, October 7, 2009, www.webdesignerdepot.com/2009/10/the-history-and-evolution-of-social-media (accessed February 17, 2010).

20. "The History of Social Media in a Blink," Windows Live, November 22, 2007, http://mbresseel.spaces.live.com/Blog/cns%2133234018BF280C82%21345.entry (accessed February 18, 2010).

21. Chapman, "The History and Evolution of Social Media."

22. Emily Schmall, "Growing Pains," *Forbes*, August 11, 2008, pp. 60–63.

23. "2009 Digital Handbook," p. 13.

24. Li and Bernoff, p. 22.

25. "Facebook: Largest, Fastest Growing Social Network," Tech Tree, August 13, 2008, www.techtree.com/India/News/Facebook_Largest_Fastest_Growing_Social_Network/551-92134-643.html (accessed January 12, 2010).

26. "2009 Digital Handbook," p. 13.

27. Nick Summers, "Heated Rivalries: #9 Facebook vs. MySpace," *NewsWeek*, www.2010.newsweek.com (accessed January 13, 2010).

28. "2009 Digital Handbook," p. 13.

29. "2009 Digital Handbook," p. 13.

30. Jack Neff, "Marketing: Prilosec Works to Become 'Sponsor of Everything'," *Advertising Age*, February 17, 2010, http://adage.com/digital/article?article_id=142150 (accessed February 18, 2010).

31. Digital Media, p. 13.

32. "2009 Digital Handbook," p. 13.

33. Alison Doyle, "LinkedIn and Your Job Search," *About.com*, http://jobsearch.about.com/od/networking/a/linkedin.htm (accessed January 8, 2010).

34. Jefferson Graham, "Cake Decorator Finds Twitter a Tweet Recipe for Success," *USA Today*, April 1, 2009, p. 5B; Mark Glaser, "Twitter Founders Thrive on Micro-Blogging Constraints," *MediaShift*, May 17, 2007, www.pbs.org/mediashift (accessed July 15, 2010).

35. "2009 Digital Handbook," p. 11.

36. Summer Busari, "Tweeting the Terror: How Social Media Reacted to Mumbai." *CNN.com*, November 28, 2008, www.cnn.com/2008/WORLD/asiapcf/11/27/mumbai.twitter/index.html?eref=rss_latest (accessed January 13, 2010).

37. Devra J. First, " 'Tweets' on the Menu Are a Sweet Deal," *Boston.com*, June 29, 2009, www.boston.com/ae/food/restaurants/articles/2009/06/29/restaurants_finding_twitter_a_cheap_effective_marketing_tool (accessed January 13, 2010).

38. Kathy Chu and Kim Thai, "Banks Jump on the Twitter Wagon," *USA Today*, May 12, 2009, p. B1.

39. Josh Tyrangiel, "Bing vs. Google: The Conquest of Twitter," *Time*, October 22, 2009, www.time.com/time/business/article/0,8599,1931532,00.html (accessed January 7, 2010).

40. "2009 Digital Handbook," p. 11.

41. Li and Bernoff, p. 43.

42. "Couldn't Stop the Spread of the Conversation in Reactions from Other Bloggers," from Hyejin Kim's May 4, 2007, blog post "Korea: Bloggers and Donuts" on the blog Global Voices at http://groundswell.forrester.com/site1-16 (accessed January 10, 2010).

43. Randy Tinseth, "Randy's Journal," Boeing, http://boeingblogs.com/randy (accessed January 10, 2010).

44. Li and Bernoff, p. 24.

45. Li and Bernoff, pp. 25–26.

46. "2009 Digital Handbook," p. 11.

47. Zeke Camusio, "Flickr Marketing—6 Awesome Tactics to Promote Your Website on Flickr," The Outsourcing Company, February 19, 2009, www.theoutsourcingcompany.com/blog/social-media-marketing/flickr-marketing-6-awesome-tactics-to-promote-your-website-on-flickr (accessed January 11, 2010).

48. Bianca Male, "How to Promote Your Business on Flickr," *The Business Insider*, December 1, 2009, www.businessinsider.com/how-to-promote-your-business-on-flickr-2009-12?utm_source=feedburner&utm_medium=feed&utm_campaign=Feed%3A+businessinsider+(The+Business+Insider) (accessed January 11, 2010).

49. "How to Market on Flickr," Small Business Search Marketing, www.smallbusinesssem.com/articles (accessed January 11, 2010).

50. "GM blogs' Photostream," Flickr, www.flickr.com/photos/gmblogs (accessed January 11, 2010); "About the Lab," The Lab, http://thelab.gmblogs.com/about (accessed January 11, 2010).

51. "Barack Obama's Photostream," Flickr, www.flickr.com/photos/barackobamadotcom (accessed January 11, 2009).

52. Sage Lewis, "Using Flickr for Marketing," YouTube, uploaded February 13, 2007. www.youtube.com/watch?v=u2Xyzkfzlug (accessed January 11, 2010).

53. Jessi Hempel, "Google (Still) Loves YouTube," *Fortune*, April 17, 2009, 37–42.

54. David Meerman Scott, *The New Rules of Marketing & PR* (Hoboken: John Wiley & Sons, 2009), p. 224; "Mainframe: The Art of the Sales, Lesson One," YouTube, www.youtube.com/watch?v=MSqXKp-00hM (accessed January 10, 2010); Ryan Rhodes, "The Mainframe: It's Like a Barn," IBM Systems, March–April 2007, www.ibmsystemsmag.com/mainframe/marchapril07/stoprun/11984p1.aspx (accessed February 18, 2010).

55. Ashlee Vance, "A Big Name in Tech Tries a Common Touch," *New York Times*, December 4, 2009, www.nytimes.com/2009/12/04/technology/04adco.html (accessed January 6, 2009).

56. "Search Giant Google to Buy YouTube for $1.65B," *FoxNews.com*, October 10, 2006, www.foxnews.com/story/0,2933,218921,00.html (accessed January 8, 2010).

57. "2009 Digital Handbook," p. 14.

58. Christopher S. Penn, "About the Financial Aid Podcast," *FinancialAidNews.com*, www.financialaidnews.com/about/ (accessed January 11, 2010).

59. "Real Cars Drive into Second Life," *CNNMoney.com*, November 18, 2006, http://money.cnn.com/2006/11/17/autos/2nd_life_cars/index.htm (accessed January 13, 2010).

60. "Sun Chief Researcher John Gage to Host Second Life's First-Ever Fortune 500 Press Conference," Oracle and Sun, October 6, 2006, www.oracle.com/us/Sun/index.html (accessed September 13, 2010).

61. "CNN enters the virtual world of Second Life," CNN.com, November 12, 2007, www.cnn.com/2007/TECH/11/12/second.life.irpt/index.html (accessed September 13, 2010).

62. Li and Bernoff, p. 41.

63. Li and Bernoff, pp. 41–42.

64. Scott, *The New Rules of Marketing and PR*, pp. 195–196.

65. Li and Bernoff, p. 44.

66. Li and Bernoff, pp. 44–45.

67. "Internet Usage Statistics," Internet World Stats, www.Internetworldstats.com/stats.htm (accessed February 22, 2010).

68. Miguel Bustillo and Geoffrey A. Fowler, "Wal-Mart Uses its Stores to Get an Edge Online," *Wall Street Journal*, December 15, 2009, p. B1.

69. "The Empire Builder," *Marketing News*, March 15, 2010, p. 19.

70. "Samsung Pushes the Right Buttons with Digital Marketing Campaign," *Zawya*, May 30, 2010, http://zawya.com/story.cfm/sidZAWYA20100530093243/Samsung%20Pushes%20the%20Right%20Buttons%20with%20Digital%20Marketing%20Campaign (accessed June 1, 2010).

71. Aaron Back, "China's Big Brands Tackle Web Sales," *Wall Street Journal*, December 1, 2009, B2.

72. "Pepsi Refreshes Digital," *Marketing News*, March 15, 2010, p. 16.

73. http://victorsandspoils.com (accessed July 16, 2010); Mark Weingarten, "'Project Runway' for The T-Shirt Crowd," *CNNMoney.com*, June 18, 2007, http://money.cnn.com/magazines/business2/business2_archive/2007/06/01/100050978/index.htm (accessed July 16, 2010); Crowdspring.com (accessed July 16, 2010).

74. Frazier, "CrowdSourcing," p. 73; "Pasta Talent Community," GrouperEye, www.groupereye.com/blog/pasta-talent-community (accessed July 16, 2010).

75. Frazier, "CrowdSourcing," p. 70.

76. Jack Neff, "P&G Embraces Facebook as Big Part of Its Marketing Plan," *Advertising Age*, January 25, 2010, http://adage.com/digital/article?article_id=141733 (accessed February 18, 2010).

77. "A Special Report on Martketing," p. 13.

78. Li and Bernoff, pp. 26–27.

79. Ryan Underwood, "Tell Us What You Really Think: Collecting Customer Feedback," *Inc.* (December 2008): pp. 52–53.

80. Noreen O'Leary, "Study: Customer Feedback Ignored." *Ad Week*, January 26, 2009, www.adweek.com/aw/content_display/news/client/e3ic96aa80f511fb30f5635f219369f11aa (accessed February 10, 2009).

81. Olivier Blanchard, "Basics of Social Media ROI," Slideshare, www.slideshare.net/ (accessed February 10, 2010).

82. Emily Steel, "Modeling Tools Stretch Ad Dollars," *Wall Street Journal*, May 18, 2009, p. B7.

83. Larry Barrett, "Data Breach Costs Surge in 2009: Study," *eSecurity Planet*, January 26, 2010, www.esecurityplanet.com/features/article.php/3860811/article.htm (accessed February 10, 2010).

84. Emily Steel, "Web Privacy Efforts Targeted," *Wall Street Journal*, June 25, 2009, B10.

85. "Facebook Takes Strong Stance Against Haiti Fraud," *Media Street*, January 19, 2010, www.media-street.co.uk/our-blog/ (accessed January 18, 2010).

86. Kara Swisher and Walt Mossberg, "All Things Digital," *Wall Street Journal*, June 2, 2009, p. R1, R6.

87. Sarah Needleman, "Social-Media Con Game," *Wall Street Journal*, October 12, 2009, http://online.wsj.com/article/SB10001424052748704471504574445502831219412.html (accessed February 18, 2010).

88. *2008 Global Software Piracy Study*, Business Software Alliance and International Data Corporation, p. 1, http://global.bsa.org/globalpiracy2008/studies/globalpiracy2008.pdf (accessed March 25, 2010).

89. Aubry R. Fowler III, Barry J. Babin, and May K. Este (2005), "Burning for Fun or Money: Illicit Consumer Behavior in a Contemporary Context," presented at the Academy of Marketing Science Annual Conference, May 27, 2005, Tampa, FL.

90. Kevin Shanahan and Mike Hyman "Motivators and Enables of SCOURing," *Journal of Business Research*, 2009.

91. "Postage ~ Postcards," iTunes Preview, http://itunes.apple.com/app/postage-postcards/id312231322?mt=8# (accessed April 22, 2010); "Welcome to Rogue Sheep," RogueSheep Website, www.roguesheep.com/ (accessed April 22, 2010); Philip Michaels, "Macworld's 2009 App Gems Awards," *Macworld*, December 15, 2009, www.macworld.com/article/145088/2009/12/appgems_2009.html?lsrc=top_1 (accessed April 22, 2010); "Company," RogueSheep Website, www.roguesheep.com/company (accessed April 22, 2010); Brier Dudley, "Rogue Sheep Wins Apple's Stamp of Approval," *The Seattle Times*, June 11, 2009, seattletimes.nwsource.com/html/brierdudley/2009325474_brier11.html (accessed April 22, 2010).

92. Brad Wilson, *Bradsdeals* homepage, http://bradsdeals.com/ (accessed April 28, 2009); Michael S. Malone, "The Twitter Revolution," *Wall Street Journal*, April 18, 2009, p. A11; Ann Meyer, "Facebook, Twitter, Other Social Media Help Drive Business for Small Firms," *Chicago Tribune*, April 27, 2009, http://articles.chicagotribune.com/ (accessed April 8, 2010); Jefferson Graham, "Cake Decorator Finds Twitter a Tweet Recipe for Success," *USA Today*, April 1, 2009, p. 5B; "A Peach of an Opportunity," *The Economist*, January 30, 2010, pp. 13–15; Courtney Rubin, "Why Social Media Is Really Worth Your Time," *Inc.*, April 23, 2010, www.inc.com/news/articles/2010/04/how-social-media-helps-small-business.html (accessed May 3, 2010); Hannah Clark Steiman, "How Twitter Helps a CEO Run His Company," July 1, 2009, www.inc.com/magazine/ (accessed May 3, 2010); Jonathan Browning and Brian Womack, "Twitter Starts Selling Advertising to Boost Revenue," *BusinessWeek*, April 13, 2010, www.businessweek.com/news/ (accessed May 5, 2010).

93. "McDonald's Delivers Another Year of Strong Results in 2009," Press Release, http://phx.corporate-ir.net/phoenix.zhtml?c=97876&p=irol-newsArticle&ID=1377920&highlight= (accessed May 4, 2010); "Canola Blend Cooking Oil," McDonald's, www.mcdonalds.com/us/en/food/food_quality/

see_what_we_are_made_of/your_questions_answered/canola_blend_oil.html (accessed May 4, 2010); "Moms' Quality Correspondents," McDonald's, www.mcdonalds.com/us/en/food/food_quality/see_what_we_are_made_of/moms_quality_correspondents.html (accessed May 4, 2010); "Arch Card," McDonald's, www.mcdonalds.com/us/en/services/arch_card.html (accessed May 4, 2010); Esther Fung, "McDonald's to Double Restaurants in China," *Wall Street Journal*, March 29, 2010, http://online.wsj.com/article/SB1000142405270230360150457515370283255686.html (accessed May 4, 2010); Meg Marco, "McDonald's Rolls Out Breakfast Dollar Menu," *The Consumerist,* August 28, 2009, http://consumerist.com/2009/08/mcdonalds-rolls-out-breakfast-dollar-menu.html (accessed May 4, 2010); "Our History," Ronald McDonald House Charities, http://rmhc.org/who-we-are/our-history (accessed May 4, 2010); Stuart Elliott, "Straight A's, with a Burger as a Prize," *New York Times*, December 6, 2007, p. C4; Janet Adamy, "Steady Diet: As Burgers Boom in Russia, McDonald's Touts Discipline," *Wall Street Journal,* October 16, 2007, p. A1.

Feature Notes

a. Kermit Pattison, "How to Market Your Business with Facebook," *New York Times,* November 12, 2009, www.nytimes.com/2009/11/12/business/smallbusiness/12guide.html (accessed November 18, 2009); www.facebook.com (accessed February 19, 2010); Kyle Austin, "5 Tips for Marketing on Facebook's New Pages," *Fast Company,* March 12, 2009, www.fastcompany.com/blog/ (accessed December 20, 2009); "Have You Tried Marketing Your Business With Facebook," *New York Times,* November 16, 2009, http://boss.blogs.nytimes.com/2009/11/16/have-you-tried-marketing-your-business-with-facebook (accessed December 20, 2009); Dan Fost, "Facebook a Friend to Small Businesses," *Chicago Tribune,* October 28, 2009, p. 47; Courtney Rubin, "Facebook Tops Google in Directing Web Traffic," *Inc.,* February 16, 2010, www.inc.com/news/articles/2010/02/facebook-tops-in-directing-web-traffic.html (accessed February 19, 2010).

b. Wailin Wong and Monica Eng, "Yelp, Other Online Review Sites Changing Consumer-Merchant Dynamics," *Chicago Tribune,* March 19, 2010, www.chicagotribune.com/business/ (accessed March 22, 2010); Max Chafkin, "In Defense of Yelp," *Inc.,* February 19, 2009, www.inc.com/staff-blog/2009/02/19/in_defense_of_yelp.html# (accessed March 22, 2010); Scott Austin, "Yelp CEO: We May Be Weird, But We Have Nothing To Hide," *Wall Street Journal,* March 1, 2010, http://blogs.wsj.com/ (accessed March 22, 2010); Jefferson Graham, "'Yelpers' Review Local Businesses," *USA Today,* June 12, 2007, www.usatoday.com/money/industries/technology/2007-06-12-yelp_N.htm (accessed March 22, 2010).

c. Care 2, www.care2.com (accessed December 17, 2009); Tree Hugger, www.treehugger.com (accessed January 16, 2010).

Chapter 11

1. Paul Ingrassia, "Taurus Takes Another Lap," *SmartMoney* (November 2009): pp. 86–87; Mike Ofiara, Amy Skogstrom, Rusty Blackwell, David Zenlea, Eric Tingwall, and Joe DeMatio, "Reviews: 2010 Ford Taurus SHO," *Automobile,* November 17, 2009, www.automobilemag.com/reviews/editors_notebook/0911_2010_ford_taurus_sho/index.html; Ann M. Job, "Ford Taurus Gets Styling and Technology Makeover," *Associated Press,* September 10, 2009, www.philly.com/philly/classifieds/cars/ (accessed November 25, 2009).

2. Michael B. Baker, "Le Meridien Dethrones Upper Upscale Leader JW Marriot," *Business Travel News,* March 8, 2010, www.btnonline.com/businesstravelnews/headlines/frontpage_display.jsp?vnu_content_id=1004073522 (accessed April 5, 2010).

3. "Company Profile," *Starbucks,* February 2010. www.starbucks.com/about-us/company-information (accessed April 5, 2010).

4. Robert Bosch, About Us, www.bosch.com/content/language2/html/2859.htm (accessed April 5, 2010)

5. "Janitorial and Housekeeping Cleaning Products: USA 2010: Market Analysis and Opportunities," The Kline Group, www.bosch.com/content/language2/html/index.htm (accessed April 5, 2010).

6. FreshPlaza.com, "Sunny Ridge Farm Launches New Product Line Extension" February 23, 2010, www.freshplaza.com/news_detail.asp?id=59361; "What's New," *SunnyRidge Farm,* March 31, 2010, www.sunnyridge.com/whatsnew.php?IDX=138.

7. William P. Putsis Jr. and Barry L. Bayus, "An Empirical Analysis of Firms' Product Line Decisions," *Journal of Marketing Research* (February 2001): pp. 110–118.

8. General Electric Website, Products & Services, www.ge.com/products_services/index.html (accessed April 7, 2010).

9. Deborah Ball, "Snack Attack: As Chocolate Sags, Cadbury Gambles on a Piece of Gum," *Wall Street Journal,* January 12, 2006, p. A1, http://online.wsj.com/.

10. Emily Bryson York, "The Cold Truth: No One Does Veggies Quite Like Birds Eye," *Advertising Age,* March 29, 2010 p. 8.

11. Brian A. Lukas and O. C. Ferrell, "The Effect of Market Orientation on Product Innovation," *Journal of the Academy of Marketing Science* (February 2000): pp. 239–247.

12. Michael D. Johnson, Andreas Herrmann, and Frank Huber, "Evolution of Loyalty Intentions," *Journal of Marketing* 70 (April 2006), via www.marketingpower.com.

13. The Dettman Group, www.doctorgadget.com (accessed April 15, 2010).

14. Narendra Rao, "The Keys to New Product Success (Part-1)—Collecting Unarticulated & Invisible Customer-Needs," *Product Management & Strategy,* June 19, 2007, http://productstrategy.wordpress.com/ (accessed April 1, 2010).

15. Gwendolyn Cuizon, "SWOT Analysis of Dell Computers," Suite101.com, March 5, 2009, http://strategic-business-planning.suite101.com/article.cfm/swot_analysis_of_dell_computers (accessed March 31, 2010).

16. Elizabeth Esfahani, "Finding the Sweet Spot," *Business 2.0,* November 2005, via money.cnn.com/magazines/business2/business2_archive/2005/11/01/8362835/index.htm (accessed April 16, 2010).

17. Dan Sewell, "P&G Testing Cheaper Tide," *AP Newswire,* July 1, 2009, via http://abcnews.go.com/Business/(accessed March 8, 2010); Jessica Noll, "Have Tides of Economy Affected P&G?" *WCPO.com,* July 16, 2009, www.wcpo.com/ (accessed April 8, 2010).

18. Jonathan Welsh, "Two Crossovers Ahead of the Class," *Wall Street Journal,* August 28, 2009, http://online.wsj.com/article/SB10001424052970203706604574378532004773694.html?KEYWORDS=crossovers (accessed April 5, 2010).

19. O. C. Ferrell and Michael Hartline, *Marketing Strategy* (Mason, OH: South-Western, 2008), pp. 172–173.

20. Sarah Kabourek & Kim Thai, "Barbie Gets a Makeover," *Fortune,* http://money.cnn.com/galleries/2009/fortune/0907/gallery.barbie_makeover.fortune/index.html (accessed March 25, 2010); Aarthi Sivaraman, "Barbie at 50: Is Mattel's Star Still in Fashion?" *Reuters,* March 6, 2009, www.reuters.com/article/lifestyleMolt/idUSTRE52603B20090307 (accessed March 25, 2010); Jessica Michault, "Looking Half Her Age: Barbie at 50," *New York Times,* January 5, 2009, www.nytimes.com/2009/01/06/style/06iht-fbarbie.1.19084850.html (accessed March 25, 2010); Louisa Lim, "Mattel Hopes Shanghai Is a

Barbie World," NPR, March 6, 2009, www.npr.org/templates/story/story.php?storyId=101479810 (accessed March 25, 2010).

21. Valerie Bauerlein, "U.S. Soda Sales Fell at Slower Rate Last Year," *Wall Street Journal*, March 25, 2010, http://online.wsj.com/article/SB10001424052748704266504575141710213338560.html (accessed April 8, 2010).

22. Adam Horowitz, Mark Athitakis, Mark Lasswell, and Owen Thomas, "101 Dumbest Moments in Business," *Business 2.0* (January/February 2005): pp. 103–112.

23. Dennis K. Berman and Ellen Byron, "P&G Sells Sure Deodorant Label to Private Firm Innovative Brands," *Wall Street Journal*, September 26, 2006, p. B2, http://online.wsj.com.

24. Adapted from Everett M. Rogers, *Diffusion of Innovations* (New York: Macmillan, 1962), pp. 81–86.

25. Arch G. Woodside and Wim Biemans, "Managing Relationships, Networks, and Complexity in Innovation, Diffusion, and Adoption Processes," *Journal of Business & Industrial Marketing* 20 (July 2005): pp. 335–338.

26. Ibid., pp. 247–250.

27. James "Dela" Delahunty, "iPod Market Share at 73.8 Percent, 225 Million iPods Sold, More Games for Touch than PSP & NDS: Apple," *After Dawn News*, September 9, 2009, www.afterdawn.com/news/article.cfm/2009/09/09/ipod_market_share_at_73_8_percent_225_million_ipods_sold_more_games_for_touch_than_psp_nds_apple (accessed April 2, 2010).

28. Horowitz, Athitakis, Lasswell, and Thomas, "101 Dumbest Moments in Business."

29. Susan Casey, "Object-Oriented: Everything I Ever Needed to Know About Business I Learned in the Frozen Food Aisle," *Business 2.0*, October 2000.

30. "McDonald's Opens First McCafe in U.S.," *Entrepreneur*, May 14, 2001, www.entrepreneur.com/franchises/franchisezone/thisjustin/article40494.html (accessed April 2, 2010); "McDonald's Poised to Rival Starbucks Nationwide Starting Today," *QSR*, May 5, 2009, www.qsrmagazine.com/articles/news/story.phtml?id=8625 (accessed April 2, 2010).

31. John Christakos, "American Furniture." *Blu Dot Website*, www.bludot.com/blu_dot_info/in_print/american_furniture (accessed April 21, 2010); "The Blu Dot Story," Blu Dot Website, www.bludot.com/blu_dot_info/the_blu_dot_story (accessed April 21, 2010); "Trade," Blu Dot Website, www.bludot.com/blu_dot_info/trade (accessed April 21, 2010); "[Stuff]," Blu Dot Website, Originally published in *Minnesota Monthly*, www.bludot.com/blu_dot_info/in_print/minnesota_monthly (accessed April 21, 2010); Carl Alviani, "Taking the Middle Ground: Massive Design for the Masses?" *Core77*, www.core77.com/reactor/07.05_mIddleground.asp (accessed April 21, 2010).

32. Justin Scheck and Niraj Sheth, "Dell Makes Phone Official," *Wall Street Journal*, January 6, 2010, blogs.wsj.com/digits/2010/01/06/dell-makes-phone-official/?KEYWORDS=Dell (accessed May 1, 2010); Michael Eggbrecht, "Smartphone Evolution: From Simon to Pre in 12 Steps," *CIO Zone*, July 17, 2009, www.ciozone.com/index.php/Mobile-and-Wireless/Smartphone-Evolution-From-Simon-to-Pre-in-12-Steps.html (accessed May 1, 2010); Justin Scheck, "Dell Reorganizes, Creating New Mobile Device Division," *Wall Street Journal*, December 5, 2009, http://online.wsj.com/article/SB10001424052748704342404575457620160069162 2.html?KEYWORDS=Dell+ (accessed May 1, 2010); http://en.community.dell.com/dell-blogs/b/direct2dell/archive/2010/01/07/dell-tablet-concept-and-more-our-products-at-ces-2010.aspx.

Feature Notes

a. Andy Stone, "The Green Giant," *Forbes*, November 2, 2009, pp. 42–44; www.novar.com (accessed January 13, 2010); Marianne Wilson, "CEOSpeak: Energy," *Chain Store Age*, January 2009, www.novar.com/Media/pdf/CEOSpeakJan.pdf (accessed January 14, 2010).

b. Laura Lorber, "Small Business Link: How Online Marketing Videos Became a Hit in Their Own Right," *The Wall Street Journal*, July 2, 2007, p. B4; Marianne Kolbasuk McGee, "YouTube Videos Stir Up New Sales For 'Will It Blend' Maker," *Information Week*, Sept. 27, 2007, www.informationweek.com; Samantha Murphy, "Blend-Worth Technology: Companies Take Online Videos to the Next Level," *Chain Store Age*, July 2007, p. 82.

c. Jeffrey A. Trachtenberg and Geoffrey A. Fowler, "Barnes & Noble Challenges Amazon's Kindle," *Wall Street Journal*, July 21, 2009, p. A1; Geoffrey A. Fowler, "Buyer's E-Morse: 'Owning' Digital Books," *Wall Street Journal*, July 23, 2009, p. A11; Michael Liedtke, "Google Makes Concessions on Digital Book Deal," www.komonews.com, November 13, 2009, www.komonews.com/news/tech/70085527.html (accessed November 29, 2009); Ginny Mies, "Skeptical Shopper: The Pros and Cons of Buying E-Books," *PCWorld*, August 21, 2009, www.pcworld.com/article/170635/skeptical_shopper_the_pros_and_cons_of_buying_ebooks.html (accessed November 29, 2009), Shira Ovide and Geoffrey A. Fowler, "Hearst Plans Digital Magazine, Newspaper Service," *Wall Street Journal*, December 4, 2009, http://online.wsj.com/article_email/SB10001424052748703735004575474290782602228-lMyQjAxMDA5MDAwNDEwNDQyWj.html (accessed December 4, 2009); www.scribd.com (accessed October 15, 2009); Jon Stokes, "The Future of Scholarship? Harvard Goes Digital with Scribd," *ars technica*, July 17, 2009, www.arstechnica.com/media/news/ (accessed October 15, 2009); Spencer E. Ante, "An E-Book Upstart with Unlikely Fans," *BusinessWeek*, June 22, 2009, p. 54; Ryan Knutson and Geoffrey A. Fowler, "Book Smarts? E-Texts Receive Mixed Reviews From Students," *Wall Street Journal*, July 16, 2009, http://online.wsj.com/article/SB10001424052970203577304574277041750084938.html.

d. "Thoughts on Music," Apple Inc.—Steve Jobs, www.apple.com/hotnews/thoughtsonmusic/, February 6, 2007 (accessed April 3, 2008); "iTunes Stores Sales Going Strong," *MacWorld*, www.macworld.com/article/54775/2007/01/sales/html, January 9, 2007 (accessed April 3, 2008).

Chapter 12

1. Anna Vander Broek, "Self-Healing Concrete," *Forbes*, November 2, 2009, pp. 46–48; Anne Minard, "Bendable Concrete Heals Itself—Just Add Water," *National Geographic News*, May 5, 2009, http://news.nationalgeographic.com/news (accessed April 11, 2010); Nicole Casal Moore, "Self-Healing Concrete for Safer, More Durable Infrastructure," *Michigan Today*, University of Michigan, April 22, 2009, http://michigantoday.umich.edu (accessed April 11, 2010); Doug Smock, "Bendable Concrete Protects Against Hurricanes," *design news*, November 4, 2007, www.designnews.com/article/3464-Bendable_Concrete_Protects_Against_Hurricanes.php (accessed April 11, 2010).

2. "Carbonated Soft Drinks in the United States 2009," Research and Markets, www.researchandmarkets.com/.../carbonated_soft_drinks_in_the_united_states.pdf (accessed March 12, 2010); Coca-Cola Press Release, "Coca-Cola North America Announces 2008 Launch of Sprite Green," December 17, 2008, www.thecoca-colacompany.com/presscenter/newproducts_sprite_green_with_truvia.html (accessed March 12, 2010).

3. "SunnyRidge Farm Launches New Product Line Extension," *Fresh Plaza*, February 23, 2010, www.freshplaza.com/news_detail.asp?id=59361 (accessed March 14, 2010).

4. "Keypads Handsets Vs. Touch Screen Mobile Phones," *TechGadgets*, August 18, 2009, www.techgadgets.in (accessed March 15, 2010).

5. Peter Cohan, "After 101 Years, Why GM Failed," *DailyFinance*, May 31, 2009, www.dailyfinance.com/story/company-news/after-101-years-why-gm-failed/19052641/ (accessed March 14, 2010).

6. Rachel Dodes, "Spanx Body Slimmers for Men Unveiled," *Wall Street Journal*, February 16, 2010, http://blogs.wsj.com/runway/2010/02/16/spanx-body-slimmers-for-men-unveiled/tab/article/ (accessed March 17, 2010).

7. Rich Jaroslovsky, "Welcome to My Mobile Hot Spot," *Bloomberg Businessweek*, February 22, 2010, p. 80.

8. "About us," *Smart USA*, www.smartusa.com (accessed March 15, 2010).

9. Leonor Vivanco, "From Mind to Menu," *Chicago Tribune*, February 21, 2010, www.chicagotribune.com/features (accessed March 17, 2010).

10. "A. G. Lafley: Procter & Gamble," *BusinessWeek*, December 19, 2005, p. 62.

11. Nadira A. Hira, "Fahreheit 212—The Innovator's Paradise," *Fortune*, December 16, 2009, http://money.cnn.com/2009/12/15/news/companies/fahrenheit_212.fortune/index.htm (accessed March 19, 2010).

12. Paul Ziobro, "Yum to Expand Test of Breakfast Menu at Taco Bell," *Nasdaq*, March 19, 2010, www.nasdaq.com (accessed March 19, 2010).

13. Jason Daley, "The Big Bounce," *Entrepreneur* (April 2010): p. 108.

14. Jack Neff, "Swiffer by Another Name," *Advertising Age*, April 11, 2005, p. 11.

15. "Scores By Industry: Full Service Restaurants," The American Consumer Satisfaction Index, www.theacsi.org (accessed April 11, 2010).

16. "Scores by Industry: Express Delivery," ACSI, www.theacsi.org (accessed April 11, 2010).

17. Press Release, The Chrysler Experience, "2010 Chrysler Town & Country and Dodge Journey Earn Pet Safe Choice Awards," February 12, 2010, www.chrysler.com/en/experience/news/articles/?guid=2010_02_12_town_n_country_journey_pet_safe_award (accessed March 26, 2010).

18. Marco Bertini, Elie Ofek, and Dan Ariely, "The Impact of Add-On Features on Consumer Product Evaluations," *Journal of Consumer Research* 36, no. 1 (June 2009): pp. 17–28.

19. Stephanie Clifford, "Condé Nast Closes Gourmet and 3 Other Magazines," *New York Times*, October 5, 2009, www.nytimes.com/2009/10/06/business/media/06gourmet.html (accessed March 26, 2010).

20. Rick Barrett, "CEO Keeping Harley Rolling through Tough Times," *Milwaukee Journal-Sentinel*, April 25, 2010, www.jsonline.com/business/92025399.html (accessed April 29, 2010); "Harley-Davidson Reports 2009 Results," Press Release, www.harley-davidson.com/wcm/Content/Pages/HD_News/Company/newsarticle.jsp?locale=en_US&articleLink=News/0632_press_release.hdnews&newsYear=2010&history=archive (accessed April 29, 2010); Rick Barrett, "A Home for Harley's Heritage," *Milwaukee Journal-Sentinel*, June 29, 2008, www.journalsentinel.com.

21. Normany Madden, "Soy-Sauce-Flavored Kit Kats? In Japan, They're No. 1," *AdAge*, March 4, 2010 http://adage.com/globalnews/article?article_id=142461 (accessed May 1, 2010); "Fad Marketing Balancing Act," *BusinessWeek*, August 6, 2007, www.businessweek.com/magazine/content/07_32/b4045055.htm (accessed May 1, 2010); W. David Marx, "Pepsi Shiso: Soda Pop Meets a Minty Japanese Herb," *CNNGO*, July 14, 2009, www.cnngo.com/tokyo/drink/pepsi-shiso-487567 (accessed May 1, 2010); Jones Soda Corporate Website: Signature Limited Edition Labels, www.jonessoda.com/files_4/limited_editions.php (accessed May 1, 2010).

Feature Notes

a. Spanx, www.spanx.com (accessed February 18, 2009); Meredith Bryan, "Spanx Me, Baby!" *The New York Observer*, December 4, 2007, www.observer.com/2007/spanx-me-baby?page=1.

b. "Elevator Pitch: Guitar Affair Is Like Netflix for High-End Guitar Rentals. Will $150,000 Help the Company go Platinum?" *Inc.* (October 2009): p. 107; www.guitaraffair.com (accessed December 18, 2009); www.myspace.com/guitaraffair (accessed April 11, 2010); "Guitar Affair: It's Netflix for Guitars," Grateful Dead Music Forum, June 2009, www.rukind.com/forum/viewtopic.php?f=346&t=6475 (accessed April 11, 2010).

c. Jeff Borden, "SunChips Lets the Sun In," *marketingnews*, September 30, 2009, pp. 10–11; www.sunchips.com (accessed April 11, 2010); Karlene Lukovitz, "SunChips Keeps Building Green Momentum," *Marketing Daily*, April 22, 2009, www.mediapost.com (accessed April 11, 2010); Charisse Jones, "Compostable SunChips Bags Part of Green Packing Trend," *USA Today*, April 16, 2009, www.usatoday.com (accessed April 11, 2010).

d. "Airborne Settles Suit Over False Claims," *NPR*, http://npr.org, January 6, 2008 (accessed April 12, 2010); "Cold Remedy Airborne Settles Lawsuit," *WebMD*, http://webmd.com, March 4, 2008 (accessed April 12, 2010); "Airborne Settles Lawsuit," *Inc.com*, http://inc.com, March 7, 2008 (accessed April 12, 2010).

Chapter 13

1. Melanie D. G. Kaplan, "Tim Zagat: Why Our Guides Are Still Relevant in the Yelp Age," *SmartPlanet.com*, March 22, 2010, www.smartplanet.com; Peter Burrows, "Yelp If You Don't Want to Go Public," *BusinessWeek*, February 15, 2010, p. 23; Max Chafkin, "You've Been Yelped," *Inc.*, February 1, 2010, www.inc.com/magazine/20100201/youve-been-yelped.html; www.angieslist.com; www.yelp.com; www.zagat.com.

2. Leonard L. Berry and A. Parasuraman, *Marketing Services: Competing through Quality* (New York: Free Press, 1991), p. 5.

3. Susan Adams, "Where the Jobs Are: Home Call-Center Workers," *Forbes.com*, October 12, 2009, www.forbes.com/.

4. Abby Ellin, "The Recession. Isn't it Romantic?" *New York Times*, February 11, 2009, www.nytimes.com/2009/02/12/fashion/12dating.html.

5. Raymond P. Fisk, Stephen J. Grove, and Joby John, *Interactive Services Marketing* (Boston: Houghton Mifflin, 2003), p. 25.

6. Ibid., p. 59.

7. The information in this section is based on K. Douglass Hoffman and John E. G. Bateson, *Services Marketing: Concepts, Strategies, and Cases*, 3rd ed. (Cincinnati, OH: Thomson/South-Western, 2006); Valarie A. Zeithaml, A. Parasuraman, and Leonard L. Berry, *Delivering Quality Service: Balancing Customer Perceptions and Expectations* (New York: Free Press, 1990).

8. Michael K. Brady, Brian L. Bourdeau, and Julia Heskel, "The Importance of Brand Cues in Intangible Service Industries: An Application to Investment Services," *Journal of Services Marketing* 19 (October 2005): pp. 401–410.

9. Don E. Schultz, "Lost in Transition," *Marketing Management* (March/April 2007): pp. 10–11.

10. Jeremy J. Sierra and Shaun McQuitty, "Service Providers and Customers: Social Exchange Theory and Service Loyalty," *Journal of Services Marketing* 19 (October 2005): pp. 392–400.

11. Steve Sizoo, Richard Plank, Wilifried Iskat, and Hendrick Serrie, "The Effect of Intercultural Sensitivity on Employee Performance in Cross-cultural Service Encounters," *Journal of Services Marketing* 29 (June 2005): pp. 245–255.

12. J. Paul Peter and James H. Donnelly, *A Preface to Marketing Management* (Burr Ridge, IL: Irwin/McGraw-Hill, 2003), p. 212.

13. Sabin Im, Charlotte H. Mason, and Mark B. Houston, "Does Innate Consumer Innovativeness Relate to New Product/Service Adoption Behavior? The Intervening Role of Social Learning via Vicarious Innovativeness," *Journal of the Academy of Marketing Science* 35 (2007): pp. 63–75.

14. Michael D. Hartline and O. C. Ferrell, "Service Quality Implementation: The Effects of Organizational Socialization and Managerial Actions of Customer Contact Employee Behavior," *Marketing Science Institute Report*, no. 93-122 (Cambridge, MA: Marketing Science Institute, 1993).

15. Terah Shelton, "Best Buy's New ROLE," *Training Magazine*, June 11, 2009, www.trainingmag.com/.

16. Fisk, Grove, and John, *Interactive Services Marketing*, p. 56.

17. Ibid., p. 91.

18. Greg Lindsay, "Flight Plan," *Fast Company* (May 2007): pp. 100–107.

19. Laura Petrecca, "More Marketers Target Baby Boomers' Eyes, Wallets," *USA Today*, February 25, 2007, www.usatoday.com.

20. Gold's Gym, "Meet the Trainers," www.goldsgym.com/gyms/trainers.php?gymID=0103 (accessed April 14, 2010).

21. Lesley Kump, "Teaching the Teachers," *Forbes*, December 12, 2005, p. 121.

22. PetSmart, banfield.petsmart.com/ (accessed April 14, 2010).

23. Ahmed Taher and Hanan El Basha, "Heterogeneity of Consumer Demand: Opportunities for Pricing of Services," *Journal of Product & Brand Management* 15 (May 2006): pp. 331–340.

24. "Microsoft Bing," *PC Magazine*, www.pcmag.com/article2/0,2817,2348065,00.asp (accessed April 14, 2010).

25. *Florian v. Wangenheim*; and Tomás Bayón, "Behavioral Consequences of Overbooking Service Capacity," *Journal of Marketing* 71 (October 2007): pp. 36–47.

26. Zeithaml, Parasuraman, and Berry, *Delivering Quality Service.*

27. Dayana Yochim, "'Customer Rage' Is on the Rise," *The Motley Fool*, November 3, 2005, via AOL.com.

28. John Gountas and Sandra Gountas, "Personality Orientations, Emotional States, Customer Satisfaction, and Intention to Repurchase," *Journal of Business Research* 60 (January 2007): pp. 72–75.

29. Valarie A. Zeithaml, "How Consumer Evaluation Processes Differ between Goods and Services," in *Marketing of Services*, eds. James H. Donnelly and William R. George (Chicago: American Marketing Association, 1981), pp. 186–190.

30. "Lawyers.com Is Most Visited Legal Site for People Seeking an Attorney," *Lawyers.com*, June 15, 2009, http:// lawyers.com.

31. A. Parasuraman, Leonard L. Berry, and Valarie A. Zeithaml, "An Empirical Examination of Relationships in an Extended Service Quality Model," *Marketing Science Institute Working Paper Services*, no. 90-112 (Cambridge, MA: Marketing Science Institute, 1990), p. 29.

32. Chana R. Schoenberger, "Will Work with Food," *Forbes*, September 18, 2006, pp. 92+.

33. Valarie A. Zeithaml, Leonard L. Berry, and A. Parasuraman, "Communication and Control Processes in the Delivery of Service Quality," *Journal of Marketing* (April 1988): pp. 35–48.

34. Valarie A. Zeithaml, Leonard L. Berry, and A. Parasuraman, "The Nature and Determinants of Customer Expectations of Service," *Journal of the Academy of Marketing Science* (Winter 1993): pp. 1–12.

35. John F. Milliman, Eric M. Olson, and Stanley F. Slater, "Courting Excellence," *Marketing Management* (March/April 2007): pp. 14–17.

36. Jose Martinez, "Voting Campaign Launched," *The [Sacramento State University] State Hornet*, November 27, 2007, media.www.statehornet.com.

37. Philip Kotler, *Marketing for Nonprofit Organizations*, 2nd ed. (Englewood Cliffs, NJ: Prentice-Hall, 1982), p. 37.

38. Ibid.

39. Eric Newman, "March of Dimes Repositions Brand to Broadcast Appeal," *Brandweek*, January 16, 2008, www.brandweek.com/bw/news/pharmaceutical/article_display.jsp?vnu_content_id=1003696958.

40. "VerticalResponse, Inc. Surveys the State of Non-Profits in America; Reports on Trends in Marketing Channel Use Across 2009 and 2010," VerticalResponse, Press Release, February 1, 2010, www.verticalresponse.com/node/1512.

41. Linda Formichelli, "A Delicate Balance," *Deliver* (September 2007): pp. 8–9.

42. VerticalResponse, Press Release.

43. "Disaster Alert: Earthquake in Haiti," Red Cross, January 13, 2010, newsroom.redcross.org.

44. Dan Reed, "Continental, Southwest Land Profits," *USA Today*, January 22, 2010, p. 2B; Tom Belden, "Baggage Fees, 'Other' Revenue Seems Here to Stay," *Philadelphia Inquirer*, January 29, 2010; Lewis Lazare, "Why Southwest Soars as Other Airlines Sag," *Chicago Sun-Times*, June 20, 2008, www.suntimes.com; Trebor Banstetter, "Southwest's Boss Shuns Fees, Aims for More Fliers," *Fort Worth Star-Telegram*, June 2, 2008, www.dfw.com; Evan Smith, "Texas Monthly Talks: Evan Smith Sits Down with Herb Kelleher," *Texas Monthly* (June 2008): pp. 78+; www.southwest.com.

45. Monée Fields-White, "Walgreen Stands to Reap Benefits of Health Care Reform," *Crain's Chicago Business*, March 24, 2010, www.chicagobusinesss.com; Ben Sutherly, "Health Care Clinics Setting Up Shop Inside Area Kroger Stores, *Dayton Daily News* (OH), March 21, 2010, www.daytondailynews.com; "In-store Clinics Build Niche in Changing Health Care System," *Chain Drug Review*, April 20, 2009, p. 71; Walecia Konrad, "A Quick Trip to the Store for Milk and a Throat Swab," *New York Times*, October 3, 2009, p. B6.

Feature Notes

a. Kathryn Rem, "More Springfield Restaurants Are Going Green," *The State Journal-Register* (Springfield, IL), March 23, 2010, www.sj-r.com/business/; Mary Landers, "Thrive Becomes Savannah's First Certified Green Restaurant," *Savannah Morning News*, March 25, 2010, savannahnow.com; Rita Cook, "Dallas-area Restaurants Make Cleaner Environment a Top Priority," *Dallas Morning News*, March 13, 2010, www.dallasnews.com/.

b. Cirque du Soleil, www.cirquedusoleil.com (accessed April 14, 2010); Douglas Belkin, "Talent Scouts for Cirque du Soleil Walk a Tightrope," *The Wall Street Journal*, September 8, 2007, p. A1; Forrest Glenn Spencer, "It's One Big Circus," *Information Outlook* (October 2007): pp. 22–23.

c. "BBB Reports Nearly One in Five Adult Americans' Trust in Business Decreased in Past Year," Better Business Bureau, Press Release, November 8, 2007, www.bbb.org/us/BBB-Press-Releases.

d. Benny Evangelista, "Technology Gives Charities New Way to Reach Out," *San Francisco Chronicle*, March 16, 2010, www.sfgate.com; Dave Choate, "Nonprofits Turn to Facebook, Twitter," *Seacoast Online (New Hampshire)*, March 21, 2010, www.seacoastonline.com; www.scouting.org; www.habitat.org.

Chapter 14

1. Michael Learmonth, "Sales Chief Bradford to Leave Yahoo," *Advertising Age*, March 15, 2010, www.adage.com; Michael Learmonth, "Tale of the Tape: The Web's Old Guard," *Advertising Age*, October 5, 2009, p. 8; Brian Morrissey,

"Elisa Steele Joins Yahoo as CMO," *Adweek Online*, March 23, 2009, www.adweek.com; Abbey Klaassen, "Women to Watch: Elisa Steele," *Advertising Age*, June 1, 2009, p. 34; www.yahoo.com.

2. "Dictionary of Marketing Terms," American Marketing Association, www.marketingpower.com.

3. Warren Church, "Investment in Brand Pays Large Dividends," *Marketing News*, November 15, 2006, p. 21.

4. Bethany McLean, "Classic Rock," *Fortune*, November 12, 2007, pp. 35–40.

5. U.S. Bureau of the Census, *Statistical Abstract of the United States, 2010*, www.census.gov (Table 754).

6. "US: Wal-Mart Taps Agentrics to Support Great Value Re-Branding, Private Label Development," *Just-Style*, January 12, 2009, www.just-style.com.

7. C. D. Simms and P. Trott, "The Perception of the BMW Mini Brand: The Importance of Historical Associations and the Development of a Model," *Journal of Product and Brand Management* 15 (2006): pp. 228–238.

8. Douglas B. Holt, *How Brands Become Icons: The Principles of Cultural Branding* (Boston: Harvard Business School Press, 2004).

9. "The Charmin(R) Restrooms Return to Times Square This Holiday Season to Help Consumers Really 'Enjoy the Go,'" Proctor & Gamble, News Release, November 23, 2009, www.pginvestor.com.

10. David A. Aaker, *Managing Brand Equity: Capitalizing on the Value of a Brand Name* (New York: Free Press, 1991), pp. 16–17.

11. Nick Bunkley, "Toyota's Sales Fall as G.M. and Ford Gain," *The New York Times*, February 2, 2010, www.nytimes.com.

12. "Coca-Cola Buys Glaceau, Maker of Vitaminwater, for $4.1 Billion," *The Star*, May 28, 2007, thestar.com.

13. "US: Wal-Mart Taps Agentrics to Support Great Value Re-Branding, Private Label Development."

14. "Store Brands Achieving New Heights of Consumer Popularity and Growth," Private Label Manufacturer's Association, plma.com (accessed April 14, 2010).

15. Chiranjeev S. Kholi, Katrin R. Harich, and Lance Leuthesser, "Creating Brand Identity: A Study of Evaluation of New Brand Names," *Journal of Business Research* 58 (2005): pp. 1506–1515.

16. Dionne Searcey, "Bye, Cingular, in AT&T Rebranding," *The Wall Street Journal*, January 12, 2007, p. B3, online.wsj.com.

17. Allison Fass, "Animal House," *Forbes*, February 12, 2007, pp. 72–75.

18. Dorothy Cohen, "Trademark Strategy," *Journal of Marketing* (January 1986): p. 63.

19. U.S. Trademark Association, "Trademark Stylesheet," no. 1A.

20. Devon Del Vecchio and Daniel C. Smith, "Brand-Extension Price Premiums: The Effects of Perceived Fit and Extension Product Category Risk," *Journal of Marketing Science* 33 (April 2005): pp. 184–196.

21. "MillerCoors Beers," MillerCoors, www.millercoors.com (accessed April 14, 2010).

22. Kenneth Hein, "BK Boxers Leads Pack of Worst Line Extensions," *Brandweek*, December 15, 2008, www.brandweek.com.

23. Shantini Munthree, Geoff Bick, and Russell Abratt, "A Framework for Brand Revitalization," *Journal of Product & Brand Management* 15 (2006): pp. 157–167.

24. Chris Pullig, Carolyn J. Simmons, and Richard G. Netemeyer, "Brand Dilution: When Do New Brands Hurt Existing Brands?" *Journal of Marketing* 70 (April 2006).

25. Sarah Jacobsson, "T-Mobile and Eric Clapton Pitch Fender Themed Phone," *PCWorld*, January 14, 2010, www.pcworld.com.

26. Thomas J. Madden, Kelly Hewett, and Martin S. Roth, "Managing Images in Different Cultures: A Cross-National Study of Color Meanings and Preferences," *Journal of International Marketing* (Winter 2000): p. 90.

27. Bruce Horovitz, "Earthbound Farm, Naked Juice to Use 100% Recycled Plastic," *USA Today*, July 9, 2009, www.usatoday.com.

28. "Will Healthy Options = Healthy Sales?" *Packaging Digest* (July 2007): pp. 28–33.

29. Joel Dresang, "Making Bacon Pop," *Milwaukee Journal-Sentinel*, November 17, 2007, www.jsonline.com.

30. Bertrand Connolly, "Innovative Food Packaging Catches the Eye—and More," *FoodProcessing.com*, February 23, 2009, www.foodprocessing.com.

31. Valerie Folkes and Shashi Matta, "The Effect of Package Shape on Consumers' Judgment of Product Volume: Attention as a Mental Contaminant," *Journal of Consumer Research* (September 2004): p. 390.

32. Steve Everly, "Regulators Target Ink Cartridges," *Tennessean.com*, January 17, 2010, www.tennessean.com.

33. "Looking for That Label," *Prepared Foods* (September 2006): p. 38.

34. Federal Trade Commission, www.ftc.gov (accessed March 31, 2010).

35. Paul Suprenard, "Climate Change in Our Own Back Yard," *St. Petersburg (Florida) Times*, March 2, 2010, p. 7A; Jennifer Wang, "Brewing Big (With a Micro Soul)," *Entrepreneur*, November 2009, www.entrepreneur.com; Robert Baun, "What's in a Name? Ask the Makers of Fat Tire," *The [Fort Collins] Coloradoan*, October 8, 2000, pp. E1, E3; Julie Gordon, "Lebesch Balances Interests in Business, Community," *The [Fort Collins] Coloradoan*, February 26, 2003; Del I. Hawkins, Roger J. Best, and Kenneth A. Coney, *Consumer Behavior: Building Marketing Strategy*, 8th ed. (Burr Ridge, IL: IrwinMcGraw-Hill, 2001); David Kemp, Tour Connoisseur, New Belgium Brewing Company, personal interview by Nikole Haiar, November 21, 2000; www.newbelgium.com; *New Belgium Brewing Company Tour* by Nikole Haiar, November 20, 2000; Lisa Sanders, "This *Beer Will Reduce Your Anxiety*," *Advertising Age*, January 17, 2005, p. 25; Bryan Simpson, "New Belgium Brewing: Brand Building Through Advertising and Public Relations," http://college.hmco.com/instructorscatalog/misc/new_belgium_brewing.pdf.

36. Jeremiah McWilliams, "PepsiCo Revamps 'Formidable' Gatorade Franchise After Rocky 2009," *The Atlanta Journal-Constitution*, March 23, 2010, www.ajc.com; Martinne Geller, "Pepsi Eyes Emerging Markets, Healthy Fare," *Reuters*, March 22, 2010, www.reuters.com; Noreen O'Leary, "Gatorade's G2 Channels All to Punch Up Its Messaging," *Brandweek*, January 4, 2010, p. 4; Emily Bryson and Natalie Zmuda, "What G Isn't Is a Sales Success," *Advertising Age*, August 10, 2009, p. 17; David Sterrett, "New Drinks in Gatorade's Playbook," *Crain's Chicago Business*, November 9, 2009, p. 1; Burt Helm, "Blowing Up Pepsi," *BusinessWeek*, April 27, 2009, p. 32; www.gatorade.com.

37. Benjamin Pimentel, "Online Photo-Processing Pioneers, A Decade Later," *Wall Street Journal*, March 29, 2010, www.wsj.com; Anne Eisenberg, "When a Greeting Card Becomes a Photo Album," *The New York Times*, October 14, 2007, p. BU4; Jefferson Graham, "At Holidays, Net Photo Business Cranks Up," *USA Today*, December 22, 2006, p. 4B; Miguel Helft, "A Dot-Com Survivor's Long Road," *The New York Times*, October 30, 2006, p. C1; Jeff Housenbold, "A Photographic Vision," *Newsweek*, October 1, 2007, p. E4; "Nickelodeon and Shutterfly to Create New Character-Customized Digital Photo Products," *Wireless News*, November 14, 2007; "Olson Eyes Shutterfly Opportunities," *Brandweek*, August 6, 2007, p. 40; Shutterfly, www.shutterfly.com; "Shutterfly Goes East," *Digital Imaging Digest*, February 2007; "Shutterfly Joins Deloitte's 2007 Technology Fast 50 & Fast 500," *Wireless News*, November 27, 2007, www.10meters.com.

Feature Notes

a. Kelly Evans, "Headwinds Threaten Campbell's Charge," *The Wall Street Journal*, February 22, 2010, http://online.wsj.com; Jon Newberry, "Battle of the Titans," *Portfolio.com*, February 2, 2010, www.portfolio.com; Jenn Abelson, "Seeking Savings, Some Ditch Brand Loyalty," *Boston Globe*, January 29, 2010, www.boston.com; Matthew Boyle, "Wal-Mart Gives Its Store Brand a Makeover," *BusinessWeek*, March 16, 2009, www.businessweek.com.

b. Debra D. Bass, "Founder of Spanx Reshapes Foundation Wear," *St. Louis Post-Dispatch*, March 27, 2007, www.stltoday.com; Allen, "The Story of Spanx," www.articlesbase.com (accessed April 15, 2010); Spanx, www.spanx.com (accessed February 5, 2008); "Spanx Banks on Its Mission," *Apparel* (August 2007): pp. 5ff.

c. Camille Sweeney, "Now, the Cosmetics Jar Matters, Too," *The New York Times*, March 24, 2010, www.nytimes.com; Michelle Maisto, "'Green' Carrier AT&T Announces New Packaging Requirements," *eWeek*, March 5, 2010, www.eweek.com; "100% Bio-Plastic Water Bottles Trickle into Marketplace," *Environmental Leader*, March 8, 2010, www.environmentalleader.com.

Chapter 15

1. "Are Happy Days Here Again for Coca-Cola India?" *India Knowledge@Wharton*, March 11, 2010, http://knowledge.wharton.upenn.edu/india/article.cfm?articleid=4457#; Carol Massar, "Muhtar Kent, CEO, Coca-Cola Company," *Bloomberg Daily Programming*, March 4, 2010, www.bloomberg.com; Jeremiah McWilliams, "Coke Shakes Up Distribution," *Atlanta Journal-Constitution*, February 26, 2010, p. A1; "How Coke's Growth Got a RED Boost," *Business Line*, February 12, 2010; "New Plant to Bottle Coca-Cola Products Opens in China's Jiangxi," *AsiaPulse News*, June 24, 2009; Martinne Geller, "Coca-Cola Aims to Double System Revenue by 2020," *Reuters*, November 16, 2009, www.reuters.com.

2. Kenneth Karel Boyer, Markham T. Frolich, G. Tomas, and M. Hult, *Extending the Supply Chain* (New York: AMACOM, 2005).

3. Ricky W. Griffin, *Principles of Management* (Mason, OH: South-Western Cengage, 2011).

4. Lisa Harrington, "Getting Service Parts Logistics Up to Speed," *Inbound Logistics*, November 2006, www.inboundlogistics.com.

5. *The Supply Chain Management Spending Report, 2007-2008*, AMR Research, www.amrresearch.com (accessed April 15, 2010).

6. Soonhong Min, John Mentzer, and Robert T. Ladd, "A Market Orientation in Supply Chain Management," *Journal of the Academy of Marketing Research* 43 (February 2006).

7. Dan Sewell, "P&G Plans Smaller, Stronger Detergent," *USAToday.com*, May 22, 2007, www.usatoday.com/money/economy/2007-05-22-2055931001_x.htm.

8. Anthony J. Dukes, Esther Gal-Or, and Kannan Srinivasan, "Channel Bargaining with Retailer Asymmetry," *Journal of Marketing Research* 43 (February 2006).

9. "W.W. Grainger, Inc.," Hoovers, http://hoovers.com/company/WW_Grainger_Inc/rrhsyi-1.html (accessed April 15, 2010).

10. Jessica Wohl, "P&G Floats Selling Products on Its Own Website," *Reuters.com*, January 15, 2010, www.reuters.com/article/idUSTRE60E2TP20100115.

11. Leo Aspinwall, "The Marketing Characteristics of Goods," in *Four Marketing Theories* (Boulder, CO: University of Colorado Press, 1961), pp. 27–32.

12. "eBay Fined in LVMH Perfume Sales Row," *BBC News*, November 30, 2009, http://news.bbc.co.uk/2/hi/business/8386390.stm.

13. Wroe Alderson, *Dynamic Marketing Behavior* (Homewood, IL: Irwin, 1965), p. 239.

14. "About Pepsi Beverages Company," PepsiCo, www.pepsico.com/Company/The-PepsiCo-Family/Pepsi-Beverages-Company.html (accessed April 17, 2010).

15. "Dell to Provide Business Process Outsourcing Services to Help USCIS Enhance More Than 60 Field Office Operations," Dell, Press Release, via *Business Wire*.

16. Vicki O'Meara, "Take a Deep Breath Before Diving into Global Outsourcing," *Inbound Logistics* (September 2007): p. 36.

17. Lee Pender, "The Basic Links of SCM," Supply Chain Management Research Center, www.itworld.com/CIO020501_basic_content (accessed April 16, 2010).

18. Cindy H. Dubin, "Moving Shoes Is No Easy Feat," *Inbound Logistics*, December 2009.

19. Claire Swedberg, "Daisy Brand Benefits from RFID Analytics," *RFID Journal*, January 18, 2008, www.rfidjournal.com/article/articleview/3860/1/1/.

20. Distribution Unlimited Inc., http://disunlt.com (accessed April 16, 2010).

21. American Eagle Outfitters, Careers, www.liveyourlifeloveyourjob.com (accessed April 16, 2010).

22. "Freight Payment Services: Boosting Invoice IQ," *Inbound Logistics*, September 2009.

23. Joseph O'Reilly, "Trends: Clorox Cleans Up," *Inbound Logistics*, January 2010.

24. "Desktop Shipping and Compliance Fact Sheet," Iron Data, transportation.irondata.com/pdf/trans/Desktopshippingoptimizationsolution.pdf (accessed April 16, 2010).

25. "Intermodal Case Study: Electrolux Sweeps Up Savings," *Inbound Logistics*, October 2009.

26. "[Case Study] Inbound Routing Compliance: L'Oreal-ity Check," *Inbound Logistics*, January 2010.

27. Joseph O'Reilly, "Global Logistics," *Inbound Logistics*, October 2009.

28. Austin Carr, "Today in Most Innovative Companies," *Fast Company*, March 30, 2010, www.fastcompany.com; Teresa Rivas, "Blockbuster in a Fix, Netflix Is a Pick," *Barron's*, March 17, 2010, online.barrons.com/article/SB126877637345963181.html; Russ Britt, "Netflix Seeks to Stay Atop Video Heap," *The Wall Street Journal*, March 17, 2010, www.wsj.com; www.netflix.com; www.redbox.com.

29. "Dell Bets on Social Commerce as Next Boom Area for Etail," *New Media Age*, March 25, 2010, p. 3; Antone Gonsalves, "AT&T to Launch Dell Smartphone," *InformationWeek*, March 23, 2010, www.informationweek.com; Fritz Nelson, "Who Is Dell?" *InformationWeek*, January 25, 2010, p. 46; Doug Woodburn, "Dell Invites Bell to Join Distribution Carnival," *CRN*, March 23, 2010; "News: Dell," *MicroScope*, November 9, 2009, www.microscope.co.uk; Mary Ellen Slayter, "How Dell Took Social Media Mainstream," *Smart Blog on Social Media*, October 2, 2009, http://smartblogs.com; Jack Ewing, "Where Dell Sells With Brick and Mortar," *BusinessWeek*, October 8, 2007, www.businessweek.com; www.dell.com.

Feature Notes

a. Daniel Fisher, "A Dirty Game," *Forbes*, March 10, 2008, pp. 38–40; Jim Rogers, "Point of View: A New Model for Energy Efficiency," *The News & Observer*, February 19, 2008; "Greenwashing," *The Dictionary of Sustainable Management*, www.sustainabilitydictionary.com/g/greenwashing.php (accessed April 16, 2010).

b. Jean E. Palmieri, "Adapt or Go Extinct," *WWD*, March 25, 2010, p. 1; Cathy Barringer, "Ben's Supercenter Manager Celebrates 25 Years," *Brown City (MI) Banner,* January 25, 2010, http://browncitybanner.mihomepaper.com/news/2010-01-25/Front_Page/Bens_Supercenter_manager_celebrates_25_years.html; "A Legacy in the Making: Nine Retailers Honored in First Annual Retail Innovators Award Program," *Hardware Retailing* (September 2009): pp. 48ff; http://kilgoretrout.com.

c. "FedEx Aims to Be First U.S. Parcel Firm to Put All-Electric Trucks in Service," *Environmental Leader,* March 29, 2010, www.environmentalleader.com; "10 Ways for the Freight Sector to Lessen Its Environmental Impact," *Environmental Leader,* March 19, 2010, www.environmentalleader.com; "Corporate Fleets Expected Early Adopters of Electric Vehicles," *Environmental Leader,* March 4, 2010, www.environmentalleader.com; "Sustainable Distribution: Patagonia's Distribution Center Takes a Green Step Forward," *Sustainable Facility* (November 2009): pp. 18ff; John M. Saulnier, "Solar Flares Green in Garden State, Generating Electricity at Hall's Warehouses," *Quick Frozen Foods International* (October 2009): pp. 138ff.

d. Lillian Kafka, "Milestone in Rail Transportation," MHW Group, November 1, 2006, www.mhwgroup.com/index.php/news/91-november-2006-martin-brower-qmilestone-in-rail-transportationq; Amanda Loudin, "Freezing Transport Costs in Their Tracks," *Inbound Logistics* (January 27, 2007): pp. 251–254, www.inboundlogistics.com/articles/casebook/casebook0107.shtml (accessed April 16, 2010).

Chapter 16

1. "Founder of Geek Squad Is Best Buy's Corporate Cisionary," *Richmond Times-Dispatch*, April 5, 2010, www2.timesdispatch.com; Vivek Kaul, "Do You Really Know Who Your Customer Is?" *Daily News & Analysis,* March 29, 2010; Jonathan Marino, "Corporates Venture Into Startups," *Investment Dealers' Digest*, March 26, 2010, p. 17; Miguel Bustillo and Christopher Lawton, "Best Buy Expands Private-Label Brands," *The Wall Street Journal*, April 27, 2009, www.wsj.com; www.bestbuy.com.

2. Jeff Clabaugh, "Black Friday Online Sales Up 11%," *South Florida Business Journal*, November 30, 2009, www.bizjournals.com/southflorida/stories/2009/11/30/daily4.html.

3. U.S. Bureau of the Census, *Statistical Abstract of the United States, 2010,* www.census.gov/compendia/statab/ (accessed April 19, 2010), Table 743.

4. "NRF Forecasts One Percent Decline in Holiday Sales," National Retail Federation, October 6, 2009, www.nrf.com/modules.php?name=news&op=viewlive&sp_id=799.

5. Walmart Corporate Fact Sheet, walmartstores.com/download/2230.pdf (accessed April 19, 2010).

6. Matthew Boyle, "Wal-Mart Moves Upmarket," *BusinessWeek.com,* June 3, 2009, www.businessweek.com/magazine/content/09_24/b4135000941856.htm?chan=innovation_branding_top+stories.

7. "U.S. Convenience Store Count," National Association of Convenience Stores, January 2010, www.nacsonline.com/NACS/News/factsheets/scopeofindustry/pages/industrystorecount.aspx (accessed April 19, 2010).

8. Seth Perlman, "Retailers Emulate Wal-Mart's Focus on Necessities," *USAToday.com*, June 4, 2009, www.usatoday.com/money/industries/retail/2009-06-03-walmart_N.htm.

9. Sam's Club Fact Sheet, Costco Wholesale Corporation Fact Sheet, B.J.'s Wholesale Club Fact Sheet, Hoover's Online, www.hoovers.com (accessed April 19, 2010).

10. Louis Llovino, "J.C. Penney Opens Non-Mall Store in Henrico," *Richmond Times Dispatch*, Mar 7, 2009, www2.timesdispatch.com.

11. Janet Adamy, "For Subway, Every Nook and Cranny on the Planet Is Possible Site for a Franchise," *The Wall Street Journal*, September 1, 2006, p. A11, http://online.wsj.com.

12. Mall of America, www.mallofamerica.com (accessed April 19, 2010).

13. Kurt Blumenau, "Are Target, Best Buy Really Upscale? Owners of 'Lifestyle' Shopping Centers Still Signing Retail Tenants," *The [Allentown, Pennsylvania] Morning Call*, May 29, 2005, via LexisNexis; Debra Hazel, "Wide-Open Spaces," *Chain Store Age* (November 2005): p. 120; "ICSC Shopping Center Definitions," International Council of Shopping Centers, http://icsc.org/srch/lib/USDefinitions.pdf (accessed April 20, 2010); Greg Lindsay, "Say Goodbye to the Mall," *Advertising Age,* October 2, 2006, p. 13.

14. Lauren B. Cooper, "Bayer Properties to Manage S.C. Shopping Center," *BizJournals.com*, May 14, 2009, www.bizjournals.com/birmingham/stories/2009/05/11/daily34.html; www.mtpleasanttownecentre.com/go/dirListing.cfm?FL=all (accessed March 4, 2010).

15. Stephanie Kang, "After a Slump, Payless Tries on Fashion for Size," *The Wall Street Journal*, February 10, 2007, p. A1, http://online.wsj.com.

16. Velitchka D. Kaltcheva and Barton A. Weitz, "When Should a Retailer Create an Exciting Store Environment?" *Journal of Marketing* 70 (January 2006).

17. "History of Ceasars Palace," *A2ZLasVegas.com,* www.a2zlasvegas.com/hotels/history/h-caesars.html.

18. Mindy Fetterman and Jayne O'Donnell, "Just Browsing at the Mall? That's What You Think," *USA Today*, September 1, 2006, www.usatoday.com.

19. Anick Bosmans, "Scents and Sensibility: When Do (In) Congruent Ambient Scents Influence Product Evaluations?" *Journal of Marketing* 70 (July 2006).

20. "DMA's 'Power of Direct Marketing' Report Finds Direct Marketing Ad Expenditures Climb to Over 54%," Direct Marketing Association, press release, October 19, 2009, www.the-dma.org/cgi/disppressrelease?article=1359.

21. "Direct Marketing an $8 Billion Auto Industry Driver," *Brandweek*, January 28, 2008, www.brandweek.com/bw/news/recent_display.jsp?vnu_content_id=1003702944.

22. Maris Halkias, "J.C. Penney's Big Catalog Soon to Be But a Memory," *TheSeattleTimes.com*, November 27, 2009, http://seattletimes.nwsource.com/html/businesstechnology/2010365217_jcpenneycatalog27.html.

23. Jack Neff, "Snuggie: An America's Hottest Brands Case Study," *AdAge.com*, November 16, 2009, http://adage.com.

24. "Additional Report to Congress: Pursuant to the Do Not Call Registry Fee Extension Act of 2007," Federal Trade Commission, December 2009, www.ftc.gov/os/2010/01/100104dncadditionalreport.pdf.

25. Sucharita Mulpuru and Peter Hult, "US Online Retail Forecast: 2009-2014," Forrester Research, March 5, 2010, www.forrester.com/rb/Research/us_online_retail_forecast%2C_2009_to_2014/q/id/56551/t/2.

26. "Direct Selling News Global 100: 2009," *Direct Selling News,* April 2010, www.directsellingnews.com/index.php/site/entries_archive_display/direct_selling_news_global_100_2009.

27. "Fact Sheet: U.S. Direct Selling in 2008," *Direct Selling Association*, www.dsa.org/research (accessed April 19, 2010).

28. "Redbox's Vending Machines Are Giving Netflix Competition," *NYTimes.com*, June 21, 2009, www.nytimes.com/2009/06/22/business/media/22redbox.html.

29. "Vending Machines Go Luxe," *BusinessWeek*, January 28, 2008, p. 17.

30. "2010 Franchise Business Economic Outlook," *International Franchise Association*, December 2009, www.franchise.org; "Franchise Industries," International Franchise Association, www.franchise.org/franchisecategories.aspx (accessed April 19, 2010).

31. Raymund Flandez, "New Franchise Idea: Fewer Rules, More Difference," *The Wall Street Journal*, September 18, 2007, online.wsj.com.

32. U.S. Bureau of the Census, *Statistical Abstract of the United States, 2010*, Table 743.

33. "Genuine Parts Company," *Hoover's Online*, www.hoovers.com/company/Genuine_Parts_Company/rfjcji-1.html (accessed April 20, 2010).

34. "Universal Corporation," *Hoover's Online*, www.hoovers.com (accessed April 20, 2010).

35. "Red River Commodities, Inc.," *Hoover's Online*, www.hoovers.com/company/Red_River_Commodities_Inc/rtkshci-1.html; Red River Commodities, Inc., www.redriv.com (accessed April 20, 2010).

36. Connie Gentry, "EMS Charts Course for Growth," *Chain Store Age* (March 2010): p. 22; Lynette Carpiet, "EMS Expands in Northeast," *Bicycle Retailer and Industry News*, May 1, 2008; Lucas Conley, "Climbing Back Up the Mountain," *Fast Company*, April 2005; Eastern Mountain Sports Climbing School, www.emsclimb.com; Drew Robb, "Eastern Mountain Sports: Getting Smarter with Each Sale," *Computer World*, September 18, 2006, www.computerworld.com; www.ems.com.

37. James Quinn, "Tesco's US Venture Sets Its Sights on Hispanic Shoppers," *The Telegraph (U.K.)*, April 7, 2010, www.telegraph.co.uk; Scott Weber, "Grocery Store Shopping Is Getting Fresher, Easier," *NBC News Los Angeles*, April 6, 2010, www.nbclosangeles.com; Kathy Gordon, "Not So Fresh & Easy for Tesco in the U.S.," *The Source (The Wall Street Journal)*, January 12, 2010, www.wsj.com; Kate Rockwood, "How Tesco Tweaked Its Fresh & Easy Concept," *Fast Company*, October 1, 2009, www.fastcompany.com; "Fresh & Easy Exec: Tesco Concept Fills Gap in U.S. Market," *Progressive Grocer*, December 13, 2009, www.progressivegrocer.com; www.freshandeasy.com.

38. Brett Molina, "Want a Used Game with Your 7-11 Slurpee?" *USA Today*, April 19, 2010, www.usatoday.com; Victor Godinez, "Movie, Book, Game Companies Fight to Survive Plunge into Internet Age," *Dallas Morning News*, April 5, 2010, www.dallasnews.com; "GameStop Launches Its First Online Video Game," *Internet Retailer*, March 31, 2010, www.internetretailer.com; Andrew Bary, "GameStop Builds a Business Selling Used Games to Teens," *Barron's Insight*, March 28, 2010, www.wsj.com; www.gamestop.com.

Feature Notes

a. Starbucks Corporation, Fiscal 2007 Annual Report, March 2008, http://media.corporate-ir.net/media_files/irol/99/99518/2007AR.pdf (accessed April 20, 2010); Bruce Horovitz, "Starbucks Aims Beyond Lattes to Extend Brand to Films, Music, and Books," *USA Today*, May 19, 2006, pp. A1, A2; Neil Merrett, "Starbucks Trims Fat to Meet Dairy Demands," *DairyReporter.com*, June 5, 2007, www.dairyreporter.com (accessed April 20, 2010).

b. Laura Paskus, "Owner Won't Melt under Stress of Ice Cream Niche Business," *New Mexico Business Weekly*, July 27—August 2, 2007, 15; "Tara's Gets Organic in New Mexico," *Ice Cream Reporter*, October 2005, www.allbusiness.com/manufacturing/food-manufacturing-dairy-product-ice-cream/592756-1.html; Tara's Organic Ice Cream, www.tarasorganic.com (accessed April 20, 2010).

c. Elaine Misonzhnik, "Swayed by Changing Consumer Patterns, More Retailers Eye Outlets," *Retail Traffic*, January 20, 2010; Rosemary Feitelberg, "Malls See Reinvention as a Survival Skill," *WWD*, April 28, 2009, p. 12; Tim Logan, "Recession Widening Gap Between Healthy Malls, Weak Ones," *St. Louis Post-Dispatch*, August 16, 2009, www.stltoday.com.

d. "Kohl's Ranks as Top Green Power Retailer," *Retain Information Systems News*, February 2, 2010, http://risnews.edgl.com: 80/home, Kim Ann Zimmermann, "Taking the LEED," *Grocery Headquarters* (January 2010): pp. 139+; Robin Pagnamenta, "Multinationals Plan to Put Their Money Behind Britain's Push for Wind Energy," *The Times (London)*, October 23, 2009, p. 42.

Chapter 17

1. Piet Levy, "La Musica to Their Ears," *Marketing News*, May 15, 2009, pp. 14–16; "State Farm's Regional Mexican Band Comes to TV," *Marketing Power*, October 30, 2009, www.marketingpower2.com/blog/marketingnews/2009/10/state_farms_regional_mexican_b.html (accessed April 8, 2010); "Branded Entertainment Winners: Hispanic Creative Advertising Awards," *AdvertisingAge*, September 19, 2009, http://adage.com (accessed April 8, 2010).

2. The Official Site of the San Diego Padres, http://sandiego.padres.mlb.com/index.jsp?c_id=sd (accessed March 27, 2010); Jordan Edelman & Kate Creveling, "Utilizing Integrated Marketing Communications with the Academic Centers for Excellence," *The Mentor: An Academic Advising Journal*, 2009, www.psu.edu/dus/mentor/090819je.htm (accessed March 27, 2010).

3. "Ford Music Video Challenge," American Idol, www.americanidol.com/ford/challenge (accessed March 27, 2010).

4. "Performance Downloads," American Idol, www.americanidol.com/itunes (accessed March 27, 2010).

5. Salvador Ruiz and María Sicilia, "The Impact of Cognitive and/or Affective Processing Styles on Consumer Response to Advertising Appeals," *Journal of Business Research* 57 (2004): pp. 657–664.

6. Deborah Swallow, "Cross Cultural Marketing Blunders," August 20, 2009, www.deborahswallow.com/2009/08/20/cross-cultural-marketing-blunders (accessed March 30, 2010).

7. Bruce Horovitz, "Betty White, Snickers Top Ad Meter; View and Rate All the Ads," *USA Today*, February 15, 2010, www.usatoday.com/money/advertising/admeter/2010admeter.htm (accessed March 31, 2010).

8. "Yoplait USA," Susan G. Komen For the Cure, ww5.komen.org/ContentHeaderOnly.aspx?id=6442451452 (accessed March 27, 2010); "Save Lids to Save Lives," www.yoplait.com/slsl (accessed March 27, 2010).

9. Aaron Baar, "Kraft, Animal Planet in Lunchables Promotion," *Marketing Daily*, February 6, 2010, www.mediapost.com/publications/?fa=Articles.showArticle&art_aid=121952 (accessed March 27, 2010).

10. Scott Davis, "Successful Brand Turnarounds Require Fearless Moves," *Advertising Age*, March 29, 2010, http://adage.com/cmostrategy/article?article_id=143025 (accessed March 31, 2010).

11. Nate Ives, "Publishers Gush Over iPad, but Their Publications Are More Restrained," *Advertising Age*, March 31, 2010, http://adage.com/mediaworks/article?article_id=143074 (accessed March 31, 2010).

12. "Nike-Reuse a Shoe," www.nikereuseashoe.com (accessed March 25, 2010).

13. Regal Crown Club, Regal Entertainment Group, http://rcc.regalcinemas.com/CrownClub/appmanager/rcc/CrownClub?_

nfpb=true&_pageLabel=CROWNCLUB (accessed March 27, 2010).

14. "2010 U.S. National Edition Rates," TIME Media Kit, www.timemediakit.com/us/timemagazine/rates/national/index.html (accessed April 6, 2010).

15. Joann Peck and Jennifer Wiggins, "It Just Feels Good: Customers' Affective Response to Touch and Its Influence in Persuasion," *Journal of Marketing* 70 (October 2006).

16. Belinda Goldsmith, "Star Power: Celebrity Endorsements Surge at Grammys," *Reuters*, February 2, 2010, www.reuters.com/article/idUSTRE61141G20100202 (accessed March 27, 2010).

17. Michael Bush, "As Media Market Shrinks, PR Passes Up Reporters, Pitches Directly to Consumers," *Advertising Age*, October 26, 2009, http://adage.com/article?article_id=139864 (accessed April 6, 2010).

18. "What Travel Goodies the Celebs Got in the $91,000 Oscars *Gift Bags*," *Jaunted*, March 8, 2010, www.jaunted.com/story/2010/3/8/105942/8794/travel/What+Travel+Goodies+the+Celebs+Got+in+the+$91,000+Oscars+Gift+Bags (accessed April 6, 2010).

19. Michelle Leder, "Goldman Discloses a New Risk: Bad Publicity," DealBook, *The New York Times*, March 1, 2010, http://dealbook.blogs.nytimes.com (accessed April 8, 2010).

20. Patricia Hurtado, "Goldman Sachs Sued by Shareholder Over Pay, Bonuses," *BusinessWeek*, January 8, 2010, www.businessweek.com/news (accessed April 6, 2010).

21. Old Navy Supermodelquin Sweepstakes, www.iwannabesuper.com/?id=tn#landing (accessed March 28, 2010).

22. Doug Brooks, "How to Balance Brand Building and Price Promotion," *Advertising Age*, December 29, 2010, http://adage.com (accessed April 6, 2010).

23. "TNS Media Intelligence Reports US Advertising Expenditures Declined 14.7 Percent in First Nine months of 2009," *Freeband TV News*, December 10, 2009, www.freebandtvnews.com (accessed April 6, 2010).

24. U.S. Census Bureau, American Community Survey, Fact Finder, factfinder.census.gov/servlet/ADPTable?_bm=y&-geo_id=01000US&-ds_name=ACS_2008_3YR_G00_&-_lang=en&-_caller=geoselect&-format= (accessed March 28, 2010).

25. Rockney G. Walters and Maqbul Jamil, "Exploring the Relationships Between Shopping Trip Type, Purchases of Products on Promotion, and Shopping Basket Profit," *Journal of Business Research* 56 (2003): pp. 17–29.

26. "Quattron Technology," www.aquos-world.com/en/product/quattron_technology.html (accessed April 6, 2010).

27. Emma Hall, "German Magazine Ditches Models for 'Real' Women," *Advertising Age*, October 6, 2009, http://adage.com/globalnews/article?article_id=139485 (accessed April 6), 2010).

28. *Florian v. Wangenheim*; and Tomás Bayón, "The Chain from Customer Satisfaction via Word-of-Mouth Referrals to New Customer Acquisition," *Journal of the Academy of Marketing Science* 35 (June 2007): pp. 233–249.

29. Pratibha A. Dabholkar, "Factors Influencing Consumer Choice of a 'Rating Web Site': An Experimental Investigation of an Online Interactive Decision Aid," *Journal of Marketing Theory and Practice* 14 (Fall 2006): pp. 259–273.

30. "Global Advertising: Consumers Trust Real Friends and Virtual Strangers the Most," *NielsenWire*, July 7, 2009, http://blog.nielsen.com/nielsenwire/consumer (accessed March 28, 2010).

31. Aarthi Sivaraman, "Barbie at 50: Is Mattel's Star Still in Fashion?" *Reuters*, March 6, 2009, www.reuters.com/article/idUSTRE52603B20090307 (accessed March 28, 2010).

32. Stuart McGurk, "2012 and How Good Viral Marketing Can Go Bad," *The Guardian*, November 14, 2009, www.guardian.co.uk/film/2009/nov/14/2012-roland-emmerich-viral-marketing (accessed March 28, 2010).

33. Jesse Grainger, "47 Outrageous Viral Marketing Examples over the Last Decade," *Ignite Social Media*, June 28, 2009, www.ignitesocialmedia.com/viral-marketing-examples (accessed March 28, 2010).

34. Adam Bluestein, "Customers Were Grumbling, Griping, Threatening to Leave. Was That Price Hike Really Such a Good Idea?" *Inc.* (March 2010): pp. 55–58.

35. "Volvo Builds Promotion Around Twilight Sequel," *Product Placement News*, October 27, 2009, www.productplacement.biz (accessed April 6, 2010).

36. Lynna Goch, "The Place to Be," *Best's Review* (February 2005): pp. 64–65.

37. "Kodak Product Placement on The Celebrity Apprentice," March 19, 2010. www.productplacement.biz (accessed April 6, 2010).

38. Erin Copple Smith, "Egregious Product Placement: The Biggest Loser," antenna, January 30, 2010, www.blog.commarts.wisc.edu/2010/01/30/egregious-product-placement-the-biggest-loser/ (accessed March 29, 2010).

39. Rupert Neate, "TV Product Placement Ban Lifted in UK," *Telegraph*, February 9, 2010, www.telegraph.co.uk/finance/newsbysector/mediatechnologyandtelecoms/media/7197867/TV-product-placement-ban-lifted-in-UK.html (accessed March 19, 2010).

40. "AT&T Drops Verizon Map Ad Lawsuit," December 2, 2009, www.theatlantic.com/business/archive/2009/12/at-t-drops-verizon-map-ad-lawsuit/31169 (accessed April 6, 2010).

41. *The Toledo Mud Hens*, www.mudhens.com (accessed July 14, 2008); *The Detroit Tigers*, http://tigers.mlb.com (accessed July 14, 2008); Sherry Chiger, "Toledo Mud Hens Score with CRM/E-mail Integration," *Direct*, April 5, 2010, 74.125.155.132/search?q=cache:http://directmag.com/email/Mud-Hens-CRM-email-0405/ (accessed April 24, 2010).

42. *One Report 2009*, downloaded from Southwest.com. 216.139.227.101/interactive/luv2009/ (accessed May 2, 2010); *PR Newswire*, "Southwest Airlines Launches New 'Grab Your Bag: It's On!' Ads," *Southwest.com*. March 15, 2010, www.southwest.com/about_swa/press/prindex.html?int=GFOOTER-ABOUT-PRESS (accessed May 2, 2010); "Airlines to Charge for Carry-on Bags," *CBS News*, April 7, 2010, www.cbsnews.com/video/watch/?id=6372838n (accessed May 2, 2010); "Southwest Airlines Unveils *Florida One*." Southwest News Release, April 23, 2010. www.swamedia.com/swamedia/floridaOneRelease.pdf (accessed May 2, 2010); "We Weren't Just Airborne Yesterday," *Southwest*.com. www.southwest.com/about_swa/airborne.html (accessed May 2, 2010); posted by NutsAboutSouthwest, "*Southwest* Airlines Bags Fly Free Commercial," September 28, 2009, www.youtube.com/ (accessed May 2, 2010); posted by NutsAboutSouthwest, "At Southwest Airlines, We Love Your Bags!" October 9, 2009, www.youtube.com/ (accessed May 2, 2010).

Feature Notes

a. imc² Clear Sky Media Tool, www.imc2.com/carbon (accessed April 11, 2010); Union Green, www.union-green.com, (accessed April 11, 2010); Greendisk, greendisk.com (accessed April 11, 2010).

b. Andrew Hampp, "Turner Agrees to Pay Boston $2 Million," *Advertising Age*, February 5, 2007, http://adage.com/mediaworks/article?article_id=114825 (accessed April 10, 2009); Suzanne Smalley and Raja Mishra, "Froth, Fear, and Fury," *The Boston Globe*, February 1, 2007, www.boston.com/news/local/massachusetts/articles/2007/02/01/froth_fear_and_fury/ (accessed July 31, 2009); John R. Ellement and Andrew Ryan, "Dr. Pepper's 'Gold Coin' Found in Historic Cemetery,"

Boston.com, February 23, 2007, www.boston.com/news/globe/city_region/breaking_news/2007/02/dr_peppers_gold.html (accessed November 29, 2010).

c. Hulu-About, www.hulu.com/about (accessed April 11, 2010); Chuck Salter, "The Unlikely Mogul," *Fast Company* (November 2009): pp. 98-105; www.hulu.com (accessed April 11, 2010); Ian Paul, "The Simpsons: Worth More on Hulu than Fox," *PCWorld*, June 25, 2009, www.pcworld.com/article/167344/the_simpsons_worth_more_on_hulu_than_fox.html (accessed April 11, 2010); Chuck Salter, "Can Hulu Save Traditional TV?" *Fast Company*, November 2009, www.fastcompany.com/magazine/140/the-unlikely-mogul.html?page=0,3 (accessed April 11, 2010).

d. "The PIVMAN System for Secure ID Checking," *Core Street*, www.corestreet.com/solutions/prod_tech/id/ (accessed April 14, 2009); *PIVMAN for First Response* comic, www.corestreet.com/about/library/other/pivman_comic-lores.pdf.

Chapter 18

1. Joe Flint, "3-D Makes the Leap to the Small Screen," *LA Times*, January 6, 2010, http://articles.latimes.com/2010/jan/06/business/la-fi-ct-3dtv6-2010jan06 (accessed April 15, 2010); Nick Parish, "Think You Need a 3-D Ad? Some Advice from Experts," *Advertising Age*, January 11, 2010, http://adage.com (accessed April 15, 2010).

2. "Foods Taste Better with McDonald's Logo, Kids Say," *Drugs.com*, www.drugs.com/news/foods-taste-better-mcdonald-s-logo-kids-say-8889.html (accessed April 7, 2010).

3. "2010 Strategic Tourism Plan Approved," August 11, 2009, www.arts.state.tx.us/index.php?option=com_content&view=article&id=296&Itemid=16 (accessed April 7, 2010).

4. Marvin E. Goldberg, Cornelia Pechmann, Guangzhi Zhao, and Ellen Thomas Reibling, "What to Convey in Antismoking Advertisements for Adolescents: The Use of Protection Motivation Theory to Identify Effective Message Themes," *Journal of Marketing* (April 2003): pp. 1–18.

5. Tanya Irwin, "American Airlines Campaign Targets Latinos," *Marketing Daily*, June 11, 2009, www.mediapost.com/publications/?fa=Articles.showArticle&art_aid=107754 (accessed March 24, 2010).

6. "E*TRADE Announces New Super Bowl® XLIV Advertisement and Evolved Marketing Campaign," http://investor.etrade.com/releasedetail.cfm?ReleaseID=437920 (accessed April 8, 2010).

7. March Blumenthal, "Census Is Counting on Ad Campaign," *GovernmentExecutive.com*, March 15, 2010, www.govexec.com/dailyfed/0310/031510nj1.htm (accessed April 8, 2010).

8. Ibid.

9. Glamour Circulation/Demographics, http://condenastmediakit.com/gla/circulation.cfm (accessed April 9, 2010).

10. Ilona A. Berney-Reddish and Charles S. Areni, "Sex Differences in Responses to Probability Markers in Advertising Claims," *Journal of Advertising* 35 (Summer 2006): pp. 7–17.

11. Daniel J. Howard and Roger A. Kerin, "The Effects of Personalized Product Recommendations on Advertisement Response Rates: The 'Try This. It Works!' Technique," *Journal of Consumer Psychology* 14, no. 3, (2004): pp. 271–279.

12. Pamela W. Henderson, Joan L. Giese, and Joseph A. Cote, "Impression Management Using Typeface Design," *Journal of Marketing* 68 (October 2004): pp. 60–72.

13. Rik Pieters and Michel Wedel, "Attention Capture and Transfer in Advertising: Brand, Pictorial, and Text-Size Effects," *Journal of Marketing* 68 (April 2004): pp. 36–50.

14. Suzanne Vranica, "After 5 Short-Lived Campaigns, Wendy's Will Focus on Freshness," *The Wall Street Journal*, October 8, 2009, http://online.wsj.com/article/SB10001424052748704252004574457611553266206.html (accessed March 29, 2010).

15. Andrew Hampp, "Outdoor Ad Industry Finally Gets Its Improved Metrics," *Advertising Age*, March 30, 2010, adage.com (accessed April 9, 2010).

16. Philip W. Sawyer, "Why Most Digital Ads Still Fail to Work," *Advertising Age*, January 27, 2010, http://adage.com/digitalnext/post?article_id=141751 (accessed April 9, 2010).

17. "Utah Launches Summer Tourism Ad Campaign," Utah Travel Industry Website, April, 6, 2009, www.utah.com/travelheadlines/2009/04/utah-launches-summer-tourism-ad.html (accessed March 29, 2010).

18. Mya Frazier, "This Ad Will Give You a Headache, but It Sells," *Advertising Age*, September 24, 2007, http://adage.com (accessed April 15, 2010).

19. Peter J. Danaher and Guy W. Mullarkey, "Factors Affecting Online Advertising Recall: A Study of Students," *Journal of Advertising Research* 43 (2003): pp. 252–267.

20. Andrew Hampp, "Schering-Plough's $10M Experiment with Digital Out-of-Home" *Advertising Age*, November 11, 2009, adage.com (accessed April 9, 2010).

21. Emily Bryson York, "Miracle Whip Ad Campaign to Spread 'Boring' Mayo Message," *Advertising Age*, March 22, 2010, adage.com (accessed March 29, 2010).

22. Alex Taylor III, "Buyer Interest in Toyota Tanks," March 22, 2010, *CNNMoney.com*, http://money.cnn.com/2010/03/22/autos/toyota_buyers.fortune (accessed April 9, 2010).

23. George E. Belch and Michael A. Belch, *Advertising and Promotion* (Burr Ridge, IL: Irwin/McGraw-Hill, 2008), p. 570.

24. "About," Real Women, Real Advice, http://realwomenrealadvice.wordpress.com/about (accessed April 9, 2010).

25. "Nike, Starbucks, and Clean Energy Companies Join Forces to Launch Nationwide 'Race' for American Jobs and Innovation," Press Release, February 16, 2010, www.nikebiz.com/media/pr/2010/02/16_raceForJobsInnovation.html (accessed April 9, 2010).

26. Belch and Belch, *Advertising and Promotion*, pp. 580–581.

27. Suman Basuroy, Subimal Chatterjee, and S. Abraham Ravid, "How Critical Are Critical Reviews? The Box Office Effects of Film Critics, Star Power, and Budgets," *Journal of Marketing*, October 2003: 103–117.

28. "Goldman Sachs Admits "Negative Publicity" Is Bad for Business," March 3, 2010, http://NewStatesman.com, www.newstatesman.com (accessed April 9, 2010).

29. [[Data to come]]

30. Jeff Bailey, "JetBlue's CEO Is 'Mortified' After Fliers Are Stranded," *The New York Times*, February 19, 2007, www.nytimes.com/2007/02/19/business/19jetblue.html (accessed April 15, 2010).

31. Vans Shoes, www.vans.com (accessed April 15, 2010); Jason Lee, "The History of Vans," Sneaker Freaker, www.sneakerfreaker.com/feature/history-of-vans/1 (accessed April 15, 2010); "Vans: 40 Years of Originality," www.vans40.com (accessed July 17, 2008).

32. "What the World's Biggest Carmaker Can Learn from Other Corporate Turnarounds," *The Economist*, December 12, 2009, p. 11; Phil LeBeau, "Toyota Issues a 2nd Recall," *The New York Times*, January 21, 2010, www.nytimes.com/2010/01/22/business/22toyota.html (accessed February 24, 2010); "Toyota Motor Corporation," *The New York Times*, February 3, 2010, http://topics.nytimes.com/top/news/business/companies/toyota_motor_corporation/index.html (accessed February 24, 2010); Hiroko Tabuchi and Nick Bunkley, "Toyota Announces Steps to Restore Confidence on Safety," *The New York Times*, February 17, 2010, www.nytimes.com/2010/02/18/business/global/18recall.html (accessed February 24, 2010); "Toyota May Recall Corolla After U.S. Investigation (Update3)", *BusinessWeek*, February 18, 2010, www.businessweek.com (accessed February 24, 2010); Daisuke Wakabayashi,

"Adherents Defend the Toyota 'Way,'" *The Wall Street Journal*, February 24, 2010, http://online.wsj.com/article/SB1000142 40527487035102045750884840073648572.html?mod=WSJ_ latestheadlines (accessed February 24, 2010). Joseph B. White, "Why Toyota Rolled Over for Its SUVs," *The Wall Street Journal*, April 21, 2010; Suzanne Vranica, "Toyota Pulls Ads, Hires P.R. Firm," *The Wall Street Journal*, January 27, 2010; "Analysis: Toyota's PR 'Lessons to Be Learned,' *just-auto.com*, March 30, 2010, www.just-auto.com/article.aspx?id=103856; Rich Thomaselli, "Incentives Boost Sales but Brand Challenge Liners on for Toyota," *AdAge*, April 12, 2010.

Feature Notes

a. Susan Gunelius, "Womenkind Uses Women to Create Ads," *Brand Curve*, November 21, 2007, www.brandcurve.com (accessed April 2, 2009); Andrew McMains, "Womenkind Opens Doors," *AdWeek*, November 16, 2007, www.adweek. com (accessed April 2, 2009); Susanne Vranica, "Ads Made for Women, by Women," *The Wall Street Journal*, November 21, 2007 p. B3.

b. Josh Bernoff, "Social Ads Must Get the Rhythm Right," *marketingnews*, June 15, 2009, p. 20; Stephen Baker, "Beware Social Media Snake Oil," *Bloomberg Businessweek*, December 14, 2009, pp. 48–51; Adam L. Penenberg, "Loop de Loop," *Fast Company* (October 2009): pp. 55–58; Spencer E. Ante, "The Real Value of Tweets," *Bloomberg Businessweek*, January 18, 2010, p. 31; Max Chafkin, "5 Ways to Actually Make Money on Twitter," *Inc.* (December 2009/January 2010): pp. 96–101.

c. Jack Neff, "Brita's Marketing Flows from Grassroots Effort," *Advertising Age*, November 16, 2009, http://adage.com (accessed April 20, 2010); Kate Stinchfield, "Is Your Bottled Water Safe?" *CNN*, July 13, 2009, www.cnn.com/2009/ HEALTH/07/13/bottled.water.safety/index.html?eref=rss_health (accessed April 20, 2010); http://FitlerforGood.com (accessed April 20, 2010).

Chapter 19

1. Jessi Hempel, "IBM's All-Star Salesman," *CNNMoney.com*, September 26, 2008, http://money.cnn.com/2008/09/23/ technology/hempel_IBM.fortune/index.htm (accessed January 27, 2009); "Challenges in OSS/BSS and Optimized Provisioning," *Sasken*, www.sasken.com/downloads/TGJ/ issue3/challenges_in_oss_bss.htm (accessed April 12, 2010); Rajesh Mahapatra, "IBM Wins Order from Vodafone's India Arm," *Washingtonpost.com*, December 10, 2007, www. washingtonpost.com/wp-dyn/content/article/2007/12/10/ AR2007121000473.html (accessed April 12, 2010).

2. Avinash Malshe and Avipreet Sohi, "What Makes Strategy Making Across the Sales-Marketing Interface More Successful?," *Journal of the Academy of Marketing Science* 37, no. 4 (Winter 2009): pp. 400–421.

3. "Research and Markets: The Cost of the Average Sales Call Today Is More Than 400 Dollars," *M2 Presswire*, February 28, 2006.

4. Jon M. Hawes, Anne K. Rich, and Scott M. Widmier, "Assessing the Development of the Sales Profession," *Journal of Personal Selling & Sales Management* 24 (Winter 2004): pp. 27–37.

5. Ed Peelena, Kees van Montfort; Rob Beltman; and Arnoud Klerkx, "An Empirical Study into the Foundation of CRM Success," *Journal of Strategic Marketing* 17, no. 6 (December 2009): pp. 453–471.

6. Eli Jones, Paul Busch, and Peter Dacin, "Firm Market Orientation and Salesperson Customer Orientation: Interpersonal and Intrapersonal Influence on Customer Service and Retention in Business-to-Business Buyer–Seller Relationships," *Journal of Business Research* 56 (2003): pp. 323–340.

7. Julie T. Johnson, Hiram C. Barksdale Jr., and James S. Boles, "Factors Associated with Customer Willingness to Refer Leads to Salespeople," *Journal of Business Research* 56 (2003): pp. 257–263.

8. Ralph W. Giacobbe, Donald W. Jackson Jr., Lawrence A. Crosby, and Claudia M. Bridges, "A Contingency Approach to Adaptive Selling Behavior and Sales Performance: Selling Situations and Salesperson Characteristics," *Journal of Personal Selling & Sales Management* 26 (Spring 2006): pp. 115–142.

9. Richard G. McFarland, Goutam N. Challagalla, and Tasadduq A. Shervani, "Influence Tactics for Effective Adaptive Selling," *Journal of Marketing* 70 (October 2006).

10. John Andy Wood, "NLP Revisted: Nonverbal Communications and Signals of Trustworthiness," *Journal of Personal Selling & Sales Management* 26 (Spring 2006): pp. 198–204.

11. Stephen S. Porter, Joshua L. Wiener, and Gary L. Frankwick, "The Moderating Effect of Selling Situation on the Adaptive Selling Strategy—Selling Effectiveness Relationship," *Journal of Business Research* 56 (2003): pp. 275–281.

12. Gary K. Hunter and William D. Perreault Jr., "Making Sales Technology Effective," *Journal of Marketing* 71 (January 2007): pp. 16–34.

13. Othman Boujena, Johnston J. Wesley, and Dwight R. Merunka, "The Benefits of Sales Force Automation: A Customer's Perspective," *Journal of Personal Selling and Sales Management*, 29, no. 2 (2009): pp. 137–150.

14. Fernando Jaramillo, Jay Prakash Mulki, and Paul Solomon, "The Role of Ethical Climate on Salesperson's Role Stress, Job Attitudes, Turnover Intention, and Job Performance," *Journal of Personal Selling & Sales Management* 26 (Summer 2006): pp. 272–282.

15. Christophe Fournier, John F. Tanner Jr., Lawrence B. Chonko, and Chris Manolis, "The Moderating Role of Ethical Climate on Salesperson Propensity to Leave," *Journal of Personal Selling and Sales Management*, 3, no. 1 (Winter 2009–2010): pp. 7–22.

16. Noah Buhayar, "IBM's Secret for Making the Sale," BNET, www.bnet.com (accessed April 7, 2010).

17. "PGI Launches Online Sales Training Program," *JCKOnline. com*, May 15, 2009, www.jckonline.com/article/286043- PGI_Launches_Online_Sales_Training_Program.php (accessed April 7, 2010).

18. Tara Burnthorne Lopez, Christopher D. Hopkins, and Mary Anne Raymond, "Reward Preferences of Salespeople: How Do Commissions Rate?" *Journal of Personal Selling & Sales Management* 26 (Fall 2006): pp. 381–390.

19. Kirk Shinkle, "All of Your People Are Salesmen: Do They Know? Are They Ready?" *Investor's Business Daily*, February 6, 2002, p. A1.

20. "100 Best Companies to Work For 2009," *Fortune*, February 2, 2009, money.cnn.com/magazines/fortune/bestcompanies/2009/ snapshots/32.html (accessed April 7, 2010).

21. Ibid.

22. John W. Barnes, Donald W. Jackson Jr., Michael D. Hutt, and Ajith Kumar, "The Role of Culture Strength in Shaping Salesforce Outcomes," *Journal of Personal Selling & Sales Management* 26 (Summer 2006): pp. 255–270.

23. Patricia Odell, "Motivating the Masses," *Promo*, September 1, 2005, http://promomagazine.com/research/pitrends/marketing_ motivating_masses/ (accessed April 16, 2010).

24. Tracy Turner, "Wendy's Newest Pitch Aimed at Online Crowd," *The Columbus Dispatch*, April 3, 2009.

25. George E. Belch and Michael A. Belch, *Advertising and Promotion* (Burr Ridge, IL: Irwin/McGraw-Hill, 2004), pp. 514–522.

26. "NCH Resource Center," NCH Marketing, www.nchmarketing. com/ResourceCenter/ (accessed April 7, 2010; Angela Sauber, "National Coupon Month," Examiner.com, September 14, 2009, www.examiner.com (accessed April 7, 2010).

27. Arthur L. Porter, "Direct Mail's Lessons for Electronic Couponers," *Marketing Management Journal* (Spring/Summer 2000): pp. 107–115.

28. Ibid.

29. Kathryn Rem, "Kathryn Rem: Internet Coupons Clipped," *Cheboygan News,* www.cheboygannews.com/lifestyle/x599189738/Kathryn-Rem-Internet-coupons-clipped (accessed April 7, 2010).

30. Brian Grow, "The Great Rebate Runaround," *BusinessWeek,* December 5, 2005, pp. 34–37.

31. "For Our Members," Hallmark, www.hallmark.com/ (accessed April 14, 2010).

32. Mya Frazier, James Tenser, and Tricia Despres, "Retail Lesson: Small Programs Best," *Advertising Age,* March 20, 2006, pp. S2–S3.

33. "Secret Weapon?" *Promo,* December 1, 2007, http://promomagazine.com/sampling/secret_weapon_trial_purchase_study/ (accessed April 16, 2010).

34. "Beverage Packaging: 2010 Coca-Cola Film Award Brings Attention to Recycling," *Packaging Digest,* March 16, 2010, www.packagingdigest.com/article/453292-Beverage_packaging_2010_Coca_Cola_film_award_brings_attention_to_recycling.php (accessed April 8, 2010).

35. Jeffrey May, "Burger King Franchisee Lacked Standing to Bring False Ad Suit Against McDonald's," *Trade Regulation Talk,* June 26, 2007, http://traderegulation.blogspot.com/2007/06/burger-king-franchisee-lacked-standing.html (accessed April 8, 2010).

36. "Kroger and Murray's Cheese Launch Partnership with Opening of First of Three Murray's Cheese Departments in Cincinnati-Area Kroger Supermarkets," November 17, 2008, www.murrayscheese.com/images_global/murrays_kroger_press_release.pdf (accessed April 23, 2010); Rosalind Resnick, "Market with Meaning," *Entrepreneur,* November 6, 2009, www.entrepreneur.com/marketing/marketingideas/article203938.html# (accessed April 23, 2010); "Murray's Press," Murray's, www.murrayscheese.com/press_main.asp (accessed April 23, 2010); Kim Severson, "Murray's Cheese Will Open 50 Locations in Kroger Markets," *The New York Times,* November 24, 2009, http://dinersjournal.blogs.nytimes.com/tag/murrays-cheese/ (accessed April 23, 2010); "Murray's Cheese Presents Cheese U Bootcamp," Murray's, www.murrayscheese.com/edu_cheeseubootcamp.asp (April 23, 2010); "The History of New York's Oldest and Best Cheese Shop," Murray's, www.murrayscheese.com/prodinfo.asp?number=ABOUT%5FMURRAYSSTORY (accessed April 23, 2010).

37. David Barboza, "Direct Selling Flourishes in China," *The New York Times,* December 25, 2009, www.nytimes.com/2009/12/26/business/global/26marykay.html?_r=1&scp=1&sq=%22direct%20selling%22&st=Search (accessed April 12, 2010); Wing-Gar Cheng and Bruce Einhorn, "Amway China Sales May Rise at Least 10% as Direct Sales Rebound," *BusinessWeek,* April 9, 2010, www.businessweek.com (accessed April 12, 2010); Amway website, www.amway.com/en (accessed April 27, 2010); Avon website, www.avon.com (accessed April 27, 2010).

38. Some of this material is adapted from "The Indy Racing League (IRL): Driving for First Place" by Don Roy. Originally published in O.C. Ferrell's and Michael D. Hartline's *Marketing Strategy,* 5th ed. (Mason, OH South-Western Cengage Learning, 2011), pp. 428–435. These facts are from "A Brief History of CART and Champ Car Racing," www.fsdb.net/champcar/history/index.htm; "Celebrities Who Are Revved Up Over Racing," *Street & Smith's Sports Business Journal,* May 22, 2006, p. 27; "Hot Wheels Announces Partnership with the IndyCar Series, Indianapolis 500," *Entertainment Newsweekly,* April 24, 2009, p. 140; Marty O'Brien, "Helio Castroneves Is Happier Making Headlines on the Race Tack," *Daily Press,* June 27, 2009; John Ourand, "IRL to Get at Least 7 Hours Weekly on Versus," *Street & Smith's Sports Business Journal,* February 23, 2009, p. 7; Jennifer Pendleton, "Danica Patrick," *Advertising Age,* November 7, 2005, p. S4; Anthony Schoettle, "IRL Ratings Continue Their Skid," *Indianapolis Business Journal,* November 1, 2004, p. 3; "Kiss Rocker Lends Voice to Indy Races," *Knight Ridder Tribune Business News,* April 1, 2006, p. 1; "Turnkey Sports Poll," *Street & Smith's Sports Business Journal,* May 22, 2006, p. 24; J. K. Wall, "Indy Racing League Sets Sights on Marketing Dollars," *Knight Ridder Tribune Business News,* May 27, 2004, p. 1; Scott Warfield, "IRL in Line to Court Young Males," *Street & Smith's Sports Business Journal,* November 29, 2004, p. 4; Jeff Wolf, "George's Ouster Clouds IRL's Future," *Las Vegas Review-Journal,* July 3, 2009; Nate Ryan, "Circuits One Again, But Gains from Split Came at Dear Cost," *USA Today,* April 17, 2008, pp. 1C-2C; Associated Press, "Rahal-Letterman Team Out of IRL, Lacks Sponsor," *ESPN Racing,* January 29, 2009, http://sports.espn.go.com/espn/wire? section=auto&id=3868795&campaign=rsssrch=irl (accessed August 27, 2009); "Team History," *Penske Racing,* 2008, www.penskeracing.com/about/index.cfm?cid=14189 (accessed August 27, 2009); "About Andretti Green," *Andretti Green,* www.andrettigreen.com (accessed August 27, 2009); Larry Hawley, "IRL: Izod, Racing Make for Unique Match," *Indy Sports Nation,* November 4, 2009, www.fox59.com/sports/ (accessed May 4, 2010).

Feature Notes

a. Timothy W. Martin, "Coupons Are Hot. Clipping Is Not," *The Wall Street Journal,* February 25, 2009, pp. D1, D8; Katy Bachman, "Younger Consumers Prefer Online Coupons," *BrandWeek,* April 2, 2009, www.brandweek.com/ (accessed December 30, 2009); "Growth of Digital Coupons Outpaces That of Printed Newspaper Coupons 10 to 1," *QSR,* February 10, 2010, www.qsrmagazine.com/ (accessed February 28, 2010); Associated Press, "P&G Ending E-Coupons for Kroger's Loyalty Cards," *OregonLive.com,* December 16, 2009, www.oregonlive.com/business/index.ssf/2009/12/pg_ending_e-coupons_for_kroger.html (accessed February 28, 2010).

b. "Hello Green Tomorrow," Avon, www.hellogreentomorrow.com/ (accessed April 12, 2010); "Hello Green Tomorrow External Engagement: Empowering a Global Women's Environmental Movement to Nurture Nature," Avon, http://responsibility.avoncompany.com/page-45-Hello-Green-Tomorrow (accessed April 12, 2010); *Avon Products, Inc.: The Avon Paper Promise,* http://responsibility.avoncompany.com/docs/Avon_Paper_Promise.pdf (accessed April 12, 2010); *PR Newswire,* "Avon Launches Hello Green Tomorrow in More Than 65 Countries: A Global Women's Environmental Movement to Nurture Nature," *Market Watch,* March 16, 2010, www.marketwatch.com/story/avon-launches-hello-green-tomorrow-in-more-than-65-countries-a-global-womens-environmental-movement-to-nurture-nature-2010-03-16?reflink=MW_news_stmp (accessed April 12, 2010).

c. Cheryl Lu-Lien Tan, "Haggelling 2.0," *The Wall Street Journal,* June 23–24, 2007, pp. P1, P3; "Haggling," Haggle Point, www.hagglepoint.com/about.html (accessed March 17, 2008); Dan Sewell, "Grocers Clip Digital Coupons," *USA Today,* January 14, 2008, http://usatoday.com/tech/products/services/2008-01-14-grocer-digital-coupons_n.htm.

Chapter 20

1. "Spotify: U.S. Launch Is Coming," *The Online Reporter*, February 5, 2010, p. 17; Ian Youngs, "Spotify Boss Sets Out Future Plans," *BBC News*, January 25, 2010, http://news.bbc.co.uk/2/hi/entertainment/8478599.stm; Ari Levy and Greg Bensinger, "LinkedIn Joins ESPN, Skype in Shifting from Free to 'Freemium,'" *BusinessWeek Online*, December 21, 2009, www.businesseek.com; Rita Chang and Michael Learmonth, "Are Your Ads Being Used to Drive Consumers to Ad-free Services?" *Advertising Age*, September 21, 2009, p. 3.

2. Rajneesh Suri and Kent B. Monroe, "The Effects of Time Constraints on Consumers' Judgements of Prices and Products," *Journal of Consumer Research* (June 2003): p. 92.

3. "Modern Trade & Barter Can Aid Economic Recovery," International Reciprocal Trade Association, March 4, 2009, www.irta.com/news.html.

4. "Hewlett-Packard," case study, Professional Pricing Society, www.pricingsociety.com/Page5024.aspx (accessed April 21, 2010).

5. Janet Adamy, "Corporate News: Starbucks—Coffee Empire Seeks to Seem Less Expensive in Recession," *The Wall Street Journal*, February 9, 2009, p. B3.

6. Steve Tilley, "Let the Price War Begin," *The Toronto Sun*, August 27, 2009, www.torontosun.com/entertainment/columnists/steve_tilley/2009/08/27/10629221-sun.html.

7. Lauren Young, "Candy's Getting Dandy," *BusinessWeek*, February 13, 2006, pp. 88–89.

8. Jim Zemlin, "Linux Can Compete With the iPad on Price, But Where's the Magic?" *The Linux Foundation*, January 28, 2010, www.linux-foundation.org/weblogs/jzemlin/2010/01/.

9. "Nintendo Cutting Wii Price by $50 to $200," *MSNBC*, September 24, 2009, www.msnbc.msn.com/id/33001544/ns/technology_and_science-games/.

10. *Dictionary of Marketing Terms*, American Marketing Association, www.marketingpower.com/_layouts/Dictionary.aspx (accessed March 3, 2008).

11. Ibid.

12. Elwin Green, "Gas Prices Aren't Slowing U.S. Motorists," *Pittsburgh Post-Gazette*, November 25, 2007, www.post-gazette.com/pg/07329/836591-28.stm.

13. Daisuke Wakabayashi, "Cost Cutting Pays Off at Sony," *The Wall Street Journal*, February 5, 2010, http://online.wsj.com.

14. Donald Lichtenstein, Nancy M. Ridgeway, and Richard G. Netemeyer, "Price Perceptions and Consumer Shopping Behavior: A Field Study," *Journal of Marketing Research* (May 1993): pp. 234–245.

15. Russell S. Winer, *Pricing* (Cambridge, MA: Marketing Science Institute, 2005), p. 20.

16. Manoj Thomas and Geeta Menon, "Internal Reference Prices and Price Expectations," *Journal of Marketing Research* XLIV (August 2007).

17. Emily Donaldson, "Why We Make Dumb Decisions," *The Toronto Star*, April 13, 2008, www.thestar.com/entertainment/article/413972.

18. Lichtenstein, Ridgway, and Netemeyer, "Price Perceptions and Consumer Shopping Behavior."

19. Piet Levy, "How to Reach the New Consumer," *Marketing News*, February 28, 2010.

20. Gerald E. Smith and Thomas T. Nagle, "A Question of Value," *Marketing Management* (July/August 2005): pp. 39–40.

21. Levy, "How to Reach the New Consumer."

22. "Coty Inc. and HSN Announce New Partnership," HSN, Press Release, April 4, 2008, www.hsni.com/releasedetail.cfm?ReleaseID=327241.

23. Matthew Keys, "Justice Department Looks Into Possible AT&T, Verizon Antitrust," *Fox40 News*, www.fox40.com/news/headlines/ktxl-news-antitrust0706,0,1225904.story.

24. Marc Levy, "Europe Studies Candy Prices of Hershey, Mars," *USA Today*, February 19, 2008, www.usatoday.com/money/industries/food/2008-02-19-candy-price-fixing_N.htm.

25. David Voreacos, "Exxon's New Jersey Franchisees Sue over Fuel Prices, Rent," *Bloomberg News*, December 10, 2009, www.bloomberg.com/apps/news?pid=20670001&sid=acvF_jEdjKME.

26. Washburn Guitar website, www.washburn.com; Washburn Guitar video.

27. Jeffrey A. Trachtenberg, "Amazon Gives Way on E-Book Pricing," *The Wall Street Journal*, April 1, 2010, www.wsj.com; Steven Musil, "Reports: Publishers to Set Amazon E-Book Prices," *CNET News*, March 31, 2010, http://news.cnet.com/8301-1023_3-20001538-93.html; Mylene Mangalindan and Jeffrey A. Trachtenberg, "IPod of E-Book Readers?" *The Wall Street Journal*, November 20, 2007, p. B1; Mylene Mangalindan, "Amazon's Latest Thriller: Growth," *The Wall Street Journal*, October. 24, 2007, p. A3; Bob Tedeschi, "Nothing Says 'Buy' Like 'Free Shipping,'" *New York Times*, October 8, 2007, p. C8; www.amazon.com.

Feature Notes

a. Arik Hesseldahl, "The iPhone Eyes Blackberry's Turf," *BusinessWeek*, June 23, 2008, p. 38; Andrea Chalupa, "Extravagant Electronics," *Portfolio.com*, December 14, 2007, http://portfolio.com; "Marketing Society Awards for Excellence: International Brand Development," *Marketing*, June 20, 2007, p. 12; "Samsung Accused of Heavy Cost-Cutting," *UPI NewsTrack*, June 5, 2007; "Samsung and LG Hear the Call for Low-End Mobiles," *Financial Times*, March 26, 2007, 21; "Vertu Rings Till for British-Made Luxury Goods," *PC Magazine Online*, July 16, 2007, www.pcmag.com; John Walko, "Q3 Cell Phone Stats," *Electronic Engineering Times*, December 3, 2007, p. 8; Interview with salesman at Exquisite Timepieces, Naples, FL, March 12, 2009.

b. Dan Sewell, "'Green' Becomes More Than Just a Marketing Pitch," *Associated Press*, April 23, 2010, http://abcnews.go.com/Business/wireStory?id=10459604; Lisa Baertlein and Dana Ford, "Companies Get Sold on Green, Consumers Wary," *Reuters*, April 14, 2010, www.reuters.com; "Sustainable Packaging: Are Americans Willing to Pay More for Green?" *Packaging Digest*, March 25, 2010, www.packagingdigest.com.

c. "Finance/Credit Companies: Long-Term Contribution Trends," OpenSecrets.org, http://opensecrets.org/industries March 3, 2008 (accessed April 7, 2008); "Plastic Money's Predatory Lenders," *The Nader Page*, http://nader.org/interest/070303.html, July 3, 2003 (accessed April 7, 2008).

d. Jason Del Rey, "How to Use Groupon to Boost Sales," *Inc.*, April 1, 2010, www.inc.com; Jessi Hempel, "Social Media Meets Retailing," *Fortune*, March 22, 2010, p. 30; Kunur Patel, "Groupon Takes Coupons into the Social-Media Age," *Advertising Age*, December 21, 2009, www.adage.com.

Chapter 21

1. Amy Wallace, "Creme de la Cell: Six-Figure Phones," *The New York Times*, April 18, 2010, p. BU-5; "Nokia Brings Cheap Corporate Phones," *CIOL*, April 14, 2010; "Nokia Wins $2 Billion Mobile Handset Orders in China," *The Information Company*, April 3, 2010; Sreejiraj Eluvangal, "India Is No. 2 in Mobile Net Use," *Daily News & Analysis*, March 31, 2010; Arik Hesseldahl, "Nokia's Kallasvuo: We Must 'Move Even Faster,'" *BusinessWeek Online*, March 18, 2010, www.businessweek.com; www.nokia.com.

2. Dominic Haber, "Abercrombie & Fitch Plans Further Price Cuts After 1Q Loss," *TopNews.com*, May 17, 2009, http://topnews.us/content/25241-abercrombie-fitch-plans-further-price-cuts-after-1q-loss.

3. Chang-Ran Kim, "Toyota to Halve Hybrid Pride, Size for Next Prius," *Reuters*, October 25, 2007, www.reuters.com/article/marketsNews/idUKT13140520071025?rpc=44&pageNumber=1&sp=true.

4. "New Bentley Pricing," *Automotive.com*, www.automotive.com/new-cars/pricing/01/Bentley/index.html (accessed April 22, 2010).

5. Piet Levy, "How to Reach the New Consumer," *Marketing News*, February 28, 2010.

6. Robert J. Frank, Jeffrey P. George, and Laxman Narasimhan, "When Your Competitor Delivers More for Less," *McKinsey Quarterly*, www.mckinseyquarterly.com (accessed April 23, 2010).

7. Wes Siler, "New Prius Vs. Fusion Hybrid Vs. Honda Insight: Which Hybrid Should You Buy?" *Jalopnik.com*, March 27, 2009, http://jalopnik.com/5186000/new-prius-vs-fusion-hybrid-vs-honda-insight-which-hybrid-should-you-buy; Ford, www.fordvehicles.com/cars/fusion/features/ (accessed April 26, 2010).

8. "Fairchild Dynamic Pricing Team," Professional Pricing Society, case study, www.pricingsociety.com/Page5023.aspx (accessed April 26, 2010).

9. Angela Moore, "Costco Shows No Fear," *MarketWatch*, December 10, 2009, www.marketwatch.com/.

10. Vera Gibbons, "Five Leading Retail Rip-Offs," *CBS News*, March 30, 2009, www.cbsnews.com/stories/2009/03/30/earlyshow/living/ConsumerWatch/main4902625.shtml.

11. Jan Sjostrom, "Demand-Based Ticket Pricing Starts at Kravis, Opera, Florida Stage," *Palm BeachDaily News*, July 26, 2009, www.palmbeachdailynews.com/arts/content/arts/2009/07/26/tickets0719.html.

12. Ricky W. Griffin, "Differential Tuition to Benefit Our Students," *Mays Business Online*, March 5, 2008, http://maysbusiness.tamu.edu/.

13. "Cutler-Hammer/Eaton Corporation," case study, Professional Pricing Society, www.pricingsociety.com/Page5022.aspx (accessed April 26, 2010).

14. Jim Downing, "Safeway Begins Broad Discount Campaign," *The Sacramento Bee*, July 23, 2009, www.sacbee.com.

15. Marla Royne Stafford and Thomas F. Stafford, "The Effectiveness of Tensile Pricing Tactics in the Advertising of Services," *Journal of Advertising* (Summer 2000:)pp. 45–56.

16. Jefferson Graham, "Kodak Printer Ads Remind Consumers of Lower Ink Costs," *USA Today*, November 30, 2009, www.usatoday.com/tech/news/2009-11-30-printers30_ST_N.htm.

17. "2011 Corvette ZR1," Chevrolet, www.chevrolet.com/corvette-zr1/competitive-comparison/ (accessed April 19, 2010).

18. Microsoft, www.microsoft.com/windows/windows-7/compare/default.aspx (accessed April 22, 2010).

19. Simona Romani, "Price Misleading Advertising: Effects on Trustworthiness Toward the Source of Information and Willingness to Buy," *Journal of Product & Brand Management* 15 (2006): pp. 130–138.

20. Earnest Cavalli, "Upcoming Xbox 360 Bundle Includes Fable II, Halo 3," *Wired.com*, April 20, 2009, www.wired.com/gamelife/2009/04/upcoming-xbox-3/.

21. Jaihak Chung and Vithala R. Rao, "A General Choice Model for Bundles with Multiple-Category Products: Application to Market Segmentation and Optimal Pricing for Bundles," *Journal of Marketing Research* (May 2003): pp. 115–130.

22. Kris Hudson, "Competing Retailers Dispute Wal-Mart Trademark Request," *The Wall Street Journal*, November 7, 2006, http://online.wsj.com; "NGA Stops Wal-Mart's EDLP Trademark Plan," *Frozen Food Age*, April 4, 2007.

23. Christine Harris and Jeffrey Bray, "Price Endings and Consumer Segmentation," *Journal of Product & Brand Management* 16 (March 2007): pp. 200–205.

24. Ralk Wagner and Kai-Stefan Beinke, "Identifying Patterns of Customer Response to Price Endings," *Journal of Product & Brand Management*, 15 (May 2006): pp. 341–351.

25. Rita Rubin, "Placebo Tests 'Costlier is Better' Notion," *USA Today*, March 4, 2008, www.usatoday.com/news/health/2008-03-04-placebo-effect_N.htm.

26. Bruce L. Alford and Brian T. Engelland, "Advertised Reference Price Effects on Consumer Price Estimates, Value Perception, and Search Intention," *Journal of Business Research* (May 2000): pp. 93–100.

27. Chris Reiter, "Smart Car Sputters in U.S. as Daimler Hunts for Partner," *Toronto Sun*, January 12, 2010, p. B6; Bernard Simon, "Daimler Discounts Smart in US," *Financial Times*, November 13, 2009, p. 21; Steve Miller, "Vroom for Two," *Brandweek*, June 2, 2008, pp. 20+; Bill Marsh, "Welcome, Little Smart Car, to the Big American Road," *The New York Times*, January 6, 2008, sec. 4, p. 3; Chris Woodyard, "America Crazy about Breadbox on Wheels Called Smart Car," *USA Today*, November 11, 2007, www.usatoday.com; Royal Ford, "Smallest Car, Biggest Market," *Boston Globe*, December 6, 2007, p. E1.

28. Yukari Iwatani Kane and Roger Cheng, "Surge in iPhone Powers Apple," *The Wall Street Journal*, April 21, 2010, www.wsj.com; Alice Z. Cuneo, "iPhone: Steve Jobs," *Advertising Age*, November 12, 2007, p. S13; Katie Hafner and Brad Stone, "iPhone Owners Crying Foul Over Price Cut," *The New York Times*, September 7, 2007, pp. C1, C7; Yukari Iwatani Kane and Nick Wingfield, "For Apple iPhone, Japan Could Be the Next Big Test," *The Wall Street Journal*, December 19, 2007, p. B1; Brad Kenney, "Apple's iPhone: IW's IT Product of the Year," *Industry Week* (December 2007): pp. 47+; Josh Krist, "The Painful Cost of First-on-the-Block Bragging Rights," *PC World*, December 2007, pp. 53+; Alex Markels, "Apple's Mac Sales Are Surging," *U.S. News & World Report*, September 26, 2007; Jon Swartz, "iPhone Helps Apple Earn Juicy Profit," *USA Today*, October 23, 2007, p. 1B.

29. Vipin V. Nair, "Tata May Beat Hyundai in India Helped by World's Cheapest Car," *BusinessWeek*, April 22, 2010, www.businessweek.com; Gail Edmondson, "The Race to Build Really Cheap Cars," *BusinessWeek*, April 23, 2007, pp. 44–48; John Murphy, "Suzuki Sets the Pace in India," *The Wall Street Journal*, December 13, 2007, p. C5; www.tatamotors.com; Steven Cole Smith, "Will Consumers Say Tata to Used Cars?" *Orlando Sentinel*, November 16, 2007, www.orlandosentinel.com; Heather Timmons, "India's Automaker of Many Faces May Land Jaguar," *The New York Times*, December 18, 2007, p. C3; Heather Timmons, "In India, a $2,500 Pace Car," *The New York Times*, October 12, 2007, pp. C1, C4.

Feature Notes

a. Dean Takahashi, "Copy This: Zynga Raises $130K for Two Charities through Social Games," *VentureBeat*, April 22, 2010, games.venturebeat.com; Ari Levy, Brian Womack and Joseph Galante, "Facebook Tests a Payment Service for Virtual Goods," *BusinessWeek*, February 25, 2010, www.businessweek.com; Mike Snider, "'Microtransactions' Add Up for Free Online Games, *USA Today*, January 19, 2010, www.usatoday.com; Elizabeth Heichler, "Money for Nothing? Virtual Goods Market Takes Off," *Computerworld*, January 8, 2010, www.computerworld.com.

b. Kelli B. Grant, "20 Ways to Save Green by Going Green," *SmartMoney*, April 22, 2010, www.smartmoney.com; Randy Lee Loftis, "Message That 'Green Is the Glue' Starts to Stick," *Dallas Morning News*, April 22, 2010, www.dallasnews.com; www.jcpenney.com.

c. Gwendolyn Bounds, "TerraCycle Fashions a New Life for Old Wrappers," *The Wall Street Journal,* July 1, 2008, p. B5; Arden Dale, "Green Products Gain from New Price Equation," *The Wall Street Journal,* June 24, 2008, p. B7; Christopher Shulgan, "The Worm Wrangler," *Maclean's,* June 4, 2007, p. 34+; www.terracycle.net (accessed February 27, 2009).

Appendix A

1. This section is adapted from William M. Pride, Robert J. Hughes, and Jack R. Kapoor, *Business* (Boston: Houghton-Mifflin, 2002), pp. A1–A9.
2. Sal Divita, "Résumé Writing Requires Proper Strategy," *Marketing News* (July 3, 1995): p. 6.
3. Andrew J. DuBrin, "Deadly Political Sins," *The Wall Street Journal*'s Managing Your Career (Fall 1993): pp. 11–13.
4. Ibid.
5. Cyndee Miller, "Marketing Research Salaries Up a Bit, but Layoffs Take Toll," *Marketing News,* June 19, 1995, p. 1.
6. Careers in Marketing, "Market Research—Salaries," www.careers-in-marketing.com/mrsal.htm (accessed November 2, 2009).
7. Payscale, www.payscale.com (accessed November 2, 2009).
8. Ibid.
9. Ibid.
10. Careers in Marketing, "Product Management—Salaries," www.careers-in-marketing.com/pmsal.htm (accessed November 2, 2009).
11. Careers in Marketing, "Advertising and Public Relations—Salaries," www.careers-in-marketing.com/adsal.htm (accessed November 2, 2009).
12. Payscale, www.payscale.com (accessed November 2, 2009).
13. Ibid.
14. *PCWorld.com,* www.pcworld.com (accessed November 2, 2009).

name index

organization index

subject index